Street by Stree

SURREY

Enlarged areas CROYDON, FARNHAM, GUILDFORD, KINGSTON UPON THAMES, WOKING

Plus Aldershot, Biggin Hill, Bracknell, Crawley, East Grinstead, Edenbridge, Farnborough, Fleet, Gatwick Airport, Heathrow Airport, Horsham, Richmond, Sutton

3rd edition February 2007
© Automobile Association Developments Limited 2007

Original edition printed May 2001

 This product includes map data licensed from Ordnance Survey® with the permission of the Controller of Her Majesty's Stationery Office. © Crown copyright 2007. All rights reserved. Licence number 100021153.

Published by AA Publishing (a trading name of Automobile Association Developments Limited, whose registered office is Fanum House, Basing View, Basingstoke, Hampshire RG21 4EA. Registered number 1878835).

Produced by the Mapping Services Department of The Automobile Association. (A02664)

A CIP Catalogue record for this book is available from the British Library.

Printed by Oriental Press in Dubai

Ref: ML119y

Key to map pages	ii-iii
Key to map symbols	iv-1
Enlarged map pages	2-11
Main map pages	12-195
Index – towns & villages	196-197
Index – streets	198-263
Index – featured places	263-276
Acknowledgements	276

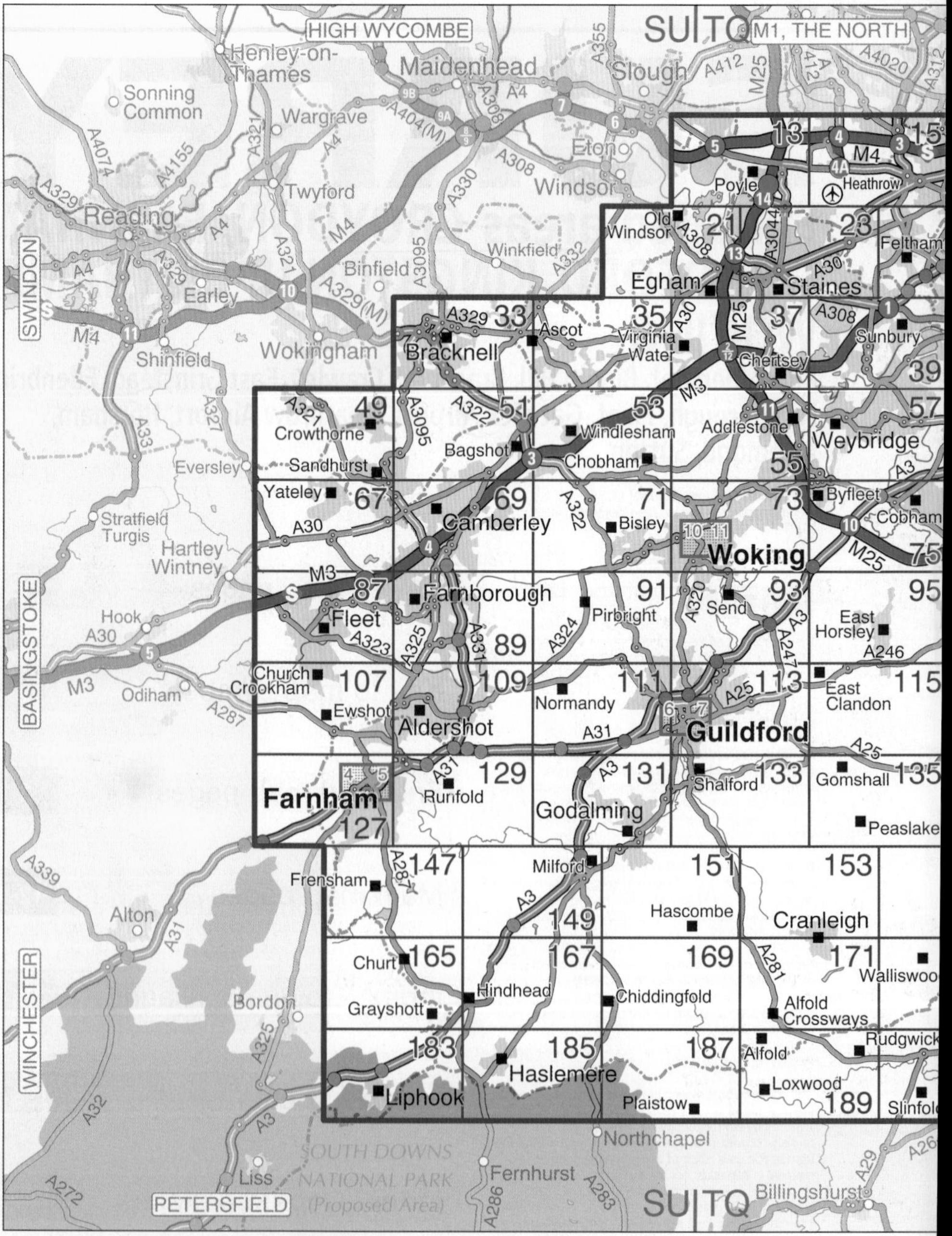

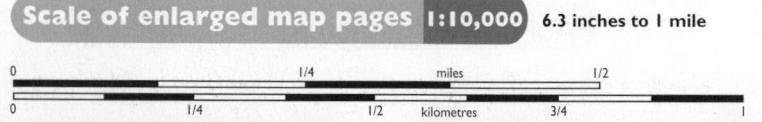

Scale of enlarged map pages 1:10,000 **6.3 inches to 1 mile**

0 — 1/4 — miles — 1/2

0 — 1/4 — 1/2 — kilometres — 3/4 — 1

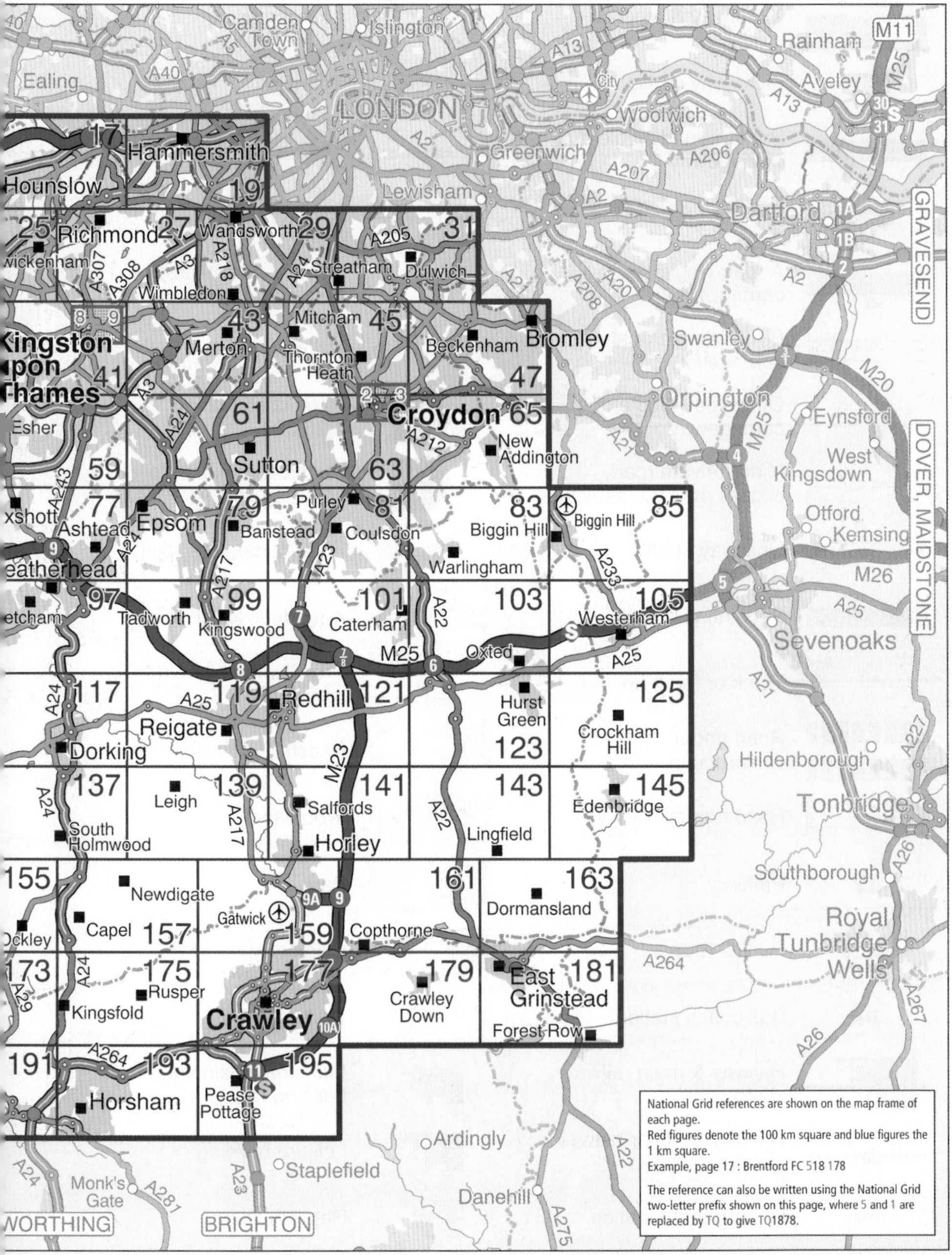

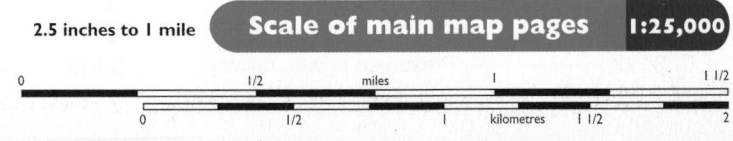

2.5 inches to 1 mile **Scale of main map pages** **1:25,000**

National Grid references are shown on the map frame of each page.
Red figures denote the 100 km square and blue figures the 1 km square.
Example, page 17 : Brentford FC 518 178

The reference can also be written using the National Grid two-letter prefix shown on this page, where 5 and 1 are replaced by TQ to give TQ1878.

iv

Junction 9	Motorway & junction
Services	Motorway service area
	Primary road single/dual carriageway
Services	Primary road service area
	A road single/dual carriageway
	B road single/dual carriageway
	Other road single/dual carriageway
	Minor/private road, access may be restricted
← ←	One-way street
	Pedestrian area
	Track or footpath
	Road under construction
	Road tunnel
P	Parking
P+	Park & Ride
	Bus/coach station
	Railway & main railway station
	Railway & minor railway station
⊖	Underground station
⊖	Light railway & station
+++++++	Preserved private railway

LC	Level crossing
●—●—●—●	Tramway
----------	Ferry route
....	Airport runway
—·—·—·—	County, administrative boundary
⊼⊼⊼⊼⊼	Mounds
17	Page continuation 1:25,000
3	Page continuation to enlarged scale 1:10,000
	River/canal, lake, pier
	Aqueduct, lock, weir
465 ▲ Winter Hill	Peak (with height in metres)
	Beach
	Woodland
	Park
	Cemetery
	Built-up area
	Industrial/business building
	Leisure building
	Retail building
	Other building
IKEA	IKEA store

Symbol	Description	Symbol	Description
City wall	Castle
A&E	Hospital with 24-hour A&E department	Historic house or building
PO	Post Office	Wakehurst Place NT — National Trust property
Public library	Museum or art gallery
i	Tourist Information Centre	Roman antiquity
i	Seasonal Tourist Information Centre	Ancient site, battlefield or monument
Petrol station, 24 hour — Major suppliers only	Industrial interest
†	Church/chapel	Garden
Public toilets	Garden Centre — Garden Centre Association Member
Toilet with disabled facilities	Garden Centre — Wyevale Garden Centre
PH	Public house — AA recommended	Arboretum
Restaurant — AA inspected	Farm or animal centre
Madeira Hotel — Hotel — AA inspected	Zoological or wildlife collection
Theatre or performing arts centre	Bird collection
Cinema	Nature reserve
Golf course	Aquarium
Camping — AA inspected	Visitor or heritage centre
Caravan site — AA inspected	Country park
Camping & caravan site — AA inspected	Cave
Theme park	Windmill
Abbey, cathedral or priory	Distillery, brewery or vineyard

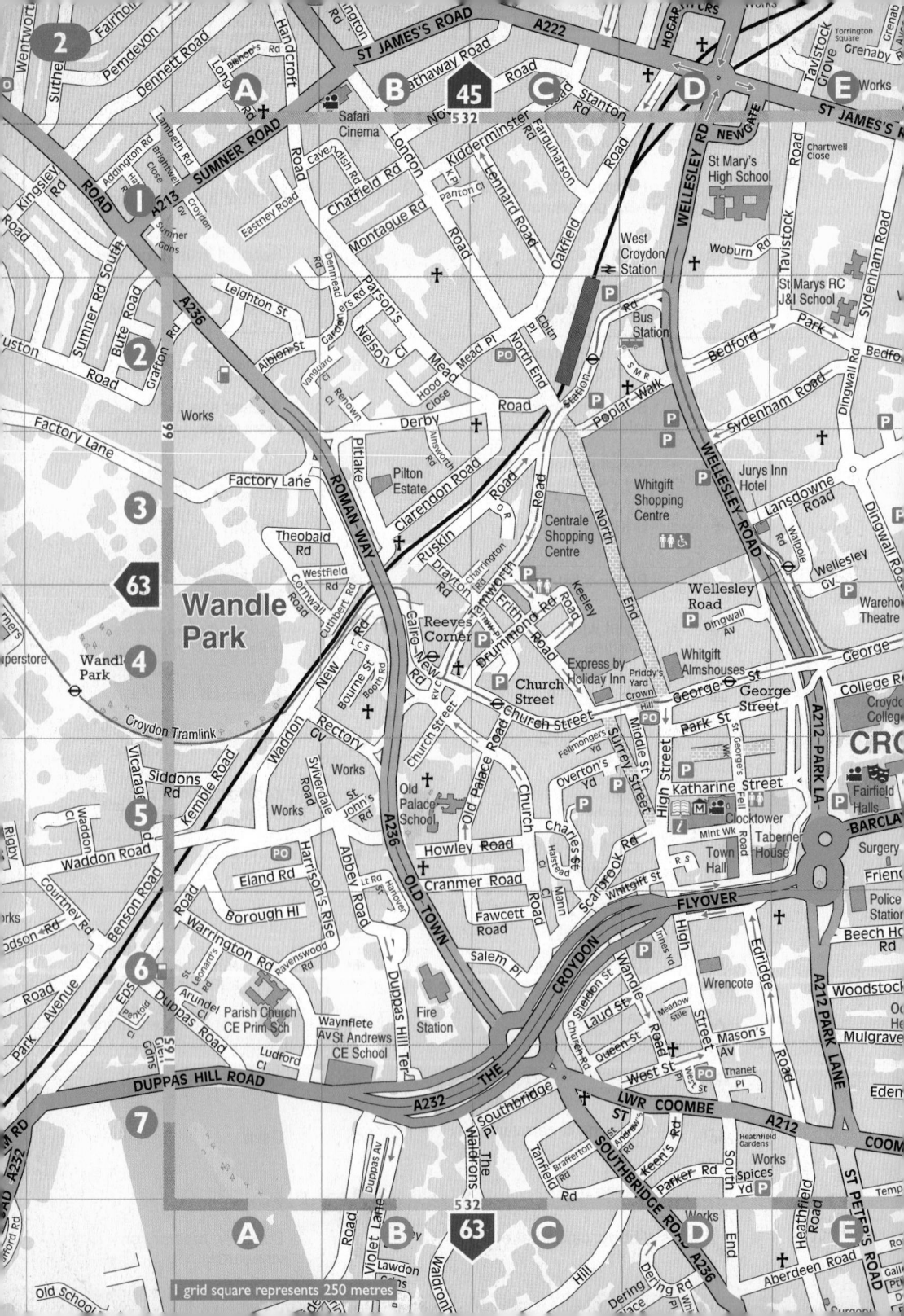

1 grid square represents 250 metres

4

A   B   **127** 483   C   D   E

The Grange

Old Park Lane

1

Castle

CASTLE

2

Friars Field   Castle Field   Lion & Lamb Shopp Centre

Surrey Institute of Art and Design

Long Gdn Wa

Larkfield Rd   Larkfield Rd

Falkner Road   The Hart   Lion an Lamb   Arur Place

3   **127**   Beavers Hill   Crondall Lane

Byworth Cl   Hill View Road   Beavers   Beavers Road   Penns Yard   Foxyd   Bishop's Table Hotel   Ad Ed Ce

Tor Rd   Byworth Road   Tor Rd   Potters Gate CE Primary School   Potters Gate   College   Farnham Museum

4   Waynflete   Lane   A325   WEST STREET   Works

Hazell Road   Marston Rd   The Chantrys   Chantry   West End Grove   Parfitts Cl   West End Grove   Bishop's Mead   Works

The Chantrys   Mt pleasant   Babbs Mead   Crosby   Brookmead Court   Pengilly Rd   Meadow Bank

5   The Chantrys   Coxbridge Maw   WEST STREET   Crosby Way   Ferns Mead   Whrlet Ct   GU9

Cemetery   Weydon MI Lane   River Wey

6   A325   Farnham Bu Park   Farnham Business Park   Weydo

7   Works   A31 FARNHAM BY-PASS   A325   The Pilg Way Pri School   Talbot Road

ALTON ROAD   ROAD   A325   483 atches   Weydon Lane   Pilgrims Cl   Grevs

A   B   **127** 483   C   D   E

The   Chest Avenu   Bards'ey   Grd   Baldreys   Way

I grid square represents 250 metres

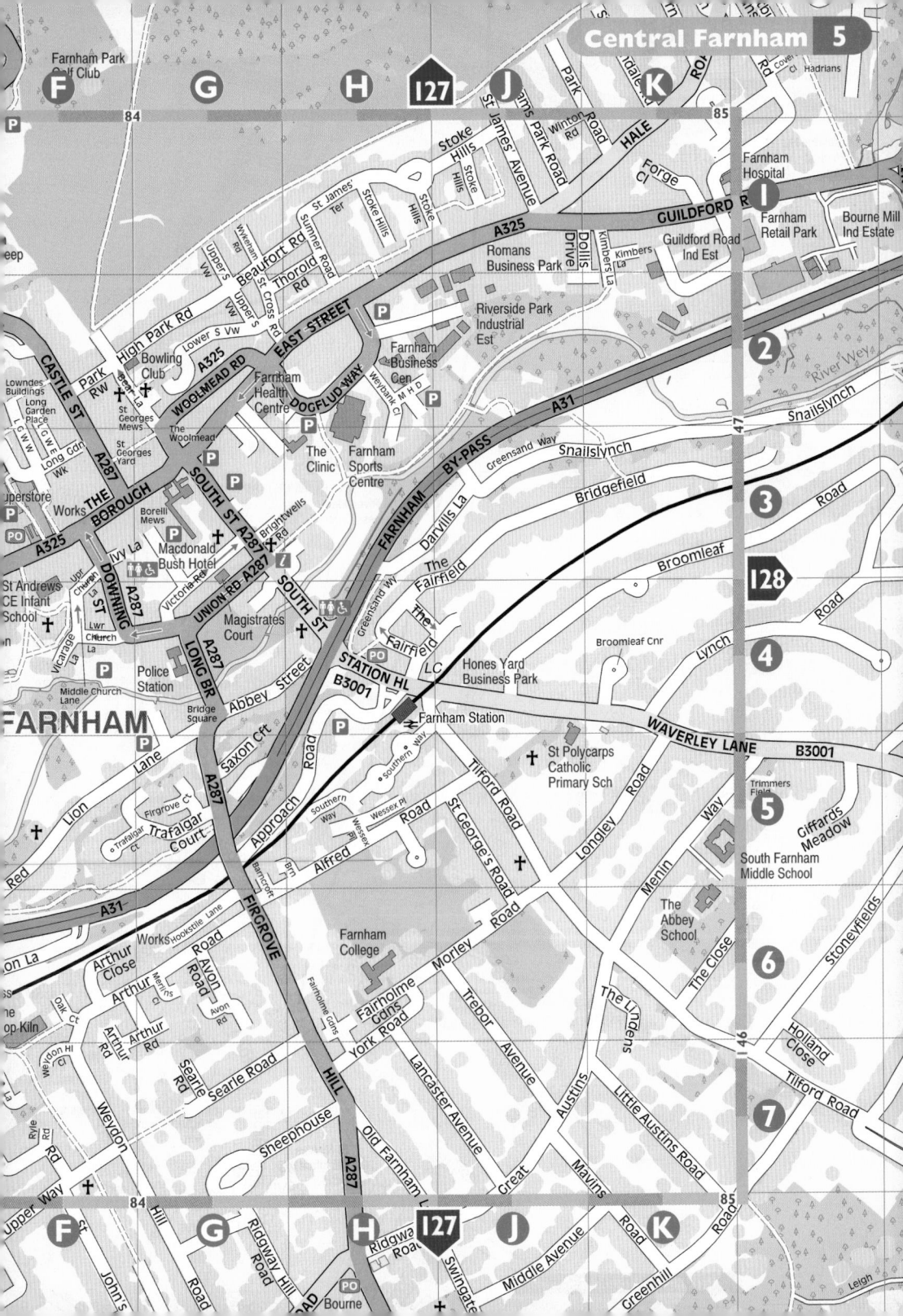

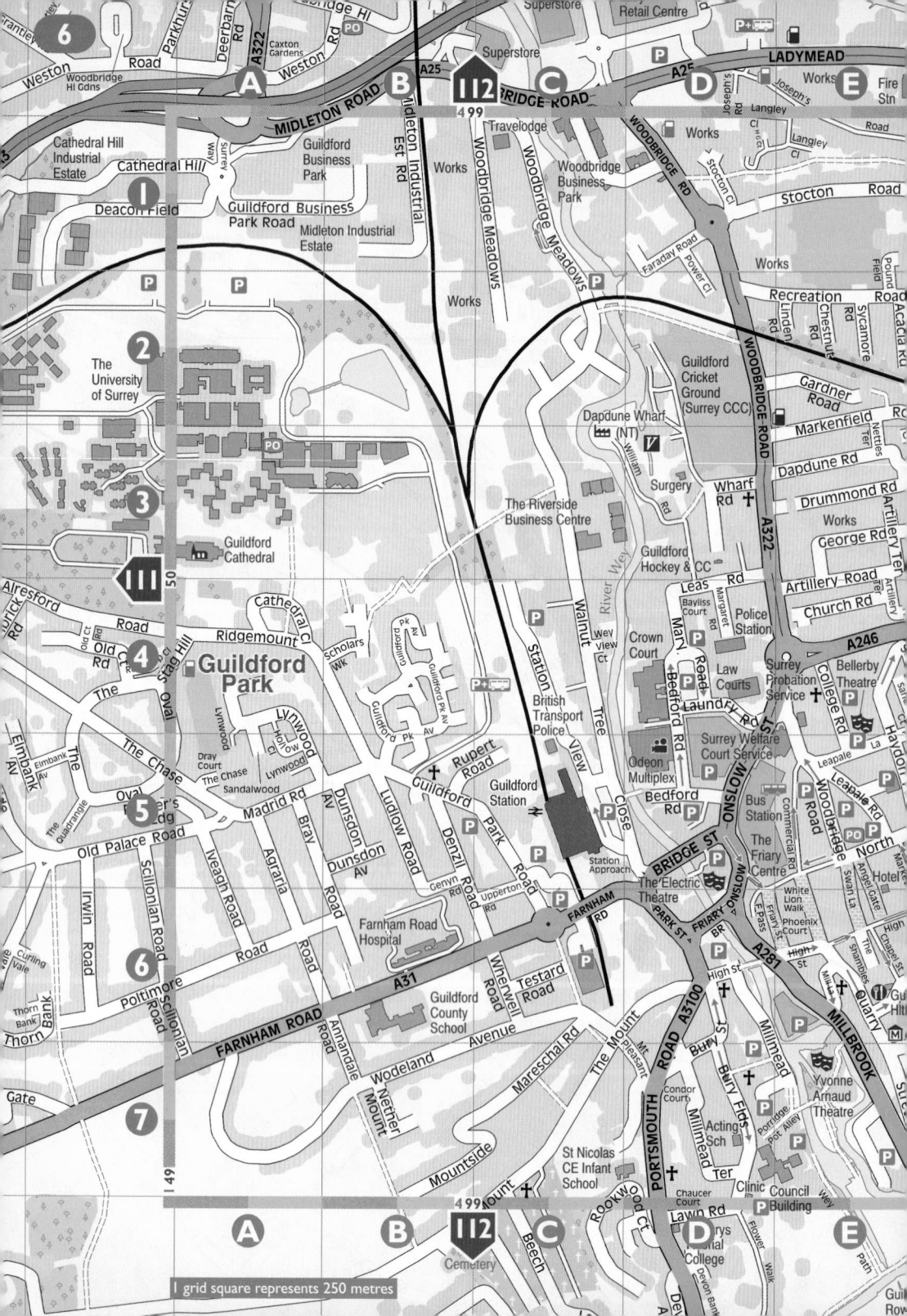

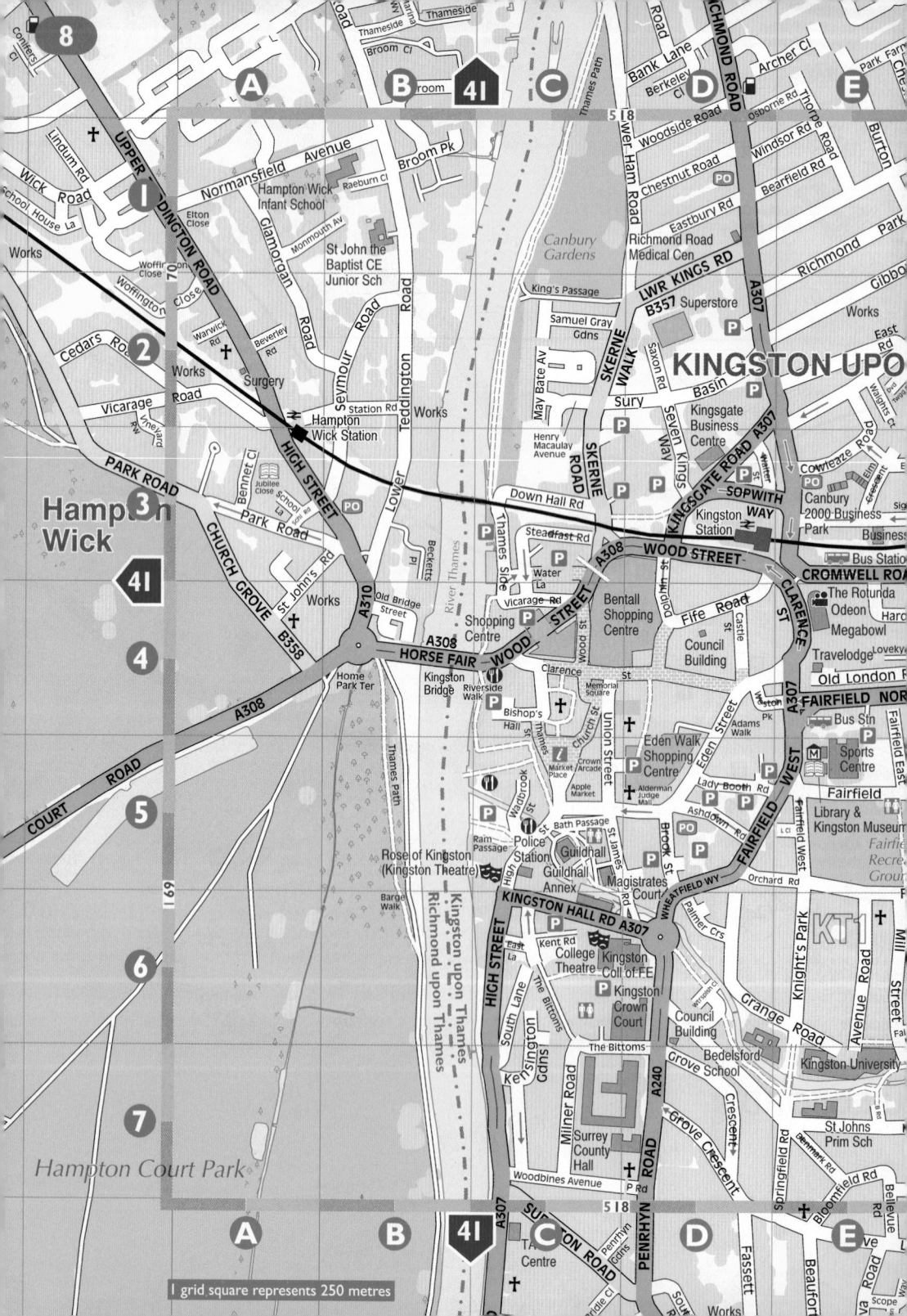

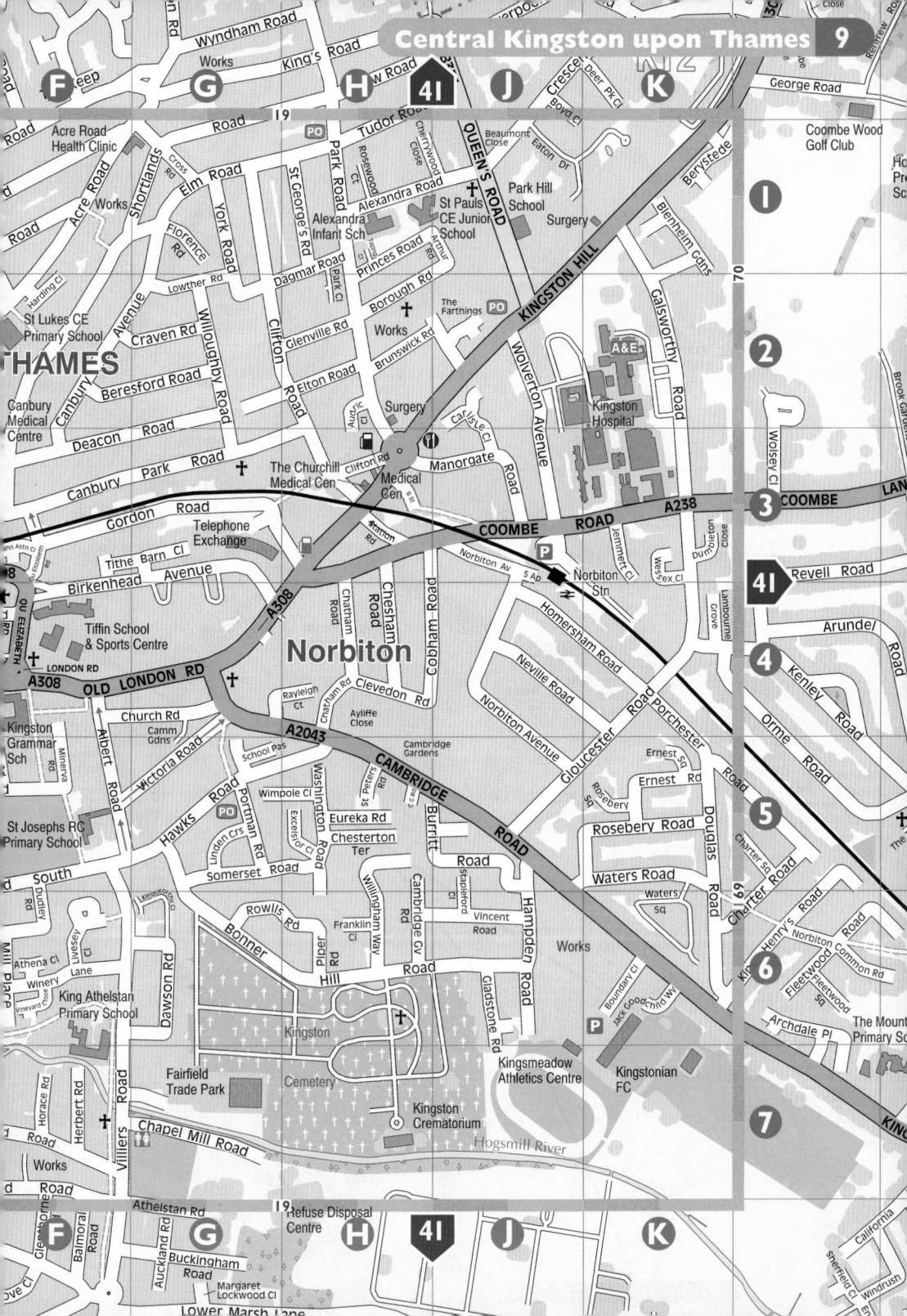

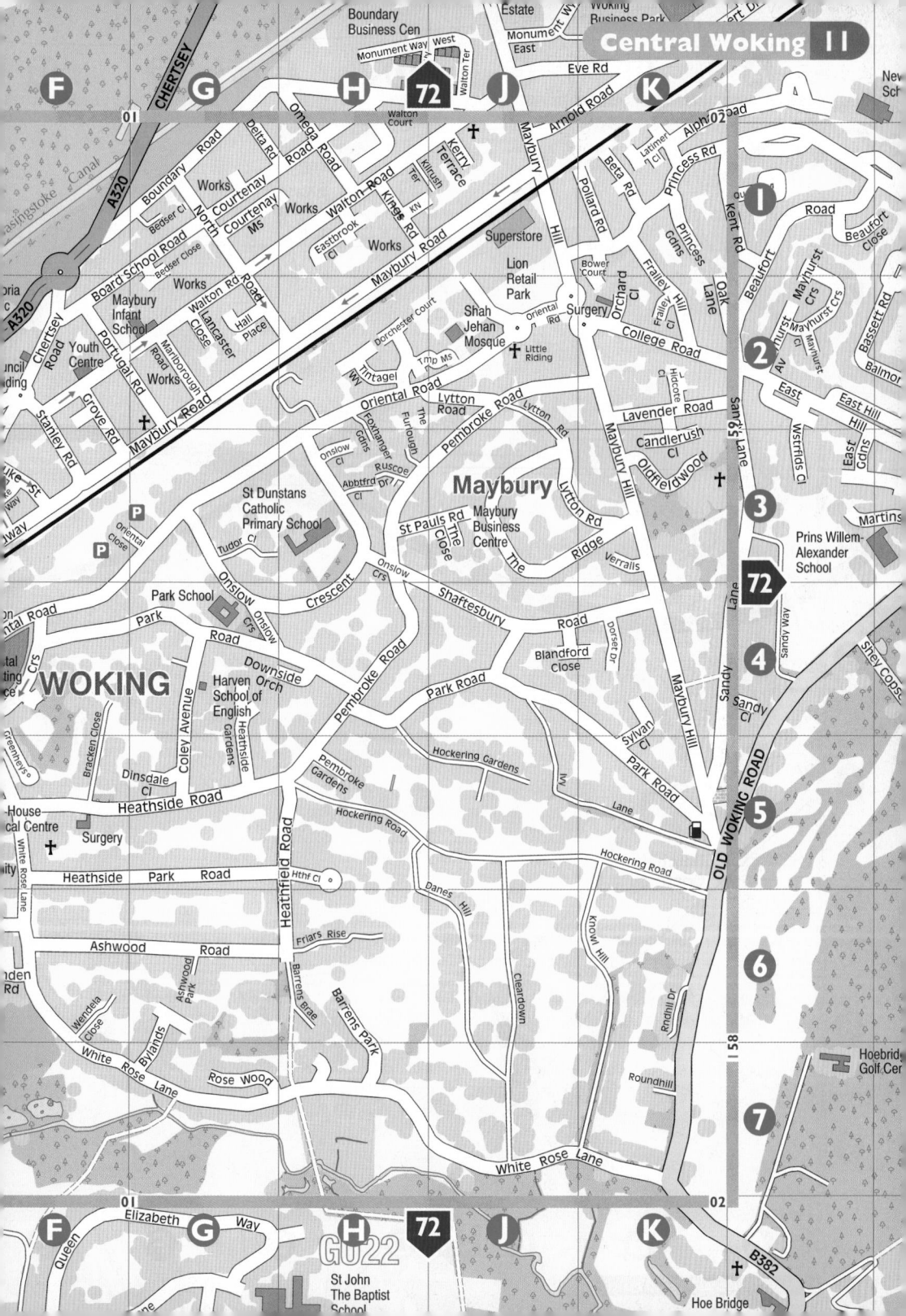

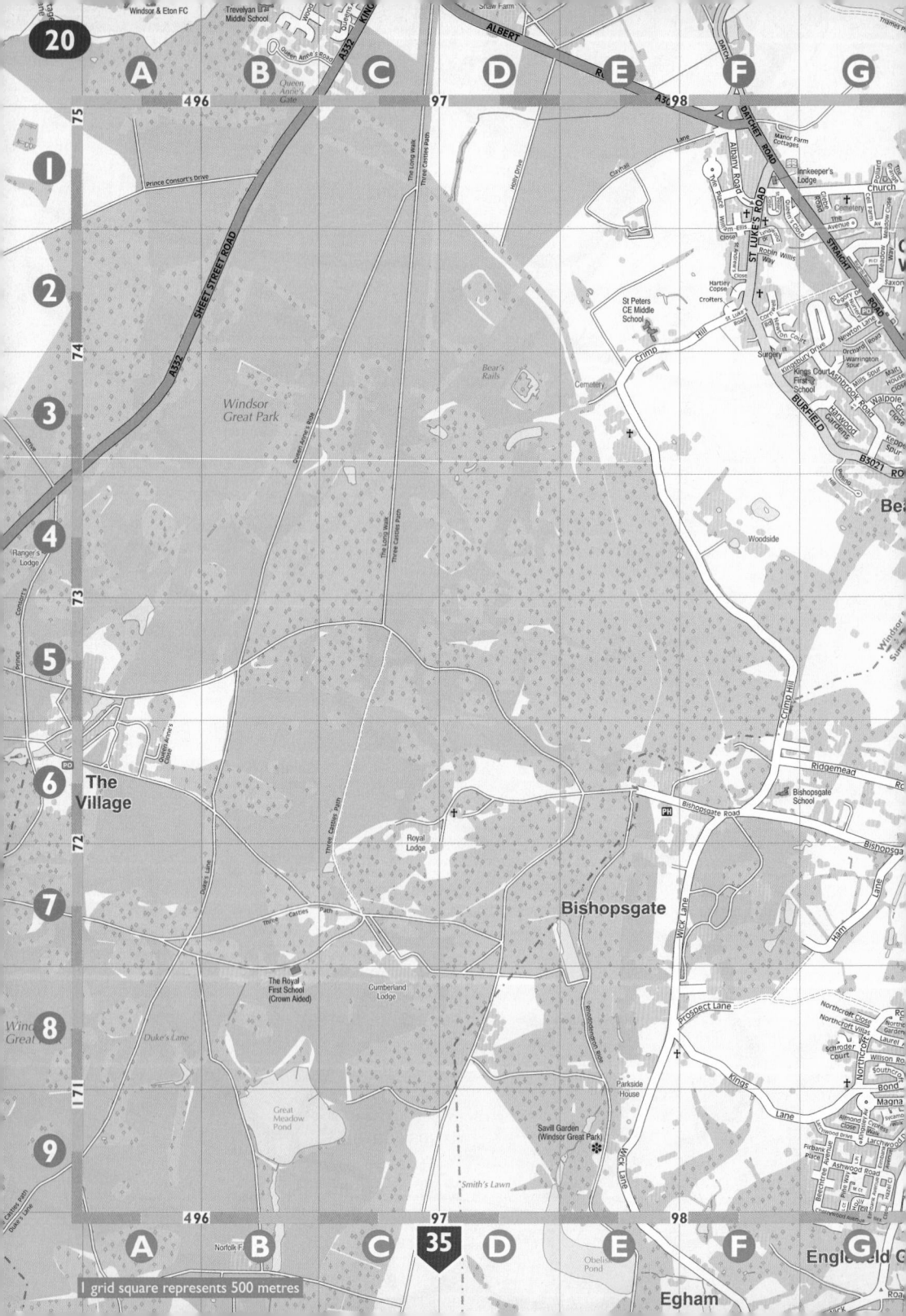

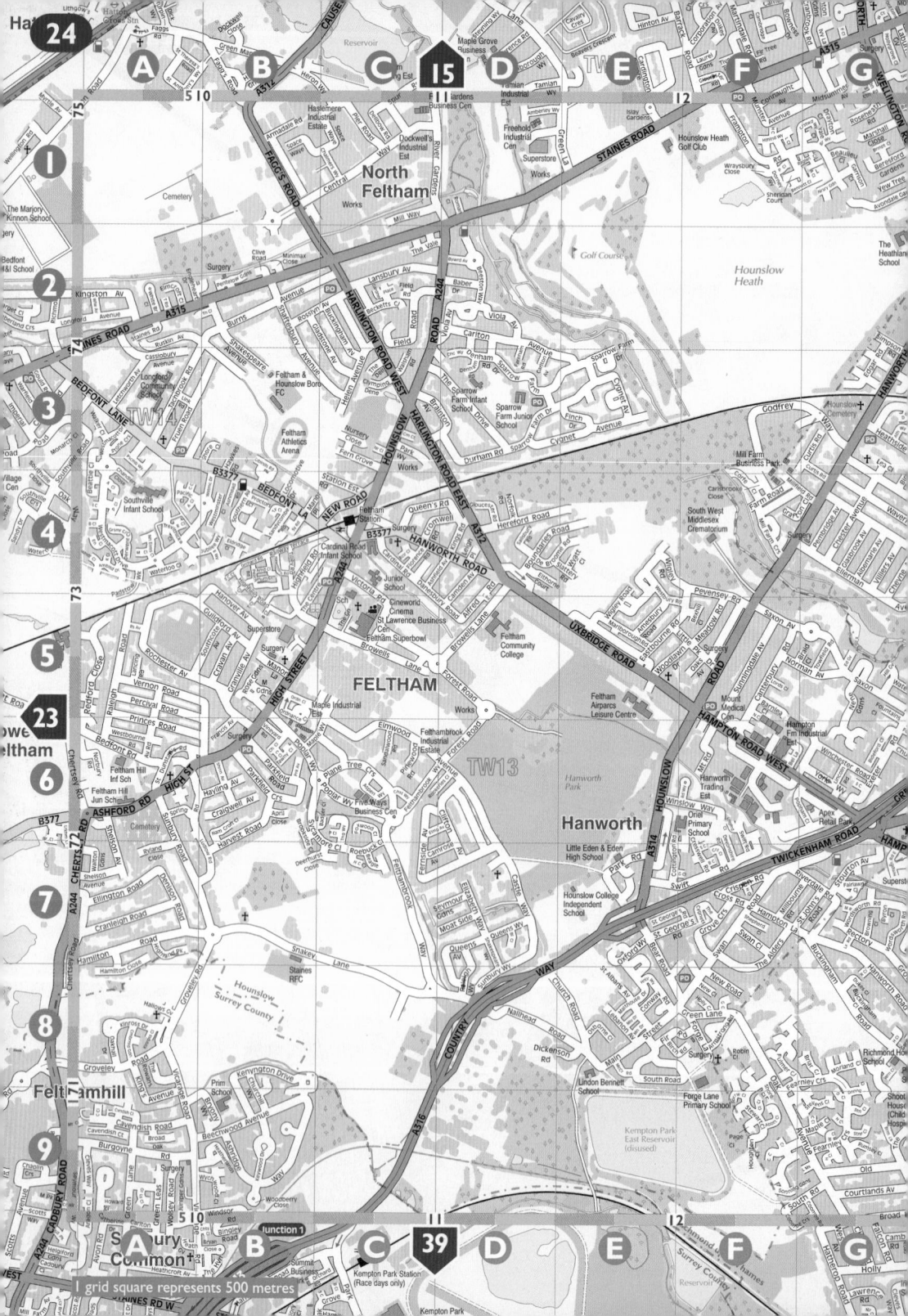

I grid square represents 500 metres

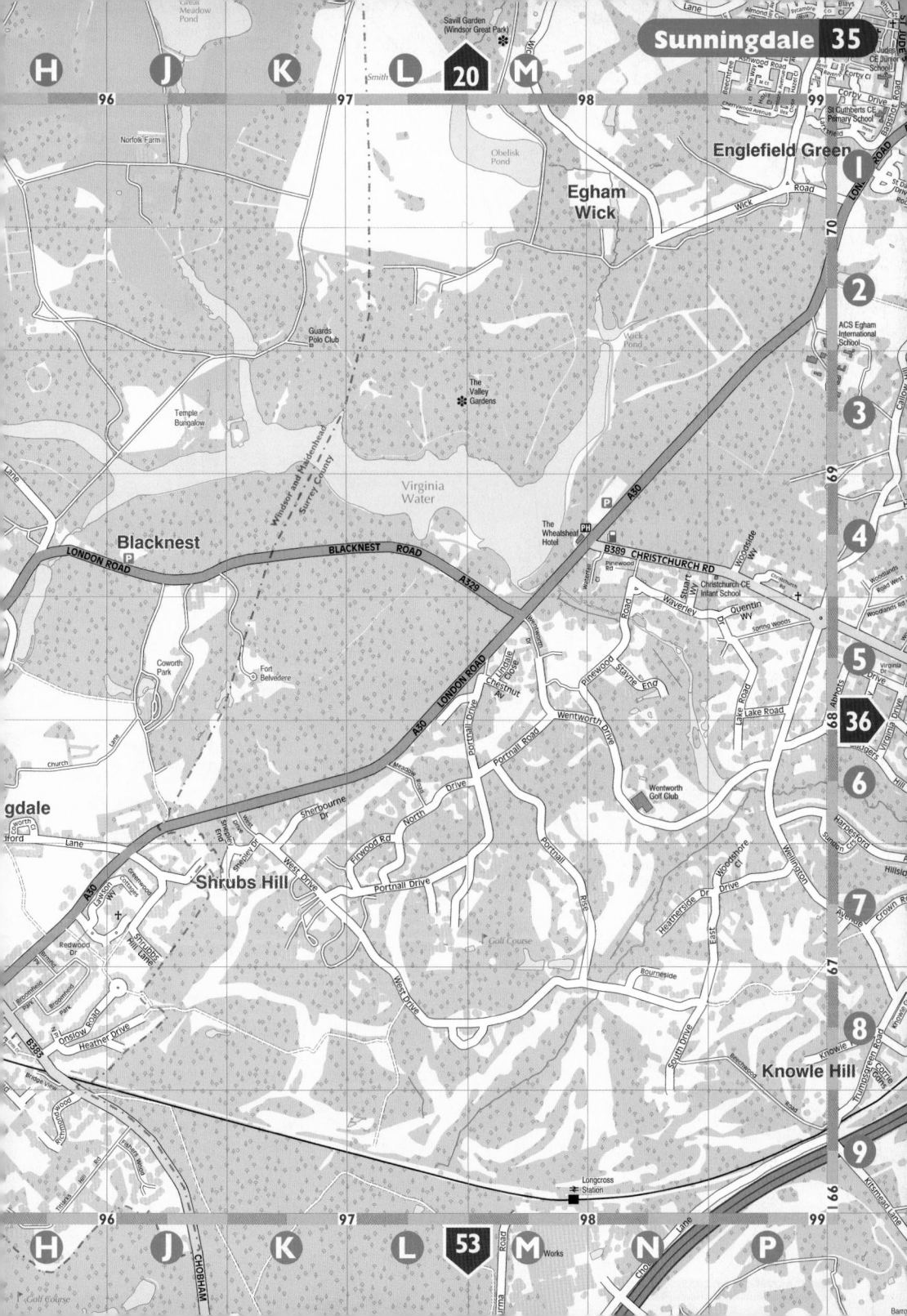

H J K L **20** M

96 97 98 99

Great
Meadow
Pond

Savill Garden
(Windsor Great Park)

Norfolk Farm

Obelisk
Pond

Englefield Green

Egham
Wick

St Cuthberts CE
Primary School

1

2

ACS Egham
International
School

Wick
Pond

Guards
Polo Club

The Valley
Gardens

3

70

Temple
Bungalow

69

4

Virginia
Water

The Wheatsheaf
Hotel

PH

LONDON ROAD

Blacknest

BLACKNEST ROAD

A329

B389 CHRISTCHURCH RD

Christchurch CE
Infant School

Coworth
Park

Fort
Belvedere

A30

LONDON ROAD

Wentworth Drive

Lake Road

68

5

36

6

Wentworth
Golf Club

gdale

Sherbourne
Dr

North
Drive

Portnail Road

Shrubs Hill

A30

Portnail Drive

West Drive

67

7

Golf Course

Bourneside

West Drive

8

Knowle Hill

66

9

96 97 98 99

H J K L **53** M N P

CHOBHAM

Longcross
Station

Works

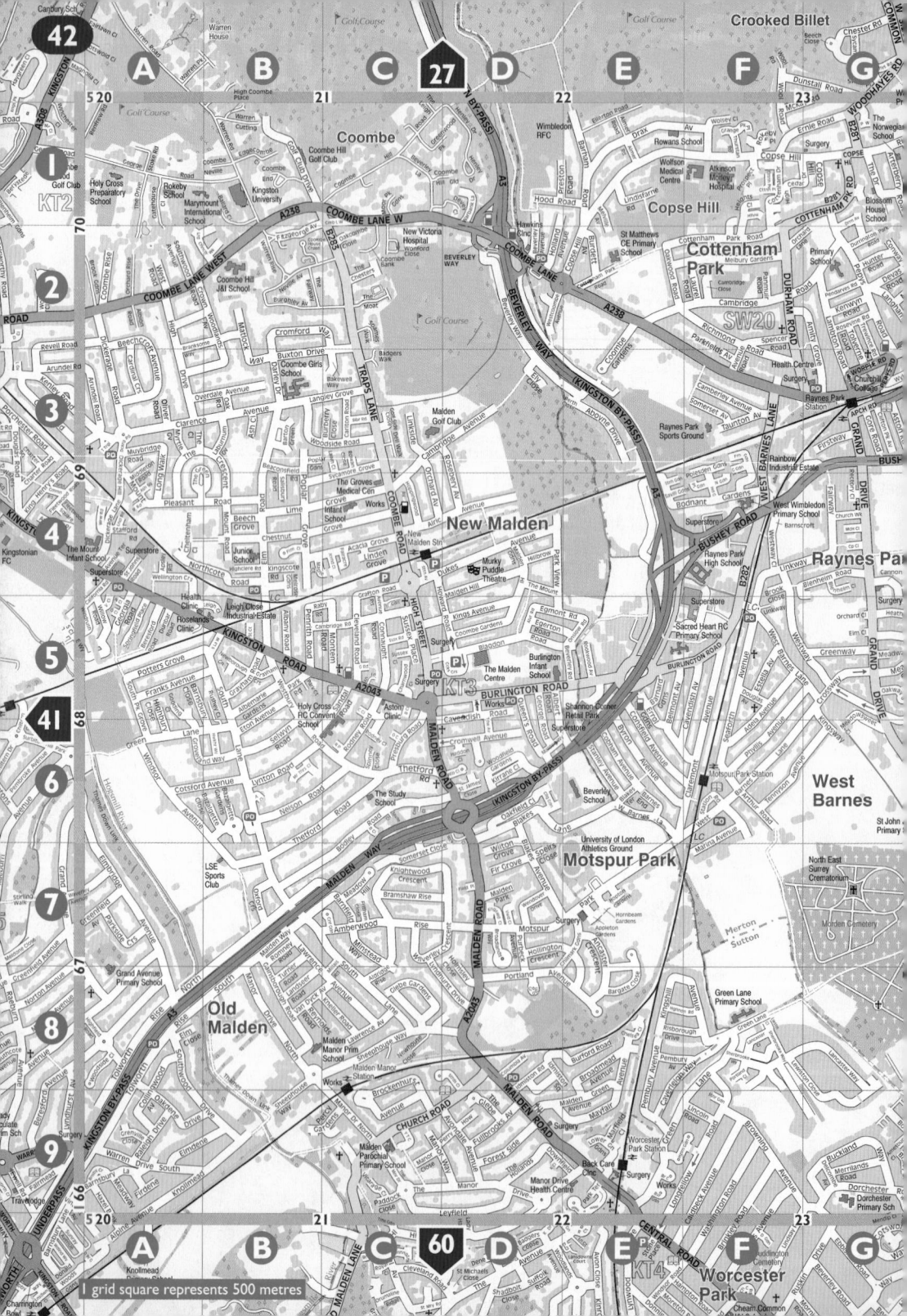

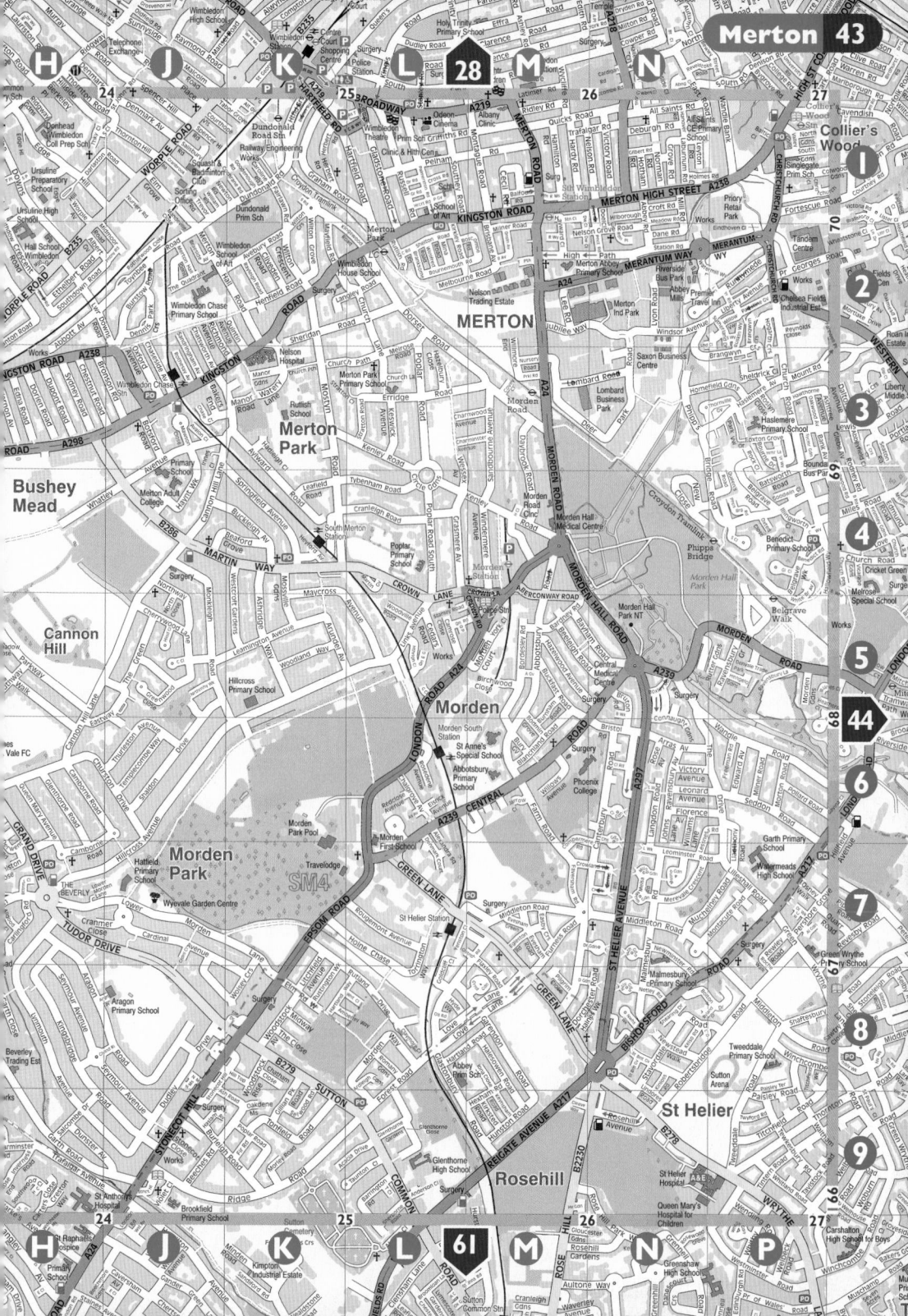

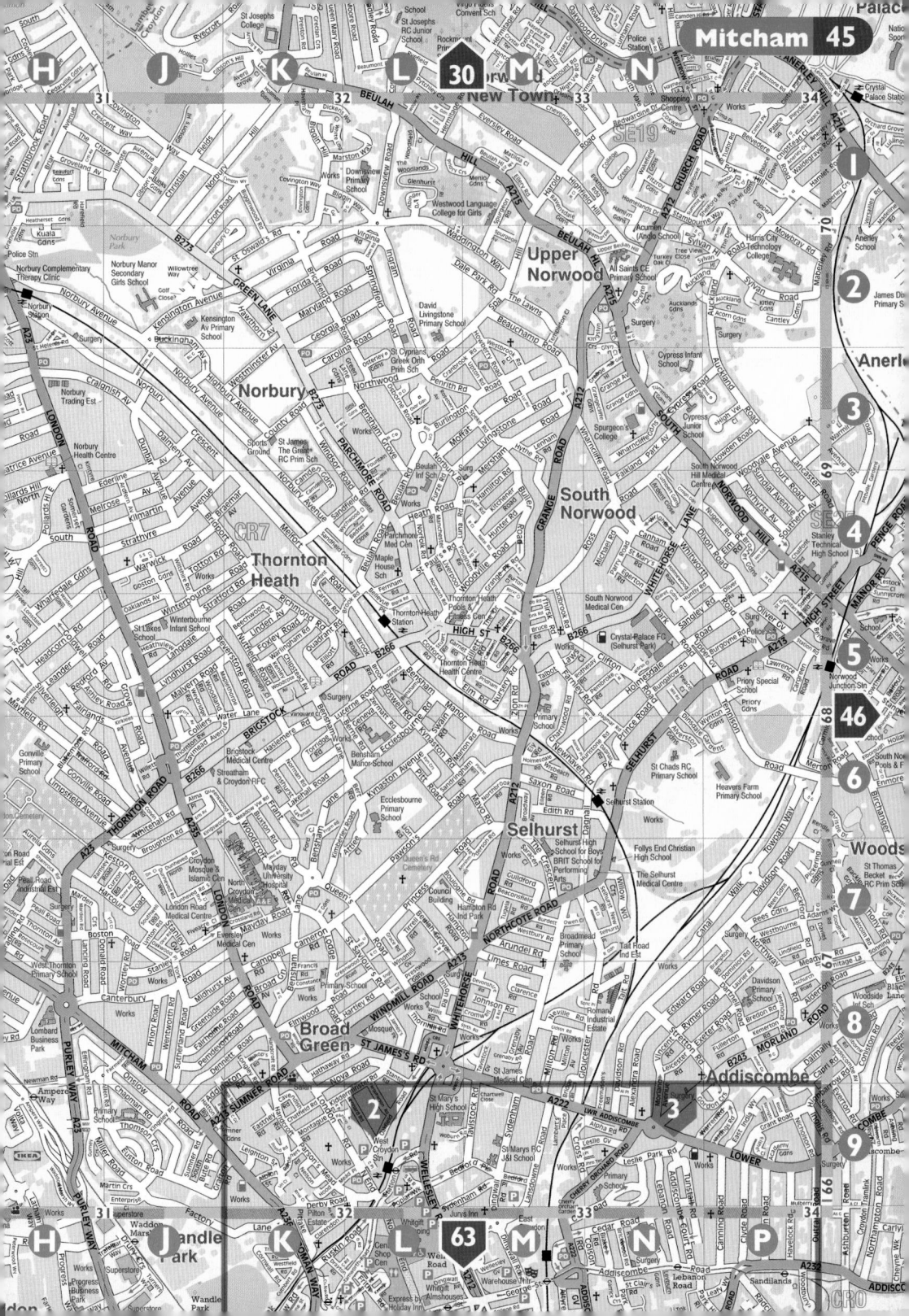

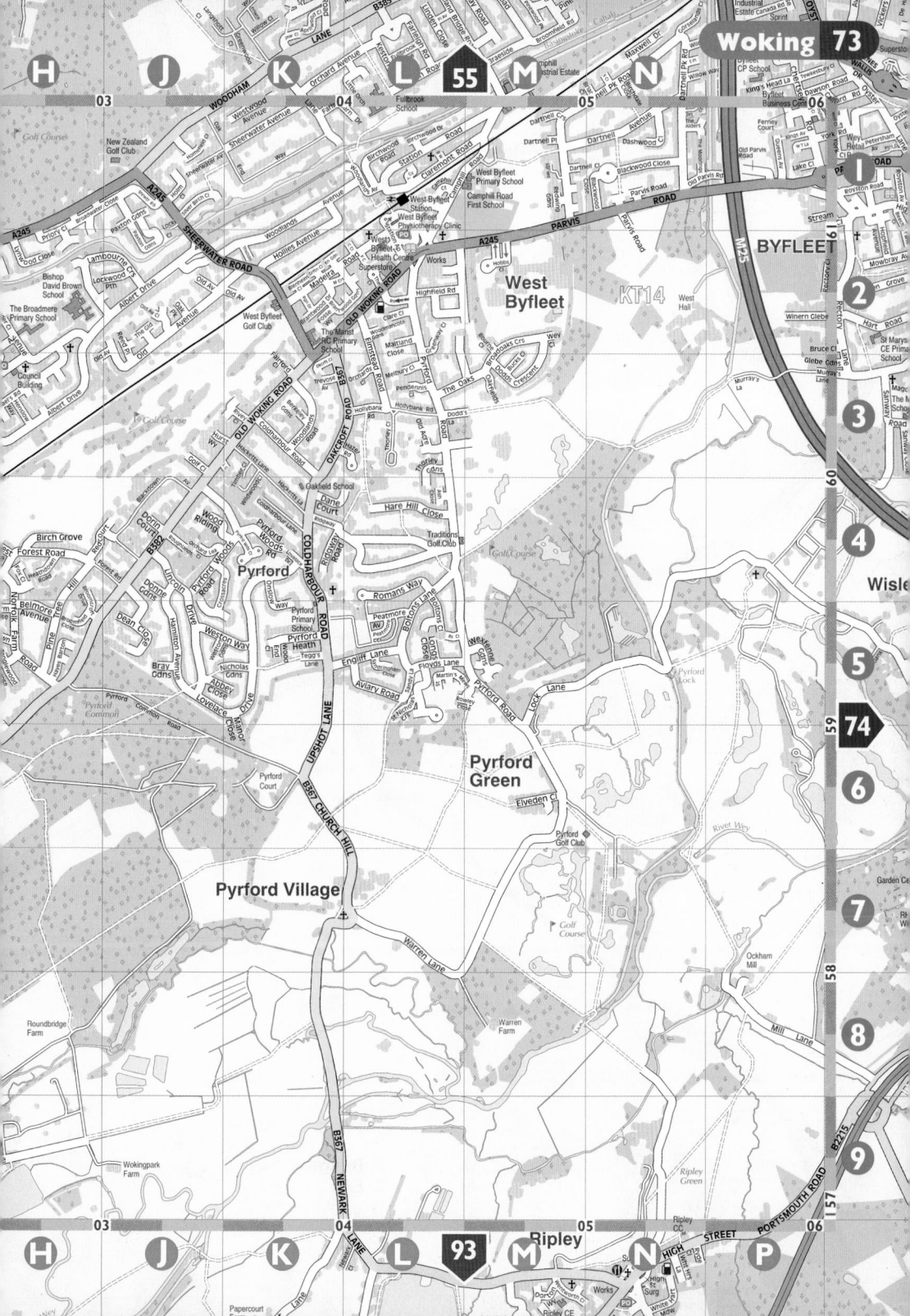

I grid square represents 500 metres

H J K L 65 M

38 39 40 41

Broom Dam Crescent

Crs

Clive Crs

Milne

Park East

Uvedale

Cator Ct

Cator Crs

Drive

Wrenches

High House Farm

Homestead Way

Fairchildes Avenue

Watch Crs

King Henry's Drive

Featherbed Lane

Fairchildes Primary School

Addington High School

Sheepbarn Lane

Jewels Hill

Mouchette

Keith Park Crescent

Crick

Harbury Drive

Saltbox Hill

Fickleshole

Park Road

Blackman's Lane

Skid Hill

Skid Hill Farm

A233

MAIN

Court

P

Fairleigh Ct

Scotshall Lane

Fairchildes Road

Victoria Cottages

Lane

Christie

Oaklands Junior School

Holt Wood

Church Lane

Heslers Road

Oaklands Infant

Whallock Close

Highfield

Ledgers Farm

Heslers Hill

Court Road

84

Beech

Hillingdale

Saltbox Close

Saltbox Road

Washpond Lane

Chelsham Road

Beddlestead Lane

Chelsham Court Farm

Northeads Lane

Bramble Close

Maxfield Road

Melody Road

Timbertop Road

Bryant

Ledgers Road

Broom Bank

Beech Farm Road

Worms Heath

ROAD

Beddlestead Farm

Limpet Hall Lane

Crosweys

Beech Farm

Shelton Av Way

Crossways

Beddles Lane

Ship

Surgery

H J K L 103 M N P

38 39 40 41

Cheverells Farm

I 61 2 3 60 4 59 5 6 7 58 8 9 57

H   J   K   L   M   N

45   46   47   48

Halstead Place School

Pratts Bottom Primary School

Norsted Manor Farm

Port Hill

Budgin's

Fairtrough Farm

Mace Farm

Fairtrough Road

Garden Centre

Park Farm

Hostye Farm

Perrys Lane

Washneys Road

Stubbs Hill

Rushmore Hill

The Washneys

Lane

Snag Lane

Mace Lane

Newyears Wood

New Years Lane

Bromley Kent County

Cemetery

Angas Home

Cacket's Farm

Raradle's

Single's Cross Lane

Pound Lane

Blueberry Farm

Harrow Rd

Cudham

Cacket's Lane

Cacket's Lane

Lett's Green

Shelleys

Blueberry Lane

The Nower

Cheventn

Shelleys Lane

Burlings

†

North Downs Way

Lane South

New Barn Farm

Horns Green

Burlings

Burlings Lane

†

St. Katharines Knockholt CE Primary School

Knockholt

Sundridge Lane

Lord Chetham's Lane

The Mount

Main Road

Sundridge Hill Farm

Stonelngs Lane

Sundridge Hill

TN14

Brasted Lane

Cudham Erith

Scott's Lodge

Shootfield

Bombers Farm

Bombers Lane

Newlands Avenue

The Nower

Horns Downs Way

Brasted Hill

Brasted

Brasted Hill Farm

Cudham Grange

Grays Road

Silversted Lane

Silversted Lane

Combe Bank Farm

1   2   3   4   5   6   7   8   9

61   60   59   58   57

45   46   47   48

I grid square represents 500 metres

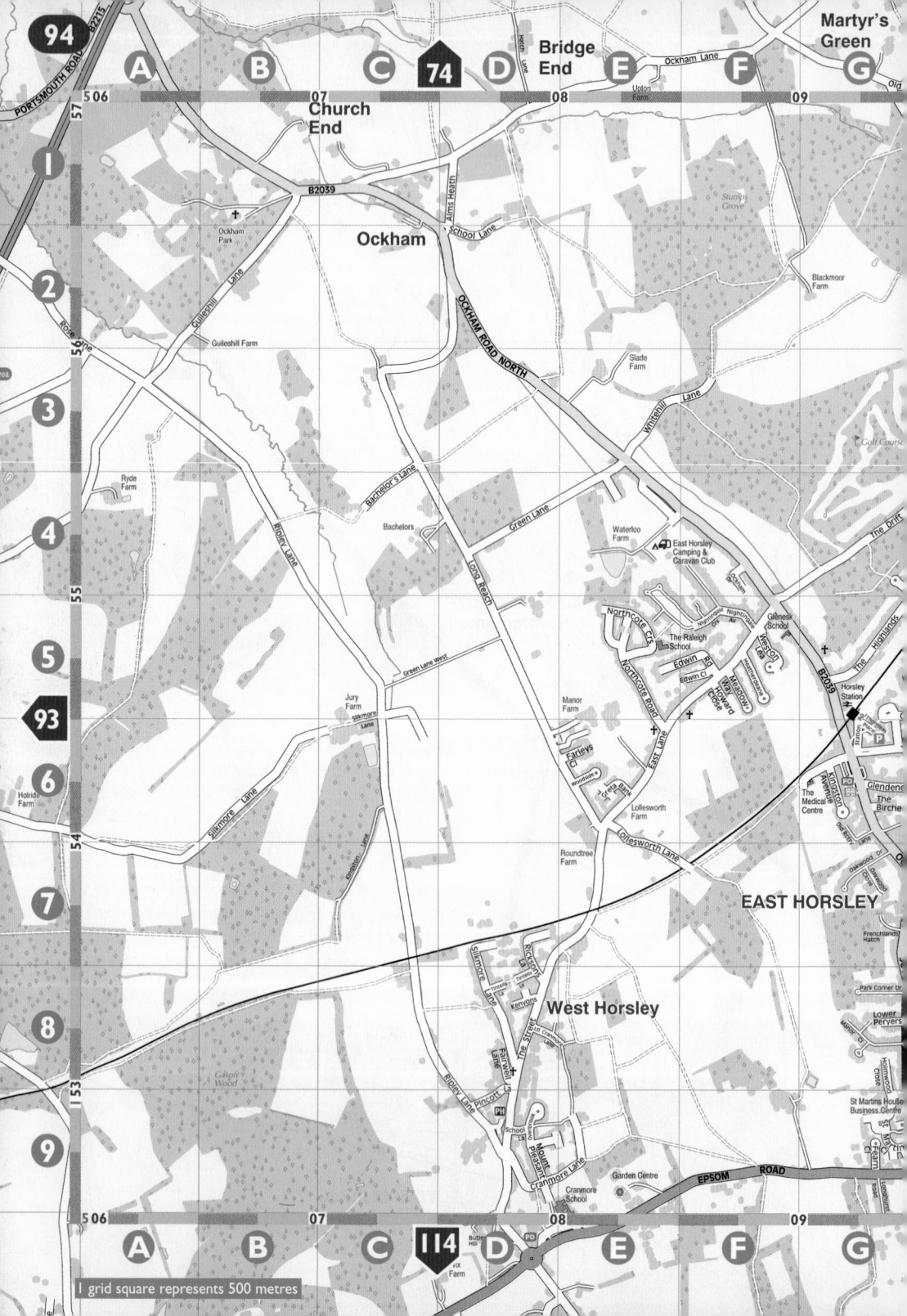

A   B   C   90   D   E   F   G

PIRBRIGHT

Henleypark Farm

492   93   94   95

Henley
Park

1

A324

PIRBRIGHT ROAD

52

School Lane

Hunts Hill Road

Longerend Farm

Whipley
Manor

ALDERSHOT ROAD

A323

Frog Grove Lane

A3

Normandy

Anchor
Close

Wells
Lane

2

Normandy Common Ln

GUILDFORD ROAD

Wyke CRP
School

A323

Normandy
Common

Mariner's
Drive

Glaziers Lane

Surgery

Willey Green

Bilse Lane

Frog Grove Lane

Wyke

51

Westwood Lane

Walden
Cottages

Nanscombe Cl

GU3

Wood S

3

Glaziers Lane

White Hart Lane

Oa

Russellplace Farm

Balles Lane

4

Westwood
Place

Broadstreet Comm

Wanborough
Station

The Paddocks

5

Breech Lane

Lane

Stado Ct   Christmaspie Av

Orchard Close

Orchard Way

Christmaspie Av

Cull's Road

Willow View

Flexford

Wanborough
Youth House

Wildfield Copse

109

50

Flexford Road

Christmaspie

West Flexford Lane

6

Green Lane East

Westwood Lane

Greencut
Copse

7

49

Wanborough
Wood

Wanborough
Manor

Flexford Ho

East Flexford Lane

8

Wanborough

Manor
Farm

Wanborough Hill

B3000

9

48

A31

Hog's   Back

PUTTENHAM HILL

B3000

3300

Puttenham

492   93   94   95

A   B   C   130   D   E   F   G

Seale

Munday's

Dark La

Puttenham
CE Infant
School

The   Street

School Lane

Puttenham
Golf Club

North Downs Way

PUTTENHAM

Cemetery

Lascombe La

1 grid square represents 500 metres

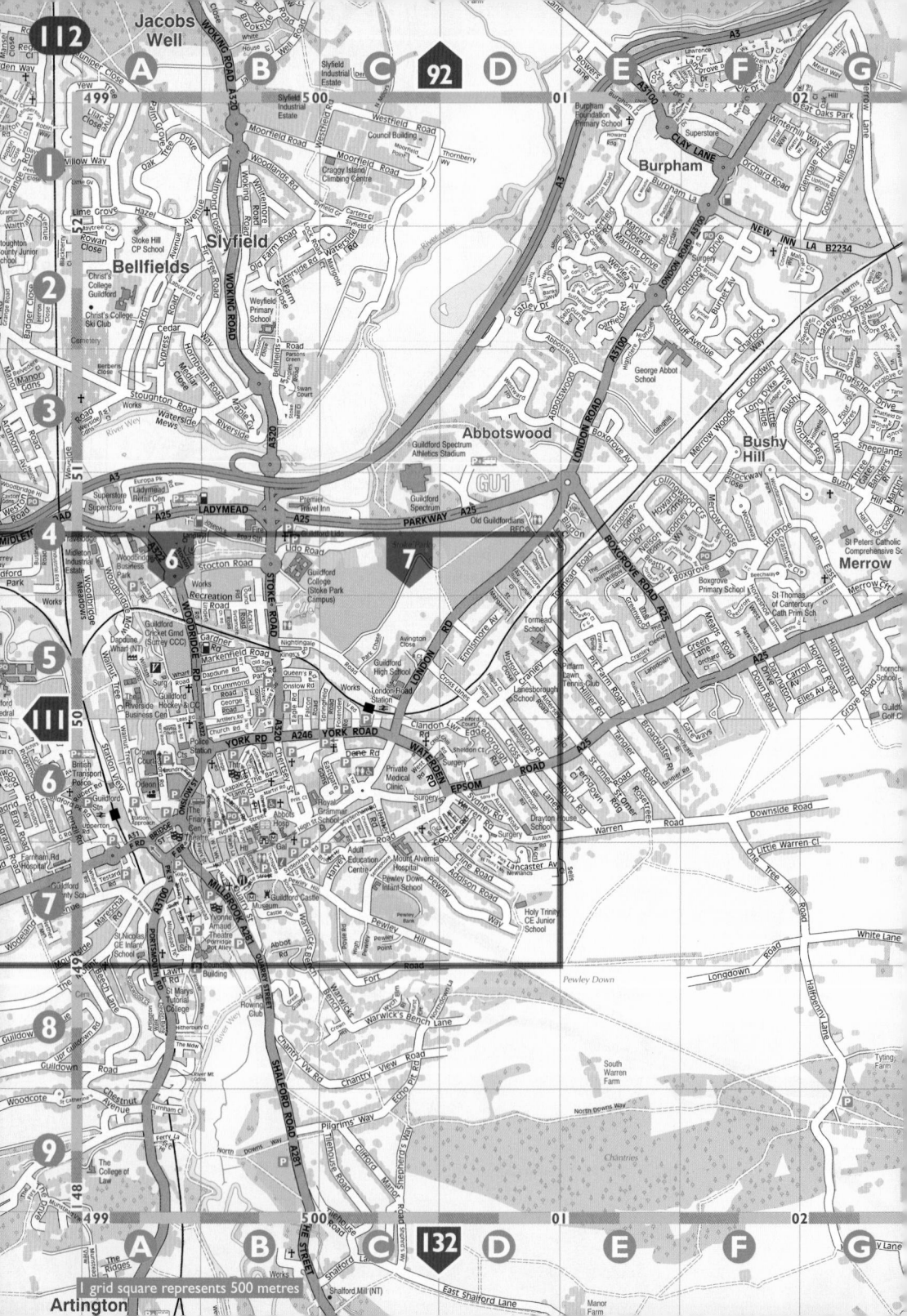

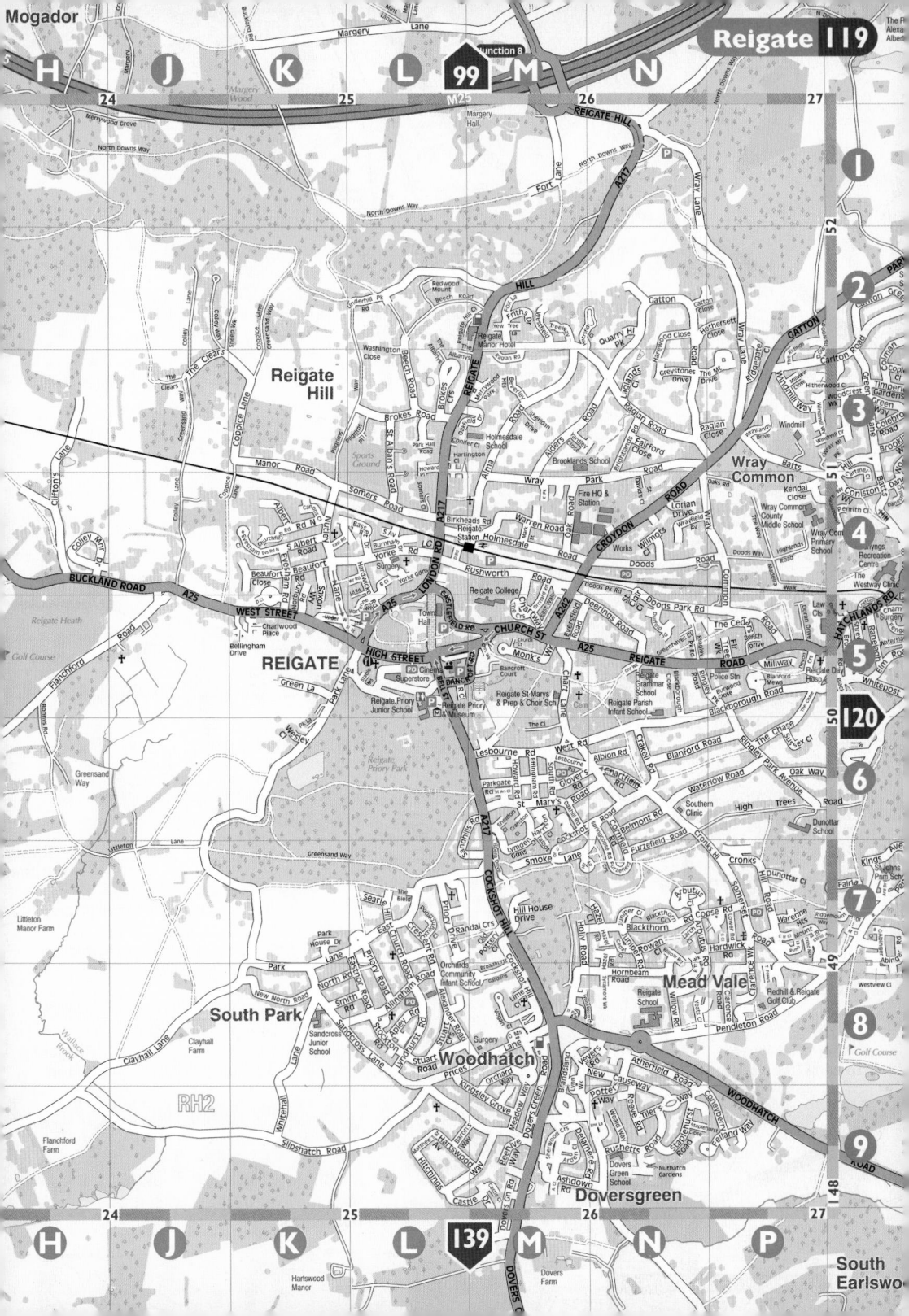

H J K L **105** M
45 46 48
52
51
50
49
48

H J K L **145** M N P

French Street
Tle Chart
The Philippines
Emmetts Garden (NT)
Emmetts Road
Horns Hill
Hosey Common Lane
Greensand Way
Scords Wood
Toy's Hill
Ide Hill
Mapleton Road
Chartwell (NT)
Chartwell
P
Scords Lane
Froghole
Froghole Lane
Puddledock Lane
Bardogs Farm
Greensand Way
Puddledock
am Hill
Tan House
Obriss Farm
Crockham Grange
Boons Park
Coakham Farm
Mapleton Road
Mapleton
Toy's Hill
Chittenden
B2042 GREEN LANE
Pootings
Roodlands Lane
Holmwood Place
Pootings Road
B269
Broxham Manor
Four Elms
Styles Croke
Roodlands Farm
Fumace H Farm
Hillcrest
Four Elms Primary School
Mowshurst
B2027
Broxham House
FOUR ELMS ROAD
Pike Fields Lane
Swan Lane

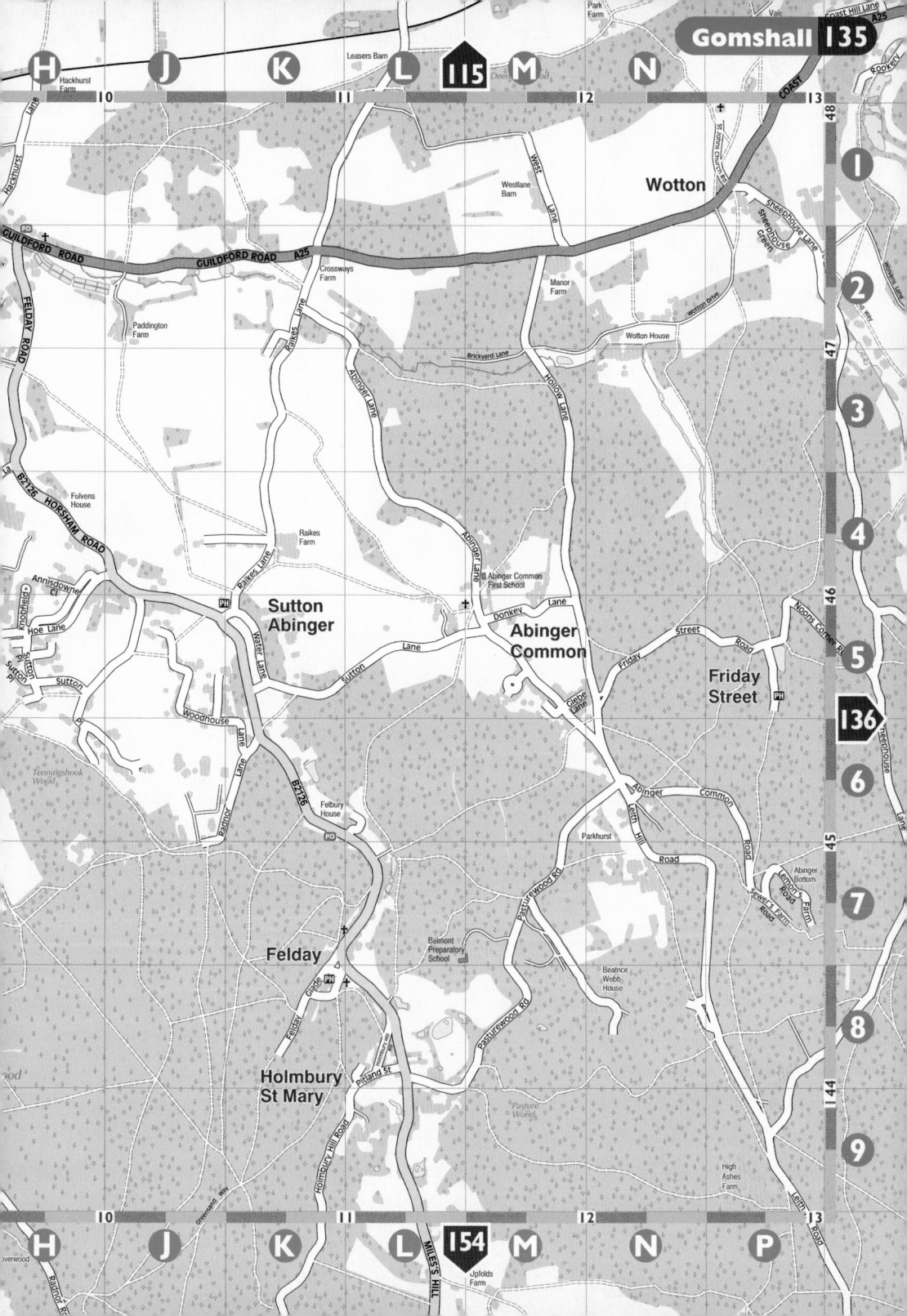

136

A25

COAST HILL

Coast Hill Lane

Greenland Way

The Hildens

Knoll Road

Ridgeway Brymer

Home Farm

Coldharbour

Pope Ct

Fir's Cr

Drive

A · B · C · **116** · D · E · F · G

48 5 13 · 14 · 15 · 16

1

Sheephouse Lane

Sheephouse Green

Vale Fields

The Rookery

Bury Hill House

47

2

Greensand Way

Wolvens Lane

Westlees Farm

Chadhurst Farm

Holmwo Farm

Logmore Green

3

Squire's Farm

Logmore Lane

Bear Hill

Redlands Farm

Redlands Lane

46

4

Noons Corner Road

Squire's Great Wood

Collickmoor Farm

Abinger Forest

Coldharbour Lane

Redlands Wood

5

135

Broadmoor

45

6

Sheephouse Lane

Wolvens Lane

Shoollands

Abinger Bottom

Leith Hill Rd

Sewer's Lane

7

Greensand Way

The Duke's Warren

Coldharbour Common

Redlands

44

8

Wotton Common

Coldharbour

Wolvens Lane

Westcott Lane

Anstie Grange

9

Leith Hill Road

Abinger Road

Broomehall Road

PO PH

Anstie Lane

The Landslip

Kitlands

Minnickfold

5 13 · 14 · 15 · 16

A · B · C · **155** · D · E · F · G · RH5

Tower Hill

Starhurst School

Stonebridge

Bushbury

The Redlands Primary School

North Holmwood

North Holmwood CC

Blackbrook

Roothill

Great Brockhamhurst

Red Lane

Mid Holmwood

Mill Works

Holmwood Common

Mid Holmwood

Brook Lodge Farm

Lodge Farm

Hawesrew Farm

Lodge

138

Oakdale

Folly Lane

Mill Road

Brookside

South Holmwood

Holmwood Park

Ewood Farm

Westwood Common

Redlands

Petersfield Farm

Ewood Lane

Swires Farm

Holmwood Corner

Vigo Farm

Grandon Lodge

Becket Wood

Capel Leyse

Bregsell's Farm

Moorhurst Lane

Holmwood Station

Reffolds Copse

The Weald CE Primary School

117

156

Coleshill Farm

Jubilee Terrace

Four Elms

Broxham
Manor

Styx Close

Four Elms
Primary
School

125

FOUR ELMS ROAD

Hill
Court

Five Fields Lane

Furnace House
Farm

Mowshurst

B2027

Broxham
House

Prettymans Lane

Owls
Court

CLINTON LANE

B2027

Swan
Lane

Union Road

Field
Drive

Wayside
Dr

ELMS ROAD

Lockhurst
LC

Prettymans
Lane

Skinners

Lane

Skinners
Farm

Medhurst Row

Whistlers

Brasted
Lands

**How
Green**

How Green Lane

Hever Road

How Green
Farm

Hever Castle
Golf Club

River Eden

Eden Valley Walk

Cemetery

The Plat

Church Street

Golf Course

Delaware
Farm

Eden Valley Walk

TN8

Warsop
Trading
Estate

Hever Road

Polebrook
Farm

Hever Castle
and Gardens

Mead Road

HILL

B2026

Brocas
Farm

Hever

Den
Cross

Old Barn
Farm

Lydens Lane

Lydens
Farm

Eden Valley Walk

Hever
Station

Hever CE
Primary School

HARTFIELD ROAD

Roman Road

Brook Street
Farm

Hill House

Hever Lane

Hever
Warren

Lickfield Lane

Pigdown

Pigdown Lane

Shernden
Farm

Howlets
Farm

**Stick
Hill**

Wilderness
Farm

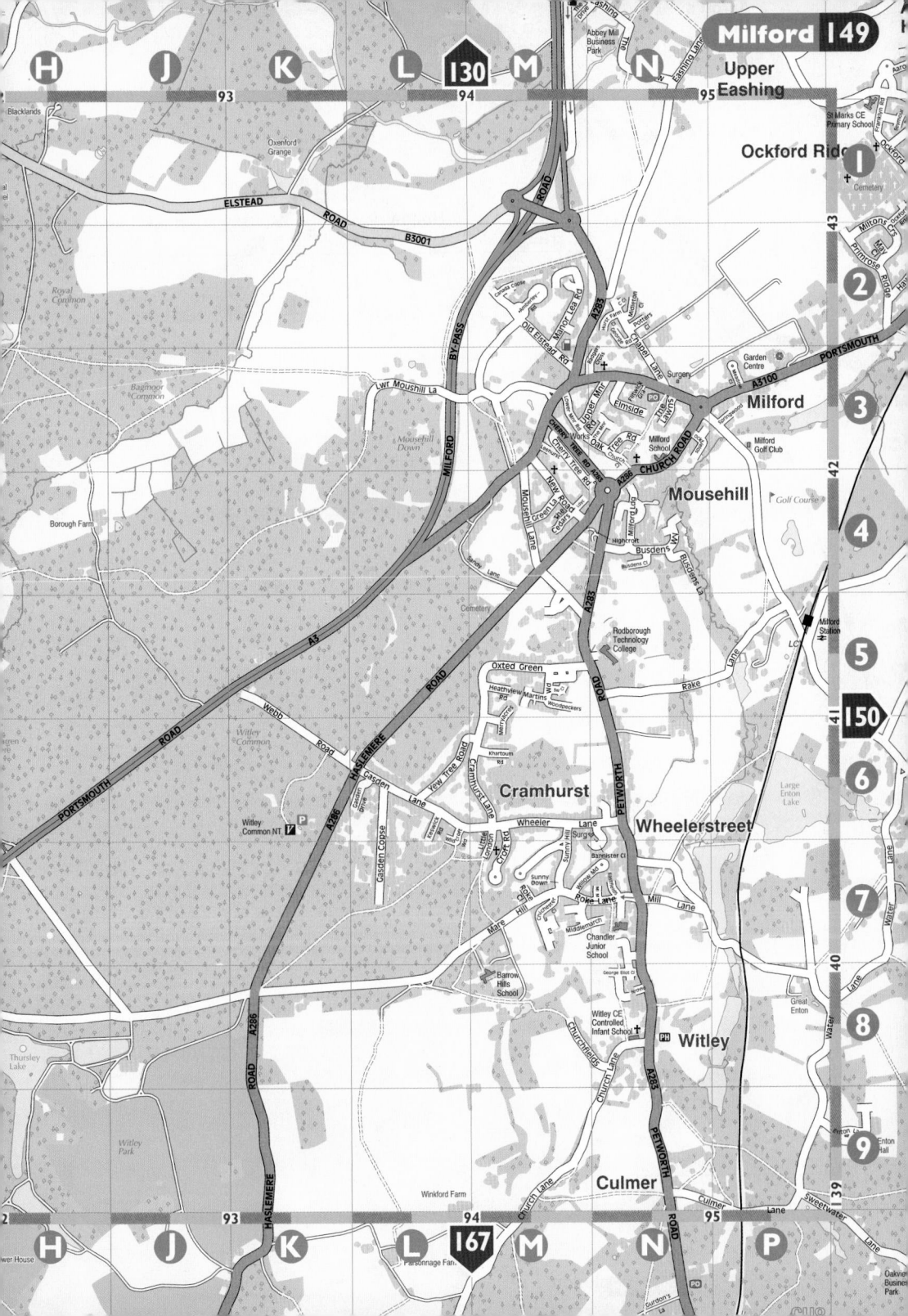

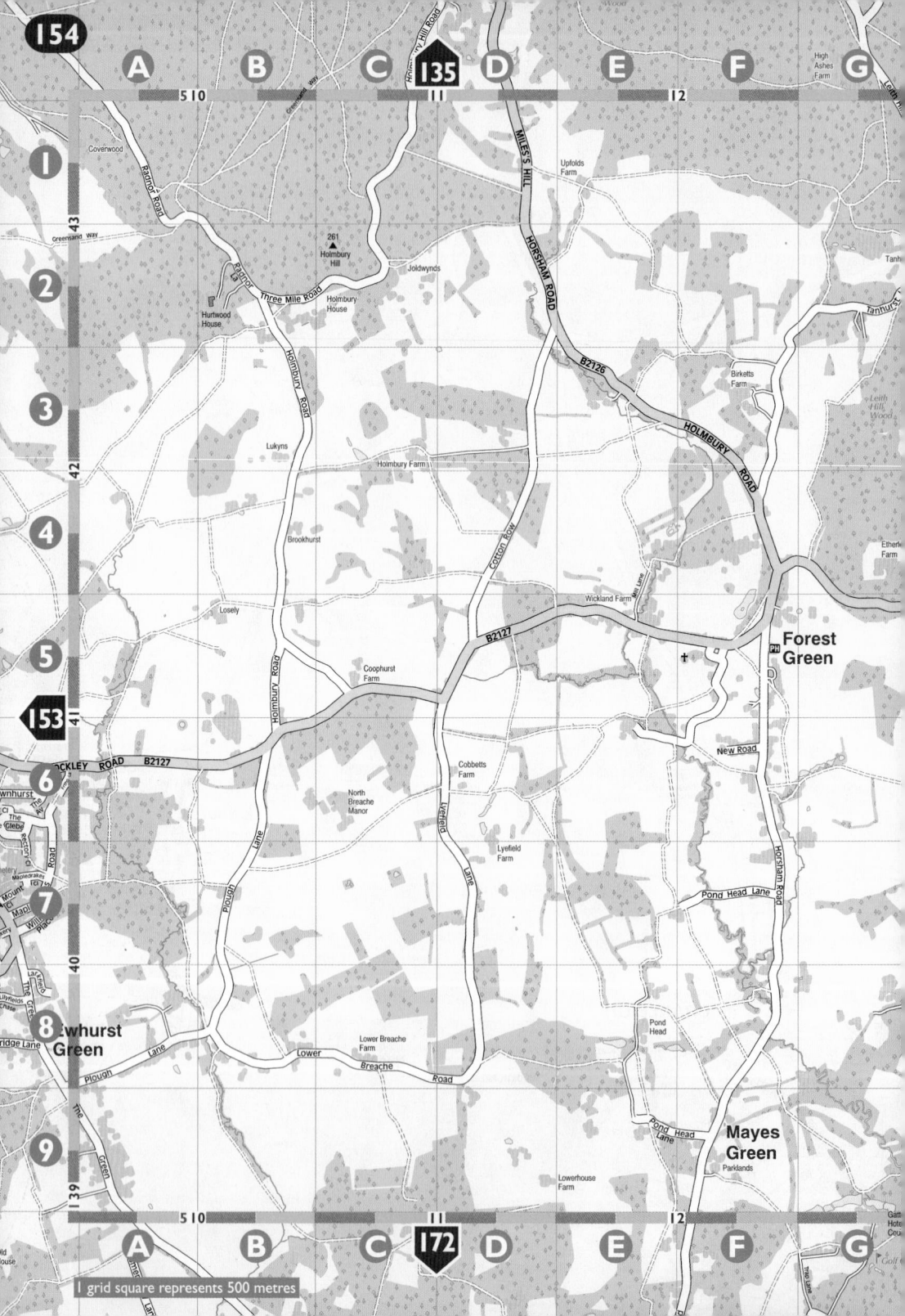

A   B   C   137   D   E   F   G

517   18   19

I

43

Moorhurst

Holmwood Station

The Weald CE Primary School
Newdigate Rd.

Beare Green

Henfold

Henfold

Gaterounds Farm

Trouts Farm

Arnolds

OCKLEY ROAD

BEAR 42 REEN ROAD

Wigmore

Wigmore

HORSHAM RD

HORSHAM ROAD

A29

A24

Works

Horsham Road

Hoyle Hill

Hoyle Farm

Seaman's Green

Thorncroft Hill

Hillhouse Farm

Trig Street

Knowle

Newdigate

Parrotite Road

Village Street

Underhill Road

Kingsland

Newdigate Endowed C Infant Scho

Winfield Gro

PH

Churc

Surger

Rusper Road

2

3

4

Riversh Lane

Horsham Road

Mizbrooks Green

Broomell's Farm

Mizbrook Farm

Peak Road

Temple Lane

Greens Farm

Tanhurst Farm

5

155

41

Youngs Farm

6

Ockley Station

Station Ap

B2126

A24

The Street

Mortimer Road

Old Ba RD

Vicarage

Lane

Scott Broadwood CE Infant School

Capel

Nursery Bake La

Aldhurst Farm

7

LANE

Woodland Drive

Coles

Bennetts Wd

The Street

Wolven Hill

Rushetts

8

Road

Grenehurst Park

Clark's Green

Temple Elfande

9

139

A24

Rusper Road

Pleystowe Farm

517   18   19

A   B   C   174   D   E   F   G

Taylors

Clock House   Clock

Parkgate

H J K L **138** M N

Becket Wood

Partridge Lane

Hales Bridge

Rickettswood Farm

Norwood

Blanks Lane

Clayhill Road

Red House

Hatchetts

Sturtwood Farm

Highworth Farm

Hornbrook Hamlet Lane

Wapecks Lane

Stanhill Court Hotel

Cudworth Lane

Burnt Oak Lane

Cudworth

Green Lane

Manor House

Partridge Lane

Burnt Oak Lane

Beam Brook

The Greenings

Breggarshouse Lane

Stan Hill

Ockley Lodge

Home Farm

Duke's Road

Cidermill Farm

Glovers Wood

Russ Hill Road

158

Russ Hill Road

Duke's Road

Duke's Road

Duke's Rd

Russ Hill

Newhouse Farm

Boothlands Farm

Charlwood La

Russ Hill

Upper Prestwood Farm

Rusper Golf Club

Melton Hall Farm

Golf Course

Ivyhouse Farm

Oaklands Park

Sussex Border Path

Chaffold's Farm

H J K L **175** M N P

Orltons

Jordans

Partridge Lane

Lower Prestwood Farm

Wood Lane

148

165

A ursley Road **B** Place **C** **D** **E** **F** **G**

Pitch Place Farm 489

39

90

91

French

1
Hyde Farm

Lower Highfield Farm

Bedford Farm

Cosford House

Heath Hall

2

Ridgeway Farm

Pitlands Farm

Bowlhead Green

Bowhe

38

Emley Farm

3

Highcomb Bottom

4

Begley Farm

Park Lane

Creedhole Farm

37

5

Boundless Copse

Witley Farm

6

Hindhead Common

Devil's Punch Bowl

High Button

Hindhead

A3 PORTSMOUTH ROAD

High Copse

7

PH

Greensand Way

The Stepping Stone School

36

8

Heather Lane

South Park Farm

135

church

9

The Royal School

Coombe Head

Grays Infant

PH

489

A **B** 90 **C** 184 **D** Weydown Common **E** 91 **F** ROAD **G**

Amesbury School

Wispers School

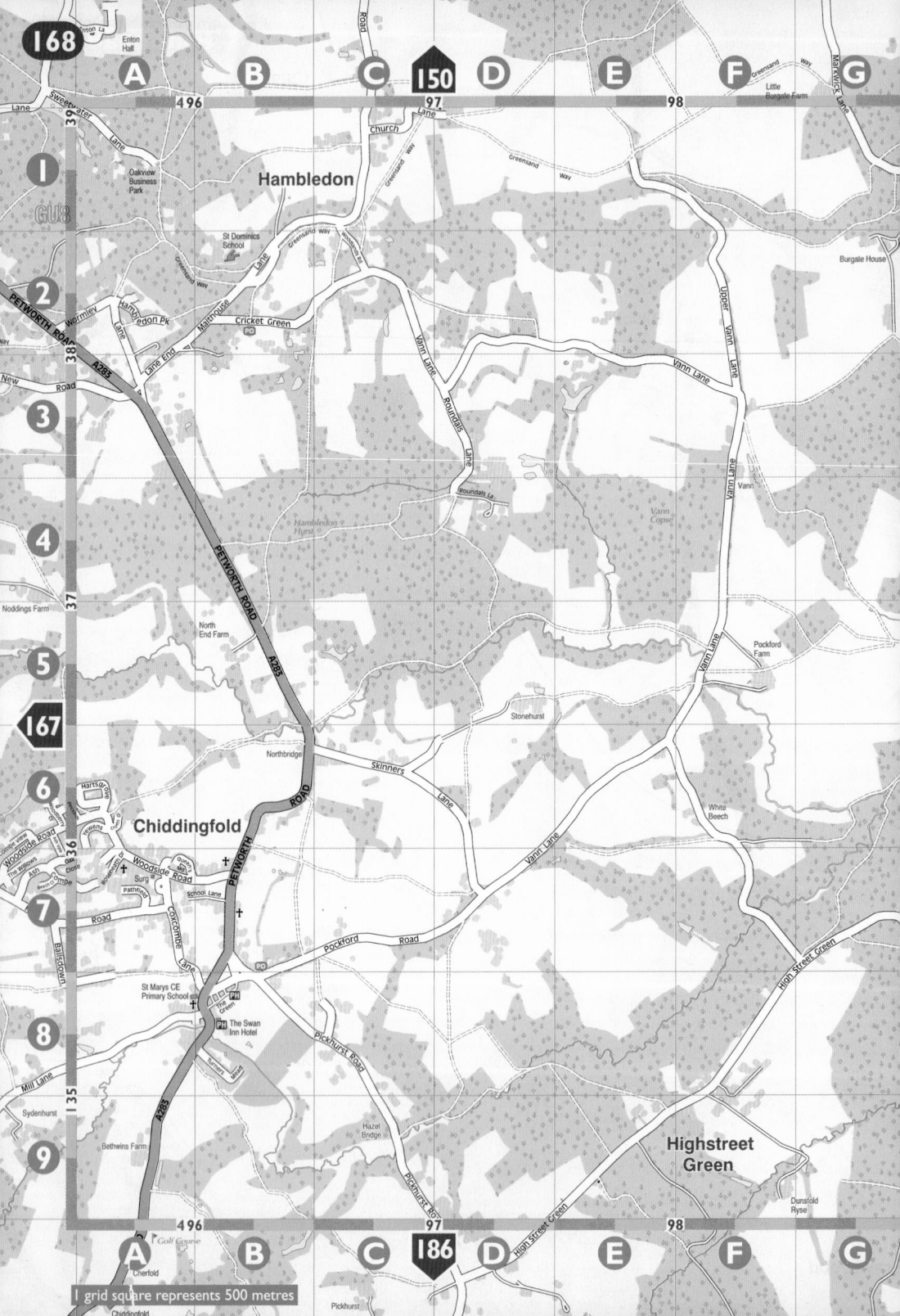

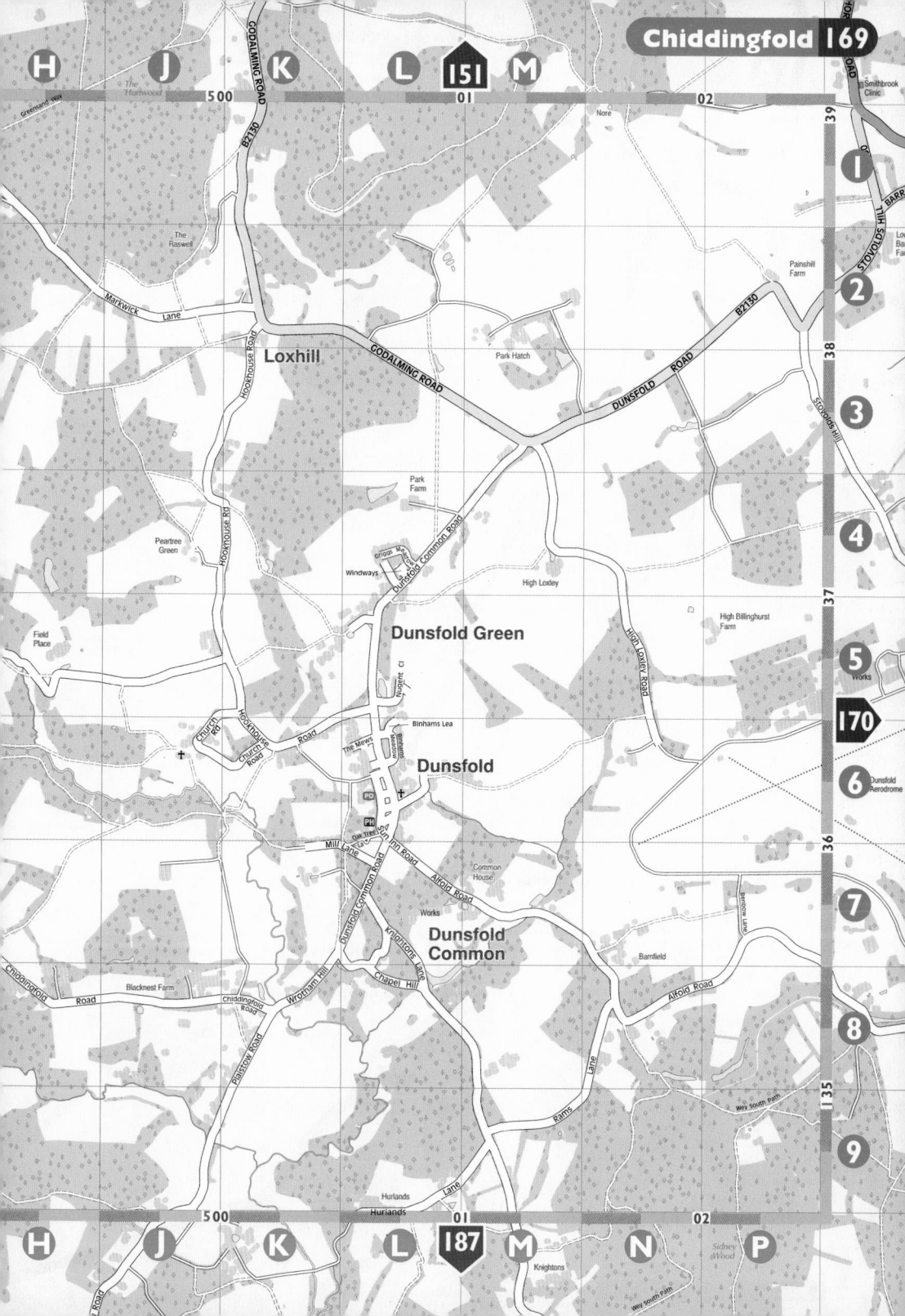

A   B   C   154   D   E   F   G

510   11   12

Pond Head Lane

MAYES Green

Old House

1

I

Somersbury Lane

39

Gat Hot Cor

Golf

2

38

Horsham Road

Froggetts Lane

Lowerhouse Farm

Walliswood Farm

Horsham Road

Standon Lane

WALLISWOOD

Church

3

Somersbury Wood

Oakfields

Oakwoo

4

37

Hillhouse Farm

Works

Smokejack Farm

Horsham Road

5

171

Broadstone Farm

Honeywood Lane

Monks

Monks Lane

6

36

Pollingfold

Pinkhurst Farm

Sussex Border Path

7

Ellen's Green

Furzen Lane

Furzen Lane

Ellens

Honeywood House

8

135

B2128

Ridge Farm

Horsham Road

9

Hermonger Lane

ox Green

Bury St Austen's

A   B   510   C   190   D   E   F   G

11   12

Sussex Border Path

Hermongers

ROWHOOK

PH

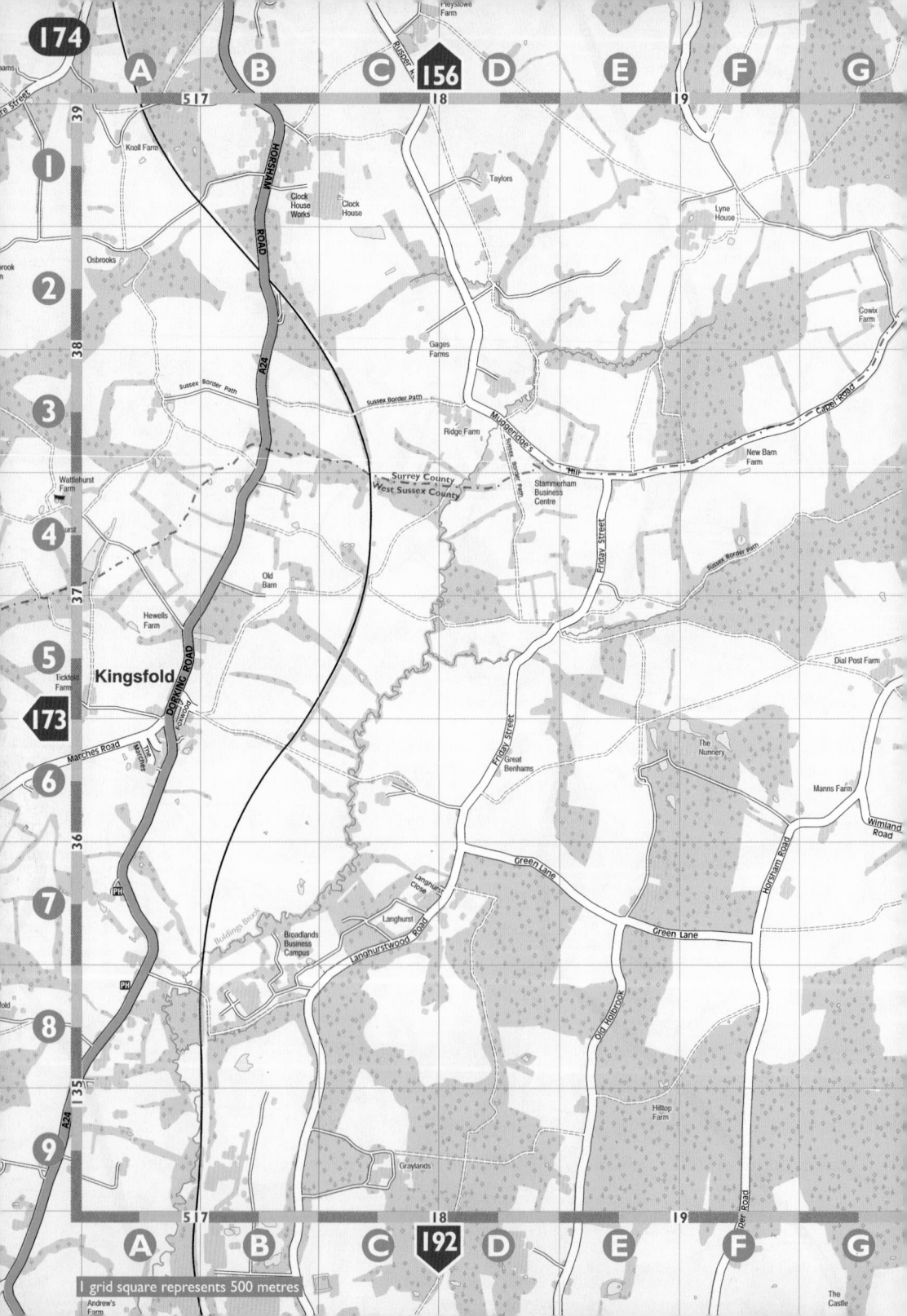

Grayswood

Trillinghurst Wood

Prestwick Farm

PITTS

West End Farm

West End Lane

Killinghurst Lane

Killinghurst

Killinghurst Lane

Imbhams Farm

Furnace Place

Holdfast

Ramsnest Common

PETWORTH

Cherfold

Chiddingfold Golf Club

Gostrode Farm

CRIPPLECRUTCH HILL

A283

Gostrode Lane

Surrey County
West Sussex County

Sussex Border Path

Chaleshurst

Lythe Hill Hotel & Spa

Ansteadbrook

PETWORTH ROAD

B2131

RODGATE LA

Dickhurst House

Broadlands

Stilland Farm

Gaston's Farm

Boxalland Farm

Surrey County
West Sussex County

Gospel Green

Fisherstreet

Eastland Farm

Tennyson's Lane

Jay's Lane

Barfold

Jay's Copse

Robson's Lane

Aldworth House

Black Down (NT)

Robson's Lane

Roundhurst Farms

Roundhurst Common

Frith Wood

Greenland Farm

Upper Diddlesfold Farm

A283

167

186

H J K L M N

93 94 95

1 2 3 4 5 6 7 8 9

34 33 32 31 30

A   B   C   168   D   E   F   G

Highstreet
Green

Bethwins Farm

Hazel
Bridge

Dunsfold
Ryse

496   97   98

ROAD

Golf Course

1   Cherfold

PETWORTH

Pickhurst

Follies Farm

Chiddingfold
Golf Club

34

2

Tingley
Wood

Gostrode
Farm

3   Robins Farm   Fisher Lane

33   Picthurst Road

Gostrode
Lane

Dunsfold
Wood

Surrey County   Fisherlane
Wood

4   West Sussex County

Palmston Rd

5   Shillinglee Road   Surrey County

Shillinglee
Home Farm   West Sussex County

185   32   Shillinglee Road   East
End Farm

6   Gaston's Farm   Newhouse
Farm

Deer
Tower

Eastland Farm

7   Haymans Farm

31   The
Lake

8   Park
Mill Farm   Birchfold
Copse

Frith Wood

9   Dale's Farm

130

496   97   98

A   B   C   D   E   F   G

Mitchell Park Fa

Upper
Frithfold Farm

I grid square represents 500 metres

170

187

A B C D E F G

5 03 04 05 A281

HORSHAM ROAD

Sachel Court

Chiddingfold Common

White Lea

Springbok Farm

Rosemary Lane

Alfold

Cemetery

Rikkyo School in England

Rosemary Lane

LOXWOOD ROAD

Sunday Border Path

Pigbush Lane

The Walled Garden

Alfold Bars

Loxwood Hall

Monckton Hook

Oakhurst Lane

Old Songhurst Farm

Oakhurst Farm

Sydney Farm

B2133

GUILDFORD

Merry Hills

Merryhills Lane

Merryhills

Sussex Border

Pond Cottage

Lane

ROAD

Pond Close

Loxwood

Loxwood Primary School

Loxwood

Road

Loxwood Road

Geese Lane

Thirteenbrown View

Hogwood Rd

Wey Road

Lane

Station Road

Loxwood Farm Place

Farm Close

HIGH STREET

Works

Wey South Path

Brewhurst Mill

Wey South Path

fold Road

Chalk Lane

The Close

The Ride

Birchwood

Brewhurst Lane

B2133

The Drive

Plaistow Road

Headfoldswood Farm

Drungewick Lane

Foxbridge Farm

xbridge lf Club

Skiff Lane

Lakers Lodge

A B C D E F G

5 03 04 05

I 88

I

34

2

3

33

4

5

32

6

7

31

8

30

9

Wephurst Wood

olf Course

1 grid square represents 500 metres

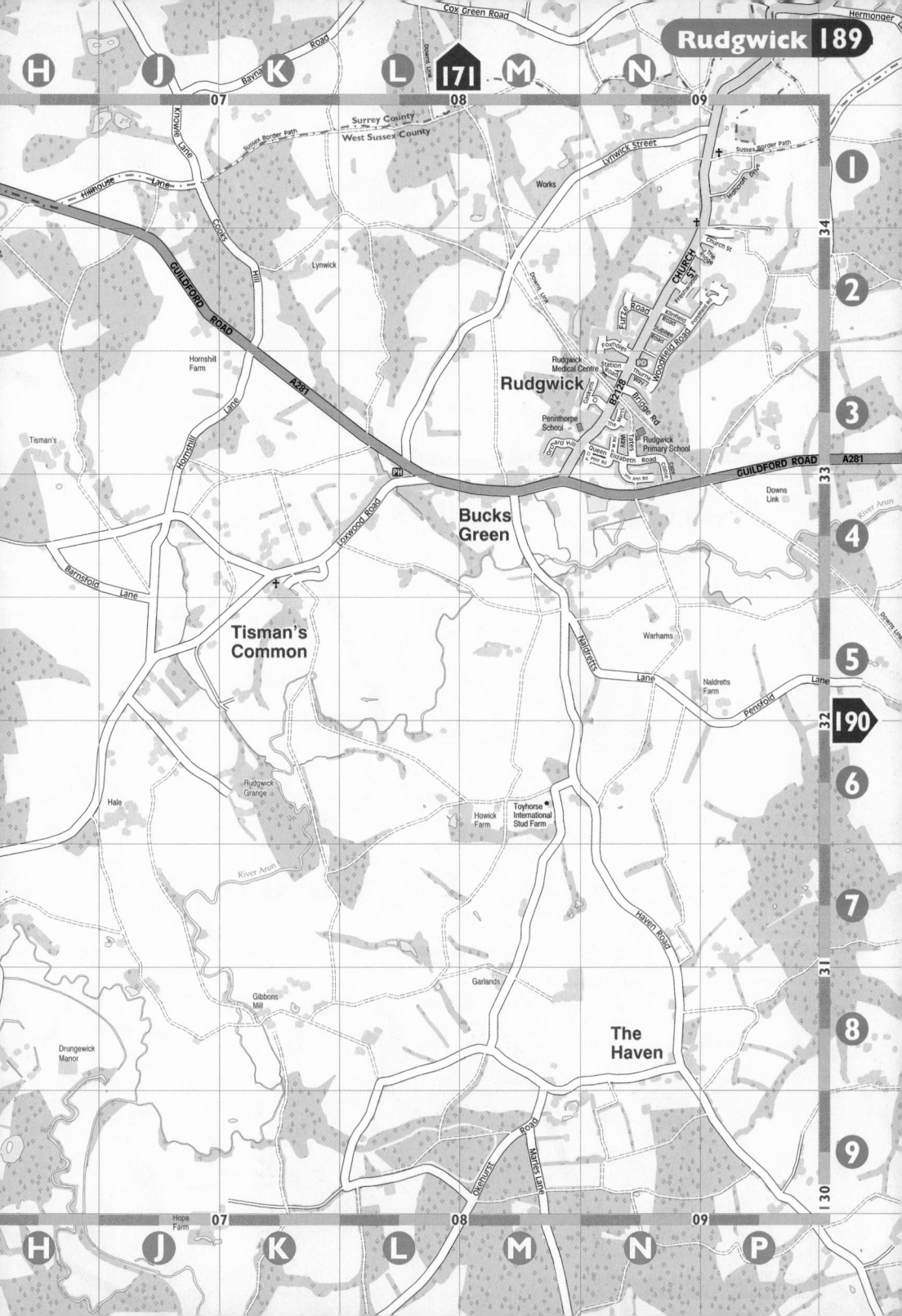

173

192

RH12

H J K L M

Warnham Lodge
Geerings
Andrew's Farm
Westbrook Hall
Sands Farm
Mayes Lane
Cider Mill Farm
Threestile Road
Knob Hill
School Lane
Station
Westons Pl
Great Daux
Warnham
Warnham CE Primary School
Freeman Rd
Lucas
Gardeners Way
Hands Way
Church St
Works
Close
PO
Farm Close
Bell Road
The Forge
PH
Friday Street
Tuggles Plat
Tillotts Lane
Byrefts Lane
Daux Hill
Strood Lane
Ends Place
Bailing Hill Farm
Warnham Court
Brookhurst Farm
Farlington School
Goosegreen
Warnham Deer Park
Strood Green
Nowhurst Lane
hurst Farm
Guildford Road
Byrefts Lane
Robin Hood Lane
Broomhall
WARNI
A281
Rapkyns
A281
Guildford Road
The Common
Park Rise
Rookwood Park
Trafalga Infant Sch
Swindon
Spencers Rd
Saxon
Alcery
Greenway School
Broadbridge Heath
Old Guildford Rd
Lawson Hunt Ind Park
PO
St Johns
Shelley Primary Sch
Swann Way
Oak Lane
Broadbridge Heath Retail Park
Cootes Avenue
Ryecroft Drive
Greenway
Mill Rd
The Plat
Greenway
Chillinghurst Wy
Kingsmead
Corsletts
Church Road
Thelton
Superstore
Guildford Rd
A281
Guildford Road
Irwin Drive
Curzon Av
Shelley Dr
Finch
A264
Broadbridge Heath Stadium
Tanbridge House School
Wickhurst Lane
River Arun
Hills Place
Meadvale
Cemetery
Arunside Prim Sch
BISHOP
Gilligan Close
Tanbridge Retail Park
Lyons Road
Lyons Farm Estate
Wellcross Grange
Pinkhurst La
hurst
A264
Old
Broadbridge Farm
Englefield
Somergate
Hills Farm
Ridgell
St Johns Catholic Prim Sch
Blackbridge Lane
Horsham CC Sports Club
Downs Lane
A264
River Arun
Granary Way
Longfield Road
Windrum Close
Parthings
Things Lane
Tower Hill
Fulfords Farm
Itchingfield Rd
PH
Rowhook Manor
BOGNOR ROAD
A29
A281
DORKING ROAD
A24
WORTHING ROAD

H J K L M N P

1 2 3 4 5 6 7 8 9

34 33 32 31 30

H J K L M

H J K L M N P

1
2
3
4
5
6
7
8
9

28 29 30

Tilgate Drive

Winchester
Oxford Rd
Salisbury Road
Constable Rd

Tilgate Drive

Tilgate Forest
Golf Centre

177

M23

Tilgate
Lake

Tilgate
Park

Tilgate Forest

M23

Oldhouse Warren

Whitely

Balcombe
Forest

Cowdray
Forest

BALCOMBE ROAD

34

B2110

Parish Lane

Mount Pleasant
Farm

Greentrees
Farm

HIGH STREET

Monks
Forest

33

Shelford Brock

Brantridge
Forest

Highbeeches
Forest

Crawley Lane

HIGH STREET

Highley
Manor

Lodgelands

Crawley Lane

32

B2110

Brantridge Forest
Farm

Redbridge
Lane

New England

Handcross Road

Great Cooper's
Corner Farm

Handcross Road

LONDON ROAD

31

BEECHES LANE

Brantridge Lane

Brantridge Park

Westup Road

Balcombe CE
Primary School

Westup
Farm

combe
tion

Newlands

30

196 Index - towns & villages

Aaron's Hill ...131 H9
Abbey Mead ...37 M7
Abbotswood ...112 D3
Abinger Common ...135 M5
Abinger Hammer ...134 G2
Acton Green ...18 B2
Addington ...64 G5
Addiscombe ...45 P8
Addlestone ...55 N4
Addlestonemoor ...55 N1
Albury ...133 N1
Albury Heath ...134 A3
Aldershot ...108 E3
Alfold ...188 C1
Alfold Bars ...188 C3
Alfold Crossways ...170 D8
Anerley ...46 A3
Ansteadbrook ...185 K5
Anthonys ...72 E1
Aperfield ...84 D6
Arford ...164 B5
Artington ...131 P1
Ascot ...34 C3
Ash ...109 J3
Ashford ...23 K7
Ashford Common ...23 N9
Ash Green ...109 N6
Ashley Park ...57 J2
Ashtead ...77 L7
Ashurst Wood ...181 K5
Ash Vale ...89 J9
Badshot Lea ...108 D8
Bagshot ...51 M6
Bagshot Heath ...51 N8
Baldwins Hill ...162 B9
Balham ...29 J3
Bandonhill ...62 F4
Banstead ...79 L5
Barford ...165 H3
Barnes ...18 F6
Barwell ...59 J6
Batt's Corner ...146 A5
Beacon Hill ...165 N4
Beare Green ...156 D2
Beaumont ...20 G4
Beckenham ...46 G3
Beddington ...62 G1
Beddington Corner ...44 C8
Bedford Park ...18 D1
Bellfields ...112 A2
Bell Green ...31 N6
Bellingham ...31 P7
Belmont ...61 L7
Benhilton ...61 M2
Berrylands ...41 M7
Berry's Green ...84 E5
Betchworth ...118 A4
Bewbush ...176 C8
Biggin Hill ...84 B5
Binscombe ...131 J5
Birch Hill ...32 E8
Birtley Green ...132 E9
Bishopsgate ...20 E7
Bisley ...71 H5
Blackbrook ...137 L3
Black Corner ...159 N8
Blackheath ...133 J4
Blacknest ...35 J4
Blackwater ...67 P4
Blackwell ...180 D1
Bletchingley ...121 M5
Blindley Heath ...142 E4
Boundstone ...127 M9
The Bourne ...127 N7
Bowlhead Green ...166 F2
Bowling Alley ...106 C6
Box Hill ...117 N3
Bracknell ...32 E4
Bramley ...132 D8
Bramshott ...182 F4
Brands Hill ...12 F5
Brasted ...105 M4
Brasted Chart ...105 M8
Brentford ...17 K4
Brentford End ...17 H4
Brewer Street ...121 L2
Brick Hill ...53 J3
Bridge End ...74 D9
Broadbridge Heath ...191 J6
Broadfield ...176 F9
Broadford ...132 A6
Broad Green ...45 K8
Broadham Green ...123 J3
Broadmoor ...136 B5
Brockham ...117 N6
Brockham Park ...138 A1
Brockley ...31 N1
Bromley ...47 P3
Bromley Park ...47 L2
Brook ...167 K2
Brook Green ...18 G1
Brooklands ...56 B7
Brookwood ...70 G9
Broomhall ...34 F8
Buchan Hill ...134 D2
Buckland ...118 E4
Bucks Green ...189 L4
Bullbrook ...33 H3
Bunce Common ...138 B3
Burgh Heath ...79 H8
Burntcommon ...93 K5
Burpham ...112 E1
Burrowhill ...53 M7
Burrows Cross ...134 D3
Burstow ...160 B5
Burwood Park ...57 J4
Busbridge ...150 F2
Bushbury ...137 N1
Bushey Mead ...43 H4
Bushy Hill ...112 F3
Byfleet ...73 P2

Camberley ...68 G1
Camelsdale ...184 B5
Cannon Hill ...43 H5
Capel ...156 C6
Carshalton ...62 A5
Carshalton Beeches ...62 B6
Carshalton on the Hill ...62 B6
Cartbridge ...92 F2
Castle Green ...71 K2
Caterham ...101 N3
Catteshall ...131 N7
Chaldon ...101 K4
Charleshill ...129 J8
Charlton ...38 E3
Charlwood ...158 C5
The Chart ...125 M1
Chattern Hill ...23 L7
Chavey Down ...33 K3
Cheam ...61 J4
Cheapside ...34 E5
Chelsham ...82 G6
Chertsey ...37 L8
Chertsey Meads ...38 A9
Chessington ...59 L5
Chiddingfold ...168 A6
Chilworth ...132 G2
Chipstead ...80 C8
Chiswick ...18 D2
Chobham ...53 K8
Christmaspie ...110 B6
Church Crookham ...106 F1
Church End ...94 B1
Church Town ...122 C2
Churt ...165 J7
Clapham Park ...29 N2
Claremont Park ...58 A6
Clark's Green ...156 B8
Claygate ...58 F5
Clock House ...80 E3
Cobham ...75 J3
Cold Ash Hill ...183 H5
Coldharbour ...136 D8
Cole Park ...25 P2
Coles Meads ...120 B2
Colgate ...193 P4
College Town ...50 A8
Collier's Wood ...43 P1
Colnbrook ...12 C6
The Common ...191 P6
Compton ...128 B4
Compton ...130 G2
Coney Hall ...65 L3
Conford ...182 C3
Coombe ...42 C1
Cooper's Hill ...21 J6
Copse Hill ...42 E1
Copthorne ...160 C9
Cottenham Park ...42 F2
Coulsdon ...80 G5
Cove ...88 A1
Cox Green ...171 P9
Cramhurst ...149 M6
Cranford ...15 J5
Cranleigh ...153 J8
Crawley ...177 H6
Crawley Down ...178 G4
Crawley Hill ...68 G3
Cricket Hill ...67 J3
Critchmere ...183 P3
Crockham Hill ...124 G4
Crondall ...106 C7
Crooked Billet ...27 N9
Crookham Village ...86 C9
Crosswater ...147 H8
Crossways ...165 H2
Crowhurst ...143 K2
Crowhurst Lane End ...122 G9
Crownpits ...150 D1
Crown Wood ...32 F7
Crowthorne ...49 J4
Croydon ...2 E5
Crystal Palace ...31 H9
Cudham ...85 H4
Cudworth ...157 K4
Culmer ...149 N9
Darby Green ...12 A7
Datchet Common ...12 A7
Dawesgreen ...138 C2
Deepcut ...89 L1
Deepdene ...117 K7
Denbies ...116 G6
Dippenhall ...127 H5
Dockenfield ...146 C6
Dogmersfield ...86 A9
Domewood ...161 J7
Donkey Town ...70 D2
Dora's Green ...106 G9
Dorking ...117 J8
Dormansland ...162 G5
Dormans Park ...162 D5
Doversgreen ...119 M9
Down Park ...179 H2
Downside ...75 K8
Dulwich ...30 G5
Dulwich Village ...30 F3
Dunsfold ...169 L6
Dunsfold Common ...169 L7
Dunsfold Green ...169 L5
Earl's Court ...19 L3
Earlsfield ...28 F4
Earlswood ...120 B7
Eashing ...130 G8
East Bedfont ...23 L5
East Clandon ...114 A2
East Dulwich ...31 H1
East Ewell ...61 H8
East Green ...126 C7
East Grinstead ...180 D1
Easthampstead ...32 D5
East Horsley ...94 F7
East Molesey ...40 C6
East Sheen ...27 J1

Edenbridge ...144 E3
Eden Park ...46 F5
Effingham ...95 M7
Egham ...21 M9
Egham Hythe ...22 A9
Egham Wick ...35 M1
Ellen's Green ...171 P7
Elm Corner ...74 C8
Elmers End ...46 D4
Elstead ...148 E1
Elvetham ...86 E2
Elvetham Heath ...86 E3
Englefield Green ...35 P1
Enton Green ...150 A6
Epsom ...78 A3
Esher ...58 C3
Eversley ...48 D9
Eversley Centre ...48 B9
Eversley Cross ...48 D9
Ewell ...60 E7
Ewhurst ...153 N6
Ewhurst Green ...153 P8
Ewshot ...106 C6
Fairlands ...111 K2
Fairmile ...75 P1
Farleigh ...82 E3
Farleigh Court ...82 G3
Farley Green ...134 A6
Farnborough ...88 C5
Farnborough Green ...88 E2
Farnborough Park ...88 F4
Farnborough Street ...88 E2
Farncombe ...131 K5
Farnham ...5 E4
Faygate ...193 K1
Felbridge ...161 N8
Felcourt ...162 B4
Felday ...135 K7
Feltham ...24 C5
Felthamhill ...23 P9
Fernhill ...159 P5
Fetcham ...96 D3
Fickleshole ...83 L3
Field Common ...39 P8
Finchampstead ...48 B6
Fisherstreet ...185 N7
Fleet ...86 G6
Flexford ...110 D5
Folly Hill ...107 L3
Force Green ...105 J4
Forestdale ...64 E7
Forest Green ...154 F5
Forest Hill ...31 L4
Four Elms ...125 L9
Fox Corner ...91 J5
Fox Lane ...68 E7
Fredley ...97 H9
French Street ...125 K1
Frensham ...146 E5
Friday Street ...135 P5
Frimley ...68 E7
Frimley Green ...69 H9
Frimley Ridge ...69 J5
Frith Hill ...131 K7
Froghole ...125 H3
Frogmore ...67 M2
Fulham ...19 H5
Furnace Green ...177 K7
Furnace Wood ...161 K9
Furzedown ...29 L7
Gadbrook ...118 B9
Gatton ...100 B8
Giggshill ...40 C8
Givons Grove ...97 K5
Godalming ...131 M9
Godstone ...122 B2
Goldworth Park ...71 N5
Gomshall ...134 E2
Goodley Stock ...124 F1
Gossops Green ...176 E6
Grafham ...151 P4
Grayshott ...165 L8
Grayswood ...185 H1
Great Bookham ...96 B6
Great Burgh ...78 G6
Great Hollands ...32 A7
Green Cross ...165 L2
Griggs Green ...182 C6
Grove Park ...18 B6
Guildford ...6 E7
Guildford Park ...6 D1
Hackbridge ...62 D1
Hale ...107 P9
Ham ...26 C6
Hambledon ...168 B1
Hammer ...183 M5
Hammer Bottom ...183 L5
Hammersmith ...18 F2
Hammerwood ...163 N9
Hamm Moor ...55 P3
Hampton ...40 B2
Hampton Hill ...25 K7
Hampton Wick ...41 H2
Hamsey Green ...82 C4
Hanworth ...24 G8
Hanworth ...32 C8
Harlington ...14 D4
Harmans Water ...32 F5
Harmondsworth ...13 N4
Hascombe ...151 K8
Haslemere ...184 E4
Hatton ...14 G3
Hatton Hill ...52 D3
The Haven ...189 N1
Hawk's Hill ...96 F4
Hawley ...68 A5
Hawley Lane ...68 B9
Haxted ...144 D5
Hayes ...47 P8
Headley ...96 A6
Headley ...164 A6
Headley Down ...164 E7
Hearn ...164 E4

Heath End ...107 P7
Heatherside ...69 K4
Heathlands ...49 K1
Herne Hill ...30 D2
Hersham ...57 L4
Heston ...15 P5
Hever ...145 N7
High Curley ...51 N9
Highstreet Green ...168 E9
Hill Park ...104 F3
Hinchley Wood ...58 F2
Hindhead ...164 G7
Hoe ...134 F5
Hog Hatch ...107 K8
Holland ...123 N4
Holloway Hill ...150 D2
Holmbury St Mary ...135 K8
Holmethorpe ...120 D5
Holmwood Corner ...137 K7
Holt Pound ...127 H9
Honor Oak ...31 L2
Honor Oak Park ...31 M2
Hook ...59 L4
Hook Heath ...71 P9
Hookwood ...158 F2
Hooley ...100 C2
Horley ...140 D8
Horne ...141 P8
Horns Green ...85 J6
Horsell ...10 B1
Horton ...12 E8
Hosey Hill ...125 M3
Hounslow ...16 A7
Hounslow West ...15 M8
How Green ...145 P3
Hurst Green ...123 L3
Hurst Park ...40 C3
Hurtmore ...130 G6
Hydestile ...150 D6
Hythe End ...21 N6
Ifield ...176 D3
Ifield Green ...176 D3
Ifieldwood ...176 A2
Ifold ...187 P7
Irons Bottom ...139 L4
Isleworth ...17 H8
Jacobs Well ...92 A9
Kenley ...81 M5
Kensington ...19 L1
Kew ...17 M5
Kingfield ...72 C9
Kingsfold ...174 A5
Kingsley Green ...184 C8
Kingston upon Thames ...8 D2
Kingston Vale ...27 P6
Kingswood ...99 K3
Knaphill ...71 J7
Knight's Hill ...30 D4
Knockholt ...85 L6
Knowle Green ...22 E8
Knowle Hill ...35 P8
Laker's Green ...170 C7
Laleham ...37 N4
Laleham Burway ...37 M6
Lambs Green ...175 L5
Lampton ...16 B6
Lane End ...146 C6
Langley ...12 D1
Langley Green ...176 E1
Langley Vale ...78 B9
Leatherhead ...96 E1
Leigh ...138 E3
Lett's Green ...85 K5
Lightwater ...52 C9
Limpsfield ...103 M7
Limpsfield Chart ...124 D2
Limpsfield Common ...123 P1
Linchmere ...183 K7
Lingfield ...143 K9
Lingfield Common ...143 K7
Liphook ...182 D7
Little Bookham ...95 N5
Littlefield Common ...91 H9
Littlehaven ...192 B7
Little Heath ...75 D5
Little Sandhurst ...49 L7
Littleton ...131 N2
Littleton Common ...38 D1
Littlewick ...71 M5
Little Woodcote ...62 G9
Logmore Green ...136 B3
Longcross ...53 P2
Long Ditton ...41 H9
Longford ...13 M6
Lordshill Common ...132 G9
Lower Ashtead ...77 J8
Lower Bourne ...128 A7
Lower Feltham ...23 P5
Lower Green ...58 B1
Lower Halliford ...38 F8
Lower Kingswood ...99 L6
Lower Sunbury ...39 J4
Lower Sydenham ...31 P5
Lowfield Heath ...159 J7
Loxhill ...169 K3
Loxwood ...188 B6
Lucas Green ...70 D4
Luxted ...84 E3
Maidenbower ...177 M7
Malden Rushett ...77 H1
Manor Royal ...176 G1
Margery ...99 L9
Marley Heights ...184 A9
Marlpit Hill ...144 F1
Marsh Green ...144 F8
Martin's Heron ...33 J4
Martyr's Green ...74 C9
Maybury ...11 J3
Mayes Green ...154 F9
Mayford ...92 A3

May's Green ...75 H9
Mead Vale ...119 N8
Meath Green ...139 P8
Medhurst Row ...145 M3
Merle Common ...123 N7
Merrow ...112 G4
Merstham ...100 D8
Merton ...43 L3
Merton Park ...43 K3
Mickleham ...97 J8
Middle Bourne ...127 N6
Mid Holmwood ...137 H5
Milford ...149 P3
Millbridge ...146 G3
Mill Lane ...106 A5
Mimbridge ...71 P2
Mitcham ...44 C4
Mogador ...99 H9
Monks Orchard ...46 E6
Montgomery Lines ...108 E2
Moorhouse Bank ...104 E8
Moor Park ...128 D4
Morden ...43 L5
Morden Park ...43 J7
Mortlake ...18 A7
Motspur Park ...43 H2
Mount Hermon ...10 C7
Mousehill ...149 N4
Mowshurst ...145 J3
Mugswell ...99 M5
Mytchett ...88 G4
Mytchett Place ...89 K5
Naldretswood ...138 G6
Nash ...65 P5
Netherne on the Hill ...100 F2
New Addington ...65 K6
New Beckenham ...31 M9
Newchapel ...161 M3
Newdigate ...156 F3
New Haw ...55 N6
Newlands Corner ...113 M7
New Malden ...42 D4
Newtown ...182 E8
Norbiton ...9 H4
Norbury ...45 K3
Nork ...79 H5
Norley Common ...133 H8
Norney ...130 D3
Normandy ...130 E7
North Ascot ...33 L3
North Camp ...88 D9
North Cheam ...61 H2
North End ...162 A8
North Feltham ...24 C1
Northgate ...177 J3
North Holmwood ...137 H3
North Hyde ...15 N2
North Looe ...78 G2
North Sheen ...17 P7
North Town ...108 G4
Norwood Green ...16 A2
Norwood Hill ...158 B1
Norwood New Town ...30 F9
Nutcombe ...165 N9
Nutfield ...121 H5
Oakhill ...192 E4
Oakwoodhill ...172 G4
Oatlands Park ...56 G3
Ockford Ridge ...149 P1
Ockham ...94 A2
Ockley ...155 L7
Old Coulsdon ...81 K9
Old Malden ...42 B8
Old Windsor ...20 G2
Old Woking ...72 F9
Onslow Village ...111 L7
Osterley ...16 C5
Ottershaw ...54 C4
Outwood ...141 L5
Owlsmoor ...49 P7
Oxshott ...76 C2
Oxted ...103 K9
Pachesham Park ...76 G5
Pains Hill ...123 M5
Palmers Cross ...151 P6
Park Barn ...111 L4
Parkgate ...138 B9
Park Langley ...47 J7
Park Street ...190 D7
Parsons Green ...19 L7
Passfield ...182 C1
Paynes Green ...173 L4
Pease Pottage ...194 D3
Peaslake ...134 F7
Peasmarsh ...132 A4
Penge ...46 C1
Peper Harow ...130 C8
Petersham ...26 D3
Pirbright ...90 F5
Pitch Place ...91 M9
Pitch Place ...148 B9
Pixham ...117 J4
Plaistow ...187 L8
Pondtail ...87 K7
Pootings ...125 J7
Pot Common ...148 D2
Pound Hill ...177 M3
Povey Cross ...158 F3
Poyle ...13 J6
Prey Heath ...91 P3
Priestwood ...32 A3
Puddledock ...125 L4
Purley ...81 J1
Putney ...28 A1
Putney Heath ...27 P3
Putney Vale ...27 M6
Puttenham ...110 B9
Pyle Hill ...92 B5
Pyrford ...73 K4
Pyrford Green ...73 M6
Pyrford Village ...73 J7
Rafborough ...88 A4

Ramsnest Common 185 N3
Ranmore Common 116 C4
Rapkyns 191 H6
Ravenswood Village
  Settlement 49 J2
Raynes Park 42 C4
Redhill 120 C3
Reigate 119 K5
Reigate Hill 119 K3
Richings Park 13 J1
Richmond 26 D1
Richmond Hill 26 D2
Ridge Green 120 C8
The Ridges 48 F5
Ripley 93 M1
The Rise 34 E2
Roehampton 27 L1
Roffey 192 F5
Rosehill 43 M9
Rose Hill 116 C7
Rotten Green 86 D2
Roundshaw 63 H5
Rowhook 190 F1
Rowledge 146 C1
Rowly 152 E6
Row Town 55 K5
Rudgwick 188 M3
Runfold 128 E2
Rushmoor 147 M5
Rushmore Hill 85 N2
Rusper 175 H4
Russell Hill 63 H8
Russ Hill 137 P7
Rydens 57 L1
Rydeshill 111 K3
St George's Hill 56 E7
St Helier 43 N9
Saint Hill 180 C7
St Johns 71 N8
St Margarets 26 B2
Salfords 140 D4
Sanderstead 64 A9
Sandhills 167 L2
Sandhurst 49 M8
Sands End 19 N6
The Sands 128 G3
Sandy Cross 129 H1
Scotswood 34 D9
Seale 129 K1
Seething Wells 41 H7
Selhurst 45 M6
Selsdon 64 C8
Send 92 C4

Send Grove 92 F6
Send Marsh 93 K3
Shackleford 130 D6
Shalford 132 D3
Shamley Green 133 J8
Sheerwater 72 C2
Sheets Heath 70 F8
Shellwood Cross 138 C5
Shepherd's Hill 184 D4
Shepperton 38 C7
Shepperton Green 38 C5
Shere 114 C9
Shipley Bridge 160 A6
Shirley 64 C1
Shortfield Common 146 E2
Shortheath 127 M7
Shortlands 47 L4
Shottermill 185 P4
Shrubs Hill 35 J7
Sidlow 139 M3
Sipson 14 B3
Slinfold 190 E7
Slyfield 112 B2
Smallfield 160 B2
South Ascot 34 A7
South Beddington 62 F5
South Croydon 63 K5
South Earlswood 140 A1
South Farnborough 88 F6
Southfields 28 D4
Southgate 176 C7
South Godstone 122 F9
South Holmwood 137 H7
South Kensington 19 N3
South Merstham 120 F1
South Norwood 45 M4
South Nutfield 120 C7
South Park 119 J8
South Street 84 D8
South Wimbledon 28 F8
Southwood 87 M4
Spitals Cross 144 G2
Spreakley 146 E4
Spring Grove 16 D6
Spring Park 64 C1
Staines 22 C7
Stanwell 22 D2
Stanwell Moor 22 D2
Stoke D'Abernon 75 N4
Stonebridge 137 K1
Stonehill 54 C5
Stoneleigh 60 D4
Stonequarry 162 F9

Stoughton 111 P2
Strawberry Hill 25 L6
Streatham 29 P8
Streatham Hill 29 P4
Streatham Park 29 M7
Streatham Vale 44 D1
Strood Green 191 J4
Stroude 36 D3
Summerstown 28 G5
Sunbury 38 G2
Sunbury Common 39 H1
Sunningdale 34 G6
Sunninghill 34 D6
Sunnymeads 12 C9
Sunnyside 180 D5
Surbiton 41 K9
Sutton 12 G3
Sutton 61 L4
Sutton Abinger 135 K5
Sutton Green 92 D5
Sydenham 31 L8
Tadworth 98 G2
Tandridge 122 G4
Tatsfield 84 B9
Teddington 25 L9
Thames Ditton 40 G8
Thorncombe Street 151 H5
Thornton Heath 45 K4
Thorpe 36 G4
Thorpe Green 36 E5
Thorpe Lea 36 G1
Three Bridges 177 J4
Thursley 168 D8
Tilford 147 N1
Tilford Common 147 L3
Tilford Reeds 147 L1
Tilgate 176 G8
Tilgate Forest Row 194 F5
Tinsley Green 159 M8
Tisman's Common 189 K5
Titsey 104 A5
Tittenhurst 34 G5
Tolworth 41 N9
Tongham 109 H8
Tooting 29 J8
Tooting Graveney 28 G8
Tower Hill 117 H9
Toy's Hill 125 N5
Troy Town 124 D9
Trumpsgreen 36 A7
Tuesley 150 B4
Tulse Hill 30 C4
Turners Hill 179 H7

Twickenham 25 M4
Tyler's Green 122 B1
Tyrrell's Wood 97 N4
Up Green 86 C2
Upper Eashing 130 C9
Upper Elmers End 46 F6
Upper Hale 107 M8
Upper Halliford 38 F5
Upper Ifold 187 M3
Upper Norwood 45 M2
Upper Shirley 64 C5
Upper Sydenham 31 H7
Upper Tooting 29 H6
Valley End 52 C4
The Village 20 A6
Virginia Water 36 A4
Waddon 62 C1
Walham Green 19 L6
Wallington 62 C4
Walliswood 172 F2
Walton-on-Thames 39 J9
Walton on the Hill 98 D4
Wanborough 110 B8
Wandle Park 2 A4
Wandsworth 19 L9
Warlingham 82 D7
Warnham 191 M2
Warren Corner 106 C7
Warwick Wold 101 J9
Wasp Green 141 L6
Waterside 143 M6
Weatherhill 141 J9
The Wells 77 M3
West Barnes 42 C6
West Bedfont 23 J3
West Brompton 19 M4
Westbrook 131 J8
West Byfleet 73 M2
West Clandon 93 M9
Westcott 116 B8
West Drayton 13 P1
West Dulwich 30 E5
West End 57 P4
West End 70 F3
West End 146 C4
Westerham 105 H7
West Ewell 60 B5
Westfield 92 D2
West Green 176 F4
West Heath 88 A2
West Hill 28 B3
West Horsley 94 D8
Westhumble 116 G2

West Kensington 19 H3
West Molesey 39 P5
West Norwood 30 D7
Weston Green 40 E9
West Wickham 47 K9
Weybourne 108 B8
Weybridge 56 C3
Wheelerstreet 149 N6
Whitebushes 140 D1
Whiteley Village 57 H7
Whitton 25 K2
Whyteleafe 81 P7
Wick Hill 32 E1
Wick Hill 48 E3
Wildridings 32 B5
Willey Green 110 D2
Wimbledon 28 B8
Wimble Hill 126 E3
Windlesham 52 B5
Winkfield Row 33 J1
Wisley 74 A4
Witley 149 N8
Woking 11 F4
Woldingham 102 G3
Woldingham
  Garden Village 102 F1
Woners 132 G6
Woodbridge Hill 111 N3
Woodcote 62 G9
Woodcote 78 B5
Woodcote Green 62 D8
Woodham 55 L8
Woodhatch 119 L8
Woodlands 16 D8
Woodmansterne 79 P4
Woodside 46 A7
Wood Street Village 110 G3
Woolmer Hill 183 M3
Worcester Park 60 F1
Wormley 167 M2
Worplesdon 91 K7
Worth 177 P6
Wotton 135 N1
Wray Common 119 P3
Wraysbury 21 L2
Wrecclesham 127 K7
The Wrythe 62 A1
Wyke 109 P5
Yateley 67 H2
York Town 68 C5

USING THE STREET INDEX

Street names are listed alphabetically. Each street name is followed by its postal town or area locality, the Postcode District, the page number, and the reference to the square in which the name is found.

Standard index entries are shown as follows:

Aaron's Hl *GODL* GU7 * **131** J9

Street names and selected addresses not shown on the map due to scale restrictions are shown in the index with an asterisk:

Abbeville Ms *CLAP* SW4 * **29** N1

GENERAL ABBREVIATIONS

ACC ....ACCESS	CTYD ......COURTYARD	HLS ....HILLS	MWY ......MOTORWAY	SE ......SOUTH EAST
ALY ....ALLEY	CUTT ......CUTTINGS	HO ....HOUSE	N ....NORTH	SER ....SERVICE AREA
AP ....APPROACH	CV ....COVE	HOL ....HOLLOW	NE ....NORTH EAST	SH ....SHORE
AR ....ARCADE	CYN ....CANYON	HOSP ......HOSPITAL	NW ......NORTH WEST	SHOP ......SHOPPING
ASS ......ASSOCIATION	DEPT ......DEPARTMENT	HRB ......HARBOUR	O/P ......OVERPASS	SKWY ......SKYWAY
AV ....AVENUE	DL ....DALE	HTH ....HEATH	OFF ....OFFICE	SMT ......SUMMIT
BCH ....BEACH	DM ....DAM	HTS ......HEIGHTS	ORCH ......ORCHARD	SOC ......SOCIETY
BLDS ......BUILDINGS	DR ....DRIVE	HVN ....HAVEN	OV ....OVAL	SP ......SPUR
BND ....BEND	DRO ......DROVE	HWY ......HIGHWAY	PAL ......PALACE	SPR ......SPRING
BNK ....BANK	DRY ......DRIVEWAY	IMP ......IMPERIAL	PAS ......PASSAGE	SQ ......SQUARE
BR ....BRIDGE	DWGS ....DWELLINGS	IN ....INLET	PAV ......PAVILION	ST ......STREET
BRK ....BROOK	E ....EAST	IND EST ...INDUSTRIAL ESTATE	PDE ......PARADE	STN ......STATION
BTM ....BOTTOM	EMB ....EMBANKMENT	INF ......INFIRMARY	PH ......PUBLIC HOUSE	STR ......STREAM
BUS ......BUSINESS	EMBY ......EMBASSY	INFO ....INFORMATION	PK ....PARK	STRD ......STRAND
BVD ......BOULEVARD	ESP ......ESPLANADE	INT ....INTERCHANGE	PKWY ......PARKWAY	SW ......SOUTH WEST
BY ....BYPASS	EST ......ESTATE	IS ....ISLAND	PL ....PLACE	TDG ......TRADING
CATH ......CATHEDRAL	EX ......EXCHANGE	JCT ......JUNCTION	PLN ......PLAIN	TER ......TERRACE
CEM ......CEMETERY	EXPY ......EXPRESSWAY	JTY ......JETTY	PLNS ......PLAINS	THWY ....THROUGHWAY
CEN ......CENTRE	EXT ......EXTENSION	KG ....KING	PLZ ......PLAZA	TNL ......TUNNEL
CFT ....CROFT	F/O ......FLYOVER	KNL ......KNOLL	POL ....POLICE STATION	TOLL ......TOLLWAY
CH ....CHURCH	FC ....FOOTBALL CLUB	L ....LAKE	PR ....PRINCE	TPK ......TURNPIKE
CHA ....CHASE	FK ....FORK	LA ....LANE	PREC ......PRECINCT	TR ....TRACK
CHYD ....CHURCHYARD	FLD ......FIELD	LDG ......LODGE	PREP ....PREPARATORY	TRL ......TRAIL
CIR ....CIRCLE	FLDS ......FIELDS	LGT ......LIGHT	PRIM ......PRIMARY	TWR ......TOWER
CIRC ......CIRCUS	FLS ......FALLS	LK ....LOCK	PROM ....PROMENADE	U/P ......UNDERPASS
CL ....CLOSE	FM ....FARM	LKS ......LAKES	PRS ......PRINCESS	UNI ......UNIVERSITY
CLFS ......CLIFFS	FT ....FORT	LNDG ......LANDING	PRT ....PORT	UPR ......UPPER
CMP ....CAMP	FTS ......FLATS	LTL ......LITTLE	PT ....POINT	V ....VALE
CNR ......CORNER	FWY ......FREEWAY	LWR ......LOWER	PTH ......PATH	VA ......VALLEY
CO ....COUNTY	FY ....FERRY	MAG ....MAGISTRATE	PZ ......PIAZZA	VIAD ......VIADUCT
COLL ......COLLEGE	GA ....GATE	MAN ......MANSIONS	QD ......QUADRANT	VIL ....VILLA
COM ......COMMON	GAL ......GALLERY	MD ....MEAD	QU ....QUEEN	VIS ......VISTA
COMM ....COMMISSION	GDN ......GARDEN	MDW ......MEADOWS	QY ....QUAY	VLG ......VILLAGE
CON ......CONVENT	GDNS ......GARDENS	MEM ......MEMORIAL	R ....RIVER	VLS ......VILLAS
COT ......COTTAGE	GLD ......GLADE	MI ....MILL	RBT ....ROUNDABOUT	VW ....VIEW
COTS ....COTTAGES	GLN ......GLEN	MKT ......MARKET	RD ....ROAD	W ....WEST
CP ....CAPE	GN ....GREEN	MKTS ......MARKETS	RDG ......RIDGE	WD ....WOOD
CPS ....COPSE	GND ......GROUND	ML ....MALL	REP ......REPUBLIC	WHF ......WHARF
CR ....CREEK	GRA ......GRANGE	MNR ......MANOR	RES ......RESERVOIR	WK ....WALK
CREM ..CREMATORIUM	GRG ......GARAGE	MS ....MEWS	RFC ...RUGBY FOOTBALL CLUB	WKS ......WALKS
CRS ......CRESCENT	GT ....GREAT	MSN ......MISSION	RI ....RISE	WLS ......WELLS
CSWY ......CAUSEWAY	GTWY ......GATEWAY	MT ....MOUNT	RP ....RAMP	WY ....WAY
CT ....COURT	GV ....GROVE	MTN ......MOUNTAIN	RW ....ROW	YD ....YARD
CTRL ......CENTRAL	HGR ......HIGHER	MTS ......MOUNTAINS	S ....SOUTH	YHA ....YOUTH HOSTEL
CTS ......COURTS	HL ....HILL	MUS ......MUSEUM	SCH ......SCHOOL	

198

POSTCODE TOWNS AND AREA ABBREVIATIONS

ACT Acton
ADL/WDHM Addlestone/Woodham
ALDT Aldershot
ASC Ascot
ASHF Ashford (Surrey)
ASHTD Ashtead
ASHV Ash Vale
BAGS Bagshot
BAL Balham
BARN Barnes
BECK Beckenham
BELMT Belmont
BF/WBF Byfleet/West Byfleet
BFOR Bracknell Forest/Windlesham
BH/WHM Biggin Hill/Westerham
BIL Billingshurst
BLKW Blackwater
BMLY Bromley
BNFD Binfield
BNSTD Banstead
BOR Bordon
BRAK Bracknell
BRKHM/BTCW Brockham/Betchworth
BROCKY Brockley
BRXN/ST Brixton north/Stockwell
BRXS/STRHM Brixton south/Streatham Hill
BRYLDS Berrylands
BTFD Brentford
BTSEA Battersea
CAR Carshalton
CAT Catford
CBLY Camberley
CHEAM Cheam
CHEL Chelsea
CHERT Chertsey
CHOB/PIR Chobham/Pirbright
CHSGTN Chessington
CHSWK Chiswick
CLAP Clapham
COB Cobham
COUL/CHIP Coulsdon/Chipstead
CRAN Cranleigh
CRAWE Crawley east
CRAWW Crawley west
CROY/NA Croydon/New Addington
CTHM Caterham
CWTH Crowthorne
DORK Dorking
DTCH/LGLY Datchet/Langley
DUL Dulwich
E/WMO/HCT East & West Molesey/Hampton Court
EA Ealing
EBED/NFELT East Bedfont/North Feltham
ECT Earl's Court
EDEN Edenbridge
EDUL East Dulwich
EGH Egham
EGRIN East Grinstead
EHSLY East Horsley
EPSOM Epsom
ESH/CLAY Esher/Claygate
EW Ewell
EWKG Wokingham east
FARN Farnborough
FELT Feltham
FLEETN Fleet north
FLEETS Fleet south
FNM Farnham
FRIM Frimley
FROW Forest Row
FSTH Forest Hill
FUL/PGN Fulham/Parsons Green
GDST Godstone
GODL Godalming
GSHT Grayshott
GT/LBKH Great Bookham/Little Bookham
GU Guildford
GUW Guildford west
HASM Haslemere
HAYES Hayes
HEST Heston
HMSMTH Hammersmith
HNHL Herne Hill
HNWL Hanwell
HOR/WEW Horton/West Ewell
HORL Horley
HORS Horsham
HPTN Hampton
HRTF Hartfield
HSLW Hounslow
HSLWW Hounslow west
HTHAIR Heathrow Airport
HTWY Hartley Wintney
HYS/HAR Hayes/Harlington
ISLW Isleworth
KENS Kensington
KUT/HW Kingston upon Thames/Hampton Wick
KUTN/CMB Kingston upon Thames north/Coombe
KWD/TDW/WH Kingswood/Tadworth/Walton on the Hill
LEW Lewisham
LHD/OX Leatherhead/Oxshott
LING Lingfield
LIPH Liphook
LTWR Lightwater
MFD/CHID Milford/Chiddingfold
MORT/ESHN Mortlake/East Sheen
MRDN Morden
MTCM Mitcham
NRWD Norwood
NWDGN Norwood Green
NWMAL New Malden
ORP Orpington
OXTED Oxted
PECK Peckham
PETW Petworth
PGE/AN Penge/Anerley
PUR/KEN Purley/Kenley
PUT/ROE Putney/Roehampton
RCH/KEW Richmond/Kew
RCHPK/HAM Richmond Park/Ham
RDKG Rural Dorking
REDH Redhill
REIG Reigate
RFNM Rural Farnham
RGUE Rural Guildford east
RGUW Rural Guildford west
RHWH Rural Haywards Heath
RPLY/SEND Ripley/Send
RSEV Rural Sevenoaks
RYNPK Raynes Park
SAND/SEL Sanderstead/Selsdon
SHB Shepherd's Bush
SHGR Shamley Green
SHPTN Shepperton
SHST Sandhurst
SKENS South Kensington
SL Slough
SNWD South Norwood
STA Staines
STRHM/NOR Streatham/Norbury
STWL/WRAY Stanwell/Wraysbury
SUN Sunbury
SURB Surbiton
SUT Sutton
SWTR Southwater
SYD Sydenham
TEDD Teddington
THDIT Thames Ditton
THHTH Thornton Heath
TOOT Tooting
TWK Twickenham
VW Virginia Water
WALW Walworth
WAND/EARL Wandsworth/Earlsfield
WARL Warlingham
WBPTN West Brompton
WDR/YW West Drayton/Yiewsley
WDSR Windsor
WEA West Ealing
WEY Weybridge
WHTN Whitton
WIM/MER Wimbledon/Merton
WKENS West Kensington
WLGTN Wallington
WNWD West Norwood
WOKN/KNAP Woking north/Knaphill
WOKS/MYFD Woking south/Mayford
WOT/HER Walton-on-Thames/Hersham
WPK Worcester Park
WWKM West Wickham
YTLY Yateley

Index - streets

1st - Alb

1

1st Av KWD/TDW/WH KT20 99 J5
2nd Av KWD/TDW/WH KT20 99 J5
3rd Av KWD/TDW/WH KT20 99 J5
4th Av KWD/TDW/WH KT20 99 J5
6th Av KWD/TDW/WH KT20 99 J5
7th Av KWD/TDW/WH KT20 99 J5
8th Av KWD/TDW/WH KT20 99 J6
9th Av KWD/TDW/WH KT20 99 J5
10th Av KWD/TDW/WH KT20 99 J6
11th Av KWD/TDW/WH KT20 99 J5
12th Av KWD/TDW/WH KT20 99 J6
13th Av KWD/TDW/WH KT20 99 J6
14th Av KWD/TDW/WH KT20 99 J6
15th Av KWD/TDW/WH KT20 99 K6
16th Av KWD/TDW/WH KT20 99 J6

A

Aaron's Hl GODL GU7 131 J9
Abbess Cl BRXS/STRHM SW2 30 C4
Abbetts La CBLY GU15 68 D5
Abbeville Ms CLAP SW4 * 29 N1
Abbeville Rd CLAP SW4 29 M2
Abbey Cha CHERT KT16 * 37 M7
Abbey Cl BRAK RG12 32 F6
WOKS/MYFD GU22 73 J5
Abbey Ct CHERT KT16 * 37 M8
Abbeydore Cl BOR GU35 164 B6
Abbey Dr STA TW18 37 N5
TOOT SW17 29 K8
Abbeyfield Cl MTCM CR4 44 A3
Abbey Gdns CHERT KT16 37 L7
HMSMTH W6 19 J4
Abbey Gn CHERT KT16 37 L7
Abbey La BECK BR3 46 G1
Abbey Ms ISLW TW7 17 H6
STA TW18 * 37 N4
Abbey Pk BECK BR3 46 G1
Abbey Pl CHERT KT16 * 37 L4
Abbey Rd CHERT KT16 37 M8
CROY/NA CR0 2 B5
SAND/SEL CR2 64 D8
SHPTN TW17 38 C9
VW GU25 36 B6
WIM/MER SW19 43 N1
WOKN/KNAP GU21 72 A6
Abbey St FNM GU9 5 G4
Abbey Wk E/WMO/HCT KT8 40 B4
Abbey Wy FARN GU14 88 E3
Abbey Wd ASC SL5 34 G8
Abbeywood ASHV GU12 * 109 K2
Abbot Cl BF/WBF KT14 55 P8
STA TW18 37 P1
Abbot Rd GU GU1 7 F7
Abbots Av HOR/WEW KT19 59 N9
Abbotsbury BRAK RG12 32 B6
Abbotsbury Ct SWTR RH13 192 D7
Abbotsbury Rd MRDN SM4 43 M5
WWKM BR4 65 M1
Abbots Cl FLEETN GU51 86 G6
GUW GU2 111 L8
Abbots Dr VW GU25 36 A5
Abbotsfield Rd
CRAWW RH11 176 A6
Abbotsford Cl
WOKS/MYFD GU22 11 H3
Abbots Gn CROY/NA CR0 64 D5
Abbots La PUR/KEN CR8 81 L5
Abbotsleigh Cl BELMT SM2 61 M6
Abbotsleigh Rd
STRHM/NOR SW16 29 M7
Abbotsmede Cl TWK TW1 25 N5
Abbots Pk BRXS/STRHM SW2 30 B4
Abbot's Ride FNM GU9 128 A5
Abbots Rd CHEAM SM3 61 J3
Abbotstone Rd
PUT/ROE SW15 18 G8
Abbots Wk CTHM CR3 102 B2
KENS W8 * 19 M1
Abbots Wy BECK BR3 46 E6
CHERT KT16 37 K8
GU GU1 113 H4
Abbotswell Rd BROCKY SE4 31 N1
Abbotswood GU GU1 112 D3
Abbotswood Cl GU GU1 112 D2
Abbotswood Dr WEY KT13 56 F8
Abbotswood Rd
STRHM/NOR SW16 29 N6
Abbott Av RYNPK SW20 43 H3
Abbott Cl HPTN TW12 24 F9
Abbotts Md
RCHPK/HAM TW10 * 26 B7
Abbotts Ri REDH RH1 120 C3
Abbotts Rd MTCM CR4 44 E5
Abbotts Tilt WOT/HER KT12 57 N2
Abelia Cl CHOB/PIR GU24 70 E2
Abercairn Rd
STRHM/NOR SW16 44 E1
Aberconway Rd MRDN SM4 43 M4
Abercorn Cl SAND/SEL CR2 82 D1
Abercorn Wy
WOKN/KNAP GU21 71 N7
Aberdare Cl WWKM BR4 65 J1
Aberdeen Rd CROY/NA CR0 63 L3
Aberdeen Ter GSHT GU26 * 165 N8
Aberfoyle Rd
STRHM/NOR SW16 44 F1
Abingdon Cl BRAK RG12 32 G6
WIM/MER SW19 28 F9
WOKN/KNAP GU21 71 P7
Abingdon Rd KENS W8 19 L1
SHST GU47 49 N9
STRHM/NOR SW16 44 G2
Abingdon Vls KENS W8 19 L1
Abinger Av BELMT SM2 60 G7
Abinger Cl CROY/NA CR0 65 J5
RDKG RH5 137 J2
WLGTN SM6 62 G4
Abinger Common Rd
RDKG RH5 135 N6
Abinger Dr NRWD SE19 45 L1
REDH RH1 120 A7
Abinger Gdns ISLW TW7 16 E8
Abinger La RDKG RH5 135 L4
Abinger Rd CHSWK W4 18 D1
RDKG RH5 155 H3
REDH RH1 120 A8
Abinger Wy RGUE GU4 92 F9
Aboyne Dr RYNPK SW20 42 E3
Aboyne Rd TOOT SW17 28 G6
Abrahams Rd CRAWW RH11 194 D1
Acacia Av BTFD TW8 17 H5
SHPTN TW17 38 C6
SHST GU47 49 P8
STWL/WRAY TW19 12 C9
WOKS/MYFD GU22 72 B9
Acacia Cl ADL/WDHM KT15 55 K8
Acacia Ct BRAK RG12 32 D4
Acacia Dr ADL/WDHM KT15 55 K9
BNSTD SM7 79 H3
CHEAM SM3 43 K9
Acacia Gdns WWKM BR4 65 J1
Acacia Gv DUL SE21 30 E5
NWMAL KT3 42 C4
Acacia Ms WDR/YW UB7 13 P4
Acacia Rd BECK BR3 46 F4
GU GU1 6 E2
HPTN TW12 25 H9
MTCM CR4 44 C3
STA TW18 22 E8
STRHM/NOR SW16 44 G2
Academy Cl CBLY GU15 50 G9
Academy Gdns CROY/NA CR0 3 K2
Academy Pl SHST GU47 68 A1
Accommodation La
WDR/YW UB7 13 N4
Accommodation Rd
CHERT KT16 54 C3
Ace Pde CHSGTN KT9 59 L2
Acer Dr CHOB/PIR GU24 70 F2
Acer Rd BH/WHM TN16 84 B5
Acfold Rd FUL/PGN SW6 19 M6
Acheulian Cl FNM GU9 127 N6
Achilles Pl WOKN/KNAP GU21 72 A6
Ackmar Rd FUL/PGN SW6 19 L6
Ackrells Md SHST GU47 49 K8
Ackroyd Rd FSTH SE23 31 L3
Acorn Cl EGRIN RH19 180 D3
HORL RH6 140 E9
HPTN TW12 25 J9
Acorn Gdns NRWD SE19 45 P2
Acorn Gv HYS/HAR UB3 15 H5
KWD/TDW/WH KT20 99 K4
WOKS/MYFD GU22 * 92 C1
Acorn Keep FNM GU9 107 P6
Acorn Rd BLKW GU17 67 M3
Acorns SWTR RH13 192 F6
The Acorns CRAWW RH11 194 E1
HORL RH6 160 C1
Acorns Wy ESH/CLAY KT10 58 C4
Acorn Wy FSTH SE23 31 L6
Acre La CAR SM5 62 C3
Acre Rd KUTN/CMB KT2 9 F1
WIM/MER SW19 28 G9
Acres Gdns
KWD/TDW/WH KT20 78 G8
Acres Platt CRAN GU6 153 J8
Acris St WAND/EARL SW18 28 F1
Acton La CHSWK W4 18 A2
Acuba Rd WAND/EARL SW18 28 E5
Adair Cl SNWD SE25 46 B4
Adair Gdns CTHM CR3 101 L1
Adam And Eve Ms KENS W8 19 L1
Adam Cl CAT SE6 31 N7
FSTH SE23 31 K5
Adams Cl BRYLDS KT5 41 M7
Adams Cft CHOB/PIR GU24 70 C9
Adams Dr FLEETN GU51 87 H6
Adams Ms LIPH GU30 182 E8
TOOT SW17 29 J5
Adamson Wy BECK BR3 47 J6
Adams Park Rd FNM GU9 127 P1
Adamsrill Rd SYD SE26 31 L7
Adams Rd BECK BR3 46 E6
Adams Wk KUT/HW KT1 8 D4
Adams Wy CROY/NA CR0 45 P7
Adam Wk FUL/PGN SW6 * 18 G5
Adare Wk STRHM/NOR SW16 29 P5
Adderley Gv BTSEA SW11 29 K1
Addington Gv SYD SE26 31 M7
Addington Rd CROY/NA CR0 45 J9
SAND/SEL CR2 64 A9
WWKM BR4 65 J3
Addington Village Rd
CROY/NA CR0 64 F5
Addiscombe Av
CROY/NA CR0 46 A8
Addiscombe Court Rd
CROY/NA CR0 3 H2
Addiscombe Gv CROY/NA CR0 3 F4
Addiscombe Rd CROY/NA CR0 3 G4
CWTH RG45 49 N5
Addison Av HSLW TW3 16 C6
Addison Bridge Pl
WKENS W14 19 J2
Addison Cl CTHM CR3 101 M2
Addison Crs WKENS W14 19 J1
Addison Gdns BRYLDS KT5 41 M5
WKENS W14 19 H1
Addison Gv CHSWK W4 18 C1
Addison Rd CTHM CR3 101 M1
FRIM GU16 68 G8
GU GU1 7 J6
SNWD SE25 46 A5
TEDD TW11 26 A9
WKENS W14 19 K1
Addison's Cl CROY/NA CR0 64 F1
Addison Ter CHSWK W4 * 18 A2
Addlestone Moor
ADL/WDHM KT15 55 N1
Addlestone Pk
ADL/WDHM KT15 55 M4
Addlestone Rd
ADL/WDHM KT15 56 B3
Adecroft Wy
E/WMO/HCT KT8 40 C4
Adela Av NWMAL KT3 42 F6
Adelaide Cl CRAWW RH11 176 G2
HORS RH12 192 E6
Adelaide Pl WEY KT13 56 F3
Adelaide Rd ASHF TW15 22 G8
HEST TW5 15 N6
NWDGN UB2 15 N2
PUT/ROE SW15 28 D1
RCH/KEW TW9 17 M9
SURB KT6 41 K6
TEDD TW11 25 N9
WOT/HER KT12 57 J2
Adelaide Ter BTFD TW8 * 17 K3
Adelina Ms BAL SW12 29 N4
Adelphi Cl CRAWE RH10 177 N7
Adelphi Rd EW KT17 78 B2
Adeney Cl HMSMTH W6 19 H4
Adenmore Rd CAT SE6 31 P3
Adie Rd HMSMTH W6 18 G1
Adlers La RDKG RH5 116 G2
Adlington Pl FARN GU14 88 G5
Admers Crs LIPH GU30 182 F8
Admiral Kepple Ct ASC SL5 * 33 N1
Admiral Rd CRAWW RH11 176 D8
Admiral's Bridge La
EGRIN RH19 180 B9
Admirals Ct GU GU1 112 F4
Admiral Sq WBPTN SW10 * 19 N6
Admiralty Rd TEDD TW11 25 N9
Admiralty Wy CBLY GU15 68 B4
Adolf St CAT SE6 31 P7
Adrian Ms WBPTN SW10 19 M4
Advance Rd WNWD SE27 30 D7
Aerodrome Wy HEST TW5 15 L4
Aerospace Bvd FARN GU14 88 C8
Agar Cl SURB KT6 59 M1
Agar Crs BNFD RG42 32 D1
Agate La HORS RH12 192 D5
Agate Rd HMSMTH W6 18 G1
Agates La ASHTD KT21 77 K7
Agincourt Pl ASC SL5 34 C4
Agnes Riley Gdns CLAP SW4 * 29 M3
Agnes Scott Ct WEY KT13 56 D2
Agnew Rd FSTH SE23 31 M3
Agraria Rd GUW GU2 6 A5
Ailsa Av TWK TW1 25 P1
Ailsa Cl CRAWW RH11 176 E8
Ailsa Rd TWK TW1 26 A1
Ainger Cl ASHV GU12 108 F4
Ainsdale Wy
WOKN/KNAP GU21 71 N6
Ainsworth Rd CROY/NA CR0 2 B3
Aintree Cl DTCH/LGLY SL3 13 J6
Aintree Rd CRAWE RH10 177 K7
Aintree St FUL/PGN SW6 19 J5
Aircraft Esp FARN GU14 88 E6
Airedale Av CHSWK W4 18 D3
Airedale Av South
CHSWK W4 * 18 D3
Airedale Rd BAL SW12 29 J3
EA W5 17 J1
Airport Wy HORL RH6 159 K4
STWL/WRAY TW19 13 L9
Aisgill Av WKENS W14 19 K3
Aisne Rd FRIM GU16 69 N7
Aiten Pl HMSMTH W6 18 E2
Aitken Cl MTCM CR4 44 B8
Aitman Dr BTFD TW8 * 17 N3
Akabusi Cl CROY/NA CR0 46 A7
Akehurst Cl CRAWE RH10 160 B9
Akehurst St PUT/ROE SW15 27 M2
Akerman Rd SURB KT6 41 J7
Alamein Rd ALDT GU11 108 D3
Alanbrooke Cl
WOKN/KNAP GU21 71 J7
Alanbrooke Rd ALDT GU11 88 F9
Alan Hilton Ct CHERT KT16 * 55 H5
Alan Rd WIM/MER SW19 28 B8
Alan Turing Rd GUW GU2 111 K5
Albain Crs ASHF TW15 23 H5
Albany Cl ESH/CLAY KT10 58 A7
FLEETN GU51 87 H7
MORT/ESHN SW14 17 P9
Albany Crs ESH/CLAY KT10 58 E5
Albany Ms SUT SM1 61 M4
Albany Pde BTFD TW8 * 17 L4
Albany Pk DTCH/LGLY SL3 13 H5
FRIM GU16 68 E7
Albany Park Rd
KUTN/CMB KT2 26 C9
LHD/OX KT22 76 G8
Albany Pl BTFD TW8 17 K4
EGH TW20 21 M7
Albany Rd BTFD TW8 17 K4
CRAWW RH11 176 F5
FLEETN GU51 86 G7
NWMAL KT3 42 B5
RCHPK/HAM TW10 * 26 E1
WDSR SL4 20 F1
WIM/MER SW19 28 E8
WOT/HER KT12 57 M3
The Albanys REIG RH2 119 L2

Albany Ter
  RCHPK/HAM TW10 * 26 E1
The Albany KUTN/CMB KT2 ....26 C9
Albatross Gdns
  SAND/SEL CR2 ....64 D9
Albemarle Av WHTN TW2......24 C4
Albemarle Gdns NWMAL KT3..42 B5
Albemarle Pk BECK BR3 * 47 H2
Albemarle Rd BECK BR3.......47 H2
Alberta Av SUT SM1 ....61 J3
Alberta Dr HORL RH6.........160 B1
Albert Ct CHERT KT16 ....37 L4
Albert Carr Gdns
  STRHM/NOR SW16 ....29 P8
Albert Dr STA TW18...........22 C8
  WIM/MER SW19 ....28 A3
  WOKN/KNAP GU21 ....72 G3
Albert Gv RYNPK SW20........43 H2
Albertine Cl EW KT17.........78 F5
Albertine Cl EW KT17 * 78 F5
Albert Ms KENS W8...........19 N1
Albert Rd ADL/WDHM KT15 ..15 P3
  ALDT GU11 ....108 D4
  ASHF TW15 ....23 J8
  ASHTD KT21 ....77 M7
  BAGS GU19 ....51 N8
  BNFD RG42 ....32 D2
  CBLY GU15 * 68 E2
  CWTH RG45 ....49 M4
  EGH TW20 ....21 J9
  EW KT17 ....78 D2
  FARN GU14 ....88 E5
  HORL RH6..................159 K1
  HPTN TW12 ....25 K8
  HSLW TW3 ....16 A9
  HYS/HAR UB3 ....14 C1
  KUT/HW KT1 ....9 F4
  MTCM CR4 ....44 D3
  NWDGN UB2 ....15 M1
  NWMAL KT3 ....42 D5
  PGE/AN SE20 ....46 D1
  RCHPK/HAM TW10 ....26 D1
  REDH RH1 ....100 E9
  SNWD SE25 ....46 B5
  SUT SM1 ....61 P4
  TEDD TW11 ....25 N9
  TWK TW1 ....26 C5
  WARL CR6..................82 E6
Albert Rd North REIG RH2 ...119 K4
Albert St FLEETN GU51 ....86 F6
Albery Cl HORS RH12.........117 N3
Albion Cl HMSMTH W6........18 F2
Albion Gdns HMSMTH W6....18 F2
Albion Ms REIG RH2 *........119 N7
Albion Pde
  WOKN/KNAP GU21 * 71 J6
Albion Pl HMSMTH W6........18 F2
  SNWD SE25 * 46 A4
Albion Rd BELMT SM2.........61 P5
  HSLW TW3 ....16 A9
  KUTN/CMB KT2 ....42 A2
  REIG RH2 ....119 N6
  SURB KT6 ....41 M9
  WHTN TW2 ....25 M4
Albion St CROY/NA CRO.......2 A2
Albion Villas Rd SYD SE26....31 K6
Albion Wy EDEN TN8.........144 C1
  HORS RH12 ....192 A8
Albion St SHGR GU5..........153 N1
Alcester Rd WLGTN SM6......62 D3
Alcock Cl WLGTN SM6........62 F6
Alcock Rd HEST TW5.........15 M5
Alcocks Cl
  KWD/TDW/WH KT20 ....79 J9
Alcocks La
  KWD/TDW/WH KT20 ....79 J9
Alcorn Cl CHEAM SM3........61 L1
Alcot Cl CWTH RG45.........49 M5
Aldenham Ter BRAK RG12....32 E7
Aldenholme WEY KT13.......56 C5
Aldensley Rd HMSMTH W6...18 F1
Alderbank Cl CWTH RG45....49 L4
Alderbrook Rd BAL SW12....29 L2
  CRAN GU6..................152 E5
Alderbury Rd BARN SW13....18 E4
Alder Cl ASHV GU12.........109 J3
  CRAWE RH10...............179 J3
  EGH TW20 ....21 K8
Aldercombe La CTHM CR3..101 N7
Alder Cl COUL/CHIP CR5.....80 G6
Alder Gv YTLY GU46.........66 C3
Alderman Judge Ml
  KUT/HW KT1 ....8 D5
Aldermary Rd BMLY BR1.....47 N2
Aldermoor Rd CAT SE6.......31 N6
Alderney Av HEST TW5.......16 B5
Alder Rd BOR GU35..........164 E5
  MORT/ESHN SW14..........18 B8
Alders Av EGRIN RH19......162 C9
Aldersbrook Dr
  KUTN/CMB KT2 ....26 E9
Alders Cl EA W5.............17 K1
Aldersey Rd GU GU1.........7 K3
Aldersgrove
  E/WMO/HCT KT8 ....40 D6
Aldershot Rd ASHV GU12...109 H5
  CHOB/PIR GU24.............90 E6
  FLEETN GU51 ....86 D7
  FLEETS GU52 ....107 J1
  RGUW GU3 ....110 E1
Alderside Wk EGH TW20......21 K8
Aldersmead Av CROY/NA CRO..46 D7

Aldersmead Rd BECK BR3.....46 E1
Alders Rd REIG RH2..........119 M3
Alderstead La REDH RH1.....100 F5
The Alders EF/WBF KT14.....73 N1
  FELT TW13 ....25 J7
  FNM GU9 ....108 C8
  HEST TW5 ....15 P4
  STRHM/NOR SW16 * 29 M7
  WWKM BR4 ....47 P9
Alders View Dr EGRIN RH19..162 D9
Aldis Ms TOOT SW17..........29 H8
Aldis St TOOT SW17..........29 H8
Aldren Rd TOOT SW17........28 F6
Aldrich Crs CROY/NA CRO....65 J7
Aldrich Gdns CHEAM SM3....61 K2
Aldrich Ter WAND/EARL SW18..28 F5
Aldridge Ri NWMAL KT3......42 C8
Aldrington Rd
  STRHM/NOR SW16 ....29 M8
Aldrin Pl FARN GU14.........87 P3
Aldwick Cl FARN GU14.......88 A5
Aldwick Rd CROY/NA CRO....63 J2
Aldworth Cl BRAK RG12......32 C5
Aldworth Gdns CWTH RG45..49 L4
Alexander Cl HAYES BR2.....47 N9
Alexander Crs CTHM CR3....101 L2
Alexander Evans Ms
  FSTH SE23 ....31 L5
Alexander Godley Cl
  ASHTD KT21 ....77 M8
Alexander Pl OXTED RH8....103 L8
Alexander Rd
  COUL/CHIP CR5 ....80 D4
  REDH RH1 ....120 B5
  REIG RH2 ....119 N7
Alexanders Wk CTHM CR3...101 P6
Alexander Wk BRAK RG12...32 D6
Alexandra Av CBLY GU15.....68 C3
  SUT SM1 ....61 L2
  WARL CR6..................82 C6
Alexandra Ct ASHF TW15....38 F1
  STA TW18 ....22 G9
  WOT/HER KT12.............57 J1
Alexandra Ct CRAWE RH10 *..176 G6
  FARN GU14 ....88 E6
Alexandra Dr BRYLDS KT5...41 N8
  NRWD SE19 ....30 F8
Alexandra Gdns CAR SM5....62 C7
  HSLW TW3 ....16 A7
  WOKN/KNAP GU21 ....71 J7
Alexandra Pl CROY/NA CRO..3 K1
  GU GU1 ....7 J6
  SNWD SE25 ....45 M6
Alexandra Rd
  ADL/WDHM KT15...........55 P3
  ALDT GU11 ....108 B4
  ASHF TW15 ....38 F1
  ASHV GU12 ....109 H5
  BH/WHM TN16.............83 P8
  BTFD TW8 * 17 K1
  CROY/NA CRO.............3 G1
  EGH TW20 ....21 H9
  EW KT17 ....78 D2
  FARN GU14 ....88 E5
  HSLW TW3 ....16 A7
  KUTN/CMB KT2.............9 H1
  MORT/ESHN SW14.........18 B8
  MTCM CR4 ....44 A1
  PGE/AN SE20 ....31 L9
  RCH/KEW TW9.............17 M7
  THDIT KT7.................40 F6
  TWK TW1 ....26 B2
  WARL CR6..................82 E6
  WIM/MER SW19 ....28 C9
Alexandra Sq MRDN SM4....43 L6
Alexandra Ter ALDT GU11 *..108 C4
  GU GU1 ....7 G4
Alexandra Wy
  HOR/WEW KT19............77 N1
Alfold By-Pass CRAN GU6...170 C5
Alfold Rd MFD/CHID GU8....169 L7
Alfonso Cl ASHV GU12.......108 E6
Alford Cl RGUE GU3..........112 D2
Alford Rd ERITH DA8 *.......107 M4
Alford Gn CROY/NA CRO.....65 K5
Alfred Cl CHSWK W4.........18 B3
  CRAWE RH10...............177 P6
  FLEETN GU51 ....86 D9
Alfred Rd FELT TW13.........24 D5
  FNM GU9 ....5 K5
  KUT/HW KT1 ....8 B6
  SNWD SE25 ....46 A6
  SUT SM1 ....61 N4
Alfreton Cl WIM/MER SW19..28 A6
Alfriston BRYLDS KT5.........41 M7
Alfriston Av CROY/NA CRO...44 G8
Alfriston Cl BRYLDS KT5......41 M7
Alfriston Rd BTSEA SW11....29 J1
Algar Rd ISLW TW7...........16 G8
Algarve Rd
  WAND/EARL SW18...........28 E4
Alice Ruston Pl
  WOKS/MYFD GU22...........72 A8
Alice Av REDH RH1...........120 C2
Alicia Av CRAWE RH10.......177 L5
Alington Gv WLGTN SM6.....62 F7
Alison Cl CROY/NA CRO......46 D8
  FARN GU14 ....88 A4
  WOKN/KNAP GU21 ....71 J7
Alison Dr CBLY GU15.........69 H3
Alison's Rd ALDT GU11......108 B4
Alison Wy ALDT GU11........108 B4
Alkerden Rd CHSWK W4.....18 C3

Allan Cl NWMAL KT3.........42 B6
Allbrook Cl TEDD TW11.......25 M8
Allcard Cl HORS RH12........192 C5
Allcot Cl CRAWW RH11.......176 D8
  EBED/NFELT TW14...........24 A4
Allden Av ASHV GU12........108 F7
Allden Gdns ASHV GU12.....108 F7
Alldens La MFD/CHID GU8...150 C2
Allder Wy SAND/SEL CR2....63 K6
Allee Dr LIPH GU30..........182 E5
Allenby Av SAND/SEL CR2...63 L7
Allenby Rd BH/WHM TN16...96 C6
  CBLY GU15..................68 C2
Allen Cl MTCM CR4...........44 D2
  SUN TW16 ....39 K2
Allendale Cl SHST GU47......49 L7
  SYD SE26...................31 L8
Allen House Pk
  WOKS/MYFD GU22...........72 A9
Allen Rd BECK BR3............46 D3
  CROY/NA CRO.............45 H8
  GT/LBKH KT23.............96 B6
  SUN TW16 ....39 K2
All Saints Crs EGRIN RH19..181 J5
All Saints St SE KENS W8....19 L1
Allestree Rd FUL/PGN SW6..30 E5
Alleyn Crs DUL SE21.........30 E5
Alleyn Pk DUL SE21..........30 E5
  NWDGN UB2.................15 P5
Alleyn Rd DUL SE21..........30 E6
Allfarthing La
  WAND/EARL SW18...........28 F2
Allgood Cl MRDN SM4........43 H7
All Hallows Av
  WOKS/MYFD GU22...........91 H2
Alliance Cl HSLWW TW4......24 C1
Allingham Rd REIG RH2......119 L8
Allington Av SHPTN TW17....38 C4
Allington Cl WIM/MER SW19..28 A8
Allison Gv DUL SE21..........30 F3
Allnutt Wy CLAP SW4.........29 L1
Alloway Cl WOKN/KNAP GU21..71 P7
All Saints Crs FARN GU14....68 A4
All Saints Ri BNFD RG42.....32 C1
All Saints' Rd ALDT GU11....18 A1
  LTWR GU18..................52 C8
  SUT SM1 ....61 M2
  WIM/MER SW19 ....43 N1
Allsmoor La BRAK RG12......33 H4
All Souls Av CHOB/PIR GU24..91 H6
All Souls Rd ASC SL5.........34 A6
Allum Gv WDR/YW/DTW KT20..38 F7
Allwood Cl SYD SE26.........31 L7
Allyington Wy CRAWE RH10..177 N6
Allyn Cl STA TW18...........22 C9
Alma Cl ASHV GU12..........108 F3
  WOKN/KNAP GU21...........71 L6
Alma Crs SUT SM1...........61 J4
Alma Gdns FNM GU16........69 M8
Alma Pl NRWD SE19..........45 P1
  THHTH CR7.................45 J6
Alma Rd BOR GU35..........164 F6
  CAR SM5....................62 A4
  ESH/CLAY KT10.............40 D9
  REIG RH2...................119 M4
  WAND/EARL SW18...........28 F1
Alma Ter KENS W8 *.........19 L1
Alma Wy FNM GU9...........107 P7
Almer Rd RYNPK SW20.......42 P1
Almners Rd CHERT KT16.....36 G8
Almsbury RGUW GU3........131 J3
Almond Cl CRAWW RH11....176 D6
  EGH TW20 ....20 D9
  FARN GU14 ....68 C9
  FELT TW13 ....11 B1
  GU GU1 ....112 B1
  SHPTN TW17................38 F4
Almond Rd HOR/WEW KT19..60 B9
Almond Wy MTCM CR4.......44 F6
Almorah Rd HEST TW5........15 M6

Alterton Cl
  WOKN/KNAP GU21...........71 N6
Alt Gv WIM/MER SW19.......43 K1
Althea St FUL/PGN SW6.....19 M7
Althorne Rd REDH RH1......120 C7
Althorp Rd TOOT SW17......29 J4
Alton Cl ISLW TW7............16 F7
Alton Gdns BECK BR3........47 H1
  WHTN TW2 ....25 L2
Alton Ride BLKW GU17.......67 N2
Alton Rd CROY/NA CRO.......63 J3
  FLEETN GU51 ....87 J6
  PUT/ROE SW15..............27 M7
  RCH/KEW TW9..............17 L9
Altyre Cl BECK BR3...........46 F6
Altyre Rd CROY/NA CRO.....3 F4
Altyre Wy BECK BR3.........46 F6
Alvernia Cl GODL GU7.......150 B2
Alverstoke Gdns ALDT GU11..108 A5
Alverstone Av
  WAND/EARL SW18...........28 D5
Alverstone Rd NWMAL KT3..42 D5
Alverston Gdns SNWD SE25..45 N6
Alvia Gdns SUT SM1.........61 N3
Alway Av HOR/WEW KT19...60 A4
Alwin Pl FNM GU9...........107 N7
Alwyn Av CHSWK W4........18 B3
Alwyn Cl CROY/NA CRO......65 H6
Alwyne Ct WOKN/KNAP GU21..10 D2
Alwyne Rd WIM/MER SW19..28 C8
Alwyns Cl CHERT KT16.......37 L7
Alwyns La CHERT KT16.......37 K7
Amalgamated Dr BTFD TW8..16 G4
Amanda Ct DTCH/LGLY SL3..12 B1
Ambarrow Crs SHST GU47...49 K8
Ambarrow La SHST GU47....49 H7
Ambassador BRAK RG12.....32 B6
Ambassador Cl HSLW TW3..15 N7
Ambercroft Wy
  COUL/CHIP CR5 ....81 K8
Amber Hl CBLY GU15.........69 J5
Amberley Cl CRAWE RH10..177 M5
  RPLY/SEND GU23............93 K5
Amberley Ct BECK BR3 *.....47 J1
  SAND/SEL CR2 ....81 M8
Amberley Dr
  ADL/WDHM KT15............55 K8
Amberley Gdns
  HOR/WEW KT19............60 D3
Amberley Gra ALDT GU11...108 B6
Amberley Gv CROY/NA CRO..45 P8
  SYD SE26...................31 J7
Amberley Rd HORS RH12...192 F4
  MFD/CHID GU8..............149 M2
  MRDN SM4 ....43 K8
Amberside Cl ISLW TW7.....25 L2
Amberwood Cl WLGTN SM6..62 G4
Amberwood Dr CBLY GU15..69 H1
Amberwood Ri NWMAL KT3..42 C7
Amblecote COB KT11.........57 M9
Ambleside BECK BR3.........46 F6
  FARN GU14 ....88 A3
  FRIM GU16 ....89 J5
  REDH RH1..................140 D1
Ambleside Crs FNM GU9....107 L8
Ambleside Dr
  EBED/NFELT TW14...........24 A4
Ambleside Gdns BELMT SM2..61 N5
  SAND/SEL CR2 ....64 D8
Ambleside Rd LTWR GU18...52 A9
Ambleside Wy EGH TW20....36 F1
Ambrey Wy WLGTN SM6.....62 F7
Amen Cnr TOOT SW17........29 K9
Amerland Rd PUT/ROE SW15..27 M7
Amersham Rd CROY/NA CRO..45 L7
Amesbury Av
  BRXS/STRHM SW2...........29 P5
Amesbury Cl WPK KT4.......43 J9
Amesbury Rd FELT TW13....24 E5
Amey Dr GT/LBKH KT23.....96 C4
Amhurst Gdns ISLW TW7....16 F6
Amis Av HOR/WEW KT19....59 N5
Amis Rd WOKN/KNAP GU21..71 J8
Amity Gv RYNPK SW20......42 G2
Amlets La CRAN GU6.........152 C7
Amner Rd BTSEA SW11.......29 K2
Amor Rd HMSMTH W6........18 G1
Ampere Wy CROY/NA CRO...44 G8
Amroth Cl FSTH SE23.........31 J4
Amstel Wy
  WOKN/KNAP GU21...........71 M7
Amundsen Rd HORS RH12...192 C4
Amyand Cottages TWK TW1..26 A2
Amyand Park Gdns TWK TW1..26 A3
Amyand Park Rd TWK TW1..25 P3
Amy Cl WLGTN SM6...........62 G6
Amy Rd OXTED RH8..........103 L9
Amyruth Rd BROCKY SE4....31 P1
Ancaster Crs NWMAL KT3...42 F7
Ancaster Dr ASC SL5.........33 N2
Ancaster Rd BECK BR3.......46 D4
Ancells Rd FLEETN GU51....87 J3
Anchorage Cl
  WIM/MER SW19 ....28 D8
Anchor Cl RGUW GU3........110 C2
Anchor Crs HORS RH12.....192 B9
Anchor Hl WOKN/KNAP GU21..71 H8
Anchor Meadow FARN GU14..88 B5
Ancill Cl HMSMTH W6........19 H4
Anders Cnr BNFD RG42......32 B2
Anderson Cl CHEAM SM3....43 J9
  HOR/WEW KT19............77 P1
Anderson Dr ASHF TW15....23 M7
Anderson Pl BAGS GU19....51 N5
Anderson Rd WEY KT13......56 F2
Anderson's Pl HSLW TW3...16 B9

Andover Cl
  EBED/NFELT TW14...........24 A4
  HOR/WEW KT19............77 N1
Andover Rd BLKW GU17......67 N2
  WHTN TW2 ....25 L4
Andover Ter HMSMTH W6 *..18 F2
Andover Wy ALDT GU11.....108 D7
Andrewartha Rd FARN GU14..88 D3
Andrew's Cl EW KT17........78 D3
  FLEETS GU52 ....86 D9
  WPK KT4....................61 H1
Andrews Rd FARN GU14.....88 A2
Andromeda Cl
  CRAWW RH11...............176 B7
Anerley Gv NRWD SE19......45 N1
Anerley Hl NRWD SE19......30 G9
Anerley Pk PGE/AN SE20....31 J9
Anerley Park Rd
  PGE/AN SE20................46 B2
Anerley Rd PGE/AN SE20....46 B2
Anerley Station Rd
  PGE/AN SE20................46 B2
Anerley V NRWD SE19.......45 P1
Anfield Cl BAL SW12.........29 M3
Angel Ga GU GU1............6 E5
Angel Hl SUT SM1...........61 M2
Angel Hill Dr SUT SM1.......61 M2
Angelica Gdns CROY/NA CRO..46 D9
Angelica Rd CHOB/PIR GU24..70 G4
  GUW GU2...................111 N1
Angel Pl REIG RH2 *.........119 M7
Angel Rd THDIT KT7..........40 C9
Angel Wk HMSMTH W6.......18 G2
Anglers Reach SURB KT6 *..41 K5
Anglesea Rd KUT/HW KT1...41 K5
Anglesey Av FARN GU14.....68 A8
Anglesey Cl ASHF TW15.....23 K7
  CRAWW RH11...............176 D4
Anglesey Court Rd CAR SM5..62 C5
Anglesey Gdns CAR SM5....62 C5
Anglesey Rd STRHM/NOR SW16..29 P7
Angles Rd STRHM/NOR SW16..29 N7
Angora Wy FLEETN GU51....87 H3
Angus Cl CHSGTN KT9.......59 N4
  HORS RH12 ....192 D4
Anlaby Rd TEDD TW11.......25 M8
Annandale Dr RFNM GU10..127 P7
Annandale Rd CHSWK W4...18 C2
  CROY/NA CRO.............64 A1
  GUW GU2...................111 N4
Anne Armstrong Cl
  ALDT GU11 ....108 F1
Anne Boleyn's Wk
  CHEAM SM3 ....61 H6
  KUTN/CMB KT2 ....26 D8
Anne Case Ms NWMAL KT3..42 B4
Annefiorde Rd BNFD RG42..32 D4
Anners Cl EGH TW20.........36 C4
Annesley Dr CROY/NA CRO..64 F2
Anne's Wk CTHM CR3........81 N9
Annett Cl SHPTN TW17.......38 G5
Annett Rd WOT/HER KT12...39 J9
Annettes Cft FLEETS GU52..106 E2
Annett Rd WOT/HER KT12...39 J9
Annie Brookes Cl STA TW18..22 A6
Anningsley Pk CHERT KT16..54 F8
Annisdowne Cl RDKG RH5..135 H4
Ann La WBPTN SW10.........19 N3
Annsworthy Av THHTH CR7..45 M4
Ansdell St KENS W8..........19 M1
Ansdell Ter KENS W8.........19 M1
Ansel Gv CAR SM5...........44 B9
  FRIM GU16 ....68 C8
  TOOT SW17 ....29 H6
Anselm Cl CROY/NA CRO.....3 J5
Anselm Rd FUL/PGN SW6...19 L4
Ansley Cl SAND/SEL CR2....81 N8
Anson Cl ALDT GU11.........108 B3
  PUR/KEN CR8...............81 M9
Anstead MFD/CHID GU8....168 B4
Anstice Cl CHSWK W4........18 C5
Ansticey Ct RDKG RH5......156 B1
Anstie La RDKG RH5.........136 F9
Anthony Pl GSHT GU26.....184 A1
Anthony Rd SNWD SE25.....46 A6
Antigua Wy CRAWW RH11..176 B7
Antlands La East HORL RH6..159 P7
Antlands La West HORL RH6..159 P6
Anton Crs SUT SM1..........61 L2
Antrobus Cl SUT SM1........61 K4
Antrobus Rd CHSWK W4.....18 B3
Anvil Cl STRHM/NOR SW16..44 E1
Anvil La COB KT11...........57 H3
Anvil Rd SUN TW16..........39 J4
Anyards Rd COB KT11........75 K3
Anzio Cl ALDT GU11.........108 C4
Anzio Gdns CTHM CR3......101 L1
Apeldoorn Dr WLGTN SM6..62 G7
Aperdele Rd LHD/OX KT22..76 D7
Aperfield Rd BH/WHM TN16..84 C6
Apers Av WOKS/MYFD GU22..92 D1
Apex Cl BECK BR3............47 J1
  WEY KT13...................56 F2
Apley Rd REIG RH2..........119 L8
Aplin Wy ISLW TW7..........16 E7
  LTWR GU18..................52 A8
Apollo Av BMLY BR1.........47 N3
Apollo Dr BOR GU35........164 C5
Apollo Pl WBPTN SW10 *...19 P5
  WOKN/KNAP GU21..........71 N8
Apollo Ri FARN GU14........87 P3
Apperley Dr
  BRKHM/BTCW RH3..........118 A6
Appleby Cl WHTN TW2.......25 L5
Appleby Gdns
  EBED/NFELT TW14...........24 A4
Appledore BRAK RG12.......32 B7
Appledore Cl HAYES BR2....47 M6
  TOOT SW17 ....29 J5

Appledore Ms FARN GU14 68 C9
Appledown Ri
COUL/CHIP CR5 80 E4
Applefield CRAWE RH10 177 H4
Apple Garth BTFD TW8 17 K2
GODL GU7 131 J6
Applegarth CROY/NA CR0 65 H6
ESH/CLAY KT10 58 F4
Applegarth Av GUW GU2 111 K5
Applegarth Rd WKENS W14 * 19 H1
Apple Gv CHSGTN KT9 59 L3
Applelands Cl RFNM GU10 127 L9
Apple Market KUT/HW KT1 8 C5
Appleton Gdns NWMAL KT3 42 E7
Apple Tree Cl LHD/OX KT22 96 C4
Appletree Cl GODL GU7 150 E2
PGE/AN SE20 46 B2
Appletree Ct RGUE GU4 113 H3
Appletree La DTCH/LGLY SL3 12 A1
Appletree Pl BNFD RG42 32 C2
Apple Trees Pl
WOKS/MYFD GU22 * 72 A8
Apple Tree Wy SHST GU47 49 P8
Appley Dr CBLY GU15 68 D3
Approach Rd ASHF TW15 23 M9
BH/WHM TN16 103 P2
E/WMO/HCT KT8 40 A6
FNM GU9 5 G5
PUR/KEN CR8 81 J1
RYNPK SW20 42 G3
The Approach EGRIN RH19 162 F6
April Cl ASHTD KT21 77 M7
CBLY GU15 68 E6
FELT TW13 24 B6
HORS RH12 192 B6
April Gln FSTH SE23 31 L6
Aprilwood Cl
ADL/WDHM KT15 55 K9
Apsey Ct BNFD RG42 32 A1
Apsley Rd NWMAL KT3 42 A4
SNWD SE25 46 B5
Aquila Cl LHD/OX KT22 97 L1
Arabella Dr PUT/ROE SW15 18 C9
Aragon Av EW KT17 60 F7
THDIT KT7 40 F6
Aragon Cl CROY/NA CR0 65 L8
SUN TW16 39 H1
Aragon Ct BRAK RG12 32 E5
Aragon Pl MRDN SM4 43 H8
Aragon Rd KUTN/CMB KT2 26 D8
MRDN SM4 43 H8
YTLY GU46 * 66 G4
Aram Ct WOKS/MYFD GU22 * 72 F4
Arbor Cl BECK BR3 47 H3
Arborfield Cl
BRXS/STRHM SW2 30 A4
Arbour Cl LHD/OX KT22 96 F3
Arbrook La ESH/CLAY KT10 58 D5
Arbutus Cl REDH RH1 119 N7
Arbutus Rd REDH RH1 119 N7
Arcade Pde CHSGTN KT9 * 59 L3
Arcadia Cl CAR SM5 62 C3
Arcadian Pl
WAND/EARL SW18 28 C3
Archbishop's Pl
BRXS/STRHM SW2 30 A2
Archdale Pl NWMAL KT3 41 P4
Archdale Rd EDUL SE22 30 G1
Archel Rd WKENS W14 19 K4
Archer Cl KUTN/CMB KT2 41 L1
Archer Rd SNWD SE25 46 B5
Arch Rd WOT/HER KT12 57 M2
Archway Cl WIM/MER SW19 28 E7
WLGTN SM6 * 62 G2
Archway Ms DORK RH4 116 G6
Archway St BARN SW13 18 C8
Arcturus Rd CRAWW RH11 176 B7
Ardbeg Rd HNHL SE24 30 E2
Arden Cl BRAK RG12 33 J3
REIG RH2 119 M9
Arden Rd CRAWE RH10 177 J7
Ardenrun LING RH7 142 G5
Ardent Cl SNWD SE25 45 N4
Ardesley Wd WEY KT13 56 G3
Ardfern Av
STRHM/NOR SW16 45 J4
Ardingly BRAK RG12 32 C7
Ardingly Cl CRAWW RH11 176 E3
CROY/NA CR0 64 D2
Ardleigh Gdns CHEAM SM3 43 L9
Ardley Cl CAT SE6 31 M6
Ardlui Rd WNWD SE27 30 D5
Ardmay Gdns SURB KT6 41 L6
Ardmore Av GUW GU2 111 P3
Ardmore Wy GUW GU2 111 P3
Ardrossan Av CBLY GU15 69 J4
Ardrossan Gdns WPK KT4 60 E2
Ardshiel Cl PUT/ROE SW15 19 H8
Ardshiel Dr REDH RH1 120 A7
Ardwell Cl CWTH RG45 49 J4
Ardwell Rd
BRXS/STRHM SW2 29 P5
Arena La ALDT GU11 108 A2
Arenal Dr CWTH RG45 49 M6
Arethusa Wy CHOB/PIR GU24 70 F5
Arford Common BOR GU35 164 D5
Arford Rd BOR GU35 164 C5
Argent Cl EGH TW20 21 P9
Argent Ct SURB KT6 * 59 N1
Argente Cl FLEETN GU51 87 H3
Argent Ter SHST GU47 * 50 A9
Argon Ms FUL/PGN SW6 19 L5
Argosy Gdns STA TW18 22 C9
Argosy La STWL/WRAY TW19 22 G3
Argus Wk CRAWW RH11 176 D8
Argyle Av HSLW TW3 25 H2
Argyle Pl HMSMTH W6 18 F2
Argyle Rd HSLW TW3 25 J1
Argyle St CHOB/PIR GU24 90 A1
Ariel Wy HSLWW TW4 15 K8
Arkell Gv NRWD SE19 45 K1
Arkwright Rd DTCH/LGLY SL3 13 J7
SAND/SEL CR2 63 P8
Arlingford Rd
BRXS/STRHM SW2 30 B2
Arlington Cl BNFD RG42 32 C2
SUT SM1 61 L1
TWK TW1 * 26 B2
Arlington Ct HYS/HAR UB3 14 F3
Arlington Dr CAR SM5 62 B1
Arlington Gdns CHSWK W4 18 A3
Arlington Ldg WEY KT13 56 D3
Arlington Rd ASHF TW15 23 J8
RCHPK/HAM TW10 26 C5
SURB KT6 41 K7
TEDD TW11 25 N7
TWK TW1 26 B2
Arlington Sq BRAK RG12 32 C3
Arlington Ter ALDT GU11 108 B4
Armadale Rd
EBED/NFELT TW14 24 B1
FUL/PGN SW6 19 L5
WOKN/KNAP GU21 71 N6
Armfield Cl E/WMO/HCT KT8 39 P6
Armfield Crs MTCM CR4 44 B3
Armitage Ct ASC SL5 34 C7
Armitage Dr FRIM GU16 69 H7
Armoury Wy
WAND/EARL SW18 28 D1
Armstrong Cl WOT/HER KT12 39 J7
Armstrong Ml FARN GU14 87 P3
Armstrong Rd EGH TW20 21 H9
FELT TW13 24 F8
Armstrong Wy FARN GU14 87 M6
Armytage Rd HEST TW5 15 M5
Arnal Crs WAND/EARL SW18 28 B3
Arncliffe BRAK RG12 32 C6
Arndale Wy EGH TW20 21 M8
Arne Cl CRAWW RH11 176 C8
Arne Gv HORL RH6 140 A8
Arnett Av EWKG RG40 48 C2
Arnewood Cl LHD/OX KT22 76 B3
PUT/ROE SW15 27 M4
Arney's La MTCM CR4 44 C7
Arnfield Cl CRAWW RH11 176 B6
Arnhem Dr CROY/NA CR0 65 K9
Arnison Rd E/WMO/HCT KT8 40 D5
Arnold Crs ISLW TW7 25 L1
Arnold Dr CHSGTN KT9 59 K5
Arnold Rd STA TW18 37 N1
TOOT SW17 44 B1
WOKN/KNAP GU21 11 J1
Arnott Cl CHSWK W4 18 B2
Arnull's Rd
STRHM/NOR SW16 30 C9
Arodene Rd
BRXS/STRHM SW2 30 A2
Arosa Rd TWK TW1 26 C2
Arragon Gdns
STRHM/NOR SW16 44 G1
WWKM BR4 65 H2
Arragon Rd TWK TW1 25 P4
WAND/EARL SW18 28 D4
Arragon Wk BF/WBF KT14 74 B2
Arran Cl CRAWW RH11 176 E8
WLGTN SM6 62 E3
Arran Wy ESH/CLAY KT10 58 B1
Arras Av MRDN SM4 43 N6
Arreton Md
WOKN/KNAP GU21 72 C3
Arrivals Rd HORL RH6 159 J4
Arrol Rd BECK BR3 46 C4
Arrow Rd FARN GU14 88 B5
Artel Cft CRAWE RH10 177 J5
Arterberry Rd RYNPK SW20 42 G1
Arthur Cl BAGS GU19 51 N8
FNM GU9 5 F6
Arthurdon Rd BROCKY SE4 31 P1
Arthur Rd BH/WHM TN16 84 A4
CRAWW RH11 176 B5
FNM GU9 5 F7
KUTN/CMB KT2 9 H1
NWMAL KT3 42 F6
SWTR RH13 192 C9
WIM/MER SW19 28 D7
Arthur's Bridge Rd
WOKN/KNAP GU21 10 A4
Arthur St ALDT GU11 108 D5
Artillery Rd ALDT GU11 108 D4
GU GU1 6 E4
Artillery Ter GU GU1 6 E3
Arundel Av EW KT17 60 F8
MRDN SM4 43 K5
SAND/SEL CR2 64 A8
Arundel Cl BTSEA SW11 29 H1
CRAWE RH10 177 M5
CROY/NA CR0 2 A6
FLEETN GU51 87 H7
HPTN TW12 25 J8
LIPH GU30 182 A2
Arundel Ct DTCH/LGLY SL3 12 B2
Arundel Pl FNM GU9 4 E3
Arundel Rd BELMT SM2 61 K6
CBLY GU15 69 L4
CROY/NA CR0 45 M7
DORK RH4 116 G7
HSLWW TW4 15 L8
KUT/HW KT1 41 P3
Arundel Ter BARN SW13 18 F4
Arunside HORS RH12 191 P9
Arun Wy SWTR RH13 192 D9
Aschurch Rd CROY/NA CR0 45 P8
Ascot Cl ALDT GU11 108 C5
Ascot Ga ASC SL5 * 34 F1
Ascot Ms WLGTN SM6 62 E7
Ascot Pk ASC SL5 * 33 N4
Ascot Rd EBED/NFELT TW14 23 K4
TOOT SW17 29 K9
Ashbourne BRAK RG12 32 B7
Ashbourne Cl ASHV GU12 109 L3
COUL/CHIP CR5 80 E7
Ashbourne Gv CHSWK W4 18 C3
EDUL SE22 30 G1
Ashbourne Rd MTCM CR4 29 K9
Ashbourne Ter
WIM/MER SW19 43 L1
Ashbrook Rd WDSR SL4 20 G3
Ashburn Gdns SKENS SW7 19 N2
Ashburnham Pk
ESH/CLAY KT10 58 C3
Ashburnham Rd
CRAWE RH10 177 K7
RCHPK/HAM TW10 26 A6
WBPTN SW10 * 19 N5
Ashburn Pl SKENS SW7 19 N2
Ashburton Av CROY/NA CR0 46 B9
Ashburton Cl CROY/NA CR0 46 A9
Ashburton Gdns
CROY/NA CR0 64 A1
Ashburton Rd CROY/NA CR0 64 A1
Ashbury Ct BMLY BR1 47 N1
Ashbury Crs RGUE GU4 112 G3
Ashbury Dr BLKW GU17 68 C7
Ashbury Pl WIM/MER SW19 28 F9
Ashby Av CHSGTN KT9 59 N5
Ashby's Cl EDEN TN8 145 H5
Ashby Wk CROY/NA CR0 45 L7
Ashby Wy WDR/YW UB7 14 C5
Ashchurch Park Vls SHB W12 18 E1
Ash Church Rd ASHV GU12 109 K4
Ashchurch Ter SHB W12 18 D1
Ash Cl ASHV GU12 109 K3
BLKW GU17 67 N3
CAR SM5 62 B1
CRAWE RH10 179 K2
DTCH/LGLY SL3 12 F1
EDEN TN8 144 F4
KWD/TDW/WH KT20 118 A2
LING RH7 143 L8
NWMAL KT3 42 B3
PGE/AN SE20 46 C3
REDH RH1 120 E1
WOKS/MYFD GU22 72 C9
WOKS/MYFD GU22 73 L4
Ash Combe MFD/CHID GU8 167 P7
Ashcombe Av SURB KT6 41 K8
Ashcombe Dr EDEN TN8 144 F1
Ashcombe Pde
WOKS/MYFD GU22 * 72 E9
Ashcombe Rd CAR SM5 62 C5
DORK RH4 116 G5
REDH RH1 100 E7
WIM/MER SW19 28 D8
Ashcombe Sq NWMAL KT3 42 A4
Ashcombe St FUL/PGN SW6 * 19 M7
Ashcombe Ter
KWD/TDW/WH KT20 78 F9
Ash Ct HOR/WEW KT19 60 A3
Ashcroft RGUE GU4 132 C3
Ashcroft Pk COB KT11 75 N1
Ashcroft Ri COUL/CHIP CR5 80 G5
Ashcroft Rd CHSGTN KT9 59 M2
Ashdale GT/LBKH KT23 96 C6
Ashdale Cl STWL/WRAY TW19 23 H5
WHTN TW2 25 J3
Ashdale Pk EWKG RG40 48 G2
Ashdene Cl ASHF TW15 * 38 E1
Ashdene Crs ASHV GU12 109 J3
Ashdene Rd ASHV GU12 109 J3
Ashdown Av FARN GU14 88 G5
Ashdown Cl BECK BR3 47 H3
BRAK RG12 33 H3
FROW RH18 181 M9
REIG RH2 119 M9
WOKS/MYFD GU22 10 C7
Ashdown Ct CRAWE RH10 * 177 J8
Ashdown Dr CRAWE RH10 177 H9
Ashdown Gdns
SAND/SEL CR2 82 B4
Ashdown Pl THDIT KT7 40 G7
Ashdown Rd EW KT17 78 D2
FROW RH18 181 L9
KUT/HW KT1 8 D5
REIG RH2 119 M9
Ashdown Vw EGRIN RH19 180 D4
Ashdown Wy TOOT SW17 29 K5
Ash Dr REDH RH1 120 C7
Ashenden Rd GUW GU2 111 M5
Ashen Gv WIM/MER SW19 28 D6
Ashen V SAND/SEL CR2 64 D7
Asher Dr ASC SL5 33 L2
Ashfield BIL RH14 187 K8
Ashfield Av FELT TW13 24 C4
Ashfield Cl BECK BR3 46 G1
RCHPK/HAM TW10 26 D4
Ashfield Gn YTLY GU46 67 K3
Ashford Av ASHF TW15 23 L9
Ashford Cl ASHF TW15 23 H7
Ashford Crs ASHF TW15 23 H6
Ashford Gdns COB KT11 75 M5
Ashford Rd ASHF TW15 38 E1
FELT TW13 23 N7
Ash Green La East
ASHV GU12 109 L6
Ash Green La West
RFNM GU10 109 H6
Ash Green Rd ASHV GU12 109 L5
Ash Gv EBED/NFELT TW14 23 P4
GUW GU2 111 N5
HEST TW5 15 M6
LIPH GU30 182 G7
PGE/AN SE20 46 C3
STA TW18 22 F9
WWKM BR4 65 J1
Ashgrove Rd ASHF TW15 23 M8
Ash Hill Rd ASHV GU12 109 L3
Ashington Rd
FUL/PGN SW6 * 19 K7
Ash Keys CRAWE RH10 177 H6
Ashlake Rd
STRHM/NOR SW16 29 P7
Ash La MFD/CHID GU8 148 D2
Ashleigh Av EGH TW20 36 G1
Ashleigh Cl HORL RH6 159 J1
Ashleigh Gdns SUT SM1 61 M1
Ashleigh Rd HORS RH12 192 B5
MORT/ESHN SW14 18 C8
PGE/AN SE20 46 B4
Ashley Av EPSOM KT18 78 B2
MRDN SM4 43 L6
Ashley Cl FRIM GU16 89 J1
GT/LBKH KT23 95 P5
RFNM GU10 106 D7
WOT/HER KT12 38 G9
Ashley Ct EPSOM KT18 78 B2
WOKN/KNAP GU21 * 71 M7
Ashley Dr BLKW GU17 67 N4
BNSTD SM7 79 L3
ISLW TW7 16 E4
WHTN TW2 25 J4
WOT/HER KT12 57 J2
Ashley Gdns
RCHPK/HAM TW10 26 C6
Ashley La CROY/NA CR0 63 K3
Ashley Park Av
WOT/HER KT12 39 H9
Ashley Park Crs
WOT/HER KT12 39 J9
Ashley Park Rd
WOT/HER KT12 57 J1
Ashley Ri WOT/HER KT12 57 J2
Ashley Rd DORK RH4 116 C8
EPSOM KT18 78 D6
FARN GU14 88 F3
HOR/WEW KT19 78 B2
HPTN TW12 40 A2
RCH/KEW TW9 17 L8
THDIT KT7 40 F7
THHTH CR7 45 H5
WIM/MER SW19 28 E9
WOKN/KNAP GU21 71 M7
WOT/HER KT12 57 H3
Ashley Wy CHOB/PIR GU24 70 D2
Ashling Rd CROY/NA CR0 46 A9
Ash Lodge Cl ASHV GU12 109 J5
Ash Lodge Dr ASHV GU12 109 J5
Ashlone Rd PUT/ROE SW15 18 G8
Ashlyn's Pk COB KT11 75 N2
Ashlyns Wy CHSGTN KT9 59 K5
Ashmead Rd
EBED/NFELT TW14 24 B4
Ashmere Av BECK BR3 47 K3
Ashmere Cl CHEAM SM3 61 H4
Ash Ms EPSOM KT18 78 C3
Ashmore La HORS RH12 175 H5
Ashmount Ter EA W5 * 17 K2
Ashness Rd BTSEA SW11 29 J1
Ashridge FARN GU14 68 B9
Ashridge Gn BNFD RG42 32 D2
Ashridge Wy MRDN SM4 43 K5
SUN TW16 24 B9
Ash Rd ASHV GU12 108 E6
BH/WHM TN16 105 H5
CHEAM SM3 43 J9
CHOB/PIR GU24 90 G6
CRAWE RH10 177 K3
CROY/NA CR0 64 G1
SHPTN TW17 38 C5
WOKS/MYFD GU22 72 C9
Ash St ASHV GU12 109 J5
Ashtead La GODL GU7 150 C2
Ashtead Woods Rd
ASHTD KT21 77 J5
Ashton Cl SUT SM1 61 L3
WOT/HER KT12 57 K5
Ashton Gdns HSLWW TW4 15 P9
Ashton Rd WOKN/KNAP GU21 71 M6
Ashtree Av MTCM CR4 43 P3
Ash Tree Cl CROY/NA CR0 46 E7
FARN GU14 87 N4
HASM GU27 184 G1
SURB KT6 41 L9
Ashtrees CRAN GU6 171 H2
Ash Tree Wy CROY/NA CR0 46 E6
Ashurst Cl HORS RH12 192 F5
LHD/OX KT22 96 G1
PGE/AN SE20 46 B2
PUR/KEN CR8 81 M4
Ashurst Dr CRAWE RH10 177 N5
KWD/TDW/WH KT20 117 P1
SHPTN TW17 38 A6
Ashurst Gdns
BRXS/STRHM SW2 * 30 B4
Ashurst Pk ASC SL5 * 34 D4
Ashurst Pl DORK RH4 117 J6
Ashurst Rd ASHV GU12 109 H2
KWD/TDW/WH KT20 98 F1
Ashurst Wk CROY/NA CR0 64 B1
Ash V MFD/CHID GU8 167 P6
Ashvale Rd TOOT SW17 29 J8
Ashview Cl ASHF TW15 23 H9
Ashview Gdns ASHF TW15 23 H8
Ashwell Av CBLY GU15 69 H2
Ashwick Cl CTHM CR3 102 A5
Ashwood WARL CR6 82 C9
Ashwood Gdns CROY/NA CR0 65 H5
HYS/HAR UB3 15 H2
Ashwood Pk LHD/OX KT22 96 C3
WOKS/MYFD GU22 11 G6
Ashwood Rd EGH TW20 20 G9
WOKS/MYFD GU22 11 F6
Ashworth Pl GUW GU2 * 111 M5
Askill Dr PUT/ROE SW15 28 B1
Aslett St WAND/EARL SW18 28 E3
Asmar Cl COUL/CHIP CR5 80 G4
Aspen Cl COB KT11 75 N5
RGUE GU4 113 H2
STA TW18 22 C6
Aspen Gdns ASHF TW15 23 M8
MTCM CR4 44 C6
Aspen Gv ASHV GU12 108 G6
Aspenlea Rd HMSMTH W6 19 H4
Aspen V CTHM CR3 81 P7
Aspen Wy BNSTD SM7 79 H3
FELT TW13 24 C6
HORS RH12 192 D6
Aspin Wy BLKW GU17 67 M3
Aspley Rd WAND/EARL SW18 28 E1
Asprey Gv CTHM CR3 102 A4
Assembly Wk CAR SM5 44 A8
Assher Rd WOT/HER KT12 57 N2
Astleham Wy SHPTN TW17 38 A4
Aston Cl ASHTD KT21 77 J7
Aston Gn HSLWW TW4 15 L7
Aston Rd ESH/CLAY KT10 58 E4
RYNPK SW20 42 G3
Aston Ter BAL SW12 * 29 L2
Astonville St
WAND/EARL SW18 28 D4
Aston Wy EPSOM KT18 78 D5
Astor Cl ADL/WDHM KT15 55 P3
KUTN/CMB KT2 26 G9
Astoria Pde ASHF TW15 * 23 K7
STRHM/NOR SW16 * 29 P6
Astrop Ms HMSMTH W6 18 G1
Astrop Ter HMSMTH W6 18 G1
Astwood Ms SKENS SW7 19 M2
Asylum Arch Rd REDH RH1 120 B8
Atalanta Cl PUR/KEN CR8 63 J8
Atalanta St FUL/PGN SW6 19 H6
Atbara Rd FLEETS GU52 106 G2
TEDD TW11 26 A9
Atcham Rd HSLW TW3 16 C9
Atfield Gv BFOR GU20 52 D5
Atheldene Rd
WAND/EARL SW18 28 E4
Athelney St CAT SE6 31 P6
Athelstan Cl CRAWE RH10 177 P5
Athelstan Rd KUT/HW KT1 41 M5
Athena Cl KUT/HW KT1 9 F6
Athenlay Rd PECK SE15 31 L1
Atherfield Rd REIG RH2 119 N8
Atherley Wy HSLWW TW4 24 G3
Atherstone Ms SKENS SW7 * 19 N2
Atherton Cl RGUE GU4 132 C2
STWL/WRAY TW19 22 G2
Atherton Dr WIM/MER SW19 28 A7
Atherton Rd BARN SW13 18 E5
Athlone ESH/CLAY KT10 58 E5
Athlone Rd
BRXS/STRHM SW2 30 A3
Atkins Cl WOKN/KNAP GU21 71 N7
Atkins Dr WWKM BR4 65 K2
Atkinson Ct HORL RH6 * 159 L2
Atkinson Rd CRAWE RH10 177 M7
Atney Rd PUT/ROE SW15 19 J9
Atrebatti Rd SHST GU47 49 N8
Attebrouche Ct BRAK RG12 32 F8
Attenborough Cl
FLEETN GU51 87 H4
Atterbury Cl BH/WHM TN16 105 H6
Attfield Cl ASHV GU12 109 H5
Attlee Cl THHTH CR7 45 L7
Attlee Gdns FLEETS GU52 106 F2
Attwood Cl SAND/SEL CR2 82 B3
Atwood GT/LBKH KT23 95 N4
Atwood Av RCH/KEW TW9 17 N7
Atwood Rd HMSMTH W6 18 F2
Aubyn Hl WNWD SE27 30 D7
Aubyn Sq PUT/ROE SW15 18 E9
Auchinleck Ct
CRAWE RH10 * 179 J4
Auchinleck Wy ALDT GU11 108 A4
Auckland Cl CRAWW RH11 176 G2
NRWD SE19 45 P2
Auckland Hl WNWD SE27 30 D7
Auckland Ri NRWD SE19 45 N2
Auckland Rd CTHM CR3 101 N2
KUT/HW KT1 41 M5
NRWD SE19 45 P2
Aucklands Gdns NRWD SE19 45 N2
Auden Pl CHEAM SM3 * 60 G3
Audley Cl ADL/WDHM KT15 55 M4
Audley Dr WARL CR6 82 C4
Audley Firs WOT/HER KT12 57 K3
Audley Pl BELMT SM2 61 M6
Audley Rd RCHPK/HAM TW10 26 E1
Audley Wy ASC SL5 33 M4
Audrey Cl BECK BR3 47 H7
Audric Cl KUTN/CMB KT2 9 H2
Augur Cl STA TW18 22 C8
Augusta Cl E/WMO/HCT KT8 39 P4
Augusta Rd WHTN TW2 25 K5
Augustine Cl DTCH/LGLY SL3 13 J8
Augustine Rd HMSMTH W6 19 H1
Augustine Wk BNFD RG42 32 G1
August La SHGR GU5 133 P6
Augustus Cl BTFD TW8 17 K5
Augustus Gdns CBLY GU15 69 L3
Augustus Rd
WIM/MER SW19 28 B4
Aultone Wy CAR SM5 62 B2
SUT SM1 61 M1
Aurelia Gdns CROY/NA CR0 45 H6
Aurelia Rd CROY/NA CR0 44 G7
Auriol Cl WPK KT4 60 C2
Auriol Park Rd WPK KT4 60 C2
Auriol Rd WKENS W14 19 J2
Aurum Cl HORL RH6 159 L2
Austen Cl EGRIN RH19 180 A2
Austen Rd FARN GU14 88 C1
GU GU1 7 K5
Austin Cl COUL/CHIP CR5 81 K7
FSTH SE23 31 M3
Austyn Gdns BRYLDS KT5 * 41 P9
Autumn Cl WIM/MER SW19 28 F9
Autumn Dr BELMT SM2 61 M7
Avalon Cl RYNPK SW20 43 J3
Avalon Rd FUL/PGN SW6 19 M6
Avarn Rd TOOT SW17 29 J9
Avebury BRAK RG12 32 C7
Avebury Cl HORS RH12 192 F3
Avebury Pk SURB KT6 * 41 K7
Avebury Rd WIM/MER SW19 43 K2
Aveley La FNM GU9 127 M6
Aveling Cl CRAWE RH10 177 M7
PUR/KEN CR8 81 H2
Aven Cl CRAN GU6 171 H1
Avening Rd
WAND/EARL SW18 28 D3

Avening Ter
WAND/EARL SW18 28 D2
Avenue C *ADL/WDHM* KT15 56 A2
Avenue Cl *HEST* TW5 15 K6
KWD/TDW/WH KT20 98 F2
LIPH GU30 182 E6
WDR/YW UB7 13 P1
Avenue Crs *HEST* TW5 15 K6
Avenue De Cagny
CHOB/PIR GU24 90 F2
Avenue Elmers *SURB* KT6 41 L6
Avenue Gdns *HEST* TW5 * 15 J5
HORL RH6 159 M2
MORT/ESHN SW14 18 C8
TEDD TW11 40 F1
Avenue One
ADL/WDHM KT15 56 A3
Avenue Pde *SUN* TW16 * 39 K4
Avenue Park Rd *WNWD* SE27 30 C5
Avenue Rd *BELMT* SM2 61 L8
BH/WHM TN16 84 C9
BNSTD SM7 79 M4
BTFD TW8 17 J3
COB KT11 75 M5
CRAN GU6 171 J2
CTHM CR3 101 M2
EPSOM KT18 78 B3
FARN GU14 88 F3
FELT TW13 24 A6
FLEETN GU51 86 F5
GSHT GU26 165 N8
HPTN TW12 40 B2
ISLW TW7 16 E6
KUT/HW KT1 8 E6
NWMAL KT3 42 C4
PGE/AN SE20 46 C2
RYNPK SW20 42 F3
SNWD SE25 46 A3
STA TW18 22 A8
STRHM/NOR SW16 44 F3
TEDD TW11 40 G1
WLGTN SM6 62 E6
Avenue South *BRYLDS* KT5 41 M8
Avenue Sucy *CBLY* GU15 68 C4
Avenue Ter *NWMAL* KT3 42 A4
The Avenue *ADL/WDHM* KT15 55 L8
ASC SL5 33 P1
ASHV GU12 108 F7
BECK BR3 47 H2
BELMT SM2 61 K7
BH/WHM TN16 104 E3
BRKHM/BTCW RH3 117 N5
BRYLDS KT5 41 M7
CAR SM5 62 C6
CBLY GU15 68 D4
CHOB/PIR GU24 53 M7
CHSWK W4 18 C1
CLAP SW4 29 L2
COUL/CHIP CR5 80 F4
CRAN GU6 153 P6
CROY/NA CR0 3 G5
CTHM CR3 82 A8
CWTH RG45 49 L4
EGH TW20 21 N7
ESH/CLAY KT10 58 E5
EW KT17 60 G6
FLEETN GU51 86 E6
GODL GU7 150 E2
GSHT GU26 165 N8
HASM GU27 184 A3
HEST TW5 15 J6
HORL RH6 159 J2
HPTN TW12 24 G9
HSLW TW3 25 J1
KWD/TDW/WH KT20 98 F2
LHD/OX KT22 76 F1
LIPH GU30 182 D6
LTWR GU18 52 A8
RCH/KEW TW9 17 M7
REDH RH1 120 G8
RFNM GU10 127 K9
RFNM GU10 146 B1
RGUW GU3 91 L7
RGUW GU3 131 J4
STA TW18 37 M2
STWL/WRAY TW19 12 C9
SUN TW16 39 K3
TWK TW1 26 B1
WDSR SL4 20 G2
WPK KT4 60 D1
WWKM BR4 47 K8
Avenue Three
ADL/WDHM KT15 56 A2
Avenue Two
ADL/WDHM KT15 56 A3
Averil Gv *STRHM/NOR* SW16 30 C9
Averill St *HMSMTH* W6 19 H4
Avern Gdns *E/WMO/HCT* KT8 40 B5
Avern Rd *E/WMO/HCT* KT8 40 B5
Avery Cl *EWKG* RG40 48 D3
Aviary Rd *WOKS/MYFD* GU22 73 L5
Aviary Wy *CRAWE* RH10 179 K2
Aviemore Cl *BECK* BR3 46 F6
Aviemore Wy *BECK* BR3 46 E6
Avington Cl *GU* GU1 7 H2
Avington Gv *PGE/AN* SE20 46 C1
Avoca Rd *TOOT* SW17 29 K7
Avocet Crs *SHST* GU47 49 P9
Avon Cl *ADL/WDHM* KT15 55 L5
ASHV GU12 109 H5
FARN GU14 68 A9
SUT SM1 61 N3
WPK KT4 60 E1
Avondale *ASHV* GU12 89 H8
Avondale Av *ESH/CLAY* KT10 58 G2
STA TW18 37 K1
WPK KT4 42 D9
Avondale Cl *HORL* RH6 140 B8
WOT/HER KT12 57 L4
Avondale Gdns *HSLWW* TW4 24 G1
Avondale Rd *ALDT* GU11 108 D6
ASHF TW15 22 G6
FLEETN GU51 86 G5
MORT/ESHN SW14 18 B8
SAND/SEL CR2 63 L5
WIM/MER SW19 28 E8
Avon Gv *BRAK* RG12 32 E1
Avonmead
WOKN/KNAP GU21 72 A7
Avonmore Av *GU* GU1 7 K1
Avonmore Gdns
WKENS W14 * 19 K2
Avonmore Pl *WKENS* W14 19 J2
Avonmore Rd *WKENS* W14 19 K2
Avon Rd *FNM* GU9 5 G6
SUN TW16 39 H1
Avon Wk *CRAWW* RH11 176 C6
Avonwick Rd *HSLW* TW3 16 B7
Avro Wy *BF/WBF* KT14 56 A8
WLGTN SM6 62 G6
Award Rd *FLEETS* GU52 106 G1
Axbridge *BRAK* RG12 32 G6
Axes La *REDH* RH1 140 E3
Axwood *EPSOM* KT18 78 A4
Ayebridges Av *EGH* TW20 36 G1
Ayesgarth *FLEETS* GU52 107 H1
Ayjay Cl *ALDT* GU11 108 D7
Aylesbury Rd *HAYES* BR2 47 N4
Aylesford Av *BECK* BR3 46 E6
Aylesham Wy *YTLY* GU46 66 F2
Aylesworth Sp *WDSR* SL4 20 G3
Aylett Rd *ISLW* TW7 16 E7
SNWD SE25 46 B5
Ayliffe Cl *KUT/HW* KT1 9 H4
Ayling Ct *FNM* GU9 108 B7
Ayling Hl *ALDT* GU11 108 B5
Ayling La *ALDT* GU11 108 B6
Aylward Rd *FSTH* SE23 31 L5
RYNPK SW20 43 K3
Aymer Cl *STA* TW18 37 J2
Aymer Dr *STA* TW18 37 J2
Aynhoe Rd *WKENS* W14 19 H2
Ayrshire Gdns *FLEETN* GU51 87 H3
Ayrton Rd *SKENS* SW7 19 P1
Aysgarth *BRAK* RG12 32 B7
Aysgarth Rd *DUL* SE21 30 E2
Ayshe Court Dr *SWTR* RH13 192 D8
Azalea Ct *WOKS/MYFD* GU22 10 A7
Azalea Dr *HASM* GU27 184 A2
Azalea Gdns *FLEETS* GU52 107 H1
Azalea Wy *CBLY* GU15 69 K2

B

Babbacombe Cl *CHSGTN* KT9 59 K4
Babbacombe Rd *BMLY* BR1 47 P2
Babbs Md *FNM* GU9 4 D5
Baber Bridge Pde
EBED/NFELT TW14 * 24 D2
Baber Dr *EBED/NFELT* TW14 24 D2
Babington Rd
STRHM/NOR SW16 29 N8
Babs Flds *RFNM* GU10 126 A8
Babylon La
KWD/TDW/WH KT20 99 M7
Bachelor's La
RPLY/SEND GU23 94 C4
Back Dr *CWTH* RG45 * 49 M6
Back Gn *WOT/HER* KT12 57 L5
Back La *BIL* RH14 187 K8
BTFD TW8 17 K5
CRAWE RH10 178 D9
MFD/CHID GU8 129 M9
RCHPK/HAM TW10 26 B6
RGUE GU4 113 P2
Backley Gdns *CROY/NA* CR0 46 A7
Back Rd *TEDD* TW11 40 E1
Bacon Cl *SHST* GU47 67 P2
Bacon La *RFNM* GU10 146 F8
Badajos Rd *ALDT* GU11 108 B3
Baden Cl *STA* TW18 37 L1
Baden Dr *HORL* RH6 140 A9
Baden Powell Cl *SURB* KT6 59 M1
Baden Rd *GUW* GU2 111 N3
Bader Cl *PUR/KEN* CR8 81 M4
Badger Cl *FELT* TW13 24 C6
GUW GU2 111 P2
HSLWW TW4 15 L8
Badger Dr *LTWR* GU18 52 A8
Badgers Cl *ASHF* TW15 * 23 J8
FLEETS GU52 86 F7
GODL GU7 131 K5
HORS RH12 192 E4
WOKN/KNAP GU21 72 A7
Badgers Copse *CBLY* GU15 68 G5
WPK KT4 60 D1
Badgers Ct *WPK* KT4 * 60 D1
Badgers Cross
MFD/CHID GU8 149 N3
Badgers Hl *VW* GU25 36 A6
Badgers Hollow *GODL* GU7 131 K4
Badgers Holt *YTLY* GU46 66 F3
Badgers La *WARL* CR6 82 C8
Badgers St *CWTH* RG45 49 K4
Badgers Wk *CTHM* CR3 81 P7
NWMAL KT3 42 C3
PUR/KEN CR8 62 E9
Badgers Wy *BIL* RH14 188 D6
BRAK RG12 33 H2
EGRIN RH19 162 D9
Badgers Wd *CTHM* CR3 101 L3
Badger Wy *ASHV* GU12 108 F3
RFNM GU10 107 H6
Badgerwood Dr *FRIM* GU16 68 F6
Badingham Dr *LHD/OX* KT22 96 E4
Badminton Rd *BAL* SW12 29 K2
Badshot Lea Rd *FNM* GU9 108 D8
Badshot Pk *FNM* GU9 108 C8
Bafton Ga *HAYES* BR2 47 P9
Bagley's La *FUL/PGN* SW6 19 M6
Bagot Cl *ASHTD* KT21 77 M5
Bagshot Gn *BAGS* GU19 51 N7
Bagshot Rd *ASC* SL5 34 B9
BRAK RG12 32 D4
CHOB/PIR GU24 53 H9
EGH TW20 36 A1
WOKN/KNAP GU21 71 H8
Bahram Rd *HOR/WEW* KT19 60 B8
Baigents La *BFOR* GU20 52 D5
Bailes La *RGUW* GU3 110 D4
Bailey Cl *FRIM* GU16 68 F8
HORS RH12 192 E3
Bailey Crs *CHSGTN* KT9 59 K6
Bailey Pl *SYD* SE26 31 K9
Bailey Rd *DORK* RH4 116 C8
Baileys Cl *BLKW* GU17 67 M4
Bailing Hl *HORS* RH12 191 M4
Baillie Rd *GU* GU1 7 J5
Bain Av *CBLY* GU15 68 D7
Bainbridge Cl
RCHPK/HAM TW10 26 D8
Baines Cl *SAND/SEL* CR2 63 M4
Bainton Md
WOKN/KNAP GU21 71 N6
Baird Cl *CRAWE* RH10 177 K2
Baird Dr *RGUW* GU3 111 H4
Baird Gdns *NRWD* SE19 30 F7
Baird Rd *FARN* GU14 88 E1
Bakehouse Barn Cl
HORS RH12 192 D3
Bakehouse Gdns
FLEETS GU52 107 H1
Bakehouse Ms *ALDT* GU11 * 108 C4
Bakehouse Rd *HORL* RH6 140 B8
Baker Cl *CRAWE* RH10 176 G7
Baker La *MTCM* CR4 44 C3
Baker's Cl *LING* RH7 143 L8
PUR/KEN CR8 81 L3
Bakers End *RYNPK* SW20 43 J3
Bakers Gdns *CAR* SM5 62 A1
Baker's La *LING* RH7 143 L9
Bakers Md *GDST* RH9 122 C1
Baker St *WEY* KT13 56 C3
Bakers Wy *RDKG* RH5 156 B7
Bakewell Wy *NWMAL* KT3 42 C3
Balaclava Rd *SURB* KT6 41 J8
Balchier Rd *EDUL* SE22 31 J2
Balchins La *DORK* RH4 116 A8
Balcombe Gdns *HORL* RH6 159 M2
Balcombe Rd *CRAWE* RH10 177 N4
CRAWE RH10 195 P1
HORL RH6 140 D9
Baldreys *FNM* GU9 127 L5
Baldry Gdns
STRHM/NOR SW16 29 P9
Baldwin Cl *CRAWE* RH10 * 177 M8
Baldwin Crs *RGUE* GU4 112 G3
Baldwin Gdns *HSLW* TW3 16 C6
Baldwins Fld *EGRIN* RH19 * 162 B8
Balfern Gv *CHSWK* W4 18 C3
Balfont Cl *SAND/SEL* CR2 82 A2
Balfour Av
WOKS/MYFD GU22 92 C2
Balfour Crs *BRAK* RG12 32 D6
Balfour Rd *CAR* SM5 62 B6
HSLW TW3 16 B8
NWDGN UB2 15 M1
SNWD SE25 46 A5
WEY KT13 56 B3
WIM/MER SW19 43 M1
Balgowan Cl *NWMAL* KT3 42 C5
Balgowan Rd *BECK* BR3 46 G4
Balham Gv *BAL* SW12 29 K3
Balham High Rd *BAL* SW12 29 L3
Balham Hl *BAL* SW12 29 L3
Balham New Rd *BAL* SW12 29 L3
Balham Park Rd *BAL* SW12 29 J4
Balham Station Rd *BAL* SW12 29 K4
Balintore Ct *SHST* GU47 67 P1
The Ballands North
LHD/OX KT22 96 E2
The Ballands South
LHD/OX KT22 96 E3
Ballantine St
WAND/EARL SW18 19 N9
Ballantyne Dr
KWD/TDW/WH KT20 99 K1
Ballantyne Rd *FARN* GU14 88 C1
Ballard Cl *KUTN/CMB* KT2 42 B1
Ballard Rd *CBLY* GU15 51 J9
Ballards Farm Rd
SAND/SEL CR2 64 A5
Ballards Gn
KWD/TDW/WH KT20 79 J8
Ballards La *OXTED* RH8 104 A9
Ballards Ri *SAND/SEL* CR2 64 A5
Ballards Wy *SAND/SEL* CR2 64 A5
Ballater Rd *SAND/SEL* CR2 63 P4
Ballencrieff Rd *ASC* SL5 34 F8
Ballfield Rd *GODL* GU7 131 K7
Ballina St *FSTH* SE23 31 L3
Ballingdon Rd *BTSEA* SW11 29 J2
Balliol Cl *CRAWE* RH10 177 M2
Balliol Wy *SHST* GU47 50 A8
Balloon Rd *FARN* GU14 88 D5
Ballsdown *MFD/CHID* GU8 167 P7
Ball & Wicket La *FNM* GU9 107 N7
Balmoral Av *BECK* BR3 46 E5
Balmoral Cl *PUT/ROE* SW15 * 28 A2
Balmoral Crs
E/WMO/HCT KT8 40 A4
FNM GU9 107 M8
Balmoral Dr *FRIM* GU16 68 G8
WOKS/MYFD GU22 72 G5
Balmoral Gdns
SAND/SEL CR2 63 M8
WEA W13 16 G1
Balmoral Ms *SHB* W12 18 D1
Balmoral Rd *ASHV* GU12 109 J2
KUT/HW KT1 41 M5
WPK KT4 60 F2
Balmoral Wy *BELMT* SM2 61 L8
Balmuir Gdns *PUT/ROE* SW15 18 G9
Balquhain Cl *ASHTD* KT21 77 K6
Baltic Cl *WIM/MER* SW19 43 P1
Balvernie Gv
WAND/EARL SW18 28 C3
Bampfylde Cl *WLGTN* SM6 62 E2
Bampton Rd *FSTH* SE23 31 L6
Bampton Wy
WOKN/KNAP GU21 71 N7
Banavie Gdns *BECK* BR3 47 H2
Banbury *BRAK* RG12 32 G8
Banbury Cl *FRIM* GU16 69 H9
Banbury Ct *BELMT* SM2 * 61 L6
Bancroft Cl *ASHF* TW15 * 23 K8
Bancroft Ct *REIG* RH2 119 M5
Bancroft Rd *CRAWE* RH10 177 N6
REIG RH2 119 L5
Banders Ri *GU* GU1 112 G4
Band La *EGH* TW20 21 L8
Bandon Ri *WLGTN* SM6 62 F5
Bangalore St *PUT/ROE* SW15 18 G8
Banim St *HMSMTH* W6 18 F1
Bank Av *MTCM* CR4 43 P3
Bankhurst Rd *CAT* SE6 31 N3
Bank La *CRAWE* RH10 176 G5
KUTN/CMB KT2 41 L1
PUT/ROE SW15 27 K1
Bank Rd *ALDT* GU11 108 F1
Bank Side *EWKG* RG40 48 D3
Bankside *FNM* GU9 108 B7
SAND/SEL CR2 63 P5
WOKN/KNAP GU21 71 P7
Bankside Cl *BH/WHM* TN16 84 A7
CAR SM5 62 A4
ISLW TW7 16 F9
MFD/CHID GU8 148 E1
Bankside Dr *THDIT* KT7 59 H1
Bank's La *EHSLY* KT24 95 K2
Banks Rd *CRAWE* RH10 177 M6
Banks Wy *RGUE* GU4 112 D2
Bank Ter *CRAWE* RH10 * 176 G6
The Bank *CRAWE* RH10 * 179 H7
Bank Willow
RCHPK/HAM TW10 26 A6
Bannacle Hill Rd
MFD/CHID GU8 167 L2
Bannister Cl
BRXS/STRHM SW2 30 B4
MFD/CHID GU8 149 N7
Bannister Gdns *HTWY* RG27 48 A9
YTLY GU46 67 K3
Bannister's Rd *GUW* GU2 111 M7
Bannow Cl *HOR/WEW* KT19 60 C3
Banstead Rd *BNSTD* SM7 79 J2
CAR SM5 61 P6
CTHM CR3 101 M2
EW KT17 60 F8
PUR/KEN CR8 63 J9
Banstead Rd South
BELMT SM2 61 N8
Banstead Wy *WLGTN* SM6 62 G4
Barbara Cl *FLEETS* GU52 87 H9
SHPTN TW17 38 D6
Barber Cl *CRAWE* RH10 177 M9
Barber Dr *CRAN* GU6 153 H8
Barberry Cl *FLEETS* GU52 86 G9
Barberry Wy *BLKW* GU17 68 B5
Barb Ms *HMSMTH* W6 18 G1
Barbon Cl *CBLY* GU15 69 M5
Barchard St
WAND/EARL SW18 28 E1
Barclay Cl *FUL/PGN* SW6 * 19 L5
LHD/OX KT22 96 B3
Barclay Rd *CROY/NA* CR0 2 E5
FUL/PGN SW6 19 L5
Barcombe Av
BRXS/STRHM SW2 29 P5
Bardney Rd *MRDN* SM4 43 M5
Bardolph Av *CROY/NA* CR0 64 F7
Bardolph Rd *RCH/KEW* TW9 17 M9
Bardon Wk
WOKN/KNAP GU21 * 71 P6
Bardsley Cl *CROY/NA* CR0 3 J5
Bardsley Dr *FNM* GU9 127 L5
Barfields *REDH* RH1 121 K4
Barford Cl *FLEETN* GU51 87 K7
Barfreston Wy *PGE/AN* SE20 46 B2
Bargate Cl *NWMAL* KT3 42 E8
Bargate Ri *GODL* GU7 131 J9
Barge Cl *ALDT* GU11 108 G1
Barge Wk *KUT/HW* KT1 8 B6
Bargrove Cl *PGE/AN* SE20 46 A1
Bargrove Crs *CAT* SE6 31 N5
Barham Cl *WEY* KT13 56 E3
Barham Rd *RYNPK* SW20 42 E1
SAND/SEL CR2 63 L3
Barhatch La *CRAN* GU6 153 J6
Barhatch Rd *CRAN* GU6 153 J8
Baring Rd *CROY/NA* CR0 46 A9
Barker Cl *CHERT* KT16 37 J8
NWMAL KT3 41 P5
Barker Rd *CHERT* KT16 37 J8
Barkers Meadow *ASC* SL5 33 M2
Barker St *WBPTN* SW10 19 N4
Barker Wk *STRHM/NOR* SW16 29 N6
Barkham Ride *EWKG* RG40 48 D2
Barkis Md *SHST* GU47 50 A7
Barkston Gdns *ECT* SW5 19 M3
Barley Cl *CRAWE* RH10 176 G6
Barley Md *BNFD* RG42 32 G1
Barley Mow Cl
WOKN/KNAP GU21 71 K6
Barley Mow Ct
BRKHM/BTCW RH3 118 A5
Barley Mow Hl *BOR* GU35 164 C5
Barley Mow La
WOKN/KNAP GU21 71 J5
Barley Mow Pas *CHSWK* W4 18 B3
Barley Mow Rd *EGH* TW20 21 H8
Barley Mow Wy *SHPTN* TW17 38 C5
Barley Wy *FLEETN* GU51 87 H2
Barlow Cl *WLGTN* SM6 62 G5
Barlow Rd *CRAWW* RH11 176 B8
HPTN TW12 40 A1
Barmouth Rd *CROY/NA* CR0 64 D1
WAND/EARL SW18 28 F2
Barnaby Pl *SKENS* SW7 19 P2
Barnard Cl *FRIM* GU16 69 H8
SUN TW16 39 K1
WLGTN SM6 62 F6
Barnard Gdns *NWMAL* KT3 42 E5
Barnard Pl *EW* KT17 60 G8
Barnard Rd *MTCM* CR4 44 C4
WARL CR6 83 H8
Barnards Pl *SAND/SEL* CR2 63 K7
Barnard Wy *ALDT* GU11 108 B3
Barnato Cl *BF/WBF* KT14 74 A1
Barnby Rd *WOKN/KNAP* GU21 71 K6
Barn Cl *BNSTD* SM7 79 P4
BRAK RG12 32 F3
CBLY GU15 68 G2
CRAWW RH11 194 E3
KWD/TDW/WH KT20 * 117 M3
Barn Ct *CRAWE* RH10 178 F1
Barn Crs *PUR/KEN* CR8 81 M2
Barncroft *FNM* GU9 5 G5
Barneby Cl *WHTN* TW2 25 M4
Barnes Av *BARN* SW13 18 E5
NWDGN UB2 15 P2
Barnes Br *CHSWK* W4 18 C7
Barnes Cl *FARN* GU14 88 F3
Barnes End *NWMAL* KT3 42 E6
Barnes High St *BARN* SW13 18 D7
Barnes Rd *FRIM* GU16 68 G8
GODL GU7 131 L5
Barnes Wallis Cl *EHSLY* KT24 95 M7
Barnes Wallis Dr
BF/WBF KT14 56 A9
Barnett Cl *LHD/OX* KT22 77 H8
SHGR GU5 132 G5
Barnett Ct *BRAK* RG12 * 32 E3
Barnett Gn *BRAK* RG12 32 D7
Barnett La *LTWR* GU18 69 P1
SHGR GU5 132 F6
Barnett Rw *RGUE* GU4 92 B9
Barnett's Shaw *OXTED* RH8 103 K7
Barnetts Wy *OXTED* RH8 103 K7
Barnett Wood La
ASHTD KT21 77 J7
Barnet Wood Rd
HAYES BR2 * 65 P2
Barn Fld *BNSTD* SM7 79 M3
Barnfield *CRAN* GU6 153 H9
NWMAL KT3 42 C7
YTLY GU46 67 H3
Barnfield Av *CROY/NA* CR0 46 C9
KUTN/CMB KT2 26 C7
MTCM CR4 44 D5
Barnfield Cl *COUL/CHIP* CR5 81 L8
TOOT SW17 28 F6
Barnfield Gdns
KUTN/CMB KT2 26 D8
Barnfield Rd *BH/WHM* TN16 84 B9
CRAWE RH10 176 G4
SAND/SEL CR2 63 N7
Barnfield Wy *OXTED* RH8 123 N4
Barnfield Wood Cl *BECK* BR3 47 K7
Barnfield Wood Rd *BECK* BR3 47 K7
Barnhill Av *HAYES* BR2 47 N6
Barnlea Cl *FELT* TW13 24 F5
Barnmead *CHOB/PIR* GU24 53 M8
Barn Meadow Cl
FLEETS GU52 106 F3
Barn Meadow La
GT/LBKH KT23 95 P4
Barnmead Rd *BECK* BR3 46 D2
Barn Rd *ADL/WDHM* KT15 55 M7
Barnsbury Cl *NWMAL* KT3 42 A5
Barnsbury Crs *BRYLDS* KT5 42 A9
Barnsbury La *BRYLDS* KT5 59 P1
Barnscroft *RYNPK* SW20 42 F4
Barnsfold La *HORS* RH12 189 H4
Barnsford Crs
CHOB/PIR GU24 70 G1
Barnsley Cl *ASHV* GU12 89 K6
Barnsnap Cl *HORS* RH12 192 C4
Barnway *EGH* TW20 21 H8
Barnwell Rd
BRXS/STRHM SW2 30 B1
Barnwood Cl *CRAWE* RH10 177 M4
GUW GU2 111 L3
Barnwood Ct *GUW* GU2 111 L3
Barnwood Rd *GUW* GU2 111 L4
The Barnyard
KWD/TDW/WH KT20 98 E4
Baron Cl *BELMT* SM2 61 M8
Baron Gv *MTCM* CR4 44 A5
Barons Court Rd *WKENS* W14 19 J3
Baronsfield Rd *TWK* TW1 * 26 A2
Baron's Hurst *EPSOM* KT18 78 A5
Barons Keep *WKENS* W14 * 19 J3
Baronsmead Rd *BARN* SW13 18 E6
The Barons *TWK* TW1 26 A2
Baron's Wk *CROY/NA* CR0 46 E7
Barons Wy *EGH* TW20 22 A9
REIG RH2 119 L9
Barossa Rd *CBLY* GU15 68 F1
Barracane Dr *CWTH* RG45 49 M5
Barrack Pth
WOKN/KNAP GU21 71 M7
Barrack Rd *ALDT* GU11 * 108 C4
GUW GU2 111 N3
HSLWW TW4 15 M9
Barrens Brae
WOKS/MYFD GU22 11 H6
Barrens Cl
WOKS/MYFD GU22 * 11 H7
Barrens Pk
WOKS/MYFD GU22 11 H6
Barrett Rd *LHD/OX* KT22 96 C5
Barrhill Rd *BRXS/STRHM* SW2 29 P5
Barricane *WOKN/KNAP* GU21 71 P8
Barrie Cl *COUL/CHIP* CR5 80 E5
Barrie Rd *FNM* GU9 107 L7
Barrihurst La *CRAN* GU6 170 A1

Barringer Sq *TOOT* SW17 ....29 K7
Barrington Ct *DORK* RH4 ....116 G8
Barrington Ldg *WEY* KT13 ....56 E4
Barrington Rd *CHEAM* SM3 ....43 L9
   CRAWE RH10 ....176 C9
   DORK RH4 * 116 G8
   PUR/KEN CR8 ....80 E1
   SWTR RH13 ....192 D8
Barrington Wk *NRWD* SE19 * 30 F9
Barrow Av *CAR* SM5 ....62 B6
Barrowgate Rd *CHSWK* W4 ....18 A3
Barrow Green Rd
   OXTED RH8 ....122 G2
Barrow Hedges Cl *CAR* SM5 ....62 A6
Barrow Hedges Wy *CAR* SM5 ....62 A6
Barrow Hl *WPK* KT4 ....60 C1
Barrow Hill Cl *WPK* KT4 ....60 C1
Barrow Rd *CROY/NA* CRO 63 J4
   STRHM/NOR SW16 ....29 N9
Barr's La *WOKN/KNAP* GU21 ....71 L5
Barry Cl *CRAWE* RH10 ....177 H8
Barry Rd *EDUL* SE22 ....31 H2
Barry Sq *BRAK* RG12 ....32 F8
Barry Ter *ASHF* TW15 * 23 J5
Barsons Cl *PGE/AN* SE20 ....46 C1
The Bars *RGUE* GU4 ....6 E5
Barston Rd *WNWD* SE27 ....30 D5
Barstow Crs
   BRXS/STRHM SW2 ....30 A4
Bartholomew Ct
   DORK RH4 * 116 G8
Bartholomew Cl
   HASM GU27 ....184 D2
   WAND/EARL SW18 ....19 N9
Bartholomew Wy
   HORS RH12 ....192 F4
Bartlett Pl *FRIM* GU16 ....89 H2
Bartlett Rd *BH/WHM* TN16 ....104 G6
Bartlett St *SAND/SEL* CR2 ....63 M4
Barton Cl *ADL/WDHM* KT15 ....55 L5
   ALDT GU11 ....108 A5
   SHST GU47 ....38 D7
Barton Crs *EGRIN* RH19 ....180 F3
Barton Gn *NWMAL* KT3 ....42 B3
Barton Pl *RGUE* GU4 * 112 C7
Barton Rd *SHGR* GU5 ....132 E7
   WKENS W14 ....19 J3
Barton's Dr *YTLY* GU46 ....67 H4
Barton St *WARL* GU14 ....67 N5
The Barton *COB* KT11 ....75 M1
Barton Wk *CRAWE* RH10 ....177 L7
Bartram Rd *BROCKY* SE4 ....31 M1
Barts Cl *BECK* BR3 ....46 G6
Barttelot Rd *HORS* RH12 ....192 B9
Barwell Cl *CWTH* RG45 ....49 K5
Barwell Ct *CHSGTN* KT9 * 59 J6
Barwell La *CHSGTN* KT9 ....59 J6
Barwood Av *WWKM* BR4 ....47 H9
Bascome St
   BRXS/STRHM SW2 ....30 B2
Basden Cl *FELT* TW13 ....25 H5
Basemoors *BRAK* RG12 ....32 G3
Bashford Wy *CRAWE* RH10 ....179 N7
Basildene Rd *HSLWW* TW4 ....15 M8
Basildon Cl *BELMT* SM2 ....61 M7
Basildon Wy *CRAWW* RH11 ....176 B8
   WNWD SE27 ....30 D8
Basil Gdns *CROY/NA* CRO 46 D9
   WNWD SE27 ....30 D8
Basingbourne Cl
   FLEETS GU52 ....86 G9
Basingbourne Rd
   FLEETS GU52 ....106 F1
Basing Cl *THDIT* KT7 ....40 B8
Basing Dr *ALDT* GU11 ....108 D7
Basingfield Rd *THDIT* KT7 ....40 B8
Basinghall Gdns *BELMT* SM2 ....61 M7
Basing Rd *BNSTD* SM7 ....79 K4
Basing Wy *THDIT* KT7 ....40 B8
Baskerville Rd
   WAND/EARL SW18 ....29 N3
Bassano St *EDUL* SE22 ....30 G1
Basset Cl *ADL/WDHM* KT15 ....55 M8
Bassett Cl *BELMT* SM2 ....61 M7
   REIG RH2 ....119 L4
Bassett Gdns *ISLW* TW7 ....16 C5
Bassett Rd *CRAWE* RH10 ....177 N8
   WOKS/MYFD GU22 ....72 G5
Bassetts Hl *LING* RH7 ....162 F2
Bassingham Rd
   WAND/EARL SW18 ....28 F3
Baston Manor Rd
   WWKM BR4 ....65 P2
Baston Rd *HAYES* BR2 ....65 P1
Basuto Rd *FUL/PGN* SW6 ....19 L6
Bat And Ball La *FNM* GU9 ....127 L7
Batavia Cl *SUN* TW16 ....39 L2
Batavia Rd *SUN* TW16 ....39 K2
Batcombe Md *BRAK* RG12 ....32 G8
Bateman Ct *CRAWE* RH10 * 177 K8
Batemans Cnr *CHSWK* W4 * 18 B3
Batemans Ct *CRAWE* RH10 ....177 K8
Bates Crs *CROY/NA* CRO 63 J5
   STRHM/NOR SW16 ....44 E1
Bateson Wy
   WOKN/KNAP GU21 ....72 G3
Bates Wk *ADL/WDHM* KT15 ....55 N5
Bathgate Rd
   WIM/MER SW19 ....28 A6
Bath House Rd *CROY/NA* CRO 44 D9
Bath Pas *KUT/HW* KT1 ....8 C5
Bath Rd *CBLY* GU15 ....68 E2
   CHSWK W4 ....18 C2
   DTCH/LGLY SL3 ....13 H6
Baths Ap *FUL/PGN* SW6 ....19 K5
Bathurst Av *WIM/MER* SW19 ....43 M2
Batley Cl *MTCM* CR4 ....44 B8
Batoum Gdns *HMSMTH* W6 ....18 G1
Batsworth Rd *MTCM* CR4 ....43 P4
Batten Av *WOKN/KNAP* GU21 ....71 L8
Battersea Br *WBPTN* SW10 ....19 P5

Battersea Church Rd
   BTSEA SW11 ....19 P6
Battersea High St
   BTSEA SW11 ....19 P7
Battersea Ri *BTSEA* SW11 ....29 H1
Battlebridge La *REDH* RH11 ....120 D1
Battle Cl *WIM/MER* SW19 ....28 D3
Batts Hl *REIG* RH2 ....119 P3
The Baulk *WAND/EARL* SW18 ....28 D3
Bavant Rd *STRHM/NOR* SW16 ....44 D3
Bawdale Rd *EDUL* SE22 ....30 G1
Bawtree Cl *BELMT* SM2 ....61 N8
Bax Cl *CRAN* GU6 ....171 H1
Baxter Av *REDH* RH1 ....120 A5
Baxter Cl *CRAWE* RH10 ....177 K7
   NWDGN UB2 ....16 B1
Bayards *WARL* CR6 ....82 C7
Bay Rd *BRAK* RG12 ....32 G3
Bays Cl *SYD* SE26 ....31 K8
Baysfarm Ct *WDR/YW* UB7 ....13 N6
Baythorn La *HORL* RH6 ....159 M3
Bay Tree Av *LHD/OX* KT22 ....76 D3
Baywood Cl *FARN* GU14 ....87 N2
Bazalgette Cl *NWMAL* KT3 ....42 A6
Bazalgette Gdns *NWMAL* KT3 ....42 B6
Beach Gv *FELT* TW13 ....25 H6
Beachy Rd *CRAWW* RH11 ....194 E1
Beacon Cl *BNSTD* SM7 ....79 H5
   RFNM GU10 ....127 L8
Beacon Ct *DTCH/LGLY* SL3 ....12 C5
   SWTR RH13 * 192 F6
Beacon Gdns *FLEETN* GU51 * 86 E9
Beacon Hl *LING* RH7 ....162 G4
   WOKN/KNAP GU21 ....72 A8
Beacon Hill Ct *GSHT* GU26 ....165 N5
Beacon Hill Pk *GSHT* GU26 * 165 L6
Beacon Hill Rd *FLEETS* GU52 * 107 H2
   GSHT GU26 ....165 N5
Beacon Pl *CROY/NA* CRO 62 G1
Beacon Rd *FARN* GU14 ....88 D7
   HTHAIR TW6 ....14 A8
Beaconsfield Cl *CHSWK* W4 ....18 B1
Beaconsfield Gdns
   ESH/CLAY KT10 ....58 E6
Beaconsfield Pl *EW* KT17 ....78 C1
Beaconsfield Rd *CHSWK* W4 ....18 B1
   CROY/NA CRO 45 M7
   EPSOM KT18 ....78 B6
   ESH/CLAY KT10 ....58 E6
   NWMAL KT3 ....42 B3
   SURB KT6 ....41 M8
   TWK TW1 ....26 A3
   WOKS/MYFD GU22 ....72 D9
Beaconsfield Terrace Rd
   WKENS W14 ....19 J1
Beaconsfield Wk
   FUL/PGN SW6 ....19 K6
Beacon View Rd
   MFD/CHID GU8 ....148 D2
Beacon Wy *BNSTD* SM7 ....79 H5
Beadles La *OXTED* RH8 ....123 K1
Beadlow Cl *CAR* SM5 ....43 P7
Beadman Pl *WNWD* SE27 * 30 C7
Beadman St *WNWD* SE27 ....30 C7
Beadnell Rd *FSTH* SE23 ....31 L4
Beadon Rd *HAYES* BR2 ....47 N5
   HMSMTH W6 ....18 G2
Beaford Gv *RYNPK* SW20 ....43 J4
Beagle Cl *FELT* TW13 ....24 C7
Beales Rd *EBED/NFELT* TW14 * 56 B7
Bealeswood La *RFNM* GU10 ....146 B6
Beam Hollow *FNM* GU9 ....107 N7
Beardell Rd *NRWD* SE19 ....30 G8
Beard's Hl *HPTN* TW12 ....40 A2
Beard's Hill Cl *HPTN* TW12 * 40 A2
Beards Rd *ASHF* TW15 ....25 P9
Beare Green Rd *RDKG* RH5 ....155 P4
Bearfield Rd *KUTN/CMB* KT2 ....8 D1
Bear La *FNM* GU9 ....5 F2
Bear Rd *FELT* TW13 ....25 H6
Bears Den
   KWD/TDW/WH KT20 ....99 K2
Bearsden Wy *HORS* RH12 ....191 L7
Bearsted Av *BROCKY* SE4 * 31 N1
Bearstead Ter *BECK* BR3 * 46 G2
Bearwood Cl
   ADL/WDHM KT15 ....55 L5
Bearwood Gdns
   FLEETN GU51 ....86 G6
Beasley's Ait *SUN* TW16 ....39 J7
Beasley's Ait La *SUN* TW16 ....39 H7
Beatrice Av
   STRHM/NOR SW16 ....45 H4
Beatrice Pl *KENS* W8 ....19 N2
Beatrice Rd *OXTED* RH8 ....103 L8
   RCHPK/HAM TW10 ....26 C2
Beattie Cl *EBED/NFELT* TW14 ....24 A4
   GT/LBKH KT23 ....96 F4
Beatty Av *GU* GU1 ....112 E4
Beauchamp Rd
   E/WMO/HCT KT8 ....40 B6
   NRWD SE19 ....45 M2
   SUT SM1 ....61 L4
   TWK TW1 ....25 P3
Beauchamp Ter *BARN* SW13 ....18 F8

Beauclare Cl *LHD/OX* KT22 ....97 K1
Beauclerc Rd *HMSMTH* W6 ....18 F1
Beauclerk Cl *FELT* TW13 ....24 C4
Beaufighter Rd *FARN* GU14 ....88 C7
Beaufort Cl *PUT/ROE* SW15 ....27 P4
   REIG RH2 ....119 K4
   WOKS/MYFD GU22 ....72 G5
Beaufort Gdns *ASC* SL5 ....33 N2
   HEST TW5 ....15 N6
   STRHM/NOR SW16 ....45 H1
Beaufort Rd *ASHV* GU12 ....89 H9
   FLEETS GU52 ....87 H8
   FNM GU9 ....5 G2
   KUT/HW KT1 ....41 L5
   RCHPK/HAM TW10 ....26 B7
   REIG RH2 ....119 K4
   TWK TW1 ....26 B3
   WOKS/MYFD GU22 ....72 G5
Beauforts *EGH* TW20 ....21 H8
Beaufort St *CHEL* SW3 ....19 P4
Beaufort Wy *EW* KT17 ....60 E6
Beaufront Cl *CBLY* GU15 ....69 J1
Beaufront Rd *CBLY* GU15 ....69 J1
Beaulieu Av *SYD* SE26 ....31 J7
Beaulieu Cl *BRAK* RG12 ....33 H4
   DTCH/LGLY SL3 ....12 A7
   HSLWW TW4 ....24 C1
   MTCM CR4 ....44 C4
   TWK TW1 ....26 C2
Beaulieu Gdns *BLKW* GU17 ....67 N3
Beaulieu Pl *CHSWK* W4 ....18 A1
Beaumaris Pde *FRIM* GU16 ....89 H5
Beaumont Av *RCH/KEW* TW9 ....17 M8
   WKENS W14 ....19 K3
Beaumont Cl *CRAWW* RH11 ....176 D6
   KUTN/CMB KT2 ....9 J1
Beaumont Crs *WKENS* W14 ....19 K3
Beaumont Dr *ASHF* TW15 ....23 N8
Beaumont Gdns *BRAK* RG12 ....32 G6
Beaumont Gv *ALDT* GU11 ....108 A4
Beaumont Pl *ISLW* TW7 ....25 N1
Beaumont Rd *CHSWK* W4 ....18 A1
   NRWD SE19 ....29 P8
   PUR/KEN CR8 ....81 J2
   WIM/MER SW19 ....28 B3
Beaumonts *REDH* RH1 ....140 B4
Beauval Rd *EDUL* SE22 ....30 G2
Beaver Cl *HORS* RH12 ....192 D4
   HPTN TW12 ....40 B2
   MRDN SM4 ....42 G8
   PGE/AN SE20 * 46 A1
Beaver La *YTLY* GU46 ....67 J3
Beavers Cl *FNM* GU9 ....4 C4
   RGUW GU3 ....111 L4
Beavers Crs *HSLWW* TW4 ....15 M9
Beavers Hl *FNM* GU9 ....4 B5
Beavers La *HSLWW* TW4 ....15 L8
Beavers Rd *FNM* GU9 ....4 B4
Beavor La *HMSMTH* W6 ....18 E2
Bechin Cl *FLEETS* GU52 ....106 D3
Beck Ct *BECK* BR3 ....46 D4
Beckenham Gv *HAYES* BR2 ....47 K3
Beckenham La *HAYES* BR2 ....47 L3
Beckenham Place Pk
   BECK BR3 ....47 H1
Beckenham Rd *WWKM* BR4 ....47 H8
Beckenham Gdns
   BNSTD SM7 ....80 A4
Becket Cl *SNWD* SE25 ....46 A7
   WIM/MER SW19 * 43 M2
Beckett Av *PUR/KEN* CR8 ....81 K4
Beckett Cha *DTCH/LGLY* SL3 ....12 D5
Becket Cl *SHTM/NOR* SW16 ....29 N5
Becketts Cl
   EBED/NFELT TW14 ....24 C2
Becketts Pl *KUT/HW* KT1 ....8 B5
Beckett Wk *BECK* BR3 ....31 M9
Beckett Wy *EGRIN* RH19 ....180 E5
Beckford Av *BRAK* RG12 ....32 D7
Beckford Rd *CROY/NA* CRO 45 P7
Beckford Wy *CRAWE* RH10 ....195 L1
Beck La *BECK* BR3 ....46 D3
Beck River Pk *BECK* BR3 ....46 F2
Beck Wy *BECK* BR3 ....46 F4
Beckway Rd
   STRHM/NOR SW16 ....44 F3
Becclands Rd *TOOT* SW17 ....29 K9
Becmead Av
   STRHM/NOR SW16 ....29 N7
Becondale Rd *NRWD* SE19 ....30 F8
Bective Rd *PUT/ROE* SW15 ....19 M9
Bedale Cl *CRAWW* RH11 ....176 F7
Beddington Farm Rd
   CROY/NA CRO 44 G8
Beddington Gdns *CAR* SM5 ....62 C5
Beddington Gv *WLGTN* SM6 ....62 F4
Beddington La *CROY/NA* CRO 44 F8
Beddington Ter
   CROY/NA CRO * 45 H8
Beddlestead La
   BH/WHM TN16 ....103 N1
Bedfont Cl *EBED/NFELT* TW14 ....23 M4
   MTCM CR4 ....44 C3
Bedfont Ct
   STWL/WRAY TW19 ....13 L8
Bedfont Green Cl
   EBED/NFELT TW14 ....23 M4
Bedfont La
   EBED/NFELT TW14 ....23 P3
Bedfont Rd
   EBED/NFELT TW14 ....23 M4
   STWL/WRAY TW19 ....23 J2
Bedford Av *FRIM* GU16 ....89 H2
Bedford Cl *CHSWK* W4 ....18 C4
   WOKN/KNAP GU21 ....72 A4

Bedford Cnr *CHSWK* W4 * 18 C2
Bedford Crs *FRIM* GU16 ....88 G1
Bedford Hl *BAL* SW12 ....29 L5
Bedford La *ASC* SL5 ....35 H6
   FRIM GU16 ....89 H1
Bedford Pk *CROY/NA* CRO 2 D2
Bedford Pl *CROY/NA* CRO 2 E2
Bedford Rd *CHSWK* W4 ....18 B1
   GU GU1 ....7 H6
   SWTR RH13 ....192 C9
   WHTN TW2 ....25 L6
   WPK KT4 ....60 C1
Bedgebury Gdns
   WIM/MER SW19 ....28 B5
Bedlow Wy *CROY/NA* CRO 63 H3
Bedser Cl *THHTH* CR7 ....45 L4
   WOKN/KNAP GU21 ....11 G2
Bedster Gdns
   E/WMO/HCT KT8 ....40 B3
Bedwardine Rd *NRWD* SE19 ....45 N1
Bedwell Gdns *HYS/HAR* UB3 ....14 G3
Beech Av *BH/WHM* TN16 ....84 B8
   BTFD TW8 ....17 H5
   CBLY GU15 ....68 F4
   EHSLY KT24 ....115 M1
   RFNM GU10 ....127 N8
   SAND/SEL CR2 ....63 N6
Beechbrook Av *YTLY* GU46 ....67 H5
Beech Cl *ASHF* TW15 ....23 N8
   ASHV GU12 ....108 G6
   BF/WBF KT14 ....74 A1
   CAR SM5 ....62 C1
   COB KT11 ....76 A1
   DORK RH4 ....116 F8
   EGRIN RH19 * 180 C1
   EHSLY KT24 ....95 M8
   LING RH7 ....162 F3
   MFD/CHID GU8 ....167 P7
   PUT/ROE SW15 ....27 M3
   STWL/WRAY TW19 ....22 G3
   SUN TW16 ....39 M3
   WDR/YW UB7 ....14 C1
   WIM/MER SW19 ....27 P9
   WOT/HER KT12 ....57 L3
Beech Close Ct *COB* KT11 ....57 P9
Beech Copse *SAND/SEL* CR2 ....63 N4
Beech Crs
   KWD/TDW/WH KT20 ....118 A1
Beechcroft Av *NWMAL* KT3 ....42 A2
   PUR/KEN CR8 ....81 M4
Beechcroft Cl *ASC* SL5 ....34 D5
   HEST TW5 ....15 N5
   LIPH GU30 ....182 A7
   STRHM/NOR SW16 ....30 A8
Beechcroft Dr *GUW* GU3 ....111 K8
Beechcroft Mnr *WEY* KT13 ....56 F2
Beechcroft Rd *CHSGTN* KT9 ....59 M3
   MORT/ESHN SW14 * 18 A8
   TOOT SW17 ....29 J6
Beechdale Rd
   BRXS/STRHM SW2 ....30 A2
Beechdene
   KWD/TDW/WH KT20 ....98 F2
Beech Dr *BLKW* GU17 ....67 P4
   KWD/TDW/WH KT20 ....99 K2
   REIG RH2 ....119 P5
   RPLY/SEND GU23 ....93 K4
Beechen Cliff Wy *ISLW* TW7 ....16 F7
Beechen La
   KWD/TDW/WH KT20 ....99 K5
Beechen Pl *FSTH* SE23 ....31 K5
The Beeches Av *CAR* SM5 ....62 A6
Beeches Cl
   KWD/TDW/WH KT20 ....99 L3
   PGE/AN SE20 * 46 B1
Beeches Crs *CRAWE* RH10 ....177 H7
Beeches Rd *CHEAM* SM3 ....43 J9
   TOOT SW17 ....29 H6
The Beeches *ASHV* GU12 ....89 H6
   BNSTD SM7 ....79 M5
   LHD/OX KT22 ....97 J2
   SHGR GU5 ....132 D7
   STA TW18 * 22 D8
Beeches Wk *BELMT* SM2 ....79 M5
Beeches Wd
   KWD/TDW/WH KT20 ....99 L2
Beechey Cl *CRAWE* RH10 ....160 C9
Beechey Wy *CRAWE* RH10 ....160 C9
Beechfield *BNSTD* SM7 ....79 M4
Beechfield Rd *CAT* SE6 ....31 N4
Beech Flds *EGRIN* RH19 ....162 E9
Beech Gdns *CRAWE* RH10 ....179 H4
   WOKN/KNAP GU21 ....72 C4
Beech Gln *BRAK* RG12 ....32 D5
Beech Gv *ADL/WDHM* KT15 ....55 M3
   CHOB/PIR GU24 ....70 C9
   CTHM CR3 ....101 N6
   EPSOM KT18 ....78 F6
   GT/LBKH KT23 ....96 C3
   GUW GU3 ....111 M5
   MTCM CR4 ....44 E4
   NWMAL KT3 ....42 B4
Beech Hall *CHERT* KT16 * 54 G6
Beech Hanger End
   GSHT GU26 ....165 L8
Beech Hl *MFD/CHID* GU8 ....166 G2
   WOKS/MYFD GU22 ....92 B3
Beech Hill Av *ASC* SL5 ....34 B3
   BOR GU35 ....164 C4
Beech Holme *CRAWE* RH10 ....179 H3
Beech Holt *LHD/OX* KT22 ....97 J2
Beech House Rd
   CROY/NA CRO 2 E6
Beeching Cl *ASHV* GU12 ....109 K3
Beeching Wy *EGRIN* RH19 ....180 C2
Beech La *GSHT* GU26 ....165 L7
   GUW GU3 ....112 A8
   RGUW GU3 ....110 A5

Beechlawn *GU* GU1 ....7 J4
Beechmeads *COB* KT11 * 75 M2
Beechmont Av *VW* GU25 ....36 B7
Beechmore Gdns
   CHEAM SM3 ....61 H1
Beechnut Dr *BLKW* GU17 ....67 M2
Beechnut Rd *ASHV* GU12 ....108 D5
Beecholme Av *MTCM* CR4 ....44 D2
Beecholme *BNSTD* SM7 * 79 J3
Beech Ride *FLEETS* GU52 ....86 F8
   SHST GU47 ....49 M9
Beech Rd *BH/WHM* TN16 ....84 A6
   EBED/NFELT TW14 ....23 P3
   EW KT17 ....78 C4
   FARN GU14 ....68 D9
   FRIM GU16 ....89 H1
   HASM GU27 ....184 D3
   HORS RH12 ....192 G5
   REDH RH1 ....100 E6
   REIG RH2 ....119 L3
   STRHM/NOR SW16 ....44 G2
   WEY KT13 ....56 F3
Beechrow *KUTN/CMB* KT2 ....26 D7
Beechside *CRAWE* RH10 ....177 H6
Beechtree Av *EGH* TW20 ....20 C9
Beech Tree Cl
   CRAWE RH10 * 176 G4
Beech Tree Dr *FNM* GU9 ....108 C9
Beech Tree La *STA* TW18 * 37 M3
Beech Tree Pl *SUT* SM1 ....61 M4
Beech V *WOKS/MYFD* GU22 ....10 E6
Beech Wk *EW* KT17 ....60 E9
Beech Wy *EW* KT17 ....78 C4
   GODL GU7 ....150 C1
   SAND/SEL CR2 ....82 D2
   WHTN TW2 ....25 H6
Beechway *GU* GU1 ....112 F4
Beechwood
   KWD/TDW/WH KT20 * 117 P2
Beechwood Av
   COUL/CHIP CR5 ....80 D4
   KWD/TDW/WH KT20 ....99 L1
   RCH/KEW TW9 ....17 N6
   STA TW18 ....22 E9
   SUN TW16 ....24 B9
   THHTH CR7 ....45 K5
   WEY KT13 ....56 G3
Beechwood Cl *ASC* SL5 ....33 N1
   FLEETN GU51 ....86 E8
   SURB KT6 ....41 J8
   WEY KT13 ....56 G3
   WOKN/KNAP GU21 ....71 L6
Beechwood Dr *COB* KT11 ....58 A8
Beechwood Gdns
   CTHM CR3 ....102 A2
Beechwood La *WARL* CR6 ....82 D8
Beechwood Mnr *WEY* KT13 ....56 G3
Beechwood Rd *LHD/OX* KT22 ....97 J1
   SAND/SEL CR2 ....63 N7
   VW GU25 ....35 P8
   WOKN/KNAP GU21 ....71 L7
Beechwood Vls *REDH* RH1 ....140 C6
Beecot La *WOT/HER* KT12 ....57 L1
Beecroft La *BROCKY* SE4 ....31 M1
Beecroft Ms *BROCKY* SE4 ....31 M1
Beecroft Rd *BROCKY* SE4 ....31 M1
Beeding Cl *HORS* RH12 ....192 F5
Beedingwood Dr
   HORS RH12 ....193 K4
Beehive Rd *STA* TW18 ....22 C8
Beehive Wy *REIG* RH2 ....119 M9
Beeleigh Rd *MRDN* SM4 ....43 M5
Beeston Wy
   EBED/NFELT TW14 ....24 D2
Beeton's Av *ASHV* GU12 ....109 J2
Beggarshouse La *HORL* RH6 ....157 P4
Beggars La *BH/WHM* TN16 ....105 H5
   CHOB/PIR GU24 ....53 J9
   RDKG RH5 ....114 C9
Beggar's Roost La *SUT* SM1 ....61 L5
Begonia Pl *HPTN* TW12 ....25 H9
Behenna Cl *CRAWW* RH11 ....176 B6
Beira St *BAL* SW12 ....29 L3
Belcroft Cl *BMLY* BR1 ....47 M1
Beldam Bridge Rd
   CHOB/PIR GU24 ....70 G2
Beldham Gdns
   E/WMO/HCT KT8 ....40 B3
Beldham Rd *FNM* GU9 ....127 K6
Belfast Rd *SNWD* SE25 ....46 B5
Belfield Rd *HOR/WEW* KT19 ....60 B7
Belfry Ms *SHST* GU47 ....49 J3
The Belfry *REDH* RH1 ....120 B4
Belgrade Rd *HPTN* TW12 ....40 A2
Belgrave Av *MTCM* CR4 ....43 N4
Belgrave Cl *WOT/HER* KT12 ....57 K3
Belgrave Ct *BLKW* GU17 ....67 P5
Belgrave Crs *SUN* TW16 ....39 K2
Belgrave Mnr
   WOKS/MYFD GU22 ....10 C7
Belgrave Rd *BARN* SW13 ....18 D5
   HSLWW TW4 ....15 P8
   MTCM CR4 ....43 P4
   SNWD SE25 ....45 P5
   SUN TW16 ....39 K2
Belgrave Wk *MTCM* CR4 ....43 P4
Belgravia Ms *KUT/HW* KT1 ....41 K5
Bellamy Cl *WKENS* W14 ....19 K3
Bellamy Rd *CRAWE* RH10 ....177 M9
Belland Dr *ALDT* GU11 ....108 A5
Bel La *FELT* TW13 ....24 F6
Bellasis Av *BRXS/STRHM* SW2 ....29 P4
Bell Av *WDR/YW* UB7 ....14 B2
Bellever Hl *CBLY* GU15 ....69 H3
Bell Cl *FARN* GU14 ....88 C5
Bell Cl *CHERT* KT16 ....37 K1
Bell Crs *COUL/CHIP* CR5 ....100 D1
Bell Dr *WAND/EARL* SW18 ....28 B3
Belleville Rd *BTSEA* SW11 ....29 J1
Belle Vue Cl *ASHV* GU12 ....108 F4
   STA TW18 ....37 J5

Bellevue Pk THHTH CR7 45 L4
Belle Vue Rd ASHV GU12 108 F5
Bellevue Rd BARN SW13 18 E7
KUT/HW KT1 8 E7
TOOT SW17 29 J3
Bellew Rd FRIM GU16 89 K1
Bellew St TOOT SW17 28 F6
Bellfield CROY/NA CR0 64 F7
Bellfields Rd GU GU1 112 B3
Bell Gn SYD SE26 31 M7
Bell Green La SYD SE26 31 N8
Bell Hammer EGRIN RH19 180 D3
Bellingham Cl CBLY GU15 69 L4
Bellingham Dr REIG RH2 119 K5
Bellingham Gn CAT SE6 31 P6
Bell La BLKW GU17 67 N3
LHD/OX KT22 96 D3
RFNM GU10 146 B1
TWK TW1 25 P4
Bell Lane Cl LHD/OX KT22 96 D3
Bellmarsh Rd
ADL/WDHM KT15 55 M3
Bell Meadow GDST RH9 122 C3
NRWD SE19 30 F7
Belloc Cl CRAWE RH10 177 L4
Belloc Ct SWTR RH13 * 192 F7
Bello Cl HNHL SE24 30 C4
Bell Pde HSLW TW3 * 16 B9
WWKM BR4 * 65 J1
Bell Pl BAGS GU19 51 P6
Bell Rd E/WMO/HCT KT8 40 D6
HASM GU27 184 B7
HORS RH12 191 P2
HSLW TW3 16 B9
Bells La DTCH/LGLY SL3 12 F8
Bell St REIG RH2 119 L5
Belltrees Gv
STRHM/NOR SW16 30 A8
Bell Vale La HASM GU27 184 C6
Bellweir Cl STWL/WRAY TW19 21 N5
Bellwether La REDH RH1 141 K5
Belmont Av GUW GU2 111 M2
NWDGN UB2 15 N1
NWMAL KT3 42 E6
Belmont Cl FARN GU14 68 B9
Belmont Gv CHSWK W4 18 B2
Belmont Ms CBLY GU15 68 E5
Belmont Ri BELMT SM2 61 K6
Belmont Rd BECK BR3 46 E3
BELMT SM2 61 L8
CBLY GU15 68 E4
CWTH RG45 49 M3
LHD/OX KT22 96 G2
REIG RH2 119 N6
SNWD SE25 46 B6
WHTN TW2 25 L5
WLGTN SM6 62 E4
Belmont Ter CHSWK W4 18 B2
Belmore Av
WOKS/MYFD GU22 73 H5
Beloe Cl PUT/ROE SW15 18 E9
Belsize Av WEA W13 17 H1
Belsize Gdns SUT SM1 61 M3
Belsize Rd FARN GU14 88 E6
Belstone Ms FARN GU14 68 C9
Beltane Dr WIM/MER SW19 28 A6
Belthorn Crs BAL SW12 29 M3
Belton Rd CBLY GU15 68 G3
Beltran Rd FUL/PGN SW6 19 M7
Belvedere Av
WIM/MER SW19 28 B8
Belvedere Cl ESH/CLAY KT10 58 B4
FLEETN GU51 86 C6
GUW GU2 111 P3
TEDD TW11 25 M8
WEY KT13 56 C4
Belvedere Ct BLKW GU17 67 P5
Belvedere Dr
WIM/MER SW19 28 B8
Belvedere Gdns
E/WMO/HCT KT8 39 P6
Belvedere Gv
WIM/MER SW19 28 B8
Belvedere Rd BH/WHM TN16 84 D7
FARN GU14 88 E5
HNWL W7 16 E1
NRWD SE19 45 P1
Belvedere Sq
WIM/MER SW19 28 B8
The Belvedere
WBPTN SW10 * 19 N6
Belvoir Cl FRIM GU16 69 H7
Belvoir Rd EDUL SE22 31 H3
Bembridge Ct CWTH RG45 49 J5
Bemish Rd PUT/ROE SW15 19 H8
Benbow La MFD/CHID GU8 169 P7
Benbow Rd HMSMTH W6 18 F1
Benbricke Gn BNFD RG42 32 C1
Benbrick Rd GUW GU2 111 N6
The Bence EGH TW20 36 F4
Bench Fld SAND/SEL CR2 63 P5
Benchfield Cl EGRIN RH19 180 G3
The Bench
RCHPK/HAM TW10 * 26 B6
Bencombe Rd PUR/KEN CR8 81 J3
Bencroft Rd
STRHM/NOR SW16 44 E1
Bencurtis Pk WWKM BR4 65 K2
Bendemeer Rd
PUT/ROE SW15 19 H8
Bendeng Cl FLEETN GU51 86 D4
Bendon Va WAND/EARL SW18 28 E3
Benedict Dr
EBED/NFELT TW14 23 N3
Benedict Gn BNFD RG42 32 G1
Benedict Rd MTCM CR4 43 P4
Benedict Whf MTCM CR4 44 A4
Benenden Gn HAYES BR2 47 N6
Benen-stock Rd
STWL/WRAY TW19 22 D2
Benett Gdns
STRHM/NOR SW16 44 G3
Benfleet Cl COB KT11 75 N1
SUT SM1 61 N2
Benham Cl BTSEA SW11 19 P8
CHSGTN KT9 59 J5
COUL/CHIP CR5 81 K7
Benham Gdns HSLWW TW4 24 G1
Benhams Dr HORL RH6 140 C8
Benhill Av SUT SM1 61 N3
Benhill Rd SUT SM1 61 P2
Benhill Wood Rd SUT SM1 61 N3
Benhilton Gdns SUT SM1 61 M2
Benhurst Cl SAND/SEL CR2 64 D8
Benhurst Gdns
SAND/SEL CR2 64 C8
Benhurst La
STRHM/NOR SW16 30 B8
Benjamin Ms BAL SW12 29 M3
Benjamin Rd CRAWE RH10 177 N7
Benn Cl OXTED RH8 123 N5
Benner La CHOB/PIR GU24 70 F1
Bennerley Rd BTSEA SW11 29 J1
Bennet Cl KUT/HW KT1 8 A3
Bennett Cl COB KT11 75 J2
CRAWE RH10 177 L9
HSLWW TW4 24 F1
Bennett Ct CBLY GU15 68 F5
Bennetts Av CROY/NA CR0 64 E1
Bennetts Cl MTCM CR4 44 D2
Bennetts Farm Pl
GT/LBKH KT23 95 P5
Bennetts Ri ALDT GU11 108 E6
Bennetts Rd SWTR RH13 192 D9
Bennett St CHSWK W4 18 C4
Bennetts Wy CROY/NA CR0 64 E1
Bennetts Wd RDKG RH5 156 B7
Bennett Wy RGUE GU4 93 L9
Bennings Cl BNFD RG42 32 C1
Bens Acre SWTR RH13 192 F8
Bensbury Cl PUT/ROE SW15 27 N3
Bensham Cl THHTH CR7 45 L5
Bensham Gv THHTH CR7 45 L3
Bensham La THHTH CR7 45 K5
Bensham Manor Rd
THHTH CR7 45 L5
Benson Cl HSLW TW3 16 A9
Benson Rd CROY/NA CR0 63 J2
CWTH RG45 49 K4
FSTH SE23 31 K4
Benson's La HORS RH12 193 H1
Benthall Gdns PUR/KEN CR8 81 L5
Bentham Av
WOKN/KNAP GU21 72 G4
Bentley Copse CBLY GU15 69 K4
Bentley Dr WEY KT13 56 C7
Benton's La WNWD SE27 30 D7
Benton's Ri WNWD SE27 30 E8
Bentsbrook Cl RDKG RH5 137 H2
Bentsbrook Pk RDKG RH5 137 H2
Bentsbrook Rd RDKG RH5 137 H2
Benwell Ct SUN TW16 * 39 J2
Ben Well Rd CHOB/PIR GU24 70 G8
Benwood Ct SUT SM1 61 P1
Beomonds Rw CHERT KT16 * 37 L8
Berberis Cl GU GU1 112 A3
Berberis Wk WDR/YW UB7 14 A2
Berber Rd BTSEA SW11 * 29 J1
Berenger Wk WBPTN SW10 * 19 P5
Bere Rd BRAK RG12 32 G7
Beresford Av BRYLDS KT5 41 P9
TWK TW1 26 B2
Beresford Cl FRIM GU16 89 H1
Beresford Gdns HSLWW TW4 24 G1
Beresford Rd BELMT SM2 61 K6
DORK RH4 117 H7
KUTN/CMB KT2 9 F2
NWMAL KT3 42 A5
Berestede Rd HMSMTH W6 18 D3
Bergenia Ct CHOB/PIR GU24 70 E2
Berghem Ms WKENS W14 19 H1
Berisford Ms
WAND/EARL SW18 28 F2
Berkeley Av HSLWW TW4 15 J6
Berkeley Cl CRAWW RH11 176 A9
FLEETN GU51 87 H6
KUTN/CMB KT2 41 L1
STWL/WRAY TW19 22 A5
Berkeley Ct WEY KT13 56 F1
WLGTN SM6 62 E2
Berkeley Crs FRIM GU16 69 J8
Berkeley Dr E/WMO/HCT KT8 39 P4
Berkeley Gdns BF/WBF KT14 73 K3
ESH/CLAY KT10 58 G6
WOT/HER KT12 39 H8
Berkeley Ms SUN TW16 39 L4
Berkeley Pl EPSOM KT18 78 B4
WIM/MER SW19 28 A9
Berkeley Rd BARN SW13 18 E6
The Berkeleys LHD/OX KT22 96 E4
SNWD SE25 * 46 A5
Berkeley Waye HEST TW5 15 N5
Berkley Cl WHTN TW2 * 25 M6
Berkley Ct GU GU1 7 H2
Berkshire Cl CTHM CR3 101 M2
Berkshire Corpse Rd
ALDT GU11 88 A8
Berkshire Rd CBLY GU15 51 H9
Berkshire Wy MTCM CR4 44 G5
Bernadine Cl BNFD RG42 32 G1
Bernard Av WEA W13 17 H1
Bernard Gdns
WIM/MER SW19 28 C8
Bernard Rd WLGTN SM6 62 D4
Bernel Dr CROY/NA CR0 64 F2
Berne Rd THHTH CR7 45 K6
Bernersh Cl SHST GU47 49 N8
Berney Rd CROY/NA CR0 45 M8
Berridge Rd NRWD SE19 30 E8
Berrington Dr EHSLY KT24 95 H4
Berrybank SHST GU47 68 A2
Berrycroft BRAK RG12 32 G4
Berrylands BRYLDS KT5 41 N6
RYNPK SW20 42 G4
Berrylands Rd BRYLDS KT5 41 M7
Berry La DUL SE21 30 E7
RGUW GU3 91 K4
Berryman's La SYD SE26 31 L7
Berry Meade ASHTD KT21 77 M6
Berry Meade Cl ASHTD KT21 77 M6
Berrymede Rd CHSWK W4 18 B1
Berryscroft Rd STA TW18 37 N1
Berry's Green Rd
BH/WHM TN16 84 F5
Berry's Hl BH/WHM TN16 84 F4
Berry's La BF/WBF KT14 55 P9
Berry Wk ASHTD KT21 77 M8
Berry Wy EA W5 17 L1
Bertal Rd TOOT SW17 28 G7
Bertie Rd SYD SE26 31 L9
Bertram Rd KUTN/CMB KT2 41 N1
Bert Rd THHTH CR7 45 L6
Berwick Cl WHTN TW2 25 H4
Berwick Gdns SUT SM1 61 N2
Berwyn Av HSLW TW3 16 B6
Berwyn Rd HNHL SE24 30 C4
RCHPK/HAM TW10 17 P9
Beryl Rd HMSMTH W6 19 H3
Berystede KUTN/CMB KT2 9 K1
Besley St STRHM/NOR SW16 29 M9
Bessant Dr RCH/KEW TW9 17 P6
Bessborough Rd
PUT/ROE SW15 27 M4
Beswick Gdns BRAK RG12 33 H2
Beta Rd CHOB/PIR GU24 53 M8
FARN GU14 88 B2
WOKS/MYFD GU22 11 K1
Beta Wy EGH TW20 36 G2
Betchets Green Rd
RDKG RH5 137 J7
Betchley Cl EGRIN RH19 162 D9
Betchworth Cl SUT SM1 61 P4
Betchworth Wy
CROY/NA CR0 65 J7
Bethany Pl
WOKN/KNAP GU21 * 10 A5
Bethany Waye
EBED/NFELT TW14 23 P3
Bethel Cl FNM GU9 107 P8
Bethel La FNM GU9 107 P8
Bethersden Cl BECK BR3 46 F1
Bethune Cl CRAWE RH10 177 N6
Bethune Rd SWTR RH13 192 D9
Betjeman Cl COUL/CHIP CR5 81 H6
Betjeman Wk YTLY GU46 66 F4
Betley Ct WOT/HER KT12 57 K2
Betony Cl CROY/NA CR0 46 D9
Bettridge Rd FUL/PGN SW6 19 K7
Betts Cl BECK BR3 46 E3
Betts Wy CRAWE RH10 176 G1
PGE/AN SE20 46 B3
SURB KT6 41 H9
Betula Cl PUR/KEN CR8 81 M4
Between Streets COB KT11 75 K3
Beulah Av THHTH CR7 * 45 L3
Beulah Crs THHTH CR7 45 L3
Beulah Gv CROY/NA CR0 45 L7
Beulah Hl NRWD SE19 30 D9
Beulah Rd SUT SM1 61 K3
THHTH CR7 45 L4
WIM/MER SW19 43 K1
Beulah Wk CTHM CR3 82 E9
Bevan Ct CROY/NA CR0 63 J4
Bevan Ga BNFD RG42 32 C2
Bevan Pk EW KT17 60 D9
Beveren Cl FLEETN GU51 87 H3
Beverley Av HSLWW TW4 15 P9
RYNPK SW20 42 D2
Beverley Cl ADL/WDHM KT15 55 P4
ASHV GU12 109 H5
BARN SW13 18 E7
BTSEA SW11 19 P9
CBLY GU15 69 L2
CHSGTN KT9 59 J3
EW KT17 60 G9
WEY KT13 56 G1
Beverley Crs FARN GU14 88 B4
Beverley Gdns BARN SW13 18 D8
WPK KT4 42 E9
Beverley Hts REIG RH2 119 M3
Beverley La KUTN/CMB KT2 42 C1
Beverley Ms CRAWE RH10 177 K6
Beverley Rd BARN SW13 18 D8
CHSWK W4 18 D3
CTHM CR3 81 N6
KUT/HW KT1 8 A2
MTCM CR4 44 F5
NWDGN UB2 15 N2
NWMAL KT3 42 E5
PGE/AN SE20 46 B3
SUN TW16 39 H2
WPK KT4 60 G1
Beverley Wy KUTN/CMB KT2 42 D2
Beverstone Rd
BRXS/STRHM SW2 30 A1
THHTH CR7 45 J5
Bevill Cl SNWD SE25 46 A4
Bevington Rd BECK BR3 47 H3
Bevin Sq TOOT SW17 29 J6
Bewbush Dr CRAWW RH11 176 C8
Bewley St WIM/MER SW19 28 F9
Bewlys Rd WNWD SE27 30 C8
Bexhill Cl FELT TW13 24 F5
Bexhill Rd BROCKY SE4 31 N2
MORT/ESHN SW14 18 A8
Beynon Rd CAR SM5 62 B4
Bicester Rd RCH/KEW TW9 17 N8
Bickersteth Rd TOOT SW17 29 J9
Bickley St TOOT SW17 29 H8
Bicknell Rd FRIM GU16 68 G6
Bickney Wy LHD/OX KT22 96 C2
Bicknoller Cl BELMT SM2 61 M8
Bidborough Cl HAYES BR2 47 M6
Biddulph Rd SAND/SEL CR2 63 L7
Bideford Cl FARN GU14 68 C9
FELT TW13 24 G6
Bidhams Crs
KWD/TDW/WH KT20 98 G1
The Bield REIG RH2 119 L7
Big Barn Gv BNFD RG42 32 F1
Big Common La REDH RH1 121 K4
Biggin Av MTCM CR4 44 B2
Biggin Cl CRAWW RH11 176 F7
Biggin Hl NRWD SE19 45 K1
Biggin Wy NRWD SE19 45 K1
Bigginwood Rd
STRHM/NOR SW16 45 K1
Bigg's Rw PUT/ROE SW15 19 H8
Bignor Cl HORS RH12 192 F4
Bilberry Cl CRAWW RH11 176 E8
Billesden Rd CHOB/PIR GU24 90 C1
Billing Av EWKG RG40 48 C3
Billing Pl WBPTN SW10 * 19 M5
Billing Rd WBPTN SW10 19 M5
Billingshurst Rd HORS RH12 191 K7
Billing St WBPTN SW10 * 19 M5
Billinton Dr CRAWE RH10 177 L5
Billockby Cl CHSGTN KT9 59 M5
Bina Gdns ECT SW5 19 N3
Binden Rd SHB W12 18 D1
Binfield Rd BF/WBF KT14 74 A1
BNFD RG42 32 C2
SAND/SEL CR2 63 P4
Bingham Dr STA TW18 37 P1
WOKN/KNAP GU21 71 M7
Bingham Rd CROY/NA CR0 46 A9
Bingley Rd SUN TW16 39 J1
Binhams Lea MFD/CHID GU8 169 L6
Binhams Meadow
MFD/CHID GU8 169 L6
Binney Ct CRAWE RH10 177 N2
Binns Rd CHSWK W4 18 C3
Binscombe GODL GU7 131 K5
Binscombe Crs GODL GU7 131 L6
Binscombe La GODL GU7 131 K5
Binstead Cl CRAWW RH11 176 E3
Binsted Dr BLKW GU17 67 P3
Binton La RFNM GU10 128 G3
Birchanger GODL GU7 131 L9
Birchanger Rd SNWD SE25 46 A6
Birch Av CTHM CR3 101 M4
FLEETN GU51 86 F6
Birch Cir GODL GU7 131 M5
Birch Cl ADL/WDHM KT15 55 P7
BTFD TW8 17 H5
CBLY GU15 50 G9
CRAWE RH10 179 K3
HSLW TW3 16 D8
RFNM GU10 127 L9
RPLY/SEND GU23 93 K5
TEDD TW11 25 P8
WOKN/KNAP GU21 72 A8
Birch Ct WLGTN SM6 62 D3
Birchcroft Cl CTHM CR3 101 L5
Birchdale Cl BF/WBF KT14 55 N9
Birch Dr BLKW GU17 67 P5
Birchend Cl SAND/SEL CR2 63 M5
Birches Cl EPSOM KT18 78 C4
MTCM CR4 44 B4
Birches Rd HORS RH12 192 G5
The Birches BLKW GU17 67 M3
CRAWE RH10 177 K4
EHSLY KT24 94 G6
FARN GU14 87 P3
HSLWW TW4 * 24 G3
WOKS/MYFD GU22 10 E5
Birchett Rd ALDT GU11 108 C4
FARN GU14 88 A2
Birchetts Cl BNFD RG42 32 D2
Birchfield Cl
ADL/WDHM KT15 55 M3
COUL/CHIP CR5 81 H5
Birchfield Gv EW KT17 60 G8
Birchfields CBLY GU15 68 E4
Birchgate Ms
KWD/TDW/WH KT20 * 98 G1
Birch Gn STA TW18 22 C7
Birch Gv BRAK RG12 32 E5
GU GU1 * 112 A2
KWD/TDW/WH KT20 99 K4
SHPTN TW17 38 G3
WOKS/MYFD GU22 73 H4
Birchgrove COB KT11 75 L3
Birch Hl CROY/NA CR0 64 D4
Birch Hill Rd BRAK RG12 32 D8
Birchington Rd BRYLDS KT5 41 M8
Birchlands Av BAL SW12 29 J3
Birch La ASC SL5 33 J2
CHOB/PIR GU24 70 D1
PUR/KEN CR8 62 G9
Birch Lea CRAWE RH10 177 K2
Bircholt Rd LIPH GU30 182 A6
Birch Platt CHOB/PIR GU24 70 D2
Birch Rd BFOR GU20 52 E5
BOR GU35 164 E5
EWKG RG40 48 E2
FELT TW13 24 E8
GODL GU7 131 M5
Birch Side CWTH RG45 49 K3
Birch Tree Av WWKM BR4 65 M6
Birch Tree Gdns EGRIN RH19 162 A9
Birch Tree Vw LTWR GU18 52 A8
Birch Tree Wy CROY/NA CR0 64 B1
Birch V COB KT11 76 A2
Birchview Cl YTLY GU46 66 G4
Birch Wk MTCM CR4 44 D2
Birch Wy ASHV GU12 89 J8
WARL CR6 82 E7
Birchway REDH RH1 120 D7
Birchwood Av BECK BR3 46 F5
WLGTN SM6 62 C2
Birchwood Cl BIL RH14 188 A7
CRAWE RH10 177 M8
HORL RH6 140 D9
MRDN SM4 43 M5
Birchwood Dr BF/WBF KT14 73 L1
LTWR GU18 52 C8
Birchwood Gv HPTN TW12 25 H9
Birchwood La CTHM CR3 101 K5
Birchwood Rd BF/WBF KT14 73 L1
TOOT SW17 29 L8
Birdham Cl CRAWW RH11 176 E3
Birdhaven RFNM GU10 127 L8
Bird House La ORP BR6 84 E3
Birdhurst Av SAND/SEL CR2 63 M3
Birdhurst Gdns
SAND/SEL CR2 63 M3
Birdhurst Ri SAND/SEL CR2 63 N4
Birdhurst Rd SAND/SEL CR2 63 N4
WAND/EARL SW18 19 N9
WIM/MER SW19 29 H9
Bird-in-Hand Ms FSTH SE23 31 K5
Bird-in-Hand Pas FSTH SE23 31 K5
Birds Gv WOKN/KNAP GU21 71 H7
Birds Hill Dr LHD/OX KT22 76 D2
Birds Hill Ri LHD/OX KT22 76 D2
Birds Hill Rd LHD/OX KT22 76 D1
Birdswood Dr
WOKN/KNAP GU21 71 L8
Bird Wk WHTN TW2 24 G4
Birdwood Cl SAND/SEL CR2 64 C9
TEDD TW11 25 M7
Birdwood Rd CBLY GU15 68 B2
Birkbeck Hl DUL SE21 30 C5
Birkbeck Pl DUL SE21 30 C4
SHST GU47 50 A8
Birkbeck Rd BECK BR3 46 D3
EA W5 17 J2
WIM/MER SW19 28 E8
Birkdale BRAK RG12 32 A7
Birkdale Dr CRAWW RH11 176 A6
Birkdale Gdns CROY/NA CR0 64 D3
Birkenhead Av KUTN/CMB KT2 9 F4
Birkenholme Cl BOR GU35 164 F7
Birkheads Rd REIG RH2 119 L4
Birkwood Cl BAL SW12 29 N3
Birnham Cl RPLY/SEND GU23 93 L4
Birtley Ri SHGR GU5 132 E8
Birtley Rd SHGR GU5 132 E8
Biscay Rd HMSMTH W6 19 H3
Biscoe Cl HEST TW5 16 A4
Bisenden Rd CROY/NA CR0 3 G3
Bisham Cl CAR SM5 44 B8
CRAWE RH10 177 N7
Bishop Cl RCHPK/HAM TW10 26 C6
Bishopdale BRAK RG12 32 C5
Bishop Duppas Pk
SHPTN TW17 38 F8
Bishop Fox Wy
E/WMO/HCT KT8 39 P5
Bishop Kings Rd WKENS W14 19 J2
Bishopric HORS RH12 192 A8
Bishopric Ct HORS RH12 192 A8
Bishop's Av FUL/PGN SW6 19 H7
Bishops Cl CHSWK W4 18 A3
COUL/CHIP CR5 81 J7
FLEETS GU52 86 G8
SUT SM1 61 L2
Bishops Dr
EBED/NFELT TW14 23 N2
Bishopsford Rd MRDN SM4 43 N8
Bishopsgate Rd EGH TW20 20 F6
Bishops Gv BFOR GU20 52 C5
HPTN TW12 24 G7
Bishop's Hall KUT/HW KT1 8 C4
Bishops Hl WOT/HER KT12 39 J8
Bishop's Md FNM GU9 4 E4
Bishopsmead Cl EHSLY KT24 95 H8
HOR/WEW KT19 60 B8
Bishopsmead Dr EHSLY KT24 95 H9
Bishop's Park Rd
FUL/PGN SW6 19 H7
STRHM/NOR SW16 44 G2
Bishop's Pl SUT SM1 61 N4
Bishop's Rd CROY/NA CR0 45 K8
FNM GU9 107 M8
FUL/PGN SW6 19 K6
Bishopsthorpe Rd SYD SE26 31 K7
Bishop Sumner Dr FNM GU9 107 N8
Bishops Wk CROY/NA CR0 64 D4
Bishops Wy EGH TW20 22 A9
Bishops Wd
WOKN/KNAP GU21 71 M6
Bisley Cl WPK KT4 42 G9
Bitmead Cl CRAWW RH11 * 176 B6
Bittams La CHERT KT16 55 H3
Bittern Cl ALDT GU11 108 C7
CRAWW RH11 176 A6
SHST GU47 49 P9
Bitterne Dr
WOKN/KNAP GU21 71 M6
Bittoms Ct KUT/HW KT1 * 8 C6
The Bittoms KUT/HW KT1 8 C7
Bixley Cl NWDGN UB2 15 P2
Blackberry Cl GU GU1 111 P2
SHPTN TW17 38 G5
Blackberry Farm Cl
HEST TW5 15 N5
Blackberry La LING RH7 162 C2
Blackberry Rd EGRIN RH19 162 B4
Blackbird Cl SHST GU47 49 P9
Blackbird Hl CRAWE RH10 179 K6
Blackborough Cl REIG RH2 119 N5
Blackborough Rd REIG RH2 119 P5
Blackbridge La HORS RH12 191 P9
Blackbridge Rd
WOKS/MYFD GU22 72 B9
Blackbrook Rd RDKG RH5 137 L3
The Blackburn GT/LBKH KT23 95 P4
Blackburn Wy GODL GU7 131 M8
Blackbush Cl BELMT SM2 61 M6
Blackbushe Pk YTLY GU46 * 66 G3
Blackbushes Rd
FLEETN GU51 86 E1
HTWY RG27 66 C7
Blackcap Cl CRAWW RH11 176 F7
Blackcap Pl SHST GU47 50 A9
Black Dog Wk CRAWE RH10 177 H3
Blackdown Av
WOKS/MYFD GU22 73 J4

204 Bla - Bra

Blackdown Cl
WOKS/MYFD GU22 72 G5
Blackdown Rd FRIM GU16 69 L9
Black Eagle Cl
BH/WHM TN16 104 G7
Blackenham Rd TOOT SW17 29 J7
Blackett Cl STA TW18 37 J3
Blackett Rd CRAWE RH10 177 M6
Blackett St PUT/ROE SW15 19 H8
Blackfold Rd CRAWE RH10 177 K6
Blackford Cl SAND/SEL CR2 63 K7
Blackheath CRAWE RH10 177 N3
Blackheath Gv SHGR GU5 132 F5
Blackheath La SHGR GU5 132 G5
Blackheath Rd FNM GU9 107 L7
Blackhills ESH/CLAY KT10 57 P7
Blackhorse La CROY/NA CR0 46 A8
KWD/TDW/WH KT20 99 M9
Blackhorse Rd
WOKS/MYFD GU22 71 K9
Black Horse Wy HORS RH12 192 B8
Blackhouse Rd SWTR RH13 193 P4
Blacklands Crs FROW RH18 181 L9
Blacklands Meadow
REDH RH1 120 G4
Black Lion La HMSMTH W6 18 E2
Blackman Gdns ALDT GU11 108 D6
Blackman's La WARL CR6 83 L3
Blackmeadows BRAK RG12 32 E7
Blackmoor Cl ASC SL5 33 M3
Blackmoor Wd ASC SL5 33 M3
Blackmore Crs
WOKN/KNAP GU21 72 G3
Blackmore's Gv TEDD TW11 25 P9
Blackness La
WOKS/MYFD GU22 10 D7
Blacknest Rd ASC SL5 35 K4
Black Pond La RFNM GU10 127 N7
Black Potts Copse
WOKS/MYFD GU22 71 P8
Black Prince Cl BF/WBF KT14 74 B3
Black Rod Cl HYS/HAR UB3 15 H1
Blackshaw Rd TOOT SW17 28 G8
Blacksmith Cl ASHTD KT21 77 M8
Blacksmith La RGUE GU4 132 G1
Blacksmith Rw
DTCH/LGLY SL3 12 E2
Blacksmiths Hl
SAND/SEL CR2 82 B2
Blacksmiths La CHERT KT16 37 L8
STA TW18 37 M4
Black's Rd HMSMTH W6 18 G3
Blackstone Cl FARN GU14 87 P1
REDH RH1 120 A6
Blackstone Hl REDH RH1 120 A5
Blackstroud La East
LTWR GU18 52 D9
Blackstroud La West
LTWR GU18 52 D9
Black Swan Cl CRAWW RH11 194 E3
Blackthorn Av WDR/YW UB7 14 C2
Blackthorn Cl CRAWW RH11 176 F3
REIG RH2 119 N7
SWTR RH13 192 E8
Blackthorn Ct HEST TW5 15 N5
Blackthorn Crs FARN GU14 68 B8
Blackthorn Dell
DTCH/LGLY SL3 12 A1
Blackthorn Dr LTWR GU18 70 B1
Blackthorne Av
CROY/NA CR0 46 C9
Blackthorne Crs
DTCH/LGLY SL3 13 J7
Blackthorne Rd
DTCH/LGLY SL3 13 J8
GT/LBKH KT23 96 C6
Blackthorn Pl GU GU1 * 112 A2
Blackthorn Rd
BH/WHM TN16 84 C5
REIG RH2 119 N7
Blackwater Cl ASHV GU12 109 J5
Blackwater La CRAWE RH10 177 M6
Blackwater Pk ASHV GU12 108 G5
Blackwater St EDUL SE22 30 G1
Blackwater Vw EWKG RG40 48 E7
Blackwater Wy ASHV GU12 108 G6
Blackwell Av GUW GU2 111 K5
Blackwell Farm Rd
EGRIN RH19 162 E9
Blackwell Hollow
EGRIN RH19 180 E1
Blackwell Rd EGRIN RH19 180 E1
Blackwood Cl BF/WBF KT14 73 N1
Bladen Cl WEY KT13 56 F5
Blades Cl LHD/OX KT22 77 K9
Bladon Cl GU GU1 112 E4
Blagdon Rd NWMAL KT3 42 D5
Blagdon Wk TEDD TW11 26 B9
Blair Av ESH/CLAY KT10 58 C1
Blair Cl HYS/HAR UB3 15 J2
Blairderry Rd
BRXS/STRHM SW2 29 P5
Blaire Pk YTLY GU46 48 F9
Blaise Cl FARN GU14 88 F4
Blake Cl CAR SM5 44 A9
CRAWE RH10 177 J9
CWTH RG45 49 N5
Blakeden Dr ESH/CLAY KT10 58 F6
Blake Gdns FUL/PGN SW6 19 L6
Blakehall Rd CAR SM5 62 B5
Blakemore Gdns BARN SW13 18 F4
Blakemore Rd
STRHM/NOR SW16 29 P6
THHTH CR7 45 H6
Blakeney Av BECK BR3 46 F2
Blakeney Cl HOR/WEW KT19 60 B9
Blakeney Rd BECK BR3 46 F2
Blake Rd CROY/NA CR0 3 G3
MTCM CR4 44 A4
Blakes Av NWMAL KT3 42 D6
Blake's Gn WWKM BR4 47 J8
Blake's La EHSLY KT24 114 B2
NWMAL KT3 42 D6
Blakes Ride YTLY GU46 66 F2
Blakes Ter NWMAL KT3 42 E6
Blakewood Cl FELT TW13 24 D7
Blanchards Hl RGUE GU4 92 C7
Blanchland Rd MRDN SM4 43 M6
Blanchman's Rd WARL CR6 82 E7
Blandfield Rd BAL SW12 29 K2
Blandford Av BECK BR3 46 E3
WHTN TW2 25 J4
Blandford Cl CROY/NA CR0 62 G2
DTCH/LGLY SL3 12 B1
WOKS/MYFD GU22 11 J4
Blandford Rd BECK BR3 46 D3
CHSWK W4 18 C1
NWDGN UB2 16 A2
TEDD TW11 25 L8
Blandford Rd North
DTCH/LGLY SL3 12 B1
Blandford Rd South
DTCH/LGLY SL3 12 B1
Blane's La ASC SL5 33 L7
Blanford Ms REIG RH2 119 P5
Blanford Rd REIG RH2 119 N6
Blanks La HORL RH6 157 M1
Blantyre St WBPTN SW10 19 P5
Blantyre Wk WBPTN SW10 * 19 P5
Blatchford Rd SWTR RH13 192 E7
Blays Cl EGH TW20 21 H9
Blay's La EGH TW20 20 G9
Blean Gv PGE/AN SE20 46 C1
Blegborough Rd
STRHM/NOR SW16 29 M9
Blencarn Cl
WOKN/KNAP GU21 71 N5
Blenheim Cl BF/WBF KT14 73 K2
CRAWE RH10 177 N1
EGRIN RH19 162 F9
RFNM GU10 108 G7
RYNPK SW20 42 G4
WLGTN SM6 62 E6
Blenheim Ct FARN GU14 88 F5
Blenheim Crs FNM GU9 107 L8
SAND/SEL CR2 63 L6
Blenheim Flds FROW RH18 181 K8
Blenheim Gdns
BRXS/STRHM SW2 30 A2
KUTN/CMB KT2 9 K1
SAND/SEL CR2 82 A1
WLGTN SM6 62 E5
WOKS/MYFD GU22 71 P8
Blenheim Pk ALDT GU11 88 E8
Blenheim Park Rd
SAND/SEL CR2 63 L7
Blenheim Pl TEDD TW11 25 N8
Blenheim Rd CHSWK W4 18 C1
DTCH/LGLY SL3 12 B2
FARN GU14 88 E8
HOR/WEW KT19 60 B9
HORS RH12 192 C5
PGE/AN SE20 46 C1
RYNPK SW20 42 G4
SUT SM1 61 L2
Blenheim Wy ISLW TW7 16 G6
Blenkarne Rd BTSEA SW11 29 J2
Bleriot Rd HEST TW5 15 L5
Bletchingley Cl REDH RH1 100 E9
Bletchingley Rd GDST RH9 122 A2
REDH RH1 100 E9
REDH RH1 121 J4
Bletchingly Cl THHTH CR7 45 K5
Bletchmore Cl HYS/HAR UB3 14 F3
Blewburton Wk BRAK RG12 32 G5
Blewfield GODL GU7 150 E2
Bligh Cl CRAWE RH10 177 J7
Blighton La RFNM GU10 128 F3
Blincoe Cl WIM/MER SW19 28 A5
Blindley Ct LING RH7 * 142 E5
Blindley Rd CRAWE RH10 177 N2
Blithfield St KENS W8 19 M1
Blondell Cl WDR/YW UB7 13 P4
Blondin Av EA W5 17 J2
Bloomfield Cl
WOKN/KNAP GU21 71 L7
Bloomfield Dr BRAK RG12 32 E1
Bloomfield Rd KUT/HW KT1 41 L5
Bloom Gv WNWD SE27 30 C6
Bloomhall Rd NRWD SE19 30 E8
Bloom Park Rd FUL/PGN SW6 19 K5
Bloomsbury Cl
HOR/WEW KT19 60 B8
Bloomsbury Wy BLKW GU17 67 N5
Bloor Cl HORS RH12 192 C3
Blossom Cl SAND/SEL CR2 63 P4
Blossom Wy WDR/YW UB7 14 C2
Blossom Waye HEST TW5 15 N4
Blount Av EGRIN RH19 180 B2
Blount Crs BNFD RG42 32 A1
Bloxham Crs HPTN TW12 39 P2
Bloxham Rd CRAN GU6 153 K9
Bloxworth Cl BRAK RG12 33 H5
WLGTN SM6 62 E2
Blue Ball La EGH TW20 21 L8
Blue Barn Wy WEY KT13 56 C9
Bluebell Cl CRAWW RH11 * 176 E8
EGRIN RH19 180 A2
HORS RH12 192 D5
SYD SE26 30 G7
WLGTN SM6 44 D9
Bluebell Ct
WOKS/MYFD GU22 * 10 A7
Bluebell Hl BRAK RG12 32 G2
Bluebell La EHSLY KT24 94 G9
Bluebell Ri LTWR GU18 52 B9
Blueberry Gdns
COUL/CHIP CR5 81 H5
Blueberry La RSEV TN14 85 N5
Blue Cedars BNSTD SM7 79 H3
Blue Cedars Pl COB KT11 75 M1
Blue Coat Wk BRAK RG12 32 F6
Bluefield Cl HPTN TW12 25 H8
Bluegates EW KT17 60 E6
Bluehouse Gdns OXTED RH8 103 N8
Bluehouse La OXTED RH8 103 L8
Blue Leaves Av
COUL/CHIP CR5 100 F2
Blue Prior Ct FLEETS GU52 106 E3
Bluethroat Cl SHST GU47 50 A9
Bluff Cove ALDT GU11 108 E3
Blundel La COB KT11 75 P5
Blundell Av HORL RH6 159 J1
Blunden Dr DTCH/LGLY SL3 12 F2
Blunden Rd FARN GU14 88 B2
Blunt Rd SAND/SEL CR2 63 M4
Blunts Av WDR/YW UB7 14 C5
Blunts Wy HORS RH12 192 B7
Blyth Cl TWK TW1 25 N2
Blythe Cl CAT SE6 31 N3
Blythe Hl CAT SE6 31 N3
Blythe Hill La CAT SE6 31 N3
Blythe Hill Pl FSTH SE23 * 31 M3
Blythe Ms WKENS W14 * 19 H1
Blythe Rd WKENS W14 19 H1
Blytheswood Pl
STRHM/NOR SW16 30 A7
Blythe V CAT SE6 31 N4
Blythewood La ASC SL5 33 M4
Blyth Rd BMLY BR1 47 M2
Blythwood Dr FRIM GU16 68 F6
The Blytons EGRIN RH19 180 A2
Board School Rd
WOKN/KNAP GU21 11 F2
Boar Hl DORK RH4 136 E4
Bockhampton Rd
KUTN/CMB KT2 41 M1
Boddicott Cl WIM/MER SW19 28 B5
Bodens Ride ASC SL5 33 P9
Bodiam Cl CRAWE RH10 177 M5
Bodiam Rd
STRHM/NOR SW16 44 F2
Bodley Cl NWMAL KT3 42 C6
Bodley Rd NWMAL KT3 42 C7
Bodmin Gv MRDN SM4 43 M5
Bodmin St WAND/EARL SW18 28 D4
Bodnant Gdns RYNPK SW20 42 E4
Boeing Wy NWDGN UB2 15 K1
Bofors Rd FARN GU14 88 C7
Bog La BRAK RG12 33 H6
Bognor Rd HORS RH12 191 H2
RDKG RH5 155 N4
RDKG RH5 173 K4
Boileau Rd BARN SW13 18 E5
Bois Hall Rd ADL/WDHM KT15 55 P4
Bolderwood Wy WWKM BR4 65 H1
Bolding House La
CHOB/PIR GU24 70 F2
Boleyn Av EW KT17 60 E8
Boleyn Cl CRAWE RH10 177 N8
STA TW18 22 B8
Boleyn Dr E/WMO/HCT KT8 39 P4
Boleyn Gdns WWKM BR4 65 H1
Boleyn Wk LHD/OX KT22 76 F9
Bolingbroke Gv BTSEA SW11 29 J2
Bolingbroke Rd WKENS W14 19 H1
Bolingbroke Wk
BTSEA SW11 * 19 P5
Bollo Bridge Rd ACT W3 17 P1
Bollo La ACT W3 17 P1
CHSWK W4 18 A2
Bolney Ct CRAWW RH11 176 C8
Bolsover Gv REDH RH1 100 G9
Bolstead Rd MTCM CR4 44 D2
Bolters La BNSTD SM7 79 K4
Bolters Rd HORL RH6 140 C8
Bolters Rd South HORL RH6 140 B8
Bolton Cl CHSGTN KT9 59 K5
Bolton Dr MRDN SM4 43 N8
Bolton Gdns ECT SW5 19 M3
TEDD TW11 25 P9
Bolton Gardens Ms
WBPTN SW10 19 M3
Bolton Rd CHSGTN KT9 59 K5
CHSWK W4 18 A5
CRAWE RH10 195 L1
Boltons Cl WOKS/MYFD GU22 73 L4
Boltons La BNFD RG42 32 A1
HYS/HAR UB3 14 E5
WOKS/MYFD GU22 73 L5
Boltons Pl ECT SW5 19 N3
The Boltons WBPTN SW10 * 19 N3
Bombers La BH/WHM TN16 85 H9
Bomer Cl WDR/YW UB7 14 C5
Bonchurch Cl BELMT SM2 61 M6
Bond Cl RSEV TN14 85 P4
Bond Gdns WLGTN SM6 62 E3
Bond Rd MTCM CR4 44 B3
SURB KT6 59 M1
WARL CR6 82 D7
Bond's La RDKG RH5 137 H4
Bond St EGH TW20 20 G9
Bond Wy BRAK RG12 32 D3
Bonehurst Rd HORL RH6 140 C6
Bone Mill La GDST RH9 122 E5
Bones La HORL RH6 142 A9
Bonham Rd
BRXS/STRHM SW2 30 A1
Bonner Hill Rd KUT/HW KT1 9 G6
Bonners Cl
WOKS/MYFD GU22 92 D2
Bonners Fld RFNM GU10 126 A8
Bonnetts La CRAWW RH11 158 D9
Bonneville Gdns CLAP SW4 29 M2
Bonnys Rd REIG RH2 119 H5
Bonser Rd TWK TW1 25 N5
Bonsey Cl WOKS/MYFD GU22 92 C1
Bonsey La WOKS/MYFD GU22 92 C1
Bonsey's La CHOB/PIR GU24 54 C7
Bonsor Dr
KWD/TDW/WH KT20 99 J2
Bookham Ct GT/LBKH KT23 95 P3
Bookham Gv GT/LBKH KT23 96 B6
Bookham Rd COB KT11 75 M9
Bookhurst Hl CRAN GU6 * 153 L8
Bookhurst Rd CRAN GU6 153 L8
Boole Hts BRAK RG12 32 C7
Booth Dr STA TW18 22 G9
Booth Rd CRAWW RH11 176 B8
CROY/NA CR0 2 B4
Booth Wy SWTR RH13 * 192 D7
Borage Cl CRAWW RH11 176 D8
Border Cha CRAWE RH10 178 B1
Border Ct EGRIN RH19 162 E8
Border Crs SYD SE26 31 J8
Border End HASM GU27 * 183 N4
Border Gdns CROY/NA CR0 65 H3
Border Ga MTCM CR4 44 A2
Border Rd HASM GU27 183 N4
SYD SE26 31 J8
Borderside YTLY GU46 66 E2
Bordesley Rd MRDN SM4 43 M5
Bordon Wk PUT/ROE SW15 27 M3
The Boreen BOR GU35 164 E6
Borelli Ms FNM GU9 5 G3
Borers Arms Rd
CRAWE RH10 160 C8
Borers Cl CRAWE RH10 * 160 D9
Borland Rd TEDD TW11 26 A9
Borneo St PUT/ROE SW15 18 G8
Borough Hl CROY/NA CR0 2 A6
Borough Rd BH/WHM TN16 104 B1
GODL GU7 131 K8
ISLW TW7 16 E6
KUTN/CMB KT2 9 H2
MTCM CR4 44 A3
The Borough
BRKHM/BTCW RH3 117 N6
FNM GU9 5 F3
RFNM GU10 106 C8
Borrodaile Rd
WAND/EARL SW18 28 E2
Borrowdale Cl
CRAWW RH11 176 E7
EGH TW20 36 F1
SAND/SEL CR2 81 P2
Borrowdale Dr
SAND/SEL CR2 81 P1
Boscombe Rd TOOT SW17 29 K9
WIM/MER SW19 43 L2
WPK KT4 42 G9
Bosham Rd CRAWE RH10 177 M8
Boshers Gdns EGH TW20 21 L9
Bosman Dr BFOR GU20 52 B2
Bostock Av HORS RH12 192 F6
Boston Gdns BTFD TW8 16 G2
CHSWK W4 18 C4
Boston Manor Rd BTFD TW8 16 G2
Boston Pde HNWL W7 * 16 G2
Boston Park Rd BTFD TW8 * 17 J4
Boston Rd CROY/NA CR0 45 H7
Boston V HNWL W7 16 G2
Boswell Rd CRAWE RH10 177 H8
THHTH CR7 45 L5
Botany Hl RFNM GU10 128 F4
Boterys Cross REDH RH1 * 121 K4
Bothwell Rd CROY/NA CR0 65 J8
Bothwell St HMSMTH W6 19 H4
Botleys Pk CHERT KT16 * 54 G4
Botsford Rd RYNPK SW20 43 J3
Bottom Harrow Rd VW GU25 36 D7
Boucher Cl TEDD TW11 25 N8
Boughton Av HAYES BR2 47 M8
Boughton Hall Av
RPLY/SEND GU23 93 K4
Bouldish Farm Rd ASC SL5 33 P6
Boulevards ALDT GU11 * 108 C4
The Boulevard CRAWE RH10 176 G5
Boulogne Rd CROY/NA CR0 45 L7
Boulters Rd ALDT GU11 108 D5
Boulthurst Wy OXTED RH8 123 N3
Boundaries Rd BAL SW12 29 J5
FELT TW13 24 D4
Boundary Cl CRAWE RH10 177 H4
KUT/HW KT1 9 K6
NWDGN UB2 16 A3
Boundary Rd ASHF TW15 22 F8
CAR SM5 62 C7
CRAWE RH10 177 H4
FARN GU14 87 N6
FARN GU14 88 E5
GSHT GU26 165 N8
RFNM GU10 146 B5
WIM/MER SW19 28 G9
WOKN/KNAP GU21 11 G1
Boundary Rd East
ADL/WDHM KT15 55 M7
Boundary Rd North
ADL/WDHM KT15 55 M7
Boundary Rd West
ADL/WDHM KT15 55 M7
Boundary Wy CROY/NA CR0 64 G4
WOKN/KNAP GU21 72 F4
Boundless La
MFD/CHID GU8 166 D4
Boundstone Cl RFNM GU10 127 M8
Boundstone Rd RFNM GU10 127 K9
Bourdon Rd PGE/AN SE20 46 C3
Bourg-de-Peage Av
EGRIN RH19 180 F2
Bourke Cl CLAP SW4 29 P2
Bourke Hl COUL/CHIP CR5 80 B7
Bourley La RFNM GU10 107 K4
Bourley Rd FLEETS GU52 107 J2
Bourne Av CHERT KT16 37 L4
HYS/HAR UB3 14 E1
Bourne Cl BF/WBF KT14 73 M2
ISLW TW7 16 E8
RGUE GU4 132 F2
THDIT KT7 58 F1
Bourne Ct ALDT GU11 108 C6
BF/WBF KT14 * 74 A2
Bourne Dene RFNM GU10 127 L8
Bourne Dr MTCM CR4 43 P3
Bournefield Rd CTHM CR3 81 P7
Bourne Firs RFNM GU10 127 P8
Bourne Gv ASHTD KT21 77 K8
RFNM GU10 128 A6
Bourne Grove Cl
RFNM GU10 128 A6
Bourne Grove Dr
RFNM GU10 128 A6
Bourne Hts FNM GU9 * 127 N5
Bourne La CTHM CR3 101 M1
Bourne Meadow EGH TW20 36 F5
Bournemouth Rd
WIM/MER SW19 43 L2
Bourne Park Cl PUR/KEN CR8 81 N5
Bourne Rd ADL/WDHM KT15 55 M7
GODL GU7 131 M5
REDH RH1 120 E1
VW GU25 36 B6
Bourneside VW GU25 35 N8
Bourneside Rd
ADL/WDHM KT15 55 P4
Bourne St CROY/NA CR0 2 B4
The Bourne FLEETS GU52 86 G9
Bourne V HAYES BR2 47 N9
Bournevale Rd
STRHM/NOR SW16 29 P7
Bourne Vw PUR/KEN CR8 81 M4
Bourne Wy ADL/WDHM KT15 55 N4
HAYES BR2 65 N1
HOR/WEW KT19 60 A3
SUT SM1 61 K4
WOKS/MYFD GU22 92 B2
Bournville Rd CAT SE6 31 P3
Bousley Ri CHERT KT16 55 H6
Bouverie Gdns PUR/KEN CR8 80 G3
Bouverie Rd COUL/CHIP CR5 80 C7
Bouverie Wy DTCH/LGLY SL3 12 C3
Boveney Rd FSTH SE23 31 L3
Bovill Rd FSTH SE23 31 L3
Bovingdon Rd FUL/PGN SW6 19 M6
Bowater Cl
BRXS/STRHM SW2 29 P2
Bowater Rdg WEY KT13 56 F8
Bowater Rd CRAWE RH10 177 M8
Bowcott Hl BOR GU35 164 C6
Bowden Cl
EBED/NFELT TW14 23 P4
Bowden Rd ASC SL5 34 C6
Bowen Dr DUL SE21 30 F6
Bowenhurst Gdns
FLEETS GU52 106 G2
Bowenhurst La RFNM GU10 106 B5
Bowenhurst Rd
FLEETS GU52 106 G1
Bowens Wd CROY/NA CR0 * 64 F7
Bowenswood CROY/NA CR0 64 F7
Bowen Wy COUL/CHIP CR5 100 F2
Bower Ct WOKS/MYFD GU22 11 K1
Bowerdean St FUL/PGN SW6 19 M6
Bower Hill Cl REDH RH1 120 G7
Bower Hill La REDH RH1 120 F6
Bowerland La LING RH7 143 K5
Bower Rd RFNM GU10 127 L8
Bowers Cl RGUE GU4 112 E1
Bowers Farm Dr RGUE GU4 112 E1
Bowers La RGUE GU4 92 E9
Bowers Pl CRAWE RH10 179 J3
Bowes Cl SWTR RH13 192 D7
Bowes Rd STA TW18 22 B9
WOT/HER KT12 57 K1
Bowfell Rd HMSMTH W6 18 G4
Bowie Cl CLAP SW4 29 N3
Bowland Dr BRAK RG12 32 G8
Bowley Cl NRWD SE19 * 30 G9
Bowley La NRWD SE19 30 G8
Bowlhead Green Rd
MFD/CHID GU8 166 G2
Bowling Aly RFNM GU10 106 C5
Bowling Court Gn FRIM GU16 68 G9
Bowling Green Cl
PUT/ROE SW15 27 N3
Bowling Green La
HORS RH12 192 C7
Bowling Green Rd
CHOB/PIR GU24 53 L7
Bowman Ct CRAWE RH10 * 176 G4
CWTH RG45 49 J5
Bowman Ms
WAND/EARL SW18 28 C4
Bowmans Lea FSTH SE23 31 K3
Bowman's Meadow
WLGTN SM6 62 D2
Bowness Crs PUT/ROE SW15 27 K8
Bowness Dr HSLWW TW4 15 N9
Bowry Dr STWL/WRAY TW19 21 L2
Bowsley Ct FELT TW13 24 B5
The Bowsprit COB KT11 75 L4
Bowyers Cl ASHTD KT21 77 M7
Bowyers Ct TWK TW1 17 H9
Bowyer Wk ASC SL5 33 N2
Boxall Rd DUL SE21 30 F2
Boxall's Gv ALDT GU11 108 C7
Boxall's La ALDT GU11 108 C7
Boxall Wk SWTR RH13 192 C9
Box Cl CRAWW RH11 194 F1
Boxford Cl SAND/SEL CR2 82 D1
Boxford Rdg BRAK RG12 32 D4
Boxgrove Av GU GU1 112 E3
Boxgrove La GU GU1 112 E4
Boxgrove Rd GU GU1 112 E4
Boxhill Rd DORK RH4 117 L5
KWD/TDW/WH KT20 118 B1
Boxhill Wy
BRKHM/BTCW RH3 117 P9
Box La EGRIN RH19 181 K5
Boxley Rd MRDN SM4 43 N5
Box Ridge Av PUR/KEN CR8 81 H1
Box Tree Wk REDH RH1 119 N8
Boxwood Wy WARL CR6 82 D6
Boyd Cl KUTN/CMB KT2 41 N1
Boyd Ct BNFD RG42 32 C2
Boyd Rd WIM/MER SW19 28 G9
Boyle Farm Rd THDIT KT7 40 G7
Brabazon Av WLGTN SM6 62 G6
Brabazon Rd HEST TW5 15 L5
Brabon Rd FARN GU14 88 B2

Brabourne Cl NRWD SE19 30 F8
Brabourne Ri BECK BR3 47 K6
Bracebridge CBLY GU15 68 C3
Bracewood Gdns
CROY/NA CR0 3 J5
Bracken Av BAL SW12 29 K2
CROY/NA CR0 64 G2
Bracken Bank ASC SL5 33 L2
Brackenbury Gdns
HMSMTH W6 18 F1
Brackenbury Rd
HMSMTH W6 18 F1
Bracken Cl CRAWE RH10 177 H3
CRAWE RH10 178 C1
GT/LBKH KT23 95 P4
SHGR GU5 132 F7
SUN TW16 * 24 A9
WHTN TW2 25 H3
WOKS/MYFD GU22 11 F5
Brackendale Cl CBLY GU15 68 G5
HSLW TW3 16 B6
Brackendale Rd CBLY GU15 68 F4
Brackendene ASHV GU12 109 L3
Brackendene Cl
WOKN/KNAP GU21 72 E4
Bracken End ISLW TW7 25 L1
Bracken Gdns BARN SW13 18 E7
Bracken Gv HORS RH12 192 G5
Brackenhill COB KT11 76 A1
Bracken Hill Cl BMLY BR1 47 M2
Bracken Hill La BMLY BR1 47 M2
Bracken La YTLY GU46 66 E2
Brackenlea GODL GU7 131 K6
Bracken Pth EPSOM KT18 77 P2
Brackenside HORL RH6 140 D9
The Brackens ASC SL5 * 33 K4
CWTH RG45 49 L2
Bracken Wy CHOB/PIR GU24 53 M8
RGUW GU3 111 L3
Brackenwood CBLY GU15 69 M3
SUN TW16 39 J2
Brackenwood Rd
WOKN/KNAP GU21 71 K8
Bracklesham Cl FARN GU14 68 C9
Brackley WEY KT13 56 F4
Brackley Cl WLGTN SM6 62 G6
Brackley Rd BECK BR3 46 F1
CHSWK W4 18 C2
Brackley Ter CHSWK W4 18 C3
Bracklyn Av EGRIN RH19 * 162 F6
Bracknell Beeches
BRAK RG12 * 32 D4
Bracknell Cl CBLY GU15 51 H8
Bracknell Rd BAGS GU19 51 M3
CBLY GU15 51 J7
CWTH RG45 49 N4
Bracondale ESH/CLAY KT10 58 C4
Bradbourne St FUL/PGN SW6 19 L7
Bradbury Cl NWDGN UB2 15 P2
Bradbury Rd CRAWE RH10 177 M8
Braddock Cl ISLW TW7 16 F8
Braddon Rd RCH/KEW TW9 17 M8
Bradenhurst Cl CTHM CR3 101 P6
Bradfield Cl RGUE GU4 112 E2
WOKS/MYFD GU22 10 D5
Bradfields BRAK RG12 32 F6
Bradford Cl SYD SE26 31 J7
Bradford Dr HOR/WEW KT19 60 D5
Brading Rd
BRXS/STRHM SW2 30 A3
CROY/NA CR0 45 H7
Brading Ter SHB W12 18 E1
Bradley Cl BELMT SM2 61 M8
Bradley La RDKG RH5 117 H3
Bradley Rd NRWD SE19 30 D9
Bradmore Park Rd
HMSMTH W6 18 F1
Bradmore Wy
COUL/CHIP CR5 80 G7
Bradshaw Cl
WIM/MER SW19 28 D9
Bradshaws Cl SNWD SE25 46 A4
Bradstock Rd EW KT17 60 F4
Braemar Av SAND/SEL CR2 63 L8
THHTH CR7 45 K4
WIM/MER SW19 28 D5
Braemar Cl FRIM GU16 69 H8
GODL GU7 150 C1
Braemar Gdns WWKM BR4 47 J9
Braemar Rd BTFD TW8 17 K4
WPK KT4 60 F2
Braeside ADL/WDHM KT15 55 M9
BECK BR3 31 P8
Braeside Av RYNPK SW20 43 J2
Braeside Cl HASM GU27 184 A2
Braeside Rd
STRHM/NOR SW16 44 E1
Braes Md REDH RH1 120 G6
Brafferton Rd CROY/NA CR0 2 C7
Bragg Rd TEDD TW11 40 E1
Braid Cl FELT TW13 24 G5
Brailsford Cl WIM/MER SW19 44 A1
Brailsford Rd
BRXS/STRHM SW2 30 B2
Brainton Av
EBED/NFELT TW14 24 C3
Brake Rd FARN GU14 88 A6
Brakey Hl REDH RH1 121 N5
Bramber Cl CRAWE RH10 177 H3
Bramber Rd WKENS W14 19 K4
Bramber Wy WARL CR6 82 F5
Bramble Acres Cl BELMT SM2 61 L6
Bramble Bank FRIM GU16 89 J1
Bramble Banks CAR SM5 62 C7
Bramble Cl BECK BR3 47 J6
CRAWE RH10 160 C9
CROY/NA CR0 64 G3
REDH RH1 120 C7
RGUW GU3 111 L3
SHPTN TW17 38 F5
Brambledene Cl
WOKN/KNAP GU21 72 A7
Brambledown STA TW18 37 M2
Brambledown Cl WWKM BR4 47 L7
Brambledown Rd CAR SM5 62 C6
SAND/SEL CR2 63 N6
Bramblegate CWTH RG45 49 L3
Bramble Hall La
KWD/TDW/WH KT20 * 117 M3
Bramble La HPTN TW12 24 G9
Bramble Ri COB KT11 75 L4
Brambles Cl ASHV GU12 109 K5
CTHM CR3 101 N2
ISLW TW7 17 H5
Brambles Pk SHGR GU5 132 D7
The Brambles CWTH RG45 49 H3
GODL GU7 131 K6
RFNM GU10 * 106 C8
SUT SM1 61 P1
WDR/YW UB7 13 P3
WIM/MER SW19 * 28 C8
Brambleton Av FNM GU9 127 M6
Brambletye La FROW RH18 181 J8
Brambletye Park Rd
REDH RH1 120 B7
Brambletye Rd
CRAWE RH10 177 K6
Bramble Wk EPSOM KT18 77 P3
REDH RH1 * 120 C7
Bramble Wy
RPLY/SEND GU23 93 K4
Bramblewood REDH RH1 100 D9
Bramblewood Cl CAR SM5 44 A9
Bramblewood Pl
FLEETN GU51 86 E6
Brambling Cl SWTR RH13 192 F9
Brambling Rd SWTR RH13 192 F9
Bramcote CBLY GU15 69 L3
Bramcote Av MTCM CR4 44 B5
Bramcote Rd PUT/ROE SW15 18 F9
Bramerton Rd BECK BR3 46 F4
Bramfield Rd BTSEA SW11 29 H2
Bramford Rd
WAND/EARL SW18 19 N9
Bramham Gdns
CHSGTN KT9 * 59 K4
ECT SW5 19 M3
Bramley Av COUL/CHIP CR5 80 E4
SHPTN TW17 38 G4
Bramley Cl CHERT KT16 37 M9
CRAWE RH10 177 J5
REDH RH1 120 A7
SAND/SEL CR2 63 K4
STA TW18 22 F9
WHTN TW2 25 K2
Bramley Gv ASHTD KT21 77 L8
CWTH RG45 49 H4
Bramley Hl SAND/SEL CR2 63 L3
Bramley Hyrst
SAND/SEL CR2 * 63 L4
Bramley La BLKW GU17 67 M3
Bramley Rd BELMT SM2 61 H7
CBLY GU15 68 D6
EA W5 17 J1
SUT SM1 61 P4
Bramley Wk HORL RH6 159 M1
Bramley Wy ASHTD KT21 77 M6
HSLWW TW4 24 G1
WWKM BR4 65 H1
Bramling Av YTLY GU46 66 F2
Brampton Gdns
WOT/HER KT12 57 L4
Brampton Rd CROY/NA CR0 45 P8
Bramshaw Ri NWMAL KT3 42 C7
Bramshot Dr FLEETN GU51 86 G6
Bramshot La FLEETN GU51 87 L2
Bramshott Ct LIPH GU30 * 182 D2
Bramshott Rd FARN GU14 87 L5
Bramston Rd MTCM CR4 44 B1
Bramswell Rd GODL GU7 131 M7
Bramwell Cl SUN TW16 39 M3
Brancaster La PUR/KEN CR8 63 L9
Brancaster Rd
STRHM/NOR SW16 29 P6
Brandlehow Rd
PUT/ROE SW15 19 K9
Brandon Cl CBLY GU15 69 M4
CRAWE RH10 177 N7
Brandon Rd FLEETS GU52 106 E2
NWDGN UB2 15 P3
SUT SM1 61 M3
Brandreth Rd TOOT SW17 29 L5
The Brandries WLGTN SM6 62 F2
Brandsland REIG RH2 119 M9
Brands Rd DTCH/LGLY SL3 12 F4
Brandy Bottom YTLY GU46 * 67 J5
Brandy Wy BELMT SM2 61 L6
Brangwyn Crs
WIM/MER SW19 43 P3
Branksea St FUL/PGN SW6 19 J5
Branksome Cl CBLY GU15 68 G2
WOT/HER KT12 57 M1
Branksome Hill Rd
SHST GU47 68 A1
Branksome Park Rd
CBLY GU15 68 G2
Branksome Rd
BRXS/STRHM SW2 29 P1
WIM/MER SW19 43 L2
Branksome Wy NWMAL KT3 42 A3
Branksomewood Rd
FLEETN GU51 86 E6
Bransby Rd CHSGTN KT9 59 L6
Branstone Rd RCH/KEW TW9 17 M6
Brantridge La RHWH RH17 195 K8
Brantridge Rd CRAWE RH10 177 J7
Brants Br BRAK RG12 32 G5
Brantwood Av ISLW TW7 16 G9
Brantwood Dr BF/WBF KT14 73 K2
Brantwood Gdns
BF/WBF KT14 73 K2
Brantwood Rd HNHL SE24 30 D1
SAND/SEL CR2 63 L7
Brasenose Dr BARN SW13 18 G4
Brassey Cl
EBED/NFELT TW14 * 24 B4
OXTED RH8 103 N9
Brassey Hl OXTED RH8 103 N9
Brassey Rd OXTED RH8 103 N9
Brasted Cl BELMT SM2 61 L8
SYD SE26 31 K7
Brasted Hl RSEV TN14 85 L9
Brasted Hill Rd
BH/WHM TN16 105 N2
Brasted La RSEV TN14 85 L8
Brasted Rd BH/WHM TN16 105 J6
Brathway Rd
WAND/EARL SW18 28 D3
Brattain Ct BRAK RG12 32 F4
Bravington Cl SHPTN TW17 38 B6
Braxted Pk
STRHM/NOR SW16 30 A9
Braybourne Dr ISLW TW7 16 F5
Braybrooke Gdns
NRWD SE19 45 N1
Braybrooke Rd BNFD RG42 32 D1
Bray Cl CRAWE RH10 177 N7
Braycourt Av WOT/HER KT12 39 L8
Braye Cl SHST GU47 49 N8
Bray Gdns WOKS/MYFD GU22 73 J5
Bray Rd COB KT11 75 N5
GUW GU2 6 A5
Braywood Av EGH TW20 21 L9
Breakfield COUL/CHIP CR5 80 G5
Breamore Cl PUT/ROE SW15 27 M4
Breamwater Gdns
RCHPK/HAM TW10 26 A6
Breasley Cl PUT/ROE SW15 18 F9
Brechin Pl SKENS SW7 19 N3
Brecon Cl FARN GU14 67 P9
MTCM CR4 44 G5
WPK KT4 60 G1
Brecon Rd HMSMTH W6 19 J4
Bredhurst Cl PGE/AN SE20 31 K9
Bredon Rd CROY/NA CR0 45 P8
Bredune PUR/KEN CR8 81 M4
Breech La
KWD/TDW/WH KT20 98 E5
The Breech SHST GU47 68 A1
Breer St FUL/PGN SW6 19 M8
Breezehurst Dr
CRAWW RH11 176 C8
Bregsells La RDKG RH5 137 K9
Bremer Rd STA TW18 22 D6
Bremner Av HORL RH6 140 B9
Bremner Rd SKENS SW7 * 19 N1
Brenchley Cl HAYES BR2 47 M6
Brenchley Gdns EDUL SE22 31 K2
Brenda Rd TOOT SW17 29 J5
Brende Gdns
E/WMO/HCT KT8 40 B5
Brendon Cl ESH/CLAY KT10 58 C5
HYS/HAR UB3 14 E5
Brendon Dr ESH/CLAY KT10 58 C5
Brendon Rd FARN GU14 67 P9
Brenley Cl MTCM CR4 44 C4
Brent Lea BTFD TW8 17 J5
Brentmoor Rd
CHOB/PIR GU24 70 C2
Brent Rd BTFD TW8 17 J4
NWDGN UB2 15 L1
SAND/SEL CR2 64 B7
Brentside BTFD TW8 17 J4
Brent Wy BTFD TW8 17 K5
Brentwick Gdns BTFD TW8 17 L2
Bret Harte Rd FRIM GU16 68 G7
Bretlands Rd CHERT KT16 55 J1
Brettgrave HOR/WEW KT19 60 A8
Brettingham Cl
CRAWW RH11 * 176 B8
Brewer Rd CRAWE RH10 176 G7
Brewers Cl FARN GU14 88 C2
Brewer St REDH RH1 121 L2
Brewery La BF/WBF KT14 74 A2
Brewery Rd
WOKN/KNAP GU21 10 B3
Brewhouse La
PUT/ROE SW15 19 J9
Brew House Rd
BRKHM/BTCW RH3 117 P9
Brewhurst La BIL RH14 188 D8
Breydon Wk CRAWE RH10 177 L7
Brian Av SAND/SEL CR2 81 N1
Briane Rd HOR/WEW KT19 60 A8
Briar Av LTWR GU18 69 P1
STRHM/NOR SW16 45 H1
Briar Bank CAR SM5 62 C7
Briar Cl BF/WBF KT14 55 M9
CRAWW RH11 176 F2
HPTN TW12 24 G8
ISLW TW7 25 N1
WARL CR6 82 G5
Briar Gdns HAYES BR2 47 M9
Briar Gv SAND/SEL CR2 82 A2
Briar Hl PUR/KEN CR8 62 G9
Briar La CAR SM5 62 C7
CROY/NA CR0 65 H3
Briar Patch GODL GU7 131 K7
Briar Rd RPLY/SEND GU23 92 F4
SHPTN TW17 38 B6
STRHM/NOR SW16 44 G4
WHTN TW2 25 M4
Briars Cl FARN GU14 87 P4
Briars Ct LHD/OX KT22 76 D3
The Briars ASHV GU12 109 K5
DTCH/LGLY SL3 12 D2
FLEETS GU52 86 C9
Briars Wd HORL RH6 140 E9
Briarswood Cl CRAWE RH10 177 N3
Briar Wk BF/WBF KT14 73 L1
PUT/ROE SW15 18 F9
Briar Wy RGUE GU4 112 F1
Briarwood Cl FELT TW13 23 P6
Briarwood Ct WPK KT4 * 42 E9
Briarwood Dr EWKG RG40 48 C3
Briarwood Rd CLAP SW4 29 N1
EW KT17 60 E5
WOKN/KNAP GU21 71 K8
Brickbarn Cl WBPTN SW10 * 19 N5
Brick Farm Cl RCH/KEW TW9 17 P6
Brickfield Cl BTFD TW8 17 J5
Brickfield La HORL RH6 158 G3
HYS/HAR UB3 14 F4
Brickfield Rd REDH RH1 141 L5
THHTH CR7 45 K2
WIM/MER SW19 28 E7
Brickfields Wy WDR/YW UB7 14 B1
Brickhouse La GDST RH9 142 C8
Brick Kiln La OXTED RH8 124 A1
Bricklands CRAWE RH10 179 J4
Brick La FLEETN GU51 86 G5
Bricksbury Hl FNM GU9 107 N7
Brickwood Cl SYD SE26 31 J6
Brickwood Rd CROY/NA CR0 3 G3
Brickyard Copse RDKG RH5 155 K8
Brickyard La CRAWE RH10 179 J3
RDKG RH5 135 M3
Brideake Cl CRAWW RH11 176 D8
Bridge Av HMSMTH W6 18 G3
Bridge Barn La
WOKN/KNAP GU21 72 A6
Bridge Cl BF/WBF KT14 74 B1
STA TW18 22 B7
WOKN/KNAP GU21 72 A5
WOT/HER KT12 39 H8
Bridge Ct WOKN/KNAP GU21 10 A4
Bridge End CBLY GU15 68 D4
Bridgefield FNM GU9 5 J3
Bridgefield Cl BNSTD SM7 78 G4
Bridgefield Rd SUT SM1 61 L5
Bridge Gdns ASHF TW15 38 E1
E/WMO/HCT KT8 40 D5
Bridgeham Cl WEY KT13 56 C4
Bridgeham Wy HORL RH6 160 C2
Bridgehill Cl GUW GU2 111 N3
Bridgelands CRAWE RH10 160 A9
Bridgelands Cl BECK BR3 46 F1
Bridge La VW GU25 36 C7
Bridgeman Rd TEDD TW11 25 P9
Bridgemead FRIM GU16 68 F8
Bridge Ms WOKN/KNAP GU21 10 A4
Bridge Pde
STRHM/NOR SW16 * 29 P8
Bridge Pk RGUE GU4 * 112 G2
Bridge Pl CROY/NA CR0 3 F1
Bridge Rd ALDT GU11 108 C6
ASC SL5 34 D6
BAGS GU19 51 N5
BECK BR3 46 F1
CBLY GU15 68 D5
CHERT KT16 37 M8
CHSGTN KT9 59 L4
COB KT11 75 K4
CRAN GU6 171 H1
E/WMO/HCT KT8 40 E5
EW KT17 78 D1
FARN GU14 88 B3
GODL GU7 131 L8
HASM GU27 184 D3
HORS RH12 189 N3
HSLW TW3 16 D8
SUT SM1 61 M5
TWK TW1 26 A2
WEY KT13 56 B3
WLGTN SM6 62 D4
Bridge Rw CROY/NA CR0 * 3 F1
Bridges Cl HORL RH6 159 N1
Bridges Ct BTSEA SW11 19 P8
Bridges La CROY/NA CR0 62 G3
Bridge Sq FNM GU9 5 G4
Bridge St CHSWK W4 18 B2
DTCH/LGLY SL3 13 H5
GODL GU7 131 L9
GU GU1 6 D5
LHD/OX KT22 96 G2
TWK TW1 26 C2
WOT/HER KT12 39 H9
Bridgetown Cl NRWD SE19 30 F8
Bridge Vw ASC SL5 35 H8
Bridgeview HMSMTH W6 18 G3
Bridge Wk YTLY GU46 67 H1
Bridgewater Ct
DTCH/LGLY SL3 12 E3
Bridgewater Rd WEY KT13 56 F5
Bridge Wy COUL/CHIP CR5 80 A8
WHTN TW2 25 K3
Bridgewood Cl PGE/AN SE20 46 B1
Bridgewood Rd
STRHM/NOR SW16 44 F1
WPK KT4 60 E4
Bridgford St
WAND/EARL SW18 28 F6
Bridgman Rd CHSWK W4 18 A1
Bridle Cl GSHT GU26 165 K8
HOR/WEW KT19 60 A3
KUT/HW KT1 41 K5
SUN TW16 39 J4
Bridle La COB KT11 76 B4
TWK TW1 26 A2
Bridle Pth CROY/NA CR0 62 G2
The Bridle Pth EW KT17 60 G8
Bridlepath Wy
EBED/NFELT TW14 23 P3
Bridle Rd CROY/NA CR0 64 G1
ESH/CLAY KT10 59 H5
EW KT17 78 D2
The Bridle Rd PUR/KEN CR8 62 G8
Bridle Wy CRAWE RH10 177 N4
CROY/NA CR0 64 G4
Bridleway Cl EW KT17 60 G8
The Bridle Wy WLGTN SM6 62 E3
Bridlington Cl BH/WHM TN16 83 P8
Bridport Rd THHTH CR7 45 J4
Brier Lea KWD/TDW/WH KT20 99 K6
Brierley CROY/NA CR0 65 H5
Brierley Cl SNWD SE25 46 A5
Brierley Rd BAL SW12 29 M5
Brierly Cl GUW GU2 111 N3
Brier Rd KWD/TDW/WH KT20 78 F8
Brigade Pl CTHM CR3 101 L2
Briggs Cl MTCM CR4 44 D2
Bright Hl GU GU1 7 G6
Brightlands Rd REIG RH2 119 N3
Brightling Rd BROCKY SE4 31 N2
Brightman Rd
WAND/EARL SW18 28 G4
Brighton Cl ADL/WDHM KT15 55 N4
Brighton Rd
ADL/WDHM KT15 55 N3
ALDT GU11 108 E6
BELMT SM2 61 M8
BNSTD SM7 79 K3
COUL/CHIP CR5 100 D1
CRAWE RH10 176 G8
CRAWW RH11 194 F3
HORL RH6 159 J1
MFD/CHID GU8 150 G3
PUR/KEN CR8 80 G3
REDH RH1 140 C4
SURB KT6 41 J7
Brighton Ter REDH RH1 * 120 B6
Brightside Av STA TW18 37 N1
Brightwell Cl CROY/NA CR0 45 J9
Brightwell Crs TOOT SW17 29 J8
Brightwells Rd FNM GU9 5 G3
Brigstock Rd COUL/CHIP CR5 80 D4
THHTH CR7 45 K6
Brimshot La CHOB/PIR GU24 53 L7
Brindle Cl ALDT GU11 108 D7
The Brindles BNSTD SM7 79 K6
Brinkley Rd WPK KT4 60 F1
Brinksway FLEETN GU51 86 G7
Brinn's La BLKW GU17 67 N3
Brinsworth Cl WHTN TW2 25 L4
Brisbane Av WIM/MER SW19 43 M2
Brisbane Cl CRAWW RH11 176 G2
Briscoe Rd WIM/MER SW19 28 G9
Brisson Cl ESH/CLAY KT10 57 P5
Bristol Cl CRAWE RH10 177 N2
STWL/WRAY TW19 23 H2
WLGTN SM6 62 G7
Bristol Rd MRDN SM4 43 N6
Bristow Rd CBLY GU15 68 D5
CROY/NA CR0 62 G3
HSLW TW3 16 B8
NRWD SE19 30 F8
Britannia La WHTN TW2 25 K3
Britannia Rd BRYLDS KT5 41 M8
FUL/PGN SW6 19 M5
Britannia Wy FUL/PGN SW6 19 M5
STWL/WRAY TW19 22 G3
British Gv HMSMTH W6 18 D3
British Grove Pas
CHSWK W4 * 18 D3
Briton Cl SAND/SEL CR2 63 N9
Briton Crs SAND/SEL CR2 63 N9
Briton Hill Rd SAND/SEL CR2 63 N8
Brittain Rd WOT/HER KT12 57 M4
Britten Cl ASHV GU12 109 K4
CRAWW RH11 176 C8
Brittens Cl GUW GU2 91 N9
Brixton Hl BRXS/STRHM SW2 30 A2
Brixton Hill Pl
BRXS/STRHM SW2 29 P3
Brixton Water La
BRXS/STRHM SW2 30 B1
Broadacre STA TW18 22 D8
Broad Acres GODL GU7 131 L5
Broadacres FLEETN GU51 86 D7
RGUW GU3 111 L3
Broadbridge Heath Rd
HORS RH12 191 L6
Broadbridge La HORL RH6 160 B2
Broad Cl WOT/HER KT12 57 M2
Broadcoombe SAND/SEL CR2 64 D6
Broadeaves Cl SAND/SEL CR2 63 N4
Broadfield Cl
KWD/TDW/WH KT20 78 G9
Broadfield Dr CRAWW RH11 176 F9
Broadfield Pk
CRAWW RH11 * 176 G9
Broadfield Pl CRAWW RH11 176 E9
Broadfield Rd SHGR GU5 134 F4
Broadfields E/WMO/HCT KT8 40 D7
Broadford La
CHOB/PIR GU24 71 L1
Broadford Pk RGUE GU4 132 B3
Broadford Rd RGUE GU4 132 B3
Broadgates Rd
WAND/EARL SW18 28 G4
Broad Green Av
CROY/NA CR0 45 K8
Broadham Green Rd
OXTED RH8 123 K4
Broadham Pl OXTED RH8 123 K3
Broad Ha'Penny
RFNM GU10 127 L8
Broad Hwy COB KT11 75 M3
Broadhurst ASHTD KT21 77 L5
FARN GU14 87 N3
Broadhurst Gdns REIG RH2 119 M8
Broadlands FARN GU14 88 C5
FELT TW13 24 G6
FRIM GU16 69 H8
HORL RH6 140 E9
Broadlands Av SHPTN TW17 38 E7
STRHM/NOR SW16 29 P5
Broadlands Cl
STRHM/NOR SW16 29 P5
Broadlands Dr ASC SL5 34 C8
WARL CR6 82 C8
Broadlands Wy NWMAL KT3 42 D7
Broad La BRAK RG12 32 E4
HPTN TW12 39 P1
RDKG RH5 138 B8
Broadley Gn BFOR GU20 52 D6
Broadmead ASHTD KT21 77 L7
CAT SE6 31 P6
FARN GU14 87 P4
HORL RH6 140 E9

REDH RH1 *...................100 E8
Broadmead Av WPK KT4.......42 E8
Broadmead CI HPTN TW12....25 H9
Broadmeads
RPLY/SEND GU23...............92 F2
Broad Oak SUN TW16.............24 A9
Broad Oaks SURB KT6.............41 P9
Broadoaks Crs BF/WBF KT14..73 M3
Broad Oaks Wy HAYES BR2.....47 M6
Broadrick Heath BNFD RG42....32 F1
Broadstone Pk FROW RH18...181 M9
Broad St CHOB/PIR GU24........70 D1
RGUW GU3........................111 K3
TEDD TW11........................25 N9
Broadview Rd
STRHM/NOR SW16..............44 F1
Broad Wk COUL/CHIP CR5....100 C2
CRAN GU6.........................171 J2
CTHM CR5.........................101 P2
EPSOM KT18......................78 G8
FRIM GU16.........................68 G6
HEST TW5..........................15 M6
RCH/KEW TW9....................17 M5
Broadwalk CRAWE RH10......176 C6
Broadwater CI
STWL/WRAY TW19..............21 K3
WOKN/KNAP GU21..............73 H1
WOT/HER KT12...................57 J4
Broadwater Ri GU GU1.........112 E6
Broadwater Rd TOOT SW17...29 H7
Broadwater Rd North
WOT/HER KT12...................57 H4
Broadwater Rd South
WOT/HER KT12...................57 J4
Broad Wy FARN GU14..............88 C7
Broadway BRAK RG12............32 D3
STA TW18.............................22 E8
SUT SM1.............................61 N3
WOKN/KNAP GU21..............71 H8
Broadway Av CROY/NA CRO...45 M6
TWK TW1............................26 A2
Broadway CI SAND/SEL CR2....82 B3
Broadway Ct
WIM/MER SW19 *...............28 D9
Broadway Gdns MTCM CR4....44 A5
The Broadway
ADL/WDHM KT15.................55 L8
CHEAM SM5........................61 J5
CRAWE RH10.....................176 D5
SHST GU47.........................67 M1
STA TW18...........................37 N4
THDIT KT7...........................40 C9
WIM/MER SW19...................28 C9
Broadwell Rd RFNM GU10....127 K7
Broadwood CI HORS RH12...192 F5
Broadwood Ri
CRAWW RH11....................194 D3
Broadwood Ter
WKENS W14 *.......................19 K2
Brock CI FRIM GU16...............69 M8
Brockenhurst
E/WMO/HCT KT8..................39 P6
Brockenhurst Av WPK KT4.....42 C9
Brockenhurst Rd
WOKN/KNAP GU21 *...........72 D3
Brockenhurst Dr YTLY GU46...67 H3
Brockenhurst Rd
ALDT GU11........................108 D6
ASC SL5............................34 B6
BRAK RG12........................33 H4
CROY/NA CRO....................46 B8
Brockenhurst Wy
STRHM/NOR SW16..............44 D1
Brockham Cl WIM/MER SW19...28 C8
Brockham Crs CROY/NA CRO...65 K6
Brockham Dr
BRXS/STRHM SW2...............30 A3
Brockham Hill Pk
KWD/TDW/WH KT20...........118 A2
Brockhamhurst Rd
BRKHM/BTCW RH5............137 P3
Brockham La
BRKHM/BTCW RH3............117 N5
Brockhill WOKN/KNAP GU21 *..71 N6
Brockhurst CI HORS RH12...191 H7
Brockhurst Ldg YTLY GU46...127 M6
Brockhurst Ldg YTLY GU46...127 M6
Brocklebank Rd
WAND/EARL SW18................28 E3
Brocklesby Rd SNWD SE25.....46 B5
Brockley Combe WEY KT13....56 F4
Brockley Hall Rd BROCKY SE4...31 M2
Brockley Ms BROCKY SE4......31 M3
Brockley Pk FSTH SE23.........31 M3
Brockley Ri FSTH SE23..........31 N3
Brockley Rd BROCKY SE4......31 N1
Brockley Vw FSTH SE23........31 M3
Brockley Wy FSTH SE23........31 L1
Brock Rd CRAWW RH11......176 D2
Brock's CI GODL GU7...........131 N8
Brocks Dr CHEAM SM5..........60 J2
RGUW GU3.......................111 J1
Brockshot CI BTFD TW8........17 K4
Brock Wy VW GU25...............36 A6
Brockway CI GU GU1............112 F4
Brockwell Av BECK BR3..........47 J6
Brockwell Park Gdns
HNHL SE24.........................30 C5
Brodie Rd GU GU1...................7 G5
Brodrick Gv GT/LBKH KT23....96 A6
Brodrick Rd TOOT SW17.........29 J4
Brograve Gdns BECK BR3.......47 H3
Broke Ct RGUE GU4..............112 G2
Brokes Crs REIG RH2............119 L3
Brokes Rd REIG RH2.............119 L3
Brokie CI FLEETS GU52.........106 E2
Bromfield PI FLEETN GU51 *...86 E4

Bromford CI OXTED RH8.......123 N4
Bromley Av BMLY BR1............47 L1
Bromley Ct BMLY BR1............47 L1
Bromley Crs HAYES BR2........47 M4
Bromley Gdns HAYES BR2.....47 M4
Bromley Gv HAYES BR2........47 K4
Bromley Hl BMLY BR1...........47 M1
Bromley Rd BECK BR3...........46 G2
HAYES BR2.........................47 L3
Brompton CI HSLWW TW4.....24 C1
Brompton Park Crs
FUL/PGN SW6....................19 J5
Bronsart Rd FUL/PGN SW6.....19 J5
Bronson Rd RYNPK SW20......43 H3
Brook Av FNM GU9..............108 B7
Brook CI DORK RH4..............117 J5
EGRIN RH19......................180 G2
FLEETN GU51....................86 D7
HOR/WEW KT19...................60 C7
RYNPK SW20.......................42 F4
SHST GU47.........................50 A8
STWL/WRAY TW19...............23 J3
TOOT SW17.........................29 K5
Brook Ct BECK BR3 *............46 F2
Brook CI BRAK RG12 *.........32 C5
Brooke End OXTED RH8 *....123 N4
Brooke Forest RGUW GU3....111 J1
Brookehowse Rd CAT SE6.....31 P5
Brookers CI ASHTD KT21.......77 J8
Brook Farm Rd COB KT11......75 M4
Brookfield GODL GU7............131 N5
WOKN/KNAP GU21 *...........71 J5
Brookfield Av SUT SM1..........62 A2
Brookfield CI ASHTD KT21.....77 L9
CHERT KT16........................55 H5
REDH RH1........................140 C2
Brookfield Gdns
CRAWE RH10 *....................58 F5
Brookfield PI COB KT11..........75 N4
Brookfield Rd ASHV GU12....108 G4
Brookfields Av MTCM CR4.....44 A6
Brook Gdns BARN SW13........18 D8
FARN GU14.........................88 B5
KUTN/CMB KT2....................42 A2
Brook Hl OXTED RH8...........123 J1
Brook La BNFD RG42.............32 B2
HSMTH W6........................18 G2
Brook Hl OXTED RH8...........123 J1
SHGR GU5.........................133 P5
Brookhill CI CRAWE RH10....160 B9
Brookhill Rd CRAWE RH10...178 B1
Brookhouse Rd FARN GU14...88 B4
Brookhurst Fld
HORS RH12 *.....................189 N2
Brookhurst Rd
ADL/WDHM KT15.................55 M5
Brooklands GDST RH9 *.......142 C3
Brooklands Av
WIM/MER SW19..................28 E5
Brooklands CI COB KT11......75 N4
FNM GU9............................107 P7
RFNM GU10.......................126 B8
SUN TW16...........................38 C2
Brooklands La WEY KT13......56 B5
Brooklands PI HPTN TW12....25 J8
Brooklands Rd
CRAWW RH11....................194 F1
FNM GU9............................108 A7
THDIT KT7............................40 F9
WEY KT13............................56 B5
Brooklands Ter SUN TW16 *...39 J5
The Brooklands ISLW TW7 *...16 D6
Brooklands Wy EGRIN RH19..180 C3
FNM GU9............................108 A7
REDH RH1..........................120 B4
Brook La CHOB/PIR GU24.....53 K9
HORS RH12........................193 J3
RPLY/SEND GU23.................93 J2
SHGR GU5.........................134 A4
Brook La North BTFD TW8....17 K3
Brookley CI RFNM GU10......128 D2
Brookleys CHOB/PIR GU24....53 M8
Brookley Gdns FLEETS GU51...87 H6
Brooklyn Av SNWD SE25.......46 B5
Brooklyn CI CAR SM5............62 A1
WOKS/MYFD GU22...............10 C7
Brooklyn Ct
WOKS/MYFD GU22...............10 C7
Brooklyn Gv SNWD SE25.......46 B5
Brooklyn Rd SNWD SE25.......46 B5
WOKS/MYFD GU22...............10 C6
Brooklyn Wy WDR/YW UB7....13 P1
Brookmead CROY/NA CRO.....44 E7
Brook Md HOR/WEW KT19.....60 C5
Brookmead Ct CRAN GU6.....171 H1
FNM GU9..............................4 D5
Brookmead Rd CROY/NA CRO..44 E7
Brook Rd BAGS GU19............51 N1
CBLY GU15..........................68 D4
HORS RH12........................192 D4
MFD/CHID GU8..................167 K3
REDH RH1..........................100 E8
REDH RH1..........................120 B6
RGUE GU4..........................132 G2
SURB KT6............................59 J7
THHTH CR7.........................45 L5
TWK TW1.............................25 P2
Brook Rd South BTFD TW8...17 K4
Brooksby CI BLKW GU17......67 M3
Brooks CI WEY KT13.............56 C8
Brookscroft CROY/NA CRO....64 F8
Brookside CAR SM5.............62 C4
CHERT KT16.........................37 J8
CRAN GU6..........................153 H9
CRAWE RH10....................160 B9
CRAWW RH11....................177 J4
DTCH/LGLY SL3....................12 G5
FNM GU9............................107 N8
GDST RH9..........................122 D9
RDKG RH5........................137 M7

RGUE GU4...........................92 B9
SHST GU47..........................67 N1
Brookside Av ASHF TW15......22 F8
STWL/WRAY TW19...............12 B8
Brookside CI FELT TW13........24 B4
Brookside Crs WPK KT4.........42 E9
Brookside Pk FARN GU14 *....68 C7
Brookside Rd CROY/NA CRO....46 D7
Brooks La CHSWK W4...........17 N3
Brook St KUT/HW KT1..............8 D5
Brookswood RGUE GU4.......132 G5
The Brook CRAWE RH10.......176 G4
Brook Wy RDKG RH5...........137 H4
Brookview CRAWE RH10......160 B9
Brookview Rd
STRHM/NOR SW16..............29 M8
Brookville Rd FUL/PGN SW6...19 K5
Brook Wy LHD/OX KT22.........76 G7
Brookwell La SHGR GU5.......151 N2
Brookwood HORL RH6..........140 D9
Brookwood Av BARN SW13....18 D8
Brookwood Rd
CHOB/PIR GU24...................71 H9
FARN GU14.........................88 C4
HAYES BR2.........................47 M5
Brookwood Lye Rd
CHOB/PIR GU24...................71 J9
Brookwood Pk HORL RH6....159 L2
Brookwood Rd FARN GU14....88 F3
HSLW TW3...........................16 B7
WAND/EARL SW18................28 C4
Broom Acres FLEETS GU52....86 F9
SHST GU47..........................49 M9
Broom Bank WARL CR6..........83 J8
Broom CI ESH/CLAY KT10.......58 B4
TEDD TW11..........................41 K1
Broomcroft Dr
WOKN/KNAP GU21................73 H4
Broomdashers Rd
CRAWE RH10......................177 J4
Broome CI EPSOM KT18.........98 B6
HORS RH12........................192 C5
YTLY GU46............................66 C1
Broome Ct BRAK RG12..........32 D4
Broomehall Rd RDKG RH5....155 L2
Broome Rd HPTN TW12..........39 P2
Broomers La CRAN GU6........153 P7
Broom Fld LTWR GU18...........70 A1
Broomfield GU GU1..............111 L4
MFD/CHID GU8...................129 N9
SUN TW16............................39 J2
Broomfield CI RGUW GU3.....111 L3
WOKS/MYFD GU22...............73 H5
Broomfield Ct WEY KT13........56 C5
Broomfield La RFNM GU10...146 D5
Broomfield Pk ASC SL5..........35 H8
DORK RH4..........................116 C8
Broomfield Ride
LHD/OX KT22.......................76 D1
Broomfield Rd
ADL/WDHM KT15.................55 M9
BECK BR3............................46 E5
RCH/KEW TW9.....................17 M3
SURB KT6............................41 M9
TEDD TW11..........................41 M9
Broomfields ESH/CLAY KT10..58 C4
Broom Gdns CROY/NA CRO...64 G2
Broomhall La ASC SL5............34 F7
WOKN/KNAP GU21...............10 D2
Broomhall Rd SAND/SEL CR2...63 M7
WOKN/KNAP GU21...............10 D2
Broomhill RFNM GU10.........107 H6
Broomhill Rd FARN GU14......87 P2
WAND/EARL SW18................28 D1
Broomhouse La
FUL/PGN SW6.....................19 L7
Broomhouse Rd
FUL/PGN SW6.....................19 L7
Broomhurst Ct DORK RH4....117 H9
Broomhurst PI
FLEETN GU51 *....................86 E4
Broomlands La OXTED RH8..104 C7
Broom La CHOB/PIR GU24.....53 L7
Broomleaf Cnr FNM GU9..........5 K4
Broomleaf Rd FNM GU9...........5 K3
Broomloan La SUT SM1.........61 L1
Broom Lock TEDD TW11 *......26 B8
Broom Pk TEDD TW11.............8 B1
Broom Rd FLEETN GU51........86 D6
CROY/NA CRO.....................64 G2
TEDD TW11.........................26 B9
Broom Water TEDD TW11......26 B8
Broom Water West
TEDD TW11.........................26 B8
Broom Wy BLKW GU17...........67 P4
WEY KT13.............................56 F3
Broomwood CI CROY/NA CRO..46 D6
Broomwood Rd BTSEA SW11...29 J2
Broomwood Wy
RFNM GU10.......................127 N7
Broseley Gv SYD SE26...........31 M8
Broster Gdns SNWD SE25......45 P4
Brougham PI FNM GU9.........107 M7
Brough CI KUTN/CMB KT2 *....26 C2
Broughton Av
RCHPK/HAM TW10................26 B7
Broughton Ms FRIM GU16......68 F7
Broughton Rd FUL/PGN SW6...19 M7
THHTH CR7..........................45 J7
Broughton Road Ap
FUL/PGN SW6 *....................19 M7
Browells La FELT TW13..........24 D5
Brown CI WLGTN SM6............62 G6
Browngraves Rd
HYS/HAR UB3......................14 E5
Browning Av SUT SM1............62 A3
WPK KT4...............................42 F9
Browning CI CBLY GU15..........69 L4

CRAWE RH10......................177 M4
HPTN TW12.........................24 G7
Brownings EDEN TN8...........144 G1
The Brownings EGRIN RH19..180 E2
Browning Wy HEST TW5.........15 L6
Brownlow Dr BNFD RG42.......32 E1
Brownlow Rd CROY/NA CRO....3 H7
REDH RH1...........................120 A5
Brownrigg Crs BRAK RG12.....32 G2
Brownrigg Rd ASHF TW15......23 J7
Brown's HI REDH RH1...........141 M3
Browns La EHSLY KT24...........95 M7
Brownsover Rd FARN GU14....87 N3
Brown's Rd BRYLDS KT5.......41 M8
Browns Wk RFNM GU10.......127 K8
Browns Wd BNFD RG42........162 D8
The Brow REDH RH1.............140 C1
Broxash Rd BTSEA SW11........29 K2
Broxholm Rd WNWD SE27.....30 B6
Brox La CHERT KT16..............55 H7
Brox Rd CHERT KT16.............54 G8
Broxted Rd FSTH SE23...........31 N5
Bruce Av SHPTN TW17............38 E7
Bruce CI BF/WBF KT14............73 P7
Bruce Dr SAND/SEL CR2.........64 D7
Bruce Rd MTCM CR4..............44 C1
SNWD SE25..........................45 M5
Brudenell Rd TOOT SW17.......29 J6
Brumana CI WEY KT13............56 D5
Brumfield Rd
HOR/WEW KT19....................60 A4
Brunel CI HEST TW5................15 K5
NRWD SE19..........................30 E8
Brunel PI CRAWE RH10........177 H6
Brunel Wk WHTN TW2.............25 H3
Brunner Ct CHERT KT16.........54 G4
Brunswick BRAK RG12............32 C6
Brunswick CI CRAWE RH10...177 K7
THDIT KT7............................40 B8
WHTN TW2...........................25 J6
WOT/HER KT12....................57 L1
Brunswick Dr
CHOB/PIR GU24...................70 D9
Brunswick Gv COB KT11.........75 L2
Brunswick Ms
STRHM/NOR SW16..............29 N9
Brunswick PI NRWD SE19.......46 A1
Brunswick Rd
CHOB/PIR GU24...................90 D1
KUTN/CMB KT2.....................9 H2
SUT SM1..............................61 L3
Bruntile CI FARN GU14...........88 F6
Brushfield Wy
WOKN/KNAP GU21...............71 J7
Brushwood Rd HORS RH12..192 F4
Brussels Rd BTSEA SW11......19 P9
Bruton Rd MRDN SM4............43 N5
Bruton Wy BRAK RG12............32 D8
Bryan CI SUN TW16................39 J1
Bryanston Av WHTN TW2.......25 J4
Bryanston CI NWDGN UB2.....15 P2
Bryanstone Av GUW GU2......111 M1
Bryanstone CI FLEETS GU52...86 C9
GUW GU2...........................111 M1
Bryanstone Gv GUW GU2.....111 M1
Bryce CI HORS RH12............192 F5
Bryce Gdns ALDT GU11........108 E7
Bryden CI SYD SE26...............31 M8
Brympton CI DORK RH4.........116 C9
Brynford CI
WOKN/KNAP GU21...............72 C4
Bryn Rd RFNM GU10.............127 K6
Bryony Rd GU GU1................112 F2
Bryony Wy SUN TW16.............39 J1
Buchan CI SUN TW16.............39 J1
Buchans Lawn
CRAWW RH11....................176 E9
The Buchan CBLY GU15..........51 J9
Bucharest Rd
WAND/EARL SW18................28 F3
Buckfast Rd MRDN SM4..........43 M5
Buckham Thorns Rd
BH/WHM TN16....................104 D6
Buckhold Rd
WAND/EARL SW18................28 D2
Buckhurst Av CAR SM5..........44 A9
Buckhurst CI EGRIN RH19....162 B9
REDH RH1...........................120 A3
Buckhurst HI BRAK RG12.......33 H5
Buckhurst La ASC SL5............34 F5
Buckhurst Rd ASC SL5...........34 F5
BH/WHM TN16....................84 F9
FRIM GU16...........................89 H1
Buckhurst Wy EGRIN RH19..162 B9
Buckingham
E/WMO/HCT KT8..................40 B3
EBED/NFELT TW14................24 C7
THHTH CR7 *........................45 J2
Buckingham Ct BELMT SM2 *..61 L7
Buckingham Dr EGRIN RH19..180 F4
Buckingham Gdns
E/WMO/HCT KT8..................40 B3
THHTH CR7 *........................45 J3
Buckingham Ga HORL RH6...159 N4
Buckingham La FSTH SE23....31 M3
Buckingham Rd HPTN TW12...24 G7
KUT/HW KT1........................41 M6
MTCM CR4...........................44 G6
RCHPK/HAM TW10...............26 B8
REDH RH1..........................137 J6
Buckingham Wy FRIM GU16...69 H8
WLGTN SM6.........................62 E7
Buckland CI FARN GU14.........68 E9
Buckland La
BRKHM/BTCW RH3............118 F2
Buckland Rd BELMT SM2......61 H6
CHSGTN KT9........................59 M4
KWD/TDW/WH KT20.............99 K9

REIG RH2............................119 H4
Bucklands Rd TEDD TW11......26 B9
Bucklands Whf KUT/HW KT1 *...8 C3
Buckland Wk MRDN SM4........43 N5
Buckland Wy WPK KT4............42 G9
Bucklebury BRAK RG12...........32 C7
Buckleigh Av RYNPK SW20....43 K4
Buckleigh Rd
STRHM/NOR SW16..............29 N9
Buckleigh Wy NRWD SE19.....46 B3
Buckler's Wy CAR SM5..........62 B2
Buckles Wy BNSTD SM7.........79 H5
Buckley PI CRAWE RH10......179 H3
Bucknalls Rd CRAWW RH11..176 G5
Bucknall Wy BECK BR3...........47 H5
Bucknills CI EPSOM KT18.......78 A3
Bucks CI BF/WBF KT14............73 M3
Buckstone CI FSTH SE23........31 K2
Buckswood Dr
CRAWW RH11....................176 D7
Buckthorne Rd BROCKY SE4..31 M2
Buckthorns BNFD RG42.........32 A1
Budebury Rd STA TW18..........22 C8
Budge La MTCM CR4.............44 B8
Budgen CI CRAWE RH10......177 N2
Budgen Dr REDH RH1...........120 C2
Budgin's HI ORP BR6.............85 M1
Budham Wy BRAK RG12.........32 D7
Buer Rd FUL/PGN SW6..........19 J7
Buff Av BNSTD SM7...............79 M4
Buffbeards La HASM GU27...183 P3
Buffers La LHD/OX KT22.........76 G8
Bug HI WARL CR6....................82 D9
Bugkingham Wy FRIM GU16...69 H7
Buiganak Rd THHTH CR7.........45 L5
Bulkeley CI EGH TW20.............21 N6
Bullard Rd TEDD TW11 *.........25 N9
Bullbeggars La GDST RH9.....122 C3
WOKN/KNAP GU21...............71 P5
Bullbrook Dr BRAK RG12........32 G3
Bullbrook Rw BRAK RG12......32 G3
Buller CI BF/WBF KT14............45 P8
Buller Rd ALDT GU11............108 D2
THHTH CR7...........................45 M4
Bullers Rd FNM GU9.............108 A8
Bullfinch CI HORL RH6..........140 A9
HORS RH12........................192 B3
SHST GU47...........................50 A9
Bullfinch Rd SAND/SEL CR2...64 D8
Bull HI LHD/OX KT22..............96 G1
Bull La BNFD RG42.................32 C2
RGUE GU4............................92 D6
Bullrush CI CAR SM5...............62 A1
CROY/NA CRO......................45 N7
Bulls Aly MORT/ESHN SW14 *..18 B2
Bull's Br NWDGN UB2.............15 K1
Bulls Bridge Rd NWDGN UB2..15 K1
Bullswater Common Rd
CHOB/PIR GU24...................90 G5
Bulstrode Av HSLW TW3..........15 M8
Bulstrode Gdns HSLW TW3....16 A8
Bulstrode Rd HSLW TW3........16 A8
Bunbury Wy EW KT17.............78 F5
Bunce Common Rd
REIG RH2............................138 B3
Bunce Dr CTHM CR5.............101 M3
Bunch La HASM GU27...........184 B3
Bunch Wy HASM GU27..........184 B4
Bundys Wy STA TW18............22 C9
Bungalow Rd FARN GU14.......88 D5
SNWD SE25.........................45 N5
The Bungalows
STRHM/NOR SW16..............44 D1
Bunting CI MTCM CR4............44 B6
SWTR RH13........................192 E7
Bunyan CI CRAWW RH11.....176 B8
Bunyard Dr
WOKN/KNAP GU21...............72 G3
Burbage Cn BRAK RG12.........33 H6
Burbage Rd HNHL SE24.........30 E2
Burbeach CI CRAWW RH11...176 E8
Burberry CI NWMAL KT3........42 C3
Burbidge Rd SHPTN TW17.....38 C5
Burbury Woods CBLY GU15....68 G2
Burchets Hollow SHGR GU5..134 F6
Burchett Coppice
EWKG RG40........................48 C2
Burchetts Wy SHPTN TW17...38 D7
Burcote Rd WAND/EARL SW18..28 G4
Burcott Gdns
ADL/WDHM KT15.................55 P5
Burcott Rd PUR/KEN CR8.......81 J3
Burden CI BTFD TW8...............17 J3
Burdenshot HI RGUW GU3.....91 N4
Burdenshott Av
RCHPK/HAM TW10................17 P7
Burdenshott Rd RGUW GU3...91 N4
Burden Wy GU GU1................112 F2
Burdett Av RYNPK SW20.........42 E2
Burdett CI CRAWE RH10.......177 N6
Burdett Rd CROY/NA CRO......45 M7
RCH/KEW TW9.....................17 M7
Burdock CI CRAWW RH11....176 D9
CROY/NA CRO......................46 D9
Burdon La BELMT SM2............61 J5
Burdon Pk BELMT SM2...........61 K7
Burfield CI TOOT SW17............28 F7
Burfield Rd WARL CR6.............82 C8
Burfield Rd WDSR SL4...........11 N1
Burford La EW KT17................60 G9
Burford Lea MFD/CHID GU8..129 N9
Burford Rd BTFD TW8..............17 L3
CAT SE6................................31 L5
CBLY GU15...........................68 C4
SUT SM1...............................61 L1
SWTR RH13........................192 D8
WPK KT4...............................42 E8
Burford Wk FUL/PGN SW6 *...19 M5
Burford Wy CROY/NA CRO......65 J6
Burge CI FARN GU14...............87 N3

Burges Gv BARN SW13 ....18 F5
Burges Rd STA TW18 ....22 D9
Burgess Cl FELT TW13 ....24 F7
Burgess Rd SUT SM1 ....61 M3
Burges Wy STA TW18 ....22 D8
Burgh Cl CRAWE RH10 ....177 N2
Burghead Cl SHST GU47 ....67 P1
Burghfield EW KT17 ....78 D4
Burgh Heath Rd EW KT17 ....78 D4
Burgh Hill Rd LIPH GU30 ....182 C3
Burghill Rd SYD SE26 ....31 L7
Burghley Av NWMAL KT3 ....42 B2
Burghley Hall Cl
WIM/MER SW19 * 28 B4
Burghley Pl MTCM CR4 ....44 B5
Burghley Rd WIM/MER SW19 ....28 B7
Burgh Mt BNSTD SM7 ....79 K4
Burgh Wd BNSTD SM7 ....79 J4
Burgos Cl CROY/NA CR0 ....63 J5
Burgoyne Rd CBLY GU15 ....69 J2
SNWD SE25 ....45 P5
SUN TW16 ....24 A9
Burham Cl PGE/AN SE20 ....46 C1
Burhill Rd WOT/HER KT12 ....57 K7
Burke Cl PUT/ROE SW15 ....18 C9
Burket Cl NWDGN UB2 ....15 N2
Burland Rd BTSEA SW11 ....29 J1
Burlands CRAWW RH11 ....176 D2
Burlea Cl WOT/HER KT12 ....57 K4
Burleigh Av WLGTN SM6 ....62 C2
Burleigh Cl ADL/WDHM KT15 ....55 M4
CRAWE RH10 ....179 J3
Burleigh Gdns ASHF TW15 ....23 M8
WOKN/KNAP GU21 * 11 F2
Burleigh La ASC SL5 ....33 N2
CRAWE RH10 ....179 K4
Burleigh Pk COB KT11 ....75 N1
Burleigh Pl PUT/ROE SW15 ....28 A1
Burleigh Rd ADL/WDHM KT15 ....55 M3
ASC SL5 ....33 N3
CHEAM SM3 ....43 J9
FRIM GU16 ....68 F8
Burleigh Wy CRAWE RH10 ....179 J3
Burley Cl BIL RH14 ....188 D6
STRHM/NOR SW16 ....44 F3
Burleys Rd CRAWE RH10 ....177 N5
Burley Wy BLKW GU17 ....67 N2
Burlingham Cl RGUE GU4 ....113 H3
Burlings La RSEV TN14 ....85 K6
The Burlings ASC SL5 ....33 N3
Burlington Av RCH/KEW TW9 ....17 N6
Burlington Cl
EBED/NFELT TW14 ....23 N3
Burlington Ct ALDT GU11 ....108 B5
BLKW GU17 ....67 N5
Burlington Gdns CHSWK W4 ....18 A3
Burlington La CHSWK W4 ....18 A5
Burlington Pl FUL/PGN SW6 ....19 J7
REIG RH2 ....119 L4
Burlington Rd CHSWK W4 * 18 A3
FUL/PGN SW6 ....19 J7
ISLW TW7 ....16 D6
NWMAL KT3 ....42 D5
THHTH CR7 ....45 L3
Burlsdon Wy BRAK RG12 ....32 G2
Burma Rd CHERT KT16 ....53 M1
Burma Ter NRWD SE19 * 30 F8
Burmester Rd TOOT SW17 ....28 F6
Burnaby Crs CHSWK W4 ....17 P4
Burnaby Gdns CHSWK W4 ....17 P4
Burnaby St WBPTN SW10 ....19 N5
Burnbury Rd BAL SW12 ....29 M4
Burn Cl ADL/WDHM KT15 ....55 P3
LHD/OX KT22 ....76 C4
Burne-Jones Dr SHST GU47 ....67 P2
Burnell Av RCHPK/HAM TW10 ....26 B8
Burnell Rd SUT SM1 ....61 M3
Burnet Av GU GU1 ....112 F2
Burnet Cl CHOB/PIR GU24 ....70 E2
Burnet Gv HOR/WEW KT19 ....78 A2
Burney Av BRYLDS KT5 ....41 M6
Burney Cl LHD/OX KT22 ....96 C5
Burney Rd RDKG RH5 ....116 G2
Burnfoot Av FUL/PGN SW6 ....19 J6
Burnham Cl
WOKN/KNAP GU21 ....71 K7
Burnham Dr REIG RH2 ....119 L4
WPK KT4 ....61 H1
Burnham Gdns CROY/NA CR0 ....45 P8
HSLWW TW4 ....15 K6
HYS/HAR UB3 ....14 F1
Burnham Gv BNFD RG42 ....32 E1
Burnham Pl SWTR RH13 * 192 C9
Burnham Rd MRDN SM4 ....43 M6
WOKN/KNAP GU21 ....71 K7
Burnhams Rd GT/LBKH KT23 ....95 N4
Burnham St KUTN/CMB KT2 ....9 H3
Burnham Wy SYD SE26 ....31 N8
WEA W13 ....17 H2
Burnhill Rd BECK BR3 ....46 G3
Burn Moor Cha BRAK RG12 ....32 G8
Burnmoor Meadow
EWKG RG40 ....48 C7
Burnsall Cl FARN GU14 ....88 D1
Burns Av EBED/NFELT TW14 ....24 B2
FLEETS GU52 ....87 H9
Burns Cl CAR SM5 ....62 C7
FARN GU14 ....88 B1
HORS RH12 ....192 D3
WIM/MER SW19 ....28 G9
Burns Dr BNSTD SM7 ....79 J3
Burnside ASHTD KT21 ....77 M7
FLEETN GU51 ....86 G6
Burnside Cl TWK TW1 ....25 P2
Burns Rd CRAWE RH10 ....177 M3
Burns Wy EGRIN RH19 ....180 B2
HEST TW5 ....15 M6
HORS RH12 ....193 P1
Burnt Common Cl
RPLY/SEND GU23 ....93 K5
Burntcommon La
RPLY/SEND GU23 ....93 L5
Burnt Hill Rd RFNM GU10 ....127 L7
Burnt Hill Wy RFNM GU10 ....127 M8
Burnthouse Gdns BNFD RG42 ....32 C1
Burnt House La HORS RH12 ....175 L4
Burnthwaite Rd
FUL/PGN SW6 ....19 K5
Burnt Oak EWKG RG40 ....48 D1
Burnt Oak La RDKG RH5 ....157 K4
Burnt Pollard La LTWR GU18 ....52 E8
Burntwood Cl CTHM CR3 ....102 A1
WAND/EARL SW18 * 28 G4
Burntwood Grange Rd
WAND/EARL SW18 ....28 G4
Burntwood La CTHM CR3 ....102 A1
TOOT SW17 ....28 G5
Burntwood Vw NRWD SE19 * 30 G8
Burnwood Park Rd
WOT/HER KT12 ....57 K3
Burpham La RGUE GU4 ....92 E9
Burrell Cl CROY/NA CR0 ....46 E7
Burrell Rd FRIM GU16 ....68 E8
Burrell Rw BECK BR3 ....46 G3
The Burrell DORK RH4 ....116 C8
Burr Hill La CHOB/PIR GU24 ....53 L7
Burritt Rd KUT/HW KT1 ....9 H5
Burroway Rd DTCH/LGLY SL3 ....12 F1
Burrow Hill Gn
CHOB/PIR GU24 ....53 K7
Burrows Cl GT/LBKH KT23 ....95 P4
GUW GU2 ....111 M4
Burrows Hill Cl
STWL/WRAY TW19 ....13 M9
Burrows La SHGR GU5 ....134 E2
Burr Rd WAND/EARL SW18 ....28 D4
Burrwood Gdns ASHV GU12 ....109 J2
Burstead Cl COB KT11 ....75 M2
Burstock Rd PUT/ROE SW15 ....19 J9
Burston Gdns EGRIN RH19 ....162 C8
Burston Rd PUT/ROE SW15 ....28 A1
Burstow Rd RYNPK SW20 ....43 J2
Burtenshaw Rd THDIT KT7 ....40 G8
Burton Cl CHSGTN KT9 ....59 K6
HORL RH6 ....159 K2
THHTH CR7 ....45 M4
Burton Gdns HEST TW5 ....15 P6
Burton Rd KUTN/CMB KT2 ....8 E1
Burtons Ct HORS RH12 * 192 B8
Burton's Rd HPTN TW12 ....25 J7
Burtwell La WNWD SE27 ....30 E7
Burwash Rd CRAWE RH10 ....177 K6
Burway Crs CHERT KT16 ....37 L5
Burwood Av HAYES BR2 ....65 P1
PUR/KEN CR8 ....81 K3
Burwood Cl GU GU1 ....112 G4
REIG RH2 ....119 P5
SURB KT6 ....41 N9
WOT/HER KT12 ....57 L5
Burwood Rd WEY KT13 ....56 F6
Bury Cl WOKN/KNAP GU21 ....10 A2
Bury Flds GUW GU2 ....6 D7
Bury Gv MRDN SM4 ....43 M6
Bury La WOKN/KNAP GU21 ....72 A5
Bury Ms GUW GU2 * 6 D7
The Burys GODL GU7 ....131 L8
Bury St GUW GU2 ....6 D7
Busbridge La GODL GU7 ....150 D1
Busch Cl ISLW TW7 ....17 H6
Busdens Cl MFD/CHID GU8 ....149 N4
Busdens La MFD/CHID GU8 ....149 N4
Busdens Wy MFD/CHID GU8 ....149 N4
Bushbury La
BRKHM/BTCW RH3 ....137 N1
Bush Cl ADL/WDHM KT15 ....55 N4
Bush Cottages
WAND/EARL SW18 ....28 D1
Bushell Cl BRXS/STRHM SW2 ....30 A5
Bushetts Gv REDH RH1 ....100 D9
Bushey Cl PUR/KEN CR8 ....81 P5
Bushey Cft OXTED RH8 ....123 J1
Bushey La SUT SM1 ....61 L2
Bushey Rd CROY/NA CR0 ....64 C1
HYS/HAR UB3 ....14 G2
RYNPK SW20 ....42 G3
SUT SM1 ....61 M3
Bushey Wy BECK BR3 ....47 K7
Bushfield BIL RH14 ....187 L8
Bushfield Dr REDH RH1 ....140 C1
Bush La RPLY/SEND GU23 ....93 H4
Bushnell Rd TOOT SW17 ....29 L5
Bush Rd RCH/KEW TW9 ....17 M4
SHPTN TW17 ....38 B6
Bushwood Rd RCH/KEW TW9 ....17 N4
Bushy Hill Dr GU GU1 ....112 G4
Bushy Park Gdns HPTN TW12 ....25 L8
Bushy Park Rd TEDD TW11 ....41 H1
Bushy Rd LHD/OX KT22 ....96 B2
TEDD TW11 ....25 M9
Bushy Shaw ASHTD KT21 ....77 J6
Busk Crs FARN GU14 ....88 B4
Bute Av RCHPK/HAM TW10 ....26 D5
Bute Gdns HMSMTH W6 ....19 H2
RCHPK/HAM TW10 * 26 D4
WLGTN SM6 ....62 E4
Bute Gdns West WLGTN SM6 ....62 E4
Bute Rd CROY/NA CR0 ....45 J9
WLGTN SM6 ....62 E3
Bute St SKENS SW7 * 19 P2
Butler Rd BAGS GU19 ....51 P7
CWTH RG45 ....49 M3
Butlers Cl HSLWW TW4 ....15 P9
Butlers Dene Rd CTHM CR3 ....82 F9
Butlers Hl EHSLY KT24 ....114 D1
Butlers Rd SWTR RH13 ....192 F6
Butt Cl CRAN GU6 ....153 H8
Buttercup Sq
STWL/WRAY TW19 * 22 G4
Butterfield CBLY GU15 ....68 D4
EGRIN RH19 ....162 A9
Butterfield Cl TWK TW1 ....25 N2
Butterfly Wk WARL CR6 ....82 C9
Butter Hl CAR SM5 ....62 C2
DORK RH4 ....116 G7
Buttermer Cl RFNM GU10 ....127 J6
Buttermere Cl
EBED/NFELT TW14 ....24 A4
FARN GU14 ....88 A3
HORS RH12 ....192 G4
MRDN SM4 ....43 H7
Buttermere Ct ASHV GU12 * 109 H2
Buttermere Dr CBLY GU15 ....69 M4
PUT/ROE SW15 ....28 B1
Buttermere Gdns BRAK RG12 ....32 E4
PUR/KEN CR8 ....81 M2
Buttermere Wy EGH TW20 ....36 F1
Buttersteep Ri ASC SL5 ....33 L9
Butterwick HMSMTH W6 ....18 G2
Butts Cl CRAWW RH11 ....176 E4
Butts Crs FELT TW13 ....25 H6
Butts Rd WOKN/KNAP GU21 ....10 C5
The Butts BTFD TW8 ....17 K4
Buxton Av CTHM CR3 ....101 N1
Buxton Crs CHEAM SM3 ....61 J3
Buxton Dr NWMAL KT3 ....42 B3
Buxton La CTHM CR3 ....101 N1
Buxton Rd ASHF TW15 ....22 G8
MORT/ESHN SW14 ....18 C8
THHTH CR7 ....45 K6
Byam St FUL/PGN SW6 ....19 N7
Byards Cft STRHM/NOR SW16 ....44 F2
Bychurch End TEDD TW11 * 25 N8
Bycroft St PGE/AN SE20 ....46 D1
Bycroft Wy CRAWE RH10 ....177 L3
Byerley Wy CRAWE RH10 ....177 P4
Byers La GDST RH9 ....142 C4
Bye Ways WHTN TW2 ....25 J6
The Byeways BRYLDS KT5 ....41 N6
The Byeway
MORT/ESHN SW14 ....18 A8
Byfeld Gdns BARN SW13 ....18 E6
Byfield Rd ISLW TW7 ....16 G8
Byfleet Rd ADL/WDHM KT15 ....55 P7
COB KT11 ....74 D1
Byfleets La HORS RH12 ....191 L5
Bygrove CROY/NA CR0 ....65 H5
Bygrove Rd WIM/MER SW19 ....28 G9
Byland Cl CAR SM5 ....43 N8
Bylands WOKS/MYFD GU22 ....11 G7
Byne Rd CAR SM5 ....62 A1
SYD SE26 ....31 K9
Bynes Rd SAND/SEL CR2 ....63 M6
By Pass Rd LHD/OX KT22 ....77 H9
Byrd Rd CRAWW RH11 ....176 C8
Byrefield Rd GUW GU2 ....111 M2
Byrne Rd BAL SW12 ....29 L4
Byron Av CBLY GU15 ....69 K5
COUL/CHIP CR5 ....80 G4
HSLWW TW4 ....15 K7
NWMAL KT3 ....42 E6
SUT SM1 ....61 P3
Byron Av East SUT SM1 ....61 P3
Byron Cl CRAWE RH10 ....177 L4
FLEETN GU51 ....86 G7
HORS RH12 ....192 D4
HPTN TW12 ....24 G7
PGE/AN SE20 * 46 B4
SYD SE26 * 31 M7
WOKN/KNAP GU21 ....71 L6
WOT/HER KT12 ....39 N9
YTLY GU46 ....66 F4
Byron Dr CWTH RG45 ....49 M6
Byron Gdns SUT SM1 ....61 P3
Byron Gv EGRIN RH19 ....180 B3
Byron Pl LHD/OX KT22 ....97 H2
Byron Rd ADL/WDHM KT15 ....55 P3
SAND/SEL CR2 ....64 B8
Byron Wy WDR/YW UB7 ....14 B2
Byton Rd TOOT SW17 ....29 J9
Byttom Hl RDKG RH5 ....97 J7
Byward Av
EBED/NFELT TW14 ....24 D2
Byways YTLY GU46 ....66 F3
The Byways HOR/WEW KT19 ....60 D3
The Byway BELMT SM2 ....61 P7
Bywood BRAK RG12 ....32 C8
Bywood Av CROY/NA CR0 ....46 C7
Bywood Cl PUR/KEN CR8 ....81 K4
Byworth Cl FNM GU9 ....4 B3
Byworth Rd FNM GU9 ....4 B4

C

Cabbell Pl ADL/WDHM KT15 ....55 N3
Cabell Rd GUW GU2 ....111 L4
Caberfeigh Cl REDH RH1 ....120 A5
Caberfeigh Pl REDH RH1 * 119 P5
Cabin Moss BRAK RG12 ....32 G8
Cabrera Av VW GU25 ....36 B6
Cabrera Cl VW GU25 ....36 A7
Cabrol Rd FARN GU14 ....88 C2
Caburn Ct CRAWW RH11 ....176 F7
Caburn Hts CRAWW RH11 ....176 F7
Cacket's La RSEV TN14 ....85 H4
The Cackstones
CRAWE RH10 * 177 N4
Cadbury Cl ISLW TW7 ....16 G6
SUN TW16 ....38 G1
Cadbury Rd SUN TW16 ....38 G1
Caddy Cl EGH TW20 ....21 M8
Cader Rd WAND/EARL SW18 ....28 F2
Cadet Wy FLEETS GU52 ....107 H2
Cadmer Cl NWMAL KT3 ....42 C5
Cadnam Cl ALDT GU11 ....108 E8
Cadogan Ct TEDD TW11 ....25 M8
Cadogan Ct BELMT SM2 ....61 M5
Cadogan Pl PUR/KEN CR8 ....81 L6
Cadogan Rd ALDT GU11 ....88 F8
SURB KT6 ....41 K6
Caenshill Ga WEY KT13 ....56 C6
Caenshill Rd WEY KT13 ....56 C6
Caenswood Hl WEY KT13 ....56 C8
Caenwood Cl WEY KT13 ....56 C5
Caen Wood Rd ASHTD KT21 ....77 J7
Caerleon Cl ESH/CLAY KT10 ....59 H6
GSHT GU26 ....165 M5
Caernarvon FRIM GU16 ....69 H8
Caernarvon Cl MTCM CR4 ....44 G4
Caesar's Camp Rd CBLY GU15 ....51 J9
Caesar's Cl CBLY GU15 ....51 J9
Caesars Ga BNFD RG42 ....32 C1
Caesars Wk MTCM CR4 ....44 B6
Caesar's Wy SHPTN TW17 ....38 F7
Caffins Cl CRAWE RH10 ....177 H3
Cage Yd REIG RH2 * 119 L5
Caillard Rd BF/WBF KT14 ....55 P9
Cain Rd BNFD RG42 ....32 A3
Cain's La EBED/NFELT TW14 ....23 N1
Cairn Cl CBLY GU15 ....69 K5
Cairndale Cl BMLY BR1 ....47 M1
Cairngorm Pl FARN GU14 ....68 A9
Cairns Rd BTSEA SW11 ....29 H1
Cairo New Rd CROY/NA CR0 ....2 B4
Caistor Rd BAL SW12 ....29 L3
Caithness Dr EPSOM KT18 ....78 B3
Caithness Rd MTCM CR4 ....44 D1
WKENS W14 ....19 H1
Calbourne Rd BAL SW12 ....29 J3
Calcott Pk YTLY GU46 ....66 G2
Caldbeck Av WPK KT4 ....60 F1
Calder Ct DTCH/LGLY SL3 ....12 D3
Calderdale Cl CRAWW RH11 ....176 E7
Calder Rd MRDN SM4 ....43 N6
Caldervale Rd CLAP SW4 ....29 N1
Calder Wy DTCH/LGLY SL3 ....13 J8
Caldwell Rd BFOR GU20 ....52 D4
Caledonian Wy HORL RH6 * 159 L4
Caledonia Rd
STWL/WRAY TW19 ....23 H4
Caledon Pl RGUE GU4 ....112 E2
Caledon Rd WLGTN SM6 ....62 C3
Calfridus Wy BRAK RG12 ....32 G4
Calidore Cl
BRXS/STRHM SW2 * 30 A2
California Cl BELMT SM2 ....61 L8
California Rd NWMAL KT3 ....42 A5
Calley Down Crs
CROY/NA CR0 ....65 K8
Callis Farm Cl
STWL/WRAY TW19 ....23 H2
Callisto Cl CRAWW RH11 ....176 B8
Callow Fld PUR/KEN CR8 ....81 J2
Callow Hl VW GU25 ....36 A3
Callow St WBPTN SW10 ....19 N4
Calluna Ct WOKS/MYFD GU22 ....10 E5
Calluna Dr CRAWE RH10 ....178 B1
Calonne Rd WIM/MER SW19 ....28 A7
Calshot Rd HTHAIR TW6 ....14 D7
Calshot Wy FRIM GU16 ....69 J9
HTHAIR TW6 ....14 C7
Calthorpe Gdns SUT SM1 ....61 N2
Calthorpe Rd FLEETN GU51 ....86 E5
Calton Av DUL SE21 ....30 F2
Calton Gdns ALDT GU11 ....108 E7
Calvecroft LIPH GU30 ....182 F6
Calverley Rd EW KT17 ....60 E5
Calvert Cl ASHV GU12 ....108 F5
Calvert Crs DORK RH4 ....117 H5
Calvert Rd DORK RH4 ....117 H5
EHSLY KT24 ....95 K8
Calvin Cl CBLY GU15 ....69 K4
Camac Rd WHTN TW2 ....25 L4
Cambalt Rd PUT/ROE SW15 ....28 A1
Camber Cl CRAWE RH10 ....177 M5
Camberley Av RYNPK SW20 ....42 F3
Camberley Cl CHEAM SM3 ....61 H2
Camberley Rd HTHAIR TW6 ....14 C8
Camborne Cl HTHAIR TW6 ....14 C8
Camborne Crs HTHAIR TW6 ....14 C8
Camborne Ms
WAND/EARL SW18 ....28 D3
Camborne Rd BELMT SM2 ....61 L6
CROY/NA CR0 ....46 A8
MRDN SM4 ....43 H7
WAND/EARL SW18 ....28 D3
Camborne Wy HEST TW5 ....16 A6
Cambray Rd BAL SW12 ....29 M4
Cambria Cl HSLW TW3 ....16 A9
Cambria Ct
EBED/NFELT TW14 ....24 C3
Cambria Gdns
STWL/WRAY TW19 ....23 H3
Cambrian Cl CBLY GU15 ....68 D3
WNWD SE27 ....30 C6
Cambrian Rd FARN GU14 ....67 P9
RCHPK/HAM TW10 ....26 E2
Cambrian Wy EWKG RG40 ....48 E1
Cambria St FUL/PGN SW6 ....19 M5
Cambridge Av NWMAL KT3 ....42 D3
Cambridge Cl HSLWW TW4 ....15 N9
RYNPK SW20 ....42 F2
WDR/YW UB7 ....13 P4
WOKN/KNAP GU21 ....71 M7
Cambridge Crs TEDD TW11 * 25 P8
Cambridge Gdns KUT/HW KT1 ....9 H5
Cambridge Gv HMSMTH W6 ....18 G2
PGE/AN SE20 * 46 B2
Cambridge Grove Rd
KUT/HW KT1 ....9 H5
Cambridge Lodge Pk
HORL RH6 * 140 C7
Cambridge Pk TWK TW1 ....26 C3
Cambridge Rd ALDT GU11 ....108 B4
ASHF TW15 ....38 E1
BARN SW13 ....18 D7
BMLY BR1 ....47 N1
CAR SM5 ....62 A5
CWTH RG45 ....49 N5
HPTN TW12 ....39 P1
HSLWW TW4 ....15 N9
KUT/HW KT1 ....9 H5
MTCM CR4 ....44 D3
NWMAL KT3 ....42 B5
PGE/AN SE20 ....46 A4
RCH/KEW TW9 ....17 N5
RYNPK SW20 ....42 F2
SHST GU47 ....50 A8
SWTR RH13 ....192 C8
TEDD TW11 ....25 P7
TWK TW1 ....26 C2
WOT/HER KT12 ....39 K7
Cambridge Rd North
CHSWK W4 ....17 P3
Cambridge Rd South
CHSWK W4 ....17 P3
Cambridge Rd West
FARN GU14 ....88 E6
Cambridgeshire Cl
BNFD RG42 ....33 H1
Cambridge Sq REDH RH1 ....120 C8
Camden Av FELT TW13 ....24 D5
Camden Gdns SUT SM1 ....61 M4
THHTH CR7 ....45 K4
Camden Hill Rd NRWD SE19 ....30 F9
Camden Rd CAR SM5 ....62 B3
LING RH7 ....162 C1
SUT SM1 ....61 M4
Camden Wk FLEETN GU51 ....87 J6
Camden Wy THHTH CR7 ....45 K4
Camel Gv KUTN/CMB KT2 ....26 C8
Camellia Ct CHOB/PIR GU24 ....70 F2
Camellia Pl WHTN TW2 ....25 J3
Camelot Cl BH/WHM TN16 ....84 A5
WIM/MER SW19 ....28 C7
Camelsdale Rd HASM GU27 ....184 A5
Camel Wy FARN GU14 ....88 C7
Camera Pl WBPTN SW10 ....19 P4
Cameron Cl CRAN GU6 ....171 H2
Cameron Pl
STRHM/NOR SW16 ....30 B6
Cameron Rd ALDT GU11 ....88 F8
CAT SE6 * 31 N5
CROY/NA CR0 ....45 K7
HAYES BR2 ....47 N6
Camilla Cl GT/LBKH KT23 ....96 B5
SUN TW16 * 23 P9
Camilla Dr RDKG RH5 ....116 G1
Camille Cl SNWD SE25 ....46 A4
Camm Gdns KUT/HW KT1 ....9 G4
THDIT KT7 ....40 E8
Camomile Av MTCM CR4 ....44 B2
Campana Rd FUL/PGN SW6 ....19 L6
Campbell Av
WOKS/MYFD GU22 ....92 D1
Campbell Cl ALDT GU11 ....108 D7
BF/WBF KT14 ....55 P9
FLEETN GU51 ....86 E6
STRHM/NOR SW16 * 29 N8
WHTN TW2 ....25 L4
YTLY GU46 ....67 K2
Campbell Crs EGRIN RH19 ....180 A2
Campbell Pl FRIM GU16 ....69 H5
Campbell Rd ALDT GU11 ....108 C3
CRAWE RH10 ....177 M7
CROY/NA CR0 ....45 K8
CTHM CR3 ....101 M1
WEY KT13 ....56 C6
WHTN TW2 ....25 L5
Campden Rd
SAND/SEL CR2 ....63 N4
Campden Ter CHSWK W4 * 18 C3
Campen Cl WIM/MER SW19 ....28 B5
Camp End Rd WEY KT13 ....74 D1
Camp Farm Rd ALDT GU11 ....108 F1
Camp Hl RFNM GU10 ....128 E5
Camphill Ct BF/WBF KT14 ....73 L1
Camphill Rd BF/WBF KT14 ....73 L1
Campion Cl BLKW GU17 ....68 B5
CROY/NA CR0 ....63 N3
Campion Dr
KWD/TDW/WH KT20 ....78 F9
Campion Rd ISLW TW7 ....16 F6
PUT/ROE SW15 ....18 G9
Camp Rd CTHM CR3 ....102 E1
FARN GU14 ....88 E7
WIM/MER SW19 ....27 N8
Camp Vw WIM/MER SW19 ....27 N8
Camrose Av FELT TW13 ....24 C7
Camrose Cl CROY/NA CR0 ....46 E8
MRDN SM4 ....43 L5
Camus Cl FLEETS GU52 ....106 D1
Canada Av REDH RH1 ....120 C9
Canada Copse
MFD/CHID GU8 ....149 M2
Canada Dr REDH RH1 ....120 C9
Canada Rd BF/WBF KT14 ....55 P9
COB KT11 ....75 L2
FRIM GU16 ....69 M8
Canada Wy LIPH GU30 ....182 F7
Canal Cl ALDT GU11 ....108 F1
Canal Wk CROY/NA CR0 ....45 N7
Canal Yd NWDGN UB2 * 15 K2
Canberra Cl CRAWW RH11 ....176 G2
HORS RH12 ....192 E6
YTLY GU46 ....66 E1
Canberra Pl HORS RH12 * 192 E5
Canberra Rd HTHAIR TW6 ....14 C8
Canberra Wy FARN GU14 ....88 B7
Canbury Av KUTN/CMB KT2 ....9 F3
Canbury Ms SYD SE26 ....31 H6
Canbury Park Rd
KUTN/CMB KT2 ....9 F3
Candleford Cl BRAK RG12 ....32 E1
Candleford Ga LIPH GU30 * 182 E6
Candler Ms TWK TW1 ....25 P3
Candlerush Cl
WOKS/MYFD GU22 ....11 K3
Candover Cl WDR/YW UB7 ....13 P5
Candy Cft GT/LBKH KT23 ....96 B6
Canewden Cl
WOKS/MYFD GU22 ....10 D7
Canford Dr ADL/WDHM KT15 ....55 M1
Canford Gdns NWMAL KT3 ....42 C7
Canford Pl TEDD TW11 ....26 B9
Canham Rd SNWD SE25 ....45 N4
Can Hatch
KWD/TDW/WH KT20 ....79 J7

Canmore Gdns
STRHM/NOR SW16 .... 44 E1
Canning Pl *KENS* W8 .... 19 N1
Canning Place Ms *KENS* W8 * . 19 N1
Canning Rd *ASHV* GU12 ... 108 F4
CROY/NA CR0 .... 3 J3
Cannizaro Rd
WIM/MER SW19 .... 27 P9
Cannon Cl *HPTN* TW12 .... 25 J9
RYNPK SW20 .... 42 G7
SHST GU47 .... 50 B9
Cannon Crs *CHOB/PIR* GU24 ... 53 L9
Cannon Gv *LHD/OX* KT22 ... 96 E2
Cannon Hl *BRAK* RG12 .... 32 E7
Cannon Hill La *RYNPK* SW20 ... 43 H6
Cannon Side *LHD/OX* KT22 ... 96 E2
Cannon Wy *E/WMO/HCT* KT8 ... 40 A5
LHD/OX KT22 .... 96 E1
Canonbie Rd *FSTH* SE23 .... 31 K3
Canons Cl *REIG* RH2 .... 119 K4
Canon's Hl *COUL/CHIP* CR5 ... 81 J7
Canons La
KWD/TDW/WH KT20 .... 79 J8
Canon's Wk *CROY/NA* CR0 ... 64 D2
Canopus Wy
STWL/WRAY TW19 .... 23 H3
Cansiron La *EGRIN* RH19 ... 181 N6
Cantelupe Ms *EGRIN* RH19 * . 180 D2
Cantelupe Rd *EGRIN* RH19 ... 180 E2
Canterbury Cl *BECK* BR3 .... 47 H2
RPLK KT4 .... 61 H1
Canterbury Ct *DORK* RH4 * ... 116 C6
Canterbury Gv *WNWD* SE27 ... 30 C6
Canterbury Rd *ASHV* GU12 ... 109 J3
CRAWE RH10 .... 177 H9
CROY/NA CR0 .... 45 H8
FARN GU14 .... 88 F5
FELT TW13 .... 24 F5
GUW GU2 .... 111 M5
MRDN SM4 .... 43 N7
The Canter *CRAWE* RH10 ... 177 P4
Cantley Gdns *NRWD* SE19 ... 45 P2
Cantley Rd *HNWL* W7 .... 16 G1
Canvey Cl *CRAWW* RH11 ... 176 C5
Cape Copse *HORS* RH12 ... 189 N3
Capel Av *WLGTN* SM6 .... 63 K4
Capel La *CRAWW* RH11 ... 176 C6
Capel Rd *HORS* RH12 ... 174 C5
Capern Rd *WAND/EARL* SW18 ... 28 F4
Capital Interchange Wy
BTFD TW8 .... 17 N3
Capper Rd *CBLY* GU15 .... 68 C1
Capricorn Cl *CRAWW* RH11 ... 176 B7
Capri Rd *CROY/NA* CR0 .... 45 P8
Capsey Rd *CRAWW* RH11 ... 176 B6
Capstans Whf
WOKN/KNAP GU21 .... 71 M7
Caradon Cl
WOKN/KNAP GU21 .... 71 P7
Caraway Cl *CRAWW* RH11 ... 176 E9
Caraway Pl *GUW* GU2 .... 91 N9
WLGTN SM6 * 62 D2
Carberry Rd *NRWD* SE19 ... 30 F9
Carbery La *ASC* SL5 .... 34 B4
Cardamom Cl *GUW* GU2 ... 111 N1
Cardiff Rd *HNWL* W7 .... 16 C1
Cardigan Cl
WOKN/KNAP GU21 .... 71 L7
Cardigan Rd *BARN* SW13 ... 18 E7
RCHPK/HAM TW10 .... 26 D2
WIM/MER SW19 .... 28 F9
Cardinal Av *KUTN/CMB* KT2 ... 26 D8
MRDN SM4 .... 43 J7
Cardinal Cl *MRDN* SM4 .... 43 J7
SAND/SEL CR2 .... 82 A2
WPK KT4 .... 60 E5
Cardinal Crs *NWMAL* KT3 ... 42 A3
Cardinal Dr *WOT/HER* KT12 ... 39 M9
Cardinal Rd *FELT* TW13 .... 24 C4
The Cardinals *BRAK* RG12 * ... 32 D5
RFNM GU10 .... 109 H7
Cardinal's Wk *HPTN* TW12 ... 40 C1
SUN TW16 .... 23 P9
Cardingham
WOKN/KNAP GU21 .... 71 N6
Cardington Sq *HSLWW* TW4 ... 15 M9
Cardross St *HMSMTH* W6 ... 18 F1
Cardwell Crs *ASC* SL5 .... 34 C6
Cardwells Keep *GUW* GU2 ... 111 N2
Carew Cl *COUL/CHIP* CR5 ... 81 K8
Carew Rd *ASHF* TW15 .... 23 M9
MTCM CR4 .... 44 C3
THHTH CR7 .... 45 K4
WLGTN SM6 .... 62 E5
Careys Copse *HORL* RH6 * ... 160 C1
Carey's Wd *HORL* RH6 .... 160 C1
Carfax *HORS* RH12 .... 192 B8
Carfax Av *ALDT* GU11 ... 108 H6
Carfax Rd *HYS/HAR* UB3 ... 15 J3
Cargate Av *ALDT* GU11 ... 108 B5
Cargate Gv *ALDT* GU11 ... 108 B5
Cargate Hl *ALDT* GU11 ... 108 B5
Cargate Ter *ALDT* GU11 ... 108 B5
Cargill Rd *WAND/EARL* SW18 ... 28 F4
Cargo Forecourt Rd
HORL RH6 .... 158 G5
Cargo Rd *HORL* RH6 .... 158 G4
Cargreen Rd *SNWD* SE25 ... 45 P5
Carholme Rd *FSTH* SE23 ... 31 N4
Carisbrook *FRIM* GU16 ... 90 A6
Carisbrooke Cl *HSLWW* TW4 ... 24 F4
Carisbrooke Rd *MTCM* CR4 ... 44 G5
Carleton Av *WLGTN* SM6 ... 62 F7
Carleton Cl *ESH/CLAY* KT10 ... 40 D9
Carlingford Rd *MRDN* SM4 ... 43 H7
Carlin Pl *CBLY* GU15 .... 68 E4
Carlinwark Dr *CBLY* GU15 ... 69 H1
Carlisle Cl *KUTN/CMB* KT2 ... 9 J2
Carlisle Rd *HPTN* TW12 ... 40 B1
RFNM GU10 .... 147 L5
SUT SM1 .... 61 K5

Carlisle Wy *TOOT* SW17 ... 29 K8
Carlos St *GODL* GU7 .... 131 L9
Carlton Av *EBED/NFELT* TW14 ... 24 D2
HYS/HAR UB3 .... 14 G2
SAND/SEL CR2 .... 63 M6
Carlton Cl *CBLY* GU15 .... 69 K5
CHSGTN KT9 .... 59 K5
WOKN/KNAP GU21 .... 72 D3
Carlton Ct *HORL* RH6 * ... 140 D8
FLEETS GU52 .... 87 H9
Carlton Crs *CHEAM* SM3 ... 61 J3
Carlton Dene *WEY* KT17 * ... 60 D4
Carlton Dr *PUT/ROE* SW15 ... 28 A1
Carlton Gn *REDH* RH1 * ... 119 N9
Carlton Pk *WEY* KT15 * 56 D5
Carlton Rd *BOR* GU35 .... 164 F2
GDST RH9 .... 142 C3
MORT/ESHN SW14 .... 42 A1
NWMAL KT3 .... 42 C3
REIG RH2 .... 119 P5
SAND/SEL CR2 .... 63 M6
SUN TW16 .... 39 H1
WALT KT12 .... 72 E3
WOT/HER KT12 .... 39 K8
Carlton Ter *SYD* SE26 .... 31 K6
Carlwell St *TOOT* SW17 ... 29 H8
Carlyle Cl *E/WMO/HCT* KT8 ... 40 B3
Carlyle Ct *WBPTN* SW10 * ... 19 N6
Carlyle Rd *CROY/NA* CR0 ... 64 A1
EA W5 .... 17 J2
STA TW18 .... 37 K1
Carlyon Cl *FARN* GU14 .... 88 E3
FRIM GU16 .... 89 H3
Carlys Cl *BECK* BR3 .... 46 D3
Carmalt Gdns *PUT/ROE* SW15 ... 18 G9
WOT/HER KT12 .... 39 L8
Carmarthen Cl *FARN* GU14 ... 68 B9
Carmel Cl
WOKS/MYFD GU22 ... 10 D6
Carmel Wy *RCH/KEW* TW9 ... 17 N7
Carmichael Cl *BTSEA* SW11 * ... 19 P8
Carmichael Rd *SNWD* SE25 ... 46 A6
Carminia Rd *TOOT* SW17 ... 29 L5
Carmino Ter *LIPH* GU30 * ... 182 E6
Carnac St *WNWD* SE27 .... 30 D6
Carnarvon Dr *HYS/HAR* UB3 ... 14 E1
Carnation Cl *EWKG* RG40 ... 49 M1
Carnegie Cl *SURB* KT6 .... 59 M1
Carnegie Pl *WIM/MER* SW19 ... 28 A4
Carnforth Cl *HOR/WEW* KT19 ... 59 P5
Carnforth Rd
STRHM/NOR SW16 .... 44 F1
Carnoustie *BRAK* RG12 .... 32 A8
Carnwath Rd *FUL/PGN* SW6 ... 19 L8
Carolina Pl *EWKG* RG40 ... 48 C2
Carolina Rd *THHTH* CR7 ... 45 K3
Caroline Cl *ISLW* TW7 .... 16 G6
STRHM/NOR SW16 .... 30 A6
Caroline Ct *ASHF* TW15 .... 23 L9
CRAWW RH11 .... 176 G6
Caroline Rd *WIM/MER* SW19 ... 43 K1
Caroline Wk *HMSMTH* W6 ... 19 J4
Caroline Wy *FNM* GU9 .... 69 H7
Carolyn Cl *WOKN/KNAP* GU21 ... 71 M8
The Carriageway
BH/WHM TN16 .... 105 P4
Carrick Cl *ISLW* TW7 .... 16 G8
Carrick Ga *ESH/CLAY* KT10 ... 58 C2
Carrick La *YTLY* GU46 .... 67 J3
Carrington Av *HSLW* TW3 ... 25 J1
Carrington Cl *CROY/NA* CR0 ... 46 D9
REDH RH1 .... 120 D4
Carrington La *ASHV* GU12 ... 89 H7
Carrington Pl
ESH/CLAY KT10 * 58 B3
Carrington Rd
RCHPK/HAM TW10 .... 17 N9
Carroll Av *GU* GU1 .... 112 F5
Carroll Crs *ASC* SL5 .... 33 P5
Carrow Rd *WOT/HER* KT12 ... 57 M2
Carshalton Gv *SUT* SM1 ... 61 P3
Carshalton Park Rd *CAR* SM5 ... 62 B5
Carshalton Rd *BNSTD* SM7 ... 80 B2
CBLY GU15 .... 51 J8
MTCM CR4 .... 44 C6
SUT SM1 .... 61 P3
Carslake Rd *PUT/ROE* SW15 ... 27 P7
Cartbridge Cl
RPLY/SEND GU23 .... 92 F5
Carter Cl *WLGTN* SM6 .... 62 F6
Carter Rd *CRAWE* RH10 ... 177 N8
WIM/MER SW19 .... 28 G8
Carters Cl *GU* GU1 .... 112 C1
WPK KT4 .... 61 H1
Carters La *WOKS/MYFD* GU22 ... 72 G9
Cartersiodge La
RHWH RH17 .... 193 P9
Cartersmead Cl *HORL* RH6 ... 140 D9
Carters Rd *EW* KT17 .... 78 D4
Carters Wk *FNM* GU9 .... 107 P6
Carters Yd
WAND/EARL SW18 * 28 G2
Carthew Rd *HMSMTH* W6 ... 18 F1
Carthew Vls *HMSMTH* W6 ... 18 F1
Carthona Dr *FLEETS* GU52 ... 86 F8
Carthouse La
WOKN/KNAP GU21 .... 71 J3
Cartmel Cl *REIG* RH2 .... 120 A4
Cartmel Gdns *MRDN* SM4 ... 43 N6
Cartwright Wy *BARN* SW13 ... 18 F5
Carver Rd *HNHL* SE24 .... 30 D2
Carville Crs *BTFD* TW8 .... 17 L3
Cascades *CROY/NA* CR0 ... 64 G8
Caselden Cl *ADL/WDHM* KT15 ... 55 N4
Casewick Rd *WNWD* SE27 ... 30 B8
Casher Rd *CRAWE* RH10 ... 177 N8
Casino Av *HNHL* SE24 .... 30 D1

Cassidy Rd *FUL/PGN* SW6 ... 19 L5
Cassilis Rd *TWK* TW1 .... 26 A2
Cassino Cl *ALDT* GU11 ... 108 D2
Cassiobury Av
EBED/NFELT TW14 .... 24 A3
Cassland Rd *THHTH* CR7 ... 45 M5
Casslee Rd *CAT* SE6 .... 31 N5
Castello Av *PUT/ROE* SW15 ... 27 P1
Castelnau *BARN* SW13 .... 18 F5
Castlands Rd *CAT* SE6 .... 31 M6
Castle Av *EW* KT17 .... 60 E7
Castle Cl *CBLY* GU15 .... 68 G3
HAYES BR2 .... 47 L4
REDH RH1 .... 121 L4
WIM/MER SW19 .... 28 A6
Castlecombe Dr
WIM/MER SW19 .... 28 A3
Castle Ct *SYD* SE26 .... 31 M7
Castlecraig Ct *SHST* GU47 * ... 67 P1
Castle Dr *HORL* RH6 .... 159 M5
REIG RH2 .... 119 L9
Castle Fld *FNM* GU9 .... 4 F7
Castlefield Rd *REIG* RH2 ... 119 L4
Castle Gdns *DORK* RH4 ... 117 M5
Castlegate *RCH/KEW* TW9 ... 17 M8
Castle Gn *WEY* KT13 .... 56 G2
Castle Grove Rd
CHOB/PIR GU24 .... 71 L1
Castle Hl *FNM* GU9 .... 4 F7
Castle Hill Av *CROY/NA* CR0 ... 65 H7
Castle Hill Rd *EGH* TW20 ... 20 C7
Castlemaine Av *EW* KT17 ... 60 F7
SAND/SEL CR2 .... 63 P4
Castle Ms *TOOT* SW17 .... 29 H7
Castle Rd *ALDT* GU11 .... 108 C2
CBLY GU15 .... 68 G4
COUL/CHIP CR5 .... 80 A9
EPSOM KT18 .... 77 P4
HORS RH12 .... 191 C1
ISLW TW7 .... 16 F7
NWDGN UB2 * 15 P1
WOKN/KNAP GU21 .... 72 C2
Castle Rw *CHSWK* W4 * ... 18 B3
Castle Sq *REDH* RH1 .... 121 L4
Castle St *FLEETS* GU52 .... 86 F8
FNM GU9 .... 5 F2
GU GU1 .... 6 E6
HOR/WEW KT19 .... 78 A2
KUT/HW KT1 .... 8 D4
REDH RH1 .... 121 K4
The Castle *HORS* RH12 ... 192 D5
Castleton Cl *BNSTD* SM7 ... 79 L4
CROY/NA CR0 .... 46 E7
Castleton Dr *BNSTD* SM7 ... 79 L4
Castleton Rd *MTCM* CR4 ... 44 F5
Castletown Rd *WKENS* W14 ... 19 J3
Castleview Rd
DTCH/LGLY SL3 .... 12 A3
Castle View Rd *WEY* KT13 ... 56 D3
Castle Wk *SUN* TW16 .... 39 L4
Castle Wy *EW* KT17 .... 60 E8
FELT TW13 .... 24 E7
WIM/MER SW19 .... 28 A6
Castle Yd *RCH/KEW* TW9 ... 17 L9
Castor Ct *FLEETS* GU52 ... 107 H1
YTLY GU46 .... 66 F7
Caswall Ride *YTLY* GU46 ... 67 J3
Caswell Cl *FARN* GU14 .... 88 B1
Catalina Rd *HTHAIR* TW6 ... 14 D8
Catalpa Cl *GU* GU1 .... 112 A3
Catena Rt *LTWR* GU18 .... 52 A8
Caterfield La *LING* RH7 ... 143 M3
Cater Gdns *GUW* GU3 ... 111 L3
Caterham By-Pass
CTHM CR3 .... 102 B2
Caterham Dr *COUL/CHIP* CR5 ... 81 L8
Caterways *HORS* RH12 ... 191 P7
Catesby Gdns *YTLY* GU46 ... 66 E1
Catford Rd *CAT* SE6 .... 31 N4
Cathcart Rd *WBPTN* SW10 * ... 19 M4
Cathedral Cl *GUW* GU2 .... 6 A4
Cathedral Hill *GUW* GU2 ... 111 N4
Cathedral Vw *GUW* GU2 ... 111 M5
Catherine Cl *BF/WBF* KT14 ... 74 A5
Catherine Dr *RCH/KEW* TW9 ... 17 L9
SUN TW16 .... 39 H1
Catherine Howard Ct
WEY KT13 * 56 D2
Catherine Rd *SURB* KT6 ... 41 K6
Catherine Wheel Rd
BTFD TW8 .... 17 K5
Cathill La *RDKG* RH5 .... 155 J9
Cathles Rd *BAL* SW12 .... 29 L2
Catlin Crs *SHPTN* TW17 ... 38 F6
Catlin Gdns *GDST* RH9 ... 122 B1
Catling Cl *FSTH* SE23 .... 31 K6
Cator Cl *CROY/NA* CR0 .... 65 L9
Cator Crs *CROY/NA* CR0 ... 65 L9
Cator La *BECK* BR3 .... 46 F3
Cator Rd *CAR* SM5 .... 62 B4
SYD SE26 .... 31 L9
Catteshall Hatch *GODL* GU7 ... 131 N7
Catteshall La *GODL* GU7 ... 131 N8
Catteshall Rd *GODL* GU7 ... 131 N7
Cauldwell Ter
WAND/EARL SW18 * 28 G2
Causeway *EBED/NFELT* TW14 ... 15 N9
The Causeway *BELMT* SM2 ... 61 N7
CAR SM5 .... 62 C2
CHSGTN KT9 .... 59 L3
ESH/CLAY KT10 .... 58 F6
HORS RH12 .... 192 B9
STA TW18 .... 21 P7
TEDD TW11 .... 25 N9
WAND/EARL SW18 .... 19 M9

WIM/MER SW19 .... 27 P8
Cautley Av *CLAP* SW4 .... 29 M1
Cavalier Wy *EGRIN* RH19 ... 180 E4
Cavalry Cl *ALDT* GU11 ... 108 A4
Cavalry Crs *HSLWW* TW4 ... 15 M9
Cavalry Gdns *PUT/ROE* SW15 ... 28 B1
Cavan's Rd *ALDT* GU11 .... 88 E9
Cavaye Pl *WBPTN* SW10 ... 19 N3
Cavell Wy *CRAWE* RH10 ... 177 M6
HOR/WEW KT19 .... 78 A2
Cavendish Av *NWMAL* KT3 ... 43 H6
HOR/WEW KT19 .... 21 J7
Cavendish Cl *HORS* RH12 ... 192 C3
SUN TW16 .... 24 A9
Cavendish Ct *ESH/CLAY* KT10 ... 58 E4
Cavendish Gdns *CLAP* SW4 * ... 29 M2
FLEETS GU52 .... 106 E1
REDH RH1 .... 120 C4
Cavendish Meads *ASC* SL5 ... 34 D7
Cavendish Pde *HSLWW* TW4 * . 15 N7
Cavendish Rd *ALDT* GU11 ... 108 C5
BELMT SM2 .... 61 J5
CHSWK W4 .... 18 A6
CLAP SW4 .... 29 L2
CROY/NA CR0 .... 45 H9
FLEETS GU52 .... 106 F2
NWMAL KT3 .... 42 D6
REDH RH1 .... 120 C5
WEY KT13 .... 56 D7
WIM/MER SW19 .... 44 A1
WOKS/MYFD GU22 .... 10 A7
Cavendish Ter *FELT* TW13 * ... 24 B5
Cavendish Wk
HOR/WEW KT19 .... 59 P9
Caverleigh Wy *WPK* KT4 ... 42 E9
Cave Rd *RCHPK/HAM* TW10 ... 26 B7
Caversham Av *CHEAM* SM3 ... 61 J1
Caversham Rd *KUT/HW* KT1 ... 9 F4
Caves Farm Cl *SHST* GU47 ... 49 L9
Cawdor Crs *HNWL* W7 .... 16 G2
Cawnpore St *NRWD* SE19 ... 30 F8
Cawsey Wy
WOKN/KNAP GU21 .... 10 D4
Caxton Cl *CRAWE* RH10 ... 176 D8
Caxton Gdns *GUW* GU3 ... 111 P4
Caxton La *OXTED* RH8 .... 124 C2
Caxton Ms *BTFD* TW8 * 17 K5
Caxton Ri *REDH* RH1 .... 120 C4
Caxton Rd *NWDGN* UB2 ... 15 M1
WIM/MER SW19 .... 28 F8
Caygill Cl *HAYES* BR2 .... 47 M5
Cayley Rd *NWDGN* UB2 ... 16 B1
Cearn Wy *COUL/CHIP* CR5 ... 81 M5
Cecil Cl *ASHF* TW15 .... 23 M9
CHSGTN KT9 .... 59 K3
Cecil Pl *MTCM* CR4 .... 44 B6
Cecil Rd *ASHF* TW15 .... 38 E1
CROY/NA CR0 .... 45 H7
HSLW TW3 .... 25 L4
SUT SM1 .... 61 K5
WIM/MER SW19 .... 43 M1
Cecil Wy *HAYES* BR2 .... 47 N9
Cedar Av *BLKW* GU17 .... 67 P3
COB KT11 .... 75 K3
WHTN TW2 .... 25 J2
Cedar Cl *ASHV* GU12 .... 108 G6
BAGS GU19 .... 51 N6
CAR SM5 .... 62 B5
CRAWW RH11 .... 176 D2
DORK RH4 .... 117 H7
DUL SE21 .... 30 D4
ESH/CLAY KT10 .... 57 P6
EW KT17 .... 78 E1
HORS RH12 .... 192 B3
KUTN/CMB KT2 .... 27 J7
REIG RH2 .... 119 N7
STA TW18 .... 37 N3
WARL CR6 .... 82 E7
Cedar Ct *EGH* TW20 .... 21 P8
MRDN SM4 .... 43 N7
Cedar Dr *ASC* SL5 .... 34 G8
BNFD RG42 .... 32 E1
EDEN TN8 .... 144 F3
FLEETN GU51 .... 87 J6
LHD/OX KT22 .... 96 E3
WOKN/KNAP GU21 .... 71 P7
Cedar Gv *CHOB/PIR* GU24 ... 70 G4
EA W5 .... 17 K1
WEY KT13 .... 56 C2
Cedar Hts *RCHPK/HAM* TW10 ... 26 D5
Cedar Hl *EPSOM* KT18 .... 78 A4
Cedarhurst *BMLY* BR1 * 47 L1
Cedarne Rd *FUL/PGN* SW6 ... 19 L5
Cedar Pk *CTHM* CR3 .... 101 N1
Cedar Rd *BELMT* SM2 .... 61 M6
COB KT11 .... 75 K3

CROY/NA CR0 .... 62 G2
KUT/HW KT1 .... 41 J2
MRDN SM4 .... 43 L5
The Cedars *BF/WBF* KT14 ... 74 B1
FLEETN GU51 .... 87 P8
GU GU1 .... 112 E2
LHD/OX KT22 .... 97 K1
MFD/CHID GU8 .... 149 M4
REIG RH2 .... 119 P5
TEDD TW11 .... 25 M8
Cedar Ter *RCH/KEW* TW9 ... 17 L9
Cedar Tree Gv *WNWD* SE27 ... 30 B8
Cedar Vw *FLEETS* GU52 ... 87 H9
Cedarville Gdns
STRHM/NOR SW16 .... 30 A3
Cedar Wk *ESH/CLAY* KT10 ... 58 F5
KWD/TDW/WH KT20 .... 99 K1
PUR/KEN CR8 .... 81 L5
Cedar Wy *DTCH/LGLY* SL3 ... 12 A2
GU GU1 .... 112 A2
SUN TW16 .... 38 G1
Cedarways *FNM* GU9 .... 127 N6
Celandine Cl *CRAWW* RH11 * ... 176 D9
CWTH RG45 .... 49 N3
Celandine Rd *WOT/HER* KT12 ... 57 N3
Celia Crs *ASHF* TW15 .... 22 G9
Cell Farm Av *WDSR* SL4 ... 20 C1
Celtic Av *HAYES* BR2 .... 47 L4
Celtic Rd *BF/WBF* KT14 .... 74 A3
Cemetery La *SHPTN* TW17 ... 38 D7
Cemetery Pales
CHOB/PIR GU24 .... 71 L3
Cemetery Rd *FLEETN* GU51 ... 86 E8
Centaur Ct *BTFD* TW8 * 17 L3
Centennial Ct *BRAK* RG12 * ... 32 C3
Central Ar *ASHF* TW15 * 23 J7
Central Av *E/WMO/HCT* KT8 ... 39 P6
HSLW TW3 .... 16 C9
WLGTN SM6 .... 62 G3
Central Hl *NRWD* SE19 .... 30 D8
Central Pde *CROY/NA* CR0 ... 65 J8
E/WMO/HCT KT8 * 39 P5
HORL RH6 * 159 K2
PGE/AN SE20 * 46 D1
STRHM/NOR SW16 .... 29 P7
SURB KT6 * 41 L7
Central Pl *SNWD* SE25 * 46 A5
Central Rd *MRDN* SM4 .... 43 M6
WPK KT4 .... 60 E1
Central Sq *E/WMO/HCT* KT8 ... 39 N5
Central Ter *BECK* BR3 * 46 D4
Central Wy *CAR* SM5 .... 62 A6
EBED/NFELT TW14 .... 24 C1
OXTED RH8 .... 103 K7
Centre Terrace Rd
FARN GU14 .... 88 C2
The Centre *FELT* TW13 .... 24 B5
Centurion Cl *SHST* GU47 ... 49 P9
Centurion Ct *WLGTN* SM6 * ... 62 C1
Century Ct
WOKN/KNAP GU21 .... 10 E2
Century Rd *EGH* TW20 .... 21 P8
Cerne Rd *MRDN* SM4 .... 43 N7
Cerotus Pl *CHERT* KT16 ... 37 K8
Ceylon Rd *WKENS* W14 .... 19 H1
Chadacre Rd *EW* KT17 .... 60 F4
Chadhurst Cl *RDKG* RH5 ... 137 K1
Chadwick Av
WIM/MER SW19 .... 28 D9
Chadwick Cl *CRAWW* RH11 ... 194 E1
PUT/ROE SW15 .... 27 L2
TEDD TW11 .... 25 N9
Chadwick Rd *SURB* KT6 .... 41 J7
Chadworth Wy
ESH/CLAY KT10 .... 58 C4
Chaffers Rd *ALDT* GU11 ... 77 M5
Chaffinch Av *CROY/NA* CR0 ... 46 D7
Chaffinch Cl *CRAWW* RH11 ... 176 G3
CROY/NA CR0 .... 46 D6
HORS RH12 .... 192 C3
SHST GU47 .... 50 A9
Chaffinch Rd *BECK* BR3 .... 46 E2
Chaffinch Wy *HORL* RH6 ... 140 A9
Chailey Cl *CRAWW* RH11 ... 176 D8
HEST TW5 .... 15 M6
Chailey Pl *WOT/HER* KT12 ... 57 N3
Chalcot Cl *BELMT* SM2 .... 61 L6
Chalcot Ms
STRHM/NOR SW16 .... 29 P6
Chalcott Gdns *SURB* KT6 * ... 41 J9
Chalcraft Cl *LIPH* GU30 ... 182 D6
Chaldon Cl *REDH* RH1 ... 120 A7
Chaldon Common Rd
CTHM CR3 .... 101 L4
Chaldon Rd *CRAWW* RH11 ... 194 F1
CTHM CR3 .... 101 M3
FUL/PGN SW6 .... 19 J5
Chaldon Wy *COUL/CHIP* CR5 ... 80 G6
Chale Rd *BRXS/STRHM* SW2 ... 29 P1
Chalfont Dr *FARN* GU14 .... 88 E5
Chalfont Ms
WAND/EARL SW18 .... 28 C4
Chalfont Wy *WEA* W13 .... 17 J1
Chalford Cl *E/WMO/HCT* KT8 ... 40 A5
Chalford Rd *DUL* SE21 .... 30 E7
Chalgrove Av *MRDN* SM4 ... 43 L6
Chalgrove Rd *BELMT* SM2 ... 61 P6
Chalice Cl *WLGTN* SM6 .... 62 F5
Chalk Hill Rd *HMSMTH* W6 ... 19 J2
Chalk La *ASHTD* KT21 .... 77 N8
EHSLY KT24 .... 115 H2
EPSOM KT18 .... 78 C5
MFD/CHID GU8 .... 130 D5
Chalkley Cl *MTCM* CR4 .... 44 B3
Chalk Paddock *EPSOM* KT18 ... 78 B4
Chalkpit La
BRKHM/BTCW RH3 .... 117 P4
DORK RH4 .... 116 G5

Chalk Pit La GT/LBKH KT23 95 P7
Chalkpit La OXTED RH8 103 J7
Chalk Pit Rd BNSTD SM7 79 L6
EPSOM KT18 78 A8
SUT SM1 61 N4
Chalkpit Ter DORK RH4 116 G5
Chalkpit Wd OXTED RH8 103 K7
Chalk Rd BIL RH14 187 P7
GODL GU7 131 L8
Chalky La CHSGTN KT9 59 K7
Challenge Ct LHD/OX KT22 77 H8
Challenge Rd ASHF TW15 23 M6
Challenor Cl EWKG RG40 48 D2
Challice Wy
BRXS/STRHM SW2 30 A4
Challin St PGE/AN SE20 46 C2
Challis Pl BNFD RG42 32 A2
Challis Rd BTFD TW8 17 K3
Challock Cl BH/WHM TN16 84 A5
Challoner Crs WKENS W14 19 K3
Challoners Cl
E/WMO/HCT KT8 40 D5
Challoner St WKENS W14 19 K3
Chalmers Cl HORL RH6 158 B6
Chalmers Rd ASHF TW15 23 L7
BNSTD SM7 79 N4
Chalmers Rd East ASHF TW15 23 L7
Chalmers Wy
EBED/NFELT TW14 24 C1
TWK TW1 17 H9
Chamberlain Crs WWKM BR4 47 H9
Chamberlain Gdns
HSLW TW3 16 C6
Chamberlain Wy SURB KT6 41 L8
Chamber La RFNM GU10 126 G5
Chambers Rd ASHV GU12 89 K9
Chambon Pl HMSMTH W6 18 E2
Chamomile Gdns FARN GU14 87 N2
Champion Crs SYD SE26 31 M7
Champion Down EHSLY KT24 95 N8
Champion Rd SYD SE26 31 M7
Champion Wy FLEETS GU52 106 G1
Champness Cl WNWD SE27 30 E7
Champney Cl DTCH/LGLY SL3 12 E8
Champneys Cl BELMT SM2 61 K6
Chancellor Gdns
SAND/SEL CR2 63 K7
Chancellor Gv DUL SE21 30 D5
Chancellor's Rd HMSMTH W6 18 G3
Chancellors St HMSMTH W6 18 G3
Chancellors Whf
HMSMTH W6 18 G4
Chancery La BECK BR3 47 H3
Chancery Ms TOOT SW17 29 H5
Chanctonbury Cha
REDH RH1 120 D6
Chanctonbury Dr ASC SL5 34 E8
Chanctonbury Gdns
BELMT SM2 61 M6
Chanctonbury Wy
CRAWW RH11 176 F7
Chandler Cl CRAWE RH10 176 G7
HPTN TW12 39 P2
Chandlers Cl
EBED/NFELT TW14 24 A3
Chandlers La YTLY GU46 66 G1
Chandlers Rd ASHV GU12 109 K2
Chandos Av EA W5 17 J2
Chandos Rd STA TW18 22 A8
Channel Cl HEST TW5 16 A6
Channings WOKN/KNAP GU21 72 C4
Chantilly Wk HOR/WEW KT19 60 A8
Chantlers Cl EGRIN RH19 180 B1
Chanton Dr BELMT SM2 60 G8
Chantrey Cl ASHTD KT21 77 J8
Chantrey Rd CRAWE RH10 177 H8
Chantreys FLEETN GU51 86 D7
Chantry Cl FNM GU9 4 B4
HORL RH6 140 B9
SUN TW16 39 J1
Chantry Hurst EPSOM KT18 78 B4
Chantry La SHGR GU5 134 B1
Chantry Rd BAGS GU19 51 M7
CHERT KT16 37 M9
CHSGTN KT9 59 M4
RGUE GU4 132 F2
Chantry Sq KENS W8 * 19 M1
The Chantrys FNM GU9 4 B5
Chantry View Rd GU GU1 112 C8
Chantry Wy MTCM CR4 43 P4
Chapel Av ADL/WDHM KT15 55 M3
CHOB/PIR GU24 91 H1
Chapel Cl MFD/CHID GU8 149 N2
Chapel Ct DORK RH4 * 116 G7
Chapel Gn PUR/KEN CR8 81 J2
Chapel Gv ADL/WDHM KT15 55 M3
EPSOM KT18 78 G8
Chapel Hl EHSLY KT24 95 M7
MFD/CHID GU8 169 L8
Chapelhouse Cl GUW GU2 111 L5
Chapel La BAGS GU19 51 M7
CHOB/PIR GU24 90 G3
CRAWE RH10 160 G8
DORK RH4 116 C8
EGRIN RH19 181 J5
FARN GU14 68 B8
GT/LBKH KT23 96 C8
MFD/CHID GU8 149 N2
Chapel Md HTWY RG27 48 C9
Chapel Mill Rd KUT/HW KT1 9 G7
Chapel Park Rd
ADL/WDHM KT15 55 M3
Chapel Rd CBLY GU15 68 D3
HORL RH6 158 B5
HORL RH6 160 C1
HSLW TW3 16 B8
KWD/TDW/WH KT20 98 G3
OXTED RH8 124 A1
REDH RH1 120 B5
RFNM GU10 146 B1
TWK TW1 26 A3
WARL CR6 82 D7
WNWD SE27 30 C7
Chapel Sq CBLY GU15 68 B2
VW GU25 36 C4
Chapel St FARN GU14 88 F1
GU GU1 6 E6
WOKN/KNAP GU21 10 E4
Chapel Vw SAND/SEL CR2 64 C6
Chapel Wk COUL/CHIP CR5 100 F2
Chapel Wy EPSOM KT18 78 G8
Chaplain's Hl CWTH RG45 49 P5
Chaplin Crs SUN TW16 23 P9
Chaplin Ms DTCH/LGLY SL3 12 D3
Chapman Cl WDR/YW UB7 14 B1
Chapman Rd CRAWE RH10 177 L9
CROY/NA CR0 45 J9
Chapman's La EGRIN RH19 180 A2
Chapman Sq WIM/MER SW19 28 A5
Chappell Cl LIPH GU30 182 F6
Chapter Wy HPTN TW12 25 H7
Chara Pl CHSWK W4 18 B4
Chardin Rd CHSWK W4 * 18 C2
Chargate Cl WOT/HER KT12 57 J5
Charlbury Cl BRAK RG12 33 H5
Charlecote Cl FARN GU14 88 F4
Charlecote Gv SYD SE26 31 J6
Charles Babbage Cl
CHSGTN KT9 59 J6
Charles Cobb Gdns
CROY/NA CR0 63 J4
Charles Dickens Ter
PGE/AN SE20 * 46 C1
Charlesfield Rd HORL RH6 140 B9
Charles Haller St
BRXS/STRHM SW2 30 B3
Charles Hl RFNM GU10 128 G7
Charles Rd STA TW18 22 G9
WIM/MER SW19 43 L2
Charles Sq BRAK RG12 32 E3
Charles St BARN SW13 18 C8
CBLY GU15 68 E3
CHERT KT16 37 K9
CROY/NA CR0 2 C5
HSLW TW3 15 P7
Charleston Cl FELT TW13 24 B6
Charleston Ct CRAWE RH10 177 L8
Charleville Circ SYD SE26 31 H8
Charleville Rd WKENS W14 19 J3
Charlmont Rd TOOT SW17 29 H9
Charlock Cl CRAWW RH11 176 D9
Charlock Wy GU GU1 112 F3
Charlotte Cl FNM GU9 107 P6
Charlotte Ct ESH/CLAY KT10 58 C4
Charlotte Gv HORL RH6 141 J9
Charlotte Ms
ESH/CLAY KT10 * 58 B3
Charlotte Pde FSTH SE23 * 31 M5
Charlotte Rd BARN SW13 18 D6
WLGTN SM6 62 E5
Charlow Cl FUL/PGN SW6 19 N7
Charlton Av WOT/HER KT12 57 K3
Charlton Cl EWKG RG40 48 D1
Charlton Ct SHST GU47 49 P8
Charlton Dr BH/WHM TN16 84 B6
Charlton Gdns
COUL/CHIP CR5 80 E7
Charlton Kings WEY KT13 56 G3
Charlton La SHPTN TW17 38 E4
Charlton Rd SHPTN TW17 38 E3
Charlwood CROY/NA CR0 64 F7
Charlwood Cl GT/LBKH KT23 96 B4
Charlwood Dr LHD/OX KT22 76 D4
Charlwood La RDKG RH5 157 M7
Charlwood Pl REIG RH2 119 K5
Charlwood Rd
CRAWW RH11 176 C1
HORL RH6 158 F4
PUT/ROE SW15 19 H9
Charlwoods Pl EGRIN RH19 162 D9
Charlwoods Rd EGRIN RH19 180 C1
Charlwood Ter
PUT/ROE SW15 19 H9
Charlwood Wk
CRAWW RH11 176 E2
Charman Rd REDH RH1 120 A5
Charmans Cl HORS RH12 * 192 G5
Charm Cl HORL RH6 140 A9
Charminster Av
WIM/MER SW19 43 L3
Charminster Rd WPK KT4 43 H9
Charnwood ASC SL5 34 F7
Charnwood Av
WIM/MER SW19 43 L3
Charnwood Cl NWMAL KT3 42 C5
Charnwood Rd SNWD SE25 45 M6
Charrington Rd CROY/NA CR0 2 B4
Charrington Wy HORS RH12 191 K7
Charta Rd EGH TW20 21 P8
Chart Cl CROY/NA CR0 45 H7
HAYES BR2 47 L2
MTCM CR4 44 B5
RDKG RH5 117 J9
Chart Downs RDKG RH5 117 J9
Charter Crs HSLWW TW4 15 N9
Charterhouse Cl BRAK RG12 32 G6
Charterhouse Rd GODL GU7 131 K7
Charter Pl STA TW18 22 D9
Charter Rd KUT/HW KT1 9 K6
Charters Cl NRWD SE19 30 F8
Charters La ASC SL5 34 D6
Charters Rd ASC SL5 34 F8
Charters Wy ASC SL5 34 F8
Charter Wk HASM GU27 * 184 D4
Chartfield Av PUT/ROE SW15 27 N1
Chartfield Rd REIG RH2 119 N6
Chartfield Sq
PUT/ROE SW15 * 28 A1
Chart Gdns RDKG RH5 137 J1
Chartham Gv WNWD SE27 30 B6
Chartham Rd SNWD SE25 46 B4
Chart House Rd ASHV GU12 89 J8
Chart La BH/WHM TN16 105 N5
DORK RH4 117 H7
REIG RH2 119 M5
Chart La South RDKG RH5 117 K9
Charts Cl CRAN GU6 171 H1
Chart Wy HORS RH12 192 B8
Chartway REIG RH2 119 M5
Chartwell FNM GU9 127 K7
FRIM GU16 88 G2
Chartwell Cl CROY/NA CR0 2 E1
Chartwell Gdns ALDT GU11 88 E8
Chartwell Pl CHEAM SM3 61 J3
EPSOM KT18 78 C3
Chartwell Wy PGE/AN SE20 46 B2
Charwood
STRHM/NOR SW16 * 30 B7
Chase Ct RYNPK SW20 43 J3
Chase End HOR/WEW KT19 78 B1
Chasefield Cl RGUE GU4 112 E2
Chasefield Rd TOOT SW17 29 J7
Chase Gdns WHTN TW2 25 L2
Chase La HASM GU27 184 F6
Chaseley Ct CHSWK W4 17 P3
Chaseley Dr SAND/SEL CR2 63 M8
Chasemore Cl MTCM CR4 44 B8
Chasemore Gdns
CROY/NA CR0 63 J4
Chase Pln GSHT GU26 * 183 M1
Chase Rd HOR/WEW KT19 78 B1
Chaseside Av RYNPK SW20 43 J2
Chaseside Gdns CHERT KT16 37 M8
The Chase ASC SL5 34 A1
ASHTD KT21 77 J7
BMLY BR1 47 P4
COUL/CHIP CR5 81 E3
CRAWE RH10 177 K6
CWTH RG45 49 L3
EHSLY KT24 95 H6
FARN GU14 88 F1
GUW GU2 111 N6
KWD/TDW/WH KT20 99 N1
LHD/OX KT22 76 C4
STRHM/NOR SW16 45 H1
SUN TW16 39 K2
WLGTN SM6 62 G4
Chatelet Cl HORL RH6 140 D9
Chatfield Cl FARN GU14 88 E5
Chatfield Ct CTHM CR3 101 M2
Chatfield Dr RGUE GU4 112 G3
Chatfield Rd BTSEA SW11 19 N8
CROY/NA CR0 2 B1
Chatfields CRAWW RH11 176 D7
Chatham Av HAYES BR2 47 N8
Chatham Cl CHEAM SM3 43 K8
Chatham Rd BTSEA SW11 29 J2
KUT/HW KT1 9 H4
Chatsfield EW KT17 60 E8
Chatsworth Av HASM GU27 184 D2
RYNPK SW20 43 J2
Chatsworth Cl CHSWK W4 * 18 A4
WWKM BR4 65 M1
Chatsworth Crs HSLW TW3 16 D9
Chatsworth Gdns
NWMAL KT3 * 42 D6
Chatsworth Gv FNM GU9 107 M8
Chatsworth Hts CBLY GU15 69 J1
Chatsworth Pl LHD/OX KT22 76 D1
MTCM CR4 44 B4
TEDD TW11 25 P7
Chatsworth Rd CHEAM SM3 61 H3
CHSWK W4 18 A4
CROY/NA CR0 3 F7
FARN GU14 88 G4
Chatsworth Wy WNWD SE27 30 D5
Chattern Hl ASHF TW15 23 L7
Chattern Rd ASHF TW15 23 M7
Chatton Rw CHOB/PIR GU24 70 G6
Chatto Rd BTSEA SW11 29 J1
Chaucer Av EGRIN RH19 180 B3
HSLWW TW4 15 K7
RCH/KEW TW9 17 N7
WEY KT13 56 C6
Chaucer Cl BNSTD SM7 79 J3
Chaucer Ct GUW GU2 6 D7
Chaucer Gdns SUT SM1 61 L3
Chaucer Gn CROY/NA CR0 46 B8
Chaucer Gv CBLY GU15 68 F3
Chaucer Rd ASHF TW15 23 H7
CRAWE RH10 177 L3
CWTH RG45 49 M5
FARN GU14 88 B1
HNHL SE24 30 C1
SUT SM1 61 L3
Chaucer Wy
ADL/WDHM KT15 55 L5
Chaundlers Cft RFNM GU10 106 D9
Chavasse Wy FARN GU14 87 P2
Chave Cft EPSOM KT18 * 78 G8
Chavecroft Ter
EPSOM KT18 * 78 G8
Chaworth Cl CHERT KT16 54 G5
Chaworth Rd CHERT KT16 54 G5
Chawton Cl FLEETN GU51 86 C4
Cheam Cl BRAK RG12 32 F6
KWD/TDW/WH KT20 98 F1
Cheam Common Rd
WPK KT4 60 F1
Cheam Park Wy CHEAM SM3 61 H5
Cheam Rd BELMT SM2 61 H7
EW KT17 60 F8
Cheapside Rd ASC SL5 34 C4
Cheeseman Cl HPTN TW12 24 F9
Cheesemans Ter
WKENS W14 * 19 K3
Cheetah Rd FARN GU14 88 D5
Chellows La LING RH7 143 M3
Chelmsford Cl BELMT SM2 61 L7
HMSMTH W6 19 H4
Chelsea Cl HPTN TW12 25 K9
WPK KT4 42 E8
Chelsea Crs WBPTN SW10 * 19 N6
Chelsea Gdns CHEAM SM3 61 J3
Chelsea Harbour Dr
WBPTN SW10 19 N6
Chelsea Park Gdns CHEL SW3 19 P4
Chelsea Sq CAR SM5 62 B7
CHEL SW3 19 P3
Chelsea Village
FUL/PGN SW6 * 19 M5
Chelsfield Gdns SYD SE26 31 K6
Chelsham Court Rd
WARL CR6 83 K7
Chelsham Rd SAND/SEL CR2 63 M6
Cheltenham Av TWK TW1 25 P3
Cheltenham Cl NWMAL KT3 42 A4
Chelverton Rd
PUT/ROE SW15 19 H9
Chelwood Cl COUL/CHIP CR5 80 E8
CRAWE RH10 177 J7
EW KT17 78 D1
Chelwood Dr SHST GU47 49 K8
Chelwood Gdns
RCH/KEW TW9 17 N7
Cheniston Cl BF/WBF KT14 73 L2
Cheniston Gdns KENS W8 * 19 M1
Chennells Wy HORS RH12 192 C5
Chepstow Cl CRAWE RH10 177 P5
PUT/ROE SW15 28 B1
Chepstow Ri CROY/NA CR0 3 H5
Chepstow Rd CROY/NA CR0 3 H5
HNWL W7 16 G1
Chequer Rd EGRIN RH19 * 180 E2
Chequers Cl HORL RH6 140 C9
KWD/TDW/WH KT20 98 E5
Chequers Ct SWTR RH13 192 D7
Chequers Dr HORL RH6 140 C9
Chequers La HTWY RG27 66 C1
KWD/TDW/WH KT20 98 E5
Chequers Pl DORK RH4 117 H7
Chequer Tree Cl
WOKN/KNAP GU21 71 L5
Cherberry Cl FLEETN GU51 87 H3
Cherbury Cl BRAK RG12 32 G4
Cherimoya Gdns
E/WMO/HCT KT8 40 B4
Cherington Wy ASC SL5 * 33 N3
Cheriton Av HAYES BR2 47 M6
Cheriton Ct WOT/HER KT12 39 L9
Cheriton Sq TOOT SW17 29 K5
Cheriton Wy BLKW GU17 67 P3
Cherkley LHD/OX KT22 * 97 K6
Cherkley Hl LHD/OX KT22 97 J6
Cherrimans Orch
HASM GU27 184 A4
Cherry Cl BNSTD SM7 79 H3
BRXS/STRHM SW2 * 30 B3
CAR SM5 62 B1
EA W5 17 K1
MRDN SM4 43 J5
Cherry Ct SWTR RH13 192 C9
Cherry Crs BTFD TW8 17 H5
Cherrydale Rd CBLY GU15 69 M3
Cherry Garth BTFD TW8 17 K2
Cherry Green Cl REDH RH1 120 D7
Cherry Hill Gdns
CROY/NA CR0 63 H3
Cherryhurst
MFD/CHID GU8 * 168 A2
Cherry La CRAWW RH11 176 F2
WDR/YW UB7 14 B2
Cherry Orch ASHTD KT21 77 P7
STA TW18 22 D8
Cherry Orchard Gdns
CROY/NA CR0 3 F2
E/WMO/HCT KT8 39 P4
Cherry Orchard Rd
CROY/NA CR0 3 F2
E/WMO/HCT KT8 40 A4
Cherry St WOKN/KNAP GU21 10 C5
Cherry Tree Av GUW GU2 111 M5
HASM GU27 184 A3
STA TW18 22 E9
Cherry Tree Cl CRAWE RH10 177 N3
FARN GU14 * 87 N2
SHST GU47 49 P8
Cherry Tree Ct
COUL/CHIP CR5 81 H7
Cherry Tree Dr BRAK RG12 32 F4
STRHM/NOR SW16 * 29 P6
Cherry Tree Gn
SAND/SEL CR2 82 B3
Cherry Tree La GODL GU7 131 K5
Cherry Tree Rd
MFD/CHID GU8 149 M3
RFNM GU10 146 B1
Cherrytrees COUL/CHIP CR5 100 F1
Cherry Tree Wk BECK BR3 46 F5
WWKM BR4 65 M3
Cherry Wk HAYES BR2 47 N9
Cherry Wy DTCH/LGLY SL3 12 G8
HOR/WEW KT19 60 B5
SHPTN TW17 38 F5
Cherrywood Av EGH TW20 20 G9
Cherrywood Cl
KUTN/CMB KT2 9 H1
Cherrywood Dr
PUT/ROE SW15 28 A1
Cherrywood La RYNPK SW20 43 J5
Cherrywood Rd FARN GU14 68 C9
Chertsey Bridge Rd
CHERT KT16 37 P8
Chertsey Cl PUR/KEN CR8 81 K4
Chertsey Crs CROY/NA CR0 65 J8
Chertsey Dr CHEAM SM3 61 J1
Chertsey La HOR/WEW KT19 77 N1
STA TW18 37 J2
Chertsey Rd
ADL/WDHM KT15 55 N2
ASHF TW15 38 F1
BF/WBF KT14 55 P9
BFOR GU20 52 E5
CHOB/PIR GU24 53 N8
SUN TW16 23 P9
WHTN TW2 25 K4
WOKN/KNAP GU21 10 E3
Chertsey St FLEETN GU51 86 E4
GU GU1 7 F4
TOOT SW17 29 K8
Chertsey Wk CHERT KT16 * 37 L8
Chervil Cl FELT TW13 24 B6
Cherwell Cl DTCH/LGLY SL3 12 F4
Cherwell Ct HOR/WEW KT19 60 A3
Cherwell Wk CRAWW RH11 176 G6
Cheryls Cl FUL/PGN SW6 19 M6
Cheselden Rd GU GU1 7 G5
Cheseman St SYD SE26 31 J6
Chesfield Rd KUTN/CMB KT2 41 L1
Chesham Cl BELMT SM2 61 J8
Chesham Crs PGE/AN SE20 46 C2
Chesham Ms GU GU1 7 H5
Chesham Rd GU GU1 7 H5
KUT/HW KT1 9 H3
KWD/TDW/WH KT20 99 K6
PGE/AN SE20 46 C3
WARL CR6 82 G5
Cheshire Cl CHERT KT16 55 H5
MTCM CR4 44 G4
Cheshire Gdns CHSGTN KT9 59 K5
Chesilton Crs FLEETS GU52 106 G2
Chesilton Rd FUL/PGN SW6 19 K6
Chesney Crs CROY/NA CR0 65 J6
Chessholme Rd ASHF TW15 23 M9
Chessington Cl
HOR/WEW KT19 60 A5
Chessington Hall Gdns
CHSGTN KT9 59 K6
Chessington Hill Pk
CHSGTN KT9 59 N5
Chessington Pde
CHSGTN KT9 * 59 K4
Chessington Rd CHSGTN KT9 59 N5
HOR/WEW KT19 60 A5
Chessington Wy WWKM BR4 65 H1
Chesson Rd WKENS W14 19 K4
Chester Av
RCHPK/HAM TW10 26 E2
WHTN TW2 24 G4
Chesterblade La BRAK RG12 32 F8
Chester Cl ASHF TW15 23 N8
ASHV GU12 109 K4
BARN SW13 * 18 F8
DORK RH4 117 J5
GUW GU2 111 M3
SUT SM1 61 L1
Chesterfield Cl EGRIN RH19 161 K8
Chesterfield Dr
ESH/CLAY KT10 58 G1
Chesterfield Gv EDUL SE22 30 G1
Chesterfield Rd ASHF TW15 23 H8
CHSWK W4 18 A4
HOR/WEW KT19 60 B6
Chester Gdns MRDN SM4 43 N6
Chester Rd ASHV GU12 109 K3
EHSLY KT24 95 K8
HSLWW TW4 15 K8
HTHAIR TW6 14 C8
WIM/MER SW19 27 P9
Chesters HORL RH6 140 A8
Chesters Rd CBLY GU15 69 K3
The Chesters NWMAL KT3 42 C2
Chesterton Cl EGRIN RH19 180 E4
WAND/EARL SW18 28 D1
Chesterton Ct SWTR RH13 192 F6
Chesterton Dr REDH RH1 100 G8
STWL/WRAY TW19 23 J4
Chesterton Sq KENS W8 19 K2
Chesterton Ter KUT/HW KT1 9 H5
Chester Wy RFNM GU10 109 H8
Chestnut Aly FUL/PGN SW6 * 19 K4
Chestnut Av ASHV GU12 108 C7
BH/WHM TN16 104 B2
BTFD TW8 17 K3
CBLY GU15 69 J2
ESH/CLAY KT10 40 D8
FNM GU9 127 L5
GUW GU2 112 A9
HASM GU27 184 D3
HOR/WEW KT19 60 C3
HPTN TW12 40 A1
MORT/ESHN SW14 * 18 B8
TEDD TW11 40 F1
VW GU25 35 M5
WEY KT13 56 E6
WOT/HER KT12 56 G7
WWKM BR4 65 L4
Chestnut Cl ADL/WDHM KT15 55 P4
ASHF TW15 23 L7
BLKW GU17 * 68 A3
CAR SM5 44 B9
EDEN TN8 144 F3
EGH TW20 20 G9
EGRIN RH19 180 G2
FLEETN GU51 87 J3
GSHT GU26 165 L8
HYS/HAR UB3 14 D5
KWD/TDW/WH KT20 99 L3
LIPH GU30 182 G7
REDH RH1 120 D7
RPLY/SEND GU23 93 L5
STRHM/NOR SW16 30 B7
SUN TW16 24 A9
Chestnut Copse OXTED RH8 123 P4
Chestnut Ct ASHV GU12 108 F4
Chestnut Dr EGH TW20 21 J9
Chestnut End BOR GU35 164 C7
Chestnut Gdns HORS RH12 192 B5
Chestnut Gv BAL SW12 29 K3
EA W5 17 K1
FLEETN GU51 87 H5
ISLW TW7 16 G9
MTCM CR4 44 F6
NWMAL KT3 42 B4
SAND/SEL CR2 64 B6
STA TW18 22 F9
WOKS/MYFD GU22 72 C9
Chestnut La CHOB/PIR GU24 53 J5
WEY KT13 56 D4
Chestnut Mnr WLGTN SM6 62 D3

Chestnut Manor Cl STA TW18...22 E8
Chestnut Md REDH RH1...120 A4
Chestnut Pl ASHTD KT21...77 L8
SYD SE26...30 C7
WEY KT13 *...54 D4
Chestnut Rd ASHF TW15...23 J7
FARN GU14...88 C2
GU GU1...6 E2
HORL RH6...140 C8
KUTN/CMB KT2...8 D1
RYNPK SW20...43 H3
WHTN TW2...25 M5
WNWD SE27...30 C6
The Chestnuts BECK BR3 *...46 D4
WOT/HER KT12...57 J1
Chestnut Ter SUT SM1 *...61 M3
Chestnut Tree Gv FARN GU14...87 N2
Chestnut Wk CRAWW RH11...176 F2
EGRIN RH19...162 B5
SHPTN TW17...38 C6
Chestnut Wy FELT TW13...24 B6
GODL GU7...150 D2
SHGR GU5...132 E9
Cheston Av CROY/NA CR0...46 E9
Cheswell Gdns FLEETS GU51...86 E9
Chesworth Crs SWTR RH13...192 B9
Chesworth Gdns
SWTR RH13...192 B9
Chesworth La SWTR RH13...192 B9
Chetwode Dr EPSOM KT18...79 H7
Chetwode Pl ASHV GU12...108 E7
Chetwode Rd EPSOM KT18...78 G8
KWD/TDW/WH KT20...79 H8
TOOT SW17...29 J6
Chetwode Ter ALDT GU11...108 B5
Chetwood Rd CRAWW RH11...176 A9
Cheveney Wk HAYES BR2...47 N4
Chevening Cl CRAWW RH11...194 F1
Chevening Rd NRWD SE19...45 M1
Cheviot Cl BELMT SM2...61 P7
BNSTD SM7...79 M4
CBLY GU15...69 L4
FARN GU14...88 A5
HYS/HAR UB3...14 F5
Cheviot Dr FLEETN GU51...87 H3
Cheviot Rd DTCH/LGLY SL3...12 E3
SHST GU47...49 K8
WNWD SE27...45 M2
Cheviot Wk CRAWW RH11 *...176 E5
Chewter La BFOR GU20...52 B6
Cheyham Gdns BELMT SM2...61 H8
Cheyham Wy BELMT SM2...61 J8
Cheylesmore Dr FRIM GU16...69 M5
Cheyne Av WHTN TW2...24 C4
Cheyne Cl BNSTD SM7...79 M4
Cheyne Ct ASHF TW15...23 N9
Cheyne Park Dr WWKM BR4...65 J2
Cheyne Rd ASHF TW15...23 N9
Cheyne Wk CROY/NA CR0...64 A1
HORL RH6...159 A2
WBPTN SW10...19 P5
Cheyne Wy FARN GU14...68 B9
Chichele Gdns CROY/NA CR0...3 H7
Chichele Rd OXTED RH8...103 L8
Chichester Cl CRAWE RH10...177 H9
DORK RH4...117 H5
HPTN TW12...24 J2
MFD/CHID GU8...149 M7
Chichester Ct EW KT17 *...60 D7
Chichester Dr PUR/KEN CR8...81 H1
Chichester Rd ASHV GU12...109 J3
CROY/NA CR0...3 J5
DORK RH4...117 H4
Chichester Ter HORS RH12...192 C8
Chichester Wy
EBED/NFELT TW14...24 C7
Chiddingfold Rd
MFD/CHID GU8...169 H8
Chiddingstone Cl BELMT SM2...61 L8
Chiddingstone St
FUL/PGN SW6...19 L7
Chilberton Dr REDH RH1...120 E1
Chilbrook Rd COB KT11...75 J7
Chilcroft La HASM GU27...184 C9
Chilcroft Rd HASM GU27...184 D9
Chilcrofts Rd HASM GU27...184 D9
Childebert Rd TOOT SW17...29 L5
Childerley St FUL/PGN SW6...19 J6
Childerstone Cl LIPH GU30...182 G6
Childs Hall Dr GT/LBKH KT23...95 P3
Childs Hall Rd GT/LBKH KT23...95 P5
Childs La NRWD SE19 *...30 F9
Child's Ms ECT SW5 *...19 L2
Child's Pl ECT SW5...19 L2
Child's Wk ECT SW5 *...19 L2
Chilham Cl FRIM GU16...69 H8
Chilham Wy HAYES BR2...47 N8
Chillerton Rd TOOT SW17...29 K8
Chillingham Wy CBLY GU15...68 E4
Chillington Dr BTSEA SW11...19 N9
Chillingworth Gdns
TWK TW1 *...25 N5
Chilmans Dr GT/LBKH KT23...96 B5
Chilmark Gdns NWMAL KT3...42 D7
REDH RH1...100 C9
Chilmark Rd
STRHM/NOR SW16...44 F3
Chilmead La REDH RH1...120 B4
Chilmead La REDH RH1...120 D3
Chilsey Green Rd CHERT KT16...37 J7
Chiltenhurst EDEN TN8...144 E3
Chiltern WOKS/MYFD GU22...92 A2
Chiltern Av FARN GU14...88 A4
WHTN TW2...24 M5
Chiltern Cl CRAWW RH11...176 L5
CROY/NA CR0...3 H6
FARN GU14...87 N3
FLEETS GU51...107 H1
HASM GU27...184 D1
STA TW18...22 D8

WPK KT4...60 G1
Chiltern Dr BRYLDS KT5...41 P7
Chiltern Gdns HAYES BR2...47 M5
Chiltern Rd BELMT SM2...61 N8
SHST GU47...49 K8
The Chilterns BELMT SM2 *...61 M7
Chilthorne Cl CAT SE6...31 N1
Chiltlee Cl LIPH GU30...182 F6
Chiltlee Mnr LIPH GU30...182 F6
Chiltley La LIPH GU30...182 G8
Chiltley Wy LIPH GU30...182 F8
Chilton Av W5...17 K2
Chilton Cl FARN GU10...170 C9
Chilton Farm Pk FARN GU14 *...87 N3
Chilton Rd RCH/KEW TW9...17 N8
Chiltons Cl BNSTD SM7...79 M4
Chilvers Cl WHTN TW2...25 M5
Chilworth Gdns SUT SM1...61 N1
Chilworth Rd SHGR GU5...133 L1
Chinchilla Dr HSLWW TW4...15 L7
Chinthurst Cl FLEETN GU51...86 C4
The Chime DORK RH4 *...117 H6
RFNM GU10...127 K8
Chingford Av FARN GU14...88 C2
Chinnock Cl FLEETS GU52...86 E8
Chinthurst La RGUE GU4...132 C3
Chinthurst Ms
COUL/CHIP CR5...80 E5
Chinthurst Pk RGUE GU4...132 C4
Chippendale Rd
CRAWW RH11...194 E1
Chipstead Av THHTH CR7...45 K5
Chipstead Cl BELMT SM2...61 M7
COUL/CHIP CR5...80 C6
NRWD SE19...45 P1
REDH RH1...99 M8
Chipstead Ct
WOKN/KNAP GU21...71 L6
Chipstead La COUL/CHIP CR5...99 M4
Chipstead Rd BNSTD SM7...79 K6
Chipstead Station Pde
COUL/CHIP CR5...80 D7
Chipstead St FUL/PGN SW6...19 L6
Chipstead Valley Rd
COUL/CHIP CR5...80 D5
Chipstead Wy BNSTD SM7...80 B6
Chirton Wk
WOKN/KNAP GU21...71 N7
Chisbury Cl BRAK RG12...32 G7
Chisholm Rd CROY/NA CR0...3 H3
RCHPK/HAM TW10...26 E2
Chislehurst Rd
RCHPK/HAM TW10...26 D2
Chislet Cl BECK BR3...46 G1
Chislett Gdns SHST GU47...49 N9
Chiswick Br CHSWK W4...18 A7
Chiswick Common Rd
CHSWK W4...18 B2
Chiswick High Rd CHSWK W4...17 P3
Chiswick House Grounds
CHSWK W4 *...18 C3
Chiswick La CHSWK W4...18 C3
Chiswick La South
CHSWK W4...18 D3
Chiswick Ml CHSWK W4...18 C4
Chiswick Pk CHSWK W4 *...18 A1
Chiswick Quay CHSWK W4...18 A6
Chiswick Sq CHSWK W4 *...18 C4
Chiswick Staithe CHSWK W4...17 P6
Chiswick Village CHSWK W4...17 N4
Chithurst La CRAWE RH10...160 F5
Chitterfield Ga WDR/YW UB7...14 C5
Chitty's Wk RGUW GU3...111 M1
Chivalry Rd BTSEA SW11...29 H1
Chivenor Gv KUTN/CMB KT2...26 C8
Chivers Dr EWKG RG40...48 C2
Chives Pl BNFD RG42...32 F1
Chobham Cl CHERT KT16...54 E5
Chobham Gdns
WIM/MER SW19...28 A5
Chobham La CHERT KT16...53 N1
Chobham Park La
CHOB/PIR GU24...73 L2
Chobham Rd ASC SL5...53 J1
CHERT KT16...54 D6
FRIM GU16...68 C6
WOKN/KNAP GU21...10 D1
Choir Gn WOKN/KNAP GU21...71 L6
Cholmeley Rd THDIT KT7...41 H7
Cholmley Ter THDIT KT7 *...41 H8
Cholseley Dr FLEETN GU51...86 E4
Chrislaine Cl
STWL/WRAY TW19...22 G2
Chrismas Av ASHV GU12...108 E5
Chrismas Pl ASHV GU12...108 E5
Christabel Cl ISLW TW7...16 E3
Christchurch Av TEDD TW11...25 P8
Christchurch Cl
FLEETS GU52...106 F2
WIM/MER SW19...43 N1
Christchurch Dr BLKW GU17...67 N2
Christ Church Mt
HOR/WEW KT19...59 P9
Christchurch Pk BELMT SM2...61 N6
Christ Church Wy
BRYLDS KT5...41 M8
EPSOM KT18...77 L1
Christchurch Rd
BRXS/STRHM SW2...30 A4
MORT/ESHN SW14...26 A1
PUR/KEN CR8...63 J8
VW GU25...35 N4
WIM/MER SW19...43 P3
Christchurch Wy
WOKN/KNAP GU21...10 E3
Christian Flds
STRHM/NOR SW16...45 J1
Christie Cl GT/LBKH KT23...95 P5
LTWR GU18...52 A8
Christie Dr CROY/NA CR0...46 A6

Christies EGRIN RH19...180 C3
Christie Wk COUL/CHIP CR5...81 K8
YTLY GU46...66 C4
Christine Cl ASHV GU12...109 H5
Christmas Hi SHGR GU5...132 F4
Christmaspie Av RGUW GU3...110 B5
Christopher Av HNWL W7...16 A2
Christopher Rd EGRIN RH19...180 D2
NWDGN UB2...15 K2
Christy Rd BH/WHM TN16...84 A4
Chrystie La GT/LBKH KT23...96 B6
Chuck's La
KWD/TDW/WH KT20...98 F4
Chudleigh Gdns SUT SM1...61 N2
Chudleigh Rd BROCKY SE4...31 N1
Chulsa Rd SYD SE26...31 J1
Chumleigh Wk BRYLDS KT5...41 M5
Church Ap DUL SE21...30 E6
EGH TW20...36 C4
Church Av BECK BR3...46 G2
FARN GU14...88 A5
MORT/ESHN SW14...18 B9
NWDGN UB2...15 N1
Church Cir FARN GU14...88 E6
Church Cl ADL/WDHM KT15...55 M3
CHOB/PIR GU24...70 F9
EW KT17 *...78 C2
HASM GU27...166 C9
HSLW TW5...15 L9
KWD/TDW/WH KT20...99 K7
LHD/OX KT22...96 D4
STA TW18...37 N4
WDR/YW UB7...14 A1
WOKN/KNAP GU21...10 E1
Church Ct FLEETS GU51...86 E6
REIG RH2...119 M5
Churchcroft Cl BAL SW12 *...29 K3
Church Dr WWKM BR4...65 L2
Church Farm La CHEAM SM3...61 J5
Church Fld EDEN TN8...145 H4
Churchfield Rd REIG RH2...119 K4
WEY KT13...56 C5
WOT/HER KT12...57 J1
Church Flds BOR GU35...164 B6
Churchfields
E/WMO/HCT KT8...40 A4
MFD/CHID GU8...149 M8
RGUE GU4...92 E9
WEY KT13...56 D5
Churchfields Av FELT TW13...24 G6
Churchfields Rd BECK BR3...46 A5
Church Gdns LHD/OX KT22 *...77 H9
Church Gn
KWD/TDW/WH KT20 *...98 E4
WOT/HER KT12...57 L5
Church Gv FLEETN GU51...86 E6
KUT/HW KT1...8 B6
Church Hams EWKG RG40...48 B3
Church HI ASHV GU12...108 D6
BH/WHM TN16...84 C4
BH/WHM TN16...104 B2
CAR SM5...62 B3
CBLY GU15...68 C3
CTHM CR3...101 P4
PUR/KEN CR8...62 G3
REDH RH1...100 D6
SHGR GU5...152 E1
WIM/MER SW19...28 C8
WOKN/KNAP GU21...10 A2
WOKS/MYFD GU22...73 K6
Church Hill Ter
RFNM GU10...106 D9
Churchill Av ASHV GU12...108 E6
HORS RH12...192 A7
Churchill Cl
EBED/NFELT TW14...24 A4
LHD/OX KT22...96 E3
WARL CR6...82 C6
Churchill Ct CRAWE RH10...177 L2
Churchill Crs BOR GU35...164 C7
FARN GU14...68 D9
Churchill Dr WEY KT13...56 E2
Churchill Rd ASC SL5...33 P3
DTCH/LGLY SL3...12 D2
GU GU1...7 H4
HOR/WEW KT19...59 N9
HORL RH6...140 F6
SAND/SEL CR2...63 N5
Churchill Wy BH/WHM TN16...84 B4
BMLY BR1...47 N3
SUN TW16...24 B8
Churchlands ALDT GU11...108 D6
Church La ASC SL5...34 D5
ASC SL5...34 A5
ASHV GU12...109 K4
BOR GU35...164 A5
CHOB/PIR GU24...70 C4
CHOB/PIR GU24...90 D2
CHSGTN KT9...59 M5
COUL/CHIP CR5...100 C2
GODL GU6...152 G9
CRAWE RH10...177 J4
CTHM CR3...101 J3
EGRIN RH19...180 E2
EPSOM KT18...98 A5
EWKG RG40...48 C5
FARN GU14...88 F2
GDST RH9...122 D3
GSHT GU26...165 M8
HASM GU27...184 D3
HORL RH6...159 P5
HORL RH6...159 P6
HORS RH12...191 L7
LIPH GU30...182 E4
MFD/CHID GU8...167 K3

MFD/CHID GU8...168 C1
OXTED RH8...103 L9
OXTED RH8...123 K1
RDKG RH5...172 G2
REDH RH1...121 M4
RFNM GU10...106 D9
RFNM GU10...126 A3
RFNM GU10...127 K6
RFNM GU10...146 B1
RGUW GU3...91 L7
RPLY/SEND GU23...92 F6
SHGR GU5...133 M1
SHGR GU5...134 C1
TEDD TW11...25 N8
THDIT KT7...40 F7
TOOT SW17...29 J8
TWK TW1...25 P4
WARL CR6...83 J5
WEY KT13...56 B6
WIM/MER SW19...43 L3
WLGTN SM6...62 F2
Church Lane Av
COUL/CHIP CR5...100 D2
Church Lane Dr
COUL/CHIP CR5...100 D2
Church La East ALDT GU11...108 E6
Church La West ALDT GU11...108 B5
Churchley Rd SYD SE26...31 J7
Church Md ADL/WDHM KT15...55 N3
Church Ms ADL/WDHM KT15...55 N3
Church Pde ASHF TW15 *...23 J7
Church Pk CRAWW RH11 *...176 D4
Church Pth ASHV GU12...109 J3
CHSWK W4...18 A1
MTCM CR4...44 A4
RYNPK SW20...43 H4
WOKN/KNAP GU21...10 E5
Church Rd ADL/WDHM KT15...55 M5
FSTH SE23...31 L4
YTLY GU46...67 H1
Church View Cl HORL RH6...159 J2
Churchview Rd WHTN TW2...25 M4
Church Wk BTFD TW8...17 J4
CRAWE RH10...176 G5
CTHM CR4...25 H4
HORL RH6...159 J2
LHD/OX KT22...97 H2
REIG RH2...119 M5
RFNM GU10...106 D9
STA TW18...22 B7
SUN TW16...39 J4
TWK TW1...25 P4
WEY KT13...56 C3
WOKS/MYFD GU22...92 G1
WOT/HER KT12...39 J9
Church St East
WOKN/KNAP GU21...10 E3
Church St West
WOKN/KNAP GU21...10 C4
Church Ter FUL/PGN SW6 *...19 M7
RCHPK/HAM TW10...25 P2
RDKG RH5...137 J7
Church V FSTH SE23...31 K5
Church vw ASHV GU12...109 J4
FSTH SE23...31 K5
YTLY GU46...67 H1
Church Vw Cl HORL RH6...159 J2
Churchview Rd WHTN TW2...25 M4
Church Wy OXTED RH8...123 M3
SAND/SEL CR2...63 P8
Churston Cl
BRXS/STRHM SW2 *...30 C4
Churston Dr MRDN SM4...43 H6
Churton Pl CHSWK W4...18 C3
Churt Rd RFNM GU10...165 J5
Churt Wynde GSHT GU26...165 N4
Chuters Cl BF/WBF KT14...74 B1
Chuters Gv EW KT17...78 D1
Cibber Rd FSTH SE23...31 K5
Cicada Rd
WAND/EARL SW18...28 E2
Cidermill Rd RDKG RH5...157 K1
Cinder Pth
WOKS/MYFD GU22...72 A8
Cinnamon Cl CROY/NA CR0 *...44 G3
Cinnamon Gdns GUW GU2...91 N9
Cintra Pk NRWD SE19...45 P1
Circle Gdns BF/WBF KT14...74 B2
WIM/MER SW19...43 L4
Circle Hill Rd CWTH RG45...49 N4
Circle Rd WOT/HER KT12...56 C8
The Circle GODL GU7...131 M7
The Circus LHD/OX KT22 *...77 H1
Cissbury Cl HORS RH12...192 F4
Cissbury Hi CRAWW RH11...176 F7
Clacket La BH/WHM TN16...104 G4
Clacy Gn BNFD RG42...32 C1
Clairvale Rd HEST TW5...15 M6
Clairview Rd
STRHM/NOR SW16...29 L8
Clairville MFD/CHID GU8 *...167 P3
Clancarty Rd FUL/PGN SW6...19 L7
Clandon Av EGH TW20...36 G1
Clandon Cl EW KT17...60 D1
Clandon Rd FARN GU14...88 F4
GU GU1...7 H4
RGUE GU4...113 H8
Clandon Ter RYNPK SW20 *...43 H3
Clanfield Ride BLKW GU17...67 P3
Clapgate La SWTR RH13...190 E6
Clapham Common North Side
CLAP SW4...29 K1
Clapham Common West Side
CLAP SW4...29 K1
Clapham Court Ter
CLAP SW4 *...29 N1
Clapham Park Est
CLAP SW4...29 N4
Clapham Park Ter
BRXS/STRHM SW2 *...29 P1
Clappers Ga CRAWE RH10...176 G4
Clappers La CHOB/PIR GU24...53 J9
Clappers Meadow
CRAN GU6...170 D9
Clappers Orch CRAN GU6...170 C2
Clare Cl BF/WBF KT14...73 L2
CRAWE RH10...177 M2
Clare Crs LHD/OX KT22...76 G7
Claredale WOKS/MYFD GU22...72 A9
Clare Gdns EGH TW20...21 M8
Clare HI ESH/CLAY KT10...58 B4

Clare Hill (No 2)
ESH/CLAY KT10 58 B4
Clare Lawn Av
MORT/ESHN SW14 27 J1
Clare Md RFNM GU10 146 C1
Clare Ms FUL/PGN SW6 19 M5
Claremont Av CBLY GU15 69 H3
ESH/CLAY KT10 57 P5
NWMAL KT3 42 F6
SUN TW16 39 K2
WOT/HER KT12 57 M3
Claremont Cl
BRXS/STRHM SW2 30 A4
SAND/SEL CR2 82 B4
WOT/HER KT12 57 L4
Claremont Ct DORK RH4 117 H8
Claremont Dr ESH/CLAY KT10 58 B6
SHPTN TW17 38 D7
WOKS/MYFD GU22 72 C8
Claremont End
ESH/CLAY KT10 58 B5
Claremont Gdns SURB KT6 41 L5
Claremont Gv CHSWK W4 18 C5
Claremont La ESH/CLAY KT10 58 B4
Claremont Park Rd
ESH/CLAY KT10 58 B5
Claremont Rd BF/WBF KT14 73 L1
CROY/NA CR0 46 A9
ESH/CLAY KT10 58 E6
REDH RH1 120 C2
STA TW18 22 A8
SURB KT6 41 L6
TEDD TW11 25 N8
TWK TW1 26 A3
Claremont Ter THDIT KT7 * 41 H8
Claremount Cl EPSOM KT18 78 G6
Claremount Gdns
EPSOM KT18 78 G6
Clarence Av CLAP SW4 29 N3
NWMAL KT3 42 A3
Clarence Cl ASHV GU12 108 E4
WOT/HER KT12 57 K3
Clarence Ct HORL RH6 * 140 F9
Clarence Crs CLAP SW4 29 N2
Clarence Dr CBLY GU15 69 K1
EGH TW20 21 H7
EGRIN RH19 180 E4
Clarence La PUT/ROE SW15 27 L2
Clarence Ms TOOT SW17 28 F6
Clarence Rd BH/WHM TN16 84 D7
CHSWK W4 17 N3
CROY/NA CR0 45 M8
FLEETN GU51 86 F7
RCH/KEW TW9 17 M6
REDH RH1 119 P8
SUT SM1 61 M3
SWTR RH13 192 C9
TEDD TW11 25 N9
WIM/MER SW19 28 E9
WLGTN SM6 62 D4
WOT/HER KT12 57 K3
Clarence St EGH TW20 21 L9
KUT/HW KT1 8 C4
NWDGN UB2 15 M1
RCH/KEW TW9 17 L9
STA TW18 22 B7
Clarence Ter HSLW TW3 16 B9
Clarence Wk REDH RH1 119 P8
Clarence Wy HORL RH6 159 N1
Clarendon Ct BLKW GU17 67 P5
Clarendon Crs WHTN TW2 25 L6
Clarendon Dr PUT/ROE SW15 18 G9
Clarendon Ga CHERT KT16 55 H5
Clarendon Gv MTCM CR4 44 B4
Clarendon Ms ASHTD KT21 * 77 L8
Clarendon Rd ASHF TW15 23 J7
CROY/NA CR0 2 B3
REDH RH1 120 B4
WIM/MER SW19 44 A1
WLGTN SM6 62 E4
Clarens St CAT SE6 31 N5
Clare Rd HSLWW TW4 15 P8
STWL/WRAY TW19 22 G4
The Clares CTHM CR3 102 A4
Claret Gdns SNWD SE25 45 N5
Clareville Gv SKENS SW7 * 19 N2
Clareville Grove Ms
SKENS SW7 * 19 N2
Clareville Rd CTHM CR3 102 A4
Clareville St SKENS SW7 19 N2
Clare Wd LHD/OX KT22 76 G7
Clarewood Dr CBLY GU15 68 G2
Clarice Wy WLGTN SM6 62 G7
Claridge Gdns LING RH7 162 F2
Claridges Md LING RH7 162 F2
Clarke Crs SHST GU47 68 A1
Clarke's Av WPK KT4 43 H9
Clark Rd CRAWW RH11 194 D1
Clarks Hl RFNM GU10 126 G3
Clarks La OXTED RH8 103 P3
Clark Wy HEST TW5 15 M5
Claude Monet Ct EDUL SE22 * 31 H1
Claudia Pl WIM/MER SW19 28 B4
Claverdale Rd
BRXS/STRHM SW2 30 A3
Claverdon BRAK RG12 32 C8
Clavering Av BARN SW13 18 F4
Clavering Cl TEDD TW11 25 P7
Claxton Gv HMSMTH W6 19 H3
Clay Av MTCM CR4 44 D3
Claybrook Rd HMSMTH W6 19 H4
Claycart Rd ALDT GU11 107 P3
Claydon Dr CROY/NA CR0 62 G3
Claydon Gdns BLKW GU17 68 C7
Claydon Rd
WOKN/KNAP GU21 71 N5
Clayford LING RH7 162 C2
Claygate Crs CROY/NA CR0 65 J5
Claygate La ESH/CLAY KT10 58 C2
THDIT KT7 40 G9
Claygate Lodge Cl
ESH/CLAY KT10 58 E6
Claygate Rd DORK RH4 117 H9
WEA W13 17 H1
Clay Hall La CRAWE RH10 160 D8
Clayhall La REIG RH2 119 J8
WDSR SL4 20 E1
Clayhanger RGUE GU4 112 G3
Clayhill Cl BRAK RG12 33 H4
REIG RH2 138 E3
Clayhill Rd REIG RH2 138 D4
Clay La EPSOM KT18 97 P4
LING RH7 161 L2
REDH RH1 120 E6
RGUE GU4 92 B8
STWL/WRAY TW19 23 J3
Claymore Cl MRDN SM4 43 L8
Claypole Dr HEST TW5 15 N6
Clayponds Av BTFD TW8 17 L2
Clayponds Gdns BTFD TW8 17 K2
Clayponds La BTFD TW8 17 L3
Clays Cl EGRIN RH19 180 D3
Clayton Barracks
ALDT GU11 108 F2
Clayton Ct FNM GU9 * 5 F4
Clayton Crs BTFD TW8 17 K3
Clayton Dr GUW GU2 111 M2
Clayton Gv BRAK RG12 32 G2
Clayton Hl CRAWW RH11 176 F7
Clayton Md GDST RH9 122 B1
Clayton Pde DTCH/LGLY SL3 * 12 E1
Clayton Rd CHSGTN KT9 59 J3
EW KT17 78 C1
FARN GU14 68 B7
ISLW TW7 16 E8
Cleardene DORK RH4 117 H7
Cleardown
WOKS/MYFD GU22 11 J6
Clearsprings LTWR GU18 51 P9
The Clears REIG RH2 119 J3
Clearwater Pl SURB KT6 41 J7
Cleave Av HYS/HAR UB3 14 G2
Cleaveland Rd SURB KT6 41 K6
Cleave Prior COUL/CHIP CR5 80 A8
Cleaverholme Cl SNWD SE25 46 B7
Cleeve Hl FSTH SE23 31 J4
Cleeve Rd LHD/OX KT22 76 G9
The Cleeve GU GU1 112 E5
Cleeve Wy PUT/ROE SW15 27 L2
SUT SM1 43 M9
Clem Attlee Ct
FUL/PGN SW6 * 19 K4
Clem Attlee Pde
FUL/PGN SW6 * 19 K4
Clement Cl CHSWK W4 18 B2
PUR/KEN CR8 81 K5
Clement Gdns HYS/HAR UB3 14 G2
Clement Rd BECK BR3 46 D3
WIM/MER SW19 28 B8
Clements Pl BTFD TW8 17 K3
Clements Rd WOT/HER KT12 57 K1
Clensham La SUT SM1 61 L1
Cleopatra Pl BNFD RG42 32 G1
Clerks Cft REDH RH1 121 M4
Clevedon WEY KT13 56 F4
Clevedon Ct FARN GU14 88 F4
FRIM GU16 69 J8
Clevedon Gdns HEST TW5 15 K7
HYS/HAR UB3 14 F1
Clevedon Rd KUT/HW KT1 9 H4
PGE/AN SE20 46 D2
TWK TW1 26 C2
Cleveland Av CHSWK W4 18 D2
HPTN TW12 39 P1
Cleveland Cl WOT/HER KT12 57 K2
Cleveland Dr STA TW18 37 M3
Cleveland Gdns BARN SW13 18 D7
WPK KT4 60 C1
Cleveland Ri MRDN SM4 43 H8
Cleveland Rd BARN SW13 18 D7
CHSWK W4 18 A1
ISLW TW7 16 G9
NWMAL KT3 42 C5
WPK KT4 60 C1
Cleves Av EW KT17 60 F7
Cleves Cl COB KT11 75 K3
Cleves Crs CROY/NA CR0 65 J9
Cleves Rd RCHPK/HAM TW10 26 B6
Cleves Wy HPTN TW12 39 P1
SUN TW16 24 A9
Cleves Wd WEY KT13 56 G2
Clewborough Dr CBLY GU15 69 K2
Clews La CHOB/PIR GU24 70 G5
Clifden Rd BTFD TW8 17 K4
TWK TW1 25 N4
Cliff End PUR/KEN CR8 81 K1
Cliffe Ri GODL GU7 150 B2
Cliffe Rd SAND/SEL CR2 63 M4
Clifford Av MORT/ESHN SW14 18 A7
RCH/KEW TW9 17 P8
WLGTN SM6 62 E3
Clifford Gdns HYS/HAR UB3 14 F2
Clifford Gv ASHF TW15 23 K7
Clifford Manor Rd
RGUE GU4 112 C9
Clifford Rd HSLWW TW4 15 M8
RCHPK/HAM TW10 26 C5
SNWD SE25 46 A5
Clifton Av BELMT SM2 61 M9
FELT TW13 24 D6
Clifton Cl ADL/WDHM KT15 55 M1
CTHM CR3 101 M3
HORL RH6 159 N1
RFNM GU10 127 L9
Clifton Ct BECK BR3 * 47 H2
Clifton Gdns CHSWK W4 18 B2
FRIM GU16 89 H1
Clifton Ga WBPTN SW10 * 19 N4
Clifton Ms SNWD SE25 45 N5
Clifton Pde FELT TW13 * 24 D7
Clifton Park Av RYNPK SW20 42 G3
Clifton Pl BNSTD SM7 79 L4
KUTN/CMB KT2 * 9 H3
WBPTN SW10 * 19 N4
Clifton Rd COUL/CHIP CR5 80 D4
CRAWE RH10 177 M6
HTHAIR TW6 * 14 D9
ISLW TW7 16 E7
KUTN/CMB KT2 9 H3
NWDGN UB2 15 N2
SNWD SE25 45 N5
TEDD TW11 25 M7
WIM/MER SW19 28 A9
WLGTN SM6 62 D4
Clifton's La REIG RH2 119 H4
Clifton Ter DORK RH4 * 117 H8
Cliftonville DORK RH4 117 H8
Clifton Wy WOKN/KNAP GU21 71 M6
Climping Rd CRAWW RH11 176 E3
Cline Rd GU GU1 7 J6
Clinton Av E/WMO/HCT KT8 40 C5
Clinton Cl WEY KT13 56 D2
WOKN/KNAP GU21 71 K7
Clinton Hl LING RH7 162 F3
Clinton La EDEN TN8 145 P2
Clinton Rd LHD/OX KT22 97 J3
Clintons Gn BNFD RG42 32 C2
Clinton Ter SUT SM1 * 61 N3
Clippesby Cl CHSGTN KT9 * 59 M5
Clipstone Rd HSLW TW3 16 A8
Clitheroe Rd BLKW GU17 67 K7
Clitherow Av HNWL W7 16 G1
Clitherow Gdns
CRAWE RH10 177 H6
Clitherow Rd BTFD TW8 17 H3
Cliveden Pl SHPTN TW17 38 D7
Cliveden Rd WIM/MER SW19 43 K2
Clive Gn BRAK RG12 32 D6
Clive Rd ASHV GU12 108 F5
DUL SE21 30 E6
EBED/NFELT TW14 24 B2
ESH/CLAY KT10 58 B3
TWK TW1 25 N7
WIM/MER SW19 29 H9
Clive Wy CRAWE RH10 177 M5
Clock Barn La
MFD/CHID GU8 150 E5
Clock House Cl BF/WBF KT14 74 B1
Clockhouse Cl
WIM/MER SW19 27 P6
Clock House Ct
HASM GU27 * 184 D4
Clockhouse La ASHF TW15 23 K7
SHGR GU5 132 D7
Clockhouse La East
EGH TW20 36 F1
Clockhouse La West
EGH TW20 36 E1
Clock House Md
LHD/OX KT22 76 B3
Clockhouse Pl
PUT/ROE SW15 28 B1
Clock House Rd BECK BR3 46 E4
Clockhouse Rd FARN GU14 88 D3
Clock Tower Rd ISLW TW7 16 F8
Clodhouse Hl
WOKS/MYFD GU22 91 K2
Cloister Cl TEDD TW11 26 A8
Cloister Gdns SNWD SE25 46 B7
The Cloisters FRIM GU16 68 F7
WOKS/MYFD GU22 92 F1
Cloncurry St FUL/PGN SW6 19 H7
Clonmel Rd FUL/PGN SW6 19 K5
TEDD TW11 25 L7
Clonmore St
WAND/EARL SW18 28 C4
The Close ASC SL5 33 M3
BECK BR3 46 E5
BF/WBF KT14 73 L2
BH/WHM TN16 * 84 F5
BIL RH14 187 P7
BRAK RG12 32 E5
BRKHM/BTCW RH3 117 P9
CAR SM5 62 A7
CHEAM SM3 43 K8
EGRIN RH19 180 C3
FNM GU9 5 K6
FRIM GU16 68 E8
GODL GU7 150 E1
HORL RH6 159 M3
ISLW TW7 16 D7
LTWR GU18 52 A8
MTCM CR4 44 B5
NWMAL KT3 42 A3
PUR/KEN CR8 63 H8
RCH/KEW TW9 17 P8
REIG RH2 119 M6
SHGR GU5 132 F6
SHST GU47 50 A9
SNWD SE25 * 46 A7
SURB KT6 41 L8
VW GU25 36 B6
WOKS/MYFD GU22 11 J3
Closeworth Rd FARN GU14 88 G7
Cloudesdale Rd TOOT SW17 29 L5
Clouston Cl WLGTN SM6 62 G4
Clouston Rd FARN GU14 88 B2
Clovelly Av WARL CR6 82 B7
Clovelly Dr GSHT GU26 165 M4
Clovelly Rd GSHT GU26 165 M5
HSLW TW3 16 A7
Clover Ct WOKS/MYFD GU22 10 A6
Cloverfields HORL RH6 140 D9
Clover Hl COUL/CHIP CR5 100 D1
Cloverlands CRAWE RH10 177 J3
Clover La YTLY GU46 66 E2
Clover Lea GODL GU7 131 L5
Clover Rd GUW GU2 111 L4
Clovers End HORS RH12 192 F5
Clovers Wy HORS RH12 193 J3
Clover Wy HORL RH6 160 D1
WLGTN SM6 44 C9
Clowders Rd CAT SE6 31 N6
Clowser Cl SUT SM1 61 N4
Club Gardens Rd HAYES BR2 47 N8
Clubhouse Rd ALDT GU11 108 B1
Club La CWTH RG45 49 P4
Clump Av
KWD/TDW/WH KT20 118 A2
Clumps Rd RFNM GU10 128 A9
The Clumps ASHF TW15 23 N7
Clunbury Av NWDGN UB2 15 P3
Cluny Ms ECT SW5 19 K2
Clyde Av SAND/SEL CR2 82 B4
Clyde Cl REDH RH1 120 C4
Clyde Flats FUL/PGN SW6 * 19 K5
Clyde Rd CROY/NA CR0 3 J3
STWL/WRAY TW19 22 G4
SUT SM1 61 L4
WLGTN SM6 62 E4
Clydesdale Cl ISLW TW7 16 F8
Clydesdale Gdns
RCHPK/HAM TW10 17 P9
Clyde Ter FSTH SE23 31 K5
Clyde V FSTH SE23 31 K5
Clymping Dene
EBED/NFELT TW14 24 C3
Clyve Wy STA TW18 37 J2
Coach House Cl FRIM GU16 68 G5
Coach House Gdns
FLEETN GU51 86 G4
Coach House La
WIM/MER SW19 28 A7
Coach House Ms FSTH SE23 31 K2
REDH RH1 * 120 B6
Coach House Yd
WAND/EARL SW18 * 19 M9
Coachlads Av GUW GU2 111 M5
Coachmans Dr
CRAWW RH11 176 E9
Coach Rd ASC SL5 33 N1
CHERT KT16 54 G5
DORK RH4 117 L5
HORL RH6 159 L5
Coalecroft Rd
PUT/ROE SW15 18 G9
Coast Hl DORK RH4 115 P9
Coast Hill La DORK RH4 116 A9
Coates Av WAND/EARL SW18 29 H2
Coates Cl THHTH CR7 45 L4
Cobalt Cl BECK BR3 46 D5
Cobb Cl DTCH/LGLY SL3 12 B6
Cobbets Rdg RFNM GU10 128 E4
Cobbets Wy EDEN TN8 144 G5
Cobbett Cl CRAWE RH10 177 M3
Cobbett Hill Rd RGUW GU3 90 E8
Cobbett Rd GUW GU2 111 L4
WHTN TW2 25 H4
Cobbetts Cl
WOKN/KNAP GU21 71 P5
Cobbetts Farm
CHOB/PIR GU24 70 G4
Cobbetts Hl WEY KT13 56 D6
Cobbett's La BLKW GU17 67 K4
Cobbetts Ms FNM GU9 * 4 E3
Cobbetts Wk
CHOB/PIR GU24 70 G5
Cobbetts Wy FNM GU9 127 K7
Cobbler's Wk TEDD TW11 40 E1
Cobbles Crs CRAWE RH10 177 H4
Cobblestone Pl CROY/NA CR0 2 C2
Cobb's Rd HSLWW TW4 15 P9
Cob Cl CRAWE RH10 179 K3
Cobden La HASM GU27 184 E3
Cobden Ms SYD SE26 31 J8
Cobden Rd SNWD SE25 46 A6
Cobham Av NWMAL KT3 42 E6
Cobham Cl BTSEA SW11 * 29 H2
WLGTN SM6 62 G5
Cobham Park Rd COB KT11 75 K6
Cobham Rd COB KT11 76 A7
HEST TW5 15 L5
KUT/HW KT1 9 J4
Cobham Wy CRAWE RH10 159 L8
EHSLY KT24 94 G5
Cobnor Cl CRAWW RH11 176 C7
Cobs Wy ADL/WDHM KT15 55 N8
Coburg Crs
BRXS/STRHM SW2 30 A4
Cob Wk CRAWW RH11 176 D6
Cochrane Pl BFOR GU20 52 D4
Cochrane Rd
WIM/MER SW19 43 J1
Cock-a-dobby SHST GU47 49 L9
Cockcrow Hl SURB KT6 * 41 K9
Cockett Rd DTCH/LGLY SL3 12 C1
Cock La LHD/OX KT22 96 C2
Cocks Crs NWMAL KT3 42 D5
Cockshot Hl REIG RH2 119 M7
Cockshot Rd REIG RH2 119 M7
Codrington Ct
WOKN/KNAP GU21 71 M7
Codrington Hl FSTH SE23 31 M3
Cody Cl ASHV GU12 109 H1
WLGTN SM6 62 F6
Cody Rd FARN GU14 88 B4
Coe Av SNWD SE25 46 A7
Coe Cl ALDT GU11 108 C5
Cokenor Wd RFNM GU10 127 K7
Cokers La DUL SE21 30 D4
Colbeck FLEETS GU52 107 H2
Colbeck Ms SKENS SW7 19 M2
Colborne Wy WPK KT4 60 G2
Colbred Cnr FLEETN GU51 87 J3
Colbrook Av HYS/HAR UB3 14 F1
Colbrook Cl HYS/HAR UB3 14 F1
Colburn Av CTHM CR3 101 P4
Colburn Crs RGUE GU4 112 E2
Colburn Wy SUT SM1 61 P2
Colby Rd NRWD SE19 30 F8
WOT/HER KT12 39 J9
Colchester V FROW RH18 181 K9
Colcokes Rd BNSTD SM7 79 L5
Coldharbour Cl EGH TW20 36 G4
Coldharbour La
CHOB/PIR GU24 52 F9
DORK RH4 116 G9
DORK RH4 136 F5
EGH TW20 36 G4
Cold Harbour La FARN GU14 68 B8
Coldharbour La
PUR/KEN CR8 63 J8
REDH RH1 121 P5
WOKS/MYFD GU22 73 K4
Coldharbour Rd
BF/WBF KT14 73 K3
CROY/NA CR0 63 J4
Coldharbour Wy
CROY/NA CR0 63 J4
Coldshott OXTED RH8 123 N4
Coldstream Gdns
WAND/EARL SW18 28 C2
Coldstream Rd CTHM CR3 101 L2
Cole Av ALDT GU11 108 B3
Colebrook CHERT KT16 55 H5
Colebrooke Pl CHERT KT16 * 54 G6
Colebrooke Rd REDH RH1 120 A3
Colebrook Ri HAYES BR2 47 L3
Colebrook Rd
STRHM/NOR SW16 44 G2
Cole Cl CRAWW RH11 194 E1
Coleford Bridge Rd
FARN GU14 88 F3
Coleford Cl FRIM GU16 89 H4
Coleford Paddocks
FRIM GU16 89 H3
Coleford Rd
WAND/EARL SW18 28 F1
Cole Gdns HEST TW5 15 J5
Coleherne Ms WBPTN SW10 19 M3
Coleherne Rd ECT SW5 19 M3
Colehill Gdns FUL/PGN SW6 * 19 J6
Colehill La FUL/PGN SW6 19 J6
Coleman Cl SNWD SE25 46 A3
Coleman Rd ASHV GU12 108 F5
Cole Park Gdns TWK TW1 25 P2
Cole Park Rd TWK TW1 25 P3
Coleridge Av SUT SM1 62 A3
YTLY GU46 67 J3
Coleridge Cl CWTH RG45 49 N5
HORS RH12 192 D4
Coleridge Crs DTCH/LGLY SL3 13 J6
Coleridge Gdns WBPTN SW10 19 N5
Coleridge Rd ASHF TW15 23 H7
CROY/NA CR0 46 C8
Coleridge Wy WDR/YW UB7 14 B2
Cole Rd TWK TW1 25 P2
Colesburg Rd BECK BR3 46 F4
Colescroft Hl PUR/KEN CR8 81 J4
Coleshill Rd TEDD TW11 25 M9
Coles La BH/WHM TN16 105 N3
RDKG RH5 155 N6
Colesmead Rd REDH RH1 120 B2
Coleson Hill Rd RFNM GU10 127 K8
Colet Gdns WKENS W14 19 H3
Colet Rd CRAWE RH10 176 G8
Coleville Rd FARN GU14 88 B2
Coley Av WOKS/MYFD GU22 11 G5
Colfe Rd FSTH SE23 31 M4
Colgate Cl CRAWW RH11 176 E3
Colin Cl CROY/NA CR0 64 F2
WWKM BR4 65 M2
Colinette Rd PUT/ROE SW15 18 G9
Colin Rd CTHM CR3 102 A3
Coliston Rd
WAND/EARL SW18 28 D3
Collamore Av
WAND/EARL SW18 29 H4
Collard Cl PUR/KEN CR8 81 M9
Collards Ga HASM GU27 * 184 E4
Collards La HASM GU27 184 E4
College Av EGH TW20 21 N9
EW KT17 78 D3
College Cl ADL/WDHM KT15 55 P2
CBLY GU15 50 F9
EGRIN RH19 180 E2
LING RH7 143 K9
RHWH RH17 194 F8
WHTN TW2 25 L4
College Crs REDH RH1 120 C2
SHST GU47 50 A9
College Dr THDIT KT7 40 E8
College Gdns FNM GU9 4 E3
NWMAL KT3 42 D6
TOOT SW17 29 H5
College Gn NRWD SE19 45 N1
College Hl GODL GU7 150 B1
HASM GU27 184 D4
College Hill Ter HASM GU27 184 D4
College La EGRIN RH19 180 E2
WOKS/MYFD GU22 72 A8
College Pl WBPTN SW10 * 19 N5
College Ride BAGS GU19 51 L7
CBLY GU15 68 F1
College Rd ASHV GU12 109 J3
BMLY BR1 47 N2
BRAK RG12 32 E5
CRAWE RH10 177 H5
CROY/NA CR0 2 E4
DUL SE21 30 F3
EW KT17 78 E3
GU GU1 6 E4
ISLW TW7 16 F6
SHST GU47 68 A1
WIM/MER SW19 28 G9
WOKS/MYFD GU22 11 K2
The College EW KT17 * 78 E4
College Wy ASHF TW15 23 J7
Collendean La HORL RH6 139 K9
Collens Fld CHOB/PIR GU24 90 E4
Colley La REIG RH2 119 J2
Colley Manor Dr REIG RH2 119 H4
Colley Wy REIG RH2 119 J2
Collier Cl FARN GU14 87 P2
HOR/WEW KT19 59 N5
Collier Rw CRAWE RH10 176 G8
Colliers CTHM CR3 102 A5
Colliers Cl WOKN/KNAP GU21 71 P6
Colliers Water La THHTH CR7 45 J6
Collier Wy RGUE GU4 113 H3

Collingdon CRAN GU6............171 J2
Collingdon Ct CRAN GU6 * 171 J2
Collingham Pl ECT SW5...........19 M2
Collingham Rd ECT SW5..........19 M2
Collingsbourne
  ADL/WDHM KT15 *..............55 M3
Collingtree Rd SYD SE26.........31 K7
Collingwood Av BRYLDS KT5....42 A9
Collingwood Ct CRAN GU14......88 G5
Collingwood Cl EGRIN RH19...180 E4
  HORL RH6.........................140 D9
Colling Wood Cl PGE/AN SE20..46 B2
Collingwood Cl WHTN TW2........25 H3
Collingwood Crs GU GU1.........172 E4
Collingwood Grange Cl
  CBLY GU15.........................51 K9
Collingwood Ri CBLY GU15.......69 J1
Collingwood Rd
  CRAWE RH10.....................177 N6
  HORS RH12.......................192 A5
  MTCM CR4..........................44 A3
  SUT SM1............................61 M4
Collins Gdns ASHV GU12.......109 K4
Collins Rd BRAK RG12............32 B1
Collyer Av CROY/NA CRO........62 G5
Collyer Rd CROY/NA CRO.........62 G5
Collyers Crs LIPH GU30........183 H6
Colman Cl EPSOM KT18..........78 G6
Colmans Hl SHGR GU5...........134 F6
Colman Wy REDH RH1...........120 A3
Colmer Rd STRHM/NOR SW16..44 C1
Colston Rd
  MORT/ESHN SW14................18 A8
Coltash Rd CRAWE RH10.......177 K6
Coltsfoot Dr GU GU1.............112 F2
  HORS RH12.......................192 D5
Coltsfoot La OXTED RH8......123 M4
Columbia Av WPK KT4............42 D8
Columbia Ct EWKG RG40.........48 C2
Columbine Av SAND/SEL CR2...63 K6
Columbus Dr FARN GU14........87 N4
Colville Gdns LTWR GU18........52 C9
Colville Rd ACT W3.................17 P1
Colvin Cl SYD SE26................31 K8
Colvin Rd THHTH CR7.............45 J6
Colwell Rd EDUL SE22...........30 C1
Colwith Rd HMSMTH W6..........18 G4
Colwood Gdns
  WIM/MER SW19....................43 P1
Colworth Rd CROY/NA CRO......46 A9
  STRHM/NOR SW16................29 M8
  YTLY GU46........................66 F2
Colwyn Cl STRHM/NOR SW16...29 M8
Colwyn Crs HSLW TW3............16 C6
Colwyn Cl WOKN/KNAP GU21 ..72 A7
Colyton La
  STRHM/NOR SW16................30 B8
Colyton Rd EDUL SE22...........31 J1
Combe La FARN GU14.............88 C1
  MFD/CHID GU8..................167 N6
  SHGR GU5.........................114 C2
  SHGR GU5.........................151 K2
  WOT/HER KT12....................57 H7
Combemartin Rd
  WAND/EARL SW18.................28 B3
Combe Ri RFNM GU10..........127 P8
Combermere Rd MRDN SM4....43 M7
Combe Rd GODL GU7.............131 L5
Combe Vw MFD/CHID GU8.....167 P7
Comeragh Cl
  WOKS/MYFD GU22...............71 N8
Comeragh Ms WKENS W14 *....19 J3
Comeragh Rd WKENS W14.......19 J3
Comet Cl ASHV GU12............109 H1
Comet Rd STWL/WRAY TW19 ..22 G3
Comforts Farm Av
  OXTED RH8.......................123 M4
Comfrey Cl FARN GU14...........87 N2
Commerce Rd BTFD TW8.........17 J4
Commerce Wy CROY/NA CRO ..63 H2
  EDEN TN8.........................144 C2
Commercial Rd ASHV GU12...108 E6
  GU GU1..............................6 C5
  STA TW18..........................22 D9
Commercial Wy
  WOKN/KNAP GU21...............10 E3
Commodore Pde
  STRHM/NOR SW16 *.............45 H1
Common Cl
  WOKN/KNAP GU21...............72 J3
Commondale PUT/ROE SW15..18 G7
Commonfield Rd BNSTD SM7 ..79 L3
Commonfields
  CHOB/PIR GU24...................70 F2
Common La ADL/WDHM KT15..55 N7
  ESH/CLAY KT10...................58 G5
Common Rd BARN SW13........18 E8
  DTCH/LGLY SL3...................12 F3
  ESH/CLAY KT10...................58 G5

  REDH RH1.........................120 B7
Common Side EPSOM KT18....77 N4
Commonside GT/LBKH KT23 ....96 A3
Commonside Ct BELMT SM2...61 M9
  COUL/CHIP CR5...................81 K9
Commonside East
  MTCM CR4..........................44 C4
Commonside West
  MTCM CR4..........................44 C4
The Common NWDGN UB2.....15 M2
Commonwealth Rd
  CTHM CR3.........................102 A3
Community Cl HEST TW5........15 K6
Como Rd FSTH SE23...............31 H5
Compass Cl ASHF TW15.........38 E1
Compass Hl
  RCHPK/HAM TW10................26 C2
Compassion Cl
  CRAWW RH11....................176 B6
Comport Cl CROY/NA CRO......83 L1
Compound Rd FARN GU14......32 A7
Compton Cl BRAK RG12.........32 A7
  ESH/CLAY KT10....................58 D5
  FLEETS GU52....................107 H1
  SHST GU47.........................49 N8
Compton Crs CHSGTN KT9.....59 L5
  CHSWK W4..........................18 A3
Compton Rd CROY/NA CRO.....46 B9
  FLEETS GU52....................107 H1
  WIM/MER SW19....................28 C3
Comptons Brow La
  SWTR RH13.......................192 E7
Comptons Ct SWTR RH13......192 E7
Comptons La SWTR RH13......192 E7
Compton Wy RFNM GU10.....128 C3
Comsaye Wk BRAK RG12........32 L6
Conaways Cl EW KT17............60 E8
Concorde Cl HSLW TW3...........16 B7
Condor Ct GU GU1...................6 D7
Condor Rd FARN GU14............88 A5
  STA TW18..........................37 M9
Conduit La DTCH/LGLY SL3.....13 J7
  SAND/SEL CR2...................64 A4
The Conduit REDH RH1.........101 M9
Coneyberry REIG RH2...........119 N9
Coneybury REDH RH1...........121 N5
Coneybury Cl WARL CR6.........82 B8
Coney Cl CRAWW RH11..........176 E3
Coney Ct HORS RH12............192 G5
Coney Hall Pde WWKM BR4 *..65 L2
Coney Hill Rd WWKM BR4.......65 L1
Coneyhurst La CRAN GU6.....153 M5
Conford Dr RGUE GU4...........132 C3
Coniers Wy RGUE GU4..........112 F2
Conifer Cl FLEETS GU52........106 F1
  REIG RH2.........................119 L5
Conifer Dr CBLY GU15.............69 J2
Conifer Gdns
  STRHM/NOR SW16................30 A6
  SUT SM1............................61 M1
Conifer La EGH TW20.............21 P8
Conifer Pk EW KT17...............60 D8
Conifers WEY KT13.................56 G5
Conifers Cl HORS RH12........192 G4
  TEDD TW11.........................41 H1
The Conifers CWTH RG45.......49 L2
Coniger Rd FUL/PGN SW6.......19 L7
Coningsby BRAK RG12............32 L5
Coningsby Rd SAND/SEL CR2..63 J7
Coniston Cl WOKN/KNAP GU21 ..71 M5
Coniston Ct BARN SW13........18 D5
  CBLY GU15..........................69 L5
  CHSWK W4..........................18 A6
  CRAWW RH11....................176 A7
  FARN GU14..........................88 A4
  HORS RH12.......................192 G5
  MRDN SM4..........................43 H7
Coniston Dr FNM GU9...........107 L8
Coniston Gdns BELMT SM2 *..61 P5
Coniston Rd COUL/CHIP CR5...80 E5
  CROY/NA CRO.....................46 A8
  WHTN TW2..........................25 J2
  WOKS/MYFD GU22...............72 F9
Coniston Wy CHSGTN KT9......59 L2
  EGH TW20...........................36 F1
  FLEETS GU52....................106 F1
  REIG RH2.........................120 A4
Connaught Av ASHF TW15......23 H7
  HSLWW TW4........................24 F1
  MORT/ESHN SW14................18 A8
Connaught Barracks
  ALDT GU11........................108 F9
Connaught Cl CWTH RG45.......49 K6
  SUT SM1............................61 P1
  YTLY GU46.........................66 F2
Connaught Crs
  CHOB/PIR GU24...................70 F9
Connaught Dr WEY KT13.........56 A6
Connaught Gdns
  CRAWE RH10.....................176 G3
  MRDN SM4..........................43 N6
Connaught Ms
  FUL/PGN SW6 *...................19 J6
Connaught Rd ASHV GU12...108 E5
  BAGS GU19..........................51 L6
  CBLY GU15..........................69 H5
  CHOB/PIR GU24...................70 F9
  FLEETN GU51......................86 G7
  NWMAL KT3.........................42 C5
  RCHPK/HAM TW10 *.............26 E1
  SUT SM1............................61 P1
  TEDD TW11..........................25 L8
Connop Wy FRIM GU16...........69 H5
Conquest Rd
  ADL/WDHM KT15...................55 L4
Conrad Dr WPK KT4................42 G9
Consfield Av NWMAL KT3.........42 E5
Consort Cl BAGS GU19............51 L1
Consort Ms ISLW TW7.............25 L2

Consort Wy HORL RH6...........159 K1
Consort Wy East HORL RH6...159 L2
Constable Gdns ISLW TW7......25 L1
Constable Rd CRAWE RH10...177 J9
Constable Wk DUL SE21.........30 G6
Constable Wy SHST GU47.......49 N8
Constance Rd CROY/NA CRO...45 K8
  SUT SM1............................61 N3
  WHTN TW2..........................25 J3
Constant Rd FARN GU14.........87 L5
Constitution HI
  WOKS/MYFD GU22...............10 D6
Control Tower Rd
  HTHAIR TW6.........................14 C8
Convent Cl BECK BR3..............47 J1
Convent Gdns EA W5..............17 J2
Convent Hl NRWD SE19..........30 D9
Convent La COB KT11..............75 H1
Convent Rd ASHF TW15..........23 L8
Convent Wy NWDGN UB2.......15 L2
Conway Dr ASHF TW15...........23 M9
  BELMT SM2........................61 M5
  FARN GU14..........................87 P2
  HYS/HAR UB3......................14 E1
Conway Gdns MTCM CR4........44 F5
Conway Rd FELT TW13...........24 G8
  HSLWW TW4........................24 G3
  RYNPK SW20......................42 G2
Conyers Cl WOT/HER KT12.....57 M4
Conyers Rd
  STRHM/NOR SW16................29 N8
Cooden Cl BMLY BR1..............47 P1
Cookes La CHEAM SM3...........61 J5
Cookham Cl NWDGN UB2........16 B1
  SHST GU47.........................49 N8
Cookham Rd BRAK RG12.........32 A3
Cook Rd CRAWE RH10...........177 H7
  HORS RH12.......................192 C4
Cooks Hl HORS RH12...........189 J1
Cooks Md HORS RH12...........175 J4
Cooks Meadow HORS RH12 ...175 J4
Cook Wy GU GU1..................111 K4
Cookson La RI CBLY GU15........69 J2
Coolgardie Rd ASHF TW15.....23 M8
Coolhurst La SWTR RH13......192 F9
Coombe Av CROY/NA CRO......63 N3
Coombe Bank KT3..................42 C2
Coombe Cl CRAWW RH11.....176 E3
  FRIM GU16..........................68 F8
  HSLW TW3..........................16 A9
Coombe Crs HPTN TW12........39 N1
Coombe Dr ADL/WDHM KT15...55 K5
  FLEETN GU51.......................87 J6
Coombe End KUTN/CMB KT2 ...42 B1
Coombefield Cl NWMAL KT3....42 C6
Coombe Gdns NWMAL KT3......42 E5
Coombe Hill Gld
  KUTN/CMB KT2....................42 C1
Coombe Hill Rd EGRIN RH19..180 B5
  KUTN/CMB KT2....................42 C1
Coombe House Cha
  NWMAL KT3.........................42 B2
Coombelands La
  RYNPK SW20......................42 G3
Coombe La CROY/NA CRO.......64 B4
  RYNPK SW20......................42 G3
Coombe Mnr CHOB/PIR GU24..71 H4
Coombe Neville
  KUTN/CMB KT2....................42 A1
Coombe Pine BRAK RG12........32 F7
Coombe Ridings
  KUTN/CMB KT2....................27 H8
Coombe Rd KUTN/CMB KT2....42 A2
  CHSWK W4..........................18 C3
  CROY/NA CRO.......................2 E7
  HPTN TW12.........................24 C9
  KUTN/CMB KT2....................42 A3
  NWMAL KT3.........................42 C4
  SAND/SEL CR2...................63 N5
  SYD SE26............................31 J7
  WEA W13............................17 H1
  YTLY GU46..........................66 F1
Coomber Wy CROY/NA CRO....44 G8
The Coombes SHGR GU5......132 E8
The Coombe
  BRKHM/BTCW RH3..............118 B2
Coombe Vls
  WAND/EARL SW18 *...............28 D3
Coombe Wy BF/WBF KT14.......74 B1
Coombe Wood Hl
  PUR/KEN CR8......................81 L1
Coombe Wood Rd
  KUTN/CMB KT2....................27 H8
Coomb Fld EDEN TN8...........144 C5
Coomer Ms FUL/PGN SW6 *....19 K4
Coomer Pl FUL/PGN SW6.......19 K4
Cooper Cl HORL RH6............160 B1
Cooper Crs CAR SM5..............62 B2
Cooper Rd BFOR GU20...........52 D6
  CROY/NA CRO.......................63 J4
  GU GU1...............................7 H6
Cooper Rw CRAWE RH10......176 G8
Cooper's CI STA TW18............37 M3
Cooper's HI HTWY RG27.........66 B5
Coopers Hill Dr
  CHOB/PIR GU24...................70 C9
Cooper's Hill Rd REDH RH1...121 H4
Coopers Ms BECK BR3............46 C3
Coopers Ri GODL GU7...........150 A1
Cooper's Yd NRWD SE19........30 F9
Cootes Av HORS RH12..........191 P7
Copelands Cl CBLY GU15.........69 P4
Copeman Cl SYD SE26...........31 K8
Copenhagen Gdns CHEL SW3 ..15 J3
Copenhagen Wy
  WOT/HER KT12....................57 K2
Cope PI KENS W8...................19 L1
Copgate Pth
  STRHM/NOR SW16................30 A9
Copleigh Dr
  KWD/TDW/WH KT20.............79 J9

Copley Cl REDH RH1.............120 A3
  WOKN/KNAP GU21...............71 L8
Copley Pk STRHM/NOR SW16..30 A9
Copley Wy
  KWD/TDW/WH KT20.............79 H9
Copnall Wy HORS RH12........192 B8
Copnard Gdns CHSGTN KT9....59 J5
Copped Hall Dr CBLY GU15.....69 L2
Copped Hall Wy CBLY GU15....69 L2
Copper Beech Cl
  WOKS/MYFD GU22...............91 P1
Copper Cl NRWD SE19...........45 P1
Copperfield CI SAND/SEL CR2..63 L9
Copperfield PI HORS RH12...192 A7
Copperfield Ri
  ADL/WDHM KT15...................55 K4
Copperfields LHD/OX KT22.....96 C2
  SUN TW16 *........................24 A9
Coppergate Cl BMLY BR1........47 P2
Copper Mill Dr ISLW TW7.......16 F7
Copper Mill La TOOT SW17.....28 F7
Coppermill Rd STWL/WRAY
  TW19..................................21 N2
Coppice Cl BECK BR3.............47 H5
  FNM GU9...........................108 A8
  GUW GU2..........................111 K4
  RYNPK SW20......................42 C4
Coppice Dr PUT/ROE SW15...27 M2
  STWL/WRAY TW19.................21 J3
Coppice Gdns CWTH RG45.....49 K4
  YTLY GU46..........................66 G3
Coppice Gn BNFD RG42..........32 B1
Coppice La REIG RH2............119 K3
Coppice PI MFD/CHID GU8.....169 K5
Coppice Rd HORS RH12.......192 F5
The Coppice ASHF TW15........23 L9
  CRAWE RH10.....................179 J3
Coppice Wk CRAWE RH10.....177 K4
Copping Cl CROY/NA CRO........3 H7
The Coppins CROY/NA CRO.....65 H5
Coppsfield E/WMO/HCT KT8....40 A4
Copse Av FNM GU9................108 A7
  WWKM BR4..........................65 H1
Copse Cl CRAWW RH11.........176 G7
  CRAWE RH10.....................179 J1
  EGRIN RH19........................162 E9
  HORS RH12.......................192 E4
  RGUW GU3.........................132 G2
  WDR/YW UB7.......................13 P1
Copse Crs CRAWW RH11......176 F4
  REDH RH1.........................120 A7
  WOKN/KNAP GU21...............71 M7
Copse Dr EW KT17..................78 D2
Copse End CBLY GU15............69 H2
Copse Gld SURB KT6..............41 K8
Copse Hl BELMT SM2............61 M6
  PUR/KEN CR8......................80 G2
  RYNPK SW20......................42 E2
Copsem Dr ESH/CLAY KT10....58 B5
Copsem La ESH/CLAY KT10....58 B5
Copsem Wy ESH/CLAY KT10...58 C5
Copse Rd WEY KT13 LHD/OX KT22..75 K2
  COB KT11............................75 J2
Copse Side GODL GU7...........131 K5
The Copse BRAK RG12 *........32 F6
  CTHM CR3.........................102 A6
  FARN GU14..........................87 P4
  LHD/OX KT22.......................96 E3
  REDH RH1.........................120 A7
  RFNM GU10......................127 K9
Copse Vw SAND/SEL CR2.......64 E7
Copse Wd LHD/OX KT22.........75 K2
Copsewood Cl BECK BR3.......46 E1
Copse Wood Wy
  NTHWD HA6 *.....................183 P1
  REDH RH1...........................99 N8
  WOKN/KNAP GU21...............71 M7
Copthorne Av BAL SW12.........29 N3
Copthorne Bank
  CRAWE RH10.....................160 C8
Copthorne Cl SHPTN TW17 ....38 E7
Copthorne Common Rd
  CRAWE RH10.....................160 D9
Copthorne Ct LHD/OX KT22 *..96 C1
Copthorne Dr LTWR GU18.......52 B8
Copthorne Ms HYS/HAR UB3...14 C2
Copthorne Ri SAND/SEL CR2...81 M1
Copthorne Rd CRAWE RH10...161 J8
  CRAWE RH10.....................177 N3
  LHD/OX KT22.......................77 H9
Copthorne Wy CRAWE RH10..176 D1
Copyhold Rd EGRIN RH19.....180 C5
Coral Re BTSEA SW11............19 N8
Corban Rd HSLW TW3............16 A3
Corbet Cl WLGTN SM6............44 C9
Corbet Rd EW KT17.................78 C4
Corbett Cl CROY/NA CRO.........83 K1
Corbett Dr LTWR GU18............69 J8
Corby Cl EGH TW20................20 D1
Corby Dr EGH TW20................21 H9
Cordelia Cft BNFD RG42.........32 D2
Cordelia Gdns ASHV GU12....109 K2
  STWL/WRAY TW19.................23 H3
Cordelia Rd
  STWL/WRAY TW19.................23 H3
Cordrey Gdns
  COUL/CHIP CR5...................80 G4
Cordwallis Rd CBLY GU15.......51 H9
Corfe Cl ASHTD KT21..............77 J7
  HSLWW TW4........................24 F4

Corfe Gdns FRIM GU16...........69 H7
Corfe Wy FARN GU14..............88 G6
Corfield Cl EWKG RG40...........48 C6
Coriander Cl FARN GU14.........87 N3
Coriander Crs GUW GU2.........91 N9
Corkran Rd SURB KT6.............41 K8
Corkscrew Hl WWKM BR4........65 L1
Cormongers La REDH RH1....120 F4
Cormorant Pl SHST GU47.......67 P1
Cornbunting Cl SHST GU47.....67 P1
Corn Cft BNFD RG42................32 F1
Cornelia Cl FARN GU14 *.........87 P4
Corner Farm Cl
  KWD/TDW/WH KT20.............98 G2
Corner Fielde
  BRXS/STRHM SW2 *.............30 A4
Cornerside ASHF TW15..........38 E1
Corney Reach Wy CHSWK W4..18 C5
Corney Rd CHSWK W4............18 C4
Cornfield Rd REIG RH2.........119 N6
Cornfields GODL GU7............131 M6
  YTLY GU46..........................66 F4
Cornflower La CROY/NA CRO...46 D9
Cornflower Ter EDUL SE22.....31 J2
Cornford Cl HAYES BR2..........47 N5
Cornford Gv BAL SW12...........29 L5
Cornhill Cl ADL/WDHM KT15....55 M1
Cornish Gv PGE/AN SE20........46 B6
Cornwall Av BF/WBF KT14.......74 B3
  ESH/CLAY KT10....................58 F6
Cornwall Cl CBLY GU15...........69 H1
Cornwall Gdns EGRIN RH19...180 C5
  SKENS SW7........................19 M1
  SNWD SE25 *.......................45 P5
Cornwall Gardens Wk
  KENS W8............................19 M1
Cornwall Gv CHSWK W4.........18 C3
Cornwallis Cl CTHM CR3.......101 L2
Cornwall Ms South
  SKENS SW7........................19 N1
Cornwall Ms West
  SKENS SW7........................19 M1
Cornwall Rd BELMT SM2.........61 K6
  CROY/NA CRO.......................2 B3
  TWK TW1.............................25 P3
Cornwall Wy STA TW18...........22 B9
Cornwell Rd WDSR SL4..........20 F2
Coronation Rd ALDT GU11....108 D7
  ASC SL5..............................34 A7
  EGRIN RH19......................180 D4
  HYS/HAR UB3......................14 G4
  YTLY GU46..........................67 H1
The Coronet HORL RH6.........159 M3
Corporation Av HSLWW TW4...15 N9
Corrib Dr SUT SM1.................62 A4
Corrie Gdns VW GU25............36 A5
Corrie Rd ADL/WDHM KT15....55 P3
  WOKS/MYFD GU22...............92 D1
Corrigan Av COUL/CHIP CR5...80 C4
Corringway FLEETS GU52........87 H9
Corry Rd GSHT GU26............165 M5
Corsair Cl STWL/WRAY TW19 ..22 G3
Corsair Rd STWL/WRAY TW19 ..23 H3
Corscombe Cl KUTN/CMB KT2..27 H8
Corsehill St
  STRHM/NOR SW16................29 M7
Corsellis Sq TWK TW1............17 H9
Corsham Wy CWTH RG45.......49 M3
Corsletts Av HORS RH12........191 L7
Cortayne Rd FUL/PGN SW6 *..19 K7
Cortis Rd PUT/ROE SW15.......27 N2
Cortis Ter PUT/ROE SW15......27 N2
Corunna Dr SWTR RH13......192 E8
Cosbycote Av HNHL SE24......30 D1
Cosdach Av WLGTN SM6........62 F6
Cosedge Crs CROY/NA CRO....63 J4
Cosford Rd MFD/CHID GU8....148 B9
Costells Meadow
  BH/WHM TN16....................105 H6
Coteford St TOOT SW17.........29 J7
Cotelands CROY/NA CRO..........3 G5
Cotford Rd THHTH CR7............45 L5
Cotherstone EW KT19.............60 B7
Cotherstone Rd
  BRXS/STRHM SW2................30 A4
Cotland Acres REDH RH1......119 P7
Cotsford CRAWW RH11.........194 E4
Cotswold Cl CRAWW RH11....176 E5
  ESH/CLAY KT10....................58 F1
  GU GU1...............................68 A9
  STA TW18............................22 D9
Cotswold Ct SWTR RH13......192 D8
Cotswold Ms BTSEA SW11 *....19 P6
  HPTN TW12.........................25 H9
  SHST GU47.........................49 K8
Cotswold St WNWD SE27.......30 C7
Cotswold Wy WPK KT4............60 C1
Cottage Cl CHERT KT16...........55 K4
  HORS RH12.......................192 C4
Cottage Farm Wy
  EGH TW20...........................36 G4
Cottage Gdns FARN GU14......88 B3
Cottage Gv SURB KT6.............41 K7
Cottage PI CRAWE RH10.......160 F9
Cottage Rd EW KT19...............60 C5
Cottenham Dr RYNPK SW20....42 F1
Cottenham PI RYNPK SW20....42 F1
Cottenhams LING RH7...........142 E5
Cotterell Cl BNFD RG42.........32 D1
Cotterill Rd SURB KT6.............59 M1
Cottesbrooke Cl
  DTCH/LGLY SL3...................13 H6
Cottesloe Cl CHOB/PIR GU24...70 F5
Cottesmore BRAK RG12.........32 C8
Cottesmore Gdns KENS W8...19 N1
Cottimore Av WOT/HER KT12...39 K8
Cottimore Crs
  WOT/HER KT12....................39 K8
Cottimore La WOT/HER KT12..39 K9

Cottimore Ter
WOT/HER KT12 39 K8
Cottingham Av HORS RH12 192 C3
Cottingham Rd PGE/AN SE20 46 D1
Cottington Rd FELT TW13 24 E7
Cotton Cl ALDT GU11 108 B3
Cottongrass Cl CROY/NA CR0 46 D9
Cotton Rw BTSEA SW11 19 N8
RDKG RH5 154 D4
Cotts Wood Dr RGUE GU4 92 E9
Couchmore Av
ESH/CLAY KT10 58 E1
Coulsdon Court Rd
COUL/CHIP CR5 81 H5
Coulsdon La COUL/CHIP CR5 80 C8
Coulsdon Pl CTHM CR3 101 M2
Coulsdon Ri COUL/CHIP CR5 80 G6
Coulsdon Rd COUL/CHIP CR5 81 H5
Coulter Rd HMSMTH W6 18 F1
Countisbury Gdns
ADL/WDHM KT15 55 M4
Country Wy FELT TW13 24 D8
County Oak La CRAWE RH10 158 G9
County Oak Wy
CRAWW RH11 176 G1
County Pde BTFD TW8 * 17 K5
County Rd THHTH CR7 45 K3
Courland Rd
ADL/WDHM KT15 55 M2
Course Rd ASC SL5 34 A4
Court Av COUL/CHIP CR5 81 J7
Court Bushes Rd CTHM CR3 82 A8
Court Cl EGRIN RH19 180 E2
LIPH GU30 182 E7
WHTN TW2 25 J6
Court Close Av WHTN TW2 25 J6
Court Crs CHSGTN KT9 59 K5
EGRIN RH19 180 F2
Court Downs Rd BECK BR3 47 H3
Court Dr CROY/NA CR0 63 H3
SUT SM1 62 A3
Courtenay Av BELMT SM2 61 L7
Courtenay Dr BECK BR3 47 K3
Courtenay Ms
WOKN/KNAP GU21 11 G1
Courtenay Rd FNM GU9 108 A8
PGE/AN SE20 46 D1
WOKN/KNAP GU21 11 G1
WPK KT4 60 G2
Court Farm Av
HOR/WEW KT19 60 B4
Court Farm Gdns
HOR/WEW KT19 * 60 B9
Court Farm Pk WARL CR6 * 82 A5
Court Farm Rd WARL CR6 82 A7
Courtfield Gdns ECT SW5 19 M2
Courtfield Ms SKENS SW7 * 19 N2
Courtfield Ri WWKM BR4 65 K2
Courtfield Rd ASHF TW15 23 L9
ECT SW5 19 N2
Court Gdns CBLY GU15 68 F3
Court Haw BNSTD SM7 80 A4
Court Hl SAND/SEL CR2 81 N1
Courthope Rd
WIM/MER SW19 28 B8
Courthope Vls
WIM/MER SW19 43 J1
Courtland Av
STRHM/NOR SW16 45 H1
Courtlands
RCHPK/HAM TW10 26 F1
Courtlands Av
DTCH/LGLY SL3 12 B2
ESH/CLAY KT10 57 P5
HAYES BR2 47 L9
HPTN TW12 24 G9
RCH/KEW TW9 17 P7
Courtlands Cl SAND/SEL CR2 63 P8
Courtlands Crs BNSTD SM7 79 L5
Courtlands Dr
HOR/WEW KT19 60 C5
Courtlands Rd BRYLDS KT5 41 N8
Court La DUL SE21 30 G3
HOR/WEW KT19 78 A2
Court Lane Gdns DUL SE21 30 F3
Courtleas COB KT11 76 A2
Court Lodge Rd HORL RH6 140 A9
Courtmead Cl HNHL SE24 30 D2
Courtmoor Av FLEETS GU52 86 F8
Courtney Cl NRWD SE19 * 30 F9
Courtney Crs CAR SM5 62 B6
Courtney Pl COB KT11 75 P1
Courtney Rd CROY/NA CR0 63 J2
HTHAIR TW6 14 C8
WIM/MER SW19 44 A1
Courtney Wy HTHAIR TW6 14 C8
Courtrai Rd FSTH SE23 31 M2
Court Rd ALDT GU11 108 C4
BNSTD SM7 79 L4
CTHM CR3 101 M3
GDST RH9 122 C2
NWDGN UB2 15 P2
SNWD SE25 45 P3
Courts Hill Rd HASM GU27 184 C4
Courtside SYD SE26 * 31 K6
Courts Mount Rd
HASM GU27 184 C4
Court St BMLY BR1 47 N3
The Court GUW GU2 * 6 D7
WARL CR6 82 E7
Court Wy WHTN TW2 25 N3
Court Wood La CROY/NA CR0 64 F8
The Courtyard BF/WBF KT14 73 L1
BH/WHM TN16 * 105 H6
CRAWE RH10 * 176 G6
EGRIN RH19 180 G2
HORS RH12 * 192 B8
Coutts Av CHSGTN KT9 59 L4
Coval Gdns
MORT/ESHN SW14 17 P9
Coval La MORT/ESHN SW14 17 P9
Coval Rd MORT/ESHN SW14 18 A9
Coveham Crs COB KT11 75 J2
Coventry Rd SNWD SE25 46 A5
Coverack Cl CROY/NA CR0 46 E8
Coverdale Gdns CROY/NA CR0 3 J5
Cove Rd FARN GU14 88 C3
FLEETN GU51 87 J4
Covert Cl CRAWE RH10 177 H4
Covert La BRAK RG12 32 E5
Coverton Rd TOOT SW17 29 H7
Coverts Cl FNM GU9 128 A1
Coverts Rd ESH/CLAY KT10 58 F6
The Covert ASC SL5 34 B8
FARN GU14 68 A8
NRWD SE19 * 45 P1
Covey Cl FARN GU14 68 C8
WIM/MER SW19 43 M3
The Covey CRAWE RH10 177 N3
Covington Gdns
STRHM/NOR SW16 45 K1
Covington Wy
STRHM/NOR SW16 30 B9
Cowbridge Meadow
CHOB/PIR GU24 90 F3
Cowden St CAT SE6 31 P7
Cowdray Cl CRAWE RH10 177 M6
Cowdrey Rd WIM/MER SW19 28 E9
Cowfold Cl CRAWW RH11 176 C8
Cowick Rd TOOT SW17 29 J7
Cow La GODL GU7 131 K9
Cowleaze Rd KUTN/CMB KT2 8 E3
Cowley Av CHERT KT16 37 K8
Cowley Cl SAND/SEL CR2 64 C7
Cowley Crs WOT/HER KT12 57 L3
Cowley La CHERT KT16 37 K8
Cowley Rd MORT/ESHN SW14 18 C8
Coworth Cl ASC SL5 35 H6
Coworth Pk ASC SL5 * 35 J4
Coworth Rd ASC SL5 34 G6
Cowper Av SUT SM1 61 P3
Cowper Cl CHERT KT16 37 K7
Cowper Gdns WLGTN SM6 62 E5
Cowper Rd KUTN/CMB KT2 26 E8
WIM/MER SW19 28 F9
Cowshot Crs CHOB/PIR GU24 70 D9
Cowslip La RDKG RH5 96 C8
Coxbridge Mdw FNM GU9 4 B5
Coxcombe La
MFD/CHID GU8 168 A7
Coxdean EPSOM KT18 78 G8
Coxes Av SHPTN TW17 * 38 C4
Coxgreen SHST GU47 67 P2
Cox Green Rd HORS RH12 171 L9
Coxheath Rd FLEETS GU52 86 E9
Cox La CHSGTN KT9 59 M3
HOR/WEW KT19 59 P4
Coxley Ri PUR/KEN CR8 81 L2
Coxmoor Cl FLEETS GU52 107 J1
Coxs Av SHPTN TW17 38 G4
Coxwell Rd NRWD SE19 45 N1
Crabbet Rd CRAWE RH10 177 L4
Crab Hl BECK BR3 47 K1
Crab Hill La REDH RH1 121 H9
Crabtree Cl GT/LBKH KT23 96 C6
Crabtree Dr LHD/OX KT22 97 H5
Crabtree Gdns BOR GU35 164 B6
Crabtree La BOR GU35 164 B6
EPSOM KT18 98 A6
FUL/PGN SW6 19 H5
GT/LBKH KT23 96 C6
RDKG RH5 116 F1
RFNM GU10 165 K1
Crabtree Rd CBLY GU15 68 D6
CRAWW RH11 176 F4
EGH TW20 36 G3
Craddocks Av ASHTD KT21 77 M5
Cradhurst Cl DORK RH4 116 C8
Craigans CRAWW RH11 176 D5
Craigen Av CROY/NA CR0 46 B9
Craignair Rd
BRXS/STRHM SW2 30 A3
Craignish Av
STRHM/NOR SW16 45 H3
Craig Rd RCHPK/HAM TW10 26 B7
Craigwell Av FELT TW13 24 B6
Craigwell Cl STA TW18 37 J2
Crakell Rd REIG RH2 119 N6
Crake Pl SHST GU47 49 P9
Cramhurst La
MFD/CHID GU8 149 M6
Crammond Cl HMSMTH W6 19 J4
Crampshaw La ASHTD KT21 77 M9
Crampton Rd PGE/AN SE20 31 K9
Cranborne Av NWDGN UB2 16 A2
SURB KT6 59 N2
Cranborne Wk CRAWE RH10 177 J7
Cranbourne Cl HORL RH6 * 140 D8
STRHM/NOR SW16 44 G4
Cranbrook Cl HAYES BR2 47 N7
Cranbrook Ct FLEETN GU51 86 G4
Cranbrook Dr ESH/CLAY KT10 40 C9
WHTN TW2 25 J4
Cranbrook Rd CHSWK W4 18 C3
HSLWW TW4 15 P9
THHTH CR7 45 L3
WIM/MER SW19 43 J1
Cranbury Rd FUL/PGN SW6 19 M7
Crane Av ISLW TW7 25 P1
Cranebank Ms TWK TW1 * 26 A1
Cranebrook WHTN TW2 25 K5
Crane Ct MORT/ESHN SW14 * 18 A9
SHST GU47 49 P9
Craneford Cl WHTN TW2 25 N3
Craneford Wy WHTN TW2 25 M3
Crane Gdns HYS/HAR UB3 15 H2
Crane Lodge Rd HEST TW5 15 K4
Crane Park Rd WHTN TW2 25 J5
Crane Rd STWL/WRAY TW19 23 K2
WHTN TW2 25 M4
Cranes Dr BRYLDS KT5 41 L5
Cranes Pk BRYLDS KT5 41 L5
Cranes Park Av BRYLDS KT5 41 L5
Cranes Park Crs BRYLDS KT5 41 M5
Craneswater HYS/HAR UB3 15 H5
Craneswater Pk NWDGN UB2 15 P3
Crane Wy WHTN TW2 25 K3
Cranfield Rd East CAR SM5 62 C7
Cranfield Rd West CAR SM5 * 62 B7
Cranford Av FLEETS GU52 106 E1
STWL/WRAY TW19 23 H3
Cranford Cl PUR/KEN CR8 81 L2
RYNPK SW20 * 42 F2
STWL/WRAY TW19 23 H3
Cranford Dr HYS/HAR UB3 15 H2
Cranford La HYS/HAR UB3 14 F4
Cranford Park Dr YTLY GU46 67 H2
Cranford Park Rd
HYS/HAR UB3 15 H2
Cranford Ri ESH/CLAY KT10 58 C4
Cranleigh Cl PGE/AN SE20 46 B3
SAND/SEL CR2 82 A1
Cranleigh Ct FARN GU14 88 B3
Cranleigh Gdns
KUTN/CMB KT2 26 E9
SAND/SEL CR2 82 A1
SNWD SE25 45 N4
SUT SM1 61 M1
Cranleigh Md CRAN GU6 171 J1
Cranleigh Rd CRAN GU6 153 N8
ESH/CLAY KT10 40 C9
FELT TW13 24 A7
SHGR GU5 132 G6
WIM/MER SW19 43 L4
Cranley Cl GU GU1 112 E5
Cranley Dene GU GU1 112 E5
Cranley Gdns SKENS SW7 19 N3
WLGTN SM6 62 E6
Cranley Ms SKENS SW7 19 N3
Cranley Pl SKENS SW7 19 P2
WOKN/KNAP GU21 * 71 K7
Cranley Rd GU GU1 7 K3
WOT/HER KT12 57 H5
Cranmer Av WEA W13 17 H1
Cranmer Cl MRDN SM4 43 H7
WARL CR6 82 E6
WEY KT13 56 C6
Cranmer Ct HPTN TW12 25 J8
Cranmer Farm Cl MTCM CR4 44 B5
Cranmer Gdns WARL CR6 82 E6
Cranmer Rd CROY/NA CR0 2 B5
HPTN TW12 25 J8
KUTN/CMB KT2 26 D8
MTCM CR4 44 B5
Cranmer Ter TOOT SW17 28 G8
Cranmore Av ISLW TW7 16 C5
Cranmore Cl ALDT GU11 108 A5
Cranmore Gdns ALDT GU11 108 A5
Cranmore La EHSLY KT24 94 D9
Cranmore Rd FRIM GU16 89 H3
Cranston Cl HSLW TW3 15 N7
REIG RH2 119 M6
Cranston Rd FSTH SE23 31 M4
Cranstoun Cl RGUW GU3 111 M1
Cranwell Gv LTWR GU18 51 P9
SHPTN TW17 38 B5
Craster Rd BRXS/STRHM SW2 30 A3
Cravan Av FELT TW13 24 B5
Craven Cl RFNM GU10 127 N7
Craven Gdns WIM/MER SW19 28 E8
Craven Rd CRAWE RH10 177 L6
CROY/NA CR0 46 B9
KUTN/CMB KT2 9 F2
The Cravens HORL RH6 160 B1
Crawford Cl ISLW TW7 16 E7
Crawford Gdns CBLY GU15 68 D3
SWTR RH13 192 D7
Crawfurd Wy EGRIN RH19 180 E1
Crawley Av CRAWE RH10 177 H3
CRAWE RH10 177 M1
CRAWW RH11 176 E4
CRAWW RH11 176 E8
Crawley Down Rd
EGRIN RH19 161 M9
Crawley Dr CBLY GU15 69 H2
Crawley Goods Yd
CRAWE RH10 * 177 L1
Crawley Hl CBLY GU15 69 H3
Crawley La CRAWE RH10 177 M4
RHWH RH17 195 N5
Crawley Rdg CBLY GU15 69 H2
Crawley Rd HORS RH12 192 E6
Crawley Wood Cl CBLY GU15 69 H3
Crawshaw Rd CHERT KT16 55 H5
Crawters Cl CRAWE RH10 177 J4
Cray Av ASHTD KT21 77 L5
Crayke Hl CHSGTN KT9 59 L6
Crayonne Cl SUN TW16 38 G2
Crealock St
WAND/EARL SW18 28 E2
Creasys Dr CRAWW RH11 194 E2
Crebor St EDUL SE22 31 H2
Credenhill St
STRHM/NOR SW16 29 M9
Crediton Wy ESH/CLAY KT10 58 G4
Credon Cl FARN GU14 88 A2
Creek Rd E/WMO/HCT KT8 40 E5
The Creek SUN TW16 39 J6
Creeland Gv CAT SE6 31 N4
Cree's Meadow BFOR GU20 * 52 D6
Crefeld Cl HMSMTH W6 19 H4
Creighton Rd EA W5 17 J1
Cremorne Est WBPTN SW10 * 19 P4
Cremorne Gdns
HOR/WEW KT19 60 B7
Cremorne Rd WBPTN SW10 19 N5
Crerar Cl FARN GU14 87 P4
Crescent Ct HORL RH6 * 159 K3
Crescent Gdns
WIM/MER SW19 28 D6
Crescent Gv MTCM CR4 44 A5
Crescent La ASHV GU12 109 K1
CLAP SW4 29 N1
Crescent Rd BECK BR3 47 H3
BMLY BR1 47 N1
CTHM CR3 102 A4
EGRIN RH19 180 C2
KUTN/CMB KT2 41 N1
REDH RH1 121 L4
REIG RH2 119 L7
RYNPK SW20 43 H2
SHPTN TW17 38 E6
The Crescent ASHF TW15 23 J8
BARN SW13 18 D7
BECK BR3 46 G2
BELMT SM2 61 L9
BRAK RG12 32 E5
CHERT KT16 37 L4
CROY/NA CR0 45 M7
CTHM CR3 102 G3
E/WMO/HCT KT8 39 P5
EGH TW20 21 L9
EGRIN RH19 162 B4
EPSOM KT18 77 N4
FARN GU14 88 E4
FLEETN GU51 86 C9
FNM GU9 107 P6
GUW GU2 111 N4
HORL RH6 159 K3
HORS RH12 191 P8
HYS/HAR UB3 14 E5
LHD/OX KT22 97 H2
NWMAL KT3 42 A3
REDH RH1 * 119 P8
REIG RH2 119 M5
SHPTN TW17 39 H8
SURB KT6 41 L6
SUT SM1 61 P4
WEY KT13 56 C2
WIM/MER SW19 28 D6
WWKM BR4 47 L7
YTLY GU46 67 H1
Crescent Wy HORL RH6 159 K3
STRHM/NOR SW16 45 H1
Crescent Wood Rd SYD SE26 31 H6
Cresford Rd FUL/PGN SW6 19 M6
Cressall Cl LHD/OX KT22 77 H9
Cressall Md LHD/OX KT22 77 H9
Cressida Cha BNFD RG42 32 G2
Cressingham Gv SUT SM1 61 N3
Cresswell Pl WBPTN SW10 19 N3
Cresswell Rd FELT TW13 24 F6
SNWD SE25 46 A5
TWK TW1 26 C2
Cressy Ct HMSMTH W6 18 F1
Cressys Cnr HSLW TW3 * 16 B8
Cresta Dr ADL/WDHM KT15 55 K8
Crest Hl SHGR GU5 134 G4
Creston Av
WOKN/KNAP GU21 71 L6
Creston Wy WPK KT4 43 H9
Crest Rd HAYES BR2 47 M8
SAND/SEL CR2 64 B6
The Crest BRYLDS KT5 41 N6
Crestway PUT/ROE SW15 27 M2
Crestwood Wy HSLWW TW4 24 G1
Creswell WOKN/KNAP GU21 * 71 K6
Creswell Cnr
WOKN/KNAP GU21 * 71 K6
Creswell Dr BECK BR3 47 H6
Crewdson Rd HORL RH6 159 L1
Crewe's Av WARL CR6 82 C5
Crewe's Cl WARL CR6 82 C5
Crewe's La WARL CR6 82 D5
Crichton Av WLGTN SM6 62 F4
Crichton Rd CAR SM5 62 B6
Cricket Ct EGRIN RH19 162 D9
Cricketers Cl CHSGTN KT9 59 K4
RDKG RH5 155 K8
Cricketers La BFOR GU20 52 D4
Cricketers Ms BAL SW12 29 L3
WAND/EARL SW18 28 E1
Cricketers Wk SYD SE26 31 K8
Cricket Field Gv CWTH RG45 49 P5
Cricket Field Rd HORS RH12 192 A9
Cricketfield Rd WDR/YW UB7 13 N2
Cricket Gn MFD/CHID GU8 168 B2
MTCM CR4 44 B5
Cricket Hl EWKG RG40 48 D7
REDH RH1 121 H7
Cricket Hill La BLKW GU17 67 H5
Cricket La BECK BR3 31 M9
RFNM GU10 127 P7
Cricketts Hl SHGR GU5 134 C1
Cricket Vw WEY KT13 56 D4
Cricket Wy WEY KT13 56 G1
Cricklade Av
BRXS/STRHM SW2 29 P5
Crieff Rd WAND/EARL SW18 28 F2
Criffel Av BRXS/STRHM SW2 29 N5
Crimea Rd ALDT GU11 108 D4
Crimp Hl WDSR SL4 20 E3
Cripley Rd FARN GU14 87 P2
Cripplecrutch Hl
MFD/CHID GU8 185 N4
Crispen Rd FELT TW13 24 F7
Crisp Gdns BNFD RG42 32 A1
Crispin Crs CROY/NA CR0 62 F2
Crisp Rd HMSMTH W6 18 G3
Cristowe Rd FUL/PGN SW6 * 19 K7
Critchmere Hl HASM GU27 183 P3
Critchmere La HASM GU27 183 P4
Critchmere V HASM GU27 183 N4
Critten La RDKG RH5 115 M3
Cricket Cl GSHT GU26 165 N5
Crocker Cl ASC SL5 33 P2
Crockers La LING RH7 142 D9
Crockerton Rd TOOT SW17 29 J5
Crockford Cl
ADL/WDHM KT15 55 N3
Crockford Park Rd
ADL/WDHM KT15 55 N4
Crockford Pl BNFD RG42 32 B1
Crockham Cl CRAWW RH11 176 F7
Crocknorth Rd EHSLY KT24 115 H2
Crocus Cl CROY/NA CR0 46 D9
Croffets KWD/TDW/WH KT20 99 H1
Croft Av DORK RH4 117 H5
WWKM BR4 47 J9
Croft Cl HYS/HAR UB3 14 E5
Croft Ct EDEN TN8 144 G4
SUT SM1 * 61 P1
Crofters WDSR SL4 20 F2
Crofters Cl FRIM GU16 69 M7
ISLW TW7 25 L1
REDH RH1 120 D7
SHST GU47 49 L9
Crofters Md CROY/NA CR0 64 F7
The Crofters WDSR SL4 * 20 F2
Croft La EDEN TN8 144 G4
RFNM GU10 106 C9
YTLY GU46 66 G1
Croftleigh Av PUR/KEN CR8 81 J5
Crofton ASHTD KT21 77 L7
Crofton Av CHSWK W4 18 A5
WOT/HER KT12 57 L2
Crofton Cl BRAK RG12 32 G6
CHERT KT16 54 G6
Crofton Gate Wy
BROCKY SE4 31 M1
Crofton Park Rd BROCKY SE4 31 N2
Crofton Ter RCH/KEW TW9 17 M9
Croft Rd ALDT GU11 108 D6
BH/WHM TN16 104 F6
CTHM CR3 102 F2
GODL GU7 131 K9
MFD/CHID GU8 149 M7
STRHM/NOR SW16 45 J1
SUT SM1 61 P4
WIM/MER SW19 43 N1
Crofts Cl MFD/CHID GU8 168 A6
The Crofts SHPTN TW17 38 G5
The Croft BNFD RG42 32 D1
CRAWW RH11 176 D5
HEST TW5 15 N5
Croft Wy FRIM GU16 69 H7
HORS RH12 191 P7
RCHPK/HAM TW10 26 A6
Croham Cl SAND/SEL CR2 63 N5
Croham Manor Rd
SAND/SEL CR2 63 N6
Croham Mt SAND/SEL CR2 63 N6
Croham Park Av
SAND/SEL CR2 63 P4
Croham Rd SAND/SEL CR2 63 N4
Croham Valley Rd
SAND/SEL CR2 64 A5
Croindene Rd
STRHM/NOR SW16 44 G2
Cromer Hyde MRDN SM4 * 43 M6
Cromer Rd HTHAIR TW6 14 C8
SNWD SE25 46 B4
TOOT SW17 29 K9
Cromer Rd West HTHAIR TW6 14 C8
Cromer Villas Rd
WAND/EARL SW18 28 C2
Cromford Rd PUT/ROE SW15 28 C1
Cromford Wy NWMAL KT3 42 B2
Crompton Flds
CRAWE RH10 177 H2
Crompton Wy CRAWE RH10 177 H3
Cromwell Av HAYES BR2 47 P4
HMSMTH W6 18 F3
NWMAL KT3 42 D6
Cromwell Cl CHSWK W4 * 17 P3
HAYES BR2 47 P5
WOT/HER KT12 39 K9
Cromwell Crs ECT SW5 19 L2
Cromwell Gdns SKENS SW7 * 19 P2
Cromwell Gv CTHM CR3 101 L1
HMSMTH W6 18 G1
Cromwell Ms SKENS SW7 19 P2
Cromwell Pl CRAN GU6 171 J2
EGRIN RH19 180 E4
MORT/ESHN SW14 18 A8
SKENS SW7 19 P2
Cromwell Rd ASC SL5 34 B5
BECK BR3 46 E3
CBLY GU15 68 F1
CROY/NA CR0 45 M8
CTHM CR3 101 L1
ECT SW5 19 M2
FELT TW13 24 C4
HSLW TW3 16 A9
KUTN/CMB KT2 8 E3
REDH RH1 120 B5
TEDD TW11 25 P9
WIM/MER SW19 28 D8
WOT/HER KT12 57 K1
WPK KT4 60 B2
Cromwell St HSLW TW3 16 A9
Cromwell Ter HSLW TW3 * 16 A9
Cromwell Wy FARN GU14 68 D9
Crondace Rd FUL/PGN SW6 19 L6
Crondall Ct CBLY GU15 68 D4
Crondall End YTLY GU46 66 G1
Crondall La RFNM GU10 126 G3
Crondall Rd FLEETN GU51 106 C3
RFNM GU10 126 E6
Cronks Hl REIG RH2 119 N6
Cronks Hill Cl REDH RH1 119 P7
Cronks Hill Rd REDH RH1 119 P7
Crookham Reach
FLEETS GU52 106 E1
Crookham Rd FLEETN GU51 86 E9
FUL/PGN SW6 19 K6
Crooksbury Rd RFNM GU10 128 D2
Crosby Cl FELT TW13 24 F7
Crosby Gdns YTLY GU46 66 E1
Crosby Hill Dr CBLY GU15 69 H1
Crosby Wy FNM GU9 4 D5
Crossacres
WOKS/MYFD GU22 73 J5
Cross Deep TWK TW1 25 N6
Cross Deep Gdns TWK TW1 25 N5
Cross Fell BRAK RG12 32 C5
Crossfield Pl WEY KT13 56 D6
Cross Gdns FRIM GU16 89 H1
Cross Gates Cl BRAK RG12 33 H4
Cross Keys CRAWE RH10 176 G5

Cross Lances Rd HSLW TW3....16 B9
Crossland Rd REDH RH1....120 C5
THHTH CR7....45 K7
Crosslands CHERT KT16....55 J2
Crosslands Av NWDGN UB2....15 P3
Crosslands Pde
 NWDGN UB2 *....16 A3
Crosslands Rd
 HOR/WEW KT19....60 B5
Cross La CHERT KT16....54 F5
 FRIM GU16....89 H1
 HORL RH6....160 D4
Cross Lanes GU GU1....7 J3
Crossley CI BH/WHM TN16....104 C6
Cross Oak La REDH RH1....140 E6
Crosspath CRAWE RH10 *....177 H4
Cross Rd ASC SL5....34 F9
 ASHV GU12....109 K3
 BELMT SM2....61 L8
 CROY/NA CR0....3 F1
 FARN GU14....88 A6
 FELT TW13....24 F7
 KUTN/CMB KT2....9 M4
 KWD/TDW/WH KT20....98 G2
 PUR/KEN CR8....81 K2
 SUT SM1....61 P4
 WEY KT13 *....56 F2
 WIM/MER SW19....43 L1
The Crossroads EHSLY KT24....95 M8
Cross St BARN SW13....18 C7
 FARN GU14....88 E7
 HPTN TW12....25 K8
Crosswater La RFNM GU10....147 H8
Crossway BRAK RG12....32 E3
 NWMAL KT3....42 C5
 WOT/HER KT12....57 K1
Crossways ASHV GU12....108 E5
 BELMT SM2....61 P7
 BH/WHM TN16....84 A9
 CRAWE RH10....177 K4
 EGH TW20....22 A9
 EHSLY KT24....95 M7
 RFNM GU10....165 H12
 SAND/SEL CR2....64 F6
 SUN TW16....39 H2
Crossways Av EGRIN RH19....180 D2
Crossways CI CRAWE RH10....177 J4
Crossways La REIG RH2....99 N8
Crossways Rd BECK BR3....46 G5
 GSHT GU26....165 N8
 MTCM CR4....44 E3
The Crossways BRYLDS KT5 *....41 P9
 COUL/CHIP CR5....81 H8
 HEST TW5....15 P5
 REDH RH1....100 D9
Crosswell CI SHPTN TW17....38 E3
Crossways GU GU2 *....6 E6
Crouch CI BECK BR3....31 P9
Crouch House Rd EDEN TN8....144 E2
Crouch Oak La ADDL KT15....55 N3
Crowberry CI CRAWW RH11....176 D9
Crowborough CI WARL CR6....82 E7
Crowborough Dr WARL CR6....82 E7
Crowborough Rd TOOT SW17....29 K8
Crowcroft CI GUW GU2....111 P1
Crowhurst CI CRAWE RH10....177 P5
Crowhurst La OXTED RH8....123 K9
Crowhurst Md GDST RH9....122 C1
Crowhurst Rd LING RH7....143 K7
Crowhurst Village Rd
 LING RH7....143 L3
Crowland Av HYS/HAR UB3....14 G2
Crowland Rd THHTH CR7 *....45 M5
Crowland Wk MRDN SM4....43 M7
Crowley Crs CROY/NA CR0....63 J4
Crown Ar KUT/HW KT1....8 C5
Crownbourne Ct SUT SM1 *....61 M3
Crown CI DTCH/LGLY SL3....12 G5
 WOT/HER KT12....39 L8
Crown Dr FNM GU9....108 C9
Crown Gdns FLEETN GU51....87 H7
Crown Hts GU GU1....112 C8
Crown HI CROY/NA CR0....2 D4
Crown Hill Ct ASC SL5....34 B6
Crown La FNM GU9....108 C9
 MRDN SM4....43 L4
 STRHM/NOR SW16....30 B8
 VW GU25....36 B7
Crown Lane Gdns
 STRHM/NOR SW16 *....30 B8
Crown Meadow
 DTCH/LGLY SL3....12 F5
Crown Pde MRDN SM4 *....43 M5
Crownpits La GODL GU7....150 D1
Crown PI SHST GU47....50 A8
Crown Ri CHERT KT16....37 K9
Crown Rd EDEN TN8....145 H2
 KUTN/CMB KT2....42 A2
 MRDN SM4....43 L5
 SUT SM1....61 M3
 TWK TW1....26 A2
 VW GU25....36 A7
Crown Rw BRAK RG12....32 F7
Crown Ter RCH/KEW TW9....17 M9
Crown Yd HSLW TW3....16 C8
Crowther Av BTFD TW8....17 L3
Crowther Rd SNWD SE25....46 A5
Crowthorne CI
 WAND/EARL SW18....28 C3
Crowthorne Rd BRAK RG12....32 B9
 SHST GU47....49 M9
Crowthorne Rd North
 BRAK RG12....32 D4

Croxden Wk MRDN SM4....43 N7
Croxted CI DUL SE21....30 D3
Croxted Rd DUL SE21....30 D5
Croyde Av HYS/HAR UB3....14 G2
Croyde CI FARN GU14....88 C1
Croydonbarn La GDST RH9....142 A9
The Croydon F/O
 CROY/NA CR0....2 C7
Croydon Gv CROY/NA CR0....2 A1
Croydon La BNSTD SM7....79 P2
Croydon La South
 BNSTD SM7....79 N3
Croydon Rd BH/WHM TN16....104 C6
 CTHM CR3....102 A2
 MTCM CR4....44 D6
 PGE/AN SE20....46 B3
 REIG RH2....119 N4
 WARL CR6....103 K2
 WLGTN SM6....62 C3
 WWKM BR4....65 L2
Croylands Dr SURB KT6....41 L8
Croysdale Av SUN TW16....39 J4
Crozier Dr SAND/SEL CR2....64 B8
Cruikshank Lea SHST GU47....68 A2
Crunden Rd SAND/SEL CR2....63 M6
Crusader Gdns CROY/NA CR0....3 H6
Crusoe Rd MTCM CR4....44 B1
Crutchfield La HORL RH6....139 L7
 WOT/HER KT12....57 K1
Crystal Palace F/O
 NRWD SE19 *....46 A1
Crystal Palace Pde
 NRWD SE19 *....30 G9
Crystal Palace Park Rd
 SYD SE26....31 H8
Crystal Palace Rd EDUL SE22....30 D2
Crystal Ter NRWD SE19....30 E9
Cubitt St CROY/NA CR0....63 H4
Cubitt Wy WOKN/KNAP GU21....71 K7
Cuckfield CI CRAWW RH11....176 D8
Cuckmere Crs CRAWW RH11....176 C4
Cuckoo La CHOB/PIR GU24....70 D2
Cuckoo V CHOB/PIR GU24....70 D2
Cuda's CI HOR/WEW KT19....60 D3
Cuddington Av
 KWD/TDW/WH KT20....78 G9
Cuddington CI
 KWD/TDW/WH KT20....78 G9
Cuddington Gln
 HOR/WEW KT19....77 N1
Cuddington Park CI
 BNSTD SM7....79 K2
Cuddington Wy BELMT SM2....79 H1
Cudham Dr CROY/NA CR0....65 H8
Cudham La North RSEV TN14....84 G3
Cudham La South RSEV TN14....84 G4
Cudham Rd BH/WHM TN16....84 D9
Cudworth La RDKG RH5....157 H3
Cudworth Pk RDKG RH5 *....157 K4
Cuffs HI CRAWE RH10....177 P9
Cullen CI YTLY GU46....66 G3
Cullens Ms ALDT GU11 *....108 C5
Cullerne Ct EW KT17....60 D2
Cullesden Rd PUR/KEN CR8....81 H1
Cull's Rd RGUW GU3....110 B5
Culmer La MFD/CHID GU8....149 N9
Culmington Rd
 SAND/SEL CR2....63 L6
Culmstock Rd BTSEA SW11....29 K1
Culsac Rd SURB KT6....59 L1
Culver Cft BNFD RG42....32 A1
Culverden Rd BAL SW12....29 M6
Culverden Ter WEY KT13 *....56 F2
Culver Dr OXTED RH8....123 L1
Culverhay ASHTD KT21....77 L5
Culverhouse Gdns
 STRHM/NOR SW16....30 A7
Culverlands Crs ASHV GU12....109 H3
Culver Av SHST GU47....49 P8
Culvers Av CAR SM5....62 B1
Culvers Retreat CAR SM5....44 B9
Culverstone CI HAYES BR2....47 M2
Culvers Wy CAR SM5....62 B2
Cumberland Av GUW GU2....91 N9
Cumberland CI
 HOR/WEW KT19....60 C8
 RYNPK SW20....43 H1
 TWK TW1....26 A2
Cumberland Dr BRAK RG12....32 F2
 CHSGTN KT9....59 L2
 ESH/CLAY KT10....58 G1
Cumberland PI SUN TW16....39 H5
Cumberland Rd ASHF TW15....22 C6
 BARN SW13....18 D6
 CBLY GU15....69 L4
 HAYES BR2....47 L5
 RCH/KEW TW9....17 N6
 SNWD SE25....46 B7
Cumberland Ter
 PGE/AN SE20 *....46 B7
Cumberlow Av SNWD SE25....46 A4
Cumbernauld Gdns
 SUN TW16....39 H1
Cumbrae Gdns SURB KT6....59 K1
Cumbria Ct FARN GU14....88 A3
Cumnor Gdns EW KT17....60 E5
Cumnor Ri PUR/KEN CR8....81 L6
Cumnor Rd BELMT SM2....61 N5
Cumnor Wy BRAK RG12....32 G5
Cunliffe CI EPSOM KT18....77 N5
Cunliffe Rd HOR/WEW KT19....60 D3
Cunliffe St STRHM/NOR SW16....29 L9
Cunningham Av GU GU1....112 E4
Cunningham CI WWKM BR4....65 H1
Cunningham Rd BNSTD SM7....79 N4
Cunnington Rd FARN GU14....88 D3
Cunnington St CHSWK W4....18 A1
Cunworth Ct BRAK RG12....32 A7
Curfew Bell Rd CHERT KT16....37 K8
Curlew CI SAND/SEL CR2....82 A6
Curlew Gdns RGUE GU4....113 H3

Curley Hill Rd LTWR GU18....69 N1
Curling CI COUL/CHIP CR5....81 H9
Curling La CRAWE RH10....111 N7
Curly Bridge CI FARN GU14....68 B8
Curnick's La WNWD SE27....30 D7
Curran Av WLGTN SM6....62 C2
Currie Hill CI WIM/MER SW19....28 C7
Curtis CI BOR GU35....164 B5
 CBLY GU15....69 L1
Curtis Field Rd
 STRHM/NOR SW16....30 A7
Curtis la BOR GU35....164 B5
Curtis Rd DORK RH4....116 F6
 HOR/WEW KT19....60 A3
 HSLWW TW4....24 C3
Curvan CI EW KT17....60 D8
Curzon Av HORS RH12....192 A8
Curzon Dr CHOB/PIR GU24....90 C2
Curzon CI BWEY KT13....56 C5
Curzon Dr FLEETS GU52....106 C1
Curzon Rd THHTH CR7....45 J7
 WEY KT13....56 C5
Cusack CI TWK TW1 *....25 N7
Cuthbert Gdns SNWD SE25....45 N4
Cuthbert Rd ALDT GU11....108 B5
 CROY/NA CR0....2 B2
Cuttinglye La CRAWE RH10....179 H2
Cutts Rd ALDT GU11....88 F8
Cyclamen CI HPTN TW12....25 H9
Cyclamen Wy
 HOR/WEW KT19....60 A4
The Cygnets FELT TW13....24 F7
 STA TW18....22 D9
Cypress Av GU GU14....68 D7
Cypress Av WHTN TW2....25 K3
Cypress CI EWKG RG40....48 E1
Cypress Ct GU GU15....36 D5
Cypress Dr FLEETN GU51....87 J6
Cypress Gdns BROCKY SE4....31 M1
Cypress Gv ASHV GU12....109 K8
Cypress Rd GU GU1....112 A3
 SNWD SE25....45 N3
Cypress Wk EGH TW20....20 C9
Cypress Wy BNSTD SM7....79 H3
 GSHT GU26....165 N9
Cyprians Av CHOB/PIR GU24....91 H1
Cyprus Rd FRIM GU16....69 M8
Cyrena Rd EDUL SE22....30 C2

D

D'Abernon CI ESH/CLAY KT10....58 A3
D'Abernon Dr COB KT11....75 N5
Dacre Rd CROY/NA CR0....44 G8
Dacres Est FSTH SE23 *....31 L6
Dacres Rd FSTH SE23....31 L6
Dade Wy NWDGN UB2....15 P3
Daffodil CI CROY/NA CR0....46 D9
 HPTN TW12....25 H9
Daffodil Dr CHOB/PIR GU24....70 G5
Dafforne Rd TOOT SW17....29 J6
Dagden Rd RGUE GU4....132 C2
Dagley La RGUE GU4....132 B3
Dagmar Rd KUTN/CMB KT2....9 G2
 NWDGN UB2....15 N1
 SNWD SE25....46 B6
Dagnall Pk SNWD SE25....45 N6
Dagnall Rd SNWD SE25....45 N6
Dagnan Rd BAL SW12....29 L3
Dahlia Gdns MTCM CR4....44 F5
Dahomey Rd
 STRHM/NOR SW16....29 M9
Daimler Wy WLGTN SM6....62 G6
Dairy CI BMLY BR1 *....47 P1
 THHTH CR7....45 L3
Dairyfields CRAWW RH11....176 D6
Dairy Gate Rd FARN GU14....88 D7
Dairy La EDEN TN8....124 F5
Dairymans Wk RGUE GU4....92 F9
Daisy CI CROY/NA CR0....46 D9
Daisy La FUL/PGN SW6....19 L8
Daisy Meadow EGH TW20....21 M8
Dakin CI CRAWE RH10....177 M9
The Dakins EGRIN RH19....180 D3
Dakota CI WLGTN SM6....63 H6
Dalberg Rd
 BRXS/STRHM SW2....30 B1
Dalby Rd WAND/EARL SW18....19 N9
Dalcross Bd RG12....32 C7
Dalcross Rd HSLWW TW4....15 N7
Dale Av ADL/WDHM KT15....55 M4
 ASC SL5....34 G6
 HORS RH12....192 E5
 RFNM GU10....127 K6
Dale Gdns SHST GU47....49 L9
Dalegarth Gdns
 PUR/KEN CR8....81 M2
Daleham Av EGH TW20....21 M9
Dale Lodge Rd ASC SL5....34 G6
Dale Park Av CAR SM5....44 B9
Dale Park Rd NRWD SE19....45 L2
Dale Rd PUR/KEN CR8....81 J1
 SUN TW16....39 H1
 SUT SM1....61 K3
 WOT/HER KT12....39 H8
Daleside Rd HOR/WEW KT19....60 B5
 STRHM/NOR SW16....29 L8
Dale St CHSWK W4....18 B3
Dale Vw EPSOM KT18....97 P3
 HASM GU27....184 A5
 WOKN/KNAP GU21....71 N7
Dalewood Gdns
 CRAWE RH10....177 J3
 WPK KT4....60 E1
Dalkeith Rd DUL SE21....30 D4
Dallas Rd CHEAM SM3....61 J5
 SYD SE26....31 J7

Dallas Ter HYS/HAR UB3....15 H1
Dallaway Gdns EGRIN RH19....180 D2
Dalley Ct SHST GU47....67 P1
Dalling Rd HMSMTH W6....18 F2
Dallington CI WOT/HER KT12....57 L5
Dalmain Rd FSTH SE23....31 L4
Dalmally Rd CROY/NA CR0....45 P8
Dalmeny Av
 STRHM/NOR SW16....45 J3
Dalmeny Crs HSLW TW3....16 D9
Dalmeny Rd CAR SM5....62 C4
 NWMAL KT3....42 E5
 WPK KT4....60 F2
Dalmore Av ESH/CLAY KT10....58 F5
Dalmore Rd DUL SE21....30 C4
Dalston CI CBLY GU15....69 M5
Dalton Av MTCM CR4....44 A3
Dalton CI CRAWW RH11....194 D3
 PUR/KEN CR8....81 M4
Damask CI CHOB/PIR GU24....70 E2
Damer Ter WBPTN SW10....19 N5
Dampier Wk CRAWW RH11 *....194 E1
Damsonwood Rd
 NWDGN UB2....16 A1
Danbrook Rd
 STRHM/NOR SW16....44 G2
Danbury Ms WLGTN SM6....62 D3
Dancer Rd FUL/PGN SW6....19 K6
 RCH/KEW TW9....17 N8
Dandridge CI DTCH/LGLY SL3....12 A1
Danebury CROY/NA CR0....65 H5
Danebury Av PUT/ROE SW15....27 L3
Dane Ct WOKS/MYFD GU22....73 K4
Danecourt Gdns CROY/NA CR0....3 K6
Danecroft Rd HNHL SE24....30 D1
Danehurst CI EGH TW20....21 K9
Danehurst Crs SWTR RH13....192 E6
Danehurst St FUL/PGN SW6....19 J6
Danemere St PUT/ROE SW15....18 G8
Danemore La GDST RH9....142 E3
Dane Rd ASHF TW15....23 N9
 WARL CR6....82 D6
 WIM/MER SW19....43 N2
Danesbury Rd FELT TW13....24 C4
Danes CI LHD/OX KT22....76 C3
Danescourt Crs SUT SM1....61 N1
Danesfield RPLY/SEND GU23....93 K3
Danesfield CI WOT/HER KT12....57 K2
Danes HI WOKS/MYFD GU22....11 H5
Daneshill La REDH RH1....120 A4
Daneshill Rd REDH RH1....120 A4
Danes Hill School Dr
 LHD/OX KT22....76 D3
Danesmead COB KT11....58 A8
Danes Wy LHD/OX KT22....7 J4
Danesrood GU GU1 *....7 H5
Danetree CI HOR/WEW KT19....60 A6
Danetree Rd HOR/WEW KT19....60 A6
Daniel CI HSLWW TW4....24 C3
 TOOT SW17....29 H9
Daniell Wy CROY/NA CR0....45 J9
Daniels La WARL CR6....82 G5
Daniel Wy BNSTD SM7....79 M3
Dan Leno Wk FUL/PGN SW6 *....19 M5
Danley La HASM GU27....183 K7
Dan Manson Dr CHSWK W4....18 B7
Danses CI RGUE GU4....113 H3
Danvers Dr FLEETS GU52....106 E2
Danvers St CHEL SW3....19 P4
Danvers Wy CTHM CR3....101 L3
Dapdune Rd GU GU1....6 E3
Daphne CI FLEETS GU52....106 E3
Daphne St WAND/EARL SW18....28 F2
Darby CI CTHM CR3....101 J3
Darby Crs SUN TW16....39 L3
Darby Gdns SUN TW16....39 L3
Darby Green La BLKW GU17....67 M3
Darby Green Rd BLKW GU17....67 L3
Darcy Av WLGTN SM6....62 E3
Darcy CI COUL/CHIP CR5....81 K8
Darcy PI ASHTD KT21....77 M6
D'Arcy Pl HAYES BR2....47 N5
Darcy Rd ASHTD KT21....77 M6
D'Arcy Rd CHEAM SM3....61 H3
Darcy Rd ISLW TW7....16 G6
 STRHM/NOR SW16....44 G3
Darell Rd RCH/KEW TW9....17 N8
Darenth Gdns
 BH/WHM TN16....105 H6
Darenth Wy HORL RH6....140 D8
Darent La BRAK RG12....33 K9
Dare's La EGRIN RH19....106 E5
Darfield Rd BROCKY SE4....31 N1
 RGUE GU4....112 C2
Darfur St PUT/ROE SW15....19 H8
Dargate CI NRWD SE19....45 N6
Darien Rd BTSEA SW11....19 N1
Dark La CHOB/PIR GU24....90 C2
Darlan Rd FUL/PGN SW6....19 K5
Darlaston Rd
 WIM/MER SW19....43 H1
Darley CI ADL/WDHM KT15....55 N4
 CROY/NA CR0....46 D7
Darleydale CRAWW RH11....176 F8
Darleydale CI SHST GU47....49 P7
Darley Dene Ct
 ADL/WDHM KT15 *....55 N5
Darley Dr NWMAL KT3....42 B3
Darley Gdns MRDN SM4....43 M7
Darleys CI BTSEA SW11 *....29 J2
Darlington Rd WNWD SE27....30 C8
Darmaine CI SAND/SEL CR2....63 M6
Darnley Pk WEY KT13....56 D2
Darracott CI CBLY GU15....51 J9
Darrell CI DTCH/LGLY SL3....12 C2
Darrell Rd EDUL SE22....30 D2
Darset Av FLEETN GU51....86 G5
Dart CI DTCH/LGLY SL3....12 F4
Dartmouth Av
 WOKN/KNAP GU21....72 C3
Dartmouth CI BRAK RG12....32 G4
Dartmouth Pl CHSWK W4....18 C4

FSTH SE23....31 K5
Dartmouth Rd HAYES BR2....47 N8
 SYD SE26....31 J6
Dartnell Av BF/WBF KT14....73 N1
Dartnell CI BF/WBF KT14....73 N1
Dartnell Crs BF/WBF KT14....73 N1
Dartnell Park Rd
 BF/WBF KT14....73 M1
Dartnell PI BF/WBF KT14....73 M1
Dartnell Rd CROY/NA CR0....46 B8
Dartrey Wk WBPTN SW10 *....19 N5
Dart Rd FARN GU14....87 P1
Darvel CI WOKN/KNAP GU21....71 N5
Darvill Hts FNM GU9....5 H3
Darvills La FNM GU9....5 H3
Darwall Dr ASC SL5....33 M3
Darwin CI HORS RH12....192 E6
Darwin Gv ALDT GU11....108 E3
Darwin Rd EA W5....17 J5
Daryngton Dr GU GU1....112 F5
Dashwood CI BF/WBF KT14....73 M2
 BRAK RG12....32 F2
 DTCH/LGLY SL3....12 A2
Dashwood Lang Rd
 ADL/WDHM KT15....56 A3
Dassett Rd WNWD SE27....30 C8
Datchet Rd CAT SE6....31 N6
 DTCH/LGLY SL3....12 D8
 Mtsdl SL4....20 F1
Dault Rd WAND/EARL SW18....28 F2
Daux HI HORS RH12....192 A2
Davenant St TEDD TW11 *....25 P9
Davenport Rd BRAK RG12....32 C2
Daventry CI DTCH/LGLY SL3....13 K6
Daventry Ct BNFD RG42....32 D3
David CI HYS/HAR UB3....14 F5
David Rd DTCH/LGLY SL3....13 K7
Davidson Rd CROY/NA CR0....3 G1
David's Rd FSTH SE23....31 K4
David Twigg CI KUTN/CMB KT2....8 E2
Davies CI CROY/NA CR0....46 C7
 GODL GU7....131 K6
Davies Wk ISLW TW7....16 D6
Davis CI CRAWW RH11....194 D1
Davis Gdns SHST GU47....68 A1
Davis Rd CHSGTN KT9....59 N3
 WEY KT13....56 A7
Davos CI WOKS/MYFD GU22....72 C8
Dawell Dr BH/WHM TN16....84 A6
Dawes Av ISLW TW7....25 P1
Dawes Ct ESH/CLAY KT10....58 B3
Dawes Rd FUL/PGN SW6....19 K5
Dawley Ride DTCH/LGLY SL3....13 J6
Dawnay Rd HYS/HAR UB3....14 G2
Dawlish Av
 WAND/EARL SW18....28 E5
Dawnay CI ASC SL5....33 P2
Dawnay Gdns
 WAND/EARL SW18....28 E5
Dawnay Rd CBLY GU15....50 D9
 GT/LBKH KT23....96 B6
 WAND/EARL SW18....28 E5
Dawn CI HSLWW TW4....15 N7
Dawney HI CHOB/PIR GU24....90 A1
Dawneys Rd CHOB/PIR GU24....90 A1
Dawn Redwood CI
 DTCH/LGLY SL3....12 E8
Dawsmere CI CBLY GU15....69 L3
Dawson Rd BF/WBF KT14....55 P9
 KUT/HW KT1....8 G6
Daybrook Rd
 WIM/MER SW19....43 M3
Daylesford Av
 PUT/ROE SW15....18 E9
Daymerslea Rdg....97 J1
Day's Acre SAND/SEL CR2....63 P7
Daysbrook Rd
 BRXS/STRHM SW2....30 A2
Dayseys HI REDH RH1....141 J5
Dayspring GUW GU2....111 P1
Deacon CI COB KT11....75 K8
 PUR/KEN CR8....81 L3
Deacon CI HORL RH7 *....143 J9
Deacon Fld GUW GU2....111 N4
Deacon Rd KUTN/CMB KT2....9 F3
Deacons Wk HPTN TW12....25 H1
Deadbrook La ASHV GU12....108 G3
Deal Rd TOOT SW17....29 K9
Dealtry Rd PUT/ROE SW15....18 G9
Dean CI WOKS/MYFD GU22....73 J5
Deanery Rd EDEN TN8....124 G5
 GODL GU7....131 L8
Deanhill Ct
 MORT/ESHN SW14 *....17 P9
Deanhill Rd
 MORT/ESHN SW14....17 P9
Dean La REDH RH1....100 E4
Deanoak La REIG RH2....139 K6
Dean Pde CBLY GU15 *....51 H9
Dean Rd CROY/NA CR0....63 M3
 GODL GU7....131 K7
 HPTN TW12....25 H8
 HSLW TW3....25 H1
Deans CI CHSWK W4....17 P4
 CROY/NA CR0....3 J5
 KWD/TDW/WH KT20....98 F4
Deans Ct BFOR GU20....52 D6
Deansfield CTHM CR3....101 P5
Deansgate BRAK RG12....32 C8
Deans Gate CI FSTH SE23....31 L5
Deans La KWD/TDW/WH KT20....98 F5
 REDH RH1....121 J4
Deans Rd REDH RH1....120 E1
 SUT SM1....61 M2
Dean Wk GT/LBKH KT23....96 B6
De'Arn Gdns MTCM CR4....44 A4
Debden CI KUTN/CMB KT2....26 C8
Deborah CI ISLW TW7....16 E6

De Broome Rd FELT TW13 ....24 D4
De Burgh Gdns
KWD/TDW/WH KT20 ....79 H8
De Burgh Pk BNSTD SM7 ....79 M4
Deburgh Rd WIM/MER SW19 ...43 N1
Decimus Cl THHTH CR7 * 45 M5
Decoutere Cl FLEETS GU52 ....106 E1
Dedisham Cl CRAWE RH10 ....177 K6
Dedswell Dr RGUE GU4 ....93 L9
Deedman Cl ASHV GU12 ....109 J4
Deepcut Bridge Rd
FRIM GU16 ....69 M7
Deepdale BRAK RG12 ....32 C5
WIM/MER SW19 ....28 A7
Deepdale Av HAYES BR2 ....47 M5
Deep Dene HASM GU27 ....183 P4
Deepdene RFNM GU10 ....127 P7
Deepdene Av CROY/NA CR0 ....3 K6
RDKG RH5 ....117 J7
Deepdene Avenue Rd
DORK RH4 ....117 J5
Deepdene Dr RDKG RH5 ....117 J6
Deepdene Gdns
BRXS/STRHM SW2 ....30 A3
DORK RH4 ....117 H6
Deepdene V DORK RH4 ....117 J5
Deepdene Wd RDKG RH5 ....117 K7
Deepfield Rd BRAK RG12 ....32 F3
Deepfields HORL RH6 ....140 B8
Deepfield Wy
COUL/CHIP CR5 ....80 C5
Deep Pool La CHOB/PIR GU24 ....71 N2
Deeprose Cl GUW GU2 ....111 P1
Deepwell Cl ISLW TW7 ....16 G6
Deep Well Dr CBLY GU15 ....68 G3
Deerbarn Rd GUW GU2 ....111 P4
Deerbrook Rd HNHL SE24 ....30 C4
Deerhurst Cl FELT TW13 ....24 B7
Deerhurst Crs HPTN TW12 ....25 K8
Deerhurst Rd
STRHM/NOR SW16 ....30 A8
Deerings Rd REIG RH2 ....119 M5
Deerleap BOR GU35 * 164 F7
Deer Leap LTWR GU18 ....52 A9
Deerleap La RSEV TN14 ....85 P2
Deerleap Rd DORK RH4 ....116 B8
Dee Rd RCH/KEW TW9 ....17 M9
Deer Park Cl KUTN/CMB KT2 ....41 P1
Deer Park Gdns MTCM CR4 * ...43 P5
Deer Park Rd
WIM/MER SW19 ....43 M3
Deer Park Wy WWKM BR4 ....65 M1
Deer Rock Hl BRAK RG12 ....32 E7
Deer Rock Rd CBLY GU15 ....69 H1
Deers Farm Cl
RPLY/SEND GU23 ....74 A5
Deerswood Cl CRAWW RH11 ..176 E4
CTHM CR3 ....102 A4
Deerswood Rd
CRAWW RH11 ....176 E4
Deeside Rd TOOT SW17 ....28 G6
Dee Wy HOR/WEW KT19 ....60 C8
Defiant Wy WLGTN SM6 ....62 G6
Defoe Av RCH/KEW TW9 ....17 N5
Defoe Cl TOOT SW17 ....29 H9
Defoe Pl TOOT SW17 ....29 H5
De Frene Rd SYD SE26 ....31 L7
De Havilland Dr WEY KT13 ....56 A9
De Havilland Rd HEST TW5 ....15 L5
De Havilland Wy
STWL/WRAY TW19 ....22 G2
Dekker Rd DUL SE21 ....30 F2
Delabole Rd REDH RH1 ....100 G9
Delaford St FUL/PGN SW6 ....19 J5
Delagarde Rd
BH/WHM TN16 ....104 G6
Delamare Crs CROY/NA CR0 ....46 C7
Delamere Rd REIG RH2 ....119 M9
RYNPK SW20 ....43 H2
Delaporte Cl EW KT17 ....78 C1
De Lara Wy
WOKN/KNAP GU21 ....10 A6
De La Warr Rd EGRIN RH19 ....180 E2
Delawyk Crs HNHL SE24 ....30 E2
Delcombe Av WPK KT4 ....42 G9
Delderfield ASHTD KT21 ....77 K9
Delfont Cl CRAWE RH10 ....177 N7
Delia St WAND/EARL SW18 ....28 E3
Delius Gdns SWTR RH13 ....192 G6
Dellbow Rd
EBED/NFELT TW14 ....24 C1
Dell Campus BRAK RG12 * 32 A3
Dell Cl HASM GU27 ....184 B3
LHD/OX KT22 ....96 D3
RDKG RH5 ....97 J7
WLGTN SM6 ....62 E3
Deller St BNFD RG42 ....32 B1
Dellfield Cl BECK BR3 ....47 J2
Dell Gv FRIM GU16 ....69 H6
Dell La EW KT17 ....60 E4
Dell Rd EW KT17 ....60 E5
EWKG RG40 ....48 E6
WDR/YW UB7 ....14 B1
The Dell BECK BR3 * 46 G1
BTFD TW8 ....17 J4
EBED/NFELT TW14 ....24 C3
EGRIN RH19 ....180 G2
FNM GU9 ....107 N7
HORL RH6 ....139 N8
HORL RH6 ....140 D9
KWD/TDW/WH KT20 ....98 G1
NRWD SE19 ....45 P2
REIG RH2 * 119 L4
WOKN/KNAP GU21 ....72 A8
YTLY GU46 ....66 G3
Dell Wk NWMAL KT3 ....42 C3
Delmey Cl CROY/NA CR0 ....3 K5
Delorme St HMSMTH W6 ....19 H4
Delta Cl CHOB/PIR GU24 ....53 M8
WPK KT4 ....60 C2
Delta Dr HORL RH6 ....159 K3
Delta Rd CHOB/PIR GU24 ....53 M8
WOKN/KNAP GU21 ....11 G1
WPK KT4 ....60 C2
Delta Wy EGH TW20 ....36 G2
Delves KWD/TDW/WH KT20 ....99 H1
Delville Cl FARN GU14 ....87 P4
Delvino Rd FUL/PGN SW6 ....19 L6
Demesne Rd WLGTN SM6 ....62 F3
De Montfort Pde
STRHM/NOR SW16 * 29 P6
De Montfort Rd
STRHM/NOR SW16 ....29 N5
De Morgan Rd FUL/PGN SW6 ...19 M8
Dempster Rd
WAND/EARL SW18 ....28 F1
Denbigh Cl SUT SM1 ....61 K4
Denbigh Gdns
RCHPK/HAM TW10 ....26 E1
Denbigh Rd HASM GU27 ....184 E5
HSLW TW3 ....16 B7
Denby Rd COB KT11 ....75 L1
Denchers Plat CRAWW RH11 ..176 G2
Dencliffe ASHF TW15 * 23 K8
Den Cl BECK BR3 ....47 K5
Dendy St BAL SW12 ....29 K4
Dene Av HSLW TW3 ....15 P8
Dene Cl ASHV GU12 ....109 L4
BRAK RG12 ....32 E2
CBLY GU15 ....51 J9
COUL/CHIP CR5 ....80 A8
HASM GU27 ....184 D4
HAYES BR2 ....47 M9
HORL RH6 ....140 A8
RFNM GU10 ....127 P7
WPK KT4 ....60 D1
Denefield Dr PUR/KEN CR8 ....81 M4
Dene Gdns THDIT KT7 ....58 G1
Denehurst Gdns
RCHPK/HAM TW10 ....17 N9
WHTN TW2 ....25 L3
Dene La RFNM GU10 ....127 P7
Dene La West RFNM GU10 ....127 P8
Dene Pl WOKN/KNAP GU21 ....71 P7
Dene Rd ASHTD KT21 ....77 M8
FARN GU14 ....88 B4
GU GU1 ....7 G4
Dene St DORK RH4 ....117 H7
Dene Street Gdns
DORK RH4 ....117 H7
The Dene BELMT SM2 ....61 K9
CROY/NA CR0 ....64 D3
E/WMO/HCT KT8 ....39 P6
Dene Tye CRAWE RH10 ....177 M4
Dene Wk RFNM GU10 ....127 P7
Denewood EW KT17 * 78 C2
Denfield DORK RH4 ....117 H9
Denham Crs MTCM CR4 ....44 B5
Denham Dr YTLY GU46 ....67 H3
Denham Gv BRAK RG12 * 32 E7
Denham Pl RDKG RH5 * 137 K9
Denham Rd
EBED/NFELT TW14 ....24 D3
EGH TW20 ....21 M7
EW KT17 ....78 D1
Denholm Gdns RGUE GU4 ....112 E2
Denison Rd FELT TW13 ....24 A7
WIM/MER SW19 ....28 G9
Denleigh Gdns THDIT KT7 * 40 E7
Denly Wy LTWR GU18 ....52 C8
Denman Cl FLEETN GU51 ....87 J6
Denman Dr ASHF TW15 ....23 L9
ESH/CLAY KT10 ....58 G4
Denmans CRAWE RH10 ....177 N4
Denmark Av WIM/MER SW19 ..43 J1
Denmark Ct MRDN SM4 ....43 L6
Denmark Gdns CAR SM5 ....62 B2
Denmark Rd BMLY BR1 ....47 P2
CAR SM5 ....62 B2
KUT/HW KT1 ....8 E7
SNWD SE25 ....46 B6
WHTN TW2 ....25 L6
WIM/MER SW19 ....28 A9
Denmark Sq ASHV GU12 ....108 G4
Denmark St ASHV GU12 ....108 F4
Denmead Ct BRAK RG12 ....32 G7
Denmead Rd CROY/NA CR0 ....2 B1
Dennan Rd SURB KT6 ....41 M9
Denne Pde HORS RH12 ....192 B9
Denne Rd CRAWW RH11 ....176 G6
HORS RH12 ....192 B9
Dennettsland Rd EDEN TN8 ....124 G5
Denning Av CROY/NA CR0 ....63 J4
Denning Cl FLEETS GU52 ....86 E8
HPTN TW12 ....24 G9
The Denningtons WPK KT4 ....60 C1
Dennis Cl REDH RH1 ....120 A3
Dennis Park Crs RYNPK SW20 ..43 J2
Dennis Reeve Cl MTCM CR4 ....44 B2
Dennis Rd E/WMO/HCT KT8 ....40 C5
Dennistoun Cl CBLY GU15 ....68 F3
Dennis Wy GU GU1 ....92 C9
Denny Rd DTCH/LGLY SL3 * 12 D2
Den Rd HAYES BR2 ....47 K4
Densham Dr PUR/KEN CR8 ....81 J3
Densole Cl BECK BR3 * 46 E2
Denton Cl REDH RH1 ....140 C1
Denton Gv WOT/HER KT12 ....57 N1
Denton Rd TWK TW1 ....26 C2
Denton St WAND/EARL SW18 ....28 E2
Denton Wy FRIM GU16 ....68 F6
WOKN/KNAP GU21 ....71 N6
Dents Gv KWD/TDW/WH KT20 ..99 K8
Dents Rd BTSEA SW11 ....29 J2
Denvale Trade Pk MTCM CR4 ..43 P5
Denvale Wk
WOKN/KNAP GU21 ....71 N7
Denzil Rd GUW GU2 ....6 B5
Deodar Rd PUT/ROE SW15 ....19 J9
Departures Rd HORL RH6 ....159 J4
Depot Rd CRAWW RH11 ....176 G2
EW KT17 ....78 C2
HSLW TW3 ....16 D8
SWTR RH13 ....192 D8
Derby Arms Rd EPSOM KT18 ....78 D6
Derby Cl EPSOM KT18 ....78 F8
Derby Hl FSTH SE23 ....31 K5
Derby Hill Crs FSTH SE23 ....31 K5
Derby Rd BRYLDS KT5 ....41 N9
CROY/NA CR0 ....2 B2
GUW GU2 ....111 M5
HASM GU27 ....184 C3
HSLW TW3 ....16 B9
MORT/ESHN SW14 ....17 P9
SUT SM1 ....61 K5
WIM/MER SW19 ....43 L1
Derbyshire Gn BNFD RG42 ....33 H1
Derby Stables Rd
EPSOM KT18 ....78 C6
Derek Av HOR/WEW KT19 ....59 N5
WLGTN SM6 ....62 D2
Derek Cl HOR/WEW KT19 ....59 P4
Derek Walcott Cl
HNHL SE24 * 30 C1
Deri Dene Cl
STWL/WRAY TW19 * 23 H2
Dering Pl CROY/NA CR0 ....63 L3
Dering Rd CROY/NA CR0 ....63 L3
Derinton Rd TOOT SW17 ....29 K7
Derley Rd NWDGN UB2 ....15 L1
Deronda Rd HNHL SE24 ....30 C4
De Ros Pl EGH TW20 ....21 M9
Deroy Cl CAR SM5 ....62 B5
Derrick Av SAND/SEL CR2 ....63 L8
Derrick Rd BECK BR3 ....46 F4
Derry Cl ASHV GU12 ....109 H1
Derrydown
WOKS/MYFD GU22 ....91 P1
Derry Rd CROY/NA CR0 ....62 G2
FARN GU14 ....68 B7
Derwent Av ASHV GU12 ....109 H2
PUT/ROE SW15 ....27 K7
Derwent Cl ADL/WDHM KT15 ....55 P4
CRAWW RH11 ....176 C6
EBED/NFELT TW14 ....24 A4
ESH/CLAY KT10 ....58 E5
FARN GU14 ....87 P3
FNM GU9 ....107 L8
HORS RH12 ....192 G4
Derwent Dr PUR/KEN CR8 ....81 M3
Derwent Rd EA W5 ....17 J1
EGH TW20 ....21 N9
LTWR GU18 ....52 B9
PGE/AN SE20 ....46 A3
RYNPK SW20 ....43 H7
WHTN TW2 ....25 J2
Derwent Yd EA W5 * 17 J1
Desborough Cl SHPTN TW17 ....38 C8
Desenfans Rd DUL SE21 ....30 F2
Desford Wy ASHF TW15 ....23 J5
Desmond Tutu Dr FSTH SE23 ....31 M4
Detillens La OXTED RH8 ....103 N9
Detling Rd CRAWW RH11 ....194 F1
Dettingen Crs FRIM GU16 ....69 M8
Dettingen Rd FRIM GU16 ....69 N8
Devana End CAR SM5 ....62 B2
Devas Rd RYNPK SW20 ....42 G2
Devenish La ASC SL5 ....34 D9
Devenish Rd ASC SL5 ....34 D7
Deveraux Cl BECK BR3 ....47 J6
De Vere Cl WLGTN SM6 ....62 G6
De Vere Ms KENS W8 * 19 N1
Devereux La BARN SW13 ....18 F5
Devereux Rd BTSEA SW11 ....29 J2
Deverills Wy DTCH/LGLY SL3 ....12 G2
Devey Cl KUTN/CMB KT2 ....42 D1
The Devil's Hwy CWTH RG45 ....49 J4
Devil's La EGH TW20 ....21 P9
LIPH GU30 ....183 H7
Devitt Cl ASHTD KT21 ....77 N5
Devoil Cl RGUE GU4 ....112 F1
Devoke Wy WOT/HER KT12 ....57 M1
Devon Av WHTN TW2 ....25 K4
Devon Bank GUW GU2 ....112 A8
Devon Cl FLEETN GU51 ....87 H3
HOR/WEW KT19 ....77 N1
PUR/KEN CR8 ....81 N5
SHST GU47 ....67 P1
Devon Crs REDH RH1 ....119 P5
Devoncroft Gdns TWK TW1 ....25 P3
Devonhurst Pl CHSWK W4 * 18 B3
Devon Rd ALDT GU11 ....88 A8
BELMT SM2 ....61 J7
REDH RH1 ....120 E1
WOT/HER KT12 ....57 L3
Devonshire Av BELMT SM2 ....61 N6
KWD/TDW/WH KT20 ....118 A2
WOKN/KNAP GU21 ....72 G3
Devonshire Ct FELT TW13 * 24 C5
Devonshire Dr CBLY GU15 ....69 H1
SURB KT6 ....41 K9
Devonshire Gdns CHSWK W4 ....18 A5
Devonshire Pl ALDT GU11 ....108 B5
KENS W8 ....19 M1
Devonshire Rd BELMT SM2 ....61 N6
CAR SM5 ....62 C3
CHSWK W4 ....18 C3
CROY/NA CR0 ....45 M8
EA W5 ....17 J1
FELT TW13 ....24 F6
FSTH SE23 ....31 L3
SWTR RH13 ....192 C8
WEY KT13 * 56 C3
WIM/MER SW19 ....44 A1
Devonshire Sq HAYES BR2 ....47 P5
Devonshire St CHSWK W4 ....18 C3
Devonshire Wy
CROY/NA CR0 ....64 F1
Devon Wy CHSGTN KT9 ....59 J3
HOR/WEW KT19 ....59 P4
Devon Waye HEST TW5 ....15 P5
Dewar Cl CRAWW RH11 * 176 B6
Dewey La BRXS/STRHM SW2 ....30 B2
Dewey St TOOT SW17 ....29 J8
Dewhurst Rd HMSMTH W6 ....19 H1
Dewlands GDST RH9 ....122 C2
Dewlands Cl CRAN GU6 ....153 H9
Dewlands La CRAN GU6 ....153 H9
Dew Pond Cl SWTR RH13 ....192 E7
Dewsbury Gdns WPK KT4 ....60 E2
Dexter Dr EGRIN RH19 ....180 D3
Dexter Wy FLEETN GU51 ....87 H3
Diamedes Av
STWL/WRAY TW19 ....22 G3
Diamond Hl CBLY GU15 ....68 G1
Diamond Rdg CBLY GU15 ....68 F1
Diamond Wy FARN GU14 ....88 A7
Diana Gdns SURB KT6 ....59 M1
Dianthus Cl CHERT KT16 ....37 J8
Dianthus Ct
WOKS/MYFD GU22 ....10 B6
Dibdin Cl SUT SM1 ....61 L2
Dibdin Rd SUT SM1 ....61 L2
Diceland Rd BNSTD SM7 ....79 K5
Dickens Cl EGRIN RH19 ....180 B2
HYS/HAR UB3 ....14 G2
RCHPK/HAM TW10 ....26 D5
Dickens Dr ADL/WDHM KT15 ....55 K5
Dickenson Rd FELT TW13 ....24 D8
Dickenson's La SNWD SE25 ....46 A7
Dickenson's Pl SNWD SE25 ....46 A7
Dickens Pl DTCH/LGLY SL3 ....13 J6
Dickens Rd CRAWE RH10 ....176 G8
Dickens Wy YTLY GU46 ....66 G4
Dickens Wood Cl NRWD SE19 ..45 K1
Dickerage Hl NWMAL KT3 ....42 A3
Dickerage La NWMAL KT3 ....42 A4
Dickerage Rd KUT/HW KT1 ....42 A2
Dick Turpin Wy
EBED/NFELT TW14 ....15 H9
Digby Pl CROY/NA CR0 ....3 K5
Digby Wy BF/WBF KT14 ....74 B1
Digdens Ri EPSOM KT18 ....78 A4
Dighton Rd
WAND/EARL SW18 ....28 F1
Dillwyn Cl SYD SE26 ....31 M7
Dilston Rd LHD/OX KT22 ....76 G8
Dilton Gdns PUT/ROE SW15 ....27 M4
Dimes Pl HMSMTH W6 ....18 F2
Dingle Cl CRAWW RH11 ....176 E4
Dingle Rd ASHF TW15 ....23 L8
The Dingle CRAWW RH11 ....176 E5
Dingley La STRHM/NOR SW16 ..29 N5
Dingley Wy FARN GU14 ....88 C7
Dingwall Av CROY/NA CR0 ....2 D4
Dingwall Rd CAR SM5 ....62 B7
CROY/NA CR0 ....2 E3
WAND/EARL SW18 ....28 F3
Dinorben Av FLEETS GU52 ....86 E8
Dinorben Beeches
FLEETS GU52 ....86 E8
Dinorben Cl FLEETS GU52 ....86 F8
Dinsdale Cl
WOKS/MYFD GU22 ....11 F5
Dinsdale Gdns SNWD SE25 ....45 N5
Dinsmore Rd BAL SW12 ....29 L3
Dinton Rd KUTN/CMB KT2 ....41 M1
WIM/MER SW19 ....28 G9
Dippenhall Rd RFNM GU10 ....126 F3
Dippenhall St RFNM GU10 ....106 E9
Dirdene Cl EW KT17 ....78 D1
Dirdene Gdns EW KT17 ....78 D1
Dirdene Gv EW KT17 ....78 C1
Dirtham La EHSLY KT24 ....95 K9
Dirty La EGRIN RH19 ....181 K5
Disbrowe Rd HMSMTH W6 ....19 J4
Discovery Pk BRAK RG12 * 32 F9
Disraeli Ct DTCH/LGLY SL3 ....12 F4
Disraeli Rd PUT/ROE SW15 ....19 J9
Distillery La HMSMTH W6 ....18 G3
Distillery Rd HMSMTH W6 ....18 G3
Ditches La COUL/CHIP CR5 ....80 F6
Ditchfield La EWKG RG40 ....48 C1
Ditchling BRAK RG12 ....32 C8
Ditchling Hl CRAWW RH11 ....176 F8
Ditton Cl THDIT KT7 ....40 G8
Dittoncroft Cl CROY/NA CR0 ....63 N3
Ditton Grange Cl SURB KT6 ....41 K9
Ditton Grange Dr SURB KT6 ....41 K9
Ditton Hl SURB KT6 ....41 J9
Ditton Hill Rd SURB KT6 ....41 J9
Ditton Lawn THDIT KT7 ....40 G9
Ditton Park Rd
DTCH/LGLY SL3 ....12 C4
Ditton Pl PGE/AN SE20 * 46 B2
Ditton Reach THDIT KT7 ....41 H7
Ditton Rd DTCH/LGLY SL3 ....12 B6
NWDGN UB2 ....15 P3
SURB KT6 ....41 L9
The Dittons EWKG RG40 ....48 C3
Dixon Dr WEY KT13 ....56 B8
Dixon Pl WWKM BR4 ....47 H9
Dixon Rd SNWD SE25 ....45 N4
Dobbins Pl CRAWW RH11 ....176 A6
Dobson Rd CRAWW RH11 ....176 G2
Dockett Eddy La
SHPTN TW17 ....38 B8
Dock Rd BTFD TW8 * 17 K5
Dockwell Cl
EBED/NFELT TW14 ....15 J9
Doctors Cl SYD SE26 ....31 K8
Doctors La CTHM CR3 ....101 J4
Dodbrooke Rd WNWD SE27 ....30 B6
Dodds Crs BF/WBF KT14 ....73 M3
Dodd's La WOKS/MYFD GU22 ....73 L3
Dodds Pk
BRKHM/BTCW RH3 ....117 P7
Dodsells Well EWKG RG40 ....48 D1
Doel Cl WIM/MER SW19 ....43 N1
Dogflud Wy FNM GU9 ....5 H2
Doggett Rd CAT SE6 ....31 P3
Doggetts Cl EDEN TN8 ....144 G5
Doghurst Av WDR/YW UB7 ....14 D5
Doghurst Dr WDR/YW UB7 ....14 D5
Doghurst La COUL/CHIP CR5 ....80 B9
Dolby Rd FUL/PGN SW6 ....19 K7
Dolby Ter HORL RH6 * 158 B6
Dollary Pde KUT/HW KT1 * 9 K6
Dollis Cl CRAWE RH10 ....177 M6
Dollis Dr FNM GU9 ....5 J1
Dolman Rd CHSWK W4 ....18 B2
Dolphin Cl HASM GU27 ....183 P4
SURB KT6 ....41 K7
Dolphin Ct BRAK RG12 ....32 E5
STA TW18 ....22 D6
Dolphin Ct North STA TW18 * ...22 D6
Dolphin Rd SUN TW16 ....38 G2
Dolphin Rd North SUN TW16 ....38 F2
Dolphin Rd South SUN TW16 ....38 F2
Dolphin Rd West SUN TW16 ....38 G2
Dolphin Sq CHSWK W4 * 18 C5
Dolphin St KUT/HW KT1 ....8 D4
Doman Rd CBLY GU15 ....68 C4
Dome Hl CTHM CR3 ....101 N7
Dome Hill Pk SYD SE26 ....30 G7
Dome Hill Peak CTHM CR3 ....101 N6
Dome Wy REDH RH1 ....120 B4
Dominion Cl HSLW TW3 ....16 D7
Dominion Rd CROY/NA CR0 ....45 P8
NWDGN UB2 ....15 N1
Donald Rd CROY/NA CR0 ....45 H7
Donald Woods Gdns
BRYLDS KT5 ....59 P1
Doncaster Wk
CRAWE RH10 * 177 K7
Doncastle Rd BRAK RG12 ....32 B4
Doneraile St FUL/PGN SW6 ....19 H7
Donkey Aly EDUL SE22 ....31 H3
Donkey La HORL RH6 ....159 N5
RDKG RH5 ....135 M5
WDR/YW UB7 ....13 N2
Donlan Dr FARN GU14 ....87 N6
Donnafields CHOB/PIR GU24 ...70 G5
Donne Cl CRAWE RH10 ....177 L3
Donne Gdns
WOKS/MYFD GU22 ....73 J4
Donne Pl MTCM CR4 ....44 D5
Donnington Cl CBLY GU15 ....68 D4
Donnington Ct
CRAWW RH11 ....176 C8
Donnington Rd WPK KT4 ....60 E1
Donnybrook BRAK RG12 ....32 C8
Donnybrook Rd
STRHM/NOR SW16 ....44 E1
Donovan Cl HOR/WEW KT19 ....60 B8
Doods Park Rd REIG RH2 ....119 N5
Doods Pl REIG RH2 * 119 N4
Doods Rd REIG RH2 ....119 N4
Doods Wy REIG RH2 ....119 P4
Doomsday Gdn SWTR RH13 ....192 E9
Doone Cl TEDD TW11 ....25 P9
Doral Wy CAR SM5 ....62 B4
Doran Dr REDH RH1 ....119 P5
Doran Gdns REDH RH1 * 119 P5
Dora Rd WIM/MER SW19 ....28 D8
Dora's Green La RFNM GU10 ....126 F3
Dorcas Ct CBLY GU15 ....68 D5
Dorchester Ct HNHL SE24 ....30 D1
WOKS/MYFD GU22 ....11 H2
Dorchester Dr
EBED/NFELT TW14 ....23 P2
HNHL SE24 ....30 D1
Dorchester Gv CHSWK W4 ....18 C4
Dorchester Ms TWK TW1 ....26 B2
Dorchester Pde
STRHM/NOR SW16 * 29 P5
Dorchester Rd MRDN SM4 ....43 M8
WEY KT13 ....56 D2
WPK KT4 ....42 G9
Doreen Cl FARN GU14 ....67 P8
Dore Gdns MRDN SM4 ....43 M8
Dorian Ct WARL CR6 * 82 B8
Dorian Dr ASC SL5 ....34 E2
Doria Rd FUL/PGN SW6 ....19 K7
Doric Dr KWD/TDW/WH KT20 ....79 K9
Dorien Rd RYNPK SW20 ....43 H3
Dorin Ct WARL CR6 * 82 B9
WOKS/MYFD GU22 ....73 J4
Doris Rd ASHF TW15 ....23 N9
Dorking Cl WPK KT4 ....61 H1
Dorking Rd ASHTD KT21 ....77 P4
EPSOM KT18 ....78 A4
GT/LBKH KT23 ....96 B7
HORS RH12 ....191 P2
KWD/TDW/WH KT20 ....98 D8
LHD/OX KT22 ....97 H3
RGUE GU4 ....133 H2
SHGR GU5 ....134 F1
Dorlcote Rd
WAND/EARL SW18 ....28 G3
Dorling Dr EW KT17 ....78 D1
Dorly Cl SHPTN TW17 ....38 G5
Dormans CRAWW RH11 ....176 D6
Dormans Av LING RH7 ....162 F2
Dorman's Cl LING RH7 ....162 F4
Dormans High St LING RH7 ....162 F5
Dormans Park Rd
EGRIN RH19 ....162 C9
Dormans Rd LING RH7 ....162 F2
Dormans Station Rd
LING RH7 ....162 F7
Dormay St WAND/EARL SW18 ..28 E1
Dormer Cl CWTH RG45 ....49 L4
Dormers Cl GODL GU7 ....131 K6
Dorncliffe Rd FUL/PGN SW6 ....19 J7
Dorney Gv WEY KT13 ....56 D1
Dorney Wy HSLWW TW4 ....24 F1
Dornford Gdns
COUL/CHIP CR5 ....81 L8
Dornton Rd BAL SW12 ....29 L5
SAND/SEL CR2 ....63 N4
Dorrington Wy BECK BR3 ....47 J6
Dorrit Crs RGUW GU3 ....111 L3
Dorset Av EGRIN RH19 ....162 B9
NWDGN UB2 ....16 A2
Dorset Dr WOKS/MYFD GU22 ....11 K4
Dorset Gdns EGRIN RH19 ....162 B9
MTCM CR4 ....45 H5
Dorset Rd ASHF TW15 ....22 G6
ASHV GU12 ....109 J1

BECK BR3 .....46 D4
BELMT SM2 .....61 L8
EA W5 .....17 J1
MTCM CR4 .....44 A3
WIM/MER SW19 .....43 L2
Dorset Wy BF/WBF KT14 .....159 P6
WHTN TW2 .....24 D1
Dorset Waye HEST TW5 .....15 P5
Dorton Rd RPLY/SEND GU23 .....93 M1
Dorville Crs HMSMTH W6 .....18 F1
Douai Cl FARN GU14 .....88 E3
Douai Gv HPTN TW12 .....40 C2
Douglas Av NWMAL KT3 .....42 F5
Douglas Cl RCUE GU4 .....92 C5
WLGTN SM6 .....62 G5
Douglas Ct CTHM CR3 * 101 L2
Douglas Dr CROY/NA CR0 .....64 G2
GODL GU7 .....131 M8
Douglas La RFNM GU10 .....127 N8
Douglas La
STWL/WRAY TW19 .....21 L1
Douglas Ms BNSTD SM7 .....79 K5
Douglas Rd ADL/WDHM KT15 .....55 M2
ESH/CLAY KT10 .....58 B1
HSLW TW3 .....16 B8
KUT/HW KT1 .....9 K5
REIG RH2 .....119 L4
STWL/WRAY TW19 .....22 C2
SURB KT6 .....59 M1
The Doultons STA TW18 .....22 D9
Dounesforth Gdns
WAND/EARL SW18 .....28 E4
Douro Pl KENS W8 .....19 M1
Dove Cl CRAWW RH11 .....176 G3
SAND/SEL CR2 .....64 D9
WLGTN SM6 .....63 H6
Dovecote Cl WEY KT13 .....56 D2
Dovedale Cl RGUE GU4 .....112 E2
SHST GU47 .....49 P7
Dovedale Crs CRAWW RH11 .....176 G3
Dovedale Ri MTCM CR4 .....44 B3
Dovedale Rd EDUL SE22 .....31 J1
Dovehouse Gn WEY KT13 .....56 F5
Dove Ms ECT SW5 .....19 N2
Dover Ct CRAN GU6 .....153 K9
Dovercourt Rd CTHM CR7 .....45 J5
Dovercourt La SUT SM1 .....61 N2
Dovercourt Rd DUL SE21 .....30 F2
Doverfield Rd
BRXS/STRHM SW2 .....29 P2
RGUE GU4 .....112 E2
Dover Gdns CAR SM5 .....62 B2
Dover House Rd
PUT/ROE SW15 .....18 E9
Dover Park Dr
PUT/ROE SW15 .....27 N2
Dover Rd NRWD SE19 .....30 B8
Dovers Green Rd REIG RH2 .....119 M9
Doversmead
WOKN/KNAP GU21 .....71 L5
Dover Ter RCH/KEW TW9 * 17 N7
Doveton Rd SAND/SEL CR2 .....63 M4
Dowdeswell Cl
PUT/ROE SW15 .....18 C9
Dowding Ct CWTH RG45 * 49 N3
Dowding Rd BH/WHM TN16 .....84 B4
Dower Av WLGTN SM6 .....62 D7
Dowlands La HORL RH6 .....160 E2
Dowlans Cl GT/LBKH KT23 .....96 A7
Dowlans Rd GT/LBKH KT23 .....96 B7
Downe Av MSKV TW6 .....14 E7
Downe Cl HORL RH6 .....140 A8
Downer Meadow GODL GU7 .....131 L5
ORP BR6 .....84 C3
Downes Cl TWK TW1 .....26 A2
Downfield WPK KT4 .....42 D9
Down Hall Rd KUT/HW KT1 .....8 C3
Downham Ct
WOT/HER KT12 * 57 L2
Downhurst Rd CRAN GU6 .....153 P6
Downing Av GUW GU2 .....111 M6
Downing St FNM GU9 .....5 F3
Downland Cl COUL/CHIP CR5 .....80 D3
EPSOM KT18 .....78 C4
Downland Dr CRAWW RH11 .....176 F7
Downland Gdns EPSOM KT18 .....78 F7
Downland Pl CRAWW RH11 .....176 F7
Downlands Rd PUR/KEN CR8 .....80 G2
Downland Wy EPSOM KT18 .....78 F7
Downmill Rd BRAK RG12 .....32 B5
Down Pl HMSMTH W6 .....18 F2
Down Rd GU GU1 .....112 F5
TEDD TW11 .....26 A9
Downs Av EPSOM KT18 .....78 D4
Downs Bridge Rd BECK BR3 .....47 K3
Downs Ct CARSH GU14 .....68 A9
Downs Court Rd
PUR/KEN CR8 .....81 L2
Downs HI BECK BR3 .....46 G2
Downs Hill Rd EPSOM KT18 * 78 C4
Downshire Wy BRAK RG12 .....32 C3
Downside BECK BR3 .....46 G2
CHERT KT16 * 37 K9
EPSOM KT18 .....78 C3
GSHT GU26 .....165 N4
SUN TW16 .....39 J2
TWK TW1 .....25 N6
Downside Bridge Rd
COB KT11 .....75 K4
Downside Cl WIM/MER SW19 .....28 F9
Downside Common
COB KT11 .....75 K7
Downside Common Rd
COB KT11 .....75 L7
Downside Orch
WOKS/MYFD GU22 .....11 G4
Downside Rd BELMT SM2 .....61 P5
COB KT11 .....75 K7
RGUE GU4 .....112 F6

Downs La LHD/OX KT22 .....97 H3
Downs Link CRAN GU6 .....152 D8
HORS RH12 .....189 M2
RGUE GU4 .....133 J1
SWTR RH13 .....132 D5
SWTR RH13 .....90 B6
Downs Lodge Ct EW KT17 * 78 C5
Downs Rd BECK BR3 .....47 H5
BELMT SM2 .....61 M9
COUL/CHIP CR5 .....80 F7
EPSOM KT18 .....78 A9
PUR/KEN CR8 .....63 K9
RDKG RH5 .....137 J8
THHTH CR7 .....45 L2
Downs Side BELMT SM2 .....61 K9
The Downs LHD/OX KT22 .....97 J5
RYNPK SW20 .....43 H1
Downs Vw DORK RH4 .....117 J5
ISLW TW7 .....16 F6
KWD/TDW/WH KT20 .....98 F1
Downsview Av
WOKS/MYFD GU22 .....92 D1
Downsview Cl COB KT11 .....75 K8
Downsview Gdns DORK RH4.....117 H4
NRWD SE19 .....45 L1
Downs View Rd
GT/LBKH KT23 .....96 C3
Downsview Rd HORS RH12 .....192 G4
NRWD SE19 .....45 L1
Downs Wy EPSOM KT18 .....78 D5
GT/LBKH KT23 .....96 C6
KWD/TDW/WH KT20 .....98 F1
OXTED RH8 .....103 L7
Downsway CTHM CR3 .....101 L2
GU GU1 .....113 H5
SAND/SEL CR2 .....63 N9
Downsway Cl
KWD/TDW/WH KT20 .....98 E1
The Downsway BELMT SM2.....61 N7
Downs Wy EPSOM KT18 .....78 F6
Downswood REIG RH2 .....119 P3
Downton Av
BRXS/STRHM SW2 .....30 A5
Downview Cl GSHT GU26 .....165 N5
Down Yhonda
MFD/CHID GU8 .....148 D1
Doyle Gdns YTLY GU46 * 66 G3
Doyle Rd SNWD SE25 .....46 A5
Draco Ga PUT/ROE SW15 * 18 G8
Dragon La WEY KT13 .....56 C8
Drake Av CTHM CR3 .....101 L2
DTCH/LGLY SL3 .....12 B2
FRIM GU16 .....89 J6
STA TW18 .....22 C8
Drake Cl BRAK RG12 .....32 C6
EWKG RG40 .....48 C2
HORS RH12 .....192 D4
Drakefield Rd TOOT SW17 .....29 K6
Drake Rd CHSGTN KT9 .....59 N4
CRAWE RH10 .....177 H8
HORL RH6 .....159 J4
CROY/NA CR0 .....45 H8
MTCM CR4 .....44 C7
Drake's Cl ESH/CLAY KT10 .....58 A4
Drakes Wy
WOKS/MYFD GU22 .....92 B2
Drakewood Rd
STRHM/NOR SW16 .....44 F1
Drax Av RYNPK SW20 .....42 W3
Draxmont WIM/MER SW19 .....28 B9
Draycot Rd SURB KT6 .....41 N9
Draycott BRAK RG12 .....32 C6
Dray Ct GUW GU2 .....6 A5
Drayhorse Dr BACS GU19 .....51 N7
Draymans Wy ISLW TW7 .....16 F8
Drayton Cl BRAK RG12 .....32 F3
HSLWW TW4 .....24 G1
LHD/OX KT22 .....96 D3
Drayton Ct WDR/YW UB7 .....14 B2
Drayton Gdns WBPTN SW10 .....19 N3
Drayton Rd CROY/NA CR0 .....2 B3
Dresden Wy WEY KT13 .....56 D4
Dressington Av BROCKY SE4 .....31 P2
Drew Pl CTHM CR3 .....101 M3
Drewstead Rd
STRHM/NOR SW16 .....29 N5
Drifters Dr FRIM GU16 .....69 M7
The Drift EHSLY KT24 .....94 C4
Drift Wy DTCH/LGLY SL3 .....12 C6
The Driftway BNSTD SM7 .....79 J2
LHD/OX KT22 .....97 J3
MTCM CR4 .....44 B3
Driftwood Dr PUR/KEN CR8.....81 L6
Drill Hall Rd CHERT KT16 .....37 L8
Drive Rd COUL/CHIP CR5 .....81 H9
Drivers Md LING RH7 .....162 B1
The Drive ASHF TW15 .....23 M7
BECK BR3 .....46 G3
BELMT SM2 .....79 K1
BIL RH14 .....188 A8
BNSTD SM7 .....79 J6
COB KT11 .....75 N3
COUL/CHIP CR5 .....80 C3
CRAN GU6 .....171 J3
CRAWE RH10 .....160 D9
EBED/NFELT TW14 .....24 C3
ESH/CLAY KT10 .....40 C9
FNM GU9 .....127 M6
GODL GU7 .....130 E9
GODL GU7 .....150 D2
GUW GU2 .....111 M5
HOR/WEW KT19 .....60 C6
HORL RH6 .....159 L2
HSLW TW3 .....16 D7
KUTN/CMB KT2 .....42 A1
KWD/TDW/WH KT20 * 99 L4
LHD/OX KT22 .....96 E2
LHD/OX KT22 .....97 L3
MRDN SM4 .....43 N6

RGUW GU3 .....111 P9
RYNPK SW20 .....42 G1
SHGR GU5 .....132 F7
STWL/WRAY TW19 .....21 J1
SURB KT6 * 41 L8
THHTH CR7 .....45 M5
WLGTN SM6 .....62 E8
WOKS/MYFD GU22 .....71 P9
WWKM BR4 .....47 M6
Dr Johnson Av TOOT SW17 .....29 L6
Drodges Cl SHGR GU5 .....132 D5
Droitwich Cl BRAK RG12 .....32 F4
Drove Rd RGUE GU4 .....113 L7
Drovers End FLEETN GU51 .....87 J3
Drovers Rd SAND/SEL CR2 .....63 M4
Drovers Wy ASHV GU12 .....109 L5
BRAK RG12 .....33 H4
FNM GU9 .....107 L8
Druce Rd DUL SE21 .....30 F2
Druid's Cl ASHTD KT21 .....77 M9
Druids Wy HAYES BR2 .....47 M4
Drumaline Rdg WPK KT4 .....60 C1
Drummond Cl BRAK RG12 .....33 H2
Drummond Rd
CRAWW RH11 .....176 B6
CROY/NA CR0 .....2 C4
GU GU1 .....6 E3
Drummonds Pl
RCH/KEW TW9 .....17 L9
Drury Cl CRAWE RH10 .....177 N7
Drury Crs CROY/NA CR0 .....63 J1
Dryad St PUT/ROE SW15 .....19 H8
Dry Arch Rd ASC SL5 .....34 F8
Dryburgh Rd PUT/ROE SW15 .....18 G9
Dryden BRAK RG12 .....32 C8
Dryden Rd FARN GU14 .....88 B1
WIM/MER SW19 .....28 F9
Dryden Wy LIPH GU30 .....182 D5
Drynham Rd WEY KT13 .....56 G2
Duchess Cl CWTH RG45 .....49 M3
SUT SM1 .....61 N3
Duchess Ct WEY KT13 .....56 F2
Duchess of Kent Barracks
ALDT GU11 .....108 D3
Duchess of Kent Cl
GUW GU2 .....111 N1
Dudley Cl ADL/WDHM KT15 .....55 M2
Dudley Dr MRDN SM4 .....43 J9
Dudley Gv EPSOM KT18 .....78 A3
Dudley Pl HYS/HAR UB3 .....14 F2
Dudley Rd ASHF TW15 .....23 J8
EBED/NFELT TW14 .....23 N4
KUT/HW KT1 .....9 F5
RCH/KEW TW9 .....17 M7
WIM/MER SW19 .....28 D9
WOT/HER KT12 .....39 J7
Dudmaston Ms CHEL SW3 .....19 P3
Dudrich Ms EDUL SE22 .....30 G1
Dudset La HEST TW5 .....15 J6
Duffield Rd
KWD/TDW/WH KT20 .....98 F4
Duffins Orch CHERT KT16 .....54 G6
Duke Cl CRAWE RH10 .....177 M9
Duke of Cambridge Cl
WHTN TW2 .....25 L2
Duke of Cornwall Av
CBLY GU15 .....50 F7
Duke of Edinburgh Rd
SUT SM1 .....61 P2
Duke Rd CHSWK W4 .....18 B3
Duke's Av CHSWK W4 .....18 B3
HSLWW TW4 .....15 N9
NWMAL KT3 .....42 C4
RCHPK/HAM TW10 .....26 D7
Dukes Cl ASHF TW15 .....23 M7
CRAN GU6 .....171 K1
FNM GU9 .....107 L8
HPTN TW12 .....24 G8
Dukes Covert BAGS GU19 .....51 N1
Duke's Dr GODL GU7 .....131 H6
Dukes Ga CHSWK W4 * 18 A2
Dukes HI BAGS GU19 .....51 N4
Dukes Pk ALDT GU11 .....108 G2
Duke's Pk ALDT GU11 * 108 G2
Dukes Ride RDKG RH5 .....137 K5
CWTH RG45 .....49 K5
WOT/HER KT12 * 57 K7
Dukesthorpe Rd SYD SE26 .....31 L7
Duke St RCH/KEW TW9 .....17 K9
SUT SM1 .....61 P3
WOKN/KNAP GU21 .....11 F5
Dukes Wy WWKM BR4 .....65 L2
Dukes Wd CWTH RG45 .....49 M4
Dulka Rd BTSEA SW11 * 29 J1
Dulverton Rd SAND/SEL CR2 .....64 D8
Dulwich Common DUL SE21 .....30 D4
The Dulwich Oaks
DUL SE21 * 30 G6
Dulwich Rd HNHL SE24 .....30 B1
Dulwich Village DUL SE21 .....30 E2
Dulwich Wood Av
NRWD SE19 .....30 F8
Dulwich Wood Pk
NRWD SE19 .....30 F7
Dumas Cl YTLY GU46 .....66 F3
Du Maurier Cl FLEETS GU52 .....106 E3
Dumbarton Av
BRXS/STRHM SW2 .....29 P2
Dumbleton Cl KUT/HW KT1 .....9 K3
Dump Rd FARN GU14 .....88 A6
Dumville Dr GDST RH9 .....122 B2
Dunally Pk SHPTN TW17 .....38 F8
Dunbar Av BECK BR3 .....46 E5
STRHM/NOR SW16 .....45 H3
Dunbar Ct WOT/HER KT12 .....57 L1
Dunbar Rd FRIM GU16 .....69 H9

NWMAL KT3 .....42 A5
Dunbar St WNWD SE27 .....30 D6
Dunboe Pl SHPTN TW17 .....38 E8
Duncan Dr GU GU1 .....112 E4
Duncan Gdns STA TW18 .....22 D9
Duncan Rd
KWD/TDW/WH KT20 .....79 J8
RCH/KEW TW9 .....17 L9
Duncombe Hl FSTH SE23 .....31 M1
Duncombe Rd GODL GU7 .....150 C2
Duncroft Cl REIG RH2 .....119 K5
Dundaff Cl CBLY GU15 .....69 J3
Dundas Gdns
E/WMO/HCT KT8 .....40 B4
Dundee Rd SNWD SE25 .....46 B6
Dundela Gdns WPK KT4 .....60 F3
Dundonald Rd
WIM/MER SW19 .....43 K1
Dunedin Dr CTHM CR3 .....101 N5
Dunelm Gv WNWD SE27 .....30 D7
Dunfee Wy BF/WBF KT14 .....74 E4
Dunford Br CHERT KT16 .....54 F9
Dunford Pl BRGH RG42 .....32 A1
Dungarvan Av
PUT/ROE SW15 .....18 E9
Dungates La
BRKHM/BTCW RH3 .....118 C4
Dungells La YTLY GU46 .....66 H4
Dungells Farm Cl YTLY GU46 .....67 H4
Dunheved Cl THHTH CR7 .....45 J7
Dunheved Rd North
THHTH CR7 .....45 J7
Dunheved Rd South
THHTH CR7 .....45 J7
Dunheved Rd West
THHTH CR7 .....45 J7
Dunkeld Rd SNWD SE25 .....45 M5
Dunkirk St WNWD SE27 * 30 D7
Dunleary Cl HSLWW TW4 .....24 C9
Dunley Dr CROY/NA CR0 .....65 J5
Dunlin Cl REDH RH1 .....140 A1
Dunlin Ri RGUE GU4 .....113 J3
Dunmail Dr PUR/KEN CR8 .....81 N3
Dunmore GUW GU2 .....111 N3
Dunmore Rd RYNPK SW20 .....42 G2
Dunmow Cl FELT TW13 * 24 F7
Dunmow Hl FLEETN GU51 .....86 G5
Dunnets WOKN/KNAP GU21 .....71 L6
Dunnings Rd EGRIN RH19 .....180 D5
Dunnymans Rd BNSTD SM7 .....79 K4
Dunoon Gdns FSTH SE23 * 31 L3
Dunoon Rd FSTH SE23 .....31 K3
Dunottar Cl REDH RH1 .....119 P7
Dunraven Av REDH RH1 .....140 D4
Dunsany Rd HMSMTH W6 .....19 H1
Dunsbury Cl BELMT SM2 .....61 M7
Dunsdon Av GUW GU2 .....6 B5
Dunsfold Cl CRAWW RH11 .....176 D6
Dunsfold Common Rd
MFD/CHID GU8 .....169 L4
Dunsfold Rd BIL RH14 .....187 K7
CRAN GU6 .....170 B8
MFD/CHID GU8 .....169 L3
MFD/CHID GU8 .....187 H3
Dunsfold Wy CROY/NA CR0.....65 H6
Dunsmore Gdns YTLY GU46 .....66 F3
Dunsmore Rd WOT/HER KT12 .....39 K6
Dunstable Rd
E/WMO/HCT KT8 .....39 P5
RCH/KEW TW9 .....17 L9
Dunstall Pk FARN GU14 .....68 C9
Dunstall Wy E/WMO/HCT KT8.....40 B4
Dunstan Rd COUL/CHIP CR5 .....80 F6
Dunstan's Gv EDUL SE22 .....31 J2
Dunstan's Rd EDUL SE22 .....31 H3
Dunster Av MRDN SM4 .....43 H9
Dunton Cl SURB KT6 .....41 L9
Dunthill Rd
WAND/EARL SW18 .....28 C4
Dunvegan Cl
E/WMO/HCT KT8 .....40 B5
Dupont Rd RYNPK SW20 .....43 H3
Duppas Av CROY/NA CR0 .....2 B7
Duppas Cl SHPTN TW17 .....38 F6
Duppas Hill La CROY/NA CR0.....63 J3
Duppas Hill Ter CROY/NA CR0 .....2 B6
Duppas Rd CROY/NA CR0 .....63 J2
Dura Den Cl BECK BR3 .....47 H1
Durban Rd BECK BR3 .....46 F3
WNWD SE27 .....30 D7
Durbin Rd CHSGTN KT9 .....59 L3
Durfold Dr REIG RH2 .....119 N5
Durfold Rd HORS RH12 .....192 D3
Durfold Wd BIL RH14 .....187 H4
Durford Crs PUT/ROE SW15 .....27 M4
Durham Av HAYES BR2 .....47 M5
HEST TW5 .....15 P4
Durham Cl CRAWE RH10 .....177 H9
GUW GU2 .....111 M3
Durham Hl BMLY BR1 .....47 N1
Durham Rd EA W5 .....17 K1
EBED/NFELT TW14 .....24 D3
HAYES BR2 .....47 M4
RYNPK SW20 .....42 F2
SHST GU47 .....49 L9
Durham Ter PGE/AN SE20 * 46 B1
Durkins Rd EGRIN RH19 .....162 C9
Durleston Park Dr
GT/LBKH KT23 .....96 C5
Durley Md BRAK RG12 .....33 H6
Durlston Cl KUTN/CMB KT2 .....26 B9
Durning Rd NRWD SE19 .....30 E8
Durnsford Av FLEETS GU52 .....86 G8
WIM/MER SW19 .....28 D5
Durnsford Rd
WIM/MER SW19 .....28 D5
Durnsford Wy CRAN GU6 .....171 J3
Durrell Rd FUL/PGN SW6 .....19 J6

Durrell Wy SHPTN TW17 .....38 F7
Durrington Park Rd
RYNPK SW20 .....42 G2
Dutch Barn Cl
STWL/WRAY TW19 .....21 L8
Dutchells Copse HORS RH12 .....192 D4
Dutch Gdns KUTN/CMB KT2 .....26 D8
Dutch Yd WAND/EARL SW18 .....28 D1
Duval Pl BAGS GU19 .....51 N6
Duxhurst La REIG RH2 .....139 M6
Dwelly La EDEN TN8 .....144 A1
Dyehouse Rd
MFD/CHID GU8 .....148 B8
Dyers Fld HORL RH6 .....160 C1
Dyer's La PUT/ROE SW15 .....18 F8
Dykes Pth WOKN/KNAP GU21 .....72 G4
Dykes Wy HAYES BR2 .....47 M4
Dymock St FUL/PGN SW6 .....19 M8
Dynevor Pl RGUW GU3 .....111 J1
Dynevor Rd
RCHPK/HAM TW10 .....26 D1
Dysart Av KUTN/CMB KT2 .....26 B8
Dyson Ct DORK RH4 * 116 C7
Dyson Wk CRAWW RH11 * 194 E1

E

Eady Cl SWTR RH13 .....192 E8
Eagle Cl CWTH RG45 .....49 L2
WLGTN SM6 .....62 G5
Eagle Hl NRWD SE19 .....30 E9
Eagle House Ms CLAP SW4 .....29 M1
Eagle Pl WBPTN SW10 .....19 N3
Eagle Rd GU GU1 .....7 F3
HTHAIR TW6 .....15 H8
Eagles Dr BH/WHM TN16 .....84 B7
Eagles Nest SHST GU47 .....49 L8
Ealing Park Gdns EA W5 .....17 J2
Ealing Rd BTFD TW8 .....17 K2
Eardley Crs ECT SW5 .....19 L3
Eardley Rd
STRHM/NOR SW16 .....29 M9
Earldom Rd PUT/ROE SW15 .....18 G9
Earle Cft BNFD RG42 .....32 E1
Earle Gdns KUTN/CMB KT2 .....41 L1
Earles Meadow HORS RH12 .....192 G4
Earlewood Cl CRAWE RH11 .....75 M1
Earleydene ASC SL5 .....34 B9
Earl of Chester Dr FRIM GU16.....69 M8
Earl Rd MORT/ESHN SW14 .....18 A9
Earlsbourne FLEETS GU52 .....107 H2
Earlsbrook Rd REDH RH1 .....120 B7
Earls Court Gdns ECT SW5 .....19 M2
Earls Court Rd ECT SW5 .....19 L2
Earl's Court Sq ECT SW5 .....19 M3
Earlsfield
WAND/EARL SW18 .....28 E4
Earls Gv CBLY GU15 .....68 G2
Earls Ms WAND/EARL SW18 .....28 F3
Earls Ter KENS W8 .....19 L1
Earlsthorpe Rd SYD SE26 .....31 L7
Earls Wk KENS W8 .....19 L1
Earlswood BRAK RG12 .....32 D8
Earlswood Av THHTH CR7 .....45 J6
Earlswood Cl SWTR RH13 .....192 E6
Earlswood Rd REDH RH1 .....120 B7
Earley Commons
CRAWE RH10 .....177 J4
Earsby St WKENS W14 .....19 J2
Easby Crs MRDN SM4 .....43 M7
Eashing La GODL GU7 .....130 F9
Easington Pl GU GU1 .....7 K4
East Av FNM GU9 .....107 P8
WLGTN SM6 .....63 H4
Eastbank Rd HPTN TW12 .....25 K8
Eastbourne Gdns
MORT/ESHN SW14 .....18 A8
Eastbourne Rd BTFD TW8 .....17 K3
CHSWK W4 .....18 A4
EGRIN RH19 .....161 N6
FELT TW13 .....24 E5
GDST RH9 .....122 C3
TOOT SW17 .....29 K9
Eastbrook Cl
WOKN/KNAP GU21 .....11 H1
Eastbury Ct BNFD RG42 .....32 B1
Eastbury Gv CHSWK W4 .....18 C3
Eastbury La RGUW GU3 .....130 C2
Eastbury Rd KUTN/CMB KT2 * 8 D1
Eastchurch Rd HTHAIR TW6 .....15 H6
Eastcote Av E/WMO/HCT KT8.....39 P6
East Ct EGRIN RH19 * 180 E1
Eastcroft Rd HOR/WEW KT19 .....60 C6
Eastdean Av EPSOM KT18 .....77 P2
East Dr CAR SM5 .....62 A7
CWTH RG45 .....35 P7
East Dulwich Gv EDUL SE22 .....30 G1
Eastern Av CHERT KT16 .....37 L4
CHOB/PIR GU24 .....91 H1
Eastern La CWTH RG45 .....50 B5
Eastern Perimeter Rd
HTHAIR TW6 .....14 G7
Eastern Rd ASHV GU12 .....108 G4
BRAK RG12 .....32 F3
Eastern Vw BH/WHM TN16 .....84 A6
Easter Wy GDST RH9 .....122 F9
Eastfield Rd REDH RH1 .....120 E7
Eastfields MFD/CHID GU8 .....149 N7
Eastfields Av
WAND/EARL SW18 .....19 L3
East Flexford La RGUW GU3 .....110 F8
East Gdns TOOT SW17 .....29 H9
WOKS/MYFD GU22 .....72 G6
Eastgate BNSTD SM7 .....79 K3
Eastgate Ct GU GU1 * 7 G5
Eastgate Gdns GU GU1 .....7 G4
East Gn BLKW GU17 .....67 N4

East Grinstead Rd LING RH7...162 C1
Easthampstead Rd
BNFD RG42....32 C3
East Hi BH/WHM TN16 ....83 P7
EGRIN RH19 ....162 D6
OXTED RH8 ....103 M9
SAND/SEL CR2 ....63 N8
WAND/EARL SW18 ....28 F1
WOKS/MYFD GU22 ....72 C5
East Hill La CRAWE RH10 ....160 E6
East Hill Rd OXTED RH8....103 L9
East Hundreds FLEETN GU51....86 E4
East India Wy CROY/NA CRO....3 J1
Eastlands Cl OXTED RH8....103 K7
Eastlands Crs EDUL SE22 ....30 C2
Eastlands Wy OXTED RH8....103 K7
East La EHSLY KT24 ....94 E6
KUT/HW KT1 ....8 C4
Eastleigh Cl BELMT SM2....61 M6
Eastleigh Wy
EBED/NFELT TW14 ....24 B4
Eastmead FARN GU14 ....88 D4
WOKN/KNAP GU21....71 P6
East Meads GUW GU2 ....111 M6
Eastmearn Rd WNWD SE27 ....30 C5
East Ms HORS RH12 * 192 B9
Eastmont Rd ESH/CLAY KT10..58 F11
Eastney Rd CROY/NA CRO....2 A1
Eastnor Pl REIG RH2....119 L7
Eastnor Rd REIG RH2....119 K7
East Pk CRAWE RH10....176 G6
East Park La LING RH7....161 K3
East Parkside WARL CR6....82 C5
East Rp WNWD SE27 ....30 D7
East Ring RFNM TW6....109 J7
East Rd EBED/NFELT TW14 ....23 N3
KUTN/CMB KT2....8 E2
REIG RH2 ....119 K4
WDR/YW UB7 ....14 A2
WEY KT13 ....56 F6
WIM/MER SW19 ....28 F9
Eastry Av HAYES BR2....47 M7
East Shalford La RGUE GU4...132 E1
East Sheen Av
MORT/ESHN SW14....27 J1
East Stanley Gn
DTCH/LGLY SL3....12 D2
East Station Rd ASHV GU12...108 D5
East Stratton Cl BRAK RG12...33 H6
East St BMLY BR1....47 N3
BTFD TW8....17 J5
CRAWE RH10....179 J7
EW KT17 ....60 D2
FNM GU9 ....5 C2
GT/LBKH KT23....96 B5
HORS RH12....175 K4
HORS RH12....192 B9
East View La CRAN GU6....152 F9
East Wk REIG RH2....119 M5
Eastway GUW GU2....111 M1
HAYES BR2 ....47 N8
HOR/WEW KT19....78 A1
HORL RH6....159 L5
MRDN SM4....43 H6
WLGTN SM6 ....62 E3
Eastwell Cl BECK BR3 ....46 E2
East Whipley La SHGR GU5...152 C6
Eastwick Dr GT/LBKH KT23...96 B4
Eastwick Park Av
GT/LBKH KT23....96 B4
Eastwick Rd GT/LBKH KT23...96 B5
WOT/HER KT12....57 K5
Eastwood CRAWE RH10....177 J5
Eastwood Rd SHGR GU5....132 D6
Eastwood St
STRHM/NOR SW16....29 M9
Eatonworth Rd CHERT KT16....37 K9
Eaton Dr KUTN/CMB KT2....9 J1
Eaton Pk COB KT11....75 N3
Eaton Park Rd COB KT11....75 N3
Eaton Rd BELMT SM2....61 P5
CBLY GU15....66 D3
HSLW TW3....16 D9
Eatonville Rd TOOT SW17....29 J5
Eatonville Vls TOOT SW17....29 J5
Eaves Cl ADL/WDHM KT15....55 N5
Ebba's Wy EPSOM KT18 ....77 P4
Ebbisham La
KWD/TDW/WH KT20....98 D1
Ebbisham Rd EPSOM KT18....77 P4
WPK KT4....60 C1
Ebenezer Wk
STRHM/NOR SW16....44 E2
Ebner St WAND/EARL SW18....28 E1
Ebsworth St FSTH SE23....31 L3
Ecclesbourne Rd THHTH CR7...45 L6
Eccleshill RDKG RH5....137 J2
Echelforde Dr ASHF TW15....23 K7
Echo Barn La RFNM GU10....127 J8
Echo Pit Rd GU GU1....111 M1
Ecob Cl RGUW GU3....111 M1
Ecton Rd ADL/WDHM KT15....55 M3
Eddeys Cl BOR GU35....164 E5
Eddeys La BOR GU35....164 E5
Eddington Hl CRAWW RH11...194 D1
Eddington Rd BRAK RG12....32 A7
Eddiscombe Rd
FUL/PGN SW6....19 K7
Eddy Rd ASHV GU12....108 G4
Eddystone Rd BROCKY SE4...31 M1
Edenbrook LING RH7....143 L9
Eden Cl ADL/WDHM KT15....55 M8
DTCH/LGLY SL3....12 E3
KENS W8....19 L1
Edencourt Rd
STRHM/NOR SW16....29 J9
Edencroft SHGR GU5....132 E6
Edenfield Gdns WPK KT4....60 D2
Eden Grove Rd BF/WBF TW14...74 A2

Edenhurst Av FUL/PGN SW6....19 K8
Eden Pde BECK BR3 *....46 E5
Eden Park Av BECK BR3....46 G6
Eden Rd BECK BR3....46 E5
CRAWW RH11....176 C7
CROY/NA CRO 2 E7
WNWD SE27....30 D8
Edenside Rd GT/LBKH KT23...95 P4
Edensor Rd CHSWK W4....18 C5
Eden St KUT/HW KT1....8 D5
Eden V EGRIN RH19....162 D8
Edenvale Rd MTCM CR4....44 C1
Edenvale St FUL/PGN SW6....19 M7
Eden Valley Wk EDEN TN8....144 D7
Eden Wy BECK BR3....46 G6
WARL CR6....82 E7
Ederline Av
STRHM/NOR SW16....45 H4
Edgar Cl CRAWE RH10....177 P6
Edgarley Ter FUL/PGN SW6 *..19 J6
Edgar Rd BH/WHM TN16....106 B3
HSLWW TW4....24 C3
SAND/SEL CR2....64 A5
Edgbarrow Ct CWTH RG45 *....49 L6
Edgbarrowhill Star
CWTH RG45....49 L6
Edgbarrow W BI SHST GU47....49 L7
Edgcumbe Park Dr
CWTH RG45....49 L4
Edgeborough Ct GU GU1 *....7 K5
Edge Cl WEY KT13....56 C6
Edgecombe Cl
KUTN/CMB KT2....42 B1
Edgecoombe SAND/SEL CR2..64 E7
Edgedale Cl CWTH RG45....49 M5
Edgefield Cl CRAN GU6....152 F8
REDH RH1 ....140 C1
Edge Hl WIM/MER SW19....43 H1
Edgehill Ct WOT/HER KT12 *...39 L9
Edgehill Rd MTCM CR4....44 C7
PUR/KEN CR8 ....63 J8
Edgeley GT/LBKH KT23....95 N4
Edgeley Cl VW GU25....36 D4
Edgell Cl VW GU25....36 C3
Edgell Rd STA TW18....22 C5
Edgel St WAND/EARL SW18...19 M9
Edgemoor Rd FRIM GU16....69 L5
Edge Point Cl WNWD SE27....30 C8
Edgewood Cl CWTH RG45....49 L2
Edgewood Gn CROY/NA CRO..46 D9
Edgeworth Cl CTHM CR3....82 A1
Edgington Rd
STRHM/NOR SW16....29 N9
Edinburgh Cl ASHV GU12....108 D5
Edinburgh Dr STA TW18....22 G9
Edinburgh Rd SUT SM1....61 N1
Edinburgh Wy EGRIN RH19...162 B4
Edison Rd HAYES BR2....47 N3
Edith Gdns BRYLDS KT5....41 N8
Edith Gv WBPTN SW10....19 N4
Edith Rd SNWD SE25....45 M6
WIM/MER SW19....28 E9
WKENS W14....19 J2
Edith Rw FUL/PGN SW6....19 M6
Edith Ter WBPTN SW10 *....19 M5
Edith Yd WBPTN SW10 *....19 K2
Edmonds Ct BRAK RG12 *....32 E2
Edmund Gv FELT TW13....25 K8
Edmund Rd MTCM CR4....44 A4
Edna Rd RYNPK SW20....43 H3
Edney Cl FLEETS GU52....87 H9
Edrich Rd CRAWW RH11....194 D1
Edridge Rd CROY/NA CRO....2 C4
MRDN SM4....43 P6
Edward Av CBLY GU15....68 C3
MRDN SM4....43 P6
Edward Cl FSTH TW12....25 K8
Edward Ct STA TW18....22 F9
Edwardes Pl WKENS W14....19 J1
Edwardes Sq KENS W8....19 K1
Edward II Av BF/WBF KT14...74 B3
Edward Rd BFOR GU20....52 D5
BH/WHM TN16....84 C7
BMLY BR1....47 P1
COUL/CHIP CR5....80 F4
CROY/NA CRO....45 N3
EBED/NFELT TW14....23 N1
FNM GU9....127 N6
HPTN TW12....25 L8
PGE/AN SE20....46 D1
Edwards Cl WPK KT4....61 H1
Edward St ALDT GU11....108 B4
Edward's Wy BROCKY SE4....31 P1
Edward Wy ASHF TW15....23 J5
Edwin Cl EHSLY KT24....94 F5
Edwin Rd EHSLY KT24....94 F5
WHTN TW2....25 M4
Eelmoor Br ALDT GU11....87 N9
Eelmoor Plain Rd
ALDT GU11....107 P2
Eelmoor Rd ALDT GU11....108 B5
FARN GU14....88 B5
Effie Pl FUL/PGN SW6....19 L5
Effie Rd FUL/PGN SW6....19 L5
Effingham Cl BELMT SM2....61 M6
Effingham Common Rd
EHSLY KT24....95 L5
Effingham Ct
WOKS/MYFD GU22 *....10 D7
Effingham La CRAWE RH10...160 H7
Effingham Pl EHSLY KT24....95 M7
Effingham Rd CROY/NA CRO..45 H8
HORL RH6....160 D6
REDH RH1....119 H6
SURB KT6....41 H8
Effort St TOOT SW17....29 H8
Effra Pde BRXS/STRHM SW2..30 B1
Effra Rd BRXS/STRHM SW2...30 B3
WIM/MER SW19....28 E9
Egerton Pl WEY KT13....56 E5
Egerton Rd NWMAL KT3....42 D5
SHST GU47....68 A2
SNWD SE25....45 N4

WEY KT13....56 E5
WHTN TW2....25 M3
Egerton Wy HYS/HAR UB3....14 D5
Eggars Hl ALDT GU11....108 C6
Eggars Rd RFNM GU10....126 D8
Eggar's Hl ALDT GU11....108 C6
Eggleton Cl FLEETS GU52....106 E1
Egham By-Pass EGH TW20....21 L7
Egham Cl CHEAM SM3....61 H2
Egham Crs CHEAM SM3....61 H2
Egham Hl EGH TW20....21 J9
Eglantine Rd
WAND/EARL SW18....28 F1
Egleston Rd MRDN SM4....43 M7
Egley Dr WOKS/MYFD GU22..92 B2
Egley Rd WOKS/MYFD GU22..92 B2
Eglinton Rd RFNM GU10....147 L6
Eglise Rd WARL CR6....82 E6
Egliston Ms PUT/ROE SW15..18 G8
Egliston Rd PUT/ROE SW15..18 G8
Egmont Av SURB KT6....41 N9
Egmont Pk
KWD/TDW/WH KT20....98 E5
Egmont Rd BELMT SM2....61 N6
NWMAL KT3....42 D5
SURB KT6....41 M9
WOT/HER KT12....39 K8
Egmont Wy
KWD/TDW/WH KT20....79 J8
Egremont Rd WNWD SE27....30 B6
Egret Gdns ALDT GU11....108 C7
Eight Acres GSHT GU26....165 M4
Eighteenth Rd MTCM CR4....44 G5
Eighth Av
KWD/TDW/WH KT20 *....99 K6
Eileen Rd SNWD SE25....45 M6
Eindhoven Cl CAR SM5....44 C9
WIM/MER SW19....43 P2
Eland Rd ASHV GU12....108 F5
CROY/NA CRO....2 A5
Elberon Av CROY/NA CRO....44 E7
Elbe St FUL/PGN SW6....19 N7
Elborough Rd SNWD SE25....46 A6
Elborough St
WAND/EARL SW18....28 D4
Elbow Meadow
DTCH/LGLY SL3 *....13 K6
Elcho Rd CHOB/PIR GU24....70 C8
Elder Cl RGUE GU4....112 E2
Eldergrove FARN GU14....88 C5
Elder Oak Cl PGE/AN SE20....46 B2
Elder Rd WNWD SE27....30 D8
WNWD SE27....30 D8
Eldersley Cl REDH RH1....120 B3
Eldersley Gdns REDH RH1....120 B3
Elderslie Cl BECK BR3....46 G5
Elderslie Rd SYD SE26....31 M7
Eldertree Wy MTCM CR4....44 D2
Elder Wy RDKG RH5....137 J2
Eldon Av CROY/NA CRO....64 C1
HEST TW5....16 A5
Eldon Dr RFNM GU10....127 P8
Eldon Pk SNWD SE25....46 B5
Eldon Rd CTHM CR3....101 M1
KENS W8....19 M1
Eldridge Cl
EBED/NFELT TW14....24 B4
Eleanora Ter SUT SM1 *....61 N4
Eleanor Av HOR/WEW KT19...60 B9
Eleanor Cl LIPH GU30....182 A2
Eleanor Gv BARN SW13....18 C8
Electra Av HTHAIR TW6....15 H8
Electric Pde SURB KT6....41 K7
Elers Rd HYS/HAR UB3....14 E2
Eleventh Av
KWD/TDW/WH KT20 *....99 K6
Elfin Gv TEDD TW11....25 N8
Elfrida Crs CAT SE6....31 P7
Elgar Av BRYLDS KT5....42 B1
CWTH RG45....49 M3
STRHM/NOR SW16....44 G4
Elgar Wy SWTR RH10....192 G6
Elger Wy CRAWE RH10....160 B8
Elgin Av ASHF TW15....23 M9
SHB W12....18 F1
Elgin Crs CTHM CR3....102 A2
HTHAIR TW6....14 C7
Elgin Gdns GU GU1....112 E4
Elgin Pl WEY KT13....56 E5
Elgin Rd BLKW GU17....67 P3
CROY/NA CRO....3 K3
SUT SM1....61 N2
WEY KT13....56 C5
WLGTN SM6....62 E5
Elgin Wy FRIM GU16....69 H9
Eliot Bank FSTH SE23....31 J5
Eliot Cl CBLY GU15....69 K1
Eliot Dr HASM GU27....183 P4
Eliot Gdns PUT/ROE SW15..18 E9
Elizabethan Wy
CRAWE RH10....177 M6
STWL/WRAY TW19....22 G3
STA TW18....22 F9
Elizabeth Barnes Ct
FUL/PGN SW6 *....19 M7
Elizabeth Cl BRAK RG12....32 E5
SUT SM1....61 K3
Elizabeth Cottages
RCH/KEW TW9....17 M6
Elizabeth Ct GODL GU7....131 L6
HORL RH6 *....160 C7
Elizabeth Crs EGRIN RH19...162 E9
Elizabeth Gdns ASC SL5....34 B6
ISLW TW7....16 G9
SUN TW16....39 L4
Elizabeth Rd GODL GU7....131 L6
NRWD SE19....45 M1
Elkins Gdns RGUE GU4....112 E2

Elkins Gv FNM GU9 *....4 A4
Ellaline Rd HMSMTH W6....19 H4
Elland Rd WOT/HER KT12....57 M1
Ellenborough Cl BRAK RG12..32 F2
Ellenborough Pl
PUT/ROE SW15....18 E9
Ellenbridge Wy
SAND/SEL CR2....63 N7
Ellen Dr FLEETN GU51....87 H3
Elleray Ct ASHV GU12....109 J1
Elleray Rd TEDD TW11....25 N9
Ellerby St FUL/PGN SW6....19 H6
Ellerdine Rd HSLW TW3....16 E9
Ellerker Gdns
RCHPK/HAM TW10....26 D2
Ellerman Av WHTN TW2....24 G4
Ellerton Rd BARN SW13 *....18 E6
RYNPK SW20....42 E1
SURB KT6....59 M1
WAND/EARL SW18....28 G4
Ellery Cl CRAN GU6....171 H2
Ellery Rd NRWD SE19....45 M1
Elles Av GU GU1....112 F5
Elles Cl FARN GU14....88 D4
Ellesfield Av BRAK RG12....32 A5
Ellesmere Av BECK BR3....47 H3
Ellesmere Dr SAND/SEL CR2..82 B3
Ellesmere Pl WOT/HER KT12..56 G4
Ellesmere Rd TWK TW1....26 B2
Ellice Rd OXTED RH8....103 M9
Ellies Ms ASHF TW15....23 J5
Ellingham Rd CHSGTN KT9...59 K5
Ellington Rd FELT TW13....24 F7
HSLW TW3....16 B7
Ellington Wy EPSOM KT18....78 F6
Elliot Cl CRAWE RH10....177 M6
Elliott Ct
WOKN/KNAP GU21 *....11 H2
Elliott Gdns SHPTN TW17....38 C5
Elliott Rd ASC SL5....33 M3
Elliott Rd CHSWK W4....18 C2
THHTH CR7....45 K5
Elliotts La BH/WHM TN16....105 N4
Ellis Av GUW GU2....111 M7
Ellis Cl COUL/CHIP CR5....81 H9
Ellis Farm Cl
WOKS/MYFD GU22....92 B2
Ellisfield Dr PUT/ROE SW15..27 L3
Ellison Gdns NWDGN UB2....15 P2
Ellison Rd BARN SW13....18 D7
STRHM/NOR SW16....44 F1
Ellison Wy RFNM GU10....109 H7
Ellora Rd STRHM/NOR SW16..29 N8
Ellson Cl CRAWW RH11....177 M7
Ellwood Pl CRAWW RH11 *...176 C5
Elm Bank CHOB/PIR GU24 *...53 J3
YTLY GU46....66 C1
Elmbank Av EKD TW20....20 C9
GUW GU2....111 N6
Elm Bank Gdns BARN SW13...18 C7
Elmbourne Rd TOOT SW17....29 L6
Elmbridge Av BRYLDS KT5....42 A7
Elmbridge La
WOKS/MYFD GU22....72 D8
Elmbridge Rd CRAN GU6....170 C1
Elmbrook Cl SUN TW16....39 K2
Elmbrook Rd SUT SM1....61 K3
Elm Cl BRYLDS KT5....41 P8
CAR SM5....44 B9
KWD/TDW/WH KT20....118 A1
LHD/OX KT22....97 H2
RPLY/SEND GU23....93 L4
RYNPK SW20....42 G5
SAND/SEL CR2....63 M5
STWL/WRAY TW19....22 C4
WARL CR6....82 D6
WHTN TW2....25 J5
WOKN/KNAP GU21....10 A6
Elm Cnr WOKN/KNAP GU21...10 A6
Elm Cft DTCH/LGLY SL3....12 A6
Elmcroft Cl CHSGTN KT9 *....96 A4
Elmcroft Ct CHSGTN KT9 *....59 L2
EBED/NFELT TW14....24 A2
FRIM GU16....69 H9
Elmcroft Dr ASHF TW15 *....23 K8
CHSGTN KT9....59 L2
Elmdene BRYLDS KT5....42 A9
Elmdene Cl BECK BR3....46 F6
Elmdene Ct
WOKS/MYFD GU22....10 D7
Elmdon Rd HSLWW TW4....15 M7
HTHAIR TW6....15 H8
Elm Dr CHOB/PIR GU24....70 G2
EGRIN RH19....180 F2
LHD/OX KT22....97 H2
SUN TW16....39 L3
Elmer Gdns ISLW TW7....16 D8
Elmer Ms LHD/OX KT22....96 C5
Elmer's Dr TEDD TW11....26 A9
Elmers End Rd BECK BR3....46 D6
Elmerside Rd BECK BR3....46 E5
Elmers Rd RDKG RH5....155 K8
SNWD SE25....45 N8
Elm Gdns GT/LBKH KT23....95 P4
MTCM CR4....44 G3
Elmfield Av MTCM CR4....44 C2
TEDD TW11....25 N8
Elmfield Pk BMLY BR1....47 N4
Elmfield Rd BMLY BR1....47 N4
NWDGN UB2....15 N1
TOOT SW17....29 L5
Elmfield Wy SAND/SEL CR2...64 B7
Elm Gdns EPSOM KT18....78 G8
ESH/CLAY KT10....58 F5

MTCM CR4....44 F5
Elmgate Av FELT TW13....24 C6
Elm Gv CHOB/PIR GU24....70 C5
CRAN GU6....152 D9
CTHM CR3....101 N2
EPSOM KT18....78 A3
FNM GU9....107 N7
KUTN/CMB KT2....8 E3
SUT SM1....61 N3
SWTR RH13....192 D9
WIM/MER SW19....43 J1
Elm Grove Cv
WOKN/KNAP GU21....71 K8
Elm Grove Pde CAR SM5....62 C2
Elm Grove Rd BARN SW13...18 E7
COB KT11....75 M5
FARN GU14....88 D3
Elmgrove Rd WEY KT13....56 C3
CROY/NA CRO....46 B8
Elmhurst Av MTCM CR4....44 C1
Elmhurst Ct GU GU1 *....7 K4
Elmhurst Dr DORK RH4....117 H9
Elmhurst Rd DTCH/LGLY SL3..12 E1
Elm La CAT SE6....31 N5
RFNM GU10....109 H6
RPLY/SEND GU23....74 B8
Elmore Rd COUL/CHIP CR5..100 B7
Elm Pk ASC SL5....34 A2
BRXS/STRHM SW2....30 A2
Elmpark Gdns SAND/SEL CR2..64 C8
Elm Park La CHEL SW3....19 P4
Elm Park Rd CHEL SW3....19 P4
PGE/AN SE20....45 P6
SNWD SE25....45 P6
Elm Pl ALDT GU11....108 E6
SKENS SW7....19 P3
Elm Rd BECK BR3....46 E3
BH/WHM TN16....105 J5
CHSGTN KT9....59 L3
EBED/NFELT TW14....23 N4
ESH/CLAY KT10....58 F5
EW KT17....60 D9
FNM GU9....107 P7
GODL GU7....131 M5
KUTN/CMB KT2....9 G1
LHD/OX KT22....97 H2
MORT/ESHN SW14....18 A8
NWMAL KT3....42 B4
PUR/KEN CR8....63 K2
REDH RH1....120 A5
THHTH CR7....45 L5
WARL CR6....82 D6
WLGTN SM6....62 B5
WOKN/KNAP GU21....10 A6
Elms Crs CLAP SW4....29 M2
Elmshaw Rd PUT/ROE SW15..27 M1
Elmshorn EW KT17....78 G6
Elmside CROY/NA CRO....65 H5
GUW GU2....111 N6
MFD/CHID GU8....149 N5
Elmsleigh Rd FARN GU14....88 C3
STA TW18....22 C8
WHTN TW2....25 L5
Elmslie Cl EPSOM KT18....78 A3
CLAP SW4....29 M1
FLEETS GU51....87 J6
Elmstead Cl HOR/WEW KT19..60 C2
Elmstead Gdns WPK KT4....60 E2
Elmstead Rd BF/WBF KT14...73 J2
The Elms BARN SW13....18 D8
BLKW GU17....67 P6
ESH/CLAY KT10 *....58 F6
RFNM GU10....109 H7
TOOT SW17 *....29 N6
WARL CR6....82 E6
WLGTN SM6 *....62 E5
Elmstone Rd FUL/PGN SW6...19 L6
Elmsway ASHF TW15....23 J8
Elmswood GT/LBKH KT23....95 P4
Elmsworth Av HSLW TW3....16 B7
Elm Tree Av ESH/CLAY KT10..40 D8
Elm Tree Cl ASHF TW15....23 L8
CHERT KT16....55 J1
HORL RH6 *....140 C9
Elmtree Cl BF/WBF KT14....74 A2
Elmtree Rd TEDD TW11....25 M8
Elm Vw ASHV GU12....109 K3
Elm Wk RYNPK SW20....42 G5
HOR/WEW KT19....60 B4
WPK KT4....60 G3
Elmwood Av FELT TW13....24 C6
Elmwood Cl EW KT17....60 E6
WLGTN SM6....62 B1
Elmwood Dr EW KT17....60 E6
Elmwood Rd CHSWK W4....18 A4
CROY/NA CRO....45 J7
HNHL SE24....30 D2
MTCM CR4....44 B4
REDH RH1....120 C1
WOKN/KNAP GU21....71 K8
Elmworth Gv DUL SE21....30 E6
Elphage Rd FLEETN GU51....86 E4
Elsdon Rd WOKN/KNAP GU21..71 N7
Elsenham St
WAND/EARL SW18....28 B4
Elsenwood Crs CBLY GU15....69 J2
Elsenwood Dr CBLY GU15....69 J2
Elsiemaud Rd BROCKY SE4...31 N1
Elsinore Av
STWL/WRAY TW19 *....23 H3
Elsinore Rd FSTH SE23....31 M4
Elsinore Wy RCH/KEW TW9...17 P8
Elsley Cl FRIM GU16....89 H1
Elsrick Av MRDN SM4....43 L6
Elstan Wy CROY/NA CRO....46 E8
Elstead Rd MFD/CHID GU8...149 J4
RFNM GU10....109 J9
Elsted Cl CRAWW RH11....176 E5

Elston Pl ASHV GU12....108 E6
Elston Rd ASHV GU12....108 E6
Elstree Hl BMLY BR1....47 L1
Elswick St FUL/PGN SW6....19 N7
Elsworthy Cl
  EBED/NFELT TW14....23 P4
Elsworthy THDIT KT7....40 E7
Elsynge Rd
  WAND/EARL SW18....28 C1
Elthiron Rd FUL/PGN SW6....19 L6
Elthorne Ct FELT TW13....24 D4
Elthorne Park Rd HNWL W7....16 F1
Elton Cl KUT/HW KT1....8 A1
Elton Rd KUTN/CMB KT2....9 H2
  PUR/KEN CR8....80 E1
Eltringham St
  WAND/EARL SW18....19 N9
Elvaston Ms SKENS SW7 *....19 N1
Elvaston Pl SKENS SW7....19 N1
Elveden Cl WOKS/MYFD GU22..73 M6
Elveden Pl
  WOKS/MYFD GU22 *....73 M6
Elveden Rd COB KT11....57 K9
Elvetham Cl FLEETS GU51....86 E4
Elvetham Crs FLEETS GU51...86 D4
Elvetham Heath Wy
  FLEETS GU51....86 E4
Elvetham Pl FLEETS GU51....86 E4
Elvetham Rd FLEETS GU51...86 E4
Elvington Gn HAYES BR2....47 M6
Elvino Rd SYD SE26....31 L8
Elwell Cl EGH TW20....21 M9
Elwill Wy BECK BR3....47 K5
Ely Cl CRAWE RH10....177 J9
  FRIM GU16....69 J9
Ely Pl CHB....42 D5
Ely Rd CROY/NA CRO....45 M6
  HTHAIR TW6....15 H7
Elysium Pl FUL/PGN SW6 *....19 J7
Elysium St FUL/PGN SW6....19 J7
Elystan Cl WLGTN SM6....62 E7
Embankment PUT/ROE SW15..19 H6
The Embankment
  STWL/WRAY TW19....21 H3
  TWK TW1....25 J4
Embassy Ct WLGTN SM6 *....62 D5
Ember Cl ADL/WDHM KT15....55 P4
Embercourt Rd THDIT KT7....40 B7
Ember Farm Av
  E/WMO/HCT KT8....40 D7
Ember Farm Wy
  E/WMO/HCT KT8....40 D6
Ember Gdns THDIT KT7....40 D8
Ember La ESH/CLAY KT10....40 D9
Ember Rd DTCH/LGLY SL3....12 F1
Emberwood CRAWW RH11 *..176 C3
Embleton Rd LEW SE13....31 H1
Embleton Rd BOR GU35....164 E5
Emden St FUL/PGN SW6....19 M6
Emerald Sq NWDGN UB2....15 M1
Emerton Rd LHD/OX KT22....76 C9
Emery Down Cl BRAK RG12...33 J4
Emily Davison Dr
  EPSOM KT18....78 F7
Emley Rd ADL/WDHM KT15...55 L2
Emlyn La LHD/OX KT22....96 G2
Emlyn Rd HORL RH6....140 G9
  REDH RH1....120 C7
Emmanuel Cl GUW GU2....111 J9
Emmanuel Rd BAL SW12....29 M4
Emma Ter RYNPK SW20 *....42 G1
Emmetts Cl
  WOKN/KNAP GU21....10 A3
Emmetts Rd BH/WHM TN16..125 N1
Emperor's Ga SKENS SW7....19 M1
Empire Vls REDH RH1....140 C6
Empress Av FARN GU14....88 D2
Empress Pl FUL/PGN SW6....19 L3
Emsworth Cl
  CRAWE RH10 *....177 M8
Emsworth St
  BRXS/STRHM SW2....30 A5
Ena Rd STRHM/NOR SW16....44 G4
Enborne Gdns BRAK RG12...32 F1
Endale Cl CAR SM5....62 B1
Endeavour Wy CROY/NA CRO..44 G8
  WIM/MER SW19....28 E7
Endlesham Rd BAL SW12....29 K3
Endsleigh Cl SAND/SEL CR2..64 C8
Endsleigh Gdns SURB KT6...41 J7
  WOT/HER KT12....57 L1
Endsleigh Rd NWDGN UB2...15 N2
Ends Pl HORS RH12 *....191 K3
Endway BRYLDS KT5....41 N8
Endymion Rd
  BRXS/STRHM SW2....30 A3
Enfield Rd ASHV GU12....109 K1
  BTFD TW8....16 F6
  CRAWW RH11....176 E9
  HTHAIR TW6....14 C7
Engadine Cl CROY/NA CRO....3 J6
Engadine St
  WAND/EARL SW18....28 C4
Engalee EGRIN RH19....180 B1
England Wy NWMAL KT3....41 P5
Englefield HORS RH12....191 N8
Englefield Cl CROY/NA CRO...45 L7
  EGH TW20....21 J8
Engleheart Dr
  EBED/NFELT TW14....24 A2
Englehurst EGH TW20....21 J9
Englemere Pk ASC SL5....33 M5
  COB KT11....76 B3
Englemere Rd BNFD RG42...32 B1
Englefield CBLY GU15....69 J3
Englewood Rd BAL SW12....29 L2
Engliff La WOKS/MYFD GU22..73 K5
English Gdns
  STWL/WRAY TW19....12 B9
Enmore Av SNWD SE25....46 A6

Enmore Gdns
  MORT/ESHN SW14....27 J1
Enmore Rd PUT/ROE SW15...18 G9
  SNWD SE25....46 A6
Ennerdale BRAK RG12....32 C5
Ennerdale Cl CRAWW RH11..176 E7
  EBED/NFELT TW14....23 N3
  SUT SM1....61 K3
Ennerdale Gv ASHV GU12....107 L8
Ennerdale Rd RCH/KEW TW9..17 M7
Ennismore Av CHSWK W4....18 C2
  GU GU1....7 J3
Ennismore Gdns THDIT KT7....40 E7
Ennismore Gardens Ms
  SKENS SW7 *....19 P1
Ensign Cl PUR/KEN CR8....63 J8
  STWL/WRAY TW19....22 C4
Ensign Wy STWL/WRAY TW19..22 C4
  WLGTN SM6....62 G6
Ensor Ms SKENS SW7....19 P3
Enterdent Rd GDST RH9....122 C2
Enterprise Ct CROY/NA CRO...45 J9
Enterprise Wy EDEN TN8....144 F2
  TEDD TW11....25 N8
  WAND/EARL SW18....19 L9
Enton La MFD/CHID GU8....150 A9
Envis Wy RGUW GU3....111 J1
Envoy Av HTHAIR TW6....15 H8
Epirus Ms FUL/PGN SW6....19 K5
Epirus Rd FUL/PGN SW6....19 K5
Epping Wk CRAWE RH10....177 J7
Epping Wy BRAK RG12....33 H5
Epple Rd FUL/PGN SW6....19 K6
Epsom Cl CBLY GU15....50 E9
Epsom La North EPSOM KT18..78 F8
Epsom La South
  KWD/TDW/WH KT20....98 C1
Epsom Rd ASHTD KT21....77 M7
  CRAWE RH10....177 K7
  CROY/NA CRO....63 J3
  EHSLY KT24....94 F9
  GU GU1....7 J2
  LHD/OX KT22....97 H1
  MRDN SM4....43 K7
  RGUE GU4....113 J4
  RGUE GU4....113 P2
Epsom Sq HTHAIR TW6 *....15 H7
Epts Rd FARN GU14....88 D7
Epworth Rd ISLW TW7....17 H5
Eresby Dr BECK BR3....46 G9
Erica Cl CHOB/PIR GU24....70 E2
Erica Ct WOKS/MYFD GU22...10 A6
Erica Gdns CROY/NA CRO....65 H3
Erica Wy CRAWE RH10....160 A9
  HORS RH12....192 C5
Ericcson Cl WAND/EARL SW18..28 D1
Eridge Cl CRAWE RH10....177 M5
Eridge Rd CHSWK W4....18 B1
Erin Cl BMLY BR1....47 L1
Eriswell Crs WOT/HER KT12...57 H5
Eriswell Rd WOT/HER KT12...57 H4
Erkenwald Cl CHERT KT16...37 J7
Erlesmere Gdns HNWL W7...16 C1
Erles Rd LIPH GU30....182 F6
Ermine Cl HSLWW TW4....15 N7
Ermyn Cl LHD/OX KT22....97 K1
Ermyn Wy LHD/OX KT22....97 K1
Erncroft Wy TWK TW1....25 N2
Ernest Av WNWD SE27....30 C7
Ernest Cl BECK BR3....46 G6
  RFNM GU10....127 H7
Ernest Gdns CHSWK W4....18 A4
Ernest Gv BECK BR3....46 F6
Ernest Rd KUT/HW KT1....9 K5
Ernest Sq KUT/HW KT1....9 K5
Ernle Rd RYNPK SW20....42 F1
Ernshaw Pl PUT/ROE SW15...28 B1
Erpingham Rd
  PUT/ROE SW15....19 J8
Erridge Rd WIM/MER SW19...43 L3
Errol Gdns NWMAL KT3....42 E4
Erskine Cl CRAWW RH11....176 B9
  SUT SM1....62 A2
Erskine Rd SUT SM1....61 P3
Esam Wy STRHM/NOR SW16..30 B8
Escombe Dr GUW GU2....91 P9
Escot Rd SUN TW16....38 C1
Escott Pl CHERT KT16....54 C5
Esher Av CHEAM SM3....61 H2
  WOT/HER KT12....39 K9
Esher Cl ESH/CLAY KT10....58 B4
Esher Cn HTHAIR TW6....15 H7
Esher Cn ESH/CLAY KT10....58 B5
Esher Green Dr
  ESH/CLAY KT10....58 A2
Esher Ms MTCM CR4....44 C4
Esher Park Av
  ESH/CLAY KT10....58 C4
Esher Place Av
  ESH/CLAY KT10....58 B3
Esher Rd CBLY GU15....51 J8
  E/WMO/HCT KT8....40 C6
  WOT/HER KT12....57 N3
Eskdale Cl DORK RH4 *....116 G9
Eskdale Gdns PUR/KEN CR8..81 M3
Eskdale Wy CBLY GU15....69 L4
Esmont Rdg NRWD SE19....45 N4
Esmond Gdns CHSWK W4 *..18 B2
Esmond St PUT/ROE SW15...19 J9
Esparto St WAND/EARL SW18..28 E3
Essendene Cl CTHM CR3....101 N3
Essendene Rd CTHM CR3...101 N3
Essenden Rd SAND/SEL CR2..63 N6
Essex Av ISLW TW7....16 E8
Essex Cl ADL/WDHM KT15...55 N3
  FRIM GU16....69 J9
  MRDN SM4....43 H8
Essex Ct BARN SW13....18 D7
Essex Dr CRAN GU6....170 C1

CRAWW RH11....176 F5
Essex Gv NRWD SE19....30 E9
Essex Pl CHSWK W4....18 B2
Essex Place Sq CHSWK W4 *..18 B2
Essex Ri BNFD RG42....33 H1
Essex Rd CHSWK W4....18 B2
Estcots Dr EGRIN RH19....180 F2
Estcourt Rd FUL/PGN SW6....19 K4
  SNWD SE25....46 B7
Estella Av NWMAL KT3....42 F5
Estoria Cl BRXS/STRHM SW2..30 B3
Estreham Rd
  STRHM/NOR SW16....29 N9
Estridge Cl HSLW TW3....16 A9
Eswyn Rd TOOT SW17....29 J7
Ethelbert Cl BMLY BR1....47 N3
Ethelbert Rd BMLY BR1....47 N4
  RYNPK SW20....43 H2
Ethel Rd ASHF TW15....23 H8
Etherley Hl RDKG RH5....155 H5
Etherow St EDUL SE22....31 H2
Etherstone Rd
  STRHM/NOR SW16....30 A7
Eton Av HEST TW5....15 P4
Eton Cl WAND/EARL SW18....28 E3
Eton Ct STA TW18....22 C8
Eton Pl FNM GU9....107 M7
Eton Rd HYS/HAR UB3....15 H5
Eton St RCH/KEW TW9....26 C1
Etton Rd HSLW TW3....25 K1
Etwell Pl BRYLDS KT5....41 M7
Eureka Rd KUT/HW KT1....9 H5
Europa Park Rd GU GU1....112 A4
Eustace Rd FUL/PGN SW6....19 L5
  RGUE GU4....113 M3
Euston Rd CROY/NA CRO....45 J9
Evans Cl CRAWE RH10....177 N6
Evans Gv FELT TW13....25 H5
Evedon BRAK RG12....32 D8
Evelina Rd PGE/AN SE20....46 C1
Eveline Rd MTCM CR4....44 B2
Evelyn Av ALDT GU11....108 B5
Evelyn Cl WHTN TW2....25 J5
  WOKS/MYFD GU22....72 B9
Evelyn Crs SUN TW16....39 H2
Evelyn Gdns GDST RH9....122 C1
  RCH/KEW TW9....17 L9
  SKENS SW7....19 N3
Evelyn Rd RCH/KEW TW9....17 L8
  RCHPK/HAM TW10....26 B6
  WIM/MER SW19....28 E8
Evelyn Ter RCH/KEW TW9....17 L8
Evelyn Wy COB KT11....75 P5
  HOR/WEW KT19....59 N9
  SUN TW16....39 H2
  WLGTN SM6....62 G3
Evelyn Woods Rd ALDT GU11..88 E8
Evenlode Wy SHST GU47....49 N9
Evenwood Cl
  PUT/ROE SW15....28 B1
Everard Av HAYES BR2....47 N9
Everatt Cl
  WAND/EARL SW18....28 C2
Everdon Rd BARN SW13....18 E4
Everest Ct WOKN/KNAP GU21..71 L5
Everest Rd CBLY GU15....50 F9
  CWTH RG45....49 M3
  STWL/WRAY TW19....22 G3
Everglade BH/WHM TN16....84 B7
The Everglades HSLW TW3 *..16 C8
Evergreen Cl PGE/AN SE20...46 C1
Evergreen Ct
  STWL/WRAY TW19 *....22 C3
Evergreen Rd FRIM GU16....69 H6
Evergreen Wy
  STWL/WRAY TW19....22 C3
Everington St HMSMTH W6...19 H4
Everlands Cl
  WOKS/MYFD GU22....10 C6
Eve Rd ISLW TW7....16 G9
  WOKN/KNAP GU21....72 F4
Eversfield Rd RCH/KEW TW9..17 M7
  REIG RH2....119 M5
  SWTR RH13....192 D9
Eversley Wk CHSWK W4....18 C1
Eversley Crs ISLW TW7....16 D6
Eversley Pk WIM/MER SW19..27 N8
Eversley Rd BRYLDS KT5....41 M5
  HTWY RG27....66 E1
  NRWD SE19....45 M1
Everton Rd CROY/NA CRO....46 B8
Evesham Cl BELMT SM2....61 L6
  REIG RH2....119 K4
Evesham Gn MRDN SM4....43 M7
Evesham Rd MRDN SM4....43 M7
  REIG RH2....119 K4
Evesham Rd North
  REIG RH2....119 K4
Evesham Ter SURB KT6 *....41 K7
Evesham Wk SHST GU47....49 N8
Ewald Rd FUL/PGN SW6....19 K7
Ewart Rd FSTH SE23....31 L3
Ewelands HORL RH6....140 E9
Ewell By-pass EW KT17....60 E6
Ewell Court Av
  HOR/WEW KT19....60 C4
Ewell Downs Rd EW KT17....60 E9
Ewell House Gv EW KT17 *....60 D8
Ewell House Pde EW KT17 *..60 D8
Ewell Park Gdns EW KT17....60 E6
Ewell Park Wy EW KT17....60 E5
Ewell Rd CHEAM SM3....60 G4
  SURB KT6....41 H8
  SURB KT6....41 M7
Ewelme Rd FSTH SE23....31 K4
Ewen Crs BRXS/STRHM SW2..30 B3
Ewhurst Av SAND/SEL CR2...63 P8
Ewhurst Cl BELMT SM2....60 G7

CRAWW RH11....176 F5
Ewhurst Rd BROCKY SE4....31 N2
  CRAN GU6....153 H9
  CRAWW RH11....176 F5
  SHGR GU5....134 F7
Ewins Cl ASHV GU12....109 J4
Ewood La RDKG RH5....137 M7
Ewshot La FLEETS GU52....106 F3
Exbury Rd CAT SE6....31 P5
Excalibur Cl CRAWW RH11...176 B5
Excelsior Cl KUT/HW KT1....9 H5
Exchange Rd ASC SL5....34 C6
  CRAWE RH10....177 H5
Exeforde Av ASHF TW15....23 K7
Exeter Cl CRAWE RH10....177 H5
Exeter Gdns YTLY GU46....66 F1
Exeter Ms FUL/PGN SW6 *....19 L5
Exeter Pl GUW GU2 *....111 M3
  CROY/NA CRO....45 N8
  FELT TW13....24 A6
  HTHAIR TW6....14 G7
Exeter Wy HTHAIR TW6....14 C7
Exhibition Rd FARN GU14....88 C7
  SKENS SW7....19 P2
Explorer Av
  STWL/WRAY TW19....23 H4
Eyhurst Cl
  KWD/TDW/WH KT20....99 K4
Eyhurst Pk
  KWD/TDW/WH KT20 *....99 N3
Eyhurst Sp
  KWD/TDW/WH KT20....99 K4
Eyles Cl HORS RH12....192 A6
Eylewood Rd WNWD SE27...30 D8
Eynella Rd DUL SE21....30 G3
Eyot Gdns HMSMTH W6....18 D3
Eyston Dr WEY KT13....56 C8

F

Fabian Rd FUL/PGN SW6....19 K5
The Facade FSTH SE23 *....31 K3
  REIG RH2....119 L4
Factory La CROY/NA CRO....2 A3
Fagg's Rd EBED/NFELT TW14..15 J9
Faircrie ISLW TW7 *....16 G6
  NWMAL KT3....42 C4
Fair Acres HAYES BR2....47 N6
  CROY/NA CRO....64 F7
  KWD/TDW/WH KT20....98 G1
  RFNM GU10 *....127 K9
Fairbairn Cl PUR/KEN CR8....81 J2
Fairbourne COB KT11....75 N3
Fairbourne Cl
  WOKN/KNAP GU21....71 N6
Fairbourne La CTHM CR3....101 L2
Fairchild Cl BTSEA SW11....19 P7
Fairchildes Av CROY/NA CRO..83 K1
Fairchildes Rd WARL CR6....83 L3
Faircross BRAK RG12....32 D4
Fairdale Gdns PUT/ROE SW15..18 F9
  HYS/HAR UB3....15 H1
Fairdene Rd COUL/CHIP CR5..80 F7
Fairey Av HYS/HAR UB3....15 H1
Fairfax BNFD RG42....32 C2
Fairfax Av EW KT17....60 E7
  REDH RH1....120 B4
Fairfax Cl OXTED RH8....123 K1
  WOT/HER KT12....39 K9
Fairfax Ms FARN GU14....88 F5
Fairfax Pl WKENS W14....19 J1
Fairfax Rd CHSWK W4....18 C1
  FARN GU14....88 D7
  TEDD TW11....25 P9
  WOKS/MYFD GU22....72 F9
Fairfield Ap
  STWL/WRAY TW19....21 J2
Fairfield Av DTCH/LGLY SL3...12 A5
  HORL RH6....159 J7
  STA TW18....22 C7
  WHTN TW2....25 J4
Fairfield Cl GT/LBKH KT23....96 B5
  HOR/WEW KT19....60 C4
  MTCM CR4....44 A1
Fairfield Cnr KUT/HW KT1 *....9 F5
Fairfield Dr DORK RH4....116 G5
  FRIM GU16....68 G5
  WAND/EARL SW18....28 E1
Fairfield East KUT/HW KT1....8 E4
Fairfield La CHOB/PIR GU24...70 F1
Fairfield North KUTN/CMB KT2..8 E3
Fairfield Pth COB KT11....75 M3
Fairfield Pl KUT/HW KT1....8 E5
Fairfield Ri GUW GU2....111 M4
Fairfield Rd BECK BR3....46 G3
  BMLY BR1....47 N1
  CROY/NA CRO....3 F5
  EGRIN RH19....180 D3
  KUT/HW KT1....8 E5
  LHD/OX KT22....97 H1
  STWL/WRAY TW19....21 J2
Fairfield South KUT/HW KT1....8 E5
Fairfield St
  WAND/EARL SW18....28 E1
The Fairfield FNM GU9....5 H4
Fairfield Wy COUL/CHIP CR5..80 F3
  HOR/WEW KT19....60 C4
Fairfield West KUT/HW KT1....8 E5
Fairford Av CROY/NA CRO....46 D6
Fairford Cl BF/WBF KT14....73 K3
  CROY/NA CRO....46 E5
  REIG RH2....119 P3
Fairford Ct BELMT SM2 *....61 M6
Fairford Gdns WPK KT4....60 D2

Fairgreen Rd THHTH CR7....45 K6
Fairhaven EGH TW20....21 L8
Fairhaven Av CROY/NA CRO..46 D7
Fairhaven Rd REDH RH1....120 C1
Fairholme EBED/NFELT TW14..23 N3
Fairholme Crs ASHTD KT21...77 J6
Fairholme Gdns FNM GU9....5 H6
Fairholme Rd ASHF TW15....23 J8
  CROY/NA CRO....45 J8
  SUT SM1....61 K5
  WKENS W14....19 J3
Fairland Cl FLEETS GU52....87 H7
Fairlands Av RGUW GU3....111 J1
  SUT SM1....61 L1
  THHTH CR7....45 J5
Fairlands Rd RGUW GU3....91 J9
Fair La COUL/CHIP CR5....99 N5
Fairlawn GT/LBKH KT23....95 P4
  WEY KT13....56 G4
Fairlawn Av CHSWK W4....18 A2
Fairlawn Cl ESH/CLAY KT10..58 F5
  FELT TW13....24 G7
  KUTN/CMB KT2....27 H9
Fairlawn Crs EGRIN RH19...180 A1
Fairlawn Dr EGRIN RH19....180 A1
  REDH RH1....120 A7
Fairlawn Gv BNSTD SM7....79 P2
  CHSWK W4....18 A2
Fairlawn Pk SYD SE26....31 M8
  WOKN/KNAP GU21....71 J4
Fairlawn Rd CAR SM5....61 N9
  WIM/MER SW19....43 K1
Fairlawns ADL/WDHM KT15..55 K9
  HORL RH6....159 L2
  SUN TW16....39 J4
Fairlawns Cl STA TW18....22 E9
Fairlie Gdns FSTH SE23....31 K3
Fairlight Cl WPK KT4....60 G3
Fairlight Rd TOOT SW17....28 G7
Fairmead BRYLDS KT5....41 P9
  WOKN/KNAP GU21....72 A7
Fairmead Cl HEST TW5....15 M5
  NWMAL KT3....42 A3
  SHST GU47....68 A1
Fairmead Ct CBLY GU15....68 E4
  EDEN TN8....124 F9
Fairmeads COB KT11....75 N2
Fairmile FLEETS GU52....86 G9
Fairmile Av COB KT11....75 N5
  STRHM/NOR SW16....29 N8
Fairmile Ct COB KT11....75 N1
Fairmile Hts COB KT11....76 A2
Fairmile La COB KT11....75 M1
Fairmile Pk Copse COB KT11..75 P1
Fairmile Pk Rd COB KT11....75 P2
Fairmount Rd
  BRXS/STRHM SW2....30 A2
Fair Oak Cl LHD/OX KT22....58 D9
Fairoak Cl PUR/KEN CR8....81 K4
Fairoak La LHD/OX KT22....58 E9
Fairoaks RGUW GU3 *....90 C9
Fairs Rd LHD/OX KT22....76 G8
Fairstone Ct HORL RH6....140 D9
Fair St HSLW TW3....16 C8
Fairtrough Rd ORP BR6....85 M2
Fairview EW KT17 *....60 G9
Fair Vw HORS RH12....191 P7
Fairview Av
  WOKS/MYFD GU22....10 D6
Fairview Cl SYD SE26 *....31 M7
  WOKS/MYFD GU22....10 E6
Fairview Dr SHPTN TW17....38 B6
Fairview Gdns FNM GU9....107 P8
Fairview Pl
  BRXS/STRHM SW2....30 A3
Fairview Rd ASHV GU12....109 K3
  BOR GU35....164 E6
  EGRIN RH19....180 C2
  STRHM/NOR SW16....45 H2
  SUT SM1....61 P4
Fairview Ter BOR GU35 *....164 D5
Fairwater Dr
  ADL/WDHM KT15....55 N7
Fairway CAR SM5....80 A7
  CHERT KT16....37 M9
  CRAWE RH10....178 C9
  CRAWW RH11....176 A6
  GU GU1....113 H5
  RYNPK SW20....42 G4
Fairway Cl CRAWE RH10....178 B1
  CROY/NA CRO....46 E6
  HOR/WEW KT19....60 A4
  LIPH GU30....182 A7
  WOKS/MYFD GU22....71 P8
Fairway Gdns BECK BR3....47 H6
Fairway Hts CBLY GU15....69 K2
Fairways ASHF TW15....23 K9
  GSHT GU26....165 L5
  ISLW TW7....16 E6
  PUR/KEN CR8....81 K1
  TEDD TW11....41 K1
The Fairways REDH RH1....119 P8
The Fairway CBLY GU15....69 J5
  E/WMO/HCT KT8....40 B4
  FARN GU14....88 B1
  FNM GU9....107 P7
  GODL GU7....150 C2
  LHD/OX KT22....97 H2
  NWMAL KT3....42 B2
  RGUW GU3....91 J4
  WEY KT13....56 C9
Farewell La EHSLY KT24....94 D8
Fareham Rd SYD SE26....31 M6
Falaise EGH TW20....21 H8
Falaise Cl ALDT GU11....108 D3
Falcon Cl CHSWK W4....17 P4
  CRAWW RH11....176 G3
  LTWR GU18....51 P9
Falcon Dr STWL/WRAY TW19..22 G2

Falconer Rd FLEETN GU51 ....86 E4
Falconhurst LHD/OX KT22 ....76 D4
Falcon Rd GU GU1 ....7 F3
HPTN TW12 ....39 P1
Falcons Cl BH/WHM TN16 ....84 B6
Falcon Wy SUN TW16 ....38 G3
YTLY GU46 * 66 F2
Falconwood EGH TW20 ....21 K8
EHSLY KT24 ....95 H4
Falcon Wd LHD/OX KT22 ....76 F9
Falconwood Rd
CROY/NA CR0 ....64 G6
Falcourt Cl SUT SM1 ....61 M4
Falkland Gv DORK RH4 ....116 G8
Falkland Park Av SNWD SE25 ..45 N4
Falkland Rd DORK RH4 ....116 G8
Falklands Dr SWTR RH13 ....192 G6
Falkner Rd FNM GU9 ....4 D3
Falkners Cl FLEETN GU51 ....87 J3
Fallow Deer Cl SWTR RH13 ....192 G7
Fallowfield FLEETN GU51 ....87 J3
YTLY GU46 ....66 F1
Fallowfield Wy HORL RH6 ....140 D9
Fallsbrook Rd
STRHM/NOR SW16 ....29 L9
Falmer Cl CRAWW RH11 ....176 G7
Falmouth Cl CBLY GU15 ....69 J4
Falmouth Rd WOT/HER KT12 ....57 L3
Falstone WOKN/KNAP GU21 ....71 P7
Fambridge Cl SYD SE26 ....31 N7
Famet Av PUR/KEN CR8 ....81 L2
Famet Cl PUR/KEN CR8 ....81 L2
Famet Wk PUR/KEN CR8 ....81 L2
Fanes Cl BNFD RG42 ....32 B2
Fane St WKENS W14 ....19 K4
Fanshawe Rd
RCHPK/HAM TW10 ....26 B7
Fanthorpe St PUT/ROE SW15 ..18 G8
Faraday Av EGRIN RH19 ....180 E5
Faraday Pl E/WMO/HCT KT8 ....40 A5
Faraday Rd CRAWE RH10 ....177 J1
E/WMO/HCT KT8 ....40 A5
FARN GU14 ....88 E1
GU GU1 ....6 D2
WIM/MER SW19 ....28 E9
Farcrosse Cl SHST GU47 ....49 N9
Farebrothers HORS RH12 * 191 N2
Fareham Dr YTLY GU46 ....66 F1
Fareham Rd
EBED/NFELT TW14 ....24 D3
Farewell Pl MTCM CR4 ....43 P2
Farhalls Crs HORS RH12 ....192 E4
Faringdon Cl SHST GU47 ....49 N8
Faringdon Dr BRAK RG12 ....32 F6
Faris Barn Dr
ADL/WDHM KT15 ....73 K1
Faris La ADL/WDHM KT15 ....55 K9
Farleigh Av HAYES BR2 ....47 M8
Farleigh Court Rd
CROY/NA CR0 ....63 H1
WARL CR6 ....82 F3
Farleigh Dean Crs
CROY/NA CR0 ....65 H9
Farleigh Rd ADL/WDHM KT15 ....55 L9
WARL CR6 ....82 E6
Farleigh Wallop Dr
FLEETN GU51 * 86 C4
Farleton Cl WEY KT13 ....56 F5
Farley Copse BNFD RG42 ....32 A2
Farley Ct FARN GU14 * 88 F5
Farleycroft BH/WHM TN16 ....104 F6
Farley Heath Rd SHGR GU5 ....133 M9
Farley La BH/WHM TN16 ....104 F7
Farley Nursery
BH/WHM TN16 ....104 G7
Farley Pk OXTED RH8 ....123 K1
Farley Pl SNWD SE25 ....46 A5
Farley Rd SAND/SEL CR2 ....64 B6
Farleys Cl EHSLY KT24 ....94 E6
Farlington Pl PUT/ROE SW15 ....27 N3
Farlow Rd PUT/ROE SW15 ....19 H8
Farlton Rd WAND/EARL SW18 ....28 E3
Farm Av HORS RH12 ....192 A7
STRHM/NOR SW16 ....29 P7
Farm Cl ASC SL5 ....34 C6
BELMT SM2 ....61 P6
BF/WBF KT14 ....74 B1
BIL RH14 ....188 D7
BNFD RG42 ....32 B2
CHERT KT16 ....36 E7
CRAWE RH10 ....177 J4
CWTH RG45 ....49 N2
EGRIN RH19 ....180 G3
EHSLY KT24 ....95 H8
FUL/PGN SW6 * 19 L5
GU GU1 ....112 B2
HORS RH12 ....191 N3
LHD/OX KT22 ....96 D4
RGUW GU3 ....91 J9
SHPTN TW17 ....38 C8
STA TW18 ....22 B8
WLGTN SM6 ....62 E8
WWKM BR4 ....65 M2
YTLY GU46 ....67 H3
Farm Ct FRIM GU16 * 69 H6
Farmdale Rd CAR SM5 ....62 A6
Farm Dr CROY/NA CR0 ....64 F1
FLEETN GU51 ....87 H3
PUR/KEN CR8 ....80 F1
WDSR SL4 ....20 G2
Farmer's Rd STA TW18 ....22 B8
Farmfield Dr HORL RH6 ....158 E4
Farm Flds SAND/SEL CR2 ....63 P9
Farmhouse Cl
WOKS/MYFD GU22 ....73 H4
Farmhouse Rd
STRHM/NOR SW16 ....44 E1
Farmington Av SUT SM1 ....61 P2
Farm La ADL/WDHM KT15 ....55 L5
ASHTD KT21 ....77 P7
CROY/NA CR0 ....64 F1
EHSLY KT24 ....95 H8
FUL/PGN SW6 ....19 L4
PUR/KEN CR8 ....62 E8
RFNM GU10 ....106 C9
RPLY/SEND GU23 ....92 G3
Farmleigh Cl CRAWE RH10 ....177 M3
Farmleigh Gv WOT/HER KT12 ..57 H4
Farm Rd ASHV GU12 ....108 G3
BELMT SM2 ....61 P6
ESH/CLAY KT10 ....40 A9
FRIM GU16 ....68 G6
HSLWW TW4 ....24 F4
MRDN SM4 ....43 M6
STA TW18 ....22 E9
WARL CR6 ....82 E8
WOKS/MYFD GU22 ....72 F9
Farmstead Dr EDEN TN8 ....144 G2
The Farm WIM/MER SW19 * 28 A3
Farmview COB KT11 ....75 M5
Farm Vw YTLY GU46 ....67 H3
Farm Wk ASHV GU12 ....109 L6
GUW GU2 ....111 M7
Farm Wy STWL/WRAY TW19 ....22 C2
WPK KT4 ....60 G2
Farnaby Rd BMLY BR1 ....47 L2
Farnan Rd STRHM/NOR SW16 ..29 P8
Farnborough Av
SAND/SEL CR2 ....64 E6
Farnborough Crs HAYES BR2 ..47 M9
SAND/SEL CR2 ....64 E7
Farnborough Ga
FARN GU14 * 68 E9
Farnborough Rd FARN GU14 ....88 D7
FARN GU14 ....88 E2
FNM GU9 ....107 P6
Farnborough St FARN GU14 ....88 F2
Farncombe Hl GODL GU7 ....131 K6
Farncombe St GODL GU7 ....131 L6
Farnell Ms ECT SW5 ....19 M3
Farnell Rd ISLW TW7 ....16 D8
STA TW18 ....22 D6
Farnham By-pass FNM GU9 ....4 B7
Farnham Cl BRAK RG12 ....32 F3
CRAWW RH11 ....194 F2
Farnham Gdns RYNPK SW20 ....42 F2
Farnham La HASM GU27 ....184 B1
Farnham Park Cl FNM GU9 ....107 M8
Farnham Rd FLEETN GU51 ....87 K6
GUW GU2 ....6 C6
MFD/CHID GU8 ....129 L9
RFNM GU10 ....146 G9
Farnhurst La CRAN GU6 ....170 C7
Farningham BRAK RG12 ....32 G4
Farningham Crs CTHM CR3 ....102 A3
Farningham Rd CTHM CR3 ....102 A3
Farnley WOKN/KNAP GU21 ....71 M6
Farnley Rd SNWD SE25 ....45 M5
Faroe Rd WKENS W14 ....19 H1
Farquhar Rd NRWD SE19 ....30 G8
WIM/MER SW19 ....28 D6
Farquharson Rd
CROY/NA CR0 ....45 L8
Farrell Cl CBLY GU15 ....68 D5
Farren Rd FSTH SE23 ....31 M5
Farriers Cl EW KT17 ....78 C1
FLEETS GU52 ....106 E4
The Farriers SHGR GU5 ....132 E8
Farrier Wk WBPTN SW10 * 19 N4
Farrington Acres WEY KT13 * ..56 F2
Farriers Rd EW KT17 ....60 C9
Farthing Flds BOR GU35 ....164 B6
Farthingham La CRAN GU6 ....153 P6
Farthings WOKN/KNAP GU21 ....71 L5
Farthings Hl HORS RH12 * 192 A9
The Farthings KUTN/CMB KT2 ....9 J2
Farthings Wy HORS RH12 ....191 N7
Farwig La BMLY BR1 ....47 N2
Fassett Rd KUT/HW KT1 ....41 L5
Fauconberg Rd CHSWK W4 ....18 A4
Faulkner Cl CRAWW RH11 ....194 F2
Faulkner Pl BAGS GU19 ....51 N5
Faulkner's Rd WOT/HER KT12 ..57 L4
Favart Rd FUL/PGN SW6 ....19 L6
Faversham Rd BECK BR3 ....46 F3
CAT SE6 ....31 N3
MRDN SM4 ....43 M7
SHST GU47 ....49 P8
Fawcett Cl BTSEA SW11 ....19 P7
STRHM/NOR SW16 ....30 B7
Fawcett Rd CROY/NA CR0 ....2 C6
Fawcett St WBPTN SW10 ....19 N4
Fawcus Cl ESH/CLAY KT10 ....58 E5
Fawe Park Rd
PUT/ROE SW15 ....19 K9
Fawler Md BRAK RG12 ....33 K6
Fawnbrake Av HNHL SE24 ....30 C1
Fawns Manor Rd
EBED/NFELT TW14 ....23 N4
Fawsley Cl DTCH/LGLY SL3 ....13 J5
Faygate La GDST RH9 ....142 E2
HORS RH12 ....175 K4
Faygate Rd
BRXS/STRHM SW2 ....30 A5
Fayland Av
STRHM/NOR SW16 ....29 M8
Fay Rd HORS RH12 ....192 B6
Fearn Cl EHSLY KT24 ....94 G9
Fearnley Crs HPTN TW12 ....24 G9
Featherbed La
SAND/SEL CR2 ....64 F6
Feathercombe La
MFD/CHID GU8 ....150 C8
Feathers La
STWL/WRAY TW19 ....21 M5
Featherstone LING RH7 ....142 D4
Featherstone Av FSTH SE23 ....31 J5
Featherstone Rd
NWDGN UB2 ....15 N1
Featherstone Ter
NWDGN UB2 ....15 N1
Fee Farm Rd ESH/CLAY KT10 ....58 F6
Felbridge Av CRAWE RH10 ....177 N4
Felbridge Cl BELMT SM2 ....61 M7
EGRIN RH19 ....162 B9
FRIM GU16 ....69 H6
STRHM/NOR SW16 ....30 B7
Felbridge Ct EGRIN RH19 ....161 P8
Felbridge Pl EGRIN RH19 * 161 P8
Felbridge Rd EGRIN RH19 ....161 L9
Felcot Rd EGRIN RH19 ....161 K9
Felcott Cl WOT/HER KT12 ....57 L2
Felcott Rd WOT/HER KT12 ....57 L2
Felcourt La EGRIN RH19 ....162 A3
Felcourt Rd EGRIN RH19 ....162 B5
Felday Gld RDKG RH5 ....135 K8
Felday Rd RDKG RH5 ....135 H2
Felden St FUL/PGN SW6 ....19 K6
The Feld EGRIN RH19 ....161 P9
Felgate Ms HMSMTH W6 ....18 F2
Felix Dr RGUE GU4 ....93 L8
Felix La SHPTN TW17 ....38 G7
Felix Pl BRXS/STRHM SW2 ....30 B1
Felix Rd WOT/HER KT12 ....39 J7
Felland Wy REIG RH2 ....119 P9
Fellbrigg Rd EDUL SE22 ....30 G1
Fellbrook RCHPK/HAM TW10 ....26 A6
Fellcott Wy HORS RH12 ....191 N9
Fellmongers Yd CROY/NA CR0 ..2 C5
Fellowes Rd CAR SM5 ....62 A2
Fellow Gn CHOB/PIR GU24 ....70 F2
Fellow Green Rd
CHOB/PIR GU24 ....70 F2
Fellows Rd FARN GU14 ....88 F6
Fell Rd CROY/NA CR0 ....2 D5
Felmingham Rd
PGE/AN SE20 ....46 C3
Felsberg Rd
BRXS/STRHM SW2 ....29 P2
Felsham Rd PUT/ROE SW15 ....18 G8
Felstead Rd HOR/WEW KT19 ....60 B9
Feltham Av E/WMO/HCT KT8 ....40 E5
Felthambrook Wy FELT TW13 ..24 C7
Feltham Hill Rd ASHF TW15 ....23 K8
Feltham Rd ASHF TW15 ....23 L7
MTCM CR4 ....44 B3
REDH RH1 ....140 B1
Fenby Cl SWTR RH13 ....192 G6
Fenchurch Rd CRAWE RH10 ....177 L7
Fencote BRAK RG12 ....32 F8
Fendall Rd HOR/WEW KT19 ....60 A4
Fenelon Pl WKENS W14 ....19 K2
Fengates Rd REDH RH1 ....120 A5
Fenhurst Cl HORS RH12 ....191 N9
Fennel Cl ASC SL5 ....34 A5
CROY/NA CR0 ....46 D9
FARN GU14 ....87 M3
GU GU1 ....112 F2
Fennel Crs CRAWW RH11 ....176 E8
Fennells Md HOR/WEW KT19 ....60 D7
Fenner Sq BTSEA SW11 * 19 P8
Fennscombe Ct
CHOB/PIR GU24 ....70 E2
Fenns La CHOB/PIR GU24 ....70 E2
Fenn's Wy WOKN/KNAP GU21 ..72 C4
Fenton Av STA TW18 ....22 F9
Fenton Cl REDH RH1 ....120 C5
Fenton Rd REDH RH1 ....120 C5
Fentum Rd GUW GU2 ....111 N3
Fenwick Cl
WOKN/KNAP GU21 ....71 P7
Fenwick Pl SAND/SEL CR2 ....63 K6
Ferbies FLEETS GU52 ....86 G9
Ferguson Av BRYLDS KT5 ....41 M6
Ferguson Cl BECK BR3 ....47 J4
Fermandy La CRAWE RH10 ....179 H2
Fermor Dr ALDT GU11 ....108 B3
Fermor Rd FSTH SE23 ....31 M4
Fern Av MTCM CR4 ....44 F5
Fernbank EWKG RG40 ....48 B3
Fernbank Av WOT/HER KT12 ....39 N8
Fernbank Crs ASC SL5 ....33 M2
Fernbank Ms BAL SW12 ....29 L2
Fernbank Pl ASC SL5 ....33 L2
Fernbank Rd
ADL/WDHM KT15 ....55 L4
ASC SL5 ....33 M3
Fernbrae Cl RFNM GU10 ....146 E2
Fern Cl CWTH RG45 ....49 M2
FRIM GU16 ....69 L5
WARL CR6 ....82 E7
Ferndale RGUW GU3 ....111 L3
Ferndale Av CHERT KT16 ....55 J2
HSLWW TW4 ....15 N8
Ferndale Rd ASHF TW15 ....22 G8
BNSTD SM7 ....79 K5
FLEETS GU52 ....106 F1
SNWD SE25 ....46 B6
WOKN/KNAP GU21 ....10 E2
Fernden La HASM GU27 ....184 D7
Fernden Ri GODL GU7 ....131 L6
Ferndown CRAWE RH10 ....177 N1
HORL RH6 ....140 C8
Ferndown Cl BELMT SM2 ....61 P5
GU GU1 ....112 E6
Ferndown Gdns COB KT11 ....75 L3
FARN GU14 ....88 A3
Fern Dr FLEETN GU51 ....86 E9
The Fernery STA TW18 ....22 B8
Ferney Ct BF/WBF KT14 ....73 P1
Ferney Meade Wy ISLW TW7 ....16 G7
Fern Gv EBED/NFELT TW14 ....24 C3
Fernham Rd THHTH CR7 ....45 L5
Fernhill LHD/OX KT22 ....76 D3
Fernhill Cl BLKW GU17 ....68 A7
BNFD RG42 ....32 B1
CRAWE RH10 ....179 J2
FNM GU9 ....107 M8
WOKS/MYFD GU22 ....72 A9
Fernhill Dr FNM GU9 ....107 M8
Fernhill Gdns KUTN/CMB KT2 ....26 C8
Fernhill La BLKW GU17 ....68 B7
FNM GU9 ....107 M7
WOKS/MYFD GU22 ....72 A9
Fernhill Pk
WOKS/MYFD GU22 ....72 A9
Fernhill Rd FARN GU14 ....68 A9
HORL RH6 ....159 N5
Fernhill Wk BLKW GU17 ....68 B7
Fernholme Rd PECK SE15 ....31 L1
Fernhurst Cl CRAWW RH11 ....176 E3
Fernhurst Rd ASHF TW15 ....23 M7
CROY/NA CR0 ....46 A8
FUL/PGN SW6 ....19 J6
Ferniehurst CBLY GU15 ....69 H4
Fernihough Cl WEY KT13 ....56 C9
Fernlands Cl CHERT KT16 ....55 J2
Fern La HEST TW5 ....15 P3
Fernlea GT/LBKH KT23 ....96 B4
Fernlea Rd BAL SW12 ....29 L4
MTCM CR4 ....44 C3
Fernleigh Cl CROY/NA CR0 ....63 J3
WOT/HER KT12 ....57 K2
Fernleigh Ri FRIM GU16 ....69 L9
Fern Rd GODL GU7 ....131 M7
Ferns Cl SAND/SEL CR2 ....64 B8
Fernshaw Cl WBPTN SW10 * 19 N4
Fernshaw Rd WBPTN SW10 ....19 N4
Fernside Av FELT TW13 ....24 C7
Fernside Rd BAL SW12 ....29 J4
Ferns Md FNM GU9 ....4 D5
The Ferns FNM GU9 * 107 N7
Fernthorpe Rd
STRHM/NOR SW16 ....29 M9
Fern Towers CTHM CR3 ....102 A5
Fern Wk ASHF TW15 ....22 G8
Fern Wy HORS RH12 ....192 C5
Fernwood Av
STRHM/NOR SW16 ....29 N7
Feroners Cl CRAWE RH10 ....177 K7
Ferrard Cl ASC SL5 ....33 M2
Ferraro Cl HEST TW5 ....16 A4
Ferrers Av WLGTN SM6 ....62 F3
Ferrers Rd STRHM/NOR SW16 ..29 N8
Ferrier St WAND/EARL SW18 ....19 M9
Ferriers Wy EPSOM KT18 ....78 G8
Ferrings DUL SE21 ....30 F5
Ferris Av CROY/NA CR0 ....64 F2
Ferry Av STA TW18 ....37 J1
Ferry La BARN SW13 ....18 D4
BTFD TW8 ....17 L4
CHERT KT16 ....37 L7
GUW GU2 ....112 A9
SHPTN TW17 ....38 C9
STA TW18 ....37 N4
STWL/WRAY TW19 ....21 N5
Ferrymoor
RCHPK/HAM TW10 ....26 A6
Ferry Rd BARN SW13 ....18 E5
E/WMO/HCT KT8 ....40 A4
TEDD TW11 ....26 A8
THDIT KT7 ....41 H7
Ferry Sq BTFD TW8 ....17 L4
Festing Rd PUT/ROE SW15 ....19 H8
Fetcham Common La
LHD/OX KT22 ....96 B1
Fetcham Park Dr
LHD/OX KT22 ....96 E3
Fettes Rd CRAN GU6 ....153 K9
Fiddicroft Av BNSTD SM7 ....79 M4
Field Cl CHSGTN KT9 ....59 J4
E/WMO/HCT KT8 ....40 B6
HSLWW TW4 ....15 K6
HYS/HAR UB3 ....14 E5
RGUE GU4 ....113 H3
SAND/SEL CR2 ....82 B3
Fieldcommon La
WOT/HER KT12 ....39 N9
Field Ct OXTED RH8 ....103 L8
Field Dr EDEN TN8 ....145 H2
Field End CHOB/PIR GU24 ....70 F2
COUL/CHIP CR5 ....80 F3
FNM GU9 ....128 B1
Fieldend HORS RH12 ....192 G5
TEDD TW11 ....25 N7
Fieldend Rd
STRHM/NOR SW16 ....44 E2
Fielden Pl BRAK RG12 ....32 F3
Fielders Gn GU GU1 ....112 E5
The Fielders HTWY RG27 ....48 C9
Fieldfare Av YTLY GU46 ....66 E2
Field House Cl ASC SL5 ....34 A9
Fieldhouse Rd BAL SW12 ....29 M4
Field Hurst DTCH/LGLY SL3 ....12 D2
Fieldhurst Cl
ADL/WDHM KT15 ....55 M4
Fielding Av WHTN TW2 ....25 K6
Fielding Gdns CWTH RG45 ....49 M5
Fielding Rd CHSWK W4 ....18 C1
SHST GU47 ....68 A2
WKENS W14 ....19 H1
The Fieldings BNSTD SM7 ....79 K6
FSTH SE23 ....31 K4
HORL RH6 ....140 D9
WOKN/KNAP GU21 ....71 M5
Field La BTFD TW8 ....17 J5
FRIM GU16 ....68 G7
GODL GU7 ....131 M6
TEDD TW11 ....25 P8
Field Pk BRAK RG12 ....32 F2
Fieldpark Gdns CROY/NA CR0 ..46 E9
Field Pl LIPH GU30 ....182 E7
NWMAL KT3 ....42 D7
Field Rd EBED/NFELT TW14 ....24 C2
FARN GU14 ....68 B7
HMSMTH W6 ....19 J4
Fieldsend Rd CHEAM SM3 ....61 J4
Field Stores Ap ALDT GU11 ....108 E3
Field Vw EGH TW20 ....21 P8
FELT TW13 ....23 N7
Fieldview HORL RH6 ....140 D9
WAND/EARL SW18 ....28 G4
Field Wk HORL RH6 ....141 L9
Field Wy ASHV GU12 ....108 G4
CROY/NA CR0 ....65 H6
RFNM GU10 ....109 H7
RPLY/SEND GU23 ....93 K5
Fieldway FLEETN GU51 ....86 D7
HASM GU27 ....184 D3
Fifehead Cl ASHF TW15 ....23 H9
Fife Rd KUT/HW KT1 ....8 D4
MORT/ESHN SW14 ....27 H1
Fife Wy GT/LBKH KT23 ....96 A5
Fifield La RFNM GU10 ....146 F2
Fifield Pth FSTH SE23 ....31 L6
Fifteenth Av
KWD/TDW/WH KT20 * 99 K6
Fifth Av
KWD/TDW/WH KT20 * 99 K6
Fifth Cross Rd WHTN TW2 ....25 L5
Figge's Rd MTCM CR4 ....44 C1
Figgswood COUL/CHIP CR5 ....100 E2
Filbert Crs CRAWW RH11 ....176 D5
Filby Rd CHSGTN KT9 ....59 M5
Filey Cl BELMT SM2 ....61 N6
BH/WHM TN16 ....83 P8
CRAWW RH11 ....176 C7
Filmer Chambers
FUL/PGN SW6 * 19 K6
Filmer Gv GODL GU7 ....131 L8
Filmer Rd FUL/PGN SW6 ....19 K6
Finborough Rd TOOT SW17 ....44 B1
WBPTN SW10 ....19 M4
Fincham End Dr CWTH RG45 ....49 K5
Finchampstead Rd
EWKG RG40 ....48 C4
Finch Av WNWD SE27 ....30 E7
Finch Cl WOKN/KNAP GU21 ....71 J6
Finch Crs CRAWE RH10 ....179 K6
Finch Dr EBED/NFELT TW14 ....24 E3
Finches Ri GU GU1 ....112 F3
Finch Rd GU GU1 ....7 F3
Findhorn Cl SHST GU47 ....67 P1
The Findings FARN GU14 ....68 A8
Findlay Dr RGUW GU3 ....111 M1
Findon Cl WAND/EARL SW18 ....28 D2
Findon Rd CRAWW RH11 ....176 E3
Findon Wy HORS RH12 ....191 L7
Finlay Gdns ADL/WDHM KT15 ..55 N3
Finlays Cl CHSGTN KT9 ....59 N4
Finlay St FUL/PGN SW6 ....19 H6
Finmere BRAK RG12 ....32 E7
Finnart Cl WEY KT13 ....56 E3
Finney Dr BFOR GU20 ....52 D5
Finsbury Cl CRAWW RH11 ....176 F9
Finstock Gn BRAK RG12 ....33 H5
Fintry Pl FARN GU14 ....68 A9
Fiona Cl GT/LBKH KT23 ....96 A4
Fir Acre Rd ASHV GU12 ....89 J9
Firbank Dr WOKN/KNAP GU21 ..71 P8
Firbank La WOKN/KNAP GU21 ..71 P8
Firbank Pl EGH TW20 ....20 G9
Fir Cl FLEETN GU51 ....86 F7
WOT/HER KT12 ....39 J8
Fir Cottage Rd EWKG RG40 ....48 C1
Fircroft Cl WOKS/MYFD GU22 ..10 E6
Fircroft Ct WOKS/MYFD GU22 ..10 E6
Fircroft Rd CHSGTN KT9 ....59 M3
TOOT SW17 ....29 J6
Fircroft Wy EDEN TN8 ....144 G2
Firdene BRYLDS KT5 ....42 A9
Fir Dr BLKW GU17 ....67 P5
Fireball Hl ASC SL5 ....34 D8
Fire Bell Aly SURB KT6 ....41 L7
Firebell Ms SURB KT6 ....41 L7
Firefly Cl WLGTN SM6 * 62 G6
Fire Station Rd ALDT GU11 ....108 D3
Fire Thorn Cl FLEETS GU52 ....86 F9
Firfield Rd ADL/WDHM KT15 ....55 L3
FNM GU9 ....127 L6
Firfields WEY KT13 ....56 D6
Firglen Dr YTLY GU46 ....67 H1
Fir Grange Av WEY KT13 ....56 D4
Fir Gv NWMAL KT3 ....42 D7
Firgrove WOKN/KNAP GU21 ....71 N8
Firgrove Ct FNM GU9 ....5 G5
Firgrove Hl FNM GU9 ....5 G6
Firgrove Pde FARN GU14 * 88 D3
Firgrove Rd FARN GU14 ....88 D3
HTWY RG27 ....66 E2
Firhill Rd CAT SE6 ....31 P6
Firlands BRAK RG12 ....32 E6
HORL RH6 ....140 D9
WEY KT13 ....56 G5
Firlands Av CBLY GU15 ....68 F3
Firle Cl CRAWE RH10 ....177 H3
Firle Ct EW KT17 * 78 D1
Firle Pl WAND/EARL SW18 ....28 F3
Fir Rd CHEAM SM3 ....43 K9
FELT TW13 ....24 E8
Firs Av MORT/ESHN SW14 ....18 A9
SHGR GU5 ....132 E7
Firsby Av CROY/NA CR0 ....46 D9
Firs Cl DORK RH4 ....116 G9
ESH/CLAY KT10 ....58 E5
EWKG RG40 ....48 D2
FARN GU14 ....88 E5
FSTH SE23 ....31 L3
MTCM CR4 ....44 D3
Firsdene Cl CHERT KT16 ....55 H5
Firs Dr HEST TW5 ....15 K5
Firs La SHGR GU5 ....133 H9
Firs Rd PUR/KEN CR8 ....81 K4
First Av ADL/WDHM KT15 ....55 M7
E/WMO/HCT KT8 ....39 P5
HOR/WEW KT19 ....60 C7
KWD/TDW/WH KT20 * 99 K6
MORT/ESHN SW14 ....18 C7
WOT/HER KT12 ....39 K7
First Cl E/WMO/HCT KT8 ....40 C5
First Cross Rd WHTN TW2 ....25 M5
The Firs BF/WBF KT14 * 73 P1
EBED/NFELT TW14 * 23 P2
GT/LBKH KT23 * 96 B5
LIPH GU30 ....182 E7
RGUW GU3 ....111 P9
Firstway RYNPK SW20 ....42 G3
Firsway GUW GU2 ....111 M4
Firswood Av HOR/WEW KT19 ..60 C4
Firth Gdns FUL/PGN SW6 ....19 J6

Fir Tree Av *HASM* GU27 .....183 N4
WDR/YW UB7 ....14 C1
Firtree Av *MTCM* CR4 ....44 C3
Fir Tree Cl *ASC* SL5 ....44 C4
CRAWW RH11 ....176 E2
ESH/CLAY KT10 ....58 C4
EW KT17 ....78 G4
HOR/WEW KT19 ....60 D3
LHD/OX KT22 ....97 J3
STRHM/NOR SW16 ....29 M8
Firtree Cl *SHST* GU47 ....49 K9
Fir Tree Gdns *CROY/NA* CR0 ..64 C3
Fir Tree Gv *CAR* SM5 ....42 B1
Fir Tree Pl *ASHF* TW15 * 23 K7
Fir Tree Rd *EW* KT17 ....78 F5
GU GU1 ....112 A2
HSLWW TW4 ....15 N9
LHD/OX KT22 ....97 J3
Fir Tree Wk *REIG* RH2 ....119 P5
Firtree Wy *FLEETS* GU52 ....87 H7
Fir Wk *CHEAM* SM3 ....61 H5
Firway *GSHT* GU26 ....165 H6
Firwood Cl
WOKN/KNAP GU21 ....71 L9
Firwood Dr *CBLY* GU15 ....68 E3
Fir Gv Wood Wd *VW* GU25 ....35 J2
Fisher Cl *CRAWE* RH10 ....177 H7
CROY/NA CR0 ....3 J2
WOT/HER KT12 ....57 K3
Fisherdene *ESH/CLAY* KT10 ..58 G6
Fisher La *MFD/CHID* GU8 .....186 F3
Fisherman Cl
RCHPK/HAM TW10 ....26 B7
Fishermen's Cl *ALDT* GU11 ...108 C1
Fisher Rowe Cl *SHGR* GU5 ....132 E7
Fishers Ct *HORS* RH12 ....192 B6
Fisher's La *CHSWK* W4 ....18 B2
Fishers Wd *ASC* SL5 ....35 J9
Fishponds Rd *TOOT* SW17 .....29 H7
Fitchet Cl *CRAWW* RH11 ....176 E5
Fitzalan Rd *ESH/CLAY* KT10 ...58 G6
SWTR RH13 ....192 F6
Fitzgeorge Av *NWMAL* KT3 ....42 B2
WKENS W14 ....19 J2
Fitzgerald Av
MORT/ESHN SW14 ....18 C8
Fitzgerald Rd
THDIT KT7 ....40 G7
Fitzhugh Gv
WAND/EARL SW18 ....28 G2
Fitzjames Av *CROY/NA* CR0 ....64 A1
WKENS W14 ....19 J2
Fitzjohn Cl *RGUE* GU4 ....112 G2
Fitzrobert Pl *EGH* TW20 ....21 M9
Fitzroy Cl *BRAK* RG12 ....32 C7
Fitzroy Crs *CHSWK* W4 * 18 B5
Fitzroy Gdns *NRWD* SE19 ......45 N1
Fitzroy Rd *FLEETN* GU51 ....86 E6
Fitzwilliam Av
RCH/KEW TW9 ....17 M7
Fitz Wygram Cl *HPTN* TW12 ...25 K8
Fiveacre Cl *CROY/NA* CR0 ......45 J7
Five Acres *CRAWE* RH10 ....177 H3
Five Fields La *EDEN* TN8 ....145 N1
Five Oaks La
WOKN/KNAP GU21 ....71 K8
Flag Cl *CROY/NA* CR0 ....46 D9
Flambard Wy *GODL* GU7 ....131 K9
Flamborough Cl
BH/WHM TN16 ....83 P8
Flamsted Hts
CRAWW RH11 * 194 E1
Flanchford Rd *REIG* RH2 ......138 C1
SHB W12 ....18 D1
Flanders Crs *TOOT* SW17 ......44 D1
Flanders Rd *CHSWK* W4 ....18 C2
Flather Cl *STRHM/NOR* SW16 ..29 M9
The Flats *BLKW* GU17 ....67 M4
Flaxley Rd *SURB* KT6 ....41 J9
Fleece Rd *SURB* KT6 ....41 J9
Fleet Cl *E/WMO/HCT* KT8 .....39 P6
Fleet Hl *EWKG* RG40 ....48 E2
Fleet Rd *FARN* GU14 ....87 N3
FLEETN GU51 ....87 K4
HTWY RG27 ....86 A2
Fleetside *E/WMO/HCT* KT8 ...39 P7
Fleetway *EGH* TW20 ....36 G4
Fleetwood Cl *CHSGTN* KT9 ....59 K6
CROY/NA CR0 ....3 J5
KWD/TDW/WH KT20 ....99 L1
Fleetwood Ct *BF/WBF* K14 .....73 L2
Fleetwood Rd *KUT/HW* KT1 ...41 P4
Fleetwood Sq *KUT/HW* KT1 ...41 P4
Fleming Cl *FARN* GU14 ....88 F1
WBPTN SW10 * 19 N4
Fleming Ct *CROY/NA* CR0 ......63 J4
Fleming Md *MTCM* CR4 ....44 A1
Fleming Wy *CRAWE* RH10 ....177 H1
ISLW TW7 ....16 F8
Flemish Fids *CHERT* KT16 ......37 L8
Flemish Pl *BNFD* RG42 ....32 F1
Fletcher Cl *CHERT* KT16 ....55 H5
CRAWE RH10 ....177 H7
Fletcher Rd *CHERT* KT16 ....55 H5
CHSWK W4 ....18 A1
Fletchers Cl *HAYES* BR2 ....47 P5
SWTR RH13 ....192 D9
Fletchers Fld *LIPH* GU30 ......182 E7
Flexford Gn *BRAK* RG12 ....32 F2
Flexford Rd *RGUW* GU3 ....110 B6
Flint Cl *BNSTD* SM7 ....79 L4
CRAWE RH10 ....177 L8
GT/LBKH KT23 ....96 C6
REDH RH1 ....120 B4
Flintgrove *BRAK* RG12 ....32 F2
Flint Hl *DORK* RH4 ....117 H9
Flint Hill Cl *DORK* RH4 ....137 H1
Flintlock Cl
STWL/WRAY TW19 ....13 L9
Flitwick Gra *MFD/CHID* GU8 ..149 N3

Flock Mill Pl
WAND/EARL SW18 ....28 E4
Flood La *TWK* TW1 * 25 P4
Flora Gdns *CROY/NA* CR0 ......65 K9
Florence Av *ADL/WDHM* KT15 ..55 L9
MRDN SM4 ....43 N6
Florence Cl *WOT/HER* KT12 ...39 K3
YTLY GU46 ....66 G2
Florence Gdns *CHSWK* W4 ....18 A4
STA TW18 ....37 M1
Florence Rd *BECK* BR3 ....46 D5
BMLY BR1 ....47 N2
CHSWK W4 ....18 B1
FELT TW13 ....24 D5
FLEETS GU52 ....87 H9
KUTN/CMB KT2 ....9 G1
NWDGN UB2 ....15 M2
SAND/SEL CR2 ....63 M7
SWTR RH13 ....192 G7
WIM/MER SW19 ....28 E9
WOT/HER KT12 ....39 K8
Florence Wy *BAL* SW12 ....29 J4
WOKN/KNAP GU21 ....71 J7
Florian Av *SUT* SM1 ....61 P3
Florian Rd *PUT/ROE* SW15 ....19 J9
Florida Rd *RGUE* GU4 ....132 C2
THHTH CR7 ....45 K2
Floss St *PUT/ROE* SW15 ....18 G7
Flower Cres *CHERT* KT16 ....54 F5
Flower La *GDST* RH9 ....102 D9
Flower Wk *GUW* GU2 ....112 A8
Floyds La *WOKS/MYFD* GU22 ..73 J4
Floyer Cl *RCHPK/HAM* TW10 ..26 E1
The Flyers Wy
BH/WHM TN16 ....105 H6
Foden La *ALDT* GU11 ....108 C5
Folder's La *BNFD* RG42 ....32 E1
Foley La *ESH/CLAY* KT10 ....58 E5
Foley Rd *BH/WHM* TN16 ....84 B7
ESH/CLAY KT10 ....58 E6
Folkestone Ct *DTCH/LGLY* SL3 ..12 E5
Follet Cl *WDSR* SL4 ....20 C2
Folly Cl *FLEETS* GU52 ....87 H9
Follyfield Rd *BNSTD* SM7 ....79 L3
Folly Hl *FNM* GU9 ....107 L9
Folly La *RDKG* RH5 ....137 H6
Folly La North *FNM* GU9 ....107 M7
Folly La South *FNM* GU9 ....107 L8
The Folly *LTWR* GU18 * 70 B1
Fontaine Rd
STRHM/NOR SW16 ....30 A9
Fontana Cl *CRAWE* RH10 .....177 N6
Fontenoy Rd *BAL* SW12 ....29 L5
Fontley Wy *PUT/ROE* SW15 ...27 M5
Fontmell Cl *ASHF* TW15 ....23 K8
Fontmell Pk *ASHF* TW15 ....23 J8
Fontwell Cl *ASHV* GU12 ....108 F4
Fontwell Rd *CRAWE* RH10 ....177 K8
The Footpath
PUT/ROE SW15 * 27 M1
Forbes Cha *SHST* GU47 ....67 P1
Forbes Cl *CRAWE* RH10 ....177 L9
Force Green La
BH/WHM TN16 ....105 H4
Fordbridge Rd *ASHF* TW15 ....23 H9
SUN TW16 ....38 C7
Ford Cl *ASHF* TW15 ....23 H9
SHPTN TW17 ....38 C6
THHTH CR7 ....45 K7
Fordingbridge Cl
CHERT KT16 ....37 M9
HORS RH12 ....192 B9
Ford La *RFNM* GU10 ....127 M7
Ford Manor Rd *LING* RH7 ....162 G2
Fordmill Rd *CAT* SE6 ....31 P5
Ford Rd *ASHF* TW15 ....23 J7
CHERT KT16 ....37 M9
CHOB/PIR GU24 ....53 J8
CHOB/PIR GU24 ....53 P1
WOKS/MYFD GU22 ....72 F9
Fordwater Rd *CHERT* KT16 ....37 M9
Fordwells Dr *BRAK* RG12 ....33 H5
Foreman Pk *ASHV* GU12 ....109 K4
Foreman Rd *ASHV* GU12 ......109 K5
Forest Cl *ASC* SL5 ....33 L4
CRAWE RH10 ....179 J5
EHSLY KT24 ....95 H5
WOKS/MYFD GU22 ....73 H4
Forest Crs *ASHTD* KT21 ....77 N5
Forestdale *GSHT* GU26 ....165 N8
Forest Dean *FLEETN* GU51 .....87 J3
Forest Dr
KWD/TDW/WH KT20 ....99 L1
RFNM GU10 ....127 N9
SUN TW16 ....39 H1
Forest End *FLEETS* GU52 ....87 J3
Forest End Rd *SHST* GU47 .....49 K8
Forester Rd *CRAWE* RH10 ....177 H7
Forest Gn *CRAWE* RH10 ....177 L2
GUW GU2 ....111 N7
Foresters Cl *WLGTN* SM6 ....62 F6
WOKN/KNAP GU21 ....71 M7
Foresters Dr *WLGTN* SM6 ......62 F6
Foresters Sq *BRAK* RG12 ....32 G4
Foresters Wy *CWTH* RG45 ......50 B2
Forestfield *CRAWE* RH10 ......177 L7
SWTR RH13 ....192 F6
Forest Ga *CRAWW* RH11 .....194 G1
Forest Gld *RFNM* GU10 ....146 A1
Forest Gn *HORS* RH12 * 193 K6
Forest Gn Rd *BRAK* RG12 ......32 F3
Forest Hill Rd *EDUL* SE22 ......31 J2
Forest Hills *CBLY* GU15 ....68 D4
Forestholme Cl *SYD* SE26 ......31 K8
Forest La *EHSLY* KT24 ....95 H4
Forest Lane Cl *LIPH* GU30 ....182 D6
Forest Ms *HORS* RH12 ....192 H5
Forest Oaks *SWTR* RH13 ......192 E5
Forest Rdg *BECK* BR3 ....46 G4
Forest Rd *CHEAM* SM3 ....43 L9
CWTH RG45 ....49 N4
EHSLY KT24 ....95 H5

WEY KT13 ....56 F4
WOKS/MYFD GU22 ....73 H4
Foxcombe *CROY/NA* CR0 ......65 H5
Foxcote *EWKG* RG40 ....48 E2
Fox Ct *ASHV* GU12 ....108 G3
Fox Covert *LHD/OX* KT22 ......96 D4
LTWR GU18 ....70 B1
Fox Covert Cl *ASC* SL5 ....34 C6
Fox Cft *FLEETS* GU52 ....106 C1
Fox Dene *GODL* GU7 ....150 B2
Foxdown Cl *CBLY* GU15 ....68 C5
Fox Dr *YTLY* GU46 ....67 H1
Foxearth Cl *BH/WHM* TN16 ...84 C7
Foxearth Rd *SAND/SEL* CR2 ...64 C8
Foxearth Sp *SAND/SEL* CR2 ...64 C7
Foxenden Rd *GU* GU1 ....8 F4
Foxes Dl *HAYES* BR2 ....47 K4
Foxes Pth *RGUE* GU4 ....92 D6
Foxglove Av *HORS* RH12 ......192 D4
Foxglove Cl
STWL/WRAY TW19 ....23 H3
Foxglove Gdns *PUR/KEN* CR8 ..62 G9
Foxglove La *CHSGTN* KT9 ......59 N3
Foxglove Wy *WLGTN* SM6 .....44 C9
Fox Gv *WOT/HER* KT12 ....39 K8
Foxgrove Av *BECK* BR3 ....47 H1
Foxgrove Dr
WOKN/KNAP GU21 ....72 D4
Foxgrove Rd *BECK* BR3 ....47 J1
Foxhanger Gdns
WOKS/MYFD GU22 ....11 H2
Fox Heath *FARN* GU14 ....87 N4
Fox Hl *NRWD* SE19 ....45 P1
Foxhill Crs *CBLY* GU15 ....51 K9
Foxhills *WOKN/KNAP* GU21 ...72 A7
Foxhills Cl *CHERT* KT16 ....54 F5
Fox Hills La *ASHV* GU12 ....109 L3
Foxholes *HORS* RH12 ....189 N2
WEY KT13 ....56 F4
Foxhurst Rd *ASHV* GU12 ......109 J1
Foxlake Rd *BF/WBF* K14 ....74 B1
Fox La *GT/LBKH* KT23 ....95 P4
HAYES BR2 ....65 P4
REIG RH2 ....119 M8
Fox La North *CHERT* KT16 ......37 K9
Fox La South *CHERT* KT16 * ...37 K9
Foxleigh Cha *HORS* RH12 ....192 E6
Foxley Cl *BLKW* GU17 ....67 N3
REDH RH1 ....140 C1
Foxley Gdns *PUR/KEN* CR8 ....81 K2
Foxley Hill Rd *PUR/KEN* CR8 ..81 J1
Foxley La *PUR/KEN* CR8 ....62 G8
Foxley Rd *PUR/KEN* CR8 ....81 K3
THHTH CR7 ....45 K5
Foxoak Hl *WOT/HER* KT12 .....56 G8
Foxon Cl *CTHM* CR3 ....101 N1
Foxon La *CTHM* CR3 ....101 M1
Foxon Lane Gdns
CTHM CR3 ....101 N1
Fox Rd *BRAK* RG12 ....32 E5
DTCH/LGLY SL3 ....12 A2
HASM GU27 ....185 P4
RFNM GU10 ....127 N7
Foxton Gv *MTCM* CR4 ....43 P3
Foxwarren *ESH/CLAY* KT10 ....58 E7
Fox Wy *RFNM* GU10 ....107 H6
Foxwood *FLEETN* GU51 ....87 J4
Foxwood Cl *FELT* TW13 ....24 C6
MFD/CHID GU8 ....167 N4
Fox Yd *FNM* GU9 ....4 E3
Foye La *FLEETS* GU52 ....107 H1
Fraily Cl *WOKS/MYFD* GU22 ...11 K1
Frailey Hl *WOKS/MYFD* GU22 ..11 K1
Framfield Cl *CRAWW* RH11 ...176 D3
Framfield Rd *MTCM* CR4 ....44 C1
Frampton Cl *BELMT* SM2 ....61 L6
Frampton Rd *HSLWW* TW4 ....24 F1
France Hill Dr *CBLY* GU15 ......68 E3
Francemary Rd *LEW* SE13 .....31 P1
Franche Court Rd
TOOT SW17 * 28 F6
Francis Av *FELT* TW13 ....24 B6
Francis Barber Cl
STRHM/NOR SW16 * 30 A7
Franciscan Rd *TOOT* SW17 ....29 J8
Frances Chichester Ct *ASC* SL5 ..34 B6
Francis Ct *HOR/WEW* KT19 ....60 B3
SHPTN TW17 * 38 C6
Francis Ct *GUW* GU2 * 111 P3
Francis Edwards Wy
CRAWW RH11 ....176 B9
Francis Gv *WIM/MER* SW19 ...43 K1
Francis Rd *CROY/NA* CR0 ......45 H9
CTHM CR3 ....101 M2
HSLWW TW4 ....15 M7
WLGTN SM6 ....62 E5
Franconia Rd *CLAP* SW4 ....29 M1
Frank Dixon Cl *DUL* SE21 ......30 F3
Frank Dixon Wy *DUL* SE21 .....30 F4
Frankfurt Rd *HNHL* SE24 ....30 D1
Frankland Rd *SKENS* SW7 .....19 P1
Franklands Dr
ADL/WDHM KT15 ....55 K6
Franklin Cl *KUT/HW* KT1 ....9 H6
WNWD SE27 ....30 C6
Franklin Ct *GUW* GU2 ....111 M5
Franklin Crs *MTCM* CR4 ....44 E5
Franklin Rd *CRAWE* RH10 ....177 M6
PGE/AN SE20 ....46 C1
Franklin Sq *WKENS* W14 ....19 K3
Franklyn Gv *WIM/MER* SW19 *28 B5
Franklyn Rd *GODL* GU7 ....150 A1
WOT/HER KT12 ....39 K7
Franks Av *NWMAL* KT3 ....41 P5
Franksfield *SHGR* GU5 ....134 G2
Franks Fld *SHGR* GU5 ....134 G2
Franks Rd *GUW* GU2 ....111 N2

Fransland Gv *SYD* SE26 ....31 J6
Frant Cl *PGE/AN* SE20 ....46 C1
Frant Fld *EDEN* TN8 ....144 G4
Frant Rd *THHTH* CR7 ....45 K6
Fraser Md *SHST* GU47 ....49 L9
Fraser Rd *BNFD* RG42 ....32 D2
Fraser St *CHSWK* W4 ....18 C3
Frays Cl *WDR/YW* UB7 ....13 P1
Frederick Cl *SUT* SM1 ....61 K3
Frederick Gdns *CROY/NA* CR0 ..45 K7
SUT SM1 ....61 K4
Frederick Rd *SUT* SM1 ....61 K4
Frederick Sanger Rd
GUW GU2 ....111 K6
Frederick St *ALDT* GU11 ....108 C4
Freeborn Wy *BRAK* RG12 ......32 G2
Freedown La *BNSTD* SM7 ......79 M2
Freelands Av *SAND/SEL* CR2 ..64 E6
Freelands Dr *FLEETS* GU52 ...106 B1
Freelands Gv *BMLY* BR1 ....47 P2
Freelands Rd *BMLY* BR1 ....47 P2
COB KT11 ....75 K3
Freeman Cl *SHPTN* TW17 ......38 F4
Freeman Dr *E/WMO/HCT* KT8 ..39 P5
Freeman Rd *HORS* RH12 .....191 M2
MRDN SM4 ....43 P6
Freemantle Rd *BAGS* GU19 ...51 P6
Freemason's Rd *CROY/NA* CR0 ..3 L1
Free Prae Rd *CHERT* KT16 ......37 L9
Freesia Dr *CHOB/PIR* GU24 ...70 G5
Freestone Yd
DTCH/LGLY SL3 * 13 H5
French St *SUN* TW16 ....39 L3
French's Wls
WOKN/KNAP GU21 ....71 P6
Frenchay Rd *FLEETN* GU51 ....87 J6
Frenchaye *ADL/WDHM* KT15 ..55 N4
Frenches Rd *REDH* RH1 ....120 C3
The Frenches *REDH* RH1 ......120 C3
French Gdns *BLKW* GU17 ....67 P4
COB KT11 ....75 L3
Frenchlands Hatch
EHSLY KT24 ....94 G7
Frenchmans Creek
FLEETS GU52 ....106 E2
French St *SUN* TW16 ....39 L3
French's Wls
WOKN/KNAP GU21 ....71 P6
Frensham *BRAK* RG12 ....32 F7
Frensham Cl *FLEETN* GU51 ....87 J6
Frensham Ct *YTLY* GU46 ....66 F2
Frensham Ct *RFNM* GU10 ....127 M9
Frensham Dr *CROY/NA* CR0 ...65 J4
PUT/ROE SW15 ....27 M6
Frensham Heights Rd
RFNM GU10 ....146 D2
Frensham La *RFNM* GU10 ....164 D1
Frensham Rd *CWTH* RG45 .....49 N1
PUR/KEN CR8 ....81 K3
RFNM GU10 ....127 P6
Frensham V *RFNM* GU10 .....127 M9
Frensham Wy *EW* KT17 ....78 G5
Frere Av *FLEETN* GU51 ....86 E8
Freshfield Bank *FROW* RH18 ..181 M4
Freshfield Cl *CRAWE* RH10 ...177 K6
Freshfields *CROY/NA* CR0 ......46 G9
Freshford St *TOOT* SW17 ....28 F6
Freshmount Gdns
HOR/WEW KT19 ....59 P9
Freshwater Cl *TOOT* SW17 .....29 K9
Freshwater Pde
HORS RH12 * 192 M3
Freshwater Rd *TOOT* SW17 ....29 K9
Freshwood Cl *BECK* BR3 ....47 H2
Freshwood Dr *YTLY* GU46 ......66 G4
Freshwoods *HORS* RH12 ......189 N2
Freshwood Wy *WLGTN* SM6 ..62 E7
Friar Ms *WNWD* SE27 ....30 C6
Friars Av *PUT/ROE* SW15 ......27 L2
Friars Cft *RGUE* GU4 ....112 G2
Friars Fld *FNM* GU9 ....4 B2
Friar's Ga *GUW* GU2 ....111 N7
Friars Keep *BRAK* RG12 ....32 D5
Friars Rch *KEN/KEW* TW9 ....17 L6
Friars Orch *LHD/OX* KT22 ......96 D1
Friars Ri *WOKS/MYFD* GU22 ..11 H4
Friars Rd *VW* GU25 ....36 B5
Friars Rookery *CRAWE* RH10 ..177 K4
Friars Stile Rd
RCHPK/HAM TW10 ....26 B2
Friars Wy *CHERT* KT16 ....37 L7
Friars Wd *CROY/NA* CR0 * 64 E7
Friarswood *CROY/NA* CR0 .....64 E7
Friary Br *GU* GU1 ....7 G6
Friary Ct *WOKN/KNAP* GU21 ..71 M7
Friary Pas *GU* GU1 ....7 G6
Friary Rd *ASC* SL5 ....34 B7
STWL/WRAY TW19 ....21 H2
The Friary *GU* GU1 * 7 G6
Friary Wy *CRAWW* RH11 ....176 B9
WDSR SL4 ....21 H2
Friday Rd *MTCM* CR4 ....44 B1
Friday St *HORS* RH12 ....192 C3
HORS RH12 ....191 M3
RDKG RH5 ....155 L8
Friday Street Rd *RDKG* RH5 ..135 N5
Friend Av *ASHV* GU12 ....108 F5
Friends Cl *CRAWW* RH11 ......176 C5
Friendship Wy *BRAK* RG12 ....32 D4
Friends' Rd *CROY/NA* CR0 ....2 E5
PUR/KEN CR8 ....81 K1
Friern Rd *EDUL* SE22 ....31 H2
Friesian Cl *FLEETN* GU51 ....87 H3
Frimley Av *WLGTN* SM6 ....63 H4
WIM/MER SW19 ....28 B5
Frimley Crs *CROY/NA* CR0 .....65 J6
Frimley Gdns *MTCM* CR4 ......44 A4
Frimley Green Rd *FRIM* GU16 ..68 G9
Frimley Grove Gdns
FRIM GU16 ....68 F7

Frimley Hall Dr CBLY GU15 69 H2
Frimley Rd ASHV GU12 89 J6
CBLY GU15 68 D4
CHSGTN KT9 59 K4
Frinton Rd TOOT SW17 29 K9
Friston St FUL/PGN SW6 19 M7
Friston Wk CRAWW RH11 176 D4
Fritham Cl NWMAL KT3 42 C7
Frith Hill Rd FRIM GU16 69 J7
GODL GU7 131 K7
Frith Knowle WOT/HER KT12 57 K4
Frith Pk EGRIN RH19 162 D9
Frith Rd CROY/NA CR0 2 C4
Friths Dr REIG RH2 119 M2
Frithwald Rd CHERT KT16 37 K8
Frobisher BRAK RG12 32 E8
Frobisher Cl PUR/KEN CR8 81 L6
Frobisher Crs
STWL/WRAY TW19 23 H3
Frobisher Gdns GU GU1 112 E4
Frodsham Wy SHST GU47 50 A7
Froggetts La RDKG RH5 172 D2
Frog Grove La RGUW GU3 110 F2
Froghole La EDEN TN8 125 J4
Frog La BRAK RG12 32 C4
RGUE GU4 92 C5
Frogmore WAND/EARL SW18 28 D1
Frogmore Cl CHEAM SM3 61 H2
Frogmore Gdns CHEAM SM3 61 J3
Frogmore Gv BLKW GU17 67 N4
Frogmore Park Dr
BLKW GU17 67 P4
Frogmore Rd BLKW GU17 67 N4
Frome Cl FARN GU14 87 P1
Fromondes Rd CHEAM SM3 61 J4
Fromow Gdns BFOR GU20 52 D5
Fromows Cnr CHSWK W4 * 18 A3
Froxfield Down BRAK RG12 33 H6
Fruen Rd EBED/NFELT TW14 24 A3
Fry Cl CRAWW RH11 194 E1
Fryday Grove Ms BAL SW12 29 M3
Fryern Wd CTHM CR3 101 L4
Fry's La YTLY GU46 67 J1
Fryston Av COUL/CHIP CR5 80 D3
CROY/NA CR0 64 A1
Fuchsia Wy CHOB/PIR GU24 70 E2
Fugelmere Rd FLEETN GU51 87 J5
Fulbourne Cl REDH RH1 120 A3
Fulbrook La MFD/CHID GU8 129 M7
Fulford Rd CTHM CR3 101 M1
HOR/WEW KT19 60 B6
Fulham Broadway
FUL/PGN SW6 19 L5
Fulham Cl CRAWW RH11 176 E9
Fulham Est FUL/PGN SW6 19 L4
Fulham High St
FUL/PGN SW6 19 J8
Fulham Palace Rd
FUL/PGN SW6 19 H5
Fulham Park Gdns
FUL/PGN SW6 19 K7
Fulham Park Rd
FUL/PGN SW6 19 K7
Fulham Rd FUL/PGN SW6 19 J7
Fullbrook Av
ADL/WDHM KT15 55 L9
Fullbrooks Av WPK KT4 42 D9
Fullers Av SURB KT6 59 M1
Fullers Farm Rd
EHSLY KT24 114 D4
Fullers Hl BH/WHM TN16 105 H6
Fullers Rd RFNM GU10 127 H9
Fullers V BOR GU35 164 C6
Fullers Wy North SURB KT6 59 M2
Fullers Wy South
CHSGTN KT9 59 L3
Fuller's Wd CROY/NA CR0 64 G4
Fullers Wood La REDH RH1 120 E5
Fullerton Cl BF/WBF KT14 74 B3
FLEETN GU51 86 C4
Fullerton Dr BF/WBF KT14 74 A3
Fullerton Rd BF/WBF KT14 74 A3
CAR SM5 62 A7
CROY/NA CR0 45 P8
WAND/EARL SW18 28 F1
Fullerton Wy BF/WBF KT14 74 A3
Fuller Wy HYS/HAR UB3 15 H3
Fullmer Wy ADL/WDHM KT15 55 K8
Fulmar Cl CRAWW RH11 * 176 A6
Fulmar Ct BRYLDS KT5 41 M7
Fulmar Dr EGRIN RH19 162 F9
Fulmead St FUL/PGN SW6 19 M6
Fulmer Cl HPTN TW12 24 F8
Fulmer Wy WEA W13 17 H1
Fulstone Cl HSLWW TW4 15 P9
Fulvens SHGR GU5 134 G5
Fulwell Park Av WHTN TW2 25 K5
Fulwell Rd TEDD TW11 25 L7
Fulwood Gdns TWK TW1 25 N2
Fulwood Wk WIM/MER SW19 28 B4
Furber St HMSMTH W6 18 F1
Furlong Cl WLGTN SM6 44 D9
Furlong Rd DORK RH4 116 C8
Furlong Wy HORL RH6 159 J4
The Furlough
WOKS/MYFD GU22 11 H2
Furmage St
WAND/EARL SW18 28 E3
Furnace Dr CRAWE RH10 177 J7
Furnace Farm Rd
CRAWE RH10 * 177 K7
EGRIN RH19 161 K9
Furnace Pde CRAWE RH10 177 K7
Furnace Pl CRAWE RH10 177 K7
Furneaux Av WNWD SE27 30 C8
Furness Rd FUL/PGN SW6 19 M7
MRDN SM4 43 M7
Furnival Cl VW GU25 36 B7
Furrows Pl CTHM CR3 101 P3
The Furrows WOT/HER KT12 57 L1
Furse Cl CBLY GU15 69 K4
Furtherfield Cl CROY/NA CR0 45 J7
Further Vell-Mead
FLEETS GU52 106 E2
Furzebank ASC SL5 34 D5
Furze Cl ASHV GU12 89 J8
REDH RH1 120 B4
Furzedown Cl EGH TW20 21 K9
Furzedown Dr TOOT SW17 29 L8
Furzedown Rd BELMT SM2 61 N9
TOOT SW17 29 L8
Furzefield CRAWW RH11 176 E4
Furze Fld LHD/OX KT22 76 D2
Furzefield Cha EGRIN RH19 162 D6
Furzefield Crs REIG RH2 119 N7
Furzefield Rd EGRIN RH19 162 C8
HORS RH12 192 G5
REIG RH2 119 N7
Furze Gv KWD/TDW/WH KT20 99 K1
Furze Hl KWD/TDW/WH KT20 99 K1
PUR/KEN CR8 62 G9
Furzehill REDH RH1 120 A4
Furze Hill Crs CWTH RG45 49 N5
Furze Hill Rd BOR GU35 164 F7
Furze La EGRIN RH19 162 A9
GODL GU7 131 M5
PUR/KEN CR8 62 G9
Furzemoors BRAK RG12 32 D6
Furzen La HORS RH12 172 B8
Furze Pl REDH RH1 * 120 B4
Furze Rd ADL/WDHM KT15 55 K5
HORS RH12 189 N2
THHTH CR7 45 L4
Furze Vale Rd BOR GU35 164 E7
Furzewood SUN TW16 39 J2
Fyfe Wy BMLY BR1 47 N3
Fyfield Cl BLKW GU17 67 P3
HAYES BR2 47 K5

G

Gable Ct SYD SE26 31 J7
Gable End FARN GU14 * 88 D3
Gables Av ASHF TW15 23 J8
Gables Cl ASHV GU12 109 J1
FARN GU14 88 C3
WOKS/MYFD GU22 72 D9
Gables Rd FLEETS GU52 106 F2
The Gables BNSTD SM7 79 K6
HORS RH12 192 C6
LHD/OX KT22 76 C1
NRWD SE19 * 45 N2
WEY KT13 56 E4
WOKS/MYFD GU22 * 10 B7
Gables Wy BNSTD SM7 79 K5
Gabriel Cl FELT TW13 24 F7
Gabriel Dr CBLY GU15 69 K4
Gabriel Rd CRAWE RH10 177 M9
Gabriel St FSTH SE23 31 L3
Gadbridge La CRAN GU6 153 P8
Gadesden Rd
HOR/WEW KT19 60 A5
Gaffney Cl ALDT GU11 88 F8
Gage Cl CRAWE RH10 179 K2
Gainsborough BRAK RG12 32 E7
Gainsborough Cl BECK BR3 46 G1
CBLY GU15 69 H1
ESH/CLAY KT10 * 40 D9
FARN GU14 88 F5
Gainsborough Ct
WOT/HER KT12 57 J3
Gainsborough Dr ASC SL5 33 M4
SAND/SEL CR2 82 A2
Gainsborough Gdns
HSLW TW3 25 L1
Gainsborough Ms DUL SE21 30 D4
SYD SE26 * 31 J6
Gainsborough Rd CHSWK W4 18 D2
CRAWE RH10 177 J9
HOR/WEW KT19 60 A8
NWMAL KT3 42 B7
RCH/KEW TW9 17 M7
Gainsborough Ter
BELMT SM2 * 61 K6
Gaist Av CTHM CR3 102 B2
Galahad Rd CRAWW RH11 176 B5
Galata Rd BARN SW13 18 E5
Gale Barracks ALDT GU11 * 108 D2
Gale Cl HPTN TW12 24 F9
MTCM CR4 43 P4
Gale Crs BNSTD SM7 79 L6
Gale Dr LTWR GU18 52 A8
Galena Rd HMSMTH W6 18 F2
Galesbury Rd
WAND/EARL SW18 28 F2
Gales Cl RGUE GU4 * 113 H2
Gales Dr CRAWE RH10 177 J5
Gales Pl CRAWE RH10 177 J5
Galgate Cl WIM/MER SW19 28 B4
The Galleries ALDT GU11 * 108 C4
Gallery Rd DUL SE21 30 E4
Galleymead Rd
DTCH/LGLY SL3 13 K6
The Gallop BELMT SM2 61 P7
SAND/SEL CR2 64 B6
YTLY GU46 67 H1
Galloway Cl FLEETN GU51 87 J3
Galloway Pth CROY/NA CR0 63 M3
Gallwey Rd ALDT GU11 108 E3
Galy Hill Rd FLEETS GU52 106 F2
Galpin's Rd THHTH CR7 44 G5
Galsworthy Rd CHERT KT16 * 37 L8
KUTN/CMB KT2 9 K2
Galton Rd ASC SL5 34 F7
Galveston Rd PUT/ROE SW15 28 C1
Galvins Cl GUW GU2 111 N2
Galway Rd YTLY GU46 * 66 G4
Gambles La RPLY/SEND GU23 93 N5
Gambole Rd TOOT SW17 29 H7
Gamlen Rd PUT/ROE SW15 19 H9
Gander Green Crs
HPTN TW12 40 A2
Gander Green La CHEAM SM3 61 J1
Gangers Hl GDST RH9 102 F7
Ganghill GU GU1 112 E3
Gapemouth Rd
CHOB/PIR GU24 89 N2
Gap Rd WIM/MER SW19 28 D8
Garbetts Wy RFNM GU10 108 G8
Garbrand Wk EW KT17 60 D7
Garden Av MTCM CR4 44 D1
Garden Cl ADL/WDHM KT15 55 P3
ASHF TW15 23 M9
BNSTD SM7 79 L4
EGRIN RH19 180 E4
FARN GU14 88 A5
HPTN TW12 24 G8
LHD/OX KT22 97 J4
PUT/ROE SW15 27 N3
SHGR GU5 133 H9
WLGTN SM6 62 G4
Gardeners Cl HORS RH12 191 M2
Gardeners Gn HORS RH12 175 H5
Gardener's Hill Rd
RFNM GU10 127 M9
Gardeners Rd CROY/NA CR0 2 B2
Gardener's Wk GT/LBKH KT23 96 B6
Garden House La
EGRIN RH19 180 E4
Gardenia Ct CHOB/PIR GU24 70 F2
Garden La BRXS/STRHM SW2 30 A4
Garden Pl HORS RH12 * 192 B6
Garden Rd BMLY BR1 47 P1
PGE/AN SE20 46 C2
RCH/KEW TW9 17 N8
WOT/HER KT12 39 K7
The Gardens BECK BR3 47 J3
CHOB/PIR GU24 90 F2
COB KT11 * 74 E8
EBED/NFELT TW14 23 N2
ESH/CLAY KT10 58 A3
RFNM GU10 109 H7
Garden Wk BECK BR3 46 F2
COUL/CHIP CR5 100 D3
CRAWW RH11 176 F5
HORS RH12 192 B6
Garden Wood Rd
EGRIN RH19 180 B2
Gardner La CRAWE RH10 179 H3
Gardner Pl EBED/NFELT TW14 24 C2
Gardner Rd GU GU1 6 E2
Garendon Gdns MRDN SM4 43 M8
Garendon Rd MRDN SM4 43 M8
Gareth Cl WPK KT4 61 H1
Garfield Rd ADL/WDHM KT15 55 N4
CBLY GU15 68 E3
TWK TW1 25 P4
WIM/MER SW19 28 F9
Garibaldi Rd REDH RH1 120 B6
Garland Ct EGRIN RH19 * 180 C2
Garland Rd EGRIN RH19 180 C2
Garlands Rd LHD/OX KT22 97 H1
REDH RH1 120 B5
Garland Wy CTHM CR3 101 M2
Garlichill Rd EPSOM KT18 78 F6
Garlies Rd FSTH SE23 31 M6
Garnet Fld YTLY GU46 66 E3
Garnet Rd THHTH CR7 45 L5
Garrad's Rd
STRHM/NOR SW16 29 N6
Garrard Rd BNSTD SM7 79 L5
Garratt Cl CROY/NA CR0 62 G3
Garratt La WAND/EARL SW18 28 E3
Garratts La BNSTD SM7 79 K5
Garratt Ter TOOT SW17 29 H7
Garrett Cl CRAWE RH10 177 M7
Garrett Rd EWKG RG40 48 C1
Garrick Cl RCH/KEW TW9 26 B1
STA TW18 37 L1
WAND/EARL SW18 19 N9
WOT/HER KT12 57 K3
Garrick Crs CROY/NA CR0 3 G4
Garrick Gdns
E/WMO/HCT KT8 40 A4
Garrick Rd RCH/KEW TW9 17 N7
Garrick Wk CRAWE RH10 177 H8
Garrick Wy FRIM GU16 88 G1
Garrison Cl HSLWW TW4 24 G1
Garrison La CHSGTN KT9 59 L6
The Garrones
CRAWE RH10 * 177 P4
Garsdale Ter WKENS W14 * 19 K3
Garside Cl HPTN TW12 40 B1
Garson La STWL/WRAY TW19 21 J3
Garson Rd ESH/CLAY KT10 57 P4
Garston La PUR/KEN CR8 81 M4
The Garstons GT/LBKH KT23 95 P5
Garswood BRAK RG12 32 F7
Garth Cl FNM GU9 127 L6
KUTN/CMB KT2 26 E8
MRDN SM4 43 H8
Garthorne Rd FSTH SE23 31 L3
Garth Rd CHSWK W4 18 B3
KUTN/CMB KT2 26 E8
MRDN SM4 43 H9
Garthside KUTN/CMB KT2 26 D8
Garth Sq BNFD RG42 32 D1
The Garth ASHV GU12 109 H5
COB KT11 75 N2
FARN GU14 88 F3
HPTN TW12 25 J9
Gartmoor Gdns
WIM/MER SW19 28 C4
Garton Cl CRAWW RH11 176 B6
Garton Pl WAND/EARL SW18 28 F2
Gartons Wy BTSEA SW11 19 N8
Gascoigne Rd CROY/NA CR0 65 J8
WEY KT13 56 D2
Gasden Copse
MFD/CHID GU8 149 L7
Gasden Dr MFD/CHID GU8 149 L6
Gasden La MFD/CHID GU8 149 L6
Gaskarth Rd BAL SW12 29 L2
Gaskyns Cl HORS RH12 189 N3
Gaspar Ms ECT SW5 19 M2
Gassiot Rd TOOT SW17 29 J7
Gassiot Wy SUT SM1 61 P2
Gasson Wood Rd
CRAWW RH11 176 B7
Gastein Rd HMSMTH W6 19 H4
Gaston Bell Cl RCH/KEW TW9 17 M8
Gaston Bridge Rd
SHPTN TW17 38 G6
Gaston Rd MTCM CR4 44 C4
Gaston Wy SHPTN TW17 38 F6
Gatcombe Crs ASC SL5 33 P2
Gateford Dr HORS RH12 192 E4
Gatehouse Cl KUTN/CMB KT2 42 A1
Gates Cl CRAWE RH10 177 M9
Gatesden Cl LHD/OX KT22 96 C3
Gatesden Rd LHD/OX KT22 96 C3
Gates Green Rd WWKM BR4 65 N3
Gateside Rd TOOT SW17 29 J6
The Gates FLEETN GU51 87 J3
Gatestone Rd NRWD SE19 30 F9
Gateways GU GU1 112 F6
The Gateways
RCH/KEW TW9 * 17 K9
The Gateway
WOKN/KNAP GU21 72 F3
Gatfield Gv FELT TW13 25 H5
Gatley Av HOR/WEW KT19 59 P4
Gatley Dr RGUE GU4 112 D2
Gatton Bottom REIG RH2 100 B8
Gatton Cl BELMT SM2 * 61 M7
REIG RH2 119 N2
Gatton Park Rd REIG RH2 119 P2
Gatton Rd REIG RH2 119 N2
TOOT SW17 29 H7
Gatwick Rd
WAND/EARL SW18 28 C3
Gatwick Wy HORL RH6 159 J4
Gauntlet Crs PUR/KEN CR8 81 M8
Gauntlett Rd SUT SM1 61 P4
Gavell Rd COB KT11 75 J2
Gaveston Cl BF/WBF KT14 74 B2
Gaveston Rd LHD/OX KT22 76 G9
Gavina Cl MRDN SM4 44 A6
Gawton Crs COUL/CHIP CR5 100 E1
Gayfere Rd EW KT17 60 E4
Gayhouse La REDH RH1 141 N6
Gayler Cl REDH RH1 121 P5
Gaynesford Rd CAR SM5 62 B6
FSTH SE23 31 L5
Gayton Cl ASHTD KT21 77 L7
Gayville Rd BTSEA SW11 29 J2
Gaywood Cl
BRXS/STRHM SW2 30 A4
Gaywood Rd ASHTD KT21 77 M7
Gearing Cl TOOT SW17 29 L7
Geary Cl HORL RH6 160 C3
Geffers Ride ASC SL5 33 N4
Gemini Cl CRAWW RH11 176 A7
Gemmell Cl PUR/KEN CR8 81 H3
Genesis Cl STWL/WRAY TW19 23 J4
Geneva Cl SHPTN TW17 38 G3
Geneva Rd KUT/HW KT1 41 L5
THHTH CR7 45 L6
Genoa Av PUT/ROE SW15 27 P1
Genoa Rd PGE/AN SE20 46 C2
Gentles La LIPH GU30 182 D1
Genyn Rd GUW GU2 6 B6
George Denyer Cl
HASM GU27 184 D3
George Eliot Cl
MFD/CHID GU8 149 N8
George Gdns ALDT GU11 108 E7
George Groves Rd
PGE/AN SE20 46 A2
Georgeham Rd SHST GU47 49 P7
George Horley Pl
RDKG RH5 * 156 G3
Georgelands
RPLY/SEND GU23 93 M1
George La HAYES BR2 47 P9
George Rd FLEETN GU51 87 H6
GODL GU7 131 L6
GU GU1 6 E3
KUTN/CMB KT2 41 P1
MFD/CHID GU8 149 N2
NWMAL KT3 42 D5
George's Rd BH/WHM TN16 84 B9
Georges Ter CTHM CR3 101 M2
George St CHOB/PIR GU24 90 A1
CROY/NA CR0 2 E4
HSLW TW3 15 P7
NWDGN UB2 15 N2
RCH/KEW TW9 26 C1
STA TW18 22 C7
Georgetown Cl NRWD SE19 30 E8
George Wyver Cl
WIM/MER SW19 28 B3
Georgian Cl CBLY GU15 68 G1
CRAWE RH10 177 N6
HAYES BR2 47 P9
STA TW18 22 E7
Georgia Rd NWMAL KT3 42 A5
THHTH CR7 45 K2
Geraldine Rd CHSWK W4 17 N4
WAND/EARL SW18 28 F1
Gerald's Gv BNSTD SM7 79 H3
Geranium Cl CWTH RG45 49 M1
Gerard Av HSLWW TW4 25 H3
Gerard Rd BARN SW13 18 D6
Germander Dr
CHOB/PIR GU24 70 G5
Gerrards Md BNSTD SM7 79 K5
Gertrude St WBPTN SW10 19 N4
Ghent St CAT SE6 31 P5
Giant Arches Rd HNHL SE24 30 D3
Gibbet La CBLY GU15 69 J1
Gibbon Rd KUTN/CMB KT2 8 E2
Gibbons Cl CRAWE RH10 * 177 M8
SHST GU47 67 N1
Gibbon Wk PUT/ROE SW15 * 18 E9
Gibb's Acre CHOB/PIR GU24 90 F3
Gibbs Av NRWD SE19 30 E9
Gibbs Brook La OXTED RH8 123 K5
Gibbs Cl EWKG RG40 48 C3
NRWD SE19 * 30 E8
Gibbs Gn WKENS W14 * 19 K3
Gibbs Sq NRWD SE19 * 30 E8
Gibbs Wy YTLY GU46 66 F4
Giblets La HORS RH12 192 E3
Giblets Wy HORS RH12 192 D3
Gibraltar Crs HOR/WEW KT19 60 C8
Gibson Cl CHSGTN KT9 * 59 J4
ISLW TW7 16 D8
Gibson Ct DTCH/LGLY SL3 12 D3
Gibson Pl STWL/WRAY TW19 22 F2
Gibson Rd SUT SM1 61 M4
Gibson's Hl
STRHM/NOR SW16 30 B9
Gidd Hl COUL/CHIP CR5 80 C5
Giffard Dr FARN GU14 88 B1
Giffard La FLEETN GU51 86 F4
Giffards Cl EGRIN RH19 180 E2
Giffards Meadow FNM GU9 128 A4
Giffard Wy GUW GU2 111 N2
Giggs Hill Gdns THDIT KT7 40 G9
Giggs Hill Rd THDIT KT7 40 G8
Gilbert Cl WIM/MER SW19 * 43 M2
Gilbert Rd BMLY BR1 47 N1
FRIM GU16 68 E7
WIM/MER SW19 43 N1
Gilbert St HSLW TW3 16 C8
Gilbert Wy DTCH/LGLY SL3 12 D3
EWKG RG40 48 C1
Gilbey Rd TOOT SW17 29 H7
Gilders Rd CHSGTN KT9 59 M6
Giles Coppice NRWD SE19 30 G7
Giles Md EPSOM KT18 * 78 C3
Giles Travers Cl EGH TW20 36 G4
Gilham La FROW RH18 181 K9
Gilham's Av BNSTD SM7 79 H1
Gilkes Crs DUL SE21 30 F2
Gilkes Pl DUL SE21 30 F2
Gill Av GUW GU2 111 L6
Gillet Ct SWTR RH13 * 192 G6
Gillett Ct SWTR RH13 192 G6
Gillett Rd THHTH CR7 45 M5
Gillham's La HASM GU27 183 K6
Gilliam Gv PUR/KEN CR8 63 J8
Gillian Av ASHV GU12 108 E6
Gillian Cl ASHV GU12 108 F6
Gillian Park Rd CHEAM SM3 43 K9
Gillian Ter BRYLDS KT5 * 41 M7
Gilliat Dr RGUE GU4 113 H3
Gilligan Cl HORS RH12 192 A8
Gilmais GT/LBKH KT23 96 C5
Gilmore Crs ASHF TW15 23 K8
Gilpin Av MORT/ESHN SW14 18 B9
Gilpin Cl MTCM CR4 44 A3
Gilpin Crs WHTN TW2 25 J3
Gilpin Wy HYS/HAR UB3 14 F5
Gilsland Rd THHTH CR7 45 M5
Gilson Ct WDSR SL4 21 H3
Gilstead Rd FUL/PGN SW6 19 M7
Gilston Rd WBPTN SW10 19 N3
Gimcrack Hl LHD/OX KT22 97 H2
Ginhams Rd CRAWW RH11 176 E5
Gipsy Hl NRWD SE19 30 F8
Gipsy La BRAK RG12 32 F4
PUT/ROE SW15 18 E8
Gipsy Rd WNWD SE27 30 E7
Gipsy Road Gdns
WNWD SE27 30 D7
Girdlers Rd HMSMTH W6 19 H2
Girdwood Rd
WAND/EARL SW18 28 B3
Girling Wy EBED/NFELT TW14 15 J8
Gironde Rd FUL/PGN SW6 19 K5
Girton Cl SHST GU47 50 A8
Girton Gdns CROY/NA CR0 64 G2
Girton Rd SYD SE26 31 L8
Gisbourne Cl WLGTN SM6 62 F2
Glade Cl SURB KT6 * 59 K1
Glade Gdns CROY/NA CR0 46 E8
Gladeside CROY/NA CR0 46 D8
Glade Sp KWD/TDW/WH KT20 99 M1
The Glades EGRIN RH19 180 G2
The Glade ASC SL5 34 C6
BELMT SM2 61 J7
BF/WBF KT14 73 J2
COUL/CHIP CR5 81 J8
CRAWE RH10 177 K7
CROY/NA CR0 46 D6
EW KT17 60 E5
FNM GU9 107 P7
FRIM GU16 89 H5
KWD/TDW/WH KT20 99 M1
LHD/OX KT22 96 B2
STA TW18 37 M1
SWTR RH13 192 F7
WWKM BR4 65 H2
Gladiator St FSTH SE23 31 M2
Gladiator Wy FARN GU14 88 C7
Gladioli Cl HPTN TW12 25 H9
Gladsmuir Cl WOT/HER KT12 57 L1
Gladstone Av
EBED/NFELT TW14 24 B2
WHTN TW2 25 L3
Gladstone Gdns HSLW TW3 16 C6
Gladstone Ms PGE/AN SE20 46 C1
Gladstone Pl
E/WMO/HCT KT8 * 40 E6
Gladstone Rd ASHTD KT21 77 K7
CHSWK W4 * 18 B1
CROY/NA CR0 45 M8
HORS RH12 192 C7
KUT/HW KT1 9 J6
SURB KT6 59 K1
WIM/MER SW19 43 L1
Gladstone Ter WNWD SE27 * 30 D7
Gladwyn Rd PUT/ROE SW15 19 H8
Glamis Cl FRIM GU16 69 H9

Glamis Crs HYS/HAR UB3.....14 E1
Glamorgan Cl MTCM CR4.....44 G4
Glamorgan Rd KUT/HW KT1.....8 A1
Glanfield Rd BECK BR3.....46 F5
The Glanty EGH TW20.....21 P7
Glanville Rd
  BRXS/STRHM SW2.....29 P4
  HAYES BR2.....47 P4
Glasbrook Av WHTN TW2.....24 G4
Glasford St TOOT SW17.....28 C1
Glassmill La HAYES BR2.....47 M3
Glastonbury Rd MRDN SM4.....43 L8
Glayshers Hl BOR GU35.....164 D5
Glazbury Rd WKENS.....19 J2
Glazebrook Cl DUL SE21.....30 E5
Glazebrook Rd TEDD TW11.....40 F1
Glaziers La RGUW GU3.....110 C4
Gleave Cl EGRIN RH19.....180 F7
Glebe Av MTCM CR4.....43 J5
Glebe Cl ALDT GU11.....108 C7
  CHSWK W4 *.....18 C3
  CRAWE RH10.....176 G4
  GT/LBKH KT23.....96 A6
  LTWR GU18.....52 C8
  SAND/SEL CR2.....81 P7
Glebe Cottages RGUE GU4.....113 M3
Glebe Ct FLEETS GU51.....86 F5
Glebe Gdns BF/WBF KT14.....73 P3
  NWMAL KT3.....42 C8
Glebe House HAYES BR2.....47 P
Glebe Hyrst SAND/SEL CR2.....81 P1
Glebeland Gdns SHPTN TW17.....38 E7
Glebeland Rd CBLY GU15.....68 B4
Glebelands BIL RH14.....188 C6
  CRAWE RH10.....179 H3
  E/WMO/HCT KT8.....40 B6
  ESH/CLAY KT10.....57 H6
Glebelands Meadow
  CRAN GU6 *.....188 C1
Glebelands Rd
  EBED/NFELT TW14.....24 B3
  RFNM GU10.....147 M7
Glebe La RDKG RH5.....135 M5
Glebe Pth MTCM CR4.....44 B4
Glebe Rd ASHTD KT21.....77 K7
  BARN SW13.....18 E4
  BELMT SM2.....61 J7
  BMLY BR1.....47 N2
  BOR GU35.....164 B6
  CAR SM5.....62 B5
  CRAN GU6.....153 H8
  DORK RH4.....116 F7
  EGH TW20.....21 P9
  FARN GU14.....88 B7
  REDH RH1.....100 C4
  RFNM GU10.....106 D8
  STA TW18.....22 E8
  WARL CR6.....82 A6
  WDSR SL4.....20 G1
Glebe Side TWK TW1.....25 N2
Glebe Sq MTCM CR4 *.....44 B4
Glebe St CHSWK W4.....18 B3
The Glebe BLKW GU17.....68 A4
  CRAN GU6.....153 P6
  CRAWE RH10.....160 C9
  EGRIN RH19.....161 P8
  HORL RH6.....159 J1
  STRHM/NOR SW16.....29 N7
  WDR/YW UB7.....14 A2
  WPK KT4.....42 D9
Glebe Wy FELT TW13.....25 H5
  SAND/SEL CR2.....81 P1
Glebewood BRAK RG12.....32 E6
Gledhow Gdns ECT SW5.....19 N2
Glebe Wd
  KWD/TDW/WH KT20.....99 M2
Gledstanes Rd WKENS W14.....19 J3
Glegg Pl PUT/ROE SW15.....19 H9
Glen Albyn Rd
  WIM/MER SW19.....28 A5
Glena Mt SUT SM1.....61 N5
Glen Av ASHF TW15.....23 K7
Glenavon Cl ESH/CLAY KT10.....58 G5
Glenavon Gdns
  DTCH/LGLY SL3.....12 A2
  YTLY GU46.....67 H4
Glenbuck Rd SURB KT6.....41 K7
Glenburnie Rd TOOT SW17.....29 J6
Glencairn Rd
  STRHM/NOR SW16.....29 N8
  KWD/TDW/WH KT20.....99 J3
  SHPTN TW17.....38 C5
Glencoe Cl FRIM GU16.....69 H8
Glencoe Rd WEY KT13.....56 C2
Glen Cl ADL/WDHM KT15.....55 K4
Glendale Cl HORS RH12.....192 F4
  WOKN/KNAP GU21.....72 A7
Glendale Dr RGUE GU4.....112 C1
  WIM/MER SW19.....28 C8
Glen Dale Ms BECK BR3.....47 H2
Glendale Pk FLEETS GU51.....86 C5
Glendale Ri PUR/KEN CR8.....81 K4
Glendarvon St
  PUT/ROE SW15.....19 H8
Glendene Av EHSLY KT24.....94 C6
Glendower Gdns
  MORT/ESHN SW14.....18 B8
Glendower Pl SKENS SW7.....19 P2
Glendower Rd
  MORT/ESHN SW14.....18 B8
Glendye Wy EGRIN RH19.....180 F3
Gleneagle Ms
  STRHM/NOR SW16.....29 N8
Gleneagle Rd
  STRHM/NOR SW16.....29 N8
Gleneagles Cl
  STWL/WRAY TW19.....22 F2
Gleneagles Ct
  CRAWE RH10 *.....176 G6

Gleneagles Dr FARN GU14.....87 N4
Gleneldon Ms
  STRHM/NOR SW16.....29 P8
Gleneldon Rd
  STRHM/NOR SW16.....29 P8
Glenelg Dr BRXS/STRHM SW2..29 P1
Glenfield Cl
  BRKHM/BTCW RH3.....117 M9
Glenfield Rd ASHF TW15.....23 L9
  BAL SW12.....29 M4
  BNSTD SM7.....79 M4
  BRKHM/BTCW RH3.....117 P9
Glen Gdns CROY/NA CRO.....63 J2
Glenheadon Cl LHD/OX KT22..97 K3
Glenheadon Ri LHD/OX KT22..97 K3
Glenhurst BFOR GU20.....52 A3
Glenhurst Cl BLKW GU17.....68 A4
Glenhurst Rd NRWD SE19.....45 L1
Glenhurst Rd BTFD TW8.....17 L2
Glen Innes SHST GU47.....50 B8
Glenister Park Rd
  STRHM/NOR SW16.....44 F1
Glenlea GSHT GU26.....183 P1
Glenlea Hollow GSHT GU26..183 P2
Glenmore Cl
  ADL/WDHM KT15.....55 M2
Glenmount Rd FRIM GU16.....89 J5
Glenn Av PUR/KEN CR8.....63 K9
Glennie Rd WNWD SE27.....30 B6
Glen Rd CHSGTN KT9.....59 L2
  FLEETN GU51.....86 F7
Glen Road End WLGTN SM6..62 D7
Glenrosa St FUL/PGN SW6.....19 N7
Glenside Cl PUR/KEN CR8.....81 M4
Glentanner Wy TOOT SW17..29 H7
Glentham Gdns BARN SW13..18 F4
Glentham Rd BARN SW13.....18 E4
Glenthorne Av CROY/NA CRO..46 C9
Glenthorne Cl CHEAM SM3.....43 L9
Glenthorne Gdns
  CHEAM SM3.....43 L9
  KUT/HW KT1.....41 M5
Glenthorne Rd MRDN SM4....41 M5
Glenthorpe Rd MRDN SM4....42 P4
Glenville Cl CRAWE RH10.....177 J3
Glenville Gdns GSHT GU26..166 A7
Glenville Rd KUTN/CMB KT2..9 H2
Glen Vue EGRIN RH19.....180 D2
Glenwood BRAK RG12.....32 F5
  RDKG RH5.....117 J9
Glenwood Rd CAT SE6.....31 N4
  EW KT17.....60 E5
  HSLW TW3.....16 D8
Glenwood Rw NRWD SE19 *..45 P2
Glenwood Wy CROY/NA CRO..46 C9
Gliddon Rd WKENS W14.....19 J2
Globe Farm La BLKW GU17..67 M3
Glorney Md FNM GU9.....108 C8
Glory Md DORK RH4.....137 J1
Glossop Rd SAND/SEL CR2....63 N7
Gloster Rd NWMAL KT3.....42 C5
  WOKS/MYFD GU22.....72 E9
Gloucester Cl FRIM GU16.....88 G1
  THDIT KT7 *.....40 G9
Gloucester Ct MTCM CR4.....44 G6
  RCH/KEW TW9 *.....17 N5
Gloucester Crs STA TW18.....22 G9
Gloucester Dr STA TW18.....22 G9
Gloucester Lea BNFD RG42..33 K1
Gloucester Pde
  HYS/HAR UB3 *.....14 E1
Gloucester Pl BNFD RG42.....33 H1
Gloucester Rd ALDT GU11....108 E7
  BAGS GU19.....51 N5
  CRAWE RH10.....177 H9
  CROY/NA CRO.....3 F1
  FELT TW13.....24 D4
  GUW GU2.....111 M3
  HPTN TW12.....40 B1
  HSLW TW4.....15 J5
  KUT/HW KT1.....9 H5
  RCH/KEW TW9.....17 N5
  REDH RH1.....120 B4
  SKENS SW7.....19 N2
  TEDD TW11.....25 M8
  WHTN TW2.....25 K4
Glovers Cl BH/WHM TN16.....83 P5
Glover's Rd HORL RH6.....158 A5
  REIG RH2.....119 N7
Glyn Cl EW KT17.....60 E7
  SNWD SE25.....45 N3
Glynde Pl HORS RH12.....192 B9
Glynde St BROCKY SE4.....31 N2
Glyn Rd WPK KT4.....61 H1
Glynswood CBLY GU15.....69 H5
  RFNM GU10.....127 L9
Goaters Rd ASC SL5.....33 L3
Goat Rd MTCM CR4.....44 C8
Coatsfield Rd BH/WHM TN16..84 A9
Goat Whf BTFD TW8.....17 L4
Godalming Av WLGTN SM6..62 G4
Godalming Rd GODL GU7.....150 G1
  MFD/CHID GU8.....169 H6
Goddard Cl CRAWE RH10.....177 L8
  GUW GU2.....111 N1
  SHPTN TW17.....38 B4
Goddard Rd BECK BR3.....46 D5
Goddards La CBLY GU15.....68 D5
Godfrey Av WHTN TW2.....25 L3
Godfrey Wy HSLW TW4.....24 F3

WAND/EARL SW18.....28 G4
Godolphin Cl BELMT SM2.....61 K9
Godolphin Ct CRAWE RH10 *..176 G6
Godolphin Rd WEY KT13.....56 F5
Godric Crs CROY/NA CRO.....65 K8
Godson Rd CROY/NA CRO.....63 J2
Godstone Green Rd
  GDST RH9.....122 B2
Godstone Hi GDST RH9.....102 B8
Godstone Mt PUR/KEN CR8 *..81 K1
Godstone Rd CTHM CR3.....143 J8
  LING RH7.....143 J8
  OXTED RH8.....123 J1
  PUR/KEN CR8.....81 K2
  REDH RH1.....121 N4
  SUT SM1.....61 N3
  TWK TW1.....25 N2
Godwin Cl HOR/WEW KT19.....60 A5
Godwin Wy SWTR RH13.....192 E6
Goffs Cl CRAWW RH11.....176 F6
Goffs La CRAWW RH11.....176 F6
Goffs Park Rd CRAWW RH11..176 F6
Goffs Rd ASHF TW15.....23 N9
Gogmore Farm Cl
  CHERT KT16.....37 J8
Gogmore La CHERT KT16.....37 L8
Goidel Cl WLGTN SM6.....62 F3
Goldcliff Cl MRDN SM4.....43 L8
Goldcrest Cl HORL RH6.....159 P9
  YTLY GU46.....66 F2
Goldcrest Wy CROY/NA CRO..65 K7
  PUR/KEN CR8.....81 L5
Gold Cup La ASC SL5.....33 M2
Golden Ct HSLW TW3.....16 C7
Goldenfield Cl LIPH GU30.....182 G7
Golden Flds LIPH GU30.....182 F7
Goldfinch Cl ALDT GU11.....108 B6
  CRAWW RH11.....176 C3
Goldfinch Gdns RGUE GU4....113 H4
Goldfinch Rd SAND/SEL CR2..64 E8
Goldhawk Rd HMSMTH W6....18 C2
Goldhill RFNM GU10.....127 N7
Golding Cl CRAWE RH10.....177 M6
The Goldings
  WOKN/KNAP GU21.....71 M5
Gold La ALDT GU11.....108 C2
Goldney Rd CBLY GU15.....69 K4
Goldrings Rd LHD/OX KT22....76 C2
Goldsmiths Cl
  WOKN/KNAP GU21.....71 K7
Goldsmith Wy CWTH RG45....49 M5
Goldstone Farm Vw
  GT/LBKH KT23 *.....96 A7
Goldsworth Orch
  WOKN/KNAP GU21.....71 N7
Goldsworth Rd
  WOKN/KNAP GU21.....10 A5
Goldwell Rd THHTH CR7.....45 H5
Gole Rd CHOB/PIR GU24.....90 D1
Golf Cl THHTH CR7.....45 J4
  WOKS/MYFD GU22.....73 J3
Golf Club Dr KUTN/CMB KT2..42 B1
Golf Club Rd WEY KT13.....56 D8
  WOKS/MYFD GU22.....71 P9
Golf Dr CBLY GU15.....69 H4
Golf Links Av GSHT GU26.....165 L5
Golf Rd PUR/KEN CR8.....81 M7
Golf Side BELMT SM2.....25 L6
  WHTN TW2.....25 L6
Golf Side NWMAL KT3.....42 C3
Gomer Gdns TEDD TW11.....25 P9
Gomer Pl TEDD TW11.....25 P9
Gomshall Av WLGTN SM6.....62 G4
Gomshall Gdns PUR/KEN CR8..81 N4
Gomshall La SHGR GU5.....134 C1
Gomshall Rd BELMT SM2.....60 G8
Gondreville Gdns
  FLEETS GU52.....106 E2
Gong Hl RFNM GU10.....146 C1
Gong Hill Dr RFNM GU10.....127 P9
Gonston Cl WIM/MER SW19...28 B5
Gonville Rd THHTH CR7.....45 H6
Gonville St FUL/PGN SW6.....19 J8
Gooden Crs FARN GU14.....88 B5
Goodenough Cl
  COUL/CHIP CR5.....81 J9
Goodenough Wy
  COUL/CHIP CR5.....81 H9
Goodhart Wy WWKM BR4.....47 L1
Goodhew Rd CROY/NA CRO..46 A7
Gooding Cl NWMAL KT3.....42 A5
Goodley Stock Rd
  BH/WHM TN16.....104 F9
Goodman Crs
  BRXS/STRHM SW2.....29 N5
Goodrich Rd EDUL SE22.....30 C2
Goodways Dr BRAK RG12.....32 E3
Goodwin Cl CRAWW RH11.....176 B8
  MTCM CR4.....43 P4
Goodwin Gdns CROY/NA CRO..63 K5
Goodwins Cl EGRIN RH19.....162 C9
Goodwood Cl CBLY GU15.....50 E9
  CRAWE RH10.....177 M6
Goodwood Pde BECK BR3 *..46 E5
Goodwood Pl FARN GU14.....88 C4
Goodwood Rd REDH RH1.....120 B4
Goodwyns Rd DORK RH4.....137 H5
Goose Gn SHGR GU5.....134 E1
Goose Green Cl HORS RH12...192 C5
Goose La WOKS/MYFD GU22..90 F2
Goose Rye Rd RGUW GU3.....91 K6
Goossens Cl SUT SM1.....61 N4
Gordon Av CBLY GU15.....68 D4
  FLEETS GU52.....106 E2
  MORT/ESHN SW14.....18 C9
  SAND/SEL CR2.....63 L8

TWK TW1.....25 P1
Gordonbrock Rd BROCKY SE4..31 P1
Gordon Cl CHERT KT16.....55 J2
  STA TW18.....22 G9
Gordon Ct REDH RH1 *.....120 B7
Gordon Crs CBLY GU15.....68 E4
  CROY/NA CRO.....3 J1
  HYS/HAR UB3.....15 J2
Gordondale Rd
  WIM/MER SW19.....28 D5
Gordon Dr CHERT KT16.....55 J2
  SHPTN TW17.....38 F7
Gordon Rd ALDT GU11.....108 C5
  ASHF TW15.....23 H6
  BECK BR3.....46 F4
  BRYLDS KT5.....41 M8
  CAR SM5.....62 B5
  CBLY GU15.....68 E4
  CTHM CR3.....101 M1
  CWTH RG45.....49 M5
  ESH/CLAY KT10.....58 E6
  FARN GU14.....88 F2
  HORS RH12.....192 C6
  HSLW TW3.....16 C9
  KUTN/CMB KT2.....9 F5
  NWDGN UB2.....15 N2
  RCH/KEW TW9.....17 M7
  REDH RH1.....120 B7
  SHPTN TW17.....38 F7
Gordons Wy OXTED RH8.....103 K8
Gordon Wy BMLY BR1.....47 N2
Gore End RYNPK SW20.....42 G5
Gore Hill La VW GU25.....36 B5
Gore Rd WIM/MER SW19.....43 H1
Gorelands La VW GU25.....36 B5
Goreslands Cl ASHV GU12....109 J1
  BOR GU35.....164 F7
Gorham Pl MTCM CR4.....44 B1
Goring Rd STA TW18.....22 A8
Goring's Md SWTR RH13.....192 G5
Gorling Cl CRAWW RH11.....176 B6
Gorringe Park Av MTCM CR4..44 B1
Gorringes Brook
  HORS RH12.....192 C1
Gorse Bank LTWR GU18 *.....52 A9
Gorse Cl CRAWE RH10.....178 C5
  CRAWW RH11.....194 E2
  KWD/TDW/WH KT20.....78 F9
  RFNM GU10.....127 L7
Gorse Ct RGUE GU4.....112 C3
Gorse Dr HORL RH6.....141 K9
Gorse End HORS RH12.....192 C3
Gorse Hill La VW GU25.....36 B5
Gorse Hill Rd VW GU25.....36 B5
Gorse La CHOB/PIR GU24.....53 L8
  RFNM GU10.....127 L7
Gorse Pl BNFD RG42.....33 K1
Gorse Ride North EWKG RG40..48 C9
Gorse Ride South
  EWKG RG40.....48 C2
Gorse Rd CROY/NA CRO.....64 G6
Gorseway FLEETS GU52.....106 E4
Gorsewood Rd
  WOKN/KNAP GU21.....71 K8
Gorst Rd BTSEA SW11.....29 J2
Gort Cl ALDT GU11.....88 G8
Gosberton Rd BAL SW12.....29 J4
Gosbury Hl CHSGTN KT9.....59 L3
Gosden Cl CRAWE RH10.....177 K6
  SHGR GU5.....132 D5
Gosden Hill Rd RGUE GU4....112 G1
Gosfield Rd HOR/WEW KT19..78 B1
Gosling Gn DTCH/LGLY SL3....12 C1
Gosling Rd DTCH/LGLY SL3....12 C1
Gosnell Cl FRIM GU16.....69 M5
Gossops Dr CRAWW RH11.....176 D6
Gossops Green La CRAWW
  RH11.....176 D6
Gostrode La MFD/CHID GU8..185 P4
Gothic Ct HYS/HAR UB3.....14 F4
Gothic Rd WHTN TW2.....25 L5
Goudhurst Cl CRAWE RH10...177 P5
Gough Rd FLEETS GU51.....86 D6
Gough's La BRAK RG12.....32 G2
Gough's Meadow SHST GU47..67 M1
Gould Ct RGUE GU4.....113 H3
Goulding Gdns THHTH CR7....45 L3
Gould Rd EBED/NFELT TW14..23 P3
  WHTN TW2.....25 M4
Government House Rd
  FARN GU14.....88 C3
Government Rd ALDT GU11..108 G2
Governor's Rd CBLY GU15.....68 B2
Govett Av SHPTN TW17 *.....38 E6
Govett Gv BFOR GU20.....52 D4
Gowan Av FUL/PGN SW6.....19 J6
Gower Pk SHST GU47.....67 P1
Gower Rd HORL RH6.....159 H1
  ISLW TW7.....16 F4
  WEY KT13.....56 F5
The Gower EGH TW20.....36 F4
Gowland Pl BECK BR3.....46 F3
Gowlland Cl CROY/NA CRO....46 A8
Gowrie Pl CTHM CR3.....101 L2
Graburn Wy E/WMO/HCT KT8..40 D4
Grace Bennett Cl
  FARN GU14.....88 C2
Gracedale Rd
  STRHM/NOR SW16.....29 L8
Gracefield Gdns
  STRHM/NOR SW16.....29 P6
Grace Rd CRAWW RH11.....194 D1
  CROY/NA CRO.....45 L7
Gracious Pond Rd
  CHOB/PIR GU24.....53 M6

The Gradient SYD SE26.....31 H7
Graemesdyke Av
  MORT/ESHN SW14.....17 P8
Graffham Cl CRAWW RH11...176 E3
Grafton Cl BF/WBF KT14.....73 K2
  HSLWW TW4.....24 F4
  WPK KT4.....60 C2
Grafton Park Rd WPK KT4....60 C5
Grafton Rd CROY/NA CRO.....45 J9
  NWMAL KT3.....42 C4
  WPK KT4.....60 B2
Grafton Wy E/WMO/HCT KT8..39 P5
Graham Av MTCM CR4.....44 C2
Graham Cl CROY/NA CRO.....64 G1
Graham Gdns SURB KT6.....41 L9
Graham Rd BFOR GU20.....52 C5
  HPTN TW12.....25 H8
  MTCM CR4.....44 C1
  PUR/KEN CR8.....81 J2
  WIM/MER SW19.....43 K1
Grainger Rd ISLW TW7.....16 F7
Grampian Cl BELMT SM2.....61 N6
  HYS/HAR UB3.....14 F5
Grampian Rd SHST GU47.....49 P1
Grampian Wy DTCH/LGLY SL3..12 E3
Granada St TOOT SW17.....29 J8
Granard Av PUT/ROE SW15...27 N2
Granard Rd BTSEA SW11.....29 J3
Granary Cl HORL RH6.....140 C8
Granary Wy HORS RH12.....191 N9
Granborough Cl
  CBLY GU15.....68 E2
Grand Dr RYNPK SW20.....42 G5
Granden Rd
  STRHM/NOR SW16.....44 G3
Grandison Rd BTSEA SW11...29 J1
  WPK KT4.....60 G1
Grand Pde CRAWE RH10 *.....176 G5
  MORT/ESHN SW14 *.....18 B8
  SURB KT6 *.....41 N9
Grand Stand Rd EPSOM KT18..78 D6
Grand Union Canal
  Wk HNWL W7.....16 E1
  NWDGN UB2.....15 K1
Grand View Av
  BH/WHM TN16.....84 A6
Granfield St BTSEA SW11 *....19 M3
Grange Av CWTH RG45.....49 M3
  SNWD SE25.....45 N3
  WHTN TW2.....25 M5
Grangecliffe Gdns
  SNWD SE25.....45 N3
Grange Cl BH/WHM TN16 *...104 G6
  CRAWE RH10.....177 K3
  E/WMO/HCT KT8.....40 B5
  EDEN TN8.....144 G4
  GODL GU7.....131 N8
  GUW GU2.....111 P1
  HEST TW5.....15 P3
  LHD/OX KT22.....77 K9
  REDH RH1.....100 D8
  REDH RH1.....121 M4
  STWL/WRAY TW19.....21 K2
Grange Ct BELMT SM2 *.....61 M6
  EGH TW20.....21 L9
  GDST RH9.....122 E9
  GUW GU2.....111 P1
  RFNM GU10 *.....108 G8
  WLGTN SM6.....62 D2
  WOT/HER KT12.....57 J1
Grange Crs CRAWE RH10.....179 J4
Grange La DUL SE21.....30 G5
Grange Meadow BNSTD SM7..79 L1
Grange Ms FELT TW13 *.....23 N6
Grangemill Rd CAT SE6.....31 P6
Grangemill Wy CAT SE6.....31 P5
Grangemount LHD/OX KT22...77 K9
Grange Pk CRAN GU6.....153 P9
Grange Park Pl RYNPK SW20..42 F1
Grange Park Rd THHTH CR7...45 N5
  WOT/HER KT12 *.....57 J1
Grange Rd ADL/WDHM KT15...55 L8
  ASHV GU12.....109 K5
  BARN SW13.....18 E4
  BELMT SM2.....61 L6
  BRAK RG12.....32 E2
  CHOB/PIR GU24.....90 D2
  CHSGTN KT9.....59 L3
  CHSWK W4.....18 C3
  CRAWE RH10.....179 H4
  CTHM CR3.....102 A5
  E/WMO/HCT KT8.....40 B5
  EGH TW20.....21 M9
  FARN GU14.....88 D8
  FLEETS GU52.....106 E2
  GUW GU2.....111 P9
  KUT/HW KT1.....8 C6
  LHD/OX KT22.....77 K9
  RFNM GU10.....108 G8
  RFNM GU10.....147 L4
  SAND/SEL CR2.....63 L8
  SNWD SE25.....45 L6
  WOKN/KNAP GU21.....72 C4
  WOT/HER KT12.....57 J1
The Grange CHOB/PIR GU24...53 L6
  CROY/NA CRO.....64 F1
  NWMAL KT3.....42 D6
  WDSR SL4.....20 G1
  WIM/MER SW19.....28 A9
  WKENS W14 *.....19 K2
  WOT/HER KT12.....57 N3

WPK KT4 ....60 B3
Grange V BELMT SM2 ....61 M6
Grangeway HORL RH6 ....160 B1
Gransden Cl BECK BR3 ....31 N9
Granson Wy CRAWE RH10 ....179 K3
Grantchester KUT/HW KT1 * ...9 H5
Grant Cl SHPTN TW17 ....38 D7
Grantham Cl CHSWK W4 ....18 C5
Grantham Rd BTSEA SW11 .....19 P8
Grantley Av SHGR GU5 ....132 F7
Grantley Cl RGUE GU4 ....132 C3
Grantley Ct FNM GU9 ....127 K7
Grantley Dr FLEETS GU52 .....86 F8
Grantley Gdns GUW GU2 ......111 N4
Grantley Pl ESH/CLAY KT10 ...58 B4
Grantley Rd GUW GU2 ....111 N4
  HSLWW TW4 ....15 L3
Granton Rd
  STRHM/NOR SW16 ....44 E2
  CROY/NA CR0 ....3 J1
  CWTH RG45 ....49 N6
Grants La EDEN TN8 ....124 B8
  OXTED RH8 ....124 A4
Grant Wk ASC SL5 ....34 E9
Grant Wy ISLW TW7 ....16 C4
Grantwood Cl REDH RH1 ......146 C2
Granville Av FELT TW13 ....24 B5
  HSLW TW3 ....25 H1
Granville Cl BF/WBF KT14 .....74 B2
  CROY/NA CR0 ....3 G5
  WEY KT13 ....56 E5
Granville Gdns
  STRHM/NOR SW16 ....45 H2
Granville Pl FUL/PGN SW6 * ..19 M5
Granville Rd BH/WHM TN16 ..104 C6
  HYS/HAR UB3 ....15 H2
  OXTED RH8 ....103 M9
  WAND/EARL SW18 ....28 D3
  WEY KT13 ....56 E6
  WIM/MER SW19 ....43 L1
  WOKS/MYFD GU22 ....29 P6
Grapsome Cl CHSGTN KT9 .....59 J6
Grasholm Wy DTCH/LGLY SL3 .12 G2
Grasmere Av HSLW TW3 ....25 J2
  PUT/ROE SW15 ....27 J7
  WIM/MER SW19 ....43 L4
Grasmere Cl
  EBED/NFELT TW14 ....24 A4
  EGH TW20 ....36 F1
  GU GU1 ....112 F4
Grasmere Gdns HORS RH12 ..192 G4
Grasmere Rd BMLY BR1 ....47 M2
  FARN GU14 ....88 A4
  FNM GU9 ....107 L8
  LTWR GU18 ....49 K8
  PUR/KEN CR8 ....63 K9
  SNWD SE25 ....46 B7
  STRHM/NOR SW16 ....30 A8
Grasmere Wy BF/WBF KT14 ...74 B1
Grasslands HORL RH6 ....160 B1
Grassmere HORL RH6 ....140 D9
Grassmount FSTH SE23 ....31 J5
  WLGTN SM6 ....62 E8
Grassway WLGTN SM6 ....62 E3
Gratton Rd WKENS W14 ....19 J1
Grattons Dr CRAWE RH10 ....177 M2
The Grattons SWTR RH13 ....190 F7
Gravel Hi CROY/NA CR0 ....64 E5
  LHD/OX KT22 ....96 H1
Gravel Hill Rd RFNM GU10 ...126 E8
Gravelly Hi CTHM CR3 ....101 P8
Gravel Pits La SHGR GU5 ....134 E1
Gravel Rd FARN GU14 ....88 F7
  FLEETS GU52 ....87 H9
  FNM TW2 ....107 M7
  THHTH CR7 ....25 M4
Gravenel Gdns TOOT SW17 * ..29 H8
Graveney Gv PGE/AN SE20 ....46 C1
Graveney Rd CRAWE RH10 ...177 M6
  TOOT SW17 ....29 H7
Gravetts La RGUW GU3 ....111 L2
Gravetye Cl CRAWE RH10 ....177 K7
Grayham Crs NWMAL KT3 .....42 B5
Grayham Rd NWMAL KT3 .....42 B5
Graylands WOKN/KNAP GU21 .10 C1
Graylands Cl
  WOKN/KNAP GU21 ....10 C2
Gray Pl CHERT KT16 ....55 H5
Grays Cl HASM GU27 ....184 F2
Grayscroft Rd
  STRHM/NOR SW16 ....44 F1
Grayshot Dr BLKW GU17 .....67 N3
Grayshott Rd BOR GU35 .....164 F6
Grays La ASHF TW15 ....23 L7
  ASHTD KT21 ....77 M8
Grays Rd BH/WHM TN16 .....104 F1
  GODL GU7 ....131 M6
Grays Wd HORL RH6 ....159 N1
Grayswood Dr FRIM GU16 .....89 J6
Grayswood Gdns
  RYNPK SW20 ....42 F3
Grayswood Ms
  HASM GU27 ....166 C9
Grayswood Rd HASM GU27 ..184 E2
Great Austins FNM GU9 .....127 N4
Great Benty WDR/YW UB7 ....14 A2
Great Brownings DUL SE21 ...30 G7
Great Chart St BTSEA SW11 ..19 N8
Great Chertsey Rd
  CHSWK W4 ....18 B6
  FELT TW13 ....24 C6
Great Church La
  HMSMTH W6 ....19 H3
Great Elshams BNSTD SM7 ...79 L5
Great Elms EW KT17 * 60 D9
Greatfield Cl FARN GU14 .....68 D8
Greatfield Rd FARN GU14 .....68 C8
Greatford Dr GU GU1 ....113 H5
Great Gatton Cl
  CROY/NA CR0 ....46 E8
Great George St GODL GU7 ..131 L9

Great Goodwin Dr GU GU1 ..112 F3
Greatham Rd CRAWE RH10 ..177 M8
Great Hollands Rd
  BRAK RG12 ....32 B7
Great Hollands Sq
  BRAK RG12 ....32 B7
Great House Ct
  EGRIN RH19 * 180 E3
Greatlake Ct HORL RH6 .....140 D9
Great Oaks Pk RGUE GU4 ....112 F1
Great Quarry GU GU1 ....112 B8
Great South-West Rd
  EBED/NFELT TW14 ....23 M3
Great Tattenhams EPSOM
  KT18 ....78 C7
Great West Rd BTFD TW8 ....17 J3
  HEST TW5 ....15 N7
  HMSMTH W6 ....18 F3
  ISLW TW7 ....16 E5
Great West Rd Chiswick
  CHSWK W4 ....18 D4
Great West Rd Ellesmere Rd
  CHSWK W4 ....18 A4
Great West Rd Hogarth La
  CHSWK W4 ....18 B4
Greatwood Cl CHERT KT16 ...54 G7
Great Woodcote Dr
  PUR/KEN CR8 ....62 F8
Great Woodcote Pk
  PUR/KEN CR8 ....62 G8
Greaves Pl TOOT SW17 ......29 H7
Grebe Ct SUT SM1 ....61 K4
Grebe Crs SWTR RH13 ......192 F9
Grebe Ter KUT/HW KT1 * 8 D6
Grecian Crs NRWD SE19 .....30 C9
Green Acre ALDT GU11 ......108 B5
Greenacre Ct EGH TW20 * 21 H9
Greenacre RFNM GU10 ....62 D1
Green Acres CROY/NA CR0 .....3 J5
Greenacres CRAWE RH10 ....177 L6
  GT/LBKH KT23 ....96 H4
  HORS RH12 ....192 B6
  KWD/TDW/WH KT20 ....99 K8
  OXTED RH8 ....103 L7
Greenacres Cl CAR GU6 .....171 J2
Green Chain Wk HAYES BR2 ..47 K1
  SYD SE26 ....31 L9
  FELT TW13 ....24 F8
  HAYES BR2 ....47 L4
Green Court Av
  CROY/NA CR0 ....64 B1
Green Court Gdns
  CROY/NA CR0 ....64 B1
Greencroft FARN GU14 ....88 D3
  GU GU1 ....112 F5
Greencroft Rd HEST TW5 .....15 P6
Green Cross La RFNM GU10 .165 K2
Green Curve BNSTD SM7 .....79 K4
Green Dene EHSLY KT24 .....114 E6
Green Dragon La BTFD TW8 ..17 L3
Green Dr RPLY/SEND GU23 ...93 K3
Greene Fielde End STA TW18 .37 P1
Green End CHSGTN KT9 ......59 K3
  YTLY GU46 ....67 H1
Green Farm Rd BAGS GU19 ..51 P6
Greenfield EDEN TN8 ....145 H4
Greenfield Av BRYLDS KT5 ...41 P8
Greenfield Cl LIPH GU30 ....182 F5
Greenfield Link
  COUL/CHIP CR5 ....80 G4
Greenfield Rd FNM GU9 .....127 K6
  SWTR RH13 ....190 E7
Greenfields EDEN TN8 ......145 H4
  HORS RH12 ....192 F4
Greenfields Pl RDKG RH5 ...137 K9
Greenfields Rd HORL RH6 ...140 A8
  HORS RH12 ....192 F5
Greenfields Wy HORS RH12 .192 F4
Green Finch Cl CWTH RG45 ..49 L2
Greenfinch Wy HORS RH12 .192 C5
Greenford Rd SUT SM1 ......61 M3
Greenham Wk
  WOKN/KNAP GU21 ....72 A7
Greenham Wd BRAK RG12 ...32 E8
Greenhanger RFNM GU10 ...165 J3
Greenhaven YTLY GU46 ......66 F5
Greenhayes Av BNSTD SM7 ..79 L4
Greenhayes Cl REIG RH2 ....119 N5
Greenhayes Gdns
  BNSTD SM7 ....79 L4
Green Hedges Av
  EGRIN RH19 ....180 C1
Green Hedges Cl
  EGRIN RH19 ....180 C1
Green Heights Ct
  WOKS/MYFD GU22 ....72 A9
Greenheys Pl
  WOKS/MYFD GU22 ....11 F4
Green HI ORP BR6 ....84 C1
Greenhill LGT SM1 ....61 N1
Greenhill Av CTHM CR3 .....102 B1
Green Hill Cl CBLY GU15 .....69 J2
Greenhill Gdns RGUE GU4 ..112 F1
Greenhill La WARL CR6 ......82 E6
Green Hill Rd CBLY GU15 ....69 J2
Greenhill Rd FNM GU9 ......127 P5
Greenholme CBLY GU15 ......69 M3
Greenhow BRAK RG12 ....32 B3
Greenhurst La OXTED RH8 ..123 N3
Greenhurst Rd WNWD SE27 .30 B8
Greening Wd GSHT GU26 * .166 A6
Greenlake Ter STA TW18 * ...37 L5

Greenland Crs NWDGN UB2 ..15 L1
Greenlands CHERT KT16 .....54 C2
  HOR/WEW KT19 ....59 P4
Greenlands Rd CBLY GU15 ...68 D7
  STA TW18 ....22 D7
  WEY KT13 ....56 D2
Greenland Wy CROY/NA CR0 .44 F8
Green La ASC SL5 ....34 C2
  ASHTD KT21 ....77 J6
  BAGS GU19 ....51 P7
  BF/WBF KT14 ....74 B1
  BLKW GU17 ....67 N3
  BLKW GU17 ....64 C1
  CHERT KT16 ....94 C1
  CHOB/PIR GU24 ....53 M8
  CHSGTN KT9 ....59 L7
  COB KT11 ....75 N1
  CRAN GU6 ....170 C7
  CRAWE RH10 ....160 C8
  CRAWE RH10 ....177 H5
  CRAWE RH10 ....176 F4
  CROY/NA CR0 ....64 F7
  CTHM CR3 ....102 G3
  EGH TW20 ....21 H7
  EW KT17 ....78 E1
  FELT TW13 ....24 C5
  FNM GU9 ....108 C8
  FRIM GU16 ....89 H1
  GDST RH9 ....122 B3
  HAYES BR2 ....47 N8
  HEST TW5 ....16 A4
  KWD/TDW/WH KT20 ....79 J8
  KWD/TDW/WH KT20 ....99 H3
  LHD/OX KT22 ....96 D4
  MFD/CHID GU8 ....168 B8
  MRDN SM4 ....43 J5
  NWMAL KT3 ....42 A4
  RCH/KEW TW9 ....26 C1
  RFNM GU10 ....128 G4
  RGUE GU4 ....112 D7
  SHGR GU5 ....133 K7
  SHST GU47 ....49 K9
  STA TW18 ....37 J2
  SUN TW16 ....39 H1
  SWTR RH13 ....190 B3
  WOT/HER KT12 ....57 K4
  WPK KT4 ....42 B9
  YTLY GU46 ....66 F1
Green Lane Av
  WOT/HER KT12 ....57 K4
Green La BF/WBF KT14 * 55 L5
  CBLY GU15 ....68 E1
  CHERT KT16 ....55 J1
Green La East RGUW GU3 ...110 A6
Green Lane Gdns THHTH CR7 .45 L3
Green La West ASHV GU12 ..109 N6
  EHSLY KT24 ....113 H9
Green Leaf Av WLGTN SM6 ..62 F3
Greenleaf Cl
  BRXS/STRHM SW2 * 30 B2
Greenlea Pk
  WIM/MER SW19 * 44 A2
Greenleas FRIM GU16 ....68 C6
Green Leas SUN TW16 ......39 H1
Greenleas Cl YTLY GU46 ....66 F1
Greenleas Ct YTLY GU46 * ..23 L9
Greenleaves Ct ASHF TW15 * 23 L9
Green Leys FLEETS GU52 ...106 F2
Greenlink Wk RCH/KEW TW9 .17 P9
Green Man La
  EBED/NFELT TW14 ....15 J9
Green Md ESH/CLAY KT10 ....57 P5
Greenmead Cl SNWD SE25 ..46 A6
Greenmeads
  WOKS/MYFD GU22 ....92 C2
Greenoak Ri BH/WHM TN16 .84 A7
Green Oaks NWDGN UB2 * ..15 M2
Greenoak Wy
  WIM/MER SW19 ....28 A7
Greenock Rd ACT W3 ....17 P1
  STRHM/NOR SW16 ....44 F2
Greeno Crs SHPTN TW17 ....38 C6
Green Pde HSLW TW3 * 25 J2
Green Pk STA TW18 ....36 F5
Greensand Rd REDH RH1 ...100 F8
Greensand Wy
  BRKHM/BTCW RH3 ....118 A6
  EDEN TN8 ....124 C2
  FNM GU9 ....5 H4
  GSHT GU26 ....166 B9
  MFD/CHID GU8 ....148 D9
  MFD/CHID GU8 ....151 K8
  OXTED RH8 ....103 L6
  RDKG RH5 ....137 H4
  REDH RH1 ....120 A3
  REDH RH1 ....121 K5
  REIG RH2 ....119 J5
  RFNM GU10 ....147 N2
Greenside CRAWE RG45 .....49 K4
  RPLY/SEND GU23 * 93 N1
Greenside Cl RGUE GU4 ....112 G3
Greenside Rd ASHTD KT21 ..77 H7
  CROY/NA CR0 ....45 J8

SHB W12 ....18 E1
Green Springs RFNM GU10 .106 D7
Greenstead Gdns
  PUT/ROE SW15 ....27 M1
Greenstede Av EGRIN RH19 .162 E9
The Green ASHF TW15 * 22 C8
  BH/WHM TN16 ....105 H6
  BH/WHM TN16 * 105 N4
  BRAK RG12 ....32 D5
  CAR SM5 ....62 C3
  CRAN GU6 ....153 P9
  CRAN GU6 ....154 A1
  CRAWW RH11 ....176 F4
  CROY/NA CR0 ....64 F7
  CTHM CR3 ....101 L5
  E/WMO/HCT KT8 ....40 B6
  EDEN TN8 ....125 N7
  EGH TW20 ....21 N8
  EW KT17 ....36 G3
  FELT TW13 ....24 F8
  FNM GU9 ....108 B8
  FNM GU9 ....127 L5
  GODL GU7 ....131 L4
  GU GU1 ....112 F5
  HASM GU27 ....184 C7
  HORL RH6 ....160 A6
  HORS RH12 ....174 D7
  HSLWW TW4 ....21 K2
  KWD/TDW/WH KT20 ....99 K6
  LHD/OX KT22 ....97 K1
  LING RH7 ....162 B1
  MFD/CHID GU8 ....149 M4
  MRDN SM4 ....43 M3
  NWMAL KT3 ....42 A6
  PGE/AN SE20 ....46 D1
  PUR/KEN CR8 ....81 J1
  RDKG RH5 ....157 J4
  REDH RH1 ....120 A3
  REDH RH1 ....140 C1
  REDH RH1 ....141 H4
  REIG RH2 ....119 K5
  RFNM GU10 ....128 F7
  RGUE GU4 ....93 L7
  RGUW GU3 ....110 C3
  RPLY/SEND GU23 ....94 D4
  SHGR GU5 ....133 K7
  SHST GU47 ....49 K9
  STA TW18 ....37 J2
  SUN TW16 ....39 H1
  THHTH CR7 ....45 K2
  WOT/HER KT12 ....57 K4
  WPK KT4 ....42 B9
  YTLY GU46 ....66 F1
Green Lane Av
  WOT/HER KT12 ....57 K4
Green Vw CHSGTN KT9 ......59 M6
Greenview Av BECK BR3 .....46 E7
Green Wk CRAWE RH10 .....177 H5
  NWDGN UB2 ....15 L1
Green Wy ASHV GU12 ......108 G3
  REDH RH1 ....120 A3
  SUN TW16 ....39 J5
Greenway BH/WHM TN16 ...84 A9
  GT/LBKH KT23 ....96 B3
  HORS RH12 ....191 P7
  RYNPK SW20 ....42 G5
  WLGTN SM6 ....62 E5
Greenway Cl BF/WBF KT14 ..73 L2
Greenway Dr STA TW18 .....37 N2
Greenway Gdns
  CROY/NA CR0 ....64 F2
Greenways BECK BR3 ....46 C5
  EGH TW20 ....21 K9
  ESH/CLAY KT10 ....58 E3
  FLEETS GU52 ....86 F9
  KWD/TDW/WH KT20 ....98 E5
  SHST GU47 ....49 M8
Greenways Dr ASC SL5 ......34 E9
The Greenway EPSOM KT18 .77 M4
  HSLWW TW4 ....15 P9
  OXTED RH8 ....123 N4
Greenwich Cl
  CRAWW RH11 ....176 F9
Green Wd ASC SL5 ....33 L2
Greenwood Cl
  ADL/WDHM KT15 ....55 K9
  MRDN SM4 ....43 J5
  THDIT KT7 ....40 C9
Greenwood Cottages
  ASC SL5 ....35 J7
Greenwood Ct
  CRAWW RH11 * 194 E1
Greenwood Dr REDH RH1 ..140 C1
Greenwood Gdns
  CTHM CR3 ....102 A5
  OXTED RH8 ....123 N5
Greenwood La HPTN TW12 ..25 J8
Greenwood Pk
  KUTN/CMB KT2 ....42 C1
Greenwood Rd
  CHOB/PIR GU24 ....90 B1
  CROY/NA CR0 ....45 K8
  CWTH RG45 ....49 L3
  ISLW TW7 ....16 E8
  MTCM CR4 ....44 F4
  THDIT KT7 ....40 C9
The Greenwood GU GU1 ....112 E5
Green Wrythe Crs CAR SM5 .44 A9
Green Wrythe La CAR SM5 ..43 P7
Gregory Cl CRAWE RH10 ...177 M9
  WOKN/KNAP GU21 ....72 A6
Gregory Dr WDSR SL4 ......20 C2
Grenaby Av CROY/NA CR0 ...45 M8
Grenaby Rd CROY/NA CR0 ..45 M8
Grenadier Cl CTHM CR3 ....101 L2
Grenadier Rd ASHV GU12 ..109 K2
Grenadiers Wy FARN GU14 ..87 N4
Grena Gdns RCH/KEW TW9 .17 N1
Grena Rd RCH/KEW TW9 ....17 M1
Grendon Cl HORL RH6 .....140 B8
Grenfell Rd TOOT SW17 .....29 J9
Grennell Cl SUT SM1 ....61 P1
Grennell Rd SUT SM1 ....61 N1
Grenside Rd WEY KT13 .....56 D2
Grenville Cl BRYLDS KT5 ....41 P8
  COB KT11 ....75 M2
  LIPH GU30 ....182 F6
Grenville Dr FLEETS GU52 ..86 E8
Grenville Gdns FRIM GU16 ..88 G1
Grenville Ms PKSENS SW7 ..19 N1
Grenville Pl SKENS SW7 ....19 N1
Grenville Rd CROY/NA CR0 ..65 J8

MFD/CHID GU8 ....130 D6
Grenville Sq BRAK RG12 ....32 E3
Gresham Av WARL CR6 ......82 E7
Gresham Cl OXTED RH8 ....103 M9
Gresham Rd BECK BR3 ......46 E3
  HPTN TW12 ....25 J9
  HSLW TW3 ....25 J1
  OXTED RH8 ....103 M9
  SNWD SE25 ....46 A5
  STA TW18 ....22 C8
Greshams Wy EDEN TN8 ...144 E5
Gresham Wk CRAWE RH10 ..177 H8
Gresham Wy FRIM GU16 .....88 G1
  WIM/MER SW19 ....28 D6
Gressenhall Rd
  WAND/EARL SW18 ....28 C2
Greswell St FUL/PGN SW6 ..19 H6
Greta Bank EHSLY KT24 .....94 E6
Greville Cl ALDT GU11 ......108 C4
  ASHTD KT21 ....77 L8
  GUW GU2 ....111 L5
  TWK TW1 ....26 A3
Greville Ct GT/LBKH KT23 ...96 C5
Greville Park Av ASHTD KT21 .77 L7
Greville Park Rd ASHTD KT21 .77 L7
Greville Rd
  RCHPK/HAM TW10 ....26 E2
Grey Alders BNSTD SM7 ....78 G3
Greybury La EDEN TN8 .....163 N1
Greycot Rd BECK BR3 ....31 N1
Greyfields Cl PUR/KEN CR8 .81 K2
Greyfriars Dr ASC SL5 ......34 B7
  CHOB/PIR GU24 ....90 F6
Greyfriars Rd
  RPLY/SEND GU23 ....93 L4
Greyhound Cl ASHV GU12 ..109 H5
Greyhound La
  STRHM/NOR SW16 ....29 P9
Greyhound Rd HMSMTH W6 .19 H4
  SUT SM1 ....62 A4
Greyhound Slip
  CRAWE RH10 ....177 N4
Greyhound Ter
  STRHM/NOR SW16 ....44 E2
Greys Ct ALDT GU11 ....108 C4
Greystead Pk RFNM GU10 ..127 J7
Greystead Rd FSTH SE23 ...31 K5
Greystock Rd BNFD RG42 ...32 F1
Greystoke Ct CWTH RG45 ...49 J5
Greystone Cl SAND/SEL CR2 .64 C8
Greystones Cl REDH RH1 ...119 P7
Greystones Dr REIG RH2 ...119 N5
Greyswood St
  STRHM/NOR SW16 ....29 L9
Greythorne Rd
  WOKN/KNAP GU21 ....71 N7
Greywaters Dr GU GU1 .....132 E7
Grice Av BH/WHM TN16 .....83 P2
Grier Cl CRAWW RH11 .....176 B6
Grierson Rd FSTH SE23 ....31 M2
Grieve Cl RFNM GU10 ......108 A6
Griffin Cl ASHTD KT21 * 77 L8
Griffin Wy GT/LBKH KT23 ...96 C6
  SUN TW16 ....39 J3
Griffiths Rd WIM/MER SW19 .43 L1
Griffon Cl FARN GU14 ....87 P4
Griggs Meadow
  MFD/CHID GU8 ....169 L4
Grimston Rd FUL/PGN SW6 .19 K7
Grimwade Av CROY/NA CR0 .64 A2
Grimwood Rd TWK TW1 .....25 N3
Grindall Cl CROY/NA CR0 ...63 K5
Grindley Gdns
  CROY/NA CR0 ....45 P7
Grindstone Crs
  WOKN/KNAP GU21 ....71 H7
Grisedale Cl CRAWW RH11 .176 F7
  PUR/KEN CR8 ....81 N3
Grisedale Gdns PUR/KEN CR8 .81 N3
Grobars Av
  WOKN/KNAP GU21 ....72 A4
Groombridge Cl
  WOT/HER KT12 ....57 K4
Groombridge Wy
  HORS RH12 ....191 H9
Groom Cl HAYES BR2 ....47 P5
Groom Crs WAND/EARL SW18 .28 C3
Groomfield Cl TOOT SW17 ..29 K7
The Grooms CRAWE RH10 ..177 N3
Grosse Wy PUT/ROE SW15 ..27 H2
Grosvenor Av CAR SM5 .....62 B5
  MORT/ESHN SW14 ....18 C8
Grosvenor Cl HORL RH6 ...159 K3
Grosvenor Ct BLKW GU17 ...67 N5
Grosvenor Gdns
  KUTN/CMB KT2 ....41 P1
  MORT/ESHN SW14 ....18 C8
  WLGTN SM6 ....62 E6
Grosvenor HI
  WIM/MER SW19 ....28 B9
Grosvenor Ms REIG RH2 ...119 M8
Grosvenor Pl WEY KT13 ....56 F2
Grosvenor Rd ALDT GU11 ..108 C4
  BTFD TW8 ....17 K4
  CHOB/PIR GU24 ....90 A5
  CHSWK W4 ....18 A3
  EGRIN RH19 ....180 C1
  EPSOM KT18 ....78 C2
  GODL GU7 ....150 D1
  HSLWW TW4 ....15 P8
  NWDGN UB2 ....15 M1
  RCHPK/HAM TW10 ....26 A1
  SNWD SE25 ....46 A5
  STA TW18 ....37 L1
  TWK TW1 ....25 N5
  WLGTN SM6 ....62 D5
  WKWM BR4 ....47 K8
Groton Rd WAND/EARL SW18 .28 E4
Grotto Rd TWK TW1 ....25 N5
  WEY KT13 ....56 E3
Grouse Rd SWTR RH13 .....193 P1

Grove Av EW KT17 78 C2
SUT SM1 61 L5
TWK TW1 25 N4
Grove Cl CRAN GU6 171 J2
EWKG RG40 49 J2
FSTH SE23 31 L4
HAYES BR2 65 N1
HOR/WEW KT19 59 N8
KUT/HW KT1 41 M5
WDSR SL4 20 G3
Grove Ct E/WMO/HCT KT8 40 D6
EGH TW20 21 M8
Grove Crs FELT TW13 24 F7
KUT/HW KT1 8 D7
WOT/HER KT12 39 K8
Grove Cross Rd FRIM GU16 68 F7
Grove End BAGS GU19 51 P5
Grove End La ESH/CLAY KT10 40 D9
Grove End Rd FNM GU9 127 M6
Grove Farm Pk FRIM GU16 * 89 H6
Grovefields Av FRIM GU16 68 F7
Grove Footpath BRYLDS KT5 41 L5
Grove Gdns TEDD TW11 25 P7
Grove Heath La
RPLY/SEND GU23 93 N4
Grove Heath North
RPLY/SEND GU23 93 M2
Grove Heath Rd
RPLY/SEND GU23 93 M3
Grovehill Rd REDH RH1 120 A5
Groveland Av
STRHM/NOR SW16 45 H1
Groveland Rd BECK BR3 46 F4
Grovelands E/WMO/HCT KT8 40 A5
RFNM GU10 128 A6
Grovelands Rd PUR/KEN CR8 81 H1
Groveland Wy NWMAL KT3 42 A6
Grove La COUL/CHIP CR5 80 D4
KUT/HW KT1 41 L5
Groveley Rd SUN TW16 24 A8
Grove Ms HMSMTH W6 18 G1
Grove Park Br CHSWK W4 18 A5
Grove Park Gdns CHSWK W4 17 P5
Grove Park Rd CHSWK W4 17 P5
Grove Park Ter CHSWK W4 17 P5
Grove Pl BAL SW12 29 L2
WEY KT13 56 E4
Grove Rd ASHTD KT21 77 M7
ASHV GU12 109 J2
BARN SW13 18 D7
BH/WHM TN16 84 A9
BTFD TW8 17 J3
CBLY GU15 68 G3
CHERT KT16 37 K7
CRAN GU6 171 J2
E/WMO/HCT KT8 40 D5
EW KT17 78 C2
FLEETS GU52 107 H1
GODL GU7 150 B1
GSHT GU26 165 M5
GU GU1 112 G5
HORL RH6 140 A9
HSLW TW3 16 B9
ISLW TW7 16 E6
LING RH7 143 L8
MTCM CR4 44 D3
RCHPK/HAM TW10 26 E2
SHPTN TW17 38 E7
SURB KT6 41 K6
SUT SM1 61 M5
THHTH CR7 45 J5
WHTN TW2 25 L6
WIM/MER SW19 43 N1
WOKN/KNAP GU21 11 F2
Groveside GT/LBKH KT23 96 A7
Groveside Cl CAR SM5 62 A1
GT/LBKH KT23 96 A7
Grovestile Waye
EBED/NFELT TW14 23 N3
Grove Ter TEDD TW11 25 P7
The Grove ADL/WDHM KT15 55 M4
ALDT GU11 108 C5
ASC SL5 33 L2
BH/WHM TN16 84 B7
COUL/CHIP CR5 80 F4
CRAWW RH11 176 F5
CTHM CR3 101 K1
EGH TW20 21 M8
EW KT17 78 C2
FARN GU14 88 F6
FRIM GU16 68 F7
GU GU1 * 7 J6
HORL RH6 159 L2
ISLW TW7 16 E6
LIPH GU30 182 E6
TEDD TW11 25 P7
WOKN/KNAP GU21 10 E2
WOT/HER KT12 39 K8
WWKM BR4 65 J2
Grove Wy ESH/CLAY KT10 40 C9
Grove Wood Hl
COUL/CHIP CR5 80 F3
Grub St OXTED RH8 104 A9
Guardian Ct MFD/CHID GU8 148 D1
Guards Av CTHM CR3 101 L2
Guards Ct ASC SL5 35 H8
Gubyon Av HNHL SE24 30 D1
Guerdon Pl BRAK RG12 32 F8
Guernsey Cl CRAWW RH11 176 D9
HEST TW5 16 A6
RGUE GU4 92 E9
Guernsey Dr FLEETN GU51 87 H3
Guernsey Farm Dr
WOKN/KNAP GU21 * 72 B4
Guernsey Gv HNHL SE24 30 D3
Guildables La EDEN TN8 124 C5
Guildcroft GU GU1 112 E5
Guildersfield Rd
STRHM/NOR SW16 44 G1
Guildford Av FELT TW13 24 B5
Guildford Business Park Rd
GUW GU2 6 A1
Guildford La SHGR GU5 113 L9
Guildford Park Av GUW GU2 6 B4
Guildford Park Rd GUW GU2 6 B5
Guildford Rd ASHV GU12 108 F7
BAGS GU19 51 N6
BIL RH14 188 C5
CHERT KT16 54 F8
CHERT KT16 55 H2
CHOB/PIR GU24 70 E1
CHOB/PIR GU24 90 F3
CRAN GU6 152 E8
CROY/NA CR0 45 M7
DORK RH4 116 B9
FLEETN GU51 87 J6
FNM GU9 5 K1
FRIM GU16 89 J2
GODL GU7 131 N7
GT/LBKH KT23 95 P8
HORS RH12 189 J2
HORS RH12 191 J4
HORS RH12 191 N7
LHD/OX KT22 96 E4
RDKG RH5 135 J2
RFNM GU10 128 C1
RGUE GU4 92 A5
SHGR GU5 133 H8
SWTR RH13 190 C3
WOKS/MYFD GU22 10 D4
Guildford Rd East FARN GU14 88 E6
Guildford Rd West
FARN GU14 88 E6
Guildford St CHERT KT16 37 L8
STA TW18 22 D9
Guildford Wy WLGTN SM6 62 G4
Guildown Av GUW GU2 111 P8
Guildown Rd GUW GU2 111 P8
Guileshill La RPLY/SEND GU23 94 A2
Guilford Av BRYLDS KT5 41 M6
Guillemont Flds FARN GU14 87 P2
Guinevere Rd CRAWW RH11 176 B5
Guinness Cl HYS/HAR UB3 14 F1
Guinness Ct CROY/NA CR0 * 3 J4
Guion Rd FUL/PGN SW6 19 K7
Gulley Rd FARN GU14 88 C7
Gumbrells Cl RGUW GU3 111 J1
Gumleigh Rd EA W5 17 J2
Gumley Gdns ISLW TW7 16 G8
Gun Hl ALDT GU11 108 D3
Gunnell Cl CROY/NA CR0 45 P7
SYD SE26 * 31 H7
Gunnersbury Av ACT W3 17 N2
Gunnersbury Cl CHSWK W4 * 17 P3
Gunners Rd
WAND/EARL SW18 28 G5
Gunning Cl CRAWW RH11 176 D8
Gunns Farm LIPH GU30 182 F8
Gun Pit Rd LING RH7 143 J9
Gunter Gv WBPTN SW10 19 N4
Gunters Md LHD/OX KT22 * 58 C9
Gunterstone Rd WKENS W14 19 J3
Gunton Rd TOOT SW17 29 K9
Gurdon's La MFD/CHID GU8 167 N1
Gurney Crs CROY/NA CR0 45 H9
Gurney Rd CAR SM5 62 C3
FUL/PGN SW6 19 N8
Gurney's Cl REDH RH1 120 B6
Guyatt Gdns MTCM CR4 44 C3
Guy Rd WLGTN SM6 62 G2
Gwalior Rd PUT/ROE SW15 19 H9
Gwendolen Av
PUT/ROE SW15 28 A1
Gwendwr Rd WKENS W14 19 J3
Gwydor Rd BECK BR3 46 D5
Gwydyr Rd HAYES BR2 47 M4
Gwyn Cl FUL/PGN SW6 19 N5
Gwynne Av CROY/NA CR0 46 D8
Gwynne Gdns EGRIN RH19 180 B1
Gwynne Rd BTSEA SW11 19 P7
CTHM CR3 101 M3
Gwynne Whf CHSWK W4 18 D4

H

Haarlem Rd WKENS W14 19 H1
Habershon Dr FRIM GU16 69 M6
Haccombe Rd
WIM/MER SW19 28 F9
Hackbridge Park Gdns
CAR SM5 62 B1
Hackbridge Rd CAR SM5 62 C1
Hackenden Cl EGRIN RH19 162 D9
Hackenden La EGRIN RH19 162 E8
Hacketts La
WOKS/MYFD GU22 73 K4
Hackhurst La RDKG RH5 135 H1
Hackington Crs BECK BR3 31 P9
Haddon Cl NWMAL KT3 42 D6
Haddon Rd SUT SM1 61 M3
Hadfield Rd
STWL/WRAY TW19 22 G2
Hadleigh Cl RYNPK SW20 43 K3
Hadleigh Dr BELMT SM2 61 L7
Hadley Gdns CHSWK W4 18 B3
NWDGN UB2 15 P3
Hadley Pl WEY KT13 56 C6
Hadley Rd MTCM CR4 44 F5
Hadleys RFNM GU10 146 B1
Hadley Wood Ri
PUR/KEN CR8 81 K4
Hadmans Cl HORS RH12 192 B9
Hadrian Cl STWL/WRAY TW19 23 H3
Hadrian Wy
STWL/WRAY TW19 22 G3
Haggard Rd TWK TW1 26 A3
Hagley Rd FLEETN GU51 86 E5
Haigh Crs REDH RH1 120 D7
Haig La FLEETS GU52 107 H1
Haig Rd ASHV GU12 108 E5
BH/WHM TN16 84 C6
CBLY GU15 68 B2
Hailes Cl WIM/MER SW19 28 F9
Hailsham Av
BRXS/STRHM SW2 30 A5
Hailsham Cl SHST GU47 49 P8
SURB KT6 41 K8
Hailsham Rd TOOT SW17 29 K9
Haines Ct WEY KT13 56 F4
Haines Wk MRDN SM4 43 M8
Haining Cl CHSWK W4 17 N3
Haining Gdns FRIM GU16 89 J4
Hainthorpe Rd WNWD SE27 30 C6
Haldane Pl WAND/EARL SW18 28 E4
Haldane Rd FUL/PGN SW6 19 K5
Haldon Rd WAND/EARL SW18 28 C2
Halebourne La
CHOB/PIR GU24 52 G8
Hale End BRAK RG12 33 H5
Hale Ends WOKS/MYFD GU22 91 P1
Hale House La RFNM GU10 165 K2
Hale Pit Rd GT/LBKH KT23 96 C6
Hale Pl FNM GU9 108 A9
Hale Reeds FNM GU9 107 P8
Hale Rd FNM GU9 5 K1
Hales Fld HASM GU27 184 D4
Hales Oak GT/LBKH KT23 96 C6
Halesowen Rd MRDN SM4 43 M8
Hale St STA TW18 22 B7
Haleswood COB KT11 75 K3
Hale Wy FRIM GU16 68 F7
Halewood BRAK RG12 32 B7
Half Acre BTFD TW8 17 K4
Half Acre Ms BTFD TW8 17 K5
Half Moon Hl HASM GU27 184 D4
Half Moon La HNHL SE24 30 E2
Halford Rd FUL/PGN SW6 19 L4
RCHPK/HAM TW10 26 D1
Halfpenny Cl RGUE GU4 133 H2
Halfpenny La ASC SL5 34 G8
RGUE GU4 112 G8
Halfway Gn WOT/HER KT12 57 K2
Halfway La GODL GU7 131 J9
Haliburton Rd TWK TW1 25 P1
Halifax Cl CRAWE RH10 177 P2
FARN GU14 88 B4
TEDD TW11 25 M9
Halifax St SYD SE26 31 J6
Halifax Wy FARN GU14 88 B8
Halimote Rd ALDT GU11 108 C5
Haling Gv SAND/SEL CR2 63 L6
Haling Park Gdns
SAND/SEL CR2 63 K5
Haling Park Rd
SAND/SEL CR2 63 K5
Haling Rd SAND/SEL CR2 63 M5
Hallam Rd GODL GU7 131 M7
Halland Cl CRAWE RH10 177 K4
Hallbrooke Gdns BNFD RG42 32 A1
Hall Cl CBLY GU15 68 G2
GODL GU7 131 L6
Hall Ct TEDD TW11 25 N8
Hall Dene Cl GU GU1 112 G4
Hall Dr FLEETS GU52 87 H9
SYD SE26 31 K8
Halley Cl CRAWW RH11 194 E1
Halley Dr ASC SL5 33 M3
Halley's Ap
WOKN/KNAP GU21 71 N7
Halley's Ct
WOKN/KNAP GU21 * 71 N7
Halley's Wk ADL/WDHM KT15 55 N6
Hall Farm Crs YTLY GU46 66 G3
Hall Farm Dr WHTN TW2 25 L3
Hallgrove Bottom
BAGS GU19 51 P4
Hall Hl OXTED RH8 123 K3
The Halliards WOT/HER KT12 39 J7
Halliford Cl SHPTN TW17 38 G4
Halliford Rd SHPTN TW17 38 G6
Hallington Cl
WOKN/KNAP GU21 71 P6
Halliwell Rd
BRXS/STRHM SW2 30 A2
Hall La HYS/HAR UB3 14 F5
YTLY GU46 66 G3
Hallmark Cl SHST GU47 50 A9
Hallmead Rd SUT SM1 61 M2
Hallowell Av CROY/NA CR0 62 G3
Hallowell Cl MTCM CR4 44 C4
Hallowes Cl GUW GU2 91 P9
Hallowfield Wy MTCM CR4 43 P4
Hallows Gv SUN TW16 24 A8
Hall Pl WOKN/KNAP GU21 11 G2
Hall Place Dr WEY KT13 56 G4
Hall Rd FARN GU14 88 D6
ISLW TW7 25 L1
SHGR GU5 132 D6
WLGTN SM6 62 D7
Halls Dr HORS RH12 193 L1
Halls Farm Cl
WOKN/KNAP GU21 71 K6
Hallsland CRAWE RH10 179 K3
Hallsland Wy OXTED RH8 123 M4
Halnaker Wk
CRAWW RH11 * 176 C8
Halsford La EGRIN RH19 180 A1
Halsford Park Rd
EGRIN RH19 180 B1
Halstead Cl CROY/NA CR0 2 C5
Halters End GSHT GU26 165 K8
Hambalt Rd CLAP SW4 29 M1
Hamble Av BLKW GU17 67 P3
Hamble Cl WOKN/KNAP GU21 71 N6
Hambledon Gdns
SNWD SE25 45 P4
Hambledon Hl EPSOM KT18 78 A5
Hambledon Pk
MFD/CHID GU8 168 A2
Hambledon Pl DUL SE21 30 G4
GT/LBKH KT23 96 A3
Hambledon Rd CTHM CR3 101 M3
MFD/CHID GU8 150 C8
WAND/EARL SW18 28 C3
Hambledon V EPSOM KT18 78 A5
Hamble St FUL/PGN SW6 19 M8
Hambleton WDSR SL4 * 21 H4
Hambleton Cl FRIM GU16 69 K5
WPK KT4 60 G1
Hambleton Hl CRAWW RH11 176 F7
Hambro Av HAYES BR2 47 N9
Hambrook Rd SNWD SE25 46 B4
Hambro Rd
STRHM/NOR SW16 29 N9
Ham Common
RCHPK/HAM TW10 26 C6
Ham Croft Cl FELT TW13 24 B6
Hamesmoor Rd FRIM GU16 88 G3
Hamesmoor Wy FRIM GU16 89 H3
Ham Farm Rd
RCHPK/HAM TW10 26 C7
Hamfield Cl OXTED RH8 103 J7
Ham Gate Av
RCHPK/HAM TW10 26 E7
Hamilton Av CHEAM SM3 61 J1
COB KT11 75 J2
SURB KT6 59 N1
WOKS/MYFD GU22 73 J5
Hamilton Cl CHERT KT16 37 K9
FELT TW13 24 A8
GUW GU2 * 91 N9
HOR/WEW KT19 78 A1
PUR/KEN CR8 81 K1
TEDD TW11 26 A9
Hamilton Crs HSLW TW3 25 J1
Hamilton Dr ASC SL5 34 E8
GUW GU2 91 N9
Hamilton Gordon Ct GU GU1 6 D1
Hamilton Ms WEY KT13 * 56 C3
Hamilton Pde FELT TW13 * 24 B7
Hamilton Pl ALDT GU11 108 B5
GUW GU2 91 N9
KWD/TDW/WH KT20 99 K3
SUN TW16 39 K1
Hamilton Rd BTFD TW8 17 K4
CHSWK W4 18 C1
FELT TW13 23 P8
FLEETS GU52 87 H9
HORS RH12 192 A7
THHTH CR7 45 M4
WHTN TW2 25 M4
WIM/MER SW19 43 M1
WNWD SE27 30 E7
Hamilton Road Ms
WIM/MER SW19 43 M1
Hamilton Wy WLGTN SM6 62 F7
Ham La EGH TW20 20 G7
MFD/CHID GU8 129 N9
WDSR SL4 12 A9
Hamlash La RFNM GU10 146 F3
Hamlet Gdns HMSMTH W6 18 E2
Hamlet Rd NRWD SE19 45 P1
Hamlet St BNFD RG42 32 G2
Hamlyn Gdns NRWD SE19 45 N1
Hamm Ct WEY KT13 56 B2
Hamm Court Est WEY KT13 56 B1
Hammelton Rd BMLY BR1 47 N2
Hammerfield Dr RDKG RH5 135 H3
Hammer Hl HASM GU27 183 M6
Hammer La GSHT GU26 165 H4
HASM GU27 183 K4
Hammersley Rd ALDT GU11 88 D8
Hammersmith Br
HMSMTH W6 18 F3
Hammersmith Bridge Rd
BARN SW13 18 F4
Hammersmith Broadway
HMSMTH W6 18 G2
Hammersmith Emb
HMSMTH W6 * 18 G4
Hammersmith F/O
HMSMTH W6 18 G3
Hammersmith Gv
HMSMTH W6 18 G2
Hammersmith Rd
HMSMTH W6 19 H2
Hammersmith Ter
HMSMTH W6 * 18 E3
Hammerwood Copse
HASM GU27 183 N5
Hammerwood Rd
EGRIN RH19 181 K5
Hammer Yd CRAWE RH10 * 176 G6
Hamm Moor La
ADL/WDHM KT15 56 A4
Hammond Av MTCM CR4 44 D3
Hammond Cl HPTN TW12 40 A2
WOKN/KNAP GU21 72 A4
Hammond Rd
CRAWW RH11 194 E2
NWDGN UB2 15 N1
WOKN/KNAP GU21 72 A4
Hammond Wy LTWR GU18 52 B8
Hamond Cl SAND/SEL CR2 63 K7
Hampden Av BECK BR3 46 E3
Hampden Cl CRAWE RH10 177 P2
Hampden Rd BECK BR3 46 E3
DTCH/LGLY SL3 12 D1
KUT/HW KT1 9 J6
Hampers La SWTR RH13 192 F8
Hampshire Cl ASHV GU12 108 F7
Hampshire Hog La
HMSMTH W6 * 18 F2
Hampshire Rd CBLY GU15 51 H9
Hampstead La DORK RH4 116 F8
Hampstead Rd DORK RH4 116 G8
Hampstead Wk
CRAWW RH11 * 176 F9
Hampton Cl FLEETS GU52 106 G2
RYNPK SW20 * 42 G1
WOKN/KNAP GU21 71 H8
Hampton Court Av
E/WMO/HCT KT8 40 D7
Hampton Court Crs
E/WMO/HCT KT8 * 40 D4
Hampton Court Est
THDIT KT7 * 40 E6
Hampton Court Rd
HPTN TW12 40 D3
Hampton Court Wy
E/WMO/HCT KT8 40 E5
ESH/CLAY KT10 58 E1
Hampton Gv EW KT17 60 D9
Hampton La FELT TW13 24 F7
Hampton Rd CROY/NA CR0 45 L7
FNM GU9 107 L8
REDH RH1 140 B1
WHTN TW2 25 L6
WPK KT4 60 E1
Hampton Rd East FELT TW13 24 G7
Hampton Rd West
FELT TW13 24 F5
Hampton Wy EGRIN RH19 180 E4
Ham Ridings
RCHPK/HAM TW10 26 E8
Hamsey Green Gdns
WARL CR6 82 C5
Hamsey Wy SAND/SEL CR2 82 B4
Ham St RCHPK/HAM TW10 26 B5
The Ham BTFD TW8 17 J5
Ham Vw CROY/NA CR0 46 E7
Hanbury Dr BH/WHM TN16 83 P2
Hanbury Rd CRAWW RH11 176 B6
Hanbury Wy CBLY GU15 68 E5
Hancock Rd NRWD SE19 30 E9
Hancocks Mt ASC SL5 34 D7
Hancombe Rd SHST GU47 49 L7
Handcroft Cl RFNM GU10 106 D6
Handcroft Rd CROY/NA CR0 45 K8
Handcross Rd RHWH RH17 195 M7
Handford La YTLY GU46 67 H4
Handley Page Rd
WLGTN SM6 63 H6
Handside Cl WPK KT4 43 H9
Hanford Cl WAND/EARL SW18 28 D4
Hangerfield Cl YTLY GU46 66 G3
Hanger Hl WEY KT13 56 D4
The Hanger BOR GU35 164 B4
Hang Grove Hl ORP BR6 84 F2
Hanley Pl BECK BR3 46 G1
Hannah Cl BECK BR3 47 H4
Hannam's Farm RFNM GU10 106 C8
Hannell Rd FUL/PGN SW6 19 J5
Hannen Rd WNWD SE27 * 30 C6
Hannibal Rd
STWL/WRAY TW19 23 H3
Hannibal Wy CROY/NA CR0 63 H4
Hanover Av FELT TW13 24 B4
Hanover Cl CHEAM SM3 61 J3
CRAWE RH10 177 J7
EGH TW20 20 G9
FRIM GU16 68 G7
RCH/KEW TW9 17 N5
REDH RH1 100 E8
YTLY GU46 67 H1
Hanover Ct DORK RH4 116 F7
WOKS/MYFD GU22 10 B7
Hanover Dr FLEETN GU51 87 J3
Hanover Gdns BRAK RG12 32 B8
FARN GU14 88 A1
Hanover Rd WIM/MER SW19 43 N1
Hanover St CROY/NA CR0 2 B5
Hanover Wk WEY KT13 56 F2
Hansler Gv E/WMO/HCT KT8 40 D6
Hansler Rd EDUL SE22 30 G1
Hansom Ter BMLY BR1 * 47 P2
Hanson Cl BAL SW12 29 L3
CBLY GU15 69 K1
MORT/ESHN SW14 18 A8
RGUE GU4 112 D2
WDR/YW UB7 14 B1
Hanworth Cl BRAK RG12 32 E7
Hanworth La CHERT KT16 37 K9
Hanworth Rd BRAK RG12 32 C8
FELT TW13 24 C4
HSLW TW3 16 B9
HSLWW TW4 24 G3
REDH RH1 140 B1
SUN TW16 39 J1
Hanworth Ter HSLW TW3 16 B9
Harberson Rd BAL SW12 29 L4
Harbledown Rd
FUL/PGN SW6 19 L6
SAND/SEL CR2 64 A9
Harbord St FUL/PGN SW6 19 H6
Harborough Rd
STRHM/NOR SW16 30 A7
Harbour Av WBPTN SW10 19 N6
Harbour Cl FARN GU14 68 C8
Harbourfield Rd BNSTD SM7 79 M4
Harbour Yd WBPTN SW10 * 19 N6
Harbridge Av PUT/ROE SW15 27 L3
Harbury Rd CAR SM5 62 A7
Harbut Rd BTSEA SW11 19 P9
Harcourt STWL/WRAY TW19 21 K2
Harcourt Av WLGTN SM6 62 D3
Harcourt Cl EGH TW20 21 P9
ISLW TW7 16 G8
Harcourt Fld WLGTN SM6 62 D3
Harcourt Rd BRAK RG12 32 D7
CBLY GU15 68 D3
THHTH CR7 45 H7
WIM/MER SW19 43 L1
WLGTN SM6 62 D3
Harcourt Ter WBPTN SW10 19 M3
Harcourt Wy GDST RH9 122 E8
Hardcastle Cl CROY/NA CR0 46 A7
Hardcourts Cl WWKM BR4 65 H3
Hardell Cl EGH TW20 21 M8
Hardel Wk BRXS/STRHM SW2 30 B3
Harden Farm Cl
COUL/CHIP CR5 100 E1
Hardham Cl CRAWW RH11 176 D3
Harding Cl CROY/NA CR0 3 K5
KUTN/CMB KT2 9 F2
Harding Rd EPSOM KT18 78 C8
Hardings La PGE/AN SE20 31 L9

Hardman Rd *KUTN/CMB* KT2.....8 E4
Hardwell Rd *BRAK* RG12.....32 C5
Hardwick Cl *LHD/OX* KT22.....76 C4
Hardwicke Av *HEST* TW5 *.....16 A4
Hardwicke Rd *CHSWK* W4.....18 A2
RCHPK/HAM TW10.....26 E7
Hardwick Rd *REIG* RH2.....119 L4
Hardwick La *CHERT* KT16.....36 C8
Hardwick Pl
STRHM/NOR SW16.....44 E1
Hardwick Rd *REDH* RH1.....119 P7
Hardwick's Wy
WAND/EARL SW18.....28 D1
Hardy Av *YTLY* GU46.....66 C4
Hardy Cl *CRAWE* RH10.....177 M4
HORL RH6.....159 H1
HORS RH12.....192 A6
RDKG RH5.....137 H2
Hardy Gn *CWTH* RG45.....49 M5
Hardy Rd *WIM/MER* SW19.....43 M1
Harebell Hl *COB* KT11.....75 M3
Harecroft *DORK* RH4 *.....116 H1
LHD/OX KT22.....96 B3
Haredon Cl *FSTH* SE23.....31 K3
Harefield *ESH/CLAY* KT10.....58 C2
Harefield Av *BELMT* SM2.....61 J7
Harefield Rd
STRHM/NOR SW16.....45 H1
Hare Hl *ADL/WDHM* KT15.....55 K5
Hare Hill Cl
WOKS/MYFD GU22.....73 L4
Harelands Cl
WOKN/KNAP GU21.....72 A6
Hare La *CRAWE* RH11.....176 E2
ESH/CLAY KT10.....58 E5
GODL GU7.....131 M7
LING RH7.....142 D8
Harendon
KWD/TDW/WH KT20.....98 C1
Hares Bank *CROY/NA* CRO.....65 K8
Harestone Dr *CTHM* CR3.....101 P5
Harestone Hl *CTHM* CR3.....101 P6
Harestone La *CTHM* CR3.....101 N5
Harestone Valley Rd
CTHM CR3.....101 P5
Harewood Cl *CRAWE* RH10.....177 K2
REIG RH2.....119 N3
Harewood Gdns
SAND/SEL CR2.....82 B4
Harewood Rd *ISLW* TW7.....16 F5
RGUE GU4.....112 G2
SAND/SEL CR2.....63 N5
WIM/MER SW19.....29 H9
Harewood Ter *NWDGN* UB2.....15 P2
Harfield Rd *SUN* TW16.....39 M5
Harkness Cl *EW* KT17.....78 G5
Harland Av *CROY/NA* CRO.....3 K5
Harland Ct *WIM/MER* SW19.....43 M4
Harlech Gdns *HEST* TW5.....15 L4
Harlech Rd *BLKW* GU17.....67 P4
Harlequin Av *BTFD* TW8.....16 G4
Harlequin Cl *ISLW* TW7.....25 M1
Harlequin Rd *TEDD* TW11.....41 H1
Harleyford *BMLY* BR1.....47 P2
Harley Gdns *WBPTN* SW10.....19 N5
Harlington Cl *HYS/HAR* UB3.....14 E5
Harlington Rd East
EBED/NFELT TW14.....24 C3
Harlington Rd West
EBED/NFELT TW14.....24 C2
Harlington Wy *FLEETN* GU51.....86 E7
Harman Pl *PUR/KEN* CR8.....63 K9
Harmans Dr *EGRIN* RH19.....180 G2
Harmans Md *EGRIN* RH19.....180 F2
Harmans Water Rd
BRAK RG12.....32 F6
Harmondsworth La
WDR/YW UB7.....14 A1
Harmondsworth Rd
WDR/YW UB7.....14 A1
Harmony Cl *CRAWW* RH11.....176 D7
WLGTN SM6.....62 G7
Harms Gv *RGUE* GU4.....112 G2
Harold Av *HYS/HAR* UB3.....15 H1
Harold Rd *CRAWE* RH10.....177 P6
NRWD SE19.....45 M9
SUT SM1.....61 P3
Haroldslea Cl *HORL* RH6.....159 P2
Haroldslea Dr *HORL* RH6.....159 N3
Harpdon Pde *YTLY* GU46.....66 F2
Harper Rd *WNWD* SE27.....30 C5
Harper Dr *CRAWE* RH10.....177 N7
Harper's Rd *ASHV* GU12.....109 L4
Harpers Yd *ISLW* TW7 *.....16 F7
Harpesford Av *VW* GU25.....36 A6
Harps Oak La *REDH* RH1.....100 B5
Harpswood Cl
COUL/CHIP CR5.....100 E2
Hampton Cl *YTLY* GU46.....67 H1
Harpurs *KWD/TDW/WH* KT20.....99 H1
Harrier Cl *CRAN* GU6.....153 H8
Harriet Cl *BRXS/STRHM* SW2.....30 B3
Harriet Gdns *CROY/NA* CRO.....64 A1
Harrington Cl *CROY/NA* CRO.....62 G1
REIG RH2.....138 E3
Harrington Gdns *SKENS* SW7.....19 M2
Harrington Rd *SKENS* SW7.....19 M2
SNWD SE25.....46 A5
Harriotts Cl *ASHTD* KT21.....77 K9
Harriotts La *ASHTD* KT21.....77 J8
Harris Cl *CRAWW* RH11.....176 E8
HSLW TW3.....16 A6
Harrison Cl *REIG* RH2.....119 H6
Harrison Ct *SHPTN* TW17 *.....38 D6
Harrison's Ri *CROY/NA* CRO.....2 A4
Harrison Wy *SHPTN* TW17.....38 D6
Harris Wy *SUN* TW16.....38 G8
Harrogate Ct *DTCH/LGLY* SL3.....12 D1
Harroway Rd *BTSEA* SW11.....19 P7

Harrow Cl *ADL/WDHM* KT15.....55 M1
CHSGTN KT9.....59 K6
DORK RH4.....116 G8
Harrowdene *CRAN* GU6.....153 H8
Harrowdene Gdns
TEDD TW11.....40 G1
Harrow Gdns *WARL* CR6.....82 F5
Harrowlands Pk *DORK* RH4.....117 H8
Harrow La *GODL* GU7.....131 L6
Harrow Rd *CAR* SM5.....62 A5
DTCH/LGLY SL3.....12 D1
EBED/NFELT TW14.....23 K4
WARL CR6.....82 F4
Harrow Rd East *DORK* RH4.....117 H9
Harrow Rd West *DORK* RH4.....116 G9
Harrowsley Ct *HORL* RH6.....140 D9
Harrow Wy *SHPTN* TW17.....38 E3
Hart Cl *BNFD* RG42.....32 C1
FARN GU14.....88 A8
REDH RH1.....121 P4
Hart Dene Ct *BAGS* GU19.....51 N6
Harte Rd *HSLW* TW5.....15 L6
Hartfield Crs *WIM/MER* SW19.....43 K1
WWKM BR4.....65 N2
Hartfield Gv *PGE/AN* SE20.....46 B2
Hartfield Rd *CHSGTN* KT9.....59 K4
EDEN TN8.....145 J8
FROW RH18.....181 M9
WIM/MER SW19.....28 C9
WWKM BR4.....65 N3
Hartford Bridge Flats
HTWY RG27.....66 A7
Hartford Ri *CBLY* GU15.....68 F2
Hartford Rd *FLEETN* GU51.....86 F4
HOR/WEW KT19.....59 N5
Hart Gdns *DORK* RH4.....117 H6
Hartham Cl *ISLW* TW7.....16 G6
Hartham Rd *ISLW* TW7.....16 G6
Harting Ct *CRAWW* RH11.....176 C8
Hartington Cl *REIG* RH2.....119 L3
Hartington Rd *REIG* RH2 *.....119 L3
Hartington Rd *CHSWK* W4.....17 P5
NWDGN UB2 *.....15 N1
TWK TW1.....26 A3
Hartismere Rd *FUL/PGN* SW6.....19 K5
Hartland Cl *ADL/WDHM* KT15.....55 N8
Hartland Pl *FARN* GU14.....68 C9
Hartland Rd
ADL/WDHM KT15.....55 L6
HPTN TW12.....25 J7
ISLW TW7.....16 G8
MRDN SM4.....43 L8
Hartley Cl *BLKW* GU17.....67 M5
Hartley Copse *WDSR* SL4.....20 F2
Hartley Down *PUR/KEN* CR8.....81 H3
Hartley Farm *PUR/KEN* CR8.....81 H4
Hartley Hl *PUR/KEN* CR8.....81 H4
Hartley Old Rd *PUR/KEN* CR8.....81 H4
Hartley Rd *BH/WHM* TN16.....105 H5
CROY/NA CRO.....2 B1
Hartley Wy *PUR/KEN* CR8.....81 H4
Hart Rd *BF/WBF* KT14.....74 A2
DORK RH4.....117 H6
Hartscroft *CROY/NA* CRO.....64 E7
Harts Gdns *GUW* GU2.....111 P2
Hartsgrove *MFD/CHID* GU8.....168 A6
Harts Hill *GUW* GU2 *.....111 K4
Harts La *GDST* RH9.....122 D7
Hartsleaf Cl *FLEETN* GU51.....86 F7
Harts Leap Cl *SHST* GU47.....49 L8
Harts Leap Rd *SHST* GU47.....49 L9
Hartspiece Rd *REDH* RH1.....120 D7
Hart Sq *MRDN* SM4 *.....43 M6
Hartswood *RDKG* RH5.....137 K1
Hartswood Av *REIG* RH2.....119 L9
Hartswood Gdns *SHB* W12 *.....18 D1
The Hart *FNM* GU9.....4 B3
Harvard Hl *CHSWK* W4.....17 P3
Harvard Rd *CHSWK* W4.....17 P3
ISLW TW7.....16 E6
SHST GU47.....49 M8
Harvest Bank Rd
WWKM BR4.....65 N2
Harvest Cl *YTLY* GU46.....66 F4
Harvest Crs *FLEETN* GU51.....87 H2
Harvester Rd
HOR/WEW KT19.....60 B8
Harvesters *HORS* RH12.....192 C6
Harvesters Cl *ISLW* TW7.....25 L1
Harvest Hl *EGRIN* RH19.....180 G4
GODL GU7.....131 K9
Harvest La *THDIT* KT7.....40 G7
Harvest Ride *BNFD* RG42.....32 C2
Harvest Rd *CRAWE* RH10.....177 M7
EGH TW20.....21 J8
FELT TW13.....24 B7
Harvestside *HORL* RH6.....140 F8
Harvey Cl *CRAWW* RH11.....194 D1
Harvey Dr *HPTN* TW12.....40 B2
Harvey Gdns *GU* GU1 *.....7 H5
Harvey Rd *DTCH/LGLY* SL3.....12 F1
FARN GU14.....87 N2
GU GU1.....7 H6
HSLWW TW4.....24 C3
WOT/HER KT12.....39 J8
Harwarden Cl *CRAWE* RH10.....179 K3
Harwood Av *BMLY* BR1.....47 P3
MTCM CR4.....44 A4
Harwood Gdns *WDSR* SL4.....20 C3
Harwood Ms *FUL/PGN* SW6 *.....19 M5
Harwood Pk *REDH* RH1.....140 C6
Harwood Rd *FUL/PGN* SW6.....19 L5
SWTR RH13.....192 D7
Harwoods Cl *EGRIN* RH19.....180 E4
Harwood's La *EGRIN* RH19.....180 E3
Harwood Ter *FUL/PGN* SW6.....19 M6
Haseley End *FSTH* SE23 *.....31 K3
Haseltine Rd *SYD* SE26.....31 N7

Haslam Av *CHEAM* SM3.....43 J9
Hasle Dr *HASM* GU27.....184 C5
Haslemere Av *HEST* TW5.....15 J7
HNWL W7.....16 G1
MTCM CR4.....43 P5
WAND/EARL SW18.....28 E5
Haslemere Cl *FRIM* GU16.....69 J5
HPTN TW12.....24 G8
WLGTN SM6.....62 G4
Haslemere Rd *HASM* GU27.....184 C8
LIPH GU30.....182 G6
MFD/CHID GU8.....167 K1
THHTH CR7.....45 K6
Haslett Av Central *CRAWE* RH10.....177 J5
Haslett Av East
CRAWE RH10.....177 K5
Haslett Av West
CRAWE RH10.....176 G6
Haslett Rd *SHPTN* TW17.....38 G3
Hassocks Cl *SYD* SE26.....31 J6
Hassocks Rd *CRAWW* RH11.....176 G4
Hassocks Rd
STRHM/NOR SW16.....44 F2
Haste Hl *HASM* GU27 *.....184 E5
Haste Hill Top *HASM* GU27.....184 E5
Hastings Cl *FRIM* GU16.....69 J3
Hastings Dr *SURB* KT6.....41 J7
Hastings Rd *CRAWE* RH10.....177 L5
CROY/NA CRO.....3 J1
Hatch Cl *ADL/WDHM* KT15.....55 M2
CRAN GU6.....170 D8
Hatch End *BFOR* GU20.....52 C5
FROW RH18.....181 L9
The Hatches *FNM* GU9.....127 K5
Hatchett Rd
EBED/NFELT TW14.....23 M4
Hatchetts Dr *HASM* GU27.....183 M4
Hatch Gdns
KWD/TDW/WH KT20.....79 H9
Hatchgate *HORL* RH6.....159 J2
Hatchgate Copse *BRAK* RG12.....32 A7
Hatch Hl *HASM* GU27.....184 C9
Hatchlands *HORS* RH12.....192 D7
Hatchlands Rd *REDH* RH1.....120 A5
Hatch La *COB* KT11.....57 H9
HASM GU27.....184 D9
REDH RH1.....141 H2
WDR/YW UB7.....13 P5
Hatch Rd *KUTN/CMB* KT2 *.....8 E4
Hatch Ride *KWRG* RG40.....49 K1
Hatch Rd *STRHM/NOR* SW16.....44 G3
Hatfield Cl *BELMT* SM2.....61 L7
BF/WBF KT14 *.....73 M1
MTCM CR4.....43 P5
Hatfield Ct *CBLY* GU15.....68 D3
Hatfield Gdns *FARN* GU14.....88 C4
Hatfield Rd *ASHTD* KT21.....77 M8
Hathaway Rd *CROY/NA* CRO.....45 K8
Hatherleigh Cl *CHSGTN* KT9.....59 K4
MRDN SM4.....43 L5
Hatherley Rd *RCH/KEW* TW9.....17 M6
Hatherop Rd *HPTN* TW12.....39 P1
Hathersham Cl *HORL* RH6.....141 J9
Hathersham La *HORL* RH6.....141 J7
Hatherwood *LHD/OX* KT22.....77 K9
YTLY GU46.....67 H1
Hatton Gdns *MTCM* CR4.....44 B6
Hatton Gn *EBED/NFELT* TW14.....15 J9
Hatton Hl *BFOR* GU20.....52 C4
Hatton Rd *CROY/NA* CRO.....45 J9
EBED/NFELT TW14.....23 M3
HTHAIR TW6.....14 F6
Hatton Rd North
HTHAIR TW6.....14 F6
Havana Rd *WIM/MER* SW19.....28 C5
Havelock Rd *CROY/NA* CRO.....3 K3
WIM/MER SW19.....28 A6
Havelock Wk *FSTH* SE23.....31 K4
Haven Cl *WIM/MER* SW19.....28 A6
Haven Ct *BRYLDS* KT5 *.....41 M7
Haven Gdns *CRAWE* RH10.....179 H2
Havengate *HORS* RH12.....192 E5
Haven Rd *ASHF* TW15.....23 L7
BIL RH14.....189 N7
The Haven *RCH/CHID* GU8 *.....168 A2
RCH/KEW TW9.....17 N8
SUN TW16.....39 J1
Haven Wy *FNM* GU9.....127 P1
Haverfield Est *BTFD* TW8.....17 L4
Haverfield Gdns
RCH/KEW TW9.....17 N5
Haverhill Rd *BAL* SW12.....29 M4
Havers Av *WOT/HER* KT12.....57 N4
Haversham Cl *CRAWE* RH10.....177 J5
TWK TW1.....26 C2
Haversham Dr *BRAK* RG12.....32 D7
Havisham Pl *NRWD* SE19.....30 C9
Hawarden Gv *HNHL* SE24.....30 D1
Hawarden Rd *CTHM* CR3.....101 L1
Hawes La *WWKM* BR4.....47 L9
Hawes Rd *BMLY* BR1.....47 P2
KWD/TDW/WH KT20.....79 H9
Haweswater Ct
ASHV GU12 *.....109 H2
Hawke Rd *NRWD* SE19.....30 E9
Hawkedon Wy *CROY/NA* CRO.....64 E7
CROY/NA CRO.....63 J5
Hawkesbourne Rd
HORS RH12.....192 E5
Hawkesbury Rd
PUT/ROE SW15.....27 N1
Hawkesfield Rd *FSTH* SE23.....31 M5
Hawkes Leap *BFOR* GU20.....52 B4
Hawkesley Cl *TWK* TW1.....25 P7
Hawkesmoore Dr
RDKG RH5.....137 J9
Hayes Barton
WOKS/MYFD GU22.....73 H5
Hayes Cha *WWKM* BR4.....47 K7
Hayes Cl *HAYES* BR2.....65 N1
Hayes Crs *CHEAM* SM3.....61 H3

MTCM CR4.....44 A2
Hawkesworth Dr *BAGS* GU19.....51 M8
Hawkewood Rd *SUN* TW16.....39 J4
Hawkhirst Rd *PUR/KEN* CR8.....81 M5
Hawkhurst *COB* KT11.....76 A3
Hawkhurst Wk
CRAWE RH10.....177 L7
WWKM BR4.....65 H1
Hawkins Cl *BRAK* RG12.....33 J3
Hawkins Gv *FLEETN* GU51.....86 D9
Hawkins Rd *CRAWE* RH10.....177 H7
TEDD TW11.....26 A9
Hawkins Wy *GSHT* GU26.....165 P9
FLEETS GU52.....87 J7
Hawk La *BRAK* RG12.....32 F5
Hawkley Gdns *WNWD* SE27.....30 C5
Hawksbrook La *BECK* BR3.....47 J7
Hawksview *CL *SYD* SE26.....182 G6
Hawkshead Cl *BMLY* BR1.....47 L2
Hawkshead Rd *CHSWK* W4.....18 C1
Hawks Hl *LHD/OX* KT22.....96 C5
Hawkshill Cl *ESH/CLAY* KT10.....58 A5
Hawks Hill Cl *LHD/OX* KT22.....96 C5
Hawkshill Pl *ESH/CLAY* KT10.....58 A5
Hawkshill Wy *ESH/CLAY* KT10.....57 P5
Hawksdale Rd *PECK* SE15.....31 L1
Hawksmoor St *HMSMTH* W6.....19 H4
Hawks Rd *KUT/HW* KT1.....9 G5
Hawkswell Cl *COB* KT11.....75 P2
Hawksway *STA* TW18.....22 C6
Hawkswell Cl
WOKN/KNAP GU21.....71 M6
Hawkswood Av *FRIM* GU16.....69 H6
Hawkwell *FLEETS* GU52.....107 H2
Hawkwood Dell
GT/LBKH KT23.....96 A5
Hawkwood Ri *GT/LBKH* KT23.....96 A6
Hawley Cl *HPTN* TW12.....24 G9
Hawley Gn *BLKW* GU17.....68 A5
Hawley Gv *BLKW* GU17.....68 B6
Hawley La *FARN* GU14.....68 D8
Hawley Rd *BLKW* GU17.....68 B5
Hawley Wy *ASHF* TW15.....23 K8
Hawmead *CRAWE* RH10.....179 K3
Haworth Rd *CRAWE* RH10.....177 L6
Hawth Av *CRAWE* RH10.....177 J7
Hawth Cl *CRAWE* RH10.....177 H7
Hawthorn Av *THHTH* CR7.....45 K2
Hawthorn Cl *ASHV* GU12.....108 G3
BNFD RG42.....32 C2
BNSTD SM7.....79 J3
CRAWW RH11.....176 F2
EDEN TN8.....144 F3
HEST TW5.....15 K5
HORS RH12.....192 B6
HPTN TW12.....25 H9
REDH RH1.....140 C1
WOKS/MYFD GU22.....72 C9
Hawthorn Crs *SAND/SEL* CR2.....64 C9
Hawthornden Cl
HAYES BR2 *.....65 M1
Hawthorndene Rd
HAYES BR2.....65 N1
Hawthorn Dr *WWKM* BR4.....65 L4
Hawthorne Av
BH/WHM TN16.....84 B4
CAR SM5.....62 C6
MTCM CR4.....43 P3
Hawthorne Ct
STWL/WRAY TW19 *.....22 G3
Hawthorne Crs *BLKW* GU17.....68 A4
Hawthorne Pl *EW* KT17.....78 C1
Hawthorne Rd *STA* TW18.....21 P8
Hawthorne Wy *RGUE* GU4.....112 F1
Hawthorn Gdns *EA* W5.....17 K3
Hawthorn Hatch *BTFD* TW8.....17 H5
Hawthorn La *RFNM* GU10.....146 C1
Hawthorn Pl *RGUE* GU4.....92 B9
RGUE GU4.....113 H3
Hawthorn Rd *BTFD* TW8.....17 H5
FELT TW13.....24 B4
FRIM GU16.....69 J2
GODL GU7.....150 A2
RPLY/SEND GU23.....93 K4
SUT SM1.....61 P4
WLGTN SM6.....62 D6
WOKS/MYFD GU22.....72 C9
Hawthorns *DTCH/LGLY* SL3.....13 K6
EW KT17.....60 D5
OXTED RH8.....123 N4
Hawthorn Ter *WEY* KT13 *.....56 C9
Hawthorn Wy
ADL/WDHM KT15.....55 M8
CRAWE RH10.....177 L1
REDH RH1.....120 D7
SHPTN TW17.....38 F5
Haxted Rd *BMLY* BR1.....47 P2
LING RH7.....143 L6
Hayburn Dr *HORS* RH12.....192 D3
Haycroft Cl *COUL/CHIP* CR5.....81 K8
Haycroft Rd
BRXS/STRHM SW2.....29 P1
SURB KT6.....59 H1
Hayden Cl *ADL/WDHM* KT15.....55 M8
Haydn Av *PUR/KEN* CR8.....81 J4
Haydon Wy
WAND/EARL SW18.....19 N9
Haye Barton
WOKS/MYFD GU22.....73 H5
Hayes Cha *WWKM* BR4.....47 K7
Hayes Cl *HAYES* BR2.....65 N1
Hayes Crs *CHEAM* SM3.....61 H3

Hayesford Park Dr
HAYES BR2.....47 M6
Hayes Gdn *HAYES* BR2.....65 N1
Hayes Hl *HAYES* BR2.....47 L9
Hayes Hill Rd *HAYES* BR2.....47 M9
Hayes La *BECK* BR3.....47 K7
PUR/KEN CR8.....81 K5
SWTR RH13.....190 D5
Hayes Mead Rd *HAYES* BR2.....47 L9
Hayes Rd *HAYES* BR2.....47 N5
NWDGN UB2.....15 K2
Hayes Wk *HORL* RH6.....141 J9
The Hayes *CROFT* KT18.....78 D8
Hayes Wk *HORL* RH6.....141 J9
Hayes Wood Av *HAYES* BR2.....47 P9
Hayfields *HORL* RH6.....140 E9
Haygarth Pl *WIM/MER* SW19.....28 A8
Haygreen Cl *KUTN/CMB* KT2.....26 D6
Haylett Gdns *KUT/HW* KT1 *.....41 K5
Hayling Av *FELT* TW13.....24 B6
Haymeads Dr *ESH/CLAY* KT10.....58 C5
Haymer Gdns *WPK* KT4.....60 E2
Hayne Rd *BECK* BR3.....46 F3
Haynes Cl *DTCH/LGLY* SL3.....12 D3
RPLY/SEND GU23.....93 J5
Haynes La *NRWD* SE19.....30 F9
Haynt Wk *RYNPK* SW20.....43 J4
Haysleigh Gdns *PGE/AN* SE20.....46 A3
Hays Wk *BELMT* SM2.....61 H8
Hayter Rd *BRXS/STRHM* SW2.....29 P1
Haywain *OXTED* RH8.....123 L2
Hayward Cl *WIM/MER* SW19.....43 M1
Haywardens *LING* RH7.....143 K8
Hayward Gdns
PUT/ROE SW15.....27 P2
Haywards *CRAWE* RH10.....178 E7
Haywood *BRAK* RG12.....32 E8
Haywood Dr *FLEETS* GU52.....86 C6
Hazel Av *FARN* GU14.....88 B5
GU GU1.....112 A1
WDR/YW UB7.....14 C1
Hazel Bank *BRYLDS* KT5.....42 A9
Hazelbank Rd *CHERT* KT16.....37 N8
Hazelbank *EWKG* RG40.....48 B3
Hazelbank Cl *LIPH* GU30.....182 G6
Hazelbourne Rd *BAL* SW12.....29 L2
Hazelbury Cl *WIM/MER* SW19.....43 L3
Hazel Cl *BTFD* TW8 *.....17 H5
CRAWE RH10.....179 K3
CRAWW RH11.....176 E4
CROY/NA CRO.....46 D8
EGH TW20.....20 F9
MTCM CR4.....44 E6
REIG RH2.....119 N7
WHTN TW2.....25 K3
Hazel Ct *COB* KT11.....75 J2
Hazeldene *ADL/WDHM* KT15.....55 N4
Hazeldene Ct *PUR/KEN* CR8.....81 M4
Hazeldene Rd *LIPH* GU30.....182 A6
Hazeldon Rd *BROCKY* SE4.....31 N1
Hazel Dr *RPLY/SEND* GU23.....93 K5
STA TW18.....22 E9
SYD SE26.....31 L7
Hazelhurst *BECK* BR3.....47 K2
HORL RH6.....140 F9
Hazelhurst Cl *RGUE* GU4.....113 J1
Hazelhurst Crs *HORS* RH12.....191 N9
Hazelhurst Dr *CRAWE* RH10.....177 P5
Hazelhurst Rd *TOOT* SW17.....28 F7
Hazell Hl *BRAK* RG12.....32 E4
Hazell Rd *FNM* GU9.....4 A4
Hazelmere Cl
EBED/NFELT TW14.....23 N2
LHD/OX KT22.....77 H8
Hazelmere Wy *HAYES* BR2.....47 N7
Hazel Pde *LHD/OX* KT22 *.....96 C2
Hazel Rd *ASHV* GU12.....109 L2
BF/WBF KT14.....73 J5
FRIM GU16.....89 J5
REIG RH2.....119 N7
Hazel Wy *COUL/CHIP* CR5.....80 B8
CRAWE RH10.....179 J3
LHD/OX KT22.....96 C3
Hazelway Cl *LHD/OX* KT22.....96 C3
Hazelwick Av *CRAWE* RH10.....177 L3
Hazelwick Mill La
CRAWE RH10.....177 L3
Hazelwood *CRAWW* RH11.....176 D5
DORK RH4 *.....117 H8
Hazelwood Av *MRDN* SM4.....43 M5
Hazelwood Cl *CRAWE* RH10.....178 G3
Hazelwood Cl *SURB* KT6.....41 L7
Hazelwood Gv *SAND/SEL* CR2.....82 B3
Hazelwood La
COUL/CHIP CR5.....80 B8
Hazelwood Rd *OXTED* RH8.....123 P3
RSEV TN14.....85 H1
WOKN/KNAP GU21.....71 J7
Hazledean Rd *CROY/NA* CRO.....2 E4
Hazledene Rd *CHSWK* W4.....18 A4
Hazlemere Gdns *WPK* KT4.....42 E9
Hazlewell Rd *PUT/ROE* SW15.....27 P1
Hazlewood *MFD/CHID* GU8.....129 N9
Hazlitt Cl *FELT* TW13.....24 F7
Hazlitt Ms *WKENS* W14 *.....19 J1
Hazlitt Rd *WKENS* W14.....19 J1
Headcorn Rd *THHTH* CR7.....45 H5
Headington Rd
WAND/EARL SW18.....28 F4
Headlam Rd *CLAP* SW4.....29 N3
Headland Wy *LING* RH7.....143 J9
Headley Av *WLGTN* SM6.....63 H4
Headley Cl *CHSGTN* KT9.....59 H5

CRAWE RH10.....................177 N2

Headley Common Rd
EPSOM KT18.........................98 B7
Headley Dr CROY/NA CRO.......65 J6
Headley Gv EPSOM KT18......78 F8
KWD/TDW/WH KT20..............78 F9
Headley Heath Ap
KWD/TDW/WH KT20.............117 P1
Headley Hill Rd BOR GU35....164 D6
Headley La LIPH GU30........164 D4
Headley Pde EPSOM KT18 * ..78 B8
Headley Rd EPSOM KT18......78 A7
GSHT GU26...........................165 J7
LHD/OX KT22..........................97 J2
LIPH GU30.............................182 D4
RDKG RH5...............................97 J9
Headway Cl
RCHPK/HAM TW10..................26 B7
The Headway EW YLT7.........60 D7
Hearmon Cl YTLY GU46........67 H2
Hearne Rd CHSWK W4...........17 N3
Hearn V BOR GU35..............164 D4
Hearnville Rd BAL SW12.......29 K4
Hearn Wk BRAK RG12...........32 G2
Hearsey Gdns BLKW GU17....67 N2
Heatham Pk WHTN TW2.........25 N3
Heath Cl BNSTD SM7............79 M3
FNM GU9................................107 N7
GSHT GU26............................165 M4
HORS RH12...........................191 M7
HYS/HAR UB3..........................14 C1
SAND/SEL CR2.........................63 K5
STWL/WRAY TW19...................22 F2
WOKS/MYFD GU22.................36 B5
Heathcote
KWD/TDW/WH KT20.................99 H2
Heathcote Cl ASHV GU12 *...109 J3
Heathcote Dr EGRIN RH19...180 A1
Heathcote Rd ASHV GU12....109 K3
CBLY GU15...............................68 E3
EPSOM KT18..........................78 B2
TWK TW1.................................26 A2
Heathcroft Av SUN TW16.....39 H1
Heathdale Av HSLWW TW4....15 N8
Heathdene
KWD/TDW/WH KT20.................79 J8
Heathdene Rd
STRHM/NOR SW16...................45 H1
WLGTN SM6............................62 D6
Heathdown Rd
WOKS/MYFD GU22...................73 H4
CHOB/PIR GU24........................70 C9
KWD/TDW/WH KT20.................98 F6
RPLY/SEND GU23......................92 F3
RYNPK SW20............................42 G5
Heathedge SYD SE26 *.........31 J5
Heatherbank Cl COB KT11.....55 M8
Heather Cl ADL/WDHM KT15..55 M8
ALDT GU11.............................108 A5
ASHV GU12............................109 K1
CRAWE RH10..........................178 C1
EWKG RG40.............................48 C2
FNM GU9...............................127 K7
GUW GU2...............................111 P5
HORS RH12............................192 C5
HPTN TW12..............................39 P2
ISLW TW7................................25 L1
KWD/TDW/WH KT20.................99 J2
REDH RH1..............................120 D2
WOKN/KNAP GU21...................72 A4
Heatherdale Cl
KUTN/CMB KT2.........................26 F9
Heatherdale Rd CBLY GU15...68 E4
Heatherdeane Av CWTH RG45..49 J5
Heatherdene Cl MTCM CR4....43 P5
Heather Dr ASC SL5.............34 B5
FLEETS GU52.........................106 F1
Heather Gdns BELMT SM2....61 L5
Heatherlands HORL RH6 * ...140 E9
SUN TW16................................24 B9
Heatherley Cl CBLY GU15.....68 D3
Heatherley Rd CBLY GU15....68 D3
Heather Md BRAK RG12.......32 C5
Heathermount Dr
CWTH RG45.............................49 K3
Heather Pl ESH/CLAY KT10....58 B3
Heatherset Cl ESH/CLAY KT10..58 C4
Heatherset Gdns
STRHM/NOR SW16...................45 H1
Heatherside Cl
GT/LBKH KT23 *.......................95 P5
Heatherside Dr VW GU25......35 N7
Heatherside Rd
HOR/WEW KT19.......................60 B6
Heathers Land DORK RH4....137 J1
The Heathers
STWL/WRAY TW19....................23 J3
Heathervale Rd
ADL/WDHM KT15.....................55 M8
Heathervale Wy
ADL/WDHM KT15.....................55 M8
Heather Wk CHOB/PIR GU24..90 D1
HORL RH6..............................160 D1
Heather Wy CHOB/PIR GU24..90 D1
GSHT GU26............................166 A7
SAND/SEL CR2..........................64 D7
Heatherway CWTH RG45.......49 L4
EGRIN RH19...........................161 N5
Heathfield COB KT11.............76 A3
CRAWE RH10..........................177 N3
Heathfield Av ASC SL5..........34 E6
WAND/EARL SW18....................28 C5
Heathfield Cl ASHTD KT21...77 J7
GODL GU7.............................150 C2
WOKS/MYFD GU22...................72 A6
Heathfield Ct FLEETN GU51...86 E8
Heathfield Dr REDH RH1.....140 A1

Heathfield Gdns CHSWK W4..18 A3
CROY/NA CRO...........................2 E8
WAND/EARL SW18....................28 C2
Heathfield North WHTN TW2..25 N3
SAND/SEL CR2..........................63 M4
WAND/EARL SW18....................28 F2
WOKS/MYFD GU22...................11 H6
WOT/HER KT12..........................57 N3
Heathfield South WHTN TW2..25 N3
Heathfield Sq
WAND/EARL SW18....................28 C5
Heathfield Ter CHSWK W4....18 A3
SAND/SEL CR2..........................64 D7
Heathfield V SAND/SEL CR2..64 D7
Heath Gdns TWK TW1............25 N4
Heath Gv PGE/AN SE20.........46 F1
SUN TW16................................39 H1
Heath Hl DORK RH4.............117 H7
RFNM GU10............................146 B9
Heath Hill Rd North
CWTH RG45.............................49 M4
Heath Hill Rd South
CWTH RG45.............................49 M4
Heath House Rd
WOKS/MYFD GU22...................91 K2
Heathhurst Rd
SAND/SEL CR2..........................63 N7
Heathlands
KWD/TDW/WH KT20.................99 H2
Heathlands Cl SUN TW16.......39 J3
TWK TW1.................................25 N5
WOKN/KNAP GU21...................72 C5
Heathlands Ct HSLWW TW4...24 F1
Heathland St ALDT GU11.....108 C4
Heathlands Wy HSLWW TW4..24 F1
Heath La FNM GU9...............107 N7
GODL GU7..............................150 F2
RFNM GU10............................106 B5
SHGR GU5..............................134 A3
Heathman's Rd
FUL/PGN SW6...........................19 K6
Heath Md WIM/MER SW19....28 A6
Heath Mill La CHOB/PIR GU24..91 J5
Heathmoors BRAK RG12........32 C5
Heathpark Dr BFOR GU20......52 E5
Heath Pl BAGS GU19 *...........51 N6
Heath Ride CWTH RG45........49 H5
EWKG RG40.............................48 F3
Heath Ridge Gn COB KT11....76 A2
Heath Ri CBLY GU15..............68 A4
DORK RH4..............................116 C9
HAYES BR2...............................47 N7
PUT/ROE SW15.........................28 A2
Heathrise RPLY/SEND GU23...93 M3
Heath Ri VW GU25................35 B5
Heath Rd BAGS GU19.............51 N6
CTHM CR3..............................101 M3
HASM GU27............................183 N5
ISLW TW7.................................25 L1
LHD/OX KT22............................76 C1
THHTH CR7..............................45 L4
TWK TW1.................................25 N4
WEY KT13................................56 C4
WOKN/KNAP GU21...................72 D4
Heathrow SHGR GU5............134 E1
Heathrow Cl WDR/YW UB7...13 N9
Heathside ESH/CLAY KT10.....58 E2
HSLWW TW4............................24 C5
WEY KT13................................56 D4
Heathside Cl ESH/CLAY KT10..58 E2
Heathside Ct
KWD/TDW/WH KT20.................98 F3
Heathside Crs
WOKS/MYFD GU22...................10 E4
Heathside Gdns
WOKS/MYFD GU22...................11 G4
Heathside La GSHT GU26.....165 N5
Heathside Pk CBLY GU15......69 L1
Heathside Park Rd
WOKS/MYFD GU22...................11 F5
Heathside Pl EPSOM KT18....79 H7
Heathside Rd
WOKS/MYFD GU22...................10 E5
The Heath CTHM CR3...........101 L4
Heathvale Bridge Rd
ASHV GU12..............................89 J9
Heath Vw EHSLY KT24...........95 J5
Heathview Gdns
PUT/ROE SW15.........................27 P3
Heathview Rd
MFD/CHID GU8.......................149 M5
THHTH CR7..............................45 J5
Heath Wy HORS RH12..........192 C5
Heathway ASC SL5................33 N2
CBLY GU15...............................68 F5
CROY/NA CRO..........................64 F2
CTHM CR3..............................101 L5
EHSLY KT24.............................95 H4
NWDGN UB2 *.........................15 M2
Heathway Cl CBLY GU15.......68 F5
Heathway Dr CBLY GU15 *.....69 G1
Heathyfields Rd FNM GU9....107 K8
Heaton La EGRIN RH19.........161 M8
Heaton Rd MTCM CR4............43 P5
Heaver Rd BTSEA SW11 *......19 P8
Hebdon Rd TOOT SW17..........29 H6
Hebron Rd HMSMTH W6.........18 F1
Heckfield Dr FLEETN GU51.....86 C4
Heckfield Pl FUL/PGN SW6....19 L5
Hectors La EGRIN RH19.......161 M8
Heddon Cl ISLW TW7.............16 C9
Heddon La FNM GU14............68 C9
Hedgecourt Pl EGRIN RH19..161 M8
Hedgecroft YTLY GU46 *........66 F2
Hedgehog La HASM GU27.....184 C5
Hedgerley Ct
WOKN/KNAP GU21...................72 A6
Hedgeside CRAWW RH11.....194 F1
Hedgeway GUW GU2............111 N7
Hedingham Cl HORL RH6.....140 E9
Hedley Rd WHTN TW2............25 H3
Heenan Cl FRIM GU16.............68 G9

Heidegger Crs BARN SW13...18 F5
Heighton Gdns CROY/NA CRO..63 K4
Heights Cl BNSTD SM7............79 J5
RYNPK SW20.............................42 F1
The Heights BECK BR3 *........47 J1
WEY KT13................................56 E1
Helby Rd CLAP SW4................29 N7
Helder St SAND/SEL CR2.......63 M5
Heldmann Cl HSLW TW3........16 C9
Helen Av EBED/NFELT TW14...24 C3
Helen Cl E/WMO/HCT KT8......40 B5
Helen Ct FARN GU14...............88 D3
Helford Wk
WOKN/KNAP GU21...................71 N7
Helgiford Gdns SUN TW16......38 G1
Helios Rd WLGTN SM6............44 C9
Helix Gdns BRXS/STRHM SW2..30 A2
Helix Rd BRXS/STRHM SW2...30 A2
Helksham Cl SHST GU47.........49 P8
Helm Cl HOR/WEW KT19........77 N1
Helme Cl WIM/MER SW19.......28 C8
Helmsdale BRAK RG12............32 G6
WOKN/KNAP GU21...................71 P7
Helmsdale Rd
STRHM/NOR SW16...................44 E2
Helvellyn Cl EGH TW20............36 F1
Helvetia St CAT SE6................31 N5
Hemingford Rd CHEAM SM3...60 D3
Hemlock Cl
KWD/TDW/WH KT20.................99 J3
Hemming Cl HPTN TW12........40 A2
Hempshaw Av BNSTD SM7.....80 B5
Hempson Av DTCH/LGLY SL3..12 A1
Hemsby Rd CHSGTN KT9........59 M5
Hemsby Wk CRAWE RH10......177 L7
Henbit Cl
KWD/TDW/WH KT20.................78 F8
Henchley Dene RGUE GU4....113 H2
Henderson Av GUW GU2.......111 P1
Henderson Rd
BH/WHM TN16...........................84 A1
CRAWE RH10...........................194 A1
CROY/NA CRO...........................45 M7
WAND/EARL SW18....................28 F3
Hendon Rd TOOT SW17...........29 H5
Hendon Av HOR/WEW KT19...59 N7
Hendon Ter ASHF TW15 *.......23 N9
Hendon Wy
STWL/WRAY TW19....................22 G1
Hendrick Av BAL SW12...........29 J2
Heneage Crs CROY/NA CRO....65 J8
Henfield Rd WIM/MER SW19...43 K2
Henfold Dr RDKG RH5...........156 O1
Henfold La RDKG RH5...........137 L6
Hengelo Gdns MTCM CR4......43 P5
Hengist Av HORS RH12..........191 P9
Hengist Wy HAYES BR2..........47 M1
Hengrave Rd FSTH SE23........31 K3
Hengrove Crs ASHF TW15......22 G6
Henhurst Cross La
RDKG RH5..............................155 P1
Henley Av CHEAM SM3...........61 J2
Henley Bank GUW GU2.........111 N7
Henley Cl CRAWE RH10........177 N8
FARN GU14...............................68 A8
ISLW TW7................................16 C5
Henley Ct WOKS/MYFD GU22..72 E9
Henley Dr FRIM GU16.............68 G9
KUTN/CMB KT2.........................42 D1
Henley Gdns YTLY GU46.........67 H3
Henley Ga CHOB/PIR GU24.....90 C7
Henley Pk RGUW GU3 *..........90 D9
Henley Wy FELT TW13.............24 E8
Hennessy Ct
WOKN/KNAP GU21...................72 G2
Henniker Ms CHEL SW3..........19 P4
Henry Doulton Dr
TOOT SW17................................29 K7
Henry Jackson Rd
PUT/ROE SW15.........................19 H8
Henry Macaulay Av
KUTN/CMB KT2...........................8 C3
Henry Peters Dr TEDD TW11...25 M8
Henryson Rd BROCKY SE4.......31 N1
Henry St BMLY BR1.................47 P2
Hensford Gdns SYD SE26........31 J7
Henshaw Cl CRAWW RH11....176 D1
Henslowe Rd EDUL SE22........31 H1
Henslow Wy
WOKN/KNAP GU21...................73 H3
Henson Rd CRAWE RH10.......177 L4
Hensworth Rd ASHF TW15......22 G9
Henty Cl CRAWW RH11.........176 B8
Henty Wk PUT/ROE SW15......27 N1
Henville Rd BMLY BR1............47 P2
Hepburn Gdns HAYES BR2.....47 M9
Hepple Cl ISLW TW7................17 H7
Hepplewhite Cl
CRAWW RH11.........................194 E1
Hepworth Cft SHST GU47.......68 A2
Hepworth Rd
STRHM/NOR SW16...................44 G1
Hepworth Wy
WOT/HER KT12..........................39 H9
Herald Gdns WLGTN SM6.......62 D2
Herbert Cl BRAK RG12.............32 D6
Herbert Crs
WOKN/KNAP GU21...................71 L7
Herbert Gdns CHSWK W4 *.....17 P4
Herbert Rd FLEETN GU51........86 E6
KUT/HW KT1...............................9 F7
WIM/MER SW19.........................43 K1
Herbs End FARN GU14............88 B6
Hereford Cl CRAWE RH10.....177 L8
EPSOM KT18............................78 B2
GU GU1..................................111 M3
STA TW18..................................37 M2
Hereford Copse
WOKS/MYFD GU22...................71 P7
Hereford Gdns WHTN TW2 *...25 K4
Hereford La FNM GU9...........107 M8

Hereford Md FLEETN GU51.....87 H3
Hereford Rd EA W5.................17 J1
FELT TW13................................24 D4
Hereford Sq SKENS SW7.........19 N2
Hereward Av PUR/KEN CR8.....63 J8
Hereward Rd TOOT SW17........29 H6
Heriot Rd CHERT KT16............37 L8
Heritage Ct EGH TW20............21 L8
Heritage Lawn HORL RH6.....140 E9
Heritage Pl
WAND/EARL SW18....................28 C2
Herlwyn Gdns TOOT SW17......29 J7
Herm Cl CRAWW RH11 *.......176 D9
ISLW TW7.................................16 C5
Hermes Cl FLEETN GU51........87 J6
Hermes Wy WLGTN SM6........62 F6
Hermitage Cl DTCH/LGLY SL3..12 A1
ESH/CLAY KT10.........................58 C5
FARN GU16...............................88 F6
RCHPK/HAM TW10....................26 C1
SHPTN TW17............................38 A3
Hermitage Dr ASC SL5............33 N3
Hermitage Gdns NRWD SE19..45 L1
Hermitage La CROY/NA CRO....45 P8
EGRIN RH19............................180 E3
STRHM/NOR SW16...................45 H1
Hermitage Rd ASC SL5............34 A4
EGRIN RH19............................162 C9
WOKN/KNAP GU21...................71 K9
Heron Ct DORK RH4 *...........116 C6
KUT/HW KT1 *...........................8 D7
Herondale BRAK RG12.............32 E8
HASM GU27............................183 P4
SAND/SEL CR2..........................64 D7
Herondale Av
WAND/EARL SW18....................28 G4
Heron Dr DTCH/LGLY SL3........12 F2
Heronfield EGH TW20.............21 K9
Heron Pl RYNPK SW20 *.........42 E5
Heron Rd CROY/NA CRO............3 H3
The Heronry WOT/HER KT12....57 J5
Herons Cl CRAWE RH10.........161 H7
Heronscourt LTWR GU18..........52 C9
Herons Cft WEY KT13..............56 E5
Heron Shaw CRAN GU6..........171 H2
Herons Lea CRAWE RH10.......161 H7
Herons Pl ISLW TW7................17 H4
Herons Wy CHOB/PIR GU24....90 D1
Heronswood Cl HORL RH6.....140 D9
Herons Wood Ct
HORL RH6...............................140 D9
Heronte Dr EGRIN RH19........180 E3
Heron Wy EBED/NFELT TW14..13 N9
SWTR RH13............................192 F8
Heron Wood Rd ASHV GU12...108 F6
Herretts Gdns ASHV GU12.....108 F5
Herrett St ASHV GU12............108 F6
Herrick Cl CRAWE RH10.........177 M3
FRIM GU16...............................69 G5
Herrings La BFOR GU20...........52 D4
Herriot Ct YTLY GU46..............66 G4
Herschell Rd FSTH SE23.........31 L5
Herschel Wk
CRAWW RH11.........................194 E1
Hersham Cl PUT/ROE SW15....27 M3
Hersham Gdns
WOT/HER KT12..........................57 N4
Hersham Rd WOT/HER KT12...57 L4
Hershell Ct
MORT/ESHN SW14 *..................17 P9
Hertford Av
MORT/ESHN SW14....................27 J1
Hertford Wy MTCM CR4...........44 G5
Hesiers Hl WARL CR6..............83 L6
Hesiers Rd WARL CR6..............83 L6
Hesketh Cl CRAN GU6...........153 H9
Heslop Rd BAL SW12................29 J4
Hesper Ms ECT SW5................19 N2
Hessle Gv EW KT17.................60 D4
Hestercombe Av
FUL/PGN SW6...........................19 J7
Hester Ter RCH/KEW TW9.......17 N8
Heston Av HEST TW5...............15 N5
Heston Grange La HEST TW5...15 P4
Heston Rd HEST TW5..............15 P4
REDH RH1...............................140 B1
Hetherington Rd
SHPTN TW17............................38 C3
Hettersett Cl REIG RH2..........119 N2
Hever La EDEN TN8................145 L8
Hever Rd EDEN TN8...............145 L6
Hevers Av HORL RH6.............140 B9

Hewers Wy
KWD/TDW/WH KT20.................78 F9
Hewitt Cl CROY/NA CRO..........64 G2
Hewlett Pl BAGS GU19............51 N6
Hewshott Gv LIPH GU30........183 H5
Hewshott La LIPH GU30........182 G5
Hexham Cl CRAWE RH10........177 P5
SHST GU47................................49 P2
Hexham Gdns ISLW TW7 *......16 C5
Hexham Rd MRDN SM4..........43 M9
WNWD SE27..............................30 E9
Hextalls La REDH RH1...........101 M8
Heybridge Av
STRHM/NOR SW16...................30 A9
Heyford Av RYNPK SW20.........43 K4
Heyford Rd MTCM CR4............44 A3
Heymede LHD/OX KT22...........97 J3
Heythorp Cl
WOKN/KNAP GU21...................71 M6
Heythorp St
WAND/EARL SW18....................28 C5
Heywood Dr BAGS GU19.........51 L7
Hibbert St BTSEA SW11...........19 N8
Hibernia Rd HSLW TW3...........16 A9
Hichisson Rd PECK SE15..........31 K1
Hickling Wk CRAWE RH10......177 L7
Hickmans Cl GDST RH9.........122 C3
Hicks La BLKW GU17...............67 M3
Hidcote Cl WOKS/MYFD GU22..72 A4
Hidcote Gdns RYNPK SW20....42 F4
Higgs La BAGS GU19..............51 M6
Highacre DORK RH4...............137 H1
Highams Hl CRAWW RH11.....176 C6
Highams La CHOB/PIR GU24....52 C5
Highbank Pl
WAND/EARL SW18....................28 E4
High Barn Rd EHSLY KT24.......95 M4
Highbarrow Rd CROY/NA CRO...3 K1
High Beech BRAK RG12...........33 H5
SAND/SEL CR2..........................63 N6
High Beeches BNSTD SM7......79 H3
FRIM GU16................................68 F6
High Beeches Cl
PUR/KEN CR8...........................62 F8
High Beeches La
RHWH RH17...........................194 G8
High Broom Crs WWKM BR4...47 H8
Highbury Av THHTH CR7..........45 J3
Highbury Cl NWMAL KT3.........42 A5
WWKM BR4...............................47 J1
Highbury Crs CBLY GU15........69 J1
Highbury Gv HASM GU27.......183 N5
Highbury Rd WIM/MER SW19..28 B8
High Cedar Dr RYNPK SW20....42 F1
Highclere ASC SL5...................34 D6
GU GU1..................................112 E3
Highclere Cl BRAK RG12..........32 C3
PUR/KEN CR8............................81 L4
Highclere Ct
WOKN/KNAP GU21...................71 J1
Highclere Gdns
WOKN/KNAP GU21...................71 J1
Highclere Rd ASHV GU12.......108 F6
NWMAL KT3.............................42 B4
WOKN/KNAP GU21...................71 J6
Highclere St SYD SE26...........31 M7
Highcliffe Dr PUT/ROE SW15...27 L2
High Coombe Pl
KUTN/CMB KT2.........................27 J9
Highcotts La RGUE GU4...........93 L6
Highcroft MFD/CHID GU8.......149 M5
SHGR GU5..............................133 J9
Highcroft Ct GT/LBKH KT23.....96 A3
Highcroft Dr HORS RH12.......189 P1
Highdaun Dr
STRHM/NOR SW16...................45 H7
Highdown FLEETN GU51.........86 C5
WPK KT4..................................60 C1
Highdown Ct CRAWE RH10....177 M3
High Down Rd BELMT SM2.......61 M9
Highdown Rd PUT/ROE SW15..27 N2
Highdown Wy HORS RH12......192 E3
High Dr CTHM CR3..................102 F2
LHD/OX KT22.............................76 D3
NWMAL KT3...............................42 A2
Higher Alham BRAK RG12........32 G8
Highercombe Rd
BARN SW13 *..........................184 F2
Higher Dr BNSTD SM7.............79 H2
EHSLY KT24...............................94 G7
PUR/KEN CR8............................81 J2
Higher Gn EW KT17.................78 E2
Highfield BNSTD SM7..............80 B6
BRAK RG12................................32 B7
RGUE GU4..............................132 D4
Highfield Av ALDT GU11.........108 C6
Highfield Cl ALDT GU11..........108 D6
GU GU1....................................88 B3
FNM GU9................................127 M6
LHD/OX KT22.............................58 D9
SURB KT6..................................41 J3
Highfield Ct FLEETN GU51......21 H9
Highfield Crs GSHT GU26......165 P7
Highfield Dr HAYES BR2...........47 L5
HOR/WEW KT19.......................60 D6
WWKM BR4...............................47 J1
Highfield Gdns ALDT GU11....108 C6
Highfield Hl NRWD SE19.........45 M1
Highfield La LIPH GU30..........182 G8
MFD/CHID GU8.......................166 C2
RGUW GU3.............................130 A2
Highfield Pth FARN GU14.........88 B3
BH/WHM TN16...........................84 A6
BRYLDS KT5...............................41 N5
CHERT KT16..............................37 L9
CTHM CR3..............................102 A2
EGH TW20.................................21 J9
EGRIN RH19............................162 C9
FARN GU14................................88 B3

FELT TW13....24 B4
ISLW TW7....16 F6
PUR/KEN CR8....63 H8
SUN TW16....39 H6
SUT SM1....62 A4
WOT/HER KT12....39 J9
High Flds ASC SL5....34 C5
Highfields ASHTD KT21....77 K8
EHSLY KT24....95 H8
FROW RH18....181 L9
LHD/OX KT22....96 D4
Highfields Rd EDEN TN8....124 C9
High Foleys ESH/CLAY KT10....59 H6
High Garth ESH/CLAY KT10....58 C5
Highgate La FARN GU14....88 E2
Highgrove FARN GU14....68 D9
Highgrove Av ASC SL5....33 P2
Highgrove Ms CAR SM5....62 A2
Highland Dr FLEETN GU51....87 H4
Highland Pk FELT TW13....24 A7
Highland Rd ASHV GU12....108 F4
BMLY BR1....47 M2
CBLY GU15....50 C9
NRWD SE19....30 F9
PUR/KEN CR8....81 J3
RDKG RH5....156 B1
Highlands Av LHD/OX KT22....97 J2
SWTR RH13....192 D8
Highlands Cl FNM GU9....107 N6
HSLW TW3....16 B6
LHD/OX KT22....97 H2
Highlands Crs SWTR RH13....192 D8
Highlands La
    WOKS/MYFD GU22....92 C1
Highlands Pk LHD/OX KT22....97 K3
Highlands Rd FNM GU9....107 N7
LHD/OX KT22....97 J2
REIG RH2....119 P4
SWTR RH13....192 E8
The Highlands EHSLY KT24....94 C5
High La HASM GU27....184 D2
WARL CR6....82 F7
High Level Dr SYD SE26....31 H7
High Limes NRWD SE19 *....30 F9
High Loxley Rd
    MFD/CHID GU8....169 N5
High Md WWKM BR4....65 K1
High Meadow Cl DORK RH4....117 H8
High Meadow Pl CHERT KT16....37 K7
High Oaks CRAWW RH11....176 E7
The High Pde
    STRHM/NOR SW16 *....29 P6
High Park Av EHSLY KT24....95 H6
High Park Rd FNM GU9....5 F2
RCH/KEW TW9....17 N6
High Pth WIM/MER SW19....43 M2
High Path Rd GU GU1....112 C5
High Pewley GU GU1....7 G7
High Pine Cl WEY KT13....56 E4
High Pines WARL CR6....82 C8
High Pitfold GSHT GU26....165 N9
Highpoint WEY KT13....56 C2
High Rdg GODL GU7....150 C2
Highridge Cl EPSOM KT18 *....78 C4
High Rd RF/WEF KT14....74 B2
    COUL/CHIP CR5....100 A4
High Standing CTHM CR3....101 L5
High St ADL/WDHM KT15....55 M3
ALDT GU11....108 D4
ASC SL5....33 P4
ASC SL5....34 D6
ASC SL5....34 C6
BAGS GU19....51 N6
BECK BR3....46 E1
BH/WHM TN16....104 C7
BH/WHM TN16....105 N4
BIL RH14....188 C7
BMLY BR1....47 N4
BNSTD SM7....79 L4
BOR GU35....164 B6
BRAK RG12....32 D5
BTFD TW8....17 K4
CAR SM5....62 B4
CBLY GU15....68 F2
CHEAM SM3....61 J5
CHOB/PIR GU24....53 L9
CHOB/PIR GU24....70 E1
COB KT11....69 L3
CRAN GU6....152 C9
CRAWE RH10....176 C6
CROY/NA CR0....2 D5
CTHM CR3....101 N3
CWTH RG45....49 N5
DORK RH4....117 H7
DTCH/LGLY SL3....12 C5
DTCH/LGLY SL3....12 G5
E/WMO/HCT KT8....40 A5
EGH TW20....21 M8
EGRIN RH19....180 E3
ESH/CLAY KT10....58 B4
ESH/CLAY KT10....58 F5
EW KT17....60 D8
FARN GU14....88 E7
FELT TW13....24 B5
GDST RH9....122 C2
GODL GU7....131 K9
GODL GU7....150 C1
GT/LBKH KT23....96 B5
GU GU1....6 E6
HASM GU27....184 D6
HEST TW5....15 K5
HOR/WEW KT19....78 B2
HORL RH6....159 L1
HORS RH12....175 H3
HPTN TW12....40 B2
HSLW TW3....16 C8
HYS/HAR UB3....14 F4
KUT/HW KT1....8 E5
KWD/TDW/WH KT20....98 C3
LHD/OX KT22....76 D2
LHD/OX KT22....97 H2
LING RH7....143 K9

NWMAL KT3....42 C5
OXTED RH8....103 P8
OXTED RH8....123 K1
PGE/AN SE20....46 C1
PUR/KEN CR8....63 J9
REDH RH1....100 D8
REDH RH1....120 B5
REDH RH1....121 H5
REDH RH1....121 M4
REIG RH2....119 L5
RFNM GU10....146 B1
RHWH RH17....195 L6
RHWH RH17....195 P4
RPLY/SEND GU23....93 N1
SHGR GU5....132 D7
SHPTN TW17....38 E2
SHST GU47....49 K9
SNWD SE25....45 P5
STA TW18....22 C7
STWL/WRAY TW19....21 K2
STWL/WRAY TW19....22 C2
SUT SM1....61 M3
TEDD TW11....25 P8
THDIT KT7....40 C8
THHTH CR7....45 L5
WDR/YW UB7....13 P4
WEY KT13....56 C3
WHTN TW2....25 K3
WIM/MER SW19....28 A8
WOKN/KNAP GU21....10 E4
WOKN/KNAP GU21....72 A5
WOKS/MYFD GU22....92 E1
WOT/HER KT12....39 J9
WWKM BR4....47 H9
High Street Collier's Wd
    WIM/MER SW19....43 P1
High Street Grn
    MFD/CHID GU8....186 D1
High Street Harlington
    HYS/HAR UB3....14 F5
High Street Ms
    WIM/MER SW19....28 B8
High Thicket Rd RFNM GU10..146 A8
High Tor Cl BMLY BR1....47 P1
High Tree Cl ADL/WDHM KT15..55 L4
High Trees BRXS/STRHM SW2..30 B4
    CROY/NA CR0....46 E9
High Trees Cl CTHM CR3....101 P2
High Trees Rd REIG RH2....119 P6
High Vw BELMT SM2....61 K9
    SHGR GU5....134 E1
Highview CTHM CR3....101 N4
    WOKN/KNAP GU21....71 L6
High View Av WLGTN SM6....63 H4
High View Cl FARN GU14....88 C3
    NRWD SE19....45 P3
High View Cl REIG RH2....119 P5
Highview Crs CBLY GU15....51 H8
High View Rd FARN GU14....88 C3
    GUW GU2....111 K8
    LTWR GU18....51 N9
    NRWD SE19....30 E9
Highway WGRA45....49 L4
Highwayman's Rdg
    BFOR GU20....52 B3
The Highway BELMT SM2....61 N7
High Weald Landscape Trail
    EGRIN RH19....180 C4
Highwold COUL/CHIP CR5....80 C7
Highwood Cl FSTH SE23....31 H4
    PUR/KEN CR8....81 L6
    YTLY GU46....66 G4
Highwoods CTHM CR3....101 N5
    LHD/OX KT22....97 J1
Highworth SWTR RH13 *....192 E9
Hilary Av MTCM CR4....44 C4
Hilary Cl FUL/PGN SW6 *....19 M5
Hilary Dr CWTH RG45....49 M3
Hilbert Rd CHEAM SM3....61 H3
Hilborough Cl
    WIM/MER SW19....43 N1
Hildenlea Pl HAYES BR2 *....47 L3
Hildenley Cl REDH RH1....100 F8
The Hildens DORK RH4....116 C6
Hilder Gdns FARN GU14....88 F4
Hilders Cl EDEN TN8....144 D1
Hilders La EDEN TN8....144 D1
The Hilders ASHTD KT21....77 P6
Hildreth St BAL SW12....29 L4
Hildyard Rd FUL/PGN SW6....19 L4
Hilfield YTLY GU46....67 K3
Hilgay GU GU1....7 J3
Hilgay Cl GU GU1....7 J3
Hiliand Ri BOR GU35....164 C7
Hillars Heath Rd
    COUL/CHIP CR5....80 G4
Hillary Cl EGRIN RH19....180 F1
    FNM GU9....127 M6
Hillary Crs WOT/HER KT12....39 L5
Hillary Dr ISLW TW7....16 F9
Hillary Rd DTCH/LGLY SL3....12 C1
    FNM GU9....127 M6
    NWDGN UB2....16 A1
Hillbarn SAND/SEL CR2....63 N9
Hillberry BRAK RG12....32 B3
Hillborne Cl HYS/HAR UB3....15 J5
Hillborough Cl
    WIM/MER SW19 *....43 N1
Hillbrook Gdns WEY KT13....56 C6
Hillbrook Rd FNM GU9....107 L8
Hillbrow NWMAL KT3....42 D4
Hillbrow Cl RGUW GU3....111 H4
Hillbrow Ct OXTED RH8....123 K1
Hillbrow Rd BMLY BR1....47 L1
    ESH/CLAY KT10....58 C3
Hillbury Cl WARL CR6....82 B7
Hillbury Gdns WARL CR6....82 C7
Hillbury Rd TOOT SW17....29 L6
    WARL CR6....82 A6
Hill Cl COB KT11....76 A1

PUR/KEN CR8....81 L1
SHGR GU5....132 F2
Hill Copse Vw BRAK RG12....32 C2
Hillcote Av
    STRHM/NOR SW16....45 J1
Hill Ct FARN GU14....68 B7
Hillcourt Rd EDUL SE22....31 J2
Hill Crs BRYLDS KT5....41 N6
    WPK KT4....60 G1
Hill Crest EGRIN RH19....162 D6
    MFD/CHID GU8....148 E1
    SURB KT6 *....41 L8
Hillcrest EDEN TN8....125 M9
    FLEETN GU51....86 E7
    FNM GU9....107 P6
    KWD/TDW/WH KT20 *....117 P2
    WEY KT13....56 D3
Hillcrest Av CHERT KT16....55 J2
Hillcrest Cl BECK BR3....46 F7
    CRAWE RH10....177 N5
    EPSOM KT18....78 D4
    SYD SE26....31 H7
Hill Crest Dr RFNM GU10....127 K7
Hillcrest Gdns ESH/CLAY KT10..58 F3
Hillcrest Rd BH/WHM TN16....84 E5
    CBLY GU15....69 K1
    CTHM CR3....81 P6
    EDEN TN8....144 C1
    GUW GU2....111 M4
    PUR/KEN CR8....81 L6
Hillcrest Vw BECK BR3....46 F7
Hillcroft Av PUR/KEN CR8....80 E2
Hillcroome Rd BELMT SM2....61 P5
Hillcross Av MRDN SM4....43 J7
Hilldale Rd SUT SM1....61 K3
Hilldeane Rd PUR/KEN CR8....63 J8
Hilldown Rd HAYES BR2....47 L9
    STRHM/NOR SW16....44 G1
Hill Dr STRHM/NOR SW16....45 H4
Hillersdon Av BARN SW13....18 E4
Hill Farm Cl HASM GU27 *....184 A5
Hillfield Av MRDN SM4....44 A1
Hillfield Cl GU GU1....112 G3
Hillfield Ct HORS RH12 *....192 C3
Hillfield Pde MRDN SM4 *....43 P7
Hillfield Rd REDH RH1....120 C5
Hilliord Pl REDH RH1....140 C2
Hillgarth GSHT GU26....165 N6
Hillgate Pl BAL SW12....29 L2
Hill Gv FELT TW13....24 G5
Hillgate Pl BAL SW12....29 L2
Hillhampton ASC SL5....34 F3
Hill House Cl CRAWE RH10....179 H7
Hill House Dr HPTN TW12....40 A2
    REIG RH2....119 M7
    WEY KT13....56 C9
Hill House Hl LIPH GU30....182 C3
Hillhouse La HORS RH12....189 H1
Hill House Ms HAYES BR2....47 M3
Hill House Rd
    STRHM/NOR SW16....30 A8
Hillhurst Gdns CTHM CR3....81 N9
Hillier Gdns CROY/NA CR0....63 J4
Hillier Pl CHSGTN KT9....59 K5
Hillier Rd BTSEA SW11....29 L2
    GU GU1....112 E5
Hillier's La CROY/NA CR0....62 G2
Hillingdale CRAWW RH11....176 B7
    CRAWW RH11....194 F1
Hillingdon Av
    STWL/WRAY TW19....23 H4
Hillingdon Trail HYS/HAR UB3..15 J3
Hillmead BRAK RG12....32 A4
Hill Md HORS RH12....191 P7
Hillmont Rd ESH/CLAY KT10....58 E2
Hillmore Gv SYD SE26....31 L8
Hillmount WOKS/MYFD GU22..10 E6
Hill Pk LHD/OX KT22 *....76 D8
Hill Park Ct LHD/OX KT22 *....76 F8
Hill Pl CRAWW RH11....176 F6
Hill Ri DORK RH4....116 G5
Hillrise DTCH/LGLY SL3....12 E4
Hill Ri ESH/CLAY KT10....59 H1
    RCHPK/HAM TW10....26 C1
Hill Rd CAR SM5....62 A5
    FNM GU9....107 P7
    GSHT GU26....165 M8
    HASM GU27....184 D4
    LHD/OX KT22....96 B2
    MTCM CR4....44 D2
    PUR/KEN CR8....81 H1
    SUT SM1....61 M4
Hillsboro Rd EDUL SE22....30 F1
Hillsborough Ct FARN GU14..68 A8
Hillsborough Pk CBLY GU15..69 L5
Hillsid School FNM GU10....127 K6
Hillside Av PUR/KEN CR8....81 K2
Hillside ASC SL5 *....34 C6
    BNSTD SM7....79 J5
    CBLY GU15....68 B1
    ESH/CLAY KT10 *....58 D8
    HORS RH12....191 P8
    VW GU25....36 A7
    WIM/MER SW19....28 A9
    WOKS/MYFD GU22....72 B9
Hillside Av PUR/KEN CR8....81 K2
Hillside Cl BNSTD SM7....79 J5
    BNSTD SM7....79 J4
    CRAN GU6....171 J3
Hillside Dr CRAWE RH10....177 N3
Hillside Gdns ADL/WDHM KT15..55 K4
    BRKHM/BTCW RH3....117 N6
    BRXS/STRHM SW2 *....30 B5
    WLGTN SM6....62 E6

Hogarth Ter CHSWK W4 *....18 C4
Hogarth Wy HPTN TW12....40 C2
Hogden La EHSLY KT24....115 N2
Hogden Rd RDKG RH5....115 N5
Hoghatch La FNM GU9....107 L8
Hogscross La
    COUL/CHIP CR5....100 B2
Hogsmill La COB KT11....75 L3
Hogsmill Wy HOR/WEW KT19..60 A4
Hogspudding La RDKG RH5...157 H2
Hogtrough Hl
    BH/WHM TN16....105 L2
Hogtrough La OXTED RH8....103 K8
    REDH RH1....120 F6
Hogwood Rd BIL RH14....187 P7
Holbeach Rd CAT SE6....31 P3
Holbeche Cl YTLY GU46....66 E3
Holbeck BRAK RG12....32 B7
Holbein Rd CRAWE RH10....177 J8
Holborn Wy MTCM CR4....44 B3
Holbreck Pl
    WOKS/MYFD GU22....10 E5
Holbrook Cl FNM GU9....108 B6
Holbrook Meadow
    EGH TW20....21 N9
Holbrook School La
    HORS RH12....192 C3
Holbrook Wy ALDT GU11....108 D7
Holcombe Cl BH/WHM TN16..105 H6
Holcombe St HMSMTH W6....18 F5
Holcon Ct REDH RH1....120 C2
Holdenby Rd BROCKY SE4....31 M1
Holder Rd ASHV GU12....109 H3
    CRAWE RH10....177 K4
The Hill CTHM CR3....101 P4
Hill Top CHEAM SM3....43 K8
Hilltop Cl ASC SL5....34 E3
    LHD/OX KT22....97 J1
    RGUW GU3....111 M1
Hilltop La REDH RH1....101 M6
Hilltop Ri GT/LBKH KT23....96 C6
Hilltop Rd CTHM CR3....81 N6
    REIG RH2....119 M7
Hilltop Vw YTLY GU46....66 F3
Hilltop Wk CTHM CR3....82 E9
Hill Vw CHOB/PIR GU24 *....53 J3
Hillview CROY/NA CR0....63 K4
    EW KT17....60 C8
Hill View Cl
    KWD/TDW/WH KT20....98 C1
    PUR/KEN CR8....63 K9
Hillview Ct
    WOKS/MYFD GU22....10 D6
Hill View Crs GU GU1....112 B1
Hillview Dr REDH RH1....120 C6
Hillview Gdns CRAWW RH11..194 F3
Hill View Rd ESH/CLAY KT10..58 C6
    FNM GU9....4 B3
    STWL/WRAY TW19....21 J2
    TWK TW1....25 P2
    WOKS/MYFD GU22....10 E6
Hillworth BECK BR3 *....47 H3
Hillworth Rd
    BRXS/STRHM SW2....30 B3
Hillybarn Rd CRAWW RH11..175 P2
Hilton Wy SAND/SEL CR2....82 B4
Himley Rd TOOT SW17....29 H8
Hinaidi Wy FARN GU14....88 B7
Hinchley Cl ESH/CLAY KT10..58 E2
Hinchley Dr ESH/CLAY KT10..58 E2
Hinchley Wy ESH/CLAY KT10..58 F2
Hindell Cl FARN GU14....68 C8
Hindhead Cl CRAWW RH11..176 F7
Hindhead Rd HASM GU27....183 P2
Hindhead Wy WLGTN SM6....62 G4
Hindmans Rd EDUL SE22....31 H1
Hindsley's Pl FSTH SE23....31 K5
Hine Cl COUL/CHIP CR5....100 E2
Hinksey Cl DTCH/LGLY SL3....12 F1
Hinstock Cl FARN GU14....88 C4
Hinton Av HSLWW TW4....15 M9
Hinton Cl CWTH RG45....49 M2
Hinton Dr CWTH RG45....49 M2
Hinton Rd WLGTN SM6....62 E5
Hipley St WOKS/MYFD GU22..72 F9
Hitchcock Cl SHPTN TW17....38 B1
Hitches La FLEETN GU51....86 C8
Hitchings Wy REIG RH2....119 L9
Hitherbury Cl GUW GU2....112 A8
Hitherfield Rd
    STRHM/NOR SW16....30 A5
Hitherhooks Hl BNFD RG42....32 A2
Hithermoor Rd
    STWL/WRAY TW19....22 D2
Hitherwood CRAN GU6....171 H1
Hitherwood Cl REIG RH2....119 P3
Hitherwood Dr NRWD SE19....30 G7
H Jones Crs ALDT GU11....108 E5
Hoadly Rd
    STRHM/NOR SW16....29 N6
Hobart Gdns THHTH CR7....45 M4
Hobart Pl RCHPK/HAM TW10..26 E3
Hobart Rd WPK KT4....60 F2
Hobbes Wk PUT/ROE SW15....27 N1
Hobbs Cl BF/WBF KT14....74 A2
Hobbs Rd CRAWW RH11....194 D1
Hobby St SHST GU47....30 D7
Hobury St WBPTN SW10....19 N4
Hocken Md CRAWE RH10....177 N3
Hockering Gdns
    WOKS/MYFD GU22....11 J5
Hockering Rd
    WOKS/MYFD GU22....11 H5
Hockford Cl CHOB/PIR GU24..91 H6
Hodges Cl BAGS GU19....51 M8
Hodgkin Cl CRAWE RH10....177 L6
Hodgson Gdns RGUE GU4....112 E2
Hoebrook Cl
    WOKS/MYFD GU22....92 C1
Hoe La MFD/CHID GU8....151 J8
    SHGR GU5....134 C6
Hoffmann Gdns
    SAND/SEL CR2....64 A5
Hofland Rd WKENS W14....19 J1
Hogarth Av ASHF TW15....23 M9
Hogarth Cl SHST GU47....68 A2
    SWTR RH13....192 E9
Hogarth Crs CROY/NA CR0....45 P7
    WIM/MER SW19....43 P2
Hogarth Gdns HEST TW5....16 A5
Hogarth Pl ECT SW5 *....19 M2
Hogarth Rd CRAWE RH10....177 J8
    ECT SW5....19 M2

Hollybush Ter NRWD SE19 *........30 F9
Hollybush Tr BFOR GU20.........51 P3
Holly Cl ASHV GU12...........108 E4
  BECK BR3.....................47 J5
  BOR GU35....................164 F6
  CHERT KT16...................53 N2
  CRAWE RH10..................177 K3
  EGH TW20.....................20 G9
  FARN GU14....................88 C3
  FELT TW13....................24 F8
  HORS RH12...................192 C5
  WOKN/KNAP GU21...............71 P8
Hollycombe Cl LIPH GU30......182 F8
Holly Ct CWTH RG45.............49 K4
Holly Crs BECK BR3.............46 F6
Hollycroft Cl SAND/SEL CR2....63 N4
  WDR/YW UB7...................14 C4
Hollycroft Gdns
  WDR/YW UB7...................14 C4
Holly Dr WDSR SL4..............20 D1
Holly Farm Rd NWDGN UB2......15 N3
Hollyfield Rd BRYLDS KT5......41 M8
Hollyfields Cl CBLY GU15......68 D5
Holly Gn WEY KT15.............56 F3
Hollygrove Cl HSLW TW5........15 P9
Holly Hedge La FRIM GU16......68 G6
Holly Hedge Rd COB KT11......75 K3
  FRIM GU16....................68 G6
Holly Hill Dr BNSTD SM7.......79 L6
Holly Hock CHOB/PIR GU24......70 G4
Holly Hough
  KWD/TDW/WH KT20.............117 P1
Holly La BNSTD SM7............79 P7
  GODL GU7....................131 J9
  RGUW GU3.....................91 K9
Holly La East BNSTD SM7......79 M5
Holly La West BNSTD SM7......79 N6
Holly Lea RCUE GU4............92 B8
Hollymead CAR SM5.............62 B2
Hollymead Rd
  COUL/CHIP CR5................80 F6
Holly Ms WBPTN SW10...........19 N3
Hollymoor La
  HOR/WEW KT19.................60 B8
Holly Pde KT11................75 K4
Hollyridge HASM GU27........184 D4
Holly Rd ASHV GU12...........108 E5
  CHSWK W4 *...................18 B2
  FARN GU14....................88 B3
  HPTN TW12....................25 K9
  HSLW TW3.....................16 B9
  REIG RH2....................119 M7
  TWK TW1......................25 P4
Holly Spring La BRAK RG12....32 F2
Hollytree Cl WIM/MER SW19....28 A4
Hollytree Gdns FRIM GU16.....68 F8
Holly Tree Rd CTHM CR3......101 N2
Hollytrees FLEETS GU51........86 E9
Holly Vis HMSMTH W6 *.........18 F1
Holly Wk BLKW GU17...........67 P4
  MTCM CR4.....................44 F5
Hollywood Ms
  WBPTN SW10 *.................19 N4
Hollywood Rd WBPTN SW10.....19 N4
Hollywoods CROY/NA CR0........64 F8
Holman Cl CRAWW RH11.........194 E2
Holman Ct EW KT17 *...........60 E7
Holman Rd BTSEA SW11..........19 P7
  HOR/WEW KT19.................59 P9
Holmbank Dr SHPTN TW17........38 G5
Holmbrook Gdns FARN GU14....87 N3
Holmbury Cl CWTH RG45.........49 K4
Holmbury Cl CRAWW RH11......176 F7
Holmbury Ct WIM/MER SW19....44 A1
Holmbury Dr RDKG RH5........137 J1
Holmbury Gv CROY/NA CR0......64 B6
Holmbury Pk CRAN GU6........154 B6
  RDKG RH5....................154 F4
Holmbush Ct HORS RH12 *.....193 N1
Holmbush Rd PUT/ROE SW15....28 B2
Holm Cl ADL/WDHM KT15........73 J1
Holmcroft CRAWE RH10........177 H6
  KWD/TDW/WH KT20.............98 F5
Holmdene Av HNHL SE24........30 D1
Holmdene Cl BECK BR3.........47 J3
Holmead Rd FUL/PGN SW6......19 M5
Holme Cl CWTH RG45...........49 L2
Holme Chase ASC SL5..........34 C7
  PUR/KEN CR8..................81 H2
  WOKS/MYFD GU22...............92 D1
Holmes Cl ASC SL5............34 C7
Holmesdale Av
  MORT/ESHN SW14...............17 P8
Holmesdale Cl GU GU1........112 F4
  SNWD SE25....................46 B4
Holmesdale Pk REDH RH1 *....121 H5
Holmesdale Rd CROY/NA CR0...45 M6
  RCH/KEW TW9..................17 M6
  RDKG RH5....................137 H2
  REDH RH1....................121 H7
  REIG RH2....................119 M4
  TEDD TW11....................41 J1
Holmesdale Ter RDKG RH5 *...137 H2
Holmesley Rd FSTH SE23.......31 M2
Holmes Rd TWK TW1............25 N5
  WIM/MER SW19.................43 N1
Holmethorpe Av REDH RH1....120 D2
Holmewood Gdns
  BRXS/STRHM SW2...............30 A3
Holmewood Rd
  BRXS/STRHM SW2...............29 P3
  SNWD SE25....................45 N4
Holmwood Cl
  ADL/WDHM KT15................55 L4
  BELMT SM2....................61 H7
  EHSLY KT24...................94 G8
Holmwood Gdns WLGTN SM6.....62 D5
Holmwood Rd BELMT SM2........60 G7
  CHSGTN KT9...................59 L4
Holmwood View Rd
  HORS RH16...................137 H4
Holne Cha MRDN SM4...........43 L7
Holroyd Rd ESH/CLAY KT10.....58 G7
  PUT/ROE SW15.................18 G9
Holsart Cl
  KWD/TDW/WH KT20..............98 F2
Holstein Av WEY KT13..........56 C3
Holsworthy Wy CHSGTN KT9.....59 J4
Holt Cl FARN GU14.............68 E9
Holton Heath BRAK RG12.......33 H5
Holt Pound La RFNM GU10....126 C8
The Holt MRDN SM4 *..........43 K6
  WLGTN SM6....................62 E4
Holtwood Rd LHD/OX KT22......76 C2
Holtye Av EGRIN RH19........162 F9
Holtye Pl EGRIN RH19........162 G9
Holtye Rd EGRIN RH19........180 E1
Holtye Wk CRAWE RH10 *......177 K7
Holwood Ct WOT/HER KT12.....57 L1
Holybourne Av
  PUT/ROE SW15.................27 M5
Holyhoke Cl CWTH RG45........49 L3
Holyoake Av
  WOKN/KNAP GU21...............72 A6
Holyoake Crs
  WOKN/KNAP GU21...............72 A6
Holyport Rd FUL/PGN SW6......18 G5
Holyrood Pl CRAWW RH11.....176 E9
Holywell Cl FARN GU14........68 C9
  STWL/WRAY TW19...............23 H4
Holywell Wy
  STWL/WRAY TW19...............23 H4
Hombrook Dr BNFD RG42........32 A2
Home Cl CAR SM5...............62 B1
  CRAWE RH10..................177 M3
  LHD/OX KT22..................96 D1
  VW GU25......................36 B7
Home Ct FELT TW13 *...........24 B4
  SURB KT6.....................41 K6
Homecroft Rd SYD SE26.........31 K8
Home Farm Cl
  BRKHM/BTCW RH3..............118 C6
  CHERT KT16...................54 E6
  EPSOM KT18...................79 H6
  ESH/CLAY KT10................58 B5
  FARN GU14....................88 F1
  SHPTN TW17...................38 G5
  THDIT KT7....................40 F8
Home Farm Gdns
  WOT/HER KT12.................57 L1
Home Farm Rd GODL GU7......150 E2
  HTWY RG27....................66 B9
Home Ct CRAWW RH11 *.......194 E1
Homefield MFD/CHID GU8 *...148 D9
Homefield Cl
  ADL/WDHM KT15................73 J1
  HORL RH6....................140 D9
  LHD/OX KT22..................94 G3
Homefield Gdns
  KWD/TDW/WH KT20.............78 G9
  WIM/MER SW19.................43 K3
Homefield Ms BECK BR3 *......46 G9
Homefield Pk SUT SM1.........61 M5
Homefield Rd CHSWK W4........18 B3
  COUL/CHIP CR5................81 K9
  WARL CR6.....................82 C8
  WIM/MER SW19.................28 B9
  WOT/HER KT12.................39 P8
The Homefield MRDN SM4 *.....43 L5
Homeland Dr BELMT SM2........61 M7
Homelands LHD/OX KT22........97 J1
Homelands Dr NRWD SE19......45 N1
Homelea Cl FARN GU14.........68 D8
Homeleigh Crs ASHV GU12......89 J7
Homeleigh Rd PECK SE15.......31 L1
Homemead CROY/NA CR0........44 E7
Home Pk OXTED RH8...........123 N2
Home Park Cl SHGR GU5......132 D7
Home Park Ct
  KUT/HW KT1 *.................41 K5
Home Park Rd
  WIM/MER SW19.................28 C7
Home Pk Ter KUT/HW KT1.......8 C4
Home Pk Wk KUT/HW KT1 *......8 C6
Homer Rd CROY/NA CR0.........46 D7
Homersham Rd KUT/HW KT1......9 J4
Homesdale Rd CTHM CR3......101 M3
Homestall GUW GU2...........111 K5
Homestall Rd EDUL SE22......31 K1
  EGRIN RH19..................181 K3
Homestead CRAN GU6.........153 J8
Homestead Gdns
  ESH/CLAY KT10................58 E4
Homestead Rd CTHM CR3......101 M3
  EDEN TN8....................124 F9
  FUL/PGN SW6..................19 K5
  STA TW18.....................22 E9
Homestead Wy
  CROY/NA CR0..................65 J9
Homewaters Av SUN TW16.......39 J2
Homewood CRAN GU6..........153 K9
Homewood Cl HPTN TW12........24 G9
Homewood Gdns
  SNWD SE25....................45 N4
Hone Hl SHST GU47............67 M1
Honeybrook Rd BAL SW12......29 M3
Honeycrock La REDH RH1.....140 C3
Honeyhill Rd BNFD RG42.......32 B1
Honeypot La EDEN TN8........144 B1
Honeypots Rd
  WOKS/MYFD GU22...............92 B2
Honeysuckle Bottom
  EHSLY KT24..................114 G5
Honeysuckle Cl CWTH RG45.....49 L2
  HORL RH6....................140 D9
  YTLY GU46....................66 E2

Honeysuckle Gdns
  CROY/NA CR0..................46 D8
Honeysuckle La BOR GU35....164 E6
  CRAWW RH11..................176 F2
Honeysuckle Wk
  HORS RH16...................192 F5
Honeywell Rd BTSEA SW11......29 H2
Honeywood La RDKG RH5......172 F6
Honeywood Rd ISLW TW7 *......16 C3
  SWTR RH13...................192 F6
Honeywood Wk CAR SM5.........62 B3
Honister Gdns FLEETN GU51....87 J5
Honister Hts PUR/KEN CR8....81 M3
Honnor Gdns ISLW TW7.........16 D7
Honnor Rd STA TW18...........22 E1
Honor Oak Pk FSTH SE23.......31 L2
Honor Oak Ri FSTH SE23.......31 K2
Honor Oak Rd FSTH SE23.......31 K4
Hood Av MORT/ESHN SW14......27 H1
Hood Cl CROY/NA CR0...........2 B2
Hood Rd RYNPK SW20...........42 D1
Hooke Rd EHSLY KT24..........95 H5
Hookfield HOR/WEW KT19.......78 A2
Hook Heath Av
  WOKS/MYFD GU22...............71 P8
Hook Heath Gdns
  WOKS/MYFD GU22...............91 M1
Hook Heath Rd
  WOKS/MYFD GU22...............91 M1
Hook Hl SAND/SEL CR2.........63 N8
Hook Hill La
  WOKS/MYFD GU22...............91 P1
Hook Hill Pk
  WOKS/MYFD GU22...............91 P1
Hookhouse Rd
  MFD/CHID GU8................169 K5
Hook La CHOB/PIR GU24........70 C2
  RGUW GU3....................130 D3
  SHGR GU5....................134 D3
Hookley Cl MFD/CHID GU8....148 F1
Hookley La MFD/CHID GU8....148 F1
Hook Mill La LTWR GU18.......52 D7
Hook Ri North SURB KT6.......59 N2
Hook Ri South CHSGTN KT9....59 M2
Hook Rd CHSGTN KT9...........59 K4
  HOR/WEW KT19.................60 A6
Hookstile La FNM GU9..........5 G6
Hookstone La
  CHOB/PIR GU24................52 F9
Hook Underpass
(Kingston By-Pass)
  CHSGTN KT9...................59 K2
Hooley La REDH RH1..........120 B6
Hope Av BRAK RG12............32 G8
Hope Cl BTFD TW8.............17 L3
  SUT SM1......................61 N4
Hope Ct CRAWW RH11 *.......194 E1
Hope Cottage Cl GUW GU2 *....69 N4
Hope Grant's Rd ALDT GU11..108 C2
Hope La FNM GU9.............107 M8
Hopeman Cl SHST GU47........67 P1
Hope Pk BMLY BR1.............47 M1
Hopes Cl HEST TW5............16 A4
Hope St BTSEA SW11...........19 P8
  MFD/CHID GU8................148 D9
Hope Wy ALDT GU11...........108 B4
Hopfield WOKN/KNAP GU21.....10 C1
Hopfield Av BF/WBF KT14......74 A1
Hop Gdn FLEETS GU51.........106 E2
Hophurst Cl CRAWE RH10.....179 J3
Hophurst Dr CRAWE RH10.....179 J3
Hophurst Hl CRAWE RH10.....179 J2
Hophurst La CRAWE RH10.....179 J2
Hopkin Cl GUW GU2...........111 P1
Hopkins Ct CRAWW RH11 *....194 E1
Hopper V BRAK RG12...........32 C7
The Hoppety
  KWD/TDW/WH KT20.............99 H2
Hoppingwood Av
  NWMAL KT3....................42 C4
Hopton Gdns NWMAL KT3........42 E7
Hopton Pde
  STRHM/NOR SW16 *............29 P8
Hopton Rd
  STRHM/NOR SW16...............29 P8
Hopwood Cl TOOT SW17........28 F6
Horace Rd KUT/HW KT1..........8 F7
Horatio Av BNFD RG42.........32 C2
Horatius Wy CROY/NA CR0......63 H5
Horder Rd FUL/PGN SW6........19 J6
Horewood Rd BRAK RG12........32 D7
Horley Lodge La REDH RH1...140 B5
Horley Rd HORL RH6..........158 D5
  REDH RH1....................140 B9
Horley Rw HORL RH6..........140 D8
Hormer Cl SHST GU47..........49 P8
Hornbeam Cl FARN GU14........87 N2
Hornbeam Gdns NWMAL KT3.....42 E7
Hornbeam Rd GU GU1..........111 N8
  REIG RH2....................119 N8
Hornby Av BRAK RG12..........32 F8
Hornchurch Cl
  KUTN/CMB KT2.................26 C8
Hornchurch Hl CTHM CR3......81 P6
Horndean Cl CRAWE RH10 *...177 H7
  PUT/ROE SW15.................27 H4
Horndean Rd BRAK RG12........33 H7
Hornecourt Hl HORL RH6.....141 P6
Horner La MTCM CR4...........43 P3
Horne Rd SHPTN TW17..........38 B5
Hornhatch RGUE GU4..........132 F3
Hornhatch Cl RGUE GU4......132 F3
Hornhatch La RGUE GU4......132 E2
Horniman Dr FSTH SE23........31 J4
Horniman Gdns FSTH SE23 *...31 J4
Horn Rd FARN GU14............88 A2
Hornshill La HORS RH12......189 J3

Horsebrass Dr BAGS GU19......51 N7
Horsecroft BNSTD SM7.........79 K6
Horsecroft Mdw
  BNSTD SM7 *..................79 L5
Horse Fair KUT/HW KT1.........8 B4
Horse Gate Ride ASC SL5......34 A7
Horse Hl HORL RH6...........139 M9
Horsell Birch
  WOKN/KNAP GU21...............71 N4
Horsell Common Rd
  WOKN/KNAP GU21...............10 A4
Horsell Ct CHERT KT16........37 M8
Horsell Moor
  WOKN/KNAP GU21...............10 A4
Horsell Park Cl
  WOKN/KNAP GU21...............10 B3
Horsell Ri WOKN/KNAP GU21...72 C4
Horsell Rise Cl
  WOKN/KNAP GU21...............10 C1
Horsell V WOKN/KNAP GU21....10 C1
Horsemoor
  CI DTCH/LGLY SL3.............12 C2
Horseshoe Bend
  GSHT GU26..................165 K8
Horseshoe Cl CBLY GU15.......51 H9
Horseshoe Crs CBLY GU15......51 H9
Horseshoe La ASHV GU12.......89 J9
  CRAN GU6....................152 F8
Horseshoe La West GU GU1...112 F4
Horseshoe Rdg WEY KT13.......56 E9
The Horseshoe BNSTD SM7.....79 K4
  COUL/CHIP CR5................80 F2
  GODL GU7....................150 B1
Horsford Rd
  BRXS/STRHM SW2...............30 A1
Horsham Gates
  SWTR RH13 *.................192 D7
Horsham Rd CRAN GU6.........152 A9
  CRAN GU6....................171 K3
  CRAWW RH11..................176 B9
  DORK RH4....................194 D4
  EBED/NFELT TW14..............23 M2
  HORS RH12...................188 F6
  HORS RH12...................188 C1
  RDKG RH5....................154 D2
  RDKG RH5....................154 F7
  RDKG RH5....................155 H8
  SHGR GU5....................152 A8
  SHGR GU5....................133 H8
Horshoe La East GU GU1.....112 F4
Horsley Cl HOR/WEW KT19.....78 B2
Horsley Dr CROY/NA CR0.......65 J6
  KUTN/CMB KT2.................26 C8
Horsley Rd BMLY BR1..........47 P1
  COB KT11.....................75 K8
Horsmonden Rd
  BROCKY SE4...................31 N1
Hortensia Rd WBPTN SW10.....19 M4
Horticultural Pl CHSWK W4....18 B3
Horton Crs HOR/WEW KT19.....59 P9
Horton Gdns
  DTCH/LGLY SL3................12 D8
  HOR/WEW KT19.................60 A9
Horton La HOR/WEW KT19.......59 N9
Horton Pl BH/WHM TN16......105 H6
Horton Rd DTCH/LGLY SL3......12 A6
  DTCH/LGLY SL3................13 J3
Hortons Wy BH/WHM TN16......105 J9
Horton Wy CROY/NA CR0.......46 D6
Horvath Cl WEY KT13..........56 F3
Hosack Rd TOOT SW17..........29 J5
Hosey Common La
  BH/WHM TN16.................125 J1
Hosey Common Rd
  BH/WHM TN16.................105 J9
Hosey Hl BH/WHM TN16.......105 J9
Hoskins Cl HYS/HAR UB3.......15 H5
Hoskins Pl EGRIN RH19......162 E8
Hoskins Rd OXTED RH8........103 L9
Hospital Bridge Rd
  WHTN TW2....................25 J5
Hospital Hl ALDT GU11......108 C3
Hospital Rd ALDT GU11......108 C3
  HSLW TW3....................16 A8
Hostel Rd FARN GU14..........88 D7
Hotham Cl E/WMO/HCT KT8.....40 A4
Hotham Rd PUT/ROE SW15......18 G8
  WIM/MER SW19.................43 N1
Houblon Rd
  RCHPK/HAM TW10...............26 D2
Houghton Cl HPTN TW12........24 F9
Houghton Rd
  CRAWE RH10..................177 M8
Houlder Crs CROY/NA CR0......63 J5
Houlton Ct BAGS GU19.........51 N7
Hound House Rd SHGR GU5....134 C9
Houndown La
  MFD/CHID GU8................148 B7
Hounslow Av HSLW TW3.........25 J1
Hounslow Gdns HSLW TW3......25 J1
Hounslow Rd
  EBED/NFELT TW14..............24 C3
  WHTN TW2....................25 J2
Houseman Rd FARN GU14........88 B1
Houston Rd FSTH SE23........31 M5
  SURB KT6.....................41 H7
Hove Gdns SUT SM1............43 M9
Howard Av EW KT17............60 E8
Howard Cl ASHTD KT21.........77 L6
  EHSLY KT24...................94 F5
  FLEETN GU51..................87 J6

  HPTN TW12....................40 C1
  KWD/TDW/WH KT20..............98 D5
  LHD/OX KT22..................97 J3
  REIG RH2.....................24 A9
Howard Dr FARN GU14.........87 M3
Howard Gdns GU GU1..........112 E4
Howard Pl REIG RH2..........119 L3
Howard Rdg RGUE GU4.........112 E1
Howard Rd BMLY BR1...........47 N1
  COUL/CHIP CR5................80 E4
  CRAWW RH11..................176 A9
  DORK RH4....................116 C2
  EHSLY KT24...................95 J2
  GT/LBKH KT23.................96 B7
  ISLW TW7.....................16 F8
  NWMAL KT3....................42 C4
  PGE/AN SE20..................46 C2
  RDKG RH5 *..................137 J2
  REIG RH2....................119 M6
  SNWD SE25....................46 B6
  SURB KT6.....................41 M7
  SWTR RH13...................192 F6
Howards Cl
  WOKS/MYFD GU22...............72 E9
Howards Crest Cl BECK BR3....47 J1
Howards La
  ADL/WDHM KT15................55 J5
  PUT/ROE SW15.................18 G9
Howards Rd
  WOKS/MYFD GU22...............72 D9
Howard St THDIT KT7..........41 H8
Howards Yd
  WAND/EARL SW18...............28 E3
Howberry Rd THHTH CR7.......45 M2
Howden Rd SNWD SE25..........45 P5
Howe Dr CTHM CR3............101 M2
Howell Hl BELMT SM2 *........60 G8
Howell Hill Gv EW KT17.......60 G7
Howes Gdns FLEETN GU51......86 E9
The Howe FARN GU14...........87 M6
Howgate Rd
  MORT/ESHN SW14...............18 B8
How Green La EDEN TN8......145 N4
Howitts Cl ESH/CLAY KT10....58 A5
How La COUL/CHIP CR5........80 C7
Howletts Rd HNHL SE24........30 D2
Howley Rd CROY/NA CR0.........2 B5
Howsman Rd BARN SW13........18 E4
Howson Ter
  RCHPK/HAM TW10...............26 D2
Hoylake Cl CRAWW RH11......176 A6
Hoylake Gdns MTCM CR4........44 E4
Hoyle Hl RDKG RH5...........156 C5
Hoyle Rd TOOT SW17...........29 H8
Hubbard Dr CHSGTN KT9........59 J5
Hubbard Rd WNWD SE27........30 D6
Hubberholme BRAK RG12........32 C4
Hubert Cl WIM/MER SW19 *....43 N2
Hubert Rd DTCH/LGLY SL3......13 H1
Huddington Gld YTLY GU46....66 E3
Huddleston Crs REDH RH1....100 F8
Hudson Cl LIPH GU30.........182 F7
Hudson Ct WIM/MER SW19 *....43 N2
Hudson Pl DTCH/LGLY SL3.....12 D5
Hudson Rd CRAWE RH10.......177 H7
  HYS/HAR UB3..................14 F1
Hudsons KWD/TDW/WH KT20....99 H1
Huggins Pl BRXS/STRHM SW2...30 A4
Hugh Dalton Av
  FUL/PGN SW6 *................19 K4
Hugh de Pont La
  FLEETN GU51 *................86 F4
Hughenden Rd WPK KT4.........42 E8
Hughes Av HSLW TW3...........38 G1
Hughes Wk CROY/NA CR0........45 L8
Hugh Gaitskell Cl
  FUL/PGN SW6 *................19 K4
Hugon Rd FUL/PGN SW6........19 M8
Huguenot Pl
  WAND/EARL SW18...............28 F1
Huitt Sq BTSEA SW11..........19 P8
Hullbrook La SHGR GU5......133 H9
Hullmead SHGR GU5...........133 J9
Hulton Cl LHD/OX KT22........97 J3
Hulverston Cl BELMT SM2......61 M8
Humber Wy DTCH/LGLY SL3.....12 E2
  SHST GU47....................49 P8
Humbolt Cl GUW GU2..........111 L5
Humbolt Rd HMSMTH W6........19 J4
Humes Av HNWL W7.............16 F1
Hummer Rd EGH TW20...........20 G8
Humphrey Cl LHD/OX KT22.....96 C2
Hungerford Cl SHST GU47.....49 N8
Hungry Hill La
  RPLY/SEND GU23..............93 N6
Hunnels Cl FLEETS GU52.....106 E3
Hunstanton Cl
  CRAWW RH11..................176 A6
  DTCH/LGLY SL3................12 C5
Hunston Rd MRDN SM4.........43 N9
Hunter Cl BAL SW12...........29 K4
  WLGTN SM6....................62 G6
Hunter Rd CRAWE RH10.......176 G8
  FARN GU14....................88 B4
  GU GU1........................7 H5
  RYNPK SW20...................42 G2
  THHTH CR7....................45 M4
Hunters Cha GDST RH9.......122 F8
  LIPH GU30...................182 E5
Hunters Cl HOR/WEW KT19.....78 A2
  CT RCH/KEW TW9...............26 C1
Hunters Ct RCH/KEW TW9 *....26 C1
Hunters Ga REDH RH1.........121 H4
Hunters Meadow
  NRWD SE19....................30 F7
Hunters Rd CHSGTN KT9.......59 L2
Hunters Wy CROY/NA CR0........3 K7
Hunters Wy EDEN TN8........144 F2
Hunting Cl ESH/CLAY KT10....58 A3

Huntingdon Cl MTCM CR4.....44 G5
Huntingdon Gdns
  CHSWK W4 *.....18 A5
  WPK KT4.....60 C2
Huntingdon House Dr
  GSHT GU26.....165 P7
Huntingdon Rd REDH RH1.....120 B5
  WOKN/KNAP GU21.....71 L6
Huntingfield CROY/NA CR0.....64 F6
Huntingfield Rd
  PUT/ROE SW15.....18 E9
Huntingfield Wy ECH TW20.....37 H1
Huntingford Cl
  GSHT GU26 *.....165 M4
Hunting Gate Dr
  CHSGTN KT9.....59 L6
Hunting Gate Ms
  WHTN TW2 *.....25 M4
Huntington Pl
  DTCH/LGLY SL3.....12 F1
Huntley Cl STWL/WRAY TW19..23 H3
Huntley Wy RYNPK SW20.....42 E3
Huntly Rd SNWD SE25.....45 N5
Hunt Rd NWDGN UB2.....16 A1
Hunts Cl GUW GU2.....111 K4
Huntsgreen Ct BRAK RG12.....32 E4
Hunts Hill Rd RGUW GU3.....110 A1
Huntsman Cl FELT TW13.....24 C7
Huntsman Cl WARL CR6.....82 C8
Huntsmans Meadow
  ASC SL5.....33 P2
Huntsman's Ms FRIM GU16..89 H3
Huntsmoor Rd
  HOR/WEW KT19.....60 B4
Huntspill St TOOT SW17.....28 G6
Hunts Slip Rd DUL SE21.....30 F6
Hurland La BOR GU35.....164 C7
Hurlands Cl FNM GU9.....128 B5
Hurlands La MFD/CHID GU8..187 L1
Hurlands Pl FNM GU9.....128 B1
Hurley Cl WOT/HER KT12.....57 K1
Hurley Gdns RGUE GU4.....112 E2
Hurlford WOKN/KNAP GU21..71 N6
Hurlingham Gdns
  FUL/PGN SW6.....19 K8
Hurlingham Pk
  FUL/PGN SW6.....19 K8
Hurlingham Rd
  FUL/PGN SW6.....19 K7
Hurlingham Sq
  FUL/PGN SW6 *.....19 L8
Hurlstone Rd SNWD SE25.....45 M6
Hurn Court Rd HSLWW TW4..15 M7
Hurnford Cl SAND/SEL CR2..63 N8
Huron Rd TOOT SW17.....29 K5
Hurricane Rd WLGTN SM6.....62 G6
Hurricane Wy FARN GU14.....88 D8
Hurst Av HORS RH12.....192 C7
Hurstbourne Rd FSTH SE23..31 M4
Hurst Cl BRAK RG12 *.....32 C6
  CHSGTN KT9.....59 N4
  CRAWW RH11.....176 C7
  EPSOM KT18.....98 A4
  HAYES BR2.....47 M9
  LIPH GU30.....182 D9
  WOKS/MYFD GU22.....72 A9
Hurst Ct HORS RH12.....192 C7
Hurstcourt Rd SUT SM1.....43 M9
Hurst Cft GU GU1.....112 C8
Hurstdene Av HAYES BR2....47 M9
  STA TW18.....22 E9
Hurst Dr KWD/TDW/WH KT20..98 E6
Hurst Farm Cl
  MFD/CHID GU8.....149 N2
Hurst Farm Rd EGRIN RH19..180 C3
Hurstfield HAYES BR2.....47 N6
Hurstfield Rd
  E/WMO/HCT KT8.....40 A4
Hurst Green Cl OXTED RH8..123 P3
Hurst Green Rd OXTED RH8..123 N3
Hurst Gv WOT/HER KT12.....39 H9
Hurstlands OXTED RH8.....123 N3
Hurst La E/WMO/HCT KT8.....40 C5
  EGH TW20.....36 D4
  EPSOM KT18.....98 B2
Hurstleigh Cl REDH RH1.....120 B5
Hurstleigh Dr REDH RH1.....120 B5
Hurstmere Cl GSHT GU26..165 N8
Hurst Rd ALDT GU11.....108 E3
  CROY/NA CR0.....63 M4
  E/WMO/HCT KT8.....40 C4
  EPSOM KT18.....98 C3
  FARN GU14.....68 D8
  HOR/WEW KT19.....60 E9
  HORL RH6.....140 A9
  HORS RH12.....192 C7
  WOT/HER KT12.....39 M5
Hurst St HNHL SE24.....30 C2
Hurst View Rd SAND/SEL CR2..63 N6
Hurst Wy SAND/SEL CR2.....63 N5
  WOKS/MYFD GU22.....73 J5
Hurstwood ASC SL5.....34 A7
Hurtmore Cha GODL GU7.....131 H5
Hurtmore Rd
  MFD/CHID GU8.....130 D7
Hurtwood Rd WOT/HER KT12..39 P8
Hurworth Av DTCH/LGLY SL3..12 A1
Huson Rd BNFD RG42.....32 E1
Hussar Ct ALDT GU11.....108 A4
Hussars Cl HSLWW TW4.....15 N8
Husseywell Crs HAYES BR2..47 N9
Hutchingson's
  CROY/NA CR0.....65 H9
Hutchins Wy HORL RH6.....140 B8
Hutton Cl BFOR GU20.....52 D6
Hutton Rd ASHV GU12.....89 J9
Huxbear St BROCKY SE4.....31 N1
Huxley Cl NWDGN UB2.....16 A1
Huxley Cl GODL GU7.....131 K6
Huxley Rd GUW GU2.....111 K6
Hyacinth Cl HPTN TW12.....25 H9
Hyacinth Rd PUT/ROE SW15..27 M4
Hyde Dr CRAWW RH11.....176 B6

Hyde Farm Ms BAL SW12.....29 N4
Hyde La MFD/CHID GU8.....166 B1
  RFNM GU10.....106 B7
  RFNM GU10.....146 D1
Hyde Park Ga SKENS SW7 *..19 N1
Hyde Rd RCHPK/HAM TW10..26 E1
  SAND/SEL CR2.....63 N7
Hyde Ter ASHF TW15.....23 P9
Hydethorpe Rd BAL SW12.....29 N4
Hyde Wk MRDN SM4.....43 L8
Hyde Wy HYS/HAR UB3.....15 H2
Hylands Cl CRAWE RH10.....177 K6
Hylands Ms EPSOM KT18.....78 A4
Hylands Rd EPSOM KT18.....78 A4
Hyndewood FSTH SE23.....31 L6
Hyndman Cl CRAWW RH11..194 E2
Hyperion Ct CRAWW RH11..176 B7
Hyperion Pl HOR/WEW KT19..60 B7
Hythe Cl BRAK RG12.....32 G6
Hythe End Rd
  STWL/WRAY TW19.....21 M5
Hythe Field Av EGH TW20.....22 B9
Hythe Park Rd EGH TW20.....21 P8
Hythe Rd STA TW18.....22 B8
  THHTH CR7.....45 M3
The Hythe STA TW18.....22 B8

I

Iberian Av WLGTN SM6.....62 F3
Iberian Wy CBLY GU15.....69 J2
Ibis La CHSWK W4.....18 A6
Ibsley Gdns PUT/ROE SW15..27 H4
Ibworth La FLEETN GU51.....86 C4
Icehouse Wd OXTED RH8.....123 M2
Icklingham Rd COB KT11.....75 L1
Iden Cl HAYES BR2.....47 L4
Idlecombe Rd TOOT SW17.....29 K9
Idmiston Rd WNWD SE27.....30 D6
  WPK KT4.....42 E8
Iffley Rd HMSMTH W6.....18 F1
Ifield Av CRAWW RH11.....176 D1
Ifield Cl REDH RH1.....120 A8
Ifield Dr CRAWW RH11.....176 D4
Ifield Gn CRAWW RH11.....176 C1
Ifield Rd CRAWW RH11.....176 C5
Ifield Rd CRAWW RH11.....176 E4
  HORL RH6.....158 B7
  WBPTN SW10.....19 M3
Ifield St CRAWW RH11.....176 C3
Ifield Wd CRAWW RH11.....176 A2
Ifold Bridge La BIL RH14.....187 P6
Ifoldhurst BIL RH14.....187 P8
Ifold Rd REDH RH1.....120 C7
Ikona Ct WEY KT13 *.....56 E4
Ilchester Pl WKENS W14.....19 L1
Ildersly Gv DUL SE21.....30 E5
Ilex Cl EGH TW20.....35 P1
  SUN TW16.....39 L3
  YTLY GU46.....67 H3
Ilex Wy STRHM/NOR SW16..30 B8
Ilkley Cl NRWD SE19 *.....30 E9
Illingworth Cl MTCM CR4.....43 P4
Illingworth Gv BRAK RG12.....33 H2
Imber Cross THDIT KT7 *.....40 F8
Imber Gv ESH/CLAY KT10.....40 D8
Imberhorne La EGRIN RH19..179 P4
Imberhorne Wy
  EGRIN RH19.....162 A9
Imber Park Rd
  ESH/CLAY KT10.....40 D9
Imjin Cl ALDT GU11.....108 D3
Imperial College Rd
  SKENS SW7.....19 P1
Imperial Gdns MTCM CR4.....44 D4
Imperial Pk LHD/OX KT22 *..76 G9
Imperial Rd
  EBED/NFELT TW14.....23 P3
  FUL/PGN SW6.....19 M6
Imperial Sq FUL/PGN SW6..19 M6
Imperial Wy CROY/NA CR0..63 J5
Imran Ct ASHV GU12.....108 E6
Ince Rd WOT/HER KT12.....56 E9
Inchwood BRAK RG12.....32 E9
  CROY/NA CR0.....65 H3
Ingatestone Rd SNWD SE25..46 B6
Ingham Cl SAND/SEL CR2.....64 D7
Ingham Rd SAND/SEL CR2..64 D7
Ingleboro Dr PUR/KEN CR8..81 M2
Inglegreen La WLGTN SM6..62 C7
Ingle Dell CBLY GU15.....68 F4
Ingle Gln EWKG RG40 *.....48 E2
Inglehurst ADL/WDHM KT15..55 K9
Inglemere Rd FSTH SE23.....31 L6
  TOOT SW17.....44 B1
Ingleside DTCH/LGLY SL3....13 J6
Ingleside Cl BECK BR3.....46 G8
Inglethorpe St FUL/PGN SW6..19 H6
Ingleton BRAK RG12.....32 C4
Ingleton Rd CAR SM5.....62 A7
Inglewood CHERT KT16.....55 K2
  CROY/NA CR0.....64 E7
  WOKN/KNAP GU21.....71 P7
Inglewood Av CBLY GU15.....69 N2
Inglis Rd CROY/NA CR0.....3 K1
Ingram Cl HORS RH12.....191 P8
Ingram Rd THHTH CR7.....45 L2
Ingrams Cl WOT/HER KT12..57 L4
Ingrave St BTSEA SW11.....19 P8
Ingress St CHSWK W4.....18 C3
Ingress V BNFD RG42 *.....32 B2
Inkerman La RDKG RH5.....137 J2
Inkerman Pde
  WOKN/KNAP GU21 *.....71 L7
Inkerman Rd
  WOKN/KNAP GU21.....71 L7
Inkerman Wy
  WOKN/KNAP GU21.....71 L7
Inman Rd WAND/EARL SW18..28 F3

Inner Park Rd
  WIM/MER SW19.....28 A5
Inner Ring East HTHAIR TW6..14 D8
Inner Ring West HTHAIR TW6..14 B7
Innes Cl RYNPK SW20.....43 J3
Innes Gdns PUT/ROE SW15..27 N2
Innes Rd HORS RH12.....192 E6
Innes Yd CROY/NA CR0.....2 D5
Innings La BNFD RG42.....32 F2
Institute Rd ASHV GU12.....108 F5
  DORK RH4.....116 C8
Instow Gdns FARN GU14.....88 A1
International Av HEST TW5..15 L3
International Wy SUN TW16..38 G2
Inval Hl HASM GU27.....184 D2
Inveresk Gdns WPK KT4.....60 D2
Inverness Rd HSLW TW3.....15 P9
  NWDGN UB2.....15 N2
  WPK KT4.....43 H9
Inverness Wy SHST GU47.....67 P3
Invicta Cl EBED/NFELT TW14..24 A4
Invincible Rd FARN GU14.....88 C4
Inwood Av COUL/CHIP CR5..81 J9
  HSLW TW3.....16 C8
Inwood Cl CROY/NA CR0.....64 E1
Inwood Rd HSLW TW3.....16 C9
Iona Cl CAT SE6.....31 P5
  CRAWW RH11.....176 E8
  MRDN SM4.....43 M9
Ipswich Rd TOOT SW17.....29 K9
Irene Rd ORP BR6.....77 B3
  FUL/PGN SW6.....19 L6
Ireton Av WOT/HER KT12.....57 H1
Iris Cl CROY/NA CR0.....46 D9
  SURB KT6.....41 M8
Iris Rd CHOB/PIR GU24.....70 C4
  HOR/WEW KT19.....59 P8
Iron La SHGR GU5.....132 C8
Iron Mill Rd
  WAND/EARL SW18 *.....28 E2
Iron Mill Rd
  WAND/EARL SW18.....28 E2
Ironsbottom REIG RH2.....139 K6
Irvine Dr FARN GU14.....68 A8
Irvine Pl VW GU25.....36 C6
Irving Rd WKENS W14.....19 H1
Irving Wk CRAWE RH10.....177 H8
Irwin Dr HORS RH12.....191 P8
Irwin Rd GUW GU2.....111 N6
Isabella Ct RCHPK/HAM TW10..26 E3
Isabella Pl KUTN/CMB KT2..26 E2
Isbells Dr REIG RH2.....119 M7
Isham Rd STRHM/NOR SW16..44 G3
Isis Cl CRAWW RH11.....176 B7
Isis St WAND/EARL SW18.....28 F5
Isis Wy SHST GU47.....49 P9
Island Cl STA TW18.....22 B7
Island Farm Av
  E/WMO/HCT KT8.....39 P6
Island Farm Rd
  E/WMO/HCT KT8.....39 P6
Island Rd MTCM CR4.....44 B1
Islay Gdns HSLWW TW4.....24 C1
Itchel La RFNM GU10.....106 B7
Itchingwood Common Rd
  OXTED RH8.....124 A4
Ivanhoe Cl CRAWW RH11.....176 C2
Ivanhoe Rd HSLWW TW4.....15 M8
Iveagh Cl CRAWW RH11.....194 F1
Iveagh Rd GUW GU2.....111 N6
Ively Rd FARN GU14.....87 N6
Iverna Ct KENS W8.....19 L1
Iverna Gdns
  EBED/NFELT TW14.....23 N1
  KENS W8.....19 L1
Ivers Wy CROY/NA CR0.....65 H6
Ives Cl YTLY GU46.....66 F1
Ives Rd DTCH/LGLY SL3.....12 E1
Ivor Cl GU GU1.....7 K4
Ivor Gv CFELT TW13.....24 B4
Ivory Wk CRAWW RH11.....176 B8
Ivybank GODL GU7.....131 L7
Ivybridge Cl TWK TW1.....25 P2
Ivychurch Cl PGE/AN SE20..46 B9
Ivy Cl SUN TW16.....39 L3
Ivy Crs CHSWK W4.....18 A2
Ivy Gdns MTCM CR4.....44 G4
Ivyday Gv STRHM/NOR SW16..30 A6
Ivydene E/WMO/HCT KT8.....39 P6
  WOKN/KNAP GU21.....71 H7
Ivydene Cl REDH RH1.....140 D1
  SUT SM1.....61 N3
Ivy Dene La EGRIN RH19.....181 J5
Ivy La HSLWW TW4.....15 N8
  WOKS/MYFD GU22.....11 J5
Ivy Mill Cl GDST RH9.....122 B3
Ivy Mill La GDST RH9.....122 A3
Ivymount Rd WNWD SE27.....30 C6
Ivy Rd ASHV GU12.....108 C4
  HSLW TW3.....16 B9
  SURB KT6 *.....59 N1
  TOOT SW17.....29 H8

J

Jacaranda Cl NWMAL KT3.....42 C4
Jackass La GDST RH9.....122 F2
  HAYES BR2.....65 P5
Jackdaw Cl CRAWW RH11.....176 D7
Jackdaw La HORS RH12.....192 D5
Jack Good Child Wy
  KUT/HW KT1.....9 K6
Jackman's La
  WOKN/KNAP GU21.....71 N8
Jackson Cl BRAK RG12.....32 D6
  EPSOM KT18.....78 B3
Jackson Rd CRAWW RH11.....194 E2
Jackson's Pl CROY/NA CR0.....3 G2
Jackson's Wy CROY/NA CR0..64 C2
Jacobean Cl CRAWE RH10..177 M6
Jacob Rd CBLY GU15.....68 C2
Jacobs Well Rd RGUE GU4..92 B9
Jaggard Wy BAL SW12.....29 J3
Jaguar Rd FARN GU14.....88 D5
Jail La BH/WHM TN16.....84 B4
Jamaica Rd THHTH CR7.....45 K7
James Rd ALDT GU11.....68 D6
  CBLY GU15.....68 B6
  RGUW GU3.....132 A4
James St HSLW TW3.....16 D8
Jameston BRAK RG12.....32 E9
James Watt Wy
  CRAWE RH10.....159 K8
James Wy CBLY GU15.....68 B6
Jamnagar Cl STA TW18.....22 C9
Janoway Hill La
  WOKN/KNAP GU21.....72 A8
Japonica Cl
  WOKN/KNAP GU21.....72 A7
Jarrett Cl BRXS/STRHM SW2..30 C4
Jarrow Cl MRDN SM4.....43 M6
Jarvis Cl HTWY RG27.....85 N5
Jarvis Rd SAND/SEL CR2.....63 M5
Jasmine Cl REDH RH1.....140 C1
  WOKN/KNAP GU21.....71 M5
Jasmine Ct HORS RH12.....192 B6
Jasmine Gdns CROY/NA CR0..65 H2
Jasmine Gv PGE/AN SE20.....46 B2
Jasmine Rd HOR/WEW KT19..59 P5
Jasmin Rd HOR/WEW KT19..59 P5
Jason Cl REDH RH1.....140 A1
  WEY KT13.....56 E4
Jasons Dr RGUE GU4.....112 G2
Jasper Rd NRWD SE19.....30 G9
Jay Av ADL/WDHM KT15 *.....56 A2
Jays Nest Cl BLKW GU17.....67 P4
Jay Wk CRAWE RH10.....179 K6
Jean Batten Cl WLGTN SM6..63 H6
Jebb Av BRXS/STRHM SW2..29 P2
Jefferies Rd EHSLY KT24.....114 C2
Jefferson Cl DTCH/LGLY SL3..12 E2
  WEA W13.....17 H1
Jeffries Pas GU GU1 *.....7 F5
Jeffs Cl HPTN TW12 *.....25 J9
Jeffs Rd SUT SM1.....61 K3
Jeff Rd BRXS/STRHM SW2..30 B1
Jemmett Cl KUTN/CMB KT2..9 K3
Jengar Cl SUT SM1.....61 M3
Jenkins' Hill London Rd
  BAGS GU19.....51 L8
Jenner Dr CHOB/PIR GU24..70 C2
Jenner Rd CRAWW RH11.....159 J9
  GU GU1.....7 G5
Jenners Cl LING RH7.....143 K9
Jenner Wy HOR/WEW KT19..59 N7
Jennett Rd CROY/NA CR0.....63 J2
Jennings Cl ADL/WDHM KT15..55 N7
  SURB KT6.....41 J8
Jennings Rd EDUL SE22.....30 G2
Jenny Wy HORL RH6.....159 N1
Jenny La LING RH7.....143 J9
Jenny's Wk YTLY GU46.....67 J2
Jennys Wy COUL/CHIP CR5..100 E3
Jenson Wy NRWD SE19.....45 P1
Jephtha Rd
  WAND/EARL SW18.....28 D2
Jeppo's La MTCM CR4.....44 B5
Jerdan Pl FUL/PGN SW6.....19 L5
Jerome Cnr CWTH RG45.....49 N6
Jerrymoor Hl EWKG RG40..48 D1
Jersey Brow RG FARN GU14..88 C5
Jersey Cl CHERT KT16.....55 K2
  FLEETN GU51.....86 E5
  RGUE GU4.....92 F9
Jersey Rd CRAWW RH11.....176 D9
  HEST TW5.....16 B6
  TOOT SW17.....44 D1
Jerviston Gdns
  STRHM/NOR SW16.....30 B9
Jesmond Cl MTCM CR4.....44 D4
Jesmond Rd CROY/NA CR0..45 P8
Jessamy Rd WEY KT13.....56 C1
Jesses La SHGR GU5.....134 E5
Jessett Dr FLEETS GU52.....106 E2
Jessica Rd WAND/EARL SW18..28 F2
Jessiman Ter SHPTN TW17..38 C6
Jessop Av NWDGN UB2.....16 A3
Jessops Wy CROY/NA CR0..44 E7
Jevington BRAK RG12.....32 B8
Jewels Hl WARL CR6.....83 N1
Jews Rw WAND/EARL SW18..19 M9
Jews Wk SYD SE26.....31 J7
Jeypore Rd
  WAND/EARL SW18.....28 F3
Jig's La South BNFD RG42..32 G2
Jillian Cl HPTN TW12.....40 A1
Jobson's La HASM GU27.....185 M8
Jocelyn Rd RCH/KEW TW9..17 L8
Jockey Md HORS RH12.....191 P9
Jock's La BNFD RG42.....32 A2
John Ash Cl HSLW TW3 *.....16 C6
John Archer Wy
  WAND/EARL SW18.....28 G2
John Austin Cl KUTN/CMB KT2..9 F1
John Cl ALDT GU11.....108 A6
John Cobb Rd WEY KT13.....56 C6
John Parker Sq
  BTSEA SW11 *.....19 P8
John Pl BNFD RG42.....32 C1
John Russell Cl GUW GU2..111 N2
John's Cl ASHF TW15.....23 M7
Johnsdale OXTED RH8.....103 M9
John's La MRDN SM4.....43 N6
John Smith Av FUL/PGN SW6..19 K5

Johnson Dr EWKG RG40.....48 F2
Johnson Rd CROY/NA CR0..45 M8
  HEST TW5.....15 L5
Johnson's Cl CAR SM5.....62 B2
Johnsons Dr HPTN TW12.....40 C2
Johnson St NWDGN UB2.....15 L1
Johnson Wk CRAWE RH10..176 G7
Johnson Wy FLEETS GU52..86 F9
John's Rd BH/WHM TN16.....84 B9
Johnston Wk GUW GU2.....111 N1
Johns Wk CHM CR3.....15 H7
  SNWD SE25.....46 A5
Johns Wk CTHM CR3.....82 A8
Joinville Pl ADL/WDHM KT15..55 P3
Jolesfield CRAWW RH11.....176 C8
Jolive Ct GU GU1 *.....112 E6
Jolliffe Rd REDH RH1.....100 E6
Jonathan Ct CHSWK W4 *....18 C2
Jones Cl CRAWE RH10.....177 J5
Jonson Cl MTCM CR4.....44 D5
Jordan Cl SAND/SEL CR2.....63 P9
Jordans Cl CRAWW RH11.....176 C3
  GU GU1.....112 E4
  REDH RH1.....140 C1
  STWL/WRAY TW19.....22 F3
Jordans Crs CRAWW RH11..176 C3
Jordans Ms WHTN TW2.....25 N5
The Jordans EGRIN RH19.....180 D3
Josephine Av
  BRXS/STRHM SW2.....30 A1
  KWD/TDW/WH KT20.....99 K5
Josephine Cl
  KWD/TDW/WH KT20.....99 K7
Joseph Locke Wy
  ESH/CLAY KT10.....58 A1
Joseph Powell Cl BAL SW12..29 M2
Joseph's Rd GU GU1.....112 B4
Joshua Cl SAND/SEL CR2.....63 K6
Jubilee Cl ASC SL5.....33 N2
  FARN GU14.....87 N3
  KUT/HW KT1.....8 B3
  STWL/WRAY TW19.....22 F3
Jubilee Crs ADL/WDHM KT15..55 P4
Jubilee Dr ASHV GU12.....89 J9
Jubilee Est SWTR RH13.....192 D6
Jubilee Hall Rd FARN GU14..88 C5
Jubilee La GSHT GU26.....165 M8
  RFNM GU10.....127 L8
Jubilee Rd ALDT GU11.....108 D7
  CHEAM SM3.....61 H5
  EWKG RG40.....48 D4
  FRIM GU16.....89 J5
  RFNM GU10.....189 N2
Jubilee Ter
  BRKHM/BTCW RH3.....118 A9
  DORK RH4.....117 H6
  FUL/PGN SW6 *.....19 J7
Jubilee Wy CHSGTN KT9.....59 P2
  EBED/NFELT TW14.....24 D4
  WIM/MER SW19.....43 L2
Judges Ter EGRIN RH19.....180 D3
Judge Wk ESH/CLAY KT10..58 E5
Julian Cl WOKN/KNAP GU21..72 A7
Julian Hl WEY KT13.....56 C6
Julian Tayler Pth FSTH SE23 *..31 J5
Julien Rd COUL/CHIP CR5..80 E4
Juliet Gdns BNFD RG42.....33 H1
Julius Hl BNFD RG42.....33 H2
Jumps Rd RFNM GU10.....147 J3
Junction Rd ASHF TW15.....23 M8
  DORK RH4.....116 G2
  EA W5.....17 J3
  LTWR GU18.....52 B8
  SAND/SEL CR2.....63 M5
June Cl COUL/CHIP CR5.....80 D3
June La REDH RH1.....140 D3
Junewood Cl
  ADL/WDHM KT15.....55 K9
Juniper BRAK RG12.....32 C9
Juniper Cl BH/WHM TN16.....84 C6
  CHSGTN KT9.....59 M5
  GU GU1.....91 P9
  OXTED RH8.....123 P4
  REIG RH2.....119 N7
Juniper Dr CHOB/PIR GU24..70 C2
  WAND/EARL SW18.....19 P8
Juniper Gdns MTCM CR4.....44 C2
  SUN TW16.....24 A9
Juniper Rd CRAWW RH11.....176 E8
  FARN GU14.....87 N2
  REIG RH2.....119 N7
Jura Cl CRAWW RH11.....176 E8
Justin Cl BTFD TW8.....17 K5
Jutland Pl EGH TW20.....21 P8
Juxon Cl CRAWW RH11.....176 C7

K

Kambala Rd BTSEA SW11.....19 P7
Kangley Bridge Rd SYD SE26..31 N8
Karen Ct BMLY BR1.....47 M2
Kashmir Cl ADL/WDHM KT15..55 P7
Katharine St CROY/NA CR0..2 D5
Katherine Cl
  ADL/WDHM KT15.....55 L5
Katherine Rd EDEN TN8.....144 G5
Kay Av ADL/WDHM KT15.....56 A2
Kay Crs BOR GU35.....164 E5
Kaye Don Wy WEY KT13.....56 C8
Kayemoor Rd BELMT SM2..62 A6
Kaynes Pk ASC SL5.....33 N5
Kaywood Cl DTCH/LGLY SL3..12 A1
Keable Rd RFNM GU10.....127 J5

Kearton Cl PUR/KEN CR8 81 L6
Keates Gn BNFD RG42 32 D2
Keats Av REDH RH1 120 C3
Keats Cl HORS RH12 192 D3
WIM/MER SW19 28 G9
Keats Pl EGRIN RH19 180 C2
Keats Wy CROY/NA CR0 46 C7
CWTH RG45 49 M2
WDR/YW UB7 14 B2
YTLY GU46 66 F4
Keble Cl CRAWE RH10 177 N2
WPK KT4 42 D9
Keble Pl BARN SW13 18 F4
Keble St TOOT SW17 28 F7
Keble Wy SHST GU47 50 A7
Kechill Gdns HAYES BR2 47 N8
Keeley Rd CROY/NA CR0 2 C4
Keens Cl STRHM/NOR SW16 29 N8
Keens La RGUW GU3 111 M1
Keens Park Rd RGUW GU3 111 M1
Keen's Rd CROY/NA CR0 2 D7
Keepers Cl RGUE GU4 113 H2
Keepers Combe BRAK RG12 32 F7
Keepers Ms TEDD TW11 26 B9
Keepers Wk VW GU25 36 B6
The Keep KUTN/CMB KT2 26 E9
Keevil Dr WIM/MER SW19 28 A3
Keith Lucas Rd FARN GU14 88 B5
Keith Park Crs
BH/WHM TN16 84 A1
Keith Rd HYS/HAR UB3 14 G1
Keldholme BRAK RG12 32 C4
Kelling Gdns CROY/NA CR0 45 K8
Kellino St TOOT SW17 29 J7
Kelly Cl SHPTN TW17 38 G3
Kelmscott Gdns SHB W12 18 E1
Kelmscott Ri CRAWW RH11 194 E2
Kelmscott Rd BTSEA SW11 29 J1
Kelsall Ms RCH/KEW TW9 17 P6
Kelsey Av EWKG RG40 48 C3
Kelsey Cl HORL RH6 159 J1
Kelsey Gv YTLY GU46 67 J3
Kelsey La BECK BR3 46 G4
Kelsey Park Av BECK BR3 47 H4
Kelsey Park Rd BECK BR3 46 G3
Kelsey Sq BECK BR3 46 G3
Kelsey Wy BECK BR3 46 G4
Kelso Cl CRAWE RH10 177 P4
Kelso Pl KENS W8 19 M1
Kelso Rd CAR SM5 43 N8
Kelvedon Av WOT/HER KT12 56 G6
Kelvedon Cl KUTN/CMB KT2 26 F9
Kelvedon Rd FUL/PGN SW6 19 K5
Kelvin Av LHD/OX KT22 76 F9
Kelvinbrook
E/WMO/HCT KT8 40 B4
Kelvin Cl HOR/WEW KT19 59 N5
Kelvin Dr TWK TW1 26 A2
Kelvin Gdns CROY/NA CR0 44 G8
Kelvin Gv CHSGTN KT9 59 K2
SYD SE26 31 J6
Kelvington Cl CROY/NA CR0 46 E8
Kelvington Rd PECK SE15 31 L1
Kelvin La CRAWE RH10 177 J1
Kelvin Wy CRAWE RH10 177 J1
Kemble Cl WEY KT13 56 F3
Kemble Rd CROY/NA CR0 2 A5
FSTH SE23 31 L4
Kembleside Rd
BH/WHM TN16 84 A7
Kemerton Rd BECK BR3 47 H3
CROY/NA CR0 45 P8
Kemishford
WOKS/MYFD GU22 91 N3
Kemnal Pk HASM GU27 184 E2
Kemp Ct BAGS GU19 51 P7
Kempe Cl DTCH/LGLY SL3 12 G2
Kemp Gdns CROY/NA CR0 45 L7
Kempsford Gdns ECT SW5 19 L3
Kempshott Rd HORS RH12 192 A6
STRHM/NOR SW16 44 G1
Kempson Rd FUL/PGN SW6 19 L6
Kempton Av SUN TW16 39 K2
Kempton Ct FARN GU14 88 B5
SUN TW16 39 K2
Kempton Pk SUN TW16 * 39 L2
Kempton Rd HPTN TW12 39 P3
Kempton Wk CROY/NA CR0 46 E7
Kemsing Cl THHTH CR7 * 45 L5
Kemsley Rd BH/WHM TN16 84 B8
Kendal Cl EBED/NFELT TW14 24 A4
FARN GU14 * 88 A3
REIG RH2 119 P4
Kendale Cl CRAWE RH10 177 M9
Kendal Gdns SUT SM1 61 N1
Kendal Gv CBLY GU15 69 M4
Kendall Av BECK BR3 46 E3
SAND/SEL CR2 63 M7
Kendall Av South
SAND/SEL CR2 63 L8
Kendall Rd BECK BR3 46 E3
ISLW TW7 16 G7
Kendal Pl PUT/ROE SW15 28 C1
Kendor Av HOR/WEW KT19 60 A9
Kendra Hall Rd
SAND/SEL CR2 63 K6
Kendrey Gdns WHTN TW2 25 M2
Kendrick Ms SKENS SW7 19 P2
Kendrick Pl SKENS SW7 19 P2
Kenilford Rd BAL SW12 29 L3
Kenilworth Av BRAK RG12 32 E2
COB KT11 76 B3
WIM/MER SW19 28 D8
Kenilworth Cl BNSTD SM7 79 M5
CRAWW RH11 176 E9
Kenilworth Crs FLEETN GU51 87 J5
Kenilworth Dr
WOT/HER KT12 57 M2
Kenilworth Gdns STA TW18 22 F8
Kenilworth Rd ASHF TW15 22 G6
EW KT17 60 E5
FARN GU14 87 N2
FLEETN GU51 87 H6
PGE/AN SE20 46 D2
Kenilworth Ter BELMT SM2 61 L6
Kenley Aerodrome
PUR/KEN CR8 81 M3
Kenley Gdns THHTH CR7 45 K5
Kenley La PUR/KEN CR8 81 L4
Kenley Rd BOR GU35 164 E6
KUT/HW KT1 41 P3
TWK TW1 25 P2
WIM/MER SW19 43 L4
Kenley Wk CHEAM SM3 61 H3
Kenlor Rd TOOT SW17 28 G8
Kenmara Cl CRAWE RH10 177 L2
Kenmara Ct CRAWE RH10 177 K1
Kenmare Dr MTCM CR4 44 B1
Kenmare Rd THHTH CR7 45 J7
Kenmore Cl FLEETS GU52 107 H1
FRIM GU16 68 F8
Kenmore Rd PUR/KEN CR8 81 K3
Kennard Ct FROW RH18 * 181 K8
Kennedy Av EGRIN RH19 162 C9
Kennedy Cl MTCM CR4 44 C3
Kennedy Rd SWTR RH13 192 C9
Kennel Av ASC SL5 33 P2
Kennel Cl LHD/OX KT22 96 C4
Kennel Gn ASC SL5 33 N2
Kennel La BFOR GU20 52 C4
BNFD RG42 32 D1
HORL RH6 158 G2
LHD/OX KT22 96 C3
RFNM GU10 146 F2
Kennel Ride ASC SL5 33 P1
Kennels La FARN GU14 87 N5
Kennel Wd ASC SL5 33 P2
Kennelwood Crs
CROY/NA CR0 65 K9
Kennet Cl ASHV GU12 109 J5
BTSEA SW11 19 P9
CRAWW RH11 176 C6
FARN GU14 87 P1
Kenneth Rd BNSTD SM7 79 P4
Kennet Rd ISLW TW7 16 F8
Kennett Rd DTCH/LGLY SL3 12 F1
Kenny Dr CAR SM5 62 C7
Kenrick Sq REDH RH1 121 N5
Kensington Av THHTH CR7 45 J2
Kensington Court Gdns
KENS W8 * 19 M1
Kensington Court Ms
KENS W8 * 19 M1
Kensington Court Pl
KENS W8 19 M1
Kensington Gdns KUT/HW KT1 8 C7
Kensington Ga KENS W8 19 N1
Kensington Hall Gdns
WKENS W14 * 19 K3
Kensington High St
WKENS W14 19 J2
Kensington Rd
CRAWW RH11 176 E9
Kensington Ter
SAND/SEL CR2 63 M6
Kent Cl MTCM CR4 44 G5
STA TW18 22 G9
Kent Dr TEDD TW11 25 M8
Kent Gate Wy CROY/NA CR0 64 F5
Kent Hatch Rd OXTED RH8 124 A1
Kent House La BECK BR3 31 M9
Kent House Rd BECK BR3 46 D1
Kentigern Dr CWTH RG45 50 A4
Kentish Wy BMLY BR1 47 P3
Kenton Av SUN TW16 39 M3
Kenton Cl BRAK RG12 32 F3
FRIM GU16 69 H6
Kenton Wy
WOKN/KNAP GU21 71 M6
Kent Rd BFOR GU20 52 D4
CHSWK W4 18 A1
E/WMO/HCT KT8 40 C5
FLEETN GU51 87 H6
KUT/HW KT1 8 C6
RCH/KEW TW9 17 N5
WOKS/MYFD GU22 11 K1
WWKM BR4 47 H9
Kent Wy SURB KT6 59 L2
Kentwode Gn BARN SW13 18 E5
Kentwyns Ri REDH RH1 121 H6
Kenway Rd ECT SW5 19 M2
Kenwith Av FLEETN GU51 87 J6
Kenwood Cl WDR/YW UB7 14 C4
Kenwood Dr BECK BR3 47 J4
WOT/HER KT12 57 K5
Kenwood Pk WEY KT13 56 F5
Kenwood Rdg PUR/KEN CR8 81 K6
Kenworth Gv LTWR GU18 51 P8
Kenwyn Rd RYNPK SW20 42 G2
Kenya Ct HORL RH6 * 140 B9
Kenyngton Dr SUN TW16 24 B8
Kenyons EHSLY KT24 94 D8
Kenyon St FUL/PGN SW6 19 H6
Keogh Barracks ASHV GU12 89 J7
Keogh Cl ASHV GU12 89 K6
Keppel Rd DORK RH4 117 H5
Keppel Sp WDSR SL4 20 G3
Kepple Pl BAGS GU19 51 N6
Kernel Ct GU GU1 * 6 C2
Kerria Wy CHOB/PIR GU24 70 F2
Kerrill Av COUL/CHIP CR5 81 J8
Kerry Cl FLEETN GU51 87 H2
Kerry Ter WOKN/KNAP GU21 11 J1
Kersey Dr SAND/SEL CR2 82 C1
Kersfield Rd PUT/ROE SW15 28 A2
Keston Av ADL/WDHM KT15 55 L9
COUL/CHIP CR5 81 J8
Keston Rd THHTH CR7 45 H7
Kestrel Av HNHL SE24 30 C1
STA TW18 22 C6
Kestrel Cl CRAWW RH11 176 F3
HOR/WEW KT19 59 N9
HORS RH12 192 D5
KUTN/CMB KT2 26 C7
RFNM GU10 107 H7
RGUE GU4 113 H3
Kestrel Rd FARN GU14 88 D5
Kestrel Wk CRAWE RH10 179 K6
Kestrel Wy CROY/NA CR0 65 K7
WOKN/KNAP GU21 71 P4
Keswick Av PUT/ROE SW15 27 K8
SHPTN TW17 38 G4
WIM/MER SW19 43 L3
Keswick Cl CBLY GU15 69 L4
CRAWW RH11 176 A7
SUT SM1 61 N3
Keswick Dr LTWR GU18 52 B9
Keswick Rd EGH TW20 36 F1
GT/LBKH KT23 96 C5
MFD/CHID GU8 149 L6
PUT/ROE SW15 28 B1
WHTN TW2 25 K2
WWKM BR4 65 L1
Kettering St
STRHM/NOR SW16 29 L9
Kettlewell Cl
WOKN/KNAP GU21 72 C4
Kettlewell Hl
WOKN/KNAP GU21 72 C4
Kevan Dr RPLY/SEND GU23 93 J5
Kevin Cl HSLWW TW4 15 M7
Kevins Dr YTLY GU46 67 J1
Kevins Gv FLEETN GU51 87 H6
Kew Br RCH/KEW TW9 17 N4
Kew Bridge Arches
CHSWK W4 * 17 N4
Kew Bridge Rd BTFD TW8 17 M4
Kew Crs CHEAM SM3 61 K2
Kew Foot Rd RCH/KEW TW9 17 L9
Kew Gardens Rd
RCH/KEW TW9 17 M5
Kew Gn RCH/KEW TW9 17 M4
Kew Meadow Pth
RCH/KEW TW9 17 N6
Kew Riverside Pk
RCH/KEW TW9 17 P5
Kew Rd RCH/KEW TW9 17 L9
RCH/KEW TW9 17 M4
Keymer Cl BH/WHM TN16 84 A5
Keymer Rd
BRXS/STRHM SW2 30 A5
CRAWW RH11 176 G7
Keynes Cl FLEETS GU52 107 H2
Keynsham Rd MRDN SM4 43 M9
Keynsham Wy SHST GU47 49 P7
Keysham Av HEST TW5 15 J6
The Key FLEETN GU51 86 D4
Keywood Dr SUN TW16 24 B9
Khama Rd TOOT SW17 29 H7
Khartoum Rd
MFD/CHID GU8 149 M6
TOOT SW17 28 G7
Kibble Gn BRAK RG12 32 E7
Kidborough Down
GT/LBKH KT23 96 A7
Kidborough Rd
CRAWW RH11 176 C7
Kidderminster Pl
CROY/NA CR0 2 B1
Kidderminster Rd
CROY/NA CR0 2 B1
Kidmans Cl HORS RH12 192 E5
Kidworth Cl HORL RH6 140 B8
Kier Pk ASC SL5 34 C4
Kilberry Cl ISLW TW7 16 D6
Kilcorral Cl EW KT17 78 E3
Kildoran Rd CLAP SW4 29 P1
Kilgour Rd FSTH SE23 31 M2
Kilkie St FUL/PGN SW6 19 N7
Killarney Rd
WAND/EARL SW18 28 F2
Killburns Mill Cl WLGTN SM6 62 D1
Killester Gdns WPK KT4 60 F3
Killicks CRAN GU6 153 J8
Killieser Av
BRXS/STRHM SW2 29 P5
Killinghurst La HASM GU27 185 K4
Kilmaine Rd FUL/PGN SW6 19 J5
Kilmarnock Pk REIG RH2 119 M4
Kilmarsh Rd HMSMTH W6 18 G2
Kilmartin Av
STRHM/NOR SW16 45 J4
Kilmartin Gdns FRIM GU16 69 H7
Kilmington Cl BRAK RG12 32 G8
Kilmington Rd BARN SW13 18 E4
Kilmiston Av SHPTN TW17 38 E7
Kilmore Dr CBLY GU15 69 K4
Kilmorey Gdns TWK TW1 26 A1
Kilmorey Rd TWK TW1 17 H9
Kilmorie Rd FSTH SE23 31 M4
Kilmuir Cl SHST GU47 67 P1
Kiln Cl HYS/HAR UB3 14 F4
Kiln Copse CRAN GU6 153 H8
Kilnfield Rd HORS RH12 189 N2
Kiln Flds HASM GU27 184 D2
Kiln La ASC SL5 34 G6
BRAK RG12 32 C3
BRKHM/BTCW RH3 117 P6
EW KT17 60 C9
HORL RH6 140 B8
RFNM GU10 127 N7
RPLY/SEND GU23 93 M4
Kilnmead CRAWE RH10 177 H4
Kilnmead Cl CRAWE RH10 177 H4
Kiln Mdw RGUW GU3 111 J1
Kiln Ms TOOT SW17 28 G8
Kiln Ride EWKG RG40 48 E2
Kiln Ride Extension
EWKG RG40 48 E3
Kiln Rd CRAWE RH10 179 J4
Kilnside BRAK RG12 * 32 E2
ESH/CLAY KT10 58 G6
The Kilns FNM GU9 * 107 P9
Kiln Wy ALDT GU11 108 D7
GSHT GU26 165 H6
Kilnwood La HORS RH12 175 M8
Kilross Rd EBED/NFELT TW14 23 N4
Kilrue La WOT/HER KT12 57 H3
Kilrush Ter WOKN/KNAP GU21 11 H1
Kilsha Rd WOT/HER KT12 39 K7
Kimbell Gdns FUL/PGN SW6 19 J6
Kimber Ct RGUE GU4 * 113 H3
Kimberley BRAK RG12 32 E9
FLEETS GU52 107 H2
Kimberley Cl DTCH/LGLY SL3 12 D2
HORL RH6 159 H1
Kimberley Pl PUR/KEN CR8 63 J9
Kimberley Ride COB KT11 76 B2
Kimberley Rd BECK BR3 46 D3
CRAWE RH10 177 L4
CROY/NA CR0 45 K7
Kimber Rd WAND/EARL SW18 28 E3
Kimbers La FNM GU9 5 K1
Kimble Rd WIM/MER SW19 28 G9
Kimmeridge BRAK RG12 32 G7
Kimpton Dr FLEETN GU51 86 C4
Kimpton Rd CHEAM SM3 61 K2
Kinburn Dr EGH TW20 21 K8
Kindersley Cl EGRIN RH19 162 G9
Kinfauns Rd
BRXS/STRHM SW2 30 B5
King Alfred Av CAT SE6 31 P7
King Charles Crs BRYLDS KT5 41 M8
King Charles' Rd BRYLDS KT5 41 M7
King Charles Wk
WIM/MER SW19 * 28 B4
Kingcup Cl CROY/NA CR0 46 D9
Kingcup Dr CHOB/PIR GU24 70 G4
King Edward Dr CHSGTN KT9 59 L2
King Edwards Cl ASC SL5 * 33 N2
King Edward's Gv
TEDD TW11 26 A9
King Edwards Ri ASC SL5 33 N2
King Edwards Rd ASC SL5 33 N2
Kingfield Cl
WOKS/MYFD GU22 72 D9
Kingfield Dr
WOKS/MYFD GU22 72 D9
Kingfield Gdns
WOKS/MYFD GU22 72 D9
Kingfield Rd
WOKS/MYFD GU22 72 D9
Kingfisher Cl CRAWE RH10 177 K2
FARN GU14 87 N1
FLEETS GU52 106 G1
WOT/HER KT12 57 N4
Kingfisher Ct DORK RH4 * 116 G6
Kingfisher Dr
RCHPK/HAM TW10 26 B7
REDH RH1 120 C2
RGUE GU4 112 G3
STA TW18 22 C7
YTLY GU46 66 F2
Kingfisher Gdns
SAND/SEL CR2 64 D8
Kingfisher La CRAWE RH10 179 K6
Kingfisher Ri EGRIN RH19 180 E3
Kingfisher Wk ASHV GU12 109 H3
Kingfisher Wy BECK BR3 46 D6
HORS RH12 192 B5
King Gdns CROY/NA CR0 63 K4
King Garth Ms FSTH SE23 31 K5
King George Av EGRIN RH19 162 B9
WOT/HER KT12 39 M9
King George Cl FARN GU14 88 F5
SUN TW16 * 23 P8
King George's Dr
ADL/WDHM KT15 55 L8
King George Sq
RCHPK/HAM TW10 26 E2
King George VI Av
MTCM CR4 44 B5
Kingham Cl
WAND/EARL SW18 28 F3
King Henry Rd
FLEETN GU51 * 86 F4
King Henry's Dr
CROY/NA CR0 65 J7
King Henry's Reach
HMSMTH W6 18 G4
King Henry's Rd KUT/HW KT1 41 P4
King John's Cl
STWL/WRAY TW19 21 H2
King John St FLEETN GU51 86 F4
Kingpost Pde RGUE GU4 * 112 F1
Kings Apartments CBLY GU15 68 E4
Kings Arbour NWDGN UB2 15 N3
Kings Av BAL SW12 29 N4
BF/WBF KT14 73 P1
CAR SM5 62 A6
CHOB/PIR GU24 70 D8
HSLW TW3 16 B6
NWMAL KT3 42 D5
REDH RH1 120 A7
RFNM GU10 108 G6
SUN TW16 24 A8
Kingsbridge Rd MRDN SM4 43 H8
NWDGN UB2 15 P2
WOT/HER KT12 39 K8
Kingsbrook LHD/OX KT22 76 G7
Kingsbury Crs STA TW18 22 A7
Kingsbury Dr WDSR SL4 20 F3
Kings Cha E/WMO/HCT KT8 40 C4
Kingsclear Pk CBLY GU15 68 F4
Kingsclere Cl PUT/ROE SW15 27 M3
Kingscliffe Gdns
WIM/MER SW19 28 C4
King's Cl STA TW18 37 P1
THDIT KT7 40 G7
WOT/HER KT12 * 39 K9
Kings Copse EGRIN RH19 * 180 E3
Kingscote Hl CRAWW RH11 176 E7
Kingscote Rd CHSWK W4 18 B1
CROY/NA CR0 46 B8
NWMAL KT3 42 B4
Kings Ct KWD/TDW/WH KT20 98 G2
RFNM GU10 108 G6
SWTR RH13 * 192 D7
Kingscourt Rd
STRHM/NOR SW16 29 N6
King's Crs CBLY GU15 50 E9
Kingscroft FLEETN GU51 86 G7
Kingscroft Rd BNSTD SM7 79 P4
LHD/OX KT22 77 H9
Kings Cross La REDH RH1 121 H8
Kingsdale Rd PGE/AN SE20 46 D2
Kingsdene
KWD/TDW/WH KT20 98 F1
Kingsdown Av SAND/SEL CR2 63 L7
Kingsdowne Rd SURB KT6 41 L8
Kingsdown Rd CHEAM SM3 61 J4
EW KT17 78 E2
Kingsdown Wy HAYES BR2 47 N7
Kings Dr BRYLDS KT5 41 N8
THDIT KT7 41 H7
The Kings Dr WOT/HER KT12 57 H7
Kings Farm Av
RCHPK/HAM TW10 17 N9
Kingsfold Ct HORS RH12 * 174 A6
Kingsgate CRAWE RH10 * 177 H5
Kings Ga HORS RH12 192 A8
Kingsgate Rd KUT/HW KT1 8 D3
Kings Gld YTLY GU46 67 K2
Kings Hall Rd BECK BR3 46 D1
King's Head La BF/WBF KT14 55 P9
Kingshill Av WPK KT4 42 E8
Kings Keep FLEETS GU52 86 G9
HAYES BR2 * 47 L4
KUT/HW KT1 * 41 L5
SHST GU47 49 M8
Kingsland RDKG RH5 156 F3
Kingsland Ct CRAWE RH10 * 177 K5
Kings La BFOR GU20 52 E4
EGH TW20 20 F8
RFNM GU10 127 K7
SUT SM1 61 P4
Kingslawn Cl PUT/ROE SW15 27 N1
Kingslea LHD/OX KT22 76 G9
SWTR RH13 192 D7
Kingsleigh Cl BTFD TW8 17 K4
Kingsleigh Pl MTCM CR4 44 B4
Kingsleigh Wk HAYES BR2 47 M5
Kingsley Av BNSTD SM7 79 L4
CBLY GU15 68 E4
EGH TW20 20 G9
HSLW TW3 16 C7
SUT SM1 61 P3
Kingsley Cl CWTH RG45 49 M6
HORL RH6 140 B8
Kingsley Dr WPK KT4 60 D1
Kingsley Gv REIG RH2 119 L8
Kingsley Ms KENS W8 * 19 M1
Kingsley Rd CRAWW RH11 176 D8
CROY/NA CR0 45 J9
FARN GU14 88 B1
HORL RH6 140 B8
HSLW TW3 16 C7
HTWY RG27 48 A9
WIM/MER SW19 28 E8
Kingsley Sq FLEETN GU51 86 C3
Kingslyn Crs NRWD SE19 45 N2
Kings Ml HMSMTH W6 * 18 G2
Kings Md HORL RH6 160 C1
REDH RH1 120 G7
Kingsmead BH/WHM TN16 84 B5
CRAN GU6 153 H9
FARN GU14 88 D3
FRIM GU16 68 G9
RCHPK/HAM TW10 26 E2
WOKN/KNAP GU21 11 H1
Kingsmead Av MTCM CR4 44 E4
SUN TW16 39 L4
SURB KT6 59 N1
WPK KT4 60 F2
Kingsmead Cl
HOR/WEW KT19 60 B6
TEDD TW11 26 A9
Kings Mead Pk
ESH/CLAY KT10 58 E6
Kingsmead Pl HORS RH12 191 K7
Kingsmead Rd
BRXS/STRHM SW2 30 B5
HORS RH12 191 K7
Kingsmere Cl PUT/ROE SW15 19 H8
Kingsmere Rd BNFD RG42 32 B2
WIM/MER SW19 28 A5
Kings Ms FRIM GU16 89 H1
HORS RH12 192 A8
Kings Mill La REDH RH1 120 F9
Kingsnympton Pk
KUTN/CMB KT2 41 P1
King's Paddock HPTN TW12 40 C2
Kings Pde CAR SM5 * 62 A2
FLEETN GU51 * 86 G5
SHB W12 * 18 E1
King's Pas KUTN/CMB KT2 8 C2
The Kings Peace
GSHT GU26 * 165 M8
Kings Pl CHSWK W4 18 A3
King's Quay WBPTN SW10 * 19 N6
King's Ride ASC SL5 33 L5
CBLY GU15 50 F8
Kings Rd ADL/WDHM KT15 55 M8
ALDT GU11 108 A5
ASC SL5 34 E6
BELMT SM2 61 L8
BH/WHM TN16 84 A6
CHEL SW3 19 P4
CHOB/PIR GU24 70 G3
CRAN GU6 171 J1
CWTH RG45 49 M5
EGH TW20 21 M7
FELT TW13 24 D4
FLEETN GU51 87 H6
FUL/PGN SW6 19 N5
GODL GU7 131 M7
HASM GU27 184 B4
HORL RH6 159 K1
KUTN/CMB KT2 8 E1
MORT/ESHN SW14 18 B8

MTCM CR4 .... 44 C4
RCHPK/HAM TW10 .... 26 E1
RGUE GU4 .... 132 C3
SHGR GU5 .... 132 F4
SNWD SE25 .... 46 A4
SURB KT6 .... 41 J9
SWTR RH13 .... 192 D7
TEDD TW11 .... 25 L8
TWK TW1 .... 26 A2
WIM/MER SW19 .... 28 D9
WOKN/KNAP GU21 .... 11 H1
WOT/HER KT12 .... 57 K1
Kings Shade Wk HOR/WEW KT19 * 78 B2
King's Rd GU GU1 .... 7 F3
Kingsthorpe Rd SYD SE26 .... 31 L7
Kingston Av CHEAM SM3 .... 61 J2
EBED/NFELT TW14 .... 23 P2
EHSLY KT24 .... 94 C6
LHD/OX KT22 .... 97 H1
Kingston Br KUT/HW KT1 .... 8 A3
Kingston By-Pass BRYLDS KT5 .... 42 A9
ESH/CLAY KT10 .... 58 E2
RYNPK SW20 .... 27 F7
SURB KT6 .... 59 M2
Kingston Cl TEDD TW11 .... 26 A9
Kingston Gdns ASHF TW15 .... 22 F8
BECK BR3 .... 47 N4
Kingston Gdns CROY/NA CRO 62 C2
Kingston Hall Rd KUT/HW KT1 .... 8 C6
Kingston Hill Pl KUTN/CMB KT2 .... 27 H7
Kingston House Gdns LHD/OX KT22 * 97 H1
Kingston La EHSLY KT24 .... 94 C7
TEDD TW11 .... 25 P8
Kingston Ldg NWMAL KT3 .... 42 C5
Kingston Ri ADL/WDHM KT15 .... 55 L8
Kingston Rd ASHF TW15 .... 23 J9
BRYLDS KT5 .... 59 P1
HOR/WEW KT19 .... 60 C4
LHD/OX KT22 .... 42 B5
NWMAL KT3 .... 42 B5
PUT/ROE SW15 .... 27 N4
RYNPK SW20 .... 43 J3
STA TW18 .... 22 D7
TEDD TW11 .... 26 A9
Kingston Sq NRWD SE19 .... 30 E8
Kingston V PUT/ROE SW15 .... 27 J7
King St CHERT KT16 .... 37 L9
EGRIN RH19 .... 180 D2
HMSMTH W6 .... 18 D2
NWDGN UB2 .... 15 N1
RCH/KEW TW9 .... 26 C1
TWK TW1 .... 25 P4
King St Cloisters HMSMTH W6 * 18 F2
King's Wk CBLY GU15 .... 68 B2
SAND/SEL CR2 .... 82 B3
Kings Warren LHD/OX KT22 .... 58 C9
Kings Wy CROY/NA CRO 63 H1
Kingsway ALDT GU11 .... 108 E5
BLKW GU17 .... 67 L3
MORT/ESHN SW14 .... 17 P8
NWMAL KT3 .... 42 C5
WOKN/KNAP GU21 .... 10 A6
WWKM BR4 .... 65 M2
Kingsway Av SAND/SEL CR2 .... 64 C7
WOKN/KNAP GU21 .... 10 S5
Kingsway Rd CHEAM SM3 .... 61 J6
Kingsway Ter WEY KT13 .... 56 C7
The Kingsway EW KT17 .... 60 D8
Kingswick Cl ASC SL5 .... 34 E5
Kingswick Dr ASC SL5 .... 34 D5
Kingswood Av HAYES BR2 .... 47 L4
HPTN TW12 .... 25 H6
HSLW TW3 .... 15 P7
SAND/SEL CR2 .... 82 A9
THHTH CR7 .... 45 J6
Kingswood Cl ASHF TW15 .... 23 M7
Kingswood Cl 21 J7
GU GU1 .... 112 C4
NWMAL KT3 .... 42 C6
SURB KT6 .... 41 L8
WEY KT13 .... 56 D6
Kingswood Creek STWL/WRAY TW19 .... 21 J1
Kingswood Dr BELMT SM2 .... 61 M7
CAR SM5 .... 44 A9
DUL SE21 .... 30 E3
Kingswood Firs GSHT GU26 .... 165 M9
Kingswood Ri EGH TW20 .... 21 J8
Kingswood Rd BRXS/STRHM SW2 .... 29 P2
CHSWK W4 .... 18 A1
HAYES BR2 .... 47 L4
KWD/TDW/WH KT20 .... 98 F1
PGE/AN SE20 .... 31 K9
Kingswood Ter CHSWK W4 .... 18 A1
Kingswood Wy SAND/SEL CR2 .... 82 D1
WLGTN SM6 .... 63 G4
Kingsworth Cl BECK BR3 .... 46 E6
Kingsworthy Cl KUT/HW KT1 .... 9 G6
Kings Worthy Rd FLEETN GU51 .... 86 C5
Kings Yd ASC SL5 .... 33 N5
PUT/ROE SW15 * 27 P2
Kinloss Rd CAR SM5 .... 43 N8
Kinnaird Av CHSWK W4 .... 18 A5
Kinnersley Mnr REIG RH2 * 139 N4
Kinnersley Wk REIG RH2 .... 139 L1
Kinnibrugh Dr LING RH7 .... 162 F3
Kinnoul Rd HMSMTH W6 .... 19 J4

Kinross Av ASC SL5 .... 33 P6
WPK KT4 .... 60 E1
Kinross Cl SUN TW16 .... 24 A8
Kinross Ct ASC SL5 .... 33 P6
Kinross Dr SUN TW16 .... 24 A8
Kintbury Cl FLEETN GU51 .... 86 D3
Kintyre Cl STRHM/NOR SW16 .... 45 H1
Kinver Rd SYD SE26 .... 31 K7
Kipling Cl CRAWE RH10 .... 177 M3
Kipling Ct SWTR RH13 .... 192 F6
Kipling Dr WIM/MER SW19 .... 28 G9
Kipling Wy EGRIN RH19 .... 180 D2
Kirby Cl HOR/WEW KT19 .... 60 D4
Kirby Rd WOKN/KNAP GU21 .... 10 A3
Kirdford Cl CRAWW RH11 .... 176 D3
Kirkdale SYD SE26 .... 31 J5
Kirkdale Cnr SYD SE26 * 31 K7
Kirkefields GUW GU2 .... 111 N2
Kirkham Cl SHST GU47 .... 49 P7
Kirk Knoll BOR GU35 .... 164 C6
Kirkland Av WOKN/KNAP GU21 .... 71 L5
Kirkland Ter BECK BR3 .... 31 P9
Kirkleas Rd SURB KT6 .... 41 L9
Kirkleas Rd THHTH CR7 .... 45 J6
Kirkley Rd WIM/MER SW19 .... 43 L2
Kirkly Cl SAND/SEL CR2 .... 63 N7
Kirkstall Gdns BRXS/STRHM SW2 .... 29 N4
Kirkstall Rd BRXS/STRHM SW2 .... 29 P4
Kirksted Rd MRDN SM4 .... 43 M9
Kirkstone Cl CBLY GU15 .... 69 M4
Kirrane Cl NWMAL KT3 .... 42 D6
Kirriemuir Gdns ASHV GU12 .... 109 M3
Kirtley Rd SYD SE26 .... 31 M7
Kirton Cl CHSWK W4 .... 18 B2
Kirton Ldg WAND/EARL SW18 * 28 C2
Kitchener Rd ALDT GU11 .... 88 F9
THHTH CR7 * 45 M4
Kites Cl CRAWW RH11 .... 176 F5
Kithurst Cl CRAWW RH11 .... 176 F7
Kitley Gdns NRWD SE19 .... 45 P1
Kitsmead CRAWE RH10 .... 178 B1
Kitsmead La CHERT KT16 .... 54 B1
Kitson Rd BARN SW13 .... 18 E6
Kittiwake Cl CRAWW RH11 .... 176 A1
VW GU25 .... 64 E8
Kitts La RFNM GU10 .... 165 J3
Klea Av CLAP SW4 .... 29 M2
Knapdale Cl FSTH SE23 .... 31 J5
Knapmill Rd CAT SE6 .... 31 P5
Knapmill Wy CAT SE6 .... 31 P5
Knapp Rd ASHF TW15 .... 23 J7
Knapton Ms TOOT SW17 .... 29 K9
Knaresborough Dr WAND/EARL SW18 * 28 C2
Knaresborough Pl ECT SW5 .... 19 M2
Kneller Gdns ISLW TW7 .... 25 L2
Kneller Rd NWMAL KT3 .... 42 C8
WHTN TW2 .... 25 L2
Knepp Cl CRAWE RH10 .... 177 M5
Knevett Ter HSLW TW3 .... 16 A9
Knight Cl FLEETN GU51 .... 86 C9
Knighton Park Rd SYD SE26 .... 31 L8
Knighton Rd REDH RH1 .... 120 C7
Knightons La MFD/CHID GU8 .... 169 J7
Knightsbridge Crs STA TW18 .... 22 E9
Knightsbridge Rd CBLY GU15 .... 68 C1
Knights Cl E/WMO/HCT KT8 .... 39 P6
FLEET20 * 22 A9
Knights Enham Dr FLEETN GU51 * 86 C4
Knight's Hl WNWD SE27 .... 30 C8
Knight's Hill Sq WNWD SE27 .... 30 C7
Knight's Pk KUT/HW KT1 .... 8 E6
Knights Pl REDH RH1 .... 120 C4
Knights Rd FNM GU9 .... 108 A7
Knightswood BRAK RG12 .... 32 D9
WOKN/KNAP GU21 .... 71 M7
Knightwood Cl REIG RH2 .... 119 L7
Knightwood Crs NWMAL KT3 .... 42 C7
Knipp Hil COB KT11 .... 75 P2
Knivet Rd FUL/PGN SW6 .... 19 L4
Knobfield RDKG RH5 .... 135 H5
Knob Hl HORS RH12 .... 191 P1
Knockhundred La GSHT GU26 .... 183 L2
Knole Cl CRAWE RH10 .... 177 N4
CROY/NA CRO * 46 C7
Knole Gv EGRIN RH19 .... 162 B9
Knole Wd ASC SL5 * 34 F9
Knoll Cl FLEETN GU51 .... 86 C5
Knoll Ct FLEETN GU51 .... 86 C5
Knollmead BRYLDS KT5 .... 42 A9
Knoll Park Rd CHERT KT16 .... 37 K9
Knoll Quarry GODL GU7 .... 131 L7
Knoll Rd CBLY GU15 .... 68 F2
DORK RH4 .... 116 G9
FLEETN GU51 .... 86 C5
GODL GU7 .... 131 K7
WAND/EARL SW18 .... 28 E1
Knolls Cl WPK KT4 .... 60 F2
The Knolls EW KT17 .... 78 C5
The Knoll BECK BR3 .... 47 H2
CHERT KT16 .... 37 K9
COB K11 .... 76 A2
HAYES BR2 .... 65 J1
LHD/OX KT22 .... 97 J1
Knoll Wd GODL GU7 .... 131 L7
Knollys Cl STRHM/NOR SW16 .... 30 C6
Knollys Rd ALDT GU11 .... 108 B3
STRHM/NOR SW16 .... 30 B6

The Knook SHST GU47 * 67 P1
Knowle Cl CRAWE RH10 .... 160 D9
Knowle Dr CRAWE RH10 .... 160 D9
Knowle Gdns BF/WBF KT14 .... 73 K2
Knowle Gn STA TW18 .... 22 D8
Knowle Gv VW GU25 .... 36 A8
Knowle Grove Cl VW GU25 .... 36 A8
Knowle Hl VW GU25 .... 35 P8
Knowle La CRAN GU6 .... 170 C3
HORS RH12 .... 189 J1
Knowle Pk COB KT11 .... 75 N4
Knowle Park Av STA TW18 .... 22 E9
Knowle Rd WHTN TW2 .... 25 M4
Knowles Av CWTH RG45 .... 49 K5
The Knowle BOR GU35 .... 164 C5
KWD/TDW/WH KT20 .... 98 F1
Knowl Hl WOKS/MYFD GU22 .... 11 K6
Knowlton Gn HAYES BR2 .... 47 M6
Knowsley Ter MFD/CHID GU8 * 167 P7
Knox Cl FLEETS GU52 .... 106 E1
Knox Rd GUW GU2 .... 91 N9
Kohat Ct ALDT GU11 * 108 B4
Kohat Rd WIM/MER SW19 .... 28 E8
Kohima Cl ALDT GU11 .... 108 D4
Koonowla Cl BH/WHM TN16 .... 84 B4
Kooringa WARL CR6 .... 82 B8
Korda Cl SHPTN TW17 .... 38 B8
Kramer Ms ECT SW5 * 19 L3
Krooner Rd CBLY GU15 .... 68 D5
Kuala Gdns STRHM/NOR SW16 .... 45 H2
Kyle Cl BRAK RG12 .... 32 D4
Kynance Ms KENS W8 .... 19 M1
Kynance Pl KENS W8 .... 19 N1
Kynaston Av THHTH CR7 .... 45 L6
Kynaston Ct CTHM CR5 .... 101 N5
Kynaston Crs THHTH CR7 .... 45 L6
Kynaston Rd THHTH CR7 .... 45 L6
Kynersley Cl CAR SM5 .... 62 B2
Kyrle Rd BTSEA SW11 .... 29 K2

L

Laburnum Av SUT SM1 .... 62 A2
Laburnum Cl GU GU1 .... 112 A2
Laburnum Crs SUN TW16 .... 39 K2
Laburnum Gdns CROY/NA CRO 46 D8
Laburnum Gv DTCH/LGLY SL3 .... 12 L4
HSLW TW3 .... 15 P9
NWMAL KT3 .... 42 B3
Laburnum Pl EGH TW20 .... 20 C9
Laburnum Rd CHERT KT16 .... 37 L9
EPSOM KT18 .... 78 C3
FNM GU9 .... 108 A7
HYS/HAR UB3 .... 15 H2
MTCM CR4 .... 44 C3
WIM/MER SW19 .... 43 N1
WOKS/MYFD GU22 .... 72 B9
The Laburnums BLKW GU17 .... 67 M3
Laburnum Wy STWL/WRAY TW19 .... 23 J4
Lacey Av COUL/CHIP CR5 .... 81 J9
Lacey Cl EGH TW20 .... 37 H1
Lacey Dr COUL/CHIP CR5 .... 81 J9
HPTN TW12 .... 39 P2
Lackford Rd COUL/CHIP CR5 .... 80 B7
Lacock Cl WIM/MER SW19 .... 28 F9
Lacrosse Wy STRHM/NOR SW16 .... 44 F2
Lacy Gn COUL/CHIP CR5 .... 81 J9
Lacy Rd PUT/ROE SW15 .... 19 H9
Ladas Rd WNWD SE27 .... 30 D8
Ladbroke Gv REDH RH1 .... 120 C4
Ladbroke Hurst LING RH7 .... 143 M2
Ladbroke Rd EPSOM KT18 .... 78 B3
HORL RH6 .... 140 C8
REDH RH1 .... 120 C3
Ladbrook Rd SNWD SE25 .... 45 M4
Ladderstile Ride KUTN/CMB KT2 .... 26 G8
Ladybank BRAK RG12 .... 32 D9
Ladybrook Rd KUT/HW KT1 .... 8 D5
Ladycross MFD/CHID GU8 .... 149 M4
Ladygate Cl CRAWW RH11 .... 176 D4
Ladygate Rd RDKG RH5 .... 117 K6
Lady Forsdyke Wy HOR/WEW KT19 .... 59 N7
Ladygate Dr GSHT GU26 .... 165 M9
Ladygrove CROY/NA CRO 64 E7
Ladygrove Dr RGUE GU4 .... 92 F9
Lady Harewood Wy HOR/WEW KT19 .... 59 N7
Lady Hay WPK KT4 .... 60 D1
Lady Margaret Rd ASC SL5 .... 34 F9
CRAWW RH11 .... 176 D4
Ladymead GU GU1 .... 112 A4
Ladymead Cl CRAWE RH10 .... 177 M8
Ladymount WLGTN SM6 .... 62 F3
Ladyship Ter EDUL SE22 * 31 J3
Ladythorpe Cl ADL/WDHM KT15 .... 55 M3
Ladywell Rd LEW SE13 .... 31 P1
Ladywood Av FARN GU14 .... 88 A1
Ladywood Rd SURB KT6 .... 59 N1
Laffan's Rd ALDT GU11 .... 108 B1
Laffan Tr ALDT GU11 .... 87 N9
Lafone Av FELT TW13 .... 24 D4
Lagham Pk GDST RH9 .... 122 E9
Lagham Rd GDST RH9 .... 122 E8
Laglands Cl REIG RH2 .... 119 N3
Laings Av MTCM CR4 .... 44 B3
Lainlock Pl HSLW TW3 .... 16 B6
Lainson St WAND/EARL SW18 .... 28 C3
Lairdale Cl DUL SE21 .... 30 D4
Laird Ct BAGS GU19 .... 51 N8
Laitwood Rd BAL SW12 .... 29 L4

Lake Cl BF/WBF KT14 .... 73 P1
Lake End Wy CWTH RG45 .... 49 L5
Lake Gdns RCHPK/HAM TW10 .... 26 A6
WLGTN SM6 .... 44 E9
Lakehall Gdns THHTH CR7 .... 45 K6
Lakehall Rd THHTH CR7 .... 45 K6
Lakehurst Rd HOR/WEW KT19 .... 60 C4
Lakeland Dr FRIM GU16 .... 68 G7
Lake La HORL RH6 .... 140 E8
Lake Rd CROY/NA CRO 64 F1
FRIM GU16 .... 69 H9
RDKG RH5 .... 155 K6
VW GU25 .... 35 P6
WIM/MER SW19 .... 28 C8
Lakers Ri BNSTD SM7 .... 80 A5
Lakes Cl RGUE GU4 .... 132 F2
Lakeside BECK BR3 .... 47 H4
BNFD RG42 .... 32 E1
HOR/WEW KT19 .... 60 C5
HORS RH12 .... 192 B5
REDH RH1 .... 120 C3
WEY KT13 .... 56 C1
WLGTN SM6 .... 62 B1
WOKN/KNAP GU21 .... 71 L8
Lakeside Cl ASHV GU12 .... 109 H2
SNWD SE25 .... 46 A3
WOKN/KNAP GU21 .... 71 L8
Lakeside Ct FLEETN GU51 .... 87 H4
Lakeside Dr HAYES BR2 .... 65 J1
Lakeside Gdns FARN GU14 .... 67 P9
Lakeside Gra WEY KT13 .... 56 E2
Lakeside Rd ASHV GU12 .... 109 H2
DTCH/LGLY SL3 .... 13 K5
FARN GU14 .... 88 C8
WKENS W14 .... 19 H1
The Lake Side BLKW GU17 .... 67 P4
Lakeview RDKG RH5 .... 137 J1
Lake View Rd EGRIN RH19 .... 161 J9
EGRIN RH19 .... 162 E7
Lakeview Rd WNWD SE27 .... 30 B8
Laleham Abbey STA TW18 * 37 N5
Laleham Cl STA TW18 .... 37 M2
Laleham Ct SUT SM1 * 61 N4
WOKN/KNAP GU21 * 10 D1
Laleham Reach CHERT KT16 .... 37 K5
Laleham Rd SHPTN TW17 .... 38 B5
STA TW18 .... 37 L3
Lalor St FUL/PGN SW6 .... 19 J6
Lamberhurst Rd WNWD SE27 .... 30 B7
Lamberhurst Wk CRAWE RH10 .... 177 K6
Lambert Av DTCH/LGLY SL3 .... 12 C1
RCH/KEW TW9 .... 17 N8
Lambert Cl BH/WHM TN16 .... 84 B5
Lambert Cts BLKW GU17 .... 67 N3
Lambert Rd BNSTD SM7 .... 79 L3
BRXS/STRHM SW2 .... 29 P1
Lambert's Pl CROY/NA CRO 3 J5
Lambert's Rd BRYLDS KT5 .... 41 L6
Lambeth Cl CRAWW RH11 .... 176 E8
Lambeth Rd CROY/NA CRO 45 J9
Lambeth Wk CRAWW RH11 * 176 E9
Lambly Hi VW GU25 .... 36 C4
Lamborne Cl SHST GU47 .... 49 J9
Lambourn Cl EGRIN RH19 .... 162 D9
Lambourne Av WIM/MER SW19 .... 28 C7
Lambourne Cl CRAWE RH10 .... 177 J7
COB KT11 .... 75 L4
Lambourne Dr BAGS GU19 .... 51 M7
COB KT11 .... 75 L4
Lambourne Gv BRAK RG12 .... 32 G3
KUT/HW KT1 .... 9 K4
Lambourne Wy RFNM GU10 .... 108 C7
Lambrook Ter FUL/PGN SW6 .... 19 J6
Lambs Crs HORS RH12 .... 192 E5
Lambs Farm Cl HORS RH12 .... 192 F5
Lambs Farm Rd HORS RH12 .... 192 E4
Lambs Green Rd HORS RH12 .... 175 L6
Lambton Rd RYNPK SW20 .... 42 G3
Lambyn Cft HORL RH6 .... 140 E9
Lamington St HMSMTH W6 .... 18 F2
Lammas Av MTCM CR4 .... 44 C3
Lammas Cl GODL GU7 .... 131 N7
STA TW18 .... 22 B6
Lammas Dr STA TW18 .... 22 A6
Lammas La ESH/CLAY KT10 .... 58 A3
Lammas Md BNFD RG42 .... 32 A1
Lammas Rd GODL GU7 .... 131 N8
RCHPK/HAM TW10 .... 26 B7
Lammermoor Rd BAL SW12 * 29 L3
Lamont Cl CRAWW RH11 .... 176 D4
Lamont Road Pas WBPTN SW10 * 19 P4
Lamorna WOKS/MYFD GU22 .... 10 D6
Lampard Cl CRAWW RH11 .... 176 C4
Lampeter Cl WOKS/MYFD GU22 .... 10 C6
Lampton Av HSLW TW3 .... 16 A6
Lampton House Cl WIM/MER SW19 .... 28 A7
Lampton Park Rd HSLW TW3 .... 16 B7
Lampton Rd HSLW TW3 .... 16 B7
Lanark Cl FRIM GU16 .... 68 G6
SWTR RH13 .... 192 D8
Lancaster Av FNM GU9 .... 5 K6
MTCM CR4 .... 44 G5
WIM/MER SW19 .... 28 A8
WNWD SE27 .... 30 C5
Lancaster Cl ASHF TW15 .... 22 G8
ASHV GU12 .... 109 H1
CRAWE RH10 .... 177 N2
EGH TW20 .... 21 J9
HAYES BR2 .... 47 M5
STWL/WRAY TW19 .... 23 H2
WOKN/KNAP GU21 .... 11 G2

WPK KT4 .... 42 F8
Lancaster Dr CBLY GU15 .... 68 F2
WOT/HER KT12 .... 39 J8
EGRIN RH19 .... 162 F9
Lancaster Gdn KUTN/CMB KT2 .... 26 C8
Lancaster Gdns KUTN/CMB KT2 .... 26 D8
WIM/MER SW19 .... 28 B8
Lancaster Ms RCHPK/HAM TW10 .... 26 D2
WAND/EARL SW18 * 28 E1
Lancaster Pk RCHPK/HAM TW10 .... 26 D1
Lancaster Pl TWK TW1 .... 25 P3
WIM/MER SW19 .... 28 A8
Lancaster Rd FARN GU14 .... 88 D6
SNWD SE25 .... 45 P3
WIM/MER SW19 .... 28 A8
Lancaster Wy FARN GU14 .... 68 E9
WPK KT4 .... 42 G6
Lancastrian Rd WLGTN SM6 .... 62 G6
Lancer Ct ALDT GU11 * 108 A4
Lancing Cl CRAWW RH11 .... 176 D5
Lancing Rd CROY/NA CRO 45 H7
FELT TW13 .... 24 A5
Landcroft Rd EDUL SE22 .... 30 G2
Landells Rd EDUL SE22 .... 30 G2
Landen Pk HORL RH6 .... 140 A8
Landford Rd PUT/ROE SW15 .... 18 G8
Landgrove Rd WIM/MER SW19 .... 28 D8
Landon Wy ASHF TW15 * 23 J8
Landridge Rd FUL/PGN SW6 .... 19 J7
Landscape Rd WARL CR6 .... 82 B7
Landseer Cl SHST GU47 .... 68 A2
WIM/MER SW19 .... 43 N2
Landseer Rd NWMAL KT3 .... 42 B8
SUT SM1 .... 61 L5
Lane Cl ADL/WDHM KT15 .... 55 L4
Lane End EPSOM KT18 .... 77 P3
MFD/CHID GU8 .... 168 A3
Lane End Dr WOKN/KNAP GU21 .... 71 J6
Lane Gdns ESH/CLAY KT10 .... 58 F6
Lanercost Rd BRXS/STRHM SW2 .... 30 B5
CRAWW RH11 .... 176 F6
The Lane BIL RH14 .... 187 L6
CHERT KT16 .... 37 L4
MFD/CHID GU8 .... 148 C8
VW GU25 .... 36 C4
Laneway PUT/ROE SW15 .... 27 N1
Lanfrey Pl WKENS W14 .... 19 K3
Langallier La LHD/OX KT22 .... 96 F1
Langbourne Wy ESH/CLAY KT10 .... 58 F5
Langcroft Cl CAR SM5 .... 62 B2
Langdale Av MTCM CR4 .... 44 B4
Langdale Cl FARN GU14 .... 88 A3
MORT/ESHN SW14 .... 17 P9
WOKN/KNAP GU21 .... 72 A5
Langdale Ct ASHV GU12 * 33 N5
Langdale Pde MTCM CR4 * 44 B4
Langdale Rd CRAWW RH11 .... 176 D3
THHTH CR7 .... 45 J5
Langdon Cl CBLY GU15 .... 69 L4
Langdon Pk TEDD TW11 .... 41 J1
Langdon Pl MORT/ESHN SW14 .... 18 A8
Langdon Rd HAYES BR2 .... 47 N4
MRDN SM4 .... 43 N6
Langdon Wk MRDN SM4 .... 43 N6
Langford Rd FUL/PGN SW6 .... 19 M7
Langham Cl GODL GU7 .... 131 M8
Langham Dene PUR/KEN CR8 .... 81 K4
Langham Gdns RCHPK/HAM TW10 .... 26 B7
Langham House Cl RCHPK/HAM TW10 .... 26 C7
Langham Pk GODL GU7 .... 131 M8
Langham Park Pl HAYES BR2 .... 47 M5
Langham Pl CHSWK W4 .... 18 C4
EGH TW20 .... 21 L8
Langham Rd RYNPK SW20 .... 42 G2
TEDD TW11 .... 26 A8
Langholm Cl BAL SW12 .... 29 N3
Langhorn Dr WHTN TW2 .... 25 M3
Langhurst Cl HORS RH12 .... 174 C7
Langhurst La CRAWW RH11 .... 175 M4
Langhurstwood Rd HORS RH12 .... 174 C7
Langland Gdns CROY/NA CRO 64 F1
Langlands Ri HOR/WEW KT19 .... 78 A2
Langley Av SURB KT6 .... 41 K9
WPK KT4 .... 61 H1
Langley Broom DTCH/LGLY SL3 .... 12 D3
Langley Cl EPSOM KT18 .... 78 B8
FLEETS GU52 .... 106 F2
Langley Ct BECK BR3 * 47 H5
Langley Crs HYS/HAR UB3 .... 15 H5
Langley Dr ALDT GU11 .... 108 C6
CRAWW RH11 .... 176 F5
Langley Gv NWMAL KT3 .... 42 B3
Langley La CRAWW RH11 .... 176 D3
Langley Oaks Av SAND/SEL CR2 .... 64 A8
Langley Pde CRAWW RH11 .... 176 F2
Langley Pk Rd BELMT SM2 .... 61 N5
Langley Pl CRAWW RH11 .... 176 F2
Langley Rd BECK BR3 .... 46 D5
DTCH/LGLY SL3 .... 12 A1
ISLW TW7 .... 16 F7
SAND/SEL CR2 .... 64 D7
STA TW18 .... 22 C9
SURB KT6 .... 41 L8

WIM/MER SW19 ......43 K2
Langley Vale Rd EPSOM KT18..78 B7
Langley Wk CRAWW RH11 ...176 F2
WOKS/MYFD GU22 ....10 C7
Langley Wy WWKM BR4........47 K9
Langley Wd BECK BR3 *........47 L6
Langmans Wy
WOKN/KNAP GU21 ....71 L5
Langmead St WNWD SE27....30 C7
Langport Ct WOT/HER KT12...39 L9
Langridge Dr EGRIN RH19...180 D3
Langridge Ms HPTN TW12.....24 C9
Langroyd Rd TOOT SW17.......29 J5
Langshott HORL RH6.........140 F9
Langshott Cl
ADL/WDHM KT15..........55 J9
Langshott La HORL RH6.....140 E9
Langside Av PUT/ROE SW15...18 E7
Langsmead LING RH7........142 E5
Langstone Cl CRAWE RH10..177 M8
Langthorne St FUL/PGN SW6..19 H6
Langton Av EW KT17..........70 D7
Langton Cl ADL/WDHM KT15..55 M7
WOKN/KNAP GU21 ....71 M6
Langton Dr BOR GU35........164 D4
Langton Ri EDUL SE22.........31 J3
Langton Rd WIM/MER SW19...29 P7
Langton St WBPTN SW10......19 N4
Langton Wy CROY/NA CRO...3 H7
EGH TW20 ....20 E9
Langtry Pl FUL/PGN SW6......19 L4
Langwood Cha TEDD TW11....26 B9
Langwood Cl ASHTD KT21....77 N6
Lanigan Dr HSLW TW3.........25 J1
Lankton Cl BECK BR3.........47 J2
Lansbury Av
EBED/NFELT TW14 ....24 C2
Lansbury Rd CRAWW RH11..194 E1
Lansdell Rd MTCM CR4........44 C3
Lansdown GU GU14.........112 E5
Lansdown Cl HORS RH12....192 G4
WOKN/KNAP GU21 ....71 M8
WOT/HER KT12 ....39 L9
Lansdowne Cl BRYLDS KT5...59 P1
RYNPK SW20 ....43 H1
TWK TW1 ....25 N4
Lansdowne Copse WPK KT4 *..60 E1
Lansdowne Ct WPK KT4.......60 E1
Lansdowne Hl WNWD SE27....30 C6
Lansdowne Pl NRWD SE19....45 P1
Lansdowne Rd ALDT GU11...108 C5
BMLY BR1 ....47 N1
CROY/NA CRO 2 B5
FRIM GU16 ....69 J8
HOR/WEW KT19..........60 A6
HSLW TW3 ....16 B8
PUR/KEN CR8 ....81 J1
RYNPK SW20 ....42 C1
STA TW18 ....37 M1
Lansdowne Wood Cl
WNWD SE27............30 C6
Lantern Cl PUT/ROE SW15...18 E9
Lanyon Cl HORS RH12......192 F4
Lanyon Ms HORS RH12 *....192 F4
Large Wood Wk FSTH SE23...31 J4
Lapwing Cl SAND/SEL CR2...64 E6
SWTR RH13 ....192 E7
Lapwing Gv RGUE GU4......113 H3
Lara Cl CHSGTN KT9.........59 L6
Larbert Rd
STRHM/NOR SW16.......44 E2
Larby Pl EW KT17............60 C8
Larch Av ASC SL5............34 E6
GU GU1 ....112 A2
Larch Cl BAL SW12..........29 L5
CBLY GU15 ....50 G8
KWD/TDW/WH KT20......99 N1
LIPH GU30 ....182 E7
REDH RH1 ....120 C8
WARL CR6 ....82 E8
Larch Crs HOR/WEW KT19....59 P5
Larch Dr CHSWK W4 *........17 N1
Larch End HORS RH12......192 A7
Larches Av
MORT/ESHN SW14 ....18 B3
The Larches EGRIN RH19...162 F8
HORS RH12 ....192 B7
WOKN/KNAP GU21 ......10 D1
Larches Wy CRAWE RH10...179 K3
Larchfield Rd FLEETS GU52..86 G8
Larch Rd BOR GU35........164 E5
Larch Tree Wy CROY/NA CRO..64 G2
Larch Wy FARN GU14........87 N4
Larchwood Cl BNSTD SM7....79 J5
Larchwood Dr EGH TW20.....20 G9
Larchwood Gld CBLY GU15...69 J1
Larchwood Rd
WOKN/KNAP GU21 ......71 K9
Larcombe Cl CROY/NA CRO...63 P3
Larges Bridge Dr BRAK RG12..32 E4
Larges La BRAK RG12........32 E3
Largewood Av SURB KT6.....59 N1
Lark Av STA TW18............22 C6
Larkbere Rd SYD SE26.......31 M7
CRAN GU6 ....153 P8
Larkfield Cl FNM GU9.........4 A2
Larkfield Ct HORL RH6......160 B1
Larkfield Rd FNM GU9.........4 A2
RCH/KEW TW9 ....17 L9
Larkhall Cl WOT/HER KT12...57 L5
Larkham Cl FELT TW13......23 P6
Larkin Cl COUL/CHIP CR5....81 H6
Larkins Rd HORL RH6.......158 C5
Lark Ri CRAWE RH10........179 K5
CRAWW RH11 ....176 F4
EHSLY KT24 ....114 G2
SLOU SL3 ....182 D5
Larksfield EGH TW20........35 P1
HORL RH6 ....140 D9
Larkspur Cl ALDT GU11.....108 C7
Larkspur Wy HOR/WEW KT19..60 A4

RDKG RH5 ....137 K1
Larks Av WOKN/KNAP GU21 ..71 J5
Larkswood Cl SHST GU47....49 L8
Larkswood Dr CWTH RG45...49 M4
Lark Wy CAR SM5 ....44 A8
Larmer Cl FLEETN GU51......86 D8
Larnach Rd HMSMTH W6......19 H4
La Roche CI DTCH/LGLY SL3...12 A1
Larpent Av PUT/ROE SW15....27 P1
Lascombe La RGUW GU3....130 A3
Lasham Rd FLEETN GU51.....86 C3
Lashmere CRAN GU6........152 D9
CRAWE RH10 ....160 E9
Latchmere CI
RCHPK/HAM TW10........26 D8
Latchmere La KUTN/CMB KT2..26 E9
Latchmere Rd
KUTN/CMB KT2 ....26 D9
Latchwood La RFNM GU10..127 P8
Lateward Rd BTFD TW8 *......17 L4
Latham Av FRIM GU16........68 G6
Latham Cl BH/WHM TN16....84 A5
Latham Rd TWK TW1 ....25 N3
Latham's Wy CROY/NA CRO...45 H9
Latimer BRAK RG12.........32 D9
Latimer Cl CRAWW RH11....176 G2
WOKS/MYFD GU22 ....11 K1
WPK KT4 ....60 F2
Latimer Ct REDH RH1......120 B7
Latimer Rd CROY/NA CRO....2 B5
GODL GU7 ....131 L9
TEDD TW11 ....25 N8
WIM/MER SW19 ....28 E9
Lattimer Pl CHSWK W4.......18 C5
Latton Cl ESH/CLAY KT10....58 B3
WOT/HER KT12 ....39 P8
Latymer Cl WEY KT13.........56 E3
Laud Dr CRAWE RH10......177 N6
Lauder CI FRIM GU16........68 G6
Lauderdale FARN GU14.......87 P5
Lauderdale Dr
RCHPK/HAM TW10........26 C6
Laud St CROY/NA CRO........2 C6
Laughton Rd HORS RH12...192 E5
Launceston Pl KENS W8......19 N1
Laundry La SHST GU47.......68 A3
Laundry Rd GU GU1...........6 D4
HMSMTH W6 ....19 J4
Laundry Wy RDKG RH5.....156 B7
Lauradale BRAK RG12........32 C5
Laurel Av EGH TW20 ....20 C8
TWK TW1 ....25 N4
Laurel Bank
CHOB/PIR GU24 * 53 L9
Laurel Bank Gdns
FUL/PGN SW6 ....19 K7
Laurel Cl CBLY GU15.........68 F4
CRAWE RH10 *..........177 K8
DTCH/LGLY SL3 ....13 J5
FARN GU14 ....87 N4
TOOT SW17 ....29 J7
Laurel Crs CROY/NA CRO.....64 G2
WOKN/KNAP GU21 ......72 G2
Laurel Dene EGRIN RH19....180 E2
Laureldene RGUW GU3......110 B5
Laurel Dr OXTED RH8.......123 M2
Laurel Gdns ALDT GU11....108 C7
HSLWW TW4 ....15 N9
Laurel Gv PGE/AN SE20......46 B1
RFNM GU10............127 K8
SYD SE26 ....31 L8
Laurel La WDR/YW UB7......14 A2
Laurel Rd BARN SW13........18 E7
HPTN TW12 ....24 E7
RYNPK SW20 ....42 G1
The Laurels BNSTD SM7......79 K6
COB KT11..............75 N4
CRAWE RH10 * 177 K2
FLEETN GU51 ....86 B5
FNM GU9 ....108 B7
Laurel Wk SWTR RH13......192 H1
Laurier Rd CROY/NA CRO....45 P8
Lauriston Cl
WOKN/KNAP GU21 ......71 K6
Lauriston Rd WIM/MER SW19..28 A9
Lauser Rd STWL/WRAY TW19..23 J2
Laustan Cl GU GU1..........113 L6
Lavant Cl CRAWW RH11......176 C6
Lavender Av MTCM CR4......44 A1
WPK KT4 ....60 G2
Lavender Cl CAR SM5........62 D4
CHEL SW3 ....19 P4
COUL/CHIP CR5 * 80 E8
CTHM CR3 ....101 L5
REDH RH1 ....140 D1
Lavender Ct E/WMO/HCT KT8..40 B4
Lavender Ga LHD/OX KT22...76 D2
Lavender Gv MTCM CR4.....44 A2
Lavender La RFNM GU10....127 K9
Lavender Park Rd
BF/WBF KT14 *..........73 L2
Lavender Rd BTSEA SW11....19 H7
CROY/NA CRO 44 G8
HOR/WEW KT19.........59 P4
SUT SM1 ....61 P3
WLGTN SM6 ....62 C4
Lavender V WLGTN SM6......62 F5
Lavengro Rd WNWD SE27....30 D5
Lavenham Rd
WAND/EARL SW18........28 C4
Laverstock Cl FLEETN GU51...86 C3
Laverstoke Gdns
PUT/ROE SW15 ....27 L3
Laverton Ms ECT SW5.......19 M2
Laverton Pl ECT SW5........19 M2
Lavington Cl CRAWW RH11..176 C4
Lavington Rd CROY/NA CRO..63 H2
Lawbrook La SHGR GU5.....134 E5
Lawday Link FNM GU9......107 L7

Lawday Pl FNM GU9.........107 L7
Lawday Place La FNM GU9...107 L7
Lawdon Gdns CROY/NA CRO..63 K3
Lawford Crs YTLY GU46.......67 H2
Lawford Gdns PUR/KEN CR8..81 L5
Lawford Rd CHSWK W4.......18 A5
Lawford's Hill Rd RGUW GU3..91 J4
Lawn Cl BMLY BR1...........47 N3
DTCH/LGLY SL3 ....12 A1
NWMAL KT3 ....42 C5
Lawn Crs RCH/KEW TW9.....17 N7
Lawn Rd BECK BR3..........46 G1
GUW GU2 ....112 A8
Lawnsmead SHGR GU5......132 F6
Lawns Rd HORS RH12......171 K8
The Lawns BELMT SM2 *......31 J6
DTCH/LGLY SL3 * 13 J1
FARN GU14 ....88 A4
MFD/CHID GU8 ....149 N3
NRWD SE19............45 M2
The Lawn DTCH/LGLY SL3 *...12 A6
NWDGN UB2............15 N2
Lawrence Av NWMAL KT3....42 C8
Lawrence La RCUE GU4.......92 F9
Lawrence Crs EDGW GU20...52 D5
Lawrence La
BRKHM/BTCW RH3.......118 F3
Lawrence Pde ISLW TW7 *....17 H8
Lawrence Rd EA W5 ....17 J2
FLEETS GU52 ....86 F7
HPTN TW12 ....39 P1
HSLWW TW4 ....15 L9
RCHPK/HAM TW10 ....26 B7
SNWD SE25 ....45 P5
WWKM BR4 ....65 K3
Lawrence Wy CBLY GU15....68 B4
Lawrie Park Av SYD SE26....31 J8
Lawrie Park Crs SYD SE26....31 J8
Lawrie Park Gdns SYD SE26...31 J7
Lawrie Park Rd SYD SE26.....31 K9
Laws Cl CRAWW RH11.......176 B6
SNWD SE25 ....45 M5
Lawson Av WIM/MER SW19...28 A6
Lawson Ter SHGR GU5 *.....132 F6
Lawson Wk CAR SM5 ....62 B7
Lawson Wy ASC SL5..........35 H7
Laws Ter ALDT GU11........108 E3
Laxton Gdns REDH RH1.....100 F8
Layard Rd THHTH CR7........45 M3
Layburn Crs DTCH/LGLY SL3..12 F4
Laybrook Rd HAYES BR2.....65 M8
WWKM BR4 ....65 L5
Layton Ct WEY KT13.........56 D3
Layton Crs CROY/NA CRO....63 J3
Layton Pl RCH/KEW TW9.....17 N6
Layton Rd BTFD TW8.........17 K3
HSLW TW3 ....16 B9
Layton's La SUN TW16........39 H5
Lazell Gdns
BRKHM/BTCW RH3.......138 A2
Leach Gv LHD/OX KT22......97 J2
Lea Cl ASHV GU12..........109 J5
CRAWW RH11 ....176 C6
FNM GU9 ....108 C8
WHTN TW2 ....24 G3
Lea Ct FNM GU9............108 B7
Leacroft ASC SL5............34 G6
Lea Cft CWTH RG45.........49 M3
Leacroft EGRIN RH19.......180 C1
STA TW18 ....22 E8
Leacroft Av BAL SW12.......29 J3
Leacroft Cl PUR/KEN CR8....81 L5
STA TW18 ....22 E7
Leaf Cl THDIT KT7...........40 E6
Leaf Gv WNWD SE27.........30 B3
Leafield Cl STRHM/NOR SW16..30 D9
WOKN/KNAP GU21 ......71 P7
Leafield Copse BRAK RG12 *..33 K4
Leafield Rd RYNPK SW20.....43 K4
SUT SM1 ....61 L1
Leafy Wy CROY/NA CRO......3 K1
Leamington Av MRDN SM4...43 K5
Leamington Cl HSLW TW3....25 L1
Leamington Rd NWDGN UB2..15 M2
Leamore St HMSMTH W6.....18 F2
Leander Rd
BRXS/STRHM SW2........30 A2
THHTH CR7 ....45 H5
Leapale La GU GU1............6 E5
Leapale Rd GU GU1...........6 E5
Lea Rd BECK BR3............46 G3
CBLY GU15 ....68 D6
NWDGN UB2............15 N2
Leas Cl CHSGTN KT9.........59 M6
Leaside CT/LBKH KT23.......96 A3
Leas La WARL CR6...........82 D7
Lea Springs FLEETN GU51....86 D8
Leas Rd GU GU1.............6 C6
WARL CR6 ....82 D7
The Leas STA TW18 *........22 D7
Lea Vw EGH TW20...........36 F1
EWKG RG40............48 C3
FLEETN GU51 ....86 E8
Leather Cl EDEN TN8.......144 G5
MTCM CR4 ....44 C3
Leatherhead By-Pass Rd
LHD/OX KT22 ....97 K2
Leatherhead Rd
BRKHM/BTCW RH3.......96 B6
LHD/OX KT22 ....76 D4
LHD/OX KT22 ....97 K1
Leather La SHGR GU5......134 E1
Leaveland Cl BECK BR3......46 G5
Leavesden Rd WEY KT13.....56 D4
Leaves Gn BRAK RG12.......32 F7
Leaview Cl FLEETN GU51....86 D8
Leawood Rd FLEETN GU51...86 E8
Lea Wood Rd FLEETN GU51..86 E8
Leazes Av CTHM CR5........101 J3
Lebanon Dr COB KT11........76 A2

Lebanon Gdns
BH/WHM TN16...........84 B6
WAND/EARL SW18........28 D2
Lebanon Pk TWK TW1.........26 A3
Lebanon Rd CROY/NA CRO....3 H2
WAND/EARL SW18........28 D1
Le Borowe FLEETS GU52....106 E2
Leckford Rd HORL RH6......159 J3
Leckford Rd
WAND/EARL SW18........28 F5
Lecky St SKENS SW7 ....19 P5
Leconfield Av BARN SW13....18 D8
Ledbury Rd CROY/NA CRO....63 L3
REIG RH2 ....119 L5
Ledger CI GU GU1...........113 J4
Ledger Dr ADL/WDHM KT15...55 K5
Ledgers Rd WARL CR6........82 C5
Ledrington Rd NRWD SE19....30 C9
Lee Acre DORK RH4 * 137 J1
Leechcroft Rd WLGTN SM6...62 C2
Leech La EPSOM KT18........98 A6
Leechpool La SWTR RH13...192 F6
Lee Ct ALDT GU11..........108 D6
Leehurst MFD/CHID GU8....149 M3
Lee Rd ALDT GU11..........108 A4
WIM/MER SW19 ....43 M2
Leeside HORS RH12 *.......175 H5
Leeson Rd HNHL SE24 *......30 B1
The Lees CROY/NA CRO......64 F1
St Lee HORL RH6 ....140 A9
Leeward Gdns
WIM/MER SW19 ....28 B9
The Leeways CHEAM SM3 *..61 J5
Leewood Wy EHSLY KT24....95 L7
Lefroy's Fld RFNM GU10....106 D6
Leger Cl FLEETS GU52......106 E1
Legge Crs ALDT GU11......108 A5
Legrace Av HSLWW TW4.....15 M7
Leicester BRAK RG12.........32 F8
Leicester Av MTCM CR4......44 G5
Leicester Cl WPK KT4.........60 G3
Leicester Rd CROY/NA CRO...45 M8
Leigham Av
STRHM/NOR SW16.......29 P6
Leigham Cl
STRHM/NOR SW16.......30 A6
Leigham Court Rd
STRHM/NOR SW16.......30 A6
Leigham Dr ISLW TW7........16 E5
Leigham Hall Pde
STRHM/NOR SW16 *.....29 P6
Leigham V
STRHM/NOR SW16.......30 B6
Leigh Cl ADL/WDHM KT15....55 K6
NWMAL KT3 ....42 B5
Leigh Court Cl COB KT11.....75 L3
Leigh Crs CROY/NA CRO......65 H6
Leigh Hill Rd COB KT11.......75 L4
Leighlands CRAWE RH10....177 M3
Leigh La FNM GU9..........128 A5
Leigh Orchard Cl
STRHM/NOR SW16.......30 A6
Leigh Pk DTCH/LGLY SL3 *...12 A5
Leigh Pl COB KT11...........75 L4
FELT TW13 ....24 C3
Leigh Place Rd COB KT11.....75 L4
Leigh Place Rd REIG RH2....138 E2
Leigh Rd BRKHM/BTCW RH3..138 A2
COB KT11..............75 K2
HSLW TW3 ....16 D9
The Leigh KUTN/CMB KT2....27 K9
Leighton Gdns SAND/SEL CR2..82 B2
Leighton St CROY/NA CRO.....2 A2
Leighton Wy EPSOM KT18....78 B3
Leinster Av
MORT/ESHN SW14 ....18 A2
Leipzig Barracks
FLEETS GU52 ....107 H4
Leipzig Rd FLEETS GU52....107 H3
Leisure La BF/WBF KT14 *....73 M1
Leith Cl CWTH RG45..........49 L2
Leithcote Gdns
STRHM/NOR SW16.......30 A7
Leithcote Pth
STRHM/NOR SW16.......30 A6
Leith Dr ALDT GU11.........108 A4
Leith Gv PGE/AN SE20........31 N8
Leith Hill Rd RDKG RH5.....135 N6
Leith La RDKG RH5 ....137 K9
Leith Rd EW KT17............78 C1
RDKG RH5 ....137 J9
Leith View RDKG RH5.......137 J9
Leith View Rd HORS RH12...192 F5
Lela Av HSLWW TW4.........15 H8
Le Marchant Rd FRIM GU16..69 H5
Le Mayr Cl HORL RH6.......140 C9
Lemington Gv BRAK RG12....32 D7
Lemmington Wy
HORS RH12 ....192 E5
Lemon's Farm Rd RDKG RH5..135 P7
Lena Gdns HMSMTH W6......18 G1
Lendore Rd FRIM GU16.......68 F8
Lenelby Rd SURB KT6.........41 N9
Len Freeman Pl
FUL/PGN SW6 ....19 K4
Lenham Rd SUT SM1........61 M3
THHTH CR7 ....45 M3
Lennard Av WWKM BR4......65 L5
Lennard Cl WWKM BR4......65 L5
Lennard Rd CROY/NA CRO.....2 C1
PGE/AN SE20 ....31 J9
Lennel Gdns FLEETS GU52....87 J9
Lennox Gdns CROY/NA CRO...63 K3
Lenten Cl SHGR GU5........134 F4
Lenton Ri RCH/KEW TW9 *....17 M6
Leominster Rd MRDN SM4....43 N7
Leominster Wk MRDN SM4....43 N7
Leonard Av MRDN SM4.......43 N6
Leonard Ct KENS W8.........19 L1
Leonard Rd NWDGN UB2....15 M1

STRHM/NOR SW16.......44 E2
Leonardslee Ct
CRAWE RH10 * 177 L8
Leonard Wy SWTR RH13....192 E8
Leopold Av FARN GU14.......88 D2
Leopold Rd CRAWW RH11...176 F5
WIM/MER SW19 ....28 D8
Le Personne Rd CTHM CR3..101 M2
Leppington BRAK RG12.......32 D9
Leppoc Rd CLAP SW4.........29 N1
Leret Wy LHD/OX KT22.......96 G1
Lerry Cl WKENS W14.........19 K4
Lesbourne Rd REIG RH2.....119 N4
Lescombe Cl FSTH SE23.....31 M6
Lescombe Rd FSTH SE23....31 M6
Leslie Gdns BELMT SM2......61 L6
Leslie Gv CROY/NA CRO.......3 G2
Leslie Grove Pl CROY/NA CRO..3 G2
Leslie Park Rd CROY/NA CRO...3 G2
Leslie Rd CHOB/PIR GU24....53 K8
DORK RH4 ....117 K5
Lessar Av CLAP SW4.........29 M1
Lessingham Av TOOT SW17..29 J7
Lessing St FSTH SE23........31 M5
Lessness Rd MRDN SM4.....43 N7
Lestock Cl SNWD SE25......46 A4
Lestock Wy FLEETS GU51....87 K9
Letchworth Av
EBED/NFELT TW14 ......24 A3
Letchworth Cl HAYES BR2....47 N6
Letchworth Dr HAYES BR2...47 N6
Letchworth St TOOT SW17...29 J7
Letcombe Sq BRAK RG12....33 H5
Letterstone Rd FUL/PGN SW6..19 K5
Lettice St FUL/PGN SW6.....19 L6
Levana Cl WIM/MER SW19....28 D4
Levendale Rd FSTH SE23....31 M5
Leveret Cl CROY/NA CRO.....65 K8
Leveret La CRAWW RH11....176 E3
Leverette Cl ASHV GU12....108 F3
Leverkusen Rd BRAK RG12...32 D4
Levern Dr FNM GU9.........107 N8
Leverson St
STRHM/NOR SW16.......29 M9
Levett Rd LHD/OX KT22......77 H9
Levignen Cl FLEETS GU52...106 D1
Levylsdene GU GU1..........113 H5
Lewes Cl CRAWE RH10......177 M5
Lewesdon Cl WIM/MER SW19..28 A4
Lewes Rd EGRIN RH19.......180 D1
FROW RH18...........181 K8
Lewin Rd MORT/ESHN SW14..18 A9
STRHM/NOR SW16.......29 N9
Lewins Rd EPSOM KT18......77 P3
Lewis Cl ADL/WDHM KT15...55 N3
Lewisham Cl CRAWW RH11..176 F9
Lewisham Wy SHST GU47...49 P8
Lewis Rd MTCM CR4.........44 A3
RCH/KEW TW9 *.........26 C1
SUT SM1 ....61 M3
Lewiston Cl WPK KT4.........42 F8
Lexden Rd MTCM CR4.........44 G5
Lexham Gdns ECT SW5......19 M2
Lexham Ms KENS W8........19 L2
Lexington Ct PUR/KEN CR8...63 N8
Lexton Gdns BAL SW12......29 M4
Leyborne Pk RCH/KEW TW9..17 N6
Leybourne Av BF/WBF KT14..74 B2
Leybourne Cl BF/WBF KT14..74 B2
CRAWW RH11 ....194 F1
HAYES BR2 ....47 N6
Leybourne Rd CRAWW RH11..194 F1
Leyburn Gdns CROY/NA CRO..3 H4
Leycester Cl BFOR GU20.....52 B3
Leyfield WPK KT4 ....60 C1
Leylands La
STWL/WRAY TW19 ....13 K9
Ley Rd FARN GU14...........68 C3
Leyside CWTH RG45..........49 L5
Leys Rd LHD/OX KT22........76 D1
The Leys WOT/HER KT12 *....57 J5
Leyton Rd WIM/MER SW19...43 P2
Liberty Av WIM/MER SW19...43 P2
Liberty Hall Rd
ADL/WDHM KT15........55 L4
Liberty La ADL/WDHM KT15...55 L5
Liberty Ri ADL/WDHM KT15...55 L5
Library Rd FARN GU14.......88 A3
Lichfields
RCH/KEW TW9 * 26 D1
Lichfield Rd HSLWW TW4.....15 M6
Lichfields BRAK RG12........32 G5
Lichfield Ter RCH/KEW TW9 *..26 D1
Lichfield Wy SAND/SEL CR2...64 D8
Lickfolds Rd RFNM GU10....146 B2
Liddell Cl EWKG RG40........49 N1
Liddell Wy ASC SL5..........35 P6
Liddington Hall Dr
RGUW GU3 ....111 L2
Liddington New Rd
RGUW GU3 ....111 L2
Lidiard Rd WAND/EARL SW18..28 F3
Lido Rd GU GU1...............7 F1
Lidsey Cl CRAWE RH10.....177 M7
Lidstone Cl
WOKN/KNAP GU21 ......71 P6
Lifford St PUT/ROE SW15....19 H9
Lightwater Meadow
LTWR GU18 ....52 B9
Lightwater Rd LTWR GU18...52 C9
Lightwood BRAK RG12.......32 F7
Lilac Av WOKS/MYFD GU22..11 K2
Lilac Cl GU GU1............112 A1
Lilac Gdns CROY/NA CRO....64 G5
EA W5 ....17 K3
Lilah Ms HAYES BR2.........65 J9
Lilian Rd STRHM/NOR SW16..44 E2
Lille Barracks ALDT GU11...108 F7
Lilleshall Rd MRDN SM4.....43 P7
Lilley Dr KWD/TDW/WH KT20..99 M2

Lillian Rd BARN SW13 18 E4
Lillie Rd BH/WHM TN16 84 B7
FUL/PGN SW6 19 H4
Lillie Yd FUL/PGN SW6 19 L4
Lilliott's La LHD/OX KT22 76 C8
Lily Cl WKENS W14 * 19 J2
Lily Dr WDR/YW UB7 13 P2
Lilyfields Cha CRAN GU6 153 P8
Lily Hill Dr BRAK RG12 32 G3
Lily Hill Rd BRAK RG12 33 H3
Lilyville Rd FUL/PGN SW6 19 K6
Lime Av CBLY GU15 69 J2
HORS RH12 192 F6
Limebush Cl
ADL/WDHM KT15 55 N7
Lime Cl CRAWE RH10 160 C9
CRAWW RH11 176 F2
REIG RH2 119 M8
RGUE GU4 93 M8
Lime Crs SUN TW16 39 L3
Limecroft YTLY GU46 66 C3
Limecroft Cl HOR/WEW KT19 60 B6
Limecroft Rd
WOKN/KNAP GU21 71 H6
Lime Dr FLEETN GU51 87 H3
Lime Gv ADL/WDHM KT15 55 L3
GU GU1 111 P1
NWMAL KT3 42 B4
RGUE GU4 93 M8
TWK TW1 25 N2
WARL CR6 82 E8
WOKS/MYFD GU22 92 C1
Lime Meadow Av
SAND/SEL CR2 82 A2
Limerick Cl BAL SW12 29 M3
BNFD RG42 32 C2
Limerston St WBPTN SW10 19 N4
Limes Av BARN SW13 18 D7
CAR SM5 44 B9
CROY/NA CR0 63 H2
HORL RH6 159 L3
PGE/AN SE20 46 B1
Limes Cl ASHF TW15 23 K8
CAR SM5 62 B1
LIPH GU30 182 F3
Limes Field Rd
MORT/ESHN SW14 18 C8
Limes Gdns
WAND/EARL SW18 28 D2
Limes Rd BECK BR3 47 H3
CROY/NA CR0 45 M7
EGH TW20 21 L8
FARN GU14 87 N2
WEY KT13 56 C3
The Limes EDEN TN8 144 G4
EGRIN RH19 161 P7
LHD/OX KT22 97 H3
WAND/EARL SW18 * 28 D2
WOKN/KNAP GU21 * 11 G2
Lime St ALDT GU11 108 B4
Lime Tree Av THDIT KT7 40 E9
Limetree Cl
BRXS/STRHM SW2 30 A4
Lime Tree Cl GT/LBKH KT23 96 A4
Lime Tree Gv CROY/NA CR0 64 F2
Limetree Pl MTCM CR4 44 D2
Lime Tree Rd HEST TW5 16 B6
Lime Tree Ter CAT SE6 * 31 N4
Lime Tree Wk VW GU25 36 C5
WWKM BR4 65 M3
Lime Wk BRAK RG12 32 E5
Limeway Ter DORK RH4 116 C5
Limewood Cl BECK BR3 47 J6
WOKN/KNAP GU21 71 K9
Limpsfield Av THHTH CR7 45 H6
WIM/MER SW19 28 A5
Limpsfield Rd SAND/SEL CR2 82 A1
WARL CR6 82 G8
Linacre Dr HORS RH12 171 M8
Lince La DORK RH4 116 D7
Linchfield Rd DTCH/LGLY SL3 12 A6
Linchmere Pl CRAWW RH11 176 D4
Linchmere Rd HASM GU27 183 M7
Lincoln Av WHTN TW2 25 K5
WIM/MER SW19 28 A5
Lincoln Cl ASHV GU12 109 J1
CBLY GU15 69 K4
CRAWE RH10 177 H8
Lincoln Dr WOKS/MYFD GU22 73 J4
Lincoln Rd DORK RH4 117 J5
FARN GU14 88 C6
FELT TW13 24 G6
GUW GU2 111 M3
MTCM CR4 44 G6
NWMAL KT3 42 A4
SNWD SE25 46 B4
WPK KT4 42 F9
Lincolnshire Gdns
BNFD RG42 32 G1
Lincolns Md LING RH7 162 B1
Lincoln Ter BELMT SM2 * 61 L6
Lincoln Wy SUN TW16 38 G2
Lindale Cl VW GU25 35 M5
Lindal Rd BROCKY SE4 31 N1
Linden Av COUL/CHIP CR5 80 D5
EGRIN RH19 180 B1
HSLW TW3 25 J1
THHTH CR7 45 K5
Linden Cl ADL/WDHM KT15 55 L9
CRAWE RH10 177 K8
HORS RH12 192 D6
KWD/TDW/WH KT20 79 H9
THDIT KT7 40 C8
Linden Ct CBLY GU15 69 H1
EGH TW20 20 G9
LHD/OX KT22 97 H1
Linden Crs KUT/HW KT1 9 G5
Linden Dr CTHM CR3 101 L4
Linden Gdns CHSWK W4 18 B3
LHD/OX KT22 97 J1
Linden Gv NWMAL KT3 42 C4
SYD SE26 31 K9
TEDD TW11 25 N8
WARL CR6 82 E7
WOT/HER KT12 57 H1
Lindenhill Rd BNFD RG42 32 B2
Linden Lea DORK RH4 * 117 J9
Linden Leas WWKM BR4 65 K1
Linden Pit Pth LHD/OX KT22 97 H1
Linden Pl EHSLY KT24 * 94 G6
EW KT17 78 C1
MTCM CR4 44 A5
Linden Rd BOR GU35 164 E6
GU GU1 6 E2
HPTN TW12 40 A2
LHD/OX KT22 97 H1
WEY KT13 56 E7
Lindens Cl EHSLY KT24 95 N8
The Lindens CHSWK W4 18 A6
CRAWE RH10 160 C9
CROY/NA CR0 65 J5
FNM GU9 5 K6
Linden Wy PUR/KEN CR8 62 E8
RPLY/SEND GU23 93 K5
SHPTN TW17 38 E6
WOKS/MYFD GU22 92 D1
Lindfield Gdns GU GU1 7 K1
Lindfield Rd CROY/NA CR0 45 P7
Lindfield Ter
WOKN/KNAP GU21 * 72 A5
Lindgren Wk
CRAWW RH11 * 194 E1
Lindisfarne Rd RYNPK SW20 42 E1
Lindley Pl RCH/KEW TW9 17 N6
Lindley Rd GDST RH9 122 C1
WOT/HER KT12 57 N2
Lindores Rd CAR SM5 43 N8
Lind Rd SUT SM1 61 N4
Lindrop St FUL/PGN SW6 19 N7
Lindsay Cl CHSGTN KT9 59 L6
HOR/WEW KT19 78 A2
STWL/WRAY TW19 22 G2
Lindsay Dr SHPTN TW17 38 F7
Lindsay Rd ADL/WDHM KT15 55 L9
HPTN TW12 25 L8
WPK KT4 60 F1
Lindsey Cl MTCM CR4 44 G5
Lindsey Gdns
EBED/NFELT TW14 * 23 N3
Lindum Dene ALDT GU11 108 C5
Lindum Rd TEDD TW11 41 J1
Lindway WNWD SE27 30 C8
Linersh Dr SHGR GU5 132 E7
Linersh Wood Cl SHGR GU5 132 E8
Linershwood Rd SHGR GU5 132 E7
Linfield Cl WOT/HER KT12 * 57 K4
Ling Crs BOR GU35 164 E5
Ling Dr LTWR GU18 69 P1
Lingfield Av KUT/HW KT1 41 L5
Lingfield Common Rd
LING RH7 143 J8
Lingfield Dr CRAWE RH10 177 P4
Lingfield Gdns
COUL/CHIP CR5 81 K8
Lingfield Rd EDEN TN8 144 E5
EGRIN RH19 162 C7
WIM/MER SW19 28 A9
WPK KT4 60 G2
Lingmala Gv FLEETS GU52 107 H1
Lingwell Rd TOOT SW17 29 H6
Lingwood BRAK RG12 32 E7
Lingwood Gdns ISLW TW7 16 E5
Link 10 CRAWE RH10 177 K2
Linkfield E/WMO/HCT KT8 40 A4
Link Fld HAYES BR2 47 N7
Linkfield Gdns REDH RH1 120 A5
Linkfield La REDH RH1 120 B4
Linkfield Rd ISLW TW7 16 F7
Linkfield St REDH RH1 120 A5
Link La WLGTN SM6 62 F5
Link Rd ADL/WDHM KT15 56 A3
DTCH/LGLY SL3 12 A5
EBED/NFELT TW14 24 A3
FARN GU14 87 P7
WLGTN SM6 44 C9
Links Av MRDN SM4 43 L5
Links Brae LHD/OX KT22 96 E3
Links Cl ASHTD KT21 77 J6
CRAN GU6 153 P6
Linkscroft Av ASHF TW15 23 L9
Links Gdns
STRHM/NOR SW16 45 J1
Links Green Wy COB KT11 76 A3
Linkside NWMAL KT3 42 C3
Linkside East GSHT GU26 165 L4
Linkside North GSHT GU26 165 L4
Linkside South GSHT GU26 165 M5
Linkside West GSHT GU26 165 L4
Links Pl ASHTD KT21 77 K6
Links Rd ASHF TW15 23 H8
ASHTD KT21 77 J6
EW KT17 78 E2
SHGR GU5 132 C6
TOOT SW17 29 K9
WWKM BR4 47 J9
The Links ASC SL5 33 N3
WOT/HER KT12 57 J1
Links View Av
BRKHM/BTCW RH3 117 N5
Linksview Ct HPTN TW12 * 25 L7
Links View Rd CROY/NA CR0 64 G2
HPTN TW12 25 K8
Links Wy BECK BR3 46 G7
FARN GU14 87 N4
GT/LBKH KT23 95 N8
The Link CRAWW RH11 176 G5
TEDD TW11 25 N9
YTLY GU46 66 C1
Link Wy RCHPK/HAM TW10 26 A5
STA TW18 22 E9
Linkway CBLY GU15 68 E4
CWTH RG45 49 K4
FLEETS GU52 86 F9
GUW GU2 111 M5
HORL RH6 159 M5
RYNPK SW20 42 F4
WOKS/MYFD GU22 72 G6
The Linkway BELMT SM2 61 N7
Linnell Cl CRAWW RH11 194 E2
Linnell Rd REDH RH1 120 C6
Linnet Cl CRAWE RH10 179 K6
SAND/SEL CR2 64 D8
Linnet Gv RGUE GU4 113 H3
Linnet Ms BAL SW12 29 K3
Linnett Cl CRAWE RH10 * 179 K5
Linsford La FRIM GU16 89 H4
Linslade Cl HSLWW TW4 24 F1
Linstead Rd FARN GU14 68 A8
Linstead Wy
WAND/EARL SW18 28 B3
Linsted La BOR GU35 164 A4
Lintaine Cl HMSMTH W6 * 19 J4
Linton Cl CAR SM5 44 B8
Linton Gld CROY/NA CR0 64 E8
Linton Gv WNWD SE27 30 C8
Linton's La EW KT17 78 C1
Lintott Ct STWL/WRAY TW19 22 G2
Lintott Gdns SWTR RH13 192 D7
Linver Rd FUL/PGN SW6 19 K7
Lion Av TWK TW1 25 N4
Lion Cl BROCKY SE4 31 P2
SHPTN TW17 38 A4
Lionel Rd North BTFD TW8 17 L1
Lionel Rd South BTFD TW8 17 M3
Lion Gate Gdns
RCH/KEW TW9 17 M8
Lion Green Rd
COUL/CHIP CR5 80 F4
Lion & Lamb Wy FNM GU9 4 E3
Lion & Lamb Yd FNM GU9 * 5 F3
Lion La CRAWE RH10 179 H7
GSHT GU26 184 A1
Lion Md HASM GU27 184 A4
Lion Park Av CHSGTN KT9 59 N3
Lion Rd CROY/NA CR0 45 L6
FARN GU14 88 D5
TWK TW1 25 N4
Lion Wy BTFD TW8 17 K5
FLEETS GU52 107 H1
Lion Wharf Rd ISLW TW7 17 H8
Liphook Crs FSTH SE23 31 K3
Liphook Rd HASM GU27 183 K6
Lipsham Cl BNSTD SM7 79 P2
Lisbon Av WHTN TW2 25 K5
Liscombe BRAK RG12 32 D8
Lisgar Ter WKENS W14 19 K2
Liskeard Dr FARN GU14 88 C1
Lisle Cl TOOT SW17 29 L7
Lismore WIM/MER SW19 * 28 C8
Lismore Cl ISLW TW7 16 G7
Lismore Crs CRAWW RH11 176 E8
Lismore Rd SAND/SEL CR2 63 N5
Lismoyne Cl FLEETN GU51 86 F5
Lissant Cl SURB KT6 41 J8
Lissoms Rd COUL/CHIP CR5 80 C7
Lister Av EGRIN RH19 180 D5
Litchfield Av MRDN SM4 43 K8
Litchfield Rd SUT SM1 61 N3
Litchfield Wy GUW GU2 111 M7
Lithgow's Rd HTHAIR TW6 14 G9
Little Acre BECK BR3 46 G4
Little Aly EDEN TN8 144 F8
Little Austins Rd FNM GU9 5 K7
Little Benty WDR/YW UB7 13 P3
Little Birch Cl
ADL/WDHM KT15 55 P7
The Little Boltons
WBPTN SW10 19 M3
Little Bookham St
GT/LBKH KT23 95 P4
Little Bornes DUL SE21 30 F7
Little Borough
BRKHM/BTCW RH3 117 N6
Littlebrook Cl CROY/NA CR0 46 D7
Little Brownings FSTH SE23 31 J5
Little Browns La EDEN TN8 144 C1
Little Chesters
KWD/TDW/WH KT20 98 E5
Little Collins REDH RH1 * 141 K6
Littlecombe Cl
PUT/ROE SW15 * 28 A2
Little Common La
REDH RH1 121 K3
Little Comptons SWTR RH13 192 F8
Little Copse FLEETS GU52 86 F8
YTLY GU46 66 G1
Littlecote Cl WIM/MER SW19 28 A3
Little Ct WWKM BR4 65 L1
Little Crabtree
CRAWW RH11 176 F4
Little Cranmore La
EHSLY KT24 94 D8
Littlecroft Rd EGH TW20 21 L8
Littledale Cl BRAK RG12 32 G4
Little Dimocks BAL SW12 29 L5
Little Ealing La EA W5 17 J2
Little East Fld
COUL/CHIP CR5 100 F1
Little Elms HYS/HAR UB3 14 F5
Little Ferry Rd TWK TW1 * 26 A4
Littlefield Cl ASHV GU12 109 J5
KUT/HW KT1 8 E5
RGUW GU3 111 K1
Littlefield Gdns ASHV GU12 109 J5
Littlefield Wy RGUW GU3 111 J1
Littleford La SHGR GU5 133 K7
Little Foxes EWKG RG40 48 E2
Little Frith EWKG RG40 48 G3
Little Grebe HORS RH12 192 B5
Little Green La CHERT KT16 55 J2
FNM GU9 127 L6
Little Gv DORK RH4 * 117 J9
Little Halliards
WOT/HER KT12 39 J7
Little Hatch HORS RH12 192 E5
Little Haven La HORS RH12 192 E5
Littlehaven La HORS RH12 192 E6
Littleheath La COB KT11 76 A3
Little Heath Rd
CHOB/PIR GU24 53 L7
Littleheath Rd SAND/SEL CR2 64 B7
Little Hide GU GU1 112 F3
Little Kiln GODL GU7 131 L5
Little King St EGRIN RH19 180 D2
Little London
MFD/CHID GU8 149 M7
SHGR GU5 134 A3
Little Lullenden LING RH7 143 K8
Little Manor Gdns
CRAN GU6 170 G1
Littlemead ESH/CLAY KT10 58 D3
Little Md WOKN/KNAP GU21 71 M5
Little Moor SHST GU47 49 N8
Little Moreton Cl
BF/WBF KT14 * 73 M1
Little Oak Cl SHPTN TW17 38 B5
Little Orch ADL/WDHM KT15 55 L9
WOKN/KNAP GU21 72 E3
Little Orchards EPSOM KT18 78 C3
Little Orchard Wy
RGUE GU4 132 C3
Little Paddock CBLY GU15 51 J9
Little Park Dr FELT TW13 24 E5
Little Platt GUW GU2 111 K4
Little Queens Rd TEDD TW11 25 N9
Little Riding
WOKS/MYFD GU22 11 J2
Little Ringdale BRAK RG12 32 G5
Little Roke Av PUR/KEN CR8 81 K3
Little Roke Rd PUR/KEN CR8 81 L3
Littlers Cl WIM/MER SW19 43 P2
Little St Leonards
MORT/ESHN SW14 18 A8
Littlestone Cl BECK BR3 31 P9
Little St GUW GU2 111 N1
Little Sutton La
DTCH/LGLY SL3 12 G3
Little Thatch GODL GU7 131 M7
Little Thurbans Cl FNM GU9 127 L7
Littleton La REIG RH2 119 J7
RGUW GU3 131 N2
SHPTN TW17 38 A6
Littleton Rd ASHF TW15 38 E1
Littleton St
WAND/EARL SW18 28 F5
Little Tumners Ct GODL GU7 131 L6
Little Vigo YTLY GU46 66 F4
Little Warren Cl RGUE GU4 112 F7
Little Wellington St
ALDT GU11 108 C4
Littlewick Rd
WOKN/KNAP GU21 71 K5
Littlewood CRAN GU6 153 J9
Littlewood Cl WEA W13 17 H1
Little Woodcote La CAR SM5 80 D1
Littleworth Av
ESH/CLAY KT10 58 D4
Littleworth Common Rd
ESH/CLAY KT10 58 D2
Littleworth La
ESH/CLAY KT10 58 D3
Littleworth Pl ESH/CLAY KT10 58 D3
Littleworth Rd
ESH/CLAY KT10 58 D4
RFNM GU10 129 H4
RGUW GU3 129 N6
Littlt Halliards
WOT/HER KT12 * 39 J7
Liverpool Rd KUTN/CMB KT2 41 N1
THHTH CR7 45 L4
Livesey Cl KUT/HW KT1 9 F6
Livingstone Rd BTSEA SW11 19 P8
CRAWE RH10 177 H7
CTHM CR3 101 M2
HSLW TW3 16 C9
SWTR RH13 192 C9
THHTH CR7 45 M3
Llanaway Cl GODL GU7 131 M7
Llanaway Rd GODL GU7 131 M7
Llangar Gv CWTH RG45 49 L4
Llanthony Rd MRDN SM4 43 P7
Llanvair Cl ASC SL5 34 A7
Llanvair Dr ASC SL5 33 P8
Lloyd Av COUL/CHIP CR5 80 C3
STRHM/NOR SW16 44 G2
Lloyd Park Av CROY/NA CR0 63 P3
Lloyd Rd WPK KT4 60 G2
Lloyds Ct CRAWE RH10 * 177 H2
Lloyds Wy BECK BR3 46 E6
Loats Rd BRXS/STRHM SW2 29 P2
Lobelia Rd CHOB/PIR GU24 70 G4
Lochaline St HMSMTH W6 18 G4
Lochinvar St BAL SW12 29 L3
Lochinver BRAK RG12 32 D8
Lock Cl ADL/WDHM KT15 73 J1
Locke-king Cl WEY KT13 56 C6
Locke King Rd WEY KT13 56 C6
Locke Rd LIPH GU30 182 G6
Lockesley Sq SURB KT6 * 41 K7
Lockestone Cl WEY KT13 56 B5
Locke Wy WOKN/KNAP GU21 11 F3
Lockfield Dr
WOKN/KNAP GU21 10 A4
Lockhart Rd COB KT11 75 L2
Lockhursthatch La
SHGR GU5 134 A7
Lock La WOKS/MYFD GU22 73 M5
Lock Rd ALDT GU11 108 F1
GU GU1 112 B1
RCHPK/HAM TW10 26 B7
Lock's La MTCM CR4 44 C2
Locksley Dr
WOKN/KNAP GU21 71 M6
Locksmeade Rd
RCHPK/HAM TW10 26 A7
Locks Meadow LING RH7 162 F3
Locks Ride ASC SL5 33 L1
Lockstone WEY KT13 56 B5
Lockswood CHOB/PIR GU24 71 H9
Lockton Cha ASC SL5 33 M4
Lockwood Cl FARN GU14 68 A8
HORS RH12 192 F5
SYD SE26 31 L7
Lockwood Ct CRAWE RH10 * 177 J3
Lockwood Pth
WOKN/KNAP GU21 73 H2
Lockwood Wy CHSGTN KT9 59 N4
Lockyer Pl BH/WHM TN16 * 105 H6
Locomotive Dr
EBED/NFELT TW14 24 B4
Loddon Cl CBLY GU15 69 J2
Loddon Rd FARN GU14 87 P1
Loddon Wy ASHV GU12 109 J5
Loder Cl WOKN/KNAP GU21 73 H2
Lodge Av CROY/NA CR0 63 H2
Lodgebottom Rd RDKG RH5 97 N7
Lodge Cl COB KT11 75 P5
CRAWW RH11 176 F5
EGH TW20 21 J8
EGRIN RH19 180 B2
EW KT17 60 C8
ISLW TW7 17 H6
LHD/OX KT22 96 D2
RDKG RH5 137 J2
WLGTN SM6 44 C9
Lodge Gdns BECK BR3 46 F6
Lodge Gv YTLY GU46 67 K2
Lodge Hl PUR/KEN CR8 81 J4
Lodge Hill Cl RFNM GU10 127 P7
Lodge Hill Rd RFNM GU10 127 P7
Lodge La BH/WHM TN16 104 G7
CROY/NA CR0 65 H6
RDKG RH5 137 M6
REDH RH1 140 A4
Lodge Pl SUT SM1 61 M4
Lodge Rd CROY/NA CR0 45 K7
LHD/OX KT22 96 C2
SUT SM1 61 M4
WLGTN SM6 62 D4
Lodge Wk WARL CR6 82 C5
Lodge Wy ASHF TW15 23 H5
SHPTN TW17 38 E3
Lodsworth FARN GU14 87 P4
Lofthouse Pl CHSGTN KT9 59 J5
Logan Cl HSLWW TW4 15 P8
Logan Ms ECT SW5 19 L2
Logan Pl ECT SW5 19 L2
Logmore La DORK RH4 136 E3
Lois Dr SHPTN TW17 38 D6
Lollesworth La EHSLY KT24 94 E6
Loman Rd FRIM GU16 89 J4
Lomas Cl CROY/NA CR0 65 J6
Lombard Rd BTSEA SW11 19 P7
WIM/MER SW19 43 M3
Lombard St MFD/CHID GU8 129 P7
Lombardy Cl
WOKN/KNAP GU21 71 M6
Lomond Gdns SAND/SEL CR2 64 E6
Loncin Mead Av
ADL/WDHM KT15 55 N7
Londlandes FLEETS GU52 106 E2
London La BMLY BR1 47 N1
SHGR GU5 134 C1
London Loop BNSTD SM7 79 K2
COUL/CHIP CR5 80 G8
CROY/NA CR0 64 D2
PUR/KEN CR8 81 N4
WWKM BR4 65 K2
London Rd ASC SL5 33 L4
BFOR GU20 52 C2
BH/WHM TN16 104 G3
BLKW GU17 68 A4
BMLY BR1 47 M1
BRAK RG12 32 F3
CHEAM SM3 61 J1
CRAWE RH10 176 G4
CROY/NA CR0 2 B1
CTHM CR3 101 M3
DTCH/LGLY SL3 12 A1
DTCH/LGLY SL3 12 A5
EGH TW20 36 A1
EGRIN RH19 180 D2
EW KT17 60 D7
FROW RH18 181 K7
FSTH SE23 31 K4
GU GU1 7 H3
HORS RH12 192 B8
ISLW TW7 16 F7
KUTN/CMB KT2 9 F4
LIPH GU30 182 F6
MRDN SM4 43 L6
MTCM CR4 44 A5
MTCM CR4 44 C8
REDH RH1 120 C2
REIG RH2 119 L4
RPLY/SEND GU23 93 J6
STA TW18 22 C7
STRHM/NOR SW16 45 H3
TWK TW1 25 P3
WLGTN SM6 62 D3
London Rd North REDH RH1 100 D4
London Rd South
REDH RH1 100 D9
London Sq GU GU1 * 7 H3
London Stile CHSWK W4 17 N3
London St CHERT KT16 37 L8
Loneacre BFOR GU20 * 52 E5
Lone Oak HORL RH6 160 C3
Lonesome La REIG RH2 119 N9
Lonesome Wy MTCM CR4 44 D2
Longacre ASHV GU12 109 J4
Long Acre CRAWE RH10 179 H3
Longacre Pl CAR SM5 * 62 C5
Long Av CHOB/PIR GU24 90 G1
Long Beech Dr FARN GU14 87 N4
Longbourne Wy CHERT KT16 37 K7
Longboyds COB KT11 75 K4
Long Br FNM GU9 5 G4
Longbridge Rd HORL RH6 159 J3
Longbridge Wk HORL RH6 159 J3

Longbridge Wy *HORL* RH6.....159 J3
Longchamp CI *HORL* RH6.....159 N1
Long Copse CI *GT/LBKH* KT23...96 B3
Longcroft *RFNM* GU10.....126 A8
Longcroft Av *BNSTD* SM7.....79 N5
Long Cross Hl *BOR* GU5.....164 B6
Longcross Rd *CHERT* KT16.....53 P2
Longdene Rd *HASM* GU27.....184 C4
Longdown *FLEETS* GU52.....86 F9
Longdown Rd *RFNM* GU10.....127 N7
Longdown La North
  EW KT17.....78 E2
Longdown La South
  EW KT17.....78 E4
Longdown Rd *CAT* SE6.....31 P7
  EW KT17.....78 E3
  RFNM GU10.....127M8
  RGUE GU4.....112 F8
  RGUE GU4.....49 L8
Long Dyke *GU* GU1.....112 F5
Longfellow Rd *WPK* KT4.....42 E9
Longfield *BMLY* BR1.....47M2
Longfield *WLGTN* SM6.....44 C9
Longfield CI *FARN* GU14.....68 C8
Longfields Crs
  SYD SE26.....78 G9
  SYD SE26.....31 K6
Longfield Dr
  MORT/ESHN SW14.....26 C1
  MTCM CR4.....44 A2
Longfield Rd *ASHV* GU12.....109 J4
  DORK RH4.....116 F8
Longfield St
  WAND/EARL SW18.....28 D3
Longford Av
  EBED/NFELT TW14.....23 P2
  STWL/WRAY TW19.....23 H4
  FELT TW13.....24 F6
  HPTN TW12.....25 H7
Longford CI *HOR/WEW* KT19...40 A5
  HPTN TW12.....25 J9
Longford Gdns *SUT* SM1.....61 N2
Longford Rd *WHTN* TW2.....25 H4
Longford Wy
  STWL/WRAY TW19.....23 H4
Long Garden Pl *FNM* GU9.....5 F2
Long Garden Wk East *FNM* GU9..5 F5
Long Garden Wk East
  FNM GU9.....5 F5
Long Garden Wk West
  FNM GU9.....5 F2
Long Garden Wy *FNM* GU9.....5 F5
Long Gore *GODL* GU7.....131 L5
Long Grove Rd
  HOR/WEW KT19.....59 P8
  PUR/KEN CR8.....62 C9
Longheath Dr *GT/LBKH* KT23..95 N4
Longheath Gdns
  CROY/NA CR0.....46 C6
  RFNM GU10.....128 C4
Long Hl Hill Rd *ASC* SL5.....33 J8
Longhope Dr *RFNM* GU10.....127 L7
Longhurst Rd *CRAWW* RH11..194 D1
  CROY/NA CR0.....46 B7
  EHSLY KT24.....94 C9
Longlands Av
  COUL/CHIP CR5.....80 D3
  CROY/NA CR0.....46 C7
  STWL/WRAY TW19.....23 J4
Longleat Sq *FARN* GU14.....88 C4
Longleat Wy
  EBED/NFELT TW14.....23 M3
  FNM GU9.....5 J5
  TOOT SW17.....29 H9
Long Lodge Dr
  WOT/HER KT12.....57 L2
Longmead *FLEETS* GU52.....86 C9
  GU GU1.....112 C5
Longmead CI *CTHM* CR3.....101 N1
Longmeadow *FRIM* GU16.....69 H5
  GT/LBKH KT23.....95 P5
Long Meadow CI *WWKM* BR4 ..47 J8
Longmead Rd
  HOR/WEW KT19.....60 C8
  THDIT KT7.....40 F8
  TOOT SW17.....29 J8
Longmere Gdns
  KWD/TDW/WH KT20.....78 G8
Longmere Rd *CRAWE* RH10..176 G3
Long Mickle *SHST* GU47.....49 L8
Longmoor Dr *LIPH* GU30.....182 A6
Longmoore St *EWKG* RG40.....48 C3
Longmore Rd *WOT/HER* KT12..57 N3
Longpoles Rd *CRAN* GU6.....171 J1
Long Reach *RPLY/SEND* GU23..94 D4
Longridge Gv
  WOKS/MYFD GU22.....73 J3
Longridge Rd *ECT* SW5.....19 L2
The Long Rdn *RFNM* GU10.....146 C1
Longs CI *WOKS/MYFD* GU22...73 L5
Longsdon Wy *CTHM* CR3.....102 A4
Long Shaw *LHD/OX* KT22.....76 G8
Longshot La *BRAK* RG12.....32 A3
Longside La *EGH* TW20.....36 C2
Longstaff Crs
  WAND/EARL SW18.....28 D2
Longstaff Rd
  WAND/EARL SW18.....28 D2
Longstone Rd *TOOT* SW17.....29 L8
Longthornton Rd
  STRHM/NOR SW16.....44 E3
Longton Av *SYD* SE26.....31 H7
Longton Gv *SYD* SE26.....31 J7
Long Wk *EPSOM* KT18.....78 G8
  NWMAL KT3.....42 A4
  WDSR SL4.....20 C1
The Long Wk *WDSR* SL4.....20 C4
Longwater La *EWKG* RG40.....48 C7

Longwater Rd *BRAK* RG12.....32 E7
  HTWY RG27.....48 D9
Longwood Av *DTCH/LGLY* SL3..12 F3
Longwood CI *WPK* KT4.....60 E1
Longwood Dr *PUT/ROE* SW15..27M2
Longwood Rd *PUR/KEN* CR8..81 M5
Longwood Vw *CRAWE* RH10..177 K8
Lonsdale Gdns *THHTH* CR7.....45 H5
Lonsdale Ms *RCH/KEW* TW9 *..17 N6
Lonsdale Rd *CHSWK* W4.....18 D2
  DORK RH4.....117 H6
  NWDGN UB2.....15 M1
  SNWD SE25.....46 B5
  WEY KT13.....56 C6
Loop Rd *EPSOM* KT18.....78 A5
  WOKS/MYFD GU22.....72 D9
Loppets Rd *CRAWE* RH10.....177 J7
Loraine Gdns *ASHTD* KT21.....77 L6
Loraine Rd *CHSWK* W4.....17 P4
Lord Chancellor Wk
  KUTN/CMB KT2.....42 A2
Lord Chatham's Ride
  RSEV TN14.....85 P6
Lord Knyvett CI
  STWL/WRAY TW19.....23 H2
Lord Knyvetts Ct
  STWL/WRAY TW19 *.....23 H2
Lord Napier Pl *HMSMTH* W6 ..18 E3
Lord Roberts Ms
  FUL/PGN SW6 *.....19 M5
Lordsbury Fld *WLGTN* SM6.....62 E8
Lords CI *DUL* SE21.....30 D5
  FELT TW13.....24 F5
Lordsgrove CI
  KWD/TDW/WH KT20.....78 F9
Lordshill Rd *SHGR* GU5.....132 G8
Lordship La *EDUL* SE22.....30 G2
Loretto CI *CRAN* GU6.....153 J9
Lorian Dr *REIG* RH2.....119 N4
Loriners *CRAWE* RH10.....176 G8
Loriners CI *COB* KT11.....75 J3
Loring Rd *ISLW* TW7.....16 F7
Loris Rd *HMSMTH* W6.....18 G1
Lorne Av *CROY/NA* CR0.....46 D8
Lorne Gdns *CROY/NA* CR0.....46 D8
  WOKN/KNAP GU21.....71 K8
Lorne Rd *RCHPK/HAM* TW10 ..26 E1
The Lorne *GT/LBKH* KT23.....96 A4
Lorraine Rd *CBLY* GU15.....51 H9
Lorry Rdg *BAGS* GU19.....51 N5
Loseberry Rd *ESH/CLAY* KT10..58 D4
Loseley Rd *GODL* GU7.....131 L5
Lothian Rd *CHOB/PIR* GU24..90 A1
Lothian Wd
  KWD/TDW/WH KT20.....98 F2
Lots Rd *WBPTN* SW10.....19 N5
Lotus Rd *BH/WHM* TN16.....84 D7
Loubet St *TOOT* SW17.....29 J5
Loudwater CI *SUN* TW16.....39 J5
Loughborough *BRAK* RG12 ....32 C7
Louisa CI *CHOB/PIR* GU24 *....43 L6
  ALDT GU11.....108 E4
Louis Flds *RGUW* GU3.....111 J1
Louisville Rd *TOOT* SW17.....29 K6
Louvaine Rd *BTSEA* SW11.....19 P9
Lovedean Ct *BRAK* RG12 *.....32 B9
Lovekyn CI *KUTN/CMB* KT2.....8 A4
Lovelace CI *EHSLY* KT24.....95 J3
Lovelace Dr
  WOKS/MYFD GU22.....73 K4
Lovelace Gdns *SURB* KT6.....41 K8
  WOT/HER KT12.....57 L4
Lovelace Rd *BRAK* RG12.....32 B7
  DUL SE21.....30 D5
  SURB KT6.....41 J8
Lovelands CI *CRAWW* RH11 ..176 D6
  KWD/TDW/WH KT20.....99 M7
Love La *CHEAM* SM3.....61 J5
  CDST RH9.....122 C5
  KWD/TDW/WH KT20.....98 E6
  MRDN SM4.....43 L8
  MTCM CR4.....44 A4
  SNWD SE25.....46 B4
  SURB KT6.....41 H9
Lovells CI *LTWR* GU18.....52 B8
Lovelock CI *PUR/KEN* CR8 ....81 L6
Lovers La *RFNM* GU10.....146 F5
Lovett Dr *CAR* SM5.....43 N8
Lovett Rd *STA* TW18.....21 N7
Lovibonds Av *ORP* BR6.....64 B9
Lowburys *DORK* RH4.....136 C1
Lowdells CI *EGRIN* RH19.....162 B8
Lowdells Dr *EGRIN* RH19.....162 B8
Lowdells La *EGRIN* RH19.....162 B9
Lowe CI *ALDT* GU11.....108 B5
  CRAWH RH11.....194 E2
Lower Addiscombe Rd
  CROY/NA CR0.....3 F1
Lower Barn CI *HORS* RH12..192 E5
Lower Barn Rd *PUR/KEN* CR8..81 L1
Lower Breache Rd
  CRAN GU6.....154 B8
Lower Bridge Rd *REDH* RH1..120 B5
Lower Broadmoor Rd
  CWTH RG45.....49 N5
Lower Canes *YTLY* GU46.....66 E1
Lower Church La *FNM* GU9 ....4 B4
Lower Church Rd *SHST* GU47..49 L8
Lower Church St
  CROY/NA CR0.....2 B4
Lower Common South
  PUT/ROE SW15.....18 F8
Lower Coombe St
  CROY/NA CR0.....2 C7
Lower Ct *HOR/WEW* KT19.....60 B9
Lower Court Rd
  HOR/WEW KT19.....60 A9
Lower Dene *EGRIN* RH19.....180 F2
Lower Downs Rd
  RYNPK SW20.....43 H2

Lower Dunnymans
  BNSTD SM7.....79 K3
Lower Eashing *GODL* GU7.....130 E9
Lower Edgeborough Rd
  GU GU1.....7 J4
Lower Farm Rd *EHSLY* KT24..95 K4
Lower Farnham Rd *ALDT*
  GU11.....108 E7
Lower Forecourt *HORL* RH6..159 L5
Lower Green Gdns *WPK* KT4..42 E9
Lower Green Rd
  ESH/CLAY KT10.....58 B1
  GU GU1.....6 E4
Lower Grove Rd
  RCHPK/HAM TW10.....26 E2
Lower Guildford Rd
  WOKN/KNAP GU21.....71 K6
Lower Ham La
  MFD/CHID GU8.....129 N9
Lower Hampton Rd
  SUN TW16.....39 M3
Lower Ham Rd
  KUTN/CMB KT2.....26 C9
Lower Hanger *HASM* GU27..183 M4
Lower Hill Rd
  HOR/WEW KT19.....77 P1
Lower House Rd
  MFD/CHID GU8.....166 G2
Lower Kings Rd
  KUTN/CMB KT2.....8 B1
Lower Manor Rd *GODL* GU7..131 J7
  MFD/CHID GU8.....149 M3
Lower Marsh La *BRYLDS* KT5..41 M5
Lower Mere *EGRIN* RH19.....180 E3
Lower Mill Fld *BAGS* GU19 ....51 L9
Lower Moor *YTLY* GU46.....67 H3
Lower Morden La *MRDN* SM4..42 G7
Lower Mortlake Rd
  RCH/KEW TW9.....17 L9
Lower Mount St
  FLEETN GU51.....86 C4
Lower Moushill La
  MFD/CHID GU8.....149 L3
Lower Newport Rd
  ASHV GU12.....108 F5
Lower Northfield *BNSTD* SM7..79 K4
Lower Park Rd
  COUL/CHIP CR5.....80 A7
Lower Peryers *EHSLY* KT24....94 G8
Lower Pillory Down *CAR* SM5..80 C2
Lower Richmond Rd
  PUT/ROE SW15.....18 G8
  RCH/KEW TW9.....17 N8
Lower Rd *GT/LBKH* KT23.....95 P6
  HASM GU27.....166 G9
  KWD/TDW/WH KT20.....98 G8
  PUR/KEN CR8.....81 K2
  REDH RH1.....119 P7
  SUT SM1.....61 P4
Lower Sandfields
  RPLY/SEND GU23.....93 H3
Lower Sand Mills *SURB* KT6....41 J8
Lower Sandhurst Rd
  EWKG RG40.....48 E7
Lower Sawleywood
  BNSTD SM7.....79 K3
Lower Shott *GT/LBKH* KT23....96 B6
Lower South St *GODL* GU7....131 K9
Lower South Vw *FNM* GU9 ....5 G2
Lower St *HASM* GU27.....184 D4
  SHGR GU5.....134 C1
Lower Sunbury Rd
  E/WMO/HCT KT8.....39 P3
Lower Tanbridge Wy
  HORS RH12.....192 A3
Lower Teddington Rd
  KUT/HW KT1.....8 B3
Lower Terrace Rd *FARN* GU14..88 C7
Lower Village Rd *ASC* SL5.....34 C6
Lower Weybourne La
  FNM GU9.....108 B8
Lower Wood Rd
  ESH/CLAY KT10.....58 C5
Lowfield CI *LTWR* GU18.....52 A9
Lowfield Heath Rd
  HORL RH6.....158 C6
Lowfield Rd *SWTR* RH13.....190 E7
Lowicks Rd *RFNM* GU10.....147 L6
Lowlands Rd *BLKW* GU17.....67 N4
  STWL/WRAY TW19.....22 G1
  FNM GU9.....108 D8
Lowndes Buildings
  FNM GU9.....5 F2
Lowry CI *SHST* GU47.....67 P2
Lowther Crs *MTCM* CR4.....44 A3
Lowther Hl *FSTH* SE23.....31 M3
Lowther Rd *BARN* SW13.....18 D6
  KUTN/CMB KT2.....8 G2
Loxford St *CTHM* CR3.....101 P5
Loxford Wy *CTHM* CR3.....101 P5
Loxley CI *SYD* SE26.....31 M5
Loxley Rd *HPTN* TW12.....24 G7
  WAND/EARL SW18.....28 C4
Loxton Rd *FSTH* SE23.....31 L4
Loxwood Av *FLEETN* GU51 ....86 E8
Loxwood CI
  EBED/NFELT TW14.....23 M2
  KWD/TDW/WH KT20.....99 L8
Loxwood Farm Pl *BIL* RH14..188 C6
Loxwood Rd *BIL* RH14.....187 M8
  BIL RH14.....188 C3
  CRAN GU6.....170 C7
Loxwood Wk *CRAWW* RH11 ..176 C4
Lucan Dr *STA* TW18.....37 P1
Lucas CI *EGRIN* RH19 *.....180 E2
  YTLY GU46.....67 H3
Lucas Fld *HASM* GU27.....183 P4
Lucas Green Rd
  EGRIN RH19.....161 L8
Lucas Rd *HORS* RH12.....191 M2
  PGE/AN SE20.....30 E9

Lucerne CI *WOKS/MYFD* GU22..72 C8
Lucerne Dr *CRAWE* RH10.....177 N7
Lucerne Rd *THHTH* CR7.....45 K6
Lucie Av *ASHF* TW15.....23 L9
Lucien Rd *TOOT* SW17.....29 K7
  WIM/MER SW19.....28 E5
Lucilina Dr *EDEN* TN8.....144 G5
Luddenham Av *VW* GU25.....36 D3
Ludford CI *CROY/NA* CR0.....2 A7
Ludlow *BRAK* RG12.....32 D8
Ludlow CI *FRIM* GU16.....69 J9
  HAYES BR2.....47 M3
Ludlow Rd *FELT* TW13.....24 B6
  GU GU1.....6 E5
Ludovick Wk *PUT/ROE* SW15..18 C9
Ludshott Gv *BOR* GU35.....164 E6
Luke Rd *ALDT* GU11.....108 A6
Luke Rd East *ALDT* GU11.....108 A6
Lullarook CI *BH/WHM* TN16..84 A5
Lullington Garth *BMLY* BR1.....47 L1
Lullington Rd *PGE/AN* SE20 ..46 A1
Lulworth Av *HEST* TW5.....16 B6
  WOKS/MYFD GU22.....72 A6
Lulworth CI *CRAWW* RH11 ..176 D8
  FARN GU14.....68 C9
Lulworth Crs *MTCM* CR4.....44 A3
Lumley Gdns *CHEAM* SM3....61 J4
Lumley Rd *CHEAM* SM3.....61 J5
  HORL RH6.....159 K1
Lunar CI *BH/WHM* TN16.....84 B5
Luna Rd *THHTH* CR7.....45 L4
Lundy CI *CRAWW* RH11.....176 F8
Lundy Dr *HYS/HAR* UB3.....14 G2
Lunghurst Rd *CTHM* CR3.....102 C1
Lunham Rd *NRWD* SE19.....30 F9
Lupin CI *BAGS* GU19.....51 L8
  BRXS/STRHM SW2.....30 C5
  CROY/NA CR0.....46 D9
  WDR/YW UB7.....13 P3
Lupin Ride *CWTH* RG45.....49 M1
Lurgan Av *HMSMTH* W6.....19 H4
Lushington Dr *COB* KT11.....75 J3
Lusted Hall La *BH/WHM* TN16..84 A4
Lusteds CI *DORK* RH4.....137 J1
Luther Ms *TEDD* TW11.....25 N8
Luther Rd *TEDD* TW11.....25 N8
Lutterworth CI *BNFD* RG42 ....32 E1
Luttrell Av *PUT/ROE* SW15 ....27 N1
Lutwyche Rd *FSTH* SE23.....31 N5
Lutyens CI *CRAWW* RH11.....176 B7
Luxemburg Gdns
  HMSMTH W6.....19 H2
Luxford CI *HORS* RH12.....192 E5
Luxfords La *EGRIN* RH19.....180 G6
Luxted Rd *ORP* BR6.....84 E1
Lyall Av *DUL* SE21.....30 G5
Lyall PI *FNM* GU9.....107M7
Lych Gate CI *SHST* GU47.....49 K9
Lyconby Gdns *CROY/NA* CR0..46 E8
Lydbury *BRAK* RG12.....33 H4
Lydden Gv *WAND/EARL* SW18..28 D3
Lydden Rd *WAND/EARL* SW18..28 D3
Lydele CI *WOKN/KNAP* GU21..72 A4
Lydens La *EDEN* TN8.....145 K7
Lydford CI *FARN* GU14 *.....68 C9
  FRIM GU16.....69 J9
Lydhurst Av
  BRXS/STRHM SW2.....30 A5
Lydney *BRAK* RG12.....32 D8
Lydney CI *WIM/MER* SW19.....28 B5
Lye Copse Av *FARN* GU14.....68 E8
Lyefield La *RDKG* RH5.....154 D6
The Lye *KWD/TDW/WH* KT20..98 G2
Lyfield *LHD/OX* KT22.....76 B3
Lyford Rd *WAND/EARL* SW18..28 G3
Lyham CI *BRXS/STRHM* SW2 ..29 P1
Lyham Rd *BRXS/STRHM* SW2..29 P1
Lyle CI *MTCM* CR4.....44 C8
Lymbourne CI *BELMT* SM2 ....61 L8
Lymden Gdns *REIG* RH2.....119M7
Lymer Av *NRWD* SE19.....30 C8
Lyme Regis Rd *BNSTD* SM7 ..79 K6
Lymescote Gdns *SUT* SM1 ....61 L1
Lyminge Gdns
  WAND/EARL SW18.....29 H4
Lymington CI *YTLY* GU46.....66 G3
Lymington CI
  STRHM/NOR SW16.....44 F3
Lymington Gdns
  HOR/WEW KT19.....60 D4
Lynams *FLEETS* GU52.....106 E3
Lynchborough Rd
  LIPH GU30.....182 A2
Lynchen CI *HEST* TW5.....15 J6
Lynchford La *FARN* GU14.....88 G6
Lynchford Rd *FARN* GU14.....88 E7
Lyncroft Gdns *EW* KT17.....60 D7
  HSLW TW3.....25 K1
Lyndale *THDIT* KT7 *.....40 E8
Lyndale CI *REDH* RH1.....120 B2
Lyndale Hampton Court Wy
  THDIT KT7.....40 E8
Lyndale Rd *REDH* RH1.....120 B2
Lyndford Ter *FLEETS* GU52 ....86 F8
Lyndhurst Av *ALDT* GU11.....108 E8
  BLKW GU17.....67 P3
  BRYLDS KT5.....41 P9
  STRHM/NOR SW16.....44 F3
  SUN TW16.....39 J4
  WHTN TW2.....24 G4
Lyndhurst CI *BRAK* RG12 ......33 J4
  CRAWW RH11.....176 C6
  CROY/NA CR0.....3 J6
  WOKN/KNAP GU21.....72 B4
Lyndhurst Ct *BELMT* SM2 *....61 L6
Lyndhurst Dr *NWMAL* KT3 ....42 C7
Lyndhurst Farm CI
  EGRIN RH19.....161 L8
Lyndhurst Leys *HAYES* BR2 *..47 K3
Lyndhurst Prior
  SNWD SE25 *.....45 N4

Lyndhurst Rd *ASC* SL5.....34 A5
  COUL/CHIP CR5.....80 C5
  FLEETN GU51.....86 C3
  REIG RH2.....119 J7
Lyndhurst Wy *BELMT* SM2.....61 L7
  CHERT KT16.....54 C6
Lyndon Av *WLGTN* SM6.....62 C2
Lyndon Yd *TOOT* SW17.....28 E7
Lyndsey CI *FARN* GU14.....87M3
Lyndwood Dr *WDSR* SL4.....20 F2
Lyndwood Pde *WDSR* SL4 *....20 F2
Lyne CI *VW* GU25.....36 D7
Lyne Crossing Rd *VW* GU25 ..36 E7
Lynegrove Av *ASHF* TW15.....23 M8
Lyneham Rd *CWTH* RG45.....49 M4
Lyne La *ECH* TW20.....36 E6
Lyne Rd *VW* GU25.....36 C7
Lynette Av *CLAP* SW4.....29 L2
Lynmead CI *EDEN* TN8.....144 F1
Lynmouth Av *MRDN* SM4.....43 H8
Lynmouth Gdns *HEST* TW5 ....15 M6
Lynn CI *ASHF* TW15.....23 M8
Lynne CI *SAND/SEL* CR2.....64 C9
Lynne Wk *ESH/CLAY* KT10 ....58 C4
Lynn Rd *BAL* SW12.....29 L3
Lynn Wk *REIG* RH2.....119 M7
Lynn Wy *FARN* GU14.....68 B9
Lynscott Wy *SAND/SEL* CR2 ..63 K7
Lynsted Ct *BECK* BR3.....46 E3
Lynton CI *CHSGTN* KT9.....59 L3
  EGRIN RH19.....180 F1
  FNM GU9.....127 L6
Lynton Park Av *EGRIN* RH19..180 F1
Lynton Rd *CROY/NA* CR0.....45 J7
  NWMAL KT3.....42 B6
Lynwick St *HORS* RH12.....189 N1
Lynwood *GUW* GU2.....6 A5
Lynwood Av *COUL/CHIP* CR5..80 D4
  DTCH/LGLY SL3.....12 B3
  ECH TW20.....21 K9
  EW KT17.....78 C5
Lynwood Cha *BRAK* RG12 ....32 E1
Lynwood Ct
  WOKN/KNAP GU21.....73 H2
Lynwood Crs *ASC* SL5.....34 E7
Lynwood Dr *FRIM* GU16.....89 J4
  WPK KT4.....60 E1
Lynwood Gdns *CROY/NA* CR0..63 K3
Lynwood Rd *EW* KT17.....78 D3
  REDH RH1.....120 C3
  THDIT KT7.....58 F1
  TOOT SW17.....29 J6
Lyon CI *CRAWE* RH10.....177 M9
Lyon Rd *CWTH* RG45.....49 N3
  WIM/MER SW19.....43 N2
  WOT/HER KT12.....57 N1
Lyons CI *SWTR* RH13.....190 E7
Lyons Ct *DORK* RH4.....117 H7
Lyonsdene
  KWD/TDW/WH KT20.....99 K7
Lyons Dr *GUW* GU2.....91 N9
Lyons Rd *SWTR* RH13.....190 F7
Lyons Wk *WKENS* W14.....19 J2
Lyon Wy *FRIM* GU16.....68 E7
Lyric CI *SHST* GU47.....49 L9
Lyric Rd *BARN* SW13.....18 D6
Lysander Gdns *SURB* KT6.....41 M7
Lysander Rd *CROY/NA* CR0 ..63 H5
Lysander Wy *FARN* GU14.....88 D2
Lysias Rd *BAL* SW12.....29 L2
Lysons Av *ASHV* GU12.....89 H7
Lysons Rd *ALDT* GU11.....108 C5
Lysons Wk *PUT/ROE* SW15 *..27 M7
Lyster Ms *COB* KT11.....75 J2
Lytchet Minster CI
  BRAK RG12.....33 H6
Lytchet Rd *BMLY* BR1.....33 M1
Lytchgate CI *SAND/SEL* CR2..63 P4
Lytcott Dr *E/WMO/HCT* KT8 ..39 P4
Lytcott Gv *EDUL* SE22.....30 G1
Lytham *BRAK* RG12.....32 A7
Lytton Dr *CRAWE* RH10.....177 N4
Lytton Gdns *WLGTN* SM6.....62 F3
Lytton Gv *PUT/ROE* SW15.....28 A1
Lytton Pk *COB* KT11.....75 P1
Lytton Rd *WOKS/MYFD* GU22..11 J3
Lyveden Rd *TOOT* SW17.....29 N1
Lywood CI
  KWD/TDW/WH KT20.....98 G2

M

Mabbotts
  KWD/TDW/WH KT20.....99 H1
Mabel St *WOKN/KNAP* GU21..10 A5
Maberley Crs *NRWD* SE19.....46 C1
Maberley Rd *BECK* BR3.....46 D4
  NRWD SE19.....45 P2
Mablethorpe Rd
  FUL/PGN SW6.....19 J5
Macadam Av *CWTH* RG45 *....49 P1
Macaulay Av *ESH/CLAY* KT10..58 E1
Macaulay Rd *CTHM* CR3.....101 N2
Macbeth Ct *BNFD* RG42.....32 G2
Macbeth St *HMSMTH* W6.....18 F3
Macclesfield Rd *SNWD* SE25..46 B6
Macdonald Rd *FNM* GU9.....107M7
  LTWR GU18.....51 P9
Macdowall Rd *GUW* GU2.....91 N9
Mace La *RSEV* TN14.....85 H2
Macfarlane La *ISLW* TW7.....16 F4

Mackenzie Rd *BECK* BR3......46 E2
Mackie Rd *BRXS/STRHM* SW2...30 B3
Mackies HI *SHGR* GU5......134 G7
Maclean Rd *FSTH* SE23......31 M2
Macleod Rd *SWTR* RH13......192 D7
Maclise Rd *WKENS* W14......19 J1
Macmillan Wy *TOOT* SW17......29 L7
Macnaghten Woods
CBLY GU15......68 C2
Macrae Rd *YTLY* GU46......66 C2
Madan Cl *BH/WHM* TN16......105 J5
Madan Rd *BH/WHM* TN16......105 H5
Maddison Cl *TEDD* TW11......25 N9
Maddox Dr *CRAWE* RH10......177 N6
Maddox La *GT/LBKH* KT23......95 N4
Maddox Pk *GT/LBKH* KT23......95 N5
Madeira Cl *CRAWW* RH11...176 C8
Madeira Av *BMLY* BR1......47 L2
HORS RH12......192 B8
Madeira Crs *BF/WBF* KT14......73 K2
Madeira Rd *BF/WBF* KT14......73 K2
MTCM CR4......44 B5
STRHM/NOR SW16......44 F2
Madeley Wk *EPSOM* KT18......78 B5
Madeley Rd *FLEETS* GU52......87 H9
Madeline Rd *PGE/AN* SE20......46 A1
Madgehole La *SHGR* GU5......133 M9
Madingley *BRAK* RG12......32 D9
Madox Brown End
SHST GU47......68 A2
Madrid Rd *BARN* SW13......18 E6
GUW GU2......6 A5
Maesmaur Rd
BH/WHM TN16......104 B1
Mafeking Av *BTFD* TW8......17 L4
Mafeking Rd
STWL/WRAY TW19......21 N5
Magazine PI *LHD/OX* KT22......97 H2
Magazine Rd *CTHM* CR3......101 K2
FARN GU14......87 P7
Magdala Rd *ISLW* TW7......16 G8
SAND/SEL CR2......63 M6
Magdalen Cl *BF/WBF* KT14...74 A3
Magdalen Crs *BF/WBF* KT14...74 A3
Magdalene Cl *CRAWE* RH10...177 M2
Magdalene Rd *SHPTN* TW17...38 B5
SHST GU47......50 B7
Magdalen Rd
WAND/EARL SW18......28 F4
Magellan Ter *CRAWE* RH10 *...177 K1
Magna Carta La
STWL/WRAY TW19......21 K4
Magna Rd *EGH* TW20......20 C9
Magnolia Cl *KUTN/CMB* KT2...26 C9
SHST GU47......49 P8
Magnolia Ct *HORL* RH6 *....159 K1
Magnolia Dr *BH/WHM* TN16...84 B5
Magnolia PI *CLAP* SW4......29 P1
GU GU1 *......112 A2
Magnolia Rd *CHSWK* W4 *...17 P4
Magnolia St *WDR/YW* UB7...13 P2
Magnolia Wy *FLEETS* GU52...86 G8
HOR/WEW KT19......60 A4
RDKG RH5......137 K1
Magnolia Whf *CHSWK* W4 *...17 P4
Magpie Cl *COUL/CHIP* CR5...80 E7
FRIM GU16......107 H6
Maguire Dr *FRIM* GU16......69 L5
RCHPK/HAM TW10......26 B7
Mahonia Cl *CHOB/PIR* GU24 *...70 F2
Maida Rd *ALDT* GU11......108 D2
Maidenbower Dr
CRAWE RH10......177 N7
Maidenbower La
CRAWE RH10......177 L7
Maidenbower PI
CRAWE RH10......177 M7
Maiden La *CRAWW* RH11...176 F3
Maidenshaw Rd
HOR/WEW KT19......78 B1
Main Dr *ASC* SL5......13 J3
DTCH/LGLY SL3......13 J1
Main Gate Rd *FARN* GU14...88 D5
Mainprize Rd *BRAK* RG12......32 C2
Main Rd *BH/WHM* TN16......84 A2
EDEN TN8......124 F9
RSEV TN14......85 L7
Mainstone Cl *FRIM* GU16......69 L9
Mainstone Crs
CHOB/PIR GU24......90 D1
Mainstone Rd
CHOB/PIR GU24......70 F5
Main St *ADL/WDHM* KT15......56 A4
FELT TW13......24 E8
Maise Webster Cl
STWL/WRAY TW19 *......22 G3
Maitland Cl *BF/WBF* KT14...73 L2
HSLWW TW4......15 P8
WOT/HER KT12......57 N1
Maitland Rd *FARN* GU14......88 D7
PGE/AN SE20......46 C1
Maitlands Cl *RFNM* GU10...108 G8
Maizecroft *HORL* RH6......140 G8
Major's Farm Rd
DTCH/LGLY SL3......12 C5
Major's HI *CRAWE* RH10......178 E7
Makepeace Rd *BNFD* RG42...32 D1
Malacca Farm *RGUE* GU4......93 M8
Malan Cl *BH/WHM* TN16......84 C6
Malcolm Rd *PUT/ROE* SW15...18 F9
Malcolm Cl *PGE/AN* SE20 *...46 C1
Malcolm Dr *SURB* KT6......41 K9
Malcolm Gdns *HORL* RH6...158 G3
Malcolm Rd *COUL/CHIP* CR5...80 F4
PGE/AN SE20......46 A1
SNWD SE25......46 A7
Malden Av *WNWD* SE27......30 D8
Malden Green Av *WPK* KT4...42 D9
Malden HI *NWMAL* KT3......42 D5
Malden Hill Gdns *NWMAL* KT3...42 D4

Malden Pk *NWMAL* KT3......42 D7
Malden Rd *CHEAM* SM3......61 H5
NWMAL KT3......42 D8
WWKM BR4......42 D8
Malden Wy *NWMAL* KT3......42 D8
Malden Rd *WLGTN* SM6......62 D4
Malet Cl *EGH* TW20 *......22 A9
Maley Av *WNWD* SE27......30 C5
Malham Cl *CRAWE* RH10...177 M8
Malham Fell *BRAK* RG12......32 C5
Malham La *FSTH* SE23......31 L4
Mallard Cl *ASHV* GU12......109 H4
HASM GU27......183 P4
HORL RH6......140 D8
HORS RH12......192 B5
REDH RH1......120 C2
WHTN TW2......25 H3
Mallard Ct *DORK* RH4 *......116 G6
Mallard PI *EGRIN* RH19......180 E5
TWK TW1......25 P6
Mallards Wy *LTWR* GU18......52 A9
Mallard Rd *SAND/SEL* CR2...64 D8
Mallard's Reach *WEY* KT13...56 F1
The Mallards *FRIM* GU16......69 H6
STA TW18......37 M3
Mallards Wy *LTWR* GU18......52 A9
Mallard Wk *BECK* BR3......46 D6
Mallard Wy *WLGTN* SM6......62 E7
YTLY GU46 *......66 F2
Malling Cl *CROY/NA* CR0 *...46 C7
Malling Gdns *MRDN* SM4......43 N7
Malling Wy *HAYES* BR2......47 M8
Mallinson Rd *BTSEA* SW11...29 H1
CROY/NA CR0......62 F2
Mallord St *CHEL* SW3 *......19 P4
Mallow Cl *CROY/NA* CR0......46 D9
HORS RH12......192 D4
KWD/TDW/WH KT20......78 F3
Mallow Crs *RGUE* GU4......112 D1
Mallowdale Rd *BRAK* RG12...32 G8
Malll Rd *HMSMTH* W6......18 F3
The Mall *MORT/ESHN* SW14...27 H1
SURB KT6......41 K6
Mall Vls *HMSMTH* W6 *......18 F3
Malmains Cl *BECK* BR3......47 K6
Malmains Wy *BECK* BR3......47 J6
Malmesbury Rd *MRDN* SM4...43 N8
Malmstone Av *REDH* RH1...100 F8
Malory Cl *BECK* BR3......46 E3
Malta Rd *FRIM* GU16......69 M8
Maltby Rd *CHSGTN* KT9......59 N5
Malt HI *EGH* TW20......21 K8
Malthouse Cl *FLEETS* GU52...106 C1
Malt House Cl *WDSR* SL4......20 C1
Malthouse Ct
CHOB/PIR GU24 *......70 F1
RGUE GU4......132 C1
Malthouse Dr *FELT* TW13......24 E8
Malthouse La
CHOB/PIR GU24......70 F1
MFD/CHID GU8......168 B2
RGUW GU3......91 J4
Malthouse Md
MFD/CHID GU8......149 N7
Malthouse Mdw *LIPH* GU30...182 G6
Malthouse Rd *CRAWE* RH10...176 G6
Maltings PI *FUL/PGN* SW6...19 M6
The Maltings *BF/WBF* KT14...74 A2
LIPH GU30......182 G6
OXTED RH8......123 M2
SNWD SE25 *......45 N4
STA TW18......22 B7
Malting Wy *ISLW* TW7......16 F8
Malus Cl *ADL/WDHM* KT15...55 K6
Malus Dr *ADL/WDHM* KT15...55 K6
Malva Cl *WAND/EARL* SW18...28 E1
Malvern Dr *FELT* TW13......24 E8
Malvern Cl *CHERT* KT16......54 C5
MTCM CR4......44 G4
SURB KT6......41 L9
Malvern Rd *BLKW* GU17......67 K7
CRAWW RH11......176 F7
FARN GU14......87 P9
HPTN TW12......40 A2
HYS/HAR UB3......14 G5
SURB KT6......59 L1
THHTH CR7......45 J5
Malwood Rd *BAL* SW12......29 L2
The Malyons *SHPTN* TW17 *...38 F7
Manbre Rd *HMSMTH* W6......18 G4
Manchester Rd *THHTH* CR7...45 L4
Manchuria Rd *BTSEA* SW11...29 K2
Mandalay Rd *CLAP* SW4......29 M1
Mandeville Cl *GUW* GU2......111 N2
WIM/MER SW19......43 J1
Mandeville Dr *SURB* KT6......41 K9
Mandeville Rd *ISLW* TW7......16 G5
SHPTN TW17......38 C6
Mandora Rd *ALDT* GU11...108 D2
Mandrake Rd *TOOT* SW17...29 K6
Mandrell Rd
BRXS/STRHM SW2......29 P1
Manfield Pk *CRAN* GU6......152 E7
Manfield Rd *ASHV* GU12......109 J4
Manford Rd *PUT/ROE* SW15...28 C1
Mangles Rd *GU* GU1......112 B3
Manley Bridge Rd
RFNM GU10......127 J9
Mannamead *EPSOM* KT18...78 C8
Mannamead Cl *EPSOM* KT18...78 C8
Mann Cl *CRAWW* RH11......194 E2
CROY/NA CR0......2 C5
Manning Cl *EGRIN* RH19......180 C1
Manning PI
RCHPK/HAM TW10......26 E1
Mannings Cl *CRAWE* RH10...177 N2
Manningtree Cl
WIM/MER SW19......28 B4
Mann's Cl *ISLW* TW7......25 N1
Manoel Rd *WHTN* TW2......25 K5
Manor Av *CTHM* CR3......101 N4
HSLWW TW4......15 M8
Manor Cha *WEY* KT13......56 D4

Manor Cl *BNFD* RG42......32 C1
EHSLY KT24......94 G8
RFNM GU10......109 H7
HASM GU27......183 P4
HORL RH6......159 J1
RFNM GU10......109 H7
RFNM GU10......109 H7
WARL CR6......82 E6
WOKS/MYFD GU22......73 K5
WPK KT4......42 C9
Manor Ct *ACT* W3 *......17 N2
E/WMO/HCT KT8......40 A5
FLEETS GU52......106 C2
HORS RH12 *......192 F6
KUTN/CMB KT2 *......9 J3
WEY KT13......56 D3
Manor Crs *BF/WBF* KT14......74 B2
BRYLDS KT5......41 N7
CHOB/PIR GU24......90 C1
GUW GU2......111 P3
HASM GU27......183 P4
HOR/WEW KT19......60 C5
HORL RH16......159 J1
WEY KT13......56 D3
Manorcrofts Rd *EGH* TW20...21 M9
Manordene Cl *THDIT* KT7......40 G9
Manor Dr *ADL/WDHM* KT15...55 L8
SWTR RH13......192 E10
FELT TW13......24 E8
HOR/WEW KT19......60 C5
HORL RH16......159 J1
Manor Dr North *NWMAL* KT3...42 B8
The Manor Dr *WPK* KT4......42 B9
Manor Farm *RGUW* GU3......110 C8
Manor Farm Av *SHPTN* TW17...38 D7
Manor Farm Cl
ASHV GU12 *......109 H5
RGUW GU3......110 B3
Manor Farm Cottages
WDSR SL4......20 F1
Manor Farm La *EGH* TW20 *...21 M8
Manor Farm La *EGH* TW20...21 M8
Manor Farm Rd
STRHM/NOR SW16......45 J3
Manorfields *CRAWW* RH11...176 A9
Manor Flds *LIPH* GU30......182 C6
Manor Gdns *ACT* W3......17 N2
EHSLY KT24......95 M8
GODL GU7......131 L6
GUW GU2......111 P3
HPTN TW12......40 B1
RCH/KEW TW9......17 M9
RGUE GU4......132 E5
RYNPK SW20......43 K3
SAND/SEL CR2......63 P5
SUN TW16......39 J2
Manorgate Rd
KUTN/CMB KT2......9 J3
Manor Green Rd
HOR/WEW KT19......78 A1
Manor Gv *BECK* BR3......47 H3
RCH/KEW TW9......17 N9
Manor HI *BNSTD* SM7......80 B4
Manor House Ct
EPSOM KT18 *......78 A2
SHPTN TW17 *......38 D8
Manor House Dr *ASC* SL5......34 A1
WOT/HER KT12......57 H4
Manor House Gdns
EDEN TN8......144 G4
Manorhouse La
GT/LBKH KT23......95 H6
Manor House Wy *ISLW* TW7...17 H8
Manor La *FELT* TW13......24 B5
HYS/HAR UB3......14 F4
KWD/TDW/WH KT20......99 L9
SHGR GU5......152 B1
SUN TW16......39 K3
SUT SM1......61 N4
Manor Lea Rd
MFD/CHID GU8......149 M2
Manor Leaze *EGH* TW20......21 N8
Manor Pk *RCH/KEW* TW9...17 M9
STA TW18......22 A6
Manor Park Cl *WWKM* BR4...47 N6
Manor Park Dr *EWKG* RG40...48 C3
HOR/WEW KT19......60 C5
Manor Park Rd *SUT* SM1......61 M4
WWKM BR4......47 N6
Manor Pl *BRKHM/BTCW* RH3...117 P6
CTHM CR3......101 P6
EBED/NFELT TW14......24 B4
GT/LBKH KT23......96 A6
MTCM CR4......44 E4
STA TW18......22 E8
SUT SM1......61 M4
Manor Rd *ALDT* GU11......108 C6
ASC SL5......34 A3
ASHV GU12......109 H5
BECK BR3......46 G3
BELMT SM2......61 K6
BH/WHM TN16......84 C9
E/WMO/HCT KT8......40 D5
EDEN TN8......144 F4
EGRIN RH19......180 D6
FARN GU14......88 F4
FNM GU9......128 A1
GUW GU2......111 P3
HORS RH12......192 E5
MTCM CR4......44 E4
RCH/KEW TW9......17 M8
REDH RH1......100 E9
REIG RH2......119 H3
RPLY/SEND GU23......93 K3
RSEV TN14......105 P4
SNWD SE25......46 A5
TEDD TW11......25 P8
WHTN TW2......25 H3
WLGTN SM6......62 D4
WOKN/KNAP GU21......72 A5
WOT/HER KT12......39 J8
WWKM BR4......65 H1

Manor Rd North
ESH/CLAY KT10......58 F2
WLGTN SM6......62 D3
Manor Rd South
ESH/CLAY KT10......58 D3
Manor Royal *CRAWE* RH10...177 H2
Manorside Cl *RFNM* GU10...109 H6
The Manor *MFD/CHID* GU8...149 N3
Manor V *BTFD* TW8......17 J5
Manor Wk *ASHV* GU12......108 D5
WEY KT13......56 D4
Manor Wy *BAGS* GU19......51 M8
BECK BR3......46 G4
BNSTD SM7......80 B2
EGH TW20......21 L9
GUW GU2......111 L8
LHD/OX KT22......76 C5
MTCM CR4......44 E4
NWDGN UB2......15 M2
PUR/KEN CR8......80 G1
SAND/SEL CR2......63 N5
WOKS/MYFD GU22......72 F9
WPK KT4......42 C9
The Manor Wy *WLGTN* SM6...62 D3
Manor Wood Rd
PUR/KEN CR8......80 C2
Manresa Rd *CHEL* SW3 *......19 P3
Mansard Beeches
TOOT SW17......29 K8
Manse Cl *HYS/HAR* UB3......14 F4
Mansel Cl *GUW* GU2......91 P9
Mansell Wy *CTHM* CR3......101 L2
Mansel Rd *WIM/MER* SW19...28 B9
Mansfield Cl *ASC* SL5......33 M3
Mansfield Crs *BRAK* RG12...32 D7
Mansfield Dr *REDH* RH1......100 F8
Mansfield PI *ASC* SL5......33 M3
Mansfield Rd *CHSGTN* KT9...59 J4
SAND/SEL CR2......63 M5
Manship Rd *MTCM* CR4......44 C2
Manson Ms *SKENS* SW7 *...19 N2
Manson Ms *SKENS* SW7......19 P2
Manston Cl *PGE/AN* SE20...46 C2
Manston Dr *BRAK* RG12......32 D7
Manston Gv *KUTN/CMB* KT2...26 C6
Manston Rd *RGUE* GU4......112 E1
Mantilla Rd *TOOT* SW17......29 K7
Mantlet Cl *STRHM/NOR* SW16...44 E1
Manton Ter
ADL/WDHM KT15 *......55 N3
Mantua St *BTSEA* SW11......19 H9
Manville Gdns *TOOT* SW17...29 L6
Manville Rd *TOOT* SW17......29 K5
Manwood Rd *BROCKY* SE4...31 N2
Manygate La *SHPTN* TW17...38 E7
Many Gates *BAL* SW12......29 L5
Maori Rd *GU* GU1......7 K3
Maple Cl *ASHV* GU12......89 H9
BLKW GU17......67 N5
CLAP SW4......29 N2
CRAWW RH11......176 F2
HORS RH12......192 F5
HPTN TW12......24 G9
MTCM CR4......44 C2
SHST GU47......49 K8
Maple Ct *ASHF* TW15......23 P8
EGH TW20......20 C9
NWMAL KT3......42 B4
Mapledrakes Cl *CRAN* GU6...153 P7
Mapledrakes Rd *CRAN* GU6...153 P7
Maple Dr *CWTH* RG45......49 N2
EGRIN RH19......180 F2
LTWR GU18......51 P9
Maple Gdns
STWL/WRAY TW19......23 H5
YTLY GU46......67 H3
Maple Gv *BTFD* TW8......17 H5
EA W5......17 K1
GU GU1......112 B3
WOKS/MYFD GU22......92 C1
Maplehatch Cl *GODL* GU7...150 D2
Maplehurst *LHD/OX* KT22...96 D3
Maplehurst Cl *KUT/HW* KT1...41 L5
Maple Leaf Cl *FARN* GU14...88 B4
Maple Ms *STRHM/NOR* SW16...30 A8
Maple PI *BNSTD* SM7......79 H5
Maple Rd *ASHTD* KT21......77 J8
EGH TW20......20 C9
REDH RH1......120 B9
RPLY/SEND GU23......93 L4
SURB KT6......41 L6
Maplestead Rd
BRXS/STRHM SW2......30 A3
The Maples *BNSTD* SM7......79 M2
ESH/CLAY KT10 *......58 G6
KUT/HW KT1 *......41 J1
Maplethorpe Rd *THHTH* CR7...45 J5
Mapleton Cl *HAYES* BR2......47 N6
Mapleton Crs
WAND/EARL SW18......28 E2
Mapleton Rd *BH/WHM* TN16...125 L0
EDEN TN8......125 L6
WAND/EARL SW18......28 E2
Maple Wk *ASHV* GU12......108 D5
Maple Wy *BOR* GU35......164 E5
COUL/CHIP CR5......100 D1
FELT TW13......24 B6
Maplin Pk *DTCH/LGLY* SL3...12 F1
Marble Hill Cl *TWK* TW1......26 A3
Marble Hill Gdns *TWK* TW1...26 A3
Marbles Wy
KWD/TDW/WH KT20......79 H8
Marbull Wy *WLGTN* SM6 *...62 E7
Marchbank Rd *WKENS* W14...19 K4
Marcheria Cl *BRAK* RG12......32 D7
Marches Rd *HORS* RH12......173 M3
The Marches *HORS* RH12...174 A6
Marchmont Rd
RCHPK/HAM TW10......26 E1
WLGTN SM6......62 E7

March Rd *TWK* TW1......25 N3
WEY KT13......56 C4
Marchside Cl *HEST* TW5......15 M6
Marcilly Rd
WAND/EARL SW18......28 G1
Marco Rd *HMSMTH* W6......18 F1
Marcus Ct
WOKS/MYFD GU22 *......10 E5
Marcuse Rd *CTHM* CR3......101 L3
Marcus Garvey Ms
EDUL SE22......31 J2
Marcus St *WAND/EARL* SW18...28 E2
Mardale *CBLY* GU15......69 L4
Mardell Rd *CROY/NA* CR0...46 D6
Marden Av *HAYES* BR2......47 N7
Marden Crs *CROY/NA* CR0...45 H7
Marden Rd *CROY/NA* CR0...45 H7
The Mardens *CRAWW* RH11...176 B4
Mare HI *MFD/CHID* GU8......149 M7
Mare La *MFD/CHID* GU8......150 D8
Mareschal Rd *GU* GU2......6 C1
Maresfield *CROY/NA* CR0......3 H5
Marfield Cl *WPK* KT4......42 E9
Marfleet Cl *CAR* SM5......62 A1
Margaret Cl *STA* TW18......37 P1
Margaret Ingram Cl
FUL/PGN SW6 *......19 K4
Margaret Lockwood Cl
KUT/HW KT1 *......41 M5
Margaret Rd *GU* GU1......7 H4
Margaret Wy *COUL/CHIP* CR5...81 K8
Margate Rd
BRXS/STRHM SW2......29 P1
Margery Gv
KWD/TDW/WH KT20......99 J9
Margery La
KWD/TDW/WH KT20......99 K9
Margin Dr *WIM/MER* SW19...28 A8
Margravine Gdns
HMSMTH W6......19 H3
Margravine Rd *HMSMTH* W6...19 H4
Marham Gdns *MRDN* SM4...43 N7
WAND/EARL SW18......28 G5
Marian Rd *STRHM/NOR* SW16...44 E2
Maria Theresa Cl *NWMAL* KT3...42 B6
Mariette Wy *WLGTN* SM6......62 G7
Marigold Cl *CWTH* RG45......49 K2
Marigold Ct *GU* GU1......112 C2
Marigold Dr *CHOB/PIR* GU24...70 G3
Marigold Wy *CROY/NA* CR0...46 D9
Marina Av *NWMAL* KT3......42 F7
Marina Cl *CHERT* KT16......37 M9
Marina Pde *STA* TW18 *......37 M2
Marina Wy *TEDD* TW11......41 K1
Marinefield Rd *FUL/PGN* SW6...19 M7
Mariner Gdns
RCHPK/HAM TW10......26 A6
Mariners Dr *FARN* GU14......88 A5
Marion Av *SHPTN* TW17......38 D6
Marion Ms *DUL* SE21......30 E6
Marion Rd *CRAWE* RH10......177 L8
THHTH CR7......45 L6
Marius Rd *TOOT* SW17......29 K5
Marjoram Cl *FARN* GU14......87 M3
GUW GU2......111 N1
Markedge La *REDH* RH1......100 B7
Markenfield Rd *GU* GU1......6 E3
Markenhorn *GODL* GU7......131 K6
Market Centre *NWDGN* UB2 *...15 K2
Market Field Rd *REDH* RH1...120 B5
Marketfield Wy *REDH* RH1...120 B5
Market La *DTCH/LGLY* SL3...12 C1
Market Pde *BMLY* BR1 *......47 N2
EW KT17 *......60 D7
FELT TW13 *......24 F5
SNWD SE25 *......46 A5
Market PI *BRAK* RG12......32 D3
BTFD TW8......17 J5
DTCH/LGLY SL3 *......12 C5
KUT/HW KT1......8 C4
Market Rd *RCH/KEW* TW9...17 N8
Market Sq *BH/WHM* TN16...104 C1
HORS RH12 *......192 B9
Market St *BRAK* RG12......32 D3
GU GU1......6 F5
Market Ter *BTFD* TW8 *......17 L4
Market Wy *BH/WHM* TN16...105 J5
Markfield *CROY/NA* CR0......64 E9
Markham Ct *CBLY* GU15......68 F2
Markham Rd *RDKG* RH5......156 B7
Markhole Cl *HPTN* TW12......39 P1
Mark Oak La *LHD/OX* KT22...96 A1
Marksbury Av *RCH/KEW* TW9...17 N8
Marks Rd *WARL* CR6......82 E7
Mark St *REIG* RH2......119 M4
Mark Ter *RYNPK* SW20 *......42 G1
Markville Gdns *CTHM* CR3...102 A5
Mark Wy *GODL* GU7......131 N5
The Markway *SUN* TW16......39 L3
Markwell Cl *SYD* SE26......31 J7
Markwick La *MFD/CHID* GU8...150 G9
Marlborough *ISLW* TW7 *......17 H5
Marlborough Cl
CRAWW RH11......176 F9
FLEETS GU51......87 K7
HORS RH12......192 C5
WIM/MER SW19......29 H9
Marlborough Crs *CHSWK* W4...18 B1
HYS/HAR UB3......14 F5
Marlborough Ms *BNSTD* SM7...79 L4
Marlborough Ri *CBLY* GU15...68 G2
Marlborough Rd *ASHF* TW15...23 H8
CHSWK W4......18 A3
DORK RH4......117 H7
DTCH/LGLY SL3......13 J5
FELT TW13......24 F5
HPTN TW12......24 G9

HYS/HAR UB3 14 F5
NWDGN UB2 15 L1
RCHPK/HAM TW10 26 D2
SAND/SEL CR2 63 L6
SUT SM1 61 L2
WIM/MER SW19 29 H9
WOKN/KNAP GU21 11 G2
Marlborough Vw FARN GU14 87 N2
The Marld ASHTD KT21 77 M7
Marler Rd FSTH SE23 31 N4
Marles La BIL RH14 189 M9
Marley Cl ADL/WDHM KT15 55 K5
Marley Combe Rd
HASM GU27 184 A5
Marley Hanger HASM GU27 184 B7
Marley La HASM GU27 183 P5
Marley Ri DORK RH4 136 G1
Marlhurst EDEN TN8 144 F1
Marlin Cl SUN TW16 23 P9
Marlingdene Cl HPTN TW12 25 H9
Marlings Cl CTHM CR3 81 N6
Marlins Cl SUT SM1 * 61 N4
Marloes Rd KENS W8 19 M1
Marlow Cl PGE/AN SE20 46 B4
Marlow Ct CRAWE RH10 176 G4
Marlow Crs TWK TW1 25 N2
Marlow Dr CHEAM SM3 61 H2
Marlowe Wy CROY/NA CR0 62 G1
Marlow Gdns HYS/HAR UB3 14 F1
Marlow Rd NWDGN UB2 15 P1
PGE/AN SE20 46 B4
Marlpit Av COUL/CHIP CR5 80 G6
Marlpit Cl EDEN TN8 144 G1
EGRIN RH19 162 D9
Marlpit La COUL/CHIP CR5 80 G6
Marl Rd WAND/EARL SW18 19 M9
Marlyns Cl RGUE GU4 112 E1
Marlyns Dr RGUE GU4 112 E2
Marmora Rd EDUL SE22 31 K2
Marmot Rd HSLWW TW4 15 M8
Marnell Wy HSLWW TW4 15 M8
Marneys Cl EPSOM KT18 77 N4
Marnfield Crs
BRXS/STRHM SW2 30 A4
Marnham Pl
ADL/WDHM KT15 55 N3
Marnock Rd BROCKY SE4 31 N1
Maroons Wy CAT SE6 31 P8
Marrick Cl PUT/ROE SW15 18 E9
Marriott Cl
EBED/NFELT TW14 23 N2
Marriott Lodge Cl
ADL/WDHM KT15 55 N2
Marrowbrook Cl FARN GU14 88 C4
Marrowbrook La FARN GU14 88 C4
Marrowells WEY KT13 56 G2
Marrow Meade FLEETN GU51 86 E4
Marryat Cl HSLWW TW4 15 P9
Marryat Pl WIM/MER SW19 28 B7
Marryat Rd WIM/MER SW19 28 A8
Marshall Cl FARN GU14 68 B9
FRIM GU16 69 M6
HSLWW TW4 24 G1
SAND/SEL CR2 82 A2
WAND/EARL SW18 28 F2
Marshall Pde
WOKS/MYFD GU22 * 73 K4
Marshall Pl ADL/WDHM KT15 55 N7
Marshall Rd CRAWE RH10 177 M7
GODL GU7 131 L7
SHST GU47 67 P1
Marshalls Cl HOR/WEW KT19 78 A2
Marshall's Rd SUT SM1 61 M3
Marsh Av HOR/WEW KT19 60 C8
MTCM CR4 44 B3
Marsh Farm Rd WHTN TW2 25 N4
Marshfield DTCH/LGLY SL3 12 A6
Marsh Green Rd EDEN TN8 144 F9
Marsh La ADL/WDHM KT15 55 M3
HTWY RG27 66 D1
Marshwood Rd LTWR GU18 52 D9
Marston HOR/WEW KT19 60 A9
Marston Av CHSGTN KT9 59 L5
Marston Ct WOT/HER KT12 * 39 L9
Marston Dr FARN GU14 68 D9
WARL CR6 82 E7
Marston Rd FNM GU9 4 B5
TEDD TW11 26 A8
WOKN/KNAP GU21 71 P6
Marston Wy ASC SL5 33 N3
NRWD SE19 45 K1
Martel Cl CBLY GU15 69 L1
Martell Rd DUL SE21 30 E6
Martens Pl GODL GU7 131 L7
Martin Cl CRAWW RH11 176 G3
SAND/SEL CR2 64 D9
WARL CR6 82 B5
Martin Crs CROY/NA CR0 45 H9
Martindale
MORT/ESHN SW14 27 H1
Martindale Av CBLY GU15 69 L5
Martindale Cl RGUE GU4 113 H3
Martindale Pl
MFD/CHID GU8 * 167 P7
Martindale Rd BAL SW12 29 L3
HSLWW TW4 15 N9
WOKN/KNAP GU21 71 M7
Martineau Cl ESH/CLAY KT10 58 D3
Martineau Dr DORK RH4 117 H9
TWK TW1 17 H9
Martingale Cl SUN TW16 39 J5
Martingale Ct ALDT GU11 108 A4
Martingales Cl
RCHPK/HAM TW10 26 C6
Martin Gv MRDN SM4 43 L4
Martin Rd GUW GU2 111 N3
Martins Cl BLKW GU17 67 P4
GU GU1 112 G4
WWKM BR4 65 K1
Martins La BRAK RG12 32 G4
Martins Pk FARN GU14 * 67 P9
Martin's Rd HAYES BR2 47 L3
The Martins CRAWE RH10 179 K3
SYD SE26 31 J8
Martins Wd MFD/CHID GU8 149 M5
Martinsyde
WOKS/MYFD GU22 72 G6
Martin Wy FRIM GU16 68 G7
MRDN SM4 43 J4
WOKN/KNAP GU21 71 N7
Martlets Cl HORS RH12 192 B5
The Martlets CRAWE RH10 177 H5
Martletts Cnr HORS RH12 * 189 N3
Marton Cl CAT SE6 31 P6
The Marts HORS RH12 189 N3
Martyns Pl EGRIN RH19 180 F3
Martyr Rd GU GU1 6 E5
Martyrs Av CRAWW RH11 176 F2
Martyrs La WOKN/KNAP GU21 72 F1
Marvell Cl CRAWE RH10 177 M3
Marville Rd FUL/PGN SW6 19 K5
Marwell BH/WHM TN16 104 F6
Marwell Cl WWKM BR4 65 M1
Marwell Rd FLEETN GU51 86 C3
Mary Adelaide Cl
PUT/ROE SW15 27 K6
Maryat Sq FUL/PGN SW6 19 J6
Maryhill Cl PUR/KEN CR8 81 L6
Maryland EWKG RG40 48 B2
Maryland Rd THHTH CR7 45 K2
Maryland Wy SUN TW16 39 J3
Mary Rd GU GU1 6 D4
Mary Rose Cl HPTN TW12 40 A2
Mary's Ter TWK TW1 25 P3
Mary V GODL GU7 150 C2
Masbro' Rd WKENS W14 19 H1
Masdar Gdns EWKG RG40 48 C3
Masefield Rd CRAWW RH11 176 B8
HPTN TW12 24 G7
Masefield Wy
STWL/WRAY TW19 23 J4
Maskall Cl
BRXS/STRHM SW2 * 30 B4
Maskell Rd TOOT SW17 28 F6
Maskell Wy FARN GU14 87 N4
Mason Cl EGRIN RH19 180 D1
HPTN TW12 39 P2
RYNPK SW20 43 H2
YTLY GU46 * 67 J3
Masonic Hall Rd CHERT KT16 37 K7
Mason Pl SHST GU47 49 K9
Mason Rd CRAWE RH10 177 H7
FARN GU14 88 A1
Mason's Av CROY/NA CR0 2 D6
Mason's Bridge Rd
REDH RH1 140 D1
Masons Ct EW KT17 * 60 E7
Masons Hl HAYES BR2 47 N4
Masons Paddock DORK RH4 116 G5
Mason's Pl MTCM CR4 44 B2
Mason Wy ALDT GU11 108 D7
Massetts Rd HORL RH6 159 J2
Massingberd Wy TOOT SW17 29 L7
Master Cl OXTED RH8 103 L9
Masters Cl STRHM/NOR SW16 29 M9
Maswell Park Crs HSLW TW3 25 K1
Maswell Park Rd HSLW TW3 25 J1
Matfield Cl HAYES BR2 47 N6
Matham Rd E/WMO/HCT KT8 40 D6
Matheson Rd WKENS W14 19 K2
Mathews Ter ALDT GU11 * 108 E4
Mathias Cl EPSOM KT18 78 A2
Mathisen Wy DTCH/LGLY SL3 13 J6
Matilda Cl NRWD SE19 45 M1
Matlock Crs CHEAM SM3 61 J3
Matlock Gdns CHEAM SM3 61 J3
Matlock Pl CHEAM SM3 61 J3
Matlock Rd CTHM CR3 101 N2
Matlock Wy NWMAL KT3 42 B2
Matthew Arnold Cl
COB KT11 75 J3
STA TW18 22 F9
Matthew Ct MTCM CR4 44 F6
Matthew Rd ALDT GU11 108 A6
Matthews Cha BNFD RG42 32 B1
Matthews Dr CRAWE RH10 177 M9
Matthew's Gdns
CROY/NA CR0 65 K9
Matthews La STA TW18 22 C7
Matthews Rd CBLY GU15 50 E9
Matthew's St REIG RH2 119 L9
Matthey Pl CRAWE RH10 177 N2
Mauleverer Rd
BRXS/STRHM SW2 29 P1
Maultway Cl CBLY GU15 51 K9
Maultway Crs CBLY GU15 51 K9
Maultway North CBLY GU15 51 K8
The Maultway CBLY GU15 51 K9
Maunsell Pk CRAWE RH10 177 L5
Maurice Av CTHM CR3 101 M2
Mavins Rd FNM GU9 5 J7
Mavis Av HOR/WEW KT19 60 C4
Mavis Cl HOR/WEW KT19 60 C4
Mawbey Rd CHERT KT16 55 H5
Mawson Cl RYNPK SW20 43 J3
Mawson La CHSWK W4 18 D4
Maxine Cl SHST GU47 49 M8
Maxton Wk CRAWW RH11 * 176 E9
Maxwell Cl CROY/NA CR0 44 G9
Maxwell Dr BF/WBF KT14 55 N9
Maxwell Rd ASHF TW15 23 M9
FUL/PGN SW6 19 M5
WDR/YW UB7 14 A2
Maxwell Wy CRAWE RH10 177 K2
Mayall Rd HNHL SE24 30 C1
May Bate Av KUTN/CMB KT2 8 C2
Maybelle Cl RDKG RH5 156 C1
Mayberry Pl BRYLDS KT5 41 M8
Maybourne Cl SYD SE26 * 31 J9
Maybourne Ri
WOKS/MYFD GU22 92 B4
Maybrick Cl SHST GU47 49 K8
Maybury Cl FRIM GU16 68 F8
KWD/TDW/WH KT20 79 J8
Maybury Hl
WOKN/KNAP GU21 11 J1
Maybury Rd
WOKN/KNAP GU21 11 G3
Maybury St TOOT SW17 29 H8
May Cl BOR GU35 164 B7
CHSGTN KT9 59 M5
GODL GU7 150 A2
SHST GU47 49 P9
May Crs ASHV GU12 108 G5
Maycross Av MRDN SM4 43 K5
Mayday Rd THHTH CR7 45 K7
Maydwell Av SWTR RH13 190 C8
Mayell Cl LHD/OX KT22 97 J3
Mayes Cl CRAWE RH10 177 M6
WARL CR6 82 D7
Mayes La HORS RH12 191 M1
Mayfair Av WHTN TW2 25 K3
WPK KT4 42 E9
Mayfair Cl BECK BR3 47 H2
SURB KT6 41 L9
Mayfield CRAWE RH10 177 N5
LHD/OX KT22 97 J1
LING RH7 162 F3
RFNM GU10 146 C1
Mayfield Av ADL/WDHM KT15 55 M8
CHSWK W4 18 C2
WEA W13 17 H1
Mayfield Cl ADL/WDHM KT15 55 N8
ASHF TW15 23 L9
CLAP SW4 29 N1
FNM GU9 108 D8
PGE/AN SE20 * 46 B2
REDH RH1 140 C2
THDIT KT7 41 H9
WOT/HER KT12 57 J3
Mayfield Ct HTWY RG27 48 B9
Mayfield Crs THHTH CR7 45 H5
Mayfield Gdns
ADL/WDHM KT15 55 M8
STA TW18 37 K1
WOT/HER KT12 57 J3
Mayfield Gn GT/LBKH KT23 96 A7
Mayfield Rd BELMT SM2 61 P5
FARN GU14 68 B9
SAND/SEL CR2 63 M7
THHTH CR7 45 H5
WEY KT13 56 B4
WIM/MER SW19 43 K2
WOT/HER KT12 57 J3
Mayflower Cl CRAWE RH10 177 N6
Mayflower Dr YTLY GU46 66 E1
Mayford Cl BAL SW12 29 J3
BECK BR3 46 D4
WOKS/MYFD GU22 92 B2
Mayford Rd BAL SW12 29 J3
Mayhurst Av
WOKS/MYFD GU22 72 G5
Mayhurst Crs
WOKS/MYFD GU22 72 G5
Maynard Cl CRAWE RH10 160 D8
FUL/PGN SW6 19 M5
Maynooth Gdns CAR SM5 44 B8
Mayo Rd CROY/NA CR0 45 M6
WOT/HER KT12 39 J8
Mayow Rd SYD SE26 31 L7
Maypole Rd EGRIN RH19 180 C1
EGRIN RH19 181 K5
May Rd WHTN TW2 25 M4
Mayroyd Av SURB KT6 59 N1
Mays Cl WEY KT13 56 B8
Mays Cft BRAK RG12 * 32 C5
Maysfield Rd
RPLY/SEND GU23 93 H3
Mays Gn COB KT11 * 75 H9
Mays Gv RPLY/SEND GU23 93 H3
May's Hill Rd HAYES BR2 47 L3
Maysoule Rd BTSEA SW11 19 P9
Mays Rd TEDD TW11 25 L8
May St WKENS W14 19 K3
Maytree Cl GU GU1 111 P2
Maytree Ct MTCM CR4 44 C4
Maytrees WOKN/KNAP GU21 71 J6
Maytree Wk
BRXS/STRHM SW2 * 30 B5
Maywater Cl SAND/SEL CR2 63 M9
Maywood Cl BECK BR3 * 47 H1
Maywood Dr CBLY GU15 69 K1
Maze Rd RCH/KEW TW9 17 N5
McAlmont Rdg GODL GU7 131 K6
McCarthy Rd FELT TW13 24 E8
McCarthy Wy EWKG RG40 48 D1
McDonough Cl CHSGTN KT9 59 L3
McDougall Ct RCH/KEW TW9 17 N7
McGrigor Barracks
ALDT GU11 108 D3
McIndoe Rd EGRIN RH19 162 C9
McIntosh Cl WLGTN SM6 62 G6
McIver Cl EGRIN RH19 161 N8
McKay Cl ALDT GU11 108 E3
McKay Rd RYNPK SW20 42 F1
McKenzie Wy
HOR/WEW KT19 59 N8
McLeod's Ms SKENS SW7 19 M1
McNair Rd NWDGN UB2 16 A1
McNaughton Cl FARN GU14 87 N4
McRae La MTCM CR4 44 B8
Mead Av REDH RH1 140 C4
Mead Cl CRAN GU6 171 H1
EGH TW20 21 N9
REDH RH1 120 C2
Mead Ct EGH TW20 21 P9
WOKN/KNAP GU21 71 L6
Mead Crs GT/LBKH KT23 96 A5
SUT SM1 62 A3
Mead Dr COUL/CHIP CR5 80 G3
Meade Cl CHSWK W4 17 N4
Mead End ASHTD KT21 77 M5
Meades Cl LING RH7 162 F3
The Meades LING RH7 162 G3
WEY KT13 * 56 F5
Meadfield Av DTCH/LGLY SL3 12 E1
Meadfield Rd DTCH/LGLY SL3 12 F1
Meadfoot Rd
STRHM/NOR SW16 44 E2
Meadhurst Pk SUN TW16 23 P9
Meadhurst Rd CHERT KT16 * 37 M9
Meadlands Dr
RCHPK/HAM TW10 26 C5
Mead La CHERT KT16 37 N9
FNM GU9 4 E4
Meadow Ap CRAWE RH10 160 B9
Meadow Av CROY/NA CR0 46 D7
Meadowbank BRYLDS KT5 41 M7
Meadow Bank EHSLY KT24 95 H7
FNM GU9 4 E5
Meadowbank Cl
FUL/PGN SW6 18 G5
Meadowbank Gdns
HEST TW5 15 J6
Meadowbank Rd LTWR GU18 52 C8
Meadowbrook OXTED RH8 123 J1
Meadowbrook Cl
DTCH/LGLY SL3 13 J7
Meadowbrook Rd
DORK RH4 116 G6
Meadow Cl ASHV GU12 89 H6
BLKW GU17 67 P4
CAT SE6 31 P8
CRAWE RH10 160 B9
ESH/CLAY KT10 58 F2
GODL GU7 131 L6
HORS RH12 192 F5
HSLWW TW4 25 H2
LIPH GU30 182 F6
MFD/CHID GU8 149 P3
PUR/KEN CR8 80 F2
RCHPK/HAM TW10 26 D4
RYNPK SW20 42 G5
WDSR SL4 20 G2
WOT/HER KT12 57 P3
Meadow Ct EPSOM KT18 78 A2
STA TW18 22 B6
Meadowcroft Cl
CRAWW RH11 176 C6
EGRIN RH19 180 B1
Meadow Croft Cl HORL RH6 159 M4
Meadow Dr RPLY/SEND GU23 93 K3
Meadow Farm La
HORS RH12 192 E3
Meadow Gdns STA TW18 22 A8
Meadow Gate Av FARN GU14 88 B5
Meadow Hl NWMAL KT3 42 C7
PUR/KEN CR8 80 E2
Meadowlands COB KT11 75 J2
CRAWW RH11 176 F5
OXTED RH8 123 N5
RGUE GU4 113 M1
Meadow La EDEN TN8 144 F1
LHD/OX KT22 96 C2
Meadowlea Cl WDR/YW UB7 13 P4
Meadow Pl CHSWK W4 * 18 C5
Meadow Ri COUL/CHIP CR5 80 F2
WOKN/KNAP GU21 71 J6
Meadow Rd ASHF TW15 23 N8
ASHTD KT21 77 L6
DTCH/LGLY SL3 12 C1
ESH/CLAY KT10 58 E4
FARN GU14 68 D9
FELT TW13 24 F5
HAYES BR2 47 L2
RGUE GU4 112 E1
SUT SM1 62 A3
VW GU25 35 L6
WIM/MER SW19 43 N1
Meadows End SUN TW16 39 J2
Meadowside GT/LBKH KT23 96 A3
HORL RH6 140 D9
TWK TW1 26 C3
WOT/HER KT12 57 L1
Meadowside Rd BELMT SM2 61 J7
Meadows Leigh Cl WEY KT13 56 E2
The Meadows GUW GU2 112 A8
RFNM GU10 165 J2
WARL CR6 82 D6
Meadow Stile CROY/NA CR0 2 D6
Meadowsweet Cl
NWMAL KT3 42 G6
The Meadow CRAWE RH10 160 B9
Meadow V HASM GU27 184 B4
Meadow Vw CHERT KT16 37 N9
FLEETS GU52 106 E1
HORL RH6 160 D1
STWL/WRAY TW19 22 C1
Meadowview Rd CAT SE6 31 P7
HOR/WEW KT19 60 C7
Meadow View Rd
THHTH CR7 45 K6
Meadow Wk EW KT17 60 D6
KWD/TDW/WH KT20 98 F4
WLGTN SM6 62 D2
Meadow Wy
ADL/WDHM KT15 55 M3
ASHV GU12 109 H3
BLKW GU17 67 N3
BNFD RG42 32 C1
CHOB/PIR GU24 70 F2
CHSGTN KT9 59 L4
EHSLY KT24 94 F5
GT/LBKH KT23 96 B3
KWD/TDW/WH KT20 79 J6
LIPH GU30 182 F5
REIG RH2 119 M9
RFNM GU10 146 C1
WDSR SL4 20 G2
Meadow Waye HEST TW5 15 N5
Mead Pth WIM/MER SW19 28 G9
Mead Pl CROY/NA CR0 2 B2
HORL RH6 160 D1
Mead Rd CRAN GU6 153 H9
CRAWE RH10 177 J4
CTHM CR3 101 P3
EDEN TN8 145 H6
GSHT GU26 166 A7
RCHPK/HAM TW10 26 B6
WOT/HER KT12 57 N3
Meadrow GODL GU7 131 M7
Meadside Cl BECK BR3 46 E2
Meads Rd GU GU1 112 F5
The Meads CHEAM SM3 61 H2
EGRIN RH19 180 D4
HASM GU27 184 A4
MRDN SM4 * 44 A6
WEY KT13 56 E5
The Mead ASHTD KT21 77 L8
BECK BR3 47 J3
DORK RH4 * 137 J1
FARN GU14 * 88 D4
LIPH GU30 182 E5
WLGTN SM6 62 F5
WWKM BR4 47 K9
Meadvale HORS RH12 191 N8
Meadvale Rd CROY/NA CR0 45 P8
Mead Wy COUL/CHIP CR5 80 G7
CROY/NA CR0 64 E1
HAYES BR2 47 N7
Meadway ASHF TW15 23 K7
BECK BR3 47 J2
BRYLDS KT5 42 A9
EHSLY KT24 95 N8
ESH/CLAY KT10 58 B7
FRIM GU16 69 H6
HASM GU27 184 A4
HOR/WEW KT19 78 A2
LHD/OX KT22 76 D3
Mead Wy RGUE GU4 92 G9
Meadway RYNPK SW20 42 G5
STA TW18 37 L1
WARL CR6 82 C5
WHTN TW2 25 L4
Meadway Cl STA TW18 37 K1
Meadway Dr
ADL/WDHM KT15 55 N6
WOKN/KNAP GU21 72 A5
The Meadway HORL RH6 159 M1
Meaford Wy PGE/AN SE20 46 B1
Meare Cl KWD/TDW/WH KT20 98 G3
Meath Green Av HORL RH6 140 B8
Meath Green La HORL RH6 140 A5
Medawar Rd GUW GU2 111 K6
Medcroft Gdns
MORT/ESHN SW14 18 A9
Mede Cl STWL/WRAY TW19 21 J4
Mede Fld LHD/OX KT22 96 D4
Medfield St PUT/ROE SW15 27 M3
Medhurst Cl CHOB/PIR GU24 53 M7
Medina Av ESH/CLAY KT10 58 E2
Medlake Rd EGH TW20 21 P9
Medland Cl WLGTN SM6 44 C9
Medlar Cl CRAWW RH11 176 F2
GU GU1 112 A3
Medlar Dr BLKW GU17 68 B5
Medonte Cl FLEETN GU51 87 H7
Medora Rd
BRXS/STRHM SW2 30 A2
Medway CRAWE RH10 179 H6
Medway Cl CROY/NA CR0 46 C7
Medway Dr EGRIN RH19 180 C5
FARN GU14 68 A9
FROW RH18 181 M9
Medway Rd CRAWW RH11 176 C6
Medwin Wy HORS RH12 192 B8
Melbourne Cl WLGTN SM6 62 E4
Melbourne Rd TEDD TW11 26 B9
WIM/MER SW19 43 L2
WLGTN SM6 62 D4
Melbourne Ter
FUL/PGN SW6 * 19 M5
Melbourne Wy HORS RH12 * 192 E5
Melbury Av NWDGN UB2 16 B1
Melbury Cl BF/WBF KT14 73 L3
CHERT KT16 37 L8
ESH/CLAY KT10 59 H5
Melbury Ct KENS W8 19 K1
Melbury Gdns RYNPK SW20 42 F2
Melbury Rd WKENS W14 19 K1
Meldon Cl FUL/PGN SW6 * 19 M6
Meldone Cl BRYLDS KT5 41 P7
Meldrum Cl OXTED RH8 123 M3
Melfont Av THHTH CR7 45 K4
Melford Cl CHSGTN KT9 59 M4
Melford Rd EDUL SE22 31 H4
Melfort Rd THHTH CR7 45 K4
Melksham Cl SWTR RH13 192 D8
Meller Cl CROY/NA CR0 62 G2
Mellersh Cl FLEETS GU52 106 E2
Mellersh Hill Rd SHGR GU5 132 F7
Mellison Rd TOOT SW17 29 H8
Melliss Av RCH/KEW TW9 17 P6
Mellor Cl WOT/HER KT12 39 P8
Mellow Cl BNSTD SM7 79 M3
Mellows Rd WLGTN SM6 62 F4
Melody Rd BH/WHM TN16 84 A7
WAND/EARL SW18 28 F2
Melrose BRAK RG12 32 D9
Melrose Av FARN GU14 87 N2
MTCM CR4 44 D1
STRHM/NOR SW16 45 H4
WHTN TW2 25 J3
WIM/MER SW19 28 C5
Melrose Gdns HMSMTH W6 18 G1
NWMAL KT3 42 B4
WOT/HER KT12 57 L4
Melrose Rd BARN SW13 18 D7
BH/WHM TN16 84 A5
COUL/CHIP CR5 80 D4
WAND/EARL SW18 28 C2
WEY KT13 56 C4
WIM/MER SW19 43 L3
Melrose Vls BECK BR3 * 46 G3
Melsa Rd MRDN SM4 43 N7
Melton Flds HOR/WEW KT19 60 B7
Melton Pl HOR/WEW KT19 60 B7
Melton Rd REDH RH1 120 E1
Melville Av FRIM GU16 69 H7
RYNPK SW20 42 E1

SAND/SEL CR2 ....63 P4
Melville Rd BARN SW13 ......18 E6
Melville Ter FNM GU9 * 4 E4
Melvin Rd PGE/AN SE20 .....46 C2
Melvinshaw LHD/OX KT22 ...97 J1
Membury Ct FRIM GU16 ....69 J9
Membury Wk BRAK RG12 ......32 C5
OXTED RH8 ....103 K7
Memorial Cl HEST TW5 ....15 P4
Memorial Sq KUT/HW KT1 ......8 C4
Mendip Cl DTCH/LGLY SL3 ...12 E3
HYS/HAR UB3 ....15 J3
SYD SE26 ....31 K7
WPK KT4 ....60 C1
Mendip Rd BRAK RG12 ....32 C6
BTSEA SW11 ....19 N8
FARN GU14 ....68 A9
Mendip Wk CRAWW RH11 ..176 C5
Mendora Rd FUL/PGN SW6 ...19 J5
Menin Wy FNM GU9 ....5 K6
Menlo Gdns NRWD SE19 .....45 M1
Meon Cl FARN GU14 ....87 P1
KWD/TDW/WH KT20 ....98 F2
Meopham Rd MTCM CR4 ......44 E2
Merantum Wy
WIM/MER SW19 ....43 N2
Mercer Cl CRWE RH10 ....177 M8
THDIT KT7 ....40 F8
Mercer Rd HORS RH12 ....192 B2
Mercers Pl HMSMTH W6 .....18 G2
Merchants Cl SNWD SE25 ...46 A5
WOKN/KNAP GU21 ....71 J6
Mercier Rd PUT/ROE SW15 ..28 E7
Mercury Cl CRAWW RH11 ...176 B8
Mercury Rd BTFD TW8 ....17 J3
Merebank RDKG RH5 ....137 K9
Merebank La WLGTN SM6 .....63 H4
Meredyth Rd BARN SW13 .....18 E7
Mere End CROY/NA CR0 ......46 D8
Merefield Gdns
KWD/TDW/WH KT20 ....79 H8
Mere Rd KWD/TDW/WH KT20 .98 F4
SHPTN TW17 * 38 D7
WEY KT13 ....56 F2
Mereside Pk ASHF TW15 * ...23 M7
Merevale Crs MRDN SM4 ......43 N7
Mereway Rd WHTN TW2 ....25 L4
Merewood Gdns
CROY/NA CR0 ....46 D8
Mereworth Cl HAYES BR2 ....47 M6
Mereworth Dr CRAWE RH10 177 N3
Meridian Cl CRAWW RH11 ..176 C8
Meridian Gv HORL RH6 ....140 E9
Merivale FLEETN GU51 ....162 E9
Merivale Rd PUT/ROE SW15 ..19 J8
FARN GU14 ....87 P4
Merredene St
BRXS/STRHM SW2 ....30 A2
Merrick Rd NWDGN UB2 ......15 P2
Merrilands Rd WPK KT4 ....42 C9
Merrilyn Cl ESH/CLAY KT10 ..58 G5
Merrington Rd FUL/PGN SW6 .19 L4
Merrin Hl SAND/SEL CR2 .....81 N1
Merritt Gdns CHSGTN KT9 ...59 J5
Merritt Rd BROCKY SE4 ......31 N1
Merrivale Gdns
WOKN/KNAP GU21 ....72 A6
Merron Cl YTLY GU46 ....66 C3
Merrow Common Rd
RGUE GU4 ....113 H2
Merrow Cha GU GU1 ....112 C5
Merrow Common Rd
RGUE GU4 ....113 H2
Merrow Copse GU GU1 ....112 F4
Merrow Ct GU GU1 * 113 H5
Merrow Cft GU GU1 ....112 G4
Merrow La RGUE GU4 ....92 G9
Merrow Pl RGUE GU4 ....113 H3
Merrow Rd BELMT SM2 ....61 H7
Merrow St RGUE GU4 ....113 H4
Merrow Wy CROY/NA CR0 ....65 J5
GU GU1 * 113 H4
Merrow Woods GU GU1 ....112 F3
Merryacres MFD/CHID GU8 149 M6
Merryfield Dr HORS RH12 ...191 P7
Merryhill Rd BNFD RG42 ......32 C2
Merryhills Cl BH/WHM TN16 .84 B5
Merryhills La BIL RH14 ....188 D5
Merrylands CHERT KT16 ......55 J2
Merrylands Farm
GT/LBKH KT23 ....95 P4
Merrylands Rd GT/LBKH KT23 95 P3
Merryman Dr CWTH RG45 .....49 K3
Merrymeet BNSTD SM7 ....80 B3
Merryweather Ct
NWMAL KT3 ....42 C6
Merrywood Gv
KWD/TDW/WH KT20 ....119 H1
Merrywood Pk CBLY GU15 ...69 H4
REIG RH2 ....119 M3
Mersham Pl PGE/AN SE20 ...46 B2
THHTH CR7 ....45 M3
Mersham Rd THHTH CR7 .....45 M4
Merstham Rd REDH RH1 .....121 J1

Merthyr Ter BARN SW13 ......18 F4
Merton Av CHSWK W4 ....18 D2
Merton Cl SHST GU47 ....50 B7
Merton Hall Gdns
RYNPK SW20 ....43 J2
Merton Hall Rd
WIM/MER SW19 ....43 J2
Merton High St
WIM/MER SW19 ....43 M1
Merton Pl WIM/MER SW19 * ...43 N2
Merton Rd CRAWW RH11 ...194 E2
SNWD SE25 ....45 P6
WAND/EARL SW18 ....28 D4
WIM/MER SW19 ....43 M1
Mervyn Rd SHPTN TW17 ......38 E8
WEA W13 ....16 C1
Metcalf Rd ASHF TW15 ....23 L8
Metcalf Wy CRAWW RH11 ...176 C1
Meteor Wy FARN GU14 ....88 C6
WLGTN SM6 ....62 G6
Meudon Av FARN GU14 ....88 A6
Mews Ct EGRIN RH19 ....180 E5
Mewsend BH/WHM TN16 .....84 B7
The Mews BECK BR3 * 46 C2
GU GU1 * 113 H5
HORS RH12 * 191 L6
MFD/CHID GU8 ....169 L6
REIG RH2 * 119 M4
STRHM/NOR SW16 * 45 J1
TWK TW1 * 26 A2
Mexfield Rd PUT/ROE SW15 ..28 C1
Meyrick Cl WOKN/KNAP GU21 71 L5
Meyrick Rd BTSEA SW11 .....19 P8
Michael Crs HORL RH6 ....159 K3
Michael Flds PER FROM RH18 181 K1
Michael La GUW GU2 ....91 P9
Michaelmas Cl RYNPK SW20 42 G4
YTLY GU46 ....67 H4
Michael Rd FUL/PGN SW6 ..19 M6
SNWD SE25 ....45 P5
Micheldever Wy BRAK RG12 33 H7
Michelet Cl LTWR GU18 ....52 B8
Micheham Gdns
KWD/TDW/WH KT20 * 78 G9
TWK TW1 * 25 N6
Michell Cl HORS RH12 ....191 P8
Mickleham Dr LHD/OX KT22 97 J2
Mickleham Gdns CHEAM SM3 61 J5
Mickleham Wy CROY/NA CR0 65 K6
Mickle Hl SHST GU47 ....49 L8
Mickleburgh Rd
FUL/PGN SW6 ....19 L4
Middle Av FNM GU9 ....127 P5
RFNM GU10 ....127 M7
Middle Bourne La
RFNM GU10 ....127 M7
Middle Church La FNM GU9 ....5 F4
Middle Cl CBLY GU15 ....69 L2
COUL/CHIP CR5 ....81 J9
EW KT17 * 78 C1
Middlemarch
MFD/CHID GU8 ....149 M7
Middlemead Cl GT/LBKH KT23 96 A5
Middlemead Rd
GT/LBKH KT23 ....95 P5
Middlemoor Rd FRIM GU16 ..68 C8
Middle Old Pk FNM GU9 ....127 K1
Middle Rd LHD/OX KT22 ......97 H1
Middlesex Rd MTCM CR4 .....44 G6
Middle St
BRKHM/BTCW RH3 ....117 P7
CROY/NA CR0 ....2 D4
HORS RH12 ....192 B8
SHGR GU5 ....134 C1
Middleton Gdns FARN GU14 88 A1
Middleton Rd CBLY GU15 .....68 C3
COB KT11 ....75 K8
HOR/WEW KT19 * 60 A3
HORS RH12 ....191 P8
MRDN SM4 ....43 N7
NWMAL KT3 ....42 A4
Midgley Rd CRAWW RH11 ..176 B6
Midholm Rd CROY/NA CR0 ...64 E2
Mid Holmwood La
RDKG RH5 ....137 J3
Midhope Cl
WOKS/MYFD GU22 ....72 C9
Midhope Gdns
WOKS/MYFD GU22 ....10 C7
Midhurst Av CROY/NA CR0 ...45 J6
Midhurst Cl CRAWW RH11 ..176 C6
Midhurst Rd HASM GU27 ....184 C5
LIPH GU30 ....182 F7
Midleton Rd MFD/CHID GU8 149 N2
Midleton Industrial Estate Rd
GUW GU2 ....111 P4
Midleton Rd GUW GU2 ....111 M5
Midmoor Rd BAL SW12 ....29 M4
WIM/MER SW19 ....43 H2
Mid St REDH RH1 ....121 H5

Midsummer Av HSLWW TW4 15 P9
Midsummer Wk
WOKN/KNAP GU21 ....10 A1
Midway CHEAM SM3 ....43 K8
Midway Av CHERT KT16 ....57 M4
EGH TW20 ....36 F4
Miena Wy ASHTD KT21 ....77 K6
Mike Hawthorn Dr FNM GU9 ..5 H2
Milbanke Ct BRAK RG12 ....32 B3
Milbanke Wy BRAK RG12 .....32 B3
Milborne Gv WBPTN SW10 ..19 N5
Milborne Rd CRAWE RH10 .177 M9
Milbrook ESH/CLAY KT10 ....58 C5
Milburn Wk EPSOM KT18 .....78 C4
Milden Cl FRIM GU16 ....89 J1
Milden Gdns FRIM GU16 ......89 J1
Mildred Av HYS/HAR UB3 .....14 F2
Mile Pth WOKS/MYFD GU22 71 P9
Mile Rd WLGTN SM6 ....44 C9
OXTED RH8 ....122 C7
Miles Pl BRYLDS KT5 * 41 M5
LTWR GU18 ....69 P1
Miles Rd ASHV GU12 ....109 K5
HOR/WEW KT19 ....78 A2
MTCM CR4 ....44 A4
Miles's Hl RDKG RH5 ....154 D1
Milestone Cl BELMT SM2 .....61 P5
RPLY/SEND GU23 ....93 L2
Milestone Rd NRWD SE19 ....30 G9
Milford By-Pass Rd
MFD/CHID GU8 ....149 L4
Milford Ct RDKG RH5 ....137 J7
Milford Gv SUT SM1 ....61 N3
Milford Ldg MFD/CHID GU8 149 N4
Milford Ms
STRHM/NOR SW16 ....30 A6
Milford Rd MFD/CHID GU8 .129 N9
Milkhouse Ga GU GU1 ....7 F6
Milking La ORP BR6 ....84 C1
Milkwood Rd HNHL SE24 ......30 C1
Millais SWTR RH13 ....192 F7
Millais Cl CRAWW RH11 .....176 B6
Millais Crs HOR/WEW KT19 ..60 A3
Millais Wy HOR/WEW KT19 ..60 A3
Millan Cl ADL/WDHM KT15 ...55 M8
Mill Bank CRAWW RH11 .....176 C6
Mill Bay La HORS RH12 ......192 A9
Millbottom La RDKG RH5 ....137 L4
Millbourne Rd FELT TW13 ...24 F7
Millbridge Rd YTLY GU46 .....48 F9
Millbrook GU GU1 * 6 E6
WEY KT13 ....56 C3
Mill Cl BAGS GU19 ....51 M6
CAR SM5 ....62 B1
EGRIN RH19 ....180 D4
GT/LBKH KT23 ....96 A5
HASM GU27 ....183 P4
HORL RH6 ....140 A9
WDR/YW UB7 ....13 P1
Millcombe Cl
WOKN/KNAP GU21 ....71 P7
Mill Copse Rd HASM GU27 .184 C6
Mill Cnr FLEETN GU51 ....87 J2
Millennium Wy BNFD RG42 ..32 D2
Miller Rd CROY/NA CR0 ....45 H9
RGUE GU4 ....112 G2
WIM/MER SW19 ....28 G8
Millers Cl STA TW18 ....22 E7
Millers Copse EPSOM KT18 ..78 B8
Miller's Ct CHSWK W4 ....18 D3
Miller's Ga HORS RH12 ....192 C4
Miller's La REDH RH1 ....141 K6
Mill Farm Av SUN TW16 ....38 G1
Mill Farm Crs HSLWW TW4 ..24 F4
Mill Farm Rd SWTR RH13 ...192 F6
Mill Fld BAGS GU19 ....51 N6
Millfield SUN TW16 ....38 F2
Millfield La
KWD/TDW/WH KT20 ....99 L5
Millfield Rd HSLWW TW4 .....24 F4
Mill Gdns SYD SE26 ....31 J7
Mill Gn BNFD RG42 ....32 A1
MTCM CR4 ....44 C8
Mill Green Rd MTCM CR4 .....44 C8
Millhedge Cl COB KT11 ....75 N5
Mill Hl BARN SW13 ....18 E8
BRKHM/BTCW RH3 ....117 P6
EDEN TN8 ....145 H6
Mill Hill La
BRKHM/BTCW RH3 ....117 P6
Mill Hill Rd BARN SW13 ....18 F6
Mill House La EGH TW20 ......36 F5
Millhouse Pl WNWD SE27 ....30 C7
Millington Rd HYS/HAR UB3 14 C1
Millins Cl SHST GU47 ....49 P8
Mill La ASC SL5 ....35 H3
BF/WBF KT14 ....74 C2
BRAK RG12 ....32 C6
CAR SM5 ....62 C3
CHOB/PIR GU24 ....90 D4
CRAWE RH10 ....160 F9
CRAWW RH11 ....176 D3
CROY/NA CR0 ....2 B4
DORK RH4 ....117 H6
DTCH/LGLY SL3 ....12 C3
EGH TW20 ....36 G5
EGRIN RH19 ....161 L7
EW KT17 ....60 D7
GODL GU7 ....131 K9
GU GU1 ....112 B5
HORL RH6 ....158 G1

LHD/OX KT22 ....96 G2
LING RH7 ....162 E2
MFD/CHID GU8 ....149 N7
MFD/CHID GU8 ....167 P6
MFD/CHID GU8 ....169 K7
OXTED RH8 ....123 M3
OXTED RH8 ....124 D2
RDKG RH5 ....138 D3
REDH RH1 ....154 E5
REDH RH1 ....120 C2
RGUW GU3 ....132 A4
RPLY/SEND GU23 ....73 P8
SHGR GU5 ....132 D7
SHGR GU5 ....133 K1
YTLY GU46 ....49 H9
Millmead
GUW GU2 ....6 C6
Mill Md STA TW18 ....22 D7
Millmead Ct GUW GU2 * 6 D7
Millmead Ter GUW GU2 ....6 D7
Millmere YTLY GU46 ....67 H1
Mill Pl DTCH/LGLY SL3 ....12 B7
KUT/HW KT1 ....9 F6
Mill Plat ISLW TW7 ....16 G8
Mill Plat Av ISLW TW7 ....16 G8
Millpond Ct ADL/WDHM KT15 56 A4
Mill Pond Rd BFOR GU20 .....52 B3
Mill Reach SHGR GU5 ....133 K1
Mill Ride ASC SL5 ....33 M2
Mill Rd COB KT11 ....75 L4
CRAWE RH10 ....177 L4
ESH/CLAY KT10 ....58 C1
EW KT17 ....78 D1
KWD/TDW/WH KT20 ....99 H3
RDKG RH5 ....137 J6
WDR/YW UB7 ....13 P1
WHTN TW2 ....25 K5
WIM/MER SW19 ....43 N1
Mill Shaw OXTED RH8 ....123 N3
Millshot Cl FUL/PGN SW6 ....18 G6
Millside CAR SM5 ....62 B1
Millside PI ISLW TW7 ....17 H7
Mills Rd WOT/HER KT12 ....57 L4
Mills Spur WDSR SL4 ....20 G3
Millstead Cl
KWD/TDW/WH KT20 ....98 F3
Mill Stream FNM GU9 ....108 A8
The Millstream HASM GU27 183 P5
Mill St BH/WHM TN16 ....105 H7
DTCH/LGLY SL3 ....13 H5
KUT/HW KT1 ....8 E6
REDH RH1 ....120 F4
Milltheorpe Rd HORS RH12 192 E6
Mill V HAYES BR2 ....47 N4
Mill Vw CRAN GU6 * 152 E9
Mill View Cl EW KT17 ....60 D6
Millview Cl REIG RH2 ....119 P3
Mill View Gdns CROY/NA CR0 64 D2
Mill Wy EBED/NFELT TW14 ..24 C1
LHD/OX KT22 ....97 M5
Millway REIG RH2 ....119 P5
Millwood CRAWE RH10 ....179 M6
Millwood Rd HSLW TW3 ....25 K1
Milman Cl BRAK RG12 ....33 H3
Milman's St WBPTN SW10 ...19 P4
Milne Cl CRAWW RH11 ....176 B8
Milne Pk East CROY/NA CR0 65 K9
Milne Pk West CROY/NA CR0 65 K9
Milner Ap CTHM CR3 ....102 A3
Milner Cl CTHM CR3 ....102 A2
Milner Dr COB KT11 ....75 P1
WHTN TW2 ....25 K2
Milner Rd CTHM CR3 ....102 A2
KUT/HW KT1 ....8 C7
MRDN SM4 ....43 P6
THHTH CR7 ....45 L4
WIM/MER SW19 ....43 M2
Milnthorpe Rd CHSWK W4 ...18 B4
Milnwood Rd HORS RH12 ...192 B7
Milo Rd EDUL SE22 ....30 D2
Milson Rd WKENS W14 ....19 J1
Milton Av CROY/NA CR0 ....45 M8
DORK RH4 ....116 D8
SUT SM1 ....61 P2
Milton Cl BRAK RG12 ....32 C7
DTCH/LGLY SL3 ....12 E8
SUT SM1 ....61 P2
Miltoncourt La DORK RH4 ...116 E7
Milton Ct EGRIN RH19 ....180 B2
Milton Dr SHPTN TW17 ....38 A5
Milton Gdns EPSOM KT18 ....78 C3
STWL/WRAY TW19 ....23 J4
Milton Mount Av
CRAWE RH10 ....177 N2
Milton Pk EGH TW20 * 36 E1
Milton Rd ADL/WDHM KT15 ..55 L5
CRAWE RH10 ....177 M4
CROY/NA CR0 ....45 M8
CTHM CR3 ....101 M1
EGH TW20 ....21 L8
HNHL SE24 ....30 C1
HPTN TW12 ....40 A1
MORT/ESHN SW14 ....18 B8
MTCM CR4 ....44 C1
SUT SM1 ....61 L2
WIM/MER SW19 ....43 N1
WLGTN SM6 ....62 E5
WOT/HER KT12 ....39 N6
Mitons Crs GODL GU7 ....150 A2
Milton St DORK RH4 ....116 D8
Miltons Yd MFD/CHID GU8 * 149 N8
Milton Wy LHD/OX KT22 ....96 C5
WDR/YW UB7 ....14 B2
Mimosa St FUL/PGN SW6 ....19 K6
Mina Rd WIM/MER SW19 ......43 L2
Minchin Cl LHD/OX KT22 ......96 C2
Mincing La CHOB/PIR GU24 53 M7

Minden Rd CHEAM SM3 ....61 J1
PGE/AN SE20 ....46 B2
Mindleheim Av EGRIN RH19 180 G1
Minehead Rd
STRHM/NOR SW16 ....30 A8
Minehurst Rd FRIM GU16 .....89 H3
Minerva Cl
STWL/WRAY TW19 * 22 D1
Minerva Rd FARN GU14 ....88 D6
KUT/HW KT1 ....9 F5
Minimax Cl
EBED/NFELT TW14 ....24 B2
Mink Ct HSLWW TW4 ....15 L7
Minley Cl FARN GU14 ....88 A3
Minley Gv FLEETN GU51 ......87 H4
Minley Rd BLKW GU17 ....87 J7
FLEETN GU51 ....87 H4
Minniedale BRYLDS KT5 ....41 M6
Minorca Av FRIM GU16 ....69 N6
Minorca Rd FRIM GU16 ....69 N6
WEY KT13 ....56 C3
Minshull Pl BECK BR3 * 46 C1
Minstead Cl BRAK RG12 ....33 H4
Minstead Dr YTLY GU46 ....66 G2
Minstead Gdns
PUT/ROE SW15 ....27 L3
Minstead Wy NWMAL KT3 ....42 C7
Minster Av SUT SM1 ....61 L3
Minster Ct CBLY GU15 * 68 B4
Minster Dr CROY/NA CR0 ....3 J7
Minster Gdns
E/WMO/HCT KT8 ....39 P5
Minsterley Av SHPTN TW17 ..38 C5
Minster Rd BMLY BR1 ....47 P1
GODL GU7 ....150 A2
Minstrel Gdns BRYLDS KT5 .41 M5
Minterne Av NWDGN UB2 .....16 A2
Mint Gdns DORK RH4 ....116 G6
Mint La KWD/TDW/WH KT20 98 F9
WLGTN SM6 ....62 D4
Mint St GODL GU7 ....131 K9
The Mint GODL GU7 ....131 K9
Mint Wk CROY/NA CR0 ....2 D5
WARL CR6 ....82 D6
WOKN/KNAP GU21 ....10 C5
Mirabel Rd FUL/PGN SW6 ...19 K5
Misbrooks Green Rd
RDKG RH5 ....156 D5
Missenden Cl
EBED/NFELT TW14 ....24 B4
Missenden Gdns MRDN SM4 43 N7
Mistletoe Cl CROY/NA CR0 ..46 D9
Mistletoe Rd YTLY GU46 ....67 H4
Mistley Gdns HORL RH6 .....158 G2
Misty's Fld WOT/HER KT12 ..39 L9
Mitcham La
STRHM/NOR SW16 ....29 M8
Mitcham Pk MTCM CR4 ....44 B5
Mitcham Rd CBLY GU15 ....51 J8
CROY/NA CR0 ....44 G4
TOOT SW17 ....29 J8
Mitchell Gdns SWTR RH13 .190 F7
Mitchells Cl RGUE GU4 ....132 C2
Mitchells Rd CRAWE RH10 .177 L5
Mitchell Wy BMLY BR1 ....47 N1
Mitchley Av PUR/KEN CR8 ...81 M2
Mitchley Gv SAND/SEL CR2 .82 B2
Mitchley Hill SAND/SEL CR2 81 P2
Mitchley Vw SAND/SEL CR2 82 A2
Mitre Cl BELMT SM2 ....61 P7
SHPTN TW17 ....38 F7
Mixbury Gv WEY KT13 ....56 E5
Mixnams La CHERT KT16 .....37 L4
Mizen Cl COB KT11 ....75 M3
Mizen Ct ASHTD KT21 ....77 J6
Moated Farm Dr
ADL/WDHM KT15 ....55 N6
Moat Rd EGRIN RH19 ....180 D1
Moat Side FELT TW13 ....24 D7
Moats La REDH RH1 ....140 C2
The Moat NWMAL KT3 ....42 C2
Moat Wk CRAWE RH10 ....177 M4
Moberly Rd CLAP SW4 ....29 N3
Moffat Rd THHTH CR7 ....45 L3
TOOT SW17 ....29 J6
Moffats Cl SHST GU47 ....49 L9
Mogador Rd
KWD/TDW/WH KT20 ....99 N1
Mogden La ISLW TW7 ....25 N1
Moir Cl SAND/SEL CR2 ....64 A7
Mole Abbey Gdns
E/WMO/HCT KT8 ....40 B4
Mole Cl CRAWW RH11 ....176 E3
FARN GU14 ....87 P1
Mole Ct HOR/WEW KT19 ......60 A3
Molember Rd
E/WMO/HCT KT8 ....40 B6
Mole Hl LHD/OX KT22 ....96 D1
WOT/HER KT12 ....57 M4
Molesey Av E/WMO/HCT KT8 39 P6
Molesey Cl WOT/HER KT12 ..57 N3
Molesey Dr CHEAM SM3 ....61 J1
Molesey Park Av
E/WMO/HCT KT8 ....40 B6
Molesey Park Cl
E/WMO/HCT KT8 ....40 B6
Molesey Park Rd
E/WMO/HCT KT8 ....40 B6
Molesey Rd E/WMO/HCT KT8 39 N6
WOT/HER KT12 ....57 P5
Molesford Rd FUL/PGN SW6 19 L6
Molesham Cl
E/WMO/HCT KT8 ....40 B4
Molesham Wy
E/WMO/HCT KT8 ....40 B4
Moles Hl LHD/OX KT22 ....58 D9
Mole Rd EDEN TN8 ....144 C3
Mole St RDKG RH5 ....155 H5
Mole Valley Pl ASHTD KT21 ..77 K8

Mollison Dr *WLGTN* SM6........................62 G6
Molly Huggins Cl *BAL* SW12..................29 M3
Molyneux Dr *TOOT* SW17.......................29 L7
Monarch Rd *BFOR* GU20............53 C2
........................131 M6
WEY KT13........................56 C3
Monahan Av *PUR/KEN* CR8.........81 H1
Monarch Cl *CRAWW* RH11...........176 D8
EBED/NFELT TW14...................23 P3
WWKM BR4...........................65 M3
Monarch Ms
STRHM/NOR SW16.....................30 B8
Monarch Pde *MTCM* CR4 *.........44 B5
Monaveen Gdns
E/WMO/HCT KT8........................40 B4
Monck's Rw
WAND/EARL SW18 *..................28 C2
Mondial Wy *HYS/HAR* UB3........14 B3
Money Av *CTHM* CR3.................101 M2
Money La *WDR/YW* UB7............13 P1
Money Rd *CTHM* CR3................101 M2
Mongers La *EW* KT17.................60 E8
Monivea Rd *BECK* BR3................46 F1
Monkleigh Rd *MRDN* SM4..........43 J4
Monks Av *E/WMO/HCT* KT8......39 P6
Monks Cl *ASC* SL5.....................34 B7
........................*FARN* GU14........88 E3
Monks Crs *ADL/WDHM* KT15....55 M4
........................*WOT/HER* KT12....39 K9
Monksdene Gdns *SUT* SM1 *......61 M2
Monks Dr *ASC* SL5.....................34 B7
Monksfield *CRAWE* RH10 *........177 J5
Monks Gn *LHD/OX* KT22...........96 C1
Monkshanger *FNM* GU9............128 A3
Monks La *EDEN* TN8.................124 B8
........................*RDKG* RH5........172 G6
Monks Orchard Rd *BECK* BR3...46 G9
Monks Ri *FLEETN* GU51.............86 D6
Monks Rd *BNSTD* SM7................79 L6
........................*VW* GU25..........36 B5
Monks Wk *BECK* BR3 *...............46 C7
........................*FNM* GU9..........128 B6
........................*REIG* RH2............119 M5
Monks Wy *BECK* BR3..................46 C7
........................*STA* TW18..........37 P1
Monks' Well *RFNM* GU10.........128 E5
Monkswell La
........................*COUL/CHIP* CR5....99 M4
Monk Ter *FSTH* SE23..................31 N5
Monkton La *FNM* GU9.............108 A3
Monmouth Av *KUT/HW* KT1........8 A1
Monmouth Cl *CHSWK* W4...........18 B1
........................*MTCM* CR4..........44 G5
Monmouth Gv *BTFD* TW8...........17 L2
Monmouth Rd *HYS/HAR* UB3....14 C2
Monro Dr *GUW* GU2..................111 P2
Monroe Dr
........................*MORT/ESHN* SW14....27 N4
Monro Pl *HOR/WEW* KT19.........59 N7
Mons Barracks *ALDT* GU11.....108 E1
Mons Cl *ALDT* GU11..................88 G8
Monson Rd *REDH* RH1.............120 B2
Mons Wk *EGH* TW20..................21 P8
Montacute Cl *FARN* GU14.........88 F3
Montacute Rd *CAT* SE6...............31 K1
........................*CROY/NA* CR0........65 J7
........................*MRDN* SM4........44 B5
Montague Av *SAND/SEL* CR2....81 N1
Montague Cl *CBLY* GU15...........68 D3
........................*LTWR* GU18..........52 A8
........................*WOT/HER* KT12....39 J8
Montague Dr *CTHM* CR3..........101 L2
Montague Rd *CROY/NA* CR0.......2 B1
........................*HSLW* TW3..........16 B8
........................*NWDGN* UB2........15 N2
........................*RCHPK/HAM* TW10....17 M9
........................*WIM/MER* SW19....43 M1
Montague Ter *HAYES* BR2 *.......47 N5
Montagu Gdns *WLGTN* SM6.......62 E3
Montagu Rd *DTCH/LGLY* SL3....12 A7
Montana Cl *SAND/SEL* CR2.......63 M8
........................*SYD* SE26........31 N4
Montana Rd *RYNPK* SW20........42 G2
........................*TOOT* SW17........29 K6
Montcalm Cl *HAYES* BR2 *.........47 N7
Monteagle La *YTLY* GU46..........66 F2
Montem Rd *FSTH* SE23.............31 N4
........................*NWMAL* KT3........42 C5
Montford Rd *SUN* TW16.............39 J5
Montfort Pl *WIM/MER* SW19......28 A4
Montfort Ri *REDH* RH1..............140 D4
Montgomerie Dr *GUW* GU2........91 N9
Montgomerie Ms *FSTH* SE23.......31 K3
Montgomery Av
........................*ESH/CLAY* KT10....58 E1
Montgomery Cl *MTCM* CR4 *.....44 G5
........................*SHST* GU47........49 N8
Montgomery Gdns
........................*BELMT* SM2........61 P6
Montgomery Rd *CHSWK* W4......18 A1
........................*FARN* GU14........88 F3
........................*WOKS/MYFD* GU22....10 D5
Montholme Rd *BTSEA* SW11......29 J2
Montolieu Gdns
........................*PUT/ROE* SW15....27 N1
Montpelier Rd *PUR/KEN* CR8....63 K8
........................*SUT* SM1........61 N3
Montpelier Rw *TWK* TW1...........26 A3
Montrave Rd *PGE/AN* SE20........31 K9
Montreal Rd
........................*BRXS/STRHM* SW2....29 P4
Montrose Av *DTCH/LGLY* SL3.....12 A5
........................*WHTN* TW2........25 J5
Montrose Cl *ASHF* TW15...........23 M9
........................*FLEETN* GU51........87 H7
........................*FRIM* GU16........68 G8
Montrose Gdns *LHD/OX* KT22...76 D1
........................*MTCM* CR4........44 B4
........................*SUT* SM1........61 M1
Montrose Rd
........................*EBED/NFELT* TW14....23 N2

Montrose Vls *HMSMTH* W6 *.....18 E3
Montrose Wk *WEY* KT13.............56 D2
Montrose Wy *DTCH/LGLY* SL3....12 B6
........................*FSTH* SE23........31 L4
Montrouge Crs *EW* KT17............78 G5
Mont St Aignan Wy
........................*EDEN* TN8........144 G4
Montserrat Cl *NRWD* SE19.........30 E8
Montserrat Rd
........................*PUT/ROE* SW15....19 J9
Monument Cl *WEY* KT13............56 D3
Monument Rd *WEY* KT13............56 D5
........................*WOKN/KNAP* GU21....72 F4
Monument Wy East
........................*WOKN/KNAP* GU21....72 F4
Monument Wy West
........................*WOKN/KNAP* GU21....72 E4
Moon Hall Rd *CRAN* GU6........153 M5
Moons Hill *RFNM* GU10............146 G2
Moon's La *LING* RH7................163 J5
........................*SWTR* RH13........192 C9
Moor Cl *EWKG* RG40.................48 C2
........................*SHST* GU47........50 A8
Moore Grove Crs *ECH* TW20.....36 C1
Moorcroft Rd *CRAWW* RH11...176 E4
Moorcroft Rd
........................*STRHM/NOR* SW16....29 P6
Mooredale Av *BNFD* RG42.........32 B1
Moore Cl *ADL/WDHM* KT15.....55 M4
........................*FLEETS* GU52........106 C1
........................*MORT/ESHN* SW14....18 A8
........................*MTCM* CR4 *.........44 D3
........................*RFNM* GU10........128 B6
Moore Park Rd *FUL/PGN* SW6...19 M5
Moore Rd *CHOB/PIR* GU24........90 B1
........................*FLEETS* GU52........106 G1
........................*NRWD* SE19........30 D9
Moore's Rd *DORK* RH4.............117 H6
Moore Wy *BELMT* SM2.............61 J7
Moorfield *HASM* GU27.............184 A5
........................*RDKG* RH5 *.........137 K6
Moorfield Point *GU* GU11........112 C1
Moorfield Rd *CHSGTN* KT9.........59 L4
........................*GU* GU1........112 C1
Moorfields Cl *STA* TW18............37 J2
Moorhayes Dr *STA* TW18...........37 N4
Moorhead Rd *HORS* RH12......192 G5
Moorholme
........................*WOKS/MYFD* GU22....10 D7
Moorhouse Rd *OXTED* RH8.....124 D1
Moorhurst La *RDKG* RH5.........136 C9
The Moorings *BF/WBF* KT14.....75 N1
........................*EGRIN* RH19........161 P9
........................*GODL* GU7........165 P8
........................*GT/LBKH* KT23........96 A5
........................*WDSR* SL4........21 H3
Moorland Cl *WHTN* TW2............25 H3
Moorland Rd *CRAWE* RH10.....177 M8
........................*WDR/YW* UB7........13 N5
Moorlands Cl *FLEETN* GU51.......87 H7
........................*GSHT* GU26........165 P7
Moorlands Rd *CBLY* GU15.........68 C4
The Moorlands
........................*WOKS/MYFD* GU22....92 D1
Moor La *CHSGTN* KT9................59 M4
........................*STA* TW18........22 B6
........................*STWL/WRAY* TW19....21 P4
........................*WDR/YW* UB7........13 N4
........................*WOKS/MYFD* GU22....92 C2
Moormead Dr
........................*HOR/WEW* KT19....60 C4
Moor Mead Rd *TWK* TW1...........25 P2
Moormede Crs *STA* TW18...........22 C7
Moor Pk *HORL* RH6 *..............159 L2
Moor Park Crs
........................*CRAWW* RH11........176 A6
Moor Park Gdns
........................*KUTN/CMB* KT2....42 C1
Moor Park La *FNM* GU9...........128 B3
Moor Park Rd *FNM* GU9..........128 B3
Moor Pl *BFOR* GU20.................52 B4
........................*EGRIN* RH19........180 C1
Moorside Cl *FARN* GU14...........68 C7
Moors La *MFD/CHID* GU8........168 C1
Moorsom Wy *COUL/CHIP* CR5...80 F6
The Moors *RFNM* GU10............109 H7
Moray Av *HYS/HAR* UB3...........15 H3
Mora Rd *CRICK* NW2................18 P1
Moray Av *SHST* GU47................67 P1
Mordaunt Dr *CWTH* RG45.........49 M6
Morden Cl *BRAK* RG12...............33 H5
........................*KWD/TDW/WH* KT20....79 H9
Morden Ct *MRDN* SM4...............43 M4
Morden Court Pde
........................*MRDN* SM4 *.........43 M4
Morden Gdns *MTCM* CR4...........43 P5
Morden Hall Rd *MRDN* SM4......43 M4
Morden Rd *WIM/MER* SW19......43 M3
Morden Wy *CHEAM* SM3...........43 L8
Morecambe Cl
........................*CRAWW* RH11........176 C2
More Cir *GODL* GU7.................131 L6
More Cl *PUR/KEN* CR8...............63 H9
........................*WKENS* W14........19 H2
Morecoombe Cl
........................*KUTN/CMB* KT2....41 P1
Morecote Cl *RGUE* GU4...........132 C3
Moreland Cl *DTCH/LGLY* SL3....12 C5
More La *ESH/CLAY* KT10............58 B2
Morella Cl *VW* GU25..................36 A6
Morella Rd *BTSEA* SW11............29 J3
Moremead Rd *CAT* SE6...............31 N7
More Rd *GODL* GU7.................131 L6
Moresby Av *BRYLDS* KT5...........41 P8
Mores Gdn *CHEL* SW3 *.............19 P4
Moretaine Rd *ASHF* TW15..........22 G6
Moreton Av *ISLW* TW7................16 G5
Moreton Cl *FLEETS* GU52.........106 F2
........................*RFNM* GU10........165 H2

Moreton Rd *SAND/SEL* CR2.......63 M4
........................*WPK* KT4........60 E1
Morgan Rd *BMLY* BR1...............47 N1
Morie St *WAND/EARL* SW18.......28 B9
Morin Rd *TOOT* SW17................29 K7
Morkyns Wk *DUL* SE21 *............30 F6
Morland Av *CROY/NA* CR0..........3 H1
Morland Cl *HPTN* TW12.............24 G8
........................*MTCM* CR4........44 A4
Morland Rd *ALDT* GU11...........108 E7
........................*CROY/NA* CR0........46 D1
........................*PGE/AN* SE20........31 K8
........................*SUT* SM1........61 N4
Morland's Rd *ALDT* GU11........108 F1
Morley Cl *YTLY* GU46................66 F3
Morley Rd *CHEAM* SM3..............43 K9
........................*FNM* GU9........5 H6
........................*SAND/SEL* CR2........63 P5
........................*SUT* SM1........61 H4
........................*TWK* TW1........26 C2
Morningside Rd *WPK* KT4..........60 F1
Mornington Av *EWKG* RG40.......48 D1
........................*WKENS* W14........19 K2
Mornington Crs *HEST* TW5.......15 K6
Mornington Rd *ASHF* TW15......23 M8
Mornington Wk
........................*RCHPK/HAM* TW10....26 B7
Morrell Av *HORS* RH12...........192 E5
Morrice Cl *DTCH/LGLY* SL3.......12 D2
Morris Cl *CROY/NA* CR0.............46 E7
Morris Gdns
........................*WAND/EARL* SW18....28 D3
Morris Rd
........................*BRXS/STRHM* SW2....29 P3
Morris La *FARN* GU14................88 F7
........................*ISLW* TW7........16 F8
........................*REDH* RH1........120 G7
Morston Cl
........................*KWD/TDW/WH* KT20....78 F9
Mortimer Cl
........................*STRHM/NOR* SW16....29 N5
Mortimer Crs *WPK* KT4..............60 B2
Mortimer Rd *BH/WHM* TN16.....84 A1
........................*DTCH/LGLY* SL3....12 B1
........................*MTCM* CR4........44 B2
........................*RDKG* RH5........56 C6
Mortlake Cl *CROY/NA* CR0.........62 G2
Mortlake Dr *MTCM* CR4.............44 A2
Mortlake High St
........................*MORT/ESHN* SW14....18 B8
Mortlake Rd *RCH/KEW* TW9......17 N5
Morton *KWD/TDW/WH* KT20.....99 H1
Morton Cl *CRAWW* RH11.........194 E2
........................*FRIM* GU16........69 H9
........................*WLGTN* SM6........63 H6
Morton Gdns *WLGTN* SM6.........62 E4
Morton Ms *ECT* SW5................19 M2
Morton Rd *EGRIN* RH19...........180 D4
........................*MRDN* SM4........43 P6
........................*WOKN/KNAP* GU21....72 A4
Morval Cl *FARN* GU14................88 A3
Morval Rd *BRXS/STRHM* SW2...30 A7
Morven Rd *TOOT* SW17.............29 J6
Moselle Cl *FARN* GU14..............87 P2
Moselle Rd *BH/WHM* TN16.......84 C7
Mosford Cl *HORL* RH6.............140 B8
Mospey Crs *EW* KT17................78 D4
Mossfield *COB* KT11.................75 J2
Moss Gdns *FELT* TW13...............24 B5
........................*SAND/SEL* CR2........64 D6
Moss La *GODL* GU7.................131 K9
Mosslea Rd *CTHM* CR3...............81 P5
........................*PGE/AN* SE20........31 K9
Mossville Gdns *MRDN* SM4.......43 K4
Moston Cl *HYS/HAR* UB3............15 H3
Mostyn Rd *WIM/MER* SW19......43 K3
Mostyn Ter *REDH* RH1.............120 C5
Moth Cl *WLGTN* SM6.................63 H6
Motspur Pk *NWMAL* KT3............42 D7
Motts Hill La
........................*KWD/TDW/WH* KT20....98 D8
Mouchotte Cl *BH/WHM* TN16...83 P1
Moulsham Copse La
........................*YTLY* GU46........66 F1
Moulsham La *YTLY* GU46...........66 E1
Moulton Av *HSLW* TW3..............15 N7
Mountacre Cl *SYD* SE26.............30 G7
Mount Adon Pk *EDUL* SE22......31 H5
Mount Angelus Rd
........................*PUT/ROE* SW15....27 L3
Mount Ararat Rd
........................*RCHPK/HAM* TW10....26 D1
Mount Ash Rd *SYD* SE26...........31 J6
Mount Av *CTHM* CR3...............101 L4
Mountbatten Cl
........................*CRAWW* RH11 *.......176 F9
........................*NRWD* SE19........30 F8
Mountbatten Ri *SHST* GU47.......49 K8
Mount Cl *CAR* SM5.....................62 C7
........................*CRAN* GU6........153 P7
........................*CRAWE* RH10........177 M4
........................*LHD/OX* KT22........96 F3
........................*PUR/KEN* CR8........81 L5
........................*WOKS/MYFD* GU22....91 P1
The Mount Cl *VW* GU25.............36 B7
Mountcombe Cl *SURB* KT6........41 L8
Mount Ct *GUW* GU2 *..............112 A6
........................*WWKM* BR4........65 L1
The Mount Dr *REIG* RH2..........119 N3
Mountearl Gdns
........................*STRHM/NOR* SW16....30 A6
Mount Ephraim La
........................*STRHM/NOR* SW16....29 N6
Mount Ephraim Rd
........................*STRHM/NOR* SW16....29 N6
Mount Felix *WOT/HER* KT12......39 H9
Mount Gdns *SYD* SE26...............31 J6
Mount Hermon Cl
........................*WOKS/MYFD* GU22....10 C6
Mount Hermon Rd
........................*WOKS/MYFD* GU22....10 B7
Mounthurst Rd *HAYES* BR2.......47 N8

Mount La *BRAK* RG12................32 E4
........................*CRAWE* RH10........179 H7
Mount Lee *EGH* TW20................21 K8
Mount Nod Rd
........................*STRHM/NOR* SW16....30 A6
Mount Pk *CAR* SM5....................62 C7
Mount Park Av
........................*SAND/SEL* CR2........63 K3
Mount Pl *GUW* GU2 *................6 B7
Mount Pleasant
........................*BH/WHM* TN16........84 B6
........................*BRAK* RG12........32 E4
........................*EHSLY* KT24........94 D9
........................*EHSLY* KT24........95 N8
........................*EW* KT17........60 D8
........................*FNM* GU9........4 C4
........................*GUW* GU2........111 P8
........................*RDKG* RH5 *.........135 H2
........................*SHST* GU47........49 L8
........................*WEY* KT13........56 C2
........................*WNWD* SE27........30 D7
Mount Pleasant Cl
........................*LTWR* GU18........52 A8
Mount Pleasant Rd
........................*ASHV* GU12........108 E4
........................*CTHM* CR3........102 A3
........................*LING* RH7........143 J9
........................*NWMAL* KT3........42 A9
........................*WIM/MER* SW19....28 D5
........................*WOKS/MYFD* GU22....21 M2
Mountsfield Cl
........................*STWL/WRAY* TW19....22 D1
Mountside *GUW* GU2....................6 B7
Mount St *DORK* RH4................116 C7
Mounts Wy *FLEETS* GU51.........86 C4
The Mount *BOR* GU35...............164 D5
........................*COUL/CHIP* CR5....80 C2
........................*CRAN* GU6........153 P7
........................*CRAN* GU6........171 H1
........................*CRAWW* RH11........175 N2
........................*ESH/CLAY* KT10....58 A5
........................*EW* KT17........60 F3
........................*EW* KT17........60 F3
........................*FLEETN* GU51........86 B4
........................*GUW* GU2........111 P8
........................*HASM* GU27........184 F2
........................*KWD/TDW/WH* KT20....99 K6
........................*NWMAL* KT3........42 D4
........................*VW* GU25........36 B7
........................*WARL* CR6........82 A8
........................*WEY* KT13........56 G1
........................*WOKS/MYFD* GU22....10 B7
Mountview Cl *REDH* RH1.........120 A7
Mountview Dr *REDH* RH1.........120 A7
Mount View Rd
........................*ESH/CLAY* KT10....59 H6
Mount Vls *WNWD* SE27.............30 C6
Mount Wy *CAR* SM5..................62 C7
Mountwood
........................*E/WMO/HCT* KT8....40 B4
Mountwood Cl
........................*SAND/SEL* CR2........64 B8
Mousehill La
........................*MFD/CHID* GU8....149 M4
Mowbray Av *BF/WBF* KT14........74 A2
Mowbray Crs *ECH* TW20............21 M8
Mowbray Dr *CRAWW* RH11.....175 P8
Mowbray Gdns *DORK* RH4......117 H5
Mowbray Rd *NRWD* SE19..........45 P2
........................*RCHPK/HAM* TW10....26 B6
Mower Pl *CRAN* GU6................153 H8
Moylan Rd *HMSMTH* W6...........19 J4
Moyne Rd *CRAWW* RH11.........176 F9
Moys Cl *CROY/NA* CR0...............44 C7
Moyser Rd
........................*STRHM/NOR* SW16....29 L8
Muchelney Rd *MRDN* SM4.........44 A6
Muckhatch La *EGH* TW20..........36 H4
Muggeridge Cl
........................*SAND/SEL* CR2........63 M4
Muggeridge's HI *RDKG* RH5....174 D3
Muirdown Av
........................*MORT/ESHN* SW14....18 A9
Muir Dr *WAND/EARL* SW18.......29 H2
Muirfield Cl *CRAWW* RH11.....176 A6
Muirfield Rd
........................*WOKN/KNAP* GU21....71 N7
Mulberry Av
........................*STWL/WRAY* TW19....23 H4
Mulberry Cl *ASHV* GU12..........109 J2
........................*CHEL* SW3........19 N5
........................*CWTH* RG45........49 N5
........................*HORS* RH12........192 B5
........................*SHST* GU47........49 N9
........................*STRHM/NOR* SW16....29 M7
........................*WEY* KT13........56 D2
........................*WOKN/KNAP* GU21....72 C3
Mulberry Crs *BTFD* TW8............17 H5
Mulberry Dr *DTCH/LGLY* SL3....12 C5
Mulberry La *CROY/NA* CR0..........3 K2
Mulberry Pl *HMSMTH* W6 *.......18 E3
........................*RDKG* RH5........157 H2
Mulberry Rd *CRAWW* RH11.....176 E2
Mulberry Trees *SHPTN* TW17...38 F8
Mulberry Wk *CHEL* SW3.............19 N5
Mulgrave Rd *BELMT* SM2...........61 K6
........................*CROY/NA* CR0........2 C6
........................*FRIM* GU16........69 H6
........................*WKENS* W14........19 K4

Mulgrave Wy
........................*WOKN/KNAP* GU21....71 L7
Mulholland Cl *MTCM* CR4.........44 D3
Mullards Cl *MTCM* CR4..............44 B9
Mullens Rd *EGH* TW20...............21 P8
Mullins Pth
........................*MORT/ESHN* SW14....18 B8
Mulroy Dr *CBLY* GU15...............69 J3
Multon Rd *WAND/EARL* SW18...28 C3
Mumford Rd *HNHL* SE24............30 C1
Muncaster Cl *ASHF* TW15..........23 K7
Muncaster Rd *ASHF* TW15.........23 L8
Mundania Rd *EDUL* SE22...........31 J2
Munday Ct *BNFD* RG42..............32 C4
Munday's Boro *RGUW* GU3.....130 A3
Munday's Boro Rd
........................*RGUW* GU3........130 B1
Mundens St *WKENS* W14...........19 K3
Mund St *WKENS* W14.................19 K3
Munnings Dr *SHST* GU47...........67 P2
Munnings Gdns *ISLW* TW7........25 L1
Munro Ter *WBPTN* SW10...........19 P5
Munro Ter *WBPTN* SW10...........19 P5
Munslow Gdns *SUT* SM1............61 N3
Munstead Heath Rd
........................*GODL* GU8........132 A9
Munstead Pk
........................*MFD/CHID* GU8....151 H1
Munstead Vw *RGUW* GU3.........111 P9
Munster Av *HSLW* TW4...............15 N9
Munster Ms *FUL/PGN* SW6 *.....19 K5
Munster Rd *FUL/PGN* SW6.........19 J5
........................*TEDD* TW11........41 J1
Murdoch Cl *STA* TW18................22 D8
Murfett Cl *WIM/MER* SW19........28 B5
Murray Av *BMLY* BR1.................47 N4
........................*HSLW* TW3........25 J1
Murray Ct *ASC* SL5....................34 C7
........................*SWTR* RH13........192 G6
Murray Rd *CHERT* KT16..............55 H5
........................*EA* W5........17 J2
........................*FARN* GU14........88 A4
........................*RCHPK/HAM* TW10....26 A5
........................*WIM/MER* SW19....28 A9
Murray's La *BF/WBF* KT14........73 P3
Murrell Rd *ASHV* GU12...........109 J3
Murrells La *CBLY* GU15..............68 D5
Murrells Wk *GT/LBKH* KT23......96 A5
Murrey Ct *SWTR* RH13 *...........192 G6
The Murreys *ASHTD* KT21..........77 K7
Musard Rd *HMSMTH* W6............19 J4
Musgrave Av *EGRIN* RH19.......180 D4
Musgrave Crs *FUL/PGN* SW6.....19 L6
Musgrave Rd *ISLW* TW7.............16 F6
Musjid Rd *BTSEA* SW11.............29 P7
Musquash Wy *HSLWW* TW4.......15 L7
Mustard Mill Rd *STA* TW18........22 C7
Mutton Hill *LING* RH7..............162 F5
Muybridge Rd *NWMAL* KT3.......42 A3
Myers Wy *FRIM* GU16...............69 M6
Mylis Cl *SYD* SE26......................31 J7
Mylne Cl *HMSMTH* W6 *............18 E3
Mylor Cl *WOKN/KNAP* GU21......72 C3
Mynn's Cl *EPSOM* KT18.............77 P3
Myrna Cl *WIM/MER* SW19..........44 A1
Myrtle Av *EBED/NFELT* TW14....14 G9
Myrtle Cl *DTCH/LGLY* SL3..........13 J6
........................*LTWR* GU18........52 B9
........................*WDR/YW* UB7........14 B2
Myrtle Dr *BLKW* GU17...............67 P4
Myrtle Gv *NWMAL* KT3.............42 A3
Myrtle Rd *CROY/NA* CR0............64 C2
........................*DORK* RH4........116 G6
........................*HPTN* TW12........25 H7
........................*HSLW* TW3........16 C7
........................*SUT* SM1........61 N4

Nailsworth Crs *REDH* RH1.......100 F3
Nairn Cl *FRIM* GU16..................68 G6
Nairn Gv *NHNL* SE24.................30 E1
Naldrett Cl *HORS* RH12...........192 E6
Naldretts La *HORS* RH12.........189 M5
Nallhead Rd *FELT* TW13.............24 D8
Namba Roy Cl
........................*STRHM/NOR* SW16....30 A7
Namton Dr *THHTH* CR7.............44 P5
Nantes Cl *WAND/EARL* SW18....19 N9
Napier Av *FUL/PGN* SW6............19 K9
Napier Cl *ALDT* GU11................88 G8
........................*CWTH* RG45........49 N5
........................*WDR/YW* UB7........14 B1
Napier Ct *CTHM* CR3...............101 N2
Napier Dr *CBLY* GU15...............69 J1
Napier Gdns *GU* GU1...............112 F4
Napier Rd *ASHF* TW15...............38 F2
........................*ISLW* TW7........16 G9
........................*SAND/SEL* CR2........63 M6
........................*SNWD* SE25........46 B5
........................*WDR/YW* UB7........13 P2
........................*WKENS* W14........19 K1
Napier Wk *ASHF* TW15...............38 F1

Napier Wy CRAWE RH10.........177 J2
Napoleon Av FARN GU14.........88 D1
Napoleon Rd TWK TW1 *.........26 A3
Napper Cl ASC SL5.........33 L3
Napper Pl CRAN GU6.........171 H2
Narbonne Av CLAP SW4.........29 M2
Narborough St FUL/PGN SW6..19 M7
Narrow La WARL CR6.........82 B8
Naseby BRAK RG12.........32 D9
Naseby Cl ISLW TW7.........16 E6
Naseby Ct WOT/HER KT12 *....57 L1
Naseby Rd NRWD SE19.........30 E9
Nash Cl FARN GU14.........88 B3
  SUT SM1.........25 P7
Nash Gdns ASC SL5.........33 M3
  REDH RH1.........120 B3
Nash Gn BMLY BR1.........47 N1
Nash Grove La EWKG RG40...48 D1
Nash La HAYES BR2.........65 N5
Nash Rd CRAWE RH10.........177 H8
  DTCH/LGLY SL3.........12 D3
Nasmyth St HMSMTH W6.........19 F1
Nassau Rd BARN SW13.........18 D6
Nasturtium Dr
  CHOB/PIR GU24.........70 G4
Natalie Cl EBED/NFELT TW14..23 N3
Natal Rd STRHM/NOR SW16...29 N9
  THHTH CR7.........45 L5
Neale Cl EGRIN RH19.........162 A9
Neal Ter FSTH SE23 *.........31 L4
Neath Gdns MRDN SM4.........43 N7
Neb La OXTED RH8.........123 J2
Needles Bank GDST RH9.........122 B2
Needles Cl HORS RH12.........192 A9
Neil Cl ASHF TW15.........23 M8
Nelgarde Rd CAT SE6.........31 P3
Nella Rd HMSMTH W6.........19 H4
Nell Ball BIL RH14.........187 K8
Nell Gwynn Av SHPTN TW17...38 F7
Nell Gwynne Av ASC SL5.........34 D5
Nell Gwynne Cl
  HOR/WEW KT19.........59 N9
Nelson Cl ASHV GU12.........108 C5
  BH/WHM TN16.........84 C6
  BRAK RG12.........32 G3
  CRAWE RH10.........177 M6
  CROY/NA CR0.........2 B2
  DTCH/LGLY SL3.........12 B5
  EBED/NFELT TW14 *.........24 A4
  FNM GU9.........107 P6
  WOT/HER KT12.........39 K9
Nelson Gdns GU GU1.........112 C4
  HSLW TW3.........25 H2
Nelson Grove Rd
  WIM/MER SW19.........43 M2
Nelson Rd ASHF TW15.........23 H8
  CTHM CR3.........101 M3
  FNM GU9.........107 P6
  HORS RH12.........192 A7
  HTHAIR TW6.........14 B6
  NWMAL KT3.........42 B6
  WHTN TW2.........25 K3
  WIM/MER SW19.........43 M1
Nelson St ALDT GU11.........108 C4
Nelson Wk HOR/WEW KT19....59 N7
Nelson Wy CBLY GU15.........68 B4
Nene Gdns FELT TW13.........24 G5
Nene Rd HTHAIR TW6.........14 D6
Nesbitt Sq NRWD SE19 *.........45 N1
Nestle's Av HYS/HAR UB3....15 H1
Netheravon Rd CHSWK W4...18 D2
Netheravon Rd South
  CHSWK W4.........18 D4
Netherbury Rd EA W5.........17 K1
Netherby Rd FSTH SE23.........31 K3
Nethercote Av
  WOKN/KNAP GU21.........71 M6
Netherfield Rd TOOT SW17...29 K6
Netherhouse Moor
  FLEETS GU51.........86 D9
The Netherlands
  COUL/CHIP CR5.........80 E8
Netherleigh Pk REDH RH1...120 C8
Nether Mt GUW GU2.........6 B7
Nethern Court Rd
  CTHM CR3.........102 C3
Netherne Dr
  COUL/CHIP CR5.........100 E2
Netherne La COUL/CHIP CR5..100 E2
Netherton Gv WBPTN SW10...19 N4
Netherton Rd TWK TW1.........25 P1
Nether Vell-mead
  FLEETS GU51.........106 E2
Netherwood CRAWW RH11...176 D8
Netherwood Pl
  HMSMTH W6 *.........19 H1
Netherwood Rd WKENS W14...19 H1
Netley Cl CHEAM SM3.........61 H4
  CRAWW RH11.........194 F2
  CROY/NA CR0.........65 J6
  SHGR GU5.........114 E9
Netley Dr WOT/HER KT12...39 P9
Netley Gdns MRDN SM4.........43 N8
Netley Rd BTFD TW8.........17 L4
  MRDN SM4.........43 N8
Netley St FARN GU14.........88 E7
Nettlecombe BRAK RG12.........32 F6
Nettlecombe Cl BELMT SM2...61 M7
Nettlefold Pl WNWD SE27...30 C6
Nettlestead Cl BECK BR3.........46 F1
Nettles Ter GU GU1.........6 E2
Nettleton Rd HTHAIR TW6...14 D6
Nettlewood Rd
  STRHM/NOR SW16.........44 F1
Neuchatel Rd CAT SE6.........31 N5

Neuman Crs BRAK RG12.........32 C7
Nevada Cl FARN GU14.........87 P4
  NWMAL KT3.........42 A5
Nevern Pl ECT SW5.........19 L2
Nevern Rd ECT SW5.........19 L2
Nevern Sq ECT SW5.........19 L2
Nevil Cl CRAWW RH11.........176 D8
Neville Av NWMAL KT3.........42 B2
Neville Cl BNSTD SM7.........79 M3
  ESH/CLAY KT10.........57 P5
  HSLW TW3.........16 A7
Neville Duke Rd FARN GU14...68 B8
Neville Gill Cl
  WAND/EARL SW18.........28 C2
Neville Rd CROY/NA CR0.........45 M8
  KUT/HW KT1.........9 J4
  RCHPK/HAM TW10.........26 B6
Neville Ter SKENS SW7 *.........19 P3
Neville Wk CAR SM5.........44 A8
Nevil Wk CAR SM5 *.........44 A8
Nevinson Cl
  WAND/EARL SW18.........28 D2
Nevis Rd TOOT SW17.........29 K5
New Acres EWKG RG40 *.........49 J2
Newall Rd HTHAIR TW6.........14 E6
Newark Cl RGUE GU4.........92 F9
  RPLY/SEND GU23.........93 K1
Newark Ct WOT/HER KT12...39 L9
Newark La RPLY/SEND GU23...73 K9
Newark Rd BFOR GU20.........52 B3
  BLKW GU17.........67 J7
  CRAWE RH10.........177 J3
  SAND/SEL CR2.........63 M5
New Barn Cl FLEETN GU51...86 D8
  WLGTN SM6.........63 H5
Newbarn La HEST TW5 *.........14 B5
New Barns Av MTCM CR4...44 F5
New Battlebridge La
  REDH RH1.........120 D1
New Berry La WOT/HER KT12...57 M4
Newbolt Av CHEAM SM3.........60 G4
Newborough Gn NWMAL KT3..42 B5
Newbridge Cl HORS RH12...191 K7
Newbury Gdns
  HOR/WEW KT19.........60 D3
Newbury Rd CRAWE RH10...177 N5
  HAYES BR2.........47 N4
  HTHAIR TW6.........14 B6
New Cswy REIG RH2.........119 M8
Newchapel Rd LING RH7.........161 P2
New Cl FELT TW13.........24 F8
  WIM/MER SW19.........43 N4
Newcombe Gdns
  HSLWW TW4.........15 P7
Newcome Gdns
  STRHM/NOR SW16.........29 P7
Newcomen Rd BTSEA SW11...19 P8
Newcome Pl ASHV GU12.........108 F7
Newcome Rd FNM GU9.........108 F7
New Coppice
  WOKN/KNAP GU21.........71 L8
New Cross Rd GUW GU2.........111 N3
New Dawn Cl FARN GU14...87 P4
Newdigate
  STRHM/NOR SW16 *.........30 B7
Newdigate Rd HORS RH12...175 J3
  RDKG RH5.........156 C2
Newenham Rd GT/LBKH KT23..96 A6
Newent Cl CAR SM5.........44 B9
New Farm Av HAYES BR2...47 N5
New Farthingdale LING RH7...162 F4
Newfield Av FARN GU14.........88 A1
Newfield Cl HPTN TW12.........40 A2
Newfield Rd ASHV GU12.........89 J9
New Forest Ride BRAK RG12..32 G8
Newfoundland Rd
  FRIM GU16.........69 M8
Newgate CROY/NA CR0.........2 D1
Newgate Cl FELT TW13.........24 F5
New Green Pl
  BRXS/STRHM SW2.........30 B3
  NRWD SE19.........30 F2
Newnhache LING RH7.........162 F7
Newhall Gdns WOT/HER KT12..57 L1
Newhaven Cl HYS/HAR UB3...15 H2
Newhaven Crs ASHF TW15...23 N8
Newhaven Rd SNWD SE25...45 M6
New Haw Rd
  ADL/WDHM KT15.........55 N5
New Heston Rd HEST TW5...15 P5
Newhouse Cl NWMAL KT3...42 B9
Newhouse House Farm La
  RGUW GU3.........111 H3
New House La REDH RH1...140 F4
New House Ter EDEN TN8 *..144 G3
Newhouse Wk MRDN SM4...43 N8
New Inn La GU GU1.........112 F2
New Kelvin Av TEDD TW11...25 M9
New King's Rd FUL/PGN SW6..19 L6
Newlands FLEETS GU51.........86 C9
  GU GU1.........7 K6
Newlands Av THDIT KT7.........40 G8
  WOKS/MYFD GU22.........92 D1
Newlands Cl HORL RH6.........160 B8
  NWDGN UB2.........15 N3
  WOT/HER KT12.........57 N5
  YTLY GU46.........67 H3
Newlands Crs EGRIN RH19...180 C1
  GU GU1.........7 K6
Newlands Dr ASHV GU12...109 K2
  DTCH/LGLY SL3.........13 J8
Newlands Pk FROW RH18 *..181 L8
Newlands Rd CBLY GU15...68 D7
  CRAWW RH11.........176 F6
  HORS RH12.........192 B6
  STRHM/NOR SW16.........44 G3
The Newlands WLGTN SM6..62 E6

Newlands Wy CHSGTN KT9...59 J4
Newlands Wd CROY/NA CR0..64 F7
Newlands Woods
  CROY/NA CR0 *.........64 F7
New La RGUE GU4.........92 D4
New Lodge Dr OXTED RH8..103 M8
Newlyn Cl GUW GU2.........138 C9
Newman Rd BMLY BR1.........47 N2
  CROY/NA CR0.........45 H8
Newmarket Rd
  CRAWE RH10.........177 K8
New Meadow ASC SL5.........33 M2
New Mile Rd ASC SL5.........34 B3
Newminster Rd MRDN SM4...43 N7
New Moorhead Dr
  HORS RH12.........193 H4
Newnham Cl THHTH CR7.........45 L3
New North Rd REIG RH2.........119 K8
New Pde ASHF TW15 *.........23 J7
  DORK RH4 *.........117 H6
  GT/LBKH KT23 *.........96 C6
New Park Rd ASHF TW15...23 M8
  BRXS/STRHM SW2.........29 P4
  CRAN GU6.........153 H9
New Pl ASC SL5 *.........34 C5
New Place Gdns LING RH7..143 L9
New Pond Rd GODL GU7...131 L4
Newport Rd ASHV GU12.........108 E5
  BARN SW13.........18 E6
  HTHAIR TW6.........14 C6
New Rd ASC SL5.........33 P1
  BAGS GU19.........51 P6
  BLKW GU17.........68 A4
  BRAK RG12.........32 F3
  BTFD TW8 *.........17 K4
  CWTH RG45.........49 N4
  DTCH/LGLY SL3.........12 B6
  DTCH/LGLY SL3.........12 E1
  E/WMO/HCT KT8.........40 A4
  EBED/NFELT TW14.........24 A4
  ESH/CLAY KT10.........58 C3
  FELT TW13.........24 F8
  FLEETS GU52.........87 H9
  HASM GU27.........184 A5
  HORL RH6.........160 C1
  HSLW TW5.........16 B9
  HTWY RG27.........66 C1
  HYS/HAR UB3.........14 E5
  KUTN/CMB KT2.........41 N1
  KWD/TDW/WH KT20.........98 C3
  LING RH7.........143 L9
  MFD/CHID GU8.........149 M4
  MFD/CHID GU8.........150 D7
  MFD/CHID GU8.........158 A4
  MTCM CR4.........44 C9
  OXTED RH8.........122 G7
  OXTED RH8.........123 P1
  RCHPK/HAM TW10.........26 B7
  RDKG RH5.........154 F6
  RFNM GU10.........109 H8
  RGUE GU4.........114 A2
  RSEV TN14.........105 P6
  SHGR GU5.........132 F5
  SHGR GU5.........133 P1
  SHPTN TW17.........38 C4
  SHST GU47.........49 L9
  STA TW18.........21 P8
  SUT SM1.........61 P4
  TEDD TW11.........25 M9
  WDSR SL4.........20 F2
  WOKN/KNAP GU21.........71 M6
  WOKS/MYFD GU22.........72 G4
  WOKS/MYFD GU22.........73 H4
Newry Rd TWK TW1 *.........16 D9
Newsham Rd
  WOKN/KNAP GU21.........71 M6
New St BH/WHM TN16.........104 G7
  CRAWE RH10.........177 K4
  STA TW18.........22 D7
  SWTR RH13.........192 C8
Newton Av WDSR SL4 *.........20 F2
Newton Cl WDSR SL4.........20 F2
Newton Gv CHSWK W4.........18 C1
Newton La WDSR SL4.........20 G2
Newton Rd CRAWE RH10...177 J1
  FARN GU14.........88 F1
  HTHAIR TW6.........14 A6
  ISLW TW7.........16 E7
  PUR/KEN CR8.........80 E1
  WIM/MER SW19.........43 J1
Newtonside Orch
  WDSR SL4 *.........20 F2
Newton's Yd
  WAND/EARL SW18.........28 D1
Newton Wd RFNM GU10...108 G7
Newton Wood Rd
  ASHTD KT21.........77 M5
New Town CRAWE RH10...160 C9
Newtown Rd LIPH GU30...182 F7
  SHST GU47.........49 M9
New Wy GODL GU7.........131 H8
New Wickham La EGH TW20...36 E1
New Wokingham Rd
  CWTH RG45.........49 L3
New Years La RSEV TN14...85 K5
New Zealand Av
  WOT/HER KT12.........39 J9
Nexus Pk ASH GU12.........89 H7
Niagara Av EA W5.........17 J2
Nicholas Gdns
  WOKS/MYFD GU22.........92 C1
Nicholas Rd CROY/NA CR0...62 G3
Nicholes Rd HSLW TW3.........16 A9
Nichol La BMLY BR1.........47 N1
Nicholsfield BIL RH14.........187 K8
Nicholson Ms EGH TW20 *...21 M8

Nicholson Rd CROY/NA CR0....3 K1
Nicholson Wk EGH TW20.........21 M8
Nickols Wk
  WAND/EARL SW18.........19 M9
Nicola Cl SAND/SEL CR2.........63 L5
Nicosia Rd WAND/EARL SW18..29 H3
Niederwald Rd SYD SE26...31 M1
Nigel Fisher Wy CHSGTN KT9..59 J6
Nigel Playfair Av
  HMSMTH W6.........18 F3
Nightingale Av EHSLY KT24...94 F5
Nightingale Cl
  BH/WHM TN16.........84 A4
  CAR SM5.........62 C1
  CHSWK W4.........18 A4
  COB KT11.........57 M9
  CRAWW RH11.........176 F3
  EGRIN RH19.........180 C4
  FARN GU14.........87 N1
  HOR/WEW KT19.........59 N5
Nightingale Ct CBLY GU15...32 E6
  EHSLY KT24.........94 F5
Nightingale Dr FRIM GU16...89 J4
  HOR/WEW KT19.........59 N5
Nightingale Gdns SHST GU47..49 M9
Nightingale La BAL SW12.........29 K2
  CRAWE RH10.........177 M6
  RCHPK/HAM TW10.........26 D3
Nightingale Ms KUT/HW KT1 *..8 C6
Nightingale Pl WBPTN SW10..19 N4
Nightingale Rd ASHV GU12...109 L3
  CAR SM5.........62 B2
  E/WMO/HCT KT8.........40 B6
  EHSLY KT24.........95 H5
  ESH/CLAY KT10.........57 P4
  GODL GU7.........131 L7
  HORS RH12.........192 C7
  HPTN TW12.........25 H9
  SAND/SEL CR2.........64 D9
  WOT/HER KT12 *.........39 L8
Nightingales CRAN GU6.........171 K2
Nightingale Shott EGRIN RH19..21 L3
Nightingale Sq BAL SW12.........29 K2
The Nightingales
  STWL/WRAY TW19.........23 J4
Nightingale Wk BAL SW12...29 J4
Nightingale Wy REDH RH1..121 N5
Nightjar Cl RFNM GU10.........107 H6
Nimbus Rd HOR/WEW KT19...60 B8
Nimrod Rd
  STRHM/NOR SW16.........29 L9
Nineacres Wy
  COUL/CHIP CR5.........80 C5
Nine Elms Cl
  EBED/NFELT TW14.........24 A4
Ninehams Cl CTHM CR3.........81 M9
Ninehams Gdns CTHM CR3...81 M9
Ninehams Rd
  BH/WHM TN16.........104 B1
  CTHM CR3.........101 M1
Nine Mile Ride BRAK RG12...32 C9
  EWKG RG40.........48 B3
  RFNM GU10.........49 H2
Nineteenth Rd MTCM CR4...44 G5
Ninth Av
  KWD/TDW/WH KT20.........99 K6
Niton Rd RCH/KEW TW9 *...17 N3
Niton St FUL/PGN SW6.........19 H5
Niven Cl CRAWE RH10.........177 N6
Noahs Cl CRAWE RH10.........179 H7
Nobel Dr HYS/HAR UB3.........14 C5
Noble Cnr HEST TW5 *.........16 A6
Nobles Wy EGH TW20.........36 C1
Noke Dr REDH RH1.........120 C4
Nonsuch Court Av EW KT17...60 F8
Nonsuch Pl CHEAM SM3 *...61 H6
Nonsuch Wk BELMT SM2.........61 H8
Nooms Corner Rd RDKG RH5..135 P5
Norbiton Av KUT/HW KT1.........9 K5
Norbiton Common Rd
  KUT/HW KT1.........41 N7
Norbury Av HSLW TW3.........25 L1
  STRHM/NOR SW16.........45 H2
Norbury Cl
  STRHM/NOR SW16.........45 J2
Norbury Court Rd
  STRHM/NOR SW16.........44 G4
Norbury Crs
  STRHM/NOR SW16.........44 G3
Norbury Cross
  STRHM/NOR SW16.........44 G4
Norbury Hl
  STRHM/NOR SW16.........45 J1
Norbury Ri
  STRHM/NOR SW16.........44 G4
Norbury Rd FELT TW13.........24 A6
  REIG RH2.........119 K5
  THHTH CR7.........45 L3
Norbury Wy GT/LBKH KT23...96 C5
Norcroft Gdns EDUL SE22...31 H2
Norcutt Rd WHTN TW2.........25 M4
Norfolk Av SAND/SEL CR2...64 A8
Norfolk Cha BNFD RG42.........33 H1
Norfolk Cl CRAWW RH11...176 B9
  HORL RH6.........159 K2
  TWK TW1 *.........26 A2
Norfolk Farm Cl
  WOKS/MYFD GU22.........72 G4
Norfolk Farm Rd
  WOKS/MYFD GU22.........73 H4
Norfolk Gdns
  WOKN/KNAP GU21 *.........71 M8
Norfolk House Rd
  STRHM/NOR SW16.........29 N6
Norfolk La RDKG RH5.........137 H4
Norfolk Rd DORK RH4.........116 C7
  ESH/CLAY KT10.........58 E4
  FELT TW13.........24 D4
  HORS RH12.........192 C8
  RDKG RH5.........137 J7
  THHTH CR7.........45 L4

WIM/MER SW19.........44 A1
Norgrove St BAL SW12.........29 K4
Norheads La BH/WHM TN16...83 N7
Norhyrst Av SNWD SE25.........45 H3
Nork Gdns BNSTD SM7.........79 J3
Nork Ri BNSTD SM7 *.........79 H4
Nork Wy BNSTD SM7.........79 H4
Norlands La EGH TW20.........37 J5
Norley V PUT/ROE SW15.........27 M4
Norman Av EW KT17.........78 D1
  FELT TW13.........24 F5
  SAND/SEL CR2.........63 L8
  TWK TW1.........25 P1
Normanby Cl PUT/ROE SW15...28 C1
Normanby Cl EPSOM KT18...78 B8
Norman Colyer Ct
  HOR/WEW KT19 *.........60 B8
Norman Crs HEST TW5.........15 M5
Normand Gdns
  WKENS W14 *.........19 J4
Normand Ms WKENS W14...19 J4
Normand Rd WKENS W14...19 K4
Normandy HORS RH12.........192 B9
Normandy Cl CRAWE RH10...177 L7
  EGRIN RH19 *.........180 E3
  FRIM GU16.........69 N8
  SYD SE26.........31 N1
Normandy Common La
  RGUW GU3.........110 B2
Normandy Gdns
  HORS RH12.........192 B9
Normandy Wk EGH TW20 *...21 P8
Normanhurst Cl
  CRAWE RH10.........177 J5
Normanhurst Dr TWK TW1...26 A1
Normanhurst Rd
  BRXS/STRHM SW2.........30 A5
  WOT/HER KT12.........57 M1
Norman Keep BNFD RG42...33 H2
Norman Rd ASHF TW15.........23 N9
  SUT SM1.........61 L4
  THHTH CR7.........45 L4
  WIM/MER SW19.........43 N1
Normansfield Av KUT/HW KT1..8 A1
Normans La EDEN TN8.........144 C5
Norman's Rd HORL RH6.........141 M4
Normanton Av
  WAND/EARL SW18.........28 D5
Normanton Rd
  SAND/SEL CR2.........63 N5
Normanton St FSTH SE23...31 L5
Normington Cl
  STRHM/NOR SW16.........30 B8
Norrels Dr EHSLY KT24.........95 H6
Norrels Ride EHSLY KT24...95 H5
Norris Br FARN GU14.........87 L7
Norris Hill Rd FLEETN GU51...87 K8
Norroy Rd PUT/ROE SW15...19 H9
Norstead Pl PUT/ROE SW15...27 M5
North Acre BNSTD SM7.........79 K5
Northampton Cl BRAK RG12...32 F4
Northampton Rd
  CROY/NA CR0.........64 A1
Northanger Rd
  STRHM/NOR SW16.........29 P9
North Av CAR SM5.........62 C6
  FNM GU9.........107 P7
  RCH/KEW TW9.........17 N6
  WOT/HER KT12.........56 B7
Northborough Rd
  STRHM/NOR SW16.........44 G3
Northbourne GODL GU7...131 M5
  HAYES BR2.........47 N8
Northbrook Copse
  BRAK RG12.........33 H7
Northbrook Rd ALDT GU11...108 D6
  CROY/NA CR0.........45 M6
Northcliffe Cl WPK KT4.........60 C2
North Cl ASHV GU12.........108 G5
  CRAWW RH11.........177 J4
  EBED/NFELT TW14.........23 N2
  FARN GU14.........88 C8
  MRDN SM4.........43 J5
  RDKG RH5.........137 J2
North Common WEY KT13...56 E3
Northcote ADL/WDHM KT15...55 P3
Northcote Av BRYLDS KT5...41 N8
  ISLW TW7.........25 P1
Northcote Crs EHSLY KT24...94 E5
Northcote La SHGR GU5.........133 J8
Northcote Rd ASHV GU12...89 J8
  CROY/NA CR0.........45 M7
  EHSLY KT24.........94 E5
  FARN GU14.........88 A1
  NWMAL KT3.........42 A4
  TWK TW1.........25 P1
Northcott BRAK RG12.........32 C9
Northcroft Gdns FARN GU14...87 P2
Northcroft Cl EGH TW20...20 C8
Northcroft Gdns EGH TW20...20 C8
Northcroft Rd EGH TW20...20 C8
  HOR/WEW KT19.........60 C6
North Cross Rd EDUL SE22...30 G1
North Dene HSLW TW3.........16 B6
North Down SAND/SEL CR2...63 M8
Northdown Cl HORS RH12...192 B6
Northdown La GU GU1.........112 E9
Northdown Rd BELMT SM2...61 L8
  CTHM CR3.........102 C5
Northdowns CRAN GU6.........171 H2
North Downs Crs
  CROY/NA CR0.........65 H8
North Downs Rd
  CROY/NA CR0.........65 H8
North Downs Wy
  BRKHM/BTCW RH3.........118 B3
  CTHM CR3.........101 M7
  GDST RH9.........102 F8
  KWD/TDW/WH KT20.........99 M6
  RDKG RH5.........115 N6
  REDH RH1.........100 H8

RFNM GU10 ....128 C3
RGUE GU4 ....112 E9
RGUW GU5 ....129 P7
WARL CR8 ....103 N3
Northdown Ter
EGRIN RH19 * 162 C9
North Dr BECK BR3 ....47 H5
CHOB/PIR GU24 ....90 C1
HSLW TW5 ....16 C2
STRHM/NOR SW16 ....29 M7
VW GU25 ....35 L6
North End CROY/NA CR0 ....2 C3
EGRIN RH19 * 162 A9
North End Gdns WKENS W14 ....19 K2
North End La ASC SL5 ....34 G8
North End Rd WKENS W14 ....19 J2
Northernhay Wk MRDN SM4 ....43 J5
Northern Perimeter Rd
HTHAIR TW6 ....14 E6
Northern Perimeter Rd (West)
WDR/YW UB7 ....13 N6
Northey Av BELMT SM2 ....61 H8
North Eyot Gdns
HMSMTH W6 * 18 D3
North Farm Rd FARN GU14 ....68 A8
Northfield LTWR GU18 ....52 B9
MFD/CHID GU8 ....149 N8
RGUE GU4 ....132 C4
Northfield Cl ASHV GU12 ....108 F5
FLEETS GU52 * 87 H9
HYS/HAR UB3 ....15 H1
Northfield Ct STA TW18 ....37 M2
Northfield Crs CHEAM SM3 ....61 J3
Northfield Pde
HYS/HAR UB5 * 15 H1
Northfield Pk HYS/HAR UB3 ....14 G1
Northfield Pl WEY KT13 ....56 D6
North Field Rd HEST TW5 ....15 M4
Northfield Rd COB KT11 ....75 J2
FLEETS GU52 ....87 H9
STA TW18 ....37 M2
Northfields ASHTD KT21 ....77 L8
EW KT17 ....60 C9
WAND/EARL SW18 ....19 L9
North Fryerne YTLY GU46 ....49 H5
Northgate Av WIM/MER SW19 ....43 P1
Northgate Dr CBLY GU15 ....68 A8
Northgate Pl CRAWE RH10 ....177 H4
Northgate Rd CRAWE RH10 ....176 A5
North Gate Rd FARN GU14 ....88 D5
Northgate Rd HORL RH6 ....159 J5
North Gn BRAK RG12 ....32 E7
North Gv CHERT KT16 ....37 K7
North Heath Cl HORS RH12 ....192 C5
North Heath La HORS RH12 ....192 C5
North Holmes Cl
HORS RH12 ....192 G5
North Hyde Gdns
HYS/HAR UB5 ....15 J1
North Hyde La NWDGN UB2 ....15 N3
North Hyde Rd
HYS/HAR UB3 ....14 G1
North Hyde Whf
NWDGN UB2 * 15 N3
Northington Cl BRAK RG12 ....33 H7
Northlands RDKG RH5 * 156 B6
Northlands Rd HORS RH12 ....191 L1
HORS RH12 ....192 D3
North La ASHV GU12 ....108 F3
TEDD TW11 ....25 N9
North Lodge Cl
PUT/ROE SW15 * 28 A1
North Lodge Dr ASC SL5 ....33 L3
North Looe EW KT17 * 78 C2
North Md FARN GU14 ....177 H5
REDH RH1 ....120 B2
Northmead FARN GU14 ....88 D3
North Moors GU GU4 ....112 C1
North Munstead La
MFD/CHID GU8 ....150 F3
Northolt Rd WDR/YW UB7 ....13 P6
North Pde CHSGTN KT9 ....59 M4
HORS RH12 ....192 B7
North Pk DTCH/LGLY SL3 ....13 J1
North Park La GDST RH9 ....102 A9
North Pas WAND/EARL SW18 ....28 D1
North Pl MTCM CR4 ....44 D1
TEDD TW11 ....25 N9
Northpoint Cl SUT SM1 ....61 N2
North Pole La HAYES BR2 ....65 N5
North Rd ALDT GU11 ....88 F8
ASC SL5 ....33 K2
ASHV GU12 ....109 H2
BMLY BR1 ....47 K7
CRAWE RH10 ....177 K4
EA W5 ....17 K1
EBED/NFELT TW14 ....23 N2
FARN GU14 ....88 F8
GUW GU2 ....111 P2
HEST TW5 ....15 L4
RCH/KEW TW9 ....17 N7
REIG RH2 ....119 K8
SURB KT6 ....41 K7
WDR/YW UB7 ....14 B1
WOKN/KNAP GU21 ....11 G1
WOT/HER KT12 ....57 L4
Northrop Rd HTHAIR TW6 ....14 C6
North Side RFNM GU10 ....109 J7
Northside Rd BMLY BR1 ....47 N2
North Side
Wandsworth Common
WAND/EARL SW18 ....28 F1
Northspur Rd SUT SM1 ....61 L1
North Station Ap
REDH RH1 * 121 H7
Northstead Rd
BRXS/STRHM SW2 ....30 B5
North St BMLY BR1 ....47 N2
CAR SM5 ....62 B3
CRAWE RH10 ....179 H7

DORK RH4 ....116 G7
EGH TW20 ....21 L8
GODL GU7 ....131 L6
GU GU1 ....6 E5
HORS RH12 ....192 C8
ISLW TW7 ....16 G8
OXTD RH8 * 96 C1
REDH RH1 ....120 B4
Northumberland Av
ISLW TW7 ....16 F6
Northumberland Cl
BNFD RG42 ....33 H1
STWL/WRAY TW19 ....23 H2
Northumberland Crs
EBED/NFELT TW14 ....23 P2
Northumberland Gdns
MTCM CR4 ....44 G6
North Verbena Gdns
HMSMTH W6 * 18 E3
North Vw WIM/MER SW19 ....27 N8
North View Crs EPSOM KT18 ....78 G6
North Wk CROY/NA CR0 ....65 H4
Northway GODL GU7 ....131 H6
GUW GU2 ....111 N3
HORL RH6 ....159 J4
MRDN SM4 ....43 J4
WLGTN SM6 ....62 E5
Northway Rd CROY/NA CR0 ....45 P7
North Weald La
KUTN/CMB KT2 ....26 B8
Northwick HTWY RG27 ....66 C1
Northwood Av
PUR/KEN CR8 ....81 J2
WOKN/KNAP GU21 ....71 K7
Northwood Pk
CRAWE RH10 * 177 K1
Northwood Rd CAR SM5 ....62 C5
FSTH SE23 ....31 N4
HTHAIR TW6 ....13 P6
THHTH CR7 ....45 L3
North Worple Wy
MORT/ESHN SW14 ....18 B8
Norton Cl BRYLDS KT5 ....41 P9
Norton Ct RGUW GU3 ....91 K7
Norton Gdns
STRHM/NOR SW16 ....44 G3
Norton Pk ASC SL5 ....34 C6
Norton Rd CBLY GU15 ....69 L4
Norwich Av CBLY GU15 ....68 C5
Norwich Rd CRAWE RH10 ....177 K7
THHTH CR7 ....45 L4
Norwood Cl EHSLY KT24 ....95 M4
NWDGN UB2 ....16 A2
WHTN TW2 ....25 L5
Norwood Crs HTHAIR TW6 ....14 B5
Norwood Farm La COB KT11 ....57 J9
Norwood Gdns NWDGN UB2 ....15 P2
Norwood Green Rd
NWDGN UB2 ....16 A2
Norwood High St
WNWD SE27 ....30 D7
Norwood Hill HORL RH6 ....158 A1
Norwoodhill Rd HORL RH6 ....158 C5
Norwood Park Rd
WNWD SE27 ....30 D8
Norwood Rd EHSLY KT24 ....95 M8
NHHL SE24 ....30 C4
NWDGN UB2 ....15 N1
Notley End EGH TW20 * 36 A1
Notson Rd SNWD SE25 ....46 B5
Nottingham Cl
WOKN/KNAP GU21 ....71 M7
Nottingham Rd ISLW TW7 ....16 F7
SAND/SEL CR2 ....63 L4
TOOT SW17 ....29 J4
Nova Ms CHEAM SM3 ....43 J8
Nova Rd CROY/NA CR0 ....2 B1
Novello St FUL/PGN SW6 ....19 L6
Nowell Rd BARN SW13 ....18 E2
Nower Rd DORK RH4 ....116 C7
The Nower BH/WHM TW16 ....85 K9
RSEV TN14 ....85 P5
Nowhurst La HORS RH12 ....191 H5
Noyna Rd TOOT SW17 ....29 J6
Nuffield Dr SHST GU47 ....50 B8
Nugee Ct CWTH RG45 ....49 M4
Nugent Cl MFD/CHID GU8 ....169 L5
Nugent Rd GUW GU2 ....111 K6
SNWD SE25 ....45 P4
Nunappleton Wy
OXTED RH8 ....123 N3
Nuneaton BRAK RG12 ....32 C7
Nunns Fld RDKG RH5 * 156 B6
Nuns Wk VW GU25 ....35 P5
Nursery Av CROY/NA CR0 ....64 D1
Nursery Cl ADL/WDHM KT15 ....55 K8
CROY/NA CR0 ....64 D1
EBED/NFELT TW14 ....24 C3
EW KT17 ....60 C8
FLEETN GU51 ....87 K7
FRIM GU16 ....69 H9
KWD/TDW/WH KT20 ....98 F5
RDKG RH5 ....156 B7
WOKN/KNAP GU21 ....72 A5
Nursery Gdns HSLWW TW4 ....24 G1
RGUE GU4 ....132 F2
STA TW18 ....37 M1
Nursery Hl SHGR GU5 ....133 H9
Nurserylands CRAWW RH11 ....176 D5
Nursery La ASC SL5 ....33 N2
HORL RH6 ....158 G2
Nursery Pl WDSR SL4 ....20 C2
Nursery Rd GODL GU7 ....131 M6
KWD/TDW/WH KT20 ....98 F5
MTCM CR4 ....44 A4
SUN TW16 ....38 D4
SUT SM1 ....61 N3
THHTH CR7 ....45 M5
WIM/MER SW19 ....43 J1
WIM/MER SW19 ....43 M5
WOKN/KNAP GU21 ....71 K6

Nursery Wy OXTED RH8 * 103 L9
STWL/WRAY TW19 ....21 J2
Nutbourne FNM GU9 ....108 A7
Nutcombe La DORK RH4 ....116 E7
GSHT GU26 ....183 P1
Nutcroft Gv LHD/OX KT22 ....96 E2
Nutfield Cl CAR SM5 ....62 A2
Nutfield Marsh Rd R
EDH RH1 ....120 G2
Nutfield Rd COUL/CHIP CR5 ....80 C5
EDUL SE22 ....30 H1
REDH RH1 ....120 D5
THHTH CR7 ....45 K5
Nuthatch Cl RFNM GU10 ....107 H7
Nuthatch Gdns REIG RH2 ....119 N9
Nuthatch Wy CRAWE RH10 ....179 K6
Nuthurst BRAK RG12 ....32 G6
Nuthurst Av
BRXS/STRHM SW2 ....30 A5
Nutley BRAK RG12 ....32 C9
Nutley Cl YTLY GU46 ....67 L1
Nutley La REIG RH2 ....119 K4
Nutmeg Ct FARN GU14 ....87 N2
Nutshell La FNM GU9 ....107 N8
Nutty La SHPTN TW17 ....38 E5
Nutwell St TOOT SW17 ....29 H8
Nutwood Av
BRKHM/BTCW RH3 ....118 A6
Nutwood Cl
BRKHM/BTCW RH3 ....118 A6
Nyefield Pk
KWD/TDW/WH KT20 ....98 E6
Nylands Av RCH/KEW TW9 ....17 N7
Nymans Cl HORS RH12 ....21 J2
Nymans Ct CRAWE RH10 * 177 L8
Nymans Gdns RYNPK SW20 ....42 F4
Nyon Gv CAT SE6 ....31 N5

O

Oakapple Cl CRAWW RH11 ....194 E1
SAND/SEL CR2 ....82 B3
Oak Av CHOB/PIR GU24 ....90 C1
CROY/NA CR0 ....64 G1
EGH TW20 ....36 D4
HEST TW5 ....15 M5
HPTN TW12 ....24 F8
SHST GU47 ....49 P8
WDR/YW UB7 ....14 C1
Oakbank CROY/NA CR0 ....65 H3
LHD/OX KT22 ....96 C3
WOKS/MYFD GU22 ....10 D7
Oakbank Av WOT/HER KT12 ....39 P8
Oakbury Rd FUL/PGN SW6 ....19 M7
Oak Cl CRAN GU6 ....153 P6
CRAN GU6 ....160 H9
GODL GU7 ....131 L5
KWD/TDW/WH KT20 ....117 P1
SUT SM1 ....61 P1
Oakcombe Cl NWMAL KT3 ....42 C2
Oak Cnr RDKG RH5 ....156 B1
Oak Cottage Cl RGUW GU3 ....111 J4
Oak Ct CRAWE RH10 * 176 G1
FNM GU9 ....5 F6
Oak Cft EGRIN RH19 ....180 F3
Oakcroft Cl BF/WBF KT14 ....73 K3
Oakcroft Rd BF/WBF KT14 ....73 K3
CHSGTN KT9 ....59 M3
Oakcroft Vis CHSGTN KT9 ....59 M3
Oakdale BRAK RG12 ....32 F7
Oakdale La EDEN TN8 ....124 G4
Oakdale Rd HOR/WEW KT19 ....60 B7
STRHM/NOR SW16 ....29 P8
WEY KT13 ....56 C2
Oakdale Wy MTCM CR4 ....44 C8
Oak Dell CRAWE RH10 ....177 M4
Oakdene ASC SL5 ....34 F7
CHOB/PIR GU24 ....90 F4
KWD/TDW/WH KT20 ....79 J9
Oakdene Av THDIT KT7 ....40 C9
Oakdene Cl
BRKHM/BTCW RH3 ....118 A7
GT/LBKH KT23 ....96 C7
Oakdene Dr BRYLDS KT5 ....42 A9
Oakdene Ms CHEAM SM3 ....43 K9
Oakdene Pl RGUW GU3 ....132 A4
Oakdene Rd
BRKHM/BTCW RH3 ....117 P7
COB KT11 ....75 K3
GODL GU7 ....150 C1
GT/LBKH KT23 ....95 P4
REDH RH1 ....120 B5
RGUW GU3 ....132 A4
Oak Dr BH/WHM TW16 ....117 P1
Oaken Coppice ASHTD KT21 ....77 N8
Oaken Copse CBLY GU15 ....69 L1
FLEETS GU52 * 107 H2
Oaken Copse Crs FARN GU14 ....68 D9
Oak End RDKG RH5 ....156 B1
Oak End Wy
ADL/WDHM KT15 ....73 J1
Oakengates BRAK RG12 ....32 C9
Oaken La ESH/CLAY KT10 ....58 E3
Oakenshaw Cl SURB KT6 ....41 L8
Oak Farm Cl BLKW GU17 ....67 N3
Oakfield BIL RH14 ....187 K7
WOKN/KNAP GU21 ....71 L5
Oakfield Cl NWMAL KT3 ....42 D6
Oakfield Dr REIG RH2 ....119 L3
Oakfield Gdns BECK BR3 ....46 G6
CAR SM5 ....44 A9
Oakfield Gld WEY KT13 ....56 E3
Oakfield Pl FARN GU14 ....88 F8
Oakfield Rd ASHF TW15 ....23 L7
ASHTD KT21 ....77 L7

BLKW GU17 ....68 A4
COB KT11 ....75 K2
CROY/NA CR0 ....2 C1
EDEN TN8 ....144 F1
WIM/MER SW19 ....28 A6
Oakfields BF/WBF KT14 ....73 M3
CBLY GU15 ....68 C3
CRAWE RH10 ....177 M4
RDKG RH5 ....172 F5
RGUW GU3 ....111 L3
WOT/HER KT12 ....39 J9
Oak HI EPSOM KT18 ....78 B5
SURB KT6 ....41 L8
Oak HI Crs SURB KT6 ....41 L8
Oak HI RGUE GU4 ....112 C1
RGUW GU3 ....110 C5
SURB KT6 ....41 L8
Oakhill Cl ASHTD KT21 ....77 J7
Oak Hill Crs SURB KT6 ....41 L9
Oakhill Gdns WEY KT13 ....56 C1
Oak Hill Gv SURB KT6 ....41 L7
Oakhill Pl PUT/ROE SW15 ....28 D1
Oakhill Rd ADL/WDHM KT15 ....55 K5
ASHTD KT21 ....77 J7
BECK BR3 ....47 J3
BOR GU35 ....164 E6
PUT/ROE SW15 ....28 C1
REIG RH2 ....119 M6
STRHM/NOR SW16 ....44 G2
SUT SM1 ....61 M3
SWTR RH13 ....192 D8
Oakhurst CHOB/PIR GU24 ....53 L7
GSHT GU26 ....165 N8
Oakhurst Cl TEDD TW11 ....25 M8
Oakhurst Gdns EGRIN RH19 ....180 B1
Oakhurst La BIL RH14 ....188 D4
Oakhurst Ms SWTR RH13 * 192 F6
Oakhurst Ri CAR SM5 ....62 A8
Oakhurst Rd HOR/WEW KT19 ....60 A5
Oakington Av HYS/HAR UB3 ....14 F2
Oakington Cl SUN TW16 ....39 L3
Oakington Dr SUN TW16 ....39 L3
Oakland Av FNM GU9 ....108 A7
Oaklands GDST RH9 ....122 E9
HASM GU27 ....184 D3
HORL RH6 ....159 M1
LHD/OX KT22 ....96 D4
PUR/KEN CR8 ....81 L5
SWTR RH13 ....192 D8
YTLY GU46 ....67 H3
Oaklands Av ESH/CLAY KT10 ....40 D9
ISLW TW7 ....16 F4
THHTH CR7 ....45 K4
WWKM BR4 ....65 H2
Oaklands Cl ASC SL5 ....33 P1
CHSGTN KT9 ....59 J3
RGUE GU4 ....113 N7
Oaklands Dr ASC SL5 ....34 A1
REDH RH1 ....140 F6
Oaklands Gdns PUR/KEN CR8 ....81 L3
Oaklands La BH/WHM TN16 ....84 A4
CWTH RG45 ....49 J3
Oaklands Rd BMLY BR1 ....47 L1
MORT/ESHN SW14 ....18 B8
Oaklands Wy
KWD/TDW/WH KT20 ....98 G2
WLGTN SM6 ....62 E6
Oakland Wy HOR/WEW KT19 ....60 B5
Oak La EGH TW20 ....21 H6
HORS RH12 ....191 M7
ISLW TW7 ....16 F6
TWK TW1 ....25 P5
WOKS/MYFD GU22 ....10 E6
Oaklawn Rd LHD/OX KT22 ....76 E7
Oaklea ASHV GU12 ....109 J1
Oak Leaf Cl HOR/WEW KT19 * 78 A1
Oakleigh Av SURB KT6 ....41 N9
Oakleigh Ct OXTED RH8 * 103 L9
Oakleigh Rd HORS RH12 ....192 E6
Oakleigh Wy MTCM CR4 ....44 D5
SURB KT6 ....41 N9
Oakley Av CROY/NA CR0 ....63 H3
Oakley Cl ADL/WDHM KT15 ....55 P3
EGRIN RH19 ....180 C4
ISLW TW7 ....16 B6
Oakley Ct CBLY GU15 ....68 C3
Oakley Dell RGUE GU4 ....112 G5
Oakley Dr FLEETN GU51 ....86 G7
Oakley Gdns BNSTD SM7 ....79 M4
BRKHM/BTCW RH3 ....138 A2
Oakley Rd CBLY GU15 ....68 C3
SNWD SE25 ....46 B6
WARL CR6 ....82 C7
Oak Lodge Cl WOT/HER KT12 ....57 L4
Oak Lodge Dr REDH RH1 ....140 C4
WWKM BR4 ....47 M6
Oak Lodge La
BH/WHM TN16 ....105 H5
Oak Md GODL GU7 ....131 K5
Oakmead Av HAYES BR2 ....47 N7
Oakmead Gdns EPSOM KT18 ....78 A4
Oakmead Pl MTCM CR4 ....44 A1
Oakmead Rd BAL SW12 ....29 L4
CROY/NA CR0 ....44 F7
Oak Park Gdns
WIM/MER SW19 ....28 A4

Oakridge CHOB/PIR GU24 ....70 D2
Oak Rdg DORK RH4 ....137 H1
Oak Rd BH/WHM TN16 ....105 H5
COB KT11 ....75 M4
CRAWW RH11 ....176 F6
CTHM CR3 ....101 N2
FARN GU14 ....88 A2
LHD/OX KT22 ....76 G8
NWMAL KT3 ....42 B3
REIG RH2 ....119 M4
Oak Rw MTCM CR4 ....44 E3
Oaks Av FELT TW13 ....24 F5
EW KT19 ....30 F8
WPK KT4 ....60 F1
Oaks Cl HORS RH12 ....192 C4
WEY KT12 ....96 C1
Oaksford Av SYD SE26 ....31 K3
Oakshade Rd LHD/OX KT22 ....76 C3
Oakshaw OXTED RH8 ....103 K7
Oakshaw Rd
WAND/EARL SW18 ....28 E3
Oakside Ct HORL RH6 ....140 E9
Oakside La HORL RH6 ....140 E9
Oaks La CROY/NA CR0 ....64 C2
RDKG RH5 ....137 H4
Oaks Pk BNSTD SM7 * 80 B1
The Oaks Pk RDKG RH5 * 156 C3
Oaks Rd CROY/NA CR0 ....64 D4
PUR/KEN CR8 ....81 L6
REIG RH2 ....119 P4
STWL/WRAY TW19 ....22 G1
Oaks Sq EPSOM KT18 * 78 B2
The Oaks BF/WBF KT14 ....73 L3
BRAK RG12 ....32 F3
CHSGTN KT9 ....59 J2
DORK RH4 * 116 G8
EGRIN RH19 ....180 F1
EPSOM KT18 ....78 C3
FELT TW13 * 24 F5
FLEETN GU51 ....86 D6
MFD/CHID GU8 * 168 A7
MRDN SM4 * 43 J3
STA TW18 * 22 C9
WOKN/KNAP GU21 * 10 C4
YTLY GU46 ....67 H3
Oaks Tr CAR SM5 ....62 C8
Oaks Wy CAR SM5 ....62 B6
EPSOM KT18 ....78 F8
PUR/KEN CR8 ....81 L3
RPLY/SEND GU23 ....93 K4
SURB KT6 ....59 K1
Oak Tree Cl ASHV GU12 ....89 H6
ASHV GU12 ....108 F6
BOR GU35 ....164 C7
EGRIN RH19 * 162 B9
RGUE GU4 ....92 A8
RGUE GU4 ....92 G9
VW GU25 ....35 N6
WOKN/KNAP GU21 ....71 H7
Oak Tree Dr DTCH/LGLY SL3 ....12 F3
EGH TW20 ....21 H8
GU GU1 ....112 A1
Oak Tree La HASM GU27 ....183 N4
MFD/CHID GU8 ....169 L6
Oak Tree Rd MFD/CHID GU8 ....148 A9
WOKN/KNAP GU21 ....71 H7
Oaktrees ASHV GU12 ....109 H5
FNM GU9 ....107 M8
Oak Tree Vw FNM GU9 ....107 P8
Oaktree Wk CTHM CR3 ....101 N2
Oaktree Wy SHST GU47 ....49 L8
Oak Tree Wy SWTR RH13 ....192 F6
Oak Vw EDEN TN8 ....144 F5
Oakview Cv CROY/NA CR0 ....46 E9
Oak Wk HORS RH12 ....175 L9
Oak Wy ASHTD KT21 ....77 N5
CRAWE RH10 ....177 H3
CROY/NA CR0 ....46 D7
EBED/NFELT TW14 ....23 M3
REIG RH2 ....119 P6
Oakway ASHV GU12 ....108 F6
HAYES BR2 ....47 K3
RFNM GU10 ....126 A9
RYNPK SW20 ....42 G5
WOKN/KNAP GU21 ....71 J8
Oakway Dr FRIM GU16 ....68 G7
Oakwood ASC SL5 ....34 A2
Oakwood FLEETS GU52 ....106 G2
GUW GU2 ....91 N9
WLGTN SM6 ....62 D7
Oakwood Av BECK BR3 ....47 J3
HAYES BR2 ....47 P4
HOR/WEW KT19 ....59 N7
MTCM CR4 ....43 P8
Oakwood Cl EHSLY KT24 ....94 G7
REDH RH1 ....120 C5
Oakwood Ct CHOB/PIR GU24 ....70 C5
WKENS W14 ....19 K1
Oakwood Dr EHSLY KT24 ....94 C7
REDH RH1 ....120 C5
Oakwood Gdns SUT SM1 ....61 L1
WOKN/KNAP GU21 ....70 C7
Oakwood La WKENS W14 ....19 K1
Oakwood Pl CROY/NA CR0 ....45 J7
Oakwood Ri CTHM CR3 ....101 N5
Oakwood Rd BFOR GU20 ....52 E5
BRAK RG12 ....32 C6
CROY/NA CR0 ....45 J7
HORL RH6 ....140 C9
REDH RH1 ....101 J9
RYNPK SW20 ....42 E2
VW GU25 ....36 A6
WOKN/KNAP GU21 ....71 L8
Oareborough BRAK RG12 ....32 G5
Oareburgh Fl F/WMO/HCT KT8 ....40 E5
Oast House Cl
STWL/WRAY TW19 ....21 K3
Oasthouse Dr FLEETN GU51 ....87 J3
Oast House La FNM GU9 ....107 P9
Oast La ALDT GU11 ....108 D7
Oast Rd OXTED RH8 ....123 M2

Oates Cl HAYES BR2 47 K4
Oates Wk CRAWE RH10 177 J8
Oatfield Rd
KWD/TDW/WH KT20 98 F1
Oatlands CRAWW RH11 176 D6
HORL RH6 140 D9
Oatlands Av WEY KT13 56 F4
Oatlands Cha WEY KT13 56 G2
Oatlands Cl WEY KT13 56 E3
Oatlands Dr WEY KT13 56 D3
Oatlands Gn WEY KT13 56 F2
Oatlands Mere WEY KT13 56 F2
Oatlands Rd
KWD/TDW/WH KT20 79 J8
Oatsheaf Pde FLEETN GU51 * 86 F7
Oban Rd THHTH CR7 45 M5
Obelisk Wy CBLY GU15 68 E2
Oberon Wy CRAWW RH11 176 B8
SHPTN TW17 38 A4
Oberstein Rd BTSEA SW11 19 P9
Oborne Cl HNHL SE24 30 C1
Observatory Rd
MORT/ESHN SW14 18 A9
Occam Rd GUW GU2 111 K5
Occupation La EA W5 17 K2
Ockenden Cl
WOKS/MYFD GU22 * 11 F6
Ockenden Gdns
WOKS/MYFD GU22 10 E6
Ockenden Rd
WOKS/MYFD GU22 10 E6
Ockfields MFD/CHID GU8 149 N3
Ockford Dr GODL GU7 150 B1
Ockford Rdg GODL GU7 150 A2
Ockford Rd GODL GU7 150 B1
Ockham Dr EHSLY KT24 94 F4
Ockham La COB KT11 75 J7
RPLY/SEND GU23 74 E9
Ockham Rd North
RPLY/SEND GU23 94 D2
Ockham Rd South
EHSLY KT24 94 G7
Ockley Ct RGUE GU4 92 F9
Ockley Rd CRAN GU6 153 P6
CROY/NA CR0 45 H8
RDKG RH5 155 J5
RDKG RH5 156 A3
STRHM/NOR SW16 29 P7
Ockleys Md GDST RH9 102 C9
O'Connor Rd ALDT GU11 88 F8
Octagon Rd WOT/HER KT12 56 G8
Octavia BRAK RG12 32 C9
Octavia Cl MTCM CR4 44 A6
Octavia Rd ISLW TW7 16 F8
Octavia Wy STA TW18 22 D9
Odard Rd E/WMO/HCT KT8 40 A5
Odeon Pde ISLW TW7 * 16 E7
Odiham Rd RFNM GU10 106 F6
Ogden Pk BRAK RG12 32 G4
O'Gorman Av FARN GU14 88 D5
Oil Mill La HMSMTH W6 18 E3
Okeburn Rd TOOT SW17 29 K8
Okingham Cl SHST GU47 49 P8
Old Acre BF/WBF KT14 73 L3
Oldacre CHOB/PIR GU24 70 F1
Old Av BF/WBF KT14 73 J3
Old Avenue Cl
WOKN/KNAP GU21 73 J2
Old Bakery Ct CRAN GU6 153 P7
Old Barn Cl BELMT SM2 61 J6
Old Barn Dr RDKG RH5 156 C6
Old Barn La CTHM CR3 81 P5
RFNM GU10 165 L1
Old Barn Rd EPSOM KT18 78 A6
Old Barn Vw GODL GU7 * 150 B2
Old Bisley Rd FRIM GU16 69 J6
Old Bracknell Cl BRAK RG12 32 D4
Old Bracknell La East
BRAK RG12 32 D4
Old Bracknell La West
BRAK RG12 32 C4
Old Brickfield Rd ALDT GU11 108 D7
Old Bridge Rd RFNM GU10 128 D1
Old Bridge St KUT/HW KT1 8 B4
Old Brighton Rd (North)
CRAWW RH11 194 F3
Old Brighton Rd (South)
CRAWW RH11 194 E5
Old Brighton Rd South
HORL RH6 159 H8
Old Brompton Rd ECT SW5 19 L3
Oldbury BRAK RG12 32 B4
Oldbury Cl FRIM GU16 69 H8
HORS RH12 192 F3
Oldbury Rd CHERT KT16 37 J8
Old Chapel La ASHV GU12 109 J4
Old Charlton Rd SHPTN TW17 38 E6
Old Char Whf DORK RH4 116 F6
Old Chertsey Rd
CHOB/PIR GU24 53 P8
Old Chestnut Av
ESH/CLAY KT10 58 A5
Old Church La FNM GU9 127 P6
Old Church Pth
ESH/CLAY KT10 58 B3
Old Church St CHEL SW3 19 P4
Old Claygate La
ESH/CLAY KT10 58 G5
Old Common COB KT11 * 75 K1
Old Common Rd COB KT11 75 K1
Old Compton La FNM GU9 128 A4
Old Convent EGRIN RH19 * 180 D1
Oldcorne Hollow YTLY GU46 66 E3
Old Cote Dr HEST TW5 16 A4
Old Ct ASHTD KT21 77 L8
Old Court Rd GUW GU2 111 N6
The Old Ctyd BMLY BR1 47 P2
Old Cove Rd FLEETN GU51 87 H4
Old Crawley Rd HORS RH12 193 H4
Old Cross Tree Wy
ASHV GU12 109 L6
Old Dairy Cl FLEETN GU51 86 G6
Old Dairy Ms BAL SW12 29 K4
Old Dean Rd CBLY GU15 68 F1
Old Deer Pk RCH/KEW TW9 * 17 M8
Old Deer Park Gdns
RCH/KEW TW9 17 L8
Old Denne Gdns HORS RH12 192 B9
Old Devonshire Rd BAL SW12 29 L3
Old Dock Cl RCH/KEW TW9 17 N4
Old Dr SHGR GU5 * 114 E9
Olde Farm Dr BLKW GU17 67 M3
Old Elstead Rd
MFD/CHID GU8 149 M2
Olden La PUR/KEN CR8 81 J1
Old Esher Cl WOT/HER KT12 * 57 M4
Old Esher Rd WOT/HER KT12 57 M4
Old Farleigh Rd
SAND/SEL CR2 64 C8
WARL CR6 82 F4
Old Farm Cl HSLWW TW4 15 P9
Old Farm Dr BRAK RG12 32 E1
Old Farmhouse Dr
LHD/OX KT22 76 D4
Old Farm Pl ASHV GU12 109 H2
Old Farm Rd GU GU1 112 B2
HPTN TW12 24 G9
Old Farnham La FNM GU9 5 H7
RFNM GU10 126 E4
Old Ferry Dr
STWL/WRAY TW19 21 H2
Oldfield Gdns ASHTD KT21 77 K8
Oldfield Rd HORL RH6 159 J3
HPTN TW12 40 A2
WIM/MER SW19 28 B9
Oldfields Rd SUT SM1 61 L1
Oldfieldwood
WOKS/MYFD GU22 11 K3
Old Forge Cl HORS RH12 193 L1
Old Forge Crs SHPTN TW17 38 D7
Old Forge End SHST GU47 67 M1
Old Fox Cl CTHM CR3 101 K1
Old Frensham Rd
RFNM GU10 127 P7
Old Green La CBLY GU15 68 E1
Old Guildford Rd FRIM GU16 89 L2
HORS RH12 191 M7
Old Haslemere Rd
HASM GU27 184 D5
Old Heath Wy FNM GU9 * 107 N7
Old Hl WOKS/MYFD GU22 72 B9
Old Holbrook HORS RH12 192 D2
Old Hollow CRAWE RH10 178 A3
Old Horsham Rd
CRAWW RH11 176 E7
RDKG RH5 137 J8
Old Hospital Cl BAL SW12 * 29 J4
Old House Cl EW KT17 60 D8
WIM/MER SW19 28 B8
Old House Gdns TWK TW1 * 26 B2
Oldhouse La BFOR GU20 52 C7
CHOB/PIR GU24 70 G3
Old House Ms HORS RH12 * 192 B8
Old Ively Rd FARN GU14 87 L7
Old Kiln Cl RFNM GU10 165 J1
Old Kiln La
BRKHM/BTCW RH3 118 A5
RFNM GU10 165 J1
Old Kingston Rd WPK KT4 60 A2
Old Lands Hl BRAK RG12 32 F2
Old La ALDT GU11 108 C7
ASHV GU12 108 G3
BH/WHM TN16 104 B1
COB KT11 74 G9
OXTED RH8 123 M1
RFNM GU10 146 B8
Olde Lane Gdns EHSLY KT24 95 H2
Old Lodge Cl GODL GU7 * 150 A1
Old Lodge La PUR/KEN CR8 81 H2
Old London Rd EPSOM KT18 78 E7
KUTN/CMB KT2 8 E4
RDKG RH5 97 J8
Old Malden La WPK KT4 60 C1
Old Malt Wy
WOKN/KNAP GU21 10 B3
Old Manor Cl CRAWW RH11 176 D3
Old Manor Dr ISLW TW7 25 K2
Old Manor Gdns RGUE GU4 132 G2
Old Manor Yd ECT SW5 * 19 M2
Old Martyrs CRAWW RH11 176 G2
Old Merrow St RGUE GU4 112 G2
Old Mill La REDH RH1 100 D8
Old Millmeads HORS RH12 192 B5
Old Mill Pl HASM GU27 184 A3
STWL/WRAY TW19 21 N2
Old Nursery Pl ASHF TW15 23 L8
Old Oak Av COUL/CHIP CR5 80 A8
Old Oak Cl COB KT11 75 K2
Old Orch BF/WBF KT14 74 B1
SUN TW16 39 L3
Old Orchards CRAWE RH10 177 P5
The Old Orch FNM GU9 127 K6
Old Palace Rd CROY/NA CR0 2 B5
GUW GU2 111 N6
WEY KT13 56 D2
Old Palace Yd RCH/KEW TW9 26 B1
Old Park Av BAL SW12 29 K2
Old Park Cl FNM GU9 107 L8
Old Park La RFNM GU10 107 K7
Old Park Ms HEST TW5 15 P5
Old Parvis Rd BF/WBF KT14 73 N1
Old Pasture Rd FRIM GU16 69 H5
Old Pharmacy Ct
CWTH RG45 * 49 N5
Old Pond Cl CBLY GU15 68 D7
Old Portsmouth Rd
CBLY GU15 69 J4
MFD/CHID GU8 148 E8
RGUW GU3 131 P4
Old Pottery Cl REIG RH2 119 M7
Old Pound Cl ISLW TW7 16 G6
Old Pumphouse Cl
FLEETN GU51 87 H5
The Old Quarry HASM GU27 184 A6
Old Rectory Cl
KWD/TDW/WH KT20 98 E4
Old Rectory Dr ASHV GU12 109 K4
Old Rectory Gdns FARN GU14 88 F3
GODL GU7 150 E2
Old Rectory La EHSLY KT24 94 G6
Old Redstone Dr REDH RH1 120 C6
Old Reigate Rd DORK RH4 117 L5
Oldridge Rd BAL SW12 29 K3
Old Rd ADL/WDHM KT15 55 K6
BRKHM/BTCW RH3 118 D4
EGRIN RH19 180 E3
Old Sawmill La CWTH RG45 49 N3
Old School Cl ASHV GU12 109 J3
BECK BR3 46 D3
FLEETN GU51 * 86 G6
GU GU1 6 E3
Old School Ct
STWL/WRAY TW19 21 L3
Old School La
BRKHM/BTCW RH3 117 N8
YTLY GU46 66 G2
Old School Ms WEY KT13 56 F3
Old School Pl CROY/NA CR0 63 J3
LING RH7 143 K9
WOKS/MYFD GU22 92 C1
Old Schools La EW KT17 60 D7
Old School Sq THDIT KT7 40 F7
Old School Ter CHEAM SM3 * 61 H6
Old Slade La DTCH/LGLY SL3 13 K3
Old Station Ap LHD/OX KT22 96 G1
Old Station Cl CRAWE RH10 179 H4
Old Station Gdns
TEDD TW11 * 25 P9
Old Station La
STWL/WRAY TW19 21 L2
Old Station Rd HYS/HAR UB3 15 H1
Old Station Wy GODL GU7 131 L7
Oldstead BRAK RG12 32 F6
The Old Surrey Ms
GDST RH9 * 122 C1
Old Swan Yd CAR SM5 62 B3
Old Town CROY/NA CR0 2 B5
Old Town Ms FNM GU9 * 4 D4
Old Tye Av BH/WHM TN16 84 C5
Old Welmore YTLY GU46 67 J3
Old Westhall Cl WARL CR6 82 C8
Old Wickhurst La
HORS RH12 191 L9
Old Wokingham Rd
CWTH RG45 49 N2
Old Woking Rd BF/WBF KT14 73 L2
WOKS/MYFD GU22 72 G9
Oldwood Cha FARN GU14 87 M4
Old York Rd
WAND/EARL SW18 28 E1
Oleander Cl CWTH RG45 49 K2
Oliver Av SNWD SE25 45 P4
Oliver Cl ADL/WDHM KT15 55 M3
CHSWK W4 17 P4
Oliver Gv SNWD SE25 45 P5
Olive Rd EA W5 17 K1
WIM/MER SW19 * 43 N1
Oliver Rd ASC SL5 34 B5
HORS RH12 191 P9
NWMAL KT3 42 A3
SUT SM1 61 P3
Olivia Dr DTCH/LGLY SL3 12 D3
Olivier Rd CRAWE RH10 177 N6
Ollerton BRAK RG12 32 C9
Olley Cl WLGTN SM6 62 G6
Olveston Wk CAR SM5 43 P7
Olyffe Dr BECK BR3 47 J2
Olympia Wy WKENS W14 19 J1
Omega Rd WOKN/KNAP GU21 72 E4
Omega Wy EGH TW20 36 G2
One Tree Cl FSTH SE23 31 K2
One Tree Hill Rd RGUE GU4 112 F7
Ongar Cl ADL/WDHM KT15 55 K5
Ongar Hl ADL/WDHM KT15 55 L5
Ongar Pl ADL/WDHM KT15 55 L5
Ongar Rd ADL/WDHM KT15 55 L4
FUL/PGN SW6 19 L4
Onslow Av BELMT SM2 61 K8
RCHPK/HAM TW10 26 D1
Onslow Cl WOKS/MYFD GU22 11 H3
Onslow Crs SKENS SW7 19 P2
WOKS/MYFD GU22 11 H3
Onslow Dr ASC SL5 34 A1
Onslow Gdns SAND/SEL CR2 82 A1
SKENS SW7 19 P3
THDIT KT7 40 E9
WLGTN SM6 62 E6
Onslow Ms CHERT KT16 37 K7
Onslow Ms East SKENS SW7 19 P2
Onslow Ms West
SKENS SW7 * 19 P2
Onslow Rd ASC SL5 35 H8
CROY/NA CR0 45 J8
GU GU1 7 F3
NWMAL KT3 42 E5
RCHPK/HAM TW10 26 D2
WOT/HER KT12 57 J3
Onslow Sq SKENS SW7 19 P2
Onslow St GU GU1 6 D6
Onslow Wy THDIT KT7 40 E9
WOKS/MYFD GU22 73 K4
Ontario Cl HORL RH6 160 B2
Ontario Wy LIPH GU30 182 F7
Openfields BOR GU35 164 B5
Openview WAND/EARL SW18 28 F4
Opladen Wy BRAK RG12 32 E6
Opossum Wy HSLWW TW4 15 L8
Opus Pk GU GU1 * 112 B1
The Orangery
RCHPK/HAM TW10 26 B5
Oratory La CHEL SW3 * 19 P3
Orbain Rd FUL/PGN SW6 19 J5
Orbit Cl EWKG RG40 48 D3
Orchard Av ADL/WDHM KT15 55 K9
ASHF TW15 23 M9
CROY/NA CR0 64 E1
EBED/NFELT TW14 23 N1
HEST TW5 15 N5
MTCM CR4 44 C9
NWMAL KT3 42 C3
THDIT KT7 40 G9
Orchard Cl ASHF TW15 23 M9
ASHV GU12 109 J1
BLKW GU17 68 B7
BNSTD SM7 79 M3
CHOB/PIR GU24 70 D2
EDEN TN8 144 F3
EHSLY KT24 95 H4
FNM GU9 108 C8
FSTH SE23 31 K2
GU GU1 112 F5
HOR/WEW KT19 * 59 P5
HORL RH6 140 B9
LHD/OX KT22 96 D2
MFD/CHID GU8 129 M9
RGUW GU3 110 B5
RYNPK SW20 42 G5
WOKS/MYFD GU22 11 K2
WOT/HER KT12 39 K8
Orchard Ct BRAK RG12 * 32 E3
WLGTN SM6 * 62 D4
WPK KT4 * 42 E9
Orchard Dr ASHTD KT21 77 K9
EDEN TN8 144 F3
SHPTN TW17 38 G4
WOKN/KNAP GU21 72 C4
Orchard End CTHM CR3 101 N2
LHD/OX KT22 96 C4
RFNM GU10 146 C1
WEY KT13 56 G1
Orchardfield Rd GODL GU7 131 M6
Orchard Gdns ASHV GU12 108 E6
CHSGTN KT9 59 L3
CRAN GU6 171 J1
EHSLY KT24 95 N8
EPSOM KT18 78 A4
Orchard Ga ESH/CLAY KT10 40 D9
SHST GU47 49 M9
Orchard Gv CROY/NA CR0 46 E8
PGE/AN SE20 46 A1
Orchard Hl BFOR GU20 52 D6
HORS RH12 189 M3
Orchard La E/WMO/HCT KT8 40 D7
RYNPK SW20 42 F2
Orchard Lea Cl
WOKS/MYFD GU22 73 J4
Orchardleigh LHD/OX KT22 97 H2
Orchard Mains
WOKS/MYFD GU22 72 A9
Orchard Mew
WOKN/KNAP GU21 71 H7
Orchard Ms TOOT SW17 28 F6
Orchard Ri CROY/NA CR0 46 E9
KUTN/CMB KT2 42 A2
RCHPK/HAM TW10 17 P9
Orchard Rd BTFD TW8 17 J4
CHSGTN KT9 59 L3
DORK RH4 117 H8
FARN GU14 88 C3
FELT TW13 24 B4
FNM GU9 108 C8
GUW GU2 111 M7
HORL RH6 160 C1
HPTN TW12 39 P1
HSLWW TW4 24 G1
KUT/HW KT1 8 D5
RCH/KEW TW9 17 N8
REIG RH2 119 M5
RGUE GU4 112 F1
RGUE GU4 132 C2
SAND/SEL CR2 82 B3
SHGR GU5 134 C1
SUN TW16 39 K1
SUT SM1 61 L4
SWTR RH13 192 D9
TWK TW1 25 P1
WDSR SL4 20 G3
Orchards Cl BF/WBF KT14 73 L3
Orchard Sq WKENS W14 * 19 K3
The Orchards CRAWW RH11 176 A6
Orchard St CRAWW RH11 176 G5
THDIT KT7 41 H9
The Orchard CHSWK W4 18 B2
EW KT17 60 D6
HASM GU27 184 A5
HORL RH6 * 159 K1
LTWR GU18 52 B9
RDKG RH5 137 J2
SWTR RH13 192 G6
VW GU25 36 C6
WEY KT13 56 D3
WOKN/KNAP GU21 71 P5
WOKS/MYFD GU22 92 C2
Orchard Wy ADL/WDHM KT15 55 M4
ASHF TW15 23 J5
ASHV GU12 108 E6
CBLY GU15 68 D6
CROY/NA CR0 46 E8
DORK RH4 117 H8
EGRIN RH19 180 D2
ESH/CLAY KT10 58 C5
KWD/TDW/WH KT20 99 J6
OXTED RH8 123 N4
REIG RH2 119 M8
RGUW GU3 * 91 K4
RGUW GU3 110 B5
RPLY/SEND GU23 92 G5
SUT SM1 61 P3
Orchid Cl CHSGTN KT9 59 J6
Orchid Ct EGH TW20 21 N7
Orchid Dr CHOB/PIR GU24 70 G4
Orchid Gdns HSLWW TW4 15 P9
Orde Cl CRAWE RH10 177 N2
Ordnance Cl FELT TW13 24 B5
Ordnance Rd ASHV GU12 108 F3
Oregano Wy GUW GU2 91 N9
Oregon Cl NWMAL KT3 42 A5
Oregon Wk EWKG RG40 48 B2
Orestan La EHSLY KT24 95 L7
Orford Gdns TWK TW1 25 N5
Oriel Cl CRAWE RH10 177 M2
MTCM CR4 44 F5
Oriel Dr BARN SW13 18 G4
Oriel Hl CBLY GU15 68 F4
Oriental Cl WOKS/MYFD GU22 11 F3
Oriental Rd ASC SL5 34 D5
WOKS/MYFD GU22 11 F4
Orion BRAK RG12 32 C9
Orlando Gdns
HOR/WEW KT19 60 B8
Orleans Rd NRWD SE19 30 E9
TWK TW1 26 A3
Orltons La HORS RH12 175 L1
Ormanton Rd SYD SE26 31 H7
Ormathwaites Cnr
BNFD RG42 32 C1
Ormeley Rd BAL SW12 29 L3
Orme Rd KUT/HW KT1 41 P3
SUT SM1 61 M5
Ormerod Gdns MTCM CR4 44 C3
Ormesby Wk CRAWE RH10 177 L7
Ormond Av HPTN TW12 40 B2
Ormond Crs HPTN TW12 40 B1
Ormond Dr HPTN TW12 40 B1
Ormonde Av HOR/WEW KT19 60 B7
Ormonde Pl WEY KT13 * 56 F5
Ormonde Rd GODL GU7 131 L7
MORT/ESHN SW14 17 P8
WOKN/KNAP GU21 72 A5
Ormond Rd
RCHPK/HAM TW10 26 C1
Ormsby BELMT SM2 * 61 M6
Ormside Wy REDH RH1 120 D1
Orpin Rd REDH RH1 120 E1
Orpwood Cl HPTN TW12 24 G9
Orville Rd BTSEA SW11 19 P7
Orwell Cl FARN GU14 68 A9
Orwell Gdns REIG RH2 119 M7
Osborne Av
STWL/WRAY TW19 23 H4
Osborne Cl BECK BR3 46 E5
FELT TW13 24 E8
Osborne Dr FLEETS GU52 87 H8
LTWR GU18 52 A9
Osborne Gdns THHTH CR7 45 L3
Osborne Rd EGH TW20 21 L9
FARN GU14 88 E7
HSLW TW3 15 P8
KUTN/CMB KT2 41 L1
REDH RH1 120 C2
THHTH CR7 45 L3
WOT/HER KT12 39 J9
Osborne Ter TOOT SW17 * 29 K8
Osborne Wy CHSGTN KT9 59 M4
Osborn La FSTH SE23 31 M3
Osborn Rd FNM GU9 127 P1
Osier Pl EGH TW20 21 P9
Osiers Rd WAND/EARL SW18 19 L9
Osier Wy BNSTD SM7 79 J3
MTCM CR4 44 A6
Osman Rd HMSMTH W6 * 18 G1
Osman's Cl BNFD RG42 33 K1
Osmond Gdns WLGTN SM6 62 E4
Osmunda Bank EGRIN RH19 162 D6
Osmund Cl CRAWE RH10 177 P5
Osnaburgh Hl CBLY GU15 68 D3
Osney Cl CRAWW RH11 176 F6
Osney Wk MRDN SM4 43 P7
Osprey Gdns ALDT GU11 108 C7
SAND/SEL CR2 64 D8
Ospringe Cl PGE/AN SE20 46 C1
Ostade Rd BRXS/STRHM SW2 30 A3
Osten Ms SKENS SW7 * 19 M1
Osterley Av ISLW TW7 16 D5
Osterley Crs ISLW TW7 16 E6
Osterley Gdns THHTH CR7 45 L3
Osterley La ISLW TW7 16 C2
Osterley Park Rd
NWDGN UB2 15 P1
Osterley Rd ISLW TW7 16 E5
Ostlers Dr ASHF TW15 23 M8
Oswald Cl BNFD RG42 32 F1
LHD/OX KT22 96 C2
Oswald Rd LHD/OX KT22 96 C2
Osward CROY/NA CR0 64 F8
Osward Rd BAL SW12 29 J5
Otford Cl CRAWW RH11 194 F2
PGE/AN SE20 46 C2
Otford Crs BROCKY SE4 31 N2
Othello Gv BNFD RG42 * 32 G2
Ottawa Dr LIPH GU30 182 F7
Otterbourne Pl
EGRIN RH19 * 180 A2
Otterbourne Rd CROY/NA CR0 2 C3
Otterburn Gdns ISLW TW7 16 G5
Otterburn St TOOT SW17 29 J9
Otter Cl CHERT KT16 54 F5
CWTH RG45 49 L2
Otterden St CAT SE6 31 P7
Ottermead La CHERT KT16 54 G5
Otto Cl CAT SE6 31 N6
SYD SE26 31 J6
Ottways Av ASHTD KT21 77 K8
Ottways La ASHTD KT21 77 L8
Otway Cl CRAWW RH11 176 C7
Oulton Wk CRAWE RH10 177 L7
Ouseley Rd BAL SW12 29 J4
STWL/WRAY TW19 21 H3
Outdowns EHSLY KT24 115 K1
Outram Pl WEY KT13 56 E4
Outram Rd CROY/NA CR0 3 K3
Outwood La
KWD/TDW/WH KT20 99 M2
REDH RH1 121 M5
The Oval BNSTD SM7 79 L3
GODL GU7 131 M6
GUW GU2 111 N6
RGUW GU3 111 H4
Ovenden Rd RSEV TN14 85 P9
Overbrae BECK BR3 31 P9

Overbrook EHSLY KT24 .... 94 D9
GODL GU7 .... 131 N8
Overbury Av BECK BR3 .... 47 H4
Overbury Crs CROY/NA CR0 .... 65 J8
Overdale ASHTD KT21 .... 77 L5
RDKG RH5 .... 117 J6
REDH RH1 .... 121 L4
Overdale Av NWMAL KT3 .... 42 A3
Overdale Ri FRIM GU16 .... 188 C5
Overdale Rd EA W5 .... 17 J1
Overdene Dr CRAWW RH11 .... 176 D5
Overdown Rd CAT SE6 .... 31 P7
Overford Cl CRAN GU6 .... 171 H1
Overford Rd CRAN GU6 .... 171 H1
Overhill WARL CR6 .... 82 C8
Overhill Rd EDUL SE22 .... 31 H3
PUR/KEN CR8 .... 63 J7
Overhill Wy BECK BR3 .... 47 K6
Overlord Ct CBLY GU15 .... 50 E9
Overlord Ct LHD/OX KT22 .... 96 D1
Overstand Cl BECK BR3 .... 46 G6
Overstone Gdns
CROY/NA CR0 .... 46 F8
Overstone Rd HMSMTH W6 .... 18 G2
Overthorpe Cl
WOKN/KNAP GU21 .... 71 L6
Overton Cl ALDT GU11 .... 108 E8
ISLW TW7 .... 16 G8
Overton Rd BELMT SM2 .... 61 L6
Overton Shaw EGRIN RH19 .... 162 D9
Overton's Yd CROY/NA CR0 .... 2 C5
Oveton Wy GT/LBKH KT23 .... 96 B6
Ovett Cl NRWD SE19 .... 30 F9
Ovington Ct
WOKN/KNAP GU21 .... 71 M5
Owen Cl CROY/NA CR0 .... 45 M7
Owen Pl LHD/OX KT22 .... 97 H2
Owen Rd BFOR GU20 .... 52 D4
GODL GU7 .... 131 M7
Owens Wy FSTH SE23 .... 31 M3
Owen Wk PGE/AN SE20 .... 46 A1
Owlbeech Wy SWTR RH13 .... 192 G6
Owl Cl SAND/SEL CR2 .... 64 D8
Owletts CRAWE RH10 .... 177 N4
Owlscastle Cl HORS RH12 .... 192 C5
Owlsmoor Rd SHST GU47 .... 49 P9
Ownstead Gdns
SAND/SEL CR2 .... 63 P9
Ownsted Hl CROY/NA CR0 .... 65 J8
Oxberry Av FUL/PGN SW6 .... 19 J7
Oxdowne Cl COB KT11 .... 76 B3
Oxenden Cl RFNM GU10 .... 108 G6
Oxenden Rd RFNM GU10 .... 108 G6
Oxenhope BRAC RG12 .... 32 C5
Oxford Av HEST TW5 .... 16 A3
HYS/HAR UB3 .... 15 H5
RYNPK SW20 .... 43 J3
Oxford Cl ASHF TW15 .... 38 E1
MTCM CR4 .... 44 E4
Oxford Crs NWMAL KT3 .... 42 B7
Oxford Gdns CHSWK W4 .... 17 N3
Oxford Ga HMSMTH W6 .... 19 H2
Oxford Rd CAR SM5 .... 62 A5
CRAWE RH10 .... 177 J9
FARN GU14 .... 88 E6
GU GU1 .... 7 F6
NRWD SE19 .... 30 E9
PUT/ROE SW15 .... 19 J9
REDH RH1 .... 120 A4
SHST GU47 .... 50 A7
SWTR RH13 .... 192 C8
TEDD TW11 .... 25 L8
Oxford Rd North CHSWK W4 .... 17 M3
Oxford Rd South CHSWK W4 .... 17 N3
Oxford Rw SUN TW16 .... 39 L4
Oxford Ter GU GU1 .... 7 F6
Oxford Wy FELT TW13 .... 24 E7
Oxleigh Cl NWMAL KT3 .... 42 C6
Oxshott Ri COB KT11 .... 75 N5
Oxshott Rd LHD/OX KT22 .... 76 F5
Oxshott Wy COB KT11 .... 75 N4
Oxted Cl MTCM CR4 .... 43 P9
Oxted Gn MFD/CHID GU8 .... 149 M5
Oxted Rd GDST RH9 .... 122 F2
Oxtoby Wy
STRHM/NOR SW16 .... 44 F2
Oyster La BF/WBF KT14 .... 55 P9

WEY KT13 .... 56 G2
Paddocks Wy ASHTD KT21 .... 77 L7
CHERT KT16 .... 37 M9
The Paddock
BH/WHM TN16 .... 104 G6
BOR GU35 .... 164 B6
BRAK RG12 .... 32 L8
CRAN GU6 .... 153 P9
CRAWE RH10 .... 177 N4
CWTH RG45 .... 49 L3
DORK RH4 .... 116 B8
GODL GU7 .... 150 E1
GSHT GU26 .... 165 K7
HASM GU27 .... 113 H4
RFNM GU10 .... 127 K9
VW GU25 .... 36 C7
Paddock Wk WARL CR6 .... 82 B8
Paddocks Wy HASM GU27 .... 167 H9
LIPH GU30 .... 182 C5
OXTED RH8 .... 123 M2
WOKN/KNAP GU21 .... 72 E3
Padley Cl CHSGTN KT9 .... 59 M4
Padstow Wk
EBED/NFELT TW14 .... 24 A4
Padua Rd PGE/AN SE20 .... 46 C2
Padwick Rd SWTR RH13 .... 192 E8
Pageant Wk CROY/NA CR0 .... 3 J6
Page Cl HPTN TW12 .... 24 F9
Page Crs CROY/NA CR0 .... 63 K4
Pagehurst Rd CROY/NA CR0 .... 46 A8
Page Rd EBED/NFELT TW14 .... 23 N2
Pages Yd CHSWK W4 .... 18 C4
Paget Av SUT SM1 .... 61 P2
Paget Cl CBLY GU15 .... 69 K1
HPTN TW12 .... 25 J1
Paget La ISLW TW7 .... 16 D8
Paget Rd DTCH/LGLY SL3 .... 12 D2
Pagewood Cl CRAWE RH10 .... 177 N7
Pagoda Av RCH/KEW TW9 .... 17 N3
Pagoda Gv WNWD SE27 .... 30 C5
Pain's Cl MTCM CR4 .... 44 D3
Pains Hl COB KT11 .... 75 H3
OXTED RH8 .... 124 A3
Pains Hill Pk COB KT11 .... 75 H2
Paisley Cl CAR SM5 .... 43 P9
Paisley Ter CAR SM5 .... 43 P9
Pakenham Cl BAL SW12 .... 29 L2
Pakenham Dr ALDT GU11 .... 108 B3
Pakenham Rd BRAK RG12 .... 32 F8
Palace Dr WEY KT13 .... 56 D2
Palace Gdns West WEY KT13 .... 56 D2
Palace Gn CROY/NA CR0 .... 64 F6
Palace Gv BMLY BR1 .... 47 P2
RDKG RH5 .... 18 A9
Palace Ms FUL/PGN SW6 .... 19 K5
Palace Rd ADL/WDHM KT15 .... 55 M7
BH/WHM TN16 .... 104 C1
BMLY BR1 .... 47 P2
BRXS/STRHM SW2 .... 30 A4
KUT/HW KT1 .... 41 K5
STRHM/NOR SW16 .... 45 P1
Palace Sq NRWD SE19 .... 30 F9
Palace Vw BMLY BR1 .... 47 P4
CROY/NA CR0 .... 64 F3
Pale La HTWY RG27 .... 86 A5
Palemead Cl FUL/PGN SW6 .... 19 H6
Palestine Gv WIM/MER SW19 .... 43 P2
Palewell Common Dr
MORT/ESHN SW14 .... 27 J1
Palewell Pk
MORT/ESHN SW14 .... 27 J1
Palgrave Rd SHB W12 .... 18 B1
Pallingham Dr CRAWE RH10 .... 177 M8
Palliser Rd WKENS W14 .... 19 J3
Palmer Av CHEAM SM3 .... 60 C3
Palmer Cl EWKG RG40 .... 48 A2
HEST TW5 .... 16 A6
REDH RH1 .... 120 C6
WWKM BR4 .... 65 K1
Palmer Crs CHERT KT16 .... 55 H5
KUT/HW KT1 .... 8 D6
Palmer Rd CRAWE RH10 .... 177 M8
Palmersfield Rd BNSTD SM7 .... 79 L3
Palmers Gv E/WMO/HCT KT8 .... 40 A5
Palmers Rd
MORT/ESHN SW14 .... 18 A8
STRHM/NOR SW16 .... 45 H3
Palmerston Cl FARN GU14 .... 87 P4
REDH RH1 .... 120 A8
WOKN/KNAP GU21 .... 72 E3
Palmerston Gv
WIM/MER SW19 .... 43 L1
Palmerston Rd ACT W3 .... 18 A1
CAR SM5 .... 62 B5
CROY/NA CR0 .... 45 M6
HSLW TW3 .... 16 C6
MORT/ESHN SW14 .... 18 A8
SUT SM1 .... 61 N4
WHTN TW2 .... 25 N2
WIM/MER SW19 .... 43 L1
Palm Gv EA W5 .... 17 L1
GU GU1 .... 92 A9
Pampisford Rd PUR/KEN CR8 .... 63 J9
Pams Wy HOR/WEW KT19 .... 60 B4
Pankhurst Cl ISLW TW7 .... 16 E8
Pankhurst Dr BRAK RG12 .... 32 F7
Pankhurst Rd WOT/HER KT12 .... 39 L8
Pankridge St CRAN GU10 .... 106 D7
Panmuir Rd RYNPK SW20 .... 42 F2
Panmure Rd SYD SE26 .... 31 J6
Pannell Cl EGRIN RH19 .... 180 C2
Pannells RFNM GU10 .... 127 P8
Pannells Ash BIL RH14 .... 187 P7
Pannells Ct GT/LBKH KT23 .... 37 K9
Pannells Ct GU GU1 .... 7 F5
Pan's Gdns CBLY GU15 .... 69 H4
Pantile Rd WEY KT13 .... 56 F3

Pantile Rw DTCH/LGLY SL3 .... 12 E2
Pantiles BOR GU35 .... 164 E6
Pantiles Cl WOKN/KNAP GU21 .... 71 P7
Panton Cl CROY/NA CR0 .... 2 B2
Papercourt La
RPLY/SEND GU23 .... 93 K2
Paper Ms DORK RH4 .... 117 H6
Papermill Ct CAR SM5 .... 62 C3
Papworth Wy
BRXS/STRHM SW2 .... 30 B3
Parade Cl RPLY/SEND GU23 .... 92 G3
Parade Ct EHSLY KT24 .... 94 G6
Parade Ms BRXS/STRHM SW2 .... 30 C5
The Parade ASHV GU12 * 109 J2
BTSEA SW11 * 104 A1
CAR SM5 .... 62 B4
CRAWE RH10 .... 177 H4
CROY/NA CR0 .... 44 G7
EGRIN RH19 .... 162 A9
EPSOM KT18 .... 78 B2
ESH/CLAY KT10 .... 58 E5
FRIM GU16 * 40 B8
GUW GU2 .... 91 P9
HORS RH12 .... 191 P7
KUT/HW KT1 * 8 E4
KWD/TDW/WH KT20 * 79 J8
LHD/OX KT22 * 96 C2
PGE/AN SE20 * 46 C2
RCH/KEW TW9 * 17 N8
STA TW18 * 22 A8
SUN TW16 .... 39 L4
SUT SM1 .... 61 K2
SYD SE26 * 31 K5
VW GU25 .... 36 B7
WLGTN SM6 * 63 H4
WOKN/KNAP GU21 * 10 C4
Paradise Rd RCH/KEW TW9 .... 26 D1
Paragon Gv BRYLDS KT5 .... 41 M7
Parbury Ri CHSGTN KT9 .... 59 L5
Parbury Rd FSTH SE23 .... 31 M2
Parchmore Rd THHTH CR7 .... 45 K5
Parchmore Wy THHTH CR7 .... 45 K3
Pares Cl WOKN/KNAP GU21 .... 10 A1
Parfitts Cl FNM GU9 .... 4 C4
Parfour Dr PUR/KEN CR8 .... 81 L5
Parfrey St HMSMTH W6 .... 18 G4
Parham Rd CRAWW RH11 .... 176 C4
Parish Cl ASHV GU12 .... 109 K5
FNM GU9 .... 107 L8
Parish La CRAWE RH10 .... 195 J4
PGE/AN SE20 .... 31 L9
Parish Rd FARN GU14 .... 88 D7
Park Av CAR SM5 .... 62 C5
CBLY GU15 .... 68 E3
CTHM CR3 .... 101 N4
EGH TW20 .... 36 G1
ECH TW20 .... 36 C1
HSLW TW3 .... 25 J2
MFD/CHID GU8 .... 130 C8
MORT/ESHN SW14 .... 18 B9
MTCM CR4 .... 44 D1
REDH RH1 .... 140 B4
STA TW18 .... 22 C9
STWL/WRAY TW19 .... 21 J1
WWKM BR4 .... 65 J1
Park Av East EW KT17 .... 60 E5
Park Av West EW KT17 .... 60 E5
Park Barn Dr GUW GU2 .... 111 L4
Park Barn East GUW GU2 .... 111 M4
Park Barn Pde GUW GU2 .... 111 L5
Park Cha GODL GU7 .... 150 D2
GU GU1 .... 7 G3
Park Cl ADL/WDHM KT15 .... 55 M8
BRKHM/BTCW RH3 .... 137 P1
CAR SM5 .... 62 B5
ECH TW20 .... 20 F8
ESH/CLAY KT10 .... 57 P5
HASM GU27 .... 184 G1
HPTN TW12 .... 40 C2
HSLW TW3 .... 25 K1
KUTN/CMB KT2 .... 8 D1
LHD/OX KT22 .... 96 D4
OXTED RH8 .... 103 M8
WKENS W14 .... 19 H1
WOT/HER KT12 .... 57 H1
Park Copse RDKG RH5 .... 117 K7
Park Corner Dr EHSLY KT24 .... 94 G8
Park Ct BF/WBF KT14 * 73 L2
DUL SE21 .... 30 E6
NWMAL KT3 .... 42 B5
SYD SE26 * 31 J9
WOKS/MYFD GU22 .... 10 D7
Park Crs ASC SL5 .... 34 C1
FROW RH18 .... 181 M9
WHTN TW2 .... 25 L4
Parkdale Crs WPK KT4 .... 60 B2
Park Dr ACT W3 .... 17 N1
ASC SL5 .... 34 F7
CRAN GU6 .... 153 J9
MORT/ESHN SW14 .... 27 H1
SHGR GU5 .... 132 D7
WEY KT13 .... 56 E6
WOKS/MYFD GU22 .... 10 E6
Park End BMLY BR1 .... 47 M2
Parker Cl CAR SM5 .... 62 B6
Parke Rd BARN SW13 .... 18 E6
SUN TW16 .... 39 J5
Parker Rd CROY/NA CR0 .... 2 D7
Parker's Cl ASHTD KT21 .... 77 L8
Parker's Hl ASHTD KT21 .... 77 L8
Parker's La ASHTD KT21 .... 77 M8
Parker Ter FSTH SE23 .... 31 N5
Park Farm Cl HORS RH12 .... 192 C3
Park Farm Rd
KUTN/CMB KT2 .... 41 L1
Parkfield GODL GU7 .... 150 D2
HORS RH12 .... 192 B7
Parkfield Av FELT TW13 .... 24 B6
MORT/ESHN SW14 .... 18 C9

Parkfield Cl CRAWW RH11 .... 176 C5
Parkfield Crs FELT TW13 .... 24 B6
Parkfield Pde FELT TW13 * 24 B6
Parkfield Rd FELT TW13 .... 24 B6
Parkfields CROY/NA CR0 .... 46 F9
LHD/OX KT22 .... 58 D9
PUT/ROE SW15 .... 18 G9
YTLY GU46 .... 67 H3
Parkfields Av RYNPK SW20 .... 42 F2
Parkfields Cl CAR SM5 .... 62 C3
Park Gdns KUTN/CMB KT2 .... 26 B8
Parkgate Cl KUTN/CMB KT2 .... 26 C9
Park Gate Ct HPTN TW12 * 25 K8
WOKS/MYFD GU22 * 10 D6
Parkgate Gdns
MORT/ESHN SW14 .... 27 J1
Parkgate Rd RDKG RH5 .... 156 C2
REIG RH2 .... 119 M6
WLGTN SM6 .... 62 C4
Park Gn GT/LBKH KT23 .... 96 A4
Park Gv BMLY BR1 .... 47 P2
Park Hall Rd DUL SE21 .... 30 E6
REIG RH2 .... 119 L3
Parkham St BTSEA SW11 .... 19 P6
Park Hl CAR SM5 .... 62 B5
CLAP SW4 .... 29 N1
FLEETS GU52 .... 106 F2
FSTH SE23 .... 31 K3
RCHPK/HAM TW10 .... 26 C7
Parkhill Cl BLKW GU17 .... 67 P4
Park Hill Cl CAR SM5 .... 62 A4
Park Hill Ri CROY/NA CR0 .... 3 J5
Parkhill Rd BLKW GU17 .... 67 P4
Park Hill Rd BLKW GU17 .... 67 P4
Park Hill Rd CROY/NA CR0 .... 3 H7
EW KT17 .... 60 D9
HAYES BR2 .... 47 L3
WLGTN SM6 .... 62 D6
Park Horsley EHSLY KT24 .... 95 J9
Park House Dr REIG RH2 .... 119 K7
Park House Gdns TWK TW1 .... 26 B1
Parkhurst HOR/WEW KT19 .... 60 A4
Parkhurst Flds RFNM GU10 .... 165 J2
Parkhurst Gv HORL RH6 .... 140 A9
Parkhurst Rd GUW GU2 .... 111 N4
HORL RH6 .... 140 A9
SUT SM1 .... 61 P3
Parkland Av DTCH/LGLY SL3 .... 12 A2
Parkland Dr BRAK RG12 .... 32 G4
Parkland Gv ASHF TW15 .... 23 K7
FNM GU9 .... 108 B6
Parkland Rd ASHF TW15 .... 23 K7
Parklands ADL/WDHM KT15 .... 55 N4
BRYLDS KT5 .... 41 M6
GT/LBKH KT23 .... 96 A3
OXTED RH8 .... 123 J2
RDKG RH5 .... 137 H2
Parklands Cl
MORT/ESHN SW14 .... 27 H1
Parklands Pde HEST TW5 * 15 M7
Parklands Pl GU GU1 .... 112 F5
Parklands Rd
STRHM/NOR SW16 .... 29 L8
Parklands Wy WPK KT4 .... 60 C1
Park La ASHTD KT21 .... 77 M7
BNFD RG42 .... 32 A1
CAR SM5 .... 62 C5
CBLY GU15 .... 68 E3
CHEAM SM3 .... 61 J5
COUL/CHIP CR5 .... 100 F1
CROY/NA CR0 .... 2 E6
DTCH/LGLY SL3 .... 12 E8
HEST TW5 .... 15 J5
LING RH7 .... 143 N9
MFD/CHID GU8 .... 168 B6
RCH/KEW TW9 .... 26 B8
RDKG RH5 .... 155 P4
RGUE GU4 .... 113 H2
TEDD TW11 .... 25 M9
Park La East REIG RH2 .... 119 K8
Parklawn Av EPSOM KT18 .... 78 A3
HORL RH6 .... 140 B8
Park Lawn Rd WEY KT13 .... 56 E3
Parkleigh Rd WIM/MER SW19 .... 43 M3
Park Ley Rd CTHM CR3 .... 82 D7
Parkleys RCHPK/HAM TW10 .... 26 C7
Parkleys Pde
RCHPK/HAM TW10 * 26 C7
Parkmead PUT/ROE SW15 .... 27 N2
Park Ms STWL/WRAY TW19 .... 23 J3
Parkpale La
BRKHM/BTCW RH3 .... 137 N1
Park Pde ACT W3 * 17 P2
Park Pl EA W5 .... 17 H2
BMLY BR1 * 47 P2
FLEETS GU52 .... 106 F1
HORS RH12 .... 192 B9
HPTN TW12 .... 25 L2
WOKS/MYFD GU22 .... 10 E6
Park Ri HORS RH12 .... 192 A6
LHD/OX KT22 .... 96 D2
Park Rise Cl LHD/OX KT22 .... 97 H1
Park Rise Rd FSTH SE23 .... 31 M4
Park Rd ALDT GU11 .... 108 D7
ASHF TW15 .... 23 L7
BECK BR3 .... 46 F1
BELMT SM2 .... 61 M7
BMLY BR1 .... 47 N2
BNSTD SM7 .... 79 N5
BRAK RG12 .... 32 F5
BRYLDS KT5 .... 41 M7
CBLY GU15 .... 69 H1
CHEAM SM3 .... 61 J5
CHSWK W4 .... 18 B5
CTHM CR3 .... 101 N3
E/WMO/HCT KT8 .... 40 B5
EGH TW20 .... 21 N8
EGRIN RH19 .... 162 D9
EGRIN RH19 .... 162 C3
ESH/CLAY KT10 .... 58 D3
FARN GU14 .... 88 D2

FELT TW13 .... 24 E7
FNM GU9 .... 127 P1
FROW RH18 .... 181 M9
GODL GU7 .... 150 C2
GU GU1 .... 6 E5
HORL RH6 .... 160 D3
HORL RH12 .... 193 L1
HPTN TW12 .... 25 K8
HSLW TW3 .... 25 K1
ISLW TW7 .... 17 H6
KUT/HW KT1 .... 8 A3
KUTN/CMB KT2 .... 26 E8
LING RH7 .... 143 L2
NWMAL KT3 .... 42 B5
OXTED RH8 .... 103 M8
PUR/KEN CR8 .... 81 L4
REDH RH1 .... 120 B3
SHGR GU5 .... 134 B3
SHPTN TW17 .... 38 C9
SHST GU47 .... 49 N5
SNWD SE25 .... 45 N5
STWL/WRAY TW19 .... 22 F2
SUN TW16 .... 39 K1
SWTR RH13 .... 190 E7
TEDD TW11 .... 40 F1
TWK TW1 .... 26 B2
WARL CR6 .... 82 C9
WIM/MER SW19 .... 28 C9
WLGTN SM6 .... 62 D1
WOKS/MYFD GU22 .... 11 G4
Park Rd North CHSWK W4 .... 18 B4
Park Rw FNM GU9 .... 5 F2
Parkshot RCH/KEW TW9 .... 17 K9
Park Side ADL/WDHM KT15 .... 55 M8
Parkside BECK BR3 * 47 J1
CHEAM SM3 .... 61 J5
CRAWE RH10 .... 177 H5
EGRIN RH19 .... 180 B2
FNM GU9 .... 107 N8
HPTN TW12 .... 25 L8
WIM/MER SW19 .... 28 C9
WOKS/MYFD GU22 .... 11 G4
Parkside Av WIM/MER SW19 .... 28 A8
Parkside Cl EHSLY KT24 .... 95 H5
PGE/AN SE20 .... 46 C1
Parkside Crs BRYLDS KT5 .... 42 A7
Parkside Gdns
COUL/CHIP CR5 .... 80 D6
WIM/MER SW19 .... 28 A7
Parkside Pl EHSLY KT24 * 94 G5
WARL CR6 .... 82 G5
Parkside PI ASC SL5 .... 34 G7
HSLW TW3 .... 25 J1
Parkstead Rd PUT/ROE SW15 .... 27 M1
Parkstone Dr CBLY GU15 .... 68 E2
Park St BAGS GU19 .... 51 N6
CBLY GU15 .... 68 E2
CROY/NA CR0 .... 2 D4
DTCH/LGLY SL3 .... 13 H6
GU GU1 .... 7 F5
HORS RH12 .... 192 C8
SLW TW7 .... 190 D7
TEDD TW11 .... 25 M9
Park Ter CAR SM5 * 62 A2
RSEV TN14 .... 105 P4
WPK KT4 .... 42 E8
Park Ter East SWTR RH13 .... 192 C5
Park Ter West HORS RH12 .... 192 C6
The Park CAR SM5 .... 62 A2
GT/LBKH KT23 .... 66 A5
Parkthorne Rd BAL SW12 .... 29 N3
Park Vw ADL/WDHM KT15 * 55 N4
BAGS GU19 .... 51 M6
CRAWW RH11 .... 176 F6
CTHM CR3 .... 102 A5
EW KT17 .... 78 E2
GT/LBKH KT23 .... 96 A5
HORL RH6 .... 159 K1
NWMAL KT3 .... 42 D4
Park View Ct
WOKS/MYFD GU22 .... 10 E7
Park View Dr MTCM CR4 .... 43 P3
Park View Gdns
EGRIN RH19 .... 162 C9
Parkview Rd CROY/NA CR0 .... 46 A9
CTHM CR3 .... 102 F2
REDH RH1 .... 140 C3
Parkview V RGUE GU4 .... 112 G2
Park Vis TOOT SW17 * 29 H8
Park Wk FUL/PGN SW6 .... 19 N4
WBPTN SW10 .... 19 N4
Park Wy CRAWE RH10 .... 177 M3
E/WMO/HCT KT8 .... 40 C4
EBED/NFELT TW14 .... 24 C3
GT/LBKH KT23 .... 96 A3
HORS RH12 .... 192 B9
Parkway CBLY GU15 .... 68 E5
CROY/NA CR0 .... 65 J7
CWTH RG45 .... 49 L4
DORK RH4 .... 116 C6
GU GU1 .... 112 C4
RYNPK SW20 .... 43 H5
The Parkway HEST TW5 .... 15 J4
BECK BR3 .... 46 C1
Parkwood Av
ESH/CLAY KT10 .... 40 C9
Park Wood Cl BNSTD SM7 .... 79 H4
Parkwood Gv SUN TW16 .... 39 J4
Park Wood Rd BNSTD SM7 .... 79 H4
Parkwood Rd
BH/WHM TN16 .... 104 C1
ISLW TW7 .... 16 F6
REDH RH1 .... 120 C4
WIM/MER SW19 .... 28 C8
Park Wood Vw BNSTD SM7 .... 78 G5
Park Works Rd REDH RH1 .... 121 H4
Parlaunt Rd DTCH/LGLY SL3 .... 12 F2
Parley Dr WOKN/KNAP GU21 .... 72 A7

Pacific Cl EBED/NFELT TW14 .... 24 A4
Packway FNM GU9 .... 127 P6
Padbrook OXTED RH8 .... 103 N9
Padbury Cl
EBED/NFELT TW14 .... 23 N4
Paddenswick Rd
HMSMTH W6 .... 18 E1
Paddock Cl CBLY GU15 .... 69 J2
LING RH7 .... 143 J9
MFD/CHID GU8 * 168 B2
OXTED RH8 .... 123 M2
RDKG RH5 .... 137 K9
SYD SE26 .... 31 L7
WPK KT4 .... 42 E9
Paddock Gdns EGRIN RH19 .... 180 D4
NRWD SE19 .... 30 F9
Paddock Gv RDKG RH5 .... 137 K9
Paddockhurst Rd
CRAWE RH10 .... 178 D9
CRAWW RH11 .... 176 D6
Paddocks Cl COB KT11 .... 75 L5
Paddocks Md
WOKN/KNAP GU21 .... 71 L5
Paddocks Rd RGUE GU4 .... 112 L1
The Paddocks EA W5 * 17 K1
GT/LBKH KT23 .... 96 B5
RGUW GU3 .... 110 C5
WEY KT13 * 56 A9

Parliamentary Rd
CHOB/PIR GU24..........90 A1
Parnell Cl CRAWE RH10...177 N7
SHB W12.................18 F1
Parnham Av LTWR GU18....52 D6
Parr Av KT17.............60 F7
Parr Cl LHD/OX KT22......76 F9
Parris Cft DORK RH4.....137 J1
Parrs Cl SAND/SEL CR2....63 M7
Parr's Pl HPTN TW12......40 A1
Parry Cl KT17...........60 E6
SWTR RH13..............193 H6
Parry Dr WFY KT13........56 C8
Parry Gn North
DTCH/LGLY SL3...........12 D2
Parry Gn South
DTCH/LGLY SL3...........12 D2
Parry Rd SNWD SE25......45 L4
Parsonage Cl WARL CR6...82 E5
Parsonage La DORK RH4...116 C8
Parsonage Rd CRAN GU6...152 C9
EGH TW20................21 J8
HORS RH12..............192 C6
Parsonage Sq DORK RH4...116 C6
Parsonage Wy FRIM GU16...68 C7
HORS RH12..............192 D6
Parsons Cl FLEETS GU52..106 F1
HASM GU27..............184 D2
HORL RH6...............140 A9
Parsons Fld SHST GU47...49 M9
Parsonsfield Cl BNSTD SM7..79 H4
Parsonsfield Rd BNSTD SM7..79 H5
Parsons Gn FUL/PGN SW6...19 L6
GU GU1.................112 B3
HASM GU27..............184 D2
Parsons Green La
FUL/PGN SW6............19 L6
Parsons La GSHT GU26...165 M5
Parson's Md CROY/NA CRO...2 B2
E/WMO/HCT KT8..........40 C4
Parsons Rd DTCH/LGLY SL3..12 D4
Parthenia Rd FUL/PGN SW6..19 L6
Parthia Cl
KWD/TDW/WH KT20........78 F8
Partridge Av YTLY GU46...66 F2
Partridge Cl FRIM GU16...68 C7
RFNM GU10..............107 H6
Partridge Knoll
PUR/KEN CR8............81 K1
Partridge La HORS RH12..175 K1
RDKG RH5...............138 B9
Partridge Md BNSTD SM7...78 C4
Partridge Pl CRAWE RH10..179 K5
Partridge Rd HPTN TW12...24 C9
Parvis Rd BF/WBF KT14....73 N1
Paschal Rd CBLY GU15.....51 H9
Passfield Rd LIPH GU30..182 B2
Pastens Rd EGRIN RH8....124 A2
Paston Cl WLGTN SM6......62 E2
The Pasture CRAWE RH10..177 M5
Pasturewood Rd RDKG RH5..183 M8
Patching Cl CRAWW RH11..176 C4
Patchings SWTR RH13.....192 F7
Paterson Cl FRIM GU16....69 L5
Pater St KENS W8.........19 L1

FSTH SE23..............31 M6
Payne Cl CRAWE RH10....177 N3
Paynesfield Av
MORT/ESHN SW14.........18 B8
Payns Wk HMSMTH W6......19 J4
Peabody Cl CROY/NA CRO..45 J8
Peabody Est FUL/PGN SW6..19 L4
HMSMTH W6 *............18 G3
HNHL SE24..............30 C4
Peabody Hl DUL SE21.....30 A4
Peabody Rd FARN GU14....88 E6
Peace Cl SNWD SE25......45 N5
Peacemaker Cl
CRAWW RH11.............176 B7
Peaches Cl BELMT SM2....61 J6
Peach Rd FELT TW13......24 B4
Peach Tree Cl FARN GU14..68 C9
Peacock Av
EBED/NFELT TW14........23 N4
Peacock Gdns SAND/SEL CR2..64 E8
Peakfield RFNM GU10....146 F5
Peak Hl SYD SE26........31 K7
Peak Hill Av SYD SE26...31 K7
Peak Hill Gdns SYD SE26..31 K7
Peak Rd GUW GU2.........111 N2
Peaks Hl PUR/KEN CR8....62 C8
Peaks Hill Ri PUR/KEN CR8..62 D8
The Peak SYD SE26.......31 K6
Peall Rd CROY/NA CRO....45 K7
Pear Av SHPTN TW17......38 C4
Pearce Cl MTCM CR4......44 C3
Pearcefield Av FSTH SE23..31 K4
Pearfield Rd FSTH SE23...31 M6
Pear Ct WOKN/KNAP GU21..71 L5
Pearmain Cl SHPTN TW17..38 D6
Pears Av SHPTN TW17 *...38 C4
Pearscroft Ct FUL/PGN SW6..19 M6
Pearscroft Rd FUL/PGN SW6..19 M7
Pearson Rd CRAWE RH10..177 L3
Pearson Wy MTCM CR4.....44 C2
Pear Tree Av FLEETS GU52..113 H5
Peartree Av TOOT SW17...29 J9
Pear Tree Cl ADL/WDHM KT15..55 L4
MTCM CR4...............44 A3
Peartree Cl SAND/SEL CR2..82 B3
Pear Tree Hl REDH RH1 *..140 C5
Pear Tree La RFNM GU10..146 C1
Pear Tree Rd
ADL/WDHM KT15..........55 L4
ASHF TW15..............23 M8
Peary Cl HORS RH12.....192 C4
Peaslake La SHGR GU5...134 F7
Peaslake Rd CRAN GU6...153 N3
Peat Common
MFD/CHID GU8...........148 D2
Peat Moor Cl FLEETN GU51..86 E5
Peatmoor Cl FLEETN GU51..86 E5
Peatmore Av
WOKS/MYFD GU22........73 L5
Peatmore Cl
WOKS/MYFD GU22........73 L5
Peatmore Dr CHOB/PIR GU24..90 C1
Pebble Cl EPSOM KT18....98 C8
Pebble Hl EHSLY KT24...114 E4
Pebblehill Rd
BRKHM/BTCW RH3........118 C1
Pebble La LHD/OX KT22....97 N2
Peckarmans Wd SYD SE26..31 H6
Peddlars Gv YTLY GU46....67 J2
Pedleaf Cl HSLW TW3.....96 C4
Peeks Brook La HORL RH6..159 P5
Peel Av FNM GU9..........69 J9
Pegasus Av HASM GU12...108 G3
Pegasus Cl HASM GU22...183 N5
Pegasus Ct BTFD TW8.....17 M3
Pegasus Rd CROY/NA CRO..63 J5
FARN GU14..............88 D5
Pegasus Wy EGRIN RH19..162 F9
Peggotty Pl SHST GU47...50 A7
Pegg Rd HEST TW5........15 M5
Pegler Wy CRAWW RH11...176 C5
Pegwell Cl CRAWW RH11..176 C7
Peket Cl STA TW18........37 J2
Pelham Ct CRAWW RH11...176 E9
HORS RH12 *............192 A8
Pelham Dr CRAWW RH11...176 F8
Pelham Pl CRAWW RH11...176 E9
RFNM GU10..............127 L9
Pelton Av BELMT SM2.....61 M8
Pemberley Cha
HOR/WEW KT19...........59 P4
Pemberley Cl
HOR/WEW KT19...........59 P4
Pemberton Pl
ESH/CLAY KT10..........58 C2
Pemberton Rd
E/WMO/HCT KT8..........40 A4
Pembley Gn CRAWE RH10..160 F9
Pembridge Av WHTN TW2...24 G4
Pembroke BRAK RG12......32 B8
Pembroke Av BRYLDS KT5...41 P6
WOT/HER KT12 *.........57 M3
Pembroke Broadway
CBLY GU15...............55 K4
Pembroke Cl ASC SL5.....34 D6
BNSTD SM7..............79 M6
Pembroke Gdns KENS W8...19 K2
WOKS/MYFD GU22........11 H5
Pembroke Gardens Cl
KENS W8.................19 K1

Pembroke Ms KENS W8.....19 L1
Pembroke Pl ISLW TW7....16 E7
KENS W8................19 L1
Pembroke Rd CRAWE RH10..177 M2
KENS W8................19 K2
MTCM CR4...............44 C3
SNWD SE25..............45 N5
WOKS/MYFD GU22........11 H4
Pembroke Sq KENS W8....19 L1
Pembroke Vls KENS W8....19 L2
Pembroke Wk KENS W8.....19 L2
Pembury Av WPK KT4......42 E9
Pembury Ct HYS/HAR UB3..15 H3
Pembury Pl ASHV GU12...108 E5
Pembury Rd SNWD SE25....46 A5
Pemdevon Rd CROY/NA CRO..45 J8
Pemerich Cl HYS/HAR UB3 *..15 H3
Penard Rd NWDGN UB2.....16 B1
Penates ESH/CLAY KT10...58 D5
Penbury Rd NWDGN UB2...15 P3
Pendarves Av RYNPK SW20..42 G2
Pendell Av HYS/HAR UB3..15 H5
Pendell Ms REDH RH1....120 E8
Pendell Rd REDH RH1....121 K2
Pendennis Cl BF/WBF KT14..73 L3
Pendennis Rd
STRHM/NOR SW16........29 P7
Penderel Rd HSLW TW3....25 H1
Pendine Pl BRAK RG12....32 D6
Pendlebury BRAK RG12....32 C8
Pendle Rd
STRHM/NOR SW16........29 L9
Pendleton Cl REDH RH1..120 B7
Pendleton Rd REDH RH1..119 P8
Pendragon Wy CBLY GU15...69 M4
Penfold Cl CROY/NA CRO..63 J2
Penfold Ct FNM GU9.....128 E3
Penfold Rd CRAWE RH10..177 L9
Penge La PGE/AN SE20....46 C1
Penge Rd SNWD SE25......46 A6
Pengilly Rd FNM GU9.....4 A4
Penhurst WOKN/KNAP GU21..72 D3
Peninsular Cl CBLY GU15..69 K1
EBED/NFELT TW14........23 N2
Penistone Rd
STRHM/NOR SW16........44 G1
Penlee Cl EDEN TN8.....144 G3
Pennant Ms KENS W8......19 L2
The Pennards SUN TW16...39 L4
Penn Cl CRAWW RH11.....176 C2
Penn Ct CRAWW RH11.....176 C1
Pennefather's Rd
ALDT GU11..............108 B3
Penner Cl WIM/MER SW19..28 B4
Penners Gdns SURB KT6...41 L8
Pennine Cl CRAWW RH11..176 E5
Pennine Wy FARN GU14....68 A9
HYS/HAR UB3............15 F5
Pennings Av GUW GU2....111 M2
Pennington Dr WEY KT13..56 C2
Penn Rd DTCH/LGLY SL3...12 D6
Penns Wd FARN GU14......88 F6
Penns Yd FNM GU9........4 E3
Pennycroft CROY/NA CRO..64 E7
Pennine Dr RGUW GU3....111 H3
Pennyfield COB KT11......75 J2
Penny La SHPTN TW17......38 G8
Pennymead Dr E/HOR KT24..95 H7
Penny Ms WAND/EARL SW18..28 D1
Pennypot La CHOB/PIR GU24..71 H2
Penrhyn Cl ASHV GU12 *..108 D5
CTHM CR3...............81 M9
Penrhyn Crs
MORT/ESHN SW14.........18 A9
Penrhyn Rd KUT/HW KT1...41 L5
Penrith Cl BECK BR3.....47 H2
PUT/ROE SW15...........28 B1
REIG RH2...............120 A4
Penrith Pl WNWD SE27....30 C5
Penrith Rd NWMAL KT3....42 B5
THHTH CR7..............45 L1
Penrith St STRHM/NOR SW16..29 M9
Penrose Ct EGH TW20.....21 J9
Penrose Rd LHD/OX KT22...96 C2
Penryn Dr BOR GU35.....164 F6
Pensfold La HORS RH12...175 K1
Pensford Av RCH/KEW TW9..17 N7
Pensford Cl CWTH RG45...49 M2
Penshurst Cl CRAWE RH10..177 N4
Penshurst Gn HAYES BR2...47 N6
Penshurst Ri FRIM GU16...69 H8
Penshurst Rd THHTH CR7..45 K6
Penshurst Wy BELMT SM2..61 L6
Pentelow Gdns
EBED/NFELT TW14........24 B2
Pentlow St PUT/ROE SW15..18 G7
Pentney Rd BAL SW12.....29 M4
RYNPK SW20.............43 J2
Penton Av STA TW18......37 J3
Penton Hall Dr STA TW18..37 L2
Penton Rd STA TW18......37 K1
Pentreath Av GUW GU2...111 M6
Penwerris Av ISLW TW7...16 C5
Penwith Dr HASM GU27...183 N6
Penwith Rd
WAND/EARL SW18........28 E5
Penwith Wk
WOKS/MYFD GU22........10 A7
Penwood End
WOKS/MYFD GU22........91 P1
Penwortham Rd
SAND/SEL CR2...........63 M8
STRHM/NOR SW16........29 L9

Penywern Rd ECT SW5.....19 L3
Peperham Rd HASM GU27..184 D2
Peper Harow La
MFD/CHID GU8...........130 C7
Peperharow Rd GODL GU7..131 J7
Peppard Rd CRAWE RH10..177 N7
Pepper Cl CTHM CR3.....101 N5
Peppercorn Cl THHTH CR7..45 M3
Peppermead Sq LEW SE13 *..31 P1
Peppermint Cl CROY/NA CRO..44 G8
Peppers Yd HORS RH12 *..192 C7
Pepys Cl ASHTD KT21.....77 N6
DTCH/LGLY SL3...........12 F4
Pepys Rd RYNPK SW20.....42 G3
Percheron Dr
WOKN/KNAP GU21........71 J8
Percival Rd FELT TW13...24 A5
Percival Wy HOR/WEW KT19..60 A3
Percy Av ASHF TW15......23 J8
Percy Bryant Rd SUN TW16..38 E1
Percy Bush Rd WDR/YW UB7..14 B1
Percy Gdns WPK KT4......42 B9
Percy Rd GUW GU2.......111 P3
HORS RH12..............192 A7
HPTN TW12..............40 A1
ISLW TW7...............16 G9
MTCM CR4...............44 C6
PGE/AN SE20............46 D2
SNWD SE25..............45 P6
WHTN TW2...............25 J4
Percy Wy WHTN TW2.......25 K4
Peregrine Gdns
CROY/NA CRO............64 E1
Peregrine Rd SUN TW16...38 C3
Peregrine Gdns
CROY/NA CRO............64 C1
Peregrine Wy
WIM/MER SW19..........42 G1
Perham Rd WKENS W14....19 J3
Perifield DUL SE21......30 D4
Perimeter Rd East
HORL RH6...............159 L5
Perimeter Rd North
HORL RH6...............158 G5
Perkin Cl HSLW TW3......16 B9
Perleybrooke La
WOKN/KNAP GU21........71 N6
Perowne St ALDT GU11...108 B4
Perran Rd BRXS/STRHM SW2..30 B5
Perrers Rd HMSMTH W6....18 F1
Perrin Cl ASHF TW15.....23 J8
Perrin Ct WOKN/KNAP GU21..72 F4
Perring Av FARN GU14....68 A8
Perring Rd FARN GU14....88 C6
Perrior Rd GODL GU7....131 L5
Perry Av EGRIN RH19....162 D9
Perry Cl GODL GU7......131 N8
Perry Dr FLEETN GU51....86 D6
Perryfield Rd CRAWW RH11..176 D6
Perryfield Wy
RCHPK/HAM TW10........26 A5
Perry Hl CAT SE6........31 N5
Perry Oaks BRAK RG12...33 J1
Perryhill Dr SHST GU47..49 M9
Perry How WPK KT4.......42 D9
Perrylands HORL RH6....160 C4
Perrylands La HORL RH6..158 C5
Perrymead St FUL/PGN SW6..19 L6
Perry Oak Dr HTHAIR TW6..13 M7
Perry Oaks BRAK RG12...32 G5
Perry Ri FSTH SE23......31 N5
Perrys La ORP BR6.......85 M2
Perry Wy BOR GU35......164 C7
BRAK RG12..............32 G3
FNM GU9................107 M7
LTWR GU18..............69 P1
Persfield Ms EW KT17....60 D8
Persfield Rd EW KT17....60 D8
Pershore Gv CAR SM5.....43 P7
Perth Cl CRAWW RH11....176 C2
RYNPK SW20.............42 E3
Perth Rd BECK BR3.......47 J3
Perth Wy HORS RH12.....192 A7
Petauel Rd TEDD TW11....25 M8
Petavel Rd TEDD TW11....25 M9
Peter Av OXTED RH8......103 K9
Peterborough Ms
FUL/PGN SW6............19 L6
Peterborough Rd CAR SM5..44 A7
CRAWE RH10.............177 N9
FUL/PGN SW6............19 L6
HARH RH12..............111 M3
Peterborough Vls
FUL/PGN SW6............19 M6
Petergate BTSEA SW11....19 N9
Peterhead Ms DTCH/LGLY SL3..12 G3
Peterhouse Cl SHST GU47..50 B7
Petersfield Av STA TW18..22 F8
Petersfield Crs
COUL/CHIP CR5..........80 G4
Petersfield Ri PUT/ROE SW15..27 N4
Petersfield Rd STA TW18..22 F8
Petersham Av BF/WBF KT14..74 A1
Petersham Cl BF/WBF KT14..74 A1
RCHPK/HAM TW10........26 B4
SUT SM1................61 K4
Petersham La SKENS SW7 *..19 N1
Petersham Ms SKENS SW7..19 N1
Petersham Pl SKENS SW7..19 N1
Petersham Rd
RCHPK/HAM TW10........26 C6
Petersham Ter
CROY/NA CRO *..........62 G2
Peterstow Cl
WIM/MER SW19..........28 B4
Peterwood Wy CROY/NA CRO..63 H1
Petley Rd HMSMTH W6....19 H4
Petridge Rd REDH RH1...140 B1
Petters Rd ASHTD KT21...77 M5

Pettiward Cl PUT/ROE SW15..18 G9
Petts La SHPTN TW17....38 C8
Petworth Cl COUL/CHIP CR5..80 E8
FRIM GU16..............69 H8
Petworth Ct CRAWW RH11..176 C8
Petworth Dr HORS RH12..192 E7
Petworth Gdns RYNPK SW20..42 F4
Petworth Rd HASM GU27..184 E5
MFD/CHID GU8...........149 N6
MFD/CHID GU8...........168 B7
Pevensey Cl CRAWE RH10..177 M6
ISLW TW7...............16 C5
Pevensey Rd FELT TW13...24 F4
TOOT SW17..............28 G8
Pevensey Wy FRIM GU16...69 J8
Peveril Rd CRAWW RH11...176 B1
Peverill Dr TEDD TW11....25 L8
Pewley Bank GU GU1......7 H6
Pewley Hl GU GU1........7 F6
Pewley Point GU GU1.....7 F7
Pewley Wy GU GU1........7 H6
Pewsey V BRAK RG12......33 H6
Pharaoh Cl MTCM CR4.....44 B9
Pheasant Cl PUR/KEN CR8..81 K2
Pheasant Copse
FLEETN GU51............86 D5
Phelps Wy HYS/HAR UB3...15 H4
Philanthropic Rd REDH RH1..120 D7
Philbeach Gdns ECT SW5..19 L3
Philip Gdns CROY/NA CRO..64 G1
Philip Rd STA TW18......22 G9
Philips Cl CAR SM5......44 C1
Philips Crs BOR GU35...164 C6
Phillimore Gardens Cl
KENS W8................19 L1
Phillimore Ter KENS W8 *..19 L1
Phillimore Wk KENS W8...19 L1
Phillips Cl BOR GU35...164 C6
CRAWE RH10.............195 L1
GODL GU7...............150 B2
RFNM GU10..............108 G6
Phillips Hatch SHGR GU5..132 C5
Phipp's Bridge Rd
WIM/MER SW19..........43 N3
Phoebeth Rd LEW SE13...31 P1
Phoenix Cl BTFD TW8.....35 P1
Phoenix Ct BTFD TW8 *...17 L3
GU GU1.................6 E6
Phoenix La EGRIN RH19...181 K5
Phoenix Pk BTFD TW8 *...17 L3
Phoenix Pl PGE/AN SE20..31 K9
Phoenix Wy HEST TW5....15 M5
Phyllis Av NWMAL KT3....42 F6
Pickering BRAK RG12.....32 C7
Pickering Gdns CROY/NA CRO..45 P7
Pickering Rd CRAWE RH10..177 M8
Pickets St BAL SW12.....29 K3
Picketts La REDH RH1...140 E5
Pickford St ALDT GU11...108 D4
Pickhurst Gn HAYES BR2..47 M1
Pickhurst La WWKM BR4...47 M1
Pickhurst Md HAYES BR2..47 M1
Pickhurst Pk HAYES BR2..47 L1
Pickhurst Ri WWKM BR4...47 L1
Pickhurst Rd
MFD/CHID GU8...........168 B8
Pickins Piece DTCH/LGLY SL3..12 E7
Pickwick Cl HSLWW TW4...24 F1
Pickwick Gdns CBLY GU15..69 K4
Pickwick Rd DUL SE21....30 E3
Picquets Wy BNSTD SM7...79 J5
Picton Cl CBLY GU15.....69 L1
Piermont Rd EDUL SE22...31 J1
Pierrefondes Av FARN GU14..88 D2
Pier Rd EBED/NFELT TW14..24 C1
Pier Ter WAND/EARL SW18..19 M9
Pigdown La EDEN TN8....145 P9
Pigeonhouse La
COUL/CHIP CR5..........99 N5
Pigeon La HPTN TW12.....25 H7
Pigeon Pass CRAWE RH10..179 K6
Pike Cl ALDT GU11.......108 E4
Pikes Hl EW KT17........78 C3
Pikes La LING RH7.......143 L4
Pilcot Rd HTWY RG27.....86 B9
Pilgrim Cl MRDN SM4.....43 M8
Pilgrim Hl WNWD SE27....30 D7
Pilgrims Cl FNM GU9.....128 C3
RDKG RH5...............116 C3
SHGR GU5...............134 C1
Pilgrims' La CTHM CR3...101 H6
OXTED RH8..............83 H8
Pilgrims Pl ASHF TW15 *..23 J7
REIG RH2...............119 L3
Pilgrims' Wy BH/WHM TN16..84 B5
BOR GU35...............164 B6
CHOB/PIR GU24..........70 C5
EDEN TN8...............145 H4
RDKG RH5...............117 H2
REIG RH2...............119 K3
RGUE RH2...............112 C9
SAND/SEL CR2...........63 L5
SHGR GU5...............134 C1
Pilsden Cl WIM/MER SW19 *..28 A3
Pimms Cl RGUE GU4.......112 F2
Pinckards MFD/CHID GU8..167 P6
Pincott La EHSLY KT24...94 E6
Pine Av CBLY GU15.......68 F4
CHOB/PIR GU24..........90 F1
WWKM BR4...............47 H9
Pine Bank GSHT GU26....165 P7
Pine Cl ADL/WDHM KT15...55 M8
ASHV GU12..............89 J9
CBLY GU15..............68 A1
CRAWW RH11.............176 F2
PGE/AN SE20............46 C2
PUR/KEN CR8............81 L6
WOKN/KNAP GU21........72 K6

Pine Coombe *CROY/NA* CR0.........64 D3
Pinecote Dr *ASC* SL5.....................8 B3
Pine Ct *FRIM* GU16 *...................89 J4
Pine Crs *CAR* SM5......................61 P9
Pine Dean *GT/LBKH* KT25.........96 B5
Pine Dr *BLKW* GU17....................68 A5
　　EWKG RG40
Pinefields *ADL/WDHM* KT15 *...55 M3
Pinefields Cl *CWTH* RG45...........49 M4
Pine Gdns *BRYLDS* KT5.............41 N7
　　HORL RH6.................................159 K2
Pine Gv *BFOR* GU20....................52 D5
　　EDEN TN8..................................144 F3
　　EGRIN RH19...............................162 A9
　　FLEETS GU52............................107 H1
　　RFNM GU10................................128 A7
　　WEY KT13.....................................56 D4
　　WIM/MER SW19............................28 C8
Pine Grove Ms *WEY* KT13 *........56 E4
Pine Hl *EPSOM* KT18...................78 B5
Pinehill Rd *CWTH* RG45..............49 M9
Pinehurst *ASC* SL5......................34 D6
　　HORS RH12................................192 B6
Pinehurst Av *GU14* GU14.............88 D5
　　KWD/TDW/WH KT20......................99 L2
Pinehurst Rd *FARN* GU14............99 L2
Pine Cl *VW* GU25........................36 C5
Pine trees Cl
　　MORT/ESHN SW14 *...................18 A9
Pine Mount Rd *CBLY* GU15.........68 F4
Pine Pk *RGUW* GU3......................90 G9
Pine Pl *BNSTD* SM7.....................79 H3
Pine Rdg *CAR* SM5.......................62 C7
Pine Ridge Dr *RFNM* GU10......127 M8
Pine Shaw *CRAWE* MYFD GU22...72 A9
Pine Shaw *CRAWE* RH10...........177 M4
Pines Rd *FLEETS* GU51..............86 B5
　　LIPH GU30..................................182 B6
The Pines *CBLY* GU15..................69 H1
　　HORS RH12................................193 H5
　　NRWD SE19 *.................................30 C9
　　PUR/KEN CR8...............................81 J7
　　SUN TW16....................................39 J4
　　WOKN/KNAP GU21......................72 D3
Pinetops *HORS* RH12.................193 H6
Pine Tree Cl *HEST* TW5...............15 K6
Pine Tree Hl
　　WOKS/MYFD GU22........................73 H5
Pine Trees *STA* TW18...................22 B8
Pinetrees Cl *CRAWE* RH10.........160 C9
Pine Vw *BOR* GU35.....................164 E5
Pine View Cl *FNM* GU9...............108 C9
　　HASM GU27.................................184 D2
　　RGUE GU4...................................133 K2
Pine Wk *BNSTD* SM7....................80 B6
　　BRYLDS KT5..................................41 N7
　　CAR SM5..61 P8
　　COB KT11.......................................75 M3
　　CTHM CR3....................................101 N2
　　EHSLY KT24....................................95 H8
　　GT/LBKH KT23..............................96 B5
Pine Wy *EGH* TW20......................20 C9
Pine Way Cl *EGRIN* RH19.........180 D4
Pine Wd *SUN* TW16.......................39 J2
Pinewood Av
　　ADL/WDHM KT15..........................55 N7
　　CWTH RG45...................................49 N3
Pinewood Cl *CROY/NA* CR0.........64 E2
　　HORS RH12.................................191 J7
　　SHST GU47.....................................49 K9
　　WOKN/KNAP GU21........................72 C3
Pinewood Crs *FARN* GU14...........87 N2
Pinewood Dr *STA* TW18 *.............22 B8
Pinewood Gdns *BAGS* GU19........51 L6
Pinewood Gv
　　ADL/WDHM KT15..........................55 M8
Pinewood Hl *FLEETN* GU51........86 C5
Pinewood Ms
　　STWL/WRAY TW19........................22 G2
Pinewood Pk
　　ADL/WDHM KT15..........................55 M9
　　FARN GU14....................................67 N9
Pinewood Rd *ASHV* GU12..........109 M3
　　FELT TW13....................................24 C6
　　HAYES BR2.....................................47 N2
　　VW GU25..35 N4
Pinfold Rd *STRHM/NOR* SW16....29 P7
Pinglestone Cl *WDR/YW* UB7....14 A5
Pinkcoat Cl *FELT* TW13................24 C5
Pinkhurst La *SWTR* RH13...........191 H8
Pinkwell Av *HYS/HAR* UB3..........14 F2
Pinkwell La *HYS/HAR* UB3...........14 F2
Piper Rd *KUT/HW* KT1....................9 H6
Pipers Cl *COB* KT11........................75 M4
Pipers Cft *FLEETS* GU52............106 F2
Pipers End *SWTR* RH13.............190 F7
　　VW GU25..36 B4
Pipers Gdns *CROY/NA* CR0.........46 E8
Piper's Green Rd
　　BH/WHM TW16.............................105 L8
Pipers La *BH/WHM* TN16...........105 L8
Pipers Patch *FARN* GU14............88 D3
Pipewell Rd *CAR* SM5...................44 A7
Pippbrook Gdns *DORK* RH4......117 H6
Pippin Cl *CROY/NA* CR0...............46 F9
Pippins Cl *WDR/YW* UB7 *...........13 P1
Pippins Ct *ASHF* TW15................23 L3
Pipsons Cl *YTLY* GU46.................67 H2
Piquet Rd *EGH* SE20.....................46 C3
Pirbright Crs *CROY/NA* CR0.........65 J5
Pirbright Rd *FARN* GU14...............88 A8
　　RGUW GU3...................................109 P2
　　WAND/EARL SW18........................28 C4
Pirbright Ter
　　CHOB/PIR GU24 *.........................90 F3
Pisley La *RDKG* RH5...................155 H7
Pitcairn Rd *MTCM* CR4.................44 B1
Pitchfont La *OXTED* RH8............103 N6
Pit Farm Rd *GU* GU1...................112 C5
Pitfold Av *HASM* GU27................183 N4

Pitfold Cl *HASM* GU27.................183 P4
Pitlake *CROY/NA* CR0.....................2 B3
Pitland St *RDKG* RH5..................135 L8
Pit La *EDEN* TN8...........................144 G1
Pitson Cl *ADL/WDHM* KT15........155 P3
Pitt Crs *WIM/MER* SW19...............28 E7
Pitt La *RFNM* GU10.....................146 D6
Pitt Pl *EW* KT17..............................78 C5
Pitt Rd *EW* KT17.............................78 C3
　　THHTH CR7....................................45 L6
Pittsmead Av *HAYES* BR2.............47 N8
Pittville Gdns *SNWD* SE25...........46 A4
Pitt Wy *FARN* GU14.......................88 B2
Pit Wood Gn
　　KWD/TDW/WH KT20.......................78 G9
Pixham La *DORK* RH4.................117 J4
Pixholme Gv *DORK* RH4.............117 J5
Pixton Wy *CROY/NA* CR0..............64 F6
Place Farm Rd *REDH* RH1.........121 M1
Placehouse La
　　COUL/CHIP CR5.............................81 H8
Plaistow Cl *BMLY* BR1...................47 P1
Plaistow La *BMLY* BR1...................47 N1
Plaistow Rd *MFD/CHID* GU8......169 K8
　　MFD/CHID GU8............................186 C5
Plaistow St *LING* RH7..................143 J7
The Planes *CHERT* KT16.............37 N8
Plane St *SYD* SE26........................31 J6
Plane Tree Crs *FELT* TW13............24 C6
Plantagenet Cl *WPK* KT4...............60 B5
Plantagenet Pk *BNFD* RG42..........33 H2
Plantain Crs *CRAWW* RH11........176 D9
Plantation La *WARL* CR6..............82 E8
The Plat *EDEN* TN8.....................145 H4
　　HORS RH12..................................191 P8
Platt Meadow *RGUE* GU4...........113 H2
The Platt *LING* RH7.....................162 A8
Plawsfield Rd *BECK* BR3..............46 D2
Plaws Hl *SHGR* GU5....................134 F7
Playfair St *HMSMTH* W6.................18 G3
Playfields Crs *EDUL* SE22.............30 F1
Playgreen Wy *CAT* SE6..................31 P7
Playground Cl *BECK* BR3...............46 C2
Pleasance Rd *PUT/ROE* SW15.....27 N1
The Pleasance
　　PUT/ROE SW15..............................18 F9
Pleasant Gv *CROY/NA* CR0...........64 F2
Pleasant Pl *WOT/HER* KT12 *......57 M5
Pleasure Pit Rd *ASHTD* KT21......77 P7
Plesman Wy *WLGTN* SM6 *..........62 G7
Plevna Rd *HPTN* TW12....................40 B2
Pleydell Av *HMSMTH* W6..............18 D1
　　NRWD SE19 *.................................30 C9
Pleydell Gdns *NRWD* SE19 *.........30 C9
Plough Cl *CRAWW* RH11............176 C6
Ploughlands *BNFD* RG42..............32 B2
Plough La *COB* KT11.......................75 J5
　　CROY/NA CR0..............................192 D5
　　EDUL SE22.....................................30 C2
　　HORS RH12..................................192 D5
　　PUR/KEN CR8.................................62 D3
　　TEDD TW11....................................25 P8
　　WIM/MER SW19..............................28 E8
Plough Lane Cl *WLGTN* SM6........62 G4
Ploughmans End *ISLW* TW7.........25 L1
Plough Rd *BTSEA* SW11...............19 P8
　　HOR/WEW KT19............................60 B6
　　HORL RH6....................................160 D1
　　LING RH7.....................................162 F2
　　YTLY GU46......................................67 J1
Plough Ter *BTSEA* SW11...............19 P9
Plover Cl *CRAWW* RH11.............176 F8
　　STA TW18.......................................22 C6
Plovers Rd *CHOB/PIR* GU24........70 F3
Plovers Rd *SWTR* RH13..............192 E7
Plum Cl *FELT* TW13.......................24 B4
Plum Garth *BTFD* TW8...................17 K2
Plummer La *MTCM* CR4.................44 B2
Plummer Rd *CLAP* SW4...............29 M2
Plumpton Wy *CAR* SM5.................61 P9
Plymouth Rd *BMLY* BR1................47 N2
Pockford Rd *MFD/CHID* GU8......168 C7
Pocock Av *WDR/YW* UB7..............14 B1
Podmore Rd
　　WAND/EARL SW18........................19 N5
Pointers Hl *DORK* RH4................116 C9
Pointers Rd *COB* KT11...................74 C9
The Pointers *ASHTD* KT21............77 L9
Point Pleasant
　　WAND/EARL SW18........................19 M5
Point Wharf La *BTFD* TW8...........17 K5
Polden Cl *FARN* GU14...................88 A9
Polecroft La *CAT* SE6....................31 N5
Polesden Gdns *RYNPK* SW20......42 F4
Polesden La
　　RPLY/SEND GU23..........................93 K3
Polesden Rd *RDKG* RH5...............96 B9
Polesden Vw *GT/LBKH* KT23........96 B7
Poles La *CRAWH* RH11..............158 F9
Polesteeple Hl
　　BH/WHM TN16..............................84 B6
Police Station Rd
　　WOT/HER KT12..............................57 L7
Polkerris Wy *FLEETS* GU52.......107 H2
Pollard Cl *WDSR* SL4.....................20 G1
Pollard Gv *CBLY* GU15..................68 F6
Pollard Rd *MRDN* SM4..................43 P6
　　WOKS/MYFD GU22.........................72 G7
Pollardrow Av *BNFD* RG42............32 B2
Pollards *CRAWW* RH11..............176 D6
Pollards Crs
　　STRHM/NOR SW16........................44 G4
Pollards Dr *SWTR* RH13.............192 E8
Pollards Hl East
　　STRHM/NOR SW16........................45 H4
Pollards Hl North
　　STRHM/NOR SW16........................45 H4
Pollards Hl South
　　STRHM/NOR SW16........................44 G4
Pollards Hl West
　　STRHM/NOR SW16........................44 G4
Pollards Oak Crs *OXTED* RH8....123 N3

Pollards Oak Rd *OXTED* RH8....123 N3
Pollards Wood Hl
　　OXTED RH8..................................123 N1
Pollards Wood Rd
　　OXTED RH8..................................123 P2
　　STRHM/NOR SW16........................44 G3
Polsted Rd *CAT* SE6......................31 K1
Polsted Rd *GUW* GU2..................111 N7
Polworth Rd
　　STRHM/NOR SW16........................29 P8
Polyanthus Wy *CWTH* RG45........49 M1
Pomeroy Cl *TWK* TW1....................17 H9
Pompadour Cl *BRWD* CM14 *
　　WOT/HER KT12...............................17 J5
Pond Copse La *BIL* RH14............188 C5
Pond Cottage La *BECK* BR3..........46 C9
Pond Cft *YTLY* GU46......................67 J2
Pond Farm Cl
　　KWD/TDW/WH KT20.......................98 F4
Pondfield Rd *GODL* GU7..............131 N7
　　HAYES BR2.....................................47 J2
　　HORS RH12...................................189 N2
　　PUR/KEN CR8.................................81 K5
Pond Head La *RDKG* RH5..........154 E9
Pond Hill Gdns *CHEAM* SM3 *....61 J5
Pond La *RFNM* GU10...................146 F8
　　SHGR GU5....................................134 G6
Pond Md *DUL* SE21........................30 D2
Pond Meadow *GUW* GU2.............111 L5
Pond Moor Rd *BRAK* RG12...........32 D6
Pond Piece *LHD/OX* KT22.............76 B2
Pond Rd *BOR* GU35.....................164 D7
　　EGH TW20......................................21 P9
　　FARN GU14....................................88 D5
Pondside Cl *HYS/HAR* UB3..........14 F5
Ponds La *SHGR* GU5...................134 A4
The Ponds *WEY* KT13....................56 F5
Pondtail Cl *FLEETS* GU51.............87 J3
　　HORS RH12..................................192 C5
Pondtail Dr *HORS* RH12..............192 C4
Pondtail Gdns *FLEETS* GU51.......87 J7
Pondtail Rd *HORS* RH12.............192 C4
Pondtail Rd *FLEETN* GU51...........87 J7
　　HORS RH12..................................192 B5
Pond Wy *EGRIN* RH19.................180 C2
Pond Wood Rd
　　CRAWE RH10................................177 K3
Poneys Cl *BRAK* RG12 *...............32 E3
Ponsonby Rd *PUT/ROE* SW15.....27 N3
Pony Cha *COB* KT11.......................75 P2
Pook Hl *MFD/CHID* GU8.............167 M8
Pool Cl *BECK* BR3..........................31 P8
　　E/WMO/HCT KT8...........................39 P4
Pool Ct *CAT* SE6............................31 P5
Poole Court Rd *HSLWW* TW4.......15 N7
Pool End Cl *SHPTN* TW17.............38 C5
Poole Rd *HOR/WEW* KT19............60 B5
　　WOKN/KNAP GU21........................10 C4
Pooles La *WBPTN* SW10 *............18 F8
Pooley Av *EGH* TW20.....................21 N8
Pooley Dr *MORT/ESHN* SW14......18 A8
Pooley Green Rd *EGH* TW20........21 N8
Pooley Rd *ALDT* GU11.................108 E2
Pootings Rd *EDEN* TN8...............125 K8
Pope Cl *EBED/NFELT* TW14..........24 A4
　　WIM/MER SW19..............................28 G8
Pope's Av *WHTN* TW2....................25 M5
Pope's Cl *DTCH/LGLY* SL5............12 C5
Popes Gv *CROY/NA* CR0...............64 F2
　　WHTN TW2......................................25 M5
Pope's La *EA* W5............................17 K1
　　OXTED RH8..................................123 M6
Popes Md *HASM* GU27................184 D3
Popincourt Cl *BRAK* RG12...........33 H7
　　FELT TW13.....................................24 F6
Popham Gdns
　　RCH/KEW TW9 *.............................17 P8
Popinjays Rw *CHEAM* SM3 *........61 H4
Poplar Av *BFOR* GU20...................52 A3
　　LHD/OX KT22.................................97 H2
　　MTCM CR4......................................44 A3
　　NWDGN UB2...................................16 B1
Poplar Cl *BRAK* RG12....................32 F4
　　CRAWW RH11..............................176 F2
　　DTCH/LGLY SL3.............................13 J6
Poplar Court Pde *TWK* TW1 *.....26 B2
Poplar Crs *HOR/WEW* KT19..........60 A5
Poplar Dr *BNSTD* SM7...................79 H3
Poplar Farm Cl
　　HOR/WEW KT19.............................60 A5
Poplar Gdns *NWMAL* KT3.............42 B3
Poplar Gv *NWMAL* KT3..................42 B3
　　WOKS/MYFD GU22........................10 D7
Poplar Rd *ASHF* TW15...................23 N7
　　CHEAM SM3...................................43 K9
　　LHD/OX KT22.................................97 H2
　　RGUE GU4....................................132 C3
　　WIM/MER SW19..............................43 L3
Poplar Rd South
　　WIM/MER SW19..............................43 L4
Poplars Cl *FARN* GU14..................87 N2
The Poplars *ASC* SL5.....................34 B6
　　SWTR RH13.................................192 D7
Poplar Wk *CROY/NA* CR0................2 C2
　　CTHM CR3....................................101 N3
　　FNM GU9.......................................107 P7
Poppy Cl *WLGTN* SM6...................44 C9
Poppyhills Rd *CBLY* GU15............51 H9
Poppy La *CROY/NA* CR0................46 D8
Porchester *ASC* SL5........................34 E4
Porchester Rd *KUT/HW* KT1...........9 K4
Porchfield Cl *BELMT* SM2..............61 M8
Porridge Pot Aly *GUW* GU2 *..........6 D7
Portal Cl *WNWD* SE27....................30 B6

Porten Rd *WKENS* W14...................19 J1
Porters Wy *WDR/YW* UB7..............14 B1
Portesbery Rd *CBLY* GU15............68 F2
Portesbery Hill Dr *CBLY* GU15.....68 F1
Porthcawe Rd *SYD* SE26..............31 M7
Port Hl *ORP* BR6............................85 M1
Portia Gv *BNFD* RG42....................32 C2
The Porticos *CHEL* SW3 *.............19 P4
Portinscale Rd
　　PUT/ROE SW15..............................28 B1
Portland Av *NWMAL* KT3...............42 F8
　　SCUP DA15.....................................40 B5
Portland Cl *WPK* KT4.....................42 F8
Portland Crs *FELT* TW13...............23 P7
Portland Dr *FLEETS* GU52..........106 F2
　　REDH RH1.....................................100 E9
Portland Pl *EW* KT17.......................78 C1
　　SNWD SE25....................................46 A5
Portland Rd *ASHF* TW15...............23 H6
　　DORK RH4....................................116 G6
　　EGRIN RH19................................180 D5
　　KUT/HW KT1......................................9 E5
　　MTCM CR4......................................44 A3
　　NWDGN UB2...................................15 P1
　　SNWD SE25....................................46 B5
Portland Ter *FNM* GU9 *..............127 P1
　　GU GU1 *..7 H5
　　RCH/KEW TW9 *.............................17 K9
Portley La *CTHM* CR3..................101 N1
Portley Wood Rd *CTHM* CR3.......101 N1
Portman Av
　　MORT/ESHN SW14........................18 B8
Portman Cl *BNFD* RG42.................32 C2
Portman Rd *KUT/HW* KT1................9 G5
Portmore Park Rd *WEY* KT13.......56 C2
Portmore Quays *WEY* KT13.........56 B3
Portmore Wy *WEY* KT13 *.............56 C2
Portnall Dr *VW* GU25......................35 L7
Portnall Ri *VW* GU25......................35 M6
Portnall Rd *VW* GU25.....................35 M6
Portnalls Cl *COUL/CHIP* CR5.......80 D5
Portnalls Ri *COUL/CHIP* CR5........80 E5
Portnalls Rd *COUL/CHIP* CR5.......80 D6
Portsmouth Av *THDIT* KT7.............40 G8
Portsmouth Rd *CBLY* GU15..........69 J2
　　COB KT11..75 J3
　　ESH/CLAY KT10...............................58 C5
　　FRIM GU16......................................68 G5
　　GSHT GU26...................................166 B7
　　GUW GU2..6 D7
　　LIPH GU30.....................................183 H5
　　MFD/CHID GU8.............................166 E1
　　PUT/ROE SW15..............................27 N4
　　RPLY/SEND GU23...........................93 L4
Portugal Gdns *WHTN* TW2 *.........25 K5
Portugal Rd
　　WOKN/KNAP GU21........................11 F2
Port Wy *CHOB/PIR* GU24.............70 G6
Portway *EW* KT17............................60 E8
Portway Crs *EW* KT17....................60 E7
Postboys Rw *COB* KT11 *..............75 J3
Post House La *GT/LBKH* KT23......96 A5
Post La *WHTN* TW2.........................25 L4
Postmill Cl *CROY/NA* CR0.............64 C2
Post Rd *NWDGN* UB2.....................16 B1
Potley Hill Rd *YTLY* GU46.............67 K3
Potter Cl *MTCM* CR4 *...................44 C2
Potteries La *FRIM* GU16................89 H4
The Potteries *CHERT* KT16............55 J5
　　FARN GU14....................................87 P1
Potterne Cl *WIM/MER* SW19..........28 A5
Potters Cl *CROY/NA* CR0................46 E9
　　MFD/CHID GU8............................149 N2
Potters Cft *SWTR* RH13..............192 E8
Potters Ga *FNM* GU9.......................4 D3
Potters La *RFNM* GU10................109 K3
Potters Rd *NWMAL* KT3.................42 A5
Potters La *RPLY/SEND* GU23.......92 F5
　　STRHM/NOR SW16........................29 N9
Potters Pl *HORS* RH12................192 B8
Potters Wy *REIG* RH2..................119 N7
Pottery La *RFNM* GU10................127 K7
Pottery Rd *BTFD* TW8...................17 L4
Poulcott *STWL/WRAY* TW19.........21 K7
Poulett Gdns *TWK* TW1.................25 N5
Poulter Pk *MRDN* SM4 *...............44 A7
Poulton Av *SUT* SM1.....................61 P2
Pound Cl *BIL* RH14.......................188 C5
　　BOR GU35....................................164 C6
　　GODL GU7....................................131 L9
　　SURB KT6..41 J9
Pound Ct *ASHTD* KT21..................77 M7
　　RGUW GU3...................................111 H3
Pound Crs *LHD/OX* KT22..............96 D1
Pound Farm La *ASHV* GU12........109 M5
　　ESH/CLAY KT10...............................40 D9
Pound Fld *GU* GU1..........................6 E1
Poundfield Gdns
　　WOKS/MYFD GU22.........................72 G9
Poundfield La *BIL* RH14..............187 N7
Pound Hl *RGUW* GU3...................111 H4
Pound Hill Pl *CRAWE* RH10........177 M5
Pound La *BFOR* GU20....................52 C5
　　GODL GU7....................................131 L9
　　HOR/WEW KT19.............................60 B9
　　RGUW GU3...................................111 H4
　　RSEV TN14.....................................85 P4
Pound Pl *RGUE* GU4.....................132 D3
Pound Place Cl *RGUE* GU4.........132 D2
Pound Rd *ASHV* GU12.................108 E5
　　BNSTD SM7....................................79 H5
　　CHERT KT16....................................37 M8
Pound St *CAR* SM5........................62 B4
Povey Cross Rd *HORL* RH6.........158 C3
Powderham Ct
　　WOKN/KNAP GU21........................71 K7
Powder Mill La *WHTN* TW2...........24 G4
Powell Cl *GUW* GU2.....................111 M7
　　HORL RH6....................................140 D9
Power Cl *GU* GU1.............................6 D1

Power Rd *CHSWK* W4....................17 N2
Powers Ct *TWK* TW1......................26 C3
Pownall Gdns *HSLW* TW3.............16 B9
Pownall Rd *HSLW* TW3..................16 B9
Poyle Gdns *BRAK* RG12................32 F2
Poyle Pk *DTCH/LGLY* SL3 *..........13 J8
Poyle Rd *DTCH/LGLY* SL3............13 J8
　　GU GU1...7 G7
　　RFNM GU10..................................109 J7
Poynders Rd *CLAP* SW4................29 M3
Poynes Rd *HORL* RH6.................140 A8
Poynings Rd *CRAWW* RH11........176 A6
Prague Pl *BRXS/STRHM* SW2......29 P1
Prairie Cl *ADL/WDHM* KT15..........55 M2
Prairie Rd *ADL/WDHM* KT15........55 M2
Pratts La *WOT/HER* KT12...............57 M3
Prebend Gdns *HMSMTH* W6.........18 D2
The Precinct *CRAN* GU6...............153 H8
Premier Pde *HORL* RH6...............159 L1
Prentice Cl *FARN* GU14................68 D8
Prentis Rd *STRHM/NOR* SW16....29 N7
Presburg Rd *NWMAL* KT3.............42 C6
Prescott *BRAK* RG12.....................32 B8
Prescott Rd *DTCH/LGLY* SL3.......13 J7
Presentation Ms
　　BRXS/STRHM SW2.........................30 A5
Prestbury Crs *BNSTD* SM7............80 B5
Preston Cl *WHTN* TW2...................25 N5
Preston Ct *WOT/HER* KT12...........39 L9
Preston Dr *HOR/WEW* KT19.........60 C5
Preston Gv *ASHTD* KT21...............77 J6
Preston La
　　KWD/TDW/WH KT20.......................78 G9
Preston Rd *NRWD* SE19................30 C9
　　RYNPK SW20..................................42 E1
　　SHPTN TW17.................................38 C6
Prestons Rd *WWKM* BR4...............65 N2
Prestwich Ter *CLAP* SW4 *............29 N1
Prestwick Cl *CRAWW* RH11........176 A6
　　NWDGN UB2...................................15 N3
Prestwick La *HASM* GU27............167 H9
　　MFD/CHID GU8.............................167 H9
Prestwood Cl *CRAWW* RH11......176 C2
Prestwood Gdns
　　CROY/NA CR0.................................45 L8
Prestwood La *CRAWH* RH11......175 P1
Pretoria Rd *CHERT* KT16...............37 K9
　　STRHM/NOR SW16........................29 L9
Pretty La *COUL/CHIP* CR5............80 F9
Pretymans La *EDEN* TN8.............145 L2
Prey Heath Cl
　　WOKS/MYFD GU22.........................92 A4
Prey Heath Rd
　　WOKS/MYFD GU22.........................91 P4
Price Cl *TOOT* SW17......................29 J6
Price Rd *CROY/NA* CR0..................63 K4
Prices La *REIG* RH2......................119 L8
Prickley Wd *HAYES* BR2................47 M9
Priddy's Yd *CROY/NA* CR0...............2 C4
Prideaux Gdns *RDKG* RH5 *........155 L3
Prides Crossing *ASC* SL5..............34 A1
Pridham Rd *THHTH* CR7................45 M5
Priest Cft Cl *CRAWW* RH11..........176 D5
Priestfield Rd *FSTH* SE23............31 M6
Priest Hl *OXTED* RH8...................103 P9
　　WDSR SL4..21 H4
Priestlands Cl *HORL* RH6............140 B9
Priest La *CHOB/PIR* GU24............70 C4
Priestley Gdns
　　WOKS/MYFD GU22.........................72 E9
Priestley Rd *GUW* GU2................111 K6
　　MTCM CR4......................................44 C3
Priestley Wy *CRAWE* RH10..........159 K9
Priests Br *MORT/ESHN* SW14......18 A8
Priestwood Av *BNFD* RG42...........32 B2
Priestwood Court Rd
　　BNFD RG42.....................................32 B2
Priestwood Sq *BNFD* RG42...........32 B2
Priestwood Ter *BNFD* RG42 *.......32 B2
Primrose Av *HORL* RH6................159 L3
Primrose Cl *CRAWW* RH11..........176 E6
　　WLGTN SM6....................................44 A7
Primrose Copse *HORS* RH12.......192 C3
Primrose Dr *CHOB/PIR* GU24.......70 G6
　　WDR/YW UB7 *...............................13 P2
Primrose Gdns *FARN* GU14...........88 A4
Primrose La *CROY/NA* CR0............46 D9
Primrose Pl *ISLW* TW7...................16 F7
Primrose Rdg *GODL* GU7.............150 A2
Primrose Rd *WOT/HER* KT12........57 L4
Primrose Wk *BRAK* RG12..............32 E6
　　EW KT17...60 C5
Primrose Wy *SHGR* GU5..............132 E8
　　SHST GU47.....................................49 K9
Prince Albert Dr *ASC* SL5..............33 M5
Prince Albert Sq *REDH* RH1........140 C1
Prince Andrew Wy *ASC* SL5..........34 A1
Prince Charles Crs
　　FARN GU14....................................68 D3
Prince Charles Wy
　　WLGTN SM6....................................62 B3
Prince Consort Dr *ASC* SL5..........33 M5
Prince Consort Rd
　　SKENS SW7.....................................19 P1
Prince Dr *SHST* GU47....................49 P1
Prince George's Av
　　RYNPK SW20...................................42 G3
Prince Georges Rd
　　WIM/MER SW19..............................43 P2
Prince of Wales Rd
　　REDH RH1.....................................141 J4
　　SUT SM1..44 A7
Prince of Wales Ter
　　CHSWK W4......................................18 C3
Prince Regent Rd *HSLW* TW3........16 C8
Prince Rd *SNWD* SE25...................45 N6
Princes Av *ACT* W3........................17 N1
　　ALDT GU11...................................108 E1
　　CAR SM5...62 B7
　　GODL GU7.....................................131 J6
　　SAND/SEL CR2...............................82 B4

SURB KT6 ....59 N1
Princes Cl BAGS GU19 ....51 N8
HPTN TW12 ....25 L7
SAND/SEL CR2 ....82 B4
Prince's Dr LHD/OX KT22 ....76 E1
Princes Gdns RGUW GU3 * 91 L7
SKENS SW7 * 19 P1
Princes Ga SKENS SW7 * 19 P1
Princes Gate Ms SKENS SW7 ....19 P1
Princes Ms HMSMTH W6 * 19 J8
Princes Rd ASHF TW15 ....23 J8
EGH TW20 ....21 L9
FELT TW13 ....24 A6
KUTN/CMB KT2 ....9 H2
MORT/ESHN SW14 ....18 B8
PGE/AN SE20 ....31 L9
RCH/KEW TW9 ....17 M6
RCHPK/HAM TW10 ....26 E1
REDH RH1 ....120 C8
TEDD TW11 ....25 L7
WEY KT13 ....56 D4
WIM/MER SW19 ....28 D9
Princess Anne Rd
HORS RH12 ....189 N4
Princess Gdns
WOKS/MYFD GU22 * 11 K1
Princess Margaret Rd
HORS RH12 ....189 N3
Princess Mary Cl GUW GU2 ....111 N1
Princess Mary's Rd
ADL/WDHM KT15 ....55 N3
Princess Rd CRAWW RH11 ....176 F5
CROY/NA CR0 ....43 J5
WOKS/MYFD GU22 ....11 K1
Prince's St RCH/KEW TW9 ......17 L9
SUT SM1 ....61 P3
Princess Wy CBLY GU15 ....68 A3
REDH RH1 ....120 C4
Princes Wy CROY/NA CR0 ....63 H4
WIM/MER SW19 ....28 A4
WWKM BR4 ....65 M3
Princethorpe Rd SYD SE26 ......31 L7
Pringle Gdns PUR/KEN CR8 ....63 H8
STRHM/NOR SW16 ....29 M7
Prior Av BELMT SM2 ....62 A6
Prior Croft Cl CBLY GU15 ....69 J4
Prior End CBLY GU15 ....69 J4
Prioress Rd WNWD SE27 ....30 C6
Prior Rd CBLY GU15 ....69 K4
Priors Cl FARN GU14 ....68 D8
GODL GU7 ....130 C4
Priors Ct WOKN/KNAP GU21 ....71 N7
Priors Cft WOKS/MYFD GU22 ....72 C8
Priorsfield Rd GODL GU7 ....130 C5
Priors Hatch La GODL GU7 ......130 F4
Priors Keep FLEETS GU52 ....87 J7
Prior's La BLKW GU17 ....67 L3
The Priors ASHTD KT21 ....77 K8
Priors Md GT/LBKH KT23 ....96 C5
Priors Wk CRAWE RH10 ....177 J5
Priors Wd CWTH RG45 ....49 H5
Priorswood RGUW GU3 ....130 F3
CHSWK W4 ....18 C1
Priory Av CHEAM SM3 ....61 H3
CHSWK W4 ....18 C1
Priory Cl ASC SL5 ....34 G8
BECK BR3 ....46 E4
DORK RH4 ....116 G9
FLEETN GU51 ....86 D7
HORL RH6 ....140 B9
HPTN TW12 ....39 P2
SUN TW16 ....39 J1
WIM/MER SW19 * 43 M2
WOKN/KNAP GU21 ....73 H2
WOT/HER KT12 ....57 J2
Priory Crs CBLY GU15 * 68 A3
REDH RH1 ....117 H9
Priory Crs CHEAM SM3 ....61 H3
NRWD SE19 ....45 L1
Priory Dr REIG RH2 ....119 L7
Priory Gdns ASHF TW15 ....23 N8
BARN SW13 ....18 D8
CHSWK W4 * 18 C2
HPTN TW12 ....39 P2
SNWD SE25 ....45 P5
Priory Gn STA TW18 ....22 E8
Priory La BNFD RG42 ....32 E1
E/WMO/HCT KT8 ....40 A5
PUT/ROE SW15 ....27 L1
RFNM GU10 ....146 C4
Priory Ms STA TW18 ....22 E8
Priory Rd ASC SL5 ....33 K2
ASC SL5 ....34 C8
CHEAM SM3 ....61 H3
CHSGTN KT9 ....59 L2
CHSWK W4 ....18 B1
CROY/NA CR0 ....45 J8
HSLW TW3 ....15 N1
REIG RH2 ....119 L7
Priory St FARN GU14 ....88 F3
The Priory CROY/NA CR0 * 63 J2
GDST RH9 ....122 B2
Priory Wk BRAK RG12 ....33 H5
WBPTN SW10 ....19 N2
Priory Wy NWDGN UB2 ....15 M1
WDR/YW UB7 ....14 A4
Probert Rd
BRXS/STRHM SW2 ....30 B1
Probyn Rd BRXS/STRHM SW2 ..30 C5
Proctor Cl CRAWE RH10 ....177 M7
MTCM CR4 ....44 C3
Proctor Gdns GT/LBKH KT23 ....96 B5
Proctors Cl
EBED/NFELT TW14 ....24 C4
Profumo Rd WOT/HER KT12 .....57 M4
Progress Wy CROY/NA CR0 ......63 H1
Promenade Approach Rd
CHSWK W4 ....18 C5
Promenade De Verdun
PUR/KEN CR8 ....62 F9

The Promenade CHSWK W4 ....18 C6
Propeller Rd FARN GU14 ....88 B5
Prospect Av FARN GU14 ....88 D1
Prospect Cl HSLW TW5 ....15 P6
SYD SE26 ....31 J7
Prospect Cottages
WAND/EARL SW18 ....19 L9
Prospect Crs WHTN TW2 ....25 K2
Prospect La EGH TW20 ....20 F8
Prospect Pl CHSWK W4 * 18 B3
CRAWW RH11 ....176 F5
EW KT17 ....78 C2
HAYES BR2 * 47 P4
RYNPK SW20 ....42 F1
STA TW18 ....22 C8
Prospect Rd ASHV GU12 ....109 J1
FARN GU14 ....88 C2
RFNM GU10 ....146 B1
SURB KT6 ....41 H9
Prossers KWD/TDW/WH KT20 ...99 H1
Prothero Rd FUL/PGN SW6 ....19 J5
Providence La HYS/HAR UB3 ....14 F5
Providence Pl
WOKS/MYFD GU22 * 73 L3
Providence Ter
CRAWE RH10 * 179 H7
Provincial Ter PGE/AN SE20 * ...46 D1
Prune Hl EGH TW20 ....36 C1
Prunus Cl CHOB/PIR GU24 ....70 E2
Puckridge Gate Rd
ALDT GU11 ....87 P9
Puckridge Hill Rd
ALDT GU11 ....108 A1
Puckshill WOKN/KNAP GU21 ....71 K6
Puckshott Wy HASM GU27 ......184 E2
Pudding La HORL RH6 ....158 B4
Puddledock La
BH/WHM TN16 ....125 L3
Puffin Cl BECK BR3 ....46 D6
Puffin Hill CRAWE RH10 ....179 K6
Puffin Rd CRAWW RH11 * 176 A6
Pulborough Rd
WAND/EARL SW18 ....28 C3
Pulborough Wy HSLWW TW4 ....15 L9
Pullman Gdns
PUT/ROE SW15 ....27 P2
Pullman La GODL GU7 ....150 B2
Pullmans Pl STA TW18 ....22 D8
Pulteney Cl ISLW TW7 ....16 C8
Pulton Pl FUL/PGN SW6 ....19 L5
Pump Al BTFD TW8 ....17 K5
Pump House Cl HAYES BR2 * 47 M3
Pumping Station Rd
CHSWK W4 ....18 C5
Pump La ASC SL5 ....34 E2
Punchbowl La RDKG RH5 ....117 K6
Punch Copse Rd
CRAWE RH10 ....177 J4
Purbeck Av NWMAL KT3 ....42 D7
Purbeck Cl REDH RH1 ....100 E9
Purbeck Dr
WOKN/KNAP GU21 ....72 D3
Purberry Gv EW KT17 * 60 D8
Purberry Shot EW KT17 * 60 D8
Purbrook Ct BRAK RG12 ....32 G8
Purcell Cl PUR/KEN CR8 ....81 L3
Purcell Crs FUL/PGN SW6 * 19 H4
Purcell Rd CRAWW RH11 ....176 C8
CWTH RG45 ....49 H7
Purcers Cross Rd
FUL/PGN SW6 ....19 K6
Purley Bury Av PUR/KEN CR8 ...63 L9
Purley Bury Cl PUR/KEN CR8 ...63 L9
Purley Cl CRAWE RH10 ....177 N8
Purley Downs Rd
SAND/SEL CR2 ....63 L8
Purley Hl PUR/KEN CR8 ....81 K1
Purley Knoll PUR/KEN CR8 ....81 H9
Purley Oaks Rd
SAND/SEL CR2 ....63 M8
Purley Pde PUR/KEN CR8 * 63 J9
Purley Park Rd PUR/KEN CR8 ...63 K8
Purley Ri PUR/KEN CR8 ....81 H1
Purley Rd SAND/SEL CR2 ....63 M6
Purley V PUR/KEN CR8 ....81 K2
Purley Wy CROY/NA CR0 ....45 H9
FRIM GU16 ....68 G3
PUR/KEN CR8 ....80 G8
Purmerend Cl FARN GU14 ....87 N2
Pursers Cross Rd
FUL/PGN SW6 * 19 K6
Pursers Hollow SHGR GU5 ......134 F6
Pursers La SHGR GU5 ....134 F6
Purton Rd HORS RH12 ....192 A6
Putney Br PUT/ROE SW15 ....19 J8
Putney Bridge Ap
FUL/PGN SW6 ....19 J8
Putney Bridge Rd
PUT/ROE SW15 ....19 J9
Putney Common
PUT/ROE SW15 ....18 G8
Putney Heath
PUT/ROE SW15 ....27 N2
Putney Heath La
PUT/ROE SW15 ....28 A2
Putney High St
PUT/ROE SW15 ....19 J9
Putney Hl PUT/ROE SW15 ....28 A3
Putney Park Av
PUT/ROE SW15 ....18 E9
Putney Park La
PUT/ROE SW15 ....18 F9
Puttenham Heath Rd RGUW GU3
150 ....110 C9
Puttenham Hl RGUW GU3 ......110 C9
Puttenham La
MFD/CHID GU8 ....130 C4
Puttenham Rd RFNM GU10 .....129 L1
Puttocks Cl HASM GU27 ....176 G8
Pye Cl CTHM CR3 ....101 M5
Pyecombe Ct CRAWW RH11 ....176 C8
Pyegrove Cha BRAK RG12 ....32 G8

Pyestock Crs FARN GU14 ....87 M3
Pylbrook Rd SUT SM1 ....61 L2
Pyle Hl WOKS/MYFD GU22 ......92 C5
Pymers Md GU2 ....92 A8
Pyne Rd SURB KT6 ....41 N9
Pyrcroft La WEY KT13 ....56 D4
Pyrcroft Rd CHERT KT16 ....37 K8
Pyrford Heath
WOKS/MYFD GU22 ....73 K5
Pyrford Rd BF/WBF KT14 ....73 L3
Pyrford Woods Cl
WOKS/MYFD GU22 ....73 K4
Pyrford Woods Rd
WOKS/MYFD GU22 ....73 K4
Pyrland Rd
RCHPK/HAM TW10 ....26 E2
Pyrmont Gv WNWD SE27 ....30 C6
Pyrmont Rd CHSWK W4 ....17 N4
Pytchley Crs NRWD SE19 ....30 D9

Q

The Quadrangle FRIM GU16 * ...68 E8
GUW GU2 ....111 N6
HNHL SE24 * 30 D1
WBPTN SW10 * 19 N6
Quadrant Ct BRAK RG12 ....32 G4
Quadrant Rd RCH/KEW TW9 ....17 K9
THHTH CR7 ....45 K5
The Quadrant ASHV GU12 ....109 J2
BELMT SM2 ....61 N5
GU GU1 * 6 D5
RCH/KEW TW9 ....17 L9
RYNPK SW20 ....43 J2
Quadrant Wy WEY KT13 ....56 B3
Quail Cl HORS RH12 ....192 C3
Quail Gdns SAND/SEL CR2 ....64 E8
Quaker La NWDGN UB2 ....16 A1
Quakers Wy RGUW GU3 ....111 J1
Qualitas BRAK RG12 ....32 B9
Quality St REDH RH1 ....100 D8
Quandock Cl CRAWW RH11 .....176 E5
DTCH/LGLY SL3 ....12 E3
HYS/HAR UB3 ....14 F2
Quarrendon St FUL/PGN SW6 ...19 L6
Quarr Rd CAR SM5 ....43 P7
Quarry Bank LTWR GU18 ....51 P9
Quarry Cl HORS RH12 ....192 E4
LHD/OX KT22 ....97 K1
OXTED RH8 ....123 L1
Quarry Gdns LHD/OX KT22 ....97 K1
Quarry Hl GODL GU7 ....150 A1
Quarry Hill Pk REIG RH2 ....119 N2
Quarry La YTLY GU46 ....67 J5
Quarry Park Rd SUT SM1 ....61 K5
Quarry Ri EGRIN RH19 ....162 F9
SUT SM1 ....61 K5
Quarry Rd GDST RH9 ....102 C8
GODL GU7 ....130 C6
OXTED RH8 ....123 L1
WAND/EARL SW18 ....28 F2
Quarry St GU GU1 ....6 E7
The Quarry
BRKHM/BTCW RH3 ....118 B3
GU GU1 * 7 F4
Quarterbrass Farm Rd
HORS RH12 ....192 C3
Quartermaine Av
WOKS/MYFD GU22 ....92 D2
Quarter Mile Rd GODL GU7 .....150 D2
Quarters Rd FARN GU14 ....88 E5
Quebec Av BH/WHM TN16 ....105 H6
Quebec Cl HORL RH6 ....160 B1
LIPH GU30 ....182 F7
Quebec Gdns BLKW GU17 ....67 P4
Queen Adelaide Rd
PGE/AN SE20 ....31 K9
Queen Alexandra's Wy
HOR/WEW KT19 ....59 N4
Queen Anne Av HAYES BR2 * 47 N4
Queen Anne Dr
ESH/CLAY KT10 ....58 E6
Queen Anne's Cl WDSR SL4 ......20 A6
WHTN TW2 ....25 L6
Queen Anne's Gdns
CHSWK W4 ....18 C1
MTCM CR4 * 44 B4
Queen Anne's Ga ENM GU9 ....107 P7
Queen Anne's Gv CHSWK W4 ....18 C1
Queen Annes Ms
LHD/OX KT22 * 97 H1
Queen Anne's Ride
WDSR SL4 ....20 B3
Queen Anne's Ter
LHD/OX KT22 * 97 H1
Queen Caroline Est
HMSMTH W6 ....19 J3
Queen Caroline St
HMSMTH W6 ....18 G3
Queendale Ct
WOKN/KNAP GU21 ....71 M5
Queen Eleanor's Rd
GUW GU2 ....111 M6
Queen Elizabeth Cl
ASHV GU12 ....109 J4
Queen Elizabeth Dr
ALDT GU11 ....108 B4
Queen Elizabeth Gdns
MRDN SM4 ....43 L1
Queen Elizabeth's Dr
CBLY GU15 ....50 F8
HORS RH12 ....189 N3
KUTN/CMB KT2 ....9 J1
Queen Elizabeth's Dr
CROY/NA CR0 ....65 K8
Queen Elizabeth's Wk
WLGTN SM6 ....62 F5

Queen Elizabeth Wk
BARN SW13 ....18 E6
Queen Elizabeth Wy
WOKS/MYFD GU22 ....72 D8
Queenhill Rd SAND/SEL CR2 .....64 D8
Queenhythe Crs RGUE GU4 ......92 B8
Queenhythe Rd RGUE GU4 ....92 B8
Queen Mary Av CBLY GU15 ......68 C3
RYNPK SW20 ....43 H6
Queen Mary Cl FLEETN GU51 ...86 C3
SURB KT6 ....59 N2
WOKS/MYFD GU22 ....72 G5
Queen Mary Rd NRWD SE19 .....30 C9
SHPTN TW17 ....38 E3
Queen Mary's Av CAR SM5 ....62 B6
Queen Mary's Dr
ADL/WDHM KT15 ....55 K8
Queens Acre CHEAM SM3 ....61 H6
Queen's Av ALDT GU11 ....88 D3
BF/WBF KT14 ....73 P1
FELT TW13 ....24 D7
Queensberry Ms West
SKENS SW7 * 19 P2
Queensberry Pl SKENS SW7 * 19 P2
Queensberry Wy
SKENS SW7 * 19 P2
Queensbridge Pk ISLW TW7 .....25 L2
Queensbury Pl BLKW GU17 ......67 N5
Queens Cl CHOB/PIR GU24 ....70 C6
ESH/CLAY KT10 ....58 B3
FARN GU14 ....88 D7
WDSR SL4 ....20 F1
WLGTN SM6 ....62 D4
Queens Club Gdns
WKENS W14 ....19 J4
Queens Club Ter
WKENS W14 * 19 K4
Queens Ct BELMT SM2 * 61 L9
FNM GU9 ....107 M7
WEY KT13 ....56 C4
WOKS/MYFD GU22 ....72 C5
Queens Court Ride COB KT11 ...75 J2
Queens Crs DORK RH4 * 116 C8
RCHPK/HAM TW10 ....26 E1
Queens Dr BRYLDS KT5 ....41 N8
GODL GU7 ....131 H6
GUW GU2 ....111 N2
LHD/OX KT22 ....58 C9
THDIT KT7 ....40 G7
Queen's Elm Sq CHEL SW3 ....19 P5
Queen's Gdns HEST TW5 ....15 N6
Queens Garth FSTH SE23 * 31 K1
Queensgate COB KT11 ....75 M1
Queens Ga HORL RH6 ....159 K4
SKENS SW7 * 19 P2
Queensgate Gdns
PUT/ROE SW15 ....18 F9
Queens Gate Gdns
SKENS SW7 * 19 N1
Queen's Gate Ms SKENS SW7 ...19 N1
Queen's Gate Pl SKENS SW7 * ...19 N1
Queen's Gate Place Ms
SKENS SW7 * 19 N1
Queen's Gate Rd FARN GU14 ....88 D8
Queen's Gate Ter SKENS SW7 ...19 N1
Queenshill Ldg ASC SL5 ....34 B4
Queen's Keep TWK TW1 * 26 B2
Queensland Av
WIM/MER SW19 ....43 M2
Queens La FNM GU9 ....107 M7
Queensmead FARN GU14 ....88 D4
LHD/OX KT22 * 58 C9
Queensmead Av EW KT17 ....60 E8
Queen's Mead Rd HAYES BR2 ...47 M3
Queensmere Cl
WIM/MER SW19 ....28 A5
Queensmere Rd
WIM/MER SW19 ....28 A5
Queensmill Rd FUL/PGN SW6 ...19 H5
Queen's Pine BRAK RG12 ....32 G7
Queen's Pl ASC SL5 ....34 A4
MRDN SM4 ....43 L5
Queen's Prom KUT/HW KT1 ....41 K5
Queen's Ride BARN SW13 ....18 F8
CWTH RG45 ....49 L2
Queen's Ri RCHPK/HAM TW10 ...26 E2
Queens Ride CWTH RG45 ....49 L1
Queens Rd ALDT GU11 ....108 B4
ASC SL5 ....34 B6
BECK BR3 ....46 E3
BELMT SM2 ....61 L8
BMLY BR1 ....47 N3
CBLY GU15 ....68 D4
CHOB/PIR GU24 ....70 C6
CROY/NA CR0 ....45 K7
EGH TW20 ....21 L9
EGRIN RH19 ....180 D2
FARN GU14 ....88 F7
FELT TW13 ....24 C4
FLEETS GU52 ....86 G8
FNM GU9 ....107 N8
GU GU1 * 7 F3
HORL RH6 ....159 K1
HORS RH12 ....192 A6
HSLW TW3 ....16 B8
KUTN/CMB KT2 ....9 J1
MORT/ESHN SW14 ....18 B8
MRDN SM4 ....43 L5
MTCM CR4 ....43 P4
NWMAL KT3 ....42 E5
RCHPK/HAM TW10 ....26 C4
TEDD TW11 ....25 N9
THDIT KT7 ....40 F6
TWK TW1 ....25 N4

WEY KT13 ....56 G4
WIM/MER SW19 ....28 E8
WLGTN SM6 ....62 D4
WOKN/KNAP GU21 ....71 J7
WOT/HER KT12 ....57 H3
Queens Sq CRAWE RH10 ....176 G5
Queens Ter ISLW TW7 ....16 B8
THDIT KT7 * 40 G7
Queensthorpe Ms SYD SE26 * ...31 L7
Queensthorpe Rd SYD SE26 .....31 L7
Queen St ASHV GU12 ....108 F4
CHERT KT16 ....37 L7
CROY/NA CR0 ....2 D7
GODL GU7 ....131 L9
SHGR GU5 ....134 E1
SWTR RH13 ....192 C9
Queensville Rd BAL SW12 ....29 N5
Queens Wk ASHF TW15 ....22 G7
Queens Wy FELT TW13 ....24 D7
Queensway CRAN GU6 ....171 J1
CRAWE RH10 ....177 H5
CROY/NA CR0 ....63 H5
EGRIN RH19 ....180 D2
FRIM GU16 ....69 J9
REDH RH1 ....120 D4
SUN TW16 ....39 K3
SWTR RH13 ....192 B9
WOT/HER KT12 ....57 K4
WWKM BR4 ....65 N3
Queensway North
WOT/HER KT12 * 57 L4
Queensway South
WOT/HER KT12 * 57 L4
Queenswood Av HPTN TW12 .....25 J9
HSLW TW3 ....15 P7
THHTH CR7 ....45 J6
WLGTN SM6 ....62 F5
Queenswood Rd FSTH SE23 .....31 M6
WOKN/KNAP GU21 ....71 J7
Quennell Cl ASHTD KT21 ....77 M8
Quennells Hl RFNM GU10 ....128 G5
Quentins Dr BH/WHM TN16 * 84 F5
Quentins Wk
BH/WHM TN16 * 84 F5
Quention Wy WOKS/MYFD 35 P5
Querrin St FUL/PGN SW6 ....19 N7
Quick Rd CHSWK W4 ....18 C3
Quicks Rd WIM/MER SW19 ....43 M1
Quiet Cl ADL/WDHM KT15 ....55 L3
The Quillot WOT/HER KT12 ....57 H4
Quince Cl ASC SL5 ....34 G8
Quince Dr CHOB/PIR GU24 ....71 H4
Quincy Rd EGH TW20 ....21 L8
Quintilis BRAK RG12 ....32 B9
Quintin Av RYNPK SW20 ....43 J4
Quinton Cl BECK BR3 ....47 J3
HEST TW5 ....15 L6
WLGTN SM6 ....62 D3
Quinton Rd THDIT KT7 ....40 G8
Quinton St WAND/EARL SW18 ...28 F5
Quintrell Cl
WOKN/KNAP GU21 ....71 P6

R

Rabies Heath Rd REDH RH1 .....122 A5
Raby Rd NWMAL KT3 ....42 B5
Raccoon Wy HSLWW TW4 ....15 L7
Racecourse Rd LING RH7 ....162 E1
Racecourse Wy HORL RH6 ....159 J5
Rachaels Lake Vw
BNFD RG42 ....32 G1
Rackfield HASM GU27 ....183 N3
Rackham Cl CRAWW RH11 ....176 C2
Rackham Ms
STRHM/NOR SW16 ....29 M9
Rackstraw Rd SHST GU47 ....49 P8
Racquets Court Hl
GODL GU7 ....131 J7
Racton Rd FUL/PGN SW6 ....19 L4
Radar Rd FARN GU14 ....87 P6
Radbourne Av EA W5 ....17 J2
Radcliffe Cl FRIM GU16 ....69 H9
Radcliffe Gdns CAR SM5 ....62 A6
Radcliffe Rd CROY/NA CR0 ....3 K4
Radcliffe Sq PUT/ROE SW15 .....28 A2
Radcliffe Wy BNFD RG42 ....32 A1
Radcot Av DTCH/LGLY SL3 ....12 F1
Radford Cl FNM GU9 ....108 A9
Radford Rd CRAWE RH10 ....159 M8
Radical Ride EWKG RG40 ....48 F8
Radipole Rd FUL/PGN SW6 ....19 K6
Radius Pk
EBED/NFELT TW14 * 15 H9
Rad La SHGR GU5 ....134 C3
Radlet Av SYD SE26 ....31 J6
Radley Cl EBED/NFELT TW14 ....24 A4
Radley Ms KENS W8 ....19 L1
Radnor Cl MTCM CR4 ....44 C6
Radnor Ct REDH RH1 ....120 A5
Radnor Gdns TWK TW1 ....25 N5
Radnor La RDKG RH5 ....135 J6
Radnor Rd BRAK RG12 ....33 H4
SHGR GU5 ....134 F7
TWK TW1 ....25 N5
WEY KT13 ....56 C2
Radnor Ter WKENS W14 ....19 L2
Radnor Wy DTCH/LGLY SL3 ....12 C2
Radolphs
KWD/TDW/WH KT20 ....99 H2
Radstock Wy REDH RH1 ....100 G9
Radstone Ct
WOKS/MYFD GU22 * 10 E6
Raeburn Av BRYLDS KT5 ....41 P7
Raeburn Cl KUT/HW KT1 ....8 A3
Raeburn Ct
WOKN/KNAP GU21 * 71 L6

Raeburn Wy SHST GU47 67 P2
Rae Rd FARN GU14 88 D6
Rafford Wy BMLY BR1 47 P3
RAF Gate Rd FARN GU14 88 D6
Rag Hill Rd BH/WHM TN16 104 B1
Raglan Cl ASHV GU12 108 E5
FRIM GU16 69 H8
HSLWW TW4 24 F1
REIG RH2 119 N3
Raglan Ct SAND/SEL CR2 63 K4
Raglan Rd REIG RH2 119 N3
WOKN/KNAP GU21 71 L7
Raikes La RDKG RH5 135 K4
Railey Rd CRAWE RH10 177 H5
Railshead Rd ISLW TW7 17 H9
Railton Rd GUW GU2 111 P1
HNHL SE24 30 B1
Railway Ap CHERT KT16 * 37 K9
EGRIN RH19 180 C2
TWK TW1 25 P3
WLGTN SM6 * 62 D5
Railway Rd TEDD TW11 25 M7
Railway Side BARN SW13 18 C8
Railway Ter BH/WHM TN16 105 H5
FELT TW13 24 B4
STA TW18 22 A8
Railway Vw DTCH/LGLY SL3 * 12 D8
Rainbow Ct
WOKN/KNAP GU21 71 L5
Rainforest Wk BRAK RG12 32 D6
Rainham Cl BTSEA SW11 29 H2
Rainville Rd HMSMTH W6 18 G4
Rake La MFD/CHID GU8 149 N5
Rakers Rdg HORS RH12 192 C5
Raleigh Av WLGTN SM6 62 F3
Raleigh Ct CRAWE RH10 * 159 K9
STA TW18 22 D7
Raleigh Dr BRYLDS KT5 42 A9
ESH/CLAY KT10 58 D4
HORL RH6 160 B1
Raleigh Gdns
BRXS/STRHM SW2 30 A2
MTCM CR4 44 B4
Raleigh Rd FELT TW13 24 A5
NWDGN UB2 15 N3
PGE/AN SE20 46 D1
RCH/KEW TW9 17 M8
Raleigh Wk CRAWE RH10 177 H7
Raleigh Wy FELT TW13 24 D8
FRIM GU16 69 H5
Ralliwood Rd ASHTD KT21 77 N8
Ralph Perring Ct BECK BR3 46 G5
Ralphs Cross GT/LBKH KT23 * 96 C6
Ralphs Ride BRAK RG12 32 G4
Rama Cl STRHM/NOR SW16 44 G1
Rambler Cl
STRHM/NOR SW16 29 M7
Rambler La DTCH/LGLY SL3 12 A1
Ramblers Wy CRAWW RH11 194 E1
Rame Cl TOOT SW17 29 K8
Ramilles Cl
BRXS/STRHM SW2 29 P2
Ramillies Cl ALDT GU11 88 G8
Ramillies Rd CHSWK W4 18 B1
Ramones Ter MTCM CR4 * 44 E5
Ramornie Cl WOT/HER KT12 57 P3
Ram Pas KUT/HW KT1 8 C5
Ramsay Cl CBLY GU15 51 K9
Ramsay Rd ACT W3 18 A1
BFOR GU20 52 E4
Ramsbury Cl BRAK RG12 32 A7
Ramsdale Rd TOOT SW17 29 K8
Ramsdell Rd FLEETN GU51 86 D4
Ramsden Ga BAL SW12 * 29 L3
Ramsden Rd BAL SW12 29 K3
GODL GU7 150 C1
Ramsey Cl HORL RH6 159 J1
HORS RH12 192 C5
Ramsey Pl CTHM CR3 101 L2
Ramsey Rd THHTH CR7 45 H7
Ramslade Rd BRAK RG12 32 E6
Rams La MFD/CHID GU8 169 M9
Ram St WAND/EARL SW18 28 E1
Randal Crs REIG RH2 119 L7
Randall Cl DTCH/LGLY SL3 12 D3
Randalls Crs LHD/OX KT22 76 G9
Randalls Park Av
LHD/OX KT22 76 G9
Randalls Park Dr
LHD/OX KT22 96 G1
Randalls Rd LHD/OX KT22 76 E9
Randalls Wy LHD/OX KT22 96 G1
Randle Rd RCHPK/HAM TW10 26 B7
Randlesdown Rd CAT SE6 31 P7
Randle's La RSEV TN14 85 P3
Randolph Cl COB KT11 76 A4
KUTN/CMB KT2 * 27 H8
WOKN/KNAP GU21 71 L6
Randolph Dr FARN GU14 87 N4
Randolph Rd DTCH/LGLY SL3 12 C2
EW KT17 78 D3
Ranelagh Av BARN SW13 18 E7
FUL/PGN SW6 19 K8
Ranelagh Crs ASC SL5 33 L2
Ranelagh Dr BRAK RG12 32 E4
TWK TW1 17 H9
Ranelagh Gdns CHSWK W4 18 A5
FUL/PGN SW6 19 J8
Ranelagh Pl NWMAL KT3 42 C6
Ranelagh Rd REDH RH1 120 A5
Ranfurly Rd SUT SM1 61 L1
Range Ride CBLY GU15 68 B1
Range Rd EWKG RG40 48 F2
FARN GU14 87 N6
The Range SHGR GU5 132 E9
Range Vw SHST GU47 50 A9
Range Wy SHPTN TW17 38 C8
Rankine Cl FNM GU9 108 C8
Ranmere St BAL SW12 29 L4
Ranmore Av CROY/NA CR0 3 K6
Ranmore Cl CRAWW RH11 194 F2
REDH RH1 120 C2
Ranmore Common Rd
RDKG RH5 116 D4
Ranmore Pl WEY KT13 * 56 E4
Ranmore Rd BELMT SM2 61 H7
RDKG RH5 116 E5
Rannoch Rd HMSMTH W6 18 G4
Ransome Cl CRAWW RH11 176 A8
Ranyard Cl CHSGTN KT9 59 M2
Rapallo Cl FARN GU14 88 E3
Raphael Dr THDIT KT7 40 F9
Rapley Cl CBLY GU15 51 H9
Rapley Gn BRAK RG12 32 E7
Rapley's Fld CHOB/PIR GU24 90 E3
Rapsley La WOKN/KNAP GU21 71 H7
Rashleigh Ct FLEETS GU52 107 H2
Rasset Md FLEETS GU52 106 E3
Rastell Av BRXS/STRHM SW2 29 N5
Ratcliffe Rd FARN GU14 68 B8
Rathbone Sq CROY/NA CR0 * 2 C7
Rathfern Rd CAT SE6 31 N4
Rathgar Cl REDH RH1 140 C1
Rathlin Rd CRAWW RH11 176 E8
Rathmell Dr CLAP SW4 29 N2
Ravelin Cl FLEETN GU51 86 E3
RFNM GU10 106 D9
Raven Cl CRAWE RH10 179 K6
YTLY GU46 66 F2
Ravendale Rd SUN TW16 39 H3
Ravenfield Rd TOOT SW17 29 J6
Raven La CRAWW RH11 176 F3
Ravenna Rd PUT/ROE SW15 28 A1
Ravens Ait SURB KT6 * 41 K6
Ravensbourne Av HAYES BR2 47 K2
STWL/WRAY TW19 23 H4
Ravensbourne Pk CAT SE6 31 P3
Ravensbourne Park Crs
CAT SE6 31 N3
Ravensbourne Rd BMLY BR1 47 N4
CAT SE6 31 N3
TWK TW1 26 B2
Ravensbury Av MRDN SM4 43 N6
Ravensbury Gv MTCM CR4 43 P5
Ravensbury La MTCM CR4 43 P5
Ravensbury Rd
WAND/EARL SW18 28 E5
Ravensbury Ter
WAND/EARL SW18 28 E5
Ravenscar Rd SURB KT6 59 M1
Ravens Cl HAYES BR2 47 M3
REDH RH1 120 B4
WOKN/KNAP GU21 71 J5
Ravenscourt SUN TW16 39 H2
Ravenscourt Av
HMSMTH W6 18 E2
Ravenscourt Gdns
HMSMTH W6 18 D2
Ravenscourt Pk
HMSMTH W6 18 E2
Ravenscourt Pl HMSMTH W6 18 F2
Ravenscourt Rd
HMSMTH W6 18 F2
Ravenscourt Sq SHB W12 18 E1
Ravenscroft Cl ASHV GU12 109 L3
Ravenscroft Rd BECK BR3 46 C3
CHSWK W4 18 A2
WEY KT13 56 E9
Ravensdale Gdns NRWD SE19 45 M1
Ravensdale Ms STA TW18 22 E9
Ravensdale Rd ASC SL5 34 A6
HSLWW TW4 15 N8
Ravensfield EGH TW20 20 G9
Ravensfield Gdns
HOR/WEW KT19 60 C4
Ravenshead Cl
SAND/SEL CR2 64 C9
Ravenslea Rd BAL SW12 29 J3
Ravensmead Rd HAYES BR2 47 K1
Ravensmede Wy CHSWK W4 18 D2
Ravenstone Rd CBLY GU15 69 M3
Ravenstone St BAL SW12 29 K4
Ravens Wold PUR/KEN CR8 81 L4
Ravenswood Av CWTH RG45 49 J4
SURB KT6 59 M1
WWKM BR4 47 J9
Ravenswood Cl COB KT11 75 M4
Ravenswood Ct
KUTN/CMB KT2 * 26 G9
WOKS/MYFD GU22 10 D5
Ravenswood Crs WWKM BR4 47 J9
Ravenswood Dr CBLY GU15 69 J3
Ravenswood Gdns ISLW TW7 16 E6
Ravenswood Rd BAL SW12 29 L3
CROY/NA CR0 2 A6
Rawlings Cl BECK BR3 47 J6
Rawlins Cl SAND/SEL CR2 64 F6
Rawlinson Rd ALDT GU11 88 E9
CBLY GU15 68 B2
Rawnsley Av MTCM CR4 43 P6
Raworth Cl CRAWE RH10 * 177 M7
Raygnoldes FLEETS GU52 106 E3
Ray La LING RH7 142 G6
Rayleigh Av TEDD TW11 25 M9
Rayleigh Ct KUT/HW KT1 9 H4
Rayleigh Ri SAND/SEL CR2 63 N5
Rayleigh Rd WIM/MER SW19 43 K2
Raymead Av THHTH CR7 45 J6
Raymead Cl LHD/OX KT22 96 E2
Raymead Wy LHD/OX KT22 96 E2
Raymer Wk HORL RH6 140 E9
Raymond Av WEA W13 16 G1
Raymond Cl DTCH/LGLY SL3 13 J6
SYD SE26 31 K8
Raymond Crs GUW GU2 111 M6
Raymond Rd BECK BR3 46 E5
DTCH/LGLY SL3 12 E2
WIM/MER SW19 28 B9
Raymond Wy
ESH/CLAY KT10 * 58 G5
Rayners Cl DTCH/LGLY SL3 12 G5
Rayner's Rd PUT/ROE SW15 28 B1
Raynham Rd HMSMTH W6 18 F2
Ray Rd E/WMO/HCT KT8 40 B6
Rays Rd WWKM BR4 47 J8
Raywood Cl HYS/HAR UB3 14 E5
Rdffye Ct HORS RH12 192 F6
The Readens BNSTD SM7 80 A5
Reading Arch Rd REDH RH1 120 B5
Reading Rd FARN GU14 88 E6
HTWY RG27 48 B9
SUT SM1 61 N4
YTLY GU46 66 F1
YTLY GU46 67 L3
Reading Rd North
FLEETN GU51 86 E6
Reading Rd South
FLEETN GU51 86 F7
Read Rd ASHTD KT21 77 K6
Reads Rest La
KWD/TDW/WH KT20 79 K8
Reapers Cl HORS RH12 192 C5
Reapers Wy ISLW TW7 25 L1
Rebecca Cl FLEETS GU52 106 E3
Reckitt Rd CHSWK W4 18 C3
Recovery St TOOT SW17 29 H8
Recreation Cl FARN GU14 68 B7
Recreation Rd GU GU1 6 D2
HAYES BR2 47 M3
NWDGN UB2 15 N2
RFNM GU10 146 B1
SYD SE26 31 L7
Recreation Wy MTCM CR4 44 G4
Rectory Cl ASHTD KT21 77 M8
BF/WBF KT14 74 A2
BRAK RG12 32 E5
CRAN GU6 153 P6
GODL GU7 150 E2
RDKG RH5 155 K3
RGUE GU4 113 H3
RYNPK SW20 42 G3
SHGR GU5 132 D7
SHPTN TW17 38 C4
SHST GU47 49 K9
SURB KT6 41 J9
Rectory Gdn CRAN GU6 * 152 G9
Rectory Gdns BECK BR3 * 46 G2
Rectory Gn BECK BR3 46 F2
Rectory Gv CROY/NA CR0 2 A4
HPTN TW12 24 G7
Rectory La ASHTD KT21 77 M7
BF/WBF KT14 74 A2
BFOR GU20 52 C6
BH/WHM TN16 104 C3
BH/WHM TN16 105 N4
BNSTD SM7 80 B4
BRAK RG12 32 D5
BRKHM/BTCW RH3 118 D3
CRAWW RH11 176 C3
GT/LBKH KT23 95 P6
HORL RH6 158 A5
LIPH GU30 182 G3
RFNM GU10 126 B9
SHGR GU5 134 B1
SURB KT6 41 J9
TOOT SW17 29 K8
WLGTN SM6 62 E3
Rectory Orch
WIM/MER SW19 28 B7
Rectory Pk SAND/SEL CR2 81 N2
Rectory Rd BARN SW13 18 E7
BECK BR3 46 G2
COUL/CHIP CR5 99 P5
FARN GU14 88 E3
HSLWW TW4 15 K7
NWDGN UB2 15 P1
SUT SM1 61 L2
Rectory Rw BRAK RG12 32 D5
Red Admiral St HORS RH12 192 D5
Red Anchor Cl CHEL SW3 * 19 P4
Redan Gdns ASHV GU12 108 E4
Redan Hill Est ASHV GU12 * 108 E4
Redan Rd ASHV GU12 108 E4
Redan St WKENS W14 19 H1
Redbarn Cl PUR/KEN CR8 63 K9
Redberry Gv SYD SE26 31 K6
Redbridge La RHWH RH17 195 L7
Redcliffe Cl ECT SW5 19 M3
Redcliffe Gdns WBPTN SW10 19 M3
Redcliffe Ms WBPTN SW10 19 M3
Redcliffe Pl WBPTN SW10 19 N4
Redcliffe Rd WBPTN SW10 19 N3
Redcliffe Sq WBPTN SW10 19 M3
Redcliffe St WBPTN SW10 * 19 M4
Redclose Av MRDN SM4 43 L6
Redcote Pl DORK RH4 117 K5
Red Cottage Ms
DTCH/LGLY SL3 12 A1
Redcourt WOKS/MYFD GU22 73 H4
Redcrest Gdns CBLY GU15 69 H3
Redcroft Wk CRAN GU6 171 H1
Red Deer Cl SWTR RH13 192 G7
Reddington Cl SAND/SEL CR2 63 M7
Reddington Dr
DTCH/LGLY SL3 12 D2
Redditch BRAK RG12 32 F8
Redditch Cl CRAWW RH11 176 B9
Reddons Rd BECK BR3 46 E1
Reddown Rd COUL/CHIP CR5 80 F7
Rede Ct WEY KT13 55 P3
Redehall Rd HORL RH6 160 C3
Redesdale Gdns ISLW TW7 16 G5
Redfern Av HSLWW TW4 25 H3
Redfield La ECT SW5 19 L2
Redfield Ms ECT SW5 19 L2
Redfields La FLEETS GU52 106 E5
Redford Av COUL/CHIP CR5 80 D4
HORS RH12 192 A6
THHTH CR7 45 H5
WLGTN SM6 62 G5
Redford Cl FELT TW13 24 A5
Redgarth Ct EGRIN RH19 162 A9
Redgate Dr HAYES BR2 65 P1
Redgate Ter PUT/ROE SW15 28 A2
Redgauntlet EWKG RG40 48 C3
Redgrave Cl CROY/NA CR0 45 P7
Redgrave Dr CRAWE RH10 177 N6
Redgrave Rd PUT/ROE SW15 19 H9
Redhearne Flds RFNM GU10 165 H1
Redhill Rd COB KT11 74 D2
Red House La
MFD/CHID GU8 148 D1
WOT/HER KT12 57 J1
Redhouse Rd
BH/WHM TN16 104 A1
Red House Rd CROY/NA CR0 44 F7
Redkiln Cl SWTR RH13 192 E7
Redkiln Wy SWTR RH13 192 E7
Redland Gdns
E/WMO/HCT KT8 * 39 P5
Redlands COUL/CHIP CR5 80 G5
RDKG RH5 137 H7
Redlands La RDKG RH5 136 G4
RFNM GU10 106 E7
Redlands Wy
BRXS/STRHM SW2 29 P3
Red La BOR GU35 164 E4
ESH/CLAY KT10 58 G5
OXTED RH8 123 P4
RDKG RH5 137 N3
Redleaves Av ASHF TW15 23 L9
Redlees Cl ISLW TW7 16 G9
Red Lion Ct HSLW TW3 * 16 B8
Red Lion La CHOB/PIR GU24 53 L7
FNM GU9 5 F6
Red Lion Rd CHOB/PIR GU24 53 L7
SURB KT6 59 M1
Red Lion Sq
WAND/EARL SW18 * 28 D1
Red Lion St RCH/KEW TW9 26 C1
Red Lodge Rd WWKM BR4 47 J9
Redmayne CBLY GU15 69 L4
Redmead Rd HYS/HAR UB3 14 G2
Redmore Rd HMSMTH W6 * 18 F2
Red Oaks RFNM GU10 * 146 B1
Red Post Hl HNHL SE24 30 E1
Red River Ct HORS RH12 * 192 A5
Red Rd LTWR GU18 70 A1
Redroofs Cl BECK BR3 47 H2
Redstart Cl CROY/NA CR0 65 K8
Redstone Hl REDH RH1 120 C5
Redstone Hollow REDH RH1 120 C6
Redstone Mnr REDH RH1 120 C5
Redstone Pk REDH RH1 120 C5
Redstone Rd REDH RH1 120 C6
Redvers Buller Rd ALDT GU11 88 E8
Redvers Rd BRAK RG12 32 D6
WARL CR6 82 D7
Redway Dr WHTN TW2 25 K3
Redwing Av GODL GU7 131 K4
Redwing Cl SAND/SEL CR2 64 D9
SWTR RH13 192 E7
Redwing Gdns BF/WBF KT14 73 M1
Redwing Ri RGUE GU4 113 H3
Redwing Rd WLGTN SM6 62 G6
Redwood EGH TW20 37 J3
Redwood Cl CRAWE RH10 177 H3
PUR/KEN CR8 63 L7
Redwood Dr ASC SL5 35 H7
CBLY GU15 69 M4
Redwood Gv RGUE GU4 132 G2
Redwood Ms ASHF TW15 * 38 F1
Redwood Mt REIG RH2 119 L2
Redwoods ADL/WDHM KT15 55 L5
Redwoods Wy FLEETS GU52 107 H2
Reece Ms SKENS SW7 19 P2
Reed Cl ALDT GU11 88 F9
Reed Dr REDH RH1 120 C8
Reedham Dr PUR/KEN CR8 81 H2
Reedham Park Av
PUR/KEN CR8 81 J5
Reedings CRAWW RH11 176 A7
Reed Pl BF/WBF KT14 73 J2
SHPTN TW17 38 B9
Reedsfield Cl ASHF TW15 23 L6
Reedsfield Rd ASHF TW15 23 L7
Reed's Hl BRAK RG12 32 D6
The Reeds Rd RFNM GU10 146 G3
Rees Gdns CROY/NA CR0 45 P7
Reeve Rd REIG RH2 119 N9
Reeves Cnr CROY/NA CR0 2 B4
Reeves Rd ASHV GU12 108 E5
Regal Ct MTCM CR4 44 B4
Regal Crs WLGTN SM6 62 D2
Regal Dr EGRIN RH19 180 E3
Regalfield Cl GUW GU2 111 N1
Regan Cl GUW GU2 91 P9
Regency Cl HPTN TW12 24 G8
Regency Ct
ADL/WDHM KT15 * 55 P3
Regency Dr BF/WBF KT14 73 K2
Regency Gdns
WOT/HER KT12 39 M9
Regency Ms BECK BR3 47 J2
Regency Ter SKENS SW7 * 19 P3
Regency Wk CROY/NA CR0 46 E7
Regent Cl ADL/WDHM KT15 55 N7
FLEETN GU51 86 G7
HSLWW TW4 15 K6
REDH RH1 100 E9
Regent Ct BAGS GU19 51 P7
GUW GU2 * 111 P3
Regent Crs REDH RH1 120 B3
Regent Pde BELMT SM2 * 61 N5
Regent Pk LHD/OX KT22 * 76 G7
Regent Pl WIM/MER SW19 28 F8
Regent Rd BRYLDS KT5 41 M6
HNHL SE24 30 C2
Regents Cl CRAWW RH11 176 F9
CTHM CR3 81 N7
SAND/SEL CR2 63 N5
Regents Ms HORL RH6 159 K1
Regents Pl SHST GU47 49 N9
Regent St CHSWK W4 17 N3
FLEETN GU51 86 G7
Regents Wk ASC SL5 34 C7
Regent Wy FRIM GU16 69 H7
Regiment Cl FARN GU14 * 87 N4
Regina Rd NWDGN UB2 15 N2
SNWD SE25 46 A4
Reid Av CTHM CR3 101 M1
Reid Cl COUL/CHIP CR5 80 D5
Reigate Av SUT SM1 43 M9
Reigate Cl CRAWE RH10 177 N2
Reigate Hl REIG RH2 119 M1
Reigate Hill Cl REIG RH2 119 L2
Reigate Rd DORK RH4 117 L5
EW KT17 60 D8
HORL RH6 158 G2
KWD/TDW/WH KT20 79 H6
LHD/OX KT22 97 J3
REDH RH1 120 B9
REIG RH2 119 N5
REIG RH2 139 N6
Reigate Wy WLGTN SM6 62 G4
Reindorp Cl GUW GU2 111 N6
Rembrandt Ct
HOR/WEW KT19 60 D5
Rembrandt Wy
WOT/HER KT12 57 K1
Rendle Cl CROY/NA CR0 45 P6
Renfree Wy SHPTN TW17 38 C8
Renfrew Rd HSLWW TW4 15 M7
The Renmans ASHTD KT21 77 M5
Renmuir St TOOT SW17 29 J9
Rennie Cl ASHF TW15 22 G6
Rennie Ter REDH RH1 120 C6
Renown Cl CROY/NA CR0 2 B2
Renton Cl
BRXS/STRHM SW2 * 30 A2
Replingham Rd
WAND/EARL SW18 28 C4
Reporton Rd FUL/PGN SW6 19 J6
Repton Av HYS/HAR UB3 14 F2
Repton Cl CAR SM5 62 A4
Repton Ct BECK BR3 47 H2
Reservoir Cl THHTH CR7 45 M4
Reservoir Rd FARN GU14 87 P6
Restmor Wy CAR SM5 62 C1
Restwell Av CRAN GU6 152 E6
Retreat Rd RCH/KEW TW9 26 C1
The Retreat BRYLDS KT5 41 M7
CRAN GU6 * 152 F8
EGH TW20 21 J9
MORT/ESHN SW14 18 C8
THHTH CR7 45 M5
WPK KT4 60 F2
Revell Cl LHD/OX KT22 96 B2
Revell Dr LHD/OX KT22 96 B2
Revell Rd KUT/HW KT1 41 P3
SUT SM1 61 K5
Revelstoke Av FARN GU14 88 D1
Revelstoke Rd
WIM/MER SW19 28 B7
Revere Wy HOR/WEW KT19 60 C7
Revesby Cl CHOB/PIR GU24 70 D2
Revesby Rd CAR SM5 44 A7
Rewell St FUL/PGN SW6 * 19 N5
Rewley Rd CAR SM5 43 P7
Rex Av ASHF TW15 23 K9
Reynard Cl HORS RH12 192 G5
Reynard Dr NRWD SE19 45 P1
Reynolds Av CHSGTN KT9 59 L6
Reynolds Cl CAR SM5 44 B9
WIM/MER SW19 43 P2
Reynolds Gn SHST GU47 67 P2
Reynolds Pl CRAWW RH11 176 F4
RCHPK/HAM TW10 26 E2
Reynolds Rd CHSWK W4 18 A1
CRAWW RH11 176 F4
NWMAL KT3 42 B8
PECK SE15 31 K1
Reynolds St FLEETN GU51 86 E3
Reynolds Wy CROY/NA CR0 3 H7
Rheingold Wy WLGTN SM6 62 G7
Rhine Banks FARN GU14 87 P2
Rhodes Cl EGH TW20 21 P8
Rhodes Ct EGH TW20 * 21 P8
Rhodes Wy CRAWE RH10 177 J7
Rhododendron Cl ASC SL5 33 N1
Rhododendron Ride
EGH TW20 20 E8
Rhododendron Rd
FRIM GU16 69 K8
Rhododendron Wk ASC SL5 33 N1
Rhodrons Av CHSGTN KT9 59 L4
Rhyll Gdns ALDT GU11 108 B5
Rialto Rd MTCM CR4 44 C3
Ribble Pl FARN GU14 88 A1
Ribblesdale Rd
STRHM/NOR SW16 29 L8
Ricardo Ct SHGR GU5 132 D8
Ricardo Rd WDSR SL4 20 G2
Ricards Rd WIM/MER SW19 28 C8
Rices Hl EGRIN RH19 180 D2
Richard Cl FLEETN GU51 86 E8
Richards Cl ASHV GU12 * 109 J1
HYS/HAR UB3 14 F4
Richards Fld HOR/WEW KT19 60 B7
Richards Rd COB KT11 76 B3
Richbell Cl ASHTD KT21 77 K7
Richborough Ct
CRAWW RH11 * 176 F5
Richens Cl HSLW TW3 16 D7
Richford Ga HMSMTH W6 * 18 G1
Richings Pl DTCH/LGLY SL3 13 J1
Richings Wy DTCH/LGLY SL3 13 K1
Richland Av COUL/CHIP CR5 80 C3
Richlands Av EW KT17 60 E3
Richmond Av
EBED/NFELT TW14 23 P2
RYNPK SW20 43 J2
Richmond Br TWK TW1 26 C1
Richmond Cl BH/WHM TN16 83 P8
EPSOM KT18 78 C3
FARN GU14 87 P4
FLEETS GU52 86 F9
FRIM GU16 69 H7
LHD/OX KT22 96 C4
Richmond Ct CRAWE RH10 177 H6

Richmond Crs STA TW18 * 22 C8
Richmond Dr SHPTN TW17 38 E7
Richmond Gn CROY/NA CR0 62 G2
Richmond Hl
RCHPK/HAM TW10 26 D2
Richmond Hill Ct
RCHPK/HAM TW10 26 D2
Richmond Pde TWK TW1 * 26 B2
Richmond Park Rd
KUTN/CMB KT2 8 E2
MORT/ESHN SW14 27 H1
Richmond Rd
COUL/CHIP CR5 80 D4
CROY/NA CR0 62 G2
GODL GU7 131 K7
HORS RH12 192 B6
ISLW TW7 16 G9
KUTN/CMB KT2 26 C8
RYNPK SW20 42 F2
SHST GU47 50 A9
STA TW18 22 C8
THHTH CR7 45 K5
TWK TW1 26 A3
Richmond Wy EGRIN RH19 180 E3
GT/LBKH KT23 96 B4
Richmondwood ASC SL5 35 H9
Rickard Cl BRXS/STRHM SW2 30 B4
WDR/YW UB7 13 P1
Rickards Cl SURB KT6 59 L1
Ricketts Hill Rd
BH/WHM TN16 84 B7
Rickett St FUL/PGN SW6 19 L4
Rickfield CRAWW RH11 176 D6
Rickford Hl RGUW GU3 91 K6
Rickman Cl BRAK RG12 32 E7
Rickman Crs
ADL/WDHM KT15 55 M2
Rickman Hl COUL/CHIP CR5 80 D6
Rickman Hill Rd
COUL/CHIP CR5 80 D7
Rickman's La BIL RH14 187 L8
Ricksons La EHSLY KT24 94 D7
Rickwood HORL RH6 140 D9
Rickwood Pk RDKG RH5 * 156 C3
Rickyard GUW GU2 111 K5
The Riddings CTHM CR3 101 P5
Riddlesdown Av
PUR/KEN CR8 81 L1
Ride La SHGR GU5 133 P6
Riders Wy GDST RH9 122 C2
The Ride BIL RH14 187 P8
BTFD TW8 17 H3
Ride Wy CRAN GU6 153 L2
Rideway Cl CBLY GU15 68 D4
Ridge Cl BRKHM/BTCW RH3 117 P9
WOKS/MYFD GU22 91 P1
Ridgegate Cl REIG RH2 119 P3
Ridge Gn REDH RH1 120 G8
Ridge Green Cl REDH RH1 120 G8
Ridgehurst Dr HORS RH12 191 N9
Ridgelands LHD/OX KT22 96 D4
Ridge Langley SAND/SEL CR2 64 A8
Ridgemead Rd EGH TW20 20 G6
Ridge Moor Cl GSHT GU26 165 P6
Ridgemount GUW GU2 6 A4
WEY KT13 56 G1
Ridgemount Av
COUL/CHIP CR5 80 D6
CROY/NA CR0 64 D1
Ridge Mount Rd ASC SL5 34 G9
Ridgemount Wy REDH RH1 119 P7
Ridge Pk PUR/KEN CR8 62 F8
Ridge Rd CHEAM SM3 43 K9
MTCM CR4 44 D1
Ridgeside CRAWE RH10 177 J5
The Ridges RGUW GU3 132 A1
The Ridge ASC SL5 * 34 G8
BRYLDS KT5 41 N6
COUL/CHIP CR5 80 G3
CTHM CR3 103 L5
EPSOM KT18 78 A7
HORS RH12 189 P2
LHD/OX KT22 96 D4
PUR/KEN CR8 62 F8
WHTN TW2 25 L3
WOKS/MYFD GU22 11 J3
Ridge Wy EDEN TN8 144 G1
FELT TW13 24 F6
VW GU25 36 C6
Ridgeway EGRIN RH19 180 D4
HAYES BR2 65 N1
HOR/WEW KT19 78 A1
WOT/HER KT12 39 H9
Ridgeway Cl CRAN GU6 153 K9
DORK RH4 116 G9
LTWR GU18 52 A9
Ridgeway Ct REDH RH1 * 120 A6
Ridgeway Dr DORK RH4 136 G1
Ridgeway Gdns
WOKN/KNAP GU21 72 B4
Ridgeway Rd DORK RH4 116 G9
ISLW TW7 16 E5
REDH RH1 120 B5
Ridgeway Rd North
ISLW TW7 16 E5
The Ridgeway ACT W3 17 N1
BRAK RG12 32 E4
CHOB/PIR GU24 70 F9
CRAN GU6 153 J9
CROY/NA CR0 63 H2
HORL RH6 159 K3
HORS RH12 192 A6
LHD/OX KT22 76 C3
LHD/OX KT22 96 D3
LTWR GU18 52 B8
The Ridge Wy SAND/SEL CR2 63 N8
Ridgewell Cl SYD SE26 31 N7
Ridgewood Dr FRIM GU16 69 M5
Ridgley Rd MFD/CHID GU8 167 P7
Ridgmount Rd
WAND/EARL SW18 28 E1
Ridgway RCHPK/HAM TW10 * 26 D2
WIM/MER SW19 42 G1
WOKS/MYFD GU22 73 K4
Ridgway Gdns
WIM/MER SW19 43 H1
Ridgway Hill Rd FNM GU9 127 N5
Ridgway Pde FNM GU9 * 127 N5
Ridgway Pl WIM/MER SW19 28 B9
Ridgway Rd FNM GU9 127 N6
WOKS/MYFD GU22 73 K4
The Ridgway BELMT SM2 61 P6
Riding Court Rd
DTCH/LGLY SL3 12 A4
Riding Hl SAND/SEL CR2 82 A2
The Ridings ADL/WDHM KT15 55 J5
ASHTD KT21 77 K6
BH/WHM TN16 84 C6
BRYLDS KT5 41 N6
COB KT11 76 A1
CRAWE RH10 177 N4
DTCH/LGLY SL3 13 K2
EHSLY KT24 94 G5
EPSOM KT18 78 C4
EW KT17 60 D7
FRIM GU16 69 K5
KWD/TDW/WH KT20 79 K9
REIG RH2 119 P3
RPLY/SEND GU23 93 D6
SUN TW16 39 J2
The Riding CRAN GU6 153 H8
WOKN/KNAP GU21 72 F3
Ridlands Gv OXTED RH8 124 C1
Ridlands La OXTED RH8 124 C1
Ridlands Ri OXTED RH8 124 C1
Ridley Av WEA W13 17 H1
Ridley Cl FLEETS GU52 86 F8
Ridley Rd HAYES BR2 47 M4
WARL CR6 82 C7
WIM/MER SW19 43 M1
Ridsdale Rd PGE/AN SE20 46 B2
WOKN/KNAP GU21 71 P6
Riesco Dr CROY/NA CR0 64 C5
Rifle Wy FARN GU14 87 N4
Rigault Rd FUL/PGN SW6 19 J7
Rigby Cl CROY/NA CR0 63 J2
Riggindale Rd
STRHM/NOR SW16 29 N8
Riley St WBPTN SW10 19 P5
Rillside CRAWE RH10 177 K8
Rill Wk EGRIN RH19 180 G2
Rimbault Cl ALDT GU11 88 F8
Rimmer Cl CRAWW RH11 194 E2
Rinaldo Rd BAL SW12 29 L3
Rindle Cl FARN GU14 87 N3
Ring Cl BMLY BR1 47 P1
Ringer's Rd BMLY BR1 47 N4
Ringford Rd
WAND/EARL SW18 28 C1
Ringley Av HORL RH6 159 K1
Ringley Oak HORS RH12 192 E6
Ringley Park Av REIG RH2 119 P6
Ringley Park Rd REIG RH2 119 N5
Ringley Rd HORS RH12 192 D6
Ringmead BRAK RG12 32 A6
Ringmer Av FUL/PGN SW6 19 J6
Ringmore Dr RGUE GU4 112 G2
Ringmore Ri FSTH SE23 31 J3
Ringmore Rd WOT/HER KT12 57 L2
Ring Rd North HORL RH6 159 L4
Ring Rd South HORL RH6 159 M5
Ringstead Rd SUT SM1 61 P3
The Ring BRAK RG12 32 D2
Ringway NWDGN UB2 15 N3
Ringwold Cl BECK BR3 46 E1
Ringwood BRAK RG12 32 B8
Ringwood Av CROY/NA CR0 44 G8
REDH RH1 120 B2
Ringwood Cl ASC SL5 34 A5
CRAWE RH10 177 H7
Ringwood Gdns
PUT/ROE SW15 27 M5
Ringwood Rd BLKW GU17 67 N2
FARN GU14 68 E9
Ringwood Wy HPTN TW12 25 H7
Ripley Av EGH TW20 21 K9
Ripley By-pass
RPLY/SEND GU23 93 J6
Ripley Cl CROY/NA CR0 65 J5
DTCH/LGLY SL3 12 C2
Ripley Gdns
MORT/ESHN SW14 18 B8
Ripley La RPLY/SEND GU23 94 B4
Ripley Rd HPTN TW12 40 A1
RPLY/SEND GU23 93 N6
Ripley Wy HOR/WEW KT19 59 N9
Ripon Cl CBLY GU15 69 M5
GUW GU2 111 M2
Ripon Gdns CHSGTN KT9 59 K4
Ripon Rd BLKW GU17 67 K7
Ripplesmere BRAK RG12 32 F6
Ripplesmore Cl SHST GU47 49 M9
Ripston Rd ASHF TW15 23 N8
Risborough Dr WPK KT4 42 E8
Riseldine Rd FSTH SE23 31 M2
Rise Rd ASC SL5 34 E7
The Rise CRAWE RH10 177 M5
CWTH RG45 49 K4
EGRIN RH19 180 E3
EHSLY KT24 94 G6
EW KT17 60 D8
KWD/TDW/WH KT20 98 G1
SAND/SEL CR2 64 C7
Ritchie Cl CRAWE RH10 177 M9
Ritchie Rd CROY/NA CR0 46 B7
Ritherdon Rd TOOT SW17 29 K5
River Av THDIT KT7 40 G8
Riverbank DORK RH4 * 116 B7
E/WMO/HCT KT8 40 E4
River Bank THDIT KT7 40 F6
Riverbank Wy BTFD TW8 17 J4
River Ct WOKN/KNAP GU21 72 G3
Rivercourt Rd HMSMTH W6 18 F2
Riverdale RFNM GU10 127 J6
Riverdale Dr
WAND/EARL SW18 28 E4
WOKS/MYFD GU22 92 D1
Riverdale Gdns TWK TW1 26 B1
Riverdale Rd FELT TW13 24 F7
TWK TW1 26 B2
Riverfield Rd STA TW18 22 C9
River Gdns CAR SM5 62 C1
EBED/NFELT TW14 24 C1
River Grove Pk BECK BR3 46 F2
Riverhead Dr BELMT SM2 61 M8
River Hl COB KT11 75 K4
Riverholme Dr
HOR/WEW KT19 60 B7
River La COB KT11 75 N5
LHD/OX KT22 76 D9
RCHPK/HAM TW10 26 C4
RFNM GU10 127 J6
River Md CRAWW RH11 176 D2
HORS RH12 192 A9
Rivermead BF/WBF KT14 74 B2
E/WMO/HCT KT8 40 C4
KUT/HW KT1 * 41 K6
Rivermead Cl
ADL/WDHM KT15 * 55 N6
TEDD TW11 26 A8
Rivermead Rd CBLY GU15 68 D6
River Meads Av WHTN TW2 25 J6
River Mt WOT/HER KT12 39 H8
River Mount Gdns
GUW GU2 112 A8
Rivernook Cl WOT/HER KT12 39 L6
River Park Av STA TW18 22 A7
Riverpark Gdns HAYES BR2 47 K1
River Reach TEDD TW11 26 B9
River Rd STA TW18 37 K2
YTLY GU46 66 F1
River Rw FNM GU9 127 K5
Rivers Cl FARN GU14 88 G6
Riversdale Rd THDIT KT7 40 G6
Riversdell Cl CHERT KT16 37 K8
Riverside CHERT KT16 * 37 L3
DORK RH4 117 K5
EDEN TN8 144 G4
FROW RH18 181 K8
GU GU1 112 B3
HORL RH6 159 K3
HORS RH12 191 P8
RCH/KEW TW9 * 17 N4
SHPTN TW17 38 G8
STWL/WRAY TW19 21 H3
SUN TW16 * 39 M3
TWK TW1 26 A4
Riverside Av
E/WMO/HCT KT8 40 D6
LTWR GU18 52 G9
Riverside Cl CHOB/PIR GU24 70 F9
FARN GU14 88 B2
KUT/HW KT1 41 K5
STA TW18 37 K2
WLGTN SM6 62 D2
Riverside Dr CHSWK W4 18 C5
ESH/CLAY KT10 58 A3
MTCM CR4 44 A6
RCHPK/HAM TW10 26 A6
SHGR GU5 132 E6
STA TW18 22 B8
Riverside Gdns HMSMTH W6 18 F3
WOKS/MYFD GU22 93 P1
Riverside Ms CROY/NA CR0 * 62 G2
Riverside Pl
STWL/WRAY TW19 22 G2
Riverside Rd STA TW18 37 K1
STWL/WRAY TW19 22 D2
TOOT SW17 28 E7
WOT/HER KT12 57 M3
The Riverside
E/WMO/HCT KT8 * 40 D4
Riverside Wk ISLW TW7 16 E8
KUT/HW KT1 8 B4
Riverside Wy CBLY GU15 68 C5
Riverside Yd TOOT SW17 28 E6
Riversmeet RFNM GU10 128 E9
River Ter HMSMTH W6 18 G3
River Vw ADL/WDHM KT15 * 55 N4
Riverview GU GU1 * 6 C2
Riverview Gdns BARN SW13 18 F4
COB KT11 75 J2
River View Gdns TWK TW1 25 N5
Riverview Pk CAT SE6 31 P5
Riverview Rd CHSWK W4 17 P5
River Wk SUN TW16 39 M3
WOT/HER KT12 39 J7
River Wy HOR/WEW KT19 60 B4
WHTN TW2 25 J5
Riverway STA TW18 37 M2
Rivett-Drake Cl GUW GU2 111 P1
Rivey Cl BF/WBF KT14 73 K3
Road House Est
WOKS/MYFD GU22 * 72 E9
Roakes Av ADL/WDHM KT15 55 M1
Robert Cl WOT/HER KT12 57 K4
Robertsbridge Rd CAR SM5 43 N8
Roberts Cl CHEAM SM3 61 H6
STWL/WRAY TW19 22 F2
THHTH CR7 45 M4
Roberts Ct CHSGTN KT9 * 59 K4
Robertson Wy ASHV GU12 109 H5
Roberts Rd ASHV GU12 108 F5
CBLY GU15 68 C2
Robert St CROY/NA CR0 2 D5
Roberts Wy EGH TW20 36 A1
Robert Wy FRIM GU16 89 H4
HORS RH12 192 E3
Robin Cl ADL/WDHM KT15 55 P4
ASHV GU12 89 H9
CRAWW RH11 176 F3
EGRIN RH19 180 D1
FELT TW13 24 F8
Robin Gdns REDH RH1 120 C3
Robin Gv BTFD TW8 17 J4
Robin Hl GODL GU7 131 K6
Robin Hill Dr CBLY GU15 69 J5
Robin Hood Cl FARN GU14 68 C9
WOKN/KNAP GU21 71 M7
Robinhood Cl MTCM CR4 44 E5
Robin Hood Crs
WOKN/KNAP GU21 71 L6
Robin Hood La HORS RH12 191 M5
PUT/ROE SW15 27 K6
RGUE GU4 92 D4
SUT SM1 61 L4
Robinhood La MTCM CR4 44 E4
Robin Hood Rd
PUT/ROE SW15 27 K7
WOKN/KNAP GU21 71 M7
Robin Hood Wy
PUT/ROE SW15 27 K7
Robinia Cl PGE/AN SE20 46 A2
Robin La SHST GU47 49 N9
Robin Rw CRAWE RH10 179 K6
Robins Dl WOKN/KNAP GU21 71 J6
Robins Gv WWKM BR4 65 N2
Robins Grove Crs YTLY GU46 66 F2
Robinson Cl
WOKS/MYFD GU22 72 G9
Robinson Rd TOOT SW17 29 H9
Robinsway WOT/HER KT12 57 L3
Robinswood Ct
HORS RH12 * 192 E6
Robin Wy GUW GU2 111 P1
STA TW18 22 C6
Robin Willis Wy WDSR SL4 20 F2
Robinwood Pl
PUT/ROE SW15 27 J7
Robson Rd WNWD SE27 30 C6
Roby Dr BRAK RG12 32 F8
Robyns Wy EDEN TN8 145 H5
Rocastle Rd BROCKY SE4 31 M1
Rochelle Cl BTSEA SW11 19 P9
Roche Rd STRHM/NOR SW16 44 G2
Rochester Av BMLY BR1 47 P3
FELT TW13 24 A5
Rochester Cl
STRHM/NOR SW16 * 44 G1
Rochester Gdns CROY/NA CR0 3 H5
CTHM CR3 101 N2
Rochester Gv FLEETN GU51 86 F7
Rochester Ms EA W5 * 17 J2
Rochester Pde FELT TW13 * 24 B6
Rochester Rd CAR SM5 62 B3
EGH TW20 22 A8
Roche Wk CAR SM5 43 P7
Rochford Wy CROY/NA CR0 44 G7
Rockall Ct DTCH/LGLY SL3 12 F1
Rock Av MORT/ESHN SW14 18 B8
Rockbourne Rd FSTH SE23 31 L4
Rock Cl MTCM CR4 43 P3
Rockdale Dr GSHT GU26 165 N8
Rockell's Pl EDUL SE22 31 J2
The Rockery FARN GU14 87 P4
Rocket Rd FARN GU14 87 P6
Rockfield Cl OXTED RH8 123 M2
Rockfield Rd OXTED RH8 123 M1
Rockfield Wy SHST GU47 * 49 P9
Rock Gdns ALDT GU11 108 B5
Rockhampton Rd
SAND/SEL CR2 63 N5
STRHM/NOR SW16 30 B7
Rock Hl DUL SE21 30 G7
Rockingham Cl
PUT/ROE SW15 18 D9
Rockland Rd PUT/ROE SW15 19 J9
Rock La RFNM GU10 127 L8
Rockmount Rd NRWD SE19 30 E9
Rockshaw Rd REDH RH1 100 E7
Rocks La BARN SW13 18 E8
The Rocks EGRIN RH19 181 H5
Rockwell Gdns NRWD SE19 30 F7
Rockwood Pk EGRIN RH19 * 180 B6
Rocky La REDH RH1 100 C9
Rocombe Crs FSTH SE23 * 31 K3
Roden Gdns CROY/NA CR0 45 N7
Rodenhurst Rd CLAP SW4 29 M3
Rodgate La HASM GU27 185 M5
Rodmel Ct FARN GU14 88 G6
Rodmill La BRXS/STRHM SW2 29 P3
Rodney Cl NWMAL KT3 42 C6
WOT/HER KT12 * 39 L9
Rodney Gdns WWKM BR4 65 N3
Rodney Pl WIM/MER SW19 43 N2
Rodney Rd MTCM CR4 44 A3
NWMAL KT3 42 C6
WHTN TW2 25 H3
WOT/HER KT12 57 L1
Rodney Wy DTCH/LGLY SL3 13 J6
GU GU1 112 E4
Rodona Rd WEY KT13 56 F9
Rodway Rd BMLY BR1 47 P2
PUT/ROE SW15 27 M3
Rodwell Rd EDUL SE22 30 G2
Roebuck Cl ASHTD KT21 77 L9
FELT TW13 24 C7
REIG RH2 119 L5
SWTR RH13 192 G6
Roebuck Rd CHSGTN KT9 59 N4
Roedean Crs PUT/ROE SW15 27 K2
Roedeer Copse HASM GU27 183 P4
Roehampton Cl
PUT/ROE SW15 18 E9
Roehampton Ga
PUT/ROE SW15 27 K2
Roehampton High St
PUT/ROE SW15 27 M3
Roehampton La
PUT/ROE SW15 27 M1
Roehampton V
PUT/ROE SW15 27 L6
Roe Wy WLGTN SM6 62 G6
Roffes La CTHM CR3 101 M5
Roffey Cl HORL RH6 159 J1
PUR/KEN CR8 81 K5
Roffey Pk HORS RH12 * 193 K4
Roffey's Cl CRAWE RH10 160 B8
Roffords WOKN/KNAP GU21 71 P6
Rogers Cl COUL/CHIP CR5 81 K7
Rogers La WARL CR6 82 F7
Rogers Md GDST RH9 122 B3
Rogers Rd TOOT SW17 28 G7
Rojack Rd FSTH SE23 31 L4
Rokeby Cl BRAK RG12 32 F3
Rokeby Pl RYNPK SW20 42 F1
Roke Cl MFD/CHID GU8 149 M7
PUR/KEN CR8 81 L3
Roke La MFD/CHID GU8 149 M7
Roke Lodge Rd
PUR/KEN CR8 81 K2
Roke Rd PUR/KEN CR8 81 L4
Rokers La MFD/CHID GU8 130 D6
Rokes Pl YTLY GU46 66 E2
Roland Gdns SKENS SW7 19 N3
Roland Wy SKENS SW7 19 N3
WPK KT4 60 D1
Rollesby Rd CHSGTN KT9 59 N5
Rolleston Rd SAND/SEL CR2 63 M6
Rollit Crs HSLW TW3 25 H1
Rollscourt Av HNHL SE24 30 D1
Rolls Royce Cl WLGTN SM6 62 G6
Romana Ct STA TW18 * 22 D7
Roman Cl EBED/NFELT TW14 24 D1
Roman Farm Rd GUW GU2 111 K4
Roman Farm Wy GUW GU2 111 K4
Romanfield Rd
BRXS/STRHM SW2 30 A3
Romanhurst Av HAYES BR2 47 L5
Romanhurst Gdns
HAYES BR2 47 L5
Roman Ride CWTH RG45 49 H4
Roman Ri NRWD SE19 30 E9
Roman Rd CHSWK W4 18 C2
DORK RH4 116 G9
EDEN TN8 145 H8
Romans Wy
WOKS/MYFD GU22 73 L4
Roman Wy BNFD RG42 33 H2
CROY/NA CR0 2 B3
FNM GU9 128 A1
Romany Gdns CHEAM SM3 43 L8
The Romany FARN GU14 87 L6
Romayne Cl FARN GU14 88 C2
Romberg Rd TOOT SW17 29 K6
Romeo Hl BNFD RG42 33 H2
Romeyn Rd
STRHM/NOR SW16 30 A6
Rommany Rd WNWD SE27 30 E7
Romney Cl ASHF TW15 23 M8
CHSGTN KT9 59 L3
Romney Rd FARN GU14 88 A6
NWMAL KT3 42 B7
Romola Rd HNHL SE24 30 C4
Romsey Cl ALDT GU11 108 E8
BLKW GU17 67 N2
DTCH/LGLY SL3 12 D1
Rona Cl CRAWW RH11 176 E8
Ronald Cl BECK BR3 46 F6
Ronalds Rd BMLY BR1 47 N2
Ronelean Rd SURB KT6 59 M2
Ronneby Cl WEY KT13 56 G2
Ronson Wy LHD/OX KT22 96 G1
Roodlands La EDEN TN8 125 P8
Rookeries Cl FELT TW13 24 C6
Rookery Cl LHD/OX KT22 96 E4
Rookery Dr DORK RH4 116 A9
Rookery Hl ASHTD KT21 77 N7
REDH RH1 141 K7
Rookery Md
COUL/CHIP CR5 100 F2
Rookery Rd STA TW18 22 E8
The Rookery
STRHM/NOR SW16 * 30 A9
Rookery Wy
KWD/TDW/WH KT20 99 K7
Rook La CTHM CR3 101 J4
Rookley Cl BELMT SM2 61 M8
Rooks Hl SHGR GU5 151 P2
Rooksmead Rd SUN TW16 39 H3
Rookstone Rd TOOT SW17 29 J8
Rookswood BNFD RG42 32 D1
Rook Wy HORS RH12 192 D4
Rookwood Av NWMAL KT3 42 E5
SHST GU47 50 A8
WLGTN SM6 62 F3
Rookwood Cl REDH RH1 100 D9
Rookwood Ct GUW GU2 112 A8
Rookwood Pk HORS RH12 191 P7
Roothill La
BRKHM/BTCW RH3 137 N2
Ropeland Wy HORS RH12 192 D3
Roper Wy MTCM CR4 44 C3
Rorkes Drift FRIM GU16 89 H3
Rosa Av ASHF TW15 23 K7
Rosalind Franklin Cl
GUW GU2 111 L6
Rosaline Rd FUL/PGN SW6 19 J5
Rosaline Ter FUL/PGN SW6 * 19 J5
Rosamond St SYD SE26 31 J6
Rosamund Cl SAND/SEL CR2 63 M3
Rosamund Rd CRAWE RH10 177 L7
Rosary Cl HSLW TW3 15 N7
Rosary Gdns ASHF TW15 23 L7
SKENS SW7 19 N2
YTLY GU46 * 67 H2
Rosaville Rd FUL/PGN SW6 19 K5
Roseacre OXTED RH8 123 N4
Roseacre Cl SHPTN TW17 38 C6
Roseacre Gdns RGUE GU4 133 K2
Roseary Cl WDR/YW UB7 13 P2
Rose Av MRDN SM4 43 N6
MTCM CR4 44 B2
Rosebank EPSOM KT18 78 A3
PGE/AN SE20 46 B1
Rosebank Cl TEDD TW11 25 P9
Rosebery Av EW KT17 78 C3
NWMAL KT3 42 D3
THHTH CR7 45 L3
Rosebery Cl MRDN SM4 43 H7

Rosebery Crs
WOKS/MYFD GU22 72 D9
Rosebery Gdns SUT SM1 61 M3
Rosebery Pde EW KT17 * 60 D6
Rosebery Rd CLAP SW4 29 P2
EPSOM KT18 78 B8
HSLW TW3 25 K1
KUT/HW KT1 9 K5
SUT SM1 61 K5
Rosebery Sq KUT/HW KT1 9 K5
Rosebine Av WHTN TW2 25 L3
Rosebriar Cl
WOKS/MYFD GU22 73 L5
Rosebriars CTHM CR3 81 N9
ESH/CLAY KT10 58 C4
Rosebury Dr CHOB/PIR GU24 70 G4
Rosebury Rd FUL/PGN SW6 19 M7
Rose Bushes EW KT17 78 G5
Rosecourt Rd CROY/NA CR0 45 H7
Rosecroft Cl BH/WHM TN16 84 D7
Rosecroft Gdns WHTN TW2 25 L4
Rosedale ASHTD KT21 77 J7
ASHV GU12 108 E4
Rosedale Cl CRAWW RH11 176 D7
Rosedale Gdns BRAK RG12 32 C6
Rosedale Rd EW KT17 60 E4
RCH/KEW TW9 17 L9
Rosedene Av CROY/NA CR0 44 G8
MRDN SM4 43 L6
STRHM/NOR SW16 30 A6
Rosedene Gdns FLEETN GU51 86 F5
Rosedene La SHST GU47 67 P1
Rosedew Rd HMSMTH W6 19 H4
Rose End WPK KT4 43 H9
Rosefield Cl CAR SM5 62 A4
Rosefield Gdns CHERT KT16 55 H5
Rosefield Rd STA TW18 22 D7
Rose Gdns EA W5 17 K1
FARN GU14 87 P4
FELT TW13 24 B5
STWL/WRAY TW19 22 G3
Roseheath Rd HSLWW TW4 24 G1
Rose Hl DORK RH4 116 G8
SUT SM1 61 M1
Rosehill ESH/CLAY KT10 58 G5
HPTN TW12 40 A2
Rose Hill Arch Ms
DORK RH4 * 116 G7
Rosehill Av SUT SM1 43 N9
WOKN/KNAP GU21 72 A5
Rosehill Court Pde
MRDN SM4 * 43 N8
Rosehill Farm Meadow
BNSTD SM7 79 M4
Rosehill Gdns SUT SM1 61 M1
Rose Hill Pk West SUT SM1 43 N9
Rosehill Rd BH/WHM TN16 84 A6
WAND/EARL SW18 28 F2
Rose La RPLY/SEND GU23 93 P2
Roselare Cl BH/WHM TN16 105 H5
Roseleigh Cl TWK TW1 26 C2
Rosemary Av ASHV GU12 89 J7
E/WMO/HCT KT8 40 A4
HSLWW TW4 15 M7
Rosemary Cl CROY/NA CR0 44 G8
FARN GU14 87 P2
OXTED RH8 123 N4
Rosemary Ct HORL RH6 * 140 A9
Rosemary Crs RGUW GU3 111 M1
Rosemary Gdns BLKW GU17 67 N3
CHSGTN KT9 59 L3
Rosemary La BLKW GU17 67 N2
EGH TW20 36 F4
HORL RH6 158 B5
HORL RH6 159 L2
MORT/ESHN SW14 18 A8
RFNM GU10 127 J9
Rosemary Rd TOOT SW17 28 E6
Rosemead CHERT KT16 37 M8
Rosemead Av FELT TW13 24 A5
MTCM CR4 44 E4
Rosemead Cl REDH RH1 119 P7
Rose Meadow
CHOB/PIR GU24 70 G2
Rosemont Rd NWMAL KT3 42 A4
RCHPK/HAM TW10 26 D2
Rosemount Av BF/WBF KT14 73 L2
Rosendale Rd HNHL SE24 30 D3
Roseneath Ct CTHM CR3 * 102 A5
Roseneath Dr
MFD/CHID GU8 168 A7
Roseneath Pl
STRHM/NOR SW16 30 B7
Roseneath Rd BTSEA SW11 29 K2
Rosenthorpe Rd PECK SE15 31 L1
The Rosery CROY/NA CR0 46 D7
Rose Sq CHEL SW3 * 19 P3
Rosetrees GU GU1 112 E6
Rose Vw ADL/WDHM KT15 * 55 N4
Roseville Av HSLW TW3 25 H1
Roseville Rd HYS/HAR UB3 15 J3
Rosevine Rd RYNPK SW20 42 G2
Rose Wk BRYLDS KT5 41 P6
CRAWW RH11 * 176 E7
FLEETN GU51 86 F5
WWKM BR4 65 K1
Rosewarne Cl
WOKN/KNAP GU21 71 N7
Roseway DUL SE21 30 E2
Rosewell Cl PGE/AN SE20 46 B1
Rose Wd WOKS/MYFD GU22 11 G7
Rosewood Ct KUTN/CMB KT2 9 H1
Rosewood Dr SHPTN TW17 38 B6
Rosewood Gv SUT SM1 61 N1
Rosewood Ter
PGE/AN SE20 * 46 C1
Rosewood Wy
CHOB/PIR GU24 70 E2
Roskell Rd PUT/ROE SW15 19 H8
Roslin Rd ACT W3 17 P1
Roslyn Cl MTCM CR4 43 P3
Ross Cl CRAWE RH10 177 J8
HYS/HAR UB3 14 F2
Rossdale SUT SM1 62 A4
Rossdale Rd PUT/ROE SW15 18 G9
Rosset Cl BRAK RG12 32 D5
Rossetti Gdns
COUL/CHIP CR5 81 H6
Rossignol Gdns CAR SM5 62 C1
Rossindel Rd HSLW TW3 25 H1
Rossiter Cl DTCH/LGLY SL3 12 C2
Rossiter Rd BAL SW12 29 L4
Rosslea BFOR GU20 52 A3
Rosslyn Av BARN SW13 18 C8
EBED/NFELT TW14 24 B2
Rosslyn Cl SUN TW16 23 P9
WWKM BR4 65 M2
Rosslyn Pk WEY KT13 56 F3
Rosslyn Rd TWK TW1 26 B2
Rossmore Cl CRAWE RH10 177 N1
Ross Pde WLGTN SM6 62 D5
Ross Rd COB KT11 75 L2
SNWD SE25 45 N4
WHTN TW2 25 K4
WLGTN SM6 62 E5
Rosswood Gdns WLGTN SM6 62 D5
Rostella Rd TOOT SW17 28 G7
Rostrevor Gdns NWDGN UB2 15 N3
Rostrevor Rd FUL/PGN SW6 19 K6
WIM/MER SW19 28 D8
Rothbury Gdns ISLW TW7 16 G5
Rother Cl SHST GU47 49 N9
Rother Crs CRAWW RH11 176 C6
Rotherfield Rd CAR SM5 62 C3
Rotherhill Av
STRHM/NOR SW16 29 N9
Rothermere Rd
CROY/NA CR0 63 H4
Rother Rd FARN GU14 88 A1
Rotherwood Cl RYNPK SW20 43 J2
Rotherwood Rd
PUT/ROE SW15 19 H8
Rothesay Av
RCHPK/HAM TW10 17 P9
RYNPK SW20 43 J3
Rothesay Rd SNWD SE25 45 M5
Rothes Rd DORK RH4 117 H6
Rothschild Rd CHSWK W4 18 A2
Rothschild St WNWD SE27 30 C7
Rotten Green Rd HTWY RG27 86 E1
Rotunda Est ALDT GU11 * 108 D4
Rougemont Av MRDN SM4 43 L7
Roughets La REDH RH1 101 N9
Rough Fld EGRIN RH19 162 C8
Roughlands
WOKS/MYFD GU22 73 J4
Rough Rew DORK RH4 137 H1
Rough Rd WOKS/MYFD GU22 91 J2
Rough Wy HORS RH12 192 E5
Rounce La CHOB/PIR GU24 70 D2
Roundals La MFD/CHID GU8 168 D4
Round Cl YTLY GU46 67 K3
Round Gv CROY/NA CR0 46 D8
Roundhay Cl FSTH SE23 31 L5
Round Hl SYD SE26 31 J5
Roundhill WOKS/MYFD GU22 11 K7
Roundhill Dr
WOKS/MYFD GU22 11 K6
Roundhill Wy COB KT11 58 B9
GUW GU2 111 M5
Round Oak Rd WEY KT13 56 B3
Roundshead Dr BNFD RG42 32 F1
Rounds Hl BNFD RG42 * 32 B2
Roundthorn Wy
WOKN/KNAP GU21 71 M5
Roundway CBLY GU15 69 L2
EGH TW20 21 P8
Roundway Cl CBLY GU15 69 L2
The Roundway
ESH/CLAY KT10 58 F5
Roundwood Vw BNSTD SM7 79 H4
Roundwood Wy BNSTD SM7 79 H4
Rounton Rd FLEETS GU52 106 G1
Roupell Rd BRXS/STRHM SW2 30 A4
Rouse Gdns DUL SE21 30 F7
Routh Rd WAND/EARL SW18 29 H3
Rowallan Rd FUL/PGN SW6 19 J5
Rowan Av EGH TW20 21 P8
Rowan Cha RFNM GU10 127 L8
Rowan Cl CBLY GU15 51 H9
CRAWE RH10 177 J5
FLEETN GU51 87 J6
GU GU1 111 P2
HORS RH12 192 G5
NWMAL KT3 42 C3
REIG RH2 119 N7
STRHM/NOR SW16 44 E2
Rowan Crs
STRHM/NOR SW16 44 E2
Rowan Dl FLEETS GU52 106 F1
Rowan Dr CWTH RG45 49 N2
Rowan Gdns CROY/NA CR0 3 K5
Rowan Gv COUL/CHIP CR5 100 D1
Rowan Md
KWD/TDW/WH KT20 78 F8
Rowan Rd BTFD TW8 17 H5
HMSMTH W6 19 H2
STRHM/NOR SW16 44 E3
WDR/YW UB7 13 P2
Rowans Cl FARN GU14 68 A7
Rowanside Cl BOR GU35 164 F7
The Rowans GSHT GU26 165 N9
SUN TW16 24 A8
WOKS/MYFD GU22 10 D6
Rowan Ter PGE/AN SE20 * 46 A2
WIM/MER SW19 * 43 J1
Rowan Wy HORS RH12 193 H5
Rowbarns Wy EHSLY KT24 115 H1
Rowberry Cl FUL/PGN SW6 19 H5
Rowbury GODL GU7 131 N6
Rowcroft Cl ASHV GU12 89 J9
Rowden Rd BECK BR3 46 E2
HOR/WEW KT19 60 A3
Rowdown Crs CROY/NA CR0 65 K7
Rowe La CHOB/PIR GU24 90 G4
Rowfant Cl CRAWE RH10 177 P5
Rowfant Rd TOOT SW17 29 K5
Row Hl ADL/WDHM KT15 55 K5
Rowhill Av ALDT GU11 108 B6
Rowhill Crs ALDT GU11 108 B6
Rowhills FNM GU9 107 P6
Rowhills Cl FNM GU9 108 B6
Rowhook Rd HORS RH12 190 G1
Rowhurst Av
ADL/WDHM KT15 55 M5
Rowland Cl CRAWE RH10 160 F7
Rowland Gv SYD SE26 31 J6
Rowland Rd CRAN GU6 152 G9
Rowlands Rd HORS RH12 192 F4
Rowland Wy ASHF TW15 38 E1
WIM/MER SW19 43 M2
Row La SHGR GU5 134 A8
Rowley Cl BRAK RG12 32 G4
WOKS/MYFD GU22 73 L5
Rowley Ct CTHM CR3 101 L2
Rowlheys Pl WDR/YW UB7 14 A1
Rowlls Rd KUT/HW KT1 9 G6
Rowly Dr CRAN GU6 152 D7
Rowly Edge CRAN GU6 152 D6
Rowntree Rd WHTN TW2 25 M4
Rowplatt La EGRIN RH19 161 M9
The Row EDEN TN8 * 144 F1
Row Town ADL/WDHM KT15 55 K6
Roxbee Cox Rd
FLEETN GU51 87 L6
Roxborough Av ISLW TW7 16 F5
Roxburgh Cl CBLY GU15 69 L4
Roxburgh Rd WNWD SE27 30 C8
Roxby Pl FUL/PGN SW6 19 L4
Roxford Cl SHPTN TW17 38 G6
Roxton Gdns CROY/NA CR0 64 F5
Royal Av WPK KT4 60 C1
Royal Circ WNWD SE27 30 B6
Royal Cl WIM/MER SW19 28 A5
WPK KT4 60 C1
Royal Dr EPSOM KT18 78 F7
Royal Earlswood Pk
REDH RH1 120 C9
Royale Cl ALDT GU11 108 E7
Royal Ms BAL SW12 29 L3
Royal Oak Cl YTLY GU46 67 J2
Royal Oak Dr CWTH RG45 49 M1
Royal Oak Ms TEDD TW11 25 P8
Royal Oak Pl EDUL SE22 31 J2
Royal Oak Rd
WOKN/KNAP GU21 72 A7
Royal Orchard Cl
WAND/EARL SW18 28 B3
Royal Pde FUL/PGN SW6 * 19 J5
Royal Rd TEDD TW11 25 L8
Royce Rd CRAWE RH10 159 K9
Roycroft Cl
BRXS/STRHM SW2 * 30 B4
Roycroft La EWKG RG40 48 C1
Roydon Ct WOT/HER KT12 57 J3
Roy Gv HPTN TW12 25 J9
Royston Av BF/WBF KT14 74 A1
SUT SM1 61 P2
WLGTN SM6 62 F3
Royston Cl CRAWE RH10 177 K1
HEST TW5 15 K6
WOT/HER KT12 39 J9
Royston Rd BF/WBF KT14 74 A1
PGE/AN SE20 46 D2
RCHPK/HAM TW10 26 D1
The Roystons BRYLDS KT5 41 P6
Rozeldene GSHT GU26 165 P8
Rubastic Rd NWDGN UB2 15 L1
Rubens St CAT SE6 31 N5
Rubus Cl CHOB/PIR GU24 70 E2
Ruckmans La RDKG RH5 173 J4
Rudd Hall Ri CBLY GU15 68 F5
Ruden Wy EW KT17 78 F4
Rudge Ri ADL/WDHM KT15 55 K4
Rudgwick Rd CRAWW RH11 176 C4
Rudloe Rd BAL SW12 29 M3
Rudsworth Cl DTCH/LGLY SL3 13 H6
Ruffetts Cl SAND/SEL CR2 64 B6
The Ruffetts SAND/SEL CR2 64 B6
Ruffetts Wy
KWD/TDW/WH KT20 79 J7
Rufford Cl FLEETS GU52 86 G9
Rufwood CRAWE RH10 179 H3
Rugby Cl SHST GU47 50 A8
Rugby La BELMT SM2 61 H7
Rugby Rd TWK TW1 25 M2
Ruggles-Brise Rd ASHF TW15 22 G8
Rugosa Rd CHOB/PIR GU24 70 E2
Ruislip St TOOT SW17 29 J7
Rumbold Rd FUL/PGN SW6 19 M5
Rumsey Cl HPTN TW12 24 G9
Runcorn Cl CRAWW RH11 176 B9
Runes Cl MTCM CR4 43 P5
Runfold-St George
RFNM GU10 108 D9
Runnemede Rd EGH TW20 21 M8
Runnymede WIM/MER SW19 43 P2
Runnymede Cl WHTN TW2 25 J2
Runnymede Ct EGH TW20 21 M7
Runnymede Crs
STRHM/NOR SW16 44 F2
Runnymede Gdns HSLW TW3 25 J2
Runnymede Rd WHTN TW2 25 J2
Runtley Wood La RGUE GU4 92 D5
Rupert Ct E/WMO/HCT KT8 * 40 A5
Rupert Rd CHSWK W4 18 C1
GUW GU2 6 B5
Rural Wy REDH RH1 120 C5
STRHM/NOR SW16 44 D1
Ruscoe Dr WOKS/MYFD GU22 11 H3
Ruscombe Wy
EBED/NFELT TW14 24 A3
Rusham Park Av EGH TW20 21 L9
Rusham Rd BAL SW12 29 J2
EGH TW20 21 L9
Rushams Rd HORS RH12 192 A8
Rush Common Ms
BRXS/STRHM SW2 29 P3
Rush Cft GODL GU7 131 N5
Rushden Cl NRWD SE19 45 M1
Rushdene Wk BH/WHM TN16 84 B6
Rushden Wy FNM GU9 107 P7
Rushett Cl THDIT KT7 41 H9
Rushett Dr DORK RH4 137 H1
Rushett La CHSGTN KT9 77 K1
Rushett Rd THDIT KT7 41 H8
Rushetts Pl CRAWW RH11 176 F2
Rushetts Rd CRAWW RH11 176 E2
REIG RH2 119 N9
Rushey Cl NWMAL KT3 42 B5
Rushey Md BROCKY SE4 31 P1
Rushford Rd BROCKY SE4 31 N2
Rushfords LING RH7 143 L7
Rushmead
RCHPK/HAM TW10 26 A6
Rushmead Cl CROY/NA CR0 3 J7
Rushmere Ct WPK KT4 60 E1
Rushmere Pl EGH TW20 21 K8
WIM/MER SW19 28 A8
Rushmon Pl CHEAM SM3 * 61 J5
Rushmoor Cl FLEETS GU52 86 G8
GUW GU2 111 M2
Rushmoor Rd ALDT GU11 108 A3
Rushmore Hl RSEV TN14 85 P3
Rusholme Gv NRWD SE19 30 F8
Rusholme Rd PUT/ROE SW15 28 A2
Rushton Av GDST RH9 122 C9
Rushworth Rd REIG RH2 119 L4
Rushy Meadow La CAR SM5 62 A1
Ruskin Av EBED/NFELT TW14 24 A3
RCH/KEW TW9 17 N5
Ruskin Cl CRAWE RH10 177 M2
Ruskin Ct CWTH RG45 * 49 K5
Ruskin Dr WPK KT4 60 F1
Ruskin Rd CAR SM5 62 C4
CROY/NA CR0 2 B3
ISLW TW7 16 F8
STA TW18 22 C9
Ruskin Wk HNHL SE24 30 D1
Ruskin Wy WIM/MER SW19 43 P3
Rusper Rd CRAWW RH11 175 M4
HORS RH12 175 J2
HORS RH12 192 E6
RDKG RH5 156 C9
RDKG RH5 156 G4
Ruspers Keep CRAWW RH11 176 C4
Russel Cl BECK BR3 47 H4
Russell Cl BRAK RG12 32 F9
KWD/TDW/WH KT20 98 E5
WOKN/KNAP GU21 72 A4
Russell Ct BLKW GU17 67 P3
LHD/OX KT22 97 H2
Russell Dr STWL/WRAY TW19 22 G2
Russell Gdns
RCHPK/HAM TW10 26 B5
WDR/YW UB7 14 C3
WKENS W14 * 19 J1
Russell Green Cl
PUR/KEN CR8 63 J8
Russell Hl PUR/KEN CR8 63 H8
Russell Hill Pl PUR/KEN CR8 63 J9
Russell Hill Rd PUR/KEN CR8 63 J8
Russell Kerr Cl CHSWK W4 * 18 A5
Russell Rd MTCM CR4 44 A4
SHPTN TW17 38 E8
WHTN TW2 25 N2
WIM/MER SW19 43 L1
WKENS W14 19 J1
WOKN/KNAP GU21 72 A4
WOT/HER KT12 39 J7
Russells KWD/TDW/WH KT20 99 H2
Russells Crs HORL RH6 159 K2
Russell Wy CRAWE RH10 177 K6
SUT SM1 61 M4
Russet Av SHPTN TW17 38 G4
Russet Cl HORL RH6 159 M1
RFNM GU10 108 G7
STWL/WRAY TW19 22 C2
WOT/HER KT12 57 M2
Russet Dr CROY/NA CR0 46 E9
Russet Gdns CBLY GU15 68 F5
Russet Gld ALDT GU11 107 P6
Russetts Cl
WOKN/KNAP GU21 72 D4
Russetts Dr FLEETN GU51 86 G7
Russet Wy RDKG RH5 137 K2
Russ Hl HORL RH6 157 M8
Russ Hill Rd HORL RH6 158 A6
Russington Rd SHPTN TW17 38 F7
Rusthall Av CHSWK W4 18 B1
Rusthall Cl CROY/NA CR0 46 C7
Rustic Av STRHM/NOR SW16 44 D1
Rustic Gln FLEETS GU52 106 F1
Rustington Wk CHEAM SM3 43 K8
Ruston Av BRYLDS KT5 41 P8
Ruston Cl CRAWE RH10 177 M8
Ruston Wy ASC SL5 33 N3
Rutford Rd
STRHM/NOR SW16 29 P8
Ruth Cl FARN GU14 87 N2
Ruthen Cl EPSOM KT18 77 P3
Rutherford Cl BELMT SM2 61 P5
Rutherford Wy
CRAWE RH10 159 K9
Rutherwick Cl HORL RH6 159 J1
Rutherwyke Cl EW KT17 60 E5
Rutherwyk Rd CHERT KT16 37 J8
Rutland Cl ALDT GU11 108 C3
ASHTD KT21 77 L6
HOR/WEW KT19 60 B8
MORT/ESHN SW14 17 P8
REDH RH1 120 B4
Rutland Dr MRDN SM4 43 L8
RCHPK/HAM TW10 26 C4
Rutland Gdns CROY/NA CR0 63 N3
Rutland Ga HAYES BR2 47 M5
Rutland Gv HMSMTH W6 18 F3
Rutland Pk CAT SE6 31 N5
Rutland Rd HYS/HAR UB3 14 F2
WHTN TW2 25 L5
WIM/MER SW19 44 A1
Rutland Wk CAT SE6 31 N5
Rutlish Rd WIM/MER SW19 43 L2
Rutson Rd BF/WBF KT14 74 B3
Rutter Gdns MTCM CR4 43 P5
Rutton Hill Rd
MFD/CHID GU8 166 F3
Ruvigny Gdns
PUT/ROE SW15 19 H8
Ruxbury Rd CHERT KT16 37 H7
Ruxley Cl HOR/WEW KT19 59 P4
Ruxley Crs ESH/CLAY KT10 59 H6
Ruxley La HOR/WEW KT19 59 P5
Ruxley Ms HOR/WEW KT19 59 P4
Ruxley Rdg ESH/CLAY KT10 58 G6
Ruxton Cl COUL/CHIP CR5 80 E4
Ryan Dr BTFD TW8 16 G4
Ryan Mt SHST GU47 49 L9
Rydal Cl CBLY GU15 69 M3
CRAWW RH11 176 A7
FARN GU14 87 P4
PUR/KEN CR8 81 M2
Rydal Dr FLEETS GU52 106 E1
WWKM BR4 65 L1
Rydal Gdns HSLW TW3 25 J2
PUT/ROE SW15 27 K8
Rydal Mt HAYES BR2 * 47 M5
Rydal Pl LTWR GU18 52 B9
Rydal Rd STRHM/NOR SW16 29 N8
Rydal Wy EGH TW20 36 F1
Ryde Cl RPLY/SEND GU23 93 N1
Ryde Heron
WOKN/KNAP GU21 71 L6
Ryde Lands CRAN GU6 153 J8
Rydens Av WOT/HER KT12 57 L1
Rydens Cl WOT/HER KT12 57 L1
Rydens Gv WOT/HER KT12 57 M3
Rydens Pde
WOKS/MYFD GU22 * 72 F9
Rydens Pk WOT/HER KT12 57 M1
Rydens Rd WOT/HER KT12 57 K2
Rydens Wy
WOKS/MYFD GU22 72 E9
Ryde Pl TWK TW1 26 B2
Ryders Wy HORS RH12 192 E3
Rydes Av GUW GU2 111 M2
Ryde's Hill Crs GUW GU2 111 M1
Ryde's Hill Rd GUW GU2 111 M3
The Ryde STA TW18 37 M2
Ryde Vale Rd BAL SW12 29 L5
Rydon's La COUL/CHIP CR5 81 L9
Rydon's Wood Cl
COUL/CHIP CR5 81 L9
Rye Ash CRAWE RH10 177 K4
Ryebeck Rd FLEETS GU52 106 G1
Rye Brook Rd LHD/OX KT22 76 G7
Rye Cl BNFD RG42 32 F1
FARN GU14 88 A1
FLEETN GU51 87 J2
GUW GU2 111 L4
Ryecotes Md DUL SE21 30 F4
Rye Cft FLEETS GU52 106 E2
Ryecroft Av WHTN TW2 25 J4
Ryecroft Dr HORS RH12 191 P7
Ryecroft Gdns BLKW GU17 68 A4
Ryecroft Rd
STRHM/NOR SW16 30 B9
Ryecroft St FUL/PGN SW6 19 M6
Ryedale EDUL SE22 31 J2
Rye Fld ASHTD KT21 77 K6
Ryefield Rd NRWD SE19 30 D9
Rye Gv CRAN GU6 * 152 D9
LTWR GU18 52 E8
Ryeland Cl FLEETN GU51 * 87 J2
Ryelands CRAWW RH11 176 D6
HORL RH6 * 140 E9
Ryelands Cl CTHM CR3 101 N1
Ryelands Ct LHD/OX KT22 76 G7
Ryelands Pl WEY KT13 56 G2
Ryelaw Rd FLEETS GU52 106 G1
Ryersh La RDKG RH5 156 B5
Rye Wk PUT/ROE SW15 28 A1
Ryfold Rd WIM/MER SW19 28 D6
Rykens La
BRKHM/BTCW RH3 138 A1
Ryland Cl FELT TW13 24 A7
Rylandes Rd SAND/SEL CR2 64 B7
Ryle Rd FNM GU9 4 E7
Rylett Crs SHB W12 18 D1
Rylston Rd FUL/PGN SW6 19 K4
Rymer Rd CROY/NA CR0 45 N8
Rymer St HNHL SE24 30 C2
Rysted La BH/WHM TN16 104 G6
Ryst Wood Rd FROW RH18 181 N9
Rythe Cl CHSGTN KT9 59 J6
Rythe Ct THDIT KT7 40 G8
Rythe Rd ESH/CLAY KT10 58 D4
The Rythe ESH/CLAY KT10 58 B8
Ryvers End DTCH/LGLY SL3 12 D1
Ryvers Rd DTCH/LGLY SL3 12 D1
Ryves Av YTLY GU46 66 E3

S

Sable Cl HSLWW TW4 15 L8
Sabre Ct ALDT GU11 108 A4
Sachel Court Rd CRAN GU6 170 A8
Sackville Av HAYES BR2 47 N9
Sackville Cl EGRIN RH19 162 B9
Sackville Ct EGRIN RH19 * 180 E3
Sackville Est
STRHM/NOR SW16 29 P6
Sackville La EGRIN RH19 162 A9
Sackville Rd BELMT SM2 61 L6
Saddleback Rd CBLY GU15 50 G9
Saddleback Wy
FLEETN GU51 87 H3

Saddlebrook Pk SUN TW16 ......38 G1
Saddler Cnr SHST GU47 ......67 M1
Saddler Rw CRAWE RH10 ...176 C8
Saddlers Ms KUT/HW KT1 *....8 A3
Saddlers Scarp GSHT GU26...165 K7
Saddlers Wy EPSOM KT18 .....44 B3
Sadler Cl MTCM CR4 ....44 B3
Sadlers Cl GU GU1 ....113 H4
Sadlers Gate Ms
  PUT/ROE SW15 ....18 G8
Sadlers Ride
  E/WMO/HCT KT8 ....40 C3
St Agatha's Cl CRAWW RH11 ...176 D8
  CROY/NA CRO 44 C7
Saffron Platt GUW GU2 ......111 N1
Saffron Rd BRAK RG12 ....32 D5
Saffron Wy SURB KT6 ....41 K9
Sage Wk BNFD RG42 ....32 F1
Sage Yd SURB KT6 * 41 M9
Sailors La MFD/CHID GU8 ....166 A1
Sainfoin Rd TOOT SW17 ....29 K5
Sainsbury Rd NRWD SE19 .....30 F8
St Agatha's Dr
  KUTN/CMB KT2 ....26 E9
St Agatha's Gv CAR SM5 .....44 B9
St Agnes Rd EGRIN RH19 .....180 D1
St Aidan's Rd EDUL SE22 .....31 J1
St Albans Av CHSWK W4 ....18 B1
  FELT TW13 ....24 E8
  WEY KT13 ....56 C2
St Albans Cl RGUW GU3 ......113 H1
St Albans Farm
  EBED/NFELT TW14 * 24 D1
St Alban's Gdns TEDD TW11 ...25 P8
St Alban's Gv CAR SM5 ....44 A8
  KENS W8 ....19 M1
St Albans Rd KUTN/CMB KT2...26 D9
  REIG RH2 ....119 L3
  SUT SM1 ....61 K3
St Albans Ter HMSMTH W6 .....19 J4
St Amunds Cl AT SE6 ....31 P7
St Andrew Av
  CHOB/PIR GU24 ....91 H1
St Andrews BRAK RG12 ....32 A7
  CRAN GU6 * 152 E9
  HORL RH6 * 159 L2
St Andrews Cl CWTH RG45 .....49 K3
  REIG RH2 ....119 M6
  SNPTN TW17 ....38 F5
  STWL/WRAY TW19 ....21 K2
  THDIT KT7 ....41 H9
  WDSR SL4 ....20 F2
  WOKN/KNAP GU21 ....72 A6
St Andrew's Crt
  WAND/EARL SW18 ....28 F5
St Andrews Gdns COB KT11 ....75 L2
St Andrews Ga
  WOKS/MYFD GU22 ....10 C5
St Andrews Ms BAL SW12 .....29 N4
St Andrews Rd CAR SM5 ......62 A2
  COUL/CHIP CR5 ....80 D5
  CRAWW RH11 ....176 A6
  CROY/NA CRO 2 C7
  SURB KT6 ....41 K7
  WKENS W14 ....19 J4
St Andrew's Sq SURB KT6 .....41 K7
St Andrew's Wk COB KT11 .....75 K4
St Andrew's Wy FRIM GU16 ....69 H9
  OXTED RH8 ....124 C2
St Anne's Av
  STWL/WRAY TW19 ....22 C3
St Annes Bvd REDH RH1 .....120 C3
St Annes Dr REDH RH1 ......120 C4
St Annes Gld BAGS GU19 .....51 M6
St Annes Mt REDH RH1 ......120 C4
St Annes Ri REDH RH1 ......120 C4
St Annes Rd CRAWE RH10 ....177 M1
  GODL GU7 ....131 N8
St Annes Wy REDH RH1 ......120 C4
St Ann's Cl CHERT KT16 ......37 K6
St Ann's Crs
  WAND/EARL SW18 ....28 E1
St Ann's Hill Rd CHERT KT16...36 C7
St Ann's Park Rd
  WAND/EARL SW18 ....28 E2
St Anns Rd BARN SW13 * 18 D7
  CHERT KT16 ....36 E5
St Anns Wy BH/WHM TN16 *....84 F5
  CROY/NA CRO 63 K5
St Aubyn's Av HSLW TW3 .....25 H1
  WIM/MER SW19 ....28 C8
St Aubyn's Rd NRWD SE19 ....30 G9
St Augustine's Av
  SAND/SEL CR2 ....63 L6
St Augustine's Cl
  ASHV GU12 ....108 C5
St Austins GSHT GU26 * 165 N8
St Barnabas Av
  CHOB/PIR GU24 ....90 C2
St Barnabas Cl BECK BR3 .....47 J3
St Barnabas' Gdns
  E/WMO/HCT KT8 ....40 A6
St Barnabas Rd MTCM CR4 ....44 C1
  SUT SM1 ....61 P4
St Bartholomew's Cl
  SYD SE26 ....31 K7
St Bartholomew's Ct GU GU1...7 J6
St Benedict's Cl ALDT GU11 ..108 C5
St Benets Cl TOOT SW17 .....29 H5
St Benet's Gv CAR SM5 ....43 N8
St Bernards CROY/NA CRO...3 G6
St Bernards Cl WNWD SE27 ...30 E7

St Bernards Rd
  DTCH/LGLY SL3 ....12 A1
St Blaise Av BMLY BR1........47 P3
St Brelades Cl DORK RH4 ....116 C9
St Brelades Ct EDEN TN8 *...144 E2
St Brelades Rd
  CRAWW RH11 ....176 C9
St Catherines WEY KT13 * 56 D2
  WOKS/MYFD GU22 ....72 A8
St Catherines Cl CHSGTN KT9...59 K5
  TOOT SW17 * 29 H5
St Catherines Ct FELT TW13 ...24 B4
St Catherine's Cross
  REDH RH1 ....121 N5
St Catherine's Dr GUW GU2...111 P9
St Catherine's Hl GUW GU2...112 A9
St Catherine's Pk GU GU1 .....7 J2
St Catherines Rd
  CRAWE RH10................177 M2
  FRIM GU16 ....69 J7
St Chad Av
  WOKS/MYFD GU22 ....91 J2
St Chads Cl SURB KT6 ....41 J8
St Charles Pl WEY KT13 ......56 C4
St Christophers LING RH7 *...143 K9
St Christophers Cl
  ASC SL5 ....33 M2
St Christopher's Ms
  WLGTN SM6 ....62 E4
St Christophers Pl
  FARN GU14 ....88 B4
St Christopher's Rd
  FARN GU14 ....88 C4
  HASM GU27 ....184 B4
St Clair Cl OXTED RH8 ......123 J1
  REIG RH2 ....119 N5
St Clair Dr WPK KT4 ....60 F2
St Clair's Rd CROY/NA CRO 3 C4
St Clement Rd
  CRAWW RH11 ....176 C9
St Clements Yd EDUL SE22 *...30 C1
St Cloud Rd WNWD SE27 .....30 D7
St Crispins Wy CHERT KT16 ...54 C7
St Cross Rd FNM GU9 ....5 G2
  FRIM GU16 ....69 J8
  RFNM GU10.................106 D9
St Cuthbert's Cl ECH TW20 ...21 J9
St Cyprian's St TOOT SW17 ...29 J7
St David's COUL/CHIP CR5 ....81 H6
St David's Cl FARN GU14 .....68 B3
  FNM GU9 ....108 A7
  REIG RH2 ....119 N4
  WWKM BR4 ....65 J7
St David's Dr ECH TW20 ......36 A1
St Denis Rd WNWD SE27 ......30 E7
St Denys Cl PUR/KEN CR8 .....63 K8
  WOKN/KNAP GU21 * 71 K7
St Dionis Rd FUL/PGN SW6 ...19 L6
St Dunstans Cl HYS/HAR UB3...15 H2
St Dunstan's Hl SUT SM1 .....61 J3
St Dunstan's Rd FELT TW13 ...24 A6
  HMSMTH W6 ....19 H3
  HSLWW TW4 ....15 L7
  SNWD SE25 ....45 P5
St Edmunds Cl
  CRAWW RH11 ....176 C2
St Edmund's La WHTN TW2 ....25 J3
St Edmunds Sq BARN SW13 ...18 C4
St Edwards Cl CROY/NA CRO ..65 K9
  EGRIN RH19 ....180 B3
St Elizabeth Dr EPSOM KT18 ...78 A3
St Faith's Rd DUL SE21 ....30 C4
St Francis Gdns
  CRAWE RH10...............160 D8
St George Av
  WOKS/MYFD GU22 ....91 H2
St Georges HORL RH6 * 159 L2
St George's Cl FNM GU9 * ...108 D8
  HORL RH6...................159 L1
  WEY KT13 ....56 E4
St Georges Cl CRAWW RH11...176 C4
  E/WMO/HCT KT8............40 D5
  EGRIN RH19 ....180 D1
St Georges Gdns EW KT17 ....78 D3
  HORS RH12.................192 D6
  SURB KT6 ....59 P1
St Georges Gv TOOT SW17 ...28 G6
St George's La ASC SL5 ......34 B4
St Georges Ms CHSWK W4 *...18 A4
  FNM GU9 ....5 F2
St Georges Pde CAT SE6 *....31 N5
St Georges Rd
  ADL/WDHM KT15............55 N3
  ASHV GU12 ....108 D5
  BECK BR3 ....47 H2
  CBLY GU15 ....68 F2
  FELT TW15 ....24 E7
  FNM GU9 ....5 J5
  FNM GU9 ....108 D8
  KUTN/CMB KT2 ....9 H1
  MTCM CR4 ....44 D4
  RCH/KEW TW9 ....17 N9
  REDH RH1 ....140 F4
  TWK TW1 ....26 A1
  WEY KT13 ....56 F5
  WIM/MER SW19 ....28 C9
  WLGTN SM6 ....62 D4
St Georges Sq NWMAL KT3 *...42 C4
St Georges Cv CROY/NA CRO...2 D4
St Gerards Cl CLAP SW4 ......29 M1
St German's Rd FSTH SE23 ...31 M4
St Gothard Rd WNWD SE27 ....30 E7
St Helena Ter
  RCH/KEW TW9 ....26 C1
St Helens THDIT KT7 * 40 E8
St Helens Crs SHST GU47 ....49 M9

  STRHM/NOR SW16 ....45 H2
St Helen's Rd
  STRHM/NOR SW16 ....45 H3
St Helier Av MRDN SM4 ....43 K5
St Helier Cl CRAWW RH11 ....176 D9
St Heliers Av HSLWW TW4 ....25 H1
St Hilda's Av ASHF TW15 .....23 H8
St Hilda's Cl CRAWE RH10 *..177 M2
  HORL RH6 ....159 L1
  TOOT SW17 ....29 H5
St Hilda's Rd BARN SW13 ....18 F4
Saint Hill Rd EGRIN RH19 ...180 A5
St Hughes Cl TOOT SW17 *....29 H5
St Hugh's Cl CRAWE RH10 ...177 M2
St Ives CRAWE RH10 * 177 M2
St James Av EW KT17 ....60 D9
  FNM GU9 ....127 P1
  SUT SM1 ....61 L4
St James Cl EPSOM KT18 .....78 C3
  NWMAL KT3 ....42 D6
  WOKN/KNAP GU21 ....71 N7
St James Ga ASC SL5 ....34 F8
St James Ms WEY KT13 ....56 D5
St James Pl CRAWE RH10 * ...177 M2
  CTHM CR3 ....102 A2
St James Rd CAR SM5 ....62 A2
  CRAWE RH10................176 E2
  EWKG RG40 ....48 C1
  FLEETN GU51 ....86 E7
  KUT/HW KT1 ....8 C4
  MTCM CR4 ....44 C1
  PUR/KEN CR8 ....63 K7
  SURB KT6 ....41 K7
  SUT SM1 ....61 L4
St James's Av BECK BR3 .....46 E4
  HPTN TW12 ....25 K8
St James's Cl TOOT SW17 * ...29 K8
  FNM GU9 ....127 P1
St James's Dr BAL SW12 .....29 J4
St James's Pl CRAN GU6 ....152 F9
St James's Rd CRAWE RH10 ...45 L8
  CROY/NA CRO 45 L8
  HPTN TW12 ....25 K8
St James's Rw CHSGTN KT9 *..59 K5
St James St HMSMTH W6 .....18 G3
St James Ter BAL SW12 ......29 K4
St Joan Cl CRAWW RH11 .....176 G2
St John Cl FUL/PGN SW6 * 19 L5
  SWTR RH13 ....192 D9
St John's RDKG RH5 ....137 J2
St Johns Av EW KT17 ....78 D1
  LHD/OX KT22 ....97 H1
  PUT/ROE SW15 ....28 A1
St Johns Church Rd
  RDKG RH5 ....135 P1
St Johns Cl BH/WHM TN16 * ...84 F4
  FUL/PGN SW6 * 19 L5
  LHD/OX KT22 ....97 H1
St Johns Cl ECH TW20 ....21 M8
  FARN GU14 * 87 P2
  GDST RH9 * 122 F9
  ISLW TW7 ....16 E3
St John's Crs HORS RH12 ...191 M7
St John's Dr
  WAND/EARL SW18 ....28 E4
  WOT/HER KT12 ....39 L9
St Johns Gv BARN SW13 * 18 D7
  FNM GU9 ....127 M6
  RCH/KEW TW9 * 17 L9
St John's Hl COUL/CHIP CR5...81 J6
St John's Hill Gv BTSEA SW11...19 P9
St John's Hill Rd
  WOKN/KNAP GU21 ....71 N8
St John's Lye (Festival Path)
  WOKN/KNAP GU21 ....71 M8
St John's Meadow LING RH7...142 D5
St Johns Ms
  WOKN/KNAP GU21 ....71 N7
St Johns Ri BH/WHM TN16 * ...84 F5
  WOKN/KNAP GU21 ....71 P8
St John's Rd ASC SL5 ....33 P1
  CAR SM5 ....62 A2
  CRAWW RH11 ....176 F5
  CROY/NA CRO 2 B5
  DORK RH4 ....116 C8
  E/WMO/HCT KT8.............40 D5
  EGRIN RH19 ....180 D5
  FARN GU14 ....88 A3
  FELT TW13 ....24 G7
  FNM GU9 ....108 A8
  GUW GU2 ....111 M6
  ISLW TW7 ....16 F7
  KUT/HW KT1 ....8 C2
  LHD/OX KT22 ....97 J1
  NWDGN UB2 ....15 N1
  NWMAL KT3 ....42 A1
  PGE/AN SE20 ....46 C1
  RCH/KEW TW9 ....17 L9
  REDH RH1 ....120 B7
  SHST GU47 ....67 M1
  SUT SM1 ....61 L1
  WIM/MER SW19 ....28 B8
  WOKN/KNAP GU21 ....71 N8
St John's St GODL GU7 .....131 M7
St John's Terrace Rd
  REDH RH1 ....120 B7
St John's Vls KENS W8 ....19 M1
St John's Wy CHERT KT16 .....55 L1
  EDEN TN8 ....144 F2
St Joseph's Rd ASHV GU12...108 C5
St Jude's Cl ECH TW20 ....21 H8
St Jude's Rd
  STRHM/NOR SW16 * 30 B7
St Julian's Farm Rd
  WNWD SE27 ....30 B7
St Katharines Rd CTHM CR3 ..102 A5
St Kitts Ter NRWD SE19 ......30 F8
St Lawrence Wy CTHM CR3 ...101 M3
St Leonards Dr CRAWE RH10..177 K8

St Leonard's Gdns HEST TW5...15 N5
St Leonard's Rd CROY/NA CRO...2 A6
  EPSOM KT18 ....78 C8
  ESH/CLAY KT10 ....58 F5
  MORT/ESHN SW14 ....18 A8
  SURB KT6 ....41 K6
  SWTR RH13 ....192 D9
  THDIT KT7 ....40 G7
St Leonards Wk
  DTCH/LGLY SL3 ....13 K1
  STRHM/NOR SW16 ....45 H1
St Louis Rd WNWD SE27 ......30 D7
St Luke's Cl SNWD SE25 .....46 B7
St Lukes Ct
  WOKN/KNAP GU21 * 72 C3
St Luke's Rd CTHM CR3 ......81 P7
  WDSR SL4 ....20 F2
St Luke's Sq GU GU1 ....7 J5
St Margaret's GU GU1 ....7 J1
St Margarets Av ASHF TW15...23 J8
  BH/WHM TN16 * 84 F5
  CHEAM SM3 ....61 H4
  EGRIN RH19 ....162 D6
St Margarets Ct
  PUT/ROE SW15 * 18 F9
St Margarets Crs
  PUT/ROE SW15 * 27 N1
St Margarets Dr EPSOM KT18...78 B3
  TWK TW1 ....25 P2
St Margaret's Gv TWK TW1 ....25 P2
St Margarets La KENS W8 *....19 M1
St Margarets Ms
  KUTN/CMB KT2 * 27 H8
St Margaret's Rd
  COUL/CHIP CR5 ....100 D1
  EGRIN RH19 ....162 E9
  TWK TW1 ....17 H9
St Mark Av CHOB/PIR GU24 ...91 H3
St Marks Cl FARN GU14 ......88 E6
  FUL/PGN SW6 * 19 L6
St Mark's Gv WBPTN SW10 ...19 M5
St Mark's Hl SURB KT6 ....41 L7
St Mark's La HORS RH12 ....192 D4
St Marks Pl FNM GU9 * 107 M7
  WIM/MER SW19 * 28 C9
St Marks Rd EPSOM KT18 ....78 C7
  HAYES BR2 ....47 P4
  MTCM CR4 ....44 C3
  SNWD SE25 ....46 A5
  TEDD TW11 ....41 H1
St Martha's Av
  WOKS/MYFD GU22 ....92 D1
St Marthas Ct RGUE GU4 ....132 F2
St Martin's Av EPSOM KT18 ...78 C3
St Martins Cl EHSLY KT24 ....94 G9
  EW KT17 * 78 D2
  WDR/YW UB7 ....13 N1
St Martin's La ASHF TW15 ....22 F8
St Martins Dr WOT/HER KT12...57 L2
St Martin's La BECK BR5 .....47 H6
St Martins Meadow
  BH/WHM TN16 ....105 N3
St Martins Ms DORK RH4 ....116 C7
  WOKS/MYFD GU22 ....73 L5
St Martin's Wy TOOT SW17 ...28 F6
St Mary Abbot's Pl KENS W8...19 K1
St Mary Abbots Ter
  WKENS W14 * 19 K1
St Mary Av WLGTN SM6 ......62 C2
St Mary's Ct * 56 F2
St Mary's Av HAYES BR2 ......47 L6
  NWDGN UB2 ....16 B2
  STWL/WRAY TW19 ....22 C3
  TEDD TW11 ....25 N9
St Mary's Cl CHSGTN KT9 ....59 M6
  EW KT17 ....60 D6
  LHD/OX KT22 ....96 C3
  OXTED RH8 ....103 L9
  SHST GU47 ....49 N9
  SUN TW16 ....39 H5
St Mary's Crs ISLW TW7 ......16 D5
St Mary's Dr CRAWE RH10 * ...23 M3
  EBED/NFELT TW14 ....23 M3
  HORS RH12 ....192 D6
St Mary's Ga KENS W8 * 19 M1
St Mary's Gv BARN SW13 .....18 F8
  BH/WHM TN16 ....84 A7
  CHSWK W4 ....18 A3
  RCH/KEW TW9 ....17 M9
St Mary's Hl ASC SL5 ....34 B7
St Mary's Mt CTHM CR3 .....101 P4
St Mary's Pl KENS W8 * 19 M1
St Mary's Rd ASC SL5 ....34 B7
  ASHV GU12 ....108 D5
  CBLY GU15 ....68 D2
  E/WMO/HCT KT8.............40 C6
  LHD/OX KT22 ....97 H2
  REIG RH2 ....119 M6
  SAND/SEL CR2 ....63 M8
  SNWD SE25 ....45 N4
  WEY KT13 ....56 F3
  WIM/MER SW19 ....28 B8
  WOKN/KNAP GU21 ....71 M8
  WPK KT4 ....60 C1
St Marys Ter GU GU1 * 6 E6
St Marys Wy GUW GU2 ......111 N6
St Matthew's Av SURB KT6 ...41 L9
St Matthew's Rd
  BRXS/STRHM SW2...........30 A1
  REDH RH1 ....120 B4
St Maur Rd FUL/PGN SW6 ....19 K6
St Michael's Av RGUW GU3 ...91 J9
St Michaels Cl FLEETN GU51...87 J7
  WOT/HER KT12 ....57 L1
St Michaels Rd ASHF TW15 ...23 K8
  ASHV GU12 ....108 D5

CBLY GU15 * 68 D3
CROY/NA CRO 2 A2
CTHM CR3 ....101 M2
EGRIN RH19 ....180 D1
FARN GU14 ....88 D1
WLGTN SM6 ....62 E5
WOKN/KNAP GU21 ....73 H3
St Mildred's Rd CAT SE6 ....112 D4
St Monica's Rd
  KWD/TDW/WH KT20 ....99 K1
St Nazaire Cl EGH TW20 * 21 P8
St Nicholas Av GT/LBKH KT23...96 B5
St Nicholas Cl FLEETN GU51 ...86 F6
St Nicholas Crs
  WOKS/MYFD GU22 ....73 L5
St Nicholas Dr SHPTN TW17 ...38 C8
St Nicholas Glebe TOOT SW17...29 K9
St Nicholas Hl LHD/OX KT22 ...97 H2
  THDIT KT7 ....40 F7
St Nicholas Wy SUT SM1 .....61 M3
St Nicolas Av CRAN GU6 ....153 H9
St Nicolas Cl CRAN GU6 ....153 H9
St Normans Wy EW KT17 .....60 E8
St Olaf's Rd FUL/PGN SW6 ...19 J5
St Olave's Cl STA TW18 ......37 K1
St Olave's Wk
  STRHM/NOR SW16 ....44 E3
St Omer Barracks
  ALDT GU11 ....108 F1
St Omer Rdg GU GU1 ....112 C6
St Omer Rd GU GU1 ....112 E6
St Oswald's Rd
  STRHM/NOR SW16 ....45 K2
St Pauls Cl ADL/WDHM KT15...55 L3
  ASHF TW15 ....23 M8
  CAR SM5 ....44 A8
  CHSGTN KT9 ....59 K3
  HSLW TW3 ....15 N7
  HYS/HAR UB3 ....14 F3
St Pauls Ms DORK RH4 .....117 H8
St Pauls Rd RCH/KEW TW9 ...17 M8
  STA TW18 ....22 A8
  THHTH CR7 ....45 L4
  WOKS/MYFD GU22 ....11 H3
St Paul's Rd East DORK RH4...117 H8
St Paul's Rd West DORK RH4..116 G8
St Peters CHERT KT16 * 54 C2
St Peters Cl BAL SW12 ....29 L3
  STA TW18 ....22 C9
  TOOT SW17 ....29 H5
  WDSR SL4 ....20 F1
St Peters Gdns RFNM GU10..127 K7
  WNWD SE27 ....30 B6
  YTLY GU46 ....67 H2
St Peter's Gv HMSMTH W6 ...18 E2
St Peter's Md ASHV GU12 ...109 K4
St Peter's Pk ALDT GU11 ...108 A6
St Peter's Rd CRAWW RH11 ...176 C6
  CROY/NA CRO 2 E7
  E/WMO/HCT KT8.............40 A5
  HMSMTH W6 ....18 E3
  KUT/HW KT1 ....9 H5
  TWK TW1 ....26 A1
  WOKS/MYFD GU22 ....92 F1
St Peter's Sq HMSMTH W6 ...18 E2
  SAND/SEL CR2 ....63 M4
St Peter's Vw HMSMTH W6 ...18 E2
St Peter's Vls HMSMTH W6 ...18 E2
St Peter's Wy CHERT KT16 ...55 J3
  FRIM GU16 ....69 H9
  HYS/HAR UB3 ....14 F3
St Philip's Av WPK KT4 ......60 F1
St Philip's Rd SURB KT6 .....41 K7
St Pier's La LING RH7 ......162 E1
St Pinnock Av STA TW18 .....37 L1
St Richards Wk
  CRAWE RH10 * 177 J5
St Sampson Rd
  CRAWW RH11 ....176 C9
St Saviour Av
  CHOB/PIR GU24 ....91 H1
St Saviour's Pl GU GU1 * 6 D3
St Saviour's Rd
  BRXS/STRHM SW2...........30 A1
  CROY/NA CRO 45 L7
Saints Cl WNWD SE27 ....30 C7
St Sebastian's Cl EWKG RG40...49 J1
St Simon's Av PUT/ROE SW15...27 P1
St Stephens Av ASHTD KT21...77 L6
St Stephens Cl ASHV GU12 ...184 D3
St Stephens Ct GDST RH9 ...122 E9
St Stephen's Crs THHTH CR7...45 J4
St Stephen's Gdns TWK TW1 ...26 B2
St Stephen's Rd HSLW TW3 ...25 H2
St Stephen's Wk
  SKENS SW7 * 19 N2
St Swithun's Cl
  EGRIN RH19 * 180 E2
St Theresa Cl EPSOM KT18 ...78 A3
St Theresa's Rd
  EBED/NFELT TW14 ....15 H9
St Thomas Cl SURB KT6 .....41 M8
  WOKN/KNAP GU21 ....72 A6
St Thomas' Rd CHSWK W4 ....18 A5
St Thomas's Rd GU GU1 * 7 J6
St Thomas's Wy
  FUL/PGN SW6 ....19 K5
St Thomas Wk
  DTCH/LGLY SL3 ....13 H5
St Vincent Cl CRAWE RH10 ..177 N6
  WNWD SE27 ....30 C8
St Vincent Rd WHTN TW2 ....25 K2
  WOT/HER KT12 ....57 K2
St Winifred's Rd
  BH/WHM TN16 ....84 D7
  TEDD TW11 ....26 A9

Salamanca CWTH RG45 .... 49 J4
Salamander CI
 KUTN/CMB KT2 .... 26 B8
Salamander Quay
 KUT/HW KT1 * 8 B3
Salbrook Rd REDH RH1 .... 140 C4
Salcombe Dr MRDN SM4 .... 43 H9
Salcombe Rd ASHF TW15 .... 17 J7
Salcot Crs CROY/NA CRO 65 J8
Salcott Rd BTSEA SW11 .... 29 J1
 CROY/NA CRO 62 C2
Salehurst Rd BROCKY SE4 .... 31 N2
 CRAWE RH10 .... 177 P5
Salem PI CROY/NA CRO 2 B6
Salerno CI ALDT GU11 .... 108 C4
Salesian Vw FARN GU14 .... 88 C7
Salford Rd BRXS/STRHM SW2 .... 29 N4
Salisbury Av BARN SW13 .... 61 K5
Salisbury CI WPK KT4 .... 60 D2
Salisbury Gdns
 WIM/MER SW19 * 43 J1
Salisbury Gv FRIM GU16 .... 89 J4
Salisbury Pavement
 FUL/PGN SW6 * 19 L5
Salisbury PI BF/WBF KT14 .... 55 N9
Salisbury Rd ASHV GU12 .... 109 J4
 BLKW GU17 .... 67 N5
 BNSTD SM7 .... 79 M4
 CAR SM5 .... 62 B5
 CRAWE RH10 .... 177 J9
 FARN GU14 .... 88 E3
 FELT TW13 .... 24 D4
 GDST RH9 .... 122 C2
 HSLWW TW4 .... 15 L8
 NWDGN UB2 .... 15 N2
 NWMAL KT3 .... 42 A5
 RCH/KEW TW9 .... 17 L9
 SNWD SE25 .... 46 A7
 WIM/MER SW19 .... 43 J1
 WOKS/MYFD GU22 .... 72 C8
 WPK KT4 .... 60 B3
Salisbury Ter FRIM GU16 .... 89 J4
Salix CI GT/LBKH KT23 .... 96 B5
 SUN TW16 .... 39 K1
Salmons La CTHM CR3 .... 81 N9
Salmons La West CTHM CR3 .... 81 N9
Salmons Rd CHSGTN KT9 .... 59 L5
 EHSLY KT24 .... 95 L9
Saltash CI SUT SM1 .... 61 K3
Saltbox HI BH/WHM TN16 .... 83 P2
Salt Box Rd RGUW GU3 .... 91 N9
Saltdean CI CRAWE RH10 .... 176 G8
Salterford Rd TOOT SW17 .... 29 K9
Salterns Rd CRAWE RH10 .... 177 M8
Salter's HI NRWD SE19 .... 30 E8
Saltire Gdns BNFD RG42 .... 32 C2
Salt La MFD/CHID GU8 .... 150 C6
Saltram Rd FARN GU14 .... 88 C5
Salvador TOOT SW17 .... 29 K8
Salvation PI LHD/OX KT22 .... 96 C4
Salvington Rd CRAWW RH11 ... 176 C8
Salvin Rd PUT/ROE SW15 .... 19 H8
Salwey CI BRAK RG12 .... 32 D7
Samaritan CI CRAWW RH11 .... 176 B7
Samarkand CI CBLY GU15 .... 69 K4
Sameis Ct HMSMTH W6 .... 18 E5
Samian PI BNFD RG42 .... 32 A1
Samos Rd PGE/AN SE20 .... 46 B3
Samphire CI CRAWW RH11 .... 176 D8
Sampleoak La RGUE GU4 .... 133 L7
Samuel Gray Gdns
 KUTN/CMB KT2 .... 8 C2
San Carlos Ap ALDT GU11 .... 108 E4
Sanctuary Rd HTHAIR TW6 .... 23 K2
Sandal Rd NWMAL KT3 .... 42 C5
Sandalwood GUW GU2 .... 6 A5
Sandalwood Av CHERT KT16 .... 55 H2
Sandalwood Rd FELT TW13 .... 24 C6
Sandbourne Av
 WIM/MER SW19 .... 43 M4
Sandcross La REIG RH2 .... 119 K8
Sandell's Av ASHF TW15 .... 23 M7
Sanders CI HPTN TW12 .... 25 K8
Sandersfield Rd BNSTD SM7 ..... 79 L4
Sanders Pde
 STRHM/NOR SW16 * 29 P9
Sanderstead CI BAL SW12 .... 29 M3
Sanderstead Court Av
 SAND/SEL CR2 .... 82 A2
Sanderstead HI
 SAND/SEL CR2 .... 63 N9
Sanderstead Rd
 SAND/SEL CR2 .... 63 N8
Sandes PI LHD/OX KT22 .... 76 C7
Sandfield Ct GU GU1 .... 6 E4
Sandfield Gdns THHTH CR7 .... 45 K4
Sandfield PI THHTH CR7 .... 45 L4
Sandfield Rd THHTH CR7 .... 45 K4
Sandfields REIG RH2 .... 119 L4
Sandfields Rd RPLY/SEND GU23 .. 93 H4
Sandfield Ter GU GU1 .... 6 E4
Sandford Ct ALDT GU11 .... 108 B5
Sandford Down BRAK RG12 .... 33 H6
Sandford Rd ALDT GU11 .... 108 B5
 FNM GU9 .... 107 M7
 HAYES BR2 .... 47 N5
Sandford St FUL/PGN SW6 .... 19 M6
Sandgate La
 WAND/EARL SW18 .... 29 H4
Sandhawes HI EGRIN RH19 .... 162 F8
Sandheath Rd GSHT GU26 .... 165 M4
Sandhi HI FARN GU14 .... 68 D9
Sandhills CI VW GU25 .... 36 C6
Sandhills La VW GU25 .... 36 C6
Sandhills Rd REIG RH2 .... 119 L7
The Sandhills WBPTN SW10 * .. 19 N4
Sandhurst Av BRYLDS KT5 .... 41 N8
Sandhurst La BLKW GU17 .... 67 M2
Sandhurst La CWTH RG45 .... 49 M6
 EWKG RG40 .... 48 F1
 YTLY GU46 .... 67 J2

Sandhurst Wy SAND/SEL CR2 ... 63 N6
Sandiford Rd CHEAM SM3 .... 61 K1
Sandiland Crs HAYES BR2 .... 65 M1
Sandilands CROY/NA CRO 64 D3
Sandilands Rd FUL/PGN SW6 ... 19 M6
Sandlands Gv
 KWD/TDW/WH KT20 .... 98 E3
Sandlands Rd
 KWD/TDW/WH KT20 .... 98 E3
Sandmartin Wy WLGTN SM6 .... 44 C9
Sandon CI ESH/CLAY KT10 .... 40 E8
Sandow Crs HYS/HAR UB3 .... 15 H1
Sandown Av ESH/CLAY KT10 .... 58 C4
Sandown Ct BLKW GU17 .... 67 P5
 HEST TW5 .... 15 J6
Sandown Ct BELMT SM2 * 61 M7
 SYD SE26 * 31 J6
Sandown Dr CAR SM5 .... 62 C7
 FRIM GU16 .... 68 F6
Sandown Ga ESH/CLAY KT10 ... 58 D1
Sandown Rd COUL/CHIP CR5 .. 80 C1
 ESH/CLAY KT10 .... 58 C5
 SNWD SE25 .... 46 B6
Sandpiper CI CRAWW RH11 .... 176 A7
Sandpiper Rd SAND/SEL CR2 ... 64 D9
 SUT SM1 .... 61 K4
Sandpit Hall Rd
 CHOB/PIR GU24 .... 71 N1
Sandpit Heath RGUW GU3 ...... 111 K1
Sandpit Rd REDH RH1 .... 120 A6
Sandpits Rd CROY/NA CRO 64 D3
 RCHPK/HAM TW10 .... 26 C5
Sandra CI HSLW TW3 .... 25 J1
Sandringham Av
 RYNPK SW20 .... 43 J2
Sandringham CI
 WIM/MER SW19 * 28 A4
 WOKS/MYFD GU22 .... 73 L5
Sandringham Dr ASHF TW15 ... 22 G7
Sandringham Gdns
 E/WMO/HCT KT8 .... 40 A5
 HEST TW5 .... 15 J6
Sandringham Ms HPTN TW12 .. 39 P2
Sandringham Pk COB KT11 ..... 75 P1
Sandringham Rd
 CRAWW RH11 .... 176 E9
 HTHAIR TW6 .... 23 H1
 THHTH CR7 .... 45 L6
 WPK KT4 .... 60 D2
Sandringham Wy FRIM GU16 ... 69 H8
Sandrock HASM GU27 .... 184 D4
Sandrock Hill Rd
 RFNM GU10 .... 127 K7
Sandrock PI CROY/NA CRO 64 D3
Sandrock Rd DORK RH4 .... 116 B9
Sandroyd Wy COB KT11 .... 76 A2
Sands CI RFNM GU10 .... 128 F3
Sands End La FUL/PGN SW6 ... 19 M6
Sands Rd RFNM GU10 .... 128 E3
Sandy CI WOKS/MYFD GU22 ... 72 G6
Sandycombe Rd
 EBED/NFELT TW14 .... 24 B4
 RCH/KEW TW9 .... 17 N7
Sandycoombe Rd TWK TW1 ... 26 B2
Sandy Ct COB KT11 .... 75 P2
Sandy Cft EW KT17 .... 60 G8
Sandy Dr COB KT11 .... 58 A9
 EBED/NFELT TW14 .... 23 P4
Sandy Hill Rd FNM GU9 .... 107 L7
 WLGTN SM6 .... 62 E7
Sandy Holt COB KT11 .... 75 P2
Sandy La ASC SL5 .... 33 L2
 ASC SL5 .... 34 E3
 BELMT SM2 .... 61 J7
 BH/WHM TN16 .... 105 H5
 BRAK RG12 .... 32 E2
 BRKHM/BTCW RH3 .... 118 C5
 CBLY GU15 .... 68 G2
 COB KT11 .... 53 L7
 COB KT11 .... 76 B2
 CRAWE RH10 .... 179 H3
 EGRIN RH19 .... 180 D2
 FARN GU14 .... 87 N1
 FLEETS GU52 .... 106 G2
 GODL GU7 .... 131 K7
 HASM GU27 .... 183 M5
 HASM GU27 .... 184 D4
 KWD/TDW/WH KT20 .... 99 L3
 MTCM CR4 .... 44 C2
 OXTED RH8 .... 103 J9
 OXTED RH8 .... 103 P7
 RCHPK/HAM TW10 .... 26 B5
 REDH RH1 .... 140 F3
 RFNM GU10 .... 146 F5
 RGUW GU3 .... 131 N1
 RPLY/SEND GU23 .... 92 G3
 SHGR GU5 .... 133 J5
 SHST GU47 .... 49 K8
 TEDD TW11 .... 40 G4
 VW GU25 .... 36 C6
 WOKS/MYFD GU22 .... 73 L5
 WOT/HER KT12 .... 39 K7
Sandy La North WLGTN SM6 ... 62 F4
Sandy La South WLGTN SM6 ... 62 E7
Sandy Md HOR/WEW KT19 ..... 59 N7
Sandy Wy CROY/NA CRO 64 G2
Sandy Wy COB KT11 .... 76 A1
 CROY/NA CRO 64 F2
 WOKS/MYFD GU22 .... 72 G6
 WOT/HER KT12 .... 39 H9
San Feliu Ct EGRIN RH19 .... 180 G1
Sanger Av CHSGTN KT9 .... 59 M4
Sanger Dr RPLY/SEND GU23 ... 92 G2
Sangers Dr HORL RH6 .... 159 J2
Sangley Rd SNWD SE25 .... 45 N5
Sangora Rd BTSEA SW11 .... 19 P9
Sankey La FLEETN GU51 .... 87 K3
Santina CI FNM GU9 .... 107 P2
Santos Rd WAND/EARL SW18 .. 28 D1

Sanway CI BF/WBF KT14 .... 74 A3
Sanway Rd BF/WBF KT14 .... 74 A3
Sappho CI WOKN/KNAP GU21 .. 71 L5
Sapte CI CRAN GU6 .... 153 K9
Saracen CI CROY/NA CRO 45 M7
Sarah Wy FARN GU14 .... 88 D3
Sarel Wy HORL RH6 .... 140 D8
Sargent CI CRAWW RH10 .... 177 J9
 HEST TW5 .... 16 A5
Sark CI CRAWW RH11 .... 176 D9
 HEST TW5 .... 16 A5
Sarsby Dr STWL/WRAY TW19 .. 21 M5
Sarsen Av HSLW TW3 .... 15 P5
Sarsfeld Rd BAL SW12 .... 29 J4
Sarum BRAK RG12 .... 32 A9
Sarum Gn WEY KT13 .... 56 G2
Saturn CI CRAWW RH11 .... 176 B7
Saunders Copse
 WOKS/MYFD GU22 .... 91 P2
Saunders La
 WOKS/MYFD GU22 .... 91 M2
Saunton Av HYS/HAR UB3 .... 15 H5
Saunton Gdns FARN GU14 ...... 88 A2
Savernake Wk CRAWE RH10 ... 177 J8
Savernake Wy BRAK RG12 ..... 33 H7
Savery Dr SURB KT6 .... 41 J8
Savile CI NWMAL KT3 .... 42 C6
 THDIT KT7 .... 40 F8
Savile Gdns CROY/NA CRO 3 K4
Savile Crs ASHF TW15 .... 23 M8
Saville Gdns CBLY GU15 .... 69 K3
Saville Rd CHSWK W4 .... 18 B1
 TWK TW1 .... 25 N4
Savill Rw HAYES BR2 .... 47 M9
Savill Gdns RYNPK SW20 .... 42 E4
Savill Ms EGH TW20 .... 21 J9
Savona CI WIM/MER SW19 .... 43 H1
Savoy Av HYS/HAR UB3 .... 14 G3
Savoy Gv BLKW GU17 .... 67 P5
Sawkins CI WIM/MER SW19 .... 28 A4
Sawyer's HI
 HAM TW10 .... 26 E3
Saxby Rd BRXS/STRHM SW2 ... 29 P5
Saxby's La LING RH7 .... 143 L8
Saxley HORL RH6 .... 140 E9
Saxon Av FELT TW13 .... 24 C5
Saxonbury Av SUN TW16 .... 39 K4
Saxonbury CI MTCM CR4 .... 43 P4
Saxon Crs HORS RH12 .... 192 A6
 RFNM GU10 .... 128 B6
Saxon Cft FNM GU9 .... 5 C5
Saxon Dr BNFD RG42 .... 33 H2
Saxonfield CI
 BRXS/STRHM SW2 .... 30 A1
Saxon HI BH/WHM TN16 * 105 H6
Saxon Rd ASHF TW15 .... 23 N9
 BMLY BR1 .... 47 N1
 CRAWE RH10 .... 177 P6
 KUTN/CMB KT2 .... 8 G7
 SNWD SE25 .... 45 M6
 WOT/HER KT12 .... 57 M2
Saxons KWD/TDW/WH KT20 .. 99 H1
Saxon Wy REIG RH2 .... 119 M8
 WDR/YW UB7 .... 13 M4
 WDSR SL4 .... 20 C2
Saxony Wy YTLY GU46 * 66 C4
Sayers CI FRIM GU16 .... 68 G9
 LHD/OX KT22 .... 96 C4
 SWTR RH13 .... 192 D8
The Sayers EGRIN RH19 .... 180 B2
Sayes Ct ALDT GU11 .... 108 G5
Sayes Court Farm Dr
 ADL/WDHM KT15 .... 55 M4
Sbac Tr ALDT GU11 .... 88 A9
Scallows CI CRAWE RH10 ...... 177 K4
Scallows Rd CRAWE RH10 ..... 177 K4
Scampton Rd
 STWL/WRAY TW19 .... 23 J2
Scarborough CI BELMT SM2 ... 61 K9
 BH/WHM TN16 .... 84 A7
Scarborough Rd HTHAIR TW6 .. 23 M2
Scarbrook Rd CROY/NA CRO ... 2 C5
Scarlet Oaks CBLY GU15 .... 68 G5
Scarlett CI WOKN/KNAP GU21 .. 71 M7
Scarlett's Rd ALDT GU11 .... 108 C3
Scarsdale PI KENS W8 .... 19 L1
Scarsdale Vls KENS W8 .... 19 L1
Scarth Rd BARN SW13 .... 18 D8
Scawen CI CAR SM5 .... 62 C3
Scholars Rd BAL SW12 .... 29 M4
Scholars Wk CHOB/PIR GU24 ... 6 B4
School CI CHOB/PIR GU24 ..... 70 F4
 GU GU1 .... 112 B5
 HORS RH12 .... 192 F4
School Fld EDEN TN8 .... 144 G3
School HI CWTH RG45 .... 49 P5
 HORS RH12 .... 191 N2
 REDH RH1 .... 100 E8
 RFNM GU10 .... 129 K7
 RFNM GU10 .... 129 K1
 SHST GU47 .... 49 L8
School House La TEDD TW11 .. 41 H1
School La ADL/WDHM KT15 .... 55 L3
 ASC SL5 .... 33 M2
 BAGS GU19 .... 51 M7
 BFOR GU20 .... 52 D5
 CHOB/PIR GU24 .... 70 E2
 DORK RH4 .... 116 D8
 EGH TW20 .... 21 M8
 EGRIN RH19 .... 181 J5
 EHSLY KT24 .... 94 D9
 FROW RH18 .... 181 L9
 KUT/HW KT1 .... 8 A3
 LHD/OX KT22 .... 76 C1
 MFD/CHID GU8 .... 130 D7
 MFD/CHID GU8 .... 168 A7
 RDKG RH5 .... 97 J7
 RFNM GU10 .... 126 B8
 RFNM GU10 .... 127 P7
 RGUE GU4 .... 114 A2

 RGUW GU3 .... 109 P2
 RGUW GU3 .... 130 C1
 RPLY/SEND GU23 .... 94 D2
 SHPTN TW17 .... 38 D7
 SURB KT6 .... 41 N9
 YTLY GU46 .... 66 F2
School Meadow GUW GU2 .... 111 L4
School Pas KUT/HW KT1 * 9 D5
School Rd ASC SL5 .... 34 D6
 ASHF TW15 .... 23 L9
 BFOR GU20 .... 52 B4
 E/WMO/HCT KT8 .... 40 D5
 GSHT GU26 .... 165 L8
 HASM GU27 .... 184 D5
 HPTN TW12 .... 25 K9
 HSLW TW3 .... 16 C8
 KUT/HW KT1 .... 8 A3
 RFNM GU10 .... 146 B1
 WDR/YW UB7 .... 13 P4
School Road Av HPTN TW12 ... 25 K9
Schroder Ct EGH TW20 .... 20 G8
Schubert Rd PUT/ROE SW15 ... 28 C1
Scillonian Rd GUW GU2 .... 111 N7
Scizdons Climb GODL GU7 .... 131 M9
Scoles Crs BRXS/STRHM SW2 .. 30 B4
Scope Wy KUT/HW KT1 .... 41 L5
Scords La BH/WHM TN16 ...... 125 N5
Scory CI CRAWW RH11 .... 176 D8
Scotia Rd BRXS/STRHM SW2 ... 30 B3
Scotland Bridge Rd
 ADL/WDHM KT15 .... 55 L9
Scotland CI ASHV GU12 .... 109 J1
Scotland Farm Rd
 ASHV GU12 .... 109 J1
Scotland HI SHST GU47 .... 49 L9
Scotland La HASM GU27 .... 184 E6
Scotlands CI HASM GU27 ...... 184 C5
Scotlands Dr HASM GU27 ..... 184 C5
Scots CI STWL/WRAY TW19 ... 22 G4
Scotsdale CI CHEAM SM3 ...... 61 J6
Scotshall La WARL CR6 .... 83 J4
Scott CI GUW GU2 .... 111 N3
 HOR/WEW KT19 .... 60 B6
 STRHM/NOR SW16 .... 45 H2
 WDR/YW UB7 .... 14 B2
Scott Farm CI THDIT KT7 .... 41 H9
Scott Gdns HEST TW5 .... 15 M5
Scott Rd CRAWE RH10 .... 177 J8
Scotts Av HAYES BR2 .... 47 K3
 SUN TW16 .... 38 G1
Scotts Ct FARN GU14 .... 68 D9
Scotts Dr HPTN TW12 .... 40 B1
Scotts Farm Rd
 HOR/WEW KT19 .... 60 A5
Scott's Grove CI
 CHOB/PIR GU24 .... 71 K2
Scott's Grove Rd
 CHOB/PIR GU24 .... 71 H3
Scott's HI HORL RH6 .... 141 M9
Scott's La HAYES BR2 .... 47 K4
Scotts Ms ASC SL5 .... 33 K2
Scotts Rd BMLY BR1 .... 47 N1
 NWDGN UB2 .... 15 L1
Scotts Wy SUN TW16 .... 38 G1
Scott Ter BRAK RG12 .... 32 G2
Scott Trimmer Wy HSLW TW5 .. 15 N7
Scutari Rd EDUL SE22 .... 31 J1
Scylla Crs HTHAIR TW6 .... 23 L3
Scylla PI WOKN/KNAP GU21 * .. 71 L8
Scylla Rd HTHAIR TW6 .... 23 K3
Seabrook Dr WWKM BR4 .... 65 L1
Seacourt Rd DTCH/LGLY SL3 .. 12 F2
Seafire Wy ALDT GU11 .... 88 A3
Seaford Rd CRAWW RH11 .... 194 D1
 HTHAIR TW6 .... 22 C1
Seaforth Av NWMAL KT3 ..... 42 F6
Seaforth Gdns
 HOR/WEW KT19 .... 60 D3
Sealand Rd HTHAIR TW6 .... 23 K2
Seale La RFNM GU10 .... 128 F1
 RGUW GU3 .... 129 P1
Seale Rd RFNM GU10 .... 129 K5
Seaman's Gn RDKG RH5 ...... 156 C4
Searchwood Rd WARL CR6 .... 82 B7
Searle Hd REIG RH2 .... 119 L7
Searle's Rd ALDT GU11 .... 108 C5
Searle's Vw HORS RH12 .... 192 E5
Seaton CI PUT/ROE SW15 ..... 27 N3
 TWK TW1 .... 25 L2
Seaton Dr ASHF TW15 .... 23 H5
Seaton Rd CBLY GU15 .... 68 D3
 HYS/HAR UB3 .... 14 F7
 MTCM CR4 .... 44 A4
 WHTN TW2 .... 25 K2
Sebastopol Rd ALDT GU11 .... 108 D4
 MFD/CHID GU8 .... 167 L3
Second Av ADL/WDHM KT15 .. 55 M7
 KWD/TDW/WH KT20 * 99 K6
 MORT/ESHN SW14 .... 18 C8
Second CI E/WMO/HCT KT8 ... 40 B5
Second Cross Rd WHTN TW2 .. 25 L5
Seddon Hl BNFD RG42 .... 32 D1
Seddon Rd MRDN SM4 .... 43 P6
Sedgefield CI CRAWE RH10 ... 177 P4
Sedgehill Rd CAT SE6 .... 31 P8
Sedgemoor FARN GU14 .... 68 D9
Sedgewick CI CRAWE RH10 ... 177 M5
Sedgewood CI HAYES BR2 ..... 47 M8
Sedleigh Rd
 WAND/EARL SW18 .... 28 C2
Sedlescombe Rd
 FUL/PGN SW6 .... 19 K4
Seebys Oak SHST GU47 .... 67 P2
Seeley Dr DUL SE21 .... 30 F7
Seely Rd TOOT SW17 .... 29 K9
Seething Wells La SURB KT6 ... 41 J7
Sefton CI CHOB/PIR GU24 .... 70 F2
Sefton Rd CROY/NA CRO 46 A9
 HOR/WEW KT19 .... 60 B8
Sefton St PUT/ROE SW15 ..... 18 G7

Segrave CI WEY KT13 .... 56 C6
Segsbury Gv BRAK RG12 .... 32 G3
Sekhon Ter FELT TW13 .... 25 H6
Selborne Av ALDT GU11 .... 108 E7
Selborne CI BLKW GU17 .... 67 N2
Selborne Gdns FNM GU9 ...... 127 L6
Selborne Rd CROY/NA CRO ... 3 C5
 NWMAL KT3 .... 42 C3
Selbourne Av
 ADL/WDHM KT15 .... 55 M8
 SURB KT6 .... 59 M1
Selbourne CI
 ADL/WDHM KT15 .... 55 M8
 CRAWE RH10 .... 177 N1
Selbourne Rd RGUE GU4 ..... 112 C2
Selbourne Sq GDST RH9 ...... 122 C1
Selby CI CHSGTN KT9 .... 59 L6
Selby Gn CAR SM5 .... 44 A8
Selby Rd ASHF TW15 .... 23 M9
 CAR SM5 .... 44 A8
 PGE/AN SE20 .... 46 A3
Selbys LING RH7 .... 143 L8
Selby Wk WOKN/KNAP GU21 .. 71 P7
Selcroft Rd PUR/KEN CR8 ..... 81 K1
Selham CI CRAWW RH11 ..... 176 D4
Selhurst CI WIM/MER SW19 ... 28 A2
 WOKN/KNAP GU21 .... 72 A6
Selhurst New Rd SNWD SE25 .. 45 N7
Selhurst PI SNWD SE25 .... 45 N7
Selhurst Rd SNWD SE25 .... 45 N6
Selkirk Rd TOOT SW17 .... 29 H7
 WHTN TW2 .... 25 J5
Sellar's HI GODL GU7 .... 131 K6
Sellincourt Rd TOOT SW17 ..... 29 H8
Sellindge CI BECK BR3 .... 46 F1
Sells CI GU GU1 .... 7 K6
Selsdon Av SAND/SEL CR2 .... 63 M5
Selsdon Crs SAND/SEL CR2 .... 64 C8
Selsdon Park Rd
 CROY/NA CRO 64 E4
Selsdon Rd ADL/WDHM KT15 .. 55 L9
 SAND/SEL CR2 .... 63 M4
 WNWD SE27 .... 30 C6
Selsey Rd CRAWW RH11 ..... 176 D9
Selsfield Rd CRAWE RH10 .... 179 J9
Seltops CI CRAN GU6 .... 171 J1
Selwood
 STWL/WRAY TW19 .... 22 F2
Selwood Gdns
 STWL/WRAY TW19 .... 22 F2
Selwood Rd SKENS SW7 .... 19 P3
 CHEAM SM3 .... 43 K9
 CHSGTN KT9 .... 59 K3
 CROY/NA CRO 64 B1
 WOKS/MYFD GU22 .... 72 F9
Selwood Ter SKENS SW7 .... 19 P3
Selworthy Rd CAT SE6 .... 31 N6
Selwyn Av RCH/KEW TW9 .... 17 M8
Selwyn CI CRAWE RH10 ..... 177 M2
 HSLWW TW4 .... 15 N9
Selwyn Dr YTLY GU46 .... 66 F2
Selwyn Rd NWMAL KT3 .... 42 B6
Semaphore Rd GU GU1 .... 7 G7
Semley Rd STRHM/NOR SW16 . 44 G3
Semper CI WOKN/KNAP GU21 .. 71 L6
Send Barns La
 RPLY/SEND GU23 .... 93 J4
Send CI RPLY/SEND GU23 ..... 92 G3
Send HI RPLY/SEND GU23 .... 92 G5
Send Marsh Rd
 RPLY/SEND GU23 .... 93 J3
Send Parade CI
 RPLY/SEND GU23 * 92 G3
Seneca Rd THHTH CR7 .... 45 L5
Senga Rd WLGTN SM6 .... 44 C9
Senhouse Rd CHEAM SM3 .... 61 H1
Sepen Meade FLEETS GU52 ... 106 E2
Sequoia Pk CRAWW RH11 .... 176 D2
Serrin Wy HORS RH12 .... 192 D5
Service Rd HORL RH6 .... 159 K5
Setley Wy BRAK RG12 .... 33 H4
Settrington Rd FUL/PGN SW6 .. 19 M7
The Sett YTLY GU46 .... 66 F3
Seven Acres CAR SM5 .... 62 A1
Seven Arches Ap WEY KT13 .. 56 B6
Seven Hills CI WOT/HER KT12 .. 56 C7
Seven Hills Rd WEY KT13 ..... 56 C6
Seven Hills Rd (South)
 COB KT11 .... 74 G2
Seven Kings Wy
 KUTN/CMB KT2 .... 8 D2
Sevenoaks CI BELMT SM2 .... 61 L8
Sevenoaks Rd BROCKY SE4 .. 31 N2
Seventh Av
 KWD/TDW/WH KT20 * 99 K6
Severn CI SHST GU47 .... 49 N9
Severn Ct RFNM GU10 .... 127 L4
Severn Dr ESH/CLAY KT10 .... 58 G1
 WOT/HER KT12 .... 57 M2
Severn Rd CRAWE RH10 ..... 177 M6
 FARN GU14 .... 88 A1
Seward Rd BECK BR3 .... 46 D3
Sewer's Farm Rd RDKG RH5 .. 135 P7
Sewill CI HORL RH6 .... 158 C5
Seymour Av CTHM CR3 .... 101 L3
 EW KT17 .... 60 C7
 MRDN SM4 .... 43 H8
Seymour CI E/WMO/HCT KT8 .. 40 A6
Seymour Ct COB KT11 * 75 N3
Seymour Dr CBLY GU15 .... 51 M9
Seymour Gdns BRYLDS KT5 ... 41 M6
 FELT TW13 .... 24 C7
 TWK TW1 .... 25 N3
Seymour Ms EW KT17 .... 60 E8
Seymour PI SNWD SE25 .... 46 B5
 WOKS/MYFD GU22 .... 11 H9
Seymour Rd BOR GU35 .... 164 F7
 CAR SM5 .... 62 C4
 CHSWK W4 .... 18 A2

CRAWW RH11........176 D9
E/WMO/HCT KT8........40 C6
GODL GU7........150 A1
HPTN TW12........25 K8
KUT/HW KT1........8 B2
MTCM CR4........44 C8
WAND/EARL SW18........28 C3
WIM/MER SW19........28 A6
Seymour Ter PGE/AN SE20........46 B2
Seymour Vls PGE/AN SE20........46 B2
Seymour Wy WBPTN SW10........19 N4
Seymour Wy SUN TW16........23 P9
Shackleford Rd
  MFD/CHID GU8........148 G1
  WOKS/MYFD GU22........72 E9
Shacklegate La TEDD TW11........25 M7
Shackleton Cl ASHV GU12........89 H9
Shackleton Rd CRAWE RH10........177 H8
Shadbolt Cl WPK KT4........60 D1
Shadyhanger GODL GU7........131 L7
Shady Nook FNM GU9........107 M8
Shaef Wy TEDD TW11........40 G1
Shaftesbury Av
  EBED/NFELT TW14........24 B2
  NWDGN UB2........16 A2
Shaftesbury Cl BRAK RG12........32 F6
Shaftesbury Crs STA TW18........37 P1
Shaftesbury Ms KENS W8........19 L1
Shaftesbury Mt BLKW GU17........67 N5
Shaftesbury Rd BECK BR3........46 F3
  CAR SM5........43 P8
  CHOB/PIR GU24........70 F5
  CRAWE RH10........177 N7
  RCH/KEW TW9........17 L8
  WOKS/MYFD GU22........11 J4
Shaftesbury Ter
  HMSMTH W6 *........18 D2
Shaftesbury Wy WHTN TW2........25 L6
Shakespeare Av
  EBED/NFELT TW14........24 B2
Shakespeare Gdns
  FARN GU14........87 P2
Shakespeare Rd
  ADL/WDHM KT15........55 P3
  HNHL SE24........30 C1
Shakespeare Ter
  RCH/KEW TW9 *........17 N8
Shakespeare Wy BNFD RG42........32 G2
  FELT TW13........24 D7
Shalbourne Ri CBLY GU15........68 F3
Shalcomb St WBPTN SW10........19 N4
Shalden Rd ASHV GU12........108 F6
Shaldon Dr MRDN SM4........43 J6
Shaldon Wy WFLEETN GU51........106 D7
  WOT/HER KT12........57 L2
Shalford La RGUE GU4........132 C1
Shalford Rd GU GU1........112 B8
Shalstone Rd
  MORT/ESHN SW14........17 P8
Shalston Vls SURB KT6........41 M7
The Shambles GU GU1........6 E6
Shamrock Cl FRIM GU16........68 F8
  LHD/OX KT22........96 D1
Shandon Rd CLAP SW4........29 M2
Shandys Cl HORS RH12........191 P9
Shanklin Ct ASHV GU12........108 C5
Shannon Cl NWDGN UB2........15 N8
Shap Crs CAR SM5........44 B9
Shardcroft Av HNHL SE24........30 C1
Shardeloes Rd BROCKY SE4 *........31 N1
Sharland Cl THHTH CR7........45 J7
Sharman Rw DTCH/LGLY SL3........12 D3
Sharney Av DTCH/LGLY SL3........12 F1
Sharon Cl CRAWE RH10........177 K8
  GT/LBKH KT23........96 A4
  HOR/WEW KT19........78 A2
  SURB KT6........41 J9
Sharon Rd CHSWK W4........18 B3
Sharpthorne Cl
  CRAWW RH11........176 C5
Shawbury Rd EDUL SE22........30 C1
Shaw Cl CHERT KT16........56 C6
  EW KT17........60 D9
  SAND/SEL CR2........81 P1
Shaw Crs SAND/SEL CR2........81 N1
Shaw Dr WOT/HER KT12........39 L8
Shawfield La ASHV GU12........109 H4
Shawfield Rd ASHV GU12........109 H4
Shawford Rd
  HOR/WEW KT19........60 B5
Shaw La KWD/TDW/WH KT20...99 J4
Shawley Crs EPSOM KT18........78 C7
Shawley Wy EPSOM KT18........78 B7
Shaw Pk CWTH RG45........49 M6
Shaw Rd BH/WHM TN16........84 B5
Shaws Cottages FSTH SE23........31 M6
Shaws Rd CRAWE RH10........177 H4
Shaw Wy WLGTN SM6........62 G6
Shaxton Crs CROY/NA CR0........65 J7
Shearing Dr CAR SM5........43 N8
Shearwater Rd SUT SM1........61 K4
Sheath La LHD/OX KT22........76 B2
Sheen Common Dr
  RCHPK/HAM TW10........17 N9
Sheen Court Rd
  RCHPK/HAM TW10........17 N9
Sheendale Rd RCH/KEW TW9...17 M9
Sheenewood SYD SE26........31 J8
Sheen Gate Gdns
  MORT/ESHN SW14........18 A9
Sheen La MORT/ESHN SW14........18 A9
Sheen Pk RCH/KEW TW9........17 M9
Sheen Rd RCH/KEW TW9........17 L9
Sheen Wy WLGTN SM6........63 H4
Sheepbarn La WARL CR6........83 K1
Sheepcote Cl HEST TW5........15 J5
Sheepfold Rd GUW GU2........111 M2
Sheephatch La RFNM GU10........128 D3
Sheephouse FNM GU9........5 G7

Sheephouse Gn RDKG RH5........135 P1
Sheephouse La RDKG RH5........135 P1
  RDKG RH5........136 A6
Sheephouse Wy NWMAL KT3...42 C8
Sheeplands Av GU GU1........112 C3
Sheep Wk REIG RH2........117 P3
Sheepwalk SHPTN TW17........38 B7
Sheep Walk Ms
  WIM/MER SW19........28 A9
Sheerwater Av
  ADL/WDHM KT15........73 K1
Sheerwater Rd
  ADL/WDHM KT15........73 J1
Sheet's Heath La
  CHOB/PIR GU24........70 G8
Sheet Street Rd WDSR SL4........20 A2
Sheffield Cl CRAWE RH10........177 L7
  FARN GU14........88 B3
Sheffield Rd HTHAIR TW6........23 M2
Sheffield Wy HTHAIR TW6........23 N1
Shelburne Dr HSLWW TW4........25 H2
Shelbury Rd EDUL SE22........31 J1
Sheldon Cl CRAWE RH10........177 N6
  PGE/AN SE20........46 B2
  REIG RH2........119 M6
Sheldon Ct GU GU1........7 J4
Sheldon St CROY/NA CR0........2 C6
Sheldrick Cl MTCM CR4........43 P5
Shelford Ri NRWD SE19........45 N1
Shelgate Rd BTSEA SW11........29 J1
Shelley Av BRAK RG12........32 G3
Shelley Cl BNSTD SM7........79 H4
  COUL/CHIP CR5........81 H6
  CRAWE RH10........177 M8
  DTCH/LGLY SL3........12 E4
  FLEETN GU51........86 G7
Shelley Ct GBLY GU15........68 E3
Shelley Crs HEST TW5........15 M6
Shelley Dr REDH RH1........191 K7
Shelley Rd EGRIN RH19........180 C2
  HORS RH12........192 F7
Shelleys Ct SWTR RH13 *........192 F7
Shelleys La RSEV TN14........85 L5
Shelley Wk YTLY GU46........66 F3
Shelley Wy WIM/MER SW19........28 G9
Shellfield Cl
  STWL/WRAY TW19........22 D1
Shellwood Dr RDKG RH5........137 J2
Shellwood Rd REIG RH2........138 B3
Shelly Ri FARN GU14........88 B1
Shellys Ct SWTR RH13 *........192 F7
Shelson Pde FELT TW13 *........24 A6
Shelton Av WARL CR6........82 C7
Shelton Cl GUW GU2........91 N9
  WARL CR6........82 C6
Shelton Rd WIM/MER SW19........43 L2
Shelvers Gn
  KWD/TDW/WH KT20........98 G1
Shelvers Hl
  KWD/TDW/WH KT20........98 F1
Shelvers Sp
  KWD/TDW/WH KT20........98 G1
Shelvers Wy
  KWD/TDW/WH KT20........98 G1
Shenfield Cl COUL/CHIP CR5...80 D8
Shenley Rd HEST TW5........15 N6
Shenstone Cl EWKG RG40........48 E1
Shenstone Pk ASC SL5........34 E5
Shepherd Cl CRAWE RH10........176 G8
  FELT TW13........24 F7
Shepherd & Flock Rbt
  FNM GU9........128 B1
Shepherd's Bush Rd
  HMSMTH W6........18 G2
Shepherds Cha BAGS GU19........51 N7
Shepherds Cl SHPTN TW17........38 D7
Shepherdsgrove La
  EGRIN RH19........163 L7
Shepherds Hl BRAK RG12........32 E2
  GUW GU2........111 N3
  HASM GU27........184 D4
  REDH RH1........100 E6
Shepherds La BFOR GU20........52 C4
  BNFD RG42........32 C1
  GUW GU2........111 M2
Shepherds' Wk EPSOM KT18...97 P1
  FARN GU14........88 D4
Shepherds Wy CWTH RG45........49 J5
  HORS RH12........192 F5
  LIPH GU30........182 G7
  RGUE GU4........112 C9
  SAND/SEL CR2........64 D6
Shepiston La HYS/HAR UB3....14 D2
Shepley Cl CAR SM5........62 C2
Shepley Dr ASC SL5........35 K7
Shepley End ASC SL5........35 J8
Sheppard Cl KUT/HW KT1........41 L5
Shepperton Court Dr
  SHPTN TW17........38 D6
Shepperton Rd STA TW18........37 P5
Sheppey Cl CRAWW RH11........176 E8
Sheraton Cl BLKW GU17........67 N5
Sheraton Dr HOR/WEW KT19...78 A2
Sheraton Wk
  CRAWW RH11 *........194 E1
Sherborne SHGR GU5........133 P1
Sherborne Dr ASC SL5........35 K6
Sherborne Gdns
  SHPTN TW17........38 G8
Sherbrooke Rd
  FUL/PGN SW6........19 K5

Sherbrooke Ter
  FUL/PGN SW6 *........19 J5
Sherbrooke Wy WPK KT4........42 F8
Shere Av BELMT SM2........60 G8
Shere Cl CHSGTN KT9........59 K4
  RDKG RH5........137 J2
Shere Rd CRAN GU6........153 N5
  EHSLY KT24........114 E1
  EHSLY KT24........114 E6
  RGUE GU4........113 M7
  RGUE GU4........114 A9
Sherfield Cl NWMAL KT3........41 P5
Sherfield Gdns
  PUT/ROE SW15........27 L2
Sheridan Cl ALDT GU11........108 C6
  EGRIN RH19........180 B2
Sheridan Ct HSLWW TW4........24 F1
Sheridan Dr REIG RH2........119 M5
Sheridan Gra ASC SL5........34 C7
Sheridan Pl HPTN TW12........40 B2
Sheridan Rd FRIM GU16........68 F8
  RCHPK/HAM TW10........26 B6
  WIM/MER SW19........43 K2
Sheridans Rd GT/LBKH KT23...96 C6
Sheridan Wk CAR SM5........62 B4
Sheridan Wy BECK BR3 *........46 G2
Sheringham Rd PGE/AN SE20...46 B3
Sherington Cl FARN GU14........88 D1
Sherland Rd TWK TW1........25 N4
Sherlock Lea HTWY RG27........66 C1
Sherlock Rd BMLY BR1........47 N2
Sherndon La EDEN TN8........144 G8
Sherriff Cl ESH/CLAY KT10......58 B1
Sherring Cl BNFD RG42........32 E1
Sherringham Av FELT TW13...24 B6
Sherrydon CRAN GU6........153 J8
Sherwin Crs FARN GU14........68 D4
Sherwood Cl BRAK RG12........33 J5
  DTCH/LGLY SL3........12 F1
  LHD/OX KT22........96 C3
  WOKN/KNAP GU21........71 L6
Sherwood Rd REIG RH2........119 M9
Sherwood Park Rd
  MTCM CR4........44 E5
  SUT SM1........61 L4
Sherwood Rd
  COUL/CHIP CR5........80 E5
  CROY/NA CR0........46 B8
  HPTN TW12........25 K8
  WIM/MER SW19........43 K1
Sherwood Wk CRAWE RH10...177 J8
Sherwood Wy WKWM BR4........65 J1
Shetland Cl CRAWE RH10........177 N8
  RGUE GU4........92 F9
Shetland Wy FLEETN GU51.....87 H3
Shewens Rd WEY KT13........56 F3
Shey Copse
  WOKS/MYFD GU22........72 G6
Shield Dr BTFD TW8........17 H4
Shield Rd ASHF TW15........23 M7
Shifford Pth FSTH SE23........31 L6
Shilburn Wy
  WOKN/KNAP GU21........71 N7
Shildon Cl CBLY GU15........69 M5
Shillinglee Rd BIL RH14........187 J7
Shilton Rd CAR SM5........44 A8
The Shimmings GU GU1........112 C3
Shinners Cl SNWD SE25........46 A6
Shinwell Wk CRAWW RH11 *...176 E9
Ship Aly FARN GU14........88 E1
Ship Field Cl BH/WHM TN16...104 A1
Ship Hl BH/WHM TN16........104 B1
Shipka Rd BAL SW12........29 L4
Ship La FARN GU14........88 E1
  MORT/ESHN SW14........18 A9
Shipley Ct LIPH GU30........182 E7
Shipley Rd CRAWW RH11........176 D5
Shipman Rd FSTH SE23........31 L5
Ship St EGRIN RH19........180 D3
Ship Yd WEY KT13........56 C2
Shirburn Cl FSTH SE23........31 K5
Shire Av FLEETN GU51........87 H4
Shire Cl BAGS GU19........51 N7
Shire Ct EW KT17........60 D6
Shires Cl ASHTD KT21........77 K8
The Shires RCHPK/HAM TW10...26 D7
Shires Wy YTLY GU46........49 H9
Shirley Av BELMT SM2........61 K8
  COUL/CHIP CR5........81 K8
  CROY/NA CR0........46 D9
  REDH RH1........140 B1
  SUT SM1........62 A3
Shirley Church Rd
  CROY/NA CR0........64 D2
Shirley Cl HSLW TW3........25 K1
Shirley Dr HSLW TW3........25 K1
Shirley Hills Rd CROY/NA CR0...64 D4
Shirley Oaks Rd
  CROY/NA CR0........46 D9
Shirley Park Rd
  CROY/NA CR0........46 B9
Shirley Pl WOKN/KNAP GU21...71 J9
Shirley Rd CROY/NA CR0........46 B9
  WLGTN SM6........62 E7
Shirley Wy CROY/NA CR0........64 E2
Shoe La ALDT GU11........108 C3
Shophouse La SHGR GU5........133 P6
Shord Hl PUR/KEN CR8........81 M5
Shore Cl EBED/NFELT TW14....24 A3
  HPTN TW12........24 F8
Shore Gv FELT TW13........25 H5
Shoreham Cl CROY/NA CR0....46 C7
  WAND/EARL SW18........28 E1

Shoreham Rd CRAWE RH10...177 M8
Shoreham Rd (East)
  HTHAIR TW6........23 H1
Shoreham Rd (West)
  HTHAIR TW6........23 H1
Shoreham Wy HAYES BR2........47 N7
Shore's Rd WOKN/KNAP GU21...72 C3
Shorrolds Rd FUL/PGN SW6....19 L5
Shortacres REDH RH1........121 H4
Short Cl CRAWW RH11........176 C5
Shortcroft Rd EW KT17........60 D6
Short Dale Rd ALDT GU11........108 E8
Shortfield Rd RFNM GU10........146 F5
Short Gallop CRAWE RH10 *...177 N4
Shortheath Crest FNM GU9...127 K7
Shortheath Rd FNM GU9........127 L7
Shortlands HMSMTH W6........19 H2
  HYS/HAR UB3........14 F4
Shortlands Gdns HAYES BR2...47 J4
Shortlands Gv HAYES BR2........47 K4
Shortlands Rd HAYES BR2........47 K4
  KUTN/CMB KT2........9 G1
Short La OXTED RH8........123 J3
  STWL/WRAY TW19........23 J5
Short Rd CHSWK W4........18 C4
  HTHAIR TW6........23 M1
Shortsfield Cl HORS RH12........192 B5
Shorts Rd CAR SM5........62 A3
Short St ALDT GU11........108 C4
Short Wy WHTN TW2........25 K3
Shortwood Av STA TW18........22 E6
Shotfield WLGTN SM6........62 D5
Shott Cl SUT SM1........61 N4
Shottendane Rd
  FUL/PGN SW6 *........19 L6
Shottermill HORS RH12........192 F3
Shottermill Pk HASM GU27 *...183 P3
Shottfield Av
  MORT/ESHN SW14........18 C9
Shovelstrode La
  EGRIN RH19........181 J3
Shrewsbury Av
  MORT/ESHN SW14........18 A9
Shrewsbury Cl SURB KT6........59 L1
Shrewsbury Rd BECK BR3........46 E4
  CAR SM5........44 A8
  HTHAIR TW6........23 M2
  REDH RH1........120 A5
Shrewton Rd TOOT SW17 *.......44 E1
Shrivenham Cl SHST GU47........49 P9
Shropshire Cl MTCM CR4........44 G5
Shropshire Gdns BNFD RG42...33 H1
Shrubbery Rd
  STRHM/NOR SW16........29 P7
The Shrubbery FARN GU14 *...87 P1
  SURB KT6 *........41 L9
Shrubbs Hl CHOB/PIR GU24....53 J7
Shrubbs Hill La ASC SL5........35 J4
Shrubbs La RFNM GU10........127 K9
Shrubland Gv WPK KT4........60 G2
Shrubland Rd BNSTD SM7........79 K5
Shrublands Av CROY/NA CR0...64 G3
Shrublands Cl SYD SE26........31 K6
Shrublands Dr LTWR GU18....52 B9
Shuters Sq WKENS W14 *........19 K3
Shuttleworth Rd
  BTSEA SW11........19 P7
Sian Cl FLEETS GU52........107 H1
Sibthorp Rd MTCM CR4 *........44 B3
Sibton Rd CAR SM5........44 A8
Sickle Rd HASM GU27........184 A5
Sidbury Cl ASC SL5........34 C6
Sidbury St FUL/PGN SW6........19 J6
Siddeley Dr HSLWW TW4........15 N8
Siddons Rd CROY/NA CR0........63 J2
  FSTH SE23........31 M5
Sidestrand Rd ALDT GU11........88 A8
Sideways La HORL RH6........158 F3
The Sidings ALDT GU11........108 E5
  STA TW18........22 E7
Sidlaws Rd FARN GU14........67 P9
Sidmouth Av ISLW TW7........16 F7
Sidney Gdns BTFD TW8........17 K4
Sidney Rd BECK BR3........46 E3
  SNWD SE25........46 A6
  STA TW18........22 D7
  TWK TW1........25 P2
  WOT/HER KT12........57 L2
Signal Ct LING RH7........143 L2
Sigrist Sq KUTN/CMB KT2........8 E3
Silbury Av MTCM CR4........44 A2
Silchester Dr CRAWW RH11...176 D8
Silistria Cl WOKN/KNAP GU21...71 J7
Silkham Rd OXTED RH8........103 K7
Silkin Wk CRAWW RH11........194 E1
Silkmore La EHSLY KT24........94 B6
Silo Cl GODL GU7........131 M5
Silo Dr GODL GU7........131 M5
Silo Rd GODL GU7........131 M5
Silverbeck Wy
  STWL/WRAY TW19........22 D1
Silver Birch Cl
  ADL/WDHM KT15........73 J1
  CAT SE6........31 P3
  FLEETS GU52........106 F1
Silver Birches Wy
  MFD/CHID GU8........148 F1
Silver Cl KWD/TDW/WH KT20...99 J4
Silver Crs CHSWK W4........17 P2
Silverdale FLEETS GU52........106 C3
  WOT/HER KT12........57 L2
Silverdale Av LHD/OX KT22......76 C3
Silverdale Cl
  BRKHM/BTCW RH3........117 P9
  SUT SM1........61 K3
Silverdale Ct STA TW18........22 G8
Silverdale Dr SUN TW16........39 K3
Silver Dene PUT/ROE SW15 *...27 L2
Silver Dr FRIM GU16........69 L1
Silverglade CHSGTN KT9........77 J1
Silverglades YTLY GU46........66 C4
Silverhall St ISLW TW7........16 G8

Silver Hl SHST GU47........50 A9
Silverlands Cl CHERT KT16 *...55 H2
Silver La PUR/KEN CR8........80 F1
  WWKM BR4........65 K1
Silverlea Gdns HORL RH6.....159 M2
Silverleigh Rd THHTH CR7........45 H5
Silvermere Rd CAT SE6........31 P7
Silvermere Rw SNWD SE25 *...46 A3
Silver Park Cl FLEETS GU52....87 H9
Silversmiths Wy
  WOKN/KNAP GU21........72 A7
Silverstone Cl REDH RH1........120 B5
Silverton Rd HMSMTH W6........19 H4
Silver Tree Cl WOT/HER KT12...57 J3
Silverwood CRAWE RH10 *.....160 G9
Silverwood Cl BECK BR3........46 G1
  CROY/NA CR0........64 F7
Silverwood Dr CBLY GU15........69 J1
Silwood BRAK RG12........32 A9
Silwood Cl ASC SL5........34 D3
Silwood Pk ASC SL5........34 F4
Silwood Rd ASC SL5........34 F5
Simmil Rd ESH/CLAY KT10........58 E4
Simmonds Cl BNFD RG42........32 A2
Simmondstone La
  RFNM GU10........164 G1
Simmons Cl DTCH/LGLY SL3 *...12 F2
Simmons Ga ESH/CLAY KT10...58 C4
Simmons Pl STA TW18........22 B8
Simmons Cl CAR SM5........62 A1
Simone Dr PUR/KEN CR8........81 L5
Simons Cl CHERT KT16........54 G5
Simons Wk EGRIN RH19........36 A1
Simplemarsh Rd
  ADL/WDHM KT15........55 L3
Simpson Rd HSLWW TW4........24 G2
  RCHPK/HAM TW10........26 B7
Simpson's Rd HAYES BR2........47 H2
Simpson Wy SURB KT6........41 J7
Simrose Ct WAND/EARL SW18...28 D2
Sinclair Cl CRAWE RH10........177 M7
Sinclair Dr BELMT SM2........61 M7
Sinclair Rd WKENS W14........19 J1
Sincots Rd REDH RH1........120 B5
Sine Cl FARN GU14........68 B3
Singles Cross RSEV TN14 *.....85 P4
Single's Cross La RSEV TN14...85 N4
Single St BH/WHM TN16........84 F4
Singleton Cl CROY/NA CR0......45 L9
  TOOT SW17........44 B1
Singleton Rd HORS RH12........191 L1
Sinhurst Rd CBLY GU15........68 D4
Sion Rd TWK TW1........26 A4
Sipson Cl WDR/YW UB7........14 C4
Sipson La HYS/HAR UB3........14 B3
Sipson Rd WDR/YW UB7........14 B1
Sir Cyril Black Wy
  WIM/MER SW19........43 K1
Sir Michael Rd MTCM CR4........29 K9
Sir Robert Ms DTCH/LGLY SL3...12 F1
Sir Thomas More Est
  CHEL SW3........19 P4
Siskin Av CRAWE RH10........179 K6
Siskin Cl HORS RH12........192 D1
Sispara Gdns
  WAND/EARL SW18........28 C2
Sissinghurst Cl CRAWE RH10...177 N4
Sissinghurst Rd
  CROY/NA CR0........46 A8
Sistova Rd BAL SW12........29 L4
Siward Rd HAYES BR2........47 N4
  SWT SW17........28 F6
Six Acres SWTR RH13........190 E8
Six Penny Cl EDEN TN8........144 G5
Sixteenth Av
  KWD/TDW/WH KT20 *........99 K6
Sixth Av
  KWD/TDW/WH KT20 *........99 K6
Sixth Cross Rd WHTN TW2........25 K6
Skeena Hl WAND/EARL SW18...28 B3
Skelbrook St
  WAND/EARL SW18........28 E5
Skelgill Rd PUT/ROE SW15........19 K9
Skelton Flds BNFD RG42........32 B1
Skelwith Rd HMSMTH W6........18 G4
Skerne Rd KUTN/CMB KT2........8 C3
Skerne Wk KUTN/CMB KT2........8 C3
Skeynes Rd EDEN TN8........144 F4
Skid Hill La WARL CR6........83 M4
Skiffington Cl
  BRXS/STRHM SW2........30 B4
Skimpedhill La BRAK RG12........32 C3
Skinners La ASHTD KT21........77 K7
  EDEN TN8........145 H5
  HEST TW5........16 B6
  MFD/CHID GU8........168 C6
Skipton Dr HYS/HAR UB3........14 E1
Skipton Wy HORL RH6........140 D8
Skylark Vw HORS RH12........192 C3
Skyport Dr WDR/YW UB7........13 P5
Slade Ct CHERT KT16........55 H5
Slade Rd CHERT KT16........55 H5
  CHOB/PIR GU24........53 J1
Slagrove Pl LEW SE13........31 P1
Slaidburn Gn BRAK RG12........32 G8
Slaidburn St WBPTN SW10......19 N4
Slattery Rd FELT TW13........24 E4
Slaugham Ct CRAWW RH11....176 C8
Sleets Rd HORS RH12........191 M7
Slim Cl ALDT GU11........88 C8
Slim Rd CBLY GU15........68 C3
Slines Oak Rd WARL CR6........82 G8
Slines Oak Rd WARL CR6........82 G8
Slinfold Wk CRAWW RH11......176 D4
Slip of Wd CRAN GU6........153 H8
Slipshatch Rd REIG RH2........119 K9
Slipshoe St REIG RH2........119 K5
The Slip BH/WHM TN16........104 G6

Sloane Wk CROY/NA CRO......46 F7
Slocock HI
  WOKN/KNAP GU21......72 A6
Sloughbrook CI HORS RH12..192 E4
Slough La
  BRKHM/BTCW RH3......118 E4
  EPSOM KT18......98 A5
Slyfield Gn GU GU1......112 C1
Smaldon CI WDR/YW UB7......14 C1
Smallberry Av ISLW TW7......16 F7
Smallfield Rd HORL RH6......159 L1
Smallmead HORL......159 L1
Smalls Hill Rd HORL......159 L4
Smalls Md CRAWW RH11......176 F5
Smallwood Rd TOOT SW17......28 C7
Smart's Heath La
  WOKS/MYFD GU22......91 N3
Smart's Heath Rd
  WOKS/MYFD GU22......91 N3
Smeaton Rd
  WAND/EARL SW18......28 D3
Smeeds CI EGRIN RH19......162 F9
Smitham Bottom La
  PUR/KEN CR8......80 F1
Smitham Downs Rd
  PUR/KEN CR8......80 G2
Smithbarn SWTR RH13......192 F7
Smithbarn CI HORL RH6......140 D9
Smith CI CRAWW RH11......176 C8
The Smithers
  BRKHM/BTCW RH3......117 P7
Smithfield La RFNM GU10....164 A2
Smith Rd REIG RH2......119 K8
Smiths La EDEN TN8......124 C4
Smith Sq BRAK RG12......32 F2
Smith St BRYLDS KT5......41 M7
Smithwood Av CRAN GU6......152 E5
Smithwood CI
  WIM/MER SW19......28 B5
Smithwood Common Rd
  CRAN GU6......152 E4
Smithy CI
  KWD/TDW/WH KT20......99 K6
Smithy La
  KWD/TDW/WH KT20......99 K6
  RFNM GU10......164 B1
Smithy's Gn BFOR GU20......52 D5
Smoke La REIG RH2......119 M7
Smollets EGRIN RH19......180 B7
Smugglers' La RDKG RH5....173 M4
Smugglers' Wy RFNM GU10..128 C5
  WAND/EARL SW18......19 M9
Snag La RSEV TN14......85 H1
Snailslynch FNM GU9......5 J3
Snakey La FELT TW13......24 B7
Snatts HI OXTED RH8......103 M9
Snell Hatch CRAWW RH11....176 G5
Snellings Rd WOT/HER KT12..57 L4
Snipe La HASM GU27......184 B9
Snowbury Rd FUL/PGN SW6..19 M7
Snowdenham La SHGR GU5..132 C8
Snowdenham Links Rd
  SHGR GU5......132 B7
Snowdon Crs HYS/HAR UB3..14 E1
Snowdon Rd FARN GU14......68 A9
Snowdon Rd West
  HTHAIR TW6......23 M2
Snowdrop CI PGE/AN SE20....46 C2
Snowdrop CI CRAWW RH11..176 D9
  HPTN TW12......25 H9
Snowdrop Wy
  CHOB/PIR GU24......70 G6
Snowerhill Rd
  BRKHM/BTCW RH3......118 D9
Snow HI CRAWE RH10......160 G9
Snowhill La CRAWE RH10....160 G2
Snows Paddock BFOR GU20..52 B3
Snows Ride BFOR GU20......52 B3
Snowy Fielder Waye
  ISLW TW7......17 H7
Snoxhall Fld CRAN GU6......170 C1
Soames Wk NWMAL KT3......42 C2
Soane CI CRAWW RH11......176 B7
Solartron Rd FARN GU14......88 C4
Soldiers Ri EWKG RG40......49 H2
Solecote GT/LBKH KT23......96 A5
Sole Farm Av GT/LBKH KT23..95 P4
Sole Farm CI GT/LBKH KT23..95 N4
Sole Farm Rd GT/LBKH KT23..95 P5
Solna Av PUT/ROE SW15......27 P9
Soloms Court Rd BNSTD SM7..79 P6
Solway CI HSLWW TW4......15 N8
Somerfield CI
  KWD/TDW/WH KT20......79 J8
Somergate HORS RH12......191 N8
Somersbury La CRAN GU6...172 A1
Somers CI REIG RH2......119 L4
Somerset Av CHSGTN KT9....59 K3
  RYNPK SW20......42 F3
Somerset CI HOR/WEW KT19..60 C8
  NWMAL KT3......42 C7
  WOT/HER KT12......57 K4
Somerset Gdns
  STRHM/NOR SW16......45 H4
  TEDD TW11......25 M8
Somerset Gv BNFD RG42......33 H1
Somerset Rd BTFD TW8......17 J4
  FARN GU14......88 B1
  KUT/HW KT1......9 G5
  REDH RH1......119 P7
  TEDD TW11......25 M8
  WIM/MER SW19......27 K4
Somerset Sq WKENS W14 *....19 J1
Somerset Waye HEST TW5......15 N5
Somers PI BRXS/STRHM SW2..30 A3
Somers Rd BRXS/STRHM SW2..30 A2
  REIG RH2......119 L4
Somerswey RGUE GU4......132 C4
Somerton Av RCH/KEW TW9..17 P8
Somerton CI PUR/KEN CR8....81 J5
Somertons CI GUW GU2......111 N1

Somerville Av BARN SW13......18 G4
Somerville Crs YTLY GU46......67 J2
Somerville Dr CRAWE RH10..177 M2
Somerville Rd COB KT11......76 A3
  PGE/AN SE20......46 D1
Sondes Farm DORK RH4 *....116 F7
Sondes Place Dr DORK RH4..116 F7
Songhurst CI CROY/NA CRO....45 H7
Sonia Gdns HEST TW5......16 A5
Sonninge CI SHST GU47......49 P9
Sonning Gdns HPTN TW12....24 F9
Sonning Rd SNWD SE25......46 A7
Soper CI FSTH SE23......31 L4
Soper Dr CTHM CR3......101 M3
Sopwith Av CHSGTN KT9......59 L4
Sopwith CI BH/WHM TN16....84 B5
  KUTN/CMB KT2......26 E8
Sopwith Dr BF/WBF KT14......56 K4
Sopwith Rd HEST TW5......15 L5
Sopwith Wy KUTN/CMB KT2....8 D1
Sorbie CI WEY KT13......56 E5
Sorrel Bank CROY/NA CRO....64 E8
Sorrel CI CRAWW RH11......176 D9
Sorrel Dr LTWR GU18......69 P1
Sorrel Rd HORS RH12......192 D5
Sorrento Rd SUT SM1......61 M2
Souldern Rd WKENS W14 *....19 H1
South Albert Rd REIG RH2....119 K4
Southall La HEST TW5......15 L3
Southampton CI BLKW GU17..67 N2
Southampton Gdns
  MTCM CR4......44 G6
Southampton Rd
  HTHAIR TW6......23 J2
Southampton St FARN GU14..88 D7
South Atlantic Dr
  ALDT GU11......108 E3
South Av CAR SM5......62 C6
  EGH TW20......21 P9
  FNM GU9......107 P8
  RCH/KEW TW9 *......17 N7
  WOT/HER KT12......56 G8
South Bank BH/WHM TN16..105 H6
  SURB KT6......41 L7
Southbank THDIT KT7......41 H8
South Bank Ter SURB KT6 *....41 L7
South Beta Rd FARN GU14....88 D5
South Black Lion La
  HMSMTH W6......18 E3
South Bolton Gdns
  WBPTN SW10 *......19 M3
The South Border
  PUR/KEN CR8......61 G9
Southborough CI SURB KT6....41 K9
Southborough Rd SURB KT6..41 L9
Southborough Rd (The Lane)
  SURB KT6......41 L9
Southbourne HAYES BR2......47 N8
Southbridge PI CROY/NA CRO..2 C7
Southbridge Rd CROY/NA CRO..2 C7
Southbrook CRAWW RH11..194 F1
Southbrook Rd
  STRHM/NOR SW16......44 G2
Southby Dr FLEETN GU51......87 H6
South CI CRAWE RH10......177 L1
  WDR/YW UB7......14 B1
  WHTN TW2......25 H6
  WOKN/KNAP GU21......72 A5
South Close Gn REDH RH1..100 D9
Southcombe St WKENS W14..19 J2
Southcote Av BRYLDS KT5....41 P8
  FELT TW13......24 B5
Southcote Dr CBLY GU15......69 J1
Southcote Rd REDH RH1....120 E1
  SAND/SEL CR2......63 N8
  SNWD SE25......46 B6
Southcroft Av WWKM BR4....65 K1
Southcroft Rd
  STRHM/NOR SW16......29 L9
South Croxted Rd DUL SE21..30 E6
Southdean Gdns
  WIM/MER SW19......28 C5
Southdown Av HNWL W7......16 G1
Southdown CI HORS RH12..192 F5
Southdown Dr RYNPK SW20..43 H1
Southdown Rd CAR SM5......62 C7
  CTHM CR3......102 F2
  RYNPK SW20......43 H2
  WOT/HER KT12......57 K3
South Downs Wy RDKG RH5..117 J5
South Dr BELMT SM2......61 J8
  BNSTD SM7......80 A2
  COUL/CHIP CR5......80 C4
  RDKG RH5......117 J7
  VW GU25......35 N8
South Eden Park Rd
  BECK BR3......47 H5
South Edwardes Sq KENS W8..19 K1
South End CROY/NA CRO......2 D7
  GT/LBKH KT23......96 B6
  KENS W8......19 M1
  SAND/SEL CR2......63 L4
Southend La SYD SE26......31 N7
South End Rw KENS W8......19 M1
Sutherland CI WEY KT13......56 E3
Southern Av
  EBED/NFELT TW14......24 B4
  REDH RH1......140 C3
  SNWD SE25......46 A4
Southern Down FELT TW13 *..24 D4
Southern Perimeter Rd
  HTHAIR TW6......23 M1
Southern Rd CBLY GU15......68 E2
Southerns La COUL/CHIP CR5..99 N4
Southern Wy FARN GU14......87 P4
  FNM GU9......5 H5
Southerton Rd
  HMSMTH W6 *......18 G2
Southey Rd WIM/MER SW19..43 L1

Southey St PGE/AN SE20......46 D1
South Farm La BAGS GU19....52 A7
Southfield Gdns TWK TW1......25 N7
Southfield PI WEY KT13......56 D6
Southfield Rd CHSWK W4......18 C1
  E/WMO/HCT KT8......40 C7
Southfields Av ASHF TW15....23 L9
Southfields Ms
  WAND/EARL SW18 *......28 D2
Southgate Av CRAWE RH10..176 G8
Southgate Dr CRAWE RH10..176 G8
South Gate Av FELT TW15......23 N7
Southgate Pde CRAWE RH10..176 G7
Southgate Rd CRAWE RH10..176 G7
South Gv CHERT KT16......37 K7
  FLEETN GU51......87 J3
  SWTR RH13......192 C9
South HI GODL GU7......131 M9
  GU GU1......7 F6
South Hill Rd BRAK RG12......32 D7
  HAYES BR2......47 L4
Southholme CI NRWD SE19....45 N2
South Holmes Rd
  SWTR RH13......192 G6
South Kensington Station Ar
  SKENS SW7 *......19 P2
Southlands EGRIN RH19......180 D4
Southlands Av HORL RH6......140 C9
Southlands CI ASHV GU12....109 J5
  COUL/CHIP CR5......81 H6
Southlands Dr
  WIM/MER SW19......28 A5
Southlands La OXTED RH8..123 H5
Southlands Rd ASHV GU12..109 J5
South La ASHV GU12......109 K5
  KUT/HW KT1......8 C7
  NWMAL KT3......42 B5
South La West NWMAL KT3....42 A5
South Lodge Av MTCM CR4....44 G5
South Lodge Rd
  WOT/HER KT12......57 J7
South Lynn Crs BRAK RG12....32 C6
South Md HOR/WEW KT19....60 D6
  REDH RH1......120 B2
South Meadow CWTH RG45....49 P6
Southmead Rd ALDT GU11..108 D6
  WIM/MER SW19......28 B4
Southmont Rd
  ESH/CLAY KT10......58 E1
South Munstead La
  MFD/CHID GU8......150 G5
South Norwood HI
  SNWD SE25......45 P4
South Oak Rd
  STRHM/NOR SW16......30 A7
South Pde CHEL SW3......19 P5
  CHSWK W4......18 B2
  HORL RH6......140 B9
  REDH RH1......100 E8
  WLGTN SM6 *......62 E5
South Park Gv NWMAL KT3....42 A5
South Park Hill Rd
  SAND/SEL CR2......63 M4
South Park La REDH RH1....122 A6
South Park Ms FUL/PGN SW6..19 M8
South Pier Rd HORL RH6....159 K5
South PI BRYLDS KT5......41 M8
South Rdg WEY KT13......56 D8
South Ri CAR SM5......62 A7
South Rd ASHV GU12......109 H2
  CHOB/PIR GU24......70 F5
  CWTH RG45......49 K3
  EA W5......17 K2
  EGH TW20......21 H9
  EWKG RG40......32 A9
  FELT TW13......24 E8
  FSTH SE23......31 L5
  GUW GU2......111 P5
  REIG RH2......119 M6
  WDR/YW UB7......14 C1
  WEY KT13......56 D8
  WHTN TW2......25 L6
  WIM/MER SW19......28 C9
South Side HMSMTH W6......18 D1
Southside Common
  WIM/MER SW19......28 A9
South Station Ap
  REDH RH1......121 H7
South St BMLY BR1......47 N3
  DORK RH4......116 G8
  EPSOM KT18......78 B2
  FARN GU14......88 C6
  FNM GU9......5 G3
  GODL GU7......131 K9
  HORS RH12......192 B8
  ISLW TW7......16 G8
  STA TW18......22 C8
South Ter DORK RH4......117 H8
  SURB KT6......41 L7
South V NRWD SE19......30 F9
South Vale Rd SURB KT6......59 L1
South View CI CRAWE RH10..160 F9
South VW TOOT SW17......28 F9
South View Crs NRWD SE19 *..45 L1
  WOKS/MYFD GU22......10 D6
Southview Gdns WLGTN SM6..62 E6
South View Rd ASHTD KT21..77 K8
Southview Rd BOR GU35......164 E6
  CTHM CR3......103 H4
  WARL CR6......82 B9

Southviews SAND/SEL CR2....64 D7
Southville CI
  EBED/NFELT TW14......23 P3
  HOR/WEW KT19......60 B7
Southville Crs
  EBED/NFELT TW14......23 P4
Southville Rd
  EBED/NFELT TW14......23 P4
  THDIT KT7......40 G8
South Wk ASHV GU12......108 F4
  REIG RH2 *......119 M5
  WWKM BR4......65 L3
Southwark CI CRAWW RH11..176 E9
Southwater CI BECK BR3......47 H1
  CRAWW RH11......176 E3
South Wy CAR SM5......61 P8
  CROY/NA CRO......64 D6
Southway CBLY GU15......68 D4
  GUW GU2......111 L5
  HAYES BR2......47 N8
  RYNPK SW20......43 H5
  WLGTN SM6......62 E3
Southway Pk GUW GU2 *....111 N3
Southways Pk
  CRAWE RH10......158 G9
Southwell Gdns SKENS SW7..19 N2
Southwell Park Rd
  CBLY GU15......68 D3
Southwell Rd CROY/NA CRO....45 J7
  SNWD SE25......45 N5
South Western Rd TWK TW1..25 P2
Southwick BAGS GU19......51 N8
Southwick CI EGRIN RH19..180 C1
Southwick Ct BRAK RG12......32 G7
Southwold KWD/TDW/WH KT20..98 A2
Southwood Av CHERT KT16....54 G6
  COUL/CHIP CR5......80 E4
  KUTN/CMB KT2......42 A2
  WOKN/KNAP GU21......71 K7
Southwood Cha CRAN GU6..171 J2
Southwood CI WPK KT4......43 H9
Southwood Crs FARN GU14....87 P4
Southwood Dr BRYLDS KT5....42 A8
Southwood Gdns
  ESH/CLAY KT10......58 G2
Southwood La FLEETN GU51..87 L4
Southwood Rd BLKW GU17....67 J7
  FARN GU14......87 P5
South Worple Wy
  MORT/ESHN SW14......18 B8
Sovereign CI PUR/KEN CR8....63 H8
Sovereign Ct
  E/WMO/HCT KT8......40 A2
Sovereign Dr CBLY GU15......69 L1
Sovereign Hts
  DTCH/LGLY SL3......12 E4
Space Wave
  EBED/NFELT TW14......24 C1
Spa CI SNWD SE25......45 N2
Spa Dr EPSOM KT18......77 N3
Spa HI NRWD SE19......45 M2
Spalding Rd TOOT SW17......29 L8
Spanish Rd
  WAND/EARL SW18......28 F1
Sparkes CI HAYES BR2......47 P5
Sparks CI HPTN TW12......24 F9
Sparrow CI HPTN TW12......24 E9
Sparrow Farm Rd EW KT17..60 E3
Sparrowhawk CI
  RFNM GU10......107 H6
Sparrow Rw CHOB/PIR GU24..53 H5
Sparrows Md REDH RH1......120 C2
Spartan CI WLGTN SM6......62 G6
Sparvell Rd
  WOKN/KNAP GU21......71 H8
Sparvells HTWY RG27......48 C9
Spats La BOR GU35......164 C3
Speakers Ct CROY/NA CRO *....2 C2
Spear Ms ECT SW5......19 L2
Speart La HEST TW5......15 N5
Speedbird Wy WDR/YW UB7..13 M5
Speedwell CI RGUE GU4......112 G2
Speedwell Wy HORS RH12..192 D5
Speer Rd THDIT KT7......40 G6
Speirs CI NWMAL KT3......42 D7
Speke Rd THHTH CR7......45 M3
Speldhurst CI HAYES BR2....47 M6
Speldhurst Rd CHSWK W4....18 B1
Spelthorne Gv SUN TW16......39 H1
Spelthorne La ASHF TW15......38 E1
Spence Av BF/WBF KT14......74 A3
Spencer CI EPSOM KT18......78 C8
  FLEETS GU52......107 J1
  FRIM GU16......88 G1
  WOKN/KNAP GU21......72 G3
Spencer Gdns ECH TW20......21 J8
  MORT/ESHN SW14......27 H1
Spencer HI WIM/MER SW19..28 B9
Spencer Hill Rd
  WIM/MER SW19......43 J1
Spencer Ms HMSMTH W6......19 J4
Spencer Pk
  WAND/EARL SW18......28 F1
Spencer Rd CROY/NA CRO....45 M8
  BMLY BR1 *......47 M1
  BNFD RG42......32 B2
  BTSEA SW11......28 F4
  CHSWK W4......18 A5
  COB KT11......75 K4
  CTHM CR3......101 M1
  DTCH/LGLY SL3......12 F5
  E/WMO/HCT KT8......40 C5
  ISLW TW7......16 C6
  MTCM CR4......44 B8
  MTCM CR4......44 C4
  RYNPK SW20......42 F2
  SAND/SEL CR2......63 N4
  TWK TW1......25 M6
Spencers La HORL RH6......158 C3
Spencers PI HORS RH12......192 A6
Spencers Rd CRAWW RH11..176 F6
  HORS RH12......192 A7

Spencer St NWDGN UB2......15 M1
Spencer Wy PUT/ROE SW15..19 H9
Spencer Wy REDH RH1......140 C1
Spenser Av WEY KT13......56 C7
Spenser Ms DUL SE21......30 E4
Spenser Rd HNHL SE24......30 C1
Spiceall RGUW GU3......131 H2
Spicer CI WOT/HER KT12......39 L7
Spicers Fld LHD/OX KT22......76 D2
Spices Yd CROY/NA CRO......2 D7
Spiers Wy HORL RH6......159 L3
Spindle Wy CRAWE RH10....177 J6
Spindlewood Gdns
  CROY/NA CRO......3 F7
Spindlewoods
  KWD/TDW/WH KT20......98 F2
Spinis BRAK RG12......32 A9
Spinner Gn BRAK RG12......32 C6
Spinney CI BECK BR3......47 H5
  COB KT11......76 G3
  CRAWE RH10......179 K3
  HORS RH12......192 G4
  NWMAL KT3......42 C6
  WPK KT4......60 D2
Spinneycroft LHD/OX KT22..76 D4
Spinney Dr
  EBED/NFELT TW14......23 M3
Spinney Gdns NRWD SE19....30 G8
Spinney HI ADL/WDHM KT15..55 K4
Spinney Oak CHERT KT16....55 H5
The Spinney ASC SL5......34 E6
  BARN SW13 *......18 F4
  CBLY GU15......60 C3
  CHEAM SM3......61 J2
  CRAWW RH11......176 E7
  EPSOM KT18......78 F8
  EWKG RG40......48 B1
  FLEETN GU51......86 D7
  GSHT GU26......165 K7
  GT/LBKH KT23......96 B4
  HASM GU27 *......185 L1
  HASM GU27......184 D2
  HORL RH6......140 C8
  LHD/OX KT22......76 C1
  PUR/KEN CR8......63 K9
  RPLY/SEND GU23......93 N7
  STRHM/NOR SW16......29 M6
  SUN TW16......39 J2
  YTLY GU46......66 G1
The Spinning Wk SHGR GU5..134 C1
Spital Heath DORK RH4......117 J6
Spitfire CI DTCH/LGLY SL3....12 E3
Spitfire Est HEST TW5 *......15 L3
Spitfire Wy FARN GU14......88 A7
  HEST TW5......15 L3
Spook La RFNM GU10......109 H7
Spokane CI ALDT GU11......108 B6
Spook HI RDKG RH5......137 H3
Spooners Rd HORS RH12....192 F6
Spooner Wk WLGTN SM6......62 G4
Spout HI CROY/NA CRO......64 G4
Spout La EDEN TN8......124 C5
  STWL/WRAY TW19......22 D1
Spout La North
  STWL/WRAY TW19......13 M9
Spratts La CHERT KT16......55 J5
Spreighton Rd
  E/WMO/HCT KT8......40 B5
Spring Av EGH TW20......21 K9
Spring Bottom La
  REDH RH1......101 L7
Springbourne Ct BECK BR3....47 J2
Springclose La CHEAM SM3..61 J5
Spring Copse BH/WHM TN16..84 B7
Springcopse Rd REIG RH2..119 N6
Spring Cnr FELT TW13 *......24 B6
Springcross Av BLKW GU17..67 P5
Springdale EWKG RG40......48 C1
Springfarm Rd HASM GU27..185 J5
Springfield EGRIN RH19......162 C8
  LTWR GU18......52 A8
  OXTED RH8......123 K1
Springfield Av HPTN TW12....25 J9
  RYNPK SW20......43 K4
Springfield CI
  WOKN/KNAP GU21......72 A4
Springfield Crs HORS RH12..192 A8
Springfield Dr LHD/OX KT22..77 J2
Springfield Gdns WWKM BR4..65 H1
Springfield Gv SUN TW16......39 J2
Springfield La FLEETN GU51..86 E6
  WEY KT13......56 D3
Springfield Mdw WEY KT13..56 D3
Springfield Pk HORS RH12 *..192 B7
Springfield Park Rd
  HORS RH12......192 A8
Springfield PI NWMAL KT3....41 P5
Springfield Ri SYD SE26......31 J6
Springfield Rd ASHF TW15....23 J8
  ASHV GU12......109 J1
  CBLY GU15......69 J3
  CRAWW RH11......176 A6
  DORK RH4......116 B8
  DTCH/LGLY SL3......12 F5
  EDEN TN8......144 F4
  EW KT17......60 C8
  GU GU1......7 G4
  HORS RH12......192 A8
  KUT/HW KT1......41 L5
  SYD SE26......31 J8
  TEDD TW11......25 P8
  THHTH CR7......45 J2
  WHTN TW2......25 L6
  WIM/MER SW19......28 C8
  WLGTN SM6......62 E4
Springfields CI CHERT KT16..37 M9
Springfield Wy
  MFD/CHID GU8......148 F1
Spring Gdns ASC SL5......34 B5
  BH/WHM TN16......84 A7
  CBLY GU15......68 E3

CRAWE RH10 .... 160 D9
E/WMO/HCT KT8 .... 40 C6
EWKG RG40 * 48 D4
FARN GU14 .... 68 C9
WLGTN SM6 .... 62 E5
Spring Gv CHSWK W4 .... 17 N3
GODL GU7 .... 131 L5
HPTN TW12 .... 40 B2
LHD/OX KT22 .... 96 B3
MTCM CR4 .... 44 C2
Spring Grove Crs HSLW TW5 .... 16 C6
Spring Grove Rd HSLW TW5 .... 16 C6
RCHPK/HAM TW10 .... 26 E1
Springhaven Cl GU GU1 .... 112 E5
Springhill MFD/CHID GU8 .... 148 F1
Spring Hl SYD SE26 .... 31 K7
Springholm Cl
BH/WHM TN16 .... 84 A7
Sorinqhurst Cl CROY/NA CRO ... 64 F3
Spring La FNM GU9 .... 107 L7
OXTED RH8 .... 123 K2
SNWD SE25 .... 46 B7
SWTR RH13 .... 190 D7
Spring La West FNM GU9 .... 107 L8
Spring Meadow BRAK RG12 .... 32 F2
Spring Park Av CROY/NA CRO .. 64 D1
Springpark Dr BECK BR3 .... 47 J4
Spring Park Rd CROY/NA CRO .. 64 D1
Spring Plat CRAWE RH10 .... 177 M5
Spring Plat Ct
CRAWE RH10 * 177 M5
Spring Ri EGH TW20 .... 21 K9
Spring Rd FELT TW13 .... 24 A6
Springvale Av BTFD TW8 .... 17 K3
Springvale Cl GT/LBKH KT23 ... 96 B6
Springvale Ter WKENS W14 .... 19 H1
Spring Wy EGRIN RH19 .... 162 F8
Springwell Rd HEST TW5 .... 15 M6
RDKG RH5 .... 156 C1
STRHM/NOR SW16 .... 30 C6
Springwood MFD/CHID GU8 .149 P3
Spring Woods FLEETS GU52 ... 86 F8
SHST GU47 .... 49 N8
VW GU25 .... 35 P5
Sprucedale Gdns
CROY/NA CRO 64 D3
WLGTN SM6 .... 62 C7
Spruce Dr LTWR GU18 .... 52 B4
Spruce Rd BH/WHM TN16 ..... 84 B5
Spruce Wy FLEETN GU51 ..... 87 K6
Spur Dr KWD/TDW/WH KT20 ..99 M1
Spurfield E/WMO/HCT KT8 .... 40 B4
Spurgeon Av NRWD SE19 ..... 45 M2
Spurgeon Cl CRAWW RH11 * .176 F4
Spurgeon Rd NRWD SE19 ..... 45 M2
Spur Rd EBED/NFELT TW14 .... 24 C1
ISLW TW7 .... 16 C5
Spurs Ct ALDT GU11 .... 108 A4
The Spur WOKN/KNAP GU21 ...71 H7
Spy La BIL RH14 .... 188 D6
Square Dr HASM GU27 .... 184 D9
The Square BH/WHM TN16 .... 84 A4
BRAK RG12 .... 32 C5
CAR SM5 .... 62 C4
CRAWE RH10 .... 176 C5
GUW GU2 .... 111 M7
HMSMTH W6 .... 18 G3
LING RH7 .... 143 J9
LIPH GU30 .... 182 E6
RCH/KEW TW9 .... 26 D1
WDR/YW UB7 .... 13 M6
Squaray St TOOT SW17 .... 28 F6
Squerryes Mede
BH/WHM TN16 * 104 C7
The Squerryes CTHM CR3 ...101 N1
Squire's Bridge Rd
SHPTN TW17 .... 38 B5
Squires Cl CRAWE RH10 ..... 179 H5
Squires Ct WIM/MER SW19 .... 28 D7
Squires Hill La RFNM GU10 ...128 E8
Squire's Rd SHPTN TW17 ..... 38 B5
Squires Wk ASHF TW15 .... 38 F1
Squirrel Cl CRAWW RH11 ..... 194 A4
HSLWW TW4 .... 15 L8
SHST GU47 .... 49 M9
Squirrel La FARN GU14 .... 88 C2
Squirrel Rdg CRAWE RH10 * ...179 J4
Squirrels Cl GODL GU7 .... 131 K4
Squirrels Dray CWTH RG45 ...49 K4
Squirrels Gn GT/LBKH KT23 ...96 A3
WPK KT4 .... 60 D1
Squirrel's Wy EPSOM KT18 ... 78 D4
Squirrel Wd BF/WBF KT14 .... 73 M1
Stable Cl CRAWE RH10 .... 177 M6
EPSOM KT18 .... 78 C8
KUTN/CMB KT2 .... 8 C1
Stable Ms REIG RH2 .... 119 L5
WWWD SE27 .... 30 D8
The Stables COB KT11 .... 75 P3
Stable Vw YTLY GU46 .... 67 H1
Stacey's Farm Rd
MFD/CHID GU8 .... 148 E1
Stacey's Meadow
MFD/CHID GU8 .... 129 L9
Stackfield Rd CRAWW RH11 .176 B6
Staddon Cl BECK BR3 .... 46 E5
Staddon Ct BECK BR3 .... 46 E5
Stadium St WBPTN SW10 .... 19 N5
Staff College Rd CBLY GU15 ..68 D2
Staffhurst Wood Rd
OXTED RH8 .... 124 A8
CTHM CR3 .... 101 P3
Stafford Cl CHEAM SM3 .... 61 J5
CTHM CR3 .... 101 P3
Stafford Gdns CROY/NA CRO ...63 H4
Stafford Lake
WOKN/KNAP GU21 .... 70 C7
Stafford Pl
RCHPK/HAM TW10 .... 26 E3
Stafford Rd CRAWW RH11 .176 D2
CROY/NA CRO 63 J3

CTHM CR3 .... 101 P3
NWMAL KT3 .... 42 A4
WLGTN SM6 .... 62 E5
Staffords Pl HORL RH6 .... 159 L2
Stafford Ter KENS W8 .... 19 L1
Staff Rd ASHV GU12 .... 108 E4
Stagbury Av COUL/CHIP CR5 ...80 A7
Stagbury Cl COUL/CHIP CR5 ...80 A8
Stagbury House
COUL/CHIP CR5 .... 80 A8
Stagelands CRAWW RH11 ....176 E2
Stag HI GUW GU2 .... 111 N6
Stag La PUT/ROE SW15 .... 27 L6
Stag Leys ASHTD KT21 .... 96 A1
Stag Leys Cl BNSTD SM7 .... 80 A4
Stags Wy ISLW TW7 .... 16 F4
Stainash Crs STA TW18 .... 22 E8
Stainash Pde STA TW18 * 22 E8
Stainbank Rd MTCM CR4 .... 44 D4
Staines Av CHEAM SM3 .... 61 H1
Staines By-pass STA TW18 ...22 B6
Staines La CHERT KT16 .... 37 K6
Staines Lane Cl CHERT KT16 ...37 K6
Staines Rd CHERT KT16 .... 37 J7
EBED/NFELT TW14 .... 23 N3
STWL/WRAY TW19 .... 21 M4
WHTN TW2 .... 25 K6
Staines Rd East SUN TW16 ...39 J1
Staines Rd West ASHF TW15 ...38 E1
SUN TW16 .... 39 H1
Stainford Cl ASHF TW15 .... 23 N8
Stainton Wk
WOKN/KNAP GU21 * 72 A7
Staiths Wy
KWD/TDW/WH KT20 .... 78 F9
Stake La FARN GU14 .... 88 C3
Stakescorner Rd
RGUW GU3 .... 131 N4
Stambourne Wy NRWD SE19 ...45 N1
Stamford Av FRIM GU16 .... 69 H7
Stamford Brook Av
HMSMTH W6 .... 18 D1
Stamford Brook Gdns
HMSMTH W6 * 18 D1
Stamford Brook Rd
HMSMTH W6 .... 18 D1
Stamford Dr HAYES BR2 .... 47 M5
Stamford Green Rd
EPSOM KT18 .... 77 P2
Stamford Rd WOT/HER KT12 ...57 M2
Stanborough Cl HPTN TW12 ...24 F9
Stanborough Rd HSLW TW3 ...16 D8
Stanbridge Cl CRAWW RH11 ...176 D6
Stanbridge Rd EDEN TN8 ....144 F3
PUT/ROE SW15 .... 18 G9
Standard Rd HSLWW TW4 .... 15 N8
Standen Cl EGRIN RH19 .... 161 P9
Standen Pl HORS RH12 .... 192 F3
Standen Rd
WAND/EARL SW18 .... 28 D3
Standinghall La
CRAWE RH10 .... 178 B9
Standish Rd HMSMTH W6 .... 18 E2
Standon La RDKG RH5 .... 172 F1
Stane Cl WIM/MER SW19 .... 43 M1
Stane St RDKG RH5 .... 173 K1
Stane Wy EW KT17 .... 60 E8
Stanford Cl HPTN TW12 .... 24 F9
Stanford Orch HORS RH12 ...191 N3
Stanford Rd SKENS W8 .... 19 M1
STRHM/NOR SW16 .... 44 F9
Stanfords Pl LING RH7 .... 162 C1
The Stanfords EW KT17 .... 78 D1
Stanford Wy HORS RH12 ....191 L7
STRHM/NOR SW16 .... 44 F3
Stanger Rd SNWD SE25 ..... 46 A5
Stangrove Rd EDEN TN8 ....144 C4
Stan HI HORL RH6 .... 157 P4
Stanhope Av HAYES BR2 .... 47 N9
Stanhope Gdns SKENS SW7 ...19 N2
Stanhope Gv BECK BR3 .... 46 F6
Stanhope Heath
STWL/WRAY TW19 .... 22 F2
Stanhope Ms East
SKENS SW7 * 19 N2
Stanhope Ms South
SKENS SW7 .... 19 N2
Stanhope Ms West
SKENS SW7 .... 19 N2
Stanhope Rd CAR SM5 .... 62 C6
CBLY GU15 .... 68 C3
CROY/NA CRO 3 G6
Stanhopes OXTED RH8 .... 103 P8
Stanhope Ter WHTN TW2 * ...25 N3
Stanhope Wy
STWL/WRAY TW19 .... 22 F2
Stanier Cl CRAWE RH10 .... 177 L6
WKENS W14 .... 19 K3
Staniland Dr WEY KT13 .... 56 B9
Stanley Av BECK BR3 .... 47 J4
NWMAL KT3 .... 42 E6
Stanley Cl COUL/CHIP CR5 ...81 H6
CRAWE RH10 .... 177 M2
Stanleycroft Cl ISLW TW7 ...16 E6
Stanley Dr FARN GU14 * 87 M4
Stanley Gdns MTCM CR4 * ...29 K9
SAND/SEL CR2 .... 82 A1
WLGTN SM6 .... 62 E5
WOT/HER KT12 .... 57 L4
Stanley Gardens Rd
TEDD TW11 .... 25 M8
Stanley Gn West
DTCH/LGLY SL3 .... 12 D2
Stanley Gv CROY/NA CRO 45 J7
Stanley HI CHOB/PIR GU24 ...90 C2
Stanley Park Rd CAR SM5 ...62 C7
Stanley Rd ACT W3 .... 17 P1
ASHF TW15 .... 23 J8
BELMT SM2 .... 61 M5

CAR SM5 .... 62 C6
CROY/NA CRO 45 J8
HSLW TW3 .... 16 C9
MORT/ESHN SW14 .... 17 P9
TEDD TW11 .... 24 C1
WHTN TW2 .... 25 M2
WIM/MER SW19 .... 43 L1
WOKN/KNAP GU21 .... 11 F2
Stanley Sq CAR SM5 .... 62 B7
Stanley St CTHM CR3 .... 101 L2
Stanley Wk BRAK RG12 .... 32 E3
SWTR RH13 .... 192 C6
Stanmore Cl ASC SL5 .... 34 A5
Stanmore Gdns
RCH/KEW TW9 .... 17 M8
SUT SM1 .... 61 N2
Stanmore Rd RCH/KEW TW9 ...17 M8
Stanmore Ter BECK BR3 .... 46 G3
Stannet Wy WLGTN SM6 ..... 62 E3
Stansfield Rd HSLWW TW4 ...15 K7
Stanstead Cl HAYES BR2 .... 47 M6
Stanstead Gv CAT SE6 .... 31 N4
Stanstead Rd CTHM CR3 ....101 N4
FSTH SE23 .... 31 M4
Stansted Rd HTHAIR TW6 .... 23 J2
Stanthorpe Cl
STRHM/NOR SW16 * 29 P8
Stanthorpe Rd
STRHM/NOR SW16 .... 29 P8
Stanton Av TEDD TW11 .... 25 M9
Stanton Cl CRAN GU6 .... 152 E9
HOR/WEW KT19 .... 59 P4
WPK KT4 .... 43 H9
Stanton Dr FLEETN GU51 ....86 B7
Stanton Rd BARN SW13 .... 18 D7
CROY/NA CRO 45 L8
RYNPK SW20 .... 43 H3
Stanton Whf SHGR GU5 .... 132 E6
Stanton Wy DTCH/LGLY SL3 ...12 C2
SYD SE26 .... 31 N7
Stanwell Cl
STWL/WRAY TW19 .... 22 G2
Stanwell Gdns
STWL/WRAY TW19 * 22 G2
Stanwell Moor Rd STA TW18 ...22 E5
WDR/YW UB7 .... 13 M6
Stanwell New Rd STA TW18 ...22 E7
Stanwell Pl
STWL/WRAY TW19 * 22 F2
Stanwell Rd ASHF TW15 ..... 23 H6
DTCH/LGLY SL3 .... 12 F8
EBED/NFELT TW14 .... 23 M3
Stanwick Rd WKENS W14 .... 19 K2
Staplecross Ct
CRAWW RH11 * 176 C9
Staplefield Cl
BRXS/STRHM SW2 * 29 P4
Stapleford Cl KUT/HW KT1 .... 9 J5
STRHM/NOR SW19 .... 28 B3
Staple HI CHOB/PIR GU24 ... 53 K5
Staplehurst BRAK RG12 .... 32 A8
Staplehurst Cl REIG RH2 ....119 N9
Staplehurst Rd CAR SM5 .... 62 A6
REIG RH2 .... 119 N9
Staple La RGUE GU4 .... 114 A4
Stapleton Gdns
CROY/NA CRO 63 J4
Stapleton Rd TOOT SW17 ... 29 K6
Starborough Rd EDEN TN8 ...144 C9
Star Cl SWTR RH13 .... 192 F6
Star & Garter HI
RCHPK/HAM TW10 .... 26 D4
Star HI RFNM GU10 .... 164 C1
Star Hill Dr RFNM GU10 ....146 C9
Star La ASHV GU12 .... 109 H4
COUL/CHIP CR5 .... 100 C2
Starling Gd CROY/NA CRO 46 E7
Star Post Rd CBLY GU15 .... 50 D5
Star Rd ISLW TW7 .... 16 D7
WKENS W14 .... 19 K4
Starrock La COUL/CHIP CR5 ...80 D8
Starrock Rd COUL/CHIP CR5 ...80 D8
Starveall Cl WDR/YW UB7 ... 14 B1
Starwood Cl BF/WBF KT14 ... 55 M4
Starwood Ct DTCH/LGLY SL3 ...12 A4
Staten Gdns TWK TW1 .... 25 N4
Statham Ct BNFD RG42 .... 32 A2
Station Ap ASHV GU12 .... 89 J8
BECK BR3 .... 46 G2
BELMT SM2 .... 61 M6
BELMT SM2 * 61 M8
BF/WBF KT14 .... 73 L1
BLKW GU17 .... 68 A4
COUL/CHIP CR5 .... 80 B7
COUL/CHIP CR5 .... 80 F5
CROY/NA CRO 3 F4
CTHM CR3 .... 82 A6
EDEN TN8 .... 144 C4
EHSLY KT24 .... 94 G3
ESH/CLAY KT10 .... 58 F2
EW KT17 .... 60 F8
FUL/PGN SW6 * 19 J8
GODL GU7 .... 131 K9
GU GU1 .... 6 C5
GU GU1 .... 7 G4
HAYES BR2 .... 47 M5
HOR/WEW KT19 .... 60 D4
HOR/WEW KT19 .... 78 B2
HORL RH6 .... 159 L1
HORS RH12 .... 193 J1
HPTN TW12 .... 40 A2
HYS/HAR UB3 .... 15 H1
KUT/HW KT1 .... 8 B2
LHD/OX KT22 .... 96 C1
LING RH7 .... 143 L8
LIPH GU30 .... 182 E8
NRWD SE19 * 45 N5
NWMAL KT3 .... 42 F6
PGE/AN SE20 .... 31 K9
PUR/KEN CR8 .... 81 L2
REDH RH1 .... 100 E3
RFNM GU10 .... 126 A9
RGUE GU4 .... 132 D6
SHPTN TW17 .... 38 E6
SNWD SE25 .... 45 P5
STWL/WRAY TW19 .... 21 L2
SUN TW16 .... 39 J1
SWTR RH13 .... 192 D8
TEDD TW11 .... 25 N6
THDIT KT7 .... 40 F8
TWK TW1 .... 25 N4
WIM/MER SW19 .... 43 N2
WOKS/MYFD GU22 .... 10 D5
WWKM BR4 .... 47 J9
Station Rd East ASHV GU12 ...89 H8
OXTED RH8 .... 103 L8
Station Rd North REDH RH1 ...100 E8
Station Rd South REDH RH1 ...100 E8
Station Rd West OXTED RH8 ...103 L9
Station Rw RGUE GU4 .... 132 C2
Station Vw ASHV GU12 .... 89 J7
GU GU1 .... 6 C4
Station Wy BRAK RG12 .... 32 E4
CHEAM SM3 .... 61 J5
CRAWE RH10 .... 176 G6

SHPTN TW17 * 38 E7
STA TW18 .... 22 D8
STRHM/NOR SW16 .... 29 N8
SUN TW16 .... 39 J2
SYD SE26 .... 31 N8
VW GU25 .... 36 B5
WEY KT13 .... 56 C2
WOKS/MYFD GU22 .... 10 E4
Station Sq CAR SM5 .... 62 B7
Station Approach Rd
CHSWK W4 .... 18 A5
COUL/CHIP CR5 .... 80 F4
HORL RH6 * 159 L4
KWD/TDW/WH KT20 .... 98 G2
Station Ap West REDH RH1 ...120 B7
Station Av CTHM CR3 .... 102 A4
HOR/WEW KT19 .... 60 C7
NWMAL KT3 .... 42 C4
WOT/HER KT12 .... 57 J8
Station Cl HPTN TW12 .... 40 B2
SWTR RH13 .... 192 C8
Station Crs ASHF TW15 .... 22 G7
Station Est BECK BR3 .... 46 D5
Station Estate Rd
EBED/NFELT TW14 .... 24 C1
Station Garage Ms
STRHM/NOR SW16 * 29 N9
Station Gdns CHSWK W4 .... 18 A5
Station HI ASC SL5 .... 34 A4
CRAWE RH10 .... 177 L4
Station La MFD/CHID GU8 ...150 A6
Station Pde ASHF TW15 ..... 23 K6
BELMT SM2 * 61 N5
BMLY BR1 * 47 N2
CHSWK W4 * 18 A2
EBED/NFELT TW14 * 24 C3
EHSLY KT24 .... 94 G6
RCH/KEW TW9 * 17 N7
STA TW18 * 36 B6
Station Ri WNWD SE27 .... 30 C5
Station Rd ADL/WDHM KT15 ...55 N3
ALDT GU11 .... 108 D4
ASC SL5 .... 34 C7
ASHF TW15 .... 23 J6
BARN SW13 .... 18 E8
BELMT SM2 .... 61 N5
BF/WBF KT14 .... 73 L1
BIL RH14 .... 188 C7
BMLY BR1 .... 47 N2
BRAK RG12 .... 32 D4
BRKHM/BTCW RH3 .... 118 B4
CAR SM5 .... 62 B3
CHERT KT16 .... 37 K9
CHOB/PIR GU24 .... 74 M1
CHSGTN KT9 .... 59 L4
COB KT11 .... 75 N6
CRAWE RH10 .... 176 G6
CRAWE RH10 .... 179 J3
CROY/NA CRO 2 C2
CTHM CR3 .... 101 P7
DORK RH4 .... 116 G7
EDEN TN8 .... 144 G2
ECH TW20 .... 21 M8
EGRIN RH19 .... 180 C2
ESH/CLAY KT10 .... 58 D1
FARN GU14 .... 88 A1
FRIM GU16 .... 68 G7
FROW RH18 .... 181 L8
GDST RH9 .... 122 C2
GODL GU7 .... 131 K9
GODL GU7 .... 131 K9
HORL RH6 .... 159 L4
HORS RH12 .... 189 N3
HORS RH12 .... 192 A2
HPTN TW12 .... 40 B2
HYS/HAR UB3 .... 14 G2
KUT/HW KT1 .... 8 B2
KUTN/CMB KT2 .... 9 H3
LHD/OX KT22 .... 96 C1
LING RH7 .... 143 L8
LIPH GU30 .... 182 E8
NWMAL KT3 .... 42 F6
PGE/AN SE20 .... 31 K9
PUR/KEN CR8 .... 81 L2
REDH RH1 .... 100 E3
RFNM GU10 .... 126 A9
RGUE GU4 .... 132 D6
SHGR GU5 .... 132 D6
SHPTN TW17 .... 38 E6
SNWD SE25 .... 45 P5
STWL/WRAY TW19 .... 21 L2
SUN TW16 .... 39 J1
SWTR RH13 .... 192 D8
TEDD TW11 .... 25 N6
THDIT KT7 .... 40 F8
TWK TW1 .... 25 N4
WIM/MER SW19 .... 43 N2
WOKS/MYFD GU22 .... 10 D5
WWKM BR4 .... 47 J9
Station Rd East ASHV GU12 ...89 H8
OXTED RH8 .... 103 L8
Station Rd North REDH RH1 ...100 E8
Station Rd South REDH RH1 ...100 E8
Station Rd West OXTED RH8 ...103 L9
Station Rw RGUE GU4 .... 132 C2
Station Vw ASHV GU12 .... 89 J7
GU GU1 .... 6 C4
Station Wy BRAK RG12 .... 32 E4
CHEAM SM3 .... 61 J5
CRAWE RH10 .... 176 G6

Station Yd ASHF TW15 * 23 J7
KWD/TDW/WH KT20 * 99 K1
PUR/KEN CR8 * 81 K1
TWK TW1 .... 25 P3
Staunton Rd KUTN/CMB KT2 ...41 M1
Staveley Gdns CHSWK W4 ...18 B6
Staveley Rd ASHF TW15 .... 23 N9
Staveley Wy
WOKN/KNAP GU21 .... 71 L6
Staverton Cl BNFD RG42 .... 32 D1
Stavordale Rd CAR SM5 .... 43 N8
Stayne End VW GU25 .... 35 N5
Stayton Rd SUT SM1 .... 61 L2
Steadfast Rd KUT/HW KT1 .... 8 C3
Steam Farm La
EBED/NFELT TW14 .... 15 H9
Steele Rd CHSWK W4 .... 18 A1
ISLW TW7 .... 16 C9
Steeles Rd ALDT GU11 .... 108 D2
Steel's La LHD/OX KT22 .... 76 C3
Steep HI CHOB/PIR GU24 ... 53 J6
CROY/NA CRO 3 G7
STRHM/NOR SW16 .... 29 N6
Steeple Cl FUL/PGN SW6 .... 19 J8
WIM/MER SW19 .... 28 B7
Steeple Heights Dr
BH/WHM TN16 .... 84 B6
Steeple Point ASC SL5 .... 34 B4
Steepways CSHT GU26 .... 165 L5
Steeres HI HORS RH12 .... 175 J1
Steerforth Copse SHST GU47 ...50 A9
Steerforth St
WAND/EARL SW18 .... 28 E5
Steers La CRAWE RH10 .... 159 M8
Steers Md MTCM CR4 .... 44 B2
Stella Rd TOOT SW17 .... 29 J9
Stembridge Rd PGE/AN SE20 ...46 B3
The Stennings EGRIN RH19 ...162 B9
Stepbridge Pth
WOKN/KNAP GU21 .... 10 B4
Stepgates CHERT KT16 .... 37 M8
Stepgates Cl CHERT KT16 * ...37 M8
Stephen Cl CRAWW RH11 ...176 G2
ECH TW20 .... 21 N9
Stephendale Rd FNM GU9 ...127 P1
FUL/PGN SW6 .... 19 M8
Stephenson Dr EGRIN RH19 ...180 G1
Stephenson Pl CRAWE RH10 ...177 L5
Stephenson Rd WHTN TW2 ...25 H3
Stephenson Wy
CRAWE RH10 .... 177 L5
Stepney Cl CRAWE RH10 ....177 M4
Stepney Wy MTCM CR4 .... 44 C2
The Steps BRAK RG12 .... 32 F4
Sterling Centre BRAK RG12 ...32 F4
Sterling Pk CRAWE RH10 ....159 L9
Sterling Pl EA W5 .... 17 L2
Sterndale Rd WKENS W14 * ...19 H1
Sternhold Av
BRXS/STRHM SW2 .... 29 N5
Sterry Dr HOR/WEW KT19 ...60 C3
THDIT KT7 .... 40 E7
Steucers La FSTH SE23 .... 31 M4
Steve Biko La CAT SE6 .... 31 P7
Steve Biko Wy HSLW TW3 ...5 L9
Stevenage Rd CRAWW RH11 ...176 B9
FUL/PGN SW6 .... 19 H6
Stevens Cl BECK BR3 .... 31 P9
EW KT17 .... 57 J3
HPTN TW12 .... 24 C9
Stevens HI YTLY GU46 .... 67 J3
Stevens' La ESH/CLAY KT10 ...58 G6
Stevens Pl PUR/KEN CR8 ....81 K2
Stewards Ri RFNM GU10 ....127 K6
Stewart KWD/TDW/WH KT20 ...99 M1
Stewart Av SHPTN TW17 ..... 38 C5
Stewart Cl HPTN TW12 .... 24 F9
Stewarts Gv CHEL SW3 .... 19 P5
Steyning Cl CRAWE RH10 ...177 H5
PUR/KEN CR8 .... 81 K5
Steyning Wy HSLWW TW4 ...15 L9
Stickle Down FRIM GU16 ....69 M8
Stidle Gdns HASM GU27 ....184 A4
Stile Hall Gdns CHSWK W4 ...17 N1
Stile Pth SUN TW16 .... 39 J4
Stile Rd DTCH/LGLY SL3 .... 12 B2
Stillers MFD/CHID GU8 * 168 A7
Stillingfleet Rd BARN SW13 ...18 E4
Stillness Rd FSTH SE23 .... 31 N2
Stilwell Cl YTLY GU46 .... 67 J3
Stirling Av SHPTN TW17 ..... 38 C4
WLGTN SM6 .... 62 G6
Stirling Cl ASHV GU12 .... 109 H1
BNSTD SM7 .... 79 K6
CRAWE RH10 .... 177 L6
FARN GU14 .... 88 C4
FRIM GU16 .... 68 G6
Stirling Dr CTHM CR3 .... 101 L1
Stirling Gv HSLW TW3 .... 16 C7
Stirling Rd ACT W3 .... 17 P1
GUW GU2 .... 111 K9
WHTN TW2 .... 25 H3
Stirling Wk BRYLDS KT5 .... 41 P7
Stirling Wy ALDT GU11 .... 87 P8
EGRIN RH19 .... 162 C9
SWTR RH13 .... 192 D8
Stirrup Wy CRAWE RH10 ....177 L5
Stites Hill Rd COUL/CHIP CR5 ...81 L9
Stoatley Hollow HASM GU27 ...184 B2
Stoatley Ri HASM GU27 ....184 B2
Stoatley River HASM GU27 ...184 B2
Stoats Nest Rd
COUL/CHIP CR5 .... 80 G4
Stockbridge Dr ALDT GU11 ...108 E8
Stockbridge Rd FLEETN GU51 ...86 D3
Stockbridge Wy YTLY GU46 ...67 H4
Stockbury Rd CROY/NA CRO ...46 C7
Stockers La
WOKS/MYFD GU22 .... 72 D9
Stockfield HORL RH6 * 140 D9

Stockfield Rd ESH/CLAY KT10 ..58 E4
　STRHM/NOR SW16 ...30 A6
Stockhams Cl SAND/SEL CR2 ..63 M8
Stock Hl BH/WHM TN16 ...84 B5
Stockhurst Cl PUT/ROE SW15..18 G7
Stockley Farm Rd
　WDR/YW UB7 ...14 D1
Stockley Rd WDR/YW UB7....14 D1
Stockport Rd
　STRHM/NOR SW16 ...44 F2
Stocks Cl FRIM RH6 ...159 L2
Stockton Av FLEETN GU51...86 F5
Stockton Pk FLEETN GU51...86 F5
Stockton Rd REIG RH2 ...119 L8
Stockwell Cl BMLY BR1 ...47 P5
Stockwell Rd EGRIN RH19...180 D5
Stockwood Ri CBLY GU15...69 L3
Stockwood Wy FNM GU9 ...108 B7
Stocton Cl GU GU1 ...6 D1
Stocton Rd GU GU1....6 E1
Stodart Rd PGE/AN SE20 ...46 C2
Stofford Cl WIM/MER SW19...28 B4
Stoke Cl COB KT11 ...75 P5
Stoke Flds GU GU1 ...6 E4
Stokeford Cl BRAK RG12....33 H6
Stoke Gv GU GU1 ...7 F3
Stoke Hills FNM GU9.....5 J1
Stoke Ms GU GU1 ...7 F3
Stoke Mill Cl GU GU1 ...112 B3
Stokenchurch St
　FUL/PGN SW6 ...19 M6
Stoke Park Ct GU GU1 * ...7 F3
Stoke Ridings
　KWD/TDW/WH KT20 * ...99 H3
Stoke Rd COB KT11 ...75 N5
　KUTN/CMB K12 ...42 A1
　WOT/HER KT12 ...57 L2
Stokesby Rd CHSGTN KT9...59 M5
Stokes Cl CRAWE RH10...177 M8
Stokes Ridings
　KWD/TDW/WH KT20 *...99 H3
Stokes Rd CROY/NA CR0....46 D7
Stompond La WOT/HER KT12..57 J1
Stonards Brow SHGR GU5 ...133 H9
Stondon Pk FSTH SE23....31 M2
Stonebanks WOT/HER KT12...39 J8
Stonebridge Ct
　HORS RH12 *....191 P8
Stonebridge Flds RGUE GU4..132 B3
Stonebridge Whf RGUE GU4..132 B3
Stonecot Cl CHEAM SM3 ...43 J9
Stonecot Hl CHEAM SM3....43 J9
Stonecourt Cl HORL RH6....159 M1
Stone Crs EBED/NFELT TW14...24 A3
Stonecroft Wy CROY/NA CR0 ...44 G8
Stonecrop Rd RGUE GU4 ...112 C5
Stonedene Cl BOR GU35 ...164 E7
　FROW RH18....181 N9
Stonefield Cl CRAWE RH10 ...176 G6
Stonegate CBLY GU15 ...69 L2
Stone Hall Gdns KENS W8 *..19 M1
Stone Hatch CRAN GU6....177 N8
Stonehill Cl E/LBKH KT23...96 A5
　MORT/ESHN SW14....27 J1
Stonehill Crs CHERT KT16....54 C5
Stonehill Ga ASC SL5 * ...34 D7
Stonehill Pk BOR GU35....164 F7
　CHERT KT16....54 C5
　CHSWK W4....17 N3
　LTWR GU18....52 A8
　MORT/ESHN SW14....27 H1
Stonehills Ct DUL SE21....30 F6
Stone House Gdns
　CTHM CR3....101 N5
Stonehouse Ri FRIM GU16..68 C7
Stonehouse Rd LIPH GU30..182 G6
Stoneings La RSEV TN14...85 K7
Stoneleigh Av WPK KT4 ...60 E2
Stoneleigh Broadway
　EW KT17....60 E1
Stoneleigh Cl EGRIN RH19..180 E1
Stoneleigh Cl FRIM GU16...60 E1
Stoneleigh Crs
　HOR/WEW KT19....60 E4
Stoneleigh Pk WEY KT13....56 E5
Stoneleigh Park Av
　CROY/NA CR0....46 D7
Stoneleigh Park Rd
　HOR/WEW KT19....60 D5
Stoneleigh Rd CAR SM5...44 A8
　OXTED RH8....124 C1
Stonell's Rd TOOT SW17...28 F6
Stone Park Av BECK BR3....46 G5
Stonepark Dr FROW RH18..181 M9
Stonepit Cl GODL GU7 ...131 H9
Stone Pl WPK KT4....60 D1
Stone Crs Cl HORL RH6 ...159 M1
Stones La DORK RH4....116 C8
Stone's Rd EW KT17....60 C9
Stone St ASHV GU12....108 F6
Stonewood Rd OXTED RH8..123 P2
Stoney Bottom GSHT GU26..165 M8
Stoney Brook GUW GU2...111 L4
Stoneybrook HORS RH12...191 N9
Stoney Cl YTLY GU46....67 H4
Stoney Cft COUL/CHIP CR5..100 C2
Stoneyfield Rd
　COUL/CHIP CR5....81 H6
Stoneyfields FNM GU9...128 C5
Stoneyland Ct EGH TW20...21 L8
Stoneylands Rd EGH TW20..21 L8
Stoney La BMFD SE19....30 C9
Stoney Rd BNFD RG42....32 C2
Stonnell's Rd BTSEA SW11...29 J1
Stonny Cft ASHTD KT21....77 M6
Stonor Rd WKENS W14....19 K2
Stony Hl ESH/CLAY KT10...57 P6
Stookes Wy YTLY GU46....66 F4

Stopham Rd CRAWE RH10...177 M8
Stormont Wy CHSGTN KT9 ...59 J4
Stornaway Rd
　DTCH/LGLY SL3....12 G2
Storrington Rd CROY/NA CR0...3 K4
Storrs La RGUW GU3....91 J4
Stott Cl WAND/EARL SW18..28 C2
Stoughton Av CHEAM SM3...61 H4
Stoughton Cl PUT/ROE SW15..27 M4
Stoughton Rd GUW GU2....111 N2
Stour Av NWDGN UB2....16 A1
Stourhead Cl FARN GU14...88 F3
　WIM/MER SW19....28 A3
Stourhead Gdns
　RYNPK SW20....42 E4
Stourton Av FELT TW13....24 G7
Stovolds Hl CRAN GU6....169 P3
Stovold's Wy ALDT GU11...108 B6
Stowell Av CROY/NA CR0....65 K8
Strachan Pl RYNPK SW20...27 P9
Stradella Rd HNHL SE24....30 D2
Stratford Rd HORS RH11...25 P3
　TWK TW1....25 J5
Straight Rd WDSR SL4....20 G2
Strand Cl CRAWE RH10....177 N7
　EPSOM KT18....78 B8
Strand Dr RCH/KEW TW9....17 P5
Strand-on-the-Green
　CHSWK W4....17 N4
Strangways Ter WKENS W14..19 K1
Stratfield BRAK RG12....32 A9
Stratford Ct NWMAL KT3....42 B5
Stratford Gv PUT/ROE SW15..19 H9
Stratford Rd ASHV GU12...89 H7
　HTHAIR TW6....23 L2
　KENS W8....19 M2
　NWDGN UB2....15 N2
　THHTH CR7....45 J5
Strathan Cl
　WAND/EARL SW18....28 A3
Strathavon Cl CRAN GU6..152 E5
Strathblaine Rd BTSEA SW11..28 G1
Strathbrook Rd
　STRHM/NOR SW16....30 A8
Strathcona Av GT/LBKH KT23..95 N8
Strathdale
　STRHM/NOR SW16....30 A8
Strathdon Dr TOOT SW17...28 G6
Strathearn Av HYS/HAR UB3..15 H5
　WHTN TW2....25 K4
Strathearn Rd SUT SM1....61 L4
　WIM/MER SW19....28 D8
Strathleven Rd
　BRXS/STRHM SW2....29 P1
Strathmore Cl CTHM CR3..101 N1
Strathmore Rd
　CRAWW RH11....176 D2
　CROY/NA CR0....45 L8
　TEDD TW11....25 M7
　WIM/MER SW19....28 D6
Strathville Rd
　WAND/EARL SW18....28 E5
Strathyre Av
　STRHM/NOR SW16....45 J4
Stratton Av WLGTN SM6...62 F7
Stratton Cl HSLW TW3....15 P6
　WIM/MER SW19....43 K3
　WOT/HER KT12 *....39 L9
Stratton Rd SUN TW16....39 H3
　WIM/MER SW19....43 L3
Stratton Ter BH/WHM TN16..104 G7
Stratton Wy GUW GU14....68 C9
Strawberry Cl
　CHOB/PIR GU24....90 D1
Strawberry Ct FRIM GU16...69 M8
Strawberry Flds
　CHOB/PIR GU24....70 G4
Strawberry Hill Rd TWK TW1 ..25 N6
Strawberry La CAR SM5....62 B2
Strawberry Ri
　CHOB/PIR GU24....70 G4
Strawberry V TWK TW1....25 N6
Straw Cl CTHM CR3....101 L3
Strawson Ct HORL RH6....140 B9
Stream Cl BF/WBF KT14....74 A1
Stream Farm Cl
　RFNM GU10....127 P6
Streamline Ms EDUL SE22...31 J4
Stream Pk EGRIN RH19....161 P9
Streamside CBLY GU15....86 G7
Streamside Cl HAYES BR2..47 N5
Stream Valley Rd
　RFNM GU10....127 N7
Streatfield EDEN TN8....145 H4
Streatham Cl
　STRHM/NOR SW16 *....29 P5
Streatham Common
　STRHM/NOR SW16....44 F1
Streatham Common North
　STRHM/NOR SW16....30 A8
Streatham Common South
　STRHM/NOR SW16....29 P9
Streatham Ct
　STRHM/NOR SW16....29 P6
Streatham Gn
　STRHM/NOR SW16....29 P7
Streatham High Rd
　STRHM/NOR SW16....29 P7
Streatham Hi
　BRXS/STRHM SW2....29 P4
Streatham Pl
　BRXS/STRHM SW2....29 P3
Streatham V
　STRHM/NOR SW16....44 E1
Streathbourne Rd TOOT SW17 ..29 K5
Streatleigh Pde
　STRHM/NOR SW16 *....29 P5
Street End HTWY RG27....86 B3
Streeters Cl GODL GU7....131 N7
Streeters La WLGTN SM6...62 F2
Streetfield Rd SWTR RH13..190 E7
Street Hl CRAWE RH10....177 P6

Streets Heath
　CHOB/PIR GU24....52 F9
The Street ASHTD KT21....77 M7
　BIL RH14....187 K8
　BRKHM/BTCW RH3....118 B5
　CRAN GU6....153 P6
　EHSLY KT24....94 D8
　EHSLY KT24....95 M7
　FLEETN GU51....106 D1
　HORL RH6....158 B5
　LHD/OX KT22....96 D2
　MFD/CHID GU8....130 D6
　MFD/CHID GU8....148 D8
　MFD/CHID GU8....151 K8
　RDKG RH5....156 C6
　RFNM GU10....109 H9
　RFNM GU10....127 J7
　RFNM GU10....128 G6
　RGUE GU4....113 L1
　RGUE GU4....113 P2
　RGUE GU4....130 B1
　RGUW GU3....130 B1
　RGUW GU3....131 H3
　SHGR GU5....132 E6
　SWTR RH13....190 E6
Stretton Rd CROY/NA CR0...45 N8
Strickland Cl FRIM GU16...69 L8
Strickland Cl CRAWW RH11..176 B6
Strickland Rw
　WAND/EARL SW18....28 C3
Stringer's Av RGUE GU4....92 B8
Stringhams Copse
　RPLY/SEND GU23....93 K4
Strode Rd FUL/PGN SW6...19 H5
Strodes College La EGH TW20..21 L8
Strode St EGH TW20....21 M7
Strond Green Gdns
　CROY/NA CR0....46 C8
Strond Green Wy
　CROY/NA CR0....46 C8
Strood La HORS RH12....191 K3
Stroude Crs PUT/ROE SW15..27 L6
Stroude Rd EGH TW20....21 M9
　VW GU25....36 C5
Stroudes Cl WPK KT4....42 D8
Strood Green Wy
　CROY/NA CR0....46 C7
Stroud La FLEETN GU51....106 C1
　SHGR GU5....152 D2
Stroudley Cl CRAWE RH10..177 L6
Stroud Rd SNWD SE25....46 A7
　WIM/MER SW19....28 A8
Stroudwater Pk WEY KT13..56 D5
Stroud Wy ASHF TW15....23 L9
Strudgate Cl CRAWE RH10..177 L7
Strudwicks Fld CRAN GU6..153 J8
Stuart Av HAYES BR2....47 K7
　WOT/HER KT12....39 L9
Stuart Cl CRAWE RH10....177 M6
　FARN GU14....88 C2
Stuart Crs CROY/NA CR0....64 F2
　REIG RH2....119 L8
Stuart Gv TEDD TW11....25 M8
Stuart Pl MTCM CR4....44 B2
Stuart Rd RCHPK/HAM TW10 ..26 C9
　REIG RH2....119 L8
　THHTH CR7....45 L5
　WARL CR6....82 B9
　WIM/MER SW19....28 D6
Stuart Wy EGRIN RH19....180 E4
　STA TW18....22 E9
　VW GU25....36 C5
Stubbs Folly SHST GU47....67 P1
Stubbs Hl ORP BR6....85 N2
Stubbs La
　KWD/TDW/WH KT20....99 K8
Stubbs Moor Rd FARN GU14..88 B2
Stubbs Wy WIM/MER SW19..43 P2
Stubfield HORS RH13....191 P7
Stubpond La LING RH7....161 L5
Stubs Cl DORK RH4....117 J9
Stubs Hl DORK RH4....117 J9
Stucley Rd HEST TW5....16 C5
Studdridge St FUL/PGN SW6..19 L7
Studios Rd SHPTN TW17....38 B4
Studland Rd BF/WBF KT14 ..74 B2
　KUTN/CMB KT2....26 D9
　SYD SE26....31 L8
Studland St HMSMTH W6....18 F2
Studley Grange Rd HNWL W7..16 A1
Stumblets CRAWE RH10....177 M4
Stumps Hill La BECK BR3....31 P9
Sturdee Ct FRIM GU16....68 C7
Sturt Av HASM GU27....184 C6
Sturt Ct RGUE GU4....112 F3
Sturt Rd FNM GU9....107 M7
　FRIM GU16....89 H2

HORL RH6....159 K2
Suffolk Combe BNFD RG42 ...33 H1
Suffolk Cl FRIM GU16....69 M8
Suffolk Dr RGUE GU4....92 F9
Suffolk Rd BARN SW13....18 D5
　SNWD SE25....45 N5
　WPK KT4....60 D1
Suffolk Vls
　WAND/EARL SW18 *....28 C3
Sugden Rd THDIT KT7....40 G9
Sulina Rd BRXS/STRHM SW2 ..29 P3
Sulivan Ct FUL/PGN SW6....19 L7
Sulivan Rd FUL/PGN SW6...19 L8
Sullington Hl CRAWW RH11 ..176 C7
Sullington Md HORS RH12..191 M7
Sullivan Cl E/WMO/HCT KT8..40 A6
　FARN GU14....88 C3
Sullivan Dr CRAWW RH11...176 B9
Sullivan Rd CBLY GU15....68 C3
Sullivans Reach
　WOT/HER KT12....39 J8
Sultan St BECK BR3....46 E3
Sumburgh Rd BAL SW12....29 K2
Summer Av E/WMO/HCT KT8..40 E6
Summer Crossing THDIT KT7..40 F6
Summerene Cl
　STRHM/NOR SW16....44 E1
Summerfield ASHTD KT21...77 K8
Summerfield La RFNM GU10..146 D2
　SURB KT6....59 K1
Summerfield Pl
　CHERT KT16 *....55 H5
Summerfields Cl
　ADL/WDHM KT15....55 K4
Summer Gdns CBLY GU15...69 L3
　E/WMO/HCT KT8....40 E6
Summerhayes Cl
　WOKN/KNAP GU21....72 C3
Summerhays COB KT11....75 M2
Summerhill Wy MTCM CR4...44 C2
Summerhouse Av HEST TW5..15 N6
Summerhouse Cl GODL GU7..131 L7
Summerhouse La
　WDR/YW UB7....13 P4
Summerhouse Rd
　GODL GU7....150 C1
Summerlands CRAN GU6....153 H8
Summerlay Cl
　KWD/TDW/WH KT20....99 J3
Summerleigh WEY KT13 *...56 F5
Summerley St
　WAND/EARL SW18....28 E5
Summer Rd E/WMO/HCT KT8..40 A6
　WEY KT13....56 C9
Summers Cl BELMT SM2....61 L6
　WEY KT13....56 C9
Summers La GODL GU7....130 C5
Summer's Rd GODL GU7....131 N5
Summerstown TOOT SW17...28 F6
Summersvere Cl
　CRAWE RH10 *....177 K2
Summerswood Cl
　PUR/KEN CR8....81 M5
Summer Trees SUN TW16...39 K5
Summerville Gdns SUT SM1..61 K5
Summerwood Rd TWK TW1...25 N2
Summit Av FARN GU14....87 N4
Summit Cl EWKG RG40....48 D3
Summit Wy NRWD SE19....45 N1
Sumner Cl LHD/OX KT22....96 C4
Sumner Gdns CROY/NA CR0..45 J9
Sumner Pl ADL/WDHM KT15..55 L4
　SKENS SW7....19 P2
Sumner Place Ms SKENS SW7..19 P2
Sumner Rd CROY/NA CR0....2 A1
　FRIM GU9....5 H1
Sumner Rd South
　CROY/NA CR0....45 J9
Summit Hl WEY KT13....56 C6
Sun Brow HASM GU27....184 A5
Sunbury Av
　MORT/ESHN SW14....18 B9
Sunbury Cl WOT/HER KT12...39 J7
Sunbury Ct SUN TW16....39 M3
Sunbury Court Rd SUN TW16..39 L3
Sunbury La BTSEA SW11....19 P6
　WOT/HER KT12....39 H7
Sunbury Rd CHEAM SM3....61 H2
　FELT TW13....24 A6
Sunbury Wy FELT TW13....24 B9
Suncroft Pl SYD SE26....31 K6
Sundale Av SAND/SEL CR2...63 P8
Sunderland Mt FSTH SE23 *..31 L5
Sunderland Rd EA W5....17 K1
　FSTH SE23....31 L5
Sundew Cl CRAWW RH11...176 D9
　LTWR GU18....52 D9
Sundial Av SNWD SE25....45 P3
Sundon Crs VW GU25....35 N5
Sundown Av SAND/SEL CR2..81 N5
Sundown Rd ASHF TW15....23 M8
Sundridge Hl RSEV TN14....85 M7
Sundridge La RSEV TN14....85 N6
Sundridge Pde BMLY BR1 *...47 P1
Sundridge Rd CROY/NA CR0..3 K1
　WOKS/MYFD GU22....72 E8
Sun Hl WOKS/MYFD GU22...91 P1
Sun Inn Rd MFD/CHID GU8..169 L8
Sunken Rd CROY/NA CR0....64 B5
Sunkist Wy WLGTN SM6....62 G7
Sunlight Cl WIM/MER SW19 *..28 F9
Sunmead Cl LHD/OX KT22...96 F2
Sunmead Pde LHD/OX KT22 *..96 G2
Sunmead Rd SUN TW16....39 K5
Sunna Gdns SUN TW16....39 K3
Sunning Av ASC SL5....34 E8
Sunningdale Av FELT TW13...24 E4
Sunningdale Cl SURB KT6....59 L1

Sunningdale Ct
　CRAWE RH10....176 G2
Sunningdale Gdns KENS W8 *..19 L1
Sunningdale Pk ASC SL5 *...34 F6
Sunningdale Rd SUT SM1....61 K2
　SURB KT6....59 L1
Sunninghill Cl ASC SL5....34 D5
Sunninghill Pk ASC SL5 *...34 D3
Sunninghill Rd ASC SL5....34 D6
　BFOR GU20....52 A2
Sunningvale Av
　BH/WHM TN16....84 A4
Sunningvale Cl
　BH/WHM TN16....84 B5
Sunny Av CRAWE RH10....179 H5
Sunnybank ASC SL5....34 A5
Sunny Bank EPSOM KT18....78 A5
　SNWD SE25....46 A5
　WARL CR6....82 E6
Sunnybank Ms ASHV GU12 *..109 K3
Sunnybank Rd FARN GU14...87 P1
Sunnycroft Rd HSLW TW3....16 B7
　SNWD SE25....46 A5
Sunnydell La FNM GU9....127 L7
Sunnydene Rd PUR/KEN CR8..81 K2
Sunnydene St SYD SE26....31 M7
Sunny Down
　MFD/CHID GU8....149 M7
Sunny Hi MFD/CHID GU8....149 M7
Sunnyhill Cl CRAWE RH10...179 H3
Sunnyhill Rd ALDT GU11....107 P4
Sunnyhill Rd
　STRHM/NOR SW16....29 P7
Sunnyhurst Cl SUT SM1....61 L2
Sunnymead CRAWE RH10 *..179 J3
　CRAWW RH11....176 G5
Sunnymead Av MTCM CR4...44 F4
Sunnymead Rd
　PUT/ROE SW15....27 N1
Sunnymede Av CAR SM5....61 P9
　HOR/WEW KT19....60 C7
Sunny Nook Gdns
　SAND/SEL CR2....63 M5
Sunny Ri CTHM CR3....101 M4
Sunnyside CAT SE6 *....31 N3
　FLEETN GU51....86 E5
　WIM/MER SW19....28 B9
　WOKN/KNAP GU21 *....71 H9
Sunnyside Pas
　WIM/MER SW19....28 A9
Sunnyside Rd BOR GU35....164 F7
　TEDD TW11....25 L7
Sunnyview Cl ALDT GU11....108 E5
Sunray Av BRYLDS KT5....59 P1
　HNHL SE24....30 E1
Sun Ray Est SHST GU47....49 K9
Sunrise Cl FELT TW13....24 G6
Sun Rd WKENS W14....19 K3
Sunset Gdns SNWD SE25....45 N3
Sunset Rd WIM/MER SW19 *..27 N8
Sunshine Wy MTCM CR4....44 B3
Sunvale Av HASM GU27....183 N4
Sunvale Cl HASM GU27....183 N4
Surbiton Ct SURB KT6....41 J7
Surbiton Crs KUT/HW KT1....41 L5
Surbiton Hall Cl KUT/HW KT1..41 L6
Surbiton Hill Pk BRYLDS KT5 ..41 M6
Surbiton Hill Rd SURB KT6...41 L5
　KUT/HW KT1....41 L5
Surrenden Ri CRAWW RH11 ..194 F12
Surrey Av CBLY GU15....68 C4
Surrey Ri BNFD RG42....33 H1
Surrey Crs CHSWK W4....17 N3
Surrey Gdns EHSLY KT24....95 H5
Surrey Gv SUT SM1....61 P2
Surrey Hills Av
　KWD/TDW/WH KT20....118 A2
Surrey Ms WNWD SE27....30 F7
Surrey Rd PECK SE15....31 L1
　WWKM BR4....47 H9
Surrey St CROY/NA CR0....2 C4
Surrey Wy GUW GU2....6 A6
Surridge Ct BAGS GU19....51 N7
Surridge Gdns NRWD SE19...30 E9
Sury Basin KUTN/CMB KT2...8 C2
Sussex Av ISLW TW7....16 E8
Sussex Border Pth
　CRAWE RH10....178 C1
　EDEN TN8....163 P4
　EGRIN RH19....180 F2
　HASM GU27....184 C9
　HORL RH6....158 F4
　HORS RH12....175 H4
　HORS RH14....188 F2
　LIPH GU30....170 C3
　MFD/CHID GU8....187 K4
　RDKG RH5....172 F6
　RDKG RH5....174 A3
Sussex Cl NWMAL KT3....42 C5
　REIG RH2....119 P6
　TWK TW1....26 A2
Sussex Crs WOKN/KNAP GU21..71 J6
Sussex Gdns CHSGTN KT9...59 K5
　FLEETN GU51....87 H3
Sussex Pl HMSMTH W6....18 G3
　NWMAL KT3....42 C5
Sussex Rd CAR SM5....62 B5
　NWDGN UB2....15 M1
　NWMAL KT3....42 C5
　SAND/SEL CR2....63 M5
　WOKN/KNAP GU21....71 J7
　WWKM BR4....47 H9
Sussex Ter PGE/AN SE20 *....46 C1
Sutherland Av
　BH/WHM TN16....84 B6
　HYS/HAR UB3....15 J2
　RGUE GU4....92 C8
　SUN TW16....39 J3
Sutherland Cha ASC SL5....33 N3
Sutherland Dr RGUE GU4....112 E2
　WIM/MER SW19....43 P2

Sutherland Gdns
MORT/ESHN SW14 ....18 C8
SUN TW16 ....39 H3
WPK KT4 ....42 F9
Sutherland Gv *TEDD* TW11 ....25 M8
Sutherland Rd *CHSWK* W4 ....18 A4
CROY/NA CR0 ....45 J8
Sutton Av *WOKN/KNAP* GU21 ...71 L8
Sutton Cl *BECK* BR3 ....47 H2
CHSWK W4 * 18 A4
Sutton Common Rd
CHEAM SM3 ....43 K8
Sutton Ct *BELMT* SM2 ....61 N6
CHSWK W4 * 18 A4
Sutton Court Rd *CHSWK* W4 ...18 A4
REDH RH1 ....100 F9
Sutton Dene *HSLW* TW3 ....16 B6
Sutton Gdns *CROY/NA* CR0 ....45 P6
REDH RH1 ....100 F9
Sutton Green Rd *RGUE* GU4 ...92 C6
Sutton Hall *HEST* TW5 ....16 A5
Sutton Hill *RGUE* GU4 ....92 C9
Sutton La *BNSTD* SM7 ....79 M1
CHSWK W4 ....18 A3
DTCH/LGLY SL3 ....12 C3
HSLW TW3 ....15 P7
RDKG RH5 ....135 K5
Sutton La South *CHSWK* W4 ..18 A4
Sutton Park Rd *SUT* SM1 .....61 M5
DTCH/LGLY SL3 ....12 C4
RDKG RH5 ....135 H5
Sutton Rd *CBLY* GU15 ....51 J8
HEST TW5 ....16 A6
Sutton Sq *HEST* TW5 ....15 P6
Sutton Wy *HEST* TW5 ....15 P6
Swaby Rd *WAND/EARL* SW18 ...28 F5
Swaffield Rd
WAND/EARL SW18 ....28 F3
Swain Cl *STRHM/NOR* SW16 ...29 L3
Swain Rd *THHTH* CR7 ....45 L6
Swains Rd *MTCM* CR4 ....44 B1
Swaledale *BRAK* RG12 ....32 C6
Swaledale Cl *CRAWW* RH11 ...176 F8
Swaledale Gdns
FLEETN GU51 ....87 H3
Swale Rd *FARN* GU14 ....87 P1
Swallands Rd *CAT* SE6 ....31 P6
Swallow Cl *MFD/CHID* GU8 ...149 M5
STA TW18 ....22 C7
YTLY GU46 ....66 F3
Swallowdale *SAND/SEL* CR2 ...64 D7
Swallowfield *EGH* TW20 ....20 C9
LING RH7 ....162 F2
Swallow Ri
WOKN/KNAP GU21 ....71 J6
Swallow Rd *CRAWW* RH11 ....176 F3
Swallow St *CRAWE* RH10 .....179 K6
Swallowtail Rd *HORS* RH12 ..192 D4
Swanage Rd
WAND/EARL SW18 ....28 F2
Swan Barn Rd *HASM* GU27 ..184 E4
Swan Cl *CROY/NA* CR0 * 45 H8
FELT TW13 ....24 F7
Swancote Gn *BRAK* RG12 .....32 D6
Swan Ct *GU* GU1 ....112 B3
Swandon Wy
WAND/EARL SW18 ....19 M9
Swan Island *TWK* TW1 * 7 J5
Swan La *EDEN* TN8 ....144 C1
GU GU1 ....6 E5
HORL RH6 ....158 C5
SHST GU47 ....67 M2
Swan Mill Gdns *DORK* RH4....117 J5
Swanns Meadow
GT/LBKH KT23 ....96 A6
Swan Md *HORS* RH12 ....191 M7
Swan Pl *BARN* SW13 ....18 D7
Swan Rdg *EDEN* TN8 ....145 H1
Swan Rd *FELT* TW13 ....24 F7
Swanscombe Rd *CHSWK* W4...18 C3
Swansea Rd *HTHAIR* TW6......23 M2
Swans Ghyll *FROW* RH18.....181 K8
Swan St *ISLW* TW7 ....17 H8
The Swansway *WEY* KT13 *...56 C2
Swanton Gdns
WIM/MER SW19 ....28 A4
Swan Wk *HORS* RH12 * 192 B8
SHPTN TW17 ....38 C8
Swan Wy *FLEETN* GU51 ......86 D8
Swanwick Cl *PUT/ROE* SW15...27 L3
Swanworth La *RDKG* RH5......97 H8
Swaynes La *GU* GU1 ....113 J5
Sweeps Ditch Cl *STA* TW18 ...37 M2
Sweeps La *EGH* TW20 ....21 L8
Sweetbriar *CWTH* RG45 * 49 L2
Sweet La *SHGR* GU5 ....134 F5
Sweetwater Cl *SHGR* GU5 ...133 H9
Sweetwater La
MFD/CHID GU8 ....149 P9
SHGR GU5 ....133 H9
Swievelands Rd
BH/WHM TN16 ....83 P8
Swift La *BAGS* GU19 ....51 P6
CRAWW RH11 ....176 C3
Swift Rd *FELT* TW13 ....24 F6
FNM GU9 ....107 M7
NWDGN UB2 ....15 P1
Swift's Cl *RFNM* GU10 ....128 C4
Swift St *FUL/PGN* SW6 ....19 J6
Swinburne Crs *CROY/NA* CR0...46 C7
Swinburne Rd
PUT/ROE SW15 ....18 E9
Swindon Rd *HORS* RH12 ......192 A6
HTHAIR TW6 ....23 M2
Swinfield Cl *FELT* TW13 ......24 F7

Swingate Rd *FNM* GU9 ....127 N5
Swinley Rd *ASC* SL5 ....33 L5
Swiss Cl *RFRM* GU10 ....127 K9
Swissland Hl *EGRIN* RH19 ....162 D6
Switchback La *RGUW/GU10*...127 K9
Swithin Cha *BNFD* RG42 ....32 C1
Swordfish Wy *FARN* GU14 ......88 A5
Swordsman's Rd *FRIM* GU16...69 M8
Swyncombe Av *EA* W5 ....17 H2
Sycamore Av *EA* W5 ....17 K1
HORS RH12 * 193 H5
Sycamore Cl *CAR* SM5 ....62 B3
CRAWW RH11 ....176 F2
FELT TW13 ....24 B6
FRIM GU16 ....68 C7
LHD/OX KT22 ....96 F2
SAND/SEL CR2 ....63 N4
SHST GU47 ....67 M1
Sycamore Ct *WEY* KT15 ....57 H2
Sycamore Crs *FLEETN* GU51...86 E9
Sycamore Dr *ASHV* GU12 ....89 H8
EGRIN RH19 ....180 F2
FRIM GU16 ....68 C7
RFNM GU10 ....127 L7
Sycamore Gdns *MTCM* CR4...43 P3
Sycamore Gv *NWMAL* KT3 .....42 C4
PGE/AN SE20 ....46 A2
Sycamore Ri *BNSTD* SM7 ....79 H3
BRAK RG12 ....32 D6
Sycamore Rd *CROY/NA* CR0 ...2 E2
GU GU1 ....6 C1
SYD SE26 ....31 L8
The Sycamores *BLKW* GU17 ...67 M3
FARN GU14 ....88 F4
GT/LBKH KT23 ....96 A6
Sycamore Wk *EGH* TW20 ....20 C9
REIG RH2 ....119 N8
Sycamore Wy *TEDD* TW11 ......26 B9
Sydenham Av *SYD* SE26 ....31 J8
Sydenham Hl *FSTH* SE23 ....31 J5
Sydenham Pk *SYD* SE26 ....31 K6
Sydenham Park Rd *SYD* SE26...31 K6
Sydenham Ri *FSTH* SE23 ....31 J5
Sydenham Rd *CROY/NA* CR0 ...2 E2
GU GU1 ....6 C1
SYD SE26 ....31 L8
Sydenham Station Ap
SYD SE26 ....31 K7
Sydmons Ct *FSTH* SE23 * 31 J5
Sydney Av *PUR/KEN* CR8 ....81 H1
Sydney Cl *CWTH* RG45 ....49 N2
SKENS SW7 ....19 P2
Sydney Crs *ASHF* TW15 ....23 L9
Sydney Loader Pl
BLKW GU17 ....67 L2
Sydney Ms *SKENS* SW7 ....19 P2
Sydney Pl *GU* GU1 ....7 J5
SKENS SW7 ....19 P2
Sydney Rd *EBED/NFELT* TW14..24 A4
GU GU1 ....7 J5
RCH/KEW TW9 ....17 L9
RYNPK SW20 ....42 F3
SUT SM1 ....61 L3
TEDD TW11 ....25 N8
Sydney Smith Av *FARN* GU14...88 D6
Sydney Ter *ESH/CLAY* KT10 *...58 F5
Syke Ings *DTCH/LGLY* SL3 .....13 J1
Sykes Dr *STA* TW18 ....22 E8
Sylvan Cl *OXTED* RH8 ....103 P9
SAND/SEL CR2 ....64 B8
WOKS/MYFD GU22 ....11 K5
Sylvan Gdns *SURB* KT6 ....41 K8
Sylvan Hl *NRWD* SE19 ....45 N2
Sylvan Rd *SHST* GU47 ....49 L8
Sylvan Rd *CRAWE* RH10 ....177 K7
NRWD SE19 ....45 P2
Sylvanus *BRAK* RG12 ....32 B8
Sylvan Wy *FLEETS* GU52 ......106 F1
REDH RH1 ....120 D6
WWKM BR4 ....65 L3
Sylverdale Rd *CROY/NA* CR0...2 A5
PUR/KEN CR8 ....81 K2
Sylverns Ct *BNFD* RG42 ....32 C1
Sylvia Ct *CHOB/PIR* GU24 .....70 C4
Syon Gate Wy *BTFD* TW8 .....17 H6
Syon La *ISLW* TW7 ....16 G5
Syon Pk *ISLW* TW7 * 17 H8
Syon Park Gdns *ISLW* TW7 ...16 G5
Syon Pl *FARN* GU14 ....88 F5
Sythwood *WOKN/KNAP* GU21...71 P6
Szabo Crs *RGUW* GU3 ....110 B5

T

Tabarin Wy *EW* KT17 ....78 C5
Tableer Av *CLAP* SW4 ....29 M1
Tabor Gdns *CHEAM* SM3 ....61 K5
Tabor Gv *WIM/MER* SW19 .....43 J1
Tabor Rd *HMSMTH* W6 ....18 F1
Tachbrook Rd
EBED/NFELT TW14 ....24 A3
NWDGN UB2 ....15 M2
Tadema Rd *WBPTN* SW10 .....19 N5
Tadley Cl *FLEETN* GU51 ....86 D8
Tadmor Cl *SUN* TW16 ....39 H5
Tadorne Rd
KWD/TDW/WH KT20 ....98 G3
Tadpole La *RFNM* GU10 ....107 H5
Tadworth Av *NWMAL* KT3 .....42 D5
Tadworth Cl
KWD/TDW/WH KT20 ....99 H2
Tadworth St
KWD/TDW/WH KT20 ....98 G3
Taffy's How *MTCM* CR4 ....44 A4
Tainters Hl *EDEN* TN8 * 145 H7
Tait Rd *CROY/NA* CR0 ....45 N8
Talavera Cl *CWTH* RG45 ....49 J5

Talbot Av *DTCH/LGLY* SL3 .....12 D1
Talbot Cl *FRIM* GU16 ....89 J3
REIG RH2 ....119 M6
Talbot La *HORS* RH12 ....192 B9
Talbot Pl *BAGS* GU19 ....51 N6
DTCH/LGLY SL3 ....12 A6
Talbot Rd *ASHF* TW15 ....22 G8
CAR SM5 ....62 C4
FNM GU9 ....4 E7
ISLW TW7 ....16 G9
LING RH7 ....162 C1
NWDGN UB2 ....15 M1
THHTH CR7 ....45 M5
Talbot Rd * 25 M4
Talcott Pth
BRXS/STRHM SW2 * 30 B4
Taleworth Cl *ASHTD* KT21 .....77 K9
Taleworth Pk *ASHTD* KT21 ....77 K9
Taleworth Rd *ASHTD* KT21 ....77 K8
Talfourd Wy *REDH* RH1 ....120 B8
Talgarth Dr *FARN* GU14 ....88 F5
Talgarth Rd *WKENS* W14 .....19 J3
Talisman Cl *CWTH* RG45 ....49 H4
Talisman Wy *EW* KT17 ....78 C5
Tall Elms Cl *HAYES* BR2 ....47 M4
Tallis Cl *CRAWW* RH11 ....176 C8
Tall Oaks *BTFD* TW8 ....17 J5
Tall Trees *DTCH/LGLY* SL3 .....13 J6
EGRIN RH19 * 180 E3
STRHM/NOR SW16 ....45 H4
Tally Rd *OXTED* RH8 ....124 C2
Talma Gdns *WHTN* TW2 ....25 M3
Talmage Cl *FSTH* SE23 ....31 K3
Talman Cl *CRAWW* RH11 * ...176 B6
Tamar Cl *CRAWE* RH10 ....177 M6
Tamarind Cl *RGUW* GU3 ....91 N9
Tamar Wy *DTCH/LGLY* SL3 .....12 F3
Tamerton Sq
WOKS/MYFD GU22 ....10 C7
Tamesis Gdns *WPK* KT4 ....60 C1
Tamian Wy *HSLWW* TW4 ....15 L9
Tamworth *BRAK* RG12 ....32 F8
Tamworth Dr *FLEETN* GU51...87 H3
Tamworth La *MTCM* CR4 ....44 D4
Tamworth Pk *MTCM* CR4 ....44 D5
Tamworth Pl *CROY/NA* CR0 ...2 C3
Tamworth Rd *CROY/NA* CR0 ...2 C3
Tamworth St *FUL/PGN* SW6 ...19 L4
Tanbridge Pk *HORS* RH12 ...191 P9
Tanbridge Pl *HORS* RH12 .....192 A9
Tandridge Gdns
SAND/SEL CR2 ....81 P2
Tandridgehill La *GDST* RH9...102 F8
Tandridge La *LING* RH7 ....142 F5
OXTED RH8 ....122 G2
Tandridge Rd *WARL* CR6 ....82 D8
Tanfield Rd *CROY/NA* CR0 .....2 C7
Tangier Rd *GU* GU1 ....112 E6
RCHPK/HAM TW10 ....17 N9
Tangier Wy
KWD/TDW/WH KT20 ....79 J6
Tangier Wd
KWD/TDW/WH KT20 ....79 J7
Tangle Oak *EGRIN* RH19 .....161 M8
Tanglewood *EWKG* RG40 ....48 E2
Tanglewood Cl *CHERT* KT16 ...55 P2
CROY/NA CR0 ....64 C2
WOKS/MYFD GU22 ....73 H5
Tanglewood Ride
CHOB/PIR GU24 ....70 D1
Tanglewood Wy *FELT* TW13 ...24 C5
Tangley Gv *PUT/ROE* SW15 ...27 L3
Tangley La *RGUW* GU3 ....111 M1
Tangley Park Rd
HPTN TW12 ....24 G8
Tanglyn Av *SHPTN* TW17 ....38 C6
Tangmere Gv *KUTN/CMB* KT2...26 C9
Tangmere Rd *CRAWW* RH11...176 C5
Tanhouse Rd *OXTED* RH8 .....123 K3
Tanhurst La *RDKG* RH5 ....154 G2
Tanker Rd *FARN* GU14 ....88 D6
Tankerton Rd *SURB* KT6 ....59 M1
Tankerton Ter
CROY/NA CR0 ....45 H8
Tankerville Rd
STRHM/NOR SW16 ....44 F1
Tank Rd *CBLY* GU15 ....68 B3
Tanners Cl *WOT/HER* KT12 ...39 K7
Tanners Dean *LHD/OX* KT22 ...97 K2
Tannersfield *RGUE* GU4 ....132 C4
Tanner's Hl
BRKHM/BTCW RH3 ....117 P7
Tanners La *HASM* GU27 ....184 D3
Tanners Meadow
BRKHM/BTCW RH3 ....117 P9
Tanners Rd *BAGS* GU19 * 51 N6
Tannery Cl *CROY/NA* CR0 .....46 D6
SWTR RH13 ....190 D7
Tannery La *RPLY/SEND* GU23...93 J2
The Tannery *REDH* RH1 ....120 A5
Tannsfeld Rd *SYD* SE26 ....31 L8
Tansy Cl *RGUE* GU4 ....112 G3
Tantallon Rd *BAL* SW12 ....29 K4
Tanyard Av *EGRIN* RH19 .....180 F3
Tanyard Cl *CRAWE* RH10 .....177 M8
SWTR RH13 ....192 D3
Tanyard Wy *HORL* RH6 ....140 D9
Tapestry Cl *BELMT* SM2 ....61 M6
Taplow Ct *MTCM* CR4 ....44 A5
Tapner's Rd
BRKHM/BTCW RH3 ....138 D2
Tapping Cl *KUTN/CMB* KT2 .....9 H2
Tara Pk *COUL/CHIP* CR5 ....80 B9
Tarbat Ct *SHST* GU47 ....49 P9
Tarbert Rd *EDUL* SE22 ....30 F1
Target Cl *EBED/NFELT* TW14...23 P2
Targett Ct *SWTR* RH13 ....192 G8
Tarham Cl *HORL* RH6 ....140 A8
Tarleton Gdns *FSTH* SE23 .....31 J4
Tarmac Wy *WDR/YW* UB7 .....13 M5

Tarnbrook Wy *BRAK* RG12 .....32 G8
Tarn Cl *FARN* GU14 ....88 A5
Tarn Rd *GSHT* GU26 ....165 N8
Tarragon Cl *FARN* GU14 ....87 N3
Tarragon Dr *GUW* GU2 ....91 N9
Tarragon Gv *SYD* SE26 ....31 L9
Tarrant Cl *BF/WBF* KT14 ....73 K2
Tarrant Gn *BNFD* RG42 ....32 E1
Tarrant Pl *BF/WBF* KT14 * 73 K2
Tarrington Cl
STRHM/NOR SW16 ....29 N7
Tartar Hl *COB* KT11 ....75 K2
Tartar Rd *COB* KT11 ....75 L2
Tasker Cl *HYS/HAR* UB3 ....14 E5
Tasso Rd *HMSMTH* W6 ....19 J4
Tate Cl *LHD/OX* KT22 ....97 J3
Tate Rd *SUT* SM1 ....61 L4
Tatnell Rd *FSTH* SE23 ....31 M2
Tatsfield La *RH/WHM* TW16...104 D1
Tattenham Corner Rd
EPSOM KT18 ....78 E6
Tattenham Crs *EPSOM* KT18...78 E7
Tattenham Wy
KWD/TDW/WH KT20 ....79 J6
Taunton Av *CTHM* CR3 ....101 P3
HSLW TW5 ....16 C7
RYNPK SW20 ....42 F3
Taunton Cl *CHEAM* SM3 ....43 L9
CRAWE RH10 ....177 L4
Taunton La *COUL/CHIP* CR5...81 J8
Tavern Cl *CAR* SM5 ....44 B8
Tavistock Cl *STA* TW18 ....37 P1
Tavistock Crs *MTCM* CR4 .....44 G5
Tavistock Gdns *FARN* GU14...68 D9
Tavistock Gv *CROY/NA* CR0 ...45 M8
Tavistock Rd *CAR* SM5 ....43 P9
CROY/NA CR0 ....2 E1
FLEETN GU51 ....86 E7
HAYES BR2 ....47 N5
Tawfield *BRAK* RG12 ....32 A8
Tawny Cl *FELT* TW13 ....24 B6
Tawny Rw *SHST* GU47 * 49 P9
Tayben Av *WHTN* TW2 ....25 M2
Tay Cl *FARN* GU14 ....88 A1
Tayles Hill Dr *EW* KT17 ....60 D8
Taylor Av *RCH/KEW* TW9 ....17 P7
Taylor Cl *HOR/WEW* KT19 .....59 M3
HPTN TW12 ....25 K8
HSLW TW3 ....16 C6
Taylor Rd *ASHTD* KT21 ....77 K6
MTCM CR4 ....44 A1
WLGTN SM6 ....62 D4
Taylors Cl *FELT* TW13 ....24 B5
Taylors Crs *CRAN* GU6 ....153 J9
Taylor's La *SYD* SE26 ....31 J7
Taylor Wk *CRAWW* RH11 .....176 F5
Taymount Ri *FSTH* SE23 ....31 K5
Taynton Dr *REDH* RH1 ....120 F1
Teal Cl *HORS* RH12 ....192 B5
SAND/SEL CR2 ....64 D9
Teal Ct *DORK* RH4 * 116 C6
Tealing Dr *HOR/WEW* KT19 ...60 B8
Teasel Cl *CRAWW* RH11 ....176 E8
Teazle Wd *CRAWE* RH10 .....179 M6
Teazlewood Pk *LHD/OX* KT22...76 D6
Tebbit Cl *BRAK* RG12 ....32 F3
Teck Cl *ISLW* TW7 ....16 G7
Tedder Cl *CHSGTN* KT9 ....59 J4
Tedder Rd *SAND/SEL* CR2 .....64 D6
Teddington Cl
HOR/WEW KT19 ....60 B8
Teddington Pk *TEDD* TW11 ...25 N8
Teddington Park Rd
TEDD TW11 ....25 N7
Tedham La *GDST* RH9 ....142 B6
Tees Cl *FARN* GU14 ....88 A1
Teesdale *CRAWW* RH11 ....176 F8
Teesdale Av *ISLW* TW7 ....16 G6
Teesdale Gdns *ISLW* TW7 .....16 G6
SNWD SE25 ....45 N3
Teevan Cl *CROY/NA* CR0 ....46 A8
Teevan Rd *CROY/NA* CR0 ....46 A8
Tegg's La *WOKS/MYFD* GU22...73 K5
Tekels Av *CBLY* GU15 ....68 C5
Tekels Wy *CBLY* GU15 ....68 D6
Telconia Cl *BOR* GU35 ....164 F7
Telegraph La *ESH/CLAY* KT10...58 F3
Telegraph Pas
BRXS/STRHM SW2 * 29 P3
Telegraph Rd *PUT/ROE* SW15...27 N3
Telegraph Tr *WLGTN* SM6 .....62 G6
Telephone Pl *WKENS* W14 * ...19 K4
Telferscot Rd *BAL* SW12 ....29 N4
Telford Av *BRXS/STRHM* SW2...29 P4
Telford Cl *NRWD* SE19 ....30 C9
Telford Ct *GU* GU1 ....7 J4
Telford Pl *CRAWE* RH10 ....177 J7
Telford Rd *WHTN* TW2 ....25 H5
Telham Ct *CRAWW* RH11 .....176 C8
Tellisford *ESH/CLAY* KT10 .....58 B3
Temeraire Pl *BTFD* TW8 ....17 M3
Tempest Rd *EGH* TW20 ....21 P9
Templar Cl *SHST* GU47 ....49 L9
Templar Pl *HPTN* TW12 ....40 A1
Temple Av *CROY/NA* CR0 ....65 H1
Temple Bar Rd
WOKN/KNAP GU21 ....71 M8
Temple Cl *CRAWE* RH10 ....177 N6
Templecombe Ms
WOKS/MYFD GU22 ....11 H2
Templecombe Wy
MRDN SM4 ....43 J6
Temple Ct *STA* TW18 ....37 M1
Temple Field Cl
ADL/WDHM KT15 ....55 M5
Temple Gdns *STA* TW18 ....37 K2
Temple La *RDKG* RH5 ....156 B6
Templeman Cl *PUR/KEN* CR8...81 J1
Temple Rd *CHSWK* W4 ....18 A1
CROY/NA CR0 ....2 E7
EA W5 ....17 K1
HOR/WEW KT19 ....78 B1
HSLW TW3 ....16 B9
RCH/KEW TW9 ....17 H7
Temple's Cl *RFNM* GU10 ....128 C4
Temple Sheen Rd
MORT/ESHN SW14 ....18 A9
Templeton Cl *NRWD* SE19 ...45 M2
Templeton Pl *ECT* SW5 .....19 L2
Temple Wood Dr
REDH RH1 ....120 B2
Ten Acre *WOKN/KNAP* GU21...71 N7
Ten Acre La *EGH* TW20 ....36 G3
Ten Acres Cl *LHD/OX* KT22 ...96 D4
Tenby Dr *ASC* SL5 ....34 D6
Tenby Rd *FRIM* GU16 ....68 E8
Tenchley's La *OXTED* RH8 ...124 B2
Tenham Av
BRXS/STRHM SW2 ....29 N5
Tenniel Cl *GUW* GU2 ....111 P3
Tennison Cl *COUL/CHIP* CR5...81 N4
Tennison Rd *SNWD* SE25 .....45 P5
Tennyson Av *NWMAL* KT3 .....42 F6
TWK TW1 ....25 N4
Tennyson Cl *CRAWE* RH10 ...177 L2
EBED/NFELT TW14 ....24 B2
HORS RH12 ....192 D4
Tennyson Ri *EGRIN* RH19 ...180 B2
Tennyson Rd
ADL/WDHM KT15 ....55 N3
ASHF TW15 ....23 H8
HSLW TW3 ....16 C9
PGE/AN SE20 ....46 D1
WIM/MER SW19 ....28 E1
Tennyson's La *HASM* GU27...184 F6
Tensing Rd *NWDGN* UB2 .....16 A1
Tentelow La *NWDGN* UB2 .....16 B1
Tenterden Gdns
CROY/NA CR0 ....46 A8
Tenterden Rd *CROY/NA* CR0 ...46 A8
Tenth Av
KWD/TDW/WH KT20 * 99 K6
Tern Rd *CRAWW* RH11 ....194 E1
Terrace Gdns *BARN* SW13 ...18 D7
Terrace Rd *WOT/HER* KT12 ...39 K3
The Terrace *ADL/WDHM* KT15...56 A4
ASC SL5 ....34 C6
BARN SW13 ....18 C5
CWTH RG45 ....68 B3
FARN GU14 ....88 F4
FSTH SE23 * 31 M3
WOKS/MYFD GU22 * 92 E1
Terrace Vls *HMSMTH* W6 .....18 E3
Terra Cotta Rd *GDST* RH9 ...122 C9
Terrace St *RCH/KEW* TW9 .....17 M9
Terry Rd *CRAWW* RH11 ....194 E1
Tesimond Dr *YTLY* GU46 ....66 E3
Testard Rd *GUW* GU2 ....6 C6
Testers Cl *OXTED* RH8 ....123 P2
Tetcott Rd *WBPTN* SW10 .....19 N5
Tetty Wy *BMLY* BR1 ....47 N2
Teviot Cl *GUW* GU2 ....111 N2
Tewkesbury Av *FSTH* SE23 ...31 J4
Tewkesbury Cl *BF/WBF* KT14...55 K8
Tewkesbury Rd *CAR* SM5 .....43 P9
Teynham Gn *HAYES* BR2 ....47 N6
Thackeray Cl *ISLW* TW7 ....16 G7
Thackeray St *KENS* W8 ....19 M1
Thakeham Cl *SYD* SE26 ....31 J8
Thames Av *CHERT* KT16 ....37 L4
WBPTN SW10 ....19 N6
Thames Bank
MORT/ESHN SW14 ....18 A7
Thames Cl *CHERT* KT16 ....37 M8
FARN GU14 ....88 A1
Thames Down Link
ASHTD KT21 ....77 M3
HOR/WEW KT19 ....60 D3
Thames Eyot *TWK* TW1 * 25 P4
Thamesfield Ct *SHPTN* TW17...38 E8
Thamesfield Ms
SHPTN TW17 * 38 E8
Thames Ga *STA* TW18 ....37 M5
Thamesgate Cl
RCHPK/HAM TW10 ....26 A1
Thameside *TEDD* TW11 ....41 K1
Thames Md *WOT/HER* KT12...39 J8
Thames Meadow
SHPTN TW17 ....38 F9
Thames Pth *BARN* SW13 .....18 E8
ISLW TW7 ....17 J5
STA TW18 ....22 B6
STWL/WRAY TW19 ....13 L1
WEY KT13 ....56 D1
WOT/HER KT12 ....39 J6
Thames Quay
WBPTN SW10 * 19 N6
Thames Reach *KUT/HW* KT1 *...8 B2
DTCH/LGLY SL3 ....8 C3
Thames Side *KUT/HW* KT1 .....8 E3
THDIT KT7 ....57 N6
Thames St *HPTN* TW12 ....40 B3
KUT/HW KT1 ....8 C4
STA TW18 ....22 B6
SUN TW16 ....39 H8
WEY KT13 ....56 B2
WOT/HER KT12 ....39 K6
Thamesvale Cl *HSLW* TW3 ...16 A7
Thames Village *CHSWK* W4 ...18 B6

256 Tha - Tre

Thanescroft Gdns
CROY/NA CR0 3 H6
Thanet Pl CROY/NA CR0 2 D7
Tharp Rd WLGTN SM6 62 F4
Thatcher Cl CRAWE RH10 176 G8
Thatchers Cl HORL RH6 140 D8
HORS RH12 192 D6
Thatchers La RGUW GU3 91 K7
Thatchers Wy ISLW TW7 25 L1
Thaxted Pl RYNPK SW20 43 H1
Thaxton Rd WKENS W14 19 K4
Thayers Farm Rd BECK BR3 46 E2
Theal Cl SHST GU47 49 P9
Theatre Rd FARN GU14 88 D7
The Beverly MRDN SM4 43 H7
The Farriers EDEN TN8 144 F2
The Green WIM/MER SW19 28 A8
Thelma Gv TEDD TW11 25 P9
Thelton Av HORS RH12 191 L7
Theobald Rd CROY/NA CR0 2 A3
Theobalds Wy FRIM GU16 69 L5
Thepps Cl REDH RH1 121 H8
Therapia La CROY/NA CR0 44 G8
Therapia Rd EDUL SE22 31 K2
Theresa Rd HMSMTH W6 18 E2
Theresa's Wk SAND/SEL CR2 63 M7
Thesiger Rd PGE/AN SE20 46 D1
Thetford Rd ASHF TW15 23 H7
NWMAL KT3 42 C6
Theydon Cl CRAWE RH10 177 K7
Thibet Rd SHST GU47 49 N9
Thicket Crs SUT SM1 61 N3
Thicket Gv PGE/AN SE20 46 A1
Thicket Rd PGE/AN SE20 46 B1
SUT SM1 61 N3
Thicket Ter PGE/AN SE20 * 46 A1
Thickthorne La STA TW18 37 N1
Third Av
KWD/TDW/WH KT20 * 99 K6
Third Cl E/WMO/HCT KT8 40 B5
Third Cross Rd WHTN TW2 25 L5
Thirlmere Cl EGH TW20 36 F1
FARN GU14 88 A3
Thirlmere Crs FLEETS GU52 106 E1
Thirlmere Rd CRAWW RH11 176 A7
STRHM/NOR SW16 29 N7
Thirsk Ct ASHV GU12 108 F4
Thirsk Rd MTCM CR4 44 C1
SNWD SE25 45 M5
Thirteenth Av
KWD/TDW/WH KT20 * 99 K6
Thistlecroft Rd
WOT/HER KT12 57 L3
Thistledene BF/WBF KT14 73 K2
THDIT KT7 40 E7
Thistledown V BIL RH14 * 188 A6
Thistle Gv WBPTN SW10 * 19 N3
The Thistles LHD/OX KT22 97 J2
Thistle Wy HORL RH6 141 L9
Thistlewood Crs
CROY/NA CR0 83 K1
Thistleworth Cl ISLW TW7 16 D5
Thistley Cl COUL/CHIP CR5 100 F2
Thistley La CRAN GU6 153 H8
Thistledown V BIL RH14 188 A6
Thomas Av CTHM CR3 101 L1
Thomas Baines Rd
BTSEA SW11 19 P8
Thomas Dean Rd SYD SE26 * 31 H7
Thomas Dr BNFD RG42 * 32 G1
Thomas La EWKG RG40 48 C1
Thomas Pl KENS W8 * 19 M1
Thomas Wall Cl SUT SM1 61 M4
Thompson Av RCH/KEW TW9 17 P8
Thompson Cl CHEAM SM3 43 L9
DTCH/LGLY SL3 12 E2
Thompson Rd EDUL SE22 30 G2
HSLW TW3 16 B9
Thompsons Cl
CHOB/PIR GU24 90 D3
Thompson's La
CHOB/PIR GU24 53 K7
Thomson Crs CROY/NA CR0 45 J9
Thorburn Cha SHST GU47 68 A2
Thorburn Wy
WIM/MER SW19 * 43 P2
Thorkhill Gdns THDIT KT7 40 G9
Thorkhill Rd THDIT KT7 41 H9
Thorley Cl BF/WBF KT14 73 L3
Thorley Gdns
WOKS/MYFD GU22 73 L3
Thornash Cl
WOKN/KNAP GU21 72 A4
Thornash Rd
WOKN/KNAP GU21 72 A5
Thornash Wy
WOKN/KNAP GU21 72 A4
Thorn Bank GUW GU2 111 N7
Thornberry Wy GU GU1 112 D1
Thornbury Av ISLW TW7 16 D5
Thornbury Cl CWTH RG45 49 M4
Thornbury Rd CLAP SW4 29 P2
ISLW TW7 16 D5
Thorncliffe Rd CLAP SW4 29 N2
NWDGN UB2 15 P3
Thorn Cl RFNM GU10 127 K9
Thorncombe Rd EDUL SE22 30 F1
Thorncombe St SHGR GU5 151 J1
Thorn Ct BELMT SM2 * 61 M6
Thorncroft EGH TW20 36 A1
Thorncroft Cl COUL/CHIP CR5 81 J8
Thorncroft Rd SUT SM1 61 M3
Thorndean St
WAND/EARL SW18 28 F5
Thorndike Cl WBPTN SW10 19 N5
Thorndon Gdns
HOR/WEW KT19 60 C3
Thorndown La BFOR GU20 52 D6
Thorndyke Cl CRAWE RH10 177 N6
Thorne Cl ASHF TW15 38 E1
CWTH RG45 49 L2
ESH/CLAY KT10 58 G6
Thorneloe Gdns
CROY/NA CR0 63 K4
Thorne's Cl BECK BR3 47 J4
Thorne St BARN SW13 18 C8
Thorney Crs BTSEA SW11 * 19 P5
Thorneycroft Cl
WOT/HER KT12 39 L7
Thorney Hedge Rd
CHSWK W4 17 P2
Thorney Mill Rd
WDR/YW UB7 13 M1
Thornfield Gn BLKW GU17 68 B5
Thornhill BRAK RG12 32 G5
Thornhill Av SURB KT6 59 L1
Thornhill Rd ALDT GU11 108 F2
CROY/NA CR0 45 L8
SURB KT6 59 L1
Thornhill Vw GSHT GU26 * 165 N8
Thornhill Wy SHPTN TW17 38 C6
Thornlaw Rd WNWD SE27 30 B7
Thornleas Pl EHSLY KT24 94 G5
Thorn Rd RFNM GU10 127 K9
Thornsett Pl PGE/AN SE20 46 B3
Thornsett Rd PGE/AN SE20 46 B3
WAND/EARL SW18 28 E5
Thornsett Ter PGE/AN SE20 * 46 B3
Thorn's Meadow
BH/WHM TN16 105 N3
Thornton Av
BRXS/STRHM SW2 29 N4
CHSWK W4 18 C2
CROY/NA CR0 45 H7
WDR/YW UB7 14 B1
Thornton Cl GUW GU2 111 N2
HORL RH6 159 H1
WDR/YW UB7 14 B1
Thornton Crs COUL/CHIP CR5 81 J8
Thornton Dene BECK BR3 46 G3
Thornton Gdns BAL SW12 29 N4
Thornton Hl WIM/MER SW19 43 J1
Thornton Pl HORL RH6 159 H1
Thornton Rd BAL SW12 29 N3
CAR SM5 43 P9
MORT/ESHN SW14 18 B8
THHTH CR7 45 J6
WIM/MER SW19 28 A9
Thornton Rw THHTH CR7 45 J6
Thornville Gv MTCM CR4 43 N3
Thornyhurst Rd FRIM GU16 89 J3
Thorold Cl SAND/SEL CR2 64 D8
Thorold Rd FNM GU9 5 G2
Thorpe By-pass EGH TW20 36 F4
Thorpe Cl CROY/NA CR0 65 J9
SYD SE26 * 31 L7
Thorpe Ct TOOT SW17 29 H7
Thorpe Lea Rd EGH TW20 36 F2
Thorpe Pk CHERT KT16 * 37 K4
Thorpe Rd CHERT KT16 37 H6
KUTN/CMB KT2 41 L1
STA TW18 22 A8
Thorpes Cl GUW GU2 111 N2
Thorpeside Cl STA TW18 37 J3
Thorpewood Av SYD SE26 31 J5
Thorsden Cl
WOKS/MYFD GU22 10 D7
Thorsden Ct
WOKS/MYFD GU22 10 D6
Thorsden Wy NRWD SE19 * 30 F8
Thrale Rd STRHM/NOR SW16 29 M8
Three Acres HORS RH12 191 P9
Three Arches Pk
REDH RH1 * 120 B9
Three Arch Rd REDH RH1 120 C9
Three Bridges Rd
CRAWE RH10 177 J5
Three Castles Pth ASC SL5 33 L4
ASC SL5 34 E1
HTWY RG27 66 E1
WDSR SL4 20 C1
Three Gates GU GU1 112 G4
Three Gates La HASM GU27 184 E3
Three Mile Rd RDKG RH5 154 B2
Three Pears Rd GU GU1 113 J5
Threestile Rd HORS RH12 191 N1
Three Stiles Rd FNM GU9 4 B2
Threshers Cnr FLEETN GU51 87 J3
Threshfield BRAK RG12 32 C6
Thriffwood SYD SE26 31 K6
Thrift La RSEV TN14 * 85 J6
Thrift V RGUE GU4 113 H2
Thrigby Rd CHSGTN KT9 59 M5
Throgmorton Rd YTLY GU46 66 E3
Throwley Rd SUT SM1 61 M4
Throwley Wy SUT SM1 61 M3
Thrupp Cl MTCM CR4 44 D3
Thrupps Av WOT/HER KT12 57 M4
Thrupps La WOT/HER KT12 57 M4
Thundery Hl RFNM GU10 129 H1
Thurbans Rd FNM GU9 127 L6
Thurbarns Hl RDKG RH5 156 D3
Thurlby Rd WNWD SE27 30 B7
Thurleigh Av BAL SW12 29 K2
Thurleigh Rd BAL SW12 29 J2
Thurleston Av MRDN SM4 43 J6
Thurlestone Cl SHPTN TW17 * 38 E7
Thurlestone Pde
SHPTN TW17 * 38 E7
Thurlestone Rd WNWD SE27 30 B6
Thurloe Pl SKENS SW7 19 P2
Thurloe Place Ms
SKENS SW7 * 19 P2
Thurloe St SKENS SW7 19 P2
Thurlow Hl DUL SE21 30 D4
Thurlow Park Rd DUL SE21 30 C5
Thurlow Wk CRAN GU6 171 H2
Thurlton Ct
WOKN/KNAP GU21 10 D1
Thurne Wy HORS RH12 189 N3
Thurnham Wy
KWD/TDW/WH KT20 79 H9
Thursby Rd
WOKN/KNAP GU21 71 N7
Thursley Crs CROY/NA CR0 65 K6
Thursley Gdns
WIM/MER SW19 28 A5
Thursley Rd MFD/CHID GU8 148 C7
RFNM GU10 147 M9
Thurso St TOOT SW17 28 G7
Thurstan Rd RYNPK SW20 42 F1
Thyme Ct FARN GU14 87 N2
RGUE GU4 112 F2
Tibbenham Pl CAT SE6 31 P5
Tibbets Cl WIM/MER SW19 28 A4
Tibbet's Ride PUT/ROE SW15 28 A3
Ticehurst Cl CRAWE RH10 177 P5
Ticehurst Rd FSTH SE23 31 M5
Tichborne Cl BLKW GU17 67 P3
Tichborne Pl ASHV GU12 108 F6
Tichbourne Cl FRIM GU16 69 H5
Tichmarsh HOR/WEW KT19 60 A8
Tickenor Dr EWKG RG40 48 D2
Tidenham Gdns CROY/NA CR0 3 H5
Tideswell Rd CROY/NA CR0 64 G2
PUT/ROE SW15 18 G9
Tideway Cl
RCHPK/HAM TW10 26 A7
Tidwells Lea BNFD RG42 32 G2
Tiepigs La WWKM BR4 65 L1
Tierney Rd BRXS/STRHM SW2 29 P4
Tierney Ter
BRXS/STRHM SW2 * 29 P4
Tiger La HAYES BR2 47 P5
Tilburstow Hill Rd GDST RH9 122 C3
Tilbury Wk DTCH/LGLY SL3 12 F1
Tildesley Rd PUT/ROE SW15 27 P2
Tile Barn Cl FARN GU14 88 C1
Tilehouse Rd RGUE GU4 112 C9
Tilehurst La RDKG RH5 117 L8
Tilehurst Rd CHEAM SM3 61 J4
WAND/EARL SW18 28 G4
Tilers Cl REDH RH1 120 E2
Tiler's Wy REIG RH2 119 N9
Tilford Av CROY/NA CR0 65 J6
Tilford Gdns WIM/MER SW19 28 A4
Tilford Rd FNM GU9 5 J5
GSHT GU26 166 A6
RFNM GU10 147 M1
RFNM GU10 147 M7
Tilford St RFNM GU10 147 M1
Tilgate Common REDH RH1 121 L4
Tilgate Dr CRAWE RH10 195 H1
Tilgate Forest Ldg
CRAWW RH11 * 194 F6
Tilgate Pde CRAWE RH10 177 H8
Tilgate Pl CRAWE RH10 177 H8
Tilgate Wy CRAWE RH10 177 H8
Tilia Cl SUT SM1 61 K4
Tilletts La HORS RH12 191 M2
Tilley La EPSOM KT18 98 A3
Tilley Rd FELT TW13 24 B4
Tillingbourne Rd RGUE GU4 132 C2
Tillingdown Hl CTHM CR3 102 B2
Tillingdown La CTHM CR3 102 B5
Tillotson Cl CRAWE RH10 177 N6
Tilney Rd NWDGN UB2 15 L2
Tilson Gdns
BRXS/STRHM SW2 29 P3
Tilt Cl COB KT11 75 N5
Tilthams Corner Rd
GODL GU7 131 P5
Tilthams Gn GODL GU7 131 P6
Tilt Meadow COB KT11 75 N5
Tilton St FUL/PGN SW6 19 J4
Tilt Rd COB KT11 75 M5
Tilt Vw COB KT11 * 75 L4
Tiltwood Dr CRAWE RH10 179 K2
Timber Bank FRIM GU16 89 J2
Timber Cl FNM GU9 * 4 E3
GT/LBKH KT23 96 C7
WOKS/MYFD GU22 73 K4
Timbercroft HOR/WEW KT19 60 C3
Timberham Farm Rd
HORL RH6 158 G4
Timber Hl ASHTD KT21 77 L8
Timber Hill Rd CTHM CR3 102 A4
Timberlands CRAWW RH11 194 E1
Timberley Pl CWTH RG45 49 J5
Timberling Gdns
SAND/SEL CR2 63 M8
Timbermill Ct HASM GU27 184 A4
Timberslip Dr WLGTN SM6 62 F7
The Timbers CHEAM SM3 * 61 J5
Timbertop Rd BH/WHM TN16 84 A7
Time Sq BRAK RG12 32 D3
Times Sq SUT SM1 * 61 M4
Timline Gn BRAK RG12 33 H3
Timperley Gdns REDH RH1 120 A3
Timsway STA TW18 22 C8
Tindal Cl YTLY GU46 67 H2
Tindale Cl SAND/SEL CR2 63 M9
Tinmans Rw COB KT11 * 75 L7
Tinsey Cl EGH TW20 21 N8
Tinsley Cl CRAWE RH10 177 K2
SNWD SE25 46 B4
Tinsley Gn CRAWE RH10 159 L9
Tinsley La CRAWE RH10 177 K2
Tinsley La North
CRAWE RH10 159 L9
Tinsley La South
CRAWE RH10 177 K3
Tintagel Cl EW KT17 78 D3
Tintagel Dr FRIM GU16 69 H7
Tintagel Rd EWKG RG40 48 E1
Tintagel Wy
WOKS/MYFD GU22 11 H2
Tintells La EHSLY KT24 94 D8
Tintern Cl PUT/ROE SW15 28 B1
WIM/MER SW19 43 N1
Tintern Rd CAR SM5 43 P9
CRAWW RH11 176 D7
Tipton Dr CROY/NA CR0 3 H7
Tirlemont Rd SAND/SEL CR2 63 L6
Tirrell Rd CROY/NA CR0 45 L7
Tisbury Cl FLEETN GU51 86 E4
Tisbury Rd
STRHM/NOR SW16 44 G3
Titan Ct BTFD TW8 17 M3
Titchfield Rd CAR SM5 43 P9
Titchfield Wk CAR SM5 43 P8
Titchwell Rd
WAND/EARL SW18 28 G3
Tite Hl EGH TW20 21 J8
Tithe Barn Cl KUTN/CMB KT2 9 F3
Tithe Cl VW GU25 36 B7
WOT/HER KT12 39 K7
Tithe Ct DTCH/LGLY SL3 12 E2
Tithe La STWL/WRAY TW19 21 L2
Tithe Orch EGRIN RH19 161 M8
Tithepit Shaw La WARL CR6 82 B6
Titlarks Hill Rd ASC SL5 35 H9
Titmus Dr CRAWE RH10 177 J8
Titness Pk ASC SL5 * 34 G4
Titsey Hl WARL CR6 103 M4
Titsey Rd OXTED RH8 103 P7
Tiverton Cl CROY/NA CR0 45 P8
Tiverton Rd HSLW TW3 16 B7
Tiverton Wy CHSGTN KT9 59 J4
Tivoli Rd HSLWW TW4 15 N9
WNWD SE27 30 D8
Toad La BLKW GU17 68 A4
HSLWW TW4 15 P9
Tobin Cl HOR/WEW KT19 59 P9
Toby Wy SURB KT6 59 P1
Todds Cl HORL RH6 140 A8
Toftwood Cl CRAWE RH10 177 M6
Toland Sq PUT/ROE SW15 27 M1
Tolldene Cl
WOKN/KNAP GU21 71 L6
Tollers La COUL/CHIP CR5 81 H8
Toll Gdns BRAK RG12 32 G4
Tollgate GU GU1 113 H4
Tollgate Av REDH RH1 140 B1
Tollgate Dr DUL SE21 30 F5
Tollgate Hl CRAWW RH11 194 F2
Tollgate Rd DORK RH4 137 H1
Tollhouse La WLGTN SM6 62 E7
Tolpuddle Wy YTLY GU46 67 K3
Tolson Rd ISLW TW7 16 G8
Tolvaddon WOKN/KNAP GU21 71 N6
Tolverne Rd RYNPK SW20 42 G2
Tolworth Broadway
SURB KT6 41 P9
Tolworth Cl SURB KT6 41 P9
Tolworth Park Rd SURB KT6 59 M1
Tolworth Ri North
BRYLDS KT5 42 A8
Tolworth Ri South
BRYLDS KT5 42 A9
Tolworth Rd SURB KT6 59 L1
Tolworth Underpass
(Kingston By-Pass)
BRYLDS KT5 59 P1
Tomlin Cl HOR/WEW KT19 60 B9
Tomlins Av FRIM GU16 69 H6
Tomlinscote Wy FRIM GU16 69 J6
Tomlinson Cl CHSWK W4 17 P3
Tomlinson Dr EWKG RG40 48 E3
Tomtit Crs CRAWE RH10 179 K6
Tonbridge Cl BNSTD SM7 80 B3
Tonbridge Rd
E/WMO/HCT KT8 39 N5
Tonfield Rd CHEAM SM3 43 K9
Tongham Mdw RFNM GU10 108 G7
Tongham Rd ASHV GU12 108 F7
RFNM GU10 128 E1
Tonsley Hl WAND/EARL SW18 28 E1
Tonsley Pl WAND/EARL SW18 28 E1
Tonsley Rd WAND/EARL SW18 28 E1
Tonsley St WAND/EARL SW18 28 E1
Tonstall Rd HOR/WEW KT19 60 B8
MTCM CR4 44 C3
Tooting Bec Gdns
STRHM/NOR SW16 29 N7
Tooting Bec Rd TOOT SW17 29 K6
Tooting Gv TOOT SW17 29 H8
Tooting High St TOOT SW17 29 H9
Tootswood Rd HAYES BR2 47 L6
Top Common BNFD RG42 32 F1
Topiary Sq RCH/KEW TW9 17 M8
The Topiary ASHTD KT21 77 L9
FARN GU14 88 A4
Toplady Pl FNM GU9 107 N7
Top Pk BECK BR3 47 L6
Topsham Rd TOOT SW17 29 J6
Top Terrace Rd FARN GU14 88 C7
Torcross Dr FSTH SE23 31 K5
Torin Ct EGH TW20 21 N8
Torland Dr LHD/OX KT22 76 D3
Tor La WEY KT13 56 F9
Tormead Cl SUT SM1 61 L5
Tormead Rd GU GU1 7 K2
Toronto Dr HORL RH6 160 B2
Torrens Rd BRXS/STRHM SW2 30 A1
Torridge Rd DTCH/LGLY SL3 12 F4
THHTH CR7 45 K6
Torridon Cl
WOKN/KNAP GU21 71 P6
Torrington Cl ESH/CLAY KT10 58 E5
Torrington Rd
ESH/CLAY KT10 58 E5
Torrington Sq
CROY/NA CR0 * 45 M8
Torrington Wy MRDN SM4 43 L8
Tor Rd FNM GU9 4 B4
Torr Rd PGE/AN SE20 46 D1
Torwood La CTHM CR3 81 P9
Torwood Rd PUT/ROE SW15 27 M1
Totford La RFNM GU10 129 N2
Totland Cl FARN GU14 88 C1
Tottenham Rd GODL GU7 131 L7
Tottenham Wk SHST GU47 49 P8
Totterdown St TOOT SW17 29 J7
Totton Rd THHTH CR7 45 J4
Tournai Cl ALDT GU11 88 G8
Tournay Rd FUL/PGN SW6 19 K5
Tovil Cl PGE/AN SE20 46 A3
Tower Cl EGRIN RH19 180 C1
HORL RH6 159 J1
PGE/AN SE20 46 B1
WOKN/KNAP GU21 10 A3
Tower Ct EGRIN RH19 * 180 D1
Tower Gdns ESH/CLAY KT10 59 H6
Tower Gv WEY KT13 56 G1
Tower Hl DORK RH4 117 H9
FARN GU14 88 C4
Towerhill SHGR GU5 134 E2
Tower Hill Ri SHGR GU5 134 E2
Tower Hill Rd DORK RH4 117 H9
Tower Ri RCH/KEW TW9 17 L8
Tower Rd GSHT GU26 165 P7
HORS RH12 193 M2
KWD/TDW/WH KT20 98 G3
LIPH GU30 182 E6
WHTN TW2 25 M6
Towers Dr CWTH RG45 49 M5
Towers Pl RCH/KEW TW9 26 D1
The Towers PUR/KEN CR8 81 L4
Towers Wk WEY KT13 56 D5
Tower Vw CROY/NA CR0 46 E9
Towfield Rd FELT TW13 24 G5
Town Barn Rd CRAWW RH11 176 F5
Townend CTHM CR3 101 N2
Town End Cl CTHM CR3 101 N2
GODL GU7 131 L9
Town End Pde KUT/HW KT1 * 8 C6
Town End St GODL GU7 131 L9
Town Farm Wy
STWL/WRAY TW19 * 22 G3
Townfield Rd DORK RH4 116 G8
Town Field Wy ISLW TW7 16 G7
Towngate COB KT11 75 N4
Townhall Av CHSWK W4 18 B3
Town Hl LING RH7 143 L9
Townholm Crs HNWL W7 16 F1
Town La STWL/WRAY TW19 22 G3
Townley Rd EDUL SE22 30 F1
Town Md CRAWW RH11 176 G4
REDH RH1 121 M4
Town Meadow BTFD TW8 17 K5
Townmead Rd FUL/PGN SW6 19 N7
RCH/KEW TW9 17 P7
Town Quay STA TW18 * 37 N4
Townsend Cl BRAK RG12 32 G6
Townsend La
WOKS/MYFD GU22 92 F1
Townsend Ms
WAND/EARL SW18 28 F5
Townsend Rd ASHF TW15 23 H8
Townshend Rd
RCH/KEW TW9 17 M9
Townshend Ter
RCH/KEW TW9 17 M9
Townshott Cl GT/LBKH KT23 96 A6
Townside Pl CBLY GU15 68 F2
Town Sq BRAK RG12 32 E3
Town Tree Rd ASHF TW15 23 K8
Town Whf ISLW TW7 * 17 H8
Towpath SHPTN TW17 38 B9
Towpath Wy CROY/NA CR0 45 P7
Towton Rd WNWD SE27 30 D5
Toynbee Rd RYNPK SW20 43 J2
Toy's Hl EDEN TN8 125 N7
The Tracery BNSTD SM7 79 M4
Tracious Cl
WOKN/KNAP GU21 71 P5
Trafalgar Av WPK KT4 43 H9
Trafalgar Chambers
CHEL SW3 * 19 P3
Trafalgar Ct COB KT11 75 J2
FNM GU9 5 G5
Trafalgar Dr WOT/HER KT12 57 K2
Trafalgar Gdns KENS W8 * 19 M1
Trafalgar Rd HORS RH12 192 B6
WHTN TW2 25 L5
WIM/MER SW19 43 M1
Trafalgar Wy CBLY GU15 68 B4
CROY/NA CR0 63 H1
Trafford Rd FRIM GU16 68 F8
THHTH CR7 45 H6
Tramway Pth MTCM CR4 44 A5
Tranmere Rd
WAND/EARL SW18 28 F5
WHTN TW2 25 J3
Tranquil Dl
BRKHM/BTCW RH3 118 D3
Transport Av BTFD TW8 16 G3
Transport Rd FARN GU14 88 D6
Trap La RDKG RH5 172 G1
Traps La NWMAL KT3 42 C3
Trasher Md DORK RH4 137 J1
Travellers Wy HSLWW TW4 15 L7
Travis La SHST GU47 67 N1
Treadcroft Dr HORS RH12 192 D5
Treadwell Rd EPSOM KT18 78 D4
Trebor Av FNM GU9 5 J6
Trebovir Rd ECT SW5 19 L3
Tredenham Cl FARN GU14 88 E7
Tredown Rd SYD SE26 31 K8
Tredwell Rd WNWD SE27 30 C7
Tree Av HASM GU27 184 A2
Treebourne Rd
BH/WHM TN16 84 A6
Treebys Av RGUE GU4 92 B8
Tree Cl RCHPK/HAM TW10 26 C4
Treelands RDKG RH5 137 J1
Treen Av BARN SW13 18 C8
Treeside Cl WDR/YW UB7 13 P2
Treeside Dr FNM GU9 108 A7
Tree Tops CTHM CR3 82 A7
Treetops GDST RH9 122 E8
Tree Tops Av CBLY GU15 51 J9
Treeview CRAWW RH11 194 F1
Tree View Cl NRWD SE19 45 N2
Tree View Ct REIG RH2 * 119 P5
Treeway REIG RH2 119 M2
Trefoil Cl HORS RH12 192 D5
Trefoil Crs CRAWW RH11 176 D9
Trefoil Rd WAND/EARL SW18 28 F1

Tregaron Gdns NWMAL KT3......42 C5
Tregarthen Pl LHD/OX KT22....97 J1
Tregarth Pl
  WOKN/KNAP GU21..........71 M6
Tregolls Dr FARN GU14..........88 E4
Tregunter Rd WBPTN SW10...19 N4
Trehaven Pde REIG RH2......119 M8
Trehern Rd
  MORT/ESHN SW14..........18 B8
Trelawn Cl CHERT KT16........54 C6
Trelawne Dr CRAN GU6......171 H1
Trelawney Av DTCH/LGLY SL3..12 C2
Trelawney Gv WEY KT13.......56 C5
Trelawn Rd
  BRXS/STRHM SW2..........30 A1
Treloar Gdns NRWD SE19....30 E9
Tremaine Rd PGE/AN SE20....46 B3
Tremayne Wk CBLY GU15.......69 L4
Tenance WOKN/KNAP GU21...71 N6
Trenchard Cl WOT/HER KT12...57 L4
Trenear Cl SWTR RH13........192 D8
Trenham Dr WARL CR6.........82 C5
Trenholme Rd PGE/AN SE20....46 B3
Trenholme Ter PGE/AN SE20...46 B1
Trent Av EA W5................17 J1
Trent Cl CRAWW RH11........176 C2
  FARN GU14..................88 A1
Trentham Crs
  WOKS/MYFD GU22..........92 E1
Trentham Rd REDH RH1......120 B7
Trentham St
  WAND/EARL SW18..........28 D4
Trenton Cl FRIM GU16.........69 J6
Trent Rd BRXS/STRHM SW2....30 A1
  DTCH/LGLY SL3..............12 B2
Trent Wy WPK KT4.............60 C2
Treport St WAND/EARL SW18...28 E3
Tresham Crs YTLY GU46......66 E3
Tresillian Wy
  WOKN/KNAP GU21..........71 N6
Tresta Wk WOKN/KNAP GU21..71 N4
Trevanion Rd HYS/HAR UB3...19 J3
Trevanne Plat CRAWE RH10..177 N4
Trevelyan BRAK RG12..........32 A8
Trevelyan Rd TOOT SW17......29 J9
Trevereux Ht EDUL SE22......27 N3
Treville St PUT/ROE SW15....27 N3
Treviscoe Cl FSTH SE23......31 L5
Trevithick Cl
  EBED/NFELT TW14..........24 A4
Trevor Cl HAYES BR2..........47 P8
  ISLW TW7...................25 N1
Trevor Rd WIM/MER SW19.....43 J1
Trevose Av BF/WBF KT14......73 K3
Trewenna Dr CHSGTN KT9....59 K4
Trewince Rd RYNPK SW20.....42 C2
Trewint St WAND/EARL SW18..28 E5
Trewsbury Rd SYD SE26.......31 L8
Treyford Cl CRAWW RH11....176 C5
The Triangle KUT/HW KT1......42 A3
  WOKN/KNAP GU21..........72 A7
Trident Pl CHEL SW3..........19 P4
Trident Wy NWDGN UB2.......15 K1
Trigg's Cl WOKS/MYFD GU22..10 A7
Trigg's La WOKN/KNAP GU21..72 A7
Trig St RDKG RH5.............156 D4
Trilby Rd FSTH SE23..........31 L5
Trimmers Cl FNM GU9........107 M7
Trimmers Fld FNM GU9......128 A4
Trimmers Wd GSHT GU26...165 N5
Trindledown BNFD RG42.......32 C1
Trindles Rd REDH RH1........121 H7
Tringham Ct KUT/HW KT16....54 C4
  WOKN/KNAP GU21..........71 J7
Trinity SHST GU47............50 A7
Trinity Church Rd
Trinity Churchward GU GU1 *...7 F6
Trinity Cl CRAWE RH10......177 M3
  HSLWW TW4.................15 N3
  SAND/SEL CR2...............63 N7
  STWL/WRAY TW19...........22 F2
Trinity Ct BNFD RG42 *.......32 B2
Trinity Crs ASC SL5...........34 G6
  TOOT SW17..................29 J5
Trinity Flds FNM GU9........107 L8
Trinity Hl FNM GU9...........107 L8
Trinity Ms HSLW TW3 *.......16 B8
Trinity Pde HSLW TW3 *......16 B8
Trinity Ri BRXS/STRHM SW2...30 C3
Trinity Rd RCH/KEW TW9 *...17 M8
  TOOT SW17..................29 J5
  WAND/EARL SW18..........28 D2
  WIM/MER SW19.............28 D9
  WOKN/KNAP GU21..........71 H7
Tritton Av CROY/NA CR0......62 C3
Tritton Rd DUL SE21..........30 D1
Trittons KWD/TDW/WH KT20...98 C1
Trodd's La RGUE GU4.........113 K6
Trojan Wy CROY/NA CR0.......63 H2
Troon Cl CRAWW RH11......176 C4
Trossachs Rd EDUL SE22.....30 F1
Trotsford Meadow
  BLKW GU17.................67 N4
Trotsworth Av VW GU25......36 C5
Trotters La CHOB/PIR GU24...71 P1
Trotter Wy HOR/WEW KT19...77 N1
Trotton Cl CRAWE RH10.....177 M8
Trotts La BH/WHM TN16.....104 C7
Trott St BTSEA SW11..........19 P6
Trotwood Cl SHST GU47......50 A7
Trouville Rd CLAP SW4.......29 M2
Trowers Wy REDH RH1.......120 D2
Trowlock Av TEDD TW11......26 B9
Trowlock Wy TEDD TW11......26 B9
Troy Ct KENS W8..............19 L1
Troy La EDEN TN8............144 D1
Troy Rd NRWD SE19..........30 D8
Trubshaw Rd NWDGN UB2....16 A1
Trumbull Rd BNFD RG42......32 C1

Trumpers Wy HNWL W7......16 F1
Trumpetshill Rd
  BRKHM/BTCW RH3.........118 C6
Trumpsgreen Av VW GU25....36 D7
Trumps Green Cl VW GU25....36 C6
Trumpsgreen Rd VW GU25....36 D7
Trundle Md HORS RH12......192 B5
Trunk Rd FARN GU14...........87 N3
Trunley Heath Rd SHGR GU5..132 A5
Truslove Rd WNWD SE27......30 B8
Truss Hill Rd ASC SL5..........34 C6
Trussley Rd HMSMTH W6......18 G1
Tryplets FLEETS GU52........106 D3
Trys Hill Longcross Rd
  CHERT KT16.................54 C2
Trystings Cl ESH/CLAY KT10...58 C5
Tucker Rd CHERT KT16.........55 H5
Tuckers Dr CRAN GU6.......152 F9
Tuckey Gv RPLY/SEND GU23..93 K4
Tudor Av HPTN TW12..........25 H9
  WPK KT4....................60 F2
Tudor Cir GODL GU7..........131 L6
Tudor Cl ASHF TW15...........22 C7
  BNSTD SM7..................79 J4
  BRXS/STRHM SW2 *........30 A2
  CHEAM SM3..................61 H5
  CHSGTN KT9................59 L4
  COB KT11....................75 P2
  COUL/CHIP CR5..............81 J7
  CRAWE RH10...............177 N6
  EGRIN RH19................180 E4
  GSHT GU26.................165 N9
  GT/LBKH KT23..............95 P6
  HORL RH6..................160 C1
  HPTN TW12..................25 K8
  SAND/SEL CR2...............82 B4
  WLGTN SM6..................62 E6
  WOKS/MYFD GU22..........11 G3
Tudor Dr KUTN/CMB KT2......26 D8
  MRDN SM4...................43 H7
  WOT/HER KT12..............39 M9
  YTLY GU46...................67 H4
Tudor Gdns BARN SW13.......18 C8
  TWK TW1....................25 N4
  WWKM BR4...................65 J2
Tudor La WDSR SL4...........21 H3
Tudor Pl MTCM CR4............44 A1
  NRWD SE19 *...............45 P1
Tudor Rd ASHF TW15..........23 N9
  BECK BR3....................47 J4
  GODL GU7..................131 L6
  HPTN TW12..................40 A1
  HSLW TW3...................16 D9
  KUTN/CMB KT2...............9 H1
  NRWD SE19..................46 A1
  NWDGN UB2.................15 M1
  SNWD SE25..................46 B6
The Tudors REIG RH2 *.......119 N2
Tudor Wk LHD/OX KT22.......76 C9
Tudor Wy FLEETS GU52.......106 C2
  WOKN/KNAP GU21..........71 J7
Tuesley Cnr GODL GU7......150 C1
Tuesley La GODL GU7........150 C1
Tufton Gdns
  E/WMO/HCT KT8............40 B3
Tugela Rd CROY/NA CR0......45 M7
Tugela St CAT SE6............31 N5
Tuggles Plat HORS RH12....191 M3
Tugwood Cl COUL/CHIP CR5..100 F1
Tulip Cl CROY/NA CR0.........46 D9
  HPTN TW12..................24 G9
Tulip Ct HORS RH12 *........192 B6
Tullett Rd CRAWE RH10......177 L9
Tulls La BOR GU35...........164 A9
Tull St CAR SM5...............44 B8
Tulse Cl BECK BR3.............47 J4
Tulse Hl BRXS/STRHM SW2....30 C4
Tulsemere Rd WNWD SE27....30 D5
Tulyar Cl KWD/TDW/WH KT20..78 F8
Tumber St EPSOM KT18........98 A4
Tumblewood Rd BNSTD SM7..79 J5
Tumbling Bay WOT/HER KT12..39 J7
Tummons Gdns SNWD SE25...45 N3
Tunbridge Crs LIPH GU30....182 E5
Tunbridge La LIPH GU30.....182 E4
Tunley Rd TOOT SW17..........29 K5
Tunnel Link Rd HTHAIR TW6...23 K1
Tunnel Rd FARN GU14..........88 A6
Tunnel Rd East WDR/YW UB7..14 D5
Tunnel Rd West
  WDR/YW UB7................14 C6
Tunnmeade CRAWW RH11...176 B6
Tunsgate GU GU1 *.............7 F6
Tunsgate Sq GU GU1 *.........7 F6
Tunstall Rd CROY/NA CR0......3 H7
Tunworth Ct FARNH GU9......88 E4
Tunworth Crs PUT/ROE SW15..27 L2
Tupwood La CTHM CR3.......102 A6
Tupwood Scrubbs Rd
  CTHM CR3.................102 A8
Turene Cl WAND/EARL SW18..19 N9
Turf Hill Rd CBLY GU15........51 H9
Turfhouse La CHOB/PIR GU24..53 L7
Turgis Rd FLEETN GU51.......86 E3
Turing Dr BRAK RG12..........32 C6
Turkey Oak Cl NRWD SE19....45 N3
Turle Rd STRHM/NOR SW16...44 G3
Turnberry BRAK RG12.........32 A7
Turner Av MTCM CR4..........44 B3
  WHTN TW2...................25 K6
Turner Cl ESH/CLAY KT10....112 D2
Turner Ct EGRIN RH19.......162 F9
Turner Ms BELMT SM2........61 N6
Turner Pl SHST GU47...........67 P2
Turner Rd BH/WHM TN16......84 A1
  NWMAL KT3.................42 B8
Turners Av FLEETS GU51......86 E3
Turners Cl STA TW18..........22 E8
Turner's Green La
  HTWY RG27..................86 D2
Turners Hill Rd CRAWE RH10..160 G9

CRAWE RH10...............177 P5
  EGRIN RH19................179 P6
Turners La WOT/HER KT12....57 K5
Turners Md MFD/CHID GU8...168 B8
Turners Meadow Wy
  BECK BR3....................46 F2
Turners Wy CROY/NA CR0.....63 J1
  FLEETN GU51...............86 D4
Turneville Rd WKENS W14....19 K4
Turney Rd DUL SE21..........30 D3
Turnham Cl GU GU2..........112 A9
Turnham Green Ter
  CHSWK W4...................18 C2
Turnham Rd BROCKY SE4....31 M1
Turnoak Av
  WOKS/MYFD GU22..........72 C9
Turnoak La
  WOKS/MYFD GU22..........72 C9
Turnpike La SUT SM1.........61 N4
Turnpike Link CROY/NA CR0....3 H4
Turnpike Pl CRAWW RH11...176 C3
Turnpike Wy ISLW TW7........16 G6
Turnstone End YTLY GU46....66 F2
Turnville Cl LGHT GU18.......52 A8
Turpin Rd EBED/NFELT TW14..24 A2
Turpins Ri BFOR GU20.........52 E5
Turpin Wy WLGTN SM6.......62 E6
Turtledove Av CRAWE RH10..179 K6
Tuscany Gdns CRAWE RH10..177 H3
Tuscany Wy YTLY GU46 *......66 G4
Tushmore Av CRAWE RH10 *..177 H3
Tushmore Ct CRAWE RH10 *..177 H3
Tushmore La CRAWE RH10...177 H3
Tushmore La CRAWE RH10...177 H3
Tussock Cl CRAWW RH11....176 D7
Tuxford Cl CRAWE RH10......176 G3
Tweed Cl FARN GU14..........88 A1
Tweeddale Rd CAR SM5.......43 P9
Tweed La
  BRKHM/BTCW RH3.........117 P9
  CRAWW RH11...............176 C2
Tweed Rd DTCH/LGLY SL3.....12 F4
Tweedsmuir Cl FARN GU14...87 P4
Tweedy Rd BMLY BR1..........47 N2
Twelve Acre Cl GT/LBKH KT23..95 P4
Twelve Acre Crs FARN GU14..87 P2
Twelve Av
  KWD/TDW/WH KT20 *......99 K6
Tweseldown Rd
  FLEETS GU52...............107 H2
Twickenham Br TWK TW1.....26 B1
Twickenham Cl CROY/NA CR0..63 H2
Twickenham Rd FELT TW13....24 G6
  ISLW TW7....................16 G9
  RCH/KEW TW9...............26 B1
  TEDD TW11...................25 P8
Twilley St WAND/EARL SW18..28 E3
Twining Av WHTN TW2.........25 K6
Twinoaks COB KT11............76 A2
Twisell Thorne FLEETS GU52..106 E2
Twitten La EGRIN RH19......161 M6
The Twitten CRAWW RH11...176 F5
  LING RH7 *..................143 K9
Two Ways BIL RH14..........188 D6
Twycross Rd GODL GU7......131 K6
Twyford Cl FLEETN GU51......86 E3
Twyford La WARL CR6..........82 C8
Twyford Rd CAR SM5...........43 P9
Twyhurst Ct EGRIN RH19....162 C1
Twyne Cl CRAWW RH11......176 C7
Twyne Cl HORL RH6...........140 E9
Twynersh Av CHERT KT16......37 K7
Tybenham Rd
  WIM/MER SW19.............43 L4
Tychbourne Dr RGUE GU4....112 C2
Tydcombe Rd WARL CR6......82 C8
Tyden Wy HORS RH12.......192 E4
Tylecroft Rd
  STRHM/NOR SW16...........44 G3
Tylehost GUW GU2...........111 N1
Tyle Pl WDSR SL4.............20 F1
Tyler Gdns ADL/WDHM KT15..55 N3
Tyler Rd CRAWE RH10........176 G8
Tylers Cl GDST RH9.............122 D1
Tylers Ct CRAN GU6...........152 C9
Tyler Wk DTCH/LGLY SL3......12 D3
Tylney Av NRWD SE19..........30 C8
Tylston Meadow LIPH GU30..182 E5
Tynan Cl EBED/NFELT TW14...24 B4
Tyndalls GDST RH9...........122 C6
Tyne Cl CRAWE RH10........177 M6
  FARN GU14..................88 A1
Tynedale Rd
  BRKHM/BTCW RH3.........117 P9
Tynemouth Rd MTCM CR4....44 C1
Tynemouth St FUL/PGN SW6..19 N7
Tynley Gv RGUE GU4...........92 B6
Tynwald Wy FUL/PGN SW6....19 N8
Tyson Gdns FSTH SE23 *......31 K3
Tyson Rd FSTH SE23...........31 K3
Tythebarns La
  RPLY/SEND GU23............93 L6
Tytherton BRAK RG12..........32 E3

U

Uckfield Gv MTCM CR4........44 C2
Uckfield La EDEN TN8........145 N8
Udney Park Rd TEDD TW11...25 P8
Uffington Dr BRAK RG12.......32 C5
Uffington Rd WNWD SE27....30 B7
Ullathorne Rd
  STRHM/NOR SW16...........29 M7
Ullswater BRAK RG12..........32 A8
Ullswater Av FARN GU14......88 A4
Ullswater Cl FNM GU9.......107 L8
  LTWR GU18..................52 B8

PUT/ROE SW15 *............27 J7
Ullswater Ct ASHV GU12 *....108 G4
Ullswater Crs COUL/CHIP CR5..80 G5
  PUT/ROE SW15.............27 J7
Ullswater Rd BARN SW13.....18 E5
  LTWR GU18..................52 B8
  WNWD SE27.................30 C6
Ulstan Cl CTHM CR3.........102 G3
Ulva Rd PUT/ROE SW15........27 P1
Ulverscroft Rd EDUL SE22....31 H1
Ulwyn Av BF/WBF KT14........74 A4
Umberstone VW GU25.........36 B7
Umbria St PUT/ROE SW15....27 M2
Underhill Cl GODL GU7.......150 D1
Underhill La FNM GU9........127 M6
Underhill Park Rd REIG RH2..119 L2
Underhill Rd EDUL SE22.......31 H1
  RDKG RH5.................156 G3
Underwood BRAK RG12........32 A7
  CROY/NA CR0................65 J5
Underwood Av ASHV GU12...108 C7
Underwood Cl CRAWE RH10..179 J3
Underwood Ct CTHM CR3....101 N5
Underwood Rd CTHM CR3...101 N5
  HASM GU27.................184 A3
Undine St TOOT SW17..........29 J8
Union Cl SHST GU47............50 A7
Union Rd CROY/NA CR0.......45 L8
  FNM GU9....................5 G4
  FRIM GU16..................69 M8
Union St ALDT GU11.........108 C4
  CHOB/PIR GU24.............90 A1
  FARN GU14..................88 C3
  KUT/HW KT1..................8 C4
Unity Cl CROY/NA CR0..........65 H7
  NRWD SE19..................30 B8
University Rd
  WIM/MER SW19.............28 G9
Unstead La SHGR GU5.......132 A6
Unwin Av EBED/NFELT TW14..23 N1
Unwin Rd ISLW TW7............16 F8
  SKENS SW7 *................19 N1
Upavon Gdns BRAK RG12.....33 H6
Upcerne Rd WBPTN SW10....19 N5
Updown Hl BFOR GU20.......52 D5
Upfield CROY/NA CR0..........64 B1
  HORL RH6..................159 K3
Upfield Cl HORL RH6..........159 J5
Upfold Cl CRAN GU6..........152 E6
Upfold La CRAN GU6..........152 F7
Upfolds Gn RGUE GU4.......112 E2
Upham Park Rd CHSWK W4...18 C2
Upland Rd BELMT SM2........61 P5
  CBLY GU15..................68 F1
  CTHM CR3.................102 B1
  EDUL SE22..................31 H1
  SAND/SEL CR2...............63 M4
Uplands ASHTD KT21..........77 K3
  BECK BR3....................46 G3
Uplands Cl HASM GU27......184 E2
  MORT/ESHN SW14..........26 C1
  SHST GU47..................49 M9
Uplands Dr LHD/OX KT22.....76 D3
Uplands Rd FNM GU9........128 A4
  PUR/KEN CR8...............81 K1
Upland Wy EPSOM KT18......78 G7
Uppark Gdns HORS RH12....192 E4
Upper Berenger Wk
  WBPTN SW10 *.............19 N5
Upper Beulah Hl NRWD SE19..45 N2
Upper Blantyre Wk
  WBPTN SW10 *.............19 N5
Upper Bourne La
  RFNM GU10................127 L8
Upper Bourne V
  RFNM GU10................127 L8
Upper Bridge Rd REDH RH1..120 A5
Upper Brighton Rd
  SURB KT6...................41 L8
Upper Broadmoor Rd
  CWTH RG45..................49 N5
Upper Butts BTFD TW8.........17 J4
Upper Charles St CBLY GU15..68 E2
Upper Chobham Rd
  CBLY GU15..................69 J5
Upper Church La FNM GU9 *...4 E4
Upper College Ride
  CBLY GU15..................50 G9
Upper Court Rd CTHM CR3...102 G3
  HOR/WEW KT19..............60 A9
Upper Dartrey Wk
  WBPTN SW10 *.............19 N5
Upper Dr BH/WHM TN16......84 A4
Upper Dunnymans
  BNSTD SM7..................79 K3
Upper Edgeborough Rd
  GU GU1......................7 K5
Upper Elmers End Rd
  BECK BR3....................46 E5
Upper Elms Rd ALDT GU11..108 C5
Upper Fairfield Rd
  LHD/OX KT22................97 H1
Upper Farm Rd
  E/WMO/HCT KT8............39 P5
Upper Forecourt HORL RH6..159 L5
Upper Gordon Rd CBLY GU15..68 F3
Upper Gn East MTCM CR4....44 B3
Upper Gn West MTCM CR4...44 B3
Upper Grotto Rd TWK TW1...25 N5
Upper Gv SNWD SE25.........45 P5
Upper Guildown Rd
  GUW GU2..................111 P8
Upper Hale Rd FNM GU9....107 M7
Upper Halliford Rd
  SHPTN TW17................38 G3
Upper Ham Rd
  RCHPK/HAM TW10...........26 C6
Upper Harestone CTHM CR3..102 A7
Upper High St EW KT17........78 C2
Upper House La SHGR GU5..152 C5
Upper Kiln DORK RH4 *......117 J9

Upper Lodge Wy
  COUL/CHIP CR5..............100 F2
Upper MI HMSMTH W6........18 E3
Upper Manor Rd GODL GU7..131 L6
  MFD/CHID GU8.............149 M3
Upper Mt HASM GU27........184 C5
Upper Mulgrave Rd
  BELMT SM2..................61 J6
Upper Old Park La FNM GU9..107 K9
Upper Park Rd BMLY BR1.....47 P2
  CBLY GU15..................68 F3
  KUTN/CMB KT2...............9 G5
Upper Pth DORK RH4 *.......117 J9
Upper Pillory Down CAR SM5..80 C2
Upper Pines BNSTD SM7......80 B6
Upper Pinewood Rd
  ASHV GU12................109 L3
Upper Queen St GODL GU7..131 L9
Upper Richmond Rd
  PUT/ROE SW15..............18 F9
Upper Richmond Rd West
  RCHPK/HAM TW10...........17 N9
Upper Rd WLGTN SM6.........62 F4
Upper Rose Hl DORK RH4...117 H8
Upper St Michael's Rd
  ALDT GU11.................108 D6
Upper Sawleywood
  BNSTD SM7..................79 K3
Upper School Dr
  HASM GU27................184 A5
Upper Selsdon Rd
  SAND/SEL CR2...............63 P7
Upper Shirley Rd
  CROY/NA CR0................64 C2
Upper South Vw FNM GU9....5 G2
Upper Springfield
  MFD/CHID GU8.............129 M9
Upper Sq ISLW TW7............16 G8
Upper Stanford Rd
  CHOB/PIR GU24..............90 F5
Upper St FLEETN GU51.........86 F6
  SHGR GU5.................114 B9
Upper Sunbury Rd
  HPTN TW12..................39 P2
Upper Sutton La HEST TW5...16 A6
Upper Terrace Rd FARN GU14..88 C7
Upperton Rd GUW GU2.........6 C1
Upper Tooting Pk
  TOOT SW17..................29 J5
Upper Tooting Rd
  TOOT SW17..................29 J7
Upper Tulse Hl
  BRXS/STRHM SW2...........30 A3
Upper Union St ALDT GU11..108 C4
Upper Union Ter
  ALDT GU11 *...............108 C4
Upper Vann La
  MFD/CHID GU8.............168 F2
Upper Vernon Rd SUT SM1...61 P4
Upper Verran Rd CBLY GU15..68 F5
Upper Village Rd ASC SL5....34 C6
Upper Wy FNM GU9..........127 M5
Upper West St REIG RH2....119 K5
Upper Weybourne La
  FNM GU9...................107 P2
Upper Whistler Wk
  WBPTN SW10 *.............19 N5
Upper Wield Dr FLEETN GU51..86 E3
Upper Woodcote Village
  PUR/KEN CR8...............80 F2
Upshire Gdns BRAK RG12.....33 H5
Upshot La WOKS/MYFD GU22..73 K6
Upton WOKN/KNAP GU21.....71 P6
Upton Cl FARN GU14...........88 F4
Upton Dene BELMT SM2.......61 M6
Upton Rd HSLW TW3...........16 A8
  THHTH CR7..................45 M3
Upwood Rd
  STRHM/NOR SW16...........44 G2
Urmston Dr WIM/MER SW19...28 B4
Usherwood Cl
  KWD/TDW/WH KT20........118 A2
Usk Rd BTSEA SW11............19 N9
Uvedale Cl CROY/NA CR0.....65 K9
Uvedale Crs CROY/NA CR0....65 K9
Uvedale Rd OXTED RH8......103 M9
Uverdale Rd WBPTN SW10...19 N5
Uxbridge Rd FELT TW15.......24 E5
  HPTN TW12..................25 J8
  KUT/HW KT1..................41 K5

V

Vachery La CRAN GU6.......171 J3
Vaillant Rd WEY KT13.........56 E3
Valan Leas HAYES BR2........47 L4
Vale Cl COUL/CHIP CR5........80 C3
  RFNM GU10................127 N9
  TWK TW1....................25 P6
  WEY KT13...................56 F2
  WOKN/KNAP GU21..........10 C1
Vale Crs PUT/ROE SW15......27 H5
Vale Ct ASC SL5................34 G8
Vale Cft ESH/CLAY KT10.......58 F6
Vale Dr HORS RH12.........192 A8
Vale Farm Rd
  WOKN/KNAP GU21..........10 C4
Valentyne Cl CROY/NA CR0...65 L9
Vale Rd ASHV GU12...........108 B3
  CBLY GU15..................68 C4
  ESH/CLAY KT10..............58 E7
  MTCM CR4...................44 F4
  SUT SM1....................61 M3
  WEY KT13...................56 F1
  WPK KT4....................60 D2
Vale Rd North SURB KT6.....59 L1
Vale St DUL SE21..............30 E6
The Vale CHEL SW3............19 P4

COUL/CHIP CR5 ....80 G3
CROY/NA CR0 ....64 D1
EBED/NFELT TW14 ....24 C2
HEST TW5 ....15 N4
SUN TW16 * 24 B9
Vale Wood Dr RFNM GU10.127 P9
Vale Wood La CSHT GU26.165 M7
Valewood Rd HASM GU27.184 D6
Valiant Rd CRAW GU14 .....87 P7
Valley End Rd
  CHOB/PIR GU24..............53 H5
Valleyfield Rd
  STRHM/NOR SW16............30 A8
Valley Gdns WIM/MER SW19..45 J1
Valley La RFNM GU10.......127 N6
Valley Rd FRIM GU16 ....69 L8
  HAYES BR2 ....47 L3
  PUR/KEN CR8 ....81 M4
  STRHM/NOR SW16.............30 A7
Valley Side LIPH GU30 ......182 E5
Valley Vw BH/WHM TN16....84 A7
  GODL GU7 ....131 K9
  SHST GU47 ....67 L1
Valley View Gdns
  PUR/KEN CR8 ....81 N4
Vallis Wy CROY/NA CR0......45 K4
Valnay St TOOT SW17 ....29 J8
Valonia Gdns
  WAND/EARL SW18.............28 C2
Valroy Cl CBLY GU15 ....68 F2
Vampire Wy FARN GU14......88 A7
Vanbrugh Cl CRAWW RH11..176 B8
Vanbrugh Dr WOT/HER KT12..59 L8
Vanbrugh Rd CHSWK W4....18 B1
Vancouver Cl
  HOR/WEW KT19 ....60 A9
Vancouver Ct HORL RH6....160 B1
Vancouver Dr CRAWW RH11..176 C2
Vancouver Rd FSTH SE23 ...31 M5
  RCHPK/HAM TW10 ....26 E7
Vanderbilt Rd
  WAND/EARL SW18.............28 E4
Van Dyck Av NWMAL KT3....42 B8
Vandyke BRAK RG12 ....32 A7
Vandyke Cl PUT/ROE SW15..28 A2
  REDH RH1 ....120 B3
Vanguard Cl CROY/NA CR0....2 C2
  THHTH CR7 ....45 K5
Vanguard Wy CROY/NA CR0...3 J7
  EDEN TN8..........................144 C7
  EGRIN RH19 ....163 M9
  HTHAIR TW6 ....14 C7
  OXTED RH8 ....105 N6
  WARL CR6 ....82 F8
  WLGTN SM6........................62 C6
Vannerk Sq PUT/ROE SW15 *..27 M1
Vanners CRAWE RH10 ....177 H4
Vanners Pde BF/WBF KT14 *..74 A2
Vann Farm Rd RDKG RH5..155 N8
Vann Lake RDKG RH5........155 N8
Vann Lake Rd RDKG RH5...155 N8
Vann La MFD/CHID GU8 ...168 C2
Vanston Pl FUL/PGN SW6....19 L5
Vantage Pl KENS W8 ....19 L1
Vant Rd TOOT SW17 ....29 J8
Vapery La CHOB/PIR GU24...90 D1
Vardens Rd BTSEA SW11....19 P9
Varley Dr TWK TW1 ....17 H9
Varley Wy MTCM CR4...........45 P3
Varna Rd FUL/PGN SW6......19 J5
  HPTN TW12 * 40 B2
Varney Cl FARN GU14...........88 A2
Varsity Dr TWK TW1 ....25 N1
Varsity Rw
  MORT/ESHN SW14.............18 A7
Vaughan Av HMSMTH W6 ...18 D2
Vaughan Rd THDT KT7.........41 H8
Vaughan Wy DORK RH4 .....116 C7
Vaux Crs WOT/HER KT12.....57 K5
Vauxhall Gdns SAND/SEL CR2..63 L5
Veals Md MTCM CR4.............44 A4
Vectis Gdns TOOT SW17 ......29 L9
Vectis Rd TOOT SW17 ....29 L9
Vegal Crs EGH TW20 ....21 H8
Vellum Dr CAR SM5 ....62 C2
Velmead Cl FLEETS GU52 ....87 H8
Velmead Rd FLEETS GU52....86 G8
Vencourt Pl HMSMTH W6....18 E3
Venner Rd SYD SE26............31 K6
Ventnor Rd BELMT SM2.......61 M6
Ventnor Ter ASHV GU12 ....108 E5
Venton Cl WOKN/KNAP GU21..71 P6
Venus Ms MTCM CR4...........44 A4
Vera Rd FUL/PGN SW6..........19 J6
Verbania Wy EGRIN RH19...180 G2
Verbena Cl WDR/YW UB7.....13 P5
Verbena Gdns HMSMTH W6..18 D3
Verdayne Av CROY/NA CR0..46 D9
Verdayne Gdns WARL CR6....82 C5
Verdun Rd BARN SW13.........18 E5
Vereker Dr SUN TW16...........39 J3
Vereker Rd WKENS W14 *......19 J3
Verge Wk ALDT GU11.........108 C7
Vermont Rd NRWD SE19.......30 E9
  SUT SM1 ....61 M3
  WAND/EARL SW18.............28 E2
Vermont Woods EWKG RG40..48 C2
Verner Cl BOR GU35 ....164 B7
The Verne FLEETS GU52 ...106 G1
Verney Rd DTCH/LGLY SL3..12 E2
Vernon Av RYNPK SW20.......43 H3
Vernon Cl CHERT KT16 ....55 H5
  HOR/WEW KT19 ....60 A6
  HORS RH12 ....192 F5
  STWL/WRAY TW19 ....23 H4
Vernon Dr ASC SL5 ....35 M3
  CTHM CR3 ....101 L2
Vernon Rd FELT TW13 ....24 A5
  MORT/ESHN SW14.............18 B9
  SUT SM1 ....61 N4
Vernon St WKENS W14 ....19 J2

Vernon Wk
  KWD/TDW/WH KT20 ....79 H9
Vernon Wy GUW GU2.........111 M4
Vern Pl BH/WHM TN16.......104 A1
Verona Dr SURB KT6............59 L1
Veronica Dr FLEETN GU51..106 D1
Veronica Gdns
  STRHM/NOR SW16............44 E2
Veronica Rd TOOT SW17 .....29 L6
Verralls WOKS/MYFD GU22..11 K3
Verran Rd BAL SW12 * 29 L3
  CBLY GU15........................68 F6
Versailles Rd PGE/AN SE20...46 A1
Verulam Av PUR/KEN CR8....80 E1
Veryan WOKN/KNAP GU21...71 N6
Vesey Cl FARN GU14..........88 C2
Vestris Rd FSTH SE23..........31 L5
Vevers Rd REIG RH2...........119 M8
Vevey St CAT SE6 ....31 N5
Vibart Gdns
  BRXS/STRHM SW2.............30 A3
Vibia Cl STWL/WRAY TW19..22 G3
Viburnum Cl CHOB/PIR GU24..70 E2
Vicarage Av EGH TW20 ....20 D8
Vicarage Cl EWKG RG40......48 D3
  FNM GU9..........................127 P6
  GT/LBKH KT23 ....96 A5
  HORS RH12 ....193 P4
  KWD/TDW/WH KT20 ....99 J4
  LING RH7 ....143 K9
  WPK KT4.............................42 C9
Vicarage Ct BECK BR3 *.......46 E4
  EGH TW20 ....21 N9
Vicarage Crs BTSEA SW11...19 P7
  EGH TW20 ....21 N9
Vicarage Dr BECK BR3..........46 C2
  MORT/ESHN SW14.............18 A9
Vicarage Farm Rd HEST TW5..15 N6
Vicarage Flds
  WOT/HER KT12 ....39 L7
Vicarage Gdns ASC SL5.......34 A6
  FLEETS GU52 ....106 F2
  GSHT GU26 ....165 M8
  MTCM CR4 ....44 A4
Vicarage Ga GUW GU2 ......111 N7
Vicarage Gate Ms
  KWD/TDW/WH KT20 *........99 J4
Vicarage La BH/WHM TN16..105 H6
  FNM GU9..........................127 P5
  FNM GU9..........................107 N7
  HASM GU27 ....184 A4
  HORL RH6.........................140 B9
  LHD/OX KT22 ....97 H2
  RDKG RH5 ....156 C6
  RPLY/SEND GU23 ....12 G8
  STA TW18 ....37 M4
  STWL/WRAY TW19 ....21 L4
  YTLY GU46 ....66 G1
Vicarage Ms CHSWK W4 * ...18 C4
Vicarage Rd BAGS GU19....51 L6
  BLKW GU17 ....68 A4
  CHOB/PIR GU24 ....53 H5
  CRAWE RH10.....................179 H4
  CROY/NA CR0 ....63 J2
  EGH TW20 ....21 N8
  KUT/HW KT1 ....8 C1
  LING RH7 ....143 K9
  MORT/ESHN SW14.............27 H1
  STA TW18 ....22 B7
  SUN TW16 ....24 A9
  SUT SM1 ....61 L3
  TEDD TW11 ....25 P8
  WHTN TW2 ....25 K2
  WOKS/MYFD GU22.............92 D1
Vicarage Wk BTSEA SW11 *..19 P6
Vicarage Wy DTCH/LGLY SL3..13 H1
Vicars Oak Rd NRWD SE19...30 F9
Vickers Cl WLGTN SM6........63 H5
Vickers Dr North WEY KT13..56 A8
Vickers Dr South WEY KT13..56 A9
Vickers Rd ASHV GU12 ......109 H1
Victoria Av CBLY GU15..........68 D3
  E/WMO/HCT KT8.................40 B6
  HSLW TW3..........................25 H1
  SAND/SEL CR2 ....63 L8
  SURB KT6 ....41 K7
  WLGTN SM6........................62 C5
Victoria Cl E/WMO/HCT KT8..40 A4
  HORL RH6.........................159 K1
  WEY KT13 ....56 F2
Victoria Cottages
  RCH/KEW TW9 ....17 M6
Victoria Ct BAGS GU19 ......51 N8
  RGUE GU3 * 132 C2
Victoria Crs NRWD SE19.....30 F9
  WIM/MER SW19 * 43 K1
Victoria Dr BLKW GU17 ......67 N1
  WIM/MER SW19 ....28 A4
Victoria Gdns BH/WHM TN16..84 A4
  FLEETN GU51 * 86 F1
  HEST TW5 ....15 N6
Victoria Hill Rd FLEETN GU51..86 E8
Victoria La HYS/HAR UB3....14 F3
Victoria Ms FLEETN GU51 *...86 F6
  WAND/EARL SW18.............28 E3
Victoria Pde FLEETN GU51 *...86 F6
  RCH/KEW TW9 * 17 M6
Victoria Pl EW KT17 ....78 C1
  RCH/KEW TW9 ....17 K5
Victoria Rd ADL/WDHM KT15..55 P5
  ALDT GU11 ....108 C4
  ASC SL5 ....34 B6
  COUL/CHIP CR5 ....80 F4
  CRAN GU6.........................152 D9
  CRAWW RH11...................176 F5
  EDEN TN8..........................144 D4
  FARN GU14.........................88 D5
  FELT TW13 ....24 C4

FLEETN GU51 ....86 E6
FNM GU9..............................5 C4
GODL GU7..........................131 L9
HORL RH6...........................159 K1
KENS W8 ....19 N1
KUT/HW KT1 ....9 G5
MORT/ESHN SW14.............18 B8
NWDGN UB2.......................15 P1
REDH RH1 ....120 C6
SHST GU47 ....64 F7
STA TW18 ....22 B8
SURB KT6 ....41 K7
SUT SM1 ....61 P4
TEDD TW11 ....25 P9
TWK TW1 ....26 A3
WEY KT13 ....56 F2
WOKN/KNAP GU21 ....10 D4
Victoria Ter DORK RH4 * ...116 C7
SWTR RH13 ....192 C8
Victoria Tr ALDT GU11 ....87 P8
Victoria Vls RCH/KEW TW9..17 M8
Victoria Wy EGRIN RH19....180 E9
  LIPH GU30 ....182 E6
  WEY KT13 ....56 F2
  WOKN/KNAP GU21 ....10 D4
Victor Rd PGE/AN SE20 ....46 D1
  TEDD TW11 ....25 M8
Victors Dr HPTN TW12 * 24 F9
Victor Wy FARN GU14...........87 N7
Victory Av MRDN SM4..........43 P6
Victory Cl STWL/WRAY TW19..23 H4
Victory Pk NRWD SE19 * 30 F9
Victory Rd CHERT KT16 ....37 L9
  HORS RH12 ....192 A7
  WIM/MER SW19 ....43 N1
Victory Wy HEST TW5............15 P4
View Cl BH/WHM TN16 ....84 A5
Viewfield Rd
  WAND/EARL SW18.............28 C2
Viewlands Av BH/WHM TN16..85 J9
Viggory La
  WOKN/KNAP GU21 ....71 P4
Vigilant Cl SYD SE26.............31 H7
Vigo La YTLY GU46 ....66 C3
Viking BRAK RG12 ....32 A6
Village Cl WEY KT13 ....56 F2
Village Gdns EW KT17...........60 D8
Village Green Av
  BH/WHM TN16....................84 C6
Village Green Wy
  BH/WHM TN16....................84 C6
Village Rd EGH TW20 ....36 G4
Village Rw BELMT SM2..........61 L6
Village St RDKG RH5...........156 C3
The Village EWKG RG40........48 C6
Village Wy ASHF TW15...........23 J7
  BECK BR3............................46 G5
  DUL SE21............................30 E2
  SAND/SEL CR2 ....82 A2
  YTLY GU46 ....67 H1
Villiers Av BRYLDS KT5.........41 M6
  WHTN TW2 ....24 C4
Villiers Cl BRYLDS KT5........41 M5
Villiers Gv BELMT SM2..........61 H6
Villiers Rd BECK BR3.............46 D3
  KUT/HW KT1 ....8 E6
  ISLW TW7 ....16 E7
  SHPTN TW17 ....38 C4
The Villiers WEY KT13 * 56 F5
Vinall Gdns HORS RH12......191 L6
Vincam Cl WHTN TW2...........25 H3
Vincennes Est WNWD SE27..30 E7
Vincent Av BRYLDS KT5.......59 P3
  CAR SM5 ....61 P9
Vincent Cl CHERT KT16 ....37 J8
  ESH/CLAY KT10...................58 B2
  HAYES BR2 ....47 P5
  LHD/OX KT22 ....96 B3
  WDR/YW UB7 ....14 C4
Vincent Dr DORK RH4 ....116 C8
  SHPTN TW17 ....38 C4
Vincent La DORK RH4.........116 C7
Vincent Ri BRAK RG12..........32 G4
Vincent Rd ACT W3...............18 A1
  CHERT KT16 ....37 J8
  COB KT11 ....75 J5
  COUL/CHIP CR5 ....80 E5
  CROY/NA CR0 ....45 N8
  DORK RH4 ....116 C7
  HSLW TW3...........................15 M8
  ISLW TW7 ....16 D6
  KUT/HW KT1 ....9 K6
Vincent Sq BH/WHM TN16...84 A2
Vincents Wk DORK RH4 * ...116 C7
Vincent Wk DORK RH4 * 116 C7
Vine Cl ALDT GU11................88 C9
  BRYLDS KT5 ....41 M7
  FNM GU9............................107 J2
  RGUW GU3 ....91 K6
  STWL/WRAY TW19 ....21 N1
  SUT SM1 ....61 N2
  WDR/YW UB7 ....14 C2
Vine House Cl FRIM GU16.....89 J4
Vine Pl HSLW TW3 ....16 B9
Vineries Cl WDR/YW UB7 ....14 C4
The Vineries CAT SE6 * 31 J1
Vine Rd BARN SW13..............18 D8
  E/WMO/HCT KT8.................40 C6
Vine Rw RCHPK/HAM TW10 * ..26 D1
Viners Cl WOT/HER KT12......39 L7
Vine Sq WKENS W14 *............19 K3
Vine St ALDT GU11..............108 C5
Vine Wy RFNM GU10...........127 L8
Vineyard Cl CAT SE6 * 31 P4

KUT/HW KT1 ....9 F6
Vineyard Hill Rd
  WIM/MER SW19 ....28 D7
Vineyard Pth
  MORT/ESHN SW14.............18 B8
Vineyard Rd FELT TW13 ....24 B6
Vineyard Rw KUT/HW KT1.....41 J2
The Vineyard
  RCHPK/HAM TW10 ....26 C1
  SUN TW16 * 39 J4
Viney Bank CROY/NA CR0....64 F7
Vintney St FLEETN GU51 ......86 D4
Viola Av EBED/NFELT TW14..24 D2
  STWL/WRAY TW19 ....23 H5
Viola Cft BNFD RG42............33 H2
Violet Cl CHEAM SM3............43 L9
  WLGTN SM6........................44 C9
Violet Gdns CROY/NA CR0....63 K9
Violet La SAND/SEL CR2......63 K4
Virginia Av WY GU25 ....36 A6
Virginia Cl ASHTD KT21........77 K7
  NWMAL KT3........................41 P5
  STA TW18............................37 N4
  WEY KT13 ....56 E5
Virginia Dr VW GU25.............36 A6
Virginia Gdns FARN GU14....88 E5
Virginia Pk VW GU25 * 36 C5
Virginia Pl COB KT11 ....75 J3
Virginia Rd THHTH CR7 ....45 L2
Viscount Cl ASHV GU12 ......109 H1
Viscount Gdns BF/WBF KT14..74 A1
Viscount Rd
  STWL/WRAY TW19 ....22 G3
Viscount Wy HTHAIR TW6....14 C9
Viveash Cl HYS/HAR UB3.....15 H1
Vivian Cl FLEETS GU52.........87 H9
Vivien Cl CHSGTN KT9 ....59 L6
Vivienne Cl CRAWW RH11...176 C2
  TWK TW1 ....26 C1
Voewood Cl NWMAL KT3.......42 D7
Vogan Cl REIG RH2.............119 M8
Volta Wy CROY/NA CR0.........45 H9
Voss Ct STRHM/NOR SW16...29 P9
Vowels La EGRIN RH19 ....179 L9
Vulcan Cl CRAWW RH11......176 F9
  FARN GU14.........................87 N7
  SHST GU47 ....67 L1
  WLGTN SM6........................62 G7

W

Wadbrook St KUT/HW KT1......8 C5
Waddington Av
  COUL/CHIP CR5 ....81 J8
Waddington Cl
  COUL/CHIP CR5 ....81 K8
  CRAWW RH11...................176 D9
Waddington Wy NRWD SE19..45 L2
Waddon Cl CROY/NA CR0.....63 J2
Waddon Court Rd
  CROY/NA CR0 ....63 J3
Waddon Marsh Wy
  CROY/NA CR0 ....45 H9
Waddon New Rd
  CROY/NA CR0 ....2 A5
Waddon Park Av
  CROY/NA CR0 ....63 J3
Waddon Rd CROY/NA CR0....63 J2
Waddon Wy CROY/NA CR0....63 J5
Wade's La CHERT KT16..........37 L8
Wadham SHST GU47 ....50 B8
Wadham Cl CRAWE RH10....177 M3
  SHPTN TW17 ....38 E8
Wadham Rd PUT/ROE SW15..19 J9
Wadhurst Cl PGE/AN SE20...46 B3
Wadhurst Rd CHSWK W4 .....18 B1
Wadlands Brook Rd
  EGRIN RH19 ....162 C7
Wagbullock Ri BRAK RG12....32 E7
Waggon Ri EGRIN RH19......180 F2
Waggon Cl GUW GU2 ....111 L4
Waggoners Hollow
  BAGS GU19 ....51 N7
Waggoners Wy
  GSHT GU26 ....165 K8
Waggoners Wells Rd
  GSHT GU26 ....165 K8
Wagtail Cl HORS RH12........192 B3
Wagtail Gdns SAND/SEL CR2..64 D8
Wagtail Wk BECK BR3...........47 J6
Waights Ct KUTN/CMB KT2....8 E2
Wain End HORS RH12.........192 C5
Wainford Cl WIM/MER SW19..28 A4
Wainwright Gv ISLW TW7......16 D9
Wainwrights CRAWE RH10...177 L5
Wake Cl GUW GU2................91 P9
Wakefield Cl BF/WBF KT14....74 A1
Wakefield Gdns NRWD SE19..45 N1
Wakefield Rd
  RCHPK/HAM TW10 ....26 C1
Wakefords Copse
  FLEETS GU52 ....107 H3
Wakefords Cnr
  FLEETS GU52 * 107 H2
Wakefords Pk FLEETS GU52..107 H3
Wakehams Green Dr
  CRAWE RH10.....................177 N2
Wakehurst Dr CRAWE RH10..176 G8
Wakehurst Ms HORS RH12..191 N9
Wakehurst Rd BTSEA SW11..29 J1
Wakely Cl BH/WHM TN16......84 A7
Walburton Rd PUR/KEN CR8..80 B2
Walbury BRAK RG12..............32 G5
Waldeck Gv NWNWD SE27...30 C6
Waldeck Rd
  MORT/ESHN SW14.............18 B9
Waldegrave Gdns TWK TW1..25 N5
Waldegrave Pk TWK TW1......25 N7

Waldegrave Rd NRWD SE19..45 P1
  TWK TW1 ....25 N5
Waldegrove CROY/NA CR0......3 J6
Waldemar Av FUL/PGN SW6..19 J6
Waldemar Rd
  WIM/MER SW19 ....28 D1
Walden Cottages
  RGUW GU3 ....110 A3
Walden Gdns THHTH CR7....45 H5
Waldenshaw Rd FSTH SE23..31 K4
Waldens Park Rd
  WOKN/KNAP GU21 ....72 A6
Waldens Rd
  WOKN/KNAP GU21 ....10 A3
Waldo Cl CLAP SW4..............29 M1
Waldo Pl MTCM CR4.............44 A1
Waldorf Cl SAND/SEL CR2....63 K7
Waldram Crs FSTH SE23......31 K4
Waldram Park Rd FSTH SE23..31 L4
Waldron Gdns HAYES BR2....47 K4
Waldron Hl BRAK RG12.........33 H2
Waldronhyrst CROY/NA CR0..63 K3
Waldron Ms CHEL SW3..........19 P4
Waldron Rd
  WAND/EARL SW18.............28 F6
The Waldrons CROY/NA CR0..63 K3
  OXTED RH8 ....123 M2
Waldy Ri CRAN GU6............153 H8
Wales Av CAR SM5.................62 B4
Walesbeech CRAWE RH10...177 K6
Waleton Acres WLGTN SM6 *..62 C5
Waley's La RDKG RH5..........173 L2
Walford Rd RDKG RH5........137 H2
Walham Green Ct
  FUL/PGN SW6 * 19 M5
Walham Gv FUL/PGN SW6....19 L5
Walham Ri WIM/MER SW19...28 B8
Walham Yd FUL/PGN SW6....19 L5
Walker Cl EBED/NFELT TW14..24 A3
  HPTN TW12 ....24 G9
Walker Rd CRAWE RH10......177 L7
Walkerscroft Md DUL SE21....30 D4
Walker's Pl PUT/ROE SW15 *..19 J9
Walker's Rdg CBLY GU15......68 G3
Walkfield Dr EPSOM KT18......78 F6
Walking Bottom SHGR GU5..134 C7
The Walk OXTED RH8............122 C4
Wallace Cl RGUW GU3.........111 J1
  SHPTN TW17 ....38 F5
Wallace Crs CAR SM5............62 B4
Wallace Flds EW KT17............78 D1
Wallace Sq COUL/CHIP CR5..100 F7
Walrus Rd PADH HDSM KT15..55 N3
Wallace Wy ALDT GU11 * 108 B3
Wallage La CRAWE RH10.....178 E5
Wallcroft Cl BNFD RG42........32 F3
The Walled Gdn BIL RH14....188 C3
  BRKHM/BTCW RH3............118 B6
  KWD/TDW/WH KT20 ....99 H2
Wallgrave Rd ECT SW5........101 P3
Wall Hill Rd EGRIN RH19......181 J6
Wallingford Cl BRAK RG12....32 G5
Wallington Rd CBLY GU15.....51 J3
Wallis Cl BTSEA SW11...........19 P8
Wallis Ct CRAWE RH10 *......177 J1
Wallis Ms LHD/OX KT22 * 96 C2
Wallis Wy SWTR RH13.........192 F6
Wallorton Gdns
  MORT/ESHN SW14.............18 B9
Walmer Cl CWTH RG45..........49 N4
  FRIM GU16 ....69 H9
Walnut Av WDR/YW UB7 ....14 C1
Walnut Cl ALDT GU11..........108 C6
  CAR SM5 ....62 B4
  EPSOM KT18 ....78 D4
  YTLY GU46 ....67 H4
Walnut Dr
  KWD/TDW/WH KT20 ....99 J4
Walnut Gv BNSTD SM7..........79 H3
Walnut La CRAWW RH11.....176 E2
Walnut Ms BELMT SM2..........61 P6
The Walnuts FLEETS GU52 *..106 D1
  HORS RH12 * 192 A9
Walnut Tree Av MTCM CR4....44 A4
Walnut Tree Cl BARN SW13..18 D6
  BNSTD SM7 ....79 J1
  GU GU1..............................111 N6
Walnut Tree Gdns
  GODL GU7..........................131 K6
Walnut Tree La BF/WBF KT14..73 P1
Walnut Tree Pk GU GU1 * 6 C2
Walnut Tree Pl
  RPLY/SEND GU23 ....93 H3
Walnut Tree Rd BTFD TW8...17 L4
  HEST TW5 ....15 P4
  SHPTN TW17 ....38 C4
Walpole Av COUL/CHIP CR5..80 B5
  RCH/KEW TW9 ....17 L2
Walpole Crs TEDD TW11......25 N8
Walpole Gdns CHSWK W4....18 A3
  WHTN TW2 ....25 M5
Walpole Pl TEDD TW11.........25 N8
Walpole Rd CROY/NA CR0......2 E3
  SURB KT6 ....41 L8
  TEDD TW11 ....25 N8
  WDSR SL4 ....20 C3
  WHTN TW2 ....25 M5
  WIM/MER SW19 ....28 G9
Walsh Av BNFD RG42............32 G1
Walsh Crs CROY/NA CR0.......83 L1
Walsingham Gdns
  HOR/WEW KT19 ....60 C3
Walsingham Rd CLAP SW4 *..29 P2
  CROY/NA CR0 ....65 J8
  MTCM CR4 ....44 B6

Walter's Md ASHTD KT21....77 L6
Walter's Rd SNWD SE25....45 N5
Walter St KUTN/CMB KT2....8 D3
Walters Wy FSTH SE23....31 L2
SWTR RH13....193 H6
Waltham Av GUW GU2....111 P2
HYS/HAR UB3....14 E1
Waltham Cl SHST GU47....49 P8
Waltham Rd CAR SM5....43 P9
CTHM CR3....102 B2
NWDGN UB2....15 N1
Walton Av CHEAM SM3....61 K2
NWMAL KT3....42 D5
Walton Bridge Rd
SHPTN TW17....38 C8
Walton Cl CROY/NA KNAP GU21....72 J4
SWTR RH13....193 H6
Walton Dr ASC SL5....33 P2
SWTR RH13....193 H6
Walton Gdns FELT TW13....24 A7
Walton Gn CROY/NA CR0....65 H7
Walton Heath CRAWE RH10....177 N5
Walton La WEY KT13....56 E1
WOT/HER KT12....38 E9
Walton Pk WOT/HER KT12....57 M1
Walton Park La
WOT/HER KT12....57 N1
Walton Rd EPSOM KT18....98 A1
WOKN/KNAP GU21....11 C2
WOT/HER KT12....39 M6
Walton St
KWD/TDW/WH KT20....98 E4
Walton Ter
WOKN/KNAP GU21....72 F4
Walton Wy MTCM CR4....44 B5
Wanborough Dr
PUT/ROE SW15....27 N4
Wanborough Hl RGUW GU3....110 C8
Wanborough La CRAN GU6....153 K8
Wandle Bank CROY/NA CR0....62 G2
WIM/MER SW19....28 G9
Wandle Cl ASHV GU12....109 J5
CRAWE RH10....177 M6
Wandle Ct HOR/WEW KT19....60 A3
Wandle Court Gdns
CROY/NA CR0....62 G2
Wandle Rd CROY/NA CR0....2 C6
MRDN SM4....43 P6
TOOT SW17....29 H5
Wandle Side CROY/NA CR0....63 H2
WLGTN SM6....62 C2
Wandle Wy MTCM CR4....44 B5
WAND/EARL SW18....28 E4
Wandon Rd FUL/PGN SW6....19 M5
Wandsdyke Cl FRIM GU16....69 H8
Wandsworth Br
WAND/EARL SW18....19 N8
Wandsworth Bridge Rd
FUL/PGN SW6....19 M6
Wandsworth Common
West Side
WAND/EARL SW18....28 F1
Wandsworth High St
WAND/EARL SW18....28 D1
Wandsworth Pln
WAND/EARL SW18....19 J6
Wanmer Ct REIG RH2 *....119 L4
Wansdown Pl FUL/PGN SW6....19 M5
Wansford Gn
WOKN/KNAP GU21....71 M6
Wanstraw Gv BRAK RG12....32 C8
Wantage Cl BRAK RG12....32 C6
CRAWE RH10....177 M8
Wantage Rd SHST GU47....49 P9
Wapiti Wy FARN GU14....87 P7
The Waplings
KWD/TDW/WH KT20 *....98 F4
Wapshott Rd STA TW18....22 B9
Warbank Cl CROY/NA CR0....65 L8
Warbank Crs CROY/NA CR0....65 L8
Warbank La KUTN/CMB KT2....42 D1
Warblers Gn COB KT11....75 P3
Warboys Ap KUTN/CMB KT2....26 G9
Warboys Rd KUTN/CMB KT2....26 G9
Warburton Cl EGRIN RH19....180 F2
Warburton Rd WHTN TW2....25 J4
Warbury La
WOKN/KNAP GU21....71 J5
War Coppice Rd CTHM CR3....101 M7
Ward Cl SAND/SEL CR2....63 N4
Ward La WARL CR6....82 C5
Wardle Cl BAGS GU19....51 N6
Wardley St
WAND/EARL SW18....28 E3
Wardo Av FUL/PGN SW6....19 J6
The Wardrobe
RCH/KEW TW9 *....26 C1
Wards Pl EGH TW20....21 P9
Wards Stone Pk BRAK RG12....32 G8
Ward St GU GU1....7 G5
Wareham Cl HSLW TW3....16 B9
Wareham Rd BRAK RG12....33 H6
Warenne Hts REDH RH1....119 P7
Warenne Rd LHD/OX KT22....96 C2
Warfield Rd BRAK RG12....32 E2
EBED/NFELT TW14....23 P3
HPTN TW12....40 B2
Wargrove Dr SHST GU47....49 P9
Warham Rd SAND/SEL CR2....63 L4
Waring St WNWD SE27....30 D7
Warkworth Gdns ISLW TW7....16 C5
Warlingham Rd THHTH CR7....45 K5
Warltersville Wy HORL RH6....159 M3
Warmington Rd HNHL SE24....30 D2
Warminster Rd SNWD SE25....46 A3
Warminster Sq SNWD SE25....46 A3
Warminster Wy MTCM CR4....44 C2
Warner Av CHEAM SM3....61 J1
Warner Cl CRAWE RH10....177 M9
HPTN TW12....24 G8
HYS/HAR UB3....14 F5
Warner Rd BMLY BR1....47 M1
Warners La SHGR GU5....134 A3

Warnham Court Ms
HORS RH12 *....172 F7
Warnham Court Rd CAR SM5....62 B6
Warnham Rd CRAWE RH10....177 K7
Warpole Pk WEY KT13....56 C6
Warramill Rd GODL GU7....131 N8
Warren Av BELMT SM2....61 K8
BMLY BR1....47 L1
RCHPK/HAM TW10....17 P9
SAND/SEL CR2....64 D6
Warren Cl DTCH/LGLY SL3....12 C1
EGRIN RH19....161 M9
ESH/CLAY KT10....58 C5
FLEETS GU52....87 H8
SHST GU47....49 L9
Warren Cnr RFNM GU10....106 C7
Warren Cutting
KUTN/CMB KT2....42 B1
Warren Down BNFD RG42....32 A2
Warren Dr CRAWW RH11....176 D4
KWD/TDW/WH KT20....99 K2
Warren Dr North BRYLDS KT5....41 P9
Warren Dr South BRYLDS KT5....42 A9
Warreners La WEY KT13....56 F7
Warren Hl EPSOM KT18....78 B5
Warren La EWKG RG40....48 B4
LHD/OX KT22....76 C1
OXTED RH8....123 N5
WOKS/MYFD GU22....73 L7
Warren Lodge Dr
KWD/TDW/WH KT20....99 J4
Warren Md BNSTD SM7....78 C4
Warrenne Rd
BRKHM/BTCW RH3....118 A7
Warrenne Wy REIG RH2....119 L5
Warren Pk KUTN/CMB KT2....27 H9
KWD/TDW/WH KT20 *....118 A2
WARL CR6....82 D7
Warren Park Rd SUT SM1....61 P5
Warren Ri FRIM GU16....68 C5
Warren Rd ASHV GU12....109 J5
CBLY GU15....68 D4
CHERT KT16....37 J7
CROY/NA CR0....3 H1
GODL GU7....131 L6
GU GU1....7 J5
HAYES BR2....65 N1
KUTN/CMB KT2....27 H9
PUR/KEN CR8....81 K1
REIG RH2....119 M4
WHTN TW2....25 L2
WIM/MER SW19....29 H9
Warren Rw ASC SL5....33 M3
The Warren ASHTD KT21....77 M9
BELMT SM2....61 P7
BRAK RG12 *....33 H5
EHSLY KT24....115 H1
FNM GU9....108 A6
HEST TW5....15 P5
KWD/TDW/WH KT20....99 J3
LHD/OX KT22....76 C1
Warren Wy WEY KT13....56 C3
Warwick Av EGH TW20....36 C2
STA TW18....22 F9
Warwick Chambers
KENS W8 *....19 L1
Warwick Cl ALDT GU11....108 E6
CBLY GU15....69 G5
HPTN TW12....40 C1
RDKG RH5....137 H6
Warwick Deeping
CHERT KT16....54 C4
Warwick Dr PUT/ROE SW15....18 F8
Warwick Gdns ASHTD KT21....77 J6
THDIT KT7....40 E6
THHTH CR7 *....45 J5
WKENS W14....19 K1
Warwick Gv BRYLDS KT5....41 M8
Warwick La
WOKN/KNAP GU21....71 N8
Warwick Pl THDIT KT7 *....40 C7
Warwick Rd ASHF TW15....23 H8
ASHV GU12....89 H6
COUL/CHIP CR5....80 E5
FARN GU14....87 P4
HSLW TW3....15 K8
KUT/HW KT1....41 K5
NWDGN UB2....15 P1
NWMAL KT3....42 A4
PGE/AN SE20....46 C3
RDKG RH5....137 J7
REDH RH1....120 C5
SUT SM1....61 N4
THDIT KT7....40 F6
THHTH CR7....45 J4
WHTN TW2....25 M4
WKENS W14....19 K2
Warwick's Bench GU GU1....7 F7
Warwick's Bench La
GU GU1....112 C8
Warwick Wold Rd
REDH RH1....101 J7
Wasdale Cl SHST GU47....49 P7
Washington Cl REIG RH2....119 L3
Washington Gdns
EWKG RG40....48 E5
Washington Rd BARN SW13....18 E5
CRAWW RH11....176 B7
KUT/HW KT1....9 H5
WPK KT4....60 F1
Washneys Rd ORP BR6....85 L2
Washpond La WARL CR6....83 J7

Wasp Green La REDH RH1....141 K5
Wassand Cl CRAWE RH10....177 K5
Wastdale Rd FSTH SE23....31 L4
Watchetts Dr CBLY GU15....68 E6
Watchetts Lake Cl CBLY GU15....68 F5
Watchetts Rd CBLY GU15....68 D5
Watchfield Ct CHSWK W4 *....18 A3
Watchmoor Point
CBLY GU15 *....68 D4
Watchmoor Rd CBLY GU15....68 C5
Watcombe Rd SNWD SE25....46 B6
Watercress Wy
WOKN/KNAP GU21....71 P6
Waterden Rd GU GU1....7 H4
Waterer Gdns
KWD/TDW/WH KT20....79 J7
Waterer Ri WLGTN SM6....62 F5
Waterers Ri
WOKN/KNAP GU21....71 K6
Waterfall Cl VW GU25....35 M4
Waterfall Cottages
WIM/MER SW19....28 C9
Waterfall Rd WIM/MER SW19....28 C9
Waterfall Ter TOOT SW17....29 H9
Waterfield
KWD/TDW/WH KT20....78 F9
Waterfield Cl SWTR RH13....192 D7
Waterfield Dr WARL CR6....82 B8
Waterfield Gdns
CRAWW RH11....176 B7
SNWD SE25....45 N5
Waterfield Gn
KWD/TDW/WH KT20....78 F9
Waterfields LHD/OX KT22....77 H8
Waterford Cl COB KT11....57 N9
Waterford Rd FUL/PGN SW6....19 M6
Waterham Rd BRAK RG12....32 D7
Waterhouse La
KWD/TDW/WH KT20....99 K1
PUR/KEN CR8....81 L8
REDH RH1....121 P5
Waterhouse Md SHST GU47....49 P7
Waterlakes EDEN TN8....144 G5
Waterlands La HORS RH12....190 F2
Water La CHOB/PIR GU24....70 E8
COB KT11....75 N4
EDEN TN8....144 B6
FARN GU14....68 C9
FNM GU9....5 J4
GDST RH9....122 D9
GT/LBKH KT23....95 N6
KUT/HW KT1....8 C3
MFD/CHID GU8....150 A8
OXTED RH8....103 N6
RCH/KEW TW9....26 C1
RDKG RH5....135 H5
SHGR GU5....113 M9
TWK TW1....25 P4
Water Lea CRAWE RH10....177 K6
Waterloo Cl CBLY GU15....69 K1
EBED/NFELT TW14....24 A4
Waterloo Pl CAR SM5 *....62 B2
CWTH RG45....49 K5
RCH/KEW TW9....17 N4
Waterloo Rd ASHV GU12....108 E5
CWTH RG45....49 L5
HOR/WEW KT19....78 B2
SUT SM1....61 P4
Waterloo Ter WEY KT13 *....56 C3
Waterlow Rd REIG RH2....119 N6
Watermans Cl
KUTN/CMB KT2....8 D1
Waterman Sq PGE/AN SE20....46 C1
Waterman St
PUT/ROE SW15....19 H8
Water Md COUL/CHIP CR5....80 B6
Watermead
EBED/NFELT TW14....23 P4
KWD/TDW/WH KT20....98 F1
WOKN/KNAP GU21....71 M5
Watermead La CAR SM5....44 B7
Watermeadow La
FUL/PGN SW6....19 N7
Watermens Sq
PGE/AN SE20 *....46 C1
Watermill Cl
RCHPK/HAM TW10....26 B6
Water Mill Wy FELT TW13....24 C5
Watermill Wy
WIM/MER SW19....43 N2
Waterperry La
CHOB/PIR GU24....53 M8
Water Rede FLEETS GU52....106 E3
Waters Dr STA TW18....22 C7
Water's Edge
FUL/PGN SW6 *....19 H6
Waterside HOR/WEW KT19....60 A3
Waterside Av BECK BR3....47 H6
Waterside Cl CRAWW RH11....176 B7
GODL GU7....131 N8
SURB KT6....59 L1
Waterside Ct FLEETS GU52....87 H6
Waterside Dr WOT/HER KT12....39 H6
Waterside La GODL GU7....150 B1
Waterside Ms FLEETS GU52....87 H6
GU GU1....112 A5
Waterside Rd GU GU1....112 C2
Waterside Wy TOOT SW17....28 F7
WOKN/KNAP GU21....71 P7
Watersmeet Cl RGUE GU4....92 E9
Watersplash Cl KUT/HW KT1....8 C5
Water Splash La ASC SL5....34 E2
Watersplash Rd SHPTN TW17....38 C5
Waters Rd KUT/HW KT1....9 K5
Water Tower Hl CROY/NA CR0....3 F7
Waterway Rd LHD/OX KT22....96 G2

Waterworks Cl FROW RH18....181 L7
Waterworks Rd
BRXS/STRHM SW2....29 P2
Watery La CHOB/PIR GU24....53 K8
FLEETS GU52....106 A3
HYS/HAR UB3....14 F3
RYNPK SW20....43 K3
Wates Wy MTCM CR4....44 B7
Watford Cl GU GU1....7 K3
Wathen Rd DORK RH4....117 H6
Watlings Cl CROY/NA CR0....46 G7
Watlington Gv SYD SE26....31 M8
Watney Cl PUR/KEN CR8....81 H2
Watney Rd
MORT/ESHN SW14....18 A8
Watneys Rd CROY/NA CR0....44 G6
Watson Av CHEAM SM3....61 J1
Watson Cl CRAWE RH10....177 M8
WIM/MER SW19....29 H9
Watson Rd DORK RH4....116 C8
Wattenden Rd PUR/KEN CR8....81 K5
Watts Cl
KWD/TDW/WH KT20 *....99 H2
Watts Common Rd
ALDT GU11....88 A8
Watt's La
KWD/TDW/WH KT20....99 H2
TEDD TW11....25 P8
Watts Lea WOKN/KNAP GU21....71 N4
Watt's Md
KWD/TDW/WH KT20....99 H2
Watts Rd FARN GU14....88 B2
THDIT KT7....40 C8
Wavel Pl SYD SE26....30 G7
Wavendene Av EGH TW20....36 C1
Wavendon Av CHSWK W4....18 B3
Waveney Wk CRAWE RH10....177 L7
Waverleigh Rd CRAN GU6....171 H2
Waverley BRAK RG12....32 A6
Waverley Av BRYLDS KT5....41 P7
PUR/KEN CR8....81 N5
SUT SM1....61 M1
WHTN TW2....24 G4
Waverley Cl CBLY GU15....69 H4
E/WMO/HCT KT8....40 A6
FNM GU9....5 J4
HYS/HAR UB3....14 D5
Waverley Ct HORS RH12 *....192 A3
WOKS/MYFD GU22....10 D5
Waverley Dr ASHV GU12....89 J9
CBLY GU15....68 G3
CHERT KT16....55 H2
VW GU25....35 N5
Waverley Gdns ASHV GU12....89 J9
Waverley La FNM GU9....5 K6
Waverley Pl LHD/OX KT22 *....97 H2
Waverley Rd BAGS GU19....51 M5
COB KT11....76 B3
EW KT17....60 F4
FARN GU14....88 B2
SNWD SE25....46 B5
Waverley Wy CAR SM5....62 A5
Waverton Rd
WAND/EARL SW18....28 F3
Waye Av HEST TW5....15 J6
Wayland Ct BRAK RG12 *....32 C4
Wayland Gdns STWL/WRAY TW19....21 K2
Waylett Pl WNWD SE27....30 C6
Wayman Rd FARN GU14....68 A8
Wayneflete Tower Av
ESH/CLAY KT10....58 A2
Waynflete La FNM GU9....4 B4
Waynflete St
WAND/EARL SW18....28 F5
Ways End CBLY GU15....68 G4
Wayside CRAWW RH11....176 B7
CROY/NA CR0....65 H5
MORT/ESHN SW14....18 A9
RDKG RH5 *....156 C6
Wayside Ct TWK TW1....25 P2
Wayside Dr EDEN TN8....145 H2
The Way REIG RH2....119 P4
Weald Cl RGUE GU4....132 C2
Weald Dr CRAWE RH10....177 K6
Wealdstone Rd CHEAM SM3....61 K1
The Weald EGRIN RH19....162 E9
Weald Wy CTHM CR3....101 N6
REIG RH2....119 N9
Weare St RDKG RH5....173 K4
Weasdale Ct
WOKN/KNAP GU21....71 M5
Weatherall Cl
ADL/WDHM KT15....55 M4
Weatherhill Cl HORL RH6....160 G1
Weatherhill Rd HORL RH6....160 D1
Weather Wy BRAK RG12....32 E3
Weaver Cl CRAWW RH11....176 B6
Weaver Moss SHST GU47....67 M1
Weavers Cl ISLW TW7....16 F9
Weavers Down LIPH GU30 *....182 A7
Weavers Gdns FNM GU9....127 K6
Weavers Ter FUL/PGN SW6 *....19 L4
Weaver Wk WNWD SE27....30 C7
Webb Cl BAGS GU19....51 N8
BNFD RG42....32 A1
CRAWW RH11....194 E1
DTCH/LGLY SL3....12 B2
Webb Rd MFD/CHID GU8....149 K5
Webb's Rd BTSEA SW11....29 J3
Webb La LHD/OX KT22....76 F5
Websters Cl
WOKS/MYFD GU22....71 N9
Weddell Rd CRAWE RH10....177 J8
Wedgwoods
BH/WHM TN16 *....104 A1
Wedgwood Wy NRWD SE19....45 L1
Weekley Sq BTSEA SW11 *....19 P8

Weighbridge Rd
ADL/WDHM KT15....55 M7
Weighton Rd PGE/AN SE20....46 B3
Weihurst Gdns SUT SM1....61 P4
Weimar St PUT/ROE SW15....19 J8
Weir Av FARN GU14....88 C4
Weirbrook CRAWE RH10....177 K8
Weir Cl FARN GU14....88 C4
Weir Pl STA TW18....37 J2
Weir Rd BAL SW12....29 M4
CHERT KT16....37 M8
FLEETN GU51....87 L5
WIM/MER SW19....28 E6
WOT/HER KT12....39 J7
Weiss Rd PUT/ROE SW15....19 H8
Welbeck BRAK RG12....32 A6
Welbeck Cl EW KT17....60 E6
FARN GU14....88 B3
NWMAL KT3....42 D6
Welbeck Rd CAR SM5....44 A8
SUT SM1....61 P2
Welcomes Rd PUR/KEN CR8....81 L4
Weldon Cl FLEETS GU52....107 H1
Weldon Dr E/WMO/HCT KT8....39 P5
Weldon Wy REDH RH1....100 F9
Welford Pl WIM/MER SW19....28 B7
Welham Rd TOOT SW17....29 M9
Welhouse Rd CAR SM5....44 A8
Welland Cl DTCH/LGLY SL3....12 E4
Wellburn Cl SHST GU47....67 M1
Well Cl CBLY GU15....68 D4
STRHM/NOR SW16....30 A7
WOKN/KNAP GU21....72 A6
Weller Cl CRAWE RH10....177 N6
Weller Dr CBLY GU15....68 E5
Wellers Cl BH/WHM TN16....104 C7
Wellesford Cl BNSTD SM7....79 K7
Wellesley Av DTCH/LGLY SL3....13 K1
HMSMTH W6....18 F1
Wellesley Cl ASHV GU12....89 H8
BAGS GU19....51 L6
Wellesley Court Rd
CROY/NA CR0 *....2 E4
Wellesley Crs WHTN TW2....25 M5
Wellesley Dr CWTH RG45....49 J5
Wellesley Gdn FNM GU9....107 N7
Wellesley Ga ASHV GU12 *....108 D5
Wellesley Gv CROY/NA CR0....2 E3
Wellesley Pde WHTN TW2 *....25 M6
Wellesley Rd ALDT GU11....107 P5
BELMT SM2....61 N3
CHSWK W4....17 N3
CROY/NA CR0....2 D1
RFNM GU10....147 L6
WHTN TW2....25 L6
Wellesley Wy STWL/WRAY TW19....12 C9
Wellesley Rd STWL/WRAY TW19....12 C9
Well Farm Rd CTHM CR3....82 A8
Wellfield EGRIN RH19....181 H4
Wellfields Gdns CAR SM5....62 A8
Wellfield Rd
STRHM/NOR SW16....29 P7
Wellhouse La
BRKHM/BTCW RH3....118 C6
Wellhouse Rd BECK BR3....46 F5
BRKHM/BTCW RH3....118 C6
Wellingham Wy HORS RH12....175 P9
Wellington Av ALDT GU11....108 A4
FLEETN GU51....87 H5
HSLW TW3....15 G5
VW GU25....35 P7
WPK KT4....60 G2
Wellington Cl CRAWE RH10....177 P2
SHST GU47....49 N9
WOT/HER KT12....39 H9
Wellington Crs NWMAL KT3....42 A4
Wellington Dr BRAK RG12....32 F6
PUR/KEN CR8....63 H8
Wellington Gdns
ALDT GU11....108 B5
WHTN TW2....25 L6
Wellingtonia Av EWKG RG40....48 F9
Wellingtonia Wy
EDEN TN8....144 G3
Wellington La FNM GU9....107 P7
Wellington Pl ASHV GU12....109 H2
COB KT11....76 A1
GODL GU7....131 L6
Wellington Rd ASHF TW15....23 H8
CROY/NA CR0....45 K8
CTHM CR3....101 L2
EBED/NFELT TW14....23 P1
HORS RH12....192 C8
HPTN TW12....25 L7
SHST GU47....49 N9
WIM/MER SW19....28 B5
Wellington Rd North
HSLW TW3....15 P8
Wellington Rd South
HSLW TW4....15 P9
Wellington St ALDT GU11....108 C4
Wellington Ter SHST GU47....49 N9
WOKN/KNAP GU21....71 L7
Wellington Town Rd
EGRIN RH19....162 C9
Wellington Wy FARN GU14....87 P8
HORL RH6....140 B8
WEY KT13....56 C8
Well La HASM GU27....184 E4
MFD/CHID GU8....167 L3
MORT/ESHN SW14....18 A9
WOKN/KNAP GU21....72 A6
Wellmeadow Rd HNWL W7....16 C2
Well Pth WOKN/KNAP GU21....72 A6
Well Rd RFNM GU10....106 C8
Wells Cl GT/LBKH KT23....96 B4
HORS RH12....191 N8
SAND/SEL CR2....63 N4
Wells Cottages FNM GU9....127 L6

Wellside Gdns
MORT/ESHN SW14 .....18 A9
Wells La ASC SL5 .....34 B5
RGUW GU3 .....110 C2
Wells Meadow EGRIN RH19 .....162 C9
Wells Park Rd SYD SE26 .....31 H6
Wells PI REDH RH1 .....120 D1
WAND/EARL SW18 .....28 F3
Wells Rd CRAWE RH10 * 177 H9
EPSOM KT18 .....77 N5
RGUE GU4 .....112 C2
Wells Wy SKENS SW7 .....19 H1
Wells Wy EPSOM KT18 .....77 N4
Wellwood Cl COUL/CHIP CR5 .....80 C5
SWTR RH13 .....192 C6
Wellwynds Rd CRAN GU6 .....171 H1
Welstead Wy CHSWK W4 .....18 D1
Weltje Rd HMSMTH W6 .....18 E3
Welwyn Av
EBED/NFELT TW14 .....24 A2
Welwyn Cl CRAWW RH11 .....176 B8
Wembley Rd HPTN TW12 .....40 A2
Wembury Pk LING RH7 .....161 M4
Wendela Cl
WOKS/MYFD GU22 .....11 F6
Wendley Dr ADL/WDHM KT15 .....55 K8
Wendling Rd SUT SM1 .....43 J2
Wendover Dr FRIM GU16 .....69 L5
NWMAL KT3 .....42 D7
Wendover PI STA TW18 .....22 A8
Wendover Rd HAYES BR2 .....47 P5
STA TW18 .....22 A8
Wendron Cl
WOKN/KNAP GU21 .....71 N7
The Wend COUL/CHIP CR5 .....80 F3
Wendy Crs GUW GU2 .....111 N3
Wenlock Cl CRAWW RH11 .....176 D7
Wenlock Edge DORK RH4 * 117 J9
Wensleydale CRAWW RH11 .....176 F8
Wensleydale Dr CBLY GU15 .....69 M5
Wensleydale Gdns
HPTN TW12 .....40 B1
Wentworth Av ASC SL5 .....33 L3
Wentworth Cl ASHF TW15 .....23 L7
ASHV GU12 .....89 J8
CWTH RG45 .....49 K3
FNM GU9 .....108 B8
HAYES BR2 * 47 L6
MRDN SM4 .....43 L8
RPLY/SEND GU23 .....93 M1
SURB KT6 .....59 K1
YTLY GU46 .....67 H3
Wentworth Crs ASHV GU12 .....89 J9
HYS/HAR UB3 .....14 F1
Wentworth Dene WEY KT13 .....56 D4
Wentworth Dr CRAWE RH10 .....177 N4
VW GU25 .....35 M5
Wentworth Rd CROY/NA CR0 .....45 J8
NWDGN UB2 .....15 L2
Wentworth Wy ASC SL5 .....33 L3
SAND/SEL CR2 .....82 A4
Werndee Rd SNWD SE25 .....46 A5
Werter Rd PUT/ROE SW15 .....19 J3
Wesley Av HSLW TW3 .....15 N7
Wesley Cl CRAWW RH11 .....176 B8
HORL RH6 .....159 J2
REIG RH2 .....119 K6
Wesley Dr EGH TW20 .....21 M9
Wessels KWD/TDW/WH KT20 .....99 H1
Wessex Av WIM/MER SW19 .....43 L3
Wessex Cl KUT/HW KT1 .....9 L3
THDIT KT7 .....58 F1
Wessex Ct BECK BR3 * 46 E2
Wessex PI FNM GU9 .....5 H5
Wessex Ter MTCM CR4 * 44 A6
Westacres ESH/CLAY KT10 .....57 P6
West Av CRAWE RH10 .....177 J5
FNM GU9 .....107 P8
REDH RH1 .....140 B2
WLGTN SM6 .....62 G4
WOT/HER KT12 .....56 G8
West Bank DORK RH4 .....116 F8
Westbank Rd HPTN TW12 .....25 K9
West Barnes La RYNPK SW20 .....42 F4
Westbourne Av CHEAM SM3 .....61 J1
Westbourne Dr FSTH SE23 .....31 L4
Westbourne Rd
CROY/NA CR0 .....45 P7
FELT TW13 .....24 A6
SHST GU47 .....68 A1
STA TW18 .....37 M1
SYD SE26 .....31 K6
Westbridge Rd BTSEA SW11 .....19 P6
Westbrook FROW RH18 * 181 K8
Westbrook Av HPTN TW12 .....39 P1
Westbrook Gdns BRAK RG12 .....32 E2
Westbrook Hl
MFD/CHID GU8 .....129 L9
Westbrook Rd HEST TW5 .....15 P5
STA TW18 .....22 C8
THHTH CR7 .....45 M2
Westbury Av ESH/CLAY KT10 .....58 F5
FLEETN GU51 .....87 K7
Westbury Cl CTHM CR3 * 81 P7
CWTH RG45 .....49 M3
FLEETN GU51 .....87 J7
SHPTN TW17 * 38 D7
Westbury Gdns
FLEETN GU51 .....87 K7
FNM GU9 .....128 A1
Westbury PI BTFD TW8 * 17 K4
Westbury Rd CROY/NA CR0 .....45 M7
FELT TW13 .....24 E4
NWMAL KT3 .....42 B5
PGE/AN SE20 .....46 D2
Westbury Ter
BH/WHM TN16 .....104 C2
Westbury Wy ASHV GU12 .....108 F4
Westcar La WOT/HER KT12 .....57 K5
West Cl ASHF TW15 .....23 H7
FNM GU9 .....107 P7

Westcombe Av
CROY/NA CR0 .....44 G7
Westcombe Cl BRAK RG12 .....32 F8
West Common Rd
HAYES BR2 .....65 N1
Westcoombe Av
RYNPK SW20 .....42 D2
Westcote Rd
STRHM/NOR SW16 .....29 M8
Westcott Cl CRAWW RH11 .....194 F2
CROY/NA CR0 .....65 H7
Westcott Rd DORK RH4 .....116 F7
Westcotts Gn BNFD RG42 .....32 F1
Westcott St DORK RH4 .....116 B8
Westcott Wy BELMT SM2 .....60 G8
Westcroft Gdns MRDN SM4 .....43 K4
Westcroft Rd CAR SM5 .....62 C3
Westcroft Ms HMSMTH W6 * 18 E2
Westcroft Sq HMSMTH W6 .....18 E2
West Cromwell Rd ECT SW5 .....19 L2
West Cross Wy BTFD TW8 .....17 H4
Westdean Cl
WAND/EARL SW18 .....28 E1
Westdene WOT/HER KT12 .....57 K4
Westdene Mdw CRAN GU6 .....152 D9
Westdene Wy WEY KT13 .....56 G2
West Down CT/LBKH KT23 .....96 B7
Westdown Rd CAT SE6 .....31 P3
West Drayton Park Av
WDR/YW UB7 .....14 A1
West Dr ADL/WDHM KT15 .....55 M8
ASC SL5 .....35 K7
BELMT SM2 .....61 H7
CAR SM5 .....61 P8
KWD/TDW/WH KT20 .....79 H7
STRHM/NOR SW16 .....29 M5
West End Gdns
ESH/CLAY KT10 .....57 P4
West End Gv FNM GU9 .....4 C3
West End La ESH/CLAY KT10 .....57 P4
HASM GU27 .....185 L2
HYS/HAR UB3 .....14 E5
RFNM GU10 .....106 E8
Westerdale Dr FRIM GU16 .....69 K5
Westerfolds Cl
WOKS/MYFD GU22 .....72 C6
Westerham Cl
ADL/WDHM KT15 .....55 N5
BELMT SM2 * 61 L8
Westerham Hl
BH/WHM TN16 .....104 F2
Westerham Rd
BH/WHM TN16 .....105 L5
OXTED RH8 .....103 N9
Westerley Crs SYD SE26 * 31 N8
Western Av CHERT KT16 .....37 L4
CHOB/PIR GU24 .....90 C1
EGH TW20 .....36 F4
Western Cl CHERT KT16 .....37 L4
Western Dr SHPTN TW17 .....38 F6
Western La BAL SW12 .....29 K3
Western Perimeter Rd
HTHAIR TW6 .....13 M8
Western PI DORK RH4 * 116 C7
Western Rd ALDT GU11 .....108 A5
BNFD RG42 .....32 A2
MTCM CR4 .....44 A2
SNWD SE25 .....46 B6
SUT SM1 .....61 L4
Western Ter HMSMTH W6 * 18 E3
West Farm Av ASHTD KT21 .....77 J7
West Farm Cl ASHTD KT21 .....77 J8
West Farm Dr ASHTD KT21 .....77 K8
Westfield RDKG RH5 .....134 C5
Westfield Av SAND/SEL CR2 .....81 M2
WOKS/MYFD GU22 .....92 C1
Westfield Cl SUT SM1 .....61 K3
WBPTN SW10 .....19 N5
Westfield Common
WOKS/MYFD GU22 .....92 C2
Westfield Dr GT/LBKH KT23 .....96 B2
Westfield Gv
WOKS/MYFD GU22 .....92 C1
Westfield La RFNM GU10 .....127 J7
Westfield Pde
ADL/WDHM KT15 * 55 P8
Westfield Rd BECK BR3 .....46 F3
CBLY GU15 .....68 D6
CRAWW RH11 .....176 E5
CROY/NA CR0 .....2 A3
GU GU1 .....112 C1
MTCM CR4 .....44 A3
SURB KT6 .....41 K6
SUT SM1 .....61 K3
WOKS/MYFD GU22 .....92 C2
WOT/HER KT12 .....39 N8
Westfields BARN SW13 .....18 D8
Westfields Av BARN SW13 .....18 C8
Westfield Wy
WOKS/MYFD GU22 .....92 C2
West Flexford La
RGUW GU3 .....110 E6
West Fryerne YTLY GU46 .....67 H1
West Gdns EW KT17 .....60 C8
TOOT SW17 .....29 H9
Westgate Rd BECK BR3 .....47 J2
SNWD SE25 .....46 B5
Westgate Ter WBPTN SW10 .....19 M3
Westglade FARN GU14 .....87 P5
West Gn YTLY GU46 .....66 F1
West Green Dr
CRAWW RH11 .....176 F5
West Gv WOT/HER KT12 .....57 K3
West Hall Rd RCH/KEW TW9 * 17 N3
Westhall Pk WARL CR6 .....82 C8
Westhall Rd WARL CR6 .....82 A7
Westhay Gdns
MORT/ESHN SW14 .....26 G1

West Heath CHOB/PIR GU24 .....90 D3
West Heath Rd FARN GU14 .....88 B3
West Hl EGRIN RH19 .....162 D6
EGRIN RH19 .....180 C3
HOR/WEW KT19 .....78 A2
OXTED RH8 .....123 K6
ORP BR6 .....84 D1
OXTED RH8 .....123 K1
SAND/SEL CR2 .....63 N7
WIM/MER SW19 .....28 A3
West Hill Av HOR/WEW KT19 .....78 A1
West Hill Bank OXTED RH8 .....123 K1
West Hill Cl CHOB/PIR GU24 .....71 H9
MFD/CHID GU8 .....148 D1
West Hill Gdns FLEETN GU51 .....86 D5
West Hill Rd
WAND/EARL SW18 .....28 C2
WOKS/MYFD GU22 .....10 B7
West Hoathly Rd
EGRIN RH19 .....180 B8
Westhorpe Rd
PUT/ROE SW15 .....18 G8
West House Cl
WIM/MER SW19 .....28 B4
Westhumble St RDKG RH5 .....117 H2
The West Hundreds
FLEETN GU51 .....86 E4
Westland Cl
STWL/WRAY TW19 * 23 H2
Westland Dr HAYES BR2 .....65 M1
Westlands Cl HYS/HAR UB3 .....15 J2
Westlands Ct EPSOM KT18 .....78 A2
Westlands Ter BAL SW12 .....29 M2
Westlands Wy OXTED RH8 .....103 K7
West La EGRIN RH19 .....180 B3
RDKG RH5 .....135 M1
Westlea Rd HNWL W7 .....16 G1
Westleas HORL RH6 .....140 A8
Westlees Cl RDKG RH5 .....137 J1
West Leigh EGRIN RH19 .....180 E4
Westleigh Av COUL/CHIP CR5 .....80 C5
PUT/ROE SW15 .....27 P1
Westmacott Dr
EBED/NFELT TW14 .....24 B4
Westmead FARN GU14 .....88 D4
West Md FNM GU9 * 4 E3
HOR/WEW KT19 .....60 C5
Westmead Dr REDH RH1 .....140 C4
Westmead Rd SUT SM1 .....61 P3
West Meads GUW GU2 .....111 M6
HORL RH6 .....159 M1
Westminster Av THHTH CR7 .....45 K3
Westminster Cl
EBED/NFELT TW14 .....24 B4
FLEETN GU51 .....86 C5
TEDD TW11 .....25 P8
Westminster Ct
WOKS/MYFD GU22 * 92 F1
Westminster Rd
CRAWE RH10 .....177 M6
SUT SM1 .....61 P1
Westmoat Cl BECK BR3 .....47 J1
Westmont Rd ESH/CLAY KT10 .....58 E1
Westmoreland Dr
BELMT SM2 .....61 M7
Westmoreland PI
BMLY BR1 * 47 N4
Westmoreland Rd
BARN SW13 .....18 D6
HAYES BR2 .....47 L6
Westmoreland Ter
PGE/AN SE20 .....46 B1
Westmore Rd BH/WHM TN16 .....84 A9
Westmorland Cl
HOR/WEW KT19 .....60 C8
TWK TW1 .....26 A2
Westmorland Dr BNFD RG42 .....33 H1
CBLY GU15 .....69 K5
Westmorland Wy MTCM CR4 .....44 F5
West Mt GUW GU2 * 6 C7
West Oak BECK BR3 .....47 K2
Weston Av ADL/WDHM KT15 .....55 L3
E/WMO/HCT KT8 .....39 P5
THDIT KT7 .....40 E8
Weston Cl COUL/CHIP CR5 .....81 H9
GODL GU7 .....131 L7
Weston Ct CTHM CR3 .....101 L1
CTHM CR3 .....102 A4
Weston Flds SHGR GU5 .....133 N1
Weston Gdns ISLW TW7 .....16 D6
WOKS/MYFD GU22 .....73 J5
Weston Gn THDIT KT7 .....40 E9
Weston Green Rd
ESH/CLAY KT10 .....40 D9
Weston Gv BAGS GU19 .....51 P7
BMLY BR1 .....47 M1
Weston Lea EHSLY KT24 .....94 F5
Weston Pk KUT/HW KT1 .....8 E4
THDIT KT7 .....40 E9
Weston Park Cl THDIT KT7 * 40 E9
Weston Rd BMLY BR1 .....47 M2
CHSWK W4 .....18 A1
EW KT17 .....60 C4
GUW GU2 .....111 N4
THDIT KT7 .....40 E9
Weston Wy
WOKS/MYFD GU22 .....73 J5
Westover Cl BELMT SM2 .....61 M7
Westover Rd FLEETN GU51 .....87 H6
WAND/EARL SW18 .....28 F2
Westow Hl NRWD SE19 .....30 F9
Westow St NRWD SE19 .....30 F9
West Pde HORS RH12 .....192 B6
West Park Av RCH/KEW TW9 .....17 N6
West Park Cl HEST TW5 .....15 P4
West Park Rd CRAWE RH10 .....160 G9
HOR/WEW KT19 .....77 M1
LING RH7 .....161 K4
RCH/KEW TW9 .....17 N6

West Parkside WARL CR6 .....82 G4
West PI NWDGN UB2 * 16 B2
WIM/MER SW19 .....27 P8
West Rp HTHAIR TW6 .....14 C6
West Rdg RFNM GU10 * 109 H9
West Ring RFNM GU10 .....109 H7
West Rd CBLY GU15 .....68 B3
CHSGTN KT9 .....59 J9
CLAP SW4 .....29 N1
EBED/NFELT TW14 .....23 N3
FARN GU14 .....68 A7
GU GU1 .....7 H4
KUTN/CMB KT2 .....42 A2
REIG RH2 .....119 H6
WDR/YW UB7 .....14 B1
WEY KT13 .....56 D7
West Sheen V RCH/KEW TW9 .....17 M9
West Side Common
WIM/MER SW19 .....27 P9
Westside Cr
CHOB/PIR GU24 * 70 E2
West St BMLY BR1 .....47 N2
CAR SM5 .....62 C3
CRAWW RH11 .....176 G6
CROY/NA CR0 .....2 D7
DORK RH4 .....116 C7
EGRIN RH19 .....180 D5
EPSOM KT18 .....78 A2
EW KT17 .....60 C8
HASM GU27 .....184 D4
HORS RH12 .....192 B8
LING RH7 .....162 F3
REIG RH2 .....119 K5
SUT SM1 .....61 P4
WOKN/KNAP GU21 .....10 E3
West Street La CAR SM5 .....62 B5
West Street PI CROY/NA CR0 .....2 D7
West Temple Sheen
MORT/ESHN SW14 .....26 G1
Westup Rd RHWH RH17 .....195 P6
West Vw EBED/NFELT TW14 .....23 M4
West View Av CTHM CR3 .....81 P7
Westview Cl REDH RH1 .....120 A8
West View Gdns
EGRIN RH19 .....180 D3
West View Rd BOR GU35 .....164 F7
WARL CR6 .....82 B8
Westville Rd SHB W12 .....18 E1
THDIT KT7 .....40 G8
Westward Ho GU GU1 .....112 C5
Westwates Cl BRAK RG12 .....32 F2
West Wy CAR SM5 .....61 P8
CRAWE RH10 .....177 K4
CROY/NA CR0 .....64 E1
TWK TW1 .....25 P6
SHPTN TW17 * 38 F7
SWTR RH13 .....190 E7
WWKM BR4 .....47 H7
Westway CRAWE RH10 .....160 B9
CTHM CR3 .....101 M2
GUW GU2 .....111 M3
HORL RH6 .....159 L5
RYNPK SW20 .....42 F5
West Way Gdns
CROY/NA CR0 .....64 D1
Westway Gdns REDH RH1 .....120 C2
Westways BH/WHM TN16 .....106 G6
EDEN TN8 .....144 G3
HOR/WEW KT19 .....60 D3
Westwell Rd
STRHM/NOR SW16 .....29 N9
Westwell Road Ap
STRHM/NOR SW16 .....29 P9
Westwick Gdns HSLWW TW15 .....15 K7
Westwood Av
ADL/WDHM KT15 .....73 K1
NRWD SE19 .....45 L1
Westwood Cl ESH/CLAY KT10 .....58 C2
Westwood Gdns BARN SW13 .....18 D8
Westwood Hl SYD SE26 .....31 H8
Westwood La RGUW GU3 .....110 A3
Westwood Pk FSTH SE23 .....31 J3
Westwood PI SYD SE26 .....31 H8
Westwood Rd BARN SW13 .....18 D8
BFOR GU20 .....52 D4
COUL/CHIP CR5 .....80 F7
Wetherby Gdns ECT SW5 .....19 N3
FARN GU14 .....88 E7
Wetherby Ms ECT SW5 .....19 N3
Wetherby PI ECT SW5 .....19 N3
Wetherby Wy CHSGTN KT9 .....59 L6
Wetton PI EGH TW20 .....21 L8
Wexfenne Gdns
WOKS/MYFD GU22 .....73 M5
Wexford Rd BAL SW12 .....29 J3
Wey Av CHERT KT16 .....37 L4
Weybank RPLY/SEND GU23 .....74 A5
Weybank Cl FNM GU9 .....108 C1
Weybarton BF/WBF KT14 .....74 B2
Weybourne PI SAND/SEL CR2 .....63 M8
Weybourne Rd FNM GU9 .....108 A9
Weybourne St
WAND/EARL SW18 .....28 F5
Weybridge Md YTLY GU46 .....67 J1
Weybridge Pk WEY KT13 .....56 D4
Weybridge Rd
ADL/WDHM KT15 .....56 B3
THHTH CR7 .....45 J5
Weybrook Dr RGUE GU4 .....92 F9
Wey Cl ASHV GU12 .....109 J5
BF/WBF KT14 .....73 M2
CBLY GU15 .....68 D7
Weycombe Rd HASM GU27 .....184 D2
Wey Ct ADL/WDHM KT15 .....55 P7
GODL GU7 .....131 N7
HOR/WEW KT19 .....60 A3
Weycrofts BNFD RG42 .....32 B1
Weydon Farm La FNM GU9 .....4 E6
Weydon Hill Cl FNM GU9 .....5 F6
Weydon Hill Rd FNM GU9 .....5 F7

Weydon Mill La FNM GU9 .....4 E6
Weydown Cl RGUW GU3 .....91 M9
WIM/MER SW19 .....28 B3
Weydown La GUW GU2 .....91 N9
Weydown Rd HASM GU27 .....184 B4
Wey Hl HASM GU27 .....184 B4
Weyland Cl LIPH GU30 .....182 F5
Weylands Pk WEY KT13 .....56 F5
Weylea Av RGUE GU4 .....112 E2
Wey Lodge Cl LIPH GU30 .....182 G6
Wey Manor Rd
ADL/WDHM KT15 .....55 P7
Weymead Cl CHERT KT16 .....37 N9
Weymouth Av EA W5 .....17 J1
Weymouth Ct BELMT SM2 * 61 M6
Wey Rd GODL GU7 .....131 N8
WEY KT13 .....56 B2
Weyside Cl BF/WBF KT14 .....74 B1
Weyside Gdns GU GU1 .....111 P3
Weyside Rd GU GU1 .....111 P4
Wey South Pth CRAN GU6 .....169 P9
GUW GU2 .....6 F7
RGUE GU4 .....132 C4
SHGR GU5 .....152 B4
Weysprings HASM GU27 .....184 A3
Weyview Cl GU GU1 .....112 A3
Wey View Ct GU GU1 .....6 C4
Weywood Cl FNM GU9 .....108 B7
Weywood La FNM GU9 .....108 A7
Wharf Bridge Rd ISLW TW7 .....17 H8
Wharfedale Gdns THHTH CR7 .....45 H5
Wharfedale St WBPTN SW10 .....19 M3
Wharfenden Wy FRIM GU16 .....89 H1
Wharf La RPLY/SEND GU23 .....92 C3
TWK TW1 * 25 P6
Wharf Rd ASHV GU12 .....109 J2
FRIM GU16 .....89 H1
GU GU1 .....6 D3
STWL/WRAY TW19 .....21 H3
Wharf St GODL GU7 .....131 L9
Wharf Ter PUT/ROE SW15 .....19 J8
Wharf Wy FRIM GU16 .....89 H1
Wharncliffe Gdns
SNWD SE25 .....45 N3
Wharncliffe Rd SNWD SE25 .....45 M3
Wharton Rd BMLY BR1 .....47 P2
Whateley Cl GUW GU2 .....91 P9
Whateley Rd EDUL SE22 .....30 C1
PGE/AN SE20 .....46 D1
Whatley Av RYNPK SW20 .....43 H4
Whatley Gn BRAK RG12 * 32 C7
Whatman Rd FSTH SE23 .....31 L3
Whatmore Cl
STWL/WRAY TW19 .....22 D2
Wheatash Rd
ADL/WDHM KT15 .....55 M1
Wheatfield Wy HORL RH6 .....140 D9
KUT/HW KT1 .....8 E6
Wheathill Rd PGE/AN SE20 .....46 B3
Wheat Knoll PUR/KEN CR8 .....81 L5
Wheatlands HEST TW5 .....16 A4
Wheatlands Rd TOOT SW17 .....29 K6
Wheatley BRAK RG12 .....32 C4
Wheatley Rd ALDT GU11 .....108 B4
ISLW TW7 .....16 G8
Wheatsheaf Cl CHERT KT16 .....55 H5
HORS RH12 .....192 D5
WOKN/KNAP GU21 .....10 D1
Wheatsheaf La FUL/PGN SW6 .....18 G5
STA TW18 .....37 K1
Wheatsheaf Pde WDSR SL4 * 20 F1
Wheatsheaf Ter
FUL/PGN SW6 * 19 K5
Wheatstone Cl CRAWE RH10 .....159 L9
WIM/MER SW19 .....43 P2
Wheeler Av OXTED RH8 .....103 K9
Wheeler La MFD/CHID GU8 .....149 M6
Wheeler PI HAYES BR2 * 47 P5
Wheeler Rd CRAWE RH10 .....177 L7
Wheelers La
BRKHM/BTCW RH3 .....117 P7
EPSOM KT18 .....78 A3
HORL RH6 .....160 B2
Wheelers Wy EGRIN RH19 .....161 M9
Wheelwrights La
GSHT GU26 .....165 K7
Wheelwrights PI
DTCH/LGLY SL3 * 12 G5
Whelan Wy WLGTN SM6 .....62 F2
Whellock Rd CHSWK W4 .....18 C1
Wherwell Rd GUW GU2 .....6 C6
Whetstone Rd FARN GU14 .....87 K1
Whimbrel Cl SAND/SEL CR2 .....63 M9
Whinfell Cl
STRHM/NOR SW16 .....29 N8
Whin Holt FLEETS GU52 .....86 G9
Whins Cl CBLY GU15 .....68 D4
Whins Dr CBLY GU15 .....68 D4
Whinshill Ct ASC SL5 .....34 G9
Whinwhistry Cl RGUE GU4 .....132 D3
Whistler Cl CRAWE RH10 .....177 J8
Whistler Gv SHST GU47 .....67 N4
Whistlers Av BTSEA SW11 * 19 P5
Whistler Wk WBPTN SW10 * 19 N5
Whistley Cl BRAK RG12 .....32 G4
Whitby Cl BH/WHM TN16 .....85 P8
FARN GU14 .....88 D5
Whitby Gdns SUT SM1 .....61 P1
Whitby Rd SUT SM1 .....61 P1
Whitchurch Cl ALDT GU11 .....108 F8
Whitchurch Rd FLEETN GU51 .....86 E4
Whitcombe Ms RCH/KEW TW9 .....17 P6
White Acres Rd FRIM GU16 .....89 H3
Whitebeam Dr REIG RH2 .....119 M8
Whitebeam Gdns
FARN GU14 .....87 N4
White Beam Wy
KWD/TDW/WH KT20 .....98 E1
Whiteberry Rd RDKG RH5 .....136 D6
White Bridge Av MTCM CR4 .....43 P5
White Bridge Cl
EBED/NFELT TW14 .....24 A2

White Bushes REDH RH1 120 C9
White City CWTH RG45 49 P4
White Cottage Cl FNM GU9 107 P8
Whitecroft Cl BECK BR3 47 K5
Whitecroft Wy BECK BR3 47 J5
Whitefield Av PUR/KEN CR8 81 J5
Whitefield Cl PUT/ROE SW15 28 B2
Whitegates
   WOKS/MYFD GU22 72 D9
Whitegate Wy
   KWD/TDW/WH KT20 78 F9
Whitehall Crs CHSGTN KT9 59 K4
Whitehall Dr CRAWW RH11 176 B5
Whitehall Farm La VW GU25 36 C4
Whitehall Gdns CHSWK W4 17 P4
Whitehall La REIG RH2 119 K9
   STWL/WRAY TW19 21 M2
   VW GU25 36 D2
Whitehall Pde EGRIN RH19 180 E3
Whitehall Park Rd
   CHSWK W4 17 P4
Whitehall Pl WLCTN SM6 62 D3
Whitehall Rd THHTH CR7 45 J6
White Hart Cl HORS RH12 192 B6
White Hart La BARN SW13 18 C7
   RGUW GU3 110 C4
White Hart Mdw
   RPLY/SEND GU23 93 N1
White Hart Rw CHERT KT16 * 37 L8
Whitehaven CI HAYES BR2 47 N5
Whitehead CI
   WAND/EARL SW18 28 F3
White Hermitage WDSR SL4 * 21 H1
White Heron Ms
   TEDD TW11 * 25 N9
White HI BFOR GU20 52 B3
   COUL/CHIP CR5 99 P3
   SAND/SEL 63 M8
Whitehill CI CBLY GU15 40 B7
Whitehill La REDH RH1 101 M7
   RPLY/SEND GU23 93 K3
Whitehill PI VW GU25 36 D2
White Horse Dr EPSOM KT18 78 A4
White Horse La EWKG RG40 48 A4
   RPLY/SEND GU23 93 N1
Whitehorse La SNWD SE25 45 N5
   HORS RH12 192 C4
Whitehouse CI FARN GU14 88 D1
Whitehouse Dr GU GU1 112 F5
White House Gdns
   YTLY GU46 66 C1
White House La RGUE GU4 92 B9
White House Wk RGUE GU4 92 B9
Whitehouse Wy
   DTCH/LGLY SL3 12 F1
White Knights Rd WEY KT13 56 E6
White Knobs Wy CTHM CR3 102 A5
Whitelands Crs
   WAND/EARL SW18 28 B3
Whitelands Dr ASC SL5 33 M2
White La ASHV GU12 109 L5
   OXTED RH8 123 P8
   RGUE GU4 112 C7
Whiteley Rd NRWD SE19 30 E8
Whiteleys Wy FELT TW13 25 H6
White Lion Wk GU GU1 6 E6
White Lion Wy YTLY GU46 67 H1
White Ldg NRWD SE19 45 K1
White Lodge CI BELMT SM2 61 N6
   ISLW TW7 5 H6
White Lodge Gdns
   REDH RH1 140 C4
Whitemore Rd GU GU1 112 B1
White Oak Dr BECK BR3 47 J3
Whiteoaks BNSTD SM7 79 M2
White Pillars
   WOKS/MYFD GU22 71 P9
Whitepost HI REDH RH1 120 A5
White Post La RFNM GU10 127 L9
White Rd CBLY GU15 68 B2
White Rose La FNM GU9 127 M6
   WOKS/MYFD GU22 10 E4
Whitestile Rd BTFD TW8 17 J3
Whitethorn Av
   COUL/CHIP CR5 80 C4
Whitethorn Gdns
   CROY/NA CRO 64 B1
Whitewater Rd FLEETN GU51 86 F3
Whitewood Cottages
   BH/WHM TN16 84 A9
Whitfield CI GUW GU2 111 N2
   HASM GU27 184 D1
Whitford Gdns MTCM CR4 44 B5
Whitgift Av SAND/SEL CR2 63 L4
Whitgift St CROY/NA CRO 2 C6
Whitland Rd CAR SM5 43 P9
Whitlet CI FNM GU9 4 E5
Whitley CI STWL/WRAY TW19 21 H2
Whitley Rd YTLY GU46 67 H4
Whitlock Dr WIM/MER SW19 28 B3
Whitmead La SAND/SEL CR2 63 M5
Whitmoor La RFNM GU10 128 C8
Whitmoor Rd BAGS GU19 51 N7
Whitmoor Vale Rd
   GSHT GU26 165 J4
Whitmore CI SHST GU47 49 P9
Whitmore Dr on FNM GU8 108 A8
Whitmore La ASC SL5 34 C6
Whitmore Rd BECK BR3 46 F4
Whitmores CI EPSOM KT18 * 78 A4
Whitmore V GSHT GU26 165 J5
White Vale Rd
   GSHT GU26 165 L7
Whitmore Wy HORL RH6 139 P9

Whitnell Wy PUT/ROE SW15 * 27 P1
Whitstable CI BECK BR3 46 F2
Whitstable PI CROY/NA CR0 63 L3
Whitstone La BECK BR3 47 H6
Whittaker Av
   RCH/KEW TW9 * 26 C1
Whittaker Rd CHEAM SM3 61 K2
Whittell Gdns SYD SE26 31 K6
Whittingstall Rd
   FUL/PGN SW6 19 K6
Whittington Rd
   CRAWE RH10 176 G8
Whittlebury CI CAR SM5 62 B6
Whittle CI ASHV GU12 109 H1
   EWKG RG40 48 C2
   SHST GU47 49 L8
Whittle Crs FARN GU14 68 B9
Whittle Rd HEST TW5 15 L5
Whitton Dene HSLW TW3 25 H2
Whitton Manor Rd
   WHTN TW2 25 K2
Whitton Rd BRAK RG12 33 H4
   HSLW TW3 16 B9
   WHTN TW2 25 M2
Whitton Waye HSLW TW3 25 H2
Whitworth Rd
   CRAWW RH11 158 C9
   SNWD SE25 45 N4
Whopshott Av
   WOKN/KNAP GU21 72 A5
Whopshott CI
   WOKN/KNAP GU21 71 P5
Whopshott Dr
   WOKN/KNAP GU21 72 A5
Whynstones Rd ASC SL5 34 A6
Whyte Av ASHV GU12 108 F7
Whytebeam Vw CTHM CR3 81 P7
Whytecliffe Rd North
   PUR/KEN CR8 63 K9
Whytecliffe Rd South
   PUR/KEN CR8 63 K9
Whytecroft HEST TW5 15 M5
Whyteleafe HI CTHM CR3 101 N8
Whyteleafe Rd CTHM CR3 101 N6
Wickers Oake NRWD SE19 * 30 G7
Wicket HI RFNM GU10 127 L7
The Wicket CROY/NA CR0 64 C4
Wickham Av CHEAM SM3 61 K5
   CROY/NA CRO 64 E1
Wickham Cha WWKM BR4 * 47 K8
Wickham CI FLEETS GU52 106 B1
   HORL RH6 140 B9
   NWMAL KT3 42 C5
Wickham Ct WWKM BR4 * 65 J1
Wickham Court Rd
   WWKM BR4 65 J1
Wickham La EGH TW20 36 B1
Wickham PI FLEETS GU52 86 E1
Wickham Rd BECK BR3 47 H4
   CBLY GU15 50 C9
   CROY/NA CR0 64 C1
   FLEETS GU52 86 E9
Wickham V BRAK RG12 32 A7
Wick Hill La EWKG RG40 48 A4
Wickhurst La HORS RH12 191 M8
Wick La EGH TW20 20 E9
Wick Rd EGH TW20 35 P1
   TEDD TW11 41 H1
Wide Wy MTCM CR4 44 H4
Widgeon Wy HORS RH12 192 B5
Widmore Rd BMLY BR1 47 P3
Wigan Rd FARN GU14 87 P7
Wiggins La RGUE GU4 * 120 C3
Wiggins La
   RCHPK/HAM TW10 26 B5
Wigley Rd FELT TW10 24 E3
Wigmore La BRAK RG5 156 B3
Wigmore Rd CAR SM5 61 P1
Wilberforce CI
   CRAWW RH11 194 F2
Wilberforce Wy BRAK RG12 32 F6
   WIM/MER SW19 28 A9
Wilbury Av BELMT SM2 61 K8
Wilbury Rd
   WOKN/KNAP GU21 10 B4
Wilcot CI CHOB/PIR GU24 70 C5
Wilcot Gdns CHOB/PIR GU24 70 C5
Wilcox Gdns SHPTN TW17 38 A4
Wilcox Rd SUT SM1 * 61 M3
   TEDD TW11 25 L7
Wildacre CI BIL RH14 188 A7
Wild Acres BF/WBF TW14 55 N9
Wild Briar EWKG RG40 48 D2
Wildcroft Dr RDKG RH5 137 K1
Wildcroft Wd
   MFD/CHID GU8 149 L6
Wilderness Ri EGRIN RH19 162 F7
Wilderness Rd FRIM GU16 68 G6
   GUW GU2 111 M4
   OXTED RH8 123 L1
The Wilderness
   E/WMO/HCT KT8 40 C6
   HPTN TW12 * 25 J9
Wilders CI BNFD RG42 32 C1
   FRIM GU16 68 F5
   WOKN/KNAP GU21 71 J7
Wilderwick Rd EGRIN RH19 162 F1
Wildfield CI RGUW GU3 131 H5
Wildgoose Dr HORS RH12 191 N7
Wildgreen North
   DTCH/LGLY SL3 12 C2
Wildgreen South
   DTCH/LGLY SL3 12 C2
Wildridings Rd BRAK RG12 32 C6
Wild Ridings Sq BRAK RG12 32 C5
Wildwood CI CRAN GU6 171 J2
   EHSLY KT24 95 H5

   WOKS/MYFD GU22 73 K4
Wildwood Gdns YTLY GU46 66 G4
Wildwood La CRAN GU6 81 H4
Wilford Rd DTCH/LGLY SL3 12 C2
Wilfred St WOKN/KNAP GU21 10 A4
Wilhelmina Av
   COUL/CHIP CR5 80 E8
Wilkes Rd BTFD TW8 17 L4
Wilkins CI HYS/HAR UB3 15 H3
   MTCM CR4 44 A2
Wilkinson Gdns SNWD SE25 45 N2
Wilkins Gdns CROY/NA CR0 46 E9
Willats CI CHERT KT16 * 37 K7
Willcocks CI CHSGTN KT9 59 L2
Willems Av ALDT GU11 108 B4
Willett Rd THHTH CR7 45 J6
Willetts Wy BIL RH14 188 C7
Willey Broom La CTHM CR3 101 J5
Willey Farm La CTHM CR3 101 L6
Willey La CTHM CR3 101 M5
William Booth Rd
   PGE/AN SE20 46 A2
William Ellis CI WDSR SL4 20 F1
William Evans Rd
   HOR/WEW KT19 59 N9
William Evelyn Ct
   RDKG RH5 * 135 P1
William Farthing CI
   ALDT GU11 108 C4
William Gdns PUT/ROE SW15 27 N1
William Morris Wy
   CRAWW RH11 194 C2
   FUL/PGN SW6 19 N8
William Rd CTHM CR3 101 M2
   GU GU1 6 D5
   SUT SM1 61 N4
   WIM/MER SW19 43 J1
Williams CI FUL/PGN SW6 19 J5
Williams Dr HSLW TW3 16 A9
Williams Gv SURB KT6 41 J7
Williams La
   MORT/ESHN SW14 18 A8
   MRDN SM4 43 N7
Williamson CI HASM GU27 184 C1
Williams PI CRAN GU6 153 P7
Williams Rd NWDGN UB2 15 P2
Williams Ter CROY/NA CR0 63 J5
Williams CI CAR SM5 62 A2
Williams Wy CRAWE RH10 177 L5
   FLEETN GU51 87 J6
Willingham Wy KUT/HW KT1 9 H5
Willington CI CBLY GU15 68 D2
Willis Av BELMT SM2 62 A5
Willis CI EPSOM KT18 77 P2
Willis Rd CROY/NA CR0 45 L8
Willmore End
   WIM/MER SW19 43 M2
Willoughby Av CROY/NA CR0 63 H3
Willoughby Rd BRAK RG12 32 B4
   DTCH/LGLY SL3 12 F1
   KUTN/CMB KT2 9 G2
   TWK TW1 26 B1
Willow Av BARN SW13 18 D7
Willow Bank
   WOKS/MYFD GU22 92 C2
Willowbank Gdns
   KWD/TDW/WH KT20 98 F2
Willow Brean HORL RH6 140 A9
Willowbrook HPTN TW12 * 25 J8
Willow Brook WDGN UB2 15 P1
   STWL/WRAY TW19 23 H4
The Willow Centre
   MTCM CR4 44 B6
Willow CI ADL/WDHM KT15 55 K9
   BTFD TW8 17 J4
   DTCH/LGLY SL3 12 C3
   EGRIN RH19 162 C9
   FRIM GU16 88 G3
   LIPH GU30 182 D7
   RDKG RH5 137 J9
Willow Cnr HORL RH6 158 C5
Willow Ct FRIM GU16 68 F7
   HORL RH6 140 D7
Willow Crs FARN GU14 68 B9
Willowdale EWKG RG40 48 D1
Willowdene CI WHTN TW2 25 K3
Willow Dr BRAK RG12 32 E2
   RGUW GU3 110 C3
   RPLY/SEND GU23 93 L4
Willow Flds ASHV GU12 109 K5
Willowford YTLY GU46 67 H2
Willow Gdns HSLW TW5 * 16 A6
Willow Gln RDKG RH5 137 J9
Willow Gn CHOB/PIR GU24 70 G2
Willowhayne Dr
   WOT/HER KT12 39 K8
Willowhayne Gdns WPK KT4 60 G3
Willow La BLKW GU17 67 P4
   GU GU1 112 E4
   MTCM CR4 44 B6
Willow Md DORK RH4 116 C6
   EGRIN RH19 180 E3
   MFD/CHID GU8 149 M7
Willowmead STA TW18 37 M2
Willowmead CI
   WOKN/KNAP GU21 71 N5
Willowmere ESH/CLAY KT10 58 C3
Willow Mt CROY/NA CR0 * 3 J7
Willow Pk ASHV GU12 109 H4
Willow Rdg CRAWE RH10 179 H8
Willow Rd DTCH/LGLY SL3 13 J7
   GODL GU7 131 M5
   HORS RH12 192 C5
   NWMAL KT3 41 P4
   REDH RH1 119 N8
   WLGTN SM6 62 D6
Willows Av MRDN SM4 43 M6
Willows End SHST GU47 49 M9
Willows Pth EPSOM KT18 77 P2
The Willows BECK BR3 * 46 G2
   BF/WBF KT14 74 A2

   ESH/CLAY KT10 58 E5
   LTWR GU18 52 F8
   MFD/CHID GU8 167 P7
   RFNM GU10 128 C2
   RGUE GU4 * 113 H3
   RGUW GU3 * 91 M9
   WEY KT13 56 C2
Willow Ter PGE/AN SE20 * 46 B2
Willow Tree CI
   WAND/EARL SW18 28 E4
Willow Tree Wk BMLY BR1 47 P2
Willowtree Wy THHTH CR7 45 J3
Willow V LHD/OX KT22 96 B3
Willow Wk WIM/MER SW19 43 P2
Willow Wk CHEAM SM3 61 K2
   EGH TW20 21 H8
   KWD/TDW/WH KT20 117 P1
   REDH RH1 140 C2
   SHST GU47 50 C1
Willow Wy ASHV GU12 108 C6
   E/WBF KT14 55 N9
   FNM GU9 107 P8
   GDST RH9 122 B3
   GU GU1 111 P1
   HOR/WEW KT19 60 B5
   SAND/SEL CR2 64 A3
   SUN TW16 39 J5
   SYD SE26 31 J6
   WHTN TW2 25 J5
Willow Wood Crs SNWD SE25 45 N7
Willow Wren Whf
   NWDGN UB2 * 15 K2
Wills Crs HSLW TW3 25 J2
Wilson Rd EGH TW20 20 G8
Wilmar Gdns WWKM BR4 47 H9
Wilmer CI KUTN/CMB KT2 26 E8
Wilmer Crs KUTN/CMB KT2 26 E8
Wilmerhatch La EPSOM KT18 77 P6
Wilmington Av CHSWK W4 18 B5
Wilmington Ct CRAWW RH11 194 D2
Wilmot Rd CAR SM5 62 B4
   PUR/KEN CR8 81 J1
Wilmots CI REIG RH2 119 N5
Wilmot's La REDH RH1 141 M6
Wilmot Wy BNSTD SM7 79 L4
   CBLY GU15 69 H5
Wilna Rd WAND/EARL SW18 28 F3
Wilson Av MTCM CR4 44 A1
Wilson CI CRAWE RH10 177 N8
   SAND/SEL CR2 63 M4
Wilson Dr CHERT KT16 54 F4
Wilson Rd ASHV GU12 108 F5
   CHSGTN KT9 59 M5
   FARN GU14 88 A4
Wilsons KWD/TDW/WH KT20 99 H1
Wilsons Rd BOR GU35 164 E6
   HMSMTH W6 19 H3
Wilson Wk CHSWK W4 * 18 D2
Wilson Wy WOKN/KNAP GU21 10 A2
Wilstrode Av BNFD RG42 32 C7
Wilton Av CHSWK W4 18 C3
Wilton CI WDR/YW UB7 13 P5
Wilton Ct FARN GU14 88 F4
Wilton Crs WIM/MER SW19 43 J3
   WOT/HER KT12 39 M9
Wilton Gdns E/WMO/HCT KT8 40 A4
   WOT/HER KT12 39 M9
Wilton Pl ADL/WDHM KT15 68 D5
Wilton Rd CBLY GU15 68 B6
   HSLW TW3 15 M8
   REDH RH1 120 B6
   WIM/MER SW19 44 A1
Wiltshire Av CWTH RG45 49 M3
Wiltshire Gdns WHTN TW2 25 J4
Wiltshire Rd THHTH CR7 45 J4
Wilverley Crs NWMAL KT3 42 C7
Wilwood Rd BNFD RG42 32 A2
Wimbart Rd
   BRXS/STRHM SW2 * 30 A3
Wimbledon Park Side
   PUT/ROE SW15 27 N3
Wimbledon Br
   WIM/MER SW19 28 C9
Wimbledon CI CBLY GU15 51 H8
Wimbledon Hill Rd
   WIM/MER SW19 28 B9
Wimbledon Park Rd
   WIM/MER SW19 28 B6
Wimbledon Park Side
   WIM/MER SW19 28 A5
Wimbledon Rd CBLY GU15 51 H8
   TOOT SW17 28 F7
Wimblehurst Rd HORS RH12 192 B6
Wimborne Av HORS RH12 192 B6
   NWDGN UB2 16 A2
   REDH RH1 140 B1
Wimborne CI EW KT17 78 C2
   WPK KT4 43 J9
Wimborne Av BECK BR3 46 D4
Wimbushes EWKG RG40 48 B3
Wimland HI HORS RH12 175 J9
Wimland Rd HORS RH12 175 J8
Wimlands La HORS RH12 175 J8
Wimpole CI KUT/HW KT1 * 9 J5
Wimshurst CI CROY/NA CR0 44 G4
Wincanton CI CRAWE RH10 177 N1
Wincanton Rd
   WAND/EARL SW18 28 C3
Winchcombe CI FLEETS GU51 86 G6
Winchcombe Rd CAR SM5 43 P8
Winchelsea CI
   PUT/ROE SW15 27 N1
Winchelsey Ri SAND/SEL CR2 63 P5
Winchendon Rd
   FUL/PGN SW6 19 K5
   TEDD TW11 25 L9
Winchester Av HEST TW5 15 P4
Winchester CI DTCH/LGLY SL3 13 J8
   ESH/CLAY KT10 58 A3
   HAYES BR2 47 M4
   KUTN/CMB KT2 41 P1
Winchester Ms WPK KT4 43 H1
Winchester Pk HAYES BR2 47 M4
Winchester Rd ASHV GU12 109 J3
   CRAWE RH10 177 H9
   FELT TW13 24 G6
   HAYES BR2 47 M4
   HYS/HAR UB3 14 C5
   RFNM GU10 147 L5
   TWK TW1 26 A2
   WOT/HER KT12 39 J9
Winchester St FARN GU14 88 E7
Winchester Wy BLKW GU17 67 N2
The Winches SWTR RH13 * 193 L6
Winchfield CI FLEETN GU51 86 E3
Winchfield CI HTWY RG27 86 A6
Winchfield Rd SYD SE26 31 M8
Winchgrove Rd BNFD RG42 32 C1
Winchilsea Crs
   E/WMO/HCT KT8 40 C3
Winchstone CI SHPTN TW17 38 B5
Windall CI NRWD SE19 46 A2
Windborough Rd CAR SM5 62 C6
Windermere Av
   WIM/MER SW19 43 M4
Windermere CI
   EBED/NFELT TW14 23 P4
   EGH TW20 21 N1
   FARN GU14 88 A4
   STWL/WRAY TW19 22 G5
Windermere Ct
   ASHV GU12 109 J2
Windermere Rd
   COUL/CHIP CR5 80 G4
   CROY/NA CR0 3 K1
   EA W5 17 J1
   LTWR GU18 52 B8
   PUT/ROE SW15 27 K7
   STRHM/NOR SW16 45 H3
   WWKM BR4 65 L1
Windermere Wy FNM GU9 107 L8
   REIG RH2 120 F3
Windfield CI SYD SE26 31 L7
Windgates RGUE GU4 112 G2
Windham Av CROY/NA CR0 65 K8
Windham Rd RCH/KEW TW9 17 M8
The Windings SAND/SEL CR2 63 P9
Windle CI CBLY GU15 69 K4
Windle CI BFOR GU20 52 C5
Windlebrook Gn BNFD RG42 32 C2
Windlesham CI BFOR GU20 52 C3
Windlesham Gv
   WIM/MER SW19 28 A4
Windlesham Rd BNFD RG42 32 A2
Windley CI FSTH SE23 31 K5
Windmill Av EW KT17 60 D8
Windmill CI CTHM CR3 101 L1
   EW KT17 78 D1
   HORL RH6 159 L1
   NWCR SE14 38 G1
   SURB KT6 41 J8
   SWTR RH13 192 F7
Windmill Ct CRAWE RH10 176 D3
Windmill Dr BOR GU35 164 E5
   CLAP SW4 29 L1
   LHD/OX KT22 97 H3
   REIG RH2 119 P3
Windmill End EW KT17 78 D1
Windmill Fld BFOR GU20 52 D5
Windmill Gv CROY/NA CR0 45 L8
Windmill La EGRIN RH19 162 D9
   EGRIN RH19 181 H4
   EW KT17 60 D9
   ISLW TW7 16 E5
   SURB KT6 41 H8
Windmill Pas CHSWK W4 * 18 C2
Windmill Ri KUTN/CMB KT2 42 A1
Windmill Rd ASHV GU12 108 E5
   BNFD RG42 32 B2
   CHSWK W4 18 C2
   CROY/NA CR0 45 L8
   HPTN TW12 25 J8
   MTCM CR4 44 B6
   SUN TW16 38 G2
   WAND/EARL SW18 28 C2
   WIM/MER SW19 27 N8
Windmill Rd West SUN TW16 38 G3
Windmill Shott EGH TW20 21 L9
Windmill Ter SHPTN TW17 * 38 C8
Windmill Wy REIG RH2 119 P3
Windrush NWMAL KT3 41 P5
Windrush Av DTCH/LGLY SL3 12 F1
Windrush CI BTSEA SW11 * 29 H1
   CHSWK W4 * 18 A5
   SHGR GU5 132 D7
Windrush Hts SHST GU47 49 M9
Windsor Av CHEAM SM3 61 J2
   E/WMO/HCT KT8 40 A4
   NWMAL KT3 41 P6
   WIM/MER SW19 43 N2
Windsor Court Rd
   CHOB/PIR GU24 53 L7
Windsor Crs FNM GU9 107 M8
Windsor Dr ASHF TW15 22 G7
Windsor Gdns ASHV GU12 109 H5
   CROY/NA CR0 63 G2
   HYS/HAR UB3 14 F1
Windsor Great Pk ASC SL5 * 34 F1
Windsor Gv WNWD SE27 30 D7
Windsor Park Rd
   HYS/HAR UB3 15 H5
Windsor PI CHERT KT16 * 37 L7
   EGRIN RH19 180 F3

Windsor Ride ASC SL5 .... 33 K6
BRAK RG12 .... 32 C9
CBLY GU15 .... 50 C9
EWKG RG40 .... 48 E2
Windsor Rd ASC SL5 .... 33 P3
CHOB/PIR GU24 .... 53 L7
FARN GU14 .... 84 A7
FARN GU14 .... 88 F6
HSLWW TW4 .... 15 K7
KUTN/CMB KT2 .... 8 D1
NWDGN UB2 .... 15 P1
RCH/KEW TW9 .... 17 M7
SUN TW16 .... 39 J1
TEDD TW11 .... 25 L8
THHTH CR7 .... 45 K3
WDSR SL4 .... 21 J4
WPK KT4 .... 60 E1
Windsor St CHERT KT16 .... 37 L7
Windsor Wk WEY KT13 .... 56 D4
Windsor Wy ALDT GU11 .... 108 D4
FRIM GU16 .... 69 H8
WKENS W14 .... 19 H2
WOKS/MYFD GU22 .... 72 C5
Winds Rdg RPLY/SEND GU23 .... 92 G5
Windways MFD/CHID GU8 .... 149 L9
Windycroft Cl PUR/KEN CR8 .... 80 F2
Windyridge CRAWW RH11 .... 176 D6
Windy Ridge Cl
WIM/MER SW19 .... 28 A8
Windy Wd GODL GU7 .... 150 B1
Winern Glebe BF/WBF KT14 .... 73 P2
Winery La KUT/HW KT1 .... 9 F6
Winey Cl CHSGTN KT9 .... 59 J6
Winfield Gv RDKG RH5 .... 156 C3
Winfrith Rd
WAND/EARL SW18 .... 28 F3
Wingate Cl ALDT GU11 .... 108 B4
Wingate Crs CROY/NA CR0 .... 44 C7
Wingate Rd HMSMTH W6 .... 18 F1
Wingfield Cl
ADL/WDHM KT15 .... 55 M8
Wingfield Gdns FRIM GU16 .... 69 M5
Wingfield Rd KUTN/CMB KT2 .... 26 B6
Wingford Rd
BRXS/STRHM SW2 .... 29 P2
Wingrave Rd HMSMTH W6 .... 18 G4
Wings Rd FNM GU9 .... 107 M8
Winifred Rd COUL/CHIP CR5 .... 80 C5
HPTN TW12 .... 25 H9
WIM/MER SW19 .... 43 L2
Winkfield Rd ASC SL5 .... 34 B1
Winkworth Pl BNSTD SM7 .... 79 K3
Winkworth Rd BNSTD SM7 .... 79 L3
Winnington Wy
WOKN/KNAP GU21 .... 71 P7
Winnipeg Cl LIPH GU50 .... 182 F7
Winscombe BRAK RG12 .... 32 A6
Winsford Rd CAT SE6 .... 31 N6
Winsham Gv BTSEA SW11 .... 29 K1
Winslade Rd
BRXS/STRHM SW2 .... 29 P1
Winslow Rd HMSMTH W6 .... 18 G4
Winslow Wy FELT TW13 .... 24 E6
WOT/HER KT12 .... 57 L2
Winstanley Cl COB KT11 .... 75 K3
Winstanley Rd BTSEA SW11 .... 19 P8
Winston Cl FRIM GU16 .... 89 H1
Winston Ct COB KT11 .... 75 N5
Winston Pl WBPTN SW10 .... 19 N4
Winston Wy
WOKS/MYFD GU22 .... 72 F9
Winterbourne HORS RH12 .... 192 E3
Winterbourne Gv WEY KT13 .... 56 E5
Winterbourne Rd CAT SE6 .... 31 N4
THHTH CR7 .... 45 J5
Winter Box Wk
RCHPK/HAM TW10 .... 26 E1
Winterbrook Rd HNHL SE24 .... 30 D2
Winterdown Gdns
ESH/CLAY KT10 .... 57 P5
Winterdown Rd
ESH/CLAY KT10 .... 57 N5
Winterfold CRAWE RH10 .... 177 K8
Winterfold Cl
WIM/MER SW19 .... 28 B5
Winter Gdns FARN GU14 .... 116 F6
Winterhill Wy RGUE GU4 .... 112 F9
Wintersells Rd BF/WBF KT14 .... 55 P8
Winters Rd THDIT KT7 .... 41 H8
Winterstoke Rd FSTH SE23 .... 31 N4
Winterton Ct SWTR RH13 .... 192 C8
Winterton Pl WBPTN SW10 .... 19 N4
Winterwell Rd
BRXS/STRHM SW2 .... 29 P1
Winthorpe Rd
PUT/ROE SW15 .... 19 J9
Winton Crs YTLY GU46 .... 67 H3
Winton Rd ALDT GU11 .... 108 C5
FNM GU9 .... 5 J1
Winton Wy
STRHM/NOR SW16 .... 30 B8
Wireless Rd BH/WHM TN16 .... 84 B4
Wire Mill La LING RH7 .... 161 M4
Wisbach Rd CROY/NA CR0 .... 45 M6
Wisborough Ct
CRAWW RH11 .... 176 D3
Wise La WDR/YW UB7 .... 13 J2
Wiseton Rd TOOT SW17 .... 29 H4
Wishanger La RFNM GU10 .... 166 F4
Wishbone Wy
WOKN/KNAP GU21 .... 71 M5
Wishmoor Cl CBLY GU15 .... 50 C9
Wishmoor Rd CBLY GU15 .... 50 C9
Wisley Gdns FARN GU14 .... 87 P5
Wisley La RPLY/SEND GU23 .... 74 A5
Wisley Rd BTSEA SW11 .... 29 J1
Wistaria La YTLY GU46 .... 66 C3
Wiston Ct CRAWW RH11 .... 176 C8

Witham Rd ISLW TW7 .... 16 D6
PGE/AN SE20 .... 46 C4
Witherby Cl CROY/NA CR0 .... 63 N4
Wither Dl HORL RH6 .... 140 A9
Witherslack Cl BOR GU35 .... 164 E7
Withew Brook HORL RH6 .... 158 G5
Witheygate Av STA TW18 .... 22 E9
Withey Mdw HORL RH6 .... 158 G3
Withies La RGUW GU3 .... 131 J3
The Withies LHD/OX KT22 .... 77 H9
WOKN/KNAP GU21 .... 71 L6
Withybed Cnr
KWD/TDW/WH KT20 .... 98 F5
Withy Cl LTWR GU18 .... 52 C8
Withypitts CRAWE RH10 .... 179 H8
Withypitts East
CRAWE RH10 .... 179 H8
Witley Crs CROY/NA CR0 .... 65 J5
Witley Gdns NWDGN UB2 .... 15 P2
Witney Pth FSTH SE23 .... 31 L6
Wittenham Rd BRAK RG12 .... 32 F5
Wittering Cl KUTN/CMB KT2 .... 26 C8
Wittmead Rd FRIM GU16 .... 89 H3
Wivenhoe Ct HSLW TW3 .... 15 P9
Wiverton Rd SYD SE26 .... 31 K9
Wix Hl EHSLY KT24 .... 114 D1
Woburn Av FARN GU14 .... 88 E7
PUR/KEN CR8 .... 63 J9
Woburn Cl FRIM GU16 .... 69 J7
WIM/MER SW19 .... 28 C1
Woburn Hl ADL/WDHM KT15 .... 55 N1
Woburn Pk
ADL/WDHM KT15 * 55 P1
Woburn Rd CAR SM5 .... 44 A9
CRAWW RH11 .... 176 D7
CROY/NA CR0 .... 2 D1
Wodeland Av GUW GU2 .... 6 B7
Woffington Cl TEDD TW11 .... 41 J2
Woking Cl PUT/ROE SW15 .... 18 D9
Wokingham Rd BNFD RG42 .... 32 B2
CWTH RG45 .... 49 J6
Wold Cl CRAWW RH11 .... 176 C7
Woldhurstlea Cl
CRAWW RH11 .... 176 C7
Woldingham Rd WARL CR6 .... 82 B9
The Wold CTHM CR3 .... 102 G2
Wolfe Cl HAYES BR2 .... 47 N7
Wolfe Rd ASHV GU12 .... 108 G5
Wolfington Rd WNWD SE27 .... 30 C7
Wolf's Hl OXTED RH8 .... 123 N1
Wolf's Rd OXTED RH8 .... 123 P1
Wolfs Wd OXTED RH8 .... 123 N3
Wolseley Av
WAND/EARL SW18 .... 28 D5
Wolseley Gdns CHSWK W4 .... 17 P4
Wolseley Rd ALDT GU11 .... 108 C5
CHSWK W4 .... 17 P4
GODL GU7 .... 131 L7
MTCM CR4 .... 44 C8
Wolsey Cl HSLW TW3 .... 16 C9
KUTN/CMB KT2 .... 41 P2
NWDGN UB2 .... 16 C1
RYNPK SW20 .... 42 F1
WPK KT4 .... 60 E5
Wolsey Crs CROY/NA CR0 .... 65 J7
MRDN SM4 .... 43 K8
Wolsey Dr KUTN/CMB KT2 .... 26 D8
WOT/HER KT12 .... 39 M9
Wolsey Gv ESH/CLAY KT10 .... 58 B3
Wolsey Rd ASHF TW15 .... 23 H7
E/WMO/HCT KT8 .... 40 D5
ESH/CLAY KT10 .... 58 B5
HPTN TW12 .... 25 J3
SUN TW16 .... 39 H1
Wolsey Wk
WOKN/KNAP GU21 .... 10 D3
Wolsey Wy CHSGTN KT9 .... 59 N4
Wolstonbury Cl
CRAWW RH11 .... 176 F7
Wolvens La RDKG RH5 .... 136 A2
RDKG RH5 .... 136 E8
Wolverton Av
KUTN/CMB KT2 .... 9 J2
Wolverton Cl HORL RH6 .... 159 J3
Wolverton Gdns
HMSMTH W6 .... 19 H2
HORL RH6 .... 159 J2
Wolves Hl RDKG RH5 .... 156 B8
Wonersh Common Rd
SHGR GU5 .... 132 F6
Wonersh Wy BELMT SM2 .... 61 H7
Wonford Cl KUTN/CMB KT2 .... 42 C2
KWD/TDW/WH KT20 .... 98 E6
Wonham La
BRKHM/BTCW RH3 .... 118 D6
Wonham Wy SHGR GU5 .... 134 F2
Wontford Rd PUR/KEN CR8 .... 81 J4
Wontner Rd BAL SW12 .... 29 J5
Woodall Cl CHSGTN KT9 .... 59 M8
The Woodbarn FNM GU9 * 5 H5
Woodbastwick Rd SYD SE26 .... 31 L9
Woodberry Cl
MFD/CHID GU8 .... 167 P6
SUN TW16 .... 24 B9
Woodbine Cl SHST GU47 .... 67 N1
WHTN TW2 .... 25 L4
Woodbine Gv PGE/AN SE20 .... 46 B1
Woodbine La WPK KT4 .... 60 F2
Woodbines Av KUT/HW KT1 .... 8 C7

Woodbridge Dr CBLY GU15 .... 68 F1
Woodbridge Gv
LHD/OX KT22 .... 76 G7
Woodbridge Hl GUW GU2 .... 111 P4
Woodbridge Hill Gdns
GUW GU2 * 111 N4
Woodbridge Mdw GU2 .... 6 C1
Woodbridge Rd BLKW GU17 .... 67 M3
Woodbury Av EGRIN RH19 .... 180 G3
Woodbury Cl BH/WHM TN16 .... 84 D7
CROY/NA CR0 .... 3 K4
EGRIN RH19 .... 180 G3
Woodbury Dr BELMT SM2 .... 61 N8
Woodhill RPLY/SEND GU23 .... 93 H6
Woodcock Ct RPLY/SEND GU23 .... 93 H5
Woodhill La SHGR GU5 .... 133 J9
Wood Cl REDH RH1 .... 140 C5
Woodcock Dr
CHOB/PIR GU24 .... 53 J6
Woodcock Hl EGRIN RH19 .... 161 N6
Woodcock La
CHOB/PIR GU24 .... 53 H6
Woodcombe Crs FSTH SE23 .... 31 K4
Woodcote CRAN GU6 .... 152 E8
GUW GU2 .... 111 P9
HORL RH6 .... 140 D9
Woodcote Av THHTH CR7 .... 45 K5
Woodcote Cl EPSOM KT18 .... 78 B3
KUTN/CMB KT2 .... 26 E8
Woodcote End EPSOM KT18 .... 78 B4
Woodcote Gn FLEETN GU51 .... 86 D7
FARN GU14 .... 86 C2
WLGTN SM6 .... 62 E7
Woodcote Green Rd
EPSOM KT18 .... 78 A5
Woodcote Grove Rd
COUL/CHIP CR5 .... 80 F4
Woodcote House Ct
EPSOM KT18 * 78 B4
Woodcote Hurst
EPSOM KT18 .... 78 A5
Woodcote La PUR/KEN CR8 .... 80 E2
Woodcote Pk
COUL/CHIP CR5 * 80 D2
Woodcote Park Av
PUR/KEN CR8 .... 80 E1
Woodcote Park Rd
EPSOM KT18 .... 78 A5
Woodcote Pl ASC SL5 .... 33 P2
WNWD SE27 * 30 C8
Woodcote Rd FROW RH18 .... 181 K9
WLGTN SM6 .... 62 D5
Woodcote Side EPSOM KT18 .... 77 P4
Woodcote Valley Rd
PUR/KEN CR8 .... 80 E2
Woodcott Gdns FARN GU14 .... 87 P3
Woodcott Ter ASHV GU12 .... 108 F6
Woodcourt CRAWW RH11 .... 194 F1
Wood Crest BELMT SM2 * 61 N6
Woodcrest Rd PUR/KEN CR8 .... 80 G2
Woodcroft Rd CRAWW RH11 .... 176 A7
THHTH CR7 .... 45 K6
Woodcut Rd RFNM GU10 .... 127 G8
Wooden Bridge Ter
WNWD SE27 * 30 C6
Wood End CWTH RG45 .... 49 K5
CHERT KT16 .... 54 F8
CRAN GU6 .... 153 J9
CRAWE RH10 .... 177 J2
ESH/CLAY KT10 .... 58 F6
Woodend
ESH/CLAY KT10 .... 58 C1
LHD/OX KT22 .... 97 J5
SUT SM1 .... 61 N1
Woodend Cl CRAWE RH10 .... 177 K3
WOKN/KNAP GU21 .... 71 N8
Wood End Cl
WOKS/MYFD GU22 .... 73 K5
Woodend Pk COB KT11 .... 75 M4
Wood End FRIM GU16 .... 69 L9
The Wood End WLGTN SM6 .... 62 D7
Woodenhill BRAK RG12 .... 32 A8
Wooderson Cl SNWD SE25 .... 45 N5
Woodfield ASHTD KT21 .... 77 K6
Woodfield Av CAR SM5 .... 62 C5
STRHM/NOR SW16 .... 29 N6
Woodfield Cl ASHTD KT21 .... 77 K6
COUL/CHIP CR5 .... 80 E6
CRAWE RH10 .... 177 H4
NRWD SE19 .... 45 L1
REDH RH1 .... 120 A4
Woodfield Gdns NWMAL KT3 .... 42 D6
Woodfield Gv
STRHM/NOR SW16 .... 29 N6
Woodfield Hl COUL/CHIP CR5 .... 80 D8
Woodfield La ASHTD KT21 .... 77 L6
Woodfield Rd ASHTD KT21 .... 77 J6
CRAWE RH10 .... 177 J3
HORS RH12 .... 189 N5
HSLWW TW4 .... 15 K7
THDIT KT7 .... 58 F1
The Woodfields
SAND/SEL CR2 .... 63 P9
Woodford Gn BRAK RG12 .... 33 H5
Woodgate FLEETN GU51 .... 87 J4
Woodgate Av CHSGTN KT9 .... 59 K4
Woodgate Dr
STRHM/NOR SW16 .... 44 F1
Woodgates Cl SWTR RH13 .... 192 E1
Woodgavil BNSTD SM7 .... 79 K5
Woodger Cl RGUE GU4 .... 112 G3
Woodhall Av DUL SE21 .... 30 G6
Woodhall Dr DUL SE21 .... 30 G6
Woodhall La ASC SL5 .... 52 C1
Woodham La
ADL/WDHM KT15 .... 55 J1
WOKN/KNAP GU21 .... 72 F2
Woodham Park Rd
ADL/WDHM KT15 .... 55 K8
Woodham Park Wy
ADL/WDHM KT15 .... 55 K9

Woodham Ri
WOKN/KNAP GU21 .... 72 E4
Woodham Waye
WOKN/KNAP GU21 .... 72 F5
Woodhatch Rd REIG RH2 .... 119 P9
Woodhatch Spinney
COUL/CHIP CR5 .... 80 G5
Woodhaw Ms
WOT/HER KT12 * 57 J3
Woodhaw ECH TW20 .... 21 N7
Woodhayes HORL RH6 .... 140 D9
Woodhayes Rd
WIM/MER SW19 .... 27 P9
Woodhill RPLY/SEND GU23 .... 93 H6
Woodhill Cl RPLY/SEND GU23 .... 93 H5
Woodhill La SHGR GU5 .... 133 J9
Woodhouse Cl HYS/HAR UB3 .... 14 G1
Woodhouse La RDKG RH5 .... 135 J5
Woodhurst La OXTED RH8 .... 123 L2
Woodhurst Pk OXTED RH8 .... 123 L1
Woodhyrst Gdns
PUR/KEN CR8 .... 81 K4
Wooding Gv CRAWW RH11 .... 194 E1
Woodland Av CRAN GU6 .... 153 J7
Woodland Cl EHSLY KT24 .... 95 H7
HOR/WEW KT19 * 60 C5
NRWD SE19 .... 30 F9
SWTR RH13 .... 192 C6
Woodland Crs BNFD RG42 .... 32 E1
FARN GU14 .... 88 C6
Woodland Dr CRAWE RH10 .... 179 J3
EDEN TN8 .... 145 H2
EHSLY KT24 .... 95 H7
RDKG RH5 .... 155 P7
RFNM GU10 .... 127 M7
Woodland Gdns ISLW TW7 .... 16 E8
SAND/SEL CR2 .... 64 C9
Woodland Gv CROY/NA CR0 .... 63 J3
OXTED RH8 .... 123 L1
Woodland Hl NRWD SE19 .... 30 F8
Woodland La SWTR RH13 .... 193 N7
Woodland Ms
STRHM/NOR SW16 .... 29 P6
Woodland Ri FLEETS GU52 .... 106 E1
OXTED RH8 .... 123 L1
Woodland Rd NRWD SE19 .... 30 F8
THHTH CR7 .... 45 J5
Woodlands ADL/WDHM KT15 .... 56 A2
ASHTD KT21 * 77 M7
CRAWE RH10 .... 177 N3
CWTH RG45 .... 49 M6
FLEETS GU51 .... 86 C7
RPLY/SEND GU23 .... 93 K5
RYNPK SW20 .... 42 G5
WOKS/MYFD GU22 .... 10 D6
YTLY GU46 .... 66 E3
Woodlands Av BF/WBF KT14 .... 73 L1
FNM GU9 .... 128 A3
NWMAL KT3 .... 42 B2
REDH RH1 .... 140 A7
WPK KT4 .... 60 C1
Woodlands Cl ASC SL5 .... 33 P7
ASHV GU12 .... 109 J1
BLKW GU17 .... 68 A7
CHERT KT16 .... 54 F8
CRAN GU6 .... 153 J7
CRAWE RH10 .... 177 N3
ESH/CLAY KT10 .... 58 F6
Woodlands Copse
ASHTD KT21 .... 77 K5
Woodlands Ct REDH RH1 * 120 B7
SHST GU47 .... 49 N9
WOKS/MYFD GU22 .... 10 D7
Woodlands Dr GDST RH9 .... 122 E8
SUN TW16 .... 39 L3
Woodlands Gdns
EPSOM KT18 .... 78 G6
Woodlands Gv
COUL/CHIP CR5 .... 80 D6
ISLW TW7 .... 16 E7
Woodlands La BFOR GU20 .... 52 F6
COB KT11 .... 76 A5
Woodlands Pde ASHF TW15 .... 23 M9
Woodlands Pk
ADL/WDHM KT15 .... 55 K4
GU GU1 .... 112 F4
KWD/TDW/WH KT20 .... 117 P2
WOKN/KNAP GU21 .... 72 B3
Woodlands Ride ASC SL5 .... 33 P7
Woodlands Rd BARN SW13 .... 18 C8
BF/WBF KT14 .... 73 K3
CBLY GU15 .... 68 B1
EGRIN RH19 .... 162 F8
EPSOM KT18 .... 95 P8
FARN GU14 .... 87 P1
GT/LBKH KT23 .... 95 P8
GU GU1 .... 112 D1
ISLW TW7 .... 16 E8
LHD/OX KT22 .... 97 J1
MFD/CHID GU8 .... 168 C2
REDH RH1 .... 120 B8
SURB KT6 .... 41 K8
Woodlands Rd East
VW GU25 .... 36 A5
Woodlands Rd West
VW GU25 .... 36 A5
The Woodlands
ESH/CLAY KT10 .... 58 C1
HORL RH6 .... 160 C1
ISLW TW7 .... 16 F7
NRWD SE19 .... 45 L5
Woodlands Wk BLKW GU17 .... 68 A7
Woodlands Wy ASHTD KT21 .... 77 N5
KWD/TDW/WH KT20 .... 118 A1
PUT/ROE SW15 .... 28 B7

CROY/NA CR0 .... 46 E9
CTHM CR3 .... 101 N8
Woodland SM4 .... 43 K5
MRDN SM4 .... 43 M8
MTCM CR4 .... 44 E5
PUR/KEN CR8 .... 81 J2
SWTR RH13 .... 192 F6
WEY KT13 .... 56 F4
WIM/MER SW19 .... 65 J2
Wood La CTHM CR3 .... 101 M4
FARN GU14 .... 88 C4
FLEETN GU51 .... 9 L1
ISLW TW7 .... 16 E4
KWD/TDW/WH KT20 .... 79 K6
RFNM GU10 .... 129 K1
WEY KT13 .... 56 E7
WOKN/KNAP GU21 .... 71 K7
Woodlark Gld CBLY GU15 .... 68 F1
Woodlawn Cl PUT/ROE SW15 .... 28 C1
Woodlawn Crs WHTN TW2 .... 25 J5
Woodlawn Dr FELT TW13 .... 24 E5
Woodlawn Gv
WOKN/KNAP GU21 .... 71 P6
Woodlawn Rd FUL/PGN SW6 .... 19 H5
Woodlea Dr HAYES BR2 .... 47 L6
Woodleigh FLEETN GU51 .... 86 C7
Woodleigh Gdns
STRHM/NOR SW16 .... 29 P6
Woodley Cl TOOT SW17 .... 44 B1
Woodley La SUT SM1 .... 61 J2
Wood Lodge La WWKM BR4 .... 65 J2
Woodmancote Gdns
BF/WBF KT14 .... 73 L1
Woodmancott Cl BRAK RG12 .... 33 H6
Woodmancourt GODL GU7 .... 131 J5
Woodman Ms RCH/KEW TW9 .... 17 P6
Woodman Rd
COUL/CHIP CR5 .... 80 D4
Woodmans HI CRAWW RH11 .... 194 F1
Woodmansterne La
BNSTD SM7 .... 79 M4
Woodmansterne Rd
CAR SM5 .... 62 A8
COUL/CHIP CR5 .... 80 E4
STRHM/NOR SW16 .... 44 E1
Woodmansterne St
BNSTD SM7 .... 80 A4
Woodmere Av CROY/NA CR0 .... 46 D8
Woodmere Cl CROY/NA CR0 .... 46 D8
Woodmere Gdns
CROY/NA CR0 .... 46 D8
Woodmere Wy BECK BR3 .... 47 K6
Wood Moor EWKG RG40 .... 48 D3
Woodpecker Cl COB KT11 .... 75 N1
RFNM GU10 .... 107 H6
Woodpecker La RDKG RH5 .... 157 H2
Woodpecker Mt
CROY/NA CR0 .... 64 E7
Woodpeckers
MFD/CHID GU8 .... 149 M5
Woodpecker Wy
CRAWE RH10 .... 179 K5
WOKS/MYFD GU22 .... 92 B3
Woodplace Cl
COUL/CHIP CR5 .... 80 E8
Woodplace La
COUL/CHIP CR5 .... 80 E9
Woodquest Av HNHL SE24 .... 30 C1
Woodridge Cl BRAK RG12 .... 32 E4
Wood Riding
WOKS/MYFD GU22 .... 73 J4
Wood Ridings WEY KT13 * 56 C5
Wood Ri GUW GU2 .... 111 L3
Wood Rd BH/WHM TN16 .... 84 A7
CBLY GU15 .... 68 D7
FNM GU9 .... 107 N7
GODL GU7 .... 131 M5
GSHT GU26 .... 165 N5
SHPTN TW17 .... 38 C5
Woodrough Copse
SHGR GU5 .... 132 E8
Woodrow Av HORL RH6 .... 159 J4
Woodroyd Gdns HORL RH6 .... 159 J6
Woodruff Av GU GU1 .... 112 G2
Woods Hill Cl EGRIN RH19 .... 181 J5
Woods Hill La EGRIN RH19 .... 181 J5
Woodshore Ct VW GU25 .... 35 P7
Woodside BLKW GU17 .... 68 B1
CBLY GU15 .... 68 B1
EHSLY KT24 .... 94 E6
KWD/TDW/WH KT20 .... 99 K8
LHD/OX KT22 .... 96 B2
SWTR RH13 .... 192 G6
WIM/MER SW19 .... 28 C8
WOT/HER KT12 .... 39 J9
Woodside Cl BRYLDS KT5 .... 42 A8
CTHM CR3 .... 101 N4
EWKG RG40 .... 48 C1
WOKN/KNAP GU21 .... 71 K6
Woodside Court Rd
CROY/NA CR0 .... 46 A8
Woodside Crs HORL RH6 .... 160 B1
Woodside Gdns SNWD SE25 .... 46 B7
Woodside Pk SNWD SE25 .... 46 A7
Woodside Rd COB KT11 .... 76 A2
CTHM CR3 .... 101 M4
CRAWE RH10 .... 177 J3
FARN GU14 .... 108 A2
FNM GU9 .... 128 A3
GUW GU2 .... 111 M4
KUTN/CMB KT2 .... 8 D1
MFD/CHID GU8 .... 167 P7
NWMAL KT3 .... 42 B3
PUR/KEN CR8 .... 80 G2
RDKG RH5 .... 156 C1
RSEV TN14 .... 105 P4

SNWD SE25 ....46 B7
SUT SM1 ....61 N2
Woodside Wy CROY/NA CR0 ...46 C7
MTCM CR4 ....44 D2
REDH RH1 ....120 C6
REDH RH1 ....140 C2
VW GU25 ....35 P4
Woodslands HORL RH6 ....140 F9
Woodsome Ldg WEY KT13 ....56 E5
Woodspring Rd
WIM/MER SW19 ....28 B5
Woodstock EGRIN RH19 ....180 B1
RGUE 93 M8
Woodstock Av CHEAM SM3 ...43 K8
DTCH/LGLY SL3 ....12 B2
ISLW TW7 ....25 P1
WEA W13 ....16 C1
Woodstock Cl CRAN GU6 ....171 J2
HORS RH12 ....192 C5
WOKN/KNAP GU21 ....10 C2
Woodstock Gdns BECK BR3 ...47 H2
Woodstock Gv GODL GU7 ......131 L6
Woodstock La North
SURB KT6 ....59 J1
Woodstock La South
ESH/CLAY KT10 ....59 H4
Woodstock Ri CHEAM SM3 ...43 K9
Woodstock Rd CAR SM5 ....62 C4
CHSWK W4 ....18 C2
COUL/CHIP CR5 ....80 D5
CROY/NA CR0 ....2 E6
Woodstocks FARN GU14 ....88 E1
Woodstock Wy MTCM CR4 ....44 E5
Woodstone Av EW KT17 ....60 E4
Wood St ASHV GU12 ....89 J9
CHSWK W4 ....18 C3
EGRIN RH19 ....180 C2
KUT/HW KT1 ....8 D3
MTCM CR4 ....44 C8
REDH RH1 ....100 E9
Woodsway LHD/OX KT22 ......76 E3
Woodsyre SYD SE26 ....23 J5
Woodthorpe Rd ASHF TW15 ...22 G8
PUT/ROE SW15 ....18 F9
Wood V FSTH SE23 ....31 J4
Woodvale Av SNWD SE25 ......45 P4
Woodview CHSGTN KT9 ....59 J9
Woodview Cl ASHTD KT21 .....77 N5
PUT/ROE SW15 ....27 J7
SAND/SEL CR2 ....82 B3
Woodville Cl BLKW GU17 ....67 M3
TEDD TW11 ....25 P7
Woodville Gdns SURB KT6 * ...41 K8
Woodville Rd LHD/OX KT22 ...77 H9
MRDN SM4 ....43 J3
RCHPK/HAM TW10 ....26 A6
THHTH CR7 ....45 M4
Woodward Cl ESH/CLAY KT10..58 F5
Woodward Rd EDUL SE22 ....30 F2
Woodwards CRAWW RH11 ..194 E1
Woodway CBLY GU15 ....68 D3
GU GU1 ....112 F4
Woodwell St
WAND/EARL SW18 ....28 F1
Woodyard La DUL SE21 ....30 F3
Woodyers Cl SHGR GU5 ......132 F6
Woolacombe Wy
HYS/HAR UB3 ....14 G2
Woolborough Cl
CRAWE RH10 ....177 H4
Woolborough La
CRAWE RH10 ....177 K3
REDH RH1 ....141 H5
Woolborough Rd
CRAWE RH10 ....176 G4
Woolford Cl BNFD RG42 ....33 K1
Woolfords La
MFD/CHID GU8 ....148 C3
Woolhampton Wy
BRAK RG12 ....32 F6
Woolhams CTHM CR3 ....101 P6
Woollards Rd ASHV GU12 ......109 J2
Woolmead Rd FNM GU9 ....5 C3
The Woolmead FNM GU9 ....5 C3
Woolmer Hill Rd
HASM GU27 ....183 M3
Woolmer La LIPH GU30 ......182 F2
Woolneigh St FUL/PGN SW6 ...19 M8
Wool Rd RYNPK SW20 ....27 N9

Woolsack Wy GODL GU7 ......131 M9
Woolstone Rd FSTH SE23 ......31 M5
Wootton Cl EPSOM KT18 ......78 C5
Worbeck Rd PGE/AN SE20 ....46 B5
Worcester Cl CROY/NA CR0 ...64 F1
FARN GU14 ....68 D9
MTCM CR4 ....44 C3
Worcester Ct WOT/HER KT12 ...57 L1
Worcester Dr ASHF TW15 ......23 L9
CHSWK W4 ....18 C1
Worcester Gdns WPK KT4 ......60 C2
Worcester Park Rd WPK KT4 ...60 A2
Worcester Rd BELMT SM2 ......61 L6
CRAWE RH10 ....177 H9
GUW GU2 ....111 M3
REIG RH2 ....119 L4
WIM/MER SW19 ....28 C8
Worcestershire Lea
BNFD RG42 ....33 H1
Wordsworth Av
PUR/KEN CR8 ....81 M4
YTLY GU46 ....66 F3
Wordsworth Cl
CRAWE RH10 ....177 L3
Wordsworth Dr CHEAM SM3 ...60 C3
Wordsworth Md REDH RH1 ...120 D3
Wordsworth Pl HORS RH12 ...192 D3
Wordsworth Ri EGRIN RH19 ..180 B2
Wordsworth Rd
ADL/WDHM KT15 ....55 P3
HPTN TW12 ....24 C7
PGE/AN SE20 ....46 D1
WLGTN SM6 ....62 E5
Wordsworth Wy
WDR/YW UB7 ....14 A2
Works Rd ADL/WDHM KT15 ...55 M7
World's End COB KT11 ....75 J3
EPSOM KT18 * 78 B5
Worlds End Hl BRAK RG12 ...33 H7
Worlds End Pas
WBPTN SW10 * 19 P5
Worlidge St HMSMTH W6 .....18 G3
Wormley La MFD/CHID GU8 ...167 P2
Worple Av ISLW TW7 ....25 P1
ISLW TW7 ....16 C9
LHD/OX KT22 ....97 H3
RYNPK SW20 ....42 G3
STA TW18 ....37 M1
Worple Cl EPSOM KT18 ....78 C3
WIM/MER SW19 ....28 C9
Worplesdon Hl
WOKS/MYFD GU22 ....91 J2
Worplesdon Rd RGUW GU3 ...91 M9
Worple St MORT/ESHN SW14..18 B8
The Worple
STWL/WRAY TW19 ....21 L2
Worple Wy
RCHPK/HAM TW10 ....26 D1
Worsfold Cl RPLY/SEND GU23..92 F3
Worslade Rd TOOT SW17 ......28 G6
Worsley Bridge Rd SYD SE26..31 N8
Worsley Rd FRIM GU16 ....89 H3
Worsopp Dr CLAP SW4 ....29 M1
Worsted Gn REDH RH1 ....100 F9
Worsted La EGRIN RH19 ......180 G4
Worthfield Cl
HOR/WEW KT19 ....60 B6
Worthing Rd HEST TW5 ....15 P4
HORS RH12 ....192 A9
Worthington Cl MTCM CR4 ...44 D5
Worthington Rd SURB KT6 ...41 M9
Worth Park Av CRAWE RH10..177 M4
Worth Rd CRAWE RH10 ......177 M5
Worthy Wy CRAWE RH10 ......177 N6
Wortley Rd CROY/NA CR0 ......45 J8
Worton Gdns ISLW TW7 ....16 D7
Worton Rd ISLW TW7 ....16 F8
Worton Rd RDKG RH5 ....135 N2
Wotton Dr RDKG RH5 ....135 N2
Wotton Wy BELMT SM2 ....60 G8
Wrabness Wy STA TW18 ....37 M2
Wray Cl EGRIN RH19 ....181 J5
Wray Common Rd REIG RH2..119 N4
Wrayfield Av REIG RH2 ....119 N4

Wrayfield Rd CHEAM SM3 ......61 H2
Wraylands Dr REIG RH2 ....119 P3
Wray La REIG RH2 ....119 N1
Wraymead Pl REIG RH2 * 119 N4
Wray Mill Pk REIG RH2 ....119 P3
Wray Park Rd REIG RH2 ......119 N4
Wray Rd BELMT SM2 ....61 J7
Wraysbury Cl HSLWW TW4 ...24 F1
Wraysbury Gdns STA TW18 ...22 B7
Wraysbury Rd
STWL/WRAY TW19 ....21 N5
Wrecclesham Hl
RFNM GU10 ....127 J8
Wrecclesham Rd FNM GU9 ...127 K5
The Wrekin FARN GU14 ....88 C6
Wren Av NWDGN UB2 ....15 P2
Wren Cl HORS RH12 ....192 C5
SAND/SEL CR2 ....64 D8
YTLY GU46 * 66 F2
Wren Ct ASHV GU12 ....109 K3
CRAWE RH10 * 177 L7
Wren Crs ADL/WDHM KT15 ...55 P4
Wren Dr WDR/YW UB7 ....13 P1
Wren's Av ASHF TW15 ....23 M8
Wren St SW CRAWE RH10 ......179 K6
Wren Wy FARN GU14 ....68 D9
Wright Cl CRAWE RH10 * 177 L9
Wright Gdns SHPTN TW17 ......38 C6
Wright Rd HEST TW5 ....15 L5
Wrights La KENS W8 * 19 L1
Wrights Rd SNWD SE25 ....45 N4
Wright's Rw WLGTN SM6 ......62 D3
Wrotham Hl MFD/CHID GU8 ..169 K8
Wroughton Rd BTSEA SW11 ...29 J2
Wroxham BRAK RG12 ....32 C5
Wroxham Wk CRAWE RH10 ...177 L7
Wrythe Gn CAR SM5 ....62 B2
Wrythe Green Rd CAR SM5 ...62 B2
Wrythe La CAR SM5 ....43 P9
Wulwyn Side CWTH RG45 ......49 L4
Wyatt Cl FELT TW13 ....24 E4
Wyatt Dr BARN SW13 ....18 F4
Wyatt Park Rd
BRXS/STRHM SW2 ....30 A5
Wyatt Rd STA TW18 ....22 D8
Wyche Cu SAND/SEL CR2 ......63 L6
Wych Elm Ri GU GU1 ....112 C8
Wychelm Rd LTWR GU18 ......52 C2
Wych Hl WOKS/MYFD GU22 ...72 A8
Wych Hill La
WOKS/MYFD GU22 ....72 C8
Wych Hill Pk
WOKS/MYFD GU22 ....10 A7
Wych Hill Ri
WOKS/MYFD GU22 ....72 A8
Wychwood BIL RH14 ....188 A7
Wychwood Av BRAK RG12 .....33 H5
THHTH CR7 ....45 L4
Wychwood Cl ASHV GU12 ......109 H4
SUN TW16 ....24 B9
Wychwood Pl CBLY GU15 ......51 K8
Wycliffe Rd WIM/MER SW19 ...28 E9
Wycombe Pl
WAND/EARL SW18 ....28 F2
Wydell Cl MRDN SM4 ....42 G7
Wydenhurst Rd
CROY/NA CR0 ....46 A8
Wycliffe Gdns REDH RH1 ....120 E1
Wye Cl ASHF TW15 ....23 L7
CRAWW RH11 ....194 F2
Wye St BTSEA SW11 ....19 P8
Wyeths Ms EW KT17 * 78 D2
Wyeth's Rd EW KT17 * 78 D2
Wyfold Rd FUL/PGN SW6 ......19 J5
Wyke Av ASHV GU12 ....109 M5
Wyke Cl ISLW TW7 ....16 E5
Wyke Gdns HNWL W7 ....16 F1
Wykeham Cl WDR/YW UB7 ...14 C4
Wykeham Rd FNM GU9 ....5 G1
GU GU1 ....113 H4
Wyke La ASHV GU12 ....109 M3
Wyke Rd RYNPK SW20 ....42 G3
Wykwood LIPH GU30 ....182 C6
Wylam BRAK RG12 ....32 B6
Wylands Rd DTCH/LGLY SL3 ...12 E3
Wyldewood ASC SL5 ....34 D7
Wyleu St FSTH SE23 ....31 M5
Wylie Rd NWDGN UB2 ....16 A1

Wymering Ct FARN GU14 ......88 F4
Wymond St PUT/ROE SW15 ...18 G8
Wyncote Wy SAND/SEL CR2 ...64 D7
Wyndham Av COB KT11 ....75 J2
Wyndham Cl BELMT SM2 ......61 L6
YTLY GU46 ....67 H1
Wyndham Crs CRAN GU6 ....152 D9
HSLWW TW4 ....24 G2
Wyndham Rd KUTN/CMB KT2...41 M1
WEA W13 ....17 H1
WOKN/KNAP GU21 ....71 J5
Wyndham St SAND/SEL CR2 ...108 E5
Wyndhurst Cl SAND/SEL CR2..63 K6
Wynell Rd FSTH SE23 ....31 L6
Wynfields FRIM GU16 ....89 H4
Wynlea Cl CRAWE RH10 ....177 H4
Wynne Gdns FLEETS GU52 ...107 H1
Wynnstay Gdns KENS W8 * ...19 L1
Wynnstow Pk OXTED RH8 ...123 M2
Wynsham Wy BFOR GU20 ......52 B4
Wynter St BTSEA SW11 ....19 N9
Wynton Gdns SNWD SE25 ...45 N6
Wynton Gv WOT/HER KT12 ...57 J2
Wyphurst Rd CRAN GU6 .....152 G8
Wyre Gv HYS/HAR UB3 ....15 H4
Wyresdale BRAK RG12 ....32 G8
Wysemead HORL RH6 ....140 E9
Wyvern Cl ASHV GU12 * 109 H1
BRAK RG12 ....32 C5
Wyvern Est NWMAL KT3 * 42 E4
Wyvern Pl ADL/WDHM KT15 *..55 M8
Wyvern Rd PUR/KEN CR8 ......63 J8

Y

Yaffle Rd WEY KT13 ....56 E8
Yale Cl HSLWW TW4 ....24 G1
SHST GU47 ....50 B7
Yarborough Rd
WIM/MER SW19 ....43 P2
Yarbridge Cl BELMT SM2 * ...61 M8
Yardley BRAK RG12 ....32 B6
Yardley Cl REIG RH2 ....119 M5
Yard Md EGH TW20 ....21 M6
Yarm Cl LHD/OX KT22 ....97 J3
Yarm Court Rd LHD/OX KT22...97 J3
Yarmouth Cl CRAWE RH10 ...177 K7
Yarm Wy LHD/OX KT22 ....97 J3
Yarrow Cl HORS RH12 ....192 D5
Yateley Rd YTLY GU46 ....67 H1
Yatesbury Cl FNM GU9 ....127 K6
Yattendon Rd HORL RH6 ......159 L1
Yaverland Dr BAGS GU19 .....51 M7
Yeats Cl REDH RH1 ....119 N8
Yeend Cl E/WMO/HCT KT8 ...40 A5
Yelland Rd HMSMTH W6 ......19 H3
Yellowcress Dr
CHOB/PIR GU24 ....70 G5
Yelverton Rd BTSEA SW11 ...19 P8
Yenston Cl MRDN SM4 ....43 L7
Yeoman Dr
STWL/WRAY TW19 ....23 H4
Yeomanry Cl EW KT17 ....78 D1
Yeomans HTWY RG27 ....66 C2
Yeomans Cl FARN GU14 ....88 C2
RFNM GU10 ....109 H6
Yeomans La LIPH GU30 ......182 D6
Yeomans Pl BOR GU35 ....164 B6
Yeomans Ter
WOKN/KNAP GU21 * 71 K6
Yeoman Wy CBLY GU15 ....68 G3
Yeoman Wy REDH RH1 ....140 D1
Yeoveney Cl
STWL/WRAY TW19 ....22 A5
Yeovil Cl FARN GU14 ....88 F6
Yeovil Rd SHST GU47 ....50 A8
Yeovilton Pl KUTN/CMB KT2...26 C8
Yetminster Rd FARN GU14 ....88 E8
Yevele Wy FARN GU14 * 81 M4
Yew Cnr BRAK RG12 ....32 E4
Yewens MFD/CHID GU8 ....168 A6
Yew La EGRIN RH19 ....162 A9
Yew Pl WEY KT13 * 57 H2
The Yews ASHF TW15 * 23 L7

BF/WBF KT14 * 74 A1
Yew Tree Bottom Rd
EW KT17 ....78 F6
Yew Tree Cl COUL/CHIP CR5...80 B8
FARN GU14 * 87 N4
HORL RH6 ....140 C8
WPK KT4 ....42 C9
Yew Tree Dr CTHM CR3 ....101 P5
GU GU1 ....91 P9
Yew Tree Gdns EPSOM KT18...78 A4
Yew Tree La REIG RH2 ....119 M2
Yewtree Rd BECK BR3 ....46 F4
Yew Tree Rd DORK RH4 ....116 G5
HORL RH6 ....158 B5
MFD/CHID GU8 ....149 L6
Yewtrees EGH TW20 ....36 G4
Yew Trees SHPTN TW17 ....38 B5
Yew Tree Wk EHSLY KT24 .....95 M7
HSLWW TW4 ....24 C1
PUR/KEN CR8 ....63 L8
Yockley Cl CBLY GU15 ....69 M5
Yolland Cl FNM GU9 ....107 N7
York Av EGRIN RH19 ....180 F5
MORT/ESHN SW14 ....18 B9
York Cl BF/WBF KT14 ....74 A1
MRDN SM4 ....43 M5
SWTR RH13 ....192 E7
York Crs ALDT GU11 ....108 B5
Yorke Gdns REIG RH2 ....119 L4
Yorke Ga CTHM CR3 ....101 M2
Yorke Rd REIG RH2 ....119 L4
York Gdns WOT/HER KT12 ...57 M1
York Hl WNWD SE27 ....30 C6
Yorke Pde BTFD TW8 * 17 K3
York Pl BTSEA SW11 ....19 N8
CBLY GU15 ....68 F1
York Rd ALDT GU11 ....108 B5
ASHV GU12 ....100 J3
BELMT SM2 ....61 L5
BF/WBF KT14 ....73 P1
BH/WHM TN16 ....83 P8
BTSEA SW11 ....19 N9
CBLY GU15 ....68 F1
CRAWE RH10 ....177 H9
CROY/NA CR0 ....45 J8
EA W5 ....17 J1
FARN GU14 ....88 B6
GU GU1 ....7 F4
KUTN/CMB KT2 ....9 G1
RCHPK/HAM TW10 ....26 D2
SAND/SEL CR2 ....64 D8
TEDD TW11 ....25 M7
WEY KT13 ....56 E4
WIM/MER SW19 ....28 E9
WOKS/MYFD GU22 ....10 B6
Yorkshire Pl BNFD RG42 ....32 G1
Yorkshire Rd MTCM CR4 ......44 C8
York St MTCM CR4 ....44 C8
TWK TW1 ....25 P4
York Terrace La CBLY GU15 *...68 C3
Yorktown Rd SHST GU47 ......67 N1
York Wy CHSGTN KT9 ....59 L6
FELT TW13 ....24 G6
SHST GU47 ....49 J3
Youlden Cl CBLY GU15 ....69 J5
Youlden Dr CBLY GU15 ....69 J5
Youngs Dr ASHV GU12 ....109 H4
Young St LHD/OX KT22 ....96 F4
Youngstroat La
CHOB/PIR GU24 ....54 C8
Yukon Rd BAL SW12 ....29 L3

Z

Zealand Av WDR/YW UB7 ......13 P5
Zennor Rd BAL SW12 ....29 M4
Zermatt Rd THHTH CR7 ....45 L5
Zig Zag Rd PUR/KEN CR8 ......81 L5
RDKG RH5 ....117 J1
Zinnia Dr CHOB/PIR GU24 ......70 G5
Zion Pl THHTH CR7 ....45 M5
Zion Rd THHTH CR7 ....45 M5

Index - featured places

Abbey Business Park
FNM GU9 ....128 B5
Abbey Industrial Estate
MTCM CR4 ....44 B6
Abbeylands School
ADL/WDHM KT15 ....55 L4
Abbey Mill Business Park
GODL GU7 ....130 E9
Abbey Mills
WIM/MER SW19 ....43 N2
Abbey Primary School
MRDN SM4 ....43 L8
The Abbey School
FNM GU9 ....5 K6
Abbey Trading Estate
SYD SE26 ....31 M8
Abbotsbury Primary School
MRDN SM4 ....43 L6
Abbots Hospital
GU GU1 ....7 F5
ABC Cinema
PUT/ROE SW15 ....19 J8

Aberdour School
KWD/TDW/WH KT20 ....79 K7
Abingdon House School
KENS W8 ....19 L1
Abinger Common
First School
RDKG RH5 ....135 M4
Abro Industrial Estate
ALDT GU11 ....108 F3
Acorn Medical Centre
TWK TW1 ....25 P4
Acorns CE School
REIG RH2 ....138 E2
The Acorns First School
BRKHM/BTCW RH3 ....118 B5
Acre Road Health Clinic
KUTN/CMB KT2 ....9 F1
ACS Egham International
School
EGH TW20 ....36 A2
Acting School
GUW GU2 ....6 D7

Acumen (Anglo School)
NRWD SE19 ....45 N2
Adamsrill Primary School
SYD SE26 ....31 M6
Addington Business Centre
CROY/NA CR0 ....65 L8
Addington Court Golf Club
CROY/NA CR0 ....64 F3
Addington Golf Club
CROY/NA CR0 ....64 F3
Addington High School
CROY/NA CR0 ....83 L1
Addington Palace Golf Club
CROY/NA CR0 ....64 E5
Addiscombe CC
CROY/NA CR0 ....64 A2
Addison Primary School
WKENS W14 ....19 H1
Addlestone Cemetery
ADL/WDHM KT15 ....55 L4
ADT College
PUT/ROE SW15 ....28 C1

Adult Education Centre
CBLY GU15 ....68 D3
FNM GU9 ....4 E4
GODL GU7 ....131 L8
GU GU1 ....7 G5
Aerodrome Hotel
CROY/NA CR0 ....63 J5
Airborne Forces Museum
ALDT GU11 ....108 C1
Airbus Coach Station
NWDGN UB2 ....14 B8
Airedale Physiotherapy
Clinic
CHSWK W4 ....18 D3
Airlinks Golf Club
NWDGN UB2 ....15 L3
Air Links Industrial Estate
HEST TW5 ....15 L3
Airport Gate Business Centre
WDR/YW UB7 ....14 B5
Airport Industrial Estate
BH/WHM TN16 ....84 B4

Albany Clinic
WIM/MER SW19 ....43 M1
Albany Park Canoe &
Sailing Club
KUTN/CMB KT2 ....26 C9
Albany Park Industrial Estate
FRIM GU16 ....68 D7
Albemarle Primary School
WIM/MER SW19 ....28 B5
Alderbrook Primary School
BAL SW12 ....29 L3
Aldershot & Farnham
County Court
ALDT GU11 ....108 D4
Aldershot Health Centre
ALDT GU11 ....108 B4
Aldershot Military Museum
ALDT GU11 ....88 E8
Aldershot Military Stadium
ALDT GU11 ....88 E8
Aldershot Outpatients
ALDT GU11 ....108 D3

Aldershot Town FC
ALDT GU11 ....108 E4
Aldro School
MFD/CHID GU8 ....130 C6
Alexander Barracks
CHOB/PIR GU24 ....90 B1
Alexander House Hotel
CRAWE RH10 ....179 K6
Alexandra Infant School
KUTN/CMB KT2 ....9 H1
PGE/AN SE20 ....46 D1
Alexandra Junior School
HSLW TW3 ....16 B7
SYD SE26 ....31 L9
The All England Lawn Tennis & Croquet Club
WIM/MER SW19 ....28 A6
Alleyns Junior School
EDUL SE22 ....30 F1
Allfarthing JMI School
WAND/EARL SW18 ....28 F2
All Hallows Catholic School
FNM GU9 ....108 B7
All Saints Benhilton CE Primary School
SUT SM1 ....61 M2
All Saints CE Infant School
LHD/OX KT22 ....76 C8
RFNM GU10 ....147 M1
All Saints CE Junior School
FLEETN GU51 ....86 D7
NRWD SE19 ....45 N2
All Saints CE Primary School
CAR SM5 ....62 C4
FUL/PGN SW6 ....19 J7
All Saints CE Primary School
HORS RH12 ....192 E4
All Saints CE Primary School
PUT/ROE SW15 ....18 G8
WIM/MER SW19 ....43 N1
Alphalingua
FNM GU9 ....127 N6
Alpine Snowsports Dry Ski Slope
ALDT GU11 ....108 E2
The Alton School
PUT/ROE SW15 ....27 L3
Ambleside Junior School
WOT/HER KT12 ....39 G1
Amen Corner Business Park
BRAK RG12 ....32 A3
The American Community School
COB KT11 ....57 M8
Amesbury School
GSHT GU26 ....183 P1
AMF Bowling
CRAWW RH11 ....176 G5
Amida Golf
FELT TW13 ....25 H6
The Andrew Ewing Primary School
HEST TW5 ....15 P5
Anerley School
NRWD SE19 ....46 A2
The Angel Posting House & Livery Hotel
GU GU1 ....6 E5
Animal Care College
ASC SL5 ....34 A4
Ansells Farm Community Centre
FLEETN GU51 ....87 J3
Apex Retail Park
FELT TW13 ....24 G6
Apostolic Nuncio
WIM/MER SW19 ....27 P6
Applegarth Primary School
CROY/NA CRO 65 H5
Apple Orchard School
SHGR GU5 ....151 N1
Aquarius Golf Club
EDUL SE22 ....31 K1
Aragon Primary School
MRDN SM4 ....43 J8
The Archbishop Lanfranc School
CROY/NA CRO 44 C7
Archbishop Tenisons CE School
CROY/NA CRO 3 J6
Archdeacon Cambridge's CE Primary School
WHTN TW2 ....25 M5
Archway Theatre
HORL RH6 ....159 K2
Arena Leisure Centre
CBLY GU15 ....68 E2
Arlington Business Park
BRAK RG12 ....32 C3
Army Golf Club
ALDT GU11 ....88 A9
Army Medical Services Museum
ASHV GU12 ....89 K6
Army Training Regiment
CHOB/PIR GU24 ....90 C1
Arndale Health Centre
WAND/EARL SW18 ....28 D2
Arnhem Barracks
ALDT GU11 ....108 C3
Arrow Industrial Estate
FARN GU14 ....88 B5
Art School
BECK BR3 ....46 E6
The Arts Educational School
CHSWK W4 ....18 C2
Arts Link Theatre Cinema
CBLY GU15 ....68 F2
Arts Theatre
PUT/ROE SW15 ....19 H9

Arun House
HORS RH12 ....192 C7
Arunside Primary School
HORS RH12 ....191 P8
Ascot Heath Infant School
ASC SL5 ....33 N1
Ascot Racecourse
ASC SL5 ....33 P4
Ashburnham Primary School
WBPTN SW10 ....19 P5
Ashburton Community School
CROY/NA CRO 46 B8
Ashburton Primary School
CROY/NA CRO 46 B7
Ashby Mill School
CLAP SW4 ....29 P1
The Ashcombe School
DORK RH4 ....117 H5
Ashdown Forest Health Centre
FROW RH18 ....181 K8
Ashford CE Primary School
ASHF TW15 ....23 J5
Ashford Clinic
ASHF TW15 ....23 H6
Ashford High School
ASHF TW15 ....23 H6
Ashford Industrial Estate
ASHF TW15 ....23 M7
Ashford Manor Golf Club
ASHF TW15 ....23 J9
Ashford Park Primary School
ASHF TW15 ....22 F7
Ash Grange CP School
ASHV GU12 ....109 K4
Ashley Centre Shopping Precinct
EPSOM KT18 ....78 B2
Ashley Primary School
WOT/HER KT12 ....39 J9
Ash Manor School
ASHV GU12 ....109 H6
Ashtead Clinic
ASHTD KT21 ....77 L6
Ashtead CC
ASHTD KT21 ....77 L6
Ashtead Hospital
ASHTD KT21 ....77 L9
Ashton House School
ISLW TW7 ....16 D6
Ashurst Wood Primary School
EGRIN RH19 ....181 K5
Ash Vale Health Centre
ASHV GU12 ....109 K2
Aspen House Secondary & Primary School
BRXS/STRHM SW2 ....29 P4
Asquith Court School
HPTN TW12 ....40 B2
Assembly Rooms
SURB KT6 ....41 L5
The Astolat Industrial Estate
RGUW GU3 ....132 A4
Aston Clinic
NWMAL KT3 ....42 C5
Astra Business Centre
REDH RH1 ....140 C6
Athelney Primary School
CAT SE6 ....31 P6
Athelstan Media School
HPTN TW12 ....40 A2
Atkinson Morley Hospital
RYNPK SW20 ....42 F1
Atlantic House (Richmond American International University)
KENS W8 ....19 M1
Atlas Medical Centre
HORL RH6 ....159 K5
Atlas Transport Estate
BTSEA SW11 ....19 N7
Atwood Primary School
SAND/SEL CR2 ....82 A3
Audley Primary School
CTHM CR3 ....101 N1
Auriol Junior School
HOR/WEW KT19 ....60 D3
The Avenue Primary School
BELMT SM2 ....61 L8
Avon Trading Estate
WKENS W14 ....19 K2
BAA Heathrow Visitor Centre
HTHAIR TW6 ....14 D6
Back Care Clinic
WPK KT4 ....42 E9
Baden Powell House
SKENS SW7 ....19 N2
Badshot Lea Village Infant School
FNM GU9 ....108 C8
Bagshot School
BAGS GU19 ....51 N6
Baldwins Hill Primary School
EGRIN RH19 ....162 B9
Balfour Business Centre
NWDGN UB2 ....15 M1
Balgowan Primary School
BECK BR3 ....46 E3
Balham Boys Preparatory Secondary School
BAL SW12 ....29 L4

Balham Girls Preparatory Secondary School
TOOT SW17 ....29 J6
Balham Health Centre
BAL SW12 ....29 L5
Balham Leisure Centre
TOOT SW17 ....29 K5
Bandon Hill Cemetery
WLGTN SM6 ....62 F4
Bandon Hill Primary School
WLGTN SM6 ....62 F4
Banstead Athletic FC
KWD/TDW/WH KT20 ....78 G9
Banstead Clinic
BNSTD SM7 ....79 L4
Banstead County Junior School
BNSTD SM7 ....79 K4
Banstead Downs Golf Club
BELMT SM2 ....61 L9
Banstead Infant School
BNSTD SM7 ....79 K4
Banstead Sports Centre
KWD/TDW/WH KT20 ....78 G9
Banstead Village Clinic
BNSTD SM7 ....79 M4
Barfield School
RFNM GU10 ....128 D2
Barn Elms Athletics Track
BARN SW13 ....18 F7
Barn Elms Water Sports Centre
PUT/ROE SW15 ....18 G7
Barnes Hospital
MORT/ESHN SW14 ....18 C8
Barnes Primary School
BARN SW13 ....18 C8
Barnes Sports Club
BARN SW13 ....18 D6
Barnett Wood Infant School
ASHTD KT21 ....77 K6
Barnsbury Junior School
WOKS/MYFD GU22 ....92 B1
Barnwood County First School
GUW GU2 ....111 K4
Barons Court Theatre
WKENS W14 ....19 J3
Barrow Hedges Primary School
CAR SM5 ....62 A6
Barrow Hills School
MFD/CHID GU8 ....149 M8
Barwell Business Park
CHSGTN KT9 ....59 K6
Basingstoke College of Technology
FLEETN GU51 ....86 F6
Baston School
HAYES BR2 ....65 P1
Bath Factory Estate
HNHL SE24 ....30 D2
Battersea Sports Centre
BTSEA SW11 ....19 P8
Battersea Tutorial College
TOOT SW17 ....29 K5
Beacon Hill CP School
GSHT GU26 ....165 M5
Beacon School
BNSTD SM7 ....79 J4
Beatrix Potter Primary School
WAND/EARL SW18 ....28 F4
Beauclerc Infant School
SUN TW16 ....39 L4
Beaufort Primary School
WOKN/KNAP GU21 ....71 M5
Beaumont Junior School
ALDT GU11 ....108 A4
Beaumont Primary School
PUR/KEN CR8 ....81 H3
Beaver Industrial Estate
LIPH GU30 ....182 F8
The Beavers Community Primary School
HSLWW TW4 ....15 L8
Beckenham Business Centre
BECK BR3 ....31 M9
Beckenham Crematorium
BECK BR3 ....46 C4
Beckenham CC
BECK BR3 ....47 H1
Beckenham Hospital
BECK BR3 ....46 F3
Beckenham Leisure Centre
BECK BR3 ....46 E2
Beckenham RFC
BECK BR3 ....46 E5
Beckenham Town FC
BECK BR3 ....46 G6
Beckmead School
BECK BR3 ....46 G9
Bective House Clinic
PUT/ROE SW15 ....19 K9
Beddington Infants School
WLGTN SM6 ....62 E2
Beddington Medical Centre
CROY/NA CRO 62 G3
Beddington Park Primary School
CROY/NA CRO 62 F2
Beddington Trading Estate
CROY/NA CRO 62 G4
Bedelsford Special School
KUT/HW KT1 ....8 D7
Bedfont Health Clinic
EBED/NFELT TW14 ....23 P3
Bedfont Industrial Park
ASHF TW15 ....23 N6
Bedfont J & I School
EBED/NFELT TW14 ....23 P2

Bedfont Lakes Country Park
EBED/NFELT TW14 ....23 M5
Bedford Lakes Office Park
EBED/NFELT TW14 ....23 M4
Bedington Infant School
STRHM SW6 ....62 E3
Beech House School
SAND/SEL CR2 ....63 P8
Beechnut Industrial Estate
ASHV GU12 ....108 D5
Beecholme Primary School
MTCM CR4 ....44 D2
Beechwood School
STRHM/NOR SW16 ....29 P6
Belfry Shopping Centre
REDH RH1 ....120 B4
Bellerby Theatre
GU GU1 ....6 E4
Belleville Primary School
BTSEA SW11 ....29 J1
Belle Vue Infant School
ASHV GU12 ....108 F4
Bell Farm Junior School
WOT/HER KT12 ....57 L3
Bell Industrial Estate
CHSWK W4 ....18 A2
Belmont Preparatory School
RDKG RH5 ....135 L7
Belmont Primary School
CHSWK W4 ....18 B2
Benedict Primary School
MTCM CR4 ....43 P4
Bensham Manor School
THHTH CR7 ....45 L6
Benson Primary School
CROY/NA CRO 64 E2
The Bentall Shopping Centre
KUT/HW KT1 ....8 C4
Bentley CE Primary School
RFNM GU10 ....126 B8
Bentley Industrial Centre
RFNM GU10 ....126 A9
The Bentley Kempinski Hotel
SKENS SW7 ....19 N2
Bentley Trimmings Business Park
RFNM GU10 ....126 B8
Benyon Primary School
HEST TW5 ....15 M4
The Berkshire Golf Club
ASC SL5 ....51 L1
Bertram House School
TOOT SW17 ....29 K5
Bessemer Grange J & I School
HNHL SE24 ....30 E1
Best Western Master Robert Hotel
HEST TW5 ....15 P6
Betchworth Park Golf Club
DORK RH4 ....117 L6
Bethlem Royal Hospital
BECK BR3 ....46 C8
Beulah Infant School
THHTH CR7 ....45 L3
Beverley School
NWMAL KT3 ....42 E6
Beverley Trading Estate
MRDN SM4 ....43 H8
Bewbush Community Primary School
CRAWW RH11 ....176 B8
Bewbush Leisure Centre
CRAWW RH11 ....176 C9
Bewbush Medical Centre
CRAWW RH11 ....176 B8
Bewhurst County First School
CRAWW RH11 ....176 C8
Biggin Hill Airport
BH/WHM TN16 ....84 A1
Biggin Hill Business Park
BH/WHM TN16 ....84 B4
Biggin Hill Primary School
BH/WHM TN16 ....84 C5
Bilton Infant School
BRAK RG12 ....32 A5
Bingham Hotel
TWK TW1 ....26 C2
Binscombe Medical Centre
GODL GU7 ....131 K5
Birches Industrial Estate
EGRIN RH19 ....161 P9
Birch Hill Medical Centre
BRAK RG12 ....32 D8
Birch Hill Primary School
BRAK RG12 ....32 E9
Bishop Challoner School
HAYES BR2 ....47 K3
Bishop David Brown School
WOKN/KNAP GU21 ....73 H2
Bishop Gilpin Primary School
WIM/MER SW19 ....28 C8
Bishop Perrin CE Primary School
WHTN TW2 ....25 J3
Bishopsgate School
EGH TW20 ....20 F6
Bishop's Table Hotel
FNM GU9 ....4 E3
Bishop Thomas Grant School
STRHM/NOR SW16 ....30 A8
Bishop Wand CE Secondary School
SUN TW16 ....39 H3
Bisley CE Primary School
CHOB/PIR GU24 ....70 C5
Blackburn Trading Estate
STWL/WRAY TW19 ....23 J2

Blackbushe Airport
BLKW GU17 ....66 E6
Blackbushe Business Park
YTLY GU46 ....66 C4
Blackdown Barracks
FRIM GU16 ....89 M1
Black Down (NT)
HASM GU27 ....185 J8
Blackwater & Hawley Leisure Centre
BLKW GU17 ....67 P5
Blackwater Industrial Estate
BLKW GU17 ....68 A3
Blackwater Trading Estate
ASHV GU12 ....108 F6
Blackwell Primary School
EGRIN RH19 ....162 D9
Bleach's Yard Industrial Estate
LIPH GU30 ....182 F8
Blenheim Business Centre
MTCM CR4 ....44 B2
Blenheim High School
HOR/WEW KT19 ....60 B8
Blenheim Shopping Centre
PGE/AN SE20 ....46 C1
Bletchingley Golf Club
REDH RH1 ....121 M4
Bloomsbury College
FUL/PGN SW6 ....19 L5
Blossom House School
RYNPK SW20 ....42 G1
Bluebell Railway
EGRIN RH19 ....179 P9
The Blue School
ISLW TW7 ....16 G8
Bocketts Farm Park
LHD/OX KT22 ....96 F5
Bohunt Manor
LIPH GU30 ....182 E7
Bohunt School
LIPH GU30 ....182 E6
Bolingbroke Hospital
BTSEA SW11 ....29 H1
Bolingbroke Primary School
BTSEA SW11 ....19 P6
Bond First School
MTCM CR4 ....44 B3
Bond Primary School
MTCM CR4 ....44 B3
Bonneville Primary School
CLAP SW4 ....29 M2
Bookham Grange Hotel
GT/LBKH KT23 ....95 P3
Bookham Industrial Estate
GT/LBKH KT23 ....95 P3
Borers Business Park
CRAWE RH10 ....160 D9
Borough Hall
GODL GU7 ....131 L8
Boston Business Park
HNWL W7 ....16 E1
Boston University
SKENS SW7 ....19 N2
Boundary Business Centre
WOKN/KNAP GU21 ....72 E4
Boundary Business Park
MTCM CR4 ....43 P3
Bourne Business Park
ADL/WDHM KT15 ....55 N1
Bourne Hall Health Centre
EW KT17 ....60 D7
Bourne Hall Museum
EW KT17 ....60 D7
Bourne Mill Industrial Estate
FNM GU9 ....128 A2
The Bourne School
RFNM GU10 ....127 P6
Bourne Tennis Club
FNM GU9 ....127 N5
Bousfield Primary School
WBPTN SW10 ....19 N3
Boxgrove Primary School
GU GU1 ....112 F4
Box Hill Country Park
KWD/TDW/WH KT20 ....117 L3
Box Hill School
RDKG RH5 ....97 H7
Brackenbury Health Centre
HMSMTH W6 ....18 F1
Brackenbury Primary School
HMSMTH W6 ....18 F1
Bracknell Business Centre
BRAK RG12 ....32 B3
Bracknell RFC
BRAK RG12 ....32 G3
Bracknell Sports Centre
BRAK RG12 ....32 E6
Bracknell Town FC
BRAK RG12 ....32 E3
Bracknell & Wokingham College
BRAK RG12 ....32 E3
Brakenhale School
BRAK RG12 ....32 D5
Brambletye Junior School
REDH RH1 ....120 C7
Brambletye School
EGRIN RH19 ....181 L7
The Bramley Business Centre
SHGR GU5 ....132 D6
Bramley CE Infant School
SHGR GU5 ....132 E7
Bramley Golf Club
SHGR GU5 ....132 C6
Bramley School
KWD/TDW/WH KT20 ....98 E5
Brandlehow Primary School
PUT/ROE SW15 ....19 K9

Brentford Business Centre
BTFD TW8 .... 17 J5
Brentford County Court
BTFD TW8 .... 17 K5
Brentford FC
London Broncos RLFC
(Griffin Park)
BTFD TW8 .... 17 K4
Brentford Fountain
Leisure Centre
BTFD TW8 .... 17 M5
Brentford Health Centre
BTFD TW8 .... 17 J4
Brentford School for Girls
BTFD TW8 .... 17 K4
Brent Knoll School
FSTH SE23 .... 31 L6
Brent Park Industrial Estate
NWDGN UB2 .... 15 K1
Brentwaters Business Park
BTFD TW8 .... 17 J5
Brewery Mews Business
Centre
ISLW TW7 .... 16 F8
Brickfields Industrial Park
BRAK RG12 .... 32 C3
Bridge Industrial Estate
HORL RH6 .... 159 L1
The Bridge Leisure Centre
SYD SE26 .... 31 N8
Bridge Medical Centre
CRAWE RH10 .... 177 K4
Brigstock Medical Centre
THHTH CR7 .... 45 K6
Bristow Infant & Nursery
School
CBLY GU15 .... 68 D6
Britannia Industrial Estate
DTCH/LGLY SL3 .... 13 J7
British Transport Police
GU GU1 .... 6 C4
BRIT School for Performing
Arts
CROY/NA CR0 .... 45 M7
Broadbridge Heath Retail
Park
HORS RH12 .... 191 M7
Broadbridge Heath
Stadium
HORS RH12 .... 191 M8
Broadfield East First
School
CRAWW RH11 .... 176 F9
Broadfield Health Centre
CRAWW RH11 .... 176 E9
Bradford Park Business
Centre
RGUE GU4 .... 132 B3
Broadlands Business
Campus
HORS RH12 .... 174 B7
HORS RH12 .... 193 N2
Broadmead Primary School
CROY/NA CR0 .... 45 M7
The Broadmere Primary
School
WOKN/KNAP GU21 .... 73 H2
Broadmoor CP School
CWTH RG45 .... 49 P5
Broadmoor Hospital
CWTH RG45 .... 50 A4
Broadwater Park Golf Club
GODL GU7 .... 131 N6
Broadwater Park Golf Club
& Driving Range
GODL GU7 .... 131 P5
Broadwater Primary School
TOOT SW17 .... 28 C7
Broadwater School
GODL GU7 .... 131 N5
Broadway Shopping Centre
HMSMTH W6 .... 18 G3
Broadway Squash & Fitness
Centre
HMSMTH W6 .... 19 H2
Brockenhurst Hotel
ASC SL5 .... 34 B7
Brockham School
BRKHM/BTCW RH3 .... 117 P7
Brocklebank Health Centre
WAND/EARL SW18 .... 28 E3
Brockley Primary School
BROCKY SE4 .... 31 N1
Brockwell Lido
HNHL SE24 .... 30 C2
Bromley Cemetery
BMLY BR1 .... 47 M1
Bromley College of Further
& Higher Education
BMLY BR1 .... 47 N2
Bromley County Court
BMLY BR1 .... 47 N2
Bromley FC
HAYES BR2 .... 47 P6
Bromley Mall Indoor Market
BMLY BR1 .... 47 N2
Bromley Road Infant School
BECK BR3 .... 47 H2
Brompton Cemetery
WBPTN SW10 .... 19 M4
Brompton Medical Centre
ECT SW5 .... 19 M5
Brookfield Primary School
CHEAM SM3 .... 43 J9
Brookham School
LIPH GU30 .... 183 H8
Brooklands Airfield (disused)
WEY KT13 .... 56 B8
Brooklands Business Park
WEY KT13 .... 56 C8
Brooklands College
WEY KT13 .... 56 C5

Brooklands Industrial Estate
WEY KT13 .... 56 A8
Brooklands Museum
WEY KT13 .... 56 C7
Brooklands School
REIG RH2 .... 119 M3
Brook Lane Business Centre
BTFD TW8 .... 17 K3
Brookmead Industrial
Estate
CROY/NA CR0 .... 44 E7
The Brook School
CRAWE RH10 .... 177 M8
The Brook Trading Estate
ASHV GU12 .... 108 C3
Brookwood Cemetery
CHOB/PIR GU24 .... 91 H2
Brookwood CP School
CHOB/PIR GU24 .... 70 G9
Broomfield House School
RCH/KEW TW9 .... 17 M6
Broomsleigh Business Park
SYD SE26 .... 31 N8
Broomwood Hall Lower
School
BAL SW12 .... 29 J2
STRHM/NOR SW16 .... 29 N6
Browning Barracks
ALDT GU11 .... 108 C1
Brunel University
ISLW TW7 .... 16 E5
TWK TW1 .... 17 H9
Brunel University
(Runnymede Campus)
EGH TW20 .... 21 J6
Brunel University Track
(Osterley Campus)
ISLW TW7 .... 16 E5
Buchan Country Park
CRAWW RH11 .... 194 B1
Buckingham Primary
School
HPTN TW12 .... 24 G8
Buckland Infant School
CHSGTN KT9 .... 59 M4
Buckland Primary School
STA TW18 .... 37 N1
Bullsbridge Industrial Estate
NWDGN UB2 .... 15 K2
Burghwood Clinic
BNSTD SM7 .... 79 K5
Burhill Golf Club
WOT/HER KT12 .... 57 J7
Burhill Infant School
WOT/HER KT12 .... 57 M5
Burleigh Infant School
CRAWE RH10 .... 179 J3
Burlington Infant School
NWMAL KT3 .... 42 D5
Burnhill Business Centre
BECK BR3 .... 46 G3
Burns Hotel
ECT SW5 .... 19 M2
Burntwood School
TOOT SW17 .... 28 G5
Burpham Foundation
Primary School
RGUE GU4 .... 112 E1
Burstow Business Centre
HORL RH6 .... 141 K8
Burstow Lodge Business
Centre
HORL RH6 .... 159 L3
Burstow Primary School
HORL RH6 .... 160 B1
Burvale Cemetery
WOT/HER KT12 .... 57 J5
Burwood Park School &
College
WOT/HER KT12 .... 57 H5
Burys Court School
REIG RH2 .... 138 G2
Busbridge CE Junior School
GODL GU7 .... 150 E1
Busbridge Infant School
GODL GU7 .... 150 E2
Bushy Hill Junior School
GU GU1 .... 113 H3
Business Aviation Centre
FARN GU14 .... 88 B8
Bute House Preparatory
School for Girls
HMSMTH W6 .... 18 G2
Butterfly House
ISLW TW7 .... 17 H6
Byfleet Business Centre
BF/WBF KT14 .... 55 P9
Byfleet CP School
BF/WBF KT14 .... 55 P9
Byfleet Industrial Estate
BF/WBF KT14 .... 55 P9
Byron Primary School
COUL/CHIP CR5 .... 80 G6
California Chalet &
Touring Park
EWKG RG40 .... 48 B2
California Country Park
EWKG RG40 .... 48 A2
Calthorpe Park School
FLEETN GU51 .... 86 C7
Calvi House Pre-preparatory
School
COB KT11 .... 74 G2
Camberley CC
CBLY GU15 .... 68 F5
Camberley County Infant
School
CBLY GU15 .... 68 D3
Camberley Health Centre
CBLY GU15 .... 68 D5
Camberley Heath Golf Club
CBLY GU15 .... 69 J4

Camberley Magistrates
Court
CBLY GU15 .... 68 F2
Camberley RFC
CBLY GU15 .... 68 E5
Camberley Town FC
CBLY GU15 .... 68 D5
Camberwell New Cemetery
PECK SE15 .... 31 L2
Cambridge Park Bowling &
Sports Club
TWK TW1 .... 26 B2
Cambridge School
HMSMTH W6 .... 18 F2
Camden Junior School
CAR SM5 .... 62 B3
Camelsdale County First
School
HASM GU27 .... 184 A5
Cameron House School
CHEL SW3 .... 19 P4
Campana Finishing School
RFNM GU10 .... 128 C4
Camphill Industrial Estate
BF/WBF KT14 .... 55 M9
Camphill Road First School
BF/WBF KT14 .... 73 M1
Campion House College
ISLW TW7 .... 16 D5
Camp Road Industrial
Estate
FARN GU14 .... 88 E7
Canbury 2000 Business
Park
KUTN/CMB KT2 .... 8 E3
Canbury Business Centre
KUTN/CMB KT2 .... 8 E5
Canbury Medical Centre
KUTN/CMB KT2 .... 9 F2
Canbury School
KUTN/CMB KT2 .... 26 G9
The Canons Leisure Centre
MTCM CR4 .... 44 B5
Capital Business Centre
MTCM CR4 .... 44 B6
SAND/SEL CR2 .... 63 M5
Caplan Estate
MTCM CR4 .... 44 E2
Cardinal Newman Catholic
Primary School
WOT/HER KT12 .... 57 M2
Cardinal Road Infant School
FELT TW13 .... 24 C4
Carew Manor School
WLGTN SM6 .... 62 F2
Carlisle Infant School
HPTN TW12 .... 25 J9
The Carlton Mitre Hotel
E/WMO/HCT KT8 .... 40 E4
Carlyle Business Centre
CHERT KT16 .... 37 L8
Carnwath Road Industrial
Estate
FUL/PGN SW6 .... 19 M8
Carrier Business Park
CRAWE RH10 .... 177 L4
Carshalton AFC
SUT SM1 .... 62 A2
Carshalton College of
Further Education
CAR SM5 .... 62 B2
Carshalton High School
for Boys
CAR SM5 .... 61 P1
Carshalton High School
for Girls
CAR SM5 .... 62 A2
Carshalton War Memorial
Hospital
CAR SM5 .... 62 B4
Carwarden House School
CBLY GU15 .... 69 J5
Casa dei Cesari Hotel
YTLY GU46 .... 67 J4
The Cassel Hospital
RCHPK/HAM TW10 .... 26 C7
Cassidy Medical Centre
FUL/PGN SW6 .... 19 L5
Castle Hill Primary School
CROY/NA CR0 .... 65 J5
Castleview Combined
School
DTCH/LGLY SL3 .... 12 B2
Casualty Plus' Clinic
BTFD TW8 .... 17 J3
The Caterham Dene
Hospital
CTHM CR3 .... 101 P3
Caterham Preparatory
School
CTHM CR3 .... 101 P6
Caterham School
CTHM CR3 .... 101 P6
Catford Cyphers CC
CAT SE6 .... 31 N5
Cator Park School for Girls
BECK BR3 .... 46 E1
Cavendish Primary School
CHSWK W4 .... 18 C5
The Cedars Primary School
HEST TW5 .... 15 M5
Centaurs Business Centre
ISLW TW7 .... 16 C4
Centenary RFC
ISLW TW7 .... 16 F4
Centrale Shopping Centre
CROY/NA CR0 .... 2 C3
Central Estate
ALDT GU11 .... 108 D5
Central London Golf Club
TOOT SW17 .... 28 G3

Central Medical Centre
MRDN SM4 .... 43 N5
Central Sussex College
CRAWE RH10 .... 177 H5
Central Sussex College
(East Grinstead Campus)
EGRIN RH19 .... 180 D2
Centre Court Shopping
Centre
WIM/MER SW19 .... 28 C9
Chaffinch Business Park
BECK BR3 .... 46 D4
Chalk Lane Hotel
EPSOM KT18 .... 78 B4
Chambers Business Park
WDR/YW UB7 .... 14 C4
Chandler Junior School
MFD/CHID GU8 .... 149 M7
Chandlers Field Primary
School
E/WMO/HCT KT8 .... 40 A6
Chandos Business Centre
WLGTN SM6 .... 62 E5
Charing Cross Hospital
HMSMTH W6 .... 19 H4
Charles Darwin School
BH/WHM TN16 .... 84 D4
Charles Kingsleys CE
Primary School
HTWY RG27 .... 48 A9
Charlwood Place
HORL RH6 .... 158 B4
Charlwoods Industrial
Estate
EGRIN RH19 .... 162 D9
Charlwood Village Infant
School
HORL RH6 .... 158 C5
Charrington Bowl
SURB KT6 .... 59 P1
Charterhouse
GODL GU7 .... 131 J7
Charterhouse School
Students Residences
GODL GU7 .... 131 H6
The Charter School
HNHL SE24 .... 30 E1
Charters School
ASC SL5 .... 34 D8
Chartfield School
PUT/ROE SW15 .... 27 N1
Chartham Park Golf Club
EGRIN RH19 .... 162 B6
Chartwell (NT)
BH/WHM TN16 .... 125 K2
Chase Bridge Primary
School
WHTN TW2 .... 25 M2
Chatsworth J & I School
HSLW TW3 .... 16 C9
Cheam Common J & I
School
WPK KT4 .... 60 F1
Cheam Fields Primary
School
CHEAM SM3 .... 61 J4
Cheam High School
CHEAM SM3 .... 61 J3
Cheam Leisure Centre
CHEAM SM3 .... 61 H3
Cheam Park Farm Junior
School
CHEAM SM3 .... 61 H1
Cheam Sports Club
CHEAM SM3 .... 61 J6
Cheapside CE Primary
School
ASC SL5 .... 34 E2
Chelsea Centre & Theatre
WBPTN SW10 .... 19 N5
The Chelsea Club Leisure
Centre
FUL/PGN SW6 .... 19 M4
Chelsea College of Art &
Design
FUL/PGN SW6 .... 19 N7
Chelsea FC
(Stamford Bridge)
FUL/PGN SW6 .... 19 M5
Chelsea Fields Industrial
Estate
WIM/MER SW19 .... 43 P2
Chelsea & Westminster
Hospital
WBPTN SW10 .... 19 N4
Chelsea Wharf
WBPTN SW10 .... 19 P5
Chennestone Community
School
SUN TW16 .... 39 K3
Cherry Lane Primary School
WDR/YW UB7 .... 14 B2
Cherry Lodge Golf Club
BH/WHM TN16 .... 84 E6
Cherry Wood Primary
School
FARN GU14 .... 88 C1
Chertsey Business Centre
CHERT KT16 .... 37 L8
Chertsey Cemetery
CHERT KT16 .... 55 L1
Chertsey Hall
CHERT KT16 .... 37 L8
Chertsey Museum
CHERT KT16 .... 37 L7
Chertsey Recreation Centre
CHERT KT16 .... 37 J9
Chertsey Town FC
CHERT KT16 .... 37 K7
Chessington CC
CHSGTN KT9 .... 59 J6

Chessington Community
College & Sports Centre
CHSGTN KT9 .... 59 K6
Chessington Golf Club
CHSGTN KT9 .... 59 K6
Chessington World of
Adventures
CHSGTN KT9 .... 59 J8
Chestnut Grove School
BAL SW12 .... 29 K4
Chesworth Junior School
SWTR RH13 .... 192 D7
Chiddingfold Golf Club
MFD/CHID GU8 .... 186 A1
Chilworth CE Infant School
RGUE GU4 .... 133 H2
Chinthurst School
KWD/TDW/WH KT20 .... 98 G3
Chipstead Golf Club
COUL/CHIP CR5 .... 80 B7
Chipstead RFC
COUL/CHIP CR5 .... 100 B1
Chipstead Valley Primary
School
COUL/CHIP CR5 .... 80 C5
Chiswick & Bedford Park
Preparatory School
CHSWK W4 .... 18 C2
Chiswick Business Park
CHSWK W4 .... 17 P2
Chiswick Community School
CHSWK W4 .... 18 B5
Chiswick House
CHSWK W4 .... 18 B4
Chobham Common National
Nature Reserve
CHOB/PIR GU24 .... 53 J2
Chobham FC
CHOB/PIR GU24 .... 71 M1
Chobham Golf Club
WOKN/KNAP GU21 .... 71 K4
Chobham RFC
CHOB/PIR GU24 .... 53 L8
Chobham St Lawrence CE
Primary School
CHOB/PIR GU24 .... 53 L9
Christ Church CE Infant
School
NWMAL KT3 .... 42 C4
Christchurch CE Infant
School
VW GU25 .... 35 N4
Christ Church CE Junior
School
NWMAL KT3 .... 42 B4
Christ Church CE Primary
School
BRXS/STRHM SW2 .... 30 A4
BRYLDS KT5 .... 41 N7
FSTH SE23 .... 31 L5
Christchurch Junior School
CHERT KT16 .... 55 H5
Christ Church Primary
School
PUR/KEN CR8 .... 63 K8
Christian Meeting Hall
BECK BR3 .... 46 G2
Christ's College Guildford
GU GU1 .... 112 A2
Christ's College Ski Club
GU GU1 .... 112 A2
Christs School
RCH/KEW TW9 .... 26 E1
Christ the King RC First
School
STWL/WRAY TW19 .... 22 G2
Chrysalis Theatre
BAL SW12 .... 29 K4
Chrysanthemum Clinic
CHSWK W4 .... 18 A5
Church Crookham Junior
School
FLEETS GU52 .... 106 G3
Churchfields Primary
School
BECK BR3 .... 46 B4
Church Hill House Hospital
BRAK RG12 .... 32 C4
Churchill Business Park
BH/WHM TN16 .... 105 M6
Churchill CE Primary
School
BH/WHM TN16 .... 104 D5
Churchill College
RYNPK SW20 .... 42 G3
The Churchill Medical
Centre
KUTN/CMB KT2 .... 9 G3
Churchill Theatre
BMLY BR1 .... 47 N3
Cineworld Cinema
FELT TW13 .... 24 C5
City Business Centre
SWTR RH13 .... 192 C9
The City Business Centre
CRAWW RH11 .... 176 G1
The City of London Academy
EDUL SE22 .... 31 H1
City of London Freemens
School
ASHTD KT21 .... 77 P8
Civic Centre & Bromley
Palace
BMLY BR1 .... 47 P3
Civil Service College
ASC SL5 .... 34 F6
Clandon CE Infant School
RGUE GU4 .... 113 L2
Clandon Park (NT)
RGUE GU4 .... 113 L3
Clandon Regis Golf Club
RGUE GU4 .... 113 M2

Clapham Park School
CLAP SW4 .... **29** N1
Clare House Primary School
BECK BR3 .... **47** J3
Claremont Fan Court School
ESH/CLAY KT10 .... **58** B5
Claremont Landscape
Garden (NT)
ESH/CLAY KT10 .... **58** A6
Clarence Road School
SWTR RH13 .... **192** C9
Clarendon Primary School
ASHF TW15 .... **23** J6
Clarendon Special School
HPTN TW12 .... **25** J9
Claygate Primary School
ESH/CLAY KT10 .... **58** E6
Claypands Hospital
BTFD TW8 .... **17** L2
Clayton Barracks
ALDT GU11 .... **108** F2
Cleves Junior School
WEY KT13 .... **57** H3
Clewborough House School
at Cheswycks
FRIM GU16 .... **89** K2
Clifton Hill School
CTHM CR3 .... **101** M4
Clifton Primary School
NWDGN UB2 .... **15** N2
Clockhouse Industrial
Estate
EBED/NFELT TW14 .... **23** L4
Cobham Bus Museum
COB KT11 .... **74** E1
The Cobham Health Centre
COB KT11 .... **75** K2
Cobham RFC
COB KT11 .... **75** M1
Cody Technology Park
FARN GU14 .... **87** N7
Colet Court
BARN SW13 .... **18** E3
Colgate Primary School
SWTR RH13 .... **193** P4
Coliseum Business Centre
CBLY GU15 .... **68** C5
College Fields Business
Centre
WIM/MER SW19 .... **44** A2
The College of Law
RGUW GU3 .... **112** A9
College of Psychic Studies
SKENS SW7 .... **19** P2
The College of Richard
Collyer
HORS RH12 .... **192** C6
The College of St Barnabas
LING RH7 .... **162** E4
College Town Infant School
SHST GU47 .... **50** A9
College Town Junior School
SHST GU47 .... **50** A9
Collingwood College
CBLY GU15 .... **51** J9
Collingwood Preparatory
School
WLGTN SM6 .... **62** D4
Collis Primary School
TEDD TW11 .... **26** A9
Colnbrook CE Primary
School
DTCH/LGLY SL3 .... **13** H6
Colnbrook Sports Club
DTCH/LGLY SL3 .... **13** K6
Coln Industrial Estate
DTCH/LGLY SL3 .... **13** K5
Coloma Convent Girls
School
CROY/NA CR0 .... **64** D2
Colonnades Leisure Park
CROY/NA CR0 .... **63** J5
Colours Sports Club
SUT SM1 .... **61** N4
Coltwood Business Centre
ALDT GU11 .... **108** D4
Comfort Inn
ECT SW5 .... **19** L2
HYS/HAR UB3 .... **14** C3
Commonwealth Institute
WKENS W14 .... **19** K1
Compton Place Business
Centre
CBLY GU15 .... **68** C4
Concorde Business Park
BH/WHM TN16 .... **84** B4
Coney Hall School
HAYES BR2 .... **65** M1
Connaught Business Centre
CROY/NA CR0 .... **63** H5
MTCM CR4 .... **44** B6
Connaught County Junior
School
BAGS GU19 .... **51** N7
The Connaught School
ASHV GU12 .... **108** G7
Conrad Hotel
WBPTN SW10 .... **19** N6
Consulate General of
Monaco
SKENS SW7 .... **19** P1
Consulate of Burkina Faso
BTSEA SW11 .... **19** N8

The Copthorne Business
Centre
CRAWE RH10 .... **160** C9
Copthorne CE Junior
School
CRAWE RH10 .... **160** C9
Copthorne Fairway Infant
School
CRAWE RH10 .... **160** C9
Copthorne Golf Club
CRAWE RH10 .... **160** D9
Copthorne Hotel
CRAWE RH10 .... **178** B1
Copthorne Hotel & Resort
Effingham Park
CRAWE RH10 .... **160** G8
Copthorne Junior School
CRAWE RH10 .... **160** C9
Copthorne Preparatory
School
CRAWE RH10 .... **160** F9
Copthorne Squash Club
CRAWE RH10 .... **178** B1
Copthorne Tara Hotel
WKENS W14 .... **19** L1
Cordwalles Junior School
CBLY GU15 .... **51** H9
Corinthian Casuals FC
SURB KT6 .... **59** N2
Cornfield School
REDH RH1 .... **140** B1
Corpus Christi RC Primary
School
BRXS/STRHM SW2 .... **30** A1
Corus Hotel
CWTH RG45 .... **49** L4
Cosmic Cycle
HORS RH12 .... **192** A8
Cottesmore Golf & Country
Club
CRAWW RH11 .... **194** B3
Cottesmore School
CRAWW RH11 .... **194** C2
Coulsdon CE Primary
School
COUL/CHIP CR5 .... **81** H7
The Coulsdon Eye Clinic
COUL/CHIP CR5 .... **80** E4
Coulsdon High School
COUL/CHIP CR5 .... **81** K9
Coulsdon Manor Golf Club
COUL/CHIP CR5 .... **81** K9
Coulsdon Sixth Form
College
COUL/CHIP CR5 .... **81** J8
Country Gardens Estate
BFOR GU20 .... **52** C1
County Mail Shopping
Centre
CRAWE RH10 .... **177** H5
County Oak Retail Park
CRAWW RH11 .... **176** G1
Court Farm Industrial
Estate
STWL/WRAY TW19 .... **23** J2
Courtfield Medical Centre
ECT SW5 .... **19** M2
Court Moor School
FLEETS GU52 .... **86** F9
Courtwood Primary School
CROY/NA CR0 .... **64** F8
Cove CC
FARN GU14 .... **88** A3
Cove Infant School
FARN GU14 .... **88** A1
Cove Junior School
FARN GU14 .... **88** A2
Cove School
FARN GU14 .... **88** A2
Coworth Flexlands School
CHOB/PIR GU24 .... **53** M9
Coxmoor Farm Light
Industrial Estate
RFNM GU10 .... **106** B4
Craggy Island Climbing
Centre
GU GU1 .... **112** C1
Cranford Community
College
HEST TW5 .... **15** K4
Cranford Infant School
HSLWW TW4 .... **15** J7
Cranford Junior School
HSLWW TW4 .... **15** K7
Cranford Park Junior School
HYS/HAR UB3 .... **15** H2
Cranleigh Golf and
Leisure Club
CRAN GU6 .... **153** J6
Cranleigh Health Centre
CRAN GU6 .... **170** C1
Cranleigh Infant School
CRAN GU6 .... **153** H9
Cranleigh Leisure Centre
CRAN GU6 .... **170** C1
Cranleigh Preparatory
School
CRAN GU6 .... **152** G8
Cranleigh School
CRAN GU6 .... **152** F7
Cranleigh Village Hospital
CRAN GU6 .... **152** G9
The Cranley Hotel
ECT SW5 .... **19** N3
Cranmer Primary School
MTCM CR4 .... **44** B5
Cranmore School
EHSLY KT24 .... **94** E9
The Craven Clinic
HMSMTH W6 .... **18** F2
Crawley College Annexe
CRAWW RH11 .... **176** F4

Crawley Down CE School
CRAWE RH10 .... **179** J3
Crawley Down Health
Centre
CRAWE RH10 .... **179** H3
Crawley Health Clinic
CRAWE RH10 .... **177** H5
Crawley Hospital
CRAWW RH11 .... **176** F5
The Crawley Lawn Tennis
Club
CRAWE RH10 .... **177** L3
Crawley Leisure Centre
Athletics Arena
CRAWE RH10 .... **177** J6
Crawley Museum
(Goffs Park House)
CRAWW RH11 .... **176** E6
Crawley RFC
CRAWW RH11 .... **176** D1
Crawley Ridge Infant
School
CBLY GU15 .... **69** H1
Crawley Swimming Pool
CRAWE RH10 .... **177** J6
Crawley Town FC
CRAWW RH11 .... **176** F9
Cricket Green School
MTCM CR4 .... **44** A4
Crockham Hill CE Primary
School
EDEN TN8 .... **124** G4
Crofton Leisure Centre
BROCKY SE4 .... **31** P2
Crofton School
BROCKY SE4 .... **31** P2
Croham Hurst Golf Club
SAND/SEL CR2 .... **63** P5
Cromwell Hospital
KENS W8 .... **19** M2
Crondall Primary School
RFNM GU10 .... **106** D8
Crookham CE Infant School
FLEETS GU52 .... **106** F2
Cross Farm Infant School
FRIM GU16 .... **88** G1
Crouch Industrial Estate
LHD/OX KT22 .... **76** G8
Crowne Plaza Hotel
WDR/YW UB7 .... **14** C2
Crown Lane Primary School
WNWD SE27 .... **30** D7
Crown Wood Primary
School
BRAK RG12 .... **32** F7
Crowthorne Business Centre
CWTH RG45 .... **49** N2
Crowthorne CE Primary
School
CWTH RG45 .... **49** M4
Croydon Airport Industrial
Estate
CROY/NA CR0 .... **63** J6
Croydon Bowling Club
SAND/SEL CR2 .... **63** L4
Croydon Cemetery
CROY/NA CR0 .... **45** H6
Croydon Clocktower Cinema
CROY/NA CR0 .... **2** D5
Croydon College
CROY/NA CR0 .... **2** E4
Croydon Crematorium
THHTH CR7 .... **44** C6
Croydon Fairfield Halls
Cinema
CROY/NA CR0 .... **2** E5
Croydon FC
SNWD SE25 .... **46** C6
Croydon High Junior School
Gdst
SAND/SEL CR2 .... **64** B9
Croydon Mosque & Islamic
Centre
THHTH CR7 .... **45** J7
Croydon Road Industrial
Estate
CROY/NA CR0 .... **46** C5
Croydon Sports Arena
SNWD SE25 .... **46** C6
Crystal Palace FC
(Selhurst Park)
SNWD SE25 .... **45** N5
Crystal Palace Museum
NRWD SE19 .... **30** G9
Cuaco Sports Ground
BECK BR3 .... **31** P9
Cuddington Cemetery
WPK KT4 .... **60** F1
Cuddington CP School
WPK KT4 .... **60** D2
Cuddington Croft Primary
School
BELMT SM2 .... **61** H7
Cuddington Golf Club
BNSTD SM7 .... **79** J2
Cudham CE Primary School
BH/WHM TN16 .... **84** E5
Culvers House Primary
School
MTCM CR4 .... **44** C9
Cumnor House School
SAND/SEL CR2 .... **63** K7
Cypress Infant School
SNWD SE25 .... **45** N3
Cypress Junior School
SNWD SE25 .... **45** N3
Cyprus College of Art
WNWD SE27 .... **30** C7
Dairy Meadow Primary
School
NWDGN UB2 .... **15** P1

D'Albiac House
HTHAIR TW6 .... **14** C7
Dalmain Primary School
FSTH SE23 .... **31** M4
Danesfield Manor School
WOT/HER KT12 .... **57** K1
Danes Hill Pre-preparatory
School
LHD/OX KT22 .... **76** C2
Danes Hill School
LHD/OX KT22 .... **76** D3
Danetree School
HOR/WEW KT19 .... **60** A6
Dapdune Wharf (NT)
GU GU1 .... **6** C2
Darell Primary School
RCH/KEW TW9 .... **17** N3
Darley Dene Infant School
ADL/WDHM KT15 .... **55** N4
Darwin Centre
SKENS SW7 .... **19** N1
Darwin Leisure Centre
BH/WHM TN16 .... **84** D5
David Game Tutorial College
SKENS SW7 .... **19** P2
David Livingstone Primary
School
THHTH CR7 .... **45** L2
David Lloyd Leisure Centre
KENS W8 .... **19** M2
Davidson Primary School
CROY/NA CR0 .... **45** P8
Dawnay CP School
GT/LBKH KT23 .... **96** A5
Days Inn Hotel
FLEETN GU51 .... **86** D3
Denbies Wine Estate
RDKG RH5 .... **117** H3
Denmead School
HPTN TW12 .... **40** A1
Desmond Anderson
Primary School
CRAWE RH10 .... **176** G9
De Stafford College
CTHM CR3 .... **101** P1
Deutsche Schule
RCHPK/HAM TW10 .... **26** C4
Devonshire Primary School
BELMT SM2 .... **61** N6
Diana Fountain
E/WMO/HCT KT8 .... **40** F3
Dockwell's Industrial Estate
EBED/NFELT TW14 .... **24** C1
Dogmersfield CE Primary
School
HTWY RG27 .... **86** A8
The Dolphin School
BTSEA SW11 .... **29** H1
Donhead (Wimbledon College
Preparatory School)
WIM/MER SW19 .... **43** H1
Donyngs Recreation Centre
REDH RH1 .... **120** A4
Doods Brow School
REDH RH1 .... **121** H4
Dorchester Primary School
WPK KT4 .... **42** G9
The Dorking Business Park
DORK RH4 .... **116** G6
Dorking Cemetery
DORK RH4 .... **117** J5
Dorking FC (Meadowbank)
DORK RH4 .... **116** G6
Dorking General Hospital
DORK RH4 .... **116** G8
Dorking Golf Club
RDKG RH5 .... **117** J8
Dorking Halls
DORK RH4 .... **117** J6
Dorking Lawn Tennis &
Squash Club
DORK RH4 .... **116** G9
Dorking Museum
DORK RH4 .... **116** G7
Dorking RFC
BRKHM/BTCW RH3 .... **117** P5
Dorking Swimming &
Sports Centre
DORK RH4 .... **117** J6
Dormansland Primary
School
LING RH7 .... **162** G3
Douglas Bader Foundation
PUT/ROE SW15 .... **27** M7
Dovers Green School
REDH RH1 .... **119** N9
Down House
ORP BR6 .... **84** E1
Downsend School-
Ashtead Lodge
ASHTD KT21 .... **77** L7
Downsend School
Epsom Lodge
EW KT17 .... **78** D2
Downsend School
Leatherhead Lodge
LHD/OX KT22 .... **77** J9
Downsview Primary School
NRWD SE19 .... **45** L1
Downs Way CP School
OXTED RH8 .... **103** L7
Drayton House School
GU GU1 .... **7** K2
Drift Golf Club
EHSLY KT24 .... **94** C3
Driving Test Centre
CRAWW RH11 .... **176** G6
Ducks Infant School
DUL SE21 .... **30** G6
Duff Miller College
SKENS SW7 .... **19** N1

Duke of Kent School
CRAN GU6 .... **153** N2
Dulwich College
DUL SE21 .... **30** F4
Dulwich College
Preparatory School
DUL SE21 .... **30** F6
Dulwich College Track
DUL SE21 .... **30** F5
Dulwich Hamlet Junior
School
HNHL SE24 .... **30** E2
Dulwich Medical Centre
EDUL SE22 .... **31** H1
Dulwich Picture Gallery
DUL SE21 .... **30** E3
Dulwich & Sydenham Hill
Golf Club
DUL SE21 .... **31** H5
Dulwich Village CE Infant
School
DUL SE21 .... **30** F2
Dundonald Primary School
WIM/MER SW19 .... **43** K1
Dunnings Squash Club
EGRIN RH19 .... **180** D5
Dunottar School
REIG RH2 .... **119** P6
Dunraven School & Upper
School
STRHM/NOR SW16 .... **30** A6
Dunsfold Aerodrome
CRAN GU6 .... **170** A6
Duppas Junior School
CROY/NA CR0 .... **63** K4
Dysart School
KUTN/CMB KT2 .... **26** C7
Dysart School
SURB KT6 .... **41** L8
Dyslexia Teaching Centre
ECT SW5 .... **19** M3
Eagle House School
SHST GU47 .... **49** L7
Eagle Trading Estate
MTCM CR4 .... **44** B7
Ealing Hammersmith &
West London College
WKENS W14 .... **19** H2
Ealing Park Health Centre
EA W5 .... **17** K2
Ealing Road Trading Estate
BTFD TW8 .... **17** K3
Eardley Primary School
STRHM/NOR SW16 .... **29** M9
Earl's Court Exhibition
Centre
FUL/PGN SW6 .... **19** L3
Earlsfield Primary School
WAND/EARL SW18 .... **28** F5
Earlswood Infant School
REDH RH1 .... **120** C6
Earth Galleries
SKENS SW7 .... **19** P1
East Berkshire College
(Langley Campus)
DTCH/LGLY SL3 .... **12** D1
East Berkshire Golf Club
CWTH RG45 .... **49** J4
East Court
EGRIN RH19 .... **180** E1
Eastern Business Centre
BRAK RG12 .... **32** F3
Eastern Business Park
HTHAIR TW6 .... **15** H7
East Grinstead Health Clinic
EGRIN RH19 .... **180** D1
East Grinstead Sports Club
EGRIN RH19 .... **180** B6
East Horsley Camping &
Caravan Club
EHSLY KT24 .... **94** E4
East Molesey CC
E/WMO/HCT KT8 .... **40** C4
East Sheen Cemetery
RCHPK/HAM TW10 .... **26** F1
East Sheen Primary School
MORT/ESHN SW14 .... **18** C9
East Surrey College
REDH RH1 .... **120** C1
East Surrey Hospital
REDH RH1 .... **120** D8
East Surrey Museum
CTHM CR3 .... **101** P4
Eastwick Infant School
GT/LBKH KT23 .... **96** B4
Eastwick Junior School
GT/LBKH KT23 .... **96** B4
Ebbisham County Infants
School
EPSOM KT18 .... **78** A3
Ebbisham Sports Club
HOR/WEW KT19 .... **78** A1
Ecclesbourne Primary
School
THHTH CR7 .... **45** L6
Echelford Primary School
ASHF TW15 .... **23** L8
Eclipse Estate
HOR/WEW KT19 .... **78** A2
Eden Walk & District Mar
Memorial Hospital
EDEN TN8 .... **144** G6
Edenbridge Golf & Country
Club
EDEN TN8 .... **144** E5
Edenbridge Leisure Centre
EDEN TN8 .... **144** G5
The Edenbridge Medical
Centre
EDEN TN8 .... **144** G5
Edenbridge Primary School
EDEN TN8 .... **144** G4

Edenham High School
CROY/NA CR0 .... 46 E8
Eden High School
FUL/PGN SW6 .... 19 K6
Eden Medical Centre
WKENS W14 .... 19 K2
Edenvale Child Health Clinic
MTCM CR4 .... 44 C1
Eden Walk Shopping Centre
KUT/HW KT1 .... 8 D5
Edes Business Park
WLGTN SM6 .... 62 C1
Edgeborrow School
CWTH RG45 .... 49 M6
Edgebarrow Sports Centre
CWTH RG45 .... 49 N6
Edgeborough School
RFNM GU10 .... 146 F1
The Edge Sports Centre
HASM GU27 .... 183 N2
Edward Pauling School
FELT TW13 .... 23 P5
Eelmoor Road Depot Trading Estate
FARN GU14 .... 88 C3
Effingham Community Sports Centre
EHSLY KT24 .... 95 N7
Effingham CC
EHSLY KT24 .... 95 K4
Effingham Golf Club
EHSLY KT24 .... 95 M8
Effingham Park Golf Club
CRAWE RH10 .... 160 G8
Effra Road Retail Park
BRXS/STRHM SW2 .... 30 B1
Egham Business Village
ECH TW20 .... 36 C3
Egham CC
ECH TW20 .... 21 N9
Egham Sports Centre
ECH TW20 .... 21 N9
Egham Town FC
ECH TW20 .... 21 P9
Electrical Trades Union College
ESH/CLAY KT10 .... 58 A3
The Electric Theatre
GU GU1 .... 6 D5
Elers Clinic
HYS/HAR UB3 .... 14 F2
Eliot Bank Primary School
FSTH SE23 .... 31 J5
Elizabeth Barracks
CHOB/PIR GU24 .... 90 A1
The Elizabeth Johnson Organisation
LIPH GU30 .... 182 A2
Ellingham Primary School
CHSGTN KT9 .... 59 K6
Elliott Industrial Park
ASHV GU12 .... 108 C4
Elliott School
PUT/ROE SW15 .... 27 P2
Elmbridge Leisure Centre
WOT/HER KT12 .... 39 K6
Elmbridge Museum
WEY KT13 .... 56 C3
Elm Court School
WNWD SE27 .... 30 C5
Elm House Business Centre
MFD/CHID GU8 .... 129 P9
Elmhurst School
SAND/SEL CR2 .... 63 M3
The Elmsleigh Centre Shopping Precinct
STA TW18 .... 22 C7
Elmwood Primary School
CROY/NA CR0 .... 45 K8
Elm Wood Primary School
DUL SE21 .... 30 E6
Elthorne Park High School
HNWL W7 .... 16 F1
Elthorne Sports Centre
HNWL W7 .... 16 F1
The Eivetham
HTWY RG27 .... 86 A2
Emanuel School
BTSEA SW11 .... 28 C1
Embassy of Armenia
KENS W8 .... 19 M1
Embassy of Bahrain
SKENS SW7 .... 19 N1
Embassy of Bulgaria
SKENS SW7 .... 19 N1
Embassy of Guatemala
WBPTN SW10 .... 19 M4
Embassy of Iraq
SKENS SW7 .... 19 N2
Embassy of Morocco
SKENS SW7 .... 19 N2
Embassy of Oman
SKENS SW7 .... 19 N1
Embassy of Paraguay
SKENS SW7 .... 19 M1
Embassy of Thailand
SKENS SW7 .... 19 N1
Embassy of the Holy See
WIM/MER SW19 .... 27 P6
Embassy of the Republic of Gabon
SKENS SW7 .... 19 N1
Embassy of Yemen
SKENS SW7 .... 19 P2
Emberhurst School
ESH/CLAY KT10 .... 40 D8
Ember Sports Club
ESH/CLAY KT10 .... 40 C9
Emerson College
FROW RH18 .... 181 N8
Emmetts Garden (NT)
RSEV TN14 .... 125 P1

Endsleigh Industrial Estate
NWDGN UB2 .... 15 N2
Englefield Green Infant School
EGH TW20 .... 21 H8
English National Ballet School
WBPTN SW10 .... 19 N5
Ensham Secondary School
TOOT SW17 .... 29 J8
Enterprise Industrial Estate
ASHV GU12 .... 89 H8
Epsom Bowls
EPSOM KT18 .... 78 C3
Epsom Business Park
EW KT17 .... 60 C9
Epsom Cemetery
EPSOM KT18 .... 78 C3
Epsom College
EW KT17 .... 78 E3
Epsom County & Magistrates Court
EPSOM KT18 .... 78 B2
Epsom Downs Racecourse
EPSOM KT18 .... 78 A7
Epsom & Ewell High School
HOR/WEW KT19 .... 60 A5
Epsom General Hospital
EPSOM KT18 .... 78 A4
Epsom Golf Club
EW KT17 .... 78 E4
Epsom Health Clinic
EPSOM KT18 .... 78 C2
Epsom Primary School
HOR/WEW KT19 .... 60 B9
Epsom Sports Club
EPSOM KT18 .... 78 B4
Eridge House Preparatory School
FUL/PGN SW6 .... 19 K7
Ernest Bevin College
TOOT SW17 .... 29 H6
Esher CE High School
ESH/CLAY KT10 .... 58 A2
Esher Church Primary School
ESH/CLAY KT10 .... 58 C5
Esher College
THDIT KT7 .... 40 E8
Esher RFC
WOT/HER KT12 .... 57 N1
Essendene Lodge School
CTHM CR3 .... 101 P2
Estcots CP School
EGRIN RH19 .... 180 F2
Eversley CC
HTWY RG27 .... 48 D9
Eversley Medical Centre
CROY/NA CR0 .... 45 J7
Evolution House
RCH/KEW TW9 .... 17 L7
Ewell Athletics Track
HOR/WEW KT19 .... 60 B5
Ewell Castle Junior School
EW KT17 .... 60 D7
Ewell Castle School
EW KT17 .... 60 D7
Ewell Grove Infant School
EW KT17 .... 60 D7
Ewhurst CE Infant School
CRAN GU6 .... 153 N7
Express by Holiday Inn
CROY/NA CR0 .... 2 C4
Fairchildes Primary School
CROY/NA CR0 .... 83 L1
Fairfax Industrial Estate
ASHV GU12 .... 108 G4
Fairfield Medical Centre
GT/LBKH KT23 .... 96 B6
Fairfield Trade Park
KUT/HW KT1 .... 9 C7
Fairholme Primary School
EBED/NFELT TW14 .... 23 N4
Fairlawn Primary School
FSTH SE23 .... 31 K3
Fairoaks Airport
CHOB/PIR GU24 .... 54 D9
Fairview Industrial Estate
OXTED RH8 .... 123 N4
Fairview Medical Centre
STRHM/NOR SW16 .... 44 G2
Falconbrook Primary School
BTSEA SW11 .... 19 P7
Falcon Hotel
FARN GU14 .... 88 E6
Falkner House School
SKENS SW7 .... 19 N3
Farleigh Court Golf Club
WARL CR6 .... 82 C1
Farleigh Primary School
WARL CR6 .... 82 D6
Farleigh Rovers FC
WARL CR6 .... 82 A6
Farlington School
HORS RH12 .... 191 J4
Farm Lane Trading Estate
FUL/PGN SW6 .... 19 L4
Farnborough Aerospace Centre
FARN GU14 .... 88 B7
Farnborough Airport
FARN GU14 .... 88 B6
Farnborough Business Centre
FARN GU14 .... 88 B5
Farnborough College of Technology
FARN GU14 .... 88 D7
FARN GU14 .... 88 E5

Farnborough Gate Retail Park
FARN GU14 .... 68 E9
Farnborough Grange Infants School
FARN GU14 .... 68 C8
Farnborough Hill School
FARN GU14 .... 88 E1
Farnborough Recreation Centre
FARN GU14 .... 88 D4
Farnborough RFC
FARN GU14 .... 88 C1
Farnborough Town FC
FARN GU14 .... 68 C8
Farncombe CC
GODL GU7 .... 131 M6
Farncombe CE Infant School
GODL GU7 .... 131 L6
Farrell House Medical Centre
HSLW TW3 .... 16 B6
Farnham Business Centre
FNM GU9 .... 4 D7
Farnham Business Park
FNM GU9 .... 4 D7
Farnham Castle Keep
FNM GU9 .... 5 H6
Farnham College
FNM GU9 .... 5 H6
Farnham Golf Club
RFNM GU10 .... 128 F3
Farnham Health Centre
FNM GU9 .... 5 G2
Farnham Heath End School
FNM GU9 .... 108 A8
Farnham Hospital
FNM GU9 .... 128 A2
Farnham House Hotel
RFNM GU10 .... 126 C5
Farnham Museum
FNM GU9 .... 4 E4
Farnham Park Golf Club
FNM GU9 .... 127 M1
Farnham Retail Park
FNM GU9 .... 128 A2
Farnham Road Hospital
GUW GU2 .... 6 B6
Farnham Sports Centre
FNM GU9 .... 5 H3
Farnham Trading Estate
FNM GU9 .... 128 B1
Faygate Business Centre
HORS RH12 .... 193 L1
Featherstone High School
NWDGN UB2 .... 15 M2
Featherstone Road Health Clinic
NWDGN UB2 .... 15 N1
Felbridge Primary School
EGRIN RH19 .... 161 N8
Felnex Trading Estate
WLGTN SM6 .... 62 C1
Feltham Airparcs Leisure Centre
FELT TW13 .... 24 E5
Feltham Athletics Arena
EBED/NFELT TW14 .... 24 B3
Felthambrook Industrial Estate
FELT TW13 .... 24 C6
Feltham Community College
FELT TW13 .... 24 D5
Feltham Hill Infant School
FELT TW13 .... 24 A6
Feltham Hill Junior School
FELT TW13 .... 24 A6
Feltham & Hounslow Boro FC
EBED/NFELT TW14 .... 24 B3
Feltham Superbowl
FELT TW13 .... 24 C5
Feltonfleet School
COB KT11 .... 74 C2
Fenstanton J & I School
BRXS/STRHM SW2 .... 30 B4
Fernhill Primary School
FARN GU14 .... 68 B7
Fernhill School
FARN GU14 .... 68 B7
Fernhill Tutors
FLEETN GU51 .... 87 J3
Ferrier Industrial Estate
WAND/EARL SW18 .... 19 M9
Fetcham Social & Sports Club
LHD/OX KT22 .... 96 E1
Fetcham Village Infant School
LHD/OX KT22 .... 96 D2
Fielding Primary School
WEA W13 .... 17 H1
Film House Cinema
RCH/KEW TW9 .... 26 C1
Finchampstead CE Primary School
EWKG RG40 .... 48 C6
Finchampstead Sports Club
EWKG RG40 .... 48 C6
Finns Industrial Park
FARN GU14 .... 106 B4
Finton House School
TOOT SW17 .... 29 J5
Fircroft Primary School
TOOT SW17 .... 29 J5
First Quarter Business Park
HOR/WEW KT19 .... 60 C9
Fishing Club House
FROW RH18 .... 180 G8

Five Ways Business Centre
FELT TW13 .... 24 C6
Fleet Business Park
FLEETS GU52 .... 107 H3
Fleet Community Hospital
FLEETN GU51 .... 86 E5
Fleet CC
FLEETN GU51 .... 86 E7
Fleet Infant School
FLEETS GU52 .... 87 H8
Fleet Town FC
FLEETN GU51 .... 86 E7
Flora Gardens Primary School
HMSMTH W6 .... 18 F2
Flutters Leisure Centre
FUL/PGN SW6 .... 19 L5
Folly Hill Infant School
FNM GU9 .... 107 L8
Follys End Christian High School
SNWD SE25 .... 45 N7
Fonthill Lodge School
EGRIN RH19 .... 180 B5
Fontigarry Farm Business Park
REIG RH2 .... 139 N5
The Foot Clinic
WIM/MER SW19 .... 28 B9
The Foot Health Centre
COUL/CHIP CR5 .... 80 F4
Fordbridge Medical Centre
ASHF TW15 .... 23 J7
Fordwater Trading Estate
CHERT KT16 .... 37 N9
Forestdale Primary School
CROY/NA CR0 .... 64 E7
Forest End Medical Centre
BRAK RG12 .... 32 D7
Foresters Primary School
WLGTN SM6 .... 62 F5
Forest Hill Business Centre
FSTH SE23 .... 31 K5
Forest Hill Industrial Estate
FSTH SE23 .... 31 K5
Forest Hill School
FSTH SE23 .... 31 L6
Forest Hill Pools
SYD SE26 .... 31 K5
Forest Row Business Park
FROW RH18 .... 181 L8
Forest Row CE Infant School
FROW RH18 .... 181 L9
Forest Row CE Primary School
FROW RH18 .... 181 L9
The Forest School
SWTR RH13 .... 192 E9
Forge Close Clinic
HAYES BR2 .... 47 N9
Forge Lane Primary School
FELT TW13 .... 24 F9
Forge Wood Industrial Estate
CRAWE RH10 .... 177 L1
Four Elms Primary School
EDEN TN8 .... 125 M9
Foxbridge Golf Club
BIL RH14 .... 187 P9
Fox Hill Primary School
BRAK RG12 .... 32 D6
Foxhills Club & Resort
CHERT KT16 .... 54 D3
Franciscan Primary School
TOOT SW17 .... 29 K7
Franklin Industrial Estate
PGE/AN SE20 .... 46 C2
Freehold Industrial Centre
HSLWW TW4 .... 24 D1
Freemantles School
CHERT KT16 .... 37 J8
Frensham Common & Country Park
RFNM GU10 .... 147 H6
Frensham Heights School
RFNM GU10 .... 146 D2
Frensham Pond Hotel
RFNM GU10 .... 146 F8
Frensham Pond Sailing Club
RFNM GU10 .... 146 F7
The Friary Centre
GU GU1 .... 6 D5
Frimley Business Park
FARN GU14 .... 68 D8
Frimley CE Junior School
FRIM GU16 .... 68 C9
Frimley Green Medical Centre
FRIM GU16 .... 89 H1
Frimley Park Hospital
CBLY GU15 .... 68 F6
Frogmore Community School
YTLY GU46 .... 67 K3
Frogmore County Infant School
BLKW GU17 .... 67 M4
Frogmore Junior School
BLKW GU17 .... 67 M3
Fulham Cemetery
FUL/PGN SW6 .... 19 H5
Fulham Clinic
FUL/PGN SW6 .... 19 K4
Fulham Cross Secondary School
FUL/PGN SW6 .... 19 H5
Fulham FC (Craven Cottage)
PUT/ROE SW15 .... 18 G6
Fulham Medical Centre
FUL/PGN SW6 .... 19 M5

Fulham Palace
FUL/PGN SW6 .... 19 H7
Fulham Preparatory School
FUL/PGN SW6 .... 19 J7
WKENS W14 .... 19 J4
Fulham Prep School
FUL/PGN SW6 .... 19 J7
Fulham Primary School
FUL/PGN SW6 .... 19 L4
Fullbrook School
ADL/WDHM KT15 .... 55 L9
Fuller Smith & Turner Sports Club
CHSWK W4 .... 18 C6
Fulwell Golf Club
HPTN TW12 .... 25 L7
Furzedown Primary School
TOOT SW17 .... 29 L9
Furzefield Primary School
REDH RH1 .... 100 F8
Gaflac Sports Ground Pavilion
SUN TW16 .... 39 J2
Garden Centre
CRAWE RH10 .... 160 G7
Gardener Industrial Estate
SYD SE26 .... 31 M8
Garden Primary School
MTCM CR4 .... 44 F4
Garfield Primary School
WIM/MER SW19 .... 28 F9
Garratt Park Secondary Special School
WAND/EARL SW18 .... 28 E6
Garth Hill College
BNFD RG42 .... 32 E2
Garth Primary School
MRDN SM4 .... 43 P6
The Garth Road Industrial Centre
MRDN SM4 .... 42 G8
Gateway Business Centre
SYD SE26 .... 31 M9
Gatton Manor Hotel Golf & Country Club
RDKG RH5 .... 172 G1
Gatton Park Business Centre
REDH RH1 .... 120 D1
Gatton School
TOOT SW17 .... 29 H7
Gatwick Airport
HORL RH6 .... 159 J5
Gatwick Gate Industrial Estate
HORL RH6 .... 159 H7
Gatwick Industrial Estate
HORL RH6 .... 158 C6
Gatwick Manor Golf Club
CRAWE RH10 .... 159 H3
Gatwick Medical Centre
HORL RH6 .... 159 L5
Gatwick Moat House Hotel
HORL RH6 .... 159 H3
Gatwick Park Hospital
HORL RH6 .... 159 H2
Gatwick Worth Hotel
CRAWE RH10 .... 178 A4
Genesis Business Centre
SWTR RH13 .... 192 E7
Genesis Business Park
WOKN/KNAP GU21 .... 72 G4
George Abbot School
GU GU1 .... 112 E3
Georgian House Hotel
HASM GU27 .... 184 E3
Gibbs Green Special School
WKENS W14 .... 19 K3
Gilbert Scott Primary School
SAND/SEL CR2 .... 64 E6
The Glades Shopping Centre
BMLY BR1 .... 47 N3
Glebelands School
CRAN GU6 .... 152 C9
Glebe School
WWKM BR4 .... 47 K9
Gleen Lecky Health Centre
PUT/ROE SW15 .... 19 H9
Glenbrook Primary School
CLAP SW4 .... 29 N2
Glendower Preparatory School
SKENS SW7 .... 19 N2
Glenesk School
EHSLY KT24 .... 94 F5
Glenlyn Medical Centre
E/WMO/HCT KT8 .... 40 C6
Glenthorne High School
CHEAM SM3 .... 43 L9
Glyn Technology School
EW KT17 .... 60 D9
Goal Farm Golf Club
CHOB/PIR GU24 .... 90 D1
The Godalming Badminton Club
GODL GU7 .... 150 C2
Godalming Business Centre
GODL GU7 .... 131 M9
Godalming College
GODL GU7 .... 150 C2
Godalming County Junior School
GODL GU7 .... 131 M8
Godalming & Guildford FC
GODL GU7 .... 131 N7
Godalming Leisure Centre
GODL GU7 .... 131 N6
Godalming Museum
GODL GU7 .... 131 K9
Godolphin & Latymer School
HMSMTH W6 .... 18 F2

Godstone Farm
  HORS RH9 ....122 C4
Godstone Village School
  GDST RH9 ....122 B3
Goethe Institute
  SKENS SW7 ....19 P1
Goldhawk Industrial Estate
  SHB W12 ....18 F1
Goldsworth CP School
  WOKN/KNAP GU21 ....72 A7
Goldsworth Park Health
  Centre
  WOKN/KNAP GU21 ....71 N6
Goldsworth Park Trading
  Estate
  WOKN/KNAP GU21 ....71 N5
Goldsworth Rd Industrial
  Estate
  WOKN/KNAP GU21 ....10 A4
Golf Driving Range
  REDH RH1 ....120 C8
Gonville Primary School
  THHTH CR7 ....45 H6
Goodrich J & I School
  EDUL SE22 ....31 H2
Good Shepherd RC Primary
  School
  CROY/NA CR0 ....65 H6
Gordonbrock Primary
  School
  BROCKY SE4 ....31 P1
Gordons School
  CHOB/PIR GU24 ....70 C1
Gorringe Park Primary
  School
  MTCM CR4 ....44 C2
Gorse Ride Infant School
  EWKG RG40 ....48 C2
Gorse Ride Junior School
  EWKG RG40 ....48 C3
Gosbury Hill Health Centre
  CHSGTN KT9 ....59 L3
Gosden House School
  SHGR GU5 ....132 C5
Gossops Green Clinic
  CRAWW RH11 ....176 C7
Gossops Green Community
  Primary School
  CRAWW RH11 ....176 D6
Grace Business Centre
  MTCM CR4 ....44 B7
Grafham Grange School
  SHGR GU5 ....151 N4
Granard Primary School
  PUT/ROE SW15 ....27 N2
Grand Avenue Primary
  School
  BRYLDS KT5 ....42 A8
The Grange Community
  Infant School
  ADL/WDHM KT15 ....55 K8
Grange Community Junior
  School
  FARN GU14 ....68 B8
The Grange Hotel
  BRAK RG12 ....32 E3
Grange Strathmore Hotel
  SKENS SW7 ....19 N1
Granton Primary School
  STRHM/NOR SW16 ....44 E1
Grasshoppers RFC
  ISLW TW7 ....16 F4
Grassroots School
  HPTN TW12 ....40 A2
Graveney School
  TOOT SW17 ....29 L9
Grayshott CE Primary
  School
  GSHT GU26 ....165 L8
Grayshott Clinic
  GSHT GU26 ....165 L7
Grayswood CE Aided Infant
  School
  HASM GU27 ....166 C9
Great Bookham County
  Infant School
  GT/LBKH KT23 ....96 A6
Great Hollands Health
  Centre
  BRAK RG12 ....32 B7
Great Hollands Primary
  School
  BRAK RG12 ....32 A6
Great Hollands Recreation
  Centre
  EWKG RG40 ....32 A9
Great West Trading Estate
  BTFD TW8 ....17 H4
Greenacre School for Girls
  BNSTD SM7 ....79 N2
Green Business Centre
  EGH TW20 ....21 P7
Green Dragon Primary
  School
  BTFD TW8 ....17 L3
Green Field Effective
  Education
  EGRIN RH19 ....180 C2
Greenfield School
  WOKS/MYFD GU22 ....10 C7
Green Lane Primary School
  WPK KT4 ....42 F8
Greenmead Primary School
  PUT/ROE SW15 ....27 N1
The Green School for Girls
  ISLW TW7 ....16 G5
Greenshaw High School
  SUT SM1 ....61 N1
Greenvale Primary School
  SAND/SEL CR2 ....64 D9
Greenvale School
  FSTH SE23 ....31 M6

Greenway School
  HORS RH12 ....192 A7
Green Wrythe Primary
  School
  CAR SM5 ....43 P7
Gresham Industrial Estate
  ASHV GU12 ....108 G4
Gresham Primary School
  SAND/SEL CR2 ....81 P1
Greville Primary School
  ASHTD KT21 ....77 M6
Grey Court School
  RCHPK/HAM TW10 ....26 C6
Grist Memorial Sports Club
  E/WMO/HCT KT8 ....40 E6
Grovebell Industrial Estate
  RFNM GU10 ....127 K6
Grove CP School
  FRIM GU16 ....68 G6
Grove House
  (Froebel College)
  PUT/ROE SW15 ....27 L2
Grove House Primary
  School for Deaf Children
  WNWD SE27 ....30 C5
Grovelands School
  WOT/HER KT12 ....39 K7
Grove Park Primary School
  CHSWK W4 ....18 A4
Grove Road Primary School
  HSLW TW3 ....16 A9
The Groves Medical Centre
  NWMAL KT3 ....42 C4
Grove Village Medical Centre
  EBED/NFELT TW14 ....23 P4
Guards Polo Club
  EGH TW20 ....35 K2
Guildford Business Park
  GUW GU2 ....6 A1
Guildford Castle
  GU GU1 ....7 F6
Guildford Cathedral
  GUW GU2 ....6 A3
Guildford College
  (Merrow Wood Campus)
  RGUW GU3 ....91 J8
Guildford College
  (Stoke Park Campus)
  GU GU1 ....7 F1
Guildford County School
  GUW GU2 ....6 B6
Guildford Crematorium
  GODL GU7 ....131 P5
Guildford Cricket Ground
  (Surrey CCC)
  GU GU1 ....6 D2
Guildford Discovery
  GU GU1 ....7 F5
Guildford Golf Club
  GU GU1 ....112 G5
Guildford Grove Primary
  School
  GUW GU2 ....111 L5
Guildford High School
  GU GU1 ....7 G3
Guildford Hockey & CC
  GU GU1 ....6 D3
Guildford House Gallery
  GU GU1 ....7 F6
Guildford Industrial Estate
  GUW GU2 ....111 N4
Guildford Lido
  GU GU1 ....7 F1
Guildford Museum
  GU GU1 ....6 E6
Guildford Natural
  Health Centre
  GU GU1 ....6 E6
The Guildford Nuffield
  Hospital
  GUW GU2 ....111 L5
Guildford Road Industrial
  Estate
  FNM GU9 ....5 K1
Guildford Rowing Club
  GU GU1 ....112 B8
Guildford Spectrum
  GU GU1 ....112 C4
Guildford Spectrum
  Athletics Stadium
  GU GU1 ....112 C3
Guillemont County Junior
  School
  BLKW GU17 ....87 N1
Gumley House Convent
  School
  ISLW TW7 ....16 G8
Gunnersbury Catholic
  School
  BTFD TW8 ....17 J3
Gunnersbury Park Museum
  ACT W3 ....17 N1
Hackbridge Primary School
  WLGTN SM6 ....44 C9
Hakim Qureshi Clinic
  NWDGN UB2 ....15 N1
Hale Primary School
  FNM GU9 ....107 M7
Haling Manor High School
  SAND/SEL CR2 ....63 K6
Hall Grove Farm Industrial
  Estate
  BAGS GU19 ....51 P4
Hall Grove School
  BAGS GU19 ....52 A4
Halliford Health Clinic
  SHPTN TW17 ....38 G5
Halliford School
  SHPTN TW17 ....38 E8

Halls Business Centre
  HYS/HAR UB3 ....15 J1
Hall School Wimbledon
  RYNPK SW20 ....43 H2
Hall School Wimbledon
  Junior Department
  PUT/ROE SW15 ....27 M6
Halsford Park Primary
  School
  EGRIN RH19 ....180 A1
Halstead Preparatory
  School
  WOKN/KNAP GU21 ....72 D4
Ham Health Clinic
  RCHPK/HAM TW10 ....26 B6
Ham House (NT)
  RCHPK/HAM TW10 ....26 B4
Hamilton Road Industrial
  Estate
  WNWD SE27 ....30 E7
Hammersmith Apollo
  HMSMTH W6 ....18 G3
Hammersmith Cemetery
  HMSMTH W6 ....19 H3
Hammersmith Industrial
  Estate
  HMSMTH W6 ....18 G4
Hammersmith
  New Cemetery
  RCH/KEW TW9 ....17 P7
Hammersmith Palais
  HMSMTH W6 ....18 G2
Hammersmith Physio &
  Sports Injury Clinic
  HMSMTH W6 ....18 G2
Hammersmith & West
  London College
  WKENS W14 ....19 J2
Hammerwood Park
  EGRIN RH19 ....181 P1
Hammond Junior School
  LTWR GU18 ....52 A8
Ham & Petersham CC
  RCHPK/HAM TW10 ....26 C7
Hampton Cemetery
  HPTN TW12 ....40 A1
Hampton Community
  College
  HPTN TW12 ....25 H8
Hampton Court House
  School
  E/WMO/HCT KT8 ....40 E3
Hampton Court Palace
  E/WMO/HCT KT8 ....40 F4
Hampton Court Palace
  Golf Club
  SURB KT6 ....41 J6
Hampton Farm Industrial
  Estate
  FELT TW13 ....24 F6
Hampton FC
  HPTN TW12 ....40 B2
Hampton Hill Junior School
  HPTN TW12 ....25 K8
Hampton Infant School
  HPTN TW12 ....39 P1
Hampton Junior School
  HPTN TW12 ....40 A2
The Hampton Medical
  Centre
  HPTN TW12 ....40 A1
Hampton Open Air Pool
  HPTN TW12 ....40 C1
Hampton Road Industrial
  Park
  CROY/NA CR0 ....45 L7
Hampton School
  HPTN TW12 ....25 H8
Hampton Wick Infant School
  KUT/HW KT1 ....8 A1
Hamsey Green Infant School
  WARL CR6 ....82 B5
Hamsey Green Junior School
  WARL CR6 ....82 B5
Handcross Park School
  RHWH RH17 ....194 G8
Handcross Primary School
  RHWH RH17 ....194 F9
Hankley Common Golf Club
  RFNM GU10 ....147 N3
Hanworth Business Park
  CHERT KT16 ....37 K9
Hanworth Trading Estate
  FELT TW13 ....24 F6
Harlington Centre
  FLEETN GU51 ....86 F7
Harlington Community
  School
  HYS/HAR UB3 ....14 F2
Harmans Water J & I School
  BRAK RG12 ....32 G6
Harris City Technology
  College
  NRWD SE19 ....45 P2
Harrodian School
  BARN SW13 ....18 D5
Hart Shopping Centre
  FLEETN GU51 ....86 F6
Hart Sports Centre
  FLEETN GU51 ....86 C7
Harven School of English
  WOKS/MYFD GU22 ....11 G4
Haseltine Primary School
  SYD SE26 ....31 N7
Haslemere Hall
  HASM GU27 ....184 D3
Haslemere Hospital &
  Health Centre
  HASM GU27 ....184 E3
Haslemere Industrial Estate
  EBED/NFELT TW14 ....24 B1
  WAND/EARL SW18 ....28 E5

Haslemere Museum
  HASM GU27 ....184 E3
Haslemere Primary School
  MTCM CR4 ....43 P5
Hastings Clinic
  BRXS/STRHM SW2 ....30 A1
Hatchlands Park (NT)
  RGUE GU4 ....114 B1
Hatch Ride Primary School
  CWTH RG45 ....49 M2
Hatfield Primary School
  MRDN SM4 ....43 J7
Havelock Primary School
  NWDGN UB2 ....15 P1
Havenbury Industrial
  Estate
  DORK RH4 ....116 G6
Hawes Down Clinic
  WWKM BR4 ....65 K1
Hawes Down Primary
  School
  WWKM BR4 ....47 K9
Hawkedale Gm School
  SUN TW16 ....39 H4
The Hawker Centre
  KUTN/CMB KT2 ....26 C8
Hawkins Clinic
  EW KT17 ....78 C4
  PUT/ROE SW15 ....19 H9
  RYNPK SW20 ....42 D2
Hawley CP School
  BLKW GU17 ....68 A5
Hawley Lane Industrial
  Estate
  FARN GU14 ....68 D8
Hawley Place School
  BLKW GU17 ....68 A7
The Hawthorns School
  REDH RH1 ....121 K2
The Hawth Theatre, Cinema
  & Conference Complex
  CRAWE RH10 ....177 J6
Hayes Grove Priory Hospital
  HAYES BR2 ....65 N1
Hayes Primary School
  HAYES BR2 ....47 P9
The Hayes Primary School
  PUR/KEN CR8 ....81 K5
Hayes School
  HAYES BR2 ....65 P1
Haysbridge Business Centre
  GDST RH9 ....142 C7
Hazelwick School
  CRAWE RH10 ....177 K3
Hazelwood School
  OXTED RH8 ....123 N2
Headley Park Country Club
  BOR GU35 ....164 A2
Headstart Montessori
  School
  TOOT SW17 ....28 F6
Heath Business Centre
  HSLW TW3 ....16 C9
  REDH RH1 ....140 D6
Heathcote Medical Centre
  KWD/TDW/WH KT20 ....99 H2
Heathermount the
  Learning Centre
  ASC SL5 ....34 D7
Heather Ridge County
  Infant School
  CBLY GU15 ....69 M4
Heatherside Junior School
  FLEETS GU52 ....86 F7
Heatherside Schools
  FLEETS GU52 ....86 G8
Heatherwood Hospital
  ASC SL5 ....33 N4
Heathfield Primary School
  WHTN TW2 ....25 H4
Heathfield School
  ASC SL5 ....33 K3
The Heathland School
  HSLWW TW4 ....24 C2
Heathmere Primary School
  PUT/ROE SW15 ....27 M4
Heathpark Golf Club
  WDR/YW UB7 ....14 C1
Heathrow Airport
  HTHAIR TW6 ....14 D7
Heathrow Airport Central
  Bus & Coach Station
  HTHAIR TW6 ....14 C8
Heathrow International
  Trading Estate
  HSLWW TW4 ....15 K8
Heathrow Medical Centre
  HYS/HAR UB3 ....14 F3
Heathrow Primary School
  WDR/YW UB7 ....14 B4
Heathrow Terminal 5
  (under construction)
  HTHAIR TW6 ....13 N8
Heathrow World Cargo
  Centre
  HTHAIR TW6 ....23 J1
Heathside School
  WEY KT13 ....56 B4
Heavers Farm Primary
  School
  SNWD SE25 ....45 P6
Heber Primary School
  EDUL SE22 ....30 G2
Heliport Industrial Estate
  BTSEA SW11 ....19 P7
Helix Business Park
  CBLY GU15 ....68 D5
Helston Court Business
  Centre
  WIM/MER SW19 ....27 N8
Henderson Hospital
  BELMT SM2 ....61 L7

Henry Cavendish Primary
  School
  BAL SW12 ....29 M4
Henry Compton School
  FUL/PGN SW6 ....19 H5
Henry Tyndale School
  FARN GU14 ....88 E1
Hermitage County First
  School
  WOKN/KNAP GU21 ....71 L8
The Hermitage School
  WOKN/KNAP GU21 ....71 L8
Herne Hill School
  HNHL SE24 ....30 D1
Herne Hill Stadium
  (Cycle Centre)
  HNHL SE24 ....30 E2
The Herons Swimming &
  Fitness Centre
  HASM GU27 ....184 A6
Heron Way Primary School
  SWTR RH13 ....192 F9
Hersham Trading Estate
  WOT/HER KT12 ....57 N1
Heston Community School
  HEST TW5 ....16 A5
Heston Community Sports
  Hall
  HEST TW5 ....16 A5
Heston Industrial Mall
  HEST TW5 ....15 P5
Heston Infant School
  HEST TW5 ....16 A5
Heston Junior School
  HEST TW5 ....16 A4
Heston Park CC
  HEST TW5 ....15 P4
Heston Swimming Baths
  HEST TW5 ....15 P4
Hever Castle and Gardens
  EDEN TN8 ....145 P6
Hever Castle Golf Club
  EDEN TN8 ....145 P4
Hever CE Primary School
  EDEN TN8 ....145 P7
Hewitts Industrial Estate
  CRAN GU6 ....152 E9
Highclere Hotel
  ASC SL5 ....34 G4
High Commission of
  Bangladesh
  SKENS SW7 ....19 N1
High Commission of
  Dominica
  ECT SW5 ....19 M2
High Commission of
  Grenada
  ECT SW5 ....19 M3
Highfield Infant School
  HAYES BR2 ....47 M5
Highfield Junior School
  HAYES BR2 ....47 L5
Highfield School
  LIPH GU30 ....183 H8
  WAND/EARL SW18 ....29 H3
High View Primary School
  BTSEA SW11 ....19 P9
Highview Primary School
  WLGTN SM6 ....62 G4
Hillbrook Primary School
  TOOT SW17 ....29 J7
Hillcrest School
  SWTR RH13 ....190 D6
Hillcroft College
  SURB KT6 ....41 L7
Hillcroft Primary School
  CTHM CR3 ....101 N3
Hillcross Primary School
  MRDN SM4 ....43 K5
Hill's Cemetery
  HORS RH12 ....191 N8
Hill School
  BH/WHM TN16 ....104 F3
Hilltop Primary School
  CRAWW RH11 ....176 F7
Hilly Fields Medical Centre
  BROCKY SE4 ....31 P1
Hinchley Wood Primary
  School
  ESH/CLAY KT10 ....58 G1
Hinchley Wood School &
  Sixth Form Centre
  ESH/CLAY KT10 ....58 G1
The Hindhead Golf Club
  GSHT GU26 ....165 L5
Hitherfield Primary School
  STRHM/NOR SW16 ....30 B5
HM Customs
  HTHAIR TW6 ....14 C6
HM Prison
  BELMT SM2 ....79 N1
  BRXS/STRHM SW2 ....29 P2
  CHOB/PIR GU24 ....70 F6
  RPLY/SEND GU23 ....93 N7
  WAND/EARL SW18 ....28 C3
HM Young Offender
  Institution
  FELT TW13 ....23 N6
Hobbs Industrial Estate
  LING RH7 ....161 L5
Hockley Industrial Centre
  REDH RH1 ....120 B6
Hoebridge Golf Centre
  WOKS/MYFD GU22 ....72 G8
Hoe Bridge Pre-preparatory
  School
  WOKS/MYFD GU22 ....72 F8
Hogan Business Centre
  WOKN/KNAP GU21 ....10 C4
Hogarth Business Park
  CHSWK W4 ....18 C4

Hogarth's House
CHSWK W4 .... 18 B4
Hogs Back Brewery
RFNM GU10 .... 109 H9
Holbeach Primary School
CAT SE6 .... 31 P5
Holborn College
Independent School
HMSMTH W6 .... 18 C3
Holbrook Primary School
HORS RH12 .... 192 C3
Holbrook Recreation
Centre
HORS RH12 .... 192 D3
Holland Park
Pre-preparatory School
WKENS W14 .... 19 K1
Hollybush Business Centre
HORL RH6 .... 160 A8
Hollybush Industrial Park
ALDT GU11 .... 108 G1
The Hollyfield School
SURB KT6 .... 41 L6
Holly Lodge Primary School
ASHV GU12 .... 89 H7
Hollymount Primary School
RYNPK SW20 .... 42 G2
Holy Spring Infant School
BRAK RG12 .... 32 C3
Hollywood Bowl
CRAWE RH10 .... 176 G4
The Holme Primary School
BOR GU35 .... 164 A5
Holmesdale School
REIG RH2 .... 119 M3
Holmethorpe Industrial
Estate
REDH RH1 .... 120 D2
Holy Cross Hospital
HASM GU27 .... 184 A3
Holy Cross Preparatory
School
KUTN/CMB KT2 .... 42 A1
Holy Cross Primary School
FUL/PGN SW6 .... 19 L6
Holy Cross RC Convent
School
NWMAL KT3 .... 42 B5
Holy Family Catholic School
DTCH/LGLY SL3 .... 12 D3
Holy Family RC Primary
School
ADL/WDHM KT15 .... 55 L4
Holy Ghost RC Primary
School
BAL SW12 .... 29 J3
Holy Trinity CE Junior School
GU GU1 .... 7 J7
WLGTN SM6 .... 62 E3
Holy Trinity CE Primary
School
ASC SL5 .... 34 G7
BRXS/STRHM SW2 .... 30 A3
CHOB/PIR GU24 .... 70 C1
RCHPK/HAM TW10 .... 17 N9
SYD SE26 .... 31 K5
The Holy Trinity CE School
CRAWW RH11 .... 176 D7
Holy Trinity Primary School
WIM/MER SW19 .... 28 D9
Homefield Preparatory
School
SUT SM1 .... 61 L4
Hones Yard Business Park
FNM GU9 .... 5 J4
Honeywell Primary School
BTSEA SW11 .... 29 J2
Honor Oak Crematorium
FSTH SE23 .... 31 L1
Honor Oak Gallery
FSTH SE23 .... 31 L2
Hook Rise South Industrial
Park
CHSGTN KT9 .... 59 M2
The Hop Kiln
FNM GU9 .... 5 F6
Horley Anderson Centre
HORL RH6 .... 159 H1
Horley Health Centre
HORL RH6 .... 159 K1
Horley Infant School
HORL RH6 .... 159 K1
The Horniman Museum &
Gardens
FSTH SE23 .... 31 J4
Horniman Primary School
FSTH SE23 .... 31 J4
Hornsby House School
BAL SW12 .... 29 K4
Horsell CE Junior School
WOKN/KNAP GU21 .... 72 A5
Horsell Village County
Infant School
WOKN/KNAP GU21 .... 10 A2
Horsham Arts Centre
HORS RH12 .... 192 B8
Horsham CC & Sports Club
HORS RH12 .... 192 A9
Horsham FC
SWTR RH13 .... 192 C9
Horsham Hospital
HORS RH12 .... 192 B7
Horsham Museum
HORS RH12 .... 192 B9
Horsham Trading Estate
SWTR RH13 .... 192 D6
Horsham YMCA FC
SWTR RH13 .... 192 C9
Horsley Sports Club
EHSLY KT24 .... 95 H7
Horton Country Park
HOR/WEW KT19 .... 59 N7

Horton Hospital
HOR/WEW KT19 .... 60 A9
Horton Park Golf & Country
Club
HOR/WEW KT19 .... 60 A6
Horton Trading Estate
DTCH/LGLY SL3 .... 12 F8
Hoskins Place Industrial
Estate
CBLY GU15 .... 68 D5
The Hotel at Chelsea
FUL/PGN SW6 .... 19 M5
Hotel Ibis
CRAWE RH10 .... 159 H9
FUL/PGN SW6 .... 19 L4
HYS/HAR UB3 .... 14 G6
Hotham Primary School
PUT/ROE SW15 .... 19 M5
Hounslow Business Park
HSLW TW3 .... 16 A9
Hounslow CC
HSLW TW3 .... 15 P7
Hounslow Cemetery
HSLWW TW4 .... 24 G3
Hounslow College
Independent School
FELT TW13 .... 24 E7
Hounslow Heath Golf Club
HSLWW TW4 .... 24 E1
Hounslow Heath Infant
School
HSLWW TW4 .... 15 N4
Hounslow Heath Junior
School
HSLWW TW4 .... 15 N8
Hounslow Manor School
HSLW TW3 .... 16 B8
Hounslow Manor Sports
Hall
HSLW TW3 .... 16 B8
Hounslow Town Primary
School
HSLW TW3 .... 16 C8
Howard of Effingham
School
EHSLY KT24 .... 95 M7
Howard Primary School
CROY/NA CR0 .... 63 L3
HSBC Sports Club
BECK BR3 .... 31 M9
Hubbard School
EGRIN RH19 .... 180 D2
Humphries Industrial
Estate
BRAK RG12 .... 32 D5
Hurlands Business Centre
FNM GU9 .... 128 B1
Hurlingham Business Park
FUL/PGN SW6 .... 19 L8
Hurlingham & Chelsea
Secondary School
FUL/PGN SW6 .... 19 L8
Hurlingham House
FUL/PGN SW6 .... 19 K8
Hurlingham Private School
PUT/ROE SW15 .... 19 K9
Hurst Green School
OXTED RH8 .... 123 N1
Hurst Lodge School
ASC SL5 .... 34 B9
Hurst Park Primary School
E/WMO/HCT KT8 .... 40 A4
Hurtmore Golf Club
GODL GU7 .... 130 F6
Hurtwood House
RDKG RH5 .... 154 B2
Hurtwood Inn Hotel
SHGR GU5 .... 134 E7
Hyland Business Centre
REDH RH1 .... 120 B5
Hythe First & Middle School
STA TW18 .... 22 A8
Ibstock Place School
PUT/ROE SW15 .... 27 K2
Ifield Golf & Country Club
CRAWW RH11 .... 176 A5
IKEA Store Croydon
CROY/NA CR0 .... 45 H9
Imber Court Trading
Estate
E/WMO/HCT KT8 .... 40 D7
Imberhorne Business
Centre
EGRIN RH19 .... 162 A9
Imberhorne School
EGRIN RH19 .... 180 A1
The Imber Sports Centre
EGRIN RH19 .... 162 C9
Immanuel CE Primary
School
STRHM/NOR SW16 .... 29 P9
Imperial College
PUT/ROE SW15 .... 19 H7
SKENS SW7 .... 19 P1
Imperial College Athletic
Ground
HYS/HAR UB3 .... 14 E4
Imperial College of Science
FUL/PGN SW6 .... 19 L4
Imperial College of Science
Technology & Medicine
ASC SL5 .... 34 F4
Independent Business Park
EGRIN RH19 .... 161 P9
Innkeeper's Lodge
BECK BR3 .... 46 G7
CBLY GU15 .... 68 G5
DTCH/LGLY SL3 .... 12 D3
FLEETN GU51 .... 87 L3
GODL GU7 .... 150 B1
REDH RH1 .... 120 C5
SAND/SEL CR2 .... 63 L7

WDSR SL4 .... 20 F1
WEY KT13 .... 56 C2
WOKN/KNAP GU21 .... 10 D2
WOT/HER KT12 .... 57 J2
Institut Francais
SKENS SW7 .... 19 P2
International School of
London
ACT W3 .... 17 N2
International Trading Estate
NWDGN UB2 .... 15 K1
Inwood Business Centre
HSLW TW3 .... 16 B9
The Islamic Grammar School
WAND/EARL SW18 .... 28 C3
Isleworth Cemetery
ISLW TW7 .... 16 G7
Isleworth Recreation Centre
ISLW TW7 .... 16 F9
Isleworth & Syon School
for Boys
ISLW TW7 .... 16 E5
Isleworth Town Primary
School
ISLW TW7 .... 16 F7
Ismaili Centre
SKENS SW7 .... 19 P2
Ithaca College
SKENS SW7 .... 19 N2
Ivybridge Primary School
TWK TW1 .... 25 N2
Ivybridge Retail Park
ISLW TW7 .... 25 N1
Ivydene Industrial Estate
EGRIN RH19 .... 181 J4
Jack & Jill School
HPTN TW12 .... 25 H9
WHTN TW2 .... 25 M5
Jack Tizard School
FUL/PGN SW6 .... 19 H6
Jacques Prevert School
HMSMTH W6 .... 19 H2
James Allens Preparatory
Girls School
HNHL SE24 .... 30 E1
James Dixon Primary
School
PGE/AN SE20 .... 46 A2
James Searle Industrial
Estate
HORS RH12 .... 192 D6
Jenner Health Centre
FSTH SE23 .... 31 M4
The Jigsaw School
FRIM GU16 .... 88 G4
John Betts Primary School
HMSMTH W6 .... 18 E1
John Nightingale School
E/WMO/HCT KT8 .... 39 P4
John Nike Athletics Stadium
BRAK RG12 .... 32 E6
John Paul II RC School
WIM/MER SW19 .... 28 A3
John Ruskin College
SAND/SEL CR2 .... 64 E6
Johnsons Industrial Estate
HYS/HAR UB3 .... 15 J1
Joseph Hood Primary
School
RYNPK SW20 .... 43 J3
Jubilee Hall Clinic
CRAWE RH10 .... 177 K5
Jubilee Primary School
BRXS/STRHM SW2 .... 30 B2
Julians Primary School
STRHM/NOR SW16 .... 30 B7
Jurys Inn Chelsea
FUL/PGN SW6 .... 19 N6
Jurys Inn Hotel
CROY/NA CR0 .... 2 D3
HTHAIR TW6 .... 15 H8
Jurys Kensington Hotel
SKENS SW7 .... 19 P2
Kangley Business Centre
BECK BR3 .... 31 N8
Kelsey Park School
BECK BR3 .... 46 G4
Kelvin Business Centre
CRAWE RH10 .... 177 J3
Kempton Park Racecourse
SUN TW16 .... 39 K1
Kendall Court Business Park
CBLY GU15 .... 68 B4
Kenley Primary School
PUR/KEN CR8 .... 81 N5
Kenley Sports Club
PUR/KEN CR8 .... 81 L3
Kensington Avenue
Primary School
THHTH CR7 .... 45 J2
The Kensington Dyslexia
Teaching Centre
KENS W8 .... 19 M1
Kensington Preparatory
School
FUL/PGN SW6 .... 19 K6
Kensington Wharf
WBPTN SW10 .... 19 P5
Kenyngton Manor Primary
School
SUN TW16 .... 24 B8
Keston Primary School
COUL/CHIP CR5 .... 81 J8
Kew Bridge Steam Museum
BTFD TW8 .... 17 M3
Kew College
RCH/KEW TW9 .... 17 N5
Kew Gardens (Royal Botanic
Gardens)
BTFD TW8 .... 17 L6
Kew Palace
RCH/KEW TW9 .... 17 L5

Kew Retail Park
RCH/KEW TW9 .... 17 P6
Kew Riverside Primary
School
RCH/KEW TW9 .... 17 P7
Kilmorie Primary School
FSTH SE23 .... 31 M5
Kiln Park Business Centre
EW KT17 .... 60 C9
Kimpton Industrial Estate
CHEAM SM3 .... 61 K1
King Athelstan Primary
School
KUT/HW KT1 .... 9 F6
King Edwards School
MFD/CHID GU8 .... 167 N2
King Fahad Academy
(Girls Upper School)
EA W5 .... 17 J2
Kingfield School
WOKS/MYFD GU22 .... 72 E9
The Kingfisher Sports Centre
KUT/HW KT1 .... 8 E5
Kings Avenue School
CLAP SW4 .... 29 P1
The Kings Centre
ALDT GU11 .... 108 C4
Kings College for the Arts
& Technology
GUW GU2 .... 111 L5
Kings College Junior School
WIM/MER SW19 .... 27 P9
Kings College School of
Medicine & Dentistry
DUL SE21 .... 30 E2
Kings Court First School
WDSR SL4 .... 20 F3
Kingscroft School
STA TW18 .... 22 D9
Kingsdale School
DUL SE21 .... 30 F6
Kingsfield Business Centre
REDH RH1 .... 120 C6
Kingsgate Business Centre
KUTN/CMB KT2 .... 8 D2
Kingsgrove Industrial Estate
FARN GU14 .... 88 C4
Kings House School
RCHPK/HAM TW10 .... 26 E1
Kings International College
for Business & the Arts
CBLY GU15 .... 68 E6
Kingsley Primary School
CROY/NA CR0 .... 45 H9
Kings Mall Shopping Centre
HMSMTH W6 .... 18 C2
Kingsmeadow Athletics
Centre
KUT/HW KT1 .... 9 J7
Kingsmead Shopping Centre
FARN GU14 .... 88 D4
Kings Road Industrial
Estate
HASM GU27 .... 184 B4
Kings School of English
BECK BR3 .... 46 F3
Kingston Business Centre
CHSGTN KT9 .... 59 L2
Kingston Cemetery
KUT/HW KT1 .... 9 H6
Kingston College of Further
Education
KUT/HW KT1 .... 8 C6
Kingston College Theatre
KUT/HW KT1 .... 8 C6
Kingston Crematorium
KUT/HW KT1 .... 9 H7
Kingston Crown Court
KUT/HW KT1 .... 8 C6
Kingston Grammar School
KUT/HW KT1 .... 9 F4
Kingston Hospital
KUTN/CMB KT2 .... 9 K2
Kingstonian FC
KUT/HW KT1 .... 9 K7
Kingstons Industrial Estate
ASHV GU12 .... 108 G4
Kingston University
BRYLDS KT5 .... 41 N6
KUT/HW KT1 .... 8 A5
KUTN/CMB KT2 .... 27 J8
KUTN/CMB KT2 .... 42 B1
PUT/ROE SW15 .... 27 L5
King Street College
HMSMTH W6 .... 18 C2
Kingsway Business Park
HPTN TW12 .... 39 P2
Kingswey Business Park
WOKN/KNAP GU21 .... 72 G3
Kingswood Golf Club
KWD/TDW/WH KT20 .... 99 L4
Kingswood House School
HOR/WEW KT19 .... 77 P2
Kingswood Primary School
KWD/TDW/WH KT20 .... 99 K8
WNWD SE27 .... 30 E7
K+K Hotel George
ECT SW5 .... 19 L2
KLC School of Design
WBPTN SW10 .... 19 N6
Knaphill Junior School
WOKN/KNAP GU21 .... 71 J7
Knaphill Lower School
WOKN/KNAP GU21 .... 71 H7
The Knightsbridge Under
School
SKENS SW7 .... 19 N2
Knollmead Primary School
BRYLDS KT5 .... 60 A1
Knowle Park Infant School
STA TW18 .... 22 D8

Knowl Hill School
CHOB/PIR GU24 .... 90 E2
Ladycross Business Park
LING RH7 .... 163 H5
The Lady Eleanor Holles
School
HPTN TW12 .... 25 J8
Lady Margaret School
FUL/PGN SW6 .... 19 L6
Ladymead Retail Centre
GU GU1 .... 112 A4
Ladywell Cemetery
BROCKY SE4 .... 31 N1
Laine Theatre Arts
EW KT17 .... 78 C2
Laker Industrial Estate
BECK BR3 .... 31 N8
Lakeside Business Park
FRIM GU16 .... 67 L1
Lakeside Country Club
FRIM GU16 .... 89 J1
Lakeside Industrial Estate
DTCH/LGLY SL3 .... 13 J5
DTCH/LGLY SL3 .... 13 L4
Lakeside International
Hotel
FRIM GU16 .... 89 J1
Lakeside Primary School
FRIM GU16 .... 69 H7
Laleham CE Primary School
STA TW18 .... 37 N3
Laleham Golf Club
CHERT KT16 .... 37 M5
Laleham Lea Preparatory
School
PUR/KEN CR8 .... 62 G8
Lambeth Academy
CLAP SW4 .... 29 M1
Lambeth Cemetery
TOOT SW17 .... 29 H1
Lambeth College
BRXS/STRHM SW2 .... 30 A1
CLAP SW4 .... 29 M1
STRHM/NOR SW16 .... 29 P5
Lambeth Crematorium
TOOT SW17 .... 28 F7
Lambs Business Park
GDST RH9 .... 122 B9
Lamont Business Centre
CROY/NA CR0 .... 44 G8
Lampton School
HSLW TW3 .... 16 A6
Langbourne Primary School
DUL SE21 .... 30 F6
Langdon Down Centre
TEDD TW11 .... 41 J1
Langford Primary School
FUL/PGN SW6 .... 19 M7
Langley Grammar School
DTCH/LGLY SL3 .... 12 D2
Langley Green Primary
School
CRAWW RH11 .... 176 F3
Langley Health Centre
DTCH/LGLY SL3 .... 12 E3
Langley Park Girls School
& Sports Centre
BECK BR3 .... 47 N6
Langley Park Golf Club
BECK BR3 .... 47 K7
Langley Park School
for Boys
BECK BR3 .... 47 H7
Langleywood School
DTCH/LGLY SL3 .... 12 C1
Langshott County Infant
School
HORL RH6 .... 159 M1
Langshott Manor Hotel
HORL RH6 .... 140 F2
The Lansbury Estate
WOKN/KNAP GU21 .... 71 K7
La Retraite RC Girl's School
BAL SW12 .... 29 M3
Larmenier Infant School
HMSMTH W6 .... 19 H2
Latchmere J & I School
KUTN/CMB KT2 .... 26 E9
The Latymer Preparatory
School
HMSMTH W6 .... 18 E3
Latymer Upper School
HMSMTH W6 .... 18 E2
Laurel Clinic
EA W5 .... 17 J2
Lavender Park Golf Club
ASC SL5 .... 33 L4
Lawn Hunt Industrial Park
HORS RH12 .... 191 L6
Lazards Sports Club
SUN TW16 .... 39 K2
Leatherhead Business Park
LHD/OX KT22 .... 77 H8
Leatherhead Clinic
LHD/OX KT22 .... 97 J1
Leatherhead CC
LHD/OX KT22 .... 96 G2
Leatherhead FC
LHD/OX KT22 .... 96 G2
Leatherhead Golf Club
LHD/OX KT22 .... 76 G5
Leatherhead Hospital
LHD/OX KT22 .... 97 J2
Leatherhead Industrial
Estate
LHD/OX KT22 .... 96 G1
Leatherhead Institute
LHD/OX KT22 .... 97 H1
Leatherhead Leisure Centre
& Water Park
LHD/OX KT22 .... 96 G3

Leatherhead Museum
LHD/OX KT22 ....97 H2
L'Ecoles des Petits School
FUL/PGN SW6 ....19 M7
Leechpool Lane Primary
School
SWTR RH13 ....192 F6
Leigh Close Industrial
Estate
NWMAL KT3 ....42 B5
Leighton House Museum
WKENS W14 ....19 K1
Leisure Centre
KUT/HW KT1 ....8 E5
Leith Hill Tower (NT)
RDKG RH5 ....155 J1
Lena Gardens Primary
School
HMSMTH W6 ....18 G1
Lewin Mead Community
Mental Health Centre
STRHM/NOR SW16 ....29 N9
Lewis Clinic
CAR SM5 ....62 C3
Liberty Middle School
MTCM CR4 ....44 A3
The Licensed Victuallers
School
ASC SL5 ....33 L3
Lightwater Country Park
LTWR GU18 ....51 P8
Lightwater Village School
LTWR GU18 ....52 A8
Lillian Bishop School of
English
SKENS SW7 ....19 P2
Limes Business Centre
HORL RH6 ....158 C6
Limpsfield CE Infant School
OXTED RH8 ....103 P9
Limpsfield Chart Golf Club
OXTED RH8 ....104 A9
Limpsfield Grange School
OXTED RH8 ....103 N7
Limpsfield Lawn Tennis
Club
OXTED RH8 ....103 N8
Linden Bridge School
WPK KT4 ....60 C2
Linden Lodge School
WIM/MER SW19 ....28 B4
Lindon Bennett School
FELT TW13 ....24 E8
Lingfield Notre Dame
School
LING RH7 ....162 E1
Lingfield Park Golf Club
LING RH7 ....162 E2
Lingfield Park Racecourse
LING RH7 ....162 E1
Lingfield Primary School
LING RH7 ....143 K9
Lingfield Squash & Leisure
Club
LING RH7 ....162 E1
The Link Day Primary
School
CROY/NA CR0 ....62 G3
The Link Secondary School
CROY/NA CR0 ....63 H3
Links Primary School
TOOT SW17 ....29 K9
Linley House School
BRYLDS KT5 ....41 M7
Linsford Business Park
FRIM GU16 ....89 H4
Lionel Road Primary School
BTFD TW8 ....17 L2
Liongate Hotel
E/WMO/HCT KT8 ....40 F4
Lion House School
PUT/ROE SW15 ....19 H9
Lion & Lamb Yard Shopping
Centre
FNM GU9 ....4 E2
Lion Retail Park
WOKS/MYFD GU22 ....11 J1
Liphook CE Junior School
LIPH GU30 ....182 D6
Liphook Infant School
LIPH GU30 ....182 D6
Lismoyne Hotel
FLEETN GU51 ....86 F2
Little Eden & Eden High
School
FELT TW13 ....24 E7
Littlehaven Infant School
HORS RH12 ....192 E5
Little Mead Industrial
Estate
CRAN GU6 ....152 E9
Littleton CE Infant School
SHPTN TW17 ....38 C4
Little Wandsworth School
TOOT SW17 ....29 K5
The Livity School
BRXS/STRHM SW2 ....29 P1
Lloyds Register CC
DUL SE21 ....30 E4
Lodge School
PUR/KEN CR8 ....80 F1
Lombard Business Centre
BTSEA SW11 ....19 P7
Lombard Business Park
CROY/NA CR0 ....45 H8
WAND/EARL SW18 ....28 C2
WIM/MER SW19 ....43 N3
London Academy of Music
& Dramatic Art
HMSMTH W6 ....19 H3
KENS W8 ....19 L2

London Cornish RFC
PUT/ROE SW15 ....27 L6
London Electronics College
ECT SW5 ....19 L3
London Irish RFC
SUN TW16 ....39 J2
London Lane Clinic
BMLY BR1 ....47 M1
London Living Theatre
SYD SE26 ....31 L7
London Oratory School
FUL/PGN SW6 ....19 L5
London Road Medical
Centre
CROY/NA CR0 ....45 J7
London Scottish Golf Club
WIM/MER SW19 ....27 N6
London Temple Visitors
Centre
LING RH7 ....161 M3
London Welsh FC
RCH/KEW TW9 ....17 L8
London Wetland Centre
BARN SW13 ....18 F6
Lonesome Primary School
MTCM CR4 ....44 D3
Longacre School
SHGR GU5 ....133 H9
The Longcroft Clinic
BNSTD SM7 ....79 N5
Long Ditton County Infant
School
SURB KT6 ....41 J9
Longford Community
School
EBED/NFELT TW14 ....24 A3
Longford Industrial Estate
HPTN TW12 ....25 J9
Longley Trading Estate
CRAWE RH10 ....177 H6
Longmead Business Centre
HOR/WEW KT19 ....60 B9
Longmead Industrial Estate
HOR/WEW KT19 ....60 B9
Longmead Primary School
WDR/YW UB7 ....13 P2
Longshot Industrial Estate
BRAK RG12 ....32 A4
Longwood Business Park
SUN TW16 ....39 H6
The Look Out Discovery
Centre
BRAK RG12 ....32 F9
Lorraine Infant School
CBLY GU15 ....51 J8
Loseley Fields Primary
School
GODL GU7 ....131 L4
Loseley Park
RGUW GU3 ....131 M2
Lovelace Primary School
CHSGTN KT9 ....59 J4
Lower Sydenham Industrial
Estate
SYD SE26 ....31 N8
Lowfield Heath Industrial
Estate
HORL RH6 ....159 H7
Lowther Primary School
BARN SW13 ....18 E4
Loxwood Primary School
BIL RH14 ....188 D6
LSE Sports Club
NWMAL KT3 ....42 B7
Ludshott Common (NT)
GSHT GU26 ....165 H8
Lyndhurst School
CBLY GU15 ....68 D3
Lyne & Longcross CE Infant
School
CHERT KT16 ....54 F1
Lynton Preparatory School
EW KT17 ....60 D9
Lyons Farm Estate
SWTR RH13 ....191 H8
Lyon Way Industrial Estate
FRIM GU16 ....68 E7
Lyric Theatre Hammersmith
HMSMTH W6 ....18 G2
Lythe Hill Hotel & Spa
HASM GU27 ....185 J5
Macdonald Bush Hotel
FNM GU9 ....5 G3
Macdonald Hotel
ASC SL5 ....34 C7
CBLY GU15 ....69 H2
DORK RH4 ....117 H7
RDKG RH5 ....117 J2
Macdonald Thames Lodge
STA TW18 ....22 B8
The Magna Carta School
EGH TW20 ....22 A9
Maidenbower First &
Middle School
CRAWE RH10 ....177 N7
Maidenbower Junior
School
CRAWE RH10 ....177 N7
Main Square Shopping
Centre
CBLY GU15 ....68 E2
Malcolm Primary School
PGE/AN SE20 ....46 C1
The Malden Centre
NWMAL KT3 ....42 D5
Malden Golf Club
NWMAL KT3 ....42 C3
Malden Manor Primary
School
NWMAL KT3 ....42 C8

Malden Parochial Primary
School
WPK KT4 ....42 C9
Malden Road Baths
CHEAM SM3 ....61 H3
Malham Road Industrial
Estate
FSTH SE23 ....31 L4
The Mall School
WHTN TW2 ....25 L6
Malmesbury Primary School
MRDN SM4 ....43 N8
Manby Lodge Infant School
WEY KT13 ....56 D3
Mancroft Primary School
EGH TW20 ....21 M9
Manor Drive Health Centre
WPK KT4 ....42 D9
Manor Farm Business
Centre
RFNM GU10 ....109 H8
Manorfield Primary School
HORL RH6 ....159 J1
Manor Green College
CRAWW RH11 ....176 D3
Manor Green Primary
School
CRAWW RH11 ....176 G1
Manor House Hotel
RGUE GU4 ....113 M6
Manor House School
GT/LBKH KT23 ....95 N7
Manor Lea School
FARN GU14 ....88 B1
Manor Mead School
SHPTN TW17 ....38 D6
Manor Park Industrial
Estate
ASHV GU12 ....108 E5
Manor Park Primary School
SUT SM1 ....61 N4
The Manor School
BF/WBF KT14 ....74 A3
Maple Grove Business
Centre
HSLWW TW4 ....15 L9
Maple House School
THHTH CR7 ....45 L4
Maple Industrial Estate
FELT TW13 ....24 B5
Maple Infant School
SURB KT6 ....41 K6
Marble Hill House
TWK TW1 ....26 B3
Marden Lodge Primary
School
CTHM CR3 ....82 B9
Margaret Roper Catholic
Primary School
PUR/KEN CR8 ....63 J8
Mariner Business Centre
CROY/NA CR0 ....63 H4
Marion Vian Primary School
BECK BR3 ....46 D6
Marish Infant School
DTCH/LGLY SL3 ....12 D1
The Marist Preparatory
School
ASC SL5 ....34 D6
The Marist RC Primary
School
BF/WBF KT14 ....73 K2
Marist Senior School
ASC SL5 ....34 D5
The Marjory Kinnon School
EBED/NFELT TW14 ....23 P1
Market Trading Estate
NWDGN UB2 ....15 K2
Marlborough County Infant
School
ALDT GU11 ....88 E8
Marlborough CC
DUL SE21 ....31 H4
Marlborough Primary School
ISLW TW7 ....16 G6
Marlborough Trading Estate
RCH/KEW TW9 ....17 P6
Marriott Hotel
DTCH/LGLY SL3 ....12 D3
ECT SW5 ....19 M2
Marsh Farm Business
Centre
RFNM GU10 ....106 D5
Marshfields CE School
CHERT KT16 ....55 J5
Marshgate Primary School
RCHPK/HAM TW10 ....26 E1
Mary Boone School
WKENS W14 ....19 J2
Marymount International
School
KUTN/CMB KT2 ....42 A1
Mary Wallace Theatre
TWK TW1 ....25 P4
Maswell Park Health Centre
HSLW TW3 ....25 K1
The Matthew Arnold School
STA TW18 ....22 F9
Maybury Business Centre
WOKS/MYFD GU22 ....11 J3
Maybury Infant School
WOKN/KNAP GU21 ....11 F2
Mayday University Hospital
THHTH CR7 ....45 K7
McKay Trading Estate
DTCH/LGLY SL3 ....13 J7
The Mead Infant School
WPK KT4 ....60 D2
Meadlands Primary School
RCHPK/HAM TW10 ....26 B7

Meadowbrook Industrial
Centre
CRAWE RH10 ....177 K2
Meadowcroft County
Infant School
CHERT KT16 ....55 K2
The Meadows (Superstores)
SHST GU47 ....68 A3
Meadow Vale Primary
School
BNFD RG42 ....32 B2
The Meads Primary School
ECRIN RH19 ....180 D4
Meath Green Infant School
HORL RH6 ....140 B8
Meath Green Junior School
HORL RH6 ....140 B8
Meath School
CHERT KT16 ....55 H6
Megabowl
KUT/HW KT1 ....8 E4
Melcombe Primary School
HMSMTH W6 ....19 H4
Melrose Special School
MTCM CR4 ....44 A4
Merland Rise Primary
School
EPSOM KT18 ....78 G8
Merlin School
PUT/ROE SW15 ....28 A1
Merrist Wood Golf Club
RGUW GU3 ....91 J9
Merrow Business Centre
RGUE GU4 ....113 H2
Merrow CE Infant School
RGUE GU4 ....113 H3
Merstham Primary School
REDH RH1 ....100 E8
Merton Abbey Primary
School
WIM/MER SW19 ....43 M2
Merton Adult College
RYNPK SW20 ....43 J4
Merton College
MRDN SM4 ....43 K7
Merton Industrial Park
WIM/MER SW19 ....43 N2
Merton Park Primary School
WIM/MER SW19 ....43 K3
Merton Road Industrial
Estate
WAND/EARL SW18 ....28 D3
Metro Business Centre
SYD SE26 ....31 N9
Metro Industrial Centre
ISLW TW7 ....16 E7
Metropolitan Police FC
E/WMO/HCT KT8 ....40 D7
Metropolitan Police Hayes
Sports Club
HAYES BR2 ....65 M1
Middle Hill Health Clinic
ALDT GU11 ....108 C3
Midleton Industrial Estate
GUW GU2 ....6 A1
Milbourne Lodge Junior
School
ESH/CLAY KT10 ....58 C4
Milbourne Lodge School
ESH/CLAY KT10 ....58 D5
Milford Golf Club
MFD/CHID GU8 ....149 P3
Milford Hospital
GODL GU7 ....150 B4
Milford School
MFD/CHID GU8 ....149 N3
Military Cemetery
CHOB/PIR GU24 ....90 F1
Millais School
SWTR RH13 ....192 E8
Millennium Bailey's Hotel
SKENS SW7 ....19 N2
Millennium Gloucester Hotel
ECT SW5 ....19 M2
Mill Farm Business Park
HSLWW TW4 ....24 F3
Mill Green Business Park
MTCM CR4 ....44 B8
Mill Lane Trading Estate
CROY/NA CR0 ....63 H2
The Mill Primary School
CRAWW RH11 ....176 D5
Mill Ride Golf Club
ASC SL5 ....33 M2
Milton Mount Primary
School
CRAWE RH10 ....177 L3
Mitcham CC
MTCM CR4 ....44 A5
Mitcham Golf Club
MTCM CR4 ....44 C6
Mitcham Industrial Estate
MTCM CR4 ....44 C2
Mitcham Vale High School
MTCM CR4 ....44 B3
The Moat School
FUL/PGN SW6 ....19 J7
Mole Business Park
LHD/OX KT22 ....96 G1
Molesey Hospital
E/WMO/HCT KT8 ....40 A6
Molesey Lock
E/WMO/HCT KT8 ....40 E4
Mollison Drive Health Centre
WLGTN SM6 ....62 G6
Monks Hill Sports Centre
SAND/SEL CR2 ....64 D6
Monks Orchard Primary
School
CROY/NA CR0 ....46 D6

Monument Bridge East
Industrial Estate
WOKN/KNAP GU21 ....72 F4
Moore Place Golf Club
ESH/CLAY KT10 ....58 A4
Moor House School
OXTED RH8 ....123 M3
Moor Lane Junior School
CHSGTN KT9 ....59 M4
Morden Cemetery
MRDN SM4 ....42 G7
Morden First School
MRDN SM4 ....43 L6
Morden Hall Medical Centre
MRDN SM4 ....43 M4
Morden Hall Park (NT)
MRDN SM4 ....43 N5
Morden Park Pool
MRDN SM4 ....43 K6
Morden Road Clinic
WIM/MER SW19 ....43 M4
Morden Road Clinic
RFNM GU10 ....146 F2
Mortimer School
STRHM/NOR SW16 ....29 N5
Mortlake Cemetery
MORT/ESHN SW14 ....18 C8
Mortlake Crematorium
RCH/KEW TW9 ....17 P7
Moss Lane School
GODL GU7 ....131 K9
Mount Alvernia Hospital
GU GU1 ....7 H6
Mount Carmel RC Primary
School
EA W5 ....17 J1
The Mount Infant School
NWMAL KT3 ....41 P4
Mount Medical Centre
FELT TW13 ....24 F5
Murky Puddle Theatre
NWMAL KT3 ....42 D4
Muschamp Primary School
CAR SM5 ....62 A4
Museum of Fulham Palace
FUL/PGN SW6 ....19 H7
Museum of Richmond
TWK TW1 ....26 C5
Museum of Rugby &
Twickenham Stadium Tours
WHTN TW2 ....25 M2
Musical Museum
BTFD TW8 ....17 L4
Mytchett Primary School
FRIM GU16 ....89 H3
Nash College of Further
Education
WWKM BR4 ....65 M2
The National Archives
RCH/KEW TW9 ....17 P5
The National Centre for
Young People with
Epilepsy
LING RH7 ....143 N9
National Physical
Laboratory
TEDD TW11 ....25 M9
National Sports Centre
NRWD SE19 ....31 H9
Natural History Museum
SKENS SW7 ....19 P1
Natural Therapy Clinic
TOOT SW17 ....29 L8
Natwest Sports Club
BECK BR3 ....31 N9
NEC Harlequins RFC
(Twickenham Stoop
Stadium)
WHTN TW2 ....25 M3
Nelson Hospital
RYNPK SW20 ....43 K3
Nelson Primary School
WHTN TW2 ....25 J2
Nelson Trading Estate
WIM/MER SW19 ....43 M2
NE Surrey College of
Technology
EW KT17 ....60 E9
New Addington Pools &
Fitness Centre
CROY/NA CR0 ....65 J8
New Brentford Cemetery
HSLW TW3 ....15 P7
New Chiswick Pool
CHSWK W4 ....18 C5
Newdigate Endowed CE
Infant School
RDKG RH5 ....156 C3
New Haw Therapy Clinic
ADL/WDHM KT15 ....55 M8
Newhouse Farm Business
Centre
HORS RH12 ....193 H3
New Kings Primary School
FUL/PGN SW6 ....19 K7
Newland House School
TWK TW1 ....25 N7
Newlands CP School
YTLY GU46 ....66 G3
New Life School
EGRIN RH19 ....180 C1
New Lodge School
DORK RH4 ....117 H4
New Monument School
WOKS/MYFD GU22 ....72 C4
Newport Junior School
CBLY GU15 ....108 F5
New School
FUL/PGN SW6 ....19 K6
New Scotland Hill Primary
School
SHST GU47 ....49 L7

New Victoria Hospital
  KUTN/CMB KT2 ....42 C2
New Victoria Theatre
  WOKN/KNAP GU21 ....10 D3
New Zealand Golf Club
  ADL/WDHM KT15 ....73 J1
Nightingale Industrial
  Estate
  HORS RH12 ....192 C7
Nightingale School
  TOOT SW17 ....29 H5
Nomad Theatre
  EHSLY KT24 ....95 H8
Nonsuch High School
  for Girls
  CHEAM SM3 ....61 H6
Nonsuch Industrial Estate
  HOR/WEW KT19 ....60 C9
Nonsuch Primary School
  EW KT17 ....60 F4
Norbury Complementary
  Therapy Clinic
  STRHM/NOR SW16 ....45 H2
Norbury Health Centre
  STRHM/NOR SW16 ....45 H3
Norbury Manor Primary
  School
  STRHM/NOR SW16 ....44 G2
Norbury Manor Secondary
  Girls School
  STRHM/NOR SW16 ....45 J3
Norbury Trading Estate
  STRHM/NOR SW16 ....45 H3
Normand Croft Community
  School
  WKENS W14 ....19 K4
Norman Park Athletics Track
  HAYES BR2 ....47 P7
North Clinic
  BMLY BR1 ....47 N2
Northcote Lodge School
  BTSEA SW11 ....29 H2
North Croydon Medical
  Centre
  THHTH CR7 ....45 K7
North Downs Golf Club
  CTHM CR3 ....102 C5
North East Surrey
  Crematorium
  NWMAL KT5 ....42 G7
North Farnborough County
  Infant School
  FARN GU14 ....88 F2
North Feltham Trading
  Estate
  EBED/NFELT TW14 ....15 K4
Northfields Prospect
  Business Centre
  PUT/ROE SW15 ....19 K9
Northgate Primary School
  CRAWE RH10 ....177 H3
North Hants Golf Club
  FLEETN GU51 ....86 G3
North Heath Lane Industrial
  Estate
  HORS RH12 ....192 C4
North Heath Primary
  School
  HORS RH12 ....192 C5
North Holmwood CC
  RDKG RH5 ....17 J4
Northlands Business Park
  HORS RH12 ....173 K7
Northolmes Junior School
  HORS RH12 ....192 F5
Northtown Trading Estate
  ASHV GU12 ....108 C5
North Weylands Industrial
  Estate
  WOT/HER KT12 ....57 N1
The Norwegian School
  WIM/MER SW19 ....42 G1
Norwood Green Infant
  School
  NWDGN UB2 ....15 N3
Norwood Green Junior
  School
  NWDGN UB2 ....15 N3
Norwood Heights Shopping
  Centre
  NRWD SE19 ....30 F9
Norwood School
  NRWD SE19 ....30 D8
Notre Dame Preparatory
  School
  COB KT11 ....57 H9
Novello Theatre
  ASC SL5 ....34 D6
Novotel
  WDR/YW UB7 ....14 C2
Novotel London West
  HMSMTH W6 ....19 H3
Nutfield Cemetery
  REDH RH1 ....120 F4
Nutfield Church CE Primary
  School
  REDH RH1 ....121 H6
Nutfield Priory Hotel
  REDH RH1 ....120 E5
Nutley Dean Business Park
  HORL RH6 ....139 J7
Oak Farm Community
  School
  FARN GU14 ....88 C4
Oakfield Junior School
  LHD/OX KT22 ....96 C3
Oakfield Preparatory School
  DUL SE21 ....30 E5
Oakfield Road Industrial
  Estate
  PGE/AN SE20 ....46 B1

Oakfield School
  WOKS/MYFD GU22 ....73 K4
Oak Hill Health Centre
  SURB KT6 ....41 L7
Oakhyrst Grange School
  CTHM CR3 ....101 M6
Oaklands Infant School
  BH/WHM TN16 ....84 A5
Oaklands Junior School
  BH/WHM TN16 ....84 A5
  CWTH RG45 ....49 L3
Oaklands School
  ISLW TW7 ....16 D8
Oak Lane Cemetery
  TWK TW1 ....25 P3
Oak Lane Medical Centre
  TWK TW1 ....26 A3
Oak Lodge JMI School
  WWKM BR4 ....47 H8
Oak Lodge School
  BAL SW12 ....29 J3
Oak Park Golf Club
  RFNM GU10 ....106 E8
The Oaks Primary School
  CRAWE RH10 ....177 J8
Oaks Sports Centre
  CAR SM5 ....62 B9
Oak Tree Clinic
  WOKN/KNAP GU21 ....71 K7
Oakview Business Park
  MFD/CHID GU8 ....168 A1
Oakwood Independent
  School
  PUR/KEN CR8 ....81 K2
Oakwood Industrial Park
  CRAWE RH10 ....177 K2
Oakwood School
  HORL RH6 ....159 L1
Oakwood Sports Centre
  HORL RH6 ....159 M1
Oast House Centre
  STA TW18 ....22 C7
Oatlands Park Hotel
  WEY KT13 ....56 E2
Oatlands School
  WEY KT13 ....56 F3
Occupational Health Centre
  CROY/NA CRO 2 E6
Odeon Cinema
  BECK BR3 ....46 C3
  ESH/CLAY KT10 ....58 B3
  EW KT17 ....78 C2
  HAYES BR2 ....47 N3
  KENS W8 ....19 K1
  KUT/HW KT1 ....8 E4
  RCH/KEW TW9 ....26 C1
  STRHM/NOR SW16 ....29 P6
  WIM/MER SW19 ....43 L1
Odeon Multiplex
  GU GU1 ....6 D5
Old Barnes Cemetery
  BARN SW13 ....18 F7
Old Barn Theatre
  CRAWW RH11 ....176 C3
Old Beckenhamian RFC
  WWKM BR4 ....65 K2
Old Bromilians CC
  HAYES BR2 ....47 P6
Old Cemetery
  EDUL SE22 ....31 J2
The Old Cottage Hospital
  EW KT17 ....78 D2
Oldfield House Special
  School
  HPTN TW12 ....39 P2
Oldfields Trading Estate
  SUT SM1 ....61 L2
Old Guildfordians RFC
  GU GU1 ....112 D4
Old Palace School
  CROY/NA CRO 2 B5
Old Thorns Hotel, Golf &
  Country Club
  LIPH GU30 ....182 A7
Old Tiffinians Sports Ground
  E/WMO/HCT KT8 ....40 E6
Old Town Hall
  CHERT KT16 ....37 L8
  CODL GU7 ....131 K8
  HORS RH12 ....192 B9
Old Vicarage School
  RCHPK/HAM TW10 ....26 D2
Old Wilsonians Sports Club
  WWKM BR4 ....47 L9
Oliver House Preparatory
  School
  CLAP SW4 ....29 L2
Olympia
  WKENS W14 ....19 J1
Ongar Place Infant School
  ADL/WDHM KT15 ....55 L5
On Sai Clinic
  ECT SW5 ....19 M2
Onslow Infant School
  GUW GU2 ....111 M7
Open University
  EGRIN RH19 ....180 D2
Orange Tree Theatre
  RCH/KEW TW9 ....17 L9
Orchard Business Centre
  BECK BR3 ....31 N8
  REDH RH1 ....140 C5
Orchard Hill College
  WLGTN SM6 ....62 D5
Orchard House School
  CHSWK W4 ....18 B2
The Orchard Junior School
  HSLWW TW4 ....16 A9
The Orchard School
  E/WMO/HCT KT8 ....40 D6

Orchards Community
  Infant School
  REIG RH2 ....119 L8
Orchard Way Primary
  School
  CROY/NA CRO 46 E8
Oriel High School
  CRAWE RH10 ....176 G5
Oriel Primary School
  FELT TW13 ....24 F6
Orleans House Gallery
  TWK TW1 ....26 A4
Orleans Infant School
  TWK TW1 ....26 A3
Osier Industrial Estate
  WAND/EARL SW18 ....19 L9
Osteopathic Clinic
  HOR/WEW KT19 ....60 B4
Osterley Park & House (NT)
  ISLW TW7 ....16 C4
Osterley RFC
  NWDGN UB2 ....16 B1
Our Lady Immaculate RC
  Primary School
  BRYLDS KT5 ....41 P9
Our Lady of the Rosary RC
  Primary School
  STA TW18 ....22 D9
Our Lady of Victories RC
  Primary School
  SKENS SW7 ....19 N2
Our Lady of Victorys RC
  Primary School
  PUT/ROE SW15 ....19 H9
Our Lady Queen of Heaven
  CP School
  CRAWW RH11 ....176 E3
Our Lady Queen of Heaven
  RC Primary School
  WIM/MER SW19 ....28 A3
Our Lady & St Johns RC
  Primary School
  BTFD TW8 ....17 J3
Our Lady & St Philip Neri RC
  Infants School
  FSTH SE23 ....31 L6
Our Lady & St Philip Neri RC
  Primary School
  SYD SE26 ....31 M7
Our Ladys Preparatory
  School
  CWTH RG45 ....49 L4
Outwood Windmill
  REDH RH1 ....141 M5
Oval Primary School
  CROY/NA CRO 3 G2
Overton Grange School
  BELMT SM2 ....61 M7
Owlsmoor Primary School
  SHST GU47 ....50 A8
Oxshott Village Sports Club
  LHD/OX KT22 ....76 C3
Oxted Health Centre
  OXTED RH8 ....103 M8
Oxted & Limpsfield Hospital
  OXTED RH8 ....103 K8
Oxted School
  OXTED RH8 ....103 M8
Pachesham Park
  Golf Centre
  LHD/OX KT22 ....76 E7
Paddock School
  PUT/ROE SW15 ....18 D9
Painshill Park
  COB KT11 ....75 J3
Paint Pots Montessori
  School
  WBPTN SW10 ....19 N4
Palmerston Business Centre
  SUT SM1 ....61 N4
Palm House
  RCH/KEW TW9 ....17 M6
Papplewick School
  ASC SL5 ....33 P2
Paray House School
  FUL/PGN SW6 ....19 K7
Parayhouse School
  WBPTN SW10 ....19 N5
Parchmore Medical Centre
  THHTH CR7 ....45 L4
Parish CE Primary School
  BMLY BR1 ....47 N1
Parish Church CE Primary
  School
  CROY/NA CRO 2 A6
Park Crematorium
  ASHV GU12 ....108 FB
Park Farm Industrial Estate
  FRIM GU16 ....68 E7
Park Hall Trading Estate
  WNWD SE27 ....30 D6
Park Hill Junior School
  CROY/NA CRO 3 G6
Park Hill School
  KUTN/CMB KT2 ....9 J1
The Park Inn Heathrow
  WDR/YW UB7 ....14 D5
Park Mead Primary School
  CRAN GU6 ....153 J8
Park Mews Small Business
  Centre
  HNHL SE24 ....30 D2
Park Primary School
  ALDT GU11 ....108 E7
Park Recreation Centre
  HORS RH12 ....192 B8
Parkside Hospital
  WIM/MER SW19 ....28 A6
Parkside School
  COB KT11 ....76 A7

Park Walk Primary School
  WBPTN SW10 ....19 P4
Parkway Trading Estate
  HEST TW5 ....15 L4
Park Wood Golf Club
  BH/WHM TN16 ....104 C2
Parlaunt Park Combined
  School
  DTCH/LGLY SL3 ....12 F1
Parsonage Business Park
  HORS RH12 ....192 D6
Parsons Green Health Clinic
  FUL/PGN SW6 ....19 L6
Parsons Mead School
  ASHTD KT21 ....77 L8
Passfield Mill Business Park
  LIPH GU30 ....182 A1
Passport Language Schools
  BMLY BR1 ....47 P2
The Patrick Doody Clinic &
  Health Centre
  WIM/MER SW19 ....43 L1
Pattinson Clinic
  RCH/KEW TW9 ....26 C1
The Paul Robeson Theatre
  HSLW TW3 ....16 B8
The Pavilion Leisure Centre
  BMLY BR1 ....47 N3
Pavilion Restaurant
  RCH/KEW TW9 ....17 L7
Pavilions in the Park
  HORS RH12 ....192 B7
Paxton Primary School
  NRWD SE19 ....30 C9
Payne Clinic
  EW KT17 ....78 E2
Peacock Cinema
  WOKN/KNAP GU21 ....10 C3
The Peacocks Shopping
  Centre
  WOKN/KNAP GU21 ....10 C3
Peall Road Industrial Estate
  CROY/NA CRO 45 H7
Peaslake School
  SHGR GU5 ....134 C6
The Peel Centre
  BRAK RG12 ....32 D3
Pelham Court Business
  Centre
  CRAWW RH11 ....176 E9
Pelham Primary School
  WIM/MER SW19 ....43 L1
Pennthorpe School
  HORS RH12 ....189 M3
Pennyhill Park Hotel &
  the Spa
  BAGS GU19 ....51 K7
Penwortham Primary
  School
  STRHM/NOR SW16 ....29 L9
Perrymount Primary School
  FSTH SE23 ....31 L5
Perrywood Business Park
  REDH RH1 ....140 D4
Peterborough Primary
  School
  FUL/PGN SW6 ....19 L7
The Petersham Hotel
  RCHPK/HAM TW10 ....26 D3
Pewley Down Infant School
  GU GU1 ....7 G6
Phoenix College
  MRDN SM4 ....43 M6
Pickhurst Infant School
  WWKM BR4 ....47 L7
Pickhurst Junior School
  WWKM BR4 ....47 M7
Pierreponte School
  RFNM GU10 ....147 N3
The Pilgrims Way Primary
  School
  FNM GU9 ....4 E7
Pilton Clinic
  CROY/NA CRO 2 B5
Pine Ridge Golf Club
  FRIM GU16 ....69 M6
Pine Ridge Infant School
  FRIM GU16 ....51 J8
The Pines Primary School
  BRAK RG12 ....32 C8
The Pines Trading Estate
  RGUW GU3 ....111 L3
Pine Trees Business Park
  STA TW18 ....22 B8
Pinewood Infant School
  FARN GU14 ....67 P9
Pinewood Leisure Centre
  EWKG RG40 ....49 M1
Pinkwell Primary School
  HYS/HAR UB3 ....14 E2
Pinnacles Cricket & Squash
  Club
  SUT SM1 ....61 L5
Pioneers Industrial Park
  CROY/NA CRO 44 G9
Pippins School
  ASHF TW15 ....23 J7
  DTCH/LGLY SL3 ....13 K6
Pirbright Camp
  CHOB/PIR GU24 ....70 B9
Pirbright Primary School
  CHOB/PIR GU24 ....90 E2
Piries Place
  HORS RH12 ....192 B8
Pitfarm Lawn Tennis Club
  GU GU1 ....112 C5
Pitwood Park Industrial
  Estate
  KWD/TDW/WH KT20 ....79 H4
Pixham School
  DORK RH4 ....117 J5

Plaistow & Kirdford
  Primary School
  BIL RH14 ....187 L7
Playhouse Cinema
  EPSOM KT18 ....78 B3
Playhouse Theatre
  EPSOM KT18 ....78 A2
Plaza Cinema
  OXTED RH8 ....103 L9
Plough Industrial Estate
  LHD/OX KT22 ....76 G9
The Point (UCI Cinema &
  Hollywood Bowl)
  BRAK RG12 ....32 D3
Polesden Lacey (NT)
  RDKG RH5 ....116 A1
Polka Theatre for Children
  WIM/MER SW19 ....28 E9
Polygon Business Centre
  DTCH/LGLY SL3 ....13 K7
Pond Meadow School
  GUW GU2 ....111 L4
Pools in the Park
  RCH/KEW TW9 ....17 K9
Poplar Primary School
  WIM/MER SW19 ....43 L4
Portesbery School
  CBLY GU15 ....68 F2
Portland Medical Centre
  SNWD SE25 ....46 B6
Potley Hill Primary School
  YTLY GU46 ....67 L3
Potters Gate CE Primary
  School
  FNM GU9 ....4 D3
Potters Industrial Park
  FLEETS GU52 ....107 J1
Potters International Hotel
  ALDT GU11 ....108 B2
Pound Hill Infant School
  CRAWE RH10 ....177 M4
Pound Hill Junior School
  CRAWE RH10 ....177 M4
The Pountney Clinic
  HSLW TW3 ....16 A8
Powell Corderoy Primary
  School
  DORK RH4 ....116 F8
Premier Cinema
  DORK RH4 ....117 J6
Premier Travel Inn
  ALDT GU11 ....108 A4
  BAGS GU19 ....51 N4
  BH/WHM TN16 ....104 C6
  BRAK RG12 ....32 D3
  BTFD TW8 ....17 L4
  CHSGTN KT9 ....59 J8
  COB KT11 ....75 L1
  CRAWE RH10 ....159 H9
  CRAWE RH10 ....159 N8
  CRAWW RH11 ....176 A6
  CRAWW RH11 ....176 F7
  CROY/NA CRO 63 J5
  CROY/NA CRO 64 A4
  ECT SW5 ....19 M2
  ECRIN RH19 ....161 P8
  EPSOM KT18 ....78 A3
  FARN GU14 ....88 A4
  FUL/PGN SW6 ....19 J8
  GU GU1 ....112 B4
  HOR/WEW KT19 ....60 C4
  HORL RH6 ....159 J3
  HORS RH12 ....192 C7
  HSLW TW3 ....16 A8
  HTHAIR TW6 ....14 C6
  HYS/HAR UB3 ....14 D2
  KWD/TDW/WH KT20 ....79 J8
  REDH RH1 ....140 C3
  SHST GU47 ....67 P1
  WHTN TW2 ....25 K4
  WIM/MER SW19 ....43 N2
  WOKN/KNAP GU21 ....72 A6
Preymead Industrial Estate
  FNM GU9 ....108 D7
Prince Consort's Library
  ALDT GU11 ....108 B3
Princes Hall
  ALDT GU11 ....108 C4
Princes Mead Shopping
  Centre
  FARN GU14 ....88 D4
Princess of Wales
  Conservatory
  RCH/KEW TW9 ....17 M5
The Princess Royal Barracks
  FRIM GU16 ....69 M9
Princess Square Shopping
  Centre
  BRAK RG12 ....32 D3
Prins Willem-Alexander
  School
  WOKS/MYFD GU22 ....72 G6
Prior Heath Infant School
  CBLY GU15 ....69 J3
Priors Field School
  GODL GU7 ....130 F4
Priory CE Primary School
  WIM/MER SW19 ....28 E8
The Priory CE Voluntary
  Aided School
  DORK RH4 ....116 F8
Priory Retail Park
  WIM/MER SW19 ....43 P1
Priory School
  BNSTD SM7 ....79 L4
Priory Special School
  CBLY GU15 ....45 P5
Progress Business Park
  CROY/NA CRO 63 H1
Prospect House School
  PUT/ROE SW15 ....28 A3

Purley Community Health Clinic
PUR/KEN CR8 ....63 J9
Purley & District War Memorial Hospital
PUR/KEN CR8 ....63 J9
Purley Downs Golf Club
SAND/SEL CR2 ....63 M9
Purley John Fisher RFC
COUL/CHIP CR5 ....81 J9
Purley Oaks Primary School
SAND/SEL CR2 ....63 M6
Purley Secretarial & Language College
PUR/KEN CR8 ....63 J9
Purley Sports Club
PUR/KEN CR8 ....62 F8
Putney Animal Hospital
PUT/ROE SW15 ....19 H9
Putney Exchange Shopping Centre
PUT/ROE SW15 ....19 H9
Putney High School
PUT/ROE SW15 ....28 A1
Putney Leisure Centre
PUT/ROE SW15 ....18 C9
Putney Lower Common Cemetery
BARN SW13 ....18 F7
Putneymead Medical Centre
PUT/ROE SW15 ....18 F9
Putney Park School
PUT/ROE SW15 ....18 F9
Putney School of Art
PUT/ROE SW15 ....19 J9
Putney Vale Cemetery
PUT/ROE SW15 ....27 M5
Putney Vale Crematorium
PUT/ROE SW15 ....27 M5
Puttenham CE Infant School
RGUW GU3 ....130 B1
Puttenham Golf Club
RGUW GU3 ....130 D1
Pyrcroft Primary School
CHERT KT16 ....37 J7
Pyrford Golf Club
WOKS/MYFD GU22 ....73 M6
Pyrford Primary School
WOKS/MYFD GU22 ....73 K5
Quality Hotel
DTCH/LGLY SL3 ....12 F4
Quarryside Business Park
REDH RH1 ....120 D1
Quebec House
BH/WHM TN16 ....105 H6
Queen Charlotte's Cottage
RCH/KEW TW9 ....17 K7
Queen Eleanor's CE Junior School
GUW GU2 ....111 M6
Queen Elizabeth Hospital
BNSTD SM7 ....79 N7
Queen Elizabeth II Silver Jubilee School
SWTR RH13 ....192 E9
Queen Elizabeth's Foundation Training College
LHD/OX KT22 ....76 D6
Queen Mary's Hospital for Children
SUT SM1 ....43 N9
Queen Mary's University Hospital
PUT/ROE SW15 ....27 M2
Queen's Building
HTHAIR TW6 ....14 D8
The Queens CE Primary School
RCH/KEW TW9 ....17 M5
Queen's Club
WKENS W14 ....19 J3
Queens Gate School
SKENS SW7 ....19 N2
Queens Manor Primary School
FUL/PGN SW6 ....18 G5
Queens Medical Centre
RCHPK/HAM TW10 ....26 E1
Queensmill School
FUL/PGN SW6 ....19 L7
Queen's Road Cemetery
CROY/NA CR0 ....45 L7
Queens Sports Centre
GODL GU7 ....131 H6
Queen Victoria Hospital
EGRIN RH19 ....162 E9
Radisson Edwardian Hotel
HYS/HAR UB3 ....14 E5
Radisson Edwardian Vanderbilt Hotel
SKENS SW7 ....19 N2
Railton Road Clinic
HNHL SE24 ....30 C1
Rainbow Industrial Estate
RYNPK SW20 ....42 F3
Rainbow Leisure Centre
EW KT17 ....78 C1
Rainbow Natural Health Centre
REDH RH1 ....120 B6
The Raleigh School
EHSLY KT24 ....94 E5
Ramada Hotel
CRAWE RH10 ....177 K3
EHSLY KT24 ....95 H9
RFARN GU10 ....109 J3
Randalls Park Crematorium
LHD/OX KT22 ....76 E9
Ranelagh School
BRAK RG12 ....32 E4

Rathfern Primary School
FSTH SE23 ....31 N4
The Ravensbourne School
HAYES BR2 ....47 P5
Ravenscourt Park Preparatory School
HMSMTH W6 ....18 E2
Ravenstone Primary School
BAL SW12 ....29 K4
Raynes Park High School
RYNPK SW20 ....42 F4
Raynes Park Sports Ground
RYNPK SW20 ....42 F4
Raynes Park Vale FC
RYNPK SW20 ....43 H6
RCA
SKENS SW7 ....19 N1
Redcliffe School
WBPTN SW10 ....19 N4
Redfields Business Park
FLEETS GU52 ....106 E4
Red Gates School
CROY/NA CR0 ....63 J4
Redhill Aerodrome
REDH RH1 ....140 G1
Redhill Business Centre
REDH RH1 ....120 B4
Redhill College
REDH RH1 ....120 D6
Redhill FC
REDH RH1 ....120 B9
Redhill & Reigate Golf Club
REDH RH1 ....119 P8
The Redlands Primary School
DORK RH4 ....137 H1
Red Lion Business Park
SURB KT6 ....59 N1
Redstone Cemetery
REDH RH1 ....120 D6
Reedham Park School
PUR/KEN CR8 ....81 J3
Reed Place Business Park
SHPTN TW17 ....38 B9
Reeds School
COB KT11 ....76 A1
Regal Cinema
CRAN GU6 ....152 F9
Regina Coeli RC Primary School
SAND/SEL CR2 ....63 K6
Reigate College
REIG RH2 ....119 M4
Reigate Day Hospital
REDH RH1 ....119 P5
Reigate Grammar School
REIG RH2 ....119 N5
Reigate Heath Golf Club
REIG RH2 ....118 C5
Reigate Hill Golf Club
REIG RH2 ....100 C8
Reigate Manor Hotel
REIG RH2 ....119 M2
Reigate Parish Infant School
REIG RH2 ....119 N5
Reigate Priory Junior School
REIG RH2 ....119 L5
Reigate Priory & Museum
REIG RH2 ....119 L5
Reigate St Marys Preparatory & Choir School
REIG RH2 ....119 M5
Reigate School
REIG RH2 ....119 N8
The Renaissance Hotel
HTHAIR TW6 ....14 E6
The Retail Business Centre
EW KT17 ....60 D8
Rewards Centre
HSLW TW3 ....16 C8
Reynard Mills Trading Estate
BTFD TW8 ....17 J3
Rhoda McGaw Theatre & Cinema
WOKN/KNAP GU21 ....10 D3
RHS Garden Wisley
RPLY/SEND GU23 ....74 A7
Ricards Lodge High School
WIM/MER SW19 ....28 C7
Richard Atkins Primary School
BRXS/STRHM SW2 ....29 P3
Richings Park Golf Club
DTCH/LGLY SL3 ....13 H2
Richings Park Sports Club
WDR/YW UB7 ....13 K1
Richmond Adult & Community College
RCH/KEW TW9 ....17 K9
Richmond American International University
RCHPK/HAM TW10 ....26 D2
The Richmond Clinic
RCH/KEW TW9 ....17 M9
Richmond Community College
TWK TW1 ....25 N4
Richmond FC
RCH/KEW TW9 ....17 K9
The Richmond Gate Hotel
RCHPK/HAM TW10 ....26 D3
The Richmond Golf Club
RCHPK/HAM TW10 ....26 D5
The Richmond Green Medical Centre
RCH/KEW TW9 ....26 C1
The Richmond Hill Hotel
RCHPK/HAM TW10 ....26 D3

Richmond House School
HPTN TW12 ....24 G8
Richmond Lock
TWK TW1 ....17 K9
Richmond Magistrates Court
RCH/KEW TW9 ....17 K9
Richmond Park Golf Club
PUT/ROE SW15 ....27 K3
Richmond Road Medical Centre
KUTN/CMB KT2 ....8 D1
Richmond Theatre
RCH/KEW TW9 ....17 K9
Richmond upon Thames College
WHTN TW2 ....25 M3
Riddlesdown High School
PUR/KEN CR8 ....81 N5
The Ridgeway Community School
CROY/NA CR0 ....127 N6
Ridgeway Primary School
SAND/SEL CR2 ....63 N7
Rikkyo School in England
HORS RH12 ....188 G2
Ripley CE Infant School
RPLY/SEND GU23 ....93 M1
Ripley Court School
RPLY/SEND GU23 ....93 N1
Ripley CC
RPLY/SEND GU23 ....93 N1
Ritz Cinema
HORS RH12 ....192 C8
River Brent Business Park
HNWL W7 ....16 E1
Riverdene Industrial Estate
WOT/HER KT12 ....57 M4
River Gardens Business Centre
EBED/NFELT TW14 ....15 K9
River Mole Business Park
ESH/CLAY KT10 ....40 A9
Riverdale Primary School
WAND/EARL SW18 ....28 D4
Riverside Business Centre
WAND/EARL SW18 ....28 E4
The Riverside Business Centre
GU GU1 ....6 C3
Riverside Business Park
WIM/MER SW19 ....43 N2
Riverside Community Health Care
WKENS W14 ....19 H1
Riverside Park Industrial Estate
FNM GU9 ....5 J2
Riverside Quarter
WAND/EARL SW18 ....19 L9
Riverside Studios Cinema
BARN SW13 ....18 F3
Riverside Wandle Trading Estate
MTCM CR4 ....44 B8
Riverview CE Primary School
HOR/WEW KT19 ....60 A3
Riverway Industrial Estate
RGUW GU3 ....132 A5
Roan Industrial Estate
MTCM CR4 ....44 A2
Robin Hood Infant School
SUT SM1 ....61 L4
Robin Hood Junior School
SUT SM1 ....61 M4
Robin Hood Lane Health Centre
SUT SM1 ....61 L4
Robin Hood Primary School
KUTN/CMB KT2 ....27 J8
The Roche School
WAND/EARL SW18 ....28 D1
Rock & Bowl Bowling Alley
EGRIN RH19 ....180 D2
Rockmount Primary School
NRWD SE19 ....30 D9
Rodborough Technology College
MFD/CHID GU8 ....149 N5
Rodd Estate
SHPTN TW17 ....38 E6
Roehampton Church School
PUT/ROE SW15 ....27 N3
The Roehampton Priory Hospital
PUT/ROE SW15 ....18 D9
Roehampton Recreation Centre
PUT/ROE SW15 ....27 L3
Roehampton University
PUT/ROE SW15 ....28 B2
Roehampton University (Digby Stuart College)
PUT/ROE SW15 ....27 L1
Roehampton University (Froebel College)
PUT/ROE SW15 ....27 L2
Roehampton University (Southlands College)
PUT/ROE SW15 ....27 L1
Roffey Park Institute
HORS RH12 ....193 L4
Roffey Social & Sports Club
HORS RH12 ....192 F5
Rokeby School
KUTN/CMB KT2 ....42 A1
Roke Primary School
PUR/KEN CR8 ....81 L3
Roker Park Golf Club
RGUW GU3 ....91 K9
Roman Industrial Estate
CROY/NA CR0 ....45 N8

Romans Business Park
FNM GU9 ....5 J1
Ronald Rose Primary School
PUT/ROE SW15 ....28 A3
Rosary RC Infant School
HEST TW5 ....15 P4
Rosebery School
EPSOM KT18 ....78 A3
Roselands Clinic
NWMAL KT3 ....42 A5
Rosemead Preparatory School
DUL SE21 ....30 D5
Rosendale Primary School
DUL SE21 ....30 D3
Rose of Kingston (Kingston Theatre)
KUT/HW KT1 ....8 B5
Rosslyn Park RFC
PUT/ROE SW15 ....18 D9
The Rotunda
KUT/HW KT1 ....8 E4
Roundshaw J & I School
WLGTN SM6 ....62 G6
Rowan High School
CLAP SW4 ....29 N2
Rowan Preparatory School
ESH/CLAY KT10 ....58 F6
Rowans School
RYNPK SW20 ....42 E1
Rowfant Business Centre
CRAWE RH10 ....178 F5
Rowledge CE (Controlled) Primary School
RFNM GU10 ....146 A1
Rowley Industrial Park
ACT W3 ....17 P1
The Royal Alexandra & Albert School
REIG RH2 ....100 A9
Royal Army Medical Corps
ALDT GU11 ....108 F2
Royal Ascot Golf Club
ASC SL5 ....34 A3
The Royal Ballet School
RCHPK/HAM TW10 ....27 J4
The Royal Berkshire Ramada Plaza Hotel
ASC SL5 ....34 G4
Royal Botanic Gardens Kew School
RCH/KEW TW9 ....17 M5
Royal Brompton & National Heart Hospitals
CHEL SW3 ....19 P3
Royal College of Music
SKENS SW7 ....19 P1
The Royal First School (Crown Aided)
WDSR SL4 ....20 B8
Royal Grammar School
GU GU1 ....7 F4
Royal Holloway University of London
EGH TW20 ....21 J9
.............36 B2
Royal Holloway University of London (Hall of Residence)
EGH TW20 ....21 J7
Royal Hospital
RCH/KEW TW9 ....17 L8
Royal Hospital for Neuro-Disability
PUT/ROE SW15 ....28 B2
Royal Hospital & Home
PUT/ROE SW15 ....27 N3
The Royal Junior School
GSHT GU26 ....183 N1
The Royal Kent CE Primary School
LHD/OX KT22 ....76 C3
Royal Logistic Corps Museum
FRIM GU16 ....69 M8
Royal Marsden Hospital
BELMT SM2 ....61 N8
CHEL SW3 ....19 P3
Royal Mid-Surrey Golf Club
RCH/KEW TW9 ....17 K8
Royal Military Academy
CBLY GU15 ....68 C1
Royal Military School of Music
WHTN TW2 ....25 L2
Royal Russell School
CROY/NA CR0 ....64 B5
The Royal School
HASM GU27 ....166 C9
Royal & Sun Alliance Sports Club
HORS RH12 ....192 D4
Royal Surrey County Hospital
GUW GU2 ....111 L5
Royal Wimbledon Golf Club
WIM/MER SW19 ....27 N8
Royston Primary School
PGE/AN SE20 ....46 D2
RSPCA HQ
HORS RH12 ....192 B9
Rudgwick Medical Centre
HORS RH12 ....189 M3
Rudgwick Primary School
HORS RH12 ....189 N3
Rufus Business Centre
WIM/MER SW19 ....28 E5
Runnymede Hospital
CHERT KT16 ....55 H2
Runnymede Hotel & Spa
EGH TW20 ....21 N6

Runnymede (NT)
EGH TW20 ....21 K6
Rural Life Centre
RFNM GU10 ....147 J1
Ruskin House School
HNHL SE24 ....30 D1
Rusper Golf Club
RDKG RH5 ....157 H8
Rusper Primary School
HORS RH12 ....175 H4
The Russell JMI School
RCHPK/HAM TW10 ....26 C5
The Russell School
RCHPK/HAM TW10 ....26 C4
Rutherford Way Industrial Estate
CRAWE RH10 ....159 K9
Rutlish School
RYNPK SW20 ....43 K3
Rydens School
WOT/HER KT12 ....57 L2
Rydes Hill Preparatory School
RGUW GU3 ....111 M3
Rydon Business Centre
LHD/OX KT22 ....76 G9
Ryebrook Business Park
LHD/OX KT22 ....76 G9
Ryelands Primary School
SNWD SE25 ....46 B6
Ryvers School
DTCH/LGLY SL3 ....12 B1
Sackville Community College
EGRIN RH19 ....180 F2
Sacred Heart Catholic Primary School
PUT/ROE SW15 ....27 M1
Sacred Heart High School
HMSMTH W6 ....18 G2
Sacred Heart Junior School
HMSMTH W6 ....19 H2
Sacred Heart RC Primary School
NWMAL KT3 ....42 E5
TEDD TW11 ....41 H1
St Agathas RC Primary School
KUTN/CMB KT2 ....26 E9
St Albans RC Aided Primary School
E/WMO/HCT KT8 ....40 B6
St Andrews Catholic School
LHD/OX KT22 ....77 J9
St Andrews CE First & Middle School
CRAWE RH11 ....177 K6
St Andrews CE Infant School
FNM GU9 ....5 F4
St Andrews CE School
CROY/NA CR0 ....2 B6
St Andrews Primary School
COB KT11 ....75 L2
St Andrew's School
WOKN/KNAP GU21 ....10 A1
St Annes Catholic Primary School
BNSTD SM7 ....79 L5
CHERT KT16 ....37 L9
St Annes CE Primary School
WAND/EARL SW18 ....28 E1
St Annes CP School
STWL/WRAY TW19 ....23 H3
St Anne's Special School
MRDN SM4 ....43 L6
St Anns Heath Junior School
VW GU25 ....36 D6
St Anselms RC Primary School
NWDGN UB2 ....15 P1
St Anslems RC Primary School
TOOT SW17 ....29 K6
St Anthonys Hospital
WPK KT4 ....43 H9
St Anthonys RC Primary School
EDUL SE22 ....31 H2
PGE/AN SE20 ....46 B2
St Augustines Primary School
FRIM GU16 ....69 H6
St Augustines RC Primary School
WKENS W14 ....19 J4
St Barnabas & Philip CE Primary
KENS W8 ....19 L1
St Bartholomews CE Primary School
SYD SE26 ....31 K7
St Bartholomews Primary School
HASM GU27 ....184 D2
St Bedes CE Junior School
RPLY/SEND GU23 ....93 M4
St Bedes RC Infant School
BAL SW12 ....29 N4
St Bedes School
REDH RH1 ....120 A2
St Bernadette Catholic Junior School
BAL SW12 ....29 M3
St Bernadettes CP School
FARN GU14 ....88 C2
St Boniface RC Primary School
TOOT SW17 ....29 J8
St Catherine's Hospice
CRAWE RH10 ....176 G7

St Catherine's Primary
School
REDH RH1 ....121 M4
St Catherines School
SHGR GU5 ....132 D6
TWK TW1 ....25 N5
St Cecilia's CE Primary
School
WAND/EARL SW18 ....28 B3
St Cecilias RC Primary
School
WPK KT4 ....61 H1
St Chads RC Primary School
SNWD SE25 ....45 N6
St Charles Borromeo RCP
School
WEY KT13 ....56 C2
St Christophers School
BECK BR3 ....47 J3
EPSOM KT18 ....78 C3
St Clare Business Park
HPTN TW12 ....25 K9
St Clements Primary School
EW KT17 ....60 D7
St Cuthbert Mayne RC
Primary School
CRAN GU6 ....153 H9
St Cuthberts CE Primary
School
EGH TW20 ....36 A1
St Cuthbert With St Matthias
CE Primary School
ECT SW5 ....19 M3
St Cyprians Greek Orthodox
Primary School
THHTH CR7 ....45 L3
St Davids College
WWKM BR4 ....47 H8
St Davids Health Centre
STWL/WRAY TW19 ....22 G3
St Davids School
ASHF TW15 ....23 J6
PUR/KEN CR8 ....63 H9
St Dominics School
MFD/CHID GU8 ....168 B2
St Dunstans Catholic
Primary School
WOKS/MYFD GU22 ....11 G3
St Dunstans CE Primary
School
CHEAM SM3 ....61 J5
St Dunstans College
CAT SE6 ....31 N4
St Ebba's Hospital
HOR/WEW KT19 ....60 A7
St Edmunds RC Primary
School
GODL GU7 ....150 E1
WHTN TW2 ....25 J5
St Edmunds School
GSHT GU26 ....165 N8
St Elizabeths CE Primary
School
RCHPK/HAM TW10 ....26 E2
St Elpheges RC Primary
School
WLGTN SM6 ....62 C5
St Faiths CE Primary School
WAND/EARL SW18 ....28 E1
St Francesca Cabrini
Primary School
FSTH SE23 ....31 K2
St Francis Catholic School
CTHM CR3 ....101 P1
St Francis of Assisi Primary
School
CRAWE RH10 ....177 H6
St Francis RC Primary School
ASC SL5 ....34 A7
St Francis, Westborough
Primary School
GUW GU2 ....111 M4
St Francis Xavier College
BAL SW12 ....29 L2
St Georges Business Park
WEY KT13 ....56 C7
St Georges College
ADL/WDHM KT15 ....55 P2
St George's College Track
ADL/WDHM KT15 ....55 P1
St George's Hill Golf Club
WEY KT13 ....56 E9
St Georges Hospital
TOOT SW17 ....29 H8
St Georges Industrial Estate
CBLY GU15 ....68 D5
KUTN/CMB KT2 ....26 C8
St Georges School
ASC SL5 ....34 B5
St Giles CE (Aided) Infant
School
ASHTD KT21 ....77 M7
St Giles School
SAND/SEL CR2 ....63 K5
St Helier Hospital
CAR SM5 ....43 N9
St Hilarys School
GODL GU7 ....150 C1
Saint Hill Manor
EGRIN RH19 ....180 B7
St Hugh of Lincoln RCP
School
WOKN/KNAP GU21 ....71 K8
St Ignatius RC Primary
School
SUN TW16 ....39 J2
St Ives School
HASM GU27 ....184 F2
St James CE Primary School
MFD/CHID GU8 ....148 D1
WEY KT13 ....56 E2

St James Independent
School
TWK TW1 ....25 P5
St James Independent
School for Senior Girls
WKENS W14 ....19 J2
St James Independent
Schools for Junior Boys
& Girls
WKENS W14 ....19 J2
St James Medical Centre
CROY/NA CR0 ....45 M8
St James RC Primary School
WHTN TW2 ....25 M6
St James the Great RC
Primary School
THHTH CR7 ....45 K3
St John Fisher RC Primary
School
RYNPK SW20 ....42 G6
St Johns Beaumont School
WDSR SL4 ....20 C5
St Johns Catholic Primary
School
HORS RH12 ....191 P9
St Johns CE Infant School
RFNM GU10 ....165 H2
St Johns CE Primary School
CROY/NA CR0 ....64 D2
KUT/HW KT1 ....8 E7
PGE/AN SE20 ....46 C1
St John's CE Walham Green
School
FUL/PGN SW6 ....19 J6
St Johns CE Primary School
CRAN GU6 ....102 B6
St Johns CP School
WOKN/KNAP GU21 ....71 L7
St John's Hospital Day
Centre
BTSEA SW11 ....19 P9
St Johns Primary School
REDH RH1 ....120 A7
St John the Baptist CE
Junior School
KUT/HW KT1 ....8 B1
St John the Baptist School
WOKS/MYFD GU22 ....72 E8
St Josephs Catholic Primary
School
ALDT GU11 ....108 C6
EPSOM KT18 ....78 A3
St Joseph's Catholic Primary
School
GUW GU2 ....111 M3
St Josephs Catholic Primary
School
REDH RH1 ....120 A4
St Josephs College
STRHM/NOR SW16 ....30 C9
St Josephs Primary School
WAND/EARL SW18 ....28 D1
St Josephs RC Infant School
NRWD SE19 ....30 D9
St Josephs RC Junior School
NRWD SE19 ....30 D9
St Josephs RC Primary
School
BRAK RG12 ....32 F3
DORK RH4 ....116 G7
KUT/HW KT1 ....9 H6
St Josephs School
CRAN GU6 ....153 J6
St Judes CE Junior School
EGH TW20 ....21 H9
St Judes CE Primary School
NHHL SE24 ....30 C2
St Katharines Knockholt CE
Primary School
RSEV TN14 ....85 M6
St Lawrence Business Centre
FELT TW13 ....24 C5
St Lawrence Catholic School
FELT TW13 ....24 C5
St Lawrence Junior School
E/WMO/HCT KT8 ....40 D4
St Lawrence Primary School
EHSLY KT24 ....95 M7
St Leonards CE Primary
School
STRHM/NOR SW16 ....29 N8
St Leonards Community
Infant School
SWTR RH13 ....192 D8
St Lukes CE Primary School
KUTN/CMB KT2 ....9 F2
WNWD SE27 ....30 D8
St Lukes School
THHTH CR7 ....45 J5
St Margaret Clitherow RC
Primary School
BRAK RG12 ....32 B8
St Margarets Business
Centre
TWK TW1 ....25 P3
St Margarets CE Primary
School
CRAWW RH11 ....176 E4
St Margaret's School
KWD/TDW/WH KT20 ....99 H1
St Marks Catholic School
HSLW TW3 ....15 P8
St Marks CE Aided Primary
School
GODL GU7 ....150 A1
St Marks CE Primary School
FARN GU14 ....88 F7
HAYES BR2 ....47 N4
SNWD SE25 ....46 A5

St Marks Primary School
MTCM CR4 ....44 B3
St Martin in the Fields High
School
BRXS/STRHM SW2 ....30 C4
St Martins CE Junior School
EPSOM KT18 ....78 B4
St Martins CE Primary
School
DORK RH4 ....116 F6
St Martins House Business
Centre
EHSLY KT24 ....94 G9
St Martins Walk Shopping
Centre
DORK RH4 ....117 H6
St Mary Magdalens Catholic
Primary School
MORT/ESHN SW14 ....18 B8
St Mary & St Peters CE
Primary School
TEDD TW11 ....25 M8
St Marys Catholic Infant
School
CROY/NA CR0 ....2 E2
St Marys CE Aided Primary
School
RFNM GU10 ....146 G5
St Marys CE First School
MFD/CHID GU8 ....130 E7
St Marys CE Infant School
LHD/OX KT22 ....97 J2
St Marys CE Junior School
OXTED RH8 ....103 L8
STWL/WRAY TW19 ....23 H2
THDT KT7 ....41 H9
St Mary's Cemetery
BTSEA SW11 ....29 H1
HORS RH12 ....192 B9
St Marys CE Primary School
BF/WBF KT14 ....74 A2
CHSGTN KT9 ....59 L5
EGRIN RH19 ....180 C1
HORS RH12 ....192 A9
MFD/CHID GU8 ....168 A8
St Mary's CE Primary School
PUT/ROE SW15 ....19 H8
St Marys CE Primary School
TWK TW1 ....25 P3
St Mary's College University
of Surrey
TWK TW1 ....25 N6
St Marys High School
CROY/NA CR0 ....2 D1
St Marys Infant School
CAR SM5 ....62 A3
St Mary's Junior School
TWK TW1 ....26 A3
St Marys Primary School
WKENS W14 ....19 H1
St Marys RC Infant School
CAR SM5 ....62 B4
St Mary's RC Primary School
CHSWK W4 ....18 C3
St Marys RC Primary School
BECK BR3 ....47 J1
CLAP SW4 ....29 M1
ISLW TW7 ....16 C8
WIM/MER SW19 ....43 L1
St Marys School Ascot
ASC SL5 ....34 B8
St Marys Tutorial College
GUW GU2 ....112 A8
St Matthews CE (Aided)
Infant School
COB KT11 ....75 K7
St Matthews CE Primary
School
REDH RH1 ....120 B5
RYNPK SW20 ....42 E2
SURB KT6 ....41 L8
St Michaels Abbey
FARN GU14 ....88 E2
St Michaels CE First School
RDKG RH5 ....97 J7
St Michaels CE Infant School
ALDT GU11 ....108 D6
St Michaels CE Junior School
ALDT GU11 ....108 D6
St Michaels CE Primary
School
ASC SL5 ....34 D6
BRAK RG12 ....32 C6
SHST GU47 ....49 J3
WAND/EARL SW18 ....28 C3
St Michaels RC School
ASHF TW15 ....23 K8
St Michaels & St Martins RC
Primary School
HSLWW TW4 ....15 P8
St Michaels Sydenham CE
Primary School
SYD SE26 ....31 N7
The St Michael Steiner
School
WAND/EARL SW18 ....28 D1
St Nicholas Centre
SUT SM1 ....61 M4
St Nicholas CE Primary
School
SHPTN TW17 ....38 D7
St Nicholas Primary School
CRAN GU6 ....152 C9
FLEETS GU52 ....106 E4
PUR/KEN CR8 ....81 J2
REDH RH1 ....100 F9
St Nicolas CE Infant School
GUW GU2 ....6 C7
St Omer Barracks
ALDT GU11 ....108 F2

St Patricks Catholic Primary
School
FARN GU14 ....88 F3
St Pauls Catholic College
SUN TW16 ....39 J2
St Pauls CE Aided Primary
School
DORK RH4 ....117 H7
St Pauls CE Infant School
RFNM GU10 ....109 J7
St Pauls CE Junior School
KUTN/CMB KT2 ....9 J1
St Pauls CE Primary School
ADL/WDHM KT15 ....55 L3
BTFD TW8 ....17 K4
CHSGTN KT9 ....59 L5
St Pauls Girls School
HMSMTH W6 ....19 H2
St Paul's Primary School
HMSMTH W6 ....18 G3
St Pauls RC Primary School
THDT KT7 ....40 E8
St Pauls School
BARN SW13 ....18 F3
St Peter & Paul CE Infant
School
CTHM CR3 ....101 J5
St Peters Catholic
Comprehensive School
GU GU1 ....112 C4
St Peters Catholic Primary
School
EGRIN RH19 ....180 B1
St Peters CE (Aided)
Primary School
FNM GU9 ....127 K6
St Peters CE Junior School
FARN GU14 ....88 E3
YTLY GU46 ....67 H2
St Peters CE Middle School
WDSR SL4 ....20 E2
St Peters CE Primary School
HMSMTH W6 ....18 E5
OXTED RH8 ....122 C4
St Peters Primary School
SAND/SEL CR2 ....63 M5
St Peters RC Primary School
LHD/OX KT22 ....77 J9
St Philips School
CHSGTN KT9 ....59 K5
SEKNS SW7 ....19 N2
St Phillips Catholic School
SYD SE26 ....31 J7
St Philomenas Catholic High
School
CAR SM5 ....62 A4
St Piers Further Education
College (NCYPE)
LING RH7 ....162 F1
St Piers School (NCYPE)
LING RH7 ....143 N9
St Polycarps Catholic
Primary School
FNM GU9 .... 5 J5
St Raphaels Hospice
WPK KT4 ....61 H1
St Richards with St Andrews
CE Primary School
RCHPK/HAM TW10 ....26 A6
St Robert Southwell
Primary School
HORS RH12 ....192 F4
St Sebastians CE Primary
School
EWKG RG40 ....49 J1
St Stephens CE Junior School
TWK TW1 ....25 P2
St Stephens CE Primary
School
GDST RH9 ....122 F8
St Teresas Preparatory
School
EHSLY KT24 ....95 M8
St Teresas School
RDKG RH5 ....115 M3
St Thomas Becket RC
Primary School
SNWD SE25 ....46 A7
St Thomas of Canterbury
Catholic Primary School
GU GU1 ....112 C5
St Thomas of Canterbury
Primary School
MTCM CR4 ....44 C4
St Thomas of Canterbury
RC Primary School
FUL/PGN SW6 ....19 K5
St Walter & St John Sports
Ground
TOOT SW17 ....29 H4
St Wilfrids RC School
CRAWW RH11 ....176 E6
St William of York Primary
School
FSTH SE23 ....31 M3
Safari Cinema
CROY/NA CR0 ....45 K8
Salesian College
CHERT KT16 ....37 L9
FARN GU14 ....88 F6
Salesian RC School
CHERT KT16 ....55 J1
Salfords Industrial Estate
REDH RH1 ....140 C4
Salfords Primary School
REDH RH1 ....140 C2
Sampson Business Park
CBLY GU15 ....68 D5
The Samuel Cody School
FARN GU14 ....88 D8
Sandcross Junior School
REIG RH2 ....119 K8

Sanderstead Junior School
SAND/SEL CR2 ....63 M7
Sandfield CP School
GU GU1 .... 6 E4
Sandhurst School
SHST GU47 ....49 P8
Sandhurst Sports Club
SHST GU47 ....67 N1
Sandown Industrial Park
ESH/CLAY KT10 ....58 A1
Sandown Park Racecourse
ESH/CLAY KT10 ....58 B2
Sandown Sports Club &
Ski Centre
ESH/CLAY KT10 ....58 B2
Sandringham Infant School
FRIM GU16 ....69 H9
Sandy Lane Primary School
BNFD RG42 ....32 D1
Satellite Business Village
CRAWE RH10 ....177 H1
Savill Garden
(Windsor Great Park)
EGH TW20 ....20 D9
Saxon Business Centre
WIM/MER SW19 ....43 N3
Saxon CP School
SHPTN TW17 ....38 B6
Sayer Clinic
CROY/NA CR0 ....63 H3
Sayes Court Junior School
ADL/WDHM KT15 ....55 M4
Science Museum
SKENS SW7 ....19 P1
Science Museum IMAX
Cinema
SKENS SW7 ....19 P1
Scott Broadwood CE Infant
School
RDKG RH5 ....156 C6
Scott Broadwood School
RDKG RH5 ....155 K8
The Screen at Reigate
REIG RH2 ....119 L5
Screen Cinema
WOT/HER KT12 ....39 J9
Seaton House School
BELMT SM2 ....61 P8
Secombe Centre
SUT SM1 ....61 M5
Selhurst High School
for Boys
CROY/NA CR0 ....45 M7
The Selhurst Medical Centre
SNWD SE25 ....45 N7
Sellincourt School
TOOT SW17 ....29 H9
Selsdon Community Centre
SAND/SEL CR2 ....64 B8
Selsdon High School
SAND/SEL CR2 ....64 D6
Selsdon Park Hotel &
Golf Course
SAND/SEL CR2 ....64 C9
Selsdon Primary School
SAND/SEL CR2 ....64 C7
Selsdon Road Industrial
Estate
SAND/SEL CR2 ....63 M6
Semaphore Tower
COB KT11 ....74 F6
Send CE Infant School
RPLY/SEND GU23 ....93 H4
Send C
RPLY/SEND GU23 ....92 F4
Sergeant Industrial Estate
WAND/EARL SW18 ....28 E2
Servite RC Primary School
WBPTN SW10 ....19 N4
Seymour First & Middle
School
CRAWW RH11 ....176 E9
Shalford Infant School
RGUE GU4 ....132 C2
Shalford Mill (NT)
RGUE GU4 ....132 C1
Shannon Corner Retail Park
NWMAL KT3 ....42 E5
Shawfield Primary School
ASHV GU12 ....109 J3
Shawley Primary School
EPSOM KT18 ....78 G7
Sheen International School
MORT/ESHN SW14 ....18 C9
Sheen Lane Health Centre
MORT/ESHN SW14 ....18 A8
Sheen Lawn Tennis &
Squash Club
MORT/ESHN SW14 ....27 H1
Sheen Mount Primary
School
RCHPK/HAM TW10 ....26 G1
Sheen Sports Centre
MORT/ESHN SW14 ....18 C9
Shelley Primary School
HORS RH12 ....191 L7
Shepperton Business Park
SHPTN TW17 ....38 E6
Shepperton Health Centre
SHPTN TW17 ....38 D6
Shepperton Studios
SHPTN TW17 ....38 B4
Sheraton Skyline Hotel
HYS/HAR UB3 ....14 F5
Shere CE Infant School
SHGR GU5 ....134 C1
Sheriglands Primary School
WAND/EARL SW18 ....28 C4
Sherwood Park School
WLGTN SM6 ....62 F2
Sherwood School
MTCM CR4 ....44 D4

The Ship Hotel
  WEY KT13 ....56 D2
Shirley Clinic
  CROY/NA CR0 ....46 C9
Shirley High School
  CROY/NA CR0 ....64 D2
Shirley Oaks Hospital
  CROY/NA CR0 ....46 C8
Shirley Park Golf Club
  CROY/NA CR0 ....64 B1
Shirley Wanderers RFC
  WWKM BR4 ....65 J3
Shooting Star House
  (Childrens Hospice)
  HPTN TW12 ....24 C9
Shortwood Infant School
  STA TW18 ....22 E6
Shotfield Health Clinic
  WLGTN SM6 ....62 D5
Shottermill Infant School
  HASM GU27 ....184 A3
Shrewsbury House School
  SURB KT6 ....59 K1
Silvergate Business Park
  COB KT11 ....74 D2
Silvermere Golf Club
  COB KT11 ....74 D2
Silver Wing Industrial Estate
  CROY/NA CR0 ....63 H5
Singlegate Primary School
  WIM/MER SW19 ....43 P1
Sir Greville Sprat Stadium
  GODL GU7 ....131 H7
Sir John Lillie Primary
  School
  HMSMTH W6 ....19 J4
Sir William Perkins School
  CHERT KT16 ....37 J9
The Sixth Form College
  FARN GU14 ....68 D9
Skimped Hill Health Centre
  BRAK RG12 ....32 D3
Sky Business Park
  EGH TW20 ....36 G3
Slinfold CE Primary School
  SWTR RH13 ....190 E6
Slinfold Park Golf &
  Country Club
  SWTR RH13 ....190 C8
Sloane Hospital
  BECK BR3 ....47 K2
Slough Community Mental
  Health Centre
  DTCH/LGLY SL3 ....12 E2
Slyfield Industrial Estate
  GU GU1 ....92 B9
Smallberry Green Primary
  School
  ISLW TW7 ....16 G7
Smallwood Primary School
  TOOT SW17 ....28 G7
Smitham Primary School
  COUL/CHIP CR5 ....80 E5
Smithbrook Clinic
  CRAN GU6 ....152 A9
Snowhill Business Centre
  CRAWE RH10 ....161 H8
Sofitel
  HORL RH6 ....159 J4
South Bookham School
  GT/LBKH KT23 ....96 C7
Southborough School
  SURB KT6 ....59 L2
South Croydon Medical
  Centre
  SAND/SEL CR2 ....63 L6
South Croydon Sports Club
  CROY/NA CR0 ....63 N4
Southern Clinic
  REIG RH2 ....119 N6
South Farnborough County
  Junior School
  FARN GU14 ....88 F5
South Farnborough Infant
  School
  FARN GU14 ....88 F7
South Farnham School
  FNM GU9 ....128 A4
The Southfields Clinic
  WAND/EARL SW18 ....28 D2
Southfields Community
  College
  WAND/EARL SW18 ....28 D4
Southfields Park Primary
  School
  HOR/WEW KT19 ....59 P8
Southgate Primary School
  CRAWE RH10 ....176 D7
South Hill Park Arts Centre
  BRAK RG12 ....32 D8
South London Crematorium
  MTCM CR4 ....44 E3
South London Liberal
  Synagogue
  STRHM/NOR SW16 ....29 N6
South London Tamil School
  CROY/NA CR0 ....45 L8
South London Theatre
  WNWD SE27 ....30 D6
Southmead Primary School
  WIM/MER SW19 ....28 B4
South Norwood Country
  Park
  SNWD SE25 ....46 C5
South Norwood Hill Medical
  Centre
  SNWD SE25 ....45 N3
South Norwood Medical
  Centre
  SNWD SE25 ....45 N5

South Norwood Pools &
  Fitness Centre
  SNWD SE25 ....46 A6
South Norwood Primary
  School
  SNWD SE25 ....46 A6
South Nutfield CC
  REDH RH1 ....121 H7
South Park Hotel
  SAND/SEL CR2 ....63 N3
Southside Shopping Centre
  WAND/EARL SW18 ....28 E2
South Thames College
  PUT/ROE SW15 ....27 L2
  PUT/ROE SW15 ....28 A1
  TOOT SW17 ....29 H8
  WAND/EARL SW18 ....28 E1
Southville Infant School
  EBED/NFELT TW14 ....24 A4
Southwark Sports Ground
  DUL SE21 ....30 G4
South West Middlesex
  Crematorium
  FELT TW13 ....24 C4
South West Surrey Business
  Centre
  GU GU1 ....7 F4
Southwood Golf Club
  FARN GU14 ....88 A5
Southwood Infant School
  FARN GU14 ....87 P4
Sparrow Farm Community
  Junior School
  EW KT17 ....60 F4
Sparrow Farm Infant School
  EBED/NFELT TW14 ....24 D3
Sparrow Farm Junior School
  EBED/NFELT TW14 ....24 D3
Spelthorne Clinic
  ASHF TW15 ....23 N9
Spelthorne Infant School
  ASHF TW15 ....23 N9
Spelthorne Leisure Centre
  STA TW18 ....22 D8
Spelthorne Sixth Form
  College
  ASHF TW15 ....23 J7
Spelthorne Sports Club
  ASHF TW15 ....38 F1
Spitfire Business Park
  CROY/NA CR0 ....63 J5
Spring Copse Business Park
  SWTR RH13 ....190 C7
Springfield Christian School
  CAT SE6 ....31 N6
Springfield Hospital
  TOOT SW17 ....29 H6
Springfield Primary School
  SUN TW16 ....38 G2
Spring Grove Primary
  School
  ISLW TW7 ....16 D7
Springlake Country Club
  ALDT GU11 ....108 G2
Spring Park Primary School
  CROY/NA CR0 ....64 G2
Springwell Infant School
  HEST TW5 ....15 N5
Springwell Junior School
  HEST TW5 ....15 N5
Sprint Industrial Estate
  BF/WBF KT14 ....55 P9
Spurgeon's College
  SNWD SE25 ....45 N3
Squerryes Court Manor
  House & Gardens
  BH/WHM TN16 ....104 G8
Squirrels Trading Estate
  HYS/HAR UB3 ....15 H1
SS Peter & Paul RC Primary
  School
  MTCM CR4 ....44 B5
Stafford Cross Business Park
  CROY/NA CR0 ....63 H4
Staines County Court
  STA TW18 ....22 D8
Staines Preparatory School
  STA TW18 ....22 D8
Staines RFC
  FELT TW13 ....24 B8
Staines Town FC
  STA TW18 ....37 L1
Stamford Clinic
  HMSMTH W6 ....18 E2
Stamford Green CP
  HOR/WEW KT19 ....77 P1
Stammerham Business
  Centre
  HORS RH12 ....174 D4
Standen (NT)
  EGRIN RH19 ....180 C7
Stanford Primary School
  STRHM/NOR SW16 ....44 F2
Stanhill Court Hotel
  HORL RH6 ....157 P3
Stanley J & I School
  TEDD TW11 ....25 M7
Stanley Park High School
  CAR SM5 ....62 C5
Stanley Park Primary School
  CAR SM5 ....62 B6
Stanley Technical High
  School
  SNWD SE25 ....45 P4
Stanton Square Industrial
  Estate
  SYD SE26 ....31 N7
Starborough Castle
  EDEN TN8 ....144 D8
Starhurst School
  RDKG RH5 ....117 J9

Station Industrial Estate
  FLEETN GU51 ....87 H4
Stepgates Community
  School
  CHERT KT16 ....37 M8
The Stepping Stone School
  CSHT GU26 ....166 A8
Stewart Fleming Primary
  School
  PGE/AN SE20 ....46 C4
Stillness Primary School
  FSTH SE23 ....31 M2
Stirling Way Industrial
  Estates
  CROY/NA CR0 ....44 G8
Stockton House School
  FLEETN GU51 ....86 F5
Stoke Hill CP School
  GU GU1 ....112 A2
Stompond Lane Track
  WOT/HER KT12 ....57 J1
Stoneleigh First School
  EW KT17 ....60 F3
Stoughton County Junior
  School
  GUW GU2 ....111 P2
Stowford College
  BELMT SM2 ....61 N6
Strand on the Green J & I
  School
  CHSWK W4 ....17 N4
Strathmore School
  RCHPK/HAM TW10 ....26 C4
Strawberry Hill Golf Club
  WHTN TW2 ....25 M6
Streatham Cemetery
  TOOT SW17 ....29 H6
Streatham & Clapham
  High School
  (Junior Department)
  BRXS/STRHM SW2 ....30 A4
Streatham & Clapham
  High School
  (Senior Department)
  STRHM/NOR SW16 ....29 M6
Streatham & Croydon RFC
  THHTH CR7 ....45 J6
Streatham Ice Rink
  STRHM/NOR SW16 ....29 P8
Streatham Leisure Centre
  STRHM/NOR SW16 ....29 P5
Streatham Modern School
  STRHM/NOR SW16 ....29 P9
Streatham Park Cemetery
  MTCM CR4 ....44 E3
Streatham Swimming Pool
  STRHM/NOR SW16 ....29 P8
Streatham Vale Sports Club
  STRHM/NOR SW16 ....44 E1
Streatham Wells Primary
  School
  BRXS/STRHM SW2 ....30 A5
Streete Court School
  GDST RH9 ....122 E1
Strodes College
  EGH TW20 ....21 L8
Stubbs Industrial Estate
  ALDT GU11 ....108 G1
Studholme Medical Centre
  ASHF TW15 ....23 J7
The Study Preparatory
  School
  WIM/MER SW19 ....28 A8
The Study School
  NWMAL KT3 ....42 C6
Sturt Priory Hospital
  KWD/TDW/WH KT20 ....98 E6
Sudbourne Primary School
  BRXS/STRHM SW2 ....30 A1
Sulivan Primary School
  FUL/PGN SW6 ....19 L7
Summit Business Park
  SUN TW16 ....39 J1
Sunbury Business Centre
  SUN TW16 ....38 G2
Sunbury Court
  SUN TW16 ....39 M3
Sunbury Golf Centre
  SHPTN TW17 ....38 E5
Sunbury Health Centre
  SUN TW16 ....39 J3
Sunbury Leisure Centre
  SUN TW16 ....39 H2
Sunbury Manor School
  SUN TW16 ....39 H2
Sun Life Trading Estate
  EBED/NFELT TW14 ....15 J8
Sunningdale Golf Club
  ASC SL5 ....34 C9
Sunningdale Ladies Golf Club
  ASC SL5 ....34 F9
Sunningdale School
  ASC SL5 ....34 C9
Sunnydown School
  CTHM CR3 ....101 N4
Sunnyhill Primary School
  STRHM/NOR SW16 ....30 A7
Surbiton Business Centre
  SURB KT6 ....41 K7
Surbiton Cemetery
  KUT/HW KT1 ....41 N5
Surbiton Golf Club
  CHSGTN KT9 ....59 H3
Surbiton High School
  KUT/HW KT1 ....41 L5
Surbiton Hospital
  SURB KT6 ....41 L7
Surbiton Natural Health
  Centre
  SURB KT6 ....41 L7
Surex Swimming Pools
  BH/WHM TN16 ....84 B4

Surrey Business Park
  EW KT17 ....60 C9
Surrey County Hall
  KUT/HW KT1 ....8 C7
Surrey Downs Golf Club
  KWD/TDW/WH KT20 ....99 N2
Surrey Heath Museum
  CBLY GU15 ....68 F2
Surrey History Centre
  WOKN/KNAP GU21 ....10 A5
Surrey Institute of Art
  & Design
  FNM GU9 ....4 E3
  HOR/WEW KT19 ....78 C1
Surrey National Golf Club
  CTHM CR3 ....101 K3
Surrey Probation Service
  GU GU1 ....6 D4
Surrey & Sussex
  Crematorium
  CRAWE RH10 ....159 N9
Surrey Welfare Court
  Service
  GU GU1 ....6 D5
Sussex Manor Business
  Park
  CRAWE RH10 ....177 K1
Sutton Alternative Health
  Centre
  SUT SM1 ....61 M4
Sutton Arena
  CAR SM5 ....43 P8
Sutton Bowling Club
  BELMT SM2 ....61 L7
Sutton Cemetery
  CHEAM SM3 ....61 K1
Sutton Civic Centre
  SUT SM1 ....61 M4
Sutton College of Learning
  for Adults
  SUT SM1 ....61 M4
Sutton General Hospital
  BELMT SM2 ....61 M8
Sutton Grammar School
  for Boys
  SUT SM1 ....61 N4
Sutton Green Golf Club
  WOKS/MYFD GU22 ....92 C2
Sutton High Junior School
  SUT SM1 ....61 M5
Sutton High School
  for Girls GDST
  SUT SM1 ....61 L5
Sutton Superbowl
  SUT SM1 ....61 M4
Sutton United FC
  SUT SM1 ....61 L3
Sutton West Centre
  SUT SM1 ....61 L4
Swaffield Primary School
  WAND/EARL SW18 ....28 F2
Swan Business Centre
  CHSWK W4 ....18 B2
The Swan Centre
  LHD/OX KT22 ....97 H1
The Swan Inn Hotel
  MFD/CHID GU8 ....168 B8
Swansmere School
  WOT/HER KT12 ....39 L9
Swan Walk Shopping
  Centre
  HORS RH12 ....192 B8
Swedish School
  BARN SW13 ....18 E4
Sybil Elgar School
  NWDGN UB2 ....15 P1
Sydenham Girls School
  SYD SE26 ....31 J6
Sydenham High Junior
  School
  SYD SE26 ....31 J7
Sydenham High Senior
  School
  SYD SE26 ....31 J8
Sydenham High School
  Sports Ground
  CAT SE6 ....31 P8
Syon House
  BTFD TW8 ....17 J6
Syon Park
  BTFD TW8 ....17 J7
Syon Park School
  ISLW TW7 ....17 H6
Sythwood Primary School
  WOKN/KNAP GU21 ....71 P5
Tabard Theatre
  CHSWK W4 ....18 C2
Taberner House
  CROY/NA CR0 ....2 D5
TA Centre
  CHERT KT16 ....37 L8
  HORS RH12 ....192 B9
Tadworth Primary School
  KWD/TDW/WH KT20 ....99 H2
Tait Road Industrial Estate
  CROY/NA CR0 ....45 N7
Talavera Junior School
  ALDT GU11 ....108 C3
Tamian Industrial Estate
  HSLWW TW4 ....15 L9
Tamworth Manor High
  School
  STRHM/NOR SW16 ....44 F4
Tanbridge House School
  HORS RH12 ....191 N8
Tanbridge Retail Park
  HORS RH12 ....192 A8

Tandem Centre
  WIM/MER SW19 ....43 P2
Tandridge Golf Club
  OXTED RH8 ....123 J2
Tasis the American School
  in England
  EGH TW20 ....36 G4
Tatsfield Primary School
  BH/WHM TN16 ....104 B1
Tattenham Health Centre
  EPSOM KT18 ....78 F7
Tavistock Infant School
  EPSOM KT18 ....86 D7
TAVR Centre
  KUT/HW KT1 ....41 K5
Teddington Business Park
  TEDD TW11 ....25 N8
Teddington Cemetery
  TEDD TW11 ....25 M7
Teddington Clinic
  TEDD TW11 ....25 M9
Teddington Lock
  TEDD TW11 ....26 A7
Teddington Memorial
  Hospital
  TEDD TW11 ....25 M9
Teddington Pool & Fitness
  Centre
  TEDD TW11 ....25 P8
Teddington School
  TEDD TW11 ....26 C9
The Teddington Theatre Club
  E/WMO/HCT KT8 ....40 D6
Telferscot Primary School
  BAL SW12 ....29 M4
Temperate House
  RCH/KEW TW9 ....17 N7
Thames Ditton & Esher
  Golf Club
  ESH/CLAY KT10 ....58 B2
Thames Ditton Infant School
  THDIT KT7 ....40 F7
Thames Ditton Junior School
  THDIT KT7 ....40 F8
Thamesmead School
  SHPTN TW17 ....38 F7
Thatched House Hotel
  SUT SM1 ....61 K5
Theatre Centre
  BECK BR3 ....47 H3
Theatre Magenta
  LHD/OX KT22 ....76 D7
Theatre of the Dispossessed
  WIM/MER SW19 ....28 A4
The Theatre on the Hill
  CTHM CR3 ....101 N2
Therapia Trading Estate
  CROY/NA CR0 ....44 F6
Therfield School
  LHD/OX KT22 ....76 E7
Thistle Hotel
  HORL RH6 ....140 C8
  WDR/YW UB7 ....13 N6
Thomas Bennett
  Community College
  CRAWE RH10 ....176 G8
Thomas London
  Independent Day School
  KENS W8 ....19 M1
Thomas More Catholic
  School
  PUR/KEN CR8 ....63 H8
Thomas' Preparatory School
  BTSEA SW11 ....19 P6
Thomas's Preparatory
  School
  BTSEA SW11 ....29 J1
Thornchace School
  GU GU1 ....112 G5
Thorncroft Manor
  LHD/OX KT22 ....96 C2
Thornton Heath Health
  Centre
  THHTH CR7 ....45 L5
Thornton Heath Pools &
  Fitness Centre
  THHTH CR7 ....45 L5
Thornton Road Industrial
  Estate
  CROY/NA CR0 ....44 G2
Thorpe CE Infant School
  EGH TW20 ....36 G4
Thorpe CC
  EGH TW20 ....36 D5
Thorpe Industrial Park
  EGH TW20 ....37 H2
Thorpe Lea Primary School
  EGH TW20 ....22 A9
Thorpe Park
  CHERT KT16 ....37 J3
Three Bridges Community
  Centre
  CRAWE RH10 ....177 K5
Three Bridges CC
  CRAWE RH10 ....177 K6
Three Bridges FC
  CRAWE RH10 ....177 K5
Three Bridges First School
  CRAWE RH10 ....177 K4
Three Bridges Junior
  School
  CRAWE RH10 ....177 J5
Three Bridges Primary
  School
  NWDGN UB2 ....16 B3
Three Counties Education
  Trust
  RFNM GU10 ....127 P2
Tiffin Girls School
  KUTN/CMB KT2 ....26 D1
Tiffin School & Sports Centre
  KUTN/CMB KT2 ....9 L4

Tilgate Forest Business Centre
CRAWW RH11 ....194 G1
Tilgate Forest Golf Centre
CRAWE RH10 ....177 K9
Tilgate Park
CRAWE RH10 ....195 J1
Tillingbourne Junior School
RGUE GU4 ....132 F3
Times Square Shopping Centre
SUT SM1 ....61 M4
Tobias School of Art
EGRIN RH19 ....180 C5
Tollgate Primary School
CROY/NA CR0 ....46 C7
Tolworth CP School
SURB KT6 ....41 M9
Tolworth Girls School
SURB KT6 ....59 K2
Tolworth Recreation Centre
SURB KT6 ....59 K2
Tomlinscote School & Sixth Form College
FRIM GU16 ....69 H6
Tooting Bec Athletics Track
TOOT SW17 ....29 L7
Tooting Leisure Centre
TOOT SW17 ....28 C7
Tooting & Mitcham United FC
MTCM CR4 ....44 C2
Tormead School
GU GU1 ....7 K2
Tower Hill Primary School
FARN GU14 ....88 B4
Tower House School
MORT/ESHN SW14 ....18 A9
Tower Industrial Estate
SNWD SE25 ....46 A5
Town Farm Primary School
STWL/WRAY TW19 ....22 G3
Townmead Business Centre
FUL/PGN SW6 ....19 N7
Toyhorse International Stud Farm
BIL RH14 ....189 M6
Traditions Golf Club
WOGS/MYFD GU22 ....73 L4
Trafalgar Community Infant School
HORS RH12 ....192 A6
Trafalgar Primary & Infant School
WHTN TW2 ....25 L5
Travelodge
BTFD TW8 ....17 L4
BTSEA SW11 ....19 N8
DORK RH4 ....117 J6
GU GU1 ....6 C1
HEST TW5 ....15 L4
HEST TW5 ....15 N4
HORL RH6 ....159 H7
KUTN/CMB KT2 ....8 E4
LHD/OX KT22 ....96 C2
LIPH GU30 ....182 C5
STA TW18 ....22 B7
The Treaty Centre
HSLW TW3 ....16 B8
Trefoil Montessori School of Arts
LING RH7 ....142 G1
Trident Business Centre
TOOT SW17 ....29 J8
Trident Industrial Estate
DTCH/LGLY SL3 ....13 J4
Trilakes Country Park
SHST GU47 ....67 K1
Trinity St Marys Primary School
BAL SW12 ....29 K4
Trinity School
CROY/NA CR0 ....64 C1
Trinity Trading Estate
HYS/HAR UB3 ....15 J1
Trumps Green Infant School
VW GU25 ....36 B7
Tudor Lodge
PUR/KEN CR8 ....62 G8
Tudor Lodge Health Centre
WIM/MER SW19 ....28 A3
Tudors Business Centre
KWD/TDW/WH KT20 ....99 K2
Turners Hill CE Primary School
CRAWE RH10 ....179 H8
Turney School
DUL SE21 ....30 D3
Turtle Key Arts Centre
FUL/PGN SW6 ....19 L4
Tweeddale Primary School
CAR SM5 ....43 P8
Twenty Nevern Square Hotel
ECT SW5 ....19 L3
Tweseldown Infant School
FLEETS GU52 ....107 H2
Twickenham Cemetery
WHTN TW2 ....25 J4
Twickenham Park Health Centre
TWK TW1 ....26 B2
Twickenham Preparatory School
HPTN TW12 ....40 B2
Twickenham Stadium
ISLW TW7 ....25 M2
Twickenham Trading Estate
TWK TW1 ....25 N2
Two Bridges Business Park
SAND/SEL CR2 ....63 M5
Two Rivers Retail Park
STA TW18 ....22 B7

Tyrrells Wood Golf Club
LHD/OX KT22 ....97 M4
UCI Cinema
SUT SM1 ....61 M4
UGC Cinema
CHEL SW3 ....19 P4
CRAWE RH10 ....176 C4
HMSMTH W6 ....18 F2
The Ullswater Business Park
COUL/CHIP CR5 ....80 G5
Ullswater Trading Estate
COUL/CHIP CR5 ....80 G5
Unicorn Primary School
BECK BR3 ....47 H6
Unicorn School
RCH/KEW TW9 ....17 M6
Unicorn Trading Estate
HASM GU27 ....184 C3
United Services Sports Ground
CHSWK W4 ....18 C6
University College for the Creative Arts at Epsom
EPSOM KT18 ....78 B3
University of London Athletics Ground
NWMAL KT3 ....42 E6
The University of Surrey
GUW GU2 ....111 N5
University of Westminster
CHSWK W4 ....18 A6
University Vandals RFC
SHPTN TW17 ....38 E8
Uplands CP School
SHST GU47 ....49 M9
Upper Tooting Independent High School
TOOT SW17 ....29 H5
Ursuline High School
RYNPK SW20 ....43 H1
Ursuline Preparatory School
RYNPK SW20 ....43 H1
The Vale Medical Centre
FSTH SE23 ....31 M5
Valence School
BH/WHM TN16 ....105 K6
Vale Primary School
EPSOM KT18 ....78 B8
The Vale School
SKENS SW7 ....19 N1
Valley End CE Infant School
CHOB/PIR GU24 ....52 C5
Valley End CC
CHOB/PIR GU24 ....52 C6
The Valley Gardens
ECH TW20 ....35 M3
Valley Primary School
HAYES BR2 ....47 M3
Velmead Community Centre
FLEETN GU51 ....106 D2
Vestry Hall
MTCM CR4 ....44 B4
Vicarage Lane Clinic
HASM GU27 ....184 A4
Victoria and Albert Museum
SKENS SW7 ....19 P1
Victoria Clinic
WOKN/KNAP GU21 ....10 E2
Victoria Junior School
FELT TW13 ....24 C4
Victor Seymour Infant School
CAR SM5 ....62 B2
Victory Business Centre
ISLW TW7 ....16 F9
The Vine Clinic
KUTN/CMB KT2 ....26 D9
Vine Medical Centre
E-/WMO/HCT KT8 ....40 C4
The Vineyard Primary School
RCHPK/HAM TW10 ....26 D2
Virgo Fidelis Convent Schools
NRWD SE19 ....30 D9
Viscount Industrial Estate
DTCH/LGLY SL3 ....13 J8
VUE Cinema
CROY/NA CR0 ....63 H1
FUL/PGN SW6 ....19 L5
STA TW18 ....22 C7
Vulcan Business Centre
CROY/NA CR0 ....65 L7
Waddon Clinic
CROY/NA CR0 ....63 J4
Waddon Infant School
CROY/NA CR0 ....63 J4
The Waldegrave Clinic
TEDD TW11 ....25 N8
Waldegrave Girls School
WHTN TW2 ....25 L6
Waldorf School of SW London
STRHM/NOR SW16 ....30 F3
Wallace Fields County Infant School
EW KT17 ....78 E2
Wallace Fields Junior School
EW KT17 ....78 E1
Wallbrook Business Centre
HSLWW TW4 ....15 K8
Wallington County Grammar School
WLGTN SM6 ....62 D2
Wallington High School for Girls
WLGTN SM6 ....62 D7
Walsh Memorial CE Infant School
ASHV GU12 ....109 H5
Walton Business Centre
WOT/HER KT12 ....39 K8

Walton Casuals FC
WOT/HER KT12 ....39 K6
Walton Community Hospital
WOT/HER KT12 ....57 K1
Walton Heath Golf Club Shop
KWD/TDW/WH KT20 ....98 F5
Walton & Hersham FC
WOT/HER KT12 ....57 J1
Walton Leigh School
WOT/HER KT12 ....56 G3
Walton-on-Thames CC
WOT/HER KT12 ....39 H9
Walton on the Hill CE Junior School
KWD/TDW/WH KT20 ....98 E5
Walton on the Hill Primary School
KWD/TDW/WH KT20 ....98 F4
Walton Swimming Pool
WOT/HER KT12 ....39 K9
Wandle Recreation Centre
WAND/EARL SW18 ....28 E2
Wandle Trading Estate
MTCM CR4 ....44 B8
Wandle Valley School
CAR SM5 ....44 A8
Wandsworth Adult College
TOOT SW17 ....29 H5
Wandsworth Cemetery
WAND/EARL SW18 ....28 E4
Wandsworth County Court
PUT/ROE SW15 ....28 B1
Wandsworth Trading Estate
WAND/EARL SW18 ....28 E3
Warehouse Theatre
CROY/NA CR0 ....2 C1
Warfield Primary School
BNFD RG42 ....32 C1
Warlingham Park School
WARL CR6 ....82 C5
Warlingham RFC & John Fisher Sports Club
WARL CR6 ....82 B5
Warlingham School
WARL CR6 ....82 B5
Warlingham Sports Club
WARL CR6 ....82 D6
War Memorial Sports Ground
SUT SM1 ....62 A3
Warnham CE Primary School
HORS RH12 ....191 N2
Warren Mead Infant School
BNSTD SM7 ....78 G4
Warren Mead Junior School
BNSTD SM7 ....79 H4
Warsop Trading Estate
EDEN TN8 ....145 H5
Warwick Quadrant & Harlequin Theatre, Cinema & Library
REDH RH1 ....120 C4
The Warwick School
REDH RH1 ....120 D4
The Watchetts Junior School
CBLY GU15 ....68 E6
Waterfield First School
CRAWW RH11 ....176 B7
Waterfront Business Park
FLEETN GU51 ....87 H5
Watermans Arts; Cinema & Theatre Centre
BTFD TW8 ....17 L4
Watermans Business Park
STA TW18 ....22 B7
Watermeads High School
MRDN SM4 ....43 P7
Watermill Museum
EDEN TN8 ....144 B5
Waterside Business Centre
ISLW TW7 ....17 H9
The Waterside Trading Centre
HNWL W7 ....16 E1
Waterside Trading Estate
ADL/WDHM KT15 ....56 A3
Wattenden Primary School
PUR/KEN CR8 ....81 K6
Wattlehurst Farm
HORS RH12 ....173 P4
The Watts Gallery
RGUW GU3 ....131 H2
The Wavell School
ALDT GU11 ....88 D8
Waverley Abbey CE School
RFNM GU10 ....128 E8
Waverley Abbey House
FNM GU9 ....128 D5
Waverley Lower Secondary School
EDUL SE22 ....31 J1
Waverley School
EDUL SE22 ....31 K1
The Weald CE Primary School
RDKG RH5 ....156 C1
Wellington Business Park
CWTH RG45 ....49 J5
Wellington College
CWTH RG45 ....49 L5
Wellingtonia Avenue (Arboretum)
CWTH RG45 ....48 G5
Wellington Primary School
HSLW TW3 ....15 P7
Wellington Shopping Centre
ALDT GU11 ....108 C4
Wellington Sports Centre
CWTH RG45 ....49 K5

Wentworth Golf Club
VW GU25 ....35 N6
West Ashtead Primary School
ASHTD KT21 ....77 K9
Westbourne Primary School
SUT SM1 ....61 L2
West Byfleet Golf Club
BF/WBF KT14 ....73 K2
West Byfleet Health Centre
BF/WBF KT14 ....73 L2
West Byfleet Physiotherapy Clinic
BF/WBF KT14 ....73 L1
West Byfleet Primary School
BF/WBF KT14 ....73 M1
Westcott CE First School
DORK RH4 ....116 C3
Westcott Leisure Centre
DORK RH4 ....116 C3
West Dene School
PUR/KEN CR8 ....81 H2
West Drayton CC
WDR/YW UB7 ....13 N2
Westend County Infant School
ALDT GU11 ....108 B5
West End Sports & Social Club
ESH/CLAY KT10 ....57 P5
Westerham Golf Club
BH/WHM TN16 ....105 K6
Western International Market
NWDGN UB2 ....15 K2
West Ewell Infant School
HOR/WEW KT19 ....60 B4
Westfield Primary School
WOKS/MYFD GU22 ....92 C1
Westfields Junior School
YTLY GU46 ....66 F3
Westfields School
BARN SW13 ....18 D7
YTLY GU46 ....66 F3
West Green First School
CRAWW RH11 ....176 F5
West Hill Golf Club
CHOB/PIR GU24 ....91 H1
West Hill Primary School
WAND/EARL SW18 ....28 D1
West Hill School
LHD/OX KT22 ....76 C7
West Kent Golf Club
ORP BR6 ....84 C1
Westland Heliport
BTSEA SW11 ....19 P8
West London County Court
WKENS W14 ....19 J2
West London Magistrates Court
HMSMTH W6 ....19 H3
West Middlesex University Hospital
ISLW TW7 ....16 G7
Westmoor Community Clinic
PUT/ROE SW15 ....27 M3
West Norwood Clinic
WNWD SE27 ....30 D5
West Norwood Crematorium
WNWD SE27 ....30 D6
Weston Green School
THDIT KT7 ....40 E9
West Park Hospital
EPSOM KT18 ....77 L1
West Ramp Coach Park
HTHAIR TW6 ....14 C6
West Surrey Golf Club
MFD/CHID GU8 ....150 A6
West Thames College
ISLW TW7 ....16 E6
West Thornton Primary School
CROY/NA CR0 ....45 H8
Westward Preparatory School
WOT/HER KT12 ....57 K1
The Westway Clinic
REDH RH1 ....120 A4
West Wickham Swimming Baths
WWKM BR4 ....47 J9
West Wimbledon Primary School
RYNPK SW20 ....42 F4
Westwood Language College for Girls
NRWD SE19 ....45 L1
Weybourne County Infant School
FNM GU9 ....108 A8
Weybridge Business Park
ADL/WDHM KT15 ....56 A3
Weybridge CC
WEY KT13 ....56 C1
Weybridge Hospital & Primary Care Centre
WEY KT13 ....56 C3
Weydon School
FNM GU9 ....127 K6
Weydown Industrial Estate
HASM GU27 ....184 D3
Weyfield Primary School
GU GU1 ....112 B2
Wey House School
SHGR GU5 ....132 C5
Wey Retail Park
BF/WBF KT14 ....74 A1
The Wheatsheaf Hotel
VW GU25 ....35 M4
White Hart Industrial Estate
BLKW GU17 ....68 A3

Whitehorse Manor Primary School
THHTH CR7 ....45 M6
The White House Preparatory School
BAL SW12 ....29 N4
Whitelands College
PUT/ROE SW15 ....27 L3
Whitgift School
SAND/SEL CR2 ....63 L4
Whitgift Shopping Centre
CROY/NA CR0 ....2 D3
Whitton Health Centre
WHTN TW2 ....25 K4
Whitton Health Clinic
WHTN TW2 ....25 J4
Whitton School
WHTN TW2 ....25 J5
Whitton Sports & Fitness Centre
WHTN TW2 ....25 J5
Whyteleafe Business Village
CTHM CR3 ....81 P6
Whyteleafe FC
CTHM CR3 ....81 P8
Whyteleafe School
CTHM CR3 ....81 P7
Wickham Court School
WWKM BR4 ....65 K3
Wickham Theatre
WWKM BR4 ....65 K2
Wide Way Health Clinic
MTCM CR4 ....44 F4
Wildridings CP School
CRAN GU6 ....170 D9
William Byrd School
HYS/HAR UB3 ....14 E4
William Cobbett Junior School
FNM GU9 ....108 A8
William Hogarth School
CHSWK W4 ....18 C4
William Morris Academy
HMSMTH W6 ....19 H3
William Morris Primary School
MTCM CR4 ....44 F4
Willington School
WIM/MER SW19 ....28 C9
Willow Business Centre
MTCM CR4 ....44 B6
Willow Business Park
SYD SE26 ....31 K6
Wilson's School
WLGTN SM6 ....62 C5
Wimbledon Chase Primary School
RYNPK SW20 ....43 J1
Wimbledon Common Golf Club
WIM/MER SW19 ....27 N8
Wimbledon Common Pre-preparatory School
WIM/MER SW19 ....27 P9
Wimbledon (Gap Road) Cemetery
WIM/MER SW19 ....28 E7
Wimbledon High School
WIM/MER SW19 ....28 B9
Wimbledon House School
WIM/MER SW19 ....43 K2
Wimbledon Lawn Tennis Museum
WIM/MER SW19 ....28 B6
Wimbledon Magistrates Court
WIM/MER SW19 ....28 D9
Wimbledon Park Athletics Track
WIM/MER SW19 ....28 C5
Wimbledon Park Golf Club
WIM/MER SW19 ....28 C6
Wimbledon Park Primary School
WIM/MER SW19 ....28 D5
Wimbledon Recreation Centre
WIM/MER SW19 ....28 E9
Wimbledon RFC
RYNPK SW20 ....42 D1
Wimbledon School of Art
WIM/MER SW19 ....43 J2
WIM/MER SW19 ....43 L1
Wimbledon Squash & Badminton Club
WIM/MER SW19 ....43 J1
Wimbledon Stadium
WIM/MER SW19 ....28 E7
Wimbledon Stadium Business Centre
WIM/MER SW19 ....28 E6
Wimbledon Theatre
WIM/MER SW19 ....43 L1
Windlemere Golf Club
CHOB/PIR GU24 ....52 E9
Windlesham Golf Club
BAGS GU19 ....51 P5
Windlesham Village Infant School
BFOR GU20 ....52 A3
The Windmill on the Common Hotel
CLAP SW4 ....29 L1
Windmill School
BRXS/STRHM SW2 ....29 P2
Windmill Trading Estate
MTCM CR4 ....44 E6
SUN TW16 ....38 F2
Winkworth Arboretum (NT)
MFD/CHID GU8 ....151 H6

The Winston Churchill School
WOKN/KNAP GU21 ....**71** L7
Winterbourne Infant School
THHTH CR7 ....**45** J5
Wishmore Cross School
CHOB/PIR GU24 ....**53** L8
Wispers School
HASM GU27 ....**184** D1
Witley CE Controlled Infant School
MFD/CHID GU8 ....**149** N8
Witley Common (NT)
MFD/CHID GU8 ....**149** K6
Witley Industrial Estate
NWDGN UB2 ....**15** P2
Woking Athletics Track
WOKN/KNAP GU21 ....**72** G2
Woking Business Park
WOKN/KNAP GU21 ....**72** F4
Woking College
WOKS/MYFD GU22 ....**72** E9
Woking Community Hospital
WOKS/MYFD GU22 ....**10** E5
Woking FC
WOKS/MYFD GU22 ....**72** D9
Woking Golf Club
WOKS/MYFD GU22 ....**71** N9
Woking High School
WOKN/KNAP GU21 ....**72** B4
Woking & Horsell CC
WOKN/KNAP GU21 ....**10** A3
Woking Hospice
WOKS/MYFD GU22 ....**10** E5

Woking Leisure Centre
WOKS/MYFD GU22 ....**10** E7
Woking Nuffield Hospital
WOKN/KNAP GU21 ....**72** C3
Woking St John's Crematorium
WOKN/KNAP GU21 ....**71** L8
Woldingham Golf Club
CTHM CR3 ....**82** D9
Woldingham School
CTHM CR3 ....**102** E5
Wolf Fields Primary School
NWDGN UB2 ....**15** P2
Wolfson Medical Centre
RYNPK SW20 ....**42** E1
Wolsey Junior School
CROY/NA CR0 ....**65** K6
Wolsey Place Shopping Centre
WOKN/KNAP GU21 ....**10** D3
Wonersh & Shamley Green CE Infant School
SHGR GU5 ....**133** H8
Woodbridge Business Park
GU GU1 ....**6** C1
Woodbrook School
BECK BR3 ....**46** F2
Woodcote High School
PUR/KEN CR8 ....**80** F2
Woodcote House School
BFOR GU20 ....**52** B4
Woodcote Park Golf Club
COUL/CHIP CR5 ....**80** E3
Woodcotes Primary School
COUL/CHIP CR5 ....**80** F3

Wooden Hill Primary School
BRAK RG12 ....**32** A8
Woodfield School
REDH RH1 ....**100** C9
Woodlands Park Hotel
COB KT11 ....**76** C6
Woodlands School
LHD/OX KT22 ....**97** J2
Wood Lane School
FUL/PGN SW6 ....**19** N6
Woodlea Primary School
CTHM CR3 ....**102** F2
Woodmansterne Primary School
BNSTD SM7 ....**80** B3
STRHM/NOR SW16 ....**44** F2
Woodmansterne Sports Club
BNSTD SM7 ....**80** A4
Woodside Health Centre
SNWD SE25 ....**46** B6
Woodside Infant School
CROY/NA CR0 ....**46** A8
Wood Street County Infant School
RGUW GU3 ....**111** J3
Woodville Junior School
LHD/OX KT22 ....**77** H9
Woolmer Hill Athletics Track
HASM GU27 ....**183** N2
Woolmer Hill Technology College
HASM GU27 ....**183** N3
World Business Centre Heathrow
HTHAIR TW6 ....**14** E6

Worlds End Place
WBPTN SW10 ....**19** N5
Worple Primary School
ISLW TW7 ....**16** G9
Worplesdon CP School
RGUW GU3 ....**111** K1
Worplesdon Golf Club
WOKS/MYFD GU22 ....**91** L2
Worsley Bridge Junior School
BECK BR3 ....**46** G1
Worton Hall Industrial Estate
ISLW TW7 ....**16** E9
Wray Common County Middle School
REIG RH2 ....**119** P4
Wray Common Primary School
REIG RH2 ....**119** P4
Wraysbury Medical Centre
STWL/WRAY TW19 ....**21** L2
Wraysbury Primary School
STWL/WRAY TW19 ....**21** K2
Wrencote
CROY/NA CR0 ....**2** D6
Wyke CP School
RGUW GU3 ....**109** P2
Wyke Green Golf Club
ISLW TW7 ....**16** F4
Yateley Common Country Park
YTLY GU46 ....**67** K5
Yateley Health Centre
YTLY GU46 ....**67** H2

Yateley Infant School
YTLY GU46 ....**67** H2
Yateley Manor School
YTLY GU46 ....**67** H1
Yateley School
YTLY GU46 ....**66** G3
Yattendon School
HORL RH6 ....**140** C9
Yehudi Menuhin School
COB KT11 ....**76** A8
YMCA Community & Sports Centre
REDH RH1 ....**120** C8
York Clinic
WOKN/KNAP GU21 ....**10** D4
York House Medical Centre
WOKS/MYFD GU22 ....**10** E5
York Town Industrial Estate
CBLY GU15 ....**68** C3
Yvonne Arnaud Theatre
GU GU1 ....**6** E7
Zennor Road Industrial Estate
BAL SW12 ....**29** M4

Acknowledgements

Schools address data provided by Education Direct.

Petrol station information supplied by Johnsons

One-way street data provided by © Tele Atlas N.V. Tele Atlas

Garden centre information provided by

Garden Centre Association — Britains best garden centres

Wyevale Garden Centres

The statement on the front cover of this atlas is sourced, selected and quoted from a reader comment and feedback form received in 2004

How do I find the perfect place?